LAWRENCE DURRELL

edited by the same author

LITERARY LIFELINES:
THE RICHARD ALDINGTON–LAWRENCE DURRELL CORRESPONDENCE

THE DURRELL–MILLER LETTERS 1935–80

Lawrence Durrell
A Biography

IAN S. MACNIVEN

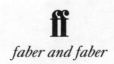

faber and faber

First published in 1998
by Faber and Faber Limited
3 Queen Square London WC1N 3AU

Photoset by Parker Typesetting Service, Leicester
Printed in England by Clays Ltd, St Ives plc

© Ian S. MacNiven, 1998

Ian S. MacNiven is hereby identified as author
of this work in accordance with Section 77
of the Copyright, Designs and Patents Act 1988

A CIP record for this book
is available from the British Library

ISBN 0–571–17248–2

2 4 6 8 10 9 7 5 3 1

This book is for Susan Steier MacNiven,
equal sharer in all that matters

Contents

Illustrations

ix

Chronology

1912 27 February: birth of Lawrence George Durrell at Jullundur.
1921 February–December 1922: attended St Joseph's College, Darjeeling.
1923 18 March: left India for England.
1924 September–June 1926: attended St Olave's and St Saviour's,
     Southwark.
1925 7 January: birth of Gerald Malcolm Durrell, Jamshedpur.
1926 September–December 1927: attended St Edmund's, Canterbury.
1928 16 April: death of Lawrence Samuel Durrell, Dalhousie.
1931 *Quaint Fragment*.
1932 *Ten Poems*.
1934 *Transition: Poems*.
1935 22 January: married Nancy Isobel Myers.
     c. 2 March: left England for Corfu.
     Pied Piper of Lovers.
1937 *Panic Spring*.
1938 *The Black Book*.
1940 4 June: birth of Penelope Berengaria Durrell, Athens.
1941 22 April: left Greece for Egypt. To October 1942: Cairo.
1942 to June 1945: Alexandria.
1943 *A Private Country*.
1945 March 1947: Rhodes.
     Prospero's Cell.
1946 *Cities, Plains and People, Zero and Asylum in the Snow: Two
     Excursions into Reality*.
1947 26 February: married Eve Cohen.
     Cefalû, republished as *The Dark Labyrinth* (1958)
     November 1947–November 1948: Cordova, Argentina.
1948 *On Seeming to Presume*.
1949 July–December 1952: Belgrade, Yugoslavia.
1950 *Sappho: A Play in Verse*.

1951 30 May: birth of Sappho Jane Durrell, Oxford.
1952 *A Key to Modern Poetry* (published in the US as *A Key to Modern British Poetry*).
1953 26 January–26 August 1956: Cyprus.
      Reflections on a Marine Venus.
1955 *The Tree of Idleness and Other Poems.*
1957 February–15 September 1958: Villa Louis, Sommières.
      Justine, White Eagles over Serbia, Bitter Lemons, Esprit de Corps.
1958 15 September–15 July 1966: Le Mazet Michel, chemin d'Engances.
      Balthazar, Mountolive, Stiff Upper Lip.
1959 *Art and Outrage* (with Alfred Perlès).
1960 *Clea* (published with *Justine, Balthazar* and *Mountolive* in a single volume as *The Alexandria Quartet*, 1962), *Collected Poems.*
1961 27 March: married Claude-Marie Vincendon.
1963 3 June: first return to Greece since 1955.
      An Irish Faustus: A Morality in Nine Scenes, Lawrence Durrell and Henry Miller: A Private Correspondence.
1964 *Acte: A Play.*
1966 *The Ikons and Other Poems, Sauve Qui Peut.*
      15 July 1966 to 1990: Mme Tartes's, route de Saussine, Sommières.
1967 1 January: death of Claude Durrell.
1968 March: first visit to the United States.
      Tunc.
1969 *Spirit of Place: Letters and Essays on Travel.*
1970 *Nunquam* (published with *Tunc* in a single volume as *The Revolt of Aphrodite*, 1974).
1971 *The Red Limbo Lingo.*
1973 November: married Ghislaine de Boysson.
      Vega and Other Poems.
1974 January–March: teaching at Caltech, Pasadena.
      Monsieur: or, The Prince of Darkness.
1978 *Livia: or, Buried Alive, The Greek Islands.*
1977 October–November: return to Egypt.
      Sicilian Carousel.
1980 *Collected Poems 1931–1974, A Smile in the Mind's Eye.*
1981 *Literary Lifelines: The Richard Aldington–Lawrence Durrell Correspondence.*
1983 *Constance: or, Solitary Practices.*
      Sebastian: or, Ruling Passions.

1985 1 February: suicide of Sappho Durrell.
      Quinx: or, The Ripper's Tale (published with *Monsieur, Livia, Constance* and *Sebastian* in a single volume as *The Avignon Quintet,* 1992).
1986 April: last visits to the United States and England.
1988 *The Durrell–Miller Letters 1935–80.*
1990 *Caesar's Vast Ghost.*
      7 November: death of Lawrence Durrell.

Preface

To understand Lawrence Durrell one must go to India, physically if possible, but otherwise at least in the imagination. One must feel the damp heat of Calcutta and the chill dawns of the high Punjab, must experience the friendly, pungent crush of the bazaars and hear the monotone trumpets of the Buddhist temples and see the creatures of the Terai forest. Above all, one must enter the vanished colonial world of the Durrell family. This world, grafted on to the trunk of India like a strange fruit united to a hospitable but overwhelming tree, instilled in Larry both pride and guilt: pride in the practical skills of his family, guilt because he could not assume a place in the machinery of Empire. He saw the role that was waiting for him, and turned away. Loving India, he felt that he belonged to it, yet he was estranged by his otherness: a white child among brown playmates, predestined to a master's position that he did not want. Even within his family, he soon discovered that he thought differently, precociously. His was not to be an unquestioning acceptance of the pattern of the more prosperous colonials: a childhood pampered by servants and followed by education abroad, the return as a master, with long hours of arduous work, whisky at the club and a small grave somewhere in the vast land. He learned to conceal his rebel thoughts, and this made him lonely while still at home, a foretaste of the loneliness that would haunt him for the rest of his life. None the less, Larry would carry with him into his lifelong exile the psychic burden of his ancestors, their aspirations and accomplishments and defeats. What he rejected outwardly remained alive inside: the lonely colonial child shadowed the cosmopolitan writer.

Durrell was early sensitive to the 'spirit of place', but Tibet and India would evolve into a state of mind more than a geographic locus for him. *The Alexandria Quartet*, the work that would gain him an international readership and fame, *Tunc* and *Nunquam*, the novels that would lose for him some of his audience and his American publisher alike, and *The Avignon Quintet*, the magisterial final sequence that would puzzle some of

xvii

his most loyal friends, are none of them set in the Orient. And yet, and yet . . . India remains the fiery shade behind Durrell's thought and work. If he succeeded – and Durrell himself was never quite sure that he had – his life's work will come to be seen as a keystone, a *clou*, a bridge linking the human physical and spiritual centres of East and West, a passage from India to the British homeland of his ancestors and back east again.

Larry's own passage would be uneasy and eventful: the bitter experiences of schoolboy exile and early loss, his discovery of Greece, the thrill of Paris in the 1930s and the shock of war, adventures in many places and with many women, the years of doubt and uncertainty, the public triumphs, the unrelaxing and unforgiving daemon driving him until the end. Durrell's ancestry and upbringing gave him a language and a tradition; India gave him a sense of otherness; England nearly broke him to harness; Greece freed him again; Egypt gave him his major subject. War, passion, divorces, disappointment, self-doubt, the temptation to suicide scorched him. Out of Durrell's drive and tensions and experiences came a range of hard-won novels, volumes of poetry, plays and non-fiction.

'Thirteen is my lucky number,' Lawrence Durrell liked to say, and at his favourite Hotel Royal in Paris he invariably reserved Room 13. It was a way of challenging Fate, of asserting that he was not bound by superstitions and accepted beliefs, while at the same time admitting to a quaint fetish. Durrell also dallied with astrology, espoused acupuncture, and played with the symbolism of the Tarot, notably in *The Alexandria Quartet*. He was fascinated by the hard sciences, including physics, astronomy and medicine, and especially by the great soft one, psychology. He could perform splendidly, whether for a single interviewer or, rarely, before a large audience, yet he was a humble, shy and intensely private man. Many contradictions were at home in Durrell's short frame. These contradictions challenged me as his biographer, and I struggled for most of the writing of this text to interpret his life in twelve chapters. Somehow, the story refused to fit; and besides, twelve seemed too biblical a number for the author of *Monsieur: or, The Prince of Darkness*. Thirteen it had to be. Here, then, is Lawrence Durrell in thirteen acts.

After writing a first novel about a boy with an Indian childhood that was clearly autobiographical, Durrell strove to distance his fiction from his own life. Yet, latterly, he threatened repeatedly to write an autobiography, or else to bring out a volume of photographs based on his disordered piles of prints and negatives. This book is in part an attempt to accomplish what

Durrell never found time for: to tell his story in his own words. Thus, I have depended heavily on Durrell's interviews, letters and published work, adding links and correctives where necessary.

Once, when Durrell was accused of remembering things 'vividly' but inaccurately, he replied to his interviewer, 'I think that's the juggling quality I have.' An astrologer had told him, he recalled, that he was characterized by 'evasion and flight and non-comprehension of what I really am and what I really feel', and Durrell had to agree that, as an 'illusionist', he often baffled himself. 'I am the supreme trickster,' he cheerfully admitted. However, in addition to his elusive quality, Durrell was a self-ironist with an enormously developed sense of play. Turning a suddenly guileless blue eye on the interviewer – who was doubtless congratulating himself on having pinned a label on to Durrell – he continued: 'But fortunately I'm not to blame. I gather it's something to do with the Fishes, to which I belong . . . . Pisceans are a bunch of liars, and when you add to that an Irish background, you have got some pretty hefty liar.' This too was disingenuous: Durrell was no habitual liar, and he was usually touchingly eager to please, to give truth-value to those who sought him out. Only, the illusionist and the joker did indeed reside within, and he was too good an actor to signal his mercurial shifts from facts as he saw them to what he called 'reality prime', from truth to the essence of truth – or to devilment.

Durrell's shyness made him shun autobiography: he rarely spoke in detail about himself, except as artist, and although he filled countless notebooks, he did not keep a regular diary. He was most consistently personal and truthful in his poetry, but his habit of evasion often made him disguise the personal even there. None the less, he distilled the sensation points of his life in his poetry, and some of these crises are heralded, as Durrell would have said, in the passages chosen for chapter headnotes.

This book springs from Durrell's contradictory nature. He was a very private person who adored good company, a recluse who had many friends and who loved many women, a spiritual man who was a sensualist. In the 1950s he was so protective of his privacy that when the publication of his and Henry Miller's letters was proposed, he suggested that only Miller's be included in the volume. As soon as *The Alexandria Quartet* appeared, Durrell began to be approached by would-be biographers. His answer was always No.

I had corresponded at widely spaced intervals with Durrell, beginning in 1970, at first mainly about the archive of his manuscripts and books that had been purchased by Southern Illinois University at Carbondale, and had visited him in France in 1975. Then in 1979 he asked me if I would like to begin assembling the material for an eventual biography, to appear after his death. He had finally resigned himself to the fact that eventually someone would write his life story, whether he wished it or not. His friends were dying off, he said, and someone might as well start collecting information. With my wife – companion and partner in my researches throughout – I began a series of visits to Durrell in his small Languedoc town of Sommières. In 1986 he spent two weeks with us in New York and Pennsylvania. He provided us with addresses of his family and of many friends, and we travelled to Bournemouth, to Greece, to Alexandria, to Yugoslavia, to Cyprus, to India. Durrell demanded no oversight of the biography and made no conditions, other than not wishing publication during his lifetime. Even this he dropped towards the end, saying, with a touch of malice, 'You have found out all there is to know about me – *why don't you write the damn thing*?'

To begin with a certainty: there is only one pronunciation of the family name. Durrell rhymes approximately with *squirrel*; it is only a shade off a monosyllable, but is melodious. It is a stubby name, fittingly like his physical form. As I began the actual writing, Durrell's first name intruded itself more and more insistently. Durrell-the-writer had a comfortable fit, but 'Durrell' sorted oddly with Larry the son, brother and centre of a circle of friends. There was also the ebullient and imposing shadow of the Other Durrell, Gerald Malcolm, Gerry, zoologist and best-selling author. Larry Durrell invited informality while maintaining his privacy: from his tightly shuttered core he would give the cue to the personality required for each occasion – Lawrence Durrell inscribing books at Hatchard's in his beautiful hand, Durrell as Director of Information Services on Cyprus, Larry the *bon vivant*, companion, lover. His books seem to me to have emanated from a source that could better be called Larry than any other part of his name. A more formal biography can Durrell him; the man himself preferred to be Larry.

The biggest obstacle that I encountered in researching this book was Larry Durrell's humility. He evinced very little interest in speaking about himself, except occasionally to spin fanciful versions of his past. I soon discovered he believed that the only important side of his story lay in his writing. He appeared to have scant concern for his reputation, yet he seemed almost naïvely grateful for any sincere attempt to understand his work – even when he disagreed: 'Oh, *thank you* for your brilliant and solacing study' was one of his standard responses to scholars. Perhaps he really meant it.

The details of Lawrence Durrell's life – his boyhood in India, his schooling, his wives, children, friendships, lovers, exploits – tended in his stated opinion to fade into an all-encompassing nebulosity that he often described with one word, 'boring'. 'Surely that's part of the record,' he would answer reproachfully to questions about his private life. He pretended to believe that some Recorder had kept a log of his movements and affairs, impersonally, along with all other lives, and that he had been simply 'lucky' in managing to write a few novels and poems and in loving a number of beautiful women.

Once, in exasperation at the contradictions that I was unearthing – and sometimes hearing from the Durrellian lips – I said, hoping to badger him into a single version of the truth, 'Larry, I know what I'm going to do: I'll write your life as a quartet, with four versions – and let the reader choose.' I should have known better. 'Yes', he replied with his most enigmatic smile, 'why *don't* you? What a splendid idea!' I retreated. I made choices.

Shortly before Larry's death in 1990, I sent him the chapter dealing with his discovery of Corfu. We spoke at length on the telephone, and he cleared up a few details. I looked forward to future consultations on the text. It was typical of his self-effacing side that he would elude me in this: two weeks later I picked up the ringing phone to hear that Larry was dead.

This, then, is one version of the life of Lawrence Durrell, composed with a good deal of love, an affection that has not compromised what I hope is an unflinching portrait of Durrell entire. I have presented as many facets of his character as I could catch, and have attempted to link the development of the man with the evolution of the artist. He did not believe in the existence of the discrete ego, the unique and indivisible personality, and this he exemplified in his own nature. I do not pretend to have written the definitive word. How could I?

Ian S. MacNiven
The Bronx, 1996

CHAPTER I

India

Once in idleness was my beginning,

Night was to the mortal boy
Innocent of surface like a new mind
Upon whose edges once he walked
In idleness, in perfect idleness.
'Cities, Plains and People'

LARRY DURRELL, christened Lawrence George Durrell to commemorate his father, his mother's father and his father's King, gazed north from the Mall, the ring road circling Observatory Hill. He stood grasping his father's hand while the town of Darjeeling rustled, rang and clopped around him. Ahead rose the stupendous peaks of the Himalayas, a delicate pink in the early morning light – Kabru, Jannu, Talung and mighty Kanchenjanga. Larry had seen the snowy Himalayas before: from Dow Hill, from Eagle's Crag, even from the upper balcony of his home in Kurseong. Here, however, by the levitation of perspective they seemed not on the horizon but above it, suspended in their own sea of perlaceous blue. Darjeeling embraced a curving ridge one thousand, two thousand feet above an immense valley tiled an enamelled green by endless tea gardens. Beyond the tea gardens the Singalela Range, a rank of mountains reduced to foothills by the enormous peaks, was lost in blackness that morning; higher still, the frozen slopes glowed in the soundless distance. The crevasses and shadows could have been etched in crystal, so well defined did they appear to the sharp eyes of childhood. A flight of pigeons lifted from a roof below the path, soared, then dropped on raised wings towards the valley. Larry's father gave his arm a tug, and they returned to the villa where they had lodged the night before.

'I would prefer to present my case in terms of biography,' said Durrell some sixty-five years later, 'for my thinking is coloured by the fact that I am a colonial, an Anglo-Indian, born into that strange world of which the only great poem is the novel *Kim* by Kipling.'[1] The romance of colonial life, the

I

glories and heartbreaks of Empire, were gospel and blood to the Durrells of India. They and Lawrence Durrell's maternal kin, the Dixies, were true believers, and they paid with their bodies, leaving their bones in the cemeteries of Mymensingh, of Roorkee, of Mussoorie, of Dalhousie – now-forgotten places of the Raj. They spoke with proprietary pride of the accomplishments of British administration in India: the suppression of thuggee, the campaigns against child marriage and suttee, the relative impartiality of British civil administration and justice, the construction of mighty railway and canal systems. Lord Curzon, most able and most arrogant of the viceroys, spoke for the Durrells too when he proclaimed near the turn of the century, 'To me the message is carved in granite, it is hewn out of the rock of doom – that our work is righteous and it shall endure.'[2] What would endure for Larry Durrell, however, was not the siren call of race and mission but a wild ache of love for the Roof of the World. Distant Tibet hit him like a blow to the chest, a challenge.

Committed to British India though the Durrells and Dixies assuredly were, they had not arrived with the imprimatur of public school and university educations, enabling them to slide easily into the commissioned ranks of the elite Indian Army or the even more exalted heights of the Indian Civil Service, the ICS. These English paragons were referred to, in a blend of envy and irony, as the Heaven-Born. Larry Durrell made no such claim for his ancestors, 'but we were real Anglo-Indians', he liked to say, turning the derogatory term into a claim of virtue; 'we spoke the languages of the places, and one of my uncles and a cousin became known as translators of Buddhist texts.'[3] Strictly speaking, 'Anglo-Indian' was a misnomer: in the census of 1911 Anglo-Indians were defined for the first time as those with mixed European and Indian ancestry, but Larry intended the term in its older, creole sense. 'The Indian Blood must have been a mistake,'[4] he told Henry Miller, who had written approvingly of his supposed mixed ancestry. Earlier, Larry had confused Miller by stating, 'I am . . . a pure Anglo-Irish-Indian ASH BLOND.'[5] The men among Larry's progenitors had come out as privates or as non-commissioned officers, survived the climate and the diseases, married the widows and daughters of other army folk, and produced children. Larry was very much aware of how rooted in the land his people were, recalling in later years that the family had 'ramified throughout India, in the police, the military, the functionaries, the technocrats'.[6] His father, Lawrence Samuel Durrell, was one of the technocrats, a railway employee who became a civil engineer and an entrepreneur. Larry insisted firmly that his family belonged to this middle rank of white society, not to the despised merchants and clerks: 'It was unthinkable to open a shop. . . . We had no box-wallahs in our family – we had several drunks and some brokes, and a few Buddhists.'[7]

Larry's father was a man who prided himself on his absolute moral rectitude, a Victorian apostle of progress endowed with a sense of self-righteous propriety, 'keen on being respectable'.[8] Once when his wife Louisa ordered a second gin and tonic at the club, he objected. Her Irish blood surged into her face and she stormed out into the night, finding her way home hours later. Her husband was coldly furious: Louisa had not been in danger, but it simply was not done for a white woman to walk out alone. To his peers Lawrence Samuel was clearly a *decenchap*, as the hero's father, John Clifton, is termed in *Pied Piper of Lovers*, Durrell's first novel and his most autobiographical fiction. The self-conscious, insecure father-figure is the major adult presence in the early third of the book, dealing with the growing up in India of a boy, Walsh – clearly modelled upon Larry himself. If Lawrence Samuel, like Clifton senior, was very concerned about appearances, it was in part because he felt vulnerable. He was afraid that others would be harsh in judging him and that this would hurt him professionally.[9] He could tick off the counts against himself: he was Indian-born and Indian-educated; he was not wealthy; and he was not by heredity a gentleman. Larry described his father as being 'bourgeois with ambitions towards the aristocracy'[10]: he wanted his first-born son to attend Oxford or Cambridge and then return to an important position in India. That, he felt, would cancel the stigma of the Indian roots.

A further clue to Lawrence Samuel Durrell's concern with status lies in the birth and marriage records of the small Suffolk towns of his progenitors. The author's great-grandmother, born Mahala Tye in 1818 at Hacheston, a tiny village set in rolling farmland north-east of Ipswich, married William Amos Durrell, a sailor, at Woodbridge in 1833. The Tyes were respectable householders and landowners, and by profession a number of the men had been wheelwrights and weavers in the sixteenth and seventeenth centuries, shoemakers in the eighteenth and nineteenth. There were two sons from the Tye-Durrell union, and then in 1844 off Yarmouth William deliberately shot himself aboard the *Reformation*, the coastal vessel he commanded. Mahala, her attractive face in the one known portrait showing both strength of character and determination, did not retire demurely into widowhood. She had dark hair, a good figure and a direct, fearless regard. Already by 1841 she had been employed as a housekeeper by Samuel Geater Stearn, a propertied farmer living at

Kettleburgh. Stearn had a wife and children in Easton, where his main farm seems to have been; and he owned other land at Wickham Market. Suicide meant scandal, especially when the bereaved widow lived in the house of a man not her husband. Stearn moved to Colchester, taking Mahala with him. By 1851 Mahala was listed in the census as residing with her father at nearby Hacheston, where she produced a son who was identified in the Register of Births as Samuel Stearn Durrell, giving rise to the conjecture that farmer Stearn, then sixty-three, had bedded the pretty widow. Exactly three months after his birth, Mahala took her son to Hacheston church to be baptized. The assistant curate penned the cruel 'illegitimate' below Samuel's name. Larry may have gotten a whiff of the scandal, but in middle age he cloaked the admission in such blarney that it could have been – and probably was – taken for a joke. Asked by a French interviewer if he was entirely Irish in ancestry, he replied, 'Ninety per cent. There was a betrayal somewhere; I think my great-grandmother betrayed the race by loving an Englishman. It's frightful to think about but . . . I am a bastard.'[11]

Village gossip bruited it about that one of Samuel Stearn's sons had fathered Mahala's baby, but later in the same year Mahala married Henry Page of Hacheston, a man eight years her junior and described as a 'labourer'. She bore Page five children over the next eleven years. Her long life was neither easy nor without tragedy, and when Mahala died in 1897, of her eight offspring only Samuel Durrell and Edward Page were left alive.[12]

Suicide and illegitimacy: not much of a legacy. Still, the Army was a great forgiver of able-bodied young men, and in 1869 at the age of eighteen Larry Durrell's grandfather joined the Fourth Regiment of Foot at Ipswich. Samuel Durrell, as he signed himself, was described as an 'agricultural labourer' in the enlistment papers. He was literate, although he surely did not have much education. Transferred to the Royal Artillery in 1872, he married Emma Cooper two years later at Portsea; two daughters were born to them in short order, and in 1876 Samuel was posted to India.

The journey to India via the Suez Canal on the Pacific and Orient Steamship Company's fast steamers meant a reasonably comfortable three weeks for commissioned officers in First Class, but Samuel Durrell was still a mere sergeant, and he and his family travelled crammed with nearly two thousand other souls aboard the troopship *Malabar*, a barque-rigged steamer. Nor did conditions improve much for them on their arrival in India. In March, near the beginning of the hot season, they moved into married quarters, a few stifling rooms with a strip of parched earth in front, and the temperatures soon topped 100° Fahrenheit daily. By the end of the year both their children had died. Two more offspring appeared but only one, a daughter, survived infancy, and Emma herself died in 1881 in Allahabad. Two years later Samuel married Dora Maria Johnstone at Lucknow, home of Kipling's Kim. By this time Samuel Durrell was using Amos as his middle name, a curious gesture towards the suicide whose last name he bore yet who was no blood kin to him. Did he know of his illegitimacy, and was this an attempt to mitigate it? Dora Maria's father, William Johnstone, was a sergeant-major in the Royal Horse Artillery, and her mother, Margaret Blaker, had come out to India in 1846 as the wife of Henry Beauchamp Blaker; after Blaker's death in 1857 she had married William Johnstone at Lahore. Many years later in London one of Larry Durrell's Blaker cousins would befriend the young man as he was trying to become a writer.

Dora Maria seems to have had a personality to match her sergeant-major father's imposing parade-ground bearing. She was a powerfully built woman with a proud aspect and a heavy face of the sort called handsome. She must also have possessed great vitality, as the stock was strong: despite all the plagues of India, seven of her eight children lived to marry and six left descendants. In her old age Dora Maria would become the formidable Big Granny of Larry's childhood.

Samuel Durrell was ordered to Fort William in the middle of the great Calcutta Maidan on the Hooghly River, which meant that he and his bride moved to the capital of the Raj. Lawrence Samuel was the first issue, in 1884, of this promising marriage. Although Samuel Durrell rose steadily through the ranks, his family grew quickly and money was always short. At about two-year intervals Lawrence Samuel's siblings arrived: Dorothy Margaret, Eleanor May, Elsie Marion, William Henry, Jessie Mahala, Muriel Florence; then there was a seven-year gap until Samuel and Dora Maria's last child, Enid Nell, appeared. This late child died in her adolescence the year Larry was born.

Following his arrival in India, Samuel Durrell had been assigned to the Bengal Unattached List as a Magazine Sergeant; then he was transferred to the Indian Ordnance Department as a Warrant Officer and in 1896 was promoted to Honorary Lieutenant. He served in the Tirah Campaign of 1897–8 and after having been wounded in action in the Boxer Rebellion was Mentioned in Dispatches in 1901. He proudly wore the China Medal, and retired as Honorary Major in 1906. He had been stationed in many of the military nerve centres of northern India: Rawalpindi, Allahabad, Dum

Dum. It had been a very respectable army career for one who had started as an enlisted man. Major Durrell continued to live in India until the last year of his life – 1914 – when, ineluctably drawn by the home country, he sailed to England and died at Portsmouth, having given his life a pleasing geographical symmetry. Dora Maria returned to India.

Samuel Durrell was apparently conscious of his own limited education. He sent his elder son to the Anglican-run La Martinière Christian Boys' College, one of the best schools in Lucknow, epicentre of the Mutiny of 1857. The school building had been the residence of General Claude Martin, who had endowed the institution in 1800, and the walls still bore scars inflicted during a British bombardment as the school was being retaken from the Mutineers.

After his graduation from La Martinière in 1902, Lawrence Samuel went to the Thomason College of Civil Engineering at Roorkee, within sight of the magnificent Solani Aqueduct of the Ganga Canal. Both the town and the school date from the construction of the canal in the mid-nineteenth century, a vast project intended to curb famines by ensuring reliable irrigation. On clear days the white peaks of the Himalayas were visible far to the north, but the terrain around Roorkee was as flat as a baking pan and could be nearly as hot.

Although Lawrence Samuel would always feel at a disadvantage because of his Indian education, he had few grounds for embarrassment academically. Thomason was the first institution of its kind in Asia, and the engineering curricula were roughly comparable to those established around the same time at Cambridge and Harvard. For instructors the college drew upon the experienced officers of the Corps of Royal Engineers and the Bengal Sappers and Miners. The massive, colonnaded old main building, in a Renaissance style and impressively domed, was surrounded by workshops of Victorian brickwork and student bungalows and barracks with thatched roofs and *kutcha* mud-and-straw walls. All the chemistry, physics, electrical and mechanical laboratories had been newly equipped, and the machinery workshop, the first of its type in India, was powered entirely by electricity.

The Thomason College enrolment of just over three hundred students was divided among three programmes: three-year degree courses in civil and electrical engineering; the Upper Subordinate Class, a two-year curriculum designed for those entering 'the higher subordinate service of the Public Works Department, Military Works Service, and the Engineering Profession generally'; and a Lower Subordinate Class, a two-year course of

6

study for Indians destined for the 'Sub-Overseer grade' in Public Works and the railways. Lawrence Samuel enrolled in the Upper Subordinate programme. Samuel Durrell apparently could not afford to pay for more than two years at the college, and this prevented his son from attempting a degree curriculum.[13] Lawrence Samuel chafed under the stigma of the inferior diploma and of its Indian origin, and he would later insist that his own sons be schooled abroad.[14] Larry was sentenced to England even before his birth.

The Upper Subordinate students adhered to a rigorous schedule of one-and-a-half hour classes in maths, sciences, materials, engineering practice, surveying and drawing, athletics and, unless they were Indians, compulsory military training. For years after the Mutiny, Thomason College had been strictly segregated, but since 1895 the division of the classes into European and Indian sections had been abolished. Nearly half of Lawrence Samuel's Upper Subordinate classmates were Indians. The messes remained separate, however, and social distinctions continued, perhaps more rigidly among the Indians than among the English: according to one estimate, an Untouchable could pollute a Nambudiri Brahman at ninety-six paces – and to a strict Brahman, an Englishman ranked with an Untouchable.[15]

Although the European-descended servants of the Raj liked to think of themselves as the bearers of scientific efficiency and civilized administration to a backward nation, those who pondered the matter honestly realized that they were all, civilians and military, men and women alike, part of an occupying force in a land that just might erupt again into open hostility. Significantly, the Mutiny had created a burgeoning demand for English wives to replace the native mistresses who had previously solaced the European empire-builders. Larry Durrell's maternal great-grandmother Louisa Boustred had ventured to India with the post-Mutiny 'Fishing Fleet' of young women seeking husbands in a booming market; those few who went back to England unclaimed were referred to as 'returned empties'. A widow and a Londoner, Louisa married Captain James H. Fairley of Roorkee. She had brought with her Georgina Nimmo, a young daughter from her first marriage, who would marry George Dixie and become Larry's Little Granny.

When Lawrence Samuel arrived in Roorkee, the Dixies were already long established and lived in The Manor House, a large, beautiful dwelling near the college. George Dixie's father-in-law, Captain Fairley, had only recently retired after teaching at Thomason for thirty years. Dixie, the Head Clerk and Works Accountant of the Canal Foundry and Workshop,

7

had a son, John, three years older than Lawrence Samuel, and another son, William, who was close to his age. The Dixie family also included a pretty and athletic teenage daughter, Louisa Florence, her younger brother Tom, and a small child, Ella. George Dixie's father, another John, had been a sergeant-major in the Sappers and Miners, and the Dixies claimed roots in County Cork. Sergeant-Major John Dixie had in 1845 married Johanna Doherty, a young widow born O'Brien in Delhi. Despite the Irish heritage, the Dixies of Roorkee were not Roman Catholics but 'God-fearing, lusty, chapel-going Mutiny stock', as Larry remembered them.[16] Larry would invariably emphasize his distant lien on Ireland, ignoring his paternal English side. This suited his rebel guise – and besides, Ireland had never had a chance to hurt him.

The hospitable Fairley and Dixie families made a lively group, and Lawrence Samuel must often have played truant from the bleak Upper Subordinate Class barracks. At the college, social life and discipline were 'permeated by the military outlook'.[17] The students were free to leave the grounds from Saturday afternoon until seven o'clock on Monday morning; however, there was little entertainment within a hundred miles for young men without large allowances. While some of the students maintained polo ponies and hunted over the weekends, Lawrence Samuel did not have much money to spend. His father's modest income of around two hundred rupees a month, approximately £20, had to be spread among eight children. The young man was fortunate indeed to gain the acceptance of two families standing high in the social circle of Roorkee. Dora Maria, ambitious for her son, seems to have pushed Lawrence Samuel into the engineering profession; and Samuel Durrell, who drove himself hard, expected much of his offspring. But a different atmosphere pervaded The Manor House. There was a sense of physical plenty, and the Dixies were characterized by a temperance, gentleness and gaiety quite exhilarating to a young man more accustomed to the rather rough military cantonment life. Georgina Nimmo Dixie was a warm, anxious mother who fussed over her children and their friends. Having grown up practically next door to the college squash and tennis courts, the Dixie boys were all good players, and Louisa took part in the games with energy and skill. Tom, sunny in manner, was a great favourite with Louisa, and Grandfather Fairley was patient and kindly. All of his daughters married Thomason engineering graduates, so that the extended family Larry was born into was broadly imbued with technical discourse. In the year of Lawrence Samuel's graduation, 1904, disease struck as if casually into the happiest home he had yet known: the child Ella died of diphtheria. The same year James Fairley also died after forty years in India.

Lawrence Samuel graduated in July, coming fifteenth in a class of thirty-six. Ten of his classmates earned honours diplomas, one qualified in photography, seven received academic silver medals in civil engineering, drawing, accounting, surveying and other specialities. There was a blank in the Remarks column after the Durrell name: the college motto, *Absque Labore Nihil* – Nothing without Labour – seemed ironically appropriate for him. Larry would often say that his father had felt at a disadvantage because of his Indian education, that he regretted having missed the cachet of Home schooling and a university accent. Lawrence Samuel's tendency to discontent would swell to major proportions in his first-born son.

A requirement of the Upper Subordinate programme was that the graduate serve a year of apprenticeship in some appropriate enterprise, and Lawrence Samuel joined the State Railway Service. Here was the fascination of steam, the romance of power and speed: wind and cinders in the face, shining brass and oiled steel, work accomplished in terms of metres of rise, tons hauled, rivers spanned in defiance of floods, strikes and pestilence. 'My father was a true Victorian and his attitude to science was, in the anthropological sense, religious,' recalled Larry.[18] He might without exaggeration have said messianic.

The hot breath of world condemnation had not yet swept over British colonialism when Lawrence Samuel was preparing himself to help bring Progress to a corner of the Empire. Lord Curzon, in one of his last speeches before he resigned the Viceroyship in 1905, admonished Englishmen in India 'to fight for the right, to abhor the imperfect, the unjust or the mean, to swerve neither to the right hand nor to the left, to care nothing for flattery, odium or abuse . . . never to let your enthusiasm be soured or your courage grow dim.'[19] Lawrence Samuel, beginning his engineering career, felt just such a sense of mission. So did a lot of Indian nationalists, but in the cause of independence, and in the same year Curzon uttered his noble sentiments, bombs killed several Englishmen in Calcutta. The pro-independence Indian National Congress, founded in 1885, became avowedly revolutionary after 1905. The spectacle of misprized Japan defeating ponderous Russia inspired Indian revolutionaries to hope that they might do the same to Britain. It is highly doubtful, however, whether the Dixies and the Durrells realized that a serious threat to the Empire lay in the future. A score of years later a desperately lonely Larry Durrell would yearn towards India: a colonial India already slipping its chains before he was born.

Lawrence Samuel's career progressed as smoothly as the trains over the track he was laying, and by early 1906 he was employed as an Assistant Engineer by the North-Western Railway, based in Lahore. The steel rails seemed to point to a secure future, but India served up another cautionary reminder that year with the death of George Dixie, Louisa's father. The Manor House in Roorkee took on a melancholy cast. Lawrence Samuel was sent to Phillour not far away to help supervise the building of a bridge over the treacherous Sutlej River. For most of the year it was a shallow ribbon of greenish water flowing over a wide sand-and-gravel bed, when it had not dried up to a series of mere pools. But when the rains came the Sutlej boiled and snarled, turning cloudy and cunningly undercutting trees, boulders and bridge piers on its way to join the mighty Indus. The bridge was more than two years in construction and by the time it was finished Lawrence Samuel had learned all the practical lessons of railway engineering: the transportation of supplies, the sinking of piers to bedrock that could lie 60, 100 or 140 feet below the surface, the cajoling and coercing of skilled and unskilled labourers in their hundreds.

When Lawrence Samuel left Phillour in April 1909, it was to take up a post as District Engineer at Karnal, a significant promotion for the young bachelor. A district engineer was responsible for virtually everything that had to be built, repaired or dismantled in his district, but Lawrence Samuel's main job turned out to be the construction of the King Edward Memorial Hospital in Karnal. His new superior was Major Cecil Henry Buck, the district Deputy Commissioner, who would become his lifelong friend. Major Buck's first wife had run off with the Austrian ambassador to India, taking her children with her, but within a month after Lawrence Samuel's arrival at Karnal, Buck was recording in his diary, 'To tea with Mr. & Miss Durrell & for a motor drive after.'[20] The next year he was to marry Lawrence Samuel's younger sister Eleanor May. Buck's diary, which he kept devotedly for his nearly thirty years in India, reveals a man methodical, decent, financially resourceful but withal unimaginative – precisely the sort of chap whose wife would leave him for a dashing Austrian diplomat. When Buck later wrote glowing testimonials for his subordinate, he tactfully omitted mentioning his family relationship to Lawrence Samuel.

With a good job and the praise of his superiors to give him confidence, Lawrence Samuel returned to Roorkee in 1910 and married Louisa Florence Dixie, five feet tall and crackling with vitality. Where Lawrence Samuel was serious and earnest, Louisa was a tease, joking and boisterous.

Her eyes were utterly candid and were set far apart in a full face, her mouth unfashionably wide and turned up at the corners even in repose. Louisa's younger sister Ella had shown precocious gifts as a clairvoyant, and Louisa herself was said to be psychic. She certainly believed in ghosts, liked them and was not a bit afraid of them. Once when Louisa was in a remote residence that bordered on a wild forest, the servants told her that there was a lonely *efreet* crying in the night. While the household staff huddled in terror, Louisa trailed out with a lantern, calling as one would to a shy animal, 'Come on, come on.'[21] She was gentle and unpretentious, said Larry: 'I think really at heart she was a Buddhist . . . I have a vague memory of two lamas kissing her feet. Apart from that, she was a bit Mrs Malaprop, with a great sense of fun.'[22] In striking contrast to Louisa, Lawrence Samuel radiated intensity of purpose. His blue eyes were lodged deeply under a high forehead; they formed his most striking feature. For the rest: strong, straight nose, small ears, assertive chin. Although half-hidden by a generous moustache, his mouth was of the sort called full and sensual by romantic novelists. He was tall, and his large, well-formed hands were those of a builder, a maker. Lawrence Samuel inspired confidence in men and adoration in women.

By his education, apprentice training and marriage, Lawrence Samuel was linked with the Punjab, that somewhat indeterminate geographical region defined by the five rivers that drain it: the Jhelum, Chenab, Ravi, Beas and Sutlej, all tributaries of the Indus. The district counted among its major cities Lahore, Lucknow, Amritsar, Jullundur and Simla. Jullundur, where Lawrence Samuel and Louisa moved after the wedding, was named after the mythical demon-king Jalandhara. It was a gritty, featureless town on a flat, featureless plain. In legend the god Siva had heaped mountains upon the fire-spitting Jalandhara, but there was nothing exciting about the actual place. The natives still say, mildly and without bitterness, 'Nothing has ever happened here. There is no past and no present.'[23] In 1912 the town consisted of a brick-and-plaster railway station, a few staff houses, a low compound of attached dwellings for subordinate railway clerks and trainmen, and a sprawl of unpaved streets wandering in every direction with little evidence of plan – people living along the railway and dependent upon it. The railway staff houses were the type of squarish bungalow built for Englishmen in the Punjab: small shuttered windows at street level, a second row of windows at ceiling height so that the terrific heat of the afternoons could exhaust itself, weakly, by convection. This living arrangement was completed by a small veranda, a flat roof on which the family could sit, a sunburnt plot of earth that could be called a garden, an outbuilding that held the kitchen and rooms for a few servants. The station was nearby across the road, and the trains could be felt passing. In such a house, nearly identical to a thousand others across the Punjab, Larry was born.

⩗ Adjacent to the civilian town sat Jullundur Cantonment, the military post, an immense spread of barracks, staff buildings, officers' quarters. All European civilians of professional status were eligible to be members of the Officers' Club, a low building with a colonnade of graceful arches, set amid the flowers of England: sweet peas, snapdragons, tea roses. At the cantonment all was space, order, studied hierarchy. The higher the rank of the officer, the larger the dwelling, the greener and more elegant the garden. St Luke's Anglican Church, dark inside and wider than it was high, with stubby pinnacles rising at every roof corner, and St Patrick's, the nearby Catholic church, stood ready to sanctify the main events of the Europeans' lives. Around the walls of St Luke's were the trophies of the dead, men of the Prince of Wales Leinster Regiment, of the Horse Artillery, of Her Majesty's Cornwall Regiment of Foot: some fallen in the Punjab campaign of 1848 or the rebellion of 1857. A plaque commemorating the wives and children of the Gordon Highlanders, buried in Jullundur over a four-year period, contained 128 names, considerably outnumbering the deceased men of the regiment. It did not speak well for the salubrity of the district.

Although Jullundur lacked pleasant distinction, and although the social opportunities offered by the neighbouring cantonment were virtually identical to those at every other British military outpost in India, Louisa and Lawrence Samuel accepted their lot. The social order was so much like the life both had long known that it had at least the comforting fit of familiarity. There was always someone in the Officers' Mess who had served with Major Samuel Durrell or Captain Fairley, or who had known George Dixie or his father John. The young Durrells acquiesced cheerfully to an established identity. It was this sense of identity that Larry Durrell, like most colonial children who were sent to the mother country, would miss so grievously.

The first two years of Louisa and Lawrence Samuel's marriage coincided with the high point of the Raj: George V and Queen Mary, the Emperor and Empress of India, visited the land for the greatest display of regal ceremony ever seen. The magnificent durbar held outside Delhi on 12 December 1911 was designed to woo the more co-operative Indians with an array of awards and honours; the announcement of the decision – carefully kept secret to heighten its impact – to move the imperial capital from British-built Calcutta to the ancient capital city, Delhi, was intended to soothe the feelings of Indian nationalists. It was public relations on a grand scale, with neither an elephant nor a peacock spared. Louisa and Lawrence Samuel almost certainly did not attend the royal durbar: she was seven months pregnant, and he was in any case far too junior to have been an invited guest. But they would have experienced all the excitement, the pre-durbar drills and projects, the post-durbar celebrations and recapitulations. 'We always had parties during the durbar,' Louisa would recall.²⁴

It turned out to be downhill for the Imperium from then on. Lawrence Samuel, along with nearly every other person of British descent in India, may not have interpreted the signs correctly, but the balance was tipping against India continuing as the most populous part of the Empire; and that shift came in the year of the birth of his first son. The official move of the capital on 1 April 1912 turned out to be, ironically, 'the beginning of the imperial retreat'.²⁵ While the shift to the new site was immensely popular in north-western India, it brought dismay to Bengal, which lost jobs and political importance. On 23 December a bomb tossed into his howdah gravely injured Viceroy Sir Charles Hardinge while he was attempting a triumphal first state entry into Delhi. Each year from then on the perceptive could tick off one or many incidents on the path to Independence. Although the British would doggedly complete Sir Edwin Lutyens' majestic red sandstone Viceregal Palace in New Delhi in 1931, the discerning had long known that the Raj was a dying animal. The Montagu-Chelmsford Reforms of 1921, granting limited self-government to India, would show that the Crown recognized it too.

IN EARLY 1912 THE GREAT EVENTS of the Raj were subjects for earnest conversation, not alarm, in the Durrell household. Louisa's pregnancy was rapidly coming to term, her short stature making her appear like a tea-cosy. 'She swallow mango seed!' joked the servants. Restless Larry began his existence as an uneasy foetus: 'I simply have no belief in my ability to follow a plotted path,' he once wrote, excusing himself. 'I was inconsistent even in the womb my mother tells me.'²⁶ Luckily for Louisa, the cool, dry Riviera season, as it was euphemistically called, was still holding. Finally, Lawrence George Durrell was born at Jullundur on the river Gumti on 27 February. Larry claimed to remember his own birth, or at least the minutes immediately following it, when he was left unattended on a bare, cold table while the doctor looked after his mother. In that shocking moment Larry glimpsed, so he maintained, a monumental loneliness, a cosmic indifference, his castaway's fate. He also claimed that his had been a forceps delivery, botched by an inexperienced woman doctor who had spoiled the shape of his head. Did his pervasive loneliness and occasional attacks of misogyny originate at birth? It seemed reasonable to him. Warming to his subject, he would tell his auditors that he had been left for dead among the bloody towels, where he was discovered, he fervently hoped, reciting the *Bhagavad-Gita*.[27] Larry liked to add that he had been born in the shadow of Mount Everest. Asked by a family friend about the truth of this last assertion, Louisa replied, 'Well, he may have been there, dear, but I certainly wasn't!'[28] To her son she would say, 'But Larry, you were born in Jullundur, a horrible place!'[29]

Like most of Larry's stories, however, his account of his birth contained elements of truth. Louisa had wanted an Indian doctor, but her husband had insisted on bringing in a white woman, who as it turned out had never before delivered a baby using forceps. Larry was quite badly cut about the face and head, and Louisa was furious. After he had been patched up, the doctor carried him back to Louisa and said, approximately, 'Here he is, all nice and clean. I'm sure you'll get used to the fact that he *only has* ten fingers and ten toes.' Louisa, exhausted and befuddled, grabbed Larry and searched for this new deformity, only to realize that the doctor was joking.[30] Fifty years later Louisa would still quiver with rage when telling the story, while throughout his life Larry would ransack Rank's *Trauma of Birth* and other texts on parturition for clues to his psychology. It became an article of faith for Larry that the violent shock of his entry into 'this munching world' – as he would write in *Monsieur* – had given him a terrifying yet privileged insight into the nature of human existence. When he came to write about the birth of his surrogate, Walsh Clifton, in *Pied Piper of Lovers*, Larry would place the event in the countryside near Akyab in Burma, site of his first conscious memories, and render it in nightmare terms. In the fictional version the mother dies, apparently during a botched Caesarean delivery performed by a woman doctor: Larry's vengeance on his mother for abandoning him, an expression of his own imagined orphaned state, and a hint of misogyny.

Shortly after Larry's birth the blistering summer began, and what breeze there was stirred only the rattle of desiccation. A fierce debate ensued about what to name the boy: one faction, evidently Lawrence Samuel and his imposing mother, wanted Samuel Amos, after Larry's paternal grandfather. Louisa resisted 'tooth and nail': 'You can't have his initials spell out SAD, can you?' She won.[31] Larry was baptized on 5 May, the hottest month of the year, in squat, solid, prosaic St Luke's, at a simple off-white marble font to the left of the main portals. This event Larry never claimed to remember.

As the Durrells well knew, restlessness was a condition of railway life. Upon completion of his contract in Jullundur, Lawrence Samuel accepted the position of Engineer-in-Chief of Construction for the Buthidaung-Maungdauw Light Railway in Arakan Burma. In October 1912, with his first-born son growing apace, Lawrence Samuel drew up a formal will. One of the two witnesses to this document was G. C. Bhattacharya, an Indian on the staff of the Jullundur Doab Railway. His choice of witness marked Lawrence Samuel as different from the run of white Anglo-Indians. 'We were completely without colour bar,' Larry always maintained.[32] Lawrence Samuel's prudence in making his will was attested to on 9 November, when Louisa's twenty-three-year-old brother Tom died of typhoid while away on assignment as an Inspector of Works for the railway. He had always been Louisa's favourite among her brothers, and his death cut across her excitement over the move to Burma.

With Lawrence Samuel's will as a nod to mortality, the Durrells departed for Buthidaung off the Bay of Bengal. Arakan Burma, a narrow strip separated from the interior by the Arakan Yoma mountains, extended some four hundred miles south along the coast from Chittagong. Louisa adapted easily to the rustic conditions in the Burmese town. As Chief Engineer, Lawrence Samuel was allotted a large, airy house, but the plumbing arrangements were primitive. All bathing was accomplished in a zinc washtub, using water dipped from a 'Pegu jar', a great earthenware vessel filled daily by water-carriers. Social intercourse was limited in the main to a handful of European families, and well-supplied shops simply did not exist. None the less, Louisa was happiest in Burma, Larry believed. For one thing, she felt drawn to Buddhism, and in the Arakan whitewashed pagodas and hundred-foot spires of stupas were everywhere, on nearly every hilltop and in even the smallest settlements. Each village was under the spiritual guidance of a yellow-robed *hpoongyi* or monk, and it seemed that a shaven-headed holy man was always ready with a blessing.

Arakan Burma was utterly different from the India Lawrence Samuel and Louisa knew. Instead of the Indo-Aryan peoples who dominated the Punjab, they were surrounded by delicately moulded Arakanese, a Burmese Mongoloid stock with rich brown skin, round faces and epicanthic eyes. It was a novel experience for Louisa to be taller than most women she saw. Men and women alike wrapped around their waists bright silk *lungyis*, ankle-length cylindrical skirts folded over at the hips and tucked in. Above their *lungyis* the men wore short single-breasted jackets in more sober hues, while the everyday uniform for the women was completed by long-sleeved white jackets. Looking like gay sunbirds, the men wrapped their heads in a *gambaung*, a strip of thin, coloured silk. Larry's own garb somewhat resembled a *lungyi*: he wore a simple shift, sometimes decorated with embroidery, pulled over his head. The infant Larry was entrusted to a shy Burmese ayah, who stared at the ground in front of her bare toes when in the company of adult Europeans. Durrell described the Burmese as 'smooth-faced, dark-eyed people', gentle, passive.[33] It was not only the bright colours worn by his ayah that Larry would remember: the warm, sweetish odour of the coconut oil with which she anointed her black hair, coiled in a cylinder on her head, became a part of his life.

Larry's father quickly discovered that constructing the Buthidaung-Maungdauw Railway was not going to be an easy task. Many cuts had to be made in the hill sections, much tunnelling through rock, but no suitable indigenous labour could be found. There were already numerous Hindu and Muslim workers from India living in Akyab, the main port and administrative centre of Arakan, but neither they nor the more slender Burmese were equal to the bone-crushing task. Lawrence Samuel imported powerful Pathan hill men from western India, splendid workers but with a reputation for unruliness. He was commended for his 'tact and gentle persuasion' in handling these men. He also found time to remedy his lack of an engineering degree by completing a series of correspondence courses offered by the University of London, and in 1913 he was admitted to Associate Membership in the Institute of Civil Engineers.

Despite their having fought three desperate wars against the British in the nineteenth century, the Burmese in the early 1900s were known for their docility. The Arakanese made delightful companions: they loved cleanliness, sports and a life of ease. They had a strong sense of honour, so that Louisa could be confident that her son would be cherished by the servants whether she was present or not. Their commitment was so absolute that ayahs and personal bearers often slept on a mat across the doorway to the child's room. The Durrells lived in greater isolation than before: mountains and the Bay of Bengal separated them from India, and the absence of trunk railways and even of serviceable roads prevented easy access to the population centres of India or to Mandalay, Rangoon and the broad inhabited plain of the Irrawaddy. The railway line Lawrence Samuel was building would run from the coast some thirty miles inland and would not connect with any other railway. In the full Conradian sense, Buthidaung was an outpost of progress, an up-country way station dependent upon Akyab. By December 1914 Lawrence Samuel had pushed Progress along to such an extent that he was able to report that the headings of the main tunnel, near the summit of the line, had been cut through the obstructing peak.

In so far as the child was aware of the outer world, there were many impressions for Larry's crib-eye perspective of Buthidaung to record. From November until February the winter monsoon blew cool and dry into the valleys from the north-east, so the boy could spend much of his time out of doors. Larry was plump and sturdy, eager to charge on his short legs into every sort of potential harm. He was learning to talk, and if anything he had too much self-confidence. His ayah was kept busy keeping him out of trouble. The world within his reach and sight was enticing indeed. He could pull the tail of the pure white cat that was part of the household. Small, bright green parrots in strictly conjugal pairs dipped and banked into the fruit trees in the garden. The vegetation was rampant and tropical: the rains usually came from June until October, and in the Arakan up to two hundred inches were likely to fall each year. There was always pent-up growth bursting into bloom. Peppermint lilies, climbing moonflowers and bird-of-paradise blooms made lavish displays. The red and orange flower spikes of bromeliads poked up from the branches of host trees. Some of the wildlife invaded the house: moths, snakes, lizards. A sudden, loud 'Tauké!', repeated half-a-dozen times and coming from any conceivable crevice of the room, would be a house gecko, a valuable self-propelled insect trap. Sometimes the child would spot the gecko disappearing in an exaggerated rubbery scuttle behind a framed portrait on the wall, or else traversing the ceiling with adhesive feet. Crickets shrilled and pye-dogs yapped and howled throughout the night; from further off sounded a deeper, more earnest note, the call of the barking deer, most common of the larger wild animals in the Arakan. These sounds would be shut off abruptly when the rain moved in with white lightning and terrific bangs of thunder. The soft slap of the ayah's feet was a welcome sound as she came in response to Larry's summons.

Their isolation blunted for the Durrells the impact of the Great War. At the top levels of the British administration, many had doubted whether the Indians would rally to the defence of the Crown. How wrong they were! The initial enthusiasm for the British cause was enormous, and the greatest support came from Larry's natal Punjab. Thousands of Indians volunteered, the native states equipped a hospital ship, and already on 24 August 1914 the first Indian Expeditionary Force sailed for France, arriving just in time for the terrible slaughter around Ypres. During all this, Lawrence Samuel kept on driving his tunnels through the rock of Burma.

The enormous rains of the Arakan seem to have remained in Larry Durrell's memory, and he would set the opening of his first novel near Akyab. The wet monsoon was menacing, turning the 'cowed earth' into a 'living clot of humidity'. The humans, 'blanch[ed]' by sheet lightning, cower behind 'flimsy matting walls', wearing 'sodden mackintosh[es]' that neither keep them dry nor protect them from chills. Larry recreated also the 'purposeless flying things, beetles, flies, moths' circling the lamps. The threatening land, he said, was 'swarming with life'.[34]

BY NOVEMBER 1915 Lawrence Samuel had returned to India proper and to the employ of the Indian State Railway system, settling in Mymensingh on the hot Gangetic plain north-east of Calcutta. He was named Executive Engineer in charge of the First Division of the Mymensingh-Bhairab line. He was responsible for constructing embankments and causeways, and his main project during 1915–17 was a bridge of nine spans of a hundred feet each over one of the older channels of the Brahmaputra. This would be memorialized as the 'tricky little swine of a bridge' that the protagonist's father builds in *Pied Piper of Lovers*. From Mymensingh rice paddies stretched to the skyline in the east, and towards Dacca the intermittent pulsing escape of steam sounded a dull, soughing note as jute fibre was separated from the pulp in rural factories. Surviving alongside the great cultivated fields, the Madhupur jungle with its population of splendid man-killing tigers extended from north of Dacca into the heart of the Mymensingh district.

Mymensingh was a much larger world for the Durrells than that represented by the thirty miles of the Buthidaung-Maungdauw light railway in Burma. For one thing, the Mymensingh-Bhairab line was not a mere feeder for a small port, but a part of the East Bengal State Railway system. It *went* somewhere: south to Bhairab, to Dacca, north-east to Shillong and on into Assam. Small electric fans blew air across blocks of ice in first-class carriages, and Larry learned to lean his nose against the edge of the ice to snuff up the cooling current. Mymensingh itself was the administrative centre for the largest geographic district in India. None of this meant anything specific to three-year-old Larry, but the people looked different to him – taller, darker – and the tidy jackets and sarongs of the

Arakanese were replaced by the loose cotton shirt-and-trousers of the house servants, the *langotis* of the porters and field labourers. The garden had a new set of hazards, some of which sounded mysterious and terrifying: 'Don't go barefoot, Larry, you'll get *hookworm*!' But his mother did not have much leisure to watch over him: she was expecting her second child any day and was also attempting to settle into their new house. He was left to the care of a new ayah, and in consequence, Larry said, 'My first language was Hindi.'[35] The Burmese tongue vanished from his memory without a trace. The ayah let him follow his whims so long as they were not too dangerous. On his entreaty she would call into the garden the itinerant 'monkey men' who signalled their presence on the road outside with the rapid pat-pat-pat-pat-pat of a pair of tiny drums on a stick, operated by a flick of the wrist. The monkey man led a pair of morose simians, usually macaques, dressed in male and female attire. In response to jerks on their neck chains they would dance to the drums for children; for adult servants, they had another act that Larry was not allowed to see.

Not sheltered as a child in England would have been, Larry grew up familiar with mortality, both fascinated and appalled. The impressions that would flesh out the grotesque elements in *Pied Piper of Lovers* were etched upon his memory: 'Under the tamarind tree, whose branches were knotted all summer in an agony of thirst', he would write, 'the trio of vultures sat, coughing and clawing at the putrescent body of the pariah. They settled their claws in the cracks of the dry earth, and ruffled their wings in an indecent ecstacy of enjoyment . . . . In the heat and the stench their soft noises took on the tones of an awful decorum.'[36] At night the vultures and kites made way for the jackals. Bickering and scavenging, they ranged from the scrub forest into Mymensingh. Their appalling cries filtered into Larry's bedroom, and according to the old hands in the English community what they said was, 'I smell the body of a dead Hindoooo! Where-where-where? Here! Here!'

The retreating monsoon winds brought relatively cool, dry weather, and on 12 November Larry's sister Margery Ruth was born. Any jealousy that Larry might have felt was soothed by his excited anticipation of Christmas. In India the true herald of Christmas in the more prosperous households was the postman delivering the Army & Navy Stores catalogue, usually by the end of October. Each family would spend hours studying the illustrated pages, circling here, underscoring there. Poorer households tended to buy from the competing Whiteaway and Laidlaw's – known as 'Right-away-and-paid-for' – which maintained emporia in Bombay and Calcutta. By the time they reached Mymensingh, the Durrells were probably Army & Navy customers. On Boxing Day, Father Christmas would come to each European community of any size, often riding a camel or an elephant unless it was a railway centre such as Mymensingh: in such cases, naturally, Santa arrived splendidly on a locomotive, amid white steam, hooting and a cloud of sparks.

Their first Christmas in Mymensingh marked a high point for Lawrence Samuel and Louisa. His job was a good one, and his superiors were men he had known and liked before the Burma venture, among them F. R. Bagley, Chief Engineer of the Mymensingh-Bhairab Railway. Cecil Buck had been promoted to Lieutenant-Colonel in the Indian Army and was acting as Deputy Commissioner at Dharmsala. The other members of the Durrell and Dixie families were once more within feasible visiting range. Larry was a sturdy and inquisitive child, and Margery, the new baby, was growing well.

Larry Durrell would cite the 'black Brahmaputra' in a poem of his maturity, 'Last Heard Of', identifying it, with a cavalier inaccuracy of fifteen hundred miles, as the place 'Where I was born and never went back again'. He would recall the dark river with 'stars printed in shining tar',[37] a broad reach of water where on rare occasions the dolphins arced upstream in schools. The upper course of the enigmatic Brahmaputra remained a mystery until the year after Larry left India to study in England, when it was finally traced to the Tibetan source and charted. For the boy, this river, which could measure six miles across near Mymensingh, provided an image of the vast scale of India; the Thames, in contrast, would seem a mere brook. In December of 1916 the Brahmaputra caused Larry's father a lot of trouble by washing out newly constructed bridge foundations and changing course. Larry would recreate this disaster in his description in *Pied Piper of Lovers* of Clifton senior's dream of the collapse of a mud-and-railway-tie embankment: 'In a sudden spasm of fear he screamed for the coolies, the overseer, everyone: and, screaming, began to prop the walls of slime with wooden sleepers . . . . With a jolt the parapet came away and spun past him in eddies of water.'[38] The next January Lawrence Samuel was rewarded for his strenuous efforts with a monthly increment of one hundred rupees, bringing his salary up to the quite substantial Rs 1050 a month, equivalent to £70. Then in March 1917 cholera broke out among the labourers and staff, and Lawrence Samuel had to assume the duties of an ailing junior assistant engineer as well as his own. Larry would remember hearing in the night the painful weak retching of a cholera victim close by the house.

Despite the outbreaks of disease, life remained generally pleasant for Louisa: she pottered about the garden, tried to keep track of the household staff, and entertained. With the birth of each baby, however, Louisa was faced with the formidable worry of keeping the child alive in a country hostile to infants. The immense marshy tract that made up the eastern part of the district was under water for eight months of the year, and it bred fevers and bacteria against which there were no vaccines. Louisa sprinkled Keating's Powder on the sheets to discourage fleas and bathed Larry with translucent Pear's Soap to relieve his prickly heat.

There was much talk of health, as Larry would remember. In his first novel, Doctor Maclean recites the Orient's deadly ailments like a litany: 'Her mind repeated the names as a child repeats verses, without meaning, even without interest: cholera, dysentery, malaria, typhoid, smallpox, bubonic plague . . . was there no end to the catalogue?'[39] Against these diseases the Durrells set the feeble arsenal of the home medicine chest: potassium permanganate, quinine, sal volatile, and for nausea, ipecacuanha wine. Margery Ruth was baptized on 6 February 1916 – and, as if to justify this preparation for a Christian Eternity, suffocated a few weeks later with diphtheria. Burial took place the same day, and the gardeners, following the local practice, collected armloads of white flowers: candytuft and fragrant tuberoses, dianthus, white bougainvillaea, gypsophila. She knew that in India babies often died, yet it was a terrific shock to Louisa: she had been trained before her marriage as a nurse, and she had evidently thought that she could at least keep *her* family healthy. More than ever, she threw her energy into the raising of her next child, Leslie Stewart, born 10 March 1917, just before the summer heat moved in and during the inevitable cholera epidemic. Leslie was indeed sickly, and was the more indulged in consequence: Larry soon recognized his brother as a serious contender for his mother's affection. Fearing for her children, Louisa focused her life increasingly on them, uneasy when social calls took her away. In future, she would make few friends outside the family.[40]

With a new-born son, cholera running its course and a bridge nearing completion, Lawrence Samuel decided that it was time to volunteer for war service. When in April 1917 he asked for a wartime commission in the Royal Engineers to take charge of a Labour Corps of Hindustani-speaking workers in France, Cecil Buck took it as a matter of course that he should do so. Despite enthusiastic endorsements from Buck and from T. R. J. Ward, Inspector-General of Irrigation in India, Lawrence Samuel was not called up to 'do [his] bit in France', as Ward phrased it.[41] Such was Lawrence Samuel's sense of duty towards the ancestral homeland he had never seen that he was probably quite disappointed.

Larry suffered many ailments while the family lived on the hot and germ-ridden plains, including earache, boils and carbuncles, but the most serious was sprue, a wasting and sometimes fatal sickness. For weeks he lost weight and did not respond to the calcium lactate and parathyroid prescribed by the European doctor. Finally Larry's father brought in an Indian physician who suggested a traditional remedy: a daily draught of chicken blood, drained into a glass from a fowl slaughtered in the kitchen. The Durrells were desperate enough to try almost anything and Indian enough not to scorn what an English-born couple might have rejected as mere super-stition. 'I had to swallow that!' Larry recalled with a shudder many years later, holding his glass of *gros rouge* up to the sunlight. Soon young Larry's condition improved, and within a month he was cured. Sahib Durrell nominated the Indian doctor to be a member of his club, but Mymensingh society would not accept what the Durrell family had, and the man was blackballed. Larry's father resigned in fury from the club.[42]

Lawrence Samuel's sponsorship of the Indian doctor was typical of him, and Louisa would gladly entertain in her home people of mixed blood as well. Eurasians were ordinarily shunned both by the pure Indians, who thought they had lost caste by a misalliance, and by the Europeans. 'In my day', Louisa testified, 'it was the Eurasians that they felt most strongly about. We wouldn't be allowed to even play with them by my grandmother. Of course, we always did.'[43] There was considerable talk of Eurasians in the Durrell household, and some of Larry's cousins were rumoured to have Indian blood: 'We were sure that was why they were so tall and handsome,' recalled Larry's sister Margaret.[44]

Little affected by questions of social propriety, the Durrells had plenty of a more ominous nature to concern themselves with. Once, when Larry opened the linen cupboard, a large cobra spread its hood level with his astonished gaze. Retelling the story years later, he would relive the event, eyes round, right hand curved palm outward, cheeks puffed: 'A cobra reared up – Bouf! – like that.'[45] Servants killed the snake, and then for weeks everyone nervously awaited the appearance of its mate. Larry was to write this event into *Pied Piper of Lovers*, except that in the book his *alter ego*, Walsh Clifton, kills the cobra. Larry also saw a mongoose fight a cobra. Such events were commonly arranged by professionals; dark, stringy bearded men in orange robes came to the house bearing baskets of snakes on long poles, with one or two leashed mongooses, their pinkish eyes gleaming, looping their weasel bodies along. The snake men would stage a performance on a small platform or else rid the premises of snakes, as requested. In either case, the confrontation was predictable: the mongoose would provoke the cobra, feint, lunge. There would be a small crunching noise as the lovely assassin bit through the cobra's skull, and then would follow the thumping of its nerve-driven body.

After the Brahmaputra bridge opened for traffic, Lawrence Samuel was assigned to direct a year-long survey of 260 miles of track. By November 1918 he had submitted his report and was ready to begin a tour as Executive Engineer of the Darjeeling-Himalayan Railway, which ran from Siliguri to terminate, fifty-one miles distant and nearly seven thousand feet higher in altitude, at the gabled station facing the Surya Mandir temple in Darjeeling. It was this railway line that was to carry the Durrells to their new home.

They went by steamer to Calcutta, a mesmerized Larry staring down at the thrashing paddle wheel until he became nauseated. Calcutta impressed Larry, both the many 'great houses . . . very tall and made of stone' and a begging leper 'whose skin had peeled off in little white flakes and to whom he gave a rupee'. From magnificence to horror, the range of impressions burned into his memory. The streets were a 'cavalcade' of 'carriages, rickshaws, and trolleys' that rendered the few motorcars almost immobile.[46] For six-year-old Larry the anticipation seemed unbearable as they waited for the evening train to pull out of Howrah Station for the overnight run to Siliguri. He was sure that he would not once close his eyes, but finally the train was moving and the monotony of the bogies tackety-clacking over the joints in the track ate into his wakefulness. Leslie was soon dozing against his mother opposite him, and Larry did not protest when his father lifted him into the hard upper berth. By the time the train was thundering across the mile-long Hardinge Bridge spanning the Ganges, he was sound asleep. On the other side, at Santahar, he suddenly found himself on his feet and being led on to the platform: they had to transfer from the broad-gauge mail train to the northern frontier railway. Larry registered the peculiar 'Boff!-clank-boff!-clank' note of the gawky-looking metre-gauge locomotive. With the dawn came Siliguri and the change to the strangest little train he had ever seen. The shriek of a steam whistle sounded and a blue-painted engine came from the machine house, all hiss and bustle on four close-set wheels, to pick up their train.

Larry decided that, with a saddle-tank for water draped like a howdah over the boiler and topped by a slender smokestack, the locomotives resembled trumpeting pachyderms. These fourteen-ton engines built by Sharp, Stewart & Co. of Glasgow were to be part of his father's charge at Kurseong: 'some ten new little elephants made of steel which he adored', said Larry. 'They were sturdy and very beautiful . . . and marvellous workers.'[47] Although the gauge was a tiny two feet – the smallest in India – the locomotives were quite wide, stood eight feet tall and could haul fifty tons up a steep gradient of one in fifteen. In 1918 the Toy Train, as it came to be called, was the lifeline of the region, and as many as thirty-five scheduled trains a day managed to pass up and down the single track by an intricate dodging in and out of sidings and station yards. The Durrells boarded a First Class coach for some dozen passengers and sat in padded armchairs. The morning heat was beginning so they propped the glass windows open. There was a tiny jerk, and they were off.

The train clicked through the yards and bazaar of Siliguri, drying clothes and market wares brushing against Larry's face as he leaned out of the window as far as his mother's restraining hand would permit. Soon they were clattering across the Mahanaddi Bridge at the top speed of fifteen miles per hour. At Sukna, where a tiger had recently disrupted services by napping on the cement slab before the ticket window, the train paused to take on water. Larry's father told him that he should keep a sharp look-out: there were still bears, wild buffalo, deer, leopards and toddy cats in the Terai forests, and elephants had been known to charge the locomotives. Larry was rewarded by the sight of monkeys in the trees and of a peacock sliding daintily through the underbrush.

After Sukna the climb began, and there was a new sharpness and urgency in the note of the steam exhaust. The firebox blower sent showers of cinders up the smokestack, and soon their hair was stiff with grit. Leslie got a cinder in his eye and howled; Larry felt complacently superior. The track was joined by the Cart Road, which would cross and recross the railway line all the way to Kurseong. The maintenance of the road as well as of the tracks would be part of Lawrence Samuel's responsibility. In the forests of the Terai it was the self-important little train that was the interloper, dwarfed by the lofty, straight trunks of the sal and toon trees, the *Bhutea frondosa*, the wide-buttressed semul hung with red pods, the many tall palms and the giant bamboo. Like the diminutive figures in a painting by Douanier Rousseau, the Durrells in their train moved through the exaggerated forest. The tea plantations, with their precise parallel rows of plants running north-south to catch the maximum sunlight, seemed threatened by the dense stands of elephant grass and the tangled cane-brakes.

24

At 2,800 feet they halted near the Tindharia railway workshops, which had only been in operation since 1914. Tea and coffee emerged on trays from a dark shop. At each stop, railway staff came to greet Lawrence Samuel; in a small way it was like a royal progress, and Larry tingled with pride. His father was very important, so he must be too. Beyond Tindharia the vegetation began to change, and occasional Sikkim pines appeared among the acacias, figs and mimosas. Far below, the Teesta and Mahanaddi rivers flashed silver in the morning light. When the train stopped at Gayabari for more water, Larry and his father got out to walk a few hundred yards up to the Pagla Jhora – 'Mad Torrent' – revetment works, where a mountain watercourse had often washed away both the track and the parallel cart road. Larry's father lifted him aboard the train as it laboured up to them. Beyond Pagla Jhora the scenery became surreal. 'The track ran through landscapes of dreams,' recalled Durrell. 'You had the snows and the mists always opening and closing upon sheer precipices.'[48] So steep were the chasms and ravines that even the laconic railway men termed them 'sensation points'.[49]

Larry found it such a *jolly* train, so tame and so friendly. Boys who lived along the track considered it a plaything, running alongside to leap and cling to the window-sills for a minute's free ride. Larry found himself staring into a grinning face a few inches away, and realized with a start that the boy had the slanting eyes of the hill folk. Like the vegetation, the population was changing with the rise in altitude. Dark Aryo-Dravidians and the Bengalis of the lower Brahmaputra and Balasun valleys gave way to a great variety of Mongol-featured folk. Nepalese women with rings in their noses carried children and produce in baskets suspended over their rumps by bands stretching down from their foreheads; short Nepalese men, the same hardy race that staffed the local police force and the Gurkha regiments, stood about, their heavy-bladed *kukris* stuck in their belts. Tibetans and aboriginal Lepchas spun prayer wheels in their right hands while they carried on their market business within a few feet of the tracks. Lepcha men and women alike often wore their hair in plaits reaching their knees, and their woven costumes were as brightly-hued as the plumage of the Impeyan pheasants that raided the terraced plots of grain. The small, high-coloured mountain women were not veiled and there was no purdah to keep them in seclusion; they gazed back at the Durrells with frank interest.

Finally the Toy Train rounded a sharp ridge and the Durrells found themselves in Kurseong, 'Land of the White Orchid', with Eagle's Crag rising in a gentle slope up to the left. The train, whistle blasting, nudged

25

through the dense pedestrian traffic: market women with loads of fruit and flowers on their heads; Bhutanese mountain porters with loads of honey, furred boots and loom-woven cloth; pack donkeys and mules carrying faggots and charcoal; Buddhist monks in magenta robes; and all the shopping population of Kurseong – Lepchas, Gurkhas, a few lanky plains dwellers, occasional white men wearing tailored military uniforms or else the khaki suits, puttees and bow ties of tea planters.

After a round of greetings at the offices of the railway, the Durrells and some of their luggage were loaded on to a pony cart for the half-mile trip to their lodgings. They followed the railway line to St Helen's Convent and turned right, taking a switchback road two hundred yards uphill, past the numbered bungalows of the European and Anglo-Indian railway staff. The driver doubled back between massive stone gateposts and before them stood Emerald Hall, 'a house as old as the Lucknow Residency' of Mutiny fame and 'very nearly as dilapidated'. Larry remembered it as 'a crumbling fortress . . . spread over a level jut of the hillside above the town, squinting down at right angles upon the pink and white straggle of newer houses'. He would describe the house as 'detached and cynical, as incongruous and striking as a museum would be in a mining colony', with 'massive cornices' and 'peeling scabs of stucco' like some 'garish relic'.[50] The house was a patchwork of various odd angles and bay windows; a wide downstairs veranda and a glassed sitting room above it both afforded slanting views of the Himalayas over a spur of Senchal Mountain. To the north-west of the house was an overgrown garden dominated by the pendant white, trumpet-shaped flowers of sentinel nightshade, and just outside the front gate was a tennis court for the railway staff. Visible through the militant cryptomeria cedars and the sensual eucalyptus planted by the British along the road, the tea gardens of the rolling Balasun valley showed a deep green through the haze. On the hill-spurs beyond, rendered tiny by the distance, Larry could descry the narrow brick houses of the tea planters who made up most of the district's permanent European population of some three thousand. Further up the slopes the vegetation changed to evergreens, and far beyond the ridge-tops, to the grey-brown rock and the white snowfields of the Himalayas.

Kurseong numbered only five thousand inhabitants, but it had a good spring-fed water supply, a library, Anglican and Catholic churches, a club with a small ballroom. One of Larry's memories of the uplands was the intensity of the storms: sheet lightning and terrific rainfall, almost as much as they had known in Burma, averaging 165 inches per year at Kurseong, with deluges of five inches in as many hours not uncommon. A more pleasant recollection was the view from Eagle's Crag, a walk of half a mile from the centre of Kurseong up through tea gardens. Spread out below the Crag like patterns on a topographical map but sounding their muffled thunder, the Balasun and Teesta rivers altered with the seasons, 'curdled and jade-green in winter, tooth-white and broad in summer' in Larry's description.[51] In the early morning the landscape tones rose with the sun 'from pastel shades of fawn and stone-grey to the sharp slate-green below the snows'.[52] A frieze of white peaks dominated the skyline. Larry could make out his own house above the railway staff section. Without being conscious of it, the boy was being trained in acute observation and opened to beauty. Like his half-forgotten Burmese nurse, his new ayah, Kasim, was Mongol-featured, but glittering and jingling with an array of ear-rings, nose-rings, silver bangles, brass anklets. She was Nepalese and she taught him songs of the hill-folk, showed him how to dissolve leeches from his limbs with a pinch of salt, and told him that the donkey urine he saw being collected in bottles was used for tanning leather. Sometimes she took him several miles up Dow Hill to the Victoria Boys' School, set in a grove of oaks.

Another walk within range of Larry's young legs was to the native cemetery, destination of the processions that passed Emerald Hall heralded by quavering blasts on conch shells. Vultures and choughs picked over the burning ghats and the exposed corpses. The ayah fled in a diminishing tinkle of jewellery when Larry found a white ankle bone among the ashes, but the boy was fascinated. To judge from his fictional re-creation of the incident, he felt that 'he had been suddenly brought face to face with the meaning of death'; it 'gave the idea of death a defined and unforgettable identity', and for weeks his mind was filled with 'morbid speculations and doubts'.[53] Although the memory would stay with Larry for the rest of his life, the tangible ankle bone seemed more real yet less appalling to the child than the Christian visions of death.

Close though Larry quickly became to Kasim, from time to time the broad cultural gulf that perforce existed between them showed itself. Once when his shadow came across the ayah's food, she angrily threw it away. To the boy, it was incomprehensible that his mere shadow could render a meal of curry and *chapattis* unclean.[54] Also he found that, when playing with Indian children – with the possible exception of those standing high in wealth and caste – there were always barriers of status and, however much he tried to deny it, of colour. The recurrence of such small events would add up to the conviction in Larry's mind that he could not be truly Indian.

Kurseong itself was a boy's paradise: there were trails to be explored, wild-looking men with great knives and muskets, new animal and insect life. There were magnificent lepidoptera to be collected, blue, yellow, brown swallowtails, admirals, fritillaries, the spectacular peacock butterfly, enormous moths. The pendulous flowers of toxic nightshade made the moths drunk on their scent, and giant flying fox bats swung down to fallen fruit at dusk. Larry became intensely aware of the fantastic life around him: 'Half a dozen different varieties of beetle, ranging from the walnut-sized coprophagous one to the sheeny grey-green rose-beetles. Caterpillars were enormous, banded with every colour of the rainbow'[55] – these were among Larry's memories. Apparently he was already conscious of the act of remembering, writing later of the young Walsh Clifton, 'he would be trapped in a mood of clear memory-images', overwhelmed by 'the terrible lucidity of his memories', the archival stuff of fiction.[56] Giving to Walsh his own sensibility, Larry would write: 'One minute he would be teasing a nest of red ants with a twig and the next he would see the whole panorama of his adventures roll out before him on the brown earth, like a picture-show . . . . His dark eyes would widen as he impressed upon himself the astonishing importance of these visions and, correspondingly, the huge importance of himself.'[57] Over all Larry's explorations and musings hovered the protecting shadow of Kasim. For his more boisterous pleasure, Larry's father bought him a small white pony and he was allowed to go on rides, escorted by a syce, with the son of an Indian hill-raja, a boy near his own age.

A threatening event for Larry was his mother's new pregnancy, becoming daily more apparent. His father seemed all too interested in the event, and was heard to exclaim, 'Oh Louie, *do* give me a girl!'[58] To Larry, perhaps grimly mindful of little Margery, dead in Mymensingh, this was nothing short of treasonous. Lawrence Samuel engaged a governess, a thin, dry Irish Catholic who was very likely the pattern for the 'gaunt' disciplinarian in *Pied Piper of Lovers*, a rather pathetic creature whose teeth 'could be levered out with the aid of a forefinger'. This humourless individual, having displaced Larry's ayah, evidently had nothing better to do than to prevent his roaming about, to give him lessons to learn and prayers to say. Larry sensed, like his creation Walsh Clifton, 'with that intuitive conviction of boyhood, that this was but the beginning'.[59] Many years later, Larry would date his 'descending' into 'the long sad river of [his] growth' from his seventh year: the end of his 'perfect idleness', of his innocence[60] – and of the beginning of his unhappiness. To be sure, there was an element of hyperbole in this pronouncement: Larry would not be unrelievedly miserable from the age of seven. However, masked by the teasing irony of his mature introspection was a very real linking of education with compulsion, with loss of freedom. Most children would have responded with a few sulks and tantrums, and then settled more or less cheerfully into the new routine. Not Larry: he turned inward, concealing his distress under a show of co-operation. His parents, he felt, had delivered him over to torment. Very well, he would harden himself and bear it, but his confidence in the father and mother whom he had trusted without reservation was subtly eroded. He was learning the defence of silence. It was the beginning not so much of his unhappiness as of the formation of a tough protective shell around his feelings, and this would have serious consequences for his adult relationships.

In fact Larry was receptive and eager for all kinds of knowledge, only it must not be dished up in such a way as to bore or confine him. Like Walsh Clifton, who 'learned to read with astonishing rapidity',[61] Larry quickly absorbed a store of printed words, and this unlocked Kipling's *Jungle Book* and the Henty, Ballantyne and other children's adventure stories on the bookshelves. In such novels as *The Lion of St Mark* and *With Clive in India*, Henty endowed the 'English boy' with the virtues of athletic skill, respect for parental authority, and adulation of 'the greatest empire the world ever saw'.[62] The 'lavishness of colour' of illustrated magazines also attracted Larry. His mother – when he could capture her attention – indulged him, but his father could be impatient. Larry has John Clifton in *Pied Piper of Lovers* slap his son for cutting pictures for his scrap-book from an unread *Times of India*, and then send the 'bewildered' boy up to his room. Very probably Larry, already an inveterate scrap-book keeper, had a similar encounter with Lawrence Samuel. Larry 'withstood downright anger fiercely', while 'gentle reproof' reduced him to 'agonized shame'. When in disgrace, Larry would slip out alone to climb a eucalyptus tree that overhung the railway. 'Little waves of shame would run over him; he would breathe more quickly, brokenly, and lay his head against the soft bark of the tree; his small arm would tighten fiercely about the trunk. At such times he seemed to draw a reserve of strength from the rustling life of the tree.' Concealed high on his leafy perch, 'the silky bark against his cheek', he would shout insults at the sand-boys clinging to the cowcatchers of the locomotives.[63] This is the common stuff of boyish rages and recoveries, but in Larry's case the sense of anger and betrayal against his father would linger past adolescence.

Larry adored and patronized his mother, confident in her love and in his ability to get his way with her. With his father he seems always to have felt insecure, and the feeling was apparently reciprocated. Larry clearly yearned for his father's companionship, and in *Pied Piper of Lovers* father and son are frequently 'arm-in-arm laughing and talking', 'hand in hand', or with Walsh 'gripping his father's wrist'. Yet in the same scenes Larry attributed to John Clifton an 'acute sense of guilt' over his son's loneliness.[64] Larry came to distrust his father's plans for him, 'smiled' and responded, like his character Walsh, with 'perfect dissimulation'.[65]

Unable to connect fully with his son, Larry's father seemed to have energy for everything active. He played tennis regularly and took part in amateur theatricals at the club. He was always ready for a costume party, and once he dressed as a pierrot and sang 'Wallah Walloo' to great applause. When Louisa did not feel like going out in the evenings, he sometimes went to dances alone, and she would chide him if she heard that he had danced with 'certain women'. Increasingly, Louisa turned to her children and called herself a 'home-body'. With their rise in status her sense of domestic propriety increased, and when Lawrence Samuel hugged her she would push him away gently and say, 'Oh, not in front of the servants, dear.'[66]

Margaret Isabel Mabel was born on 4 May 1919, and Lawrence Samuel gained the daughter he had wanted. More and more, Larry was given over to the governess, who made him read and work out sums daily. When she chastised him he would fly into a choking, white-faced rage. Remembering the woman and his dislike of her, Durrell has Walsh settle the score with *his* governess: 'She had smacked him fiercely on several occasions and once he had retaliated, hitting her on the nose with his chubby fist.'[67] It seems likely that during this period Larry also attended some lessons at Goethals' Memorial School, about half a mile and a half up the railway line from the Durrells' home.[68]

The governess was not the only blemish on Larry's happiness. His 'Big Granny', Dora Maria Durrell, arrived in a *dandy*, carried up from the station on the shoulders of a pair of grunting Bhutanese. She horrified him, from her plump, purplish hands to her constant talk about death and her invocations of God. Maliciously, Larry would later sketch her portrait in *Pied Piper of Lovers*:

With the summer came Grandmamma, and with Grandmamma came the plague; both calamities, coming as they did, at exactly the same time, became indissolubly linked in the boy's mind as a double-headed evil . . . . Grandmamma was . . . securely entrenched behind the illusory fiction of her God . . . . She was squat, immense, and obese. . . . She walked, like a spirit of parasitic evil, about the house, murmuring texts and maxims.[69]

This fictional Grandmamma told her grandson to 'sit near your old granny who hasn't got long to live' and explained to him that it took ten years for the worms to eat through the coffin. Larry's Big Granny would hug him against her Twilfit corset, tell him that he was a little sinner for whom hell had exquisitely painful torments, and then make him kneel down to pray. As soon as he could, he would escape to scour the traces of powder from his face. She would give him tracts to read in which 'the questions revolted him nearly as much as the thought of God did'.[70] The boy feared and hated her, and in retaliation Durrell-the-writer would wonder, 'Why did Grandmamma smell like a lama?'[71]

Big Granny was not the only domineering woman in the family. Larry must have been apprehensive when he was told that Aunt Muriel, his father's youngest surviving sister, was coming for a visit. In due course the boy heard an uproar at the gate, a woman's shrill, angry voice cutting through the plaintive responses of a native. Safely concealed behind a bush, Larry watched while the newcomer, her full face red and perspiring, berated the carriers, in Hindi and English, for wanting to charge her an extra two annas for the ride uphill from the station. Finally she lashed out with her umbrella, putting the Bhutanese porters to flight. Then she spotted Larry and advanced on him, her outsized breasts swaying, calling him by name. He fled to the house, hoping that this alarming creature was not his aunt. Never had he been more wrong in a first impression: Muriel Pearce turned out to be immense fun. Warm, generous, broad-minded, outspoken, she soon won Larry's confidence, and he would give her a guardian spirit's role as Walsh's Aunt Brenda in *Pied Piper of Lovers*.

Between bouts of shyness, Larry was naturally gregarious. When he was about seven he told his mother that he had a girl-friend, and that she accompanied him on his explorations. His parents were amused to hear him explain to the girl, in the most serious voice, 'I'm so sorry I can't walk you on Sunday, but I have to take my family out.'[72]

Lawrence Samuel took his family on many excursions: rides and walks in the Teesta Valley, visits to Buddhist monasteries on days of special services, and once as far as Kalimpong on the old trading route to Sikkim.[73] Sometimes he arranged a family outing to Ghoom, where he had a work party easing the track gradient by constructing the Batasia Loop, in which the track circled back once over itself in a spectacular feat of railway engineering.[74] Ghoom was a small village at the apex of the Toy Train's run, and it was an important market centre for the region, serving even the herders and craftsmen from Bhutan. The Bhutias, as Larry always called the Bhutanese, fascinated him: burly men and large-boned women, both sexes with their hair cropped short. They were a turbulent, noisy, cheerful people who loved gambling. The men sported ear-rings and wore wide-sleeved mantles, snow boots and fur-trimmed caps of every conceivable shape. The women were festooned with gold and silver worked into turquoise-studded belts, necklaces, bangles and chains. To Larry, Ghoom seemed Himalayan, and he was to draw the scene in all its cultural variety in *Pied Piper of Lovers*:

The mountaineers were there, great swarthy fellows, swaggering about in their sheepskin cloaks and boots: whose lives were spent driving their caravans back and forth through the heavy passes into the remotest parts of Tibet and Nepal; the Lepchas had covered the main street with a forest of poles upon the tops of which fluttered the strips of calico covered with propitiatory prayers to the demons. The grave-faced lamas walked in deep meditation; clicking their beads, or muttering. If you listened carefully you could hear the clicking of the Chinese tongue being spoken by some of these as they walked down the crowded bazaar among the chattering Nepalese women with their Mongoloid faces a-glitter with rings.[75]

Followed by a bearer balancing Louisa's heavy tiffin basket on his head, the Durrells would double back along the railway track and leave Ghoom, taking a well-defined path up past a small Buddhist monastery. An immense prayer-wheel stood under a painted roof in the forecourt of the temple, and from behind the red doors of the monastery often came the droning notes of straight copper tubas and the deep quarter-tones of the chanting monks. Two miles of fairly steep uphill gradients through pastures and pine forests brought them to the grassy truncated ridge of Senchal Mountain – 'Hill of Mists' in Tibetan – where a few years previously there had been an army barracks. Only the water tank of the cantonment remained. Now, improbably, the nine holes of the Ghoom golf links lay before them on the sloping plateau. Lawrence Samuel would urge his family across the fairways and on for another mile through chestnuts, laurels, magnolias and rhododendrons up towards the summit of Tiger Hill at 8,515 feet. Just below the peak they would pause at a brick-sided reservoir that formed a reflecting pond for a shrine. A path led a hundred yards around the hillside to several grottoes decorated with tridents, the sign of Siva the Destroyer and also the Generator, the god of Fire and Sun. Tiny golden ground squirrels and greenish-brown birds fed boldly on the rice left for the deity. Banded cuckoos, angling their quizzical heads for a better view, watched them from the tree rhododendrons. Such was the peacefulness of the place that it would cost them an effort of will to leave the sheltering twilight of the grottoes and ascend the remaining few hundred yards. Half the horizon was ringed by the white ranges of Sikkim, Nepal and Bhutan, of the Chola peaks and, farther still, Chumularhi Mountain in Tibet. When luck was with them they would see Everest glowing through a window in the clouds over one hundred miles distant, beyond armchair-shaped Makalu Peak. Below and to the south lay the Teesta, Balasun, Mahanaddi and Mechi rivers; to the north, the Rangeet River cut through its own deep valley, seven thousand feet down. Durrell was speaking for his younger self when he gave to Walsh Clifton, standing on Senchal Mountain, a halting realization of the magnificence of the Himalayan borderlands: 'It's so enormous, isn't it? I never realized the . . . the whole country was so lovely before . . . I . . . should like to live here all my life.'[76]

WHILE THE DURRELLS WERE LIVING an idyllic existence in Kurseong, a significant shift was occurring in British-Indian relations. Ironically, it was their loyal service in the First World War that gave the Indians a new perspective on their overlords. The stories that the survivors brought back from muddy France and little England damaged irreparably the mystique of the imperial masters: Europeans fought with the same barbaric savagery that they condemned in India; and England was not the vast and impressive country that the durbars staged in India had led them to expect – it boasted no wild elephants, no Himalayas, no Taj Mahal or Golden Temple, no Ganges. Then in 1919, just after the Armistice and following the beating of an English woman doctor, Brigadier-General Reginald Dyer ordered his troops to open fire on an unarmed crowd of pilgrims in Amritsar, holy city of the Sikhs: by the time he gave the cease-fire, 1,650 rounds had been expended, 1,500 persons lay dead or injured. Dyer and his troops had been rushed to Amritsar from the Jullundur Cantonment that the Durrells knew so well. Rabindranath Tagore renounced his knighthood and Gandhi returned his Kaiser-i-Hind – Emperor of India – and Zulu War medals, declaring his *satyagraha* or 'insistence on truth' movement. The Congress Party ceased to co-operate with the government. From then on, the days of the Raj were counted in protests, strikes and boycotts. The same year, too late to deflect the more radical nationalist aspirations, the India Act outlined a gradual progression to self-government along Dominion lines.

In 1920, the year after the Amritsar massacre, Larry's father resigned from the Darjeeling-Himalayan Railway and moved the family to Jamshedpur, centre of India's fledgeling steel industry, where that September he established a construction firm. The Parsee industrialist Sir Jamsetji N. Tata, after whom the town had been named, would devote a good part of his fortune to developing the Indian steel industry. When Lawrence Samuel chose Jamshedpur, he had picked the right industry, the right associations and the right time for his venture: Sir Thomas Holland, Director of the Geological Survey of India, was to declare in 1923 that 'without steel manufacture on a large scale and, therefore, for the near future at least without the Tata Steel Company, there can be no national India, and all political reforms must be non-productive'.[77] In 1922 the Tata company would benefit from the imperial government's policy of encouraging and protecting certain developing Indian industries against home country competition. A special act shielded tin plate products against imports from Wales, and Lawrence Samuel would be awarded the contract to build the Tinplate Company factory in Jamshedpur. For entrepreneur Lawrence Samuel, it was a chance to do well for himself yet, ironically, at the same time to move India towards the industrial independence that would speed the end of British India, the system that had nurtured him.

Lawrence Samuel chose as two of his business partners a pair of Sikhs, Buradur Singh and Sardar Kundan Singh, and he invited his brother-in-law John Dixie, also an engineer, to make up a fourth. Sardar Kundan Singh was a wealthy man who was already in the construction business, and it is probable that the two Indian partners put up most of the capital. 'Sardar' was an honorific title that Kundan Singh wore with as much dignity and ease as his immaculate turban, and he and the stern-faced Lawrence Samuel made an impressive pair. Many of the Sikhs were big men, and their turbans made them look even taller. They tended to be fanatically neat about their personal appearance, and drinking and smoking were against their religion. Sikhs were known for their technical aptitude and many became mechanics, locomotive engineers and electricians for the British. It was a Sikh contemporary of Durrell & Co., Sardar Sohan Singh Sokhi, who held the vital ice-making franchise for Jamshedpur.[78] What would life at the Club be like without cool tonics and whisky and sodas? Strong men blanched at the thought.

The move to Jamshedpur was significant for the entire family: a new job and independent responsibilities for Lawrence Samuel, a shift from an established community to a raw, unfinished town for Louisa. They would have to give up the comfort and beauty of hill-station life for the hot plains four hours by train east of Calcutta. The only hills visible near Jamshedpur were some low natural ridges and the growing heap of slag from the steel-processing plants. The railway cuttings west of the town revealed the ore-bearing red clays that drove the creation of the town. Large sections of the planned residential section were little more than roughed-out road crowns and lines of surveyor's stakes when the Durrells arrived. To shield him from the fierce sun of the plains, Larry was kitted out with an enormous and heavy pith helmet. A short-sleeved white shirt, a pair of wide shorts, knee-length socks and solid leather shoes completed his garb. Sweat soaked into his helmet-band and plastered his shirt to his back, but he stayed well covered out of doors: the dangers of sunstroke and sunburn had been drummed into him. There was a rough frontier atmosphere to Jamshedpur, and the wildlife had not yet vanished. One of the engineers became something of a local legend when he emerged from his tent early one morning, shaving mug in hand, to be accosted by a striped hyena which he dispatched with his revolver.

Lawrence Samuel knew that it was time for his first-born to pick up some regular schooling, and he resolved to place Larry at St Joseph's College, the Jesuit-run school in Darjeeling. As Lawrence Samuel no doubt presented the case to Louisa, sending Larry to St Joseph's would contribute to his education and coincidentally to his good health: Larry had indeed been ill down in the plains at Mymensingh, and Jamshedpur, although somewhat higher and much drier, was still subject to extreme heat. Darjeeling was known as 'the children's paradise' because the young were reputed to be healthier there than anywhere else in India.[79] Not having a rebuttal for this, Louisa acquiesced. Larry's own thoughts about being sent away to school must have been sombre indeed. Clearly, he knew that it would mean a further erosion of his freedom, a submission to the discipline of strangers, and above all the loss of the family circle. His mother had let him down, he felt, and he turned a fierce jealousy against Leslie and Margaret who would remain with her.

DESPITE HIS FOREBODINGS, when the trip to Darjeeling actually began Larry must have felt a tremendous excitement at returning to the hills, at recognizing and hailing friends as the Toy Train fought its gallant way up to Ghoom and beyond. From the station in Darjeeling his school trunk, a wooden box with the lid secured by a hasp, was loaded on to a pony cart for the gently sloping downhill run two miles around the ridge to the school. On 28 February 1921, the day after his ninth birthday, Larry was enrolled in the Third Standard of the Primary Department, skipping the lower standards: apparently the lessons of the governess had done some good.

St Joseph's College was situated on a large terrace cut into the slope of North Point Ridge and the boys proudly referred to themselves as North Pointers. While the school motto *Sursum Corda* – 'Lift up your hearts' – came from the Holy Mass, the words must have struck Protestant Larry as being wildly appropriate to the place. The school faced a whole panorama of Himalayan peaks. Down below St Joseph's was Bhutia Basti, the village of the Bhutanese on the Rangeet Road, and near it rose a large *chorten* or Buddhist shrine ringed with prayer-flags on tall bamboo poles. Further on stood a Buddhist monastery bright with reds, yellows and greens and fronted by ranks of prayer wheels. Here dwelt some of the lamas Larry saw passing the gates of St Joseph's on their way to the shrines and temples of Darjeeling, and it was from a lama at the Bhutia Basti monastery that, two years before, W. Y. Evans-Wentz had procured the manuscript of the *Bardo Thödol*, the Tibetan *Book of the Dead*, that he would edit and help translate into English. Larry the schoolboy probably had no inkling of this, but in later years after the *Bardo Thödol* had become important to his thought, the adult man would ascribe great significance to his glancing contacts with the Bhutanese holy men.

The school was a safe mile through a forest from the edge of the town itself; while the older boys might slip off for whatever adventures they could rouse in Darjeeling, it is doubtful that young Larry often got away from St Joseph's except on arranged outings up Birch Hill Road to the Natural History Museum, to the Lloyd Botanical Garden, and to athletics meetings at St Paul's School. None the less, the contact that he did have with the important hill station impressed Larry.

Darjeeling was five times the size of Kurseong and far more cosmopolitan. The town contained a turreted Victorian Government House, an American Methodist Mission besides the usual churches and a mosque, and a large Amusement Club with a ballroom and stage; and it had the jewellers, tailors and millinery shops that went with a fashionable resort. With his parents, Larry visited the Planters' Club set on a ridge overlooking the town, where guests took tea under the mouldering dark heads of hunting trophies. Some of the newer hotels were quite grand, especially the Mount Everest, with half-timbered dormer windows surmounting three storeys of elegant rooms.

Many of the vacation villas of Indian Civil Service personnel and of wealthy English businessmen were frank imitations of cottages set in rural retreats in the home country, and the gardens stressed English flowers in preference to native varieties. Beds of bright violets, scarlet anemones, yellow primroses, petunias and pansies surrounding stands of tea roses were given pride of place over bird-of-paradise and flowering ginger, over baskets of yellow cymbidium and lavender vanda orchids. Imported cedars grew beside towering native magnolias and golden rain trees.

The tame English gardens presided over by English wives served to emphasize by contrast Darjeeling's frontier location. The Tibetan New Year was celebrated by the Tibetans and Bhutanese during February with 'devil dances' to round, two-faced drums, exhibitions of swordsmanship and potations of *kudo*, a liquor distilled from millet seed, and of potent *chang*, fermented from barley. The devil dancers themselves stalked about the streets, older men with pleated, fanned-out head-dresses and striped shawls, in gowns with long, loose sleeves that made them resemble giant birds when they whirled and strutted. The grimacing masks they donned for the ceremonies seemed to Larry more comic than terrifying. Lamas swung by in robes reaching down to their boot-tops, round or conical hats fixed above inset eyes. 'It was an uncanny world of strangely conflicting emanations in feeling, thought, atmosphere,' said Larry. 'You smelt Tibet!'[80]

Non-Catholics were given a 'strictly secular and not religious instruction' at St Joseph's. 'We were about forty Protestants, Taoists, Indians, and so on,' Larry would recall. 'So I can say I was brought up by Jesuits, though only as an out-patient so to speak!'[81] Protestant boarders were supposed to attend the Church of England Sunday services up the hill in Darjeeling proper. The college itself was not broodingly parochial and there were few religious decorations: a winged angel guarding a boy stood on a varnished wooden pedestal in a shallow alcove in the Small Dorm where Larry slept, and a blue-robed Mary held the Child under a window arch facing the centre courtyard. Then one day Larry wandered into the 'chill and hallowed semi-darkness'[82] of the small chapel and was confronted by a 'life-size figure of Christ crucified hanging over the altar, liberally blotched with blood and perfectly pig-sticked and thorn-hatted'. The gloom and the echoing shadows added to his horror. Not rationally but intuitively, he suspected that Christians who invoked this 'doom-laden symbol' were 'sadists and cannibals'.[83] This sentiment gained force with the years, as Larry confirmed his early rejection of Christianity.

The Jesuit fathers themselves, however, were kindly, tolerant, conscientious. While the strap could on occasion be employed by the Prefect of Discipline, caning had disappeared from St Joseph's in the 1890s. In middle age Larry was still referring fondly to Father Joseph de Gheldere, the Rector, and to Father J. Paulus, the Procurator, Belgians like all the Jesuits at the college – the Belgian Jesuits had been given charge of Catholic education in northern India. All but two of the nineteen fathers wore beards, and there was a warm humanity in the black-robed men that Larry would later discover in many Greek Orthodox priests. Father de Gheldere had become Rector the year before Larry enrolled; he was only forty-four, a tall figure who ran the school from a bare, frigid office on the ground floor. He was known not only for his firmness but also for the personal interest he took in all the students. Father Paulus wore round glasses, and his white Vandyke beard, melancholy visage and long nose gave him the air of a martyr in a painting by El Greco. Yet to Larry he was the 'small boy's hero', for he could whistle, tell outrageous jokes with a straight face, and carve boats using his bone-handled knife. Another popular master, Father Denis Laenen, was a cheerful man with disproportionately short legs who had the habit of addressing each and every student as 'my best friend', only to enquire as the lad retreated, 'What is that boy's name?'[84] He may have been Durrell's inspiration for the comic Brother Gossamer, 'a little crow of a man', in *Pied Piper of Lovers*.[85] It was Edward H. Fitzgerald, however, secular bachelor and long-time Master of the Lower Standard, who had direct charge of young Larry. Everything was pinched and spare about Fitzgerald: receding hairline, narrow face tapering down from a high forehead, scarce-visible sandy eyebrows over stern, sorrowful eyes, glasses with black wire frames, little moustache, sloping shoulders. He lived in a pair of tiny cubicles opening on to the Small Dorm, a large room into which were crowded, iron bedstead touching iron bedstead, more than a hundred students, their ages running from seven to eleven. School legend has it that Mr Fitzgerald was never known to smile, and no doubt he had his reasons: in 1921 one of them was the measles epidemic that swept the Small Dorm. Larry remembered him as 'morose' and said that 'he was a bit too silent to be really popular'.[86]

Although the Primary Department was run quite separately from the rest of the school, everyone followed practically the same schedule six days of the week. The rising call came at 5.45, and the young boys began the day by washing at some fifty cold-water enamelled sinks under the windows facing west on to an inner court. At 6,800 feet, even though it rarely snowed, cold-water ablutions were no joke. The students dressed from clothes lockers that stood in a straight double rank, back-to-back, behind the sinks. Reveille was followed half an hour later by morning prayers and at 7 by *chota hazri*, a 'small meal'. Then until 3.30 in the afternoon there were classes, study periods and two gymnasium sessions – all this, with only one 'breakfast-recreation' hour-and-a-half starting at 11. Two and a half hours were set aside in the afternoon for dinner and recreation, and at 6 began another two hours of study and reading until supper time. At 6.30 Larry, with the entire Primary Department, was marched off for 'Music'. On Wednesday, Saturday and Sunday afternoons an hour was designated for hot baths. Even on Sundays the planned activities ran from 7.30 in the morning for twelve hours and included two study-and-drawing classes. Visitors were allowed on Wednesdays, Saturdays and Sundays, but only during specified hours. Any 'light literature' brought in was subject to the approval of the Prefect, and even then it was not supposed to be shared. The routine and the control must have come as a shock to Larry.

The boys in Primary had their own classrooms and refectory. There was supervised homework in the Primary Standard Study Hall, where each student had a desk with a top hinged in two halves like a cantilever bridge, the books stored under padlock. Some boys kept enormous stag beetles in their desks, and a favourite prank was to attach one of these to the back of the master's gown; then everyone would watch in suspense as the insect laboriously climbed towards his neck. The desks and varnished benches were fixed to the floor in double rows, and the front of each straight-backed seat folded up for access. The Rules demanded that in study rooms 'perfect silence will be strictly enforced',[87] an impossible goal for a hundred boys, each within a foot of his neighbour.

The Primary Standard athletic field, the level expanse between the main façade of the college and the steep bank rising up North Point Ridge, was devoid of grass, and there were skinned knees from falls on the packed sand. A steep grassy bank near by made an impromptu slide, and it was so popular among the younger boys that North Pointers were identifiable by the shiny greenish seats to their otherwise neat uniforms. The mandatory games and informal exercise did not prevent Larry from retaining the plump physique so evident in the class picture taken during his first year. One reason for his rotundity was the arrival on Wednesdays of the 'box-wallah' with a 'huge purple cabin trunk of tin'. This the box-wallah opened with a long key in the middle of the playing field, revealing tray upon tray of sweetmeats. 'The taste of those "jelabys" (how spelt) still remains with me,' wrote Larry. 'Only my mother could make them quite as well.'[88]

The curriculum was rigorously applied and was equivalent to that offered at the better English public schools. Larry must have attempted the full programme for the Third Standard. This meant that he was subjected to Longman's *Junior School Grammar*, Chambers' *Readers*, the first volume of *The Golden Book of English Verse*, Vere Foster's *Copy Books*, Pendlebury's *Arithmetic*, *The Granville History Reader* and *The Raleigh Geography Reader V*. As a non-Catholic, Larry was excused from Catechism, and he was not importuned with proselytizing either.

St Joseph's may have been run by Belgians, but the boys were made aware of the close ties that held India to England. They were encouraged to see England, and indeed all Europe, as wondrous places, almost akin to Heaven. During Larry's first year at the college, Father de Gheldere dedicated a magnificent new marble altar to the old boys killed in the Great War. The list of the fallen amounted to twenty-six names on two brass plaques, mostly lieutenants of the first or second rank who had 'gallantly rallied to the call of the Mother Country' and had died in France or in Mesopotamia. It was a long roll of honour for a small school.

The pedagogy was very sound, but the most telling impression Larry carried away was of the distant peaks: 'Each morning through the dormitory windows the Himalayas would loom up out of the shadows. It was a surprise every time. How could one ever get used to that?' The early sun tinted the snows with the most delicate rose and amber shades, set against a sky of the purest blue. Even more unforgettable were the rare double rainbows, reflected from the hovering clouds. Larry liked to claim, 'I have seen the peak of Everest from the foot of my bed in a gaunt dormitory in Darjeeling!'[89] Sometimes he added a qualifying statement: 'Mount Everest was always behind its shield of clouds. I can't have seen the Roof of the World more than twice a year.'[90] Here was an innocent example of fiction revising reality: Larry *wanted* to remember it that way. Everest is not visible from any point in Darjeeling, and although Kanchenjanga and many other summits can indeed be seen from the north-facing Upper Form dormitory windows, Larry's Primary Standard dormitory faced away from the peaks, east on to the playing fields and down a deep valley.

The first holiday visit to Jamshedpur, near the end of 1921, was a great event. St Joseph's closed early owing to a severe cold snap that was blamed for seven cases of influenzal pneumonia, one of which ended fatally, a tragedy that would be reflected in the death of Walsh Clifton's schoolmate in *Pied Piper of Lovers*. Larry, probably in the care of a personal bearer or someone appointed by the school, took the Toy Train down to the main junction at Siliguri. Many of his schoolmates were on the same train, heading home to see their parents for the first time in nine months. A roguish, festive spirit prevailed, and the boys competed with one another in tossing small explosive torpedoes at the tin sheds sheltering the switchmen, laughing at the curses shouted after them. As before, it was metre gauge from Siliguri to Santahar, the broad-gauge Mail Express to Calcutta. In the early dawn the Howrah Station, pink Victorian stucco with gables and gingerbread, loomed on the west bank of the Hooghly. Larry would have been thirsty, but he knew to avoid the water-carriers crying out '*Hindi pani, Mussulman pani*', offering water to Hindus and Muslims separately. Neither was for him. He must find the man selling '*Tahsa char, garumi garum*!' – glasses of hot, fresh tea, which would be made safely with boiling milk-and-water.

YOUNG LARRY AT FAMILY REUNIONS was surrounded by a comfortable phalanx of aunts, uncles and cousins. Having been on his own for nine months, Larry could take stock of his relatives from a fresh perspective, so to speak. He soon discovered that his siblings, Leslie and Margaret, could be valuable allies when it came to attacking family tyrants. Tired of being admonished to 'pray and chant', little Margo told their grandmother, 'Go back to your own bungalow!'[91] Margaret recalled, 'I remember Leslie and me trying to do our governess in, having successfully removed Big Granny with insults.'[92] They would put dust in the governess's food, and then 'creep to the door to see if she was still breathing'. Eventually they got rid of her too: 'we were so awful to her that she left', recalled Larry's sister.[93] But this was years after Larry had departed for England.

While Larry might have hated Big Granny, he and indeed the whole family adored Little Granny or 'Auntie Georgie', Georgina Nimmo Dixie, a tiny droll person much like her daughter. Louisa brimmed with the same puck-like humour as ever, and her fixed belief in the goodness of all children was unaltered. She seemed to Larry dangerously weak-minded in dealing with Leslie, who had learned to make use of his health to get his own way. Larry was sure that his brother was inventing his earaches and other complaints. Denied something, Leslie would hold his breath until he turned blue, whereupon Louisa would cave in. Larry would take his revenge on his brother with invective and teasing. However, as Larry himself had to admit, 'I was terribly spoilt by my mother in India. Being exiled to England severed that bond.'[94]

Stella and John Dixie lived at Chaibassa, only forty miles away, and there were frequent visits back and forth by motor car. Larry's Uncle John was an austere, silent man with a bristling moustache and a smouldering temper who was not affectionate even with his own children. During parties held at his home he would frequently withdraw behind a book, but he did have a quirky sense of humour. An avid hunter, he encouraged his three surviving children to have pets – including a deer named Jennifer Jean – and once he came home with a young hare concealed in his jacket. He told his daughter Glory to reach into his pocket for a surprise gift, and then laughed when the leveret bit her. He could also be sensitive to others' feelings, however, and when he took his younger daughter, Diana, along on a hunt, knowing that she could not bear to see dead things, he did not fire a shot as the beaters drove game past them, but pointed out the various animals. Later in life he gave up shooting animals in favour of photographing them.

Five years older than Larry, Glory – called Sally – was the beauty of the Dixie family, and he was teased for being smitten with his cousin. Glory in turn idolized Lawrence Samuel, frankly preferring him to her own father. Uncle Lawrence was so friendly, so skilful in charades, singing and dancing. Diana was born the same year as Leslie, and Douglas Dixie was near Larry's age. Every encounter produced a glorious romp.

Larry was proud of his father, now an acknowledged leader in the extended family. Lawrence Samuel's son and namesake remembered him as 'a virtuous and rather upright Victorian gentleman, without being pompous'.[95] He bore himself towards the outside world with a military correctness, the self-conscious pose of a determined man on the way up and anxious to make a good impression. 'Dead-eye' Davis, the Deputy Commissioner of Singhbhum in the late 1920s, recalled Lawrence Samuel as quiet and soft-spoken, not overly fond of the social life of Jamshedpur.[96] Davis's picture of a reserved Lawrence Samuel need not cast doubt on the family memories of him playing charades and dancing. Larry too would develop strikingly contradictory public and private personalities.

With the confidence of his rising prosperity, Lawrence Samuel had relaxed towards his immediate family, and Larry was allowed to become quite giddy from the tawny port served on special occasions: 'How grand it was to sit there with that core of warmth and mellowness inside one!' he would recall.[97] None the less, Durrell's portrait of Walsh Clifton's father emphasizes the 'puzzled problems of relationship',[98] showing a man reluctant to 'indulge in personal confidences'.[99] Walsh is told the rudiments of sexuality by a young Indian boy, and is warned off asking his father for further explanations.[100] Clearly, some of the contradictory tendencies that would manifest themselves in Larry's character were evident in his father: the shy, reserved man who could, with an effort, produce himself, entertain, act the extrovert. Also, for father as later for son, frank indulgence in alcohol was part of the ritual of good fellowship, and a *peg* – either *chota* or *burra*, big – was the usual prescription for stress. There always seemed to be plenty of that in India.

Sometimes Larry could feel very close to his father, swimming with him in a mountain stream, staying up late to greet him when he came home from work, but he also often felt uneasy in the presence of this patently well-meaning man. Partly it was a first-born son's resentment of the male authority figure in the family, but doubtless the failure to connect was also due to traditional British reserve between father and son compounded by the colonial servant structure. Servants dealt with white children in the most intimate and emotional situations, the many small crises of childhood. When fathers saw their sons, they expected behaviour consistent with the conviction that their stock was born to rule India. One could not lower one's guard. Larry picked this up early, and the tendency would remain with him, doing battle with his wild inner rebellion and with his urge to express his feelings. Larry liked to think that his own personality was an amalgam of his parents' natures: 'From my mother I inherited the Irish side of my character: laziness and bohemianism,' he said. 'From my father I acquired two qualities, quite foreign to the Irish: a love of order and a sense of responsibility.'[101] Larry would attempt to mirror his father's order and responsibility, and their mutual reserve prevented intimacy.

Lawrence Samuel's professional associates described him as being 'energetic and ambitious', possessing 'great energy and capacity for work', 'of sober habit and exceptionally hard-working . . . perfectly honest. . . . has tact in dealing with natives. . . . [and] with his subordinates', 'keen and efficient'. Lawrence Samuel's energy, engineering proficiency, organizational ability and obvious skill in handling work-forces translated into considerable success for Durrell & Co. One year after founding the company, Lawrence Samuel, the managing director, was overseeing the construction of the Tata Iron and Steel buildings at Jamshedpur, a complex that included a general office building, a hospital, a sand-lime and brick plant, a tinplate mill, fifty-eight bungalows in the Tata company's 'European town' and 386 housing units in the Indian quarter. During the same period the company was also assigned to lay thirty miles of track in a 'doubling construction' project – the addition of a parallel line of track – around Purulia, and to begin work on the Barkakhana-Chandil extension of the Bengal-Nagpur Railway.[102] A. P. MacDermid, District Engineer for the railway in Purulia, certified following the completion of the doubling construction: 'I can confidently recommend Messrs. Durrell and Company as qualified Engineers and Contractors, with ample capital and trained organization reserves to justify them taking up any size of contract they tender for.'[103] Nearly every testimonial stressed that contracts were completed in relatively short times, despite difficulties with supply, transport, disease and climate. Lawrence Samuel was the driving force behind the company. For the young engineer-entrepreneur it was reasonable to project a future of considerable riches and a record of public service capped, not inconceivably, by one of the distinguished orders of the British Empire. The Durrell & Co. brochure put out in 1926 by Lawrence Samuel ran to ninety-four pages, testifying to his enormous energy and resourcefulness, boasting of the many projects completed in Jamshedpur, as well as the railway bridges and embankments and locomotive repair facilities constructed. The total value of the completed contracts was Rs 9,200,000 or approximately £690,000, a very substantial sum at the time and an especially impressive figure considering the trade depression dating from 1921 that had caused a number of firms in India to go bankrupt.[104]

With great pride, Larry's father took him to see the construction site of the Tinplate Company rolling mill. Although the roof was not yet in place, the production of steel had begun, and the boy watched the giant assembly at work: 'It was a fascinating and frightening sight, these long gold ribbons passing through the rollers, giving off tremendous heat, and being chopped off like carrots by the machines,' Larry recalled.[105] The hot steel bars were next rolled into thin sheets of various thicknesses, again cut to size, etched in an acid bath, washed and dipped in molten tin. Larry understood his father's enthusiasm, but he could not honestly tell himself he really *liked* the tinplate mill: it was too hot, too noisy, and the acrid smells burned his nostrils. Machines did not really interest him.

Although he had dipped into Dickens and found *Pickwick* dull, Larry was reading Buchan, Surtees and Ella Wheeler Wilcox at home, and he had already discovered that writing school essays came easily to him. Rider Haggard's *She* was a favourite tale and, Larry would recall, '*Kim* was our bedside book'.[106] Lawrence Samuel recognized Larry's bent and did not try to push his son into uncongenial studies, but he must have felt a pang of disappointment at not seeing in Larry a future engineer.

Lawrence Samuel, busy as he was, tried to give time to his family. He went against the prevailing pattern, which accepted long separations when the man of the house had to travel, and often took his family along when he was overseeing distant construction projects. 'We lived under canvas a lot of the time, in real pioneer fashion,' remembered Larry.[107] By Boy Scout standards it was easy living. All the gear was loaded on to a rail car or else elephants and a bullock cart; not only a complete kitchen range and a cook went with them, but even marquees, fitted carpets and a small piano. The carpets were not mere swank: Louisa feared that a hamadryad or other dangerous snake might crawl into the tents during the night. Wall-to-wall carpeting fastened to a tent-base of his own devising would prevent this, Lawrence Samuel assured his wife. There were hardships, to be sure, as when one of the draught elephants got loose and in consequence no clean sheets could be had for three days. 'Your father was most annoyed,' Louisa reminisced much later to her children.[108] In the evenings the family would gather around a Primus lamp to play the piano and indulge in a sing-song: 'I'm Forever Blowing Bubbles' and 'Keep the Home Fires Burning' would roll out into the night. Larry began to learn to sight-read music, but as soon as he discovered that he could improvise harmonic chords to a simple melody, he gave that up. Reading scores was too much like work and too little fun. No discipline was imposed on him, yet he acquired a facility at the keyboard that would attract admirers and even earn him a few pounds later on. Like so much else in his early life, music came easily. So did the laughter, 'such pealing, profitless laughter', he would call it,[109] as family and friends vied with each other in teasing and mild ribaldry.

Larry did not see his home life as differing substantially from the common run. 'Our life in India was typically colonial, i.e. very much family-oriented,' he would recall.[110] When he was a boarding pupil in Darjeeling, he lived with other colonial children and he was still only a day and a half by rail from home. He began to realize something else as a result of his time away at school: he had learned a few facts and had experienced much that was new to his family, and he found that he could hold their attention – for a few minutes at least – by describing events. He was becoming a story-teller, and he enjoyed the sense of power that it gave him. Especially, he liked to talk about the strange mountain folk, about the Bhutias, the Tibetans, the lamas who had come over the glacier fields. His father promised that some day he would have a chance to travel over the high passes into Sikkim and Tibet. Still, Larry seems to have thought of himself as a 'solitary little devil'[111]: already the sense of difference and loneliness had set in.

It was perhaps during this vacation that Larry was sent to stay with his Uncle Henry, William Henry Durrell, who lived in a 'strange sinister rambling house' in Ranchi. Uncle Henry was the great hunter in the family, and Larry was to be given instruction in this necessary manly accomplishment. One of Uncle Henry's responsibilities was elephant control, and the back veranda was lined with a dozen skulls of elephants that had gone mad and that he had in consequence shot. This he did with immense regret. Uncle Henry carefully trepanned each skull in an attempt to find evidence for his theory that the insanity was due to brain tumours. Struck that his uncle kept referring to the skulls as 'beautiful', Larry would remember them as 'huge and grave, like a Greek chorus'. One of the rogue elephants was survived by an infant. Named Sadu, this elephant child was being trained for work when Larry arrived, and it became his playmate. Or rather, small Larry was a stand-in for the grown men the elephant would have to lift in later years: 'They hold out their trunks curled up at the end like a human hand; you put your foot into it and presto you are raised in the air, and placed securely on the animal's back, between those two fantastic ears, the signs of supernormal spirituality, they say.' Larry added, 'They have a singular floating walk, a little humorous, like a drunken Irishman.'[112]

Soon it was time for Larry to return to St Joseph's College. Father de Gheldere had recommended that Larry spend a second year in Third Standard: perhaps his previous preparation had not been sufficiently strong, or he may have missed too many classes in his first year due to illness. Durrell himself expressed only fond memories for St Joseph's, many years later thanking the school for 'its wise and kindly tuition', adding, 'I first learned to love poetry and literature in general thru my English classes at North Point.'[113] The term seems to have passed without incident. Larry was well liked by the staff, for towards the end of this second year, when his housemaster Edward Fitzgerald was given the Kaiser-i-Hind Medal, the ten-year-old boy was selected for the honour of delivering the presentation address. He prepared the speech himself, and an excerpt was published in the school yearbook, the *North Point Calendar*. The editor identified the sly encomium as being by 'Larry Durrell, as sturdy a young scamp as any in the Primary Department':

King George has sent you the King-Emperor's Medal, because you have been so good to us. Everyone who is good to us, gets rewarded, either in this world or the next. We are glad that the King did not make you wait till you got to the other world, because we might not be there. Surely they have told him what Sir is to his small boys. He is all the world to us, and a bit more besides, and the Primary Department is our home. The class-room and the play-ground, the dormitory and the dining-room are all bits of home. Sir is always with us. From the moment we awake till we close our eyes in sleep, Sir is there to tell us. When we tell our own Daddies this, they smile a knowing smile, and say, 'Now that's just what we told your grandpapas a quarter of a century ago. And in the great big world outside today we are striving still to play the game, Sir taught us once to play so well in school.'

After this we are going to be very good boys. When the King hears this, he might send you another medal. If he thinks of it, he might send us all medals, because we are so good.[114]

This was evidently Larry's first published prose, and the whole event formed a satisfying conclusion to his time at St Joseph's. None the less, he would recall with regret that the wheels of the Toy Train had sounded 'Never come back . . . Never come back' as he dropped down to Siliguri for the last time.[115]

In *Pied Piper of Lovers* Durrell gives to Walsh Clifton a resigned acceptance that he would be sent 'home' to England. Lawrence Samuel was determined that Larry should receive an English education and return with a university accent, 'no longer a *petit bourgeois* but a great man with an expensive dinner jacket!'[116] The speech consideration alone demanded that he be sent to England before he was much older – according to his sister Margaret, before the 'chee-chee' English of the Anglo-Indian became ineradicably etched upon his tongue. Chee-chee was also a term for Eurasians and came from their sing-song intonation, supposedly derived from their having learned English from Welsh missionaries. So conscious were many of the Europeans in India of the stigma attached to the accent that they ordered their servants, many of whom spoke a serviceable but chee-chee English, to use their own native languages instead of English when addressing white children. 'No one with an accent is well-bred' was an adage among some members of the Durrell family.[117] It is also possible that Lawrence Samuel was moved to his decision on English schooling by his son's two years in Third Standard: he may have decided that Larry was not making satisfactory progress. Subject for subject, it is clear that Larry would have been given as sound an education at St Joseph's as at most

English public schools. The Special Department at St Joseph's was even authorized to administer the Cambridge Higher School Certificate Examination, so that Larry, had he stayed at North Point until the age of eighteen, could have attempted to qualify for admission to a major English university. Perhaps a more pressing consideration for Lawrence Samuel was the prejudice against hiring the Indian-educated for important positions in the bureaucracy; the ICS and the Provincial Civil Service promised well for the talented young. Lawrence Samuel could cite two English-educated brothers-in-law and a second cousin who had distinguished themselves: Cecil Henry Buck, George Pearce – married to his sisters Eleanor May and Muriel respectively – and Richard Henry Blaker, who had retired recently as Keeper of the Records for India.

Larry himself thought that the pressure on his father to send him to England came from considerations of snobbery and social caste, that he had merely acquiesced in the prevailing current. This acquiescence was not shared by Louisa Durrell, and to Larry the word *home* 'applied to England . . . meant less than nothing',[118] although the awe with which almost every white person he knew spoke of England aroused his intense curiosity. Louisa attacked English schooling in an emotional outburst. 'My mother was against the idea,' Larry remembered. 'She said I was too young, that it was cruel to send me so far away.' The substance of these arguments had less effect on Larry than the emotional wrench caused by the quarrel: 'It was the first time I had witnessed a really heated argument at home; it was so calm as a rule. Seeing my mother cry was a real body-blow.'[119] When it came to assigning blame he was less charitable: he thought that his mother could have fought harder on his behalf. Up to the last, Larry must have expected her to save him. Irrationally, he held it against her, far more than against his father, that he was 'exiled' to England. His father was only doing what seemed right to his limited male vision. Larry's mother knew better, understood his emotional need to remain in India, but she had not been able to carry her point. Women let one down, he decided. Larry stored away the bitter lesson in his memory, and when he came to write in *Pied Piper* about Walsh being sent to England, he gave the decision not to Walsh's father but to his Aunt Brenda: evidently he preferred to lay the blame on a woman.

Larry was not sent back to St Joseph's for the 1923 term, since he would be leaving in a few months for England. The Durrells had moved into one of the staff bungalows built by Lawrence Samuel. Designated a D-6 type, it was identical to at least five others in Jamshedpur, with a veranda behind a pair of graceful arches, high ceilings, and kitchen and servants' quarters in a separate building to the rear. Pushing the thought of England to the backs of their minds, Larry and his family made the most of their time together, entertaining one another and taking in the rich ambience. 'I have seen the Rope Trick when I was ten, and distinctly felt the power of the conjuror over us as we sat round him in a circle,' Durrell would remember. 'I have been followed from tree-top to tree-top by sportive monkeys which pelted me with nuts and stones.'[120] What spectacles could England produce to compare with these?

Mother, family and culture tied Larry to India; father, custom and ambition pushed him towards England. Larry would come to recognize how powerfully both countries worked to shape him: 'In my case India was just as important to me as England was.'[121] A factor beyond pride, tradition and ambition for his son may have influenced Lawrence Samuel in his decision to send Larry to England in 1923. Conspiracies abounded around the agitation to replace English officials with Indian. An inoffensive Englishman was shot in Calcutta because the assassin mistook him for a police official. Brahman rule was being challenged, Gandhi was trying to raise the Untouchables, and there were the first beginnings of a feminist movement. Ironically, Lawrence Samuel benefited from the labour unrest because Durrell & Co. enjoyed good employee relations and gained contracts for that reason. In July 1922 the Durrell company provided two thousand workers to complete the Amda-Jamda construction project for the Bengal-Nagpur Railway after strikes had halted work by the government crew.

The political developments were discussed in the Durrell family, and educated young Europeans in India during the 1920s commonly gave the Raj no more than another twenty-five years to run, a most accurate estimate as events would prove. The Durrells may have been sympathetic to at least some of Gandhi's aims, but they recognized the threat to British colonial rule and to concerns run by non-Indians. Lawrence Samuel's choice of Indian business partners had shown considerable foresight, yet he may also have thought that prudence dictated the transfer of his children from the field of conflict. He also laid plans to have the sons of his Sikh associates educated in England.

The exodus of members of the extended Durrell family began, surprisingly, with Cecil Henry Buck, who as Deputy Commissioner of the Kangra district of the Punjab, India's richest area, held one of the choice middle-level ICS positions. His resignation, followed by his move to England in May 1922, undoubtedly owed something to a legal clash that would have been unthinkable a generation earlier. Buck had been travelling through a village under his jurisdiction, when some 'small boys' threw 'pebbles' at him. When his tormentors went unpunished, Buck pressed charges. The first trial ended with the conviction of the accused, but an appeal was made to a higher court. The new case for the defence was argued by a pair of Indian lawyers, a local jurist acting in conjunction with a prominent barrister from Delhi. They put Mrs Buck – Larry's Aunt May – on the stand, and the old scandal of the divorce was raked over. The magistrate hearing the case was an Englishman qualified to preside over both civil and military cases. 'I'm going to have to find against you, Buck,' he told Larry's uncle over drinks at the club.[122] The acquittal of the boys was cause for jubilation among the Indian population, and while the verdict increased respect for the fairness of British justice, it was an omen that would not have been lost on Lawrence Samuel. His first patron, friend and brother-in-law had been publicly humiliated. Two years later E. M. Forster would publish *A Passage to India*, in which the acquittal of a native would similarly embarrass the English.

Larry did not go to England alone, for his parents had decided to take advantage of the work slow-down during the summer monsoon. On 18 March the Durrells boarded the *City of London* at Calcutta for the long voyage to England. Larry went with decidedly mixed feelings. He was already nostalgic for the India that he sensed he was losing. Still, he was caught up by the sense of present adventure, and he had no concrete reason yet to dislike England. Durrell would recall years later, 'I was optimistic and eager to see this marvellous distant paradise upon which we had all depended morally for so long.' He added, 'I felt as pleased as a Jew, belonging to the chosen race, and I was eager to affront the problems with good grace.' His deepest regret was that he had not been given the promised trip to Tibet. All his life Tibet – as much as India – would haunt him. 'I was really trying to find my way back to India,' he said in old age, by way of explaining his intellectual and spiritual odyssey.[123]

When Larry left for England at the age of eleven many ties were sundered. It was not only being torn beyond reach of his family circle and losing sight of the Himalayas, the passing Buddhist lamas, the hill folk. He was never again to be a part of that settled yet exotic world that was the Raj. When called upon to describe his early years, he liked to state the facts simply: 'I was born in India. Went to school there – under the Himalayas. The most wonderful memories – a brief dream of Tibet until I was eleven.'[124] That dream was over.

CHAPTER 2

Pudding Island

But he for whom steel and running water
Were roads, went westward only
To the prudish cliffs and the sad green home
Of Pudding Island o'er the Victorian foam.
'Cities, Plains and People'

LAWRENCE DURRELL was disappointed by his first sight of England, and he gave his own feelings to Walsh Clifton in *Pied Piper of Lovers* as the boy watched the land materialize:

It would perhaps be impossible to define accurately the feeling of disappointment he experienced as he stood on the deck of the liner and watched the pearly cliffs insinuate themselves out of the light sea-haze; at any rate, he was not impressed by what he saw, and as he leaned his chin upon the rail, he told himself bitterly that it was *smaller* than he had imagined![1]

Like Walsh, Larry felt 'galled by his own lack of excitement: by his own apathy', and 'sick with an undefined regret, as though the beauty of the hills which he had left behind forever still worked in him'.[2] This sense of India left 'forever' compromised Larry's natural interest in everything new. His parents were beset by no such misgivings. This was the Promised Land that they had imagined from the Pisgah of the Northern Frontier. Louisa eagerly took in the marvellous English gardens, the stately homes, the fashionable shops. Lawrence Samuel Durrell, thirty-nine-year-old railway engineer and contractor, found England in the summer of 1923 exhilarating. Here was the home of the scientific and industrial progress that he had been trying with messianic fervour to bring to India. The English trains moved with crisp clicking sounds, chanting, according to Larry, God Save The King, God Save The King,[3] over track laid as true as glass. The streets of London were packed with motor cars and soon Lawrence Samuel bought a little 'bullnose' Morris Cowley. The family visited the Bucks at 'lax unmanning Eastbourne', as Larry was much later to call it.[4] But he was delighted to see Aunt May and Uncle Cecil and to hear all the familiar talk about India. There were visits to other relatives, including Lawrence Samuel's cousins Harry and Elsie Rickwood in London, but all too soon it was time for Larry's parents to return to Durrell & Co. in Jamshedpur. They left towards the end of September, lending the Morris Cowley to Cecil Buck and placing Larry at a school in Tunbridge Wells, a favourite retirement spot for those returned from service in India.[5]

For the year Larry spent at Tunbridge Wells he felt rather in limbo, in suspension: he was not assigned to a specific form or syllabus, but was supposed to pick up a few subjects until he could be placed permanently.[6] He had dropped behind a year by repeating a form at St Joseph's, and he had lost another half-year by being kept out of school while the family prepared for the trip to England – evidence of Louisa's indulgence of her son, and also of her reluctance to be parted from him.

Larry's impressions of England were not improving: 'I immediately sensed the hypocrisy there and the puritanism,' he would recall.[7] The damp cold, and even more the darkness, of the English winter depressed him. Most important, there was the severance of his attachment to his mother: the geographic gulf between them seemed unbridgeable. When he had been at St Joseph's he had known that a rapid train journey could restore him to his family – would, in an emergency, bring his mother to him. In England, he could die before his parents even knew he was ill. Or they could die! He felt the wrenching agony of the child sent far from home.

Looking back from a safe distance of forty-five years, Durrell claimed that his feelings towards England had been determined by his parents. Admitting that he hated England, he said, 'I can give a Freudian explanation for it! Here goes! It was my father who decided to send me to England. . . . I attack England because I identify it with my father.' He continued, 'I reacted with everything I had against England, primarily in order to break my father's will.'[8] Only, Larry the schoolboy could not say that his reaction to England was part of an unacknowledged duel with his father. England he could react against; the underlying *reason* had to remain a secret, probably at the time even from himself. Introspection and subterfuge became habitual: silent thoughts and misleading utterances. These factors were uniting to turn him into a writer. The replacement of maternal India by paternal England would bruise Larry into a cry of anguish, one eventually channelled into a literature that would strive constantly to escape England. The writer about exotic places would spring from the adolescent sick for India.

Larry's depression was not alleviated next summer by a visitor from

India: Big Granny was in Eastbourne by early June. She was clad, typically, in black silk with soiled lace at the wrists,[9] and she was still ranting about God and death. Her face and hands were like dough and were covered with age spots. Larry would record the ravages of time in his description in *Pied Piper of Lovers* of 'Grandmamma' as she appeared to Walsh in London: 'The blank light moulded her heavy, loose-fleshed face, setting the pouches wide about the sagging mouth, and the blue loops of skin about her eyes.'[10]

By September 1924 Larry was lodged with Mrs E. M. Dyson at 36 Hillsborough Road in Dulwich, a spacious south London suburb a reasonable commuting distance from the school that Larry was to attend, St Olave's and St Saviour's in Southwark. Dulwich was defined by the substantial yet self-deprecating middle-class homes with their dark, circumspect parlours and gloomy stairwells, creating an air of *pudeur*. A few streets from Mrs Dyson's stood Dulwich College, which was 'a fair candidate for the wildest nineteenth century building in the whole of London', with 'a crazy Dostoevskian gleam in its eye'.[11] In nearby Dulwich Park Larry would note a 'cold toy lake' that was home to 'a few bedraggled swans'.[12] Picture all this covered with a liberal patina of soot from bituminous coal and view it through a winter drizzle, and you will have a fair idea of why London appalled the boy from India. The raw, grey climate and the drab faces he saw matched Larry's feeling of having been abandoned.

Mrs Dyson was quite likely related to R. C. Dyson, a consulting engineer for railways to the Government of India in Calcutta, and an associate of Lawrence Samuel's, so an Indian connection may have existed.[13] However, Mrs Dyson was not a sympathetic presence. She was characterized by 'ferocious probity and total lack of sensibility or imagination', said Larry, and she was only one of a type common in Dulwich. 'Here I found actually the world of Dickens still in force', he continued, 'with caricature figures giving off waves of guilt one could literally smell like BO.'[14] In old age Durrell would decide that a major difference between himself and the native English lay in this guilt: 'They have such a sense of sin which I don't have.' Defiantly, he added, 'I believe in original innocence.'[15] Fortunately, there was a fellow-sufferer at Mrs Dyson's, a boarding boy of Larry's age named Malcolm Ayres. They became friends, and Larry admired Joan, Malcolm's 'very beautiful' older sister.

While he may have denied having a sense of sin, Larry carried a considerable burden of guilt which had nothing to do with social or sexual morality: he was very conscious of the money that was being spent on him *to make him English*, and with a part of himself he felt that the goal was hopeless, much as he wanted to fit in and please his parents. A code had been impressed upon him: 'he was to be a man' who would not cry when hurt; he must 'endeavour to live up to' being English; he must enjoy and be grateful for his English schooling. He projected his feelings on to Walsh Clifton, newly arrived in England: 'He was abjectly, slavishly intent on becoming English; and indeed, if you had seen him dressed in his sober school clothes, with his immaculate, washable rubber-composition collar, and his hair soothed back off his forehead, you might have mistaken him for one of your own.'[16] The smug ambience of Dulwich, however, worked against Larry's assimilation.

From Mrs Dyson's home Larry went by tram or train to Southwark, then walked along Tooley Street to St Olave's and St Saviour's, an old-fashioned grammar school, where he was enrolled in Class II, with boys about two years his junior. St Olave's, now South London College, was housed in a red brick three-storey Victorian structure set amid dockyards and warehouses on the south bank of the Thames, across the river from the Tower of London. The school was '*socially*, very small fry compared to a real public school,' Larry would come to recognize.[17] The plan was for Larry to pick up enough subjects to be able to pass the Common Entrance Examination, a prerequisite for his admission to a reputable public school, and he studied at St Olave's until four each afternoon with that aim. He had a 'marvellous english teacher'[18] who took his pupils on tours to the sites of the Rose and Swan theatres and other nearby places of the Elizabethan renaissance. 'We learned our Shakespeare on the spot,' Larry recalled. 'We felt very much part of the Shakespearean scene, so to speak.' A few streets beyond Southwark Cathedral the Globe Playhouse had stood, and beyond that Larry could walk along Bear Gardens Lane to the Thames. 'It was great fun', he said, 'to realize that Shakespeare and company had been trotting around there the whole time.' Although many of the masters spoke 'a good deal of cockney', Larry found them very good, and the discipline was not brutal: 'We used to get slippered a great deal for minor offences, but a slipper over the bottom, a couple of whacks, is not really an execution.' Larry would maintain that 'the grammar schools were always much better than the public schools, their curricula and everything else were much more serious: it was just the snobbery of the class structure.'[19] Precisely this higher class structure was what Lawrence Samuel wanted his son to enter. The egalitarian air of St Olave's moved Larry subtly away from the snobbery of class and money; and the space between father and son widened.

Larry told his family that he wanted to become a writer. Perhaps to his surprise, his father did not object:

He said that was okay but that I must go to Oxford first. His view was that all writers should go to Oxford where they made very influential friends who helped them to become successful afterwards. Perhaps this was not so silly as it then seemed. But he had read in the paper that Bernard Shaw had three Rolls-Royces and Kipling two – he wanted me to enjoy this sort of success; but I wanted a typewriter and if such a thing had been possible, an elephant.

This seemed a perfectly reasonable shopping list. Larry 'got the typewriter for Christmas, and a complete Shakespeare', but no elephant.[20]

Larry's father also bought him a set of Dickens: here was another writer who had made a good living by his pen.[21] Larry, who had found Dickens dull in India, now read him with appreciation. Just off nearby Borough High Street was Lant Street, where Dickens had lodged in his boyhood while his father was in the debtors' cells of the Marshalsea, birthplace of Little Dorrit. Although the gloomy prison had been demolished in Dickens's lifetime, various settings for his novels were still extant and were well within the range of Larry's lunchtime patrols. It was on the steps leading from the carriageway of London Bridge down to the river that Noah Claypole in *Oliver Twist*, hiding behind a pilaster, eavesdropped on the conversation that would lead to Nancy's murder by Bill Sikes. Lizzie Hexam in *Our Mutual Friend* rowed her father between the Southwark and London bridges in his nightly search for the bodies of the drowned. And it was in the yard of the White Horse Inn off Borough High Street that Mr Pickwick met Sam Weller cleaning boots. English literature was coming alive for Larry in a way that modern England, suffering from the comparison with India, could not.

Although Larry was appreciative of Dickensian London, it was the Elizabethans and the Jacobeans who gained his lifelong allegiance. Sometimes the schoolboys were taken to Southwark Cathedral for services: 'They were always occasions of some sort or other – the Lord Mayor, accompanied . . . by a display, the guilds, for example, in uniform, and that was very colourful.' The boys of St Olave's were lined up to march in procession. The pageantry of it all attracted Larry: 'Very picturesque – the English have a good sense of theatre, you know', he added parenthetically, 'and one could see that the Elizabethan theatre must have had that thoroughness of function.'[22] As a member of the school debating society, Larry argued – and was judged to have won his point – for continuing the tradition of the Lord Mayor's Show.

Larry's future scheme for an Elizabethan book was born on the very ground, here in Southwark. Some days he hurried east along Tooley Street to spend his lunch hour in Southwark Cathedral, and his visits lengthened into truancy. There were many intriguing monuments to muse over. Richard Humble, a Jacobean notable, was sculpted kneeling on top of his sarcophagus, with his two wives in like pious pose ranked behind him. Lancelot Andrewes, seventeenth-century Bishop of Winchester, reposed under a magnificent gilded wooden canopy. Perhaps the brilliance and graphic detail of the painted monuments, then recently restored, reminded the lonely boy of India, and seemed a promise that the world of light and colour he had known had not been utterly vanquished by black and grey London. Roguish carved faces grinned down from the roof bosses in the wooden ceiling. He particularly admired the green and red painted tomb – bright as any Hindu shrine – of John Gower, friend of Chaucer.

When his English teacher discovered where the boy was hiding during lesson time, instead of punishment he suggested, without a trace of irony, that since Master Durrell liked the farded monuments of Old England so much, he should read the literature of the past. Larry's evaluation for 1924 states, 'He has a genuine taste for English literature, and reads much on his own account.'[23] Thus grew Larry's acquaintance with the writers of the English renaissance, a passion he pursued so avidly that he would claim, with perhaps only a modicum of exaggeration, that by the age of seventeen he had read every surviving Elizabethan work.[24] Certainly he adopted their adoration of spectacle and their word-love. As he would announce a decade later to Henry Miller, 'Words I carry in my pocket where they breed like white mice . . . . Words belonging to trades stick to my tongue. I'm a fiendish reader for mere syllables.'[25] Larry's general progress was judged satisfactory, and he was moved up to Class III for the new year.

LOUISA DURRELL ARRIVED IN 1925 for another visit. Travelling with Leslie, Margaret, the three-month-old Gerry and a nurse, she had left by P & O steamer from Bombay on 28 March for the three-week run to London.[26] Lawrence Samuel had too much work in hand to take a long vacation and would not come to England until mid-summer. Not long before, he and John Dixie had quarrelled violently over a construction accident. A wall had collapsed, and there was loss of life. Dixie blamed the cost-cutting measures of the Indian partners for the mishap, while Lawrence Samuel supported the two Sikhs, maintaining that they should remain partners in the company. 'Then I'm leaving!' John Dixie said. While

Louisa, Stella and their children stood aghast, the two men shouted recriminations at one another on the platform of the railway station in Jamshedpur. Although Stella Dixie and her two daughters would slip over occasionally to Jamshedpur to see Louisa, the men did not become reconciled and John withdrew from the company.[27] The break with his friend and brother-in-law dulled Lawrence Samuel's pleasure in the five-year accomplishments of the firm.

What Lawrence Samuel found after he had rejoined his family 'got him very excited', as it had before, Larry remembered. In August they all travelled from London down to Eastbourne to see the Bucks. Larry's father loved England in a way that his eldest son could not. For Lawrence Samuel it was wonderful to explore the country: his scientific mind thrilled to the factories and the industrial exhibitions; and he discovered the heady excitement of the London stage – as his son would a few years later. In any event, he had 'got fed up' with India and 'the limitations of Indian life'.[28] The construction industry was slowing down and the agitations of the nationalists were continuing. He began to think seriously of leaving India, moving to England, and taking up a stage career. He would partner Evelyn Laye, he dreamed! Before returning to India, Louisa and Lawrence Samuel enrolled Leslie as a day boy at Dulwich; later he would attend Caldicott, a Wesleyan Methodist school. Larry's dislike of formal education seemed to be growing, and he dropped from eleventh to twenty-first in a class of thirty-three. Still, he was not a discipline problem at school, and the report at the end of the year noted that he was eager to please but 'frivolous': 'He *very* frequently answers the question that is *not* asked,' wrote his form master.[29]

Leslie was by now a virtual stranger to Larry, who looked upon his brother – when he was forced to include the much younger boy in his games – as a pest. His delicate health had made Leslie his mother's pet, which Larry resented passionately. Leslie was miserable. He hated his lessons and did not develop Larry's compensating interest in literature, but searched the magazines for accounts of hunting and pictures of guns, subjects that reminded him of India. Speaking for himself, Larry recalled, 'I was a savage,' and when a classmate ventured to tease him about 'swotting' – being too studious – he would simply punch him on the nose and go back to his books – which were, to be sure, usually not school set books.[30] Leslie, who according to Larry 'might have been a very good painter', found that the tough schoolboy world scorned such activities as sketching and painting. He lacked the vitality and the precocious intelligence of his older brother and was thus more vulnerable, but like Larry he had a fierce temper and lashed out with his fists when crossed. Soon he too turned into a young savage, but one whose wildness was unrelieved by intellectual interests. Fighting became an end in itself for Leslie. During one of his brawls he sustained a beating that left him with a ruptured ear-drum and permanent deafness. Of Dulwich and its inhabitants Larry would recall, 'I hated it and them but as I was tough, resilient and innocent-sexy I was not as much damaged by this Pentonville period as my brother Leslie.'[31] Pentonville Prison became Larry's metaphor for his London school years.

The next summer, taking advantage of the slowing down of construction work during the monsoons, the Durrells were back in England. In June 1926, before leaving India, Lawrence Samuel had produced an impressive illustrated brochure outlining in nearly a hundred pages the achievements of Durrell & Co., and he was sure that he could sell his interest in the firm for a good sum. In any case, after initially planning to move his headquarters to Calcutta, he had decided to relocate in Lahore, far to the west. He still considered leaving India permanently, and bought an eight-bedroom house in Dulwich at 48 Alleyn Park Road. The house was spacious, with high ceilings in the downstairs rooms, and it was set back a reasonable distance from the road in a long garden. There was the usual round of visits: the Rickwoods in Dulwich, the Bucks in Eastbourne. Louisa was shocked by Leslie's battered condition and convinced her husband that they should take him back to India with them.

The family visits do not seem to have created an improved understanding between Larry and his father. Larry was still not happy to be at school in England, but he did not voice his complaints. Lawrence Samuel, on his part, was disappointed by his son's academic performance, especially his apparent inability to master the rudiments of mathematics, but he did not lecture him nor call him to account. 'He took me out and fed me buns,' Larry said, evasively, when asked whether his father had scolded him.[32]

On the surface, Larry was on the way to becoming what his father wanted: an Empire-builder in the making, scarcely distinguishable in manners and speech from thousands of other sons of respectable and ambitious folk. There was an inward change too, but it was not one of which Lawrence Samuel would have approved, had he detected the signs – which he almost certainly did not. Throughout most of his time in India, Larry had been confident of his abilities and quite assured about his future. He had felt equally at home in Anglo-Indian society and in the native bazaars.

When I was only 9 or 10
I felt more secure than many men,[33]

he would write in 1940, adding a wry comment on the blows that 'fate' had dealt him in the intervening years. These blows had begun to fall during his first year in England, and he responded with some of the means at his disposal: pretence, silence, lies. At the age of fourteen he was still only four feet seven, and he compensated for his shortness with bravura and pugnacity. If survival and independence meant developing an easy outward show to protect his emotional vulnerability, to shield his fantasies against ridicule, so be it. To his father he professed contentment, even happiness.

Before Lawrence Samuel left England in September, he enrolled Larry in the Fourth Form, Grade B, at St Edmund's School, established in Canterbury by the Clergy Orphan Society. Since beginning Fourth Formers were usually thirteen or fourteen years old, this meant that Larry was not appreciably behind in his studies, despite his later claims. He was lodged in Watson House, where most of the pupils were in the Senior School.

Although not one of the famous public schools, St Edmund's was sufficiently respectable. Eton, Harrow, or any other top-ranked school was out of the question: Larry's education had been too spotty, his mathematical and science preparation too weak, and there were no influential Old Boys in the family to put in a word for him. Larry was certainly neither a clergyman's son nor an orphan, but this did not bother the St Edmund's trustees, who were content to supplement the rolls of the charity boarders with the sons of colonial gentlemen. Larry was among the few fee-paying non-foundationers, so that, as at St Joseph's, he belonged to an insignificant minority. This time, however, he was not to be excused from religious instruction and chapel services: the school had strong Anglican affiliations, and preparation for confirmation was part of the curriculum.

Larry must have noted the pleasing coincidence of his having begun his education in London at the starting point of Chaucer's great pilgrimage, and then continued it in Canterbury. Larry remembered the place as 'a most beautiful public school . . . whose architecture and atmosphere resembled very closely the school I had quitted in Darjeeling.'[34] Neo-Gothic St Edmund's rose towards the sky in rough Kentish ragstone pierced by narrow mullioned windows, the rooms darkened by wooden balustrades, benches, and tables rendered the colour of treacle through many decades of varnish. The loveliness of the place remained with Larry: 'From this static harmony he drew some intimate recognition of beauty, some taste that seemed parent to the taste of cold wind and sheer unhampered distance which had governed his child-mind.' Not that the students were encouraged to look: most of the classroom windows were set near the ceiling to deny the students the distraction of gazing out during what Larry would call 'the horrible lessons'.[35] A quiet country road led a mile and a half downhill into Canterbury. The austere main school building stood amid green lawns and playing fields on St Thomas's Hill with the cathedral massively visible below in the centre of the town. Becket's Canterbury might as well have been in the next county so far as the St Edmund's boys were concerned: they were rarely allowed to walk into the town, and then only for a specific reason, in their best clothes and carrying passes.

Larry was shown to his space in the long dormitory close under the slate roof, the dark beams making a geometric pattern overhead. Small dormer windows afforded views of Canterbury across the rolling downs. Along either side of the room stood a row of narrow beds, heads under the sloping eaves, feet towards the centre walkway, which was split by a rank of individual washstands without running water. By the head of each bed was a small chest of drawers. Larry dreaded the winter nights: 'The windows had to be kept open, so that often the snow was blowing in on to your bed.'[36] Some mornings Larry had to break a pane of ice covering his basin for the obligatory face-neck-and-ears ablution. There were other discomforts, including 'the icy plunge into the swimming-bath at seven sharp every morning'.[37] 'It was really quite a tough business,' Larry would remember. 'But you were in a much better state of health because of it. The only thing was that you had a running nose the whole time from the cold; you know, like a dog.'[38] *Tumo*, the Tibetan Buddhist method for defeating the cold through a meditative state, came to Larry's rescue, or so he would claim.[39]

St Edmund's academic syllabus was rigorous, and slanted towards the humanities. The headmaster, the Reverend Canon Walter Fletcher Burnside, projected his own passionate love for the Classics on to the curriculum. Of the twelve masters, four – counting the Head – were classics, two Junior School, and one each drawing, maths, modern languages, music and science. The remaining master had combined maths and science responsibilities. 'Divinity, Latin, English, French, Mathematics and Science are taught throughout the school,' proclaimed the St Edmund's brochure of Larry's time. The order in which the subjects were listed was significant, given Canon Burnside's proclivities. From the fourth form on, 'extra French, Maths and English are alternative with Greek'.[40] Larry opted for Greek during his last term at the school. There were four classes each morning, six mornings a week, and Burnside himself taught classics during all but one of these periods. Some idea of the level of the science instruction can be guessed from the fact that in 1922, after physics and chemistry had been part of the curriculum for fifteen years, A. D. McDonald, the newly appointed science master, discovered that the total laboratory equipment for chemistry consisted of a single flask and some lengths of glass tubing. When McDonald applied to Burnside for funds to rectify this staggering deficiency in equipment, he was given £10 and told to make do. Not surprisingly, most of the boys admitted to the universities from St Edmund's qualified in classics rather than the sciences. Larry often spoke of his inability to handle technical subjects in qualifying examinations, and part of the reason – assuming that Larry ever attempted university entry-level examinations – probably had a lot to do with the low priority given to the subjects at St Edmund's.

The tyranny of prefects and housemasters, the seemingly pointless classes, the victimizing of the studious 'swots' by the 'hairy ones' – the playing-field bullies – weighed upon Larry. He was probably writing autobiographically when he had Walsh Clifton find his first experience of a boarding school 'bewildering' and 'unspeakably horrible'. Larry described his fictional double as 'a child of space, and that is as true an approximation of his qualities as words can give; lustiness, an aptitude for sheer sensual appreciation, a secret self-immolating zest for raw life' – all threatened by the dour outlook of the school.[41] Housemasters who were all smiles for visiting parents could swing the chastising cane with, it seemed to him, self-righteous satisfaction. Like Walsh in *Pied Piper of Lovers* before his English schooling, Larry had never been beaten, and he reacted with blind rage when his turn came. His uncowed zest for life was remembered by an older schoolfellow, the Right Reverend Headley Sparks, who described him as having been 'something of a pickle'.[42] At the end of his first term he ranked fourteenth out of sixteen in 'General Order' – which included conduct.

Larry still seems to have sent 'lying letters' home, 'in which he advertised his life as an ideal one, and himself as rapturously happy'. In *Pied Piper* Larry was to write editorially, 'Displays of this kind are common to us all', and they were motivated in part by 'warm pity for his well-meaning father who was so remote from the actualities of this new life'.[43] Whatever happened, he was determined not to let his father down.

Letters from India in turn probably followed the tenor of those Larry ascribed to Walsh's father in *Pied Piper*: 'Your reports haven't been too good. However, old man, I feel I can always trust you to do the right thing and be a decent chap.' And the impact of these letters on young Larry also must have matched those attributed to Walsh: 'In the few closing phrases had been summed up all those things for which he was beginning to feel nothing but a bitter contempt – the awful ignorance of the Empire Builder, the would-be altruist, the dreary stupidity of the "team spirit".'[44] The idea of becoming part of the team of Empire was now repugnant, yet England was not providing him with a new set of aspirations and beliefs. Estranged from both India and England, he felt more lonely than ever.

St Edmund's consisted of 160 boys divided into four houses, each under a master and a monitor. The shared classes, the sufferings and the general lack of privacy made for easy intimacy: 'I made good friends,' Larry would claim in middle life,[45] but these attachments do not appear to have long survived his departure from the school, and he would describe his fictional double Walsh as a loner at school: despite the 'rough and ready fellowship'[46] that tempered his loneliness somewhat, 'He could not claim one really close friend.'[47] A digressive episode in *Pied Piper of Lovers* suggests that Larry's awakening sexuality may have brought him into contact with 'a small clique' given to 'curious ways' and 'appetites' – those boys who secretly resisted the headmaster's standard lecture against 'smut'. Rather defensively, Larry prefaced this account with the editorial assertion that 'the boy is a dirty little animal, not a eunuch nor an angel', and he has Walsh conclude, 'It was purely and simply a sort of *experimental* attitude – like tasting a new drink. I didn't like it, that's all.'[48] Perhaps Durrell felt that this was as close as he could then come to hinting at group masturbation or adolescent homosexual behaviour, whether or not either applied to him in real life.

Canon Burnside had been headmaster since 1908 and he maintained, in speech and in writing, that he and his staff existed to do their duty towards the school 'regardless of anything else'.[49] Burnside had handsome, direct eyes set wide over a full, even generous, mouth that seemed always on the verge of a smile. He had a face that promised both kindness and unflinching sternness. Certainly he was capable of both. He disapproved of smoking in public but enjoyed cigarettes. He feared the 'Trade Union spirit' that he thought stood in the way of the kind of service he expected from others; and he dreaded a future in which 'religious teaching should not be the basis of the whole of the education of this country'.[50] This was the man who had charge of Larry's education during one of the most rebellious periods of his adolescence, and he would write a searing caricature of Burnside as 'the immaculate one' in *Pied Piper of Lovers*.

Larry benefited, however, from the conscientious teaching that Canon Burnside demanded. 'The masters, like the Jesuits, were honest and lively and most competent,' Larry would recall, stressing their honesty outside matters of religion. 'My French master for example on learning that I wanted to learn French and become a writer immediately took a subscription to *Le Monde* for me – the weekly literary pages . . . . This kindly and delightful man was mad about France and French literature and encouraged my interest. His name was Mr Hollingsworth . . . he taught me my first words of the language.'[51] Larry's memory failed him – *Le Monde* did not commence publication until 1944 – yet he did rise from 13th out of 16 in French to first place in his form. He also studied the piano, and made the Pass List on the instrument.

Larry hated the religiosity of the school. Burnside must have seemed an agent of Big Granny, calling down Granny's God on the heads of the young sinners bowing their pale faces in the chapel, yet paradoxically and perhaps hypocritically – to Larry – allowing tantalizing glimpses of the wonderful pagan world of the ancient Mediterranean. 'I realized that I was in the middle of a lot of liars, and self-righteous like hell,' Larry would say later, his voice taking on a cutting edge.[52] He reacted with 'a morbid reluctance to attend chapel' and a yearning for exuberant paganism.[53] 'I saw through what I could see around me – in the Christian thing.'[54] The twice-daily chapel services probably inspired his description of the 'ordeals' suffered by Walsh Clifton, with 'the organ groaning loudly above the uproar in lachrymose anguish . . . groaning and invoking *Granny's God* . . . . Meantime he must try not to listen: *he must not listen.*'[55] In the classical world so adored by that good Christian, Canon Burnside, Larry found an appealing antidote to Granny's God: he responded with 'the erection (in private) of altars to Apollo, Aphrodite, or another [god]'.[56]

Between the influences of Big Granny and St Edmund's, Larry was cured of formal Christianity for good. In 1935, accusing his Quaker friend Alan Thomas of 'pussy-footing it with the anglican jesus', Larry struck out at Jehovah: 'As for me, I think, JAH will always be a Ya! of derision.'[57] Many years later still, when he was asked whether he believed in God, Larry replied, echoing Voltaire, 'Of course I do – but in every kind of God. It is religion I don't believe in'.[58] Larry was developing this view at St Edmund's, and by the time he left he was already becoming interested in Buddhism, but not as a ritual of incense and chants: 'It's after all a philosophy, not a religion in the other sense.' Larry had never really felt himself a Christian in any case: 'I didn't have a nervous breakdown or anything, I didn't have a change of faith.'[59] None the less, schoolboy Larry desired to please both his parents and Canon Burnside, and on 3 December 1926 the young sinner endured confirmation by the Archbishop of Canterbury in the great cathedral. He was fascinated by the place, the mediaeval darkness, the ancient martyrdom of Thomas Becket. Doubtless the solemnity of the present occasion also impressed him, but religious acceptance did not penetrate his sceptical hide.

It was not only Christianity that young Larry turned away from: he learned to *put up with*, not to accept, Pudding Island. Larry wrote of Walsh's early experience of England, 'But far above everything else it was teaching him to put up with the life of a narrow, ignorant, and conservative society in which practically none of the rules (unwritten) and regulations (printed) were not wholly idiotic.'[60] Like Walsh, Larry was not becoming truly English: 'You're not a damned Englander yet,' Walsh is told. 'They haven't got you yet.'[61] Clearly, Larry was also speaking for himself. His housemaster tried to convince him to study hard and to excel at games so as to reflect credit on the house. Larry played football and 'got all [his] house colours', he claimed,[62] but he was not good enough in any sport to receive school colours.[63] He was, however, an apt pupil for the boxing lessons offered by the physical training instructor, and fought for his form in the ring with 'huge ferocity'. Gradually he lost the child-plumpness that had marked him in India and, although still short for his years, became lean and hard-bodied.

At the end of his first term, Larry was ranked near the bottom of his form in every area but the Division of History and English, and even there he was only 10th out of 16. However, he became popular with some of the masters and he was trusted to help reproduce examination papers on the mimeograph, 'on parole not to look at the texts'. The temptation was too great: 'Needless to say . . . I was a clever lad,' he admitted[64] – although whether his opportunities had anything to do with the later improvement in his marks, he never revealed.

Larry's studies during his rather haphazard schooling cannot be measured by curricula and school terms. For one thing, he always claimed to be unable to pursue a subject that did not interest him. Larry would have Walsh Clifton say to a scolding housemaster: 'It's not a question of working. It's just that I cannot do anything that doesn't interest me.'[65] Larry was really educating himself, and he evolved his own techniques. He 'developed the deplorable habit of underlining those sentences in books which stated views with which he agreed'.[66] He also kept a volume of aphorisms, a black notebook in which he jotted down cryptic notes and copied passages, sometimes cutting out paragraphs and pictures from magazines, and even books, and pasting them in. This practice he would continue throughout his life.

Larry's parents did not come to England during 1927, and he attended St Edmund's during the summer term. A seaside visit, possibly with his aunt, Muriel Pearce, buoyed his spirits considerably, and would furnish an important episode in *Pied Piper of Lovers*. If the fictional parallel holds, Larry met a girl at the beach, fell in love, and parted from her: but there is no direct evidence. In his recreating (or imagining) the embrace, Larry would attempt, parenthetically and in italics, to catch the mindless surrender of a first love:

If you shut your eyes and allowed your lulled senses to swirl you forward until you hung limp against her warmth, limp against her body like a swallow on a wall . . . It was as if you were being gently chloroformed . . . It was as if you grew slowly into her, that essential her . . . grafting your body on to her . . . merging your sense and will voluptuously into her . . . until her breasts seemed to grow into you, firm and piercing. . . .[67]

The male *passivity* is noteworthy, the swooning unto death of a man who desires to give himself up to woman: here I am, take me, cherish me! The childlike dependent clinging to the woman, significantly without sexual consummation, suggests Larry's loneliness and insecurity, both as an adolescent and when he came to write these lines, at the age of twenty-two. Images of heartbreak and loss would dominate Larry's earliest extant poetry, as in 'Sonnet Astray', published when he was nineteen but possibly written as many as three years earlier:

> And I,
> Bewilderingly wonder at my great foolishness
> To leave you forever alone that night by a star swept sea,
> With the laughter of the dark surf in your eyes . . .[68]

It is quite likely that both the novel and the poem reflected the same event.

A calendar year and one school term made up all his experience of St Edmund's, and at the end of the autumn term in December 1927 Larry left school. He had not failed his exams, nor was he expelled for disciplinary reasons. He had not distinguished himself, but he had completed a year in the Cadet Force, he had advanced in the Fourth Form from Grade B to Grade A, and his performance had improved considerably: in English and History he had climbed to second out of eighteen. In General Science and

Greek he stood second among eight. Only in Maths was he still near the bottom. Clearly, his attitude towards the school had improved, for in General Order he now held second place out of eighteen.

His official record concludes, 'Went to Wratting Park: for Coaching.'[69] Like his father at Roorkee, Larry did not end up with a single academic, athletic or other kind of award noted after his name. 'My father's obsession was to get me to a university, you see, and I wasn't going fast enough,' Larry recalled; 'I had faulted on the age thing, and I was way behind in my studies.' Partly it was the class code – the move up to the 'officer and gentleman' social level to which Lawrence Samuel aspired – but, as Larry knew, 'It wasn't just simply a snob thing; it was also tied up with job hunting.'[70] A degree from Cambridge or Oxford would open many doors. These considerations seemed too abstract, and too far in the future. He was bored with most of his classes, so Larry made no objection when his parents resolved to take him out of St Edmund's; in fact, leaving school may have been his own idea. He was certainly impatient to get on with his life.

IN LATER YEARS, Larry was to recall almost exclusively good things about his instructors at his three main schools, St Joseph's, St Olave's and St Saviour's, and St Edmund's – a fine gallery of saints – crediting each institution, to various interrogators, with instilling in him a love of literature. It was also part of his interviewing personality to speak well of others; that is, when he was not riding a hobby-horse such as the horrors of Pudding Island. When he was lashing out at schooling in *Pied Piper of Lovers*, all the masters with one exception, the man who encourages Walsh's reading, are portrayed as bloodless hypocrites, as ineffectual plodders and petty tyrants blind to the true purposes of education. Larry certainly possessed, from a very early age, an extraordinary ability to get along with people when he wanted to: it was part of his response to the terror of finding himself, a youngster away from home, at the mercy of others. Like many abused children – although Larry seems never to have been abused in any serious physical sense – he placated his tormentors. Whatever his real opinions of his schoolmasters, it is clear that they had not failed him except in maths. Certainly, when he left St Edmund's he possessed an ingrained habit of wide reading and careful notation, a grasp of English literature and history, a love of classical Greece, a grounding in French, an indifferent knowledge of Latin and less Greek: these would serve him well.

After St Edmund's, Larry was placed with various professional crammers in an attempt to bring him up to standard in the subjects he would face in university entrance examinations. In early 1928 he was sent to board at West Wratting near Cambridge, apparently with a tutor. Nothing came of it.

A university education was not to young Larry's liking – not, at least, the concentrated study needed to get into and through a university. 'Neither my brother [Gerald] nor I could ever pass an examination,' he would often remark, ignoring Leslie's existence.[71] Larry could never let the matter drop, however. He liked to analyse his declared inability to get into a university. 'At seventeen or eighteen, I was anti-everything,' he would recall. Then he would add modestly:

And yet I should have liked to have gone to Oxford, if only to give my father some pleasure. Intellectually I was brilliant, but like all Irishmen I was dreadfully lazy. And above all my subconscious was set on proving to my father . . . that it was unfair to send me back to prison. So in spite of my capabilities I fluffed all the exams; three, four, five times . . . . Of course I hadn't read Freud at the time, or had anything to do with psychiatrists as I do now; it was a natural complex: I deliberately failed the exams, because of a subconscious resentment, in order to prove that the initial decision was wrong.

As the university prospect faded, Larry's commitment to writing grew: 'It was then that I decided to write,' he claimed. 'Before long I had joined the world of London bums.'[72] How far Larry believed his own account is debatable, and he contradicted himself freely: although he would repeat his claim about failing entrance examinations, he would date his decision to write seriously anywhere from his pre-teens to the publication of his first novel in 1935.

During his school years and tutorial period there were a couple of holiday trips across the Channel for Larry, and on one occasion he thrilled to the beauty of Lausanne and Vevey, stopping in Paris on his return. He identified as his poetic initiation a copy of Philippe Soupault's study of Lautréamont, which he picked up by chance on the *quais* and read beside the Seine.[73] When his French would not suffice he turned to Richard Aldington's essays and translations of French poetry and fiction.[74] These short excursions, free from official oversight and free from the social codes governing the behaviour of youth in England, confirmed Larry's early instinct that in escape from Pudding Island lay his main chance of joy and even of survival. He was also learning to escape into verse: by the time of his sixteenth birthday, he had begun seriously to write. 'I suspect it was an enjoyment of my own privacy,' he would recall many years later. 'If you're very lonely, it's very useful to write poetry. It keeps you company, like a pet parrot.'[75]

Early in 1928, far away in Lahore, Larry's father developed severe headaches and started to act irrationally: 'He began to drink the ink instead of the whisky,' Larry was told.[76] Hoping that a period of rest in a cool climate would set him to rights, the family went to Dalhousie, an Indian hill station near the present border with Pakistan. It was only a short day's journey by motor car for the Durrells. The road climbed steadily in a long series of switchbacks after Pathankot, and soon they were among the pines and cedars above 6,000 feet. Dalhousie existed mainly as a health resort, with a climate so cool that tea would not grow on the nearby slopes. Snow and hail were fairly common in February and March, and huge sacred langurs with magnificent grizzled pelts lounged about the town in the red tree rhododendrons, chewing reflectively on the blossoms. The Durrells rented a two-storey house off a small road junction called Charing Cross, one of the two main circuses of Dalhousie, and moved in with chauffeur, governess, ayah and bearers. The street name seemed to mock Lawrence Samuel's hopes for England. He realized his need of help, and his proud nature had become 'very amenable' at times. He could still walk, yet 'you couldn't trust him', his daughter remembered.[77] Terrifying his family, he fought against his headaches and loss of control, but eventually he had to be admitted to the tiny English Cottage Hospital on the edge of a ridge facing the Himalayas. Louisa moved with him into the hospital. Leslie, Margaret and three-year-old Gerald stayed in the house with their Irish governess, who walked them along every day in melancholy procession to visit their parents, stopping coming and going at St Mary's Church. Margaret recalled that, as the governess 'was an ardent Catholic, we did a mighty lot of praying'.[78] She had a stock of religious pictures and bottles of holy water from Lourdes, and she told the children that if anything happened on the road, they were to run for the priest, not the police or the doctor.[79]

Neither the relatively primitive medicine practised in Dalhousie nor the prayers proved efficacious. Lawrence Samuel Durrell died during a violent storm on 16 April, six days after entering the hospital. His malady was described by the family as 'a tumour on the brain'[80], and the Dalhousie official register named as the immediate cause of death a cerebral haemorrhage. He was only forty-three years old. Larry was informed by cable. A brief service was held in the small slate-roofed Anglican church in Dalhousie, mossy under the cedars, and a burial party of soldiers took Lawrence Samuel to the English cemetery[81] on an evergreen-covered hillside sloping steeply down towards the Punjab, the vast theatre of his railway-building and engineering efforts. His children were not permitted to attend the funeral. The minister, the Reverend Pryce-Jones, seemed to Louisa cold and supercilious. It was the nuns at St Mary's Convent who consoled the shattered widow, and so warmly that Louisa nearly turned Roman Catholic in the days following.[82]

LARRY DURRELL'S LIFELONG RETICENCE about speaking of his father suggests that his response to his death may have resembled Walsh's under similar circumstances in *Pied Piper of Lovers*: 'He felt guilty and ill at ease under the bland expressions of condolence – guilty because he was capable of feeling nothing but his overwhelming dumbness.' Larry's various partings from his parents, coupled with the schoolboy code that demanded the concealment of suffering, whether physical or emotional, had taught him to avoid any public display of his emotions. Now, with his father's death, he was expected to show grief, but he found himself turned to stone, 'heavy and dull', unable to weep.[83]

The shock none the less hit Larry hard. So much of what he had done in England had been conditioned by the presumed approval or disapproval of his father that Larry felt suddenly rudderless. He had very much wanted to please his father, even while he was bent upon proving that it had been wrong to send him to England. The disappearance of Lawrence Samuel in his guise as a figure of utter moral rectitude cast Larry adrift. Gradually Larry came to understand how much of what he had done, in England as in India, had been tempered by considerations such as 'Dad would be pleased', or 'He wouldn't like this.' Suddenly Larry realized that there was no one whose approval or censure *really* mattered: he was free, yes, but he felt the burden of his responsibility for himself crash down upon him. Despairing and empty and lonely, 'for want of company' Larry apparently attempted to find solace with 'one of the salvarsan cuties', he would later confess.[84] The episode found its way into *Pied Piper of Lovers*: Walsh, lonely and sad after the death of his father, 'took a bus to the nearest town; for the first and the last time in his life he went with a woman', a paid one.[85]

This banal liaison may have been Larry's sexual initiation. Often in the future, when faced with a crisis, he would seek comfort and release in sensuality, would 'get carried off in sex, the ambulance', as he was to write later in a poem. His sexual precocity, however, did not appear to be evidence of emotional maturity. Rather, cut off from his mother and from other older women to whom he might have confided his distress, he had thrown himself on the mercy of the first female who would hold and caress him. It marked the beginning of a pattern. Richard Pine, in his monograph on Durrell's 'Mindscape', identifies the two poles of Larry's quest as being 'sexual curiosity' and 'metaphysical speculation': the former, as defined by Freud, being irrevocably linked with the quest for knowledge, the second a main feature of Aldous Huxley's *Point Counter Point*,[86] which appeared the year of Lawrence Samuel's death, and which was much discussed in Larry's London circle shortly after he left St Edmund's. Here, in the first great impact of death upon Larry, the sexual and the speculative impulses came together for him.

The effect of Lawrence Samuel's death on the entire family was immediate and profound: within two months Louisa left India, never to return, and from then on devoted herself entirely to her offspring. The old tension between husband and livelihood in India, children at school in the Home Country – the lot of most colonial wives with families – ended with Louisa's move to London. The Alleyn Park Road house in Dulwich required a large and expensive staff, so Louisa evidently renewed an older lease to her brother-in-law Harry Rickwood.[87] Then she purchased a service flat in the Queens Hotel in Upper Norwood just south of Dulwich. The Browns, a matriarchal clan consisting of Grandmother Richardson, her daughter Mrs Brown, and two granddaughters, were Louisa's only good friends in England, and they already lived in the hotel. One of the girls, Dorothy, became Margaret's particular friend.

Without the stern authority of her husband behind her, the mild and unassertive Louisa could not control her strongly independent children. Leslie was a terror, Margaret was showing the unconventional, headstrong Durrell nature, and even little Gerald, only three years old, was already horrifying his mother by bringing into the house every insect and animal he could catch. Larry was still grappling with the implications of his father's death when he was writing *Pied Piper of Lovers* six years later, and in the novel he analyses the impact on a family of the loss of a dominant husband: 'He had harnessed and directed [the wife's] energies with the gentleness of his own magnificent largeness and strength.'[88] With Lawrence Samuel and the established social pattern of India bracing her, Louisa had been quite an effective parent and household manager, a woman secure in her place. All that changed after his death and her departure from India. Larry too missed the stability that his father had represented: he was not ready to assume responsibility for himself, yet there was no one to shoulder that responsibility for him. If only he could be eleven again, back in India, with his father still presiding over his destiny! An eleven-year-old was not expected to behave responsibly at all times, and in crises during the rest of his life Larry would not infrequently lose himself in pre-adolescent behaviour, lashing out with tongue and, occasionally, fists.

It was not finances that caused the Durrells to drop out of schools and give up the prospect of a university education. Lawrence Samuel's Indian partners dealt honourably with the widow; Larry recalled his mother saying, 'Thank goodness the Indian partners were so straight.'[89] Although a depression in the construction industry in India had somewhat diminished the profits of Durrell & Co., there was enough money for school fees, a large house, a few servants, even a chauffeur. Stone, the chauffeur, referred to as 'the family manservant', worked on Larry's boxing skills, sparring with him.

Inheritances were to become an important theme in *Pied Piper of Lovers*, where, although they may have promised well, they always turned out to be disappointingly small. Walsh's friend Gordon, speaking of his patrimony, says, 'It was a lot when I first got it; but most of the securities were so rocky that they crumpled up.'[90] In Louisa's case, a portion of the wealth that Lawrence Samuel left was in Japanese gold shares, and these collapsed. Walsh, when his father dies in India, says, 'I have an idea that when my father's estate is cleared up there will not be much money – certainly I think not enough for me to return to school.'[91] While this may not have been the case for Larry, within a few years the family's circumstances had declined appreciably. Like most Victorian women, Louisa was totally unused to handling money in larger than household amounts: women were not *expected* to know anything about investments, interest and mortgages. Larry was to claim with some bitterness that his mother, ill-advised, had squandered a quite satisfactory competence. The squandering began at the hotel in Upper Norwood.

The Queens Hotel was in Church Road, near the old Crystal Palace, and it housed, apart from the Durrells, an assortment of odd characters, some of whom would appear but slightly disguised in *The Black Book*. Down the corridor was a dining room 'like an aquarium', full of retired people 'out of work and on the shelf', old colonels 'a little bit soft in the head and chain-smoking and old ladies with irresistible giggles and dropped wombs'. Larry did not confine himself to the Queens Hotel 'geriatric scene', as he called

71

it.[92] 'This was when he was having his times with the negresses and all that,' Larry's first wife Nancy recalled disapprovingly.[93] The Queens Hotel would become the Hotel Regina in *The Black Book*, and Larry admitted that a couple of his caricatures in the book were 'somewhat libellous – very, in fact'.[94]

While Larry was storing up events and character notes for his writing, his siblings and the two Brown girls terrorized the hotel: once they decorated the discreet, sentimental statuary in the main hallway and lobby with underwear; another time they rearranged the shoes left for polishing outside the room doors – ladies' shoes in front of men's rooms and vice versa. Mrs Hocking, the proprietress, soon knew whose doors to knock upon whenever any outrage was discovered. 'Now, dears, you really *mustn't* do such things. What will the neighbours think?' Louisa kept telling her brood.[95]

Larry wandered disconsolately about Upper Norwood and Dulwich. Everything seemed grey: the buildings, the rain, the faces. The Crystal Palace, originally built for the Great Exhibition of 1851, 'glittered' with 'grimy glass' in the 'sooty darkness', and its towers were 'two black phalloi'.[96] Louisa went to the family solicitor for advice about Larry: place him with an Army crammer, the man said. The service will straighten the lad out, and he can make a career in the Indian Army! Soldiering had done well for his grandfather. However, India no longer looked so good to Larry – his roots had been dislodged – and going into the Army was 'the last thing he wanted to do'.[97] Consequently, Larry did badly with this tutor as well, but he made a friend among his fellow-victims, Cecil Jeffries, who like Larry had no intention of being crammed into the military.

By the summer of 1929 Larry was very much at a loose end: he had given up on the university, and he had refused to join the Army. He had learned to drive to some extent – enough to take Louisa's car out and smash it rather badly, as an angry Uncle Cecil Buck discovered when he came in December to borrow the car.[98] In 1930 Larry managed a trip to Amsterdam where he 'felt the benediction of rebirth', as he wrote in his poem 'Happy Vagabond'.[99] Larry's antics and strange acquaintances became a bit much, even for the tolerant Louisa: 'You can be as Bohemian as you like', she told him, 'but *not in the house*'.[100] 'I only feel that I am losing something by not being understood,' Larry would write when his fictional counterpart Walsh departed the family home in similar circumstances.[101] All his life Larry would be haunted by the conviction that neither in his writing nor in his person was he properly understood. Louisa, baffled, again asked the family solicitor for advice. He happened to have a friend who was an estate agent in Leytonstone, east London: young Durrell could work there as an unarticled trainee. Larry could see a glimmer of advantage: this would give a colouring of mundane purpose to his move to London. His mother agreed to give him a weekly allowance. Packing a guitar with the rest of his kit, Larry escaped towards the heart of the great city.

He knew he did not want to live in Leytonstone, a dull, middle-class area that could almost have been Upper Norwood. He found rooms off Charlotte Street in Bloomsbury – most promisingly, he thought, in a house where Verlaine was reputed to have lived. Not far away, at 5 Old Compton Street, Verlaine and Rimbaud had drunk absinthe. Leytonstone was a world away: some days a reluctant Larry inspected property and dunned tenants for back rent. Dogs strained to get at him, people slammed doors in his face, and he learned what it meant to *distrain chattels*. Leytonstone Road intersected with Henniker Street – the name Larry was to give forty years later to an elderly brothel-keeper in *The Revolt of Aphrodite*. His desultory work around Leytonstone was a stage in his own revolt.

Although Larry at various times smoothed over his early life in England – St Edmund's was beautiful, the masters were kindly, he was treated with understanding – the sum total of his memories and remarks adds up to a negative: 'Then that mean, shabby little island up there wrung my guts out of me and tried to destroy anything singular and unique in me,' he once stated.[102] The whole ambience was wrong: 'I very much hoped that England was going to be Surtees' England – a vulgar, jolly, roistering England, not especially aesthetic or cultivated or delicate in any sense, but something with its vulgar roots in food, sex, and good living.'[103] He certainly did not find the England of Surtees' *Jorrocks's Jaunts and Jollities*, Handley Cross and Mr Soapey Sponge. However, Master Durrell the schoolboy, Lawrence G. Durrell the failed candidate for a university education, was struggling to become Larry Durrell: Larry to his friends, Durrell to the literary world. Durrell the writer would eventually come to terms with England; Larry never would.

LARRY BECAME FRIENDLY with his second cousin, the novelist Richard Sidney Blaker, who was earning a modest popular recognition. Blaker had an uncle living in Upper Norwood, and the family was on visiting terms with the Durrells and the Bucks. Larry liked Blaker's *Scabby Dichson*, and his *Medal Without Bar*, which appeared in 1930, was ranked by some as being among the best novels to have emerged from the First World War.

While Blaker had not exactly lit up the literary skies, his friend the writer Louis Golding said that 'his sense of people ranks him with Arnold Bennett and [his] sense of things is as consummate as Rudyard Kipling's'.[104] Blaker was born in 1893 in India, and had inhaled mustard gas on the Western Front. His health had never fully recovered, but he had received his MA in Classics at Queen's College, Oxford. He was a handsome man with thin, curving lips, a long arched nose, wavy hair and an air of quizzical detachment. Here was someone for Larry to emulate, and in fact Blaker gave him his first real encouragement towards authorship.[105] India, a touch of Kipling, and Oxford seemed to add up to success in writing. Larry felt that he had two parts of the equation in hand, and he was sure he could finesse the third if he would only throw himself into the task. *Scabby Dichson*, with its many echoes of Kipling, would provide Larry with suggestions for *Pied Piper of Lovers*. In both novels a half-orphaned boy attends an Indian boarding school and is self-consciously alone, superior and proud; a character named Turnbull is also a friend and mentor to the hero in each book. Scabby Dichson's mother is eventually found hanging from a punkah-rope in a seedy neighbourhood of Lahore: the image of a hanged woman would spring up in Larry's last major fiction.

Blaker was considerate and kind, even to the point of letting Larry use his vacation caravan near Cadnam in the New Forest, for 'a couple of tough winters in Robin Hood like circs', Larry would recall: 'No girls alas.'[106] Perhaps Larry found his cousin too elegant, too genteel, his writing too ironically detached. At any rate, the personal connection did not long continue, and Blaker would be dead by 1941.

However, Larry kept up his friendship with Cecil Jeffries, who had acquired a small press. Within a year, in 1931, *Quaint Fragment: Poems Written between the Ages of Sixteen and Nineteen* was printed by Jeffries, who had asked Larry for something to practise on. The subject matter of the seventeen poems tends towards past passions, loss and death, the tone towards sweet melancholy: whiffs of precocious decadence, but without the bite of Rimbaud. In 'A Dedication' Larry announced the poems to be 'lame and halting parodies/ Of greater, better poems'. However, he demonstrated a fine ear for the cadences of English: 'There is a great heart-break in an evening sea', he began one poem.[107] This rarest of Durrell's *incunabula* – only a few are known to have survived – had a very limited print run, and the London bookseller Joseph A. Allen, who co-operated with Jeffries on the venture, thought that fewer than a dozen copies had been printed before the type was dispersed.[108]

Wʜᴇɴ ᴛʜᴇ ʙʀᴏᴡɴs ᴍᴏᴠᴇᴅ to Bournemouth in March 1930, Louisa Durrell decided to follow them. 'Somebody told her the sun shone here more than anywhere else in England, and as we always seem to chase the sun . . .' recalled Margaret, leaving her sentence unfinished.[109] Louisa bought Berridge House, an imposing place in Parkstone, next to Bournemouth, and in 1932 she sold the Alleyn Park residence. In fact, Louisa's children accused their distracted mother of believing that she had bought in Bournemouth itself. Larry's anger at estate agents was reflected in *Pied Piper of Lovers*, in which 'a bland and accomplished ruffian' hoodwinks Aunt Brenda into a foolish purchase.[110] True to form, Louisa Durrell bought above her needs and beyond her means. It became an adage with her that 'when people find out it's only a woman they have to deal with they take advantage.'[111] The house was a rambling three-storey building set close to the road but with a large back garden sloping downhill to a tennis court.

Larry did not move with the family, but dashed down from London for weekends and holidays, either borrowing his mother's car or taking the train. He disliked Parkstone/Bournemouth from the first: it was another 'geriatric ward',[112] but he complained about the children as well. Larry's young cousins Phyllis and Molly Rickwood learned to ride bicycles on the lawn, screaming with laughter when they fell. Larry, sitting in an upstairs room trying to write, would lean out of the window periodically to shout, 'Stop that bloody row!' The cousins remembered Gerald as a beautiful little boy, gentle and great fun. He had a secret hideout high in a tree, to which they dared not follow him, and he terrified them by playing with glow-worms, allowing the insects to crawl around his fingers. Margaret enjoyed Parkstone and was doing well in her studies at Malvern. Only Leslie seemed to be unable to get a grip on himself. He drove his mother mad by lounging in bed till noon and then slouching about; and he was moody and would sometimes turn on the younger children.[113] Only when there was a party did he show the warm, engaging side of his nature. Fortunately, almost anything could become an excuse for a party at Berridge House. Once someone decided to have a bonfire, and when the pile of brushwood was slow to light, Louisa said, 'Leslie, there's a bottle of spirits under the sink – fetch it, would you, dear?' Leslie dashed out waving a bottle, and the flames rose with a whoosh. Only then did they discover that he had poured an entire bottle of whisky over the damp wood.[114]

For about a year there was a staff at Berridge House that included a butler, a housekeeper named Lottie, and one or two other servants; then

Louisa's banker stepped in to inform her that she was living well beyond her income. The Great Depression that continued for years after the US stock market crash of 1929 was eating further into her capital. Berridge House was sold at a loss and Louisa bought again, a smaller but still very substantial dwelling set in a garden with tall evergreens and shrubs. She christened the new house at 18A Wimborne Road 'Dixie Lodge' and settled in, retaining the services of Lottie. Louisa was finally in Bournemouth, where she thought she wanted to be.

BY MID-1932 LARRY HAD MET a young woman who was attracted to him in part because she had seen him driving a large, dark maroon saloon car, his mother's new Hillman. Nancy Isobel Myers, an art student at the Slade, was intrigued by this compact young man whose small stature and round face made him seem even younger than his twenty years, made him seem to need mothering. Larry played up his boyish looks by amusing Nancy with baby-talk: 'I'se only ickle baby,' he clowned.[115] It was not entirely joking on Larry's part: a side of him still wanted the security of a woman who would look after him. Irrationally, he felt betrayed by his mother,[116] abandoned by Aunt Muriel. In Nancy he perceived an attractive young woman who also seemed very capable, poised, moving in her circle with verve and assurance. Nancy was a few months younger than Larry, five feet eight inches tall, slender, and wore her blonde hair in a modish bob. She dressed carefully and was so lovely that people turned to stare: Larry was smitten. Nancy was very conscious of the need to establish an identity: 'You had to *shed* your family and everything,' she recalled. 'You became an *artist* or you became something or other like that.'[117] Larry was eager to help her shedding and becoming process – he was doing the same himself. When he attacked with repartee and laughter, probing her ideas and prejudices, she responded with passionate argument. Nancy's family, more so than Larry's, boasted a sufficiently formal and formidable respectability to need shedding, or so it seemed to the young artist. One grandfather and a great-uncle were reverend ministers, and her maternal great-grandfather, William Green, had been Governor of Durham Prison. The Greens were entitled to a coat-of-arms with 'three stags trippant argent' and they were proud of their somewhat ambivalent motto, *Semper Viridis* – Eternally Green. Financial reverses had left Nancy's parents dependent on her father's small provincial dental practice, and her grandfather had paid for her schooling at Lincoln High School.

Nancy may have talked about casting off her family in order to find herself as an artist, but her manner and accent were part of her being, a class badge. Although not really a snob, Nancy felt herself very much a lady and took herself seriously. Her father certainly did not take her art studies seriously, and he was horrified when she said that she might become an actress. Socially, the Durrells were down a peg or two. Louisa and Larry's aunts and uncles were quite *proper*, but they were not quite *it*. Larry was fully aware that they bore a colonial stigma: they wore funny hats, and in Anglo-Indian accents compared everything in England to India – usually to the detriment of England. He exploited their foibles for comic effect when he was with Nancy.

Nancy and her friends prided themselves on their knowledge of advanced literature and read D. H. Lawrence and Aldous Huxley. She had been consorting with a nest of progressive Wykehamists in the Fitzrovia of Augustus John and Nina Hamnett. Nancy took Larry, her new acquaintance, in tow. Thus Larry met Peter Bull, not yet properly launched on his acting career; the Honourable Nicholas Phipps, a 'sort of Noël Cowardish' young man; and George Curwen Wilkinson. Bull was large and bulky – among his roles would be Pozzo in *Waiting for Godot* and 'the boxing champion of the world' in another play – but his heavy, brooding face masked a frolicking sense of humour and a tendency towards high-pitched, hysterical laughter. Fitzroy Square was considered arty, and a generation earlier Virginia Woolf had held her Thursday evening gatherings there, 'where long-legged young men would sit in long basket-chairs smoking pipes and talking', as Lady Ottoline Morrell had described the scene.[118]

George Wilkinson had just the long legs to fit Mrs Woolf's Bloomsbury tableau, and he smoked a curved briar and cultivated a Strachey air. He felt the self-conscious intellectual superiority of a Winchester boy – his was a far more prestigious school than Larry's St Edmund's. A left-handed fencer, he had taken the bronze medal in the public school championships. Then George's father had died, leaving him a small income on which he could barely subsist in London. His Curwen relatives on his mother's side were prominent Cumberland folk and his great-grandfather had founded the Curwen Press. For a time during 1932 Larry moved into George's bed-sitter at 6 Fitzroy Square, where he met Pamela Black, the young actress who was to become Mrs Wilkinson two years later. Larry would write this scene into *Pied Piper of Lovers*: Pam in a bathing costume cooking – and burning – the supper, George stretched at full length pontificating. Pam was small, pretty in a puckish way, with a quick laugh, and she wore her corn-golden hair in an Eton crop, shorn close at the back. Larry struck her as 'a short and good-looking man' whose snub nose 'made him look very young and cherub-like'. She thought him a 'brilliant talker' and liked his 'charm and enthusiasm'.[119] Larry found Pam very attractive, and would give the character based on her in *Pied Piper* Nancy's middle name, Isobel.

In those early days Wilkinson took the lead and Larry, somewhat awed by his friend's sophistication, danced attendance. George was very thin and very tall, had a pleasant face, spoke with sardonic humour, 'like the driest of dry sherries', and he peered at the world through tortoise-shell glasses.[120] He worked as secretary for A. J. A. Symons at The First Editions Club; he spoke in measured tones and twiddled a signet ring on his elegant finger. George had a neat, pointed brown beard that he liked to stroke downwards: 'such a *pubic-looking* affair' Larry would term it.[121] On one occasion George stroked Nancy's breast as a connoisseur might, 'and then gave a sort of judgement like a wine-taster .... "*Very* nice"'.[122] Sarcastically, Larry would say of Russell, the Wilkinson act-alike in *Pied Piper of Lovers*, 'He . . . fancies himself as a seducer.'[123]

George, Larry and Nancy frequented the Bloomsbury bookshop of Joseph Allen at 16 Grenville Street. The shop had been a post office and bore the caduceus of Hermes on either side of the door, so Allen named his small printing venture the Caduceus Press. Allen was a jaunty dresser, a short, stocky man with the self-confident stance of a boxer or a jockey. Only a few years older than Larry, he cast an interested eye on Nancy and decided she was a passionate number. Coolly, he speculated that sex and jealousy were behind the quarrels he witnessed early on between Nancy and Larry. Larry showed all the traditional signs of being in love with Nancy: he was, in rapid succession, tender, cruel, entertaining, boorish, courtly and possessive.[124] He was revolted by the easy sexuality of the young in Bloomsbury. Full-blooded lust was fine, but not the thin couplings of casual revellers. 'Lust was something too fine-tempered, too supple, to be blunted and soiled by a mob of chattering starlings,' of 'thumb-sucking apes', he would write.[125]

Larry took Nancy to Bournemouth to meet his family, but not before he had dramatized and exaggerated their deficiencies: his mother was 'mad', she drank and threw her money away; his brothers and sister were 'ridiculous' and 'spoiled'. Nancy was intrigued, never having heard anyone speak in quite this way about his family, but she immediately loved the entire household. It had an air of craziness that appealed: 'It looked like people sort of playing at keeping house rather than really keeping house,' she thought.[126] No one was forced into a mould; people could – and were apt to – say anything. Leslie, Margaret and Larry introduced Nancy to bicycle polo and the concomitant risks of skinned knees and torn stockings. Gerald, then about seven, reminded her of Christopher Robin. He was enrolled in Wickwood School, but seldom went. His technique for avoiding lessons was to develop a 'school pain' every Monday morning,[127] and if that did not work, to cling screaming to the playground railings until his mother relented and took him home. For a time, he had a tutor at home.

Nancy's visit ended in a terrific row with Louisa Durrell when Larry *and* Gerry jumped into bed with Nancy the first morning, and the luckless girl was accused of corrupting a mere child. Nancy and Larry were welcomed back a fortnight later by a cheerful Louisa who simply adopted Nancy, deciding that she was too thin and trying to fatten her with butter, cream and pastries, and finally inviting Nancy to join her sipping tea laced with gin.

Nancy had been absolutely broke and was staying in borrowed lodgings in Charlotte Street when she met Larry. Then she became part of the cast of *Children in Uniform*, a drama based on Christa Winsloe's *Child Manuela: Mädchen in Uniform*, at a salary of thirty shillings a week. This allowed her to pay eighteen and sixpence weekly for bed and breakfast with a Mr and Mrs Lang. Larry at this time had two rooms off Charlotte Street on the Bertorelli or west side. Mr Lang was a very proper gentleman – he had expelled his previous tenant, an impoverished Yorkshire Labour MP, for entertaining a lady in his room – and Nancy was nearly given the same treatment when Lang caught her 'canoodling and kissing' in the stairwell with Larry. Eventually Nancy left for a room in Calthorpe Street near Lamb's Conduit Street. If these various lodgings had anything in common it was that they were drab, cheerless and under-furnished.

Nancy had met a cadaverous poet named John Gawsworth through a friend at the Slade, and she introduced Larry to him at the Windmill Café, where Larry usually waited in the evenings for her to emerge from *Children in Uniform*. Larry was impressed by Gawsworth, whom he was to label 'my first Real Writer – a professional living by his books', completely ignoring his more financially successful cousin Richard Blaker. Gawsworth was not living very well to be sure, but 'inhabited an old attic' with crumbling beams and a rotting floor up three flights at 6 Denmark Street. Percival Mackay's jazz band rehearsed downstairs,[128] and a music publisher shared the building. Gawsworth took Larry and Nancy to his rooms where he displayed his treasures: his correspondence with de la Mare, Drinkwater and Wyndham Lewis; a skull-cap that had belonged to Dickens, a pen of

Thackeray's. Soon Larry was showing Gawsworth poems for criticism. Larry would walk over from his new flat at 106 Guilford Street near Russell Square. Gawsworth worked very hard indeed at being a literary gent. In fact, he even wrote under three sets of names, sometimes using his real name, Terence Ian Fytton-Armstrong, and at least once as Orpheus Scrannel. To Nancy he seemed '*incredibly* Grub Street': spiderlike in his dark chambers, he appeared emaciated, very white, with a long, thin face and a 'very pointed nose, sharp little black eyes'[129] – Larry said his eyes were 'brown and bright'. His broken nose, Larry thought, was not a disfigurement but 'gave his face a touch of Villonesque foxiness'.[130] From one corner of his mouth drooped a cigarette, and this he could slant up towards a simultaneously cocked eyebrow. During those early days his poverty did not prevent him from dressing with infallible neatness and keeping his shoes well shined.

Gawsworth, whose brother was the Jacobite Earl of Gawsworth, loved ceremony and valued the elegant gesture: even when almost penniless he would buy a large white rose on the anniversary of Charles I's execution and place it reverently at the foot of the king's statue in Whitehall. He was well aware that Nancy cut a striking figure and he liked to be seen with her at the Café Royal. On one occasion Larry and Gawsworth resolved to have a duel of words over her and orated most of the night while a bored Nancy drank tea and dozed. With the coming of daylight Gawsworth conceded defeat: 'Lawrence, the best man has won, and may you take the fair lady.'[131] Soon Larry and Nancy were sharing lodgings and funds. She encouraged him to give up entirely his estate agent apprenticeship, and Larry persuaded Nancy to pass her part in *Children in Uniform* on to Pam Black.

Gawsworth's painstaking criticism of a small handful of Larry's poems – the collection that would be published as *Ten Poems* towards the end of 1932 by the Caduceus Press – shows that he was an acute judge. 'A few of these are hardly printable yet,' he wrote, 'first because they show too many echoes (which is an adolescent failing of us all) and second because though splendidly musical – bless you! – they are yet in places very obscure.' Larry must not be rushed 'when ten days might make ten verses into ten poems!' Gawsworth was quite specific on influences, but with a prescription for correction: 'First, you must rid yourself of echoes. I take it as a very great compliment,' continued Gawsworth tactfully, 'that after reading me (as you evidently have!) you use quite unconsciously my phrases in parts. Frankly that is not allowable.' Gawsworth was not angry over the borrowings from his *Kingcup*, but he worried that reviewers would pick them up and chastise Larry: 'Eliot is the only man who bluffs through "stealing" consistently.' Gawsworth invited Larry to come over next Tuesday at 11 o'clock, 'and we'll spend the morning on them'. Above all, Larry should 'grip the pen in hand' and remember that 'there's lots to be thankful for'.[132] Nancy, in turn, took her pen in hand to design a graceful device for the cover, a male lutenist in a long robe.

Larry was humbly grateful for Gawsworth's critiques, and his literary advice was accompanied by exhibitions of practical lifemanship: his 'bibliographic breakfasts' were a revelation to Larry. Gawsworth had an amazing memory for titles, and when short of funds he would sniff with his fox-like nose over the threepenny bargain boxes on the pavement in Charing Cross Road, then plunge in and emerge with a *Frankenstein* first edition or a rare Edward Carpenter. The next step was to peddle his finds for a respectable sum at Foyle's.

Gawsworth was a valuable friend, for he was as much a confirmed Londoner as Dr Johnson, Dickens or Leigh Hunt, and he could guide Larry to the haunts of Goldsmith, Arthur Machen or Ouida, scattering dates, titles and anecdotes as they walked. As a chronicler of the ancient past, the recent past and the present, Gawsworth offered Larry an informal lecture series in literary associations. Gawsworth had met Hardy, Yeats and Wyndham Lewis; he disliked the work of Eliot, Auden and Spender; and it was inspiring to Larry that someone only a few months older than he was a published, respected author: Gawsworth's poem sequence *Kingcup* had gained him a prize and election to the Royal Society of Literature.

Larry may have stood in some awe of Gawsworth, but he soon asserted his independence: Dowson and the 1890s were not for Larry. As *Kingcup* faded in his judgement, he would transfer his admiration to Yeats and Lawrence, to Auden and Spender and Eliot – precisely those poets Gawsworth charged with polluting English poetry.

There was much that Larry admired in Gawsworth as a person, especially his generosity and his total commitment to literature. He had a passion for helping old and forgotten authors, the more eccentric the better, and spent months getting some of Matthew Phipps Shiel's books reissued. Like Gawsworth, Shiel – author of *The Purple Cloud* and twenty-three other novels – was a confirmed royalist, but the old man even claimed a kingdom for his own, the tiny island of Redonda in the West Indies, which he asserted the Crown had stolen from his father. What really intrigued Larry was the rumour that Shiel's father had made a lot of money mining guano – which Larry referred to quite accurately as 'booby shit'.[133] How wonderful to convert excrement into gold! Many years later in *Monsieur*, Larry would define gold in satiric terms as 'the apotheosis of the human turd'.[134]

Another of Larry's new friends was the poet George Barker, soon to be associated with Dylan Thomas and the New Apocalyptics. Barker adopted a wild and violent pose in his life and his poetry, a Byronic attitude towards adventure and towards women – the former largely in theory, the latter very much in practice. His face was an attractive blend of the sensitive, the sensual and the athletic. A small scar on his right cheek enhanced his air of raffish strength. He concerned himself in his poetry with love, sex, lust, the fathering of children – and indeed over the years he would father more than a dozen offspring, both in and out of wedlock.[135] Sometimes in his London days Barker would borrow Larry's typewriter and bang out poems directly on to the machine, while Larry, who could never write poetry on a typewriter, assumed that he was writing letters home. Like Larry, Barker was mainly self-educated. He concealed behind his combative arrogance and bombast a knowledge of the classics and a deep acquaintance with Villon and Baudelaire, behind his passion and irony a tempering tenderness. His tenderness embraced Larry, but not his writing: near the end of his long life, Barker was dismissive about his friend's poetry, shouting, 'It's the *man* I love!'[136] This sentiment mirrored perfectly Larry's own regard for Barker. 'He is such a sweet and sensitive person,' Larry would recall, 'always shying away and twinkling off into the deserts of his own private life like a bushman's totem. A difficult, painful man, much in need of air uncontaminated by Englishry.'[137]

As the end of 1932 approached, Larry struck out against Christianity, the family and the commercial spirit with 'The Ballade of Slow Decay', his first comic poem, printed by Caduceus as an anti-Christmas greeting:

> This business grows more dreary year by year,
> The season with its seasonable joys.

Lest anyone mistake his attitude, Larry ended a string of mock-serious complaints ('It makes me want to stamp and make a noise') with,

> How can a man withstand the atmosphere,
> This hell compounded of such strange alloys?

Even 'Grandma', 'too old to do a thing but leer,/ And call the home-made mince-pies "saveloys"', does not elude him.[138]

ONE OF THE GATHERING SPOTS for Larry and his friends was the Fitzroy Tavern in Charlotte Street, with its large saloon bar and friendly proprietor, Papa Kleinfeld. The artist Nina Hamnett, who had known Modigliani and whose nude torso had been sculpted by Gaudier-Brzeska, had returned from Paris years earlier and had searched throughout London for the right combination of ambience, cheapness and an amiable publican. The Fitzroy was it. By the time Larry came on the scene, the 'old ladies with shawls and bonnets, old men with walrus moustaches' who came for the Monday night loan club were being edged out by slumming socialites, by the art and medical students bent on a night of thrifty drinking and of ogling the 'characters'.[139] From Fitzroy Square south along Charlotte Street the neighbourhood was becoming dangerously fashionable for the artistic set, and in his *Black Book* Larry would refer scathingly to the 'goitered belles of Charlotte Street, and the flat-chested winnies of the Fitzroy Tavern'.[140] But there were still enough interesting people: the Indian novelist Mulk Raj Anand could be encountered in various pubs; also Hamnett was still much in evidence and so was her friend Anna Wickham. Hamnett liked to remind people of her famous Gaudier-Brzeska bust, at the time 'in the V and A with me left tit knocked off'.[141]

Among Larry's stranger acquaintances on the margins of literary London were a pair of Polish royalists, Geoffrey and Cedric Potocki de Montalk, claimants to the throne of Poland. Geoffrey and Cedric were born in New Zealand, but apparently they did have some connection with the Polish aristocracy. Both were pale, slender, blue-eyed and gentle-looking. The elder brother went by the title and name of Count Geoffrey Wladislas Vaile, and he sometimes dashed about Bloomsbury in kilts. Nancy would recall going with Larry to their tiny flat near Lamb's Conduit Street. On the door was a sign, 'Communists and racial enemies please abstain from calling.'[142] Geoffrey in his customary red robe, Cedric in a deep blue one, were on their hands and knees on the floor, crawling over an enormous map of Poland and quarrelling violently about how the country was to be divided between them. They were right-wing to the point of fascism, anti-Semitic and intolerant, but Larry cherished them as true eccentrics.

Both Potockis were utterly courageous, willing to risk tumult or gaol in support of their various causes. When Larry met him in the early summer of 1933, Count Geoffrey had been recently in prison for libel, and the first surviving communiqué to Larry includes a request that he check on the delivery of various copies of Potocki's *Prison Poems*. Count Geoffrey asked Larry to discover 'whether the die of my coronet has been found, which was wrapped in paper with the coronet embossed, and thrust into a matchbox. Also what has happened to my peasant chairs, mirror, books, etc.'[143]

This matchbox royalist swept about London and Paris in his long red cape, with a golden cross worthy of an archbishop banging against his navel. He also wrote and published poetry and essays that got him into trouble for their sexual explicitness and their defamatory nature. Nor did Potocki confine his exuberance to print, for he confided to Larry, 'Mr Lennon says the Police are after me for a maintenance order, but it *is* ridiculous as I haven't created any bastards, except for the disputed child of Minnie —, who slept with other men beside myself.'[144] Potocki was an exotic addition to his collection of characters, but from the first Larry was cautious, circling the embossed crown on Potocki's envelope and adding an annotation in green ink, 'Beware. High Voltage.' Larry's instinct, ingrained since his school days, was to avoid trouble from those in authority. Not Count Geoffrey. Later he would found *The Right Review* to be his political voice, and much later still would launch the Melissa Press to print his own ribald poetry and occasional pieces of questionable propriety for his friends.

During the 1930s Larry managed to appear singularly apolitical. This was to become known as 'The Pink Decade', when a majority of English intellectuals lined up on the left, but Larry came close to avoiding anything beyond a predictably personal stand: the world was going mad, he said, and the madness was threatening to get in the way of his life and his art. He was intent on becoming a Writer, and he happily talked socialism and Communism with his left-leaning friends, royalism with the Potockis. In fact, he was already developing that disbelief in the efficacy of political institutions that he would express so fully in *Bitter Lemons*. Pressed to choose, Larry would confess to a conservative bias.

Larry's caution did not prevent him from expressing his opinions of others' writing. He enjoyed firing off squibs, twitting his elders. His first target was George Bernard Shaw. In 1933 the Caduceus Press published a slender hardback book with a mock eighteenth-century title page: *Bromo Bombastes: A fragment from a laconic drama* by Gaffer Peeslake, 'which same being a brief extract from his Compendium of Lisson Devices'. In this booklet Larry slyly pokes fun at Shaw's *The Adventures of the Black Girl in Her Search for God*, written the year before. For the entire six pages of the text a Reporter interviews a Silly Black Girl, identified by the initials SBG.

> What did you seek so far away
> In Chesapeake, Kabul, Bombay . . . ?

asks the Reporter, to which the SBG answers:

> Strange as it seems I was seeking God,
> Treading the paths his feet have trod.

The SBG concludes 'that God resides in Whitehall Court'.[145] Only the pseudonym Gaffer Peeslake appeared on the title page, and Shaw gave no sign of knowing that he had been under fire.

Bromo Bombastes was more significant for Larry's development than either the conservative dramatic form or the mild satire would indicate. The stage directions show Larry's first experiments with surrealism: '*Here is a pause during which* [the Reporter] *makes symbols on a roseleaf, in goat's blood.*'[146] While ostensibly attacking him, Larry must have realized that Shaw, in favouring the merciful and humane God of Micah over the 'Bogey Man' God of Noah and Job, was also repudiating 'Granny's God'. Shaw, an Irishman with an English reputation, seemed to Larry almost a father-figure, and Larry would later appeal to him on behalf of Henry Miller for backing in a censorship battle.

THE ACQUAINTANCE WITH LONDON'S BOHEMIAN fringe would provide Larry with settings and colour for long sections of his first three novels. In retrospect, he liked to emphasize the hardships of his Bloomsbury existence: 'I was on my uppers at the time. . . . All we ate was chips, washed down with a couple of pints of beer, when we could borrow the dough. I was perfectly capable of sleeping in the street.'[147] This was sheer romancing: Larry assuredly never spent a night on a park bench, although he *might* have been tempted to do so to prove a point. True, he could not afford many luxuries, and according to Nancy he could not follow a budget. The monthly sum Larry got from his mother was not quite sufficient, even for the marginal life that Larry and Nancy chose to live. The couple tried every expedient they could imagine to add to their income. When his friend Jeff – Cecil Jeffries – opened the Blue Peter, a none too respectable nightspot lit with dim blue lights in St Martin's Lane near Leicester Square, Larry put in a few evenings a week playing the piano. He still could not reliably read music but he could 'strum quite gaily' such popular numbers as 'Trees' and 'Smoke Gets in Your Eyes'.[148] Accompanying himself, Larry sang in a pleasant light tenor 'dance tunes' of his own composition, among them 'Two of a Kind' and 'Out of the Blue'. 'Love, you're a peach', Larry would croon. Sometimes he had help on the vocals from a singer named Dixie Lee.[149] Nancy was 'incensed' when Harold Nicolson turned up with several male friends and, putting his hands on Larry's shoulders, murmured, 'Do, darling, do play "Trees" again.'[150] The Blue Peter is the flag raised by ships on the point of departure, and at this stage Larry and Nancy seemed always on the verge of departure for somewhere. One such departure was accelerated by the police, who terminated Larry's performing career by raiding the place, and he had to escape from the second storey by sliding down an outside drainpipe – his years of tree-climbing in Kurseong came in handy. During this period Larry spent a couple of weeks as an apprentice racing car driver for the Morris Garages team. He had a few practice sessions in the beautiful 'racing cars with strapped-down bonnets',[151] but was never to drive in competition.

When he was not attempting some ploy or other to augment his tiny income, Larry was often found under the great dome of the British Museum reading room. He read rapidly, recording passages and writing observations in a ruled notebook. Unlike Nancy, Larry was not keen on art exhibitions, but he developed a passion for Turner's landscapes. When they had funds Larry and Nancy went to shows like *Funny Face* and *Charlot*. Or they braved a night club to hear Leslie Hutchinson, 'the divine Hutch', play the piano and sing 'Life Is Just a Bowl of Cherries'. Sometimes the chilly London dawn caught them walking back hand in hand from the south bank across Westminster Bridge.

Living in London had shown Larry what could be done with only a little money, and he was alarmed by the rate at which his mother was spending the capital his father had left. He set out to persuade her to settle on him what he figured was his share of the estate. His confrontation with Louisa Durrell went something like this: 'You're chucking it down the drain. In another few years there won't be any left. I want my bit now.'[152] His 'bit' amounted to capital that would produce three pounds a week, enough for mere subsistence in London. He and Nancy wanted more than a bare minimum, so they continued to try various shifts to make money. The most promising venture that the pair undertook was to open a photography studio. After Nancy left *Children in Uniform* she had gone to work for a commercial photographer off Charing Cross Road. 'This seems to be a piece of cake,' she told Larry. All they would have to do was to take photographs and flog them around. On Larry's suggestion they applied to Nancy's father for a loan to establish Witch Photos. Thomas Cyril Myers, sole issue of the Reverend Thomas Myers, had never been happy with his daughter's stage career, which he had angrily called 'kicking your legs up on the stage' – never mind that *Children in Uniform* was a rather highbrow drama about a girls' school.[153] Around February 1933 he doled out £300 that would in any case be Nancy's by right in a few months' time on her twenty-first birthday. Her grandfather the Reverend Thomas Myers had settled sufficient money on her so that even after her school fees and various family living expenses had come out of it, there was still around £3000 remaining. Also, her second cousin Harold Fielding Hall, author of *The Soul of a People*, had left her the respectable sum of £1000. Nancy and Larry leased a large basement below Sheffey's, a small café off Lamb's Conduit Street. They moved in a few pieces of second-hand furniture and called it home. The area had literary resonances: Gawsworth told Larry that it had been one of Dr Johnson's haunts. Sheffey herself claimed to be a gypsy; at any rate, she took to her new neighbours and when Nancy was not cooking they ate their meals with her, often joined by Joseph Allen, Cecil Jeffries, George Wilkinson and other friends. Sheffey was a local character, with a dangling cigarette, a deep croaking voice, rouged cheeks, dyed black ringlets held in loose order by a scarf.[154] *The New Statesman* would publish an obituary when she was killed by a bomb during the coming war.

Larry set himself up as the proprietor of Witch Photos, located in a loft on Millman Street: he bought a roll-top desk, 'an enormous imitation leather armchair', a condenser enlarger and a stock of Amidol developer, and sat back to wait for clients. Nancy's parents gave her a silver fox fur on 8 May, her birthday, and the young couple felt themselves speeding along the high road to affluence. George Wilkinson was able to steer A. J. A. Symons, then finishing his *Quest for Corvo*, to Witch Photos for a sitting. Unluckily, Pike the dark-room technician had either loaded the film plates backwards or had speckled them with acid during the processing, for Larry had to ask Symons back for a second sitting. This time Symons ordered a dozen of the 'serious compton-mackenzie-esque photographs'.[155] Their friend Peter Bull was the other paying customer – there were only these two that Nancy could recall – although there was a non-paying one, a '*very* vulgar man' who wanted to market pictures he took of Nancy and Pam Black 'in camiknickers'.[156] Larry and Nancy tried to get together a portfolio in a bid for a contract to photograph underwear for British Celanese, British licensee for the new DuPont synthetic fabrics, and they persuaded Joan Reed, daughter of the Managing Director of Reed Paper and studying at the Slade, to model for them. Both Larry and Nancy took endless exposures of Joan, amid much hilarity. For most of the summer Joan practically lived with them. She admired Nancy immensely: to the 'charming spoilt baby' Larry, Nancy was 'mother and manager, his muse of course', his 'equal in intelligence and his superior in character'. Larry was 'endearing', and he and Nancy worked together in great harmony.[157] Joan was especially struck by 'his intense curiosity and interest in other people & therefore their sex'.[158] Nothing came of their efforts to break into advertising, and finally even Larry had to admit that Witch Photos was a failure. He shrugged it off but Nancy felt *bürgerlich* guilt at wasted capital.

Larry had not neglected his writing while sitting at his roll-top desk, and had produced a number of poems. One project that occupied him and his friends was the translation of the Comte de Lautréamont's *Les Chants de Maldoror*. 'My share was to supply the "poetry" to the text,' Larry recalled.[159] Le Comte de Lautréamont was important to Larry in other ways as well: his example encouraged Larry's natural drive towards early accomplishment. The author was a double being with an invented name, for his legal name was Isidore Ducasse; also, like Larry he was an expatriate, born to European parents in Montevideo. The imaginings of *Maldoror* suggest the hallucinations of a brilliant madman, and the precocity of the author – Lautréamont was only twenty-four when he died – recall Rimbaud, another of Larry's icons. Author and character sometimes appear to merge, but at other times Lautréamont speaks at odds with Maldoror the character, setting rational hope against Maldoror's blank despair. Madness, the author-character relationship, Manichean dualism all became preoccupations for Larry. Also, the effort of translation threw Larry deeper than ever before into French literature. No publisher would touch the translation, but both the surrealism and the extravagant language of *Maldoror* point towards the prose fantasies 'Asylum in the Snow' and 'Zero' that Larry was to write for Henry Miller and Anaïs Nin.

There were a lot of high jinks to break up the serious effort. 'I remember Larry and Nancy . . . Peter Bull, myself and George enjoying life in London,' said Pam Wilkinson.[160] In his mother's Hillman saloon, Larry drove his friends on various excursions outside the city. 'One night we all motored down to Sussex and swam in an old pig pond and ended up in my mother's cottage at Ditchling,' recalled Pam. Nancy did not think it had been a very glamorous plunge, but this wild night suggested to the two couples that life in a cottage might beat life in Bloomsbury. They began to search for an 'old beamy cottage' and soon turned up Chestnut Mead, nearly a mile outside Loxwood in Sussex, which they could have for a pound a week.[161] Each was to contribute five shillings. Cassell had offered a prize of £300 for a first novel and Larry and George decided to submit entries. Larry planned to write a *roman à clef* based on his early life, with a protagonist who was himself in a thin disguise – only a *tall* boy: Larry felt he was entitled to that. Larry, Nancy and George were to live permanently at the cottage, while Pam was more often than not away on tour with the Birmingham Repertory Company in the cast of *Children in Uniform*.[162] They bought, very cheaply, two beds, a few chairs and a table. George climbed a narrow oak staircase to his bedroom-cum-study and Larry spread over the rest of the house, writing on the table in the ground floor sitting room. Nancy bought Larry a second-hand Challen baby grand piano for £60. George had a set of drums and cymbals, and in the evenings they held jazz sessions. Larry renamed the house Little Songhurst Cottage in honour of the songs sung and the marvellous poetry still to be written there.

Nancy did most of the housekeeping and cooking – and tried to concentrate on her painting. She had two cookery books, one Italian and one of a distinctly health-food cast: her cuisine ran to strange concoctions involving lentils, beans, rice and fried onions; and she stewed a *carbonnade* in beer. All in all, it was a significant improvement over fish-and-chips eaten out of a fold of newspaper. George did the washing up and Larry occasionally emptied the Elsan earth closet – which would turn up in the Scobie passages of the future *Alexandria Quartet* – kept in the outdoor privy. They took baths in the kitchen almost as a matter of principle: they thought themselves too advanced to need privacy. *No shame* was the motto Larry would give Walsh Clifton,[163] and the Songhurst denizens tried to make it theirs as well. Shame was an invention of Pudding Island. 'It might be a really exciting *refinement* to have one's dinner cooked by a nude wench,' Larry would write in his novel.[164] Nakedness became part of their statement of revolt. The Loxwood villagers called them 'the three sketches' and, except for the parson, left them strictly alone.[165] That gentleman called once and spent twenty minutes in earnest conversation with the trio before retreating, his upper lip stiff with disapproval.

Larry was not only on the receiving end when it came to criticism, moral or literary. Reginald Hutchings, a Bloomsbury friend, had shown Larry various poems in typescript, and wanted him to look at some more recent work on his coming visit to Little Songhurst Cottage. He wrote to Larry, 'The value I place upon your criticism is such that I propose to postpone discussion until I see you.' Larry must have been chastising him on his borrowings, for Hutchings defended himself: 'I am convinced there is little of Eliot in my work.' What appeared to be direct influence was more likely due to the fact that he was interested in the same writers who had influenced Eliot: the lesser Elizabethans as well as Mallarmé, Valéry, Laforgue. Hutchings had almost given up reading his contemporaries' work, and had found the early Elizabethans 'my first and only constant love'. Larry considered the Elizabethans enough *his* property to bristle. Hutchings continued, 'Marsh, myself, our respective mistresses, and Anand (possibly)', were going 'next weekend' to see Count Cedric Potocki in Philip Marsh's car, and then he would drop in on Larry. Some months later Larry handed Hutchings' letter to a new friend, Alan G. Thomas, with the scornful comment, 'Hutchings' wee note should give you a hell of a laugh.'[166] Larry was quick to winnow his friendships: many he cast off quickly; where he found some indefinable kinship nothing else mattered. He was well aware that a web of influential connections among the London creative and journalistic set was a powerful aid to the construction of a literary reputation, but he had a visceral hatred of what he termed 'bum-sucking'.

At Little Songhurst Cottage George and Larry would write well, live cheaply and walk in the quiet countryside, so their theory went. Larry was not one to languish in a pool of quiet, however, and there were tensions within the *ménage*. Nancy was intense in her opinions and quick to jump into any verbal fray. Pam's happy-go-lucky gaiety could have made her a tempering influence, but she was away much of the time. George was very meticulous and very orderly, traits that Larry possessed only at odd moments. Larry could not resist the temptation to bait the schoolmasterly George. The Wine and Food Society had just been founded by Symons, George's benefactor, and one day while he and George were chopping wood, Larry delivered a magnificent tirade against it. And there were other disputes, usually with Nancy joining in stridently. Following one particularly intense wrangle, George wrote:

My Dear Larry,

After a morning spent in pondering on the inadvisability of early morning reprisals, I am moved to take up a pen. My criticism was not only ill-timed but ill-considered. I feel sure that with a little mutual effort we shall contrive to live without much friction. But you must bear in mind that I am a slow-witted plodder & find it difficult to follow your voltes-face.

It is probably your spouse who is more in need of reassuring than you. The way she thrusts her stones down my throat was unmistakable. Please carry Nancy my apologies & return her stones; I don't want to eat them, I want to cook on them.

We must keep the cottage safe for Democracy.

I think the cabbages are dying.

Yours ever

George

The cabbages may have succumbed but the friendship survived.

An important cause of the tension at the cottage was that George, desperately eager to become a writer, lacked the gift, and felt threatened by the litter of typescript pages around Larry's machine after a morning of writing.[167] Although he used only two fingers he typed rapidly, and the syncopations of his machine, clattering through the small cottage, sounded to George like the volleys of an enfilade. Quickly, the scattered sheets were forming into *Pied Piper of Lovers*. The book was to be a memorial to the Kim aspect of Larry's past. He was making the first third a paean to an idealized India: here was the great, fecund land, kaleidoscopic in colour and symphonic in sound, that had given birth to him and that he had lost. Curiously, though, while Larry praised the 'hill servants', he portrayed the run of the lowland natives in caricaturing terms that would have amused the most *pukka* sahib: they were thieving, grovelling 'sons and daughters of sows' with 'raised . . . black paws', and they beat their wives.[168] Two sides of his personality were striving with each other to take over the narrative: the modern romantic who pierced through the great façade of Empire, and the colonial boy who still saw with his dead father's eyes.

As he reached back into his memory, Larry realized that his father stood at the crux of his early life, and that he had to come to terms with his vanished parent. In particular, Durrell-the-author revisited perceived wrongs inflicted upon him by his parent. In these re-creations, Larry showed the father-figure remorseful for misleading his son about promised school holidays, riven with guilt for allowing him to grow up lonely. He constructed passages in which Walsh triumphs over his father when he thinks himself disciplined unjustly. In fact, so often does Walsh triumph over his various adversaries through the perfect retort or the well-timed punch to the nose – the way most people wish after the event that they had said or made the perfect rejoinder – that the book suffers from a sense of *post facto* revision.

More than a mere revision of the events of his early life, *Pied Piper* was an important attempt by Larry at auto-analysis. He had been reading Freud diligently by 1934 and dabbling in the psychoanalysis of his family and friends. Larry has Walsh, ironically called '*Gipsy Clifton, skilled psychologist*', examining his teachers: 'In a week Walsh had discovered that his housemaster was suffering from a repressed libido; that Binhook had a very marked shin-fetish; and that the head master was in possession of a "marked psychic derangement".' Whenever exactly Larry started reading Freud, it was as dangerous as giving explosives to an anarchist. 'If it's true,' Larry wrote, 'then none of us can be really responsible for our actions – .'[169] The entire issue of moral judgement threatened to come loose. 'Very roughly', Larry wrote, 'it amounts to what you feel being right, and what you know being wrong.' Somewhere in the back of Larry's mind stood D. H. Lawrence, with his call for trusting instinctual 'blood knowledge' over mind knowledge. Larry was discovering for himself 'the majesty of living, the greatness of the body'.[170] He tried to convince himself that he was a true Dionysian, writing of his surrogate, Walsh, '*All philosophy seems to lead me towards a perfect spiritual detachment – a divorce from the world, and therefore towards sterility and deadness. Let me be content to say: I am, and content to "be" as fully as possible.*'[171]

Continuing his dialogue with his dead father, Larry would still have him die, but in a more dramatic way than his real death had been. In *Pied Piper* the son dreams, prophetically, that his father is killed by a hamadryad, a king cobra: Walsh, who had himself earlier killed a cobra, thus earns the right – which he does not want – to succeed to his dead father's place in the family.

Nor was Larry able to assume his father's place, even though his mother was apparently willing to heed his advice, to follow his lead. There was the money-guilt, the sahib-guilt: Larry had wasted his father's hard-earned money in a vain assault on schooling, and at an age when his father had been leading hundreds of men in bridge-building crews, Larry led no one. Rationally, Larry could write in scorn of the vast number of senseless things that he had been forced to study, and of the empty values of the Empire Builder, yet in his fully conscious other self he felt that he was letting his father down. However, he *had* to turn against his father's world, to reject his father's plans for him: there was to be no return to India as a doer, as 'a great man in a dinner jacket'. 'He would have liked to explain the whole matter, gently and clearly, to his father,' Larry wrote of Walsh. Once Larry had killed off John Clifton, *Pied Piper* weakened in intensity. Because his father had let him down by dying, Larry felt that his own growth had been arrested: he would never be able to explain himself to his father and thus ease his conscience. In any case, like many young men, 'He was not certain of his path.'[172] As though by design, Larry had remained short, almost a boy in height, an adolescent in visage. The conflict with adult responsibilities remained.

Larry used the event of John Clifton's death to mark a watershed in the development of Walsh, and he digressed from the plot structure of the novel to probe what was emerging as his own dark obsession, the carefully hidden side of his character. Larry/Walsh 'realized more clearly the huge, heart-breaking doom of living; the pathos of a perpetual search which must always end; of a mind loaded with eagerness to find something – it could not tell what – and broken by the weight of that load, and by its own inability to do anything but become involved in speculations and quests which seemed to lead it farther away from its unknown objective.' If Larry did not take the escape offered – his father's occupational route, the equally narrow route of writing-for-money, any mundane goal, it did not matter which – then, he realized, his would be the doom and the grief of living without boundaries, making the *search* his object, a search that must end, not with a finding but with death. 'He had outgrown the shams,' Larry wrote with what he must have hoped was a personal fit. Larry did not claim this as an unexampled predicament:

He saw, too, with the detachment of unspoken grief, that the burden was laid not only across him, but across the whole of mankind . . . and that there was for him as for them, one escape and one only; and that was towards the illusions of a narrow life, towards the fear of a fickle and futile opinion, towards mental sterility and cowardice and the thousand and one dreary shams of middle-class society.[173]

Often Larry was impelled to consider the security of a plotted route, yet time after time he hesitated. His decision would hinge upon the state of his self-confidence at the moment: if he really did possess some rare talent, then he should not give in. If he did not . . . well, the sooner he sold out the better! 'Was it simply the same idiot hunger after beauty that everyone experienced?' he asked bitterly. 'Or was it some unique private gift, vouchsafed only to the few chosen ones?'[174] This was not the first time he had asked himself these questions, nor would it be the last.

One self-discovery that Larry had indeed made was that he needed to be a *maker*, a doer, whether a poet or an iron-founder.[175] Now he had to be concerned with *what* and *how*. 'I have discovered that each progression in my life brings a new battery of guns against me,' Larry wrote in reflection of his own dilemmas, the conflicting demands of family and of artistic freedom.[176] Clearly he was not going to turn iron-founder: that would be

93

too close to his father's career. How was he to write, then, about his preoccupations, the plastic lusts that shadowed his speculations? 'I could . . . chatter on for pages of the marvellous properties of the flesh – flesh limp, flesh supple, flesh sun-pink, flesh tender, flesh lustrous, flesh taut, flesh everything and flesh nothing whatsoever,' Larry wrote. He wondered whether sculpture might not be the best medium in which to express himself. 'Space against Time curves and stresses, structures and dimensions,' he said, borrowing from theoretical physics. 'How in hell can I express the *volume* of things by daubing ink on paper?'[177] Larry needed a literary form that would have architectural bulk and shape, but that would have to wait until he was ready to write *The Alexandria Quartet*.

In making fiction out of his inner struggles, Larry prefigured the Pursewarden/Darley relationship in *The Alexandria Quartet*: just as Larry has Robin Ames lecture Walsh as 'my good ass' in *Pied Piper of Lovers*, more than two decades later Larry would delineate the friendly but condescending confidences of Pursewarden to 'Brother Ass'. Even this early, his own inner dialogues were conducted in two voices: the critical wiser self and the mawkish naïf. This was also early evidence of Larry's disbelief in the discrete ego: the ironic observer and the observed could, he well understood, reside in the same skin.

While the main events in the Indian chapters remained highly autobiographical, Larry omitted nearly all of the family relationships that he had grown up with. Through Walsh's widowed Aunt Brenda, Larry was able to set down the sufferings of his own widowed mother: 'There had been the months of retrenchment', he wrote, 'behind the aegis of cheap novels, cheap gossip, tea-parties and prayers.' Then just as Louisa had pulled herself together to look after her children, Larry gave Brenda a new role in caring for Walsh.[178] The rest of the novel flowed quite naturally, if less poignantly, from his school life at St Edmund's and from his years in Fitzrovia and in the Reading Room of the British Museum. Fragments and echoes of the Eng. Lit. curriculum of his school years appeared: Marlowe, Swift, Pepys, Gray's 'Elegy', William Morris, Masefield's 'Cargoes', Rupert Brooke, Petrarch. Echoes of his wide reading crowded into the book. Petronius, Rabelais, Rimbaud and Verlaine hinted at the scandalous. Gerard Manley Hopkins and Ezra Pound were among the poetic godfathers.

Larry presented the bohemian world of central London around the British Museum in terms of the clichés of urban degradation, which he none the less professed to find life-giving 'after the soulless, empty ugliness of Dulwich'.[179] The landlords seemed all to be Jews who 'grappled' their 'hard hands together' as they made 'grasping demands'. 'The women were mostly Jewesses', Larry wrote, 'with black, weary-looking eyes, and their bodies under their coloured coats supple as greyhounds.'[180] Jews were 'sallow' and 'pallid'; 'their coats were padded out about the shoulders to give them the appearance of physique which they did not possess'. While Larry does not give them specific criminal activities, they are clearly predatory, like underworld cartoons from Dickens or Henty. In contrast, Larry's sympathetic portrait of a 'tall negress' with a 'beautiful silver-coated whippet on a lead' suggests direct observation. The woman hums in a 'very melancholy but not displeasing' voice.[181] Larry reserved the right to be selective in his middle-class prejudices, some of them prejudices that he would later repudiate.

Soon Larry was typing the Epilogue, and near the end he has the heroine call Walsh Clifton 'De Gourmont's faun',[182] an indication that Larry was already familiar with Rémy de Gourmont's *The Natural Philosophy of Love*, a book that would echo through Larry's novels all the way to *The Alexandria Quartet*.[183] Larry ended his first novel with a major personal apprehension that would spur on his hedonism and add urgency to all his striving: it was 'mental dynamite', the realization that 'I am and quite soon I will not be.'[184] This awareness of the ridiculous brevity of life produced the companion thought, 'What a desperate frolic life is.'[185] Of course these are among the oldest of all human speculations, but they hit Larry early and hard. Also, they had the effect of focusing him upon his 'Inself', as he called it: 'My sensibility is the only laboratory in which work is carried out that interests me at all,' he wrote.[186] The outer world was secondary to his mental life, and he was soon to express this inner world in terms of his own Heraldic Universe.

Larry's later hand-wringing about *Pied Piper of Lovers* was to an extent justified. The title is wildly inappropriate to a death-haunted book; the novel is a prosaic tale of growing up, rendered interesting in the first third by the Indian setting; the occasional editorial voice is intrusive; the characters tend towards caricature, or are simply flat; the dialogue is often stilted; and so on. However, Larry's disclaimers and all cavils to the contrary, *Pied Piper* was an important beginning. He established death as the great counterpoise to love in his writing – metaphysical speculation against sexual curiosity, if you will; like his beloved Elizabethans and Jacobeans, Larry worked in a blend of the tragic and the humorous; he struck a vein of Gothic horror; he proclaimed a personal ethic – 'No shame'

– that would for better or worse last him a lifetime; he sketched in at least a part of the symbolic structure, including the serpent motif, that would recur in his writing until his final fiction; he provided glimpses of the mastery of place that would distinguish his mature prose.

For Larry himself, *Pied Piper of Lovers* functioned in yet another manner: to an extent, it laid the ghost of his father. Larry had felt guilty over the death of his father *because he had willed it*, although doubtless unconsciously. Lawrence Samuel, suffering from a brain tumour, had died first in the mind, the ultimate willed death. His father's death had freed Larry in all the classical Freudian senses, but it also freed him to live as he wanted to live, not along the lines his father expected. When asked late in his life why he had written almost nothing else dealing with India, Larry replied, perhaps disingenuously, 'So rapidly I became a European that my source material ran out. And anyway, Forster had done it so much better than one could hope to do.'[187] Larry also realized how much he had revealed in the novel: that is perhaps the unadmitted reason why he would not permit its republication, why he would never write another Indian novel, and why he was reticent about India. His father's ghost had to stay buried.

As summer approached, Larry was working on the final revisions of *Pied Piper of Lovers*, but George was still floundering. He and Pam decided to get married and, for a honeymoon, bicycle to Corfu. Peter Bull, now in the cast of *Escape Me Never*, was their best man at the Kensington Register Office.

It was June when the Wilkinsons left, and Larry and Nancy stayed on at Loxwood for the few weeks the lease had to run. Along came Count Cedric Potocki, the younger de Montalk, bringing his oversized American mistress and her young daughter. He walked up to the door in his rippling robes, suffering from toothache, his head bound in a white scarf knotted on top, and moved in. When the lease on Little Songhurst ended, Larry had had enough of Potocki and went to visit his mother in Bournemouth; Nancy moved to an even more primitive cottage to stay with Count Cedric and 'Madame', as the Count insisted his lady be called. Immediately Nancy came down with measles. She got a message through to Larry, who came post-haste, and together they retreated to Dixie Lodge and Louisa's care.

DURING THE TIME AT LOXWOOD, Larry had done more than write fiction and argue. He had composed a number of passable poems and had sent a fan letter to Richard Aldington, whom he particularly admired.

Much to his surprise, Aldington replied in September with a friendly letter discussing D. H. Lawrence and Aldous Huxley. Uncharacteristically, Larry did not reply. 'I was too unsure of myself, too diffident,' he recalled many years later; Aldington had seemed to him, if not quite one of the giants, a top-rate man of letters, and Larry had worried about seeming to curry favour.[188] Also, he no more wanted to follow in Aldington's footsteps than he did in Richard Blaker's.

Larry's failure to respond to Aldington meant more than just the diffidence that he claimed, although his modesty was genuine enough. Larry knew that, intellectually, he had been a league ahead of most of his schoolfellows; he also knew that he was a good writer and could perhaps become a fine one. However, he was unsure – and would remain so for the rest of his life – how far his talent would carry him. He was also terribly afraid of appearing to assume that he *deserved* patronage, nor did he want success on those terms: he had too much pride. Three decades later he would worry about being exposed as a 'charlatan', and in this too he would be sincere. The self-confidence that would lead him to make pronouncements suggestive of the most glaring hubris could evaporate in a flicker. Was he indeed merely a bumptious colonial brat, Larry would wonder, in between flashes of powerful belief in himself.

Larry's move to Bournemouth would bring him two major blessings, one indirect and one evident. It provided him with a second focus, after London, for his anger at England and sent him off in the direction of Greece. The landladies and the tourists and the retired civil servants showed him his ancestral countrymen at their least sympathetic. One senses his desperation in the thoughts given to Horace Gregory in the future *Black Book*: 'In Bournemouth, walking the streets, while the rain pronged the lights and houses, the whole shape of my future rose up and choked me.'[189] For relief Larry went almost every day, usually accompanied by Nancy, to the H. G. Commins Bookshop, owned by Ernest Cooper. There he met the owner's chief assistant, a tall, angular, aesthetic young man named Alan Gradon Thomas. Apart from his passion for literature and his luminous sense of humour, Alan seemed the antithesis of Larry. Raised a Quaker, Alan was shy, introverted, careful, deliberate, orderly, precise. He was also a passionate, self-educated mediaevalist – and he looked the part, with his long jaw and narrow aquiline beak. Whereas Larry had learned to project infinite confidence despite his inner doubts, Alan could be painfully self-deprecating. He was to become Larry's longest-standing friend as well as his bibliographer and the preserver of his library and files during the upheavals of war, divorce and other misadventures. Alan would always be available as a reliable sea-anchor, to be called upon whenever Larry felt that he needed to be headed into the wind.

Soon Alan was spending most of his evenings and his weekends with the expanded Durrell family. He wrote an eyewitness account of the Durrells at home:

All six members of the family were remarkable in themselves, but in lively reaction to each other the whole was greater than the sum of the parts. Amid the gales of Rabelaisian laughter, the wit, Larry's songs accompanied by piano or guitar, the furious arguments and animated conversations going on far into the night, I felt that life had taken on a new dimension. Larry was writing, Nancy painting, Leslie crooning, like a devoted mother, over his collection of unlicensed firearms. . . . Every basin in the house was unusable because Gerry, then only a little boy, but already an animal collector, had filled them with newts, tadpoles and such-like; he roped me in to serve as a giant in the circus which he organized in the garage. Margaret, realizing that book-learning was no part of her world, was rebelling against returning to school, and soon succeeded, backed by the rest of the family, in staying put.

Although all the Durrells had been born in supposedly non-violent India, their tempers were Irish and the rows were frequent. Once Larry, in order to wash, had pulled the plug on one of Gerald's impromptu aquariums. Almost speechless with rage and searching for the most insulting word he could imagine, Gerry attacked: 'You, you . . . you AUTHOR, YOU!'[190]

Alan introduced Larry to Patrick Evans, whose father had built a house on the edge of Sway in the New Forest, not far from Bournemouth, after his retirement from the headmastership of Leighton Park, known as 'The Little Eton of the Society of Friends'. Pat, who studied at Oxford when he was not at Sway, was in rebellion against his parents, the Quakers and the university when Larry met him. Tall and fine-looking, he was a good jazz pianist and he was also classically trained. Pat, Alan and Larry tried their hands at writing jazz and popular songs, aided by Leslie.[191] Pat composed his own tunes for foxtrots and waltzes, sometimes providing 'doggerel' to go with them, and also set down the notes for the melodies Larry improvised on the piano, after which Larry would make up verses to go with the music.[192] One of Larry's efforts was a set of lyrics for a waltz, 'Three Pawnbroker's Balls':

> Look how they're getting me down –
> Had to sell everything out of my flat,

My wife, her mother, the dog and the cat,
Now what do you think is the cause of that?
Why, Balls, Balls, Balls.[193]

Sometimes Larry tried to milk a frankly sentimental muse: 'When you go, I know it's Paradise lost.'[194]

Another pianist Larry met was Evelyn Lewton-Brain, a classical performer and music teacher only a year or two older than Larry. They got together for composing sessions, with Larry providing words and scratch melodies, Evelyn working out and setting down the counterpoint. She was a small, attractive woman and although he introduced her to his family, Larry did not include her in the circle of his other Bournemouth friends.[195] They all dreamed of making easy money by writing a few hits. Larry would project this dream into *Panic Spring*, his second novel: Walsh Clifton, shown a year or so older than he was at the end of *Pied Piper of Lovers*, is able to support himself on the Greek island of Mavrodaphne by writing tunes to accompany 'greasy' lyrics.

Guided by Pat, Larry and Alan took long Sunday walks through the New Forest, 'dew on the nose and rime i' the boots', stopping at small village pubs for beer and a game of shove-ha'penny.[196] Then would come the long haul uphill to the Evans home. Pat recited satiric verses of his own composition about their acquaintances:

She was not chaste, but then she was not willing,
He didn't like it, but he had to lump it.
But now he finds himself, Ah me how thrilling,
Playing a hot tune on the muted strumpet.[197]

Nancy found such ribaldry distasteful, although she loved the Durrell family and the cultural life of Bournemouth after the hermit existence at Loxwood. Both Larry and Nancy enjoyed a visit to the home of Mrs Penry, a wealthy American lady who was the Commins Bookshop's best customer. Once Nancy admired a fine volume on Byzantine painting and Mrs Penry gave it to her on the spot. After a long and appreciative browse through her exquisite library, Larry sank into a chair, sighing, 'I'm glutted!'[198]

Larry also kept up his London connections, visiting friends and talking literary shop. On one visit he saw in a pub – but did not speak to – T. E. Lawrence, and subsequently sketched from memory in pen and water-colours the author of *The Seven Pillars of Wisdom*. 'I've lost every shred of interest I had in him. . . . Poor little fellow', Larry later commented to Alan

Thomas.[199] Through Joseph Allen and the Caduceus Press, Larry arranged to have a small collection of poetry privately printed towards the end of 1934 under the title *Transition: Poems*. Mrs Penry bought a copy and a somewhat abashed Larry inscribed it to her: 'For Mrs Penry who, after collecting one of the finest libraries in England, chose, of her own free will, to place this minnow among the tritons.'[200] If not exactly prize fish, some of the poems in the volume showed a real advance in individual voice over *Quaint Fragment* and *Ten Poems*, although still there is some straining for effect in the manner of the Metaphysicals:

> A smile is an expression of despairs,
> With mouth a hanging flap,
> A slip of skin twiddled by subcutaneous hairs,
> A juggling parody of what you say.[201]

In a rare nod to the brother he often teased, Larry dedicated *Transition* to 'LESLIE WHO LIKED ONE', the poem 'Wheat-Field'. 'I have been rooted wheat,' Larry wrote, standing grain that a 'man in a red coat . . . . destroys/ Under a dancing sun'.[202] The images of destruction appealed to Leslie.

By mid-July 1934 George Wilkinson was writing from the Tyrol, where he and Pam were pausing on their bicycle trip to Corfu via Trieste. George and Pam were to ride some 1115 miles all told, and when they finally arrived on the island, they discovered that their heavy baggage had been sent via the Cape of Good Hope and was still somewhere in transit. George gave a comic recital of the drawbacks of life on Corfu: the lavatory smelled and the mosquitoes bit. Larry and Nancy might in other circumstances have taken George's complaints seriously, but Bournemouth increasingly struck Larry as 'bloody', so when George suggested, 'Why not come out here for a spell?' Larry began to consider moving. Living was cheap, George said; they were having a boat built for £8 and shoes made for fifteen shillings.[203] Then George added that he was writing well and had finished 18,000 words of a travel book to be illustrated by the photographs Pam had taken en route. Cassell, meanwhile, had communicated not a peep to Larry about *Pied Piper of Lovers*, and in a typically absolute judgement he assumed that he had failed in England.

Larry's letter in response to George's invitation announced that they would come, and enquired about schooling for Gerald. George fired back in some alarm, 'D'you all intend coming (!) and how many is all?' The answer was quite simply *all* of them. Larry did a lot of complaining about his mother and siblings, but the ties were powerful. It was as if he could not bear to repeat the long Indian separation. He rejected the head of the family role, but he needed the warm circle that Louisa provided. His mother, Leslie, Margo and little Gerry must come along.

Years later Larry would attempt somewhat disingenuously to rationalize his decision: 'I had decided to drop everything, and the only place where one could live on next to nothing then was Greece, especially the islands. . . . It was quite by chance that Corfu was the first place I went to. I might easily have picked some more remote Greek island.'[204] Writing at the time to George, Larry was less tepid:

Corfu is the ideal place to use as a base for Mediterranean exploration: Nancy is rabid to examine the traces of early Byzantine painting down that coast of Greece, while I am mad to get to Knossos and examine the traces of a Minoan civilization, of which by this time I'm quite sure, my ancestors were a part. Do you know that the average height of the race was five four? Think it over. They were sturdy and lustful . . . .[205]

Larry would list his height in his 1935 passport, generously, as five feet four inches, but in a later passport, in 1944, a ruthlessly accurate clerk would set him down as five feet two. Although he pretended that it did not matter, Larry remained conscious of his shortness.

Larry used the financial argument to convince his mother to live abroad. Louisa, whether following her whims or heeding the financial advice of bankers and solicitors, had continued to lose capital. Larry declared that it would be a good idea to move to inexpensive Corfu for a few years to give the exchequer a chance to recover. For once, Larry's siblings took his side unanimously, and Louisa said, 'Yes, dear, I suppose you're right.'[206] Larry wrote to George, 'Being too timid to tackle foreign landscapes herself, she wants to be shown around the Mediterranean by us.' Privately, Larry had doubts. He was apprehensive about the strategic role the Balkan region would play in a European conflict: Corfu was too close to Albania for comfort, and Britain would want to use Greece as a base of operations for protecting the Suez route. 'What I want to know is, will you, Wilkinson, give your life for gallant little Greece, our gallant little ally? I thought not. Then move a few islands south.'[207] Larry also worried about the instability of Greek politics, what with the talk of restoring the monarchy. George reminded him that in their Loxwood days they had decided that 'if you want to avoid war Tristan da Cunha is the only place'. He added sarcastically, 'Cooks'll put you onto a good sea route to it, no doubt.'[208]

By January, Larry's doubts had diminished, and to lard his resolve, he got an unemployed Bournemouth schoolmaster, Stooks, to refresh his Greek.[209] The Wilkinsons wrote with advice about steamers versus rail transport: 'Don't send your excess luggage over land . . . . Bring warm clothes for winter: it doesn't last long but what there is of it is cold & wet.' This letter ends with a friendly summons: 'We, and I think I may say that I speak for the island, await your arrival impatiently.'[210]

NOT ONE OF THE DURRELLS, Indian transplants that they were, seems to have felt at home in England. Louisa thought most of her neighbours, whether in Dulwich, in Parkstone or in Bournemouth, stiff and unfriendly. Leslie had not done well scholastically. Margaret was still boarding at Malvern, and although her marks were good and she was at the top of the tennis team, she was restless. She had come home for the Christmas holidays with a bad cold and was determined not to return. Her siblings agreed, contending that education was useless. Alan Thomas was present when her eiderdown, mailed in a huge parcel by the school, was carried in by the postman. 'Look!' exclaimed Larry. 'Here comes the manuscript of my novel, back from the publishers!'[211] And Gerry had *never* liked school: his zoological avocation had always struck him as far more important than sitting on a hard bench listening to incomprehensible nonsense. Louisa, arguing for stability, responsibility and propriety, was outnumbered and seriously out-gunned.

After months of haunting the letterbox for news from Cassell or Spencer Curtis Brown, the literary agent he had been lucky enough to acquire, Larry had given up hope. Still, he consoled himself that the *writing* had been useful for him, although he considered himself a poet, not a novelist. He had composed the novel partly for exercise, partly to give colouring to his year at Loxwood and in part for the chance of prize money. He later said that 'I wrote *Pied Piper of Lovers* to prove to my family that I was a writer.'[212] Larry's enigmatic dedication, scrawled as an apparent after-thought on the typescript in lieu of his intended literary epigraph, reads: 'For my mother, but for whom . . . '[213] In fact, the novel was a valuable exercise for the young writer: it was proof of discipline and accomplishment, and it purged from Larry's literary system his nostalgically recalled childhood in India. He needed distance from India in order to comprehend England and the Continent.

WITH CORFU TO LOOK FORWARD TO in the spring and with the strain of writing *Pied Piper of Lovers* behind them, Larry and Nancy passed a good winter in Bournemouth. Alan infected Larry with his own love of classical music and introduced him to Jack Crawshaw, a remarkable amateur musician. Crawshaw played his piano for them and encouraged them to appreciate César Franck's Sonata for Violin and Piano. Larry and Nancy went to concerts many weekdays, with Alan joining them for Celebrity Concerts on Saturdays. They heard a succession of renowned soloists, among them Cortot, Myra Hess and Rubinstein. The most memorable performance, Nancy thought, was of Beethoven's Piano Concerto No. 4, played by Moiseiwitsch. Larry and Nancy bought a Ginn gramophone and collected a few records: Beethoven's Second, Fourth, and Fifth piano concerti, Ravel's *Daphnis and Chloë*, Myra Hess playing 'Jesu, Joy of Man's Desiring' – but no Mozart and no Tchaikovsky. Bournemouth had an active theatrical programme, and they saw Noël Coward's *Hay Fever*, Somerset Maugham's *The Circle*, and whatever else the Bournemouth repertory theatre produced. Alan enticed Larry and Nancy to what he considered uplifting lectures on literary subjects, including a series on literary 'Giants', but Alan finally had to conclude that 'Larry was never very keen on uplift.'[214]

Larry may have been loud in his complaints about England, loud in his mockery, yet he was conscious also of the good times. In the New Year's inscription he wrote for 1935 in Alan Thomas's copy of *Transition: Poems*, everything he said was accurate except, characteristically, the spelling of Alan's name: 'To my dear Allen, in poignant memory of a boiled egg, huge laughter, sunburn, wine, the renaissance, a César Franck canon, Beethoven's 7th, despair, dancing, rain, Christ-Church Priory, bellyache, G.K's satires, lovely books, enthusiasm, train-rides, Bournemouth, and a post-Christmas Constipation.'[215] It was a fitting summary of his time in Bournemouth.

In contrast to such private admissions, Larry's public pronouncements on Pudding Island were less kind, yet like another fugitive writer, D. H. Lawrence, he was indelibly marked by England. He had gathered a great load of useful impedimenta to carry into exile: he had been shaped in part by his English education, by his memories of south London, Kent and Sussex, by the British Museum and the Fitzroy Tavern, by Turner's paintings. Perhaps because the inoculation of Englishness began only after an exotic and often idyllic colonial boyhood, Larry would take a centrifugal course, fleeing England, while Lawrence remained a son of the Midlands, centripetal, looking back towards England with mixed scorn and yearning. Larry was quick, however, to identify with Lawrence: 'When I first started to write I was very struck by one of D. H. Lawrence's essays which showed up just how that country treated its writers. That was what made me resolve always to swim against the current.'[216]

Between the ages of eleven and twenty-three Larry had crowded a great deal into his life, layering experiences in his memory like pledges in a pawnshop, some to be redeemed in fiction, others to lie forgotten: bad debts. Larry's memories of England would focus on people. Later, in a nostalgic mood on Corfu, Larry would write two stanzas of verse headed 'England, my England', probably referring to Lawrence's short story. The narrator will not remember England, wrote Larry, for her rivers, moorlands, 'The weeping weeping scourges of the rain', or even for her 'heroes', Chaucer and Shakespeare. Rather, 'as a lover must', he will remember four women, 'Four faces . . . fixed in your seasons'. He describes them in order: the 'slender April woman with the leaning mouth', 'that summer kingcup beauty', a 'selfless and melancholy autumn girl', and 'Even the poor December one I dare not think upon'. The poet-persona promises, 'I will remember them, all of them, in you – .' There is a risk in reading these lines as straight autobiography, with Nancy as the 'you' addressed. Larry's eye ranged over other women, and there are persistent hints that he had known an unidentified woman who died young. Such a figure appears in almost every Durrell novel, beginning with the doomed Ruth of *Pied Piper of Lovers*, and in various poem drafts of the 1930s.

Larry and Nancy decided to get married before leaving for Corfu. Perhaps it was because George Wilkinson had told them he thought honeymooners could get an eighty per cent fare reduction on Italian rail tickets. The wedding was kept secret from the family, for reasons known only to the principals: maybe they saw it as striking their emancipated colours, or Larry simply shied away from the fuss he knew his mother would make. The young couple did not fear opposition. Louisa was fond of Nancy, and was indeed delighted when they chose to tell her some weeks later. Alan was originally to be one of the witnesses, but Larry said he was worried that tall Nancy and tall Alan, who looked such a perfect couple, would find that the registrar had hitched them up by mistake. An attempt to get a pair of midgets from a local carnival to act as witnesses failed when the employer refused to let his star attractions go. Alan was pressed back into service, and Larry told him to find, as the requisite second witness, 'someone who knows nothing about us'. Alan picked Jack Watts, who had just arrived in Bournemouth to take a job in an office across the street from the Commins Bookshop. There was a mutual shock of recognition between witness and bridegroom before the marriage proceeded: Watts had lived in Bloomsbury, where he had known all of Larry's London circle. Larry wanted the registrar to use a copy of Rabelais instead of the Bible for the oaths, and the man was quite insulted. 'You're taking this deeply serious thing very lightly,' he scolded an unabashed Larry.[217] Then Larry discovered that he had left his ring and Nancy's on Louisa's mantelpiece.

The threatened flight of the Durrells to Corfu was a blow to Alan, so much had the social evenings at Wimborne Road, the shared concerts and the walks in the New Forest meant to him. As a consolation, Leslie promised to do his best to write from Greece with ideas for songs. Larry had a solution, of course: Alan should come too.

Alan Thomas, later to become one of England's leading antiquarian booksellers, was already an expert on mediaeval architecture and monumental brass. He took Larry a last time to Christchurch Priory, a few miles east of Bournemouth, and pointed out the Norman sections built by Ranulph Flambard, who had gone on to design Durham Cathedral. Alan and Larry ascended the bell tower, Alan ducking his tall form carefully under the lintels and Larry bounding up the tight spiral stairs. Then they followed the dark passages between the vaulting and the timbers out on to the roof itself, from which they could view town, harbour, the water-meadows, the Stour and Avon broadening and uniting at the sea. It was a Saturday afternoon and dusk found them still aloft, vivid with plans and speculations. The vespers bell before evensong rocked the very tower on which they stood and hurried them off. 'It was from this point of departure', said Alan, 'that we each set out in different directions, he into the future, I back into the past.'[218] Larry too was aware that they had reached personal epiphanies, as he wrote to Alan from Corfu in a letter that would later appear in *The Black Book*:

I was thinking tonight of those summer days in the shadow of the priory. They seem to belong to another world – a world of shapes which included such colours as warmth, charity, love, etc. A whole dormant Platonic principle which, in its essence, is England – the marrow and bone of England. This is a very necessary valediction, not only to England, but, if you like, to the world. It will hurt you, but it is the truth. I have looked into my account – the account that seemed so full and heavy with new cash – and found hardly a coin that will ring properly on wood. There was nothing for it but to empty my wallet into the dust and take the road again: without dramatics this time, without heroics . . . . It is queer to remember that this decision was already shaping itself that afternoon, when we stood on the southern tower of the priory, hanging in the breeze, breathless and exulting like sea birds. All that was the island then, was represented in that humorous razored profile of yours – the predatory nose of the Middle Ages, the Goth singing in your blood, the music you gathered up in those nervous fingers and transmitted, crazy with your own enthusiasm. . . . It was in that time that I began dimly to see the equation which was finally printed in my brain here, over the Ionian. It was the temptation of the devil, the vision of the cities offered to me from an immense mountaintop. The devil! What should be more plausible than that you should be the Black Saint himself – panurgic, long-nosed, calculating bastard that you are! You were offering me, in your oblique way, the whole of England – the masques, the viols, the swans, the mists, the doom, the fogs: you were offering me a medieval death in which I could live forever, stifled in the pollen of breviaries, noctuaries, bestiaries: split silk and tumbrils, aesthetic horses and ruined Abbeys.[219]

Larry did not escape completely from the devil's temptation, although he had come to realize that he could never be rootedly English, that he must escape England: 'I am, and I remain, an expatriate', he was to tell Marc Alyn almost four decades later; 'that vague sense of exile has never quite left me'.[220] At the end of *Pied Piper of Lovers* Larry had Walsh say of England, 'I feel I've been imprisoned for a long time.'[221] In retrospect, the decision might appear to have been an easy one for Larry. In the event it was not. Despite his frequent protestations of unhappiness, England had gained a powerful hold upon his being, and upon his affections: Platonic and scholastic England, Chaucer's England, Shakespeare's and Turner's England, even the mundane England of convivial pubs and pork sausages for breakfast. For all this Alan, lean aesthetic lover of the many Englands, was no mean advocate. Still, Larry had set his mind on exile and escape.

Larry got his passport with only two days to spare, listing his profession as 'Journalist'. 'Just managed to catch bus, train, boat, breakfast, taxi and whatnot –' wrote Nancy to Alan; 'looks as though we're all going to be real pals and one big family on this boat'.[222] "Never Come Back" is our epitaph, our requiem, our good-bye', Larry had written in *Pied Piper*, as his hero and heroine leave England.[223] Larry might have believed that he was done with Britain: none the less, Christchurch Priory, Southwark Cathedral, a jury of Elizabethan writers, and the suavely tempting form of the devil himself travelled along in his packing case. In *The Avignon Quintet*, especially in the first volume, *Monsieur, or, The Prince of Darkness*, Larry was to revisit the Middle Ages of his friend Alan. But that was many years away when Larry and Nancy slipped past Grays on the Thames and the present crowded upon them.

CHAPTER 3

Corfu

Other countries may offer you discoveries in manners or
lore or landscape; Greece offers you something harder –
the discovery of yourself.

Prospero's Cell

LARRY AND NANCY sailed on the SS *Oronsay*, made a rough passage
down the Channel and sampled a shrewish mood of the Atlantic until
Gibraltar, whence Larry mailed two poems to Alan Thomas. In context, the
titles are eloquent: 'The Traveller's Invocation to Sea-Gulls' and 'Grace
Before Meat'. In the first, Larry wrote:

> Dive, my desperate darlings, sheer,
> Sheer on my soup and kidney-pie and beer.

'I'm rather tired tonight so to hell with news,' he wrote tersely. 'The sea-
gulls could tell you some yarns though.'[1] By 14 March he and Nancy had
traversed the Mediterranean and had been stranded for some days at the
Hotel Internazionale in a bitterly cold and wet Brindisi, staring south-east
across the Adriatic in the direction of Corfu. Italy is a nation of waiters,
Larry complained, and they all serve from the wrong side. There were
bookshops, however, and Larry offered to get Alan 'a copy of the infamous
Lady Chatterly for 14 liras – about 5/-'. The only local nightspot, 'apart
from the more obvious houses of Venus for the soldiers', had an amateur
band that played atrocious music in concert with a tinny gramophone. 'Still,
I bear up well under the stacks of local vino I am forced to consume,' sighed
Larry. 'I'm developing a paunch like a channel buoy.' He set down a song
idea for Pat Evans to consider: 'Title: "Once upon a time" – a little girl and a
little boy – like a story-book love etc. etc. Ending – but that was – – "Once
upon a time".'[2] Twenty-five years later he would end *The Alexandria
Quartet* with the same phrase, 'Words which presage simply the old story of
an artist coming of age.'[3] This is what he hoped to accomplish on Corfu,
and he chafed at the delay. Sitting impatiently in the lounge of the

Internationale, he wrote the first pages of what would become *Panic Spring*, in which the protagonist is held up in Brindisi by a revolution.[4]

There were rumours of a coup d'état in Greece and the ferry service had been stopped, so Larry claimed, to prevent the return of a rebel general from Italy 'disguised as a cargo of garlic'.[5] Soon Larry discovered a skipper who promised to land them on Corfu some time in the middle of the coming night. The Greek sailors made a favourable impression on him: long noses, curly hair, quick dark eyes. And the language stirred echoes in his mind of the few words of Greek he knew: it was 'crisp and melodious, full of pebble-like dentals'.[6] This was beginning to look like a real adventure, but he was far from admitting it: 'I'm too bored and the pen is too bad to write more. If I perish in the revolution you might save this letter as an example of what Italy can do to a gallant Englishman.'[7] Larry followed this letter with a humorous description of the attempted coup: bombs deliberately dropped at sea, troops on both sides firing into the air so as not to hurt their friends, the 'Greek fleet' captured by 'five petulant officers . . . while the population slumbered'.[8] The real Greek civil war, when it came ten years later, would prove no joke.

Corfu rose like a drowsy sea monster off the starboard bow, and soon they were in the narrowing channel separating it from the mainland. Rounded Pantokrator – the word meant 'the Almighty' and was used by the Orthodox to refer to Christ in majesty – at almost three thousand feet was the highest peak on the island, and it was cloaked lower down in grey-green olive groves that changed to vineyards and finally to sunburnt pastures near the summit. Larry preferred to describe the scene in secular terms: 'the gilded snout of Pantokrator bulwarked the horizon like a hippopotamus sunk in mud'.[9] Corfu, 'an ante-room to Aegean Greece' he would call it,[10] lay clenched like a sickle against the brooding mountains of Albania, just over a mile away at the closest point. Larry and Nancy landed at the curving harbour of Corfu town, past the enormous ramparts of the sixteenth-century Venetian fort, the Old Fort, into the port lined with stately four-storey buildings of more recent Venetian vintage, somewhat shabby and in want of paint but decorated with elegant mouldings.[11] Outnumbering the few motor taxis at the dock was a throng of fiacres, the horses wearing straw hats with holes cut for their ears, which made them look like illustrations from a comic bestiary. Somehow Larry and Nancy got through the port formalities and made their way into the town. They found a room at the Pension Suisse, a couple of streets away from the immense green sweep of the Esplanade, the town plaza.

Their baggage had not arrived, so Larry went out to buy some exercise books 'to do some notes for the next novel'. 'Believe it or not they *weighed* them!' he roared to Alan, 'On a great swivelling baggage weigher – like they have in the customs.'[12] Raw prose by the pound had mantic implications for him. As he walked out under the grotesque heads capping the arches of the pension, he was struck at once by the strangeness as much as by the beauty of the town. The decadent grace of eighteenth-century Venetian architecture and a row of soaring arcades facing the Esplanade and dating from the Napoleonic occupation contrasted sharply with the few stolid public buildings erected by the British during their control of the island. The wild variation in styles set the old port apart from the more typical Greek island towns with their stark white shapes, irregular angles, and eastern domes. The street outside the pension would barely let a car through – there was no question of two-way traffic – but there were very few cars trying to pass. The first car on the island had been the 1907 Renault belonging to the family of Maki Aspioti, a young Corfiot who was soon to become a good friend, and in 1935 automobiles were still rather rare. One of these was to become vital to the extended Durrell family: an open Dodge touring car, owned and cherished by Spiros Chalikiopoulos, a taxi driver who combined 'the air of a chief conspirator with a voice like a bass viol'.[13] He was known throughout Corfu as Spiro Americanos because he had learned his present-tense and sibilant English in Brooklyn. Spiro became the self-appointed guardian, factotum and chauffeur of Louisa Durrell, and it was he who periodically retrieved Larry and Nancy from their remoter residences. Spiro stood out even on an island of individualists, with his stentorian delivery, his white peaked cap stuck precariously on the side of his head, cigarette under a scarred upper lip, brown eyes almost hidden amid wrinkles.

There was a lot to explore in Corfu town itself. The Old Fort was in good repair, although the ramparts of the town had been blown up by the British as an exhortation to pacifism before they turned the island over to the Greek monarchy in 1864. The patron saint of the island, Spiridion, slumbered in a silver-chased casket beside the altar of the fine dark church named for him. The good saint had saved Corfu so often from plagues and attackers that half the men on the island seemed to be named after him. 'I went to church last Sunday (!)', wrote Larry to Alan, 'and heard some very fine unaccompanied singing – polyphonic I think. Like those Palestrina things we heard: very deep and sure and robust, with queer little "breaks" in unison.'[14]

The Archaeological Museum – then housed in a ponderous structure of white limestone from Malta, erected in 1816 as a residence for the governor during the British occupation of the island – stood at one end of the Esplanade, convenient to a row of cafés under the shade of the arcades. The centrepiece of the museum, and Larry's favourite exhibit, was a magnificent temple pediment of 570 BC, featuring a Medusa with bulging mad eyes and protruding tongue. Most of the surviving ancient treasures of Corfu are portable objects in the museum rather than the ranks of columns and walls that awe the traveller elsewhere in Greece. This is due in part to the many destructive wars and invasions that had afflicted the island from the time of the Peloponnesian War. The pattern of destruction would continue: modern Corfu possessed one of the finest libraries in the Mediterranean, but it was to be destroyed in the coming world war. When Larry and Nancy arrived the catalogue listed some 40,000 volumes, many from the private collection of the philhellene Lord Guilford.

Corfu town was equally attractive on a more mundane level. The faded pastels of the residences were set off by the brilliant colours of the laundry that was everywhere strung across the narrow streets. There were many pleasant tavernas to investigate, even one over the mole of the Old Fort. The island, as used to tourists as it was to conquerors, took in Larry and Nancy without question. Had Corcyra not been courtesan to Tiberius, to Pompey, to Caesar, to Byron, to Gladstone, to The Duse and D'Annunzio? Noël Coward had been devoured by fleas in the same villa where the great Italian writer had consummated his affair with The Duse, so Coward was to tell Larry years later.[15] Larry made it a point not to drink at Kardaki, the town's sacred spring, an act that would ensure he would always return to the island: 'I do not like being bound by charms,' he maintained.[16]

Soon Larry and Nancy settled into the villa that George and Pam Wilkinson had found for them next to their own in Perama, a few miles south of Corfu town. Larry christened their cottage the Villa Bumtrinket, after the maid, mentioned in Dekker, who 'has a privy fault: she farts in her sleep'.[17] It was a tiny box with a bedroom on one side, a sitting room on the other, and a kitchen at the rear. There were little windows opening on to a huge landscape of olives and the sea, 'a mere fifty yard scramble down the hill and splash!'[18] The beach was mostly stones, but what Larry would call the 'Greek sea's curly head'[19] never ceased to invite them for a nude plunge – they swam naked whenever there were no natives around to be offended. Pam commented gaily that the way to tell a real blonde was by the colour of her pubic hair. 'My God though, to sit in the shade of the olive tree and watch the fishing boats with ochre sails and drowse!' Larry exulted, ignoring the distraction afforded by occasionally nude Pam. 'In a way it's a pity I came, because I'll never be able to write about it all without a sense of inadequacy: positively it stuns me.'[20] Not far away and just off the coast lay Pondikonisi, a minute island with a monastery as its sole structure. Pondikonisi, also called Mouse Island, is in local tradition the Phaeacian ship turned to stone by Poseidon in revenge for aid given to Odysseus. Here was Homer on the Durrell doorstep!

The Wilkinsons took Larry and Nancy on hikes and excursions, and in the evenings there were gramophone concerts of Beethoven in the moonlit garden and, of course, a resumption of the High Discourse of the Little Songhurst Cottage days. George awed the Corfiots with his aesthetic mien; Pam's impish grin had not been altered by marriage either. Nancy engaged a maid, Agape, a pleasant old woman with a 'very craggy lined face'.[21] Nancy's painter's eye was caught by the brilliant colours worn by women in the south of Corfu: flower-printed skirts, bodices and scarves, set off with tight, dark bolero jackets.

The arrival less than a week later of Louisa Durrell and Larry's three siblings shattered the tranquillity of the advance guard. 'The family crawled ashore today and took us in bed so to speak, and wrung my withers with the news,' wrote Larry.[22] The momentous tidings, relayed by Alan via Naples to Louisa, announced the acceptance by Cassell of *Pied Piper of Lovers*. The book had not won the prize for Best First Novel, but the firm liked Larry's story and would publish it in the autumn. An advance of £50 would be paid! Larry was staggered: 'The suckers! To take a rotten book like that. I can do much much better.' None the less, a delighted Larry thanked Alan for his congratulations: 'I suck them up like spaghetti.'[23]

When he summed up his young career for Henry Miller a few years later, with a few exaggerations calculated to amuse the author of *Tropic of Cancer*, he ascribed considerable significance to the acceptance of his first novel, although not to *Pied Piper of Lovers* itself:

My so called up-bringing was quite an uproar. I have always broken stable when I was unhappy. The list of schools I've been to would be a yard long. I failed every known civil service exam. I hymned and whored in London – playing jazz in a nightclub, composing jazz songs, working in real estate. Never really starved – but I wonder whether thin rations are not another degree of starvation – I met Nancy in an equally precarious position and we struck up an incongruous partnership: a dream of broken bottles, sputum, tinned food, rancid meat, urinals, the smell of the lock-hospitals. And so – well we did a bit of drinking and dying. The second lesson according to St Paul. Ran a photographic studio together. It crashed. Tried posters, short stories, journalism – everything short of selling our bottoms to a clergyman. I wrote a cheap novel. Sold it – well that altered things. Here was a stable profession for me to follow. Art for money's sake. I began.[24]

True, the £45 remaining after Curtis Brown's commission had been deducted was not much money, but compared to Larry's £3 weekly stipend, the sum was significant.

Larry and Nancy had planned more carefully for Corfu than it appeared from his off-hand comments. Before leaving Bournemouth he had written to George that he was collecting 'a huge small library' to bring along, and was 'planning a specialized essay on Elizabethan writers'. Besides poetry, philosophy and art books, he had purchased a facsimile Shakespeare fourteen inches tall, 'which ought to sink the boat'. He had not included many moderns, adding that 'for about the last three months I've not read a single contemporary thing'.[25]

Larry made the most of *Pied Piper of Lovers* in his arguments with his siblings: 'They couldn't deny a published book,' he would say years later.[26] Except to his immediate family, however, Larry took an exceedingly deprecatory stance about *Pied Piper*. In the years to come he would usually not admit to having written any novels before *The Black Book* in 1938. He would steadfastly refuse to permit *Pied Piper* to be reissued and professed relief that most of the remaining stock – less than two hundred copies were sold – had been destroyed in the London Blitz. While Larry was not always sure when he had written especially well, he was confident that he could judge when he had written badly. In 1935 he needed evidence that he was an author even more than he needed the £45 that *Pied Piper* brought in, so he permitted the publication of a book that he knew was flawed. Later on he would cull drafts of novels, plays and poems that he judged really bad.

There was little time at the moment for gloating over the news from Cassell: lodgings had to be found for the family, lodgings which included that prime necessity for civilized English expatriate life: a water closet. Right near by, Larry turned up the Villa Agazini, the 'Strawberry Pink Villa' of Gerald Durrell's *My Family and Other Animals*. Then furniture had to be bought and Louisa and her brood had to be settled in. The family had had a rougher trip than Larry and Nancy's across the Bay of Biscay. Leslie wrote Alan Thomas a graphic description of walking Gerry's dog Roger on the top deck with the ship pitching violently: '*God* what a time we had, what with the dog piddling all over the place and the snow coming down, the cold wind blowing like *hell*.'[27]

The painful memories of the journey quickly receded for the Durrells.

Larry's impressions of Corfu were so vivid that he forgot to appear blasé or bored, writing in one of his typically undated letters to Alan:

I've told you how unique it is up here, stuck on the hillside, haven't I? Well, multiply that by four. Today we rose to a gorgeous sunlight and breakfasted in it. Our breakfast table looks out plumb over the sea, and the fishing boats go swirling past the window. There's a faint mist over Albania today but here the heat is paralysing. Bees and lizards and tortoises (yesterday I caught a tortoise eavesdropping on us) are making hay; and the peasants together with those animals who cannot make hay are making water beautifully and indiscriminately. Soon I'll send you some photographs – but even they can't do justice to it all. Sometimes I almost suspect the whole thing; I don't think I can yet really believe in it.

The Corfiot wines 'are not as brilliant as Italy', but 'there is a good peasant wine which tastes and looks like iced blood. It costs 6 dracks – 3^d per bottle. What more does one want? In England I couldn't buy a bottle of horse-piss for 3^d.' And the food passed muster as well: 'Yesterday we dined very royally on red mullet – as you know a most epicurean dish – it cost 10^d.'[28] Restaurants were comparably inexpensive. The cheapness of dining out was matched by the retail prices of most staples, and since small houses cost less than two pounds a month and maidservants less than one, Larry's and Nancy's incomes, combined, seemed quite adequate. In fact, with the drachma at 517 to the pound they felt positively rich. They quickly adopted a peasant diet: great loaves of greyish bread, a sort of *bouillabaisse* of various small fish with potatoes, onions, garlic and a bit of carrot or other vegetable. Macaroni was a staple, and Nancy's Italian cookbook of the Loxwood days was unpacked. A vestige of their English diet lingered in the many cakes and jams Nancy and Pam made for their daily teas, but above all, they began to appreciate the elemental nature of their lives: 'You began to taste your olive oil', Larry recalled; 'you began to taste your bread, because it had been manufactured in front of you'. The Greek appreciation of cool water from favoured wells came to them with the first hot, thirsty days. Imperceptibly, they began to adapt to peasant life: 'It proved other things for me', Larry said, 'that you don't need a lot of clubber to live, that you can live with one knife, one fork, one teaspoon, and one glass.'[29] To the end of his days, he would never lose this basic urge to simplicity.

Their exploration of the island continued, sometimes in the Wilkinsons' small sailing boat. Once they were nearly shipwrecked on the skittish April seas, George confessed to Alan: 'The wind was too much for our ignorance of sailing & the current for Larry's excavation type of rowing.' Soon they had smashed the rudder on a rock and found themselves marooned on an exposed beach, from which they were rescued by a party of grinning Greek villagers – 'ignominious but instructive', sighed George.[30] A safer and less strenuous entertainment was provided by the Shakespeare Reading Society of four that Larry, Nancy, George, and Pam formed, and Alan was asked to send a set of the plays in the Temple pocket edition.

One brilliant day in early summer the two couples walked across the island, some fifteen miles through the fertile Plain of Rópa to Paleocastrizza on the west coast, and met with hospitality that showed Zeus still to be patron of strangers on Corfu. Chairs were fetched for them in one isolated village, they were fed figs and cheese, and a heated discussion went on among the womenfolk over whether Nancy and Pam, with cropped hair and wearing only shorts and halter tops such as had never been seen there before, were boys or girls. Shifting winds brought the fragrance of lemon and orange groves, the aroma of pines, the herbal odours of the maquis – bay, myrtle, ilex. The evening was alive with the clonk of goat bells and, on occasion, with the quarter-tones of a goatherd's flute. It was easy to see why Larry soon decided that this magic terrain, covered in flowers and lulled by cicadas, and reminding him of *The Tempest*, could have been Prospero's abode: 'the isle is full of noises,/ Sounds and sweet airs, that give delight and hurt not.'

Larry set about collecting old legends and constructing new myths about Corfu. The beauty of the island is a cliché that goes back beyond Edward Lear, who spent five winters sketching there beginning in 1856. Appreciation of Corfu extends back at least to Homer if we accept Larry's contention that Kerkyra, Corcyra, Scheria, was ancient Phaeacia, the meeting place of Odysseus and Nausicaä.[31] Larry would appropriate the Homeric legend into his own mythology, and he would eventually compile an anthology of Lear's Corfu letters. Both for its strategic situation and for its gentle fruitfulness, Corfu has been much valued. The island had been invaded, raided and often sacked over the millennia by Spartans, Sicilians, Illyrians, Romans, Vandals, Goths, Byzantines, Genoese, Venetians, Catalans, Turks, French, Italians. Taking stock of his new domain, Larry approved the 'smoke-grey volcanic turtle-backs lying low against the ceiling of heaven'. He continued, 'Corcyra is all Venetian blue and gold – and utterly spoilt by the sun. Its richness cloys and enervates.'[32] Enervating or not, Corfu was to be one of Larry's most productive places. The brilliant Greek light illuminated the reds and yellows of the southern valleys, the smoky purplish-pink of the Judas trees in blossom, even the waving sea-grass fathoms deep. While Nancy produced 'lazy pleasant paintings',[33] Larry roughed out poems in wine- and sea-stained notebooks and wrote *Panic Spring* and *The Black Book*. He also toyed with his projected study of the Elizabethans, savouring them in the many books he had brought along, and influences spilled into his poetry: 'O per se O, I sing on' in 'Carol on Corfu' repeats Thomas Dekker's title 'O per se O'; and in 'Spring', entitled 'Ye Springe' in a later version, Larry wrote verse reminiscent of the Metaphysicals:

> All you beauties are my patient fuel,
> Dear fever's febrifuge, agony's anodyne.
> You, sap-drenched spring things springing
> In tepid April, the ding-dong lemon-time.

Towards the end of 1935 Larry listed in random order the writers he would like to have met, indicating some of his favourite reading: Shakespeare; Donne; Sir John Harington, Elizabethan translator of Ariosto; Rabelais; Skelton; Fabre; and Sir Thomas Urquhart, Jacobean translator of Rabelais. Under these influences Larry's mood became nostalgic. When the sirocco roared in and the sea turned ugly, he and Nancy recalled Little Songhurst Cottage where the English spring came 'like showers of blessings'. He could not forgive Bournemouth, however, and sent Alan a ten-thousand-word essay, 'Provincial Jeremiad'.[34] By then, the Greek sun had already invaded Larry's poetry and the island ambience was eventually to edge the Elizabethans off centre stage, with such local images as those in the unpublished 'Card-Players: Still Life', in which men 'snooze' with rows of 'formal melons in sunlight' behind them. The visitor can 'slough the creeping pale-skinned north' and become 'one among the brown men'.[35] Larry's assimilation of Greece was well under way, but to the sound of Beethoven's Piano Concerto No. 4 played over and over 'in this quiet room above the sea'.[36] He was not about to give up his northern culture.

His first novel was coming out, the family was in his hair, select specimens escaped from Gerry's menagerie were nesting in his typewriter, the luggage hadn't arrived, the paint on the newly purchased furniture in the Villa Agazini was still drying; yet by April Larry was bursting to get back to writing and announced to Alan, 'I am in pod again and am pupping a novel: but it's too upsidedown here as yet to really work. God but the sun. I've written a lovely poem which I transcribe for you on the back of this.' 'What sweet white meat our bodies are', proclaimed Larry in 'A Lyric of Bodies'.[37]

The novel Larry was pupping would be published as *Panic Spring*, with the name of a pseudonymous mother, Charles Norden, on the title page. *Pied Piper of Lovers* had sold only a few copies by the time *Panic Spring* was ready for the press, and since the new novel was to be Larry's first with Faber and Faber, the editors suggested a pseudonym. Larry derived his *nom de plume* from Van Norden, a character in *Tropic of Cancer* – so it amounted to a Jolly Roger at the masthead of the book, at least in the eyes of the very few who had read *Tropic*.

There was to be little in *Panic Spring* that would reflect the implied godfather, but Larry in 1935 was already chafing under the demands of British readers and publishers. *Pied Piper of Lovers* was in the galley stage, and Alan had volunteered to read proofs. Larry was soon in a rage with Cassell because 'some grubby minion' had deleted without his prior knowledge the phrase 'going with a strange woman'. He had written to the firm 'to find out for certain whether the Holy Ghost Itself is proof-reader for Cassell's'. Larry was keen to be published, but would rather not see the book come out at all than have it silently castrated, and without his permission: 'If the shits don't cultivate better manners I'm going to break the contract and find another publisher who doesn't wear crepe next to the navel.' Although Alan was complimentary about *Pied Piper*, Larry typed, 'O but its a bad book.' Even after he had sealed the envelope he could not resist a Parthian shot written on the flap in ink green as the guts of a caterpillar: 'And a great stinging hunk of Merde to the British Bourgeoisie.'[38]

He had not expected a fight over *Pied Piper of Lovers*, and in any case he did not think the book was worth an immense fracas. After the proofs arrived he was sure. Curtis Brown had written 'that it would be better to elide the dirty-dirties', Larry reported, adding that 'I was prepared to get hot about [it] when, damn it, your parcel arrived and I began to read the thing, with my belly going hollow and sick and my gorge going slimy in me.' The problem of squeamish publishers and finicky readers remained, however: 'There's your formula for a book', he told Alan later, 'rinse the baby's napkins into the soup-plates of the public and they love it. But as to the stark and lovely offal of reality – just a flavouring, please M^r So and So – God it makes me SICK! "Offal to taste" as the cookery book says.' Still quivering over the limit of 'flavouring' allowed, he fired a brief postcard to Alan: 'Went with a strange woman!!!! My bloody God!' Nancy had drawn an adroit cover showing a harlequin Pied Piper, and this gave Larry an idea: he would ask Cassell to 'issue a dummy book with Nancy's dust-wrapper. It would give me a reputation right away. The title is good, and the cover is good. But . . . . [39]

ONE OF LARRY'S MOST REWARDING FRIENDSHIPS began at the Villa Agazini in Perama. Late in 1934 Wilkinson had met an apparition among the olive groves between Analypsis and Kanoni: a distinguished-looking man with a pointed blond beard, fastidiously dressed in a tweed suit and a grey Homburg, but carrying a knapsack festooned with entomological collecting gear and bobbing smartly up and down. He turned out to be gathering wild mushrooms. George took it for granted that this unusual specimen would speak English and started a conversation. It was Dr Theodore Stephanides, the English-Greek radiologist, man of science and writer, who was to become a lifelong friend and mentor to two Durrells, Gerry and Larry. Stephanides had bright blue eyes, a chiselled profile that would have made Praxiteles sigh, and an improbable small giggle. Months later George brought Stephanides to the Villa Agazini one afternoon. Following a pleasant tea during which the good doctor was introduced to Louisa Durrell, to Leslie, Margo, Gerry, and to Roger, described by Stephanides as 'a large & friendly black dog of rather uncertain pedigree', Larry and Nancy appeared. Stephanides recalled, 'What first struck me on meeting Lawrence was his jauntiness & self-assurance (a quality I have always lacked); also his bubbling energy. He seemed to be in every corner of the little house at once, throwing off advice & suggestions like a machine-gun & arranging to undertake everything from the arrangement of the furniture to the planting out of the garden.' To Stephanides it seemed that there was no question in Larry's mind about his future: 'From the very beginning he was determined to become a great writer. He was quite certain that he would be one & after I had known him for a short while, I was equally convinced that he would succeed in his aim.'[40]

Larry may have been able to project confidence, but he was having private doubts. From the first he detested his second-born fiction, writing to Alan Thomas on 20 July, 'I'm in the 40,000 of a novel: so inconceivably bloody that I squitter with disgust when I think on it.'[41] Larry hoped to make some money with *Panic Spring*, so he set out to write an innocuous romance, an idyll about a handful of sophisticated castaways who become guests of Rumanades, the wealthy Greek owner of the fictitious island of Mavrodaphne. An early working title, 'Phoenix and the Nightingale', implied an arch and arty tone.

Despite his disparaging remarks about *Panic Spring*, Larry threw himself

LAWRENCE DURRELL

into the task of writing it with considerable gusto. His excitement comes through in the first of his vivid set pieces, Dr Fonvisin's tale of the mummified wife who walks from her sepulchre on a wolf-haunted night. 'Embalming is my subject,' says the gloomy Russian doctor by way of introduction, and then gives a meticulous description of the 'evisceration per anum' of the corpse and its suspension in a bath of spiced oils, set in a mausoleum in the garden.[42] That night the wolves come, the husband, Fonvisin's friend, rushes out with a shotgun, he sees the figure of his wife standing as if waiting for him outside the door of the tomb, the gun goes off in his startled hand – and she drops, dead a second time. Wolf-tracks punctuate the snow. Larry chose a dark August night on the shore-side rocks to read this episode 'by the light of a guttering candle' to Nancy and Theodore. 'Under these circumstances', recalled Stephanides, 'the tale was doubly gruesome, & I think that Nancy & I cast a good many shuddering glances over our shoulders into the surrounding shadows.'[43]

It was not merely love of the Gothic that prompted Larry to conjure up gruesome images: his fascination with death was already clear in *Pied Piper of Lovers* where the boy Walsh learns from his grandmother that 'it takes ten years for the worms to eat through the coffin' and dreams that the mounted specimens in an insect collection have come to life. Larry was equally concerned with the afterlife and with rebirth, but the Christian variety was closed to him: life after death would have to follow the Egyptian recipe of mummification or the Tibetan ritual of the *Bardo Thödol*, freely translated as 'Liberation by Hearing on the After-Death Plane'.[44] *Bar-do* in Tibetan means 'between two', and expresses the idea that death is a state between two passages through life. That the Buddhists generally deny the continuing existence of a *personal*, individual soul would contribute to Larry's rejection of the existence of the discrete ego among the living. Behind him was the horror of the father who had faded away into insanity and death. 'Tibet hangs like a sphinx over the revisited childhood which my dreams offer me', Larry would write near the end of *The Black Book*.[45]

Meanwhile he kept up a steady barrage of typescripts launched in the direction of London, usually to Curtis Brown but on occasion to John Gawsworth who passed them over to his own agent, John Farquharson. Gawsworth's tale of frenetic activity – he had finished a collaboration with Matthew Phipps Shiel on *The Invisible Voices*, had procured for the impoverished Shiel a Civil List pension, had edited a 'monstrous horror book', had 180 letters to answer – must have made Larry doubly glad to be far from literary London. Larry wanted his mail, nevertheless, and chastised Alan for not writing: 'Try a bit of telegraphese, if you like, but give me a little news. Has the novel come out? Shit. The reviews were bad? Good. Is there a virginal typist anywhere round you for my next? Bugger.'[46]

Encouragement, however, did come from England. Pat Evans thought that the Noah passage in Larry's unfinished 'Elegy on Time' was unique in post-war English poetry, and that there was nothing comparable back until the Elizabethans. This overvalued Larry's effort – perhaps justly, the 'Elegy' was never to see publication – but there was also in the headstrong air of Larry's circle in England an undervaluing of the rising modernists: Evans voiced the heresies and Larry was far from rebutting them. Evans spoke disparagingly of Pound: 'One or two lovely things; but isn't he piddling?' Eliot fared just as badly: 'No doubt Pound *is* just his cup of tea. Balls and balls.'[47] All this while Larry on Corfu was filling notebooks with verse that attempted faithful recordings of the scenes at hand, as if he were following the advice of the old master Imagist, Ezra Pound. Larry wrote, 'Bees brown with a flash of sun-flaming gold/ Whirl murmurous against a cypress screen', images coined to give a 'sinewy answer' to 'Pen, ink, books: lonely at the window-sill.'[48] Poetry, to be sure, was not likely to produce an income, and Larry proposed that Alan place a classified advertisement in *Time and Tide*: YOUNG POET OF CONSIDERABLE PROMISE AND MODERATE ACHIEVEMENT DESIRES PATRON. STRICTLY FINANCIAL. LACK OF INTELLIGENCE NO BAR. ROLL UP YOU SIDNEYS. IT'S YOUR MONEY I WANT. 'No', wrote Alan in the margin.[49]

The picture of Larry Durrell charging single-mindedly ahead in the cultivation of his art amid the rocky and enchanted olive groves and beaches of Corfu is misleading. Dedicated he clearly was, yet Durrell the aspiring author was frequently ready to desert his Underwood to become Larry the faun, Larry the devotee of Pan, for a hike or a swim or a long lunch or a night of singing and talking. He also made sporadic efforts to act like the head of the Durrell family, but it was an independent crew he had to deal with. Leslie adored hunting and firearms of all types, and the garden echoed with the reports of his target practice, followed occasionally by the thin wail of a ricocheting bullet. Margaret, short, blonde, pretty, and with the liveliest eyes in the family, took to tanning herself in a two-piece bathing suit – revolutionary on Corfu – and brought home a succession of acquaintances ranging from aspiring swains to a pair of itinerant Greek musicians. Larry and his mother decided in April that it was time Gerry's schooling was resumed. Larry suggested that he be put on a course of

Rabelais: 'Good, clean fun; it's important that he gets sex in its right perspective now.'[50] Gerry was ten. This proposal was vetoed; George Wilkinson was offered the post of tutor, and both needing the money and having a theory of education to test, he accepted. Gerry resisted George's programme of literature and world history, but learned from him a workable method of orderly scientific notation. Not a day passed without his bearing up to his bedroom a jar or cardboard box containing 'some wonderful new animal or insect or snake'. With the family and guests seated at tea, Larry hazarded a prediction: 'Gerry will do better than all of us one day.'[51] Later he added thoughtfully, 'Even if he does swim with one toe on the bottom.'[52]

Larry made a great show of taking Gerry's education lightly, but in fact he evidently wanted to see that his brother enjoyed an adventurous, unconventional upbringing. Recalling his own loss of freedom, Larry was determined that Gerry should not be surrendered to the schoolmasters.[53] Years later in *Tunc* Larry would write that those deprived of a true childhood would react with sterility towards the world.

Louisa Durrell acquiesced to a casual education for her youngest son, but she did not share Larry and Nancy's euphoria about Corfu. 'Don't believe a word they tell you about this smelly island', she complained to Alan Thomas. The countryside might be beautiful, but 'as for the town the less said the better'.[54] Within months Louisa moved from the cramped Villa Agazini to the Villa Anemoyanni – Gerry dubbed it the 'Daffodil-Yellow Villa' – at Sotiriotissa near Govina Bay, four miles north of Corfu town. The three-storey mansion, tall, square, Venetian, was set in an overgrown park of olive, lemon, orange, tangerine, and cypress trees. Arbutus and other shrubs were allowed to flourish unclipped. The house was a faded yellow, with green shutters and a red roof. Larry and Nancy moved from Perama to live at the Villa Anemoyanni in a bright, airy room with two large windows shaded by a vine that covered the entire side of the house. As Larry surged ahead with *Panic Spring*, the room became cluttered with 'books, dictionaries, files & manuscript sheets which, as usual, soon overflowed into every nook & corner', observed Stephanides.[55] Around June the galley proofs of *Pied Piper of Lovers* arrived and demanded attention. Larry and his mother became locked in an endless battle, she determined to straighten up his room, he equally adamant that she should *not*.

Boisterous games, 'the rougher the better', delighted the male members of the family. Often visitors expecting a quiet tea were pressed into service on one of the opposing sides attacking or defending 'the Fort', a small rise in the grounds of the villa. Larry, Gerry and Leslie, the many sons of the Greek gardener, and even suited and booted Dr Stephanides were regular participants. Sometimes Margaret joined the fray, but the other ladies complained about the amount of time they had to spend repairing the strife-torn clothing of the men and boys. Pliable cypress bows, cones and chunks of dried earth were the only weapons allowed and aiming for the face was prohibited, but even so one or the other of them, Larry included, would often turn up at tea with a bruise or a shiner. 'I can still remember with a thrill after all those years,' wrote Stephanides, 'how we all enjoyed tearing around, shouting & yelling & throwing cypress cones & earth clods at each other – although Lawrence was 25 & I 40 years old at the time'.[56]

The fort game had its ominous counterparts in the outer world. Italy was threatening Ethiopia and the eruption of conflict seemed likely. 'Shall I be seeing you in the next trench to mine defending Addis Ababa?' queried John Gawsworth. Mindful of the slaughter of the young in the First World War, Gawsworth in closing caught the sense of limited time felt by many: 'Thine, for the short span of life still allotted to us.'[57] Larry, nearer to Italy and to Africa than Gawsworth was, told Alan that he was making more concrete contingency plans: 'Hot nuts, eh? But the show is damn serious for us here. I'm going to try and kick my mother off to Athens. Ourselves, we'll have to sail across the straits and try to make Janninah if there's trouble. Brigands and whatnot on the mainland, too, so I'm sure to be raped all the way home.'[58] Job-like, Larry had also broken out in 'nasty' sores that kept him from writing, and when he went shooting at Antiniotissa with Leslie these were scraped open by the brambles.

Neither Larry's discomfort nor the threat of war could prevent the Durrells from enjoying themselves. 'Concentrating on life just at present,' wrote Larry. 'Not much of it left as far as I can gather.'[59] When the weather would not permit outdoor activities, they would dance in the large ground-floor sitting room of the Villa Anemoyanni, an aromatic fire of olive and cypress wood blazing in the hearth. One wet afternoon Stephanides brought over a gramophone record of the *Pendozali*, a lively Cretan folk dance, and taught the steps to the entire family. Ranged in a circle, hands on each other's shoulders, they whirled about the room. This dance was followed by the *Kalamatiano*, the *Syrtos* and the *Trata*. The same physical coordination that had made Larry a good public-school athlete was shared by the rest of the family, and they were all soon competent in Greek dances.

With stimulated appetites they sat down to one of Louisa Durrell's characteristic Indian curries, redolent with the scent of herbs.

Larry had mailed the unique copy of *Panic Spring* – he hated the buttery feel of carbons and so never made any – in sections beginning around October to Alan, who arranged to have a clean draft typed and then corrected the manuscript himself. Larry included detailed directions to the typist: on the insertion of 'riders', on margins, even on the quality of the paper: 'I'll stand the extra cost.' The contretemps with Cassell over *Pied Piper of Lovers* served to make Larry cautious in *Panic Spring*. 'Where you see xxx – it means asterisks,' he informed Alan; 'I've cut down the original number of *fucks* to a modest number. By God this time they give me asterisks or they can go play with the bishop of London's twat.'[60]

By December Larry had posted to Alan the last of the *Panic Spring* typescript, under the title 'Music in Limbo'. Alan was severe. Larry thanked him for his 'damn good criticism', which Nancy endorsed 'wholeheartedly', and Larry added: 'I myself make as if to vomit when I think of the book, but somehow I can't alter it as yet. Unless everyone turns it down I'll let it stand. I'm never going to tinker with stuff any more. Either it'll come out all in a piece or I'll burn it.'[61] This resolve would come back to haunt Larry, as various books would be returned for rewriting over the years. Mrs Alfred Knopf, the American publisher's wife, read the manuscript before it was submitted to Faber and Faber. She did not make an offer for US publication.

Larry paid little attention to the fate of *Panic Spring*. He was eager to begin his next novel, and announced to Alan: 'Got another germ spreading. No more tragi-heroic epics for me. Something different. More insane.'[62] Having deliberately held himself within the bounds of propriety in *Panic Spring* – there were to be no *fucks* in the published version – he decided he had earned the right to compose as he wished in his next: 'LOVER ANUBIS', he announced to Alan, was about ready to 'uncoil' inside him. With studied calm he asked, 'By the way, would your typist mind typing a *phallic* novel?'[63] Larry sent his Ben Jonson and his Rochester volumes to Bournemouth so Alan could sell them for him, an indication that he was losing enthusiasm, temporarily at least, for his planned historical monograph. True, he needed the money, but it was more than that: he felt unsettled, and wrote that he was 'no longer keen on books as *possessions*'.[64]

LIFE WAS SO EASY, THE TOYS and distractions were so many, the friends were so entertaining, that the wonder is Durrell-the-writer could ever rein in Larry-the-life-celebrant. Yet the evidence of hard labour abounds: enough poetry for a couple of volumes, two novels, several essays. Larry's power of concentration allowed him to work under the most trying circumstances, and in this he resembled one of his principal literary influences, D. H. Lawrence, who could write with equally sharp focus in a miner's crowded kitchen or under an olive tree. Larry's mind seemed to be able to operate on at least two tracks simultaneously: he would break off in the middle of a conversation, dash to his typewriter, stab furiously at the keys for ten minutes, then return to pick up his conversational thread exactly where he had left off. Prey to what he termed 'that awful contamination of restlessness',[65] he would pace about the Villa Ane-moyanni, stepping absent-mindedly over Gerry's animals, Leslie's guns and Margaret's beauty aids, all the while mulling over plots and dialogue. During one such evening session he froze, his eyes fixed on two white skulls staring back at him from the wall. The spectres resolved themselves into a pair of large Death's Head moths – *Acherontia atropos* – so called from the markings on the wings. Somewhat shaken, he picked one up, only to drop it when it emitted a high-pitched shriek. Theodore was happy to inform him that this was the only European moth that could produce such a sound, but Larry was not mollified: 'Why didn't you tell me that before I picked the damn thing up & had it scare the life out of me!'[66]

There was a fine irony in Larry's choice of Corfu as an escape from Pudding Island: Corfu, as capital of the United States of the Ionian Islands confederation, had been under a fairly benevolent English rule from 1814 to 1864, and traces remained in the cricket pitch on the Esplanade and the Anglophilia of many of the local gentry – Dr Constantine Paliatano who had studied in England and whose family was in *Burke's Peerage*, the Aspiotis who spoke perfect English. Various members of the local gentry whose English was not so good were still happy to entertain Louisa and her children, who gleefully collected linguistic howlers: 'Please come undressed because we are in the family way,' wrote one hostess.[67] Spiro Americanos was also staunchly pro-British, announcing on one occasion, 'Honest to Gods, Mrs Durrell, you cut me opes you finds the Union Jack inside.'[68] Cricket on Corfu was embellished with such English rituals as the sale among the spectators of 'tsintsinbeera' – ginger beer – and drop scones, keeping company with native lemonade, anise-flavoured water and highly sweetened ices. Two club teams, Corfu Gymnastikos and the Byron Cricket Club, played the game at a commendable level, an attraction for Larry who 'adored' – his word – village cricket. Some of the finer country homes showed the influence of English architecture; *Mon Repos* in Kanoni, built for a British governor, was the country residence of the Greek royal family, and Philip Schleswig-Holstein-Sonderburg-Glücksberg, who would take the name Mountbatten before he married the future Queen Elizabeth, had been born there in 1921. (Two years later Nancy would suggest 'Mon Repos' as the title for Larry's 'Asylum in the Snow'.) And there were many smaller villas inhabited by retired English civil servants and military officers. In fact, there was a staid and smug aspect of Corfu that, horror of horrors, was reminiscent of Bath, Brighton or Bournemouth. Larry, however, claimed that 'It wasn't the Englishness that mattered, but the communications, the postal service, the degree of civilization.'[69] To show his adopted Greekness, Larry closed a letter to Alan, 'Kali mera sas: i.e. good morning to you.'[70]

The Italian colouring of Corfu also appealed strongly to the Durrells: 'Compared to Athens,' Larry said much later, 'Corfu was like . . . Florence.' He found on Corfu 'the remains of a Venetian aristocracy', the sort of cultural leavening he would appreciate also in Alexandria and on Rhodes: 'There too you come across strata of different cultures – forgotten, overlayed, covered up; people shut away in huge, deserted villas; barons, countesses, their hearts beating weakly to the rhythm of the past. Romanticism!'[71]

ALTHOUGH LARRY HAD CLAIMED NOT to be reading his contemporaries, Barclay Hudson, a new American friend on Corfu, loaned him a recently published book that was to influence his writing and lead, ultimately, to his staunchest literary friendship. 'It's the first book which honours natural man since Villon. NATURAL. Sans conditioning, heredity, upbringing', he raved to Alan about *Tropic of Cancer*. The book was inexhaustible, like a great poem; Larry had read *Tropic* ten times over, 'and it's still giving me'. Henry Miller had rejected 'every artificial formula', all 'flummery', and had 'arrived at the stage when he can see men, actions[,] as Fabre sees insects'. Then Larry came up with a formula of his own that would prove a motif in all his major novels from *The Black Book* on: 'Chaos is the score on which reality is written.'[72]

In August 1935, with *Panic Spring* well advanced, Larry had written his first letter to Miller, a fan letter such as any ignored genius would be ecstatic to receive: 'I have just read *Tropic of Cancer* again and feel I'd like to write you a line about it. It strikes me as being the only really man-sized piece of work which this century can really boast of.' After this promising beginning, Larry's letter was not mere gush to Miller's ears, but compared him – favourably – to an author Miller admired and was indeed already writing about, D. H. Lawrence: '*Tropic* is something they've been trying to do since the war. It's the final copy of all those feeble, smudgy rough drafts – *Chatterly*, *Ulysses*, *Tarr* etc.' Larry echoed Miller's language, announcing that the book 'finds the way out of the latrines at last. Funny that no one should have thought of slipping out via the pan during a flush, instead of crowding the door.'[73] Miller replied with the sweetest of all words to a fledgeling author's ear: 'Your letter is so vivid, so keen, that I am curious to know if you are not a writer yourself.'[74] Was he not! Thus was joined the second of Larry's artistic lifelines: the first tied his self-discovery in primitive Greece and in his own poetry to literary London; this later one would link Larry to fiction under the inspiration of the expatriate Paris of Miller, Anaïs Nin and Alfred Perlès, the Viennese-born writer who was Miller's most frequent companion and court jester.

Henry Miller had first visited France in 1928 with his second wife, June, well after the wave of American writers that included Sherwood Anderson, Kay Boyle, Hart Crane, Dos Passos, Fitzgerald, Hemingway. In a frantic nine months they had travelled about Europe, going as far east as Czernowitz on the Russian frontier; had bicycled to Marseille; and in Paris had met many figures in the cultural world, both important and peripheral, including Ossip Zadkine, Oskar Kokoschka, Hans Reichel and Perlès. It was not until March 1930, unceremoniously dispatched from New York by June, that Miller returned to take up the precarious residence in Paris chronicled in *Tropic of Cancer*. By the next year Henry had met and had fallen in love with Anaïs Nin, daughter of the Cuban-born pianist Joaquín Nin and wife of the American banker Hugh Parker Guiler.

Larry took up Miller as a cause and recommended *Tropic of Cancer* to his friends, lecturing them from the lofty pinnacle of his life knowledge: 'This is the book for our generation,' he wrote to Alan. 'Of course it may shake you a bit on the physical side, because you don't really know every inch of physical passion, and your experience in the world of the body is limited as yet. . . . In the meantime read it for what you can get out of it, and really salt yourself to it.'[75] Alan did not like *Tropic* and for months avoided mentioning the book despite Larry's exclamations: 'My God! man this is a new bible,'[76] he wrote, demanding in every letter to know what his friend thought of Miller. Soon Henry had enlisted Larry in his latest scheme, a plan to print at his own cost, in a volume to be called 'The Banned Book', the 'important' letters and reviews concerning *Tropic of Cancer*: the best 'testimonials' thus far had come from Barclay Hudson,

Blaise Cendrars and Larry, so Henry asserted. And he had letters from Eliot, Huxley, Orwell, Pound . . . . Larry asked Alan to become the receiving centre for letters of support yet to be solicited.

Larry and Nancy moved around October to Kalami, a hamlet of four or five houses on the north-east coast of the island. It may come as a disappointment to readers of Gerald Durrell's *My Family and Other Animals*, but Larry did not live for any extended periods with his family on Corfu. Usually he and Nancy stayed at Kalami, or near Paleocastrizza, or at the Pension Suisse in Corfu town. The shift to Kalami came about after a wonderful tea served by Mrs Gennatas, a stony-faced, solid old lady who spoke English with a Liverpool accent. Her house, fashioned from an ancient Venetian *fortalice*, was situated on the promontory that shielded the tiny Kouloura harbour north of Kalami. Nancy was 'terribly keen' on living in the wildest, most untamed place possible.[77] The remote north appealed to Larry because it was 'much more bristly and rocky and male', with stands of scrub and holm-oak, and the prospect of spending a 'daring and lonely' winter there was alluring.[78] Nancy said, 'The quietness alone makes it another country.'[79]

Probably the experience of the cheerful chaos of Louisa Durrell's household at the Villa Agazini and the Villa Anemoyanni convinced Larry of the advantages of putting half the island between himself and his family. A decisive factor was Gerry's growing menagerie of entomological and zoological curiosities. Larry claimed it was the episode of the medicinal leeches that finally broke his nerve. Stephanides had helped Gerry collect a large container of the creatures, *Hirudo medicinalis*, but unluckily the jar was knocked from a table and the leeches disappeared. 'These were magnificent specimens', wrote Theodore admiringly, 'about 75 mm (3 in.) long, with a bright longitudinal red & green stripe on each side of the body.' Gerry and Larry both regretted their escape, each for his own reason. 'Lawrence gave me a harrowing description of how he lay awake night after night feeling leeches crawling all over him & expecting to find the bedsheets drenched with crimson blood in the morning,' Theodore reported.[80] It was easy to tell Larry that such leeches could not survive an hour out of water, but he would not be convinced. Spiro Americanos was set on to the problem of finding Larry and Nancy an abode: 'Don't you worries, Larrys, I'll soon fixes it,' he rumbled.[81] Spiro located what came to be called 'The White House' in Kalami. A week that Larry and Nancy spent with Barclay and Jane Hudson at Mangkephali, a rocky cape south of Kalami, confirmed their decision to move. Larry and Nancy competed with the Hudsons in diving from jutting rocks far above the sea, a stunt that would resurface as 'the Leap' episode in *Panic Spring*. 'Barclay is nice for all the reasons and attributes that he would be horrified to know he possessed,' Larry later told Miller. 'And we fight like hell, which I enjoy.'[82]

The White House was then a low structure gleaming with whitewash; it included three bedrooms, a dining room, and even – very rare in a peasant home – 'a quite respectable loo'.[83] A rough-finished room contained a stone olive press that made an impressive crunching sound. Larry and Nancy rented two bedrooms, with the right to use the kitchen and dining room. Their landlords, Eleni, 'delicately-formed in a deep silken olive-colour',[84] and Anastasius 'Totsa' Athenaios, a thin, quiet, resourceful man, and their young daughters, Frosso and Tihouli, occupied the rest of the house. It was perched on a series of slanting rock ledges three to twelve feet above the bay, and 'the sea fairly licks up at the drawing room windows', Larry remarked. Moving in became an adventure when their books arrived by caïque, with 'confusion, adjectives, smoke, and the deafening pumping of the wheezy Diesel engine'.[85] This same twice-weekly caïque was their main conveyor of provisions; it stopped regularly at Agni, a mile by footpath to the south, but would put in at Kalami on request.

Diesel engines and Spiro's Dodge touring car notwithstanding, Kalami and Guimari, the nearest village accessible by road from Corfu town, were closer to ancient Greece than to modern Europe in 1935: centuries-old graded, stone-paved paths staggered up the terraced hills to Vigla, to Portais, to Sinies, to Kokini, even to the summit of Pantokrator. Women still carried water up to the villages from springs in the valleys, bent nearly double under the weight of huge clay jars roped to their backs. The dull thud of their heavy footsteps echoed long after they were out of sight. Some of the older men clung to the traditional magpie-hued garb of the north: white stockings, baggy dark blue trousers, fitted black waistcoats. The olive groves were everywhere, the trees perhaps the tallest in Greece, rising unpruned to fifty feet. An enlightened Venetian government had turned Corfu into an orchard by paying a subsidy of ten pieces of gold for each hundred trees planted. The Corfiots thought the Venetians a bit daft to dole out hard cash for saplings but plant they did: olives on the slopes, lemons, oranges, peaches, apricots, pears in the valleys and plains. The decay and dropping off of occasional limbs, a natural occurrence that does not harm the olive tree, had over the centuries turned Corfu's olives into massive columns of lattice work, loopholed with head-sized irregular openings, windows for nymphs and dryads. Nowhere else in Greece have the olives such individual character; nowhere else are they so powerfully alive.

Albania was a tantalizing presence across the straits: a river with an abandoned fort on its estuary, high mountains rising inland. During the summer months Kalami meant isolation after the manner of Thoreau at Walden Pond: plenty of seclusion and natural beauty close at hand, literate friends and the amenities of civilization within fairly easy reach. Corfu town was nineteen miles by road, eight by boat. In the winter, Larry wrote, when the 'thunder walked with great thumps up and down the house',[86] it was another matter: 'Once the rains started in autumn the roads were cut. There was no way of getting anywhere, either by road or by sea: the fishing boats stopped going out. So one had to make do for oneself. It was harsh, but the harshness made it enjoyable.'[87] 'Time means nothing here,' Larry wrote to Joseph Allen. 'There is a word with which the Greeks deal with every demand of life. Perhaps, to be more accurate a phrase δεν πειράζει αύριο – Doesn't matter – tomorrow. And so the petty pace creeps on and I neglect my friends and my creditors – meaning you.'[88]

In retrospect Larry exaggerated the seclusion of Kalami, for he was far too interested in his mail and his friends to remain isolated for long, even by landslides and stormy seas. Often, he visited the family or invited friends to stay. George Wilkinson walked from Kalami up to Sinies, which Larry called 'the surprising crater under the very chin of old man Panto',[89] to observe the polling for the 3 November 1935 plebiscite, held to endorse the return of the monarchy. Other guests found out Kalami, most important among them Theodore, who lived for the month of August 1936 with Larry and Nancy while observing Peltier's Comet. Visible to the naked eye only as a faint blur, the comet, seen through Theodore's excellent prism binoculars, presented a striking luminosity with a short tail. Larry set out to write a poem on the comet but destroyed his effort when it did not please him.

Larry had brought from England the *Encyclopaedia Britannica* in the 14th edition, and he set out to read 'all' the articles on science. This was partly due to the influence of Theodore, who seemed to know everything scientific, but mainly it was Larry's own need to comprehend how the universe fitted together – even if only in its broad outlines. In fact, he read wherever his interests took him. Into his notebooks and his correspondence went specific references to *Britannica* articles on astrology, Indian philosophy, Chinese art.[90]

Throughout his Kalami days, Larry gave as his mailing address the

Ionian Bank in Corfu town: 'The Greek postal service was so unreliable, there was no point in giving a private address.'[91] Despite Larry's complaints about the mail, he usually received letters from London in under a week. Alan was frequently commissioned to buy and forward books and magazines for various members of the Durrell family. Two months after they arrived on Corfu, Leslie wrote to him asking that a weekly parcel containing the *Daily Mirror* and the overseas edition of 'any other newspaper' be mailed (Alan sent *The Times*); for himself Leslie ordered *The American Rifleman* and *Game and Gun*, for Gerry *Puck* and *Crackers*, for his mother *Stitchcraft* and *Good Housekeeping*. Larry's requests included journals, books, catalogues, a manual on repairing sailboats, a cheap fountain pen; for Stephanides Larry bought ten volumes of Benn's sixpenny poets – Belloc, Binyon, de la Mare, Drinkwater, Sassoon and so on; two friends on Corfu wanted facsimile Shakespeares like his own. Larry procured from Paris and forwarded to Alan on request three copies of the banned *Lady Chatterley's Lover*. He judged the novel 'not really worth reading'. 'If Lawrence had written it about the same people, and let the theory of it come out naturally it would have been good; but he plugs away so hard and so long that one gets tired of the gamekeeper's outsize in balls, and the sumptuous bottom of the heroine.' Then Larry made a statement that expressed his personal view of didacticism in fiction: 'Novels built on theoretical crusading simply won't do. That's what was wrong with Aldington's last don't you think? And (sweeping generalizations are in fashion these days), by the way, that's what's wrong with Wagner, Eliot, Spender, Brahms, and the early Durrell: excess of cerebration.'[92]

Larry also felt that he did not have much sympathy to spare for Oliver Mellors and Connie Chatterley: he had his own worries. There was a commission of a highly private nature that must have caused quiet bachelor Alan some anguish: an order for a 'Provace Occlusive Cap, with spring rim, size O' and, because the customs had taken to opening his parcels, special mailing instructions: 'for Godsake wrap it in a stout collection of Time and Tides, bend it up flat so that you can't see by looking at it that it's got anything inside.'[93] Barclay Hudson had taken months trying to get 'his machine' past Customs. 'We, for the time being, are most nervous and rather pious. We watch and spray.'[94] When there was no immediate compliance on Alan's part, Larry prodded him:

No don't write, you're a busy man. But, dear me, *do* send me an occlusive cap will yeu. Nancy catches babies like 'flu and I'm as fertile as a Turk or a Jew.

Grrrrr – I can see my metaphysical beast
of a self growling out of the
undergrowth. Io Io Io
Io.[95]

In his next letter to Alan, Larry's enquiries after the 'anti-baby device' took on a frantic tone: 'Do hurry, dear friend, before my inquisitive spermatozoa nose their way up into old Fallopia and meet an ova – despite olive oil and shifts.'[96] The fecundity around him was alarming: 'Life is very beautiful and drunken. The lamb has foaled white fluff and soft bones: Totsa has had a man-child with a girl's teats and the features of a toothless but knowing mandarin: and – sacré nom d'anything you like – Nancy's period is 37 days overdue. Pattering feet? Curse this tropical air. It makes me as fertile as the stoats. . . . P.S. *Are* stoats fertile?'[97]

Meanwhile, on 17 October 1935 *Pied Piper of Lovers* had appeared in England, and Larry awaited the reviews less anxiously than he did Nancy's period. He sent a copy to the Browns, and Granny Richardson commented, 'Now that you've told the world that you know all about sex, why don't you write a decent book?'[98] The few press notices were tepid at best – the *Times Literary Supplement* noted the adolescent tone and was condescending about the author's sincerity – and Larry ignored them until he discovered a 'terrific attack on the author of Piper' in *Janus*. 'I was amazed,' he wrote to Alan, 'until I looked closely and saw that my old friends? Reggie Hutchings, Philip Marsh, Ena Douglas, and the Galloping Potocki were running it'[99] – 'the assorted Potockis of Pilawa and Hogwash'.[100] Larry threatened to send a limerick response on a postcard:

I've just read a review in your Janus,
Which it seems is intended to pain us.
But the joke's in your title,
What an endless recital
Not of head, my dear Hutchings, but anus.[101]

In fact, Larry was mainly angry with himself because the book was made up of 'self-pitying little whines',[102] and so he felt he could not retaliate. 'My wretched 1st novel got fairly badly barbed', he wrote to Joseph Allen, 'but I don't complain coz it *was* a bad book . . . . Only I'm furious about the review in *Janus* . . . that wasn't about the book – about which anyone can say anything – but about me.'[103] He was right: John Mair begins his review by stating that 'By a Pavlovian Predestination the first novels of the young are always the same,' and are autobiographical. Then, although he never names the author, he describes a generic first-novelist in terms too close to Larry for mere coincidence: 'He is quiet and reserved[,] reading *The Spectator*, Propertius, and Aldous Huxley; he is bad at most games, but very good at boxing . . . . One wonders how many were really boxers.' Mair sums up the 'bohemian life' of such novels in a few phrases: 'Real gin . . . is drunk out of bottles, mass copulations take place under divans, and all ends in vomit. Usually the hero is driven to reflect on the Futility of Human Greatness.'[104] Larry asked Allen for some clue to explain the tone of Mair's piece: 'This very superior young gingerbread giant Mair I have not met and am at loss to account for his spite.' Larry threatened to come to England soon to 'renew a lot of old acquaintanceships'. Meanwhile, he begged for news about 'your sane world as well as the pimply green-socked world of the HIGHER THINKERS'.[105] He might pretend indifference to the Bloomsbury world that he had scorned and fled, yet he disliked being bitten by its denizens. He worried that Alan Thomas had actually sold five copies of *Pied Piper*: 'Now who the fuck wants *that* bloody book in the house. . . . Don't let my enemies get hold of it.'[106]

Pregnancy scare or carping critics, the literary life had to go on. In fact, there was now a new urgency to make money: Nancy really was pregnant. Both Larry and Nancy were 'terrified' at the thought of producing a child. Finally, the gynaecologist at the local clinic decided that, since Nancy was 'anaemic and not strong', he could legally recommend terminating the pregnancy. Curettage was performed successfully, but it had been a terrific strain on the pair of them. 'I'm still 24 but I've aged,' Larry wrote to Alan, 'I must be a very old gentleman in my soul.' More than ever Larry wanted his friends around him – Pat Evans was driving from England to replace Wilkinson as Gerry's tutor – and he ended the letter: 'My dear man, be an opportunist for once. Bust, smash, swivel, twist, truncate your scruples and material complexities for once and break out like a rash across Europe with Pat. What will it cost you? You owe it to your immortal soul . . . . *COME*.'[107]

Larry kept writing furiously. He and Theodore collaborated on two short stories, 'Red David' and 'A Pair of Blue Eyes'. Larry sent Curtis Brown another short story, 'The Monk and the Walnut Tree' along with 'two playlets'. Nothing came of any of these. He finished a longer play, 'The Ancient Britons', which Brown rejected in May because the characters talked too much: 'Good idea but bad dramaticks', Larry admitted.[108] Years later, Larry would confess that the short story made him feel 'uncomfortable . . . like a wooden leg'. Either they tried to extend themselves in his imagination to novella length, or they shrank to two-page squibs.[109] This genre, a money-maker for many novelists, would remain off limits to Larry.

If he was not unduly concerned over the fate of his short stories and plays, it was because 'Lover Anubis' was seething in his imagination. Later he abbreviated the provisional title to 'Anubis', then changed it to 'Anabasis' and finally to *The Black Book*.[110] By May 1936 he was cautiously describing 'my dear Black Book' to Alan: 'It's a bit queer. I'm not driving myself to it – just writing a bit when I feel like it.' He had finished Part One and he wanted Nancy and Alan to be the first to see it, 'because you two have been my first real backers'. He was clear in his own mind that this book would prove different in kind from his other fiction: 'Whatever else it's the first book which makes me feel I am almost touching the hem of the master's garment. I begin to feel the virtue going out of me.'[111] He did not specify any particular master, but Larry recognized the influence of Henry Miller and of the major Russian writers he had been reading recently – Chekhov and especially Dostoevsky. More importantly, he thought, it was 'conceived and written in a state of *poem* not prose', although he had not consciously written the sentences in scansion. The book became a hopper for the outpourings of his crowded mind: any subject from Chaucer to Nancy's Provace Occlusive Cap was likely to appear. 'She wears a thick rubber washer on her vagina', Larry wrote of a barmaid in the book.[112] While an autobiographical element exists in *The Black Book*, just as in *Pied Piper* and *Panic Spring* he had 'furnished it imaginatively': 'The people are real but filtered through the ego.'[113] John Gawsworth, for instance, probably inspired Larry's portrait of Horace Gregory, who, like Gawsworth, was a small, spidery man with pretences to elegance, writing and living in rented rooms.

As if to symbolize his new direction in writing, Larry sprouted a blond beard, but soon shaved it off – the real change was within. He worried to Alan about his diction: 'What are the twelve forbidden words? Print I mean: shit fuck cunt cock ??? What else. I want to know. My language is really awful these days. You see these things no longer mean anything.' Sex, however, 'still strikes me as better than the best novel'.[114]

A recent accomplishment by Wilkinson contributed to Larry's unease. George had finished a 'very sound and bright novel which simply must get published', Larry said, and to celebrate this event George, Pam and Larry crossed to Albania to see the Roman theatre at Butrinto. Larry wrote to Alan a clipped description that omitted the antiquities: 'Tropical undergrowth with malaria swamps. Huge spiders which are nearly as bad as scorpions across all the paths. Vipers. . . . Albanians with little white pith fezzes. Queer bony faces as animated as wooden masks. I like their queer craking language.'[115] More disturbing voices came from the artillery they had heard rumbling in the distant mountains: practice for the coming war.

The weather seemed to conspire against Larry, and even the island was failing to please: he headed a letter to Thomas 'CORFU OF GODSCURSE'. 'The south Alan dear?' he wrote. 'Fuck bugger and blast the south with its burning what have you. Oranges stiff and hard on their trees and rain blowing up from the south. Lagoon like black crepe. Funereal Ionian.' As an emblem of his black mood, Larry closed his letter with an echo of ancient Sappho:

> Lie down alone. The weeping Pleiades wester,
> Loneliness is my cold cash under these stars
> And Time like a wound in me pouring, pouring.
>   Orion
> Sits glum among his bars.[116]

IN THE LIGHT OF THE EVIDENCE, Larry's much later memories of the early life at Kalami are as understated as a sea cucumber: 'I did nothing else [but write],' he would claim. 'I swam a great deal, I went out with the fishermen. We ate what we fished, anything that we managed to pull out of the sea. . . . During the winter we kept each other warm. I had married very young.'[117] This was about as true as his description to Miller of his early life in England: the main elements were true, but the aggregate was so incomplete as to constitute a lie. His need to disguise, to conceal, to protect his privacy led him to invent a bland wash to obscure the darker pigments.

Larry did, however, almost live in the water. The summer sun blazed but the sea was brilliantly clear and cold; 'its chill hurts the back of the throat like an iced wine,' he wrote. Larry and Nancy discovered the tiny shrine of Saint Arsenius half a mile south of Kalami, built in the last century after a fisherman named Manoli had found an icon of the saint washed up there after a storm. Accessible only from the sea, the red brick, tile-roofed cubicle, about three yards square, sat on a swirl of volcanic rock over two fathoms of water. Larry and Nancy threw cherries to the sandy bottom where they 'loom like drops of blood. N. has been going in for them like an otter and bringing them up in her lips.' Near the shrine was a small cave with two entrances, one at water level, one below the surface. Half a dozen people could hide in the green light of the cave's single chamber. Larry was careful to keep the lamp in the shrine filled with clear olive oil: 'Saint Arsenius guards our bathing.'[118] The pleasing ritual of votive lights for the Orthodox saint hearkened back to pagan days. More than ever, Larry felt himself a classical pagan.

Where the sea was so translucent and the most inviting beaches were inaccessible by road, something larger than their rowboat was clearly a necessity, and in the early summer of 1936 Nancy posted a note from Corfu town to her husband in Kalami: 'Dear fainéant, dearest lazybones', she began, 'I have bought us a twenty-foot cutter, carvel built, and Bermuda rigged.'[119] The little sloop had been an auxiliary to an immense private yacht, but it had been left behind in Corfu for repairs and never reclaimed. With Henry Miller's blessing they christened it the *Van Norden*. They repainted the black hull, polished the brasswork, and a Swiss artist friend, Berlincourt, 'who lived on no money and gallons of porridge', decorated the interior.[120] The little sloop had a deep, heavy keel and a cuddy cabin, and was fast if somewhat tricky to handle: 'Now you will be able to prove if you are the stern deep-sea character you pretend to be', commented Nancy.[121] The *Van Norden* was seaworthy enough for excursions across the straits to Albania or around the northern tip of Corfu to Mathraki Island.

The Durrell flotilla quickly expanded. Leslie purchased a motor boat and, for the sum of three pounds, a small skiff which he and Pat Evans fitted out as a sailboat. Leslie offered to deliver Larry and Nancy back to Kalami in his new motor boat, with his mother, Gerry and Pat coming along for the ride. Leslie took the tiller, standing in his usual braced position, 'legs stretched out, head on one side and eyes closed against the smoke of his cigarette'.[122] The seas rose higher and higher, and waves crashed over the boat. Pat clung like a mollusc to the foredeck; Larry, Nancy, Gerry, and Louisa tried to take refuge under a blanket but were soon soaked. In his unique orthography, Leslie described the trip to Alan: 'The boat did a beautiful rool and sent gallons of sea water over us,' whereupon Mother Durrell insisted on an immediate return home for dry clothes and a stiff tot of whisky. Another excursion was more successful: Leslie took Larry and Nancy to the Antiniotissa Lagoon on the northern tip of Corfu. 'It's a grand place,' Leslie exulted, 'the lake is full of snakes and other vile creatures, we are going again soon for a shoot'.[123]

At the White House Larry and Nancy spent evenings practising Greek with Eleni and Totsa, or singing and chatting with villagers who came out of curiosity to see 'the English' and to drink the innumerable small cups of coffee served by Eleni, the glasses of wine and ouzo poured by Totsa. Sometimes Nancy would open a tin of imported tea biscuits or sweets, much appreciated for their novelty. Larry and Nancy picked up demotic Greek very rapidly, and Theodore, who at first had been much in demand as their translator, soon found they understood the local patois better than he.

These conversations were welcome. 'The voice of a man up there in the dusk under the olives disturbs and quickens one like the voice of conscience itself,' Larry would write in *Prospero's Cell*.

And now the stars are shining down frostblown and taut upon this pure Euclidian surface. It is so still that we have dinner under the cypress tree to the light of a candle. And after it, while we are drinking coffee and eating grapes on the edge of the mirror a wind comes: and the whole of heaven stirs and trembles – a great branch of blossoms melting and swaying. Then as the candle draws breath and steadies everything hardens slowly back into the image of a world in water, so that Theodore can point into the water at our feet and show us the Pleiades burning.[124]

The starry image continued to haunt Larry; in 1953 he would publish the poem 'Lesbos', beginning 'The Pleiades are sinking calm as paint',[125] and the bemused, quiet voice of Theodore carried across the intervening years.

After a breakfast of grapes, Hymettos honey, eggs and black coffee, Larry, Nancy and Theodore would often take a rowing boat north past the crescent of Kouloura – 'Ring' – harbour to a shingle beach christened Fig Tree Point by Larry because an immense fig overarched the landward end of several gently inclined slabs of rock. A low limestone cliff shielded the beach. The star-burst shapes of a few velvety-brown spiny sea urchins punctuated the ochre and cream tones of the pebbles. The sun raised seawater to blood heat in shallow rock pools: soaking in these and then plunging naked into the icy spring-fed currents a few yards away 'stimulated his brain', claimed Larry.[126] 'We were so absolutely mad on taking off our clothes', Nancy recalled, 'I wanted just to absolutely drown myself in the sun and the sea'.[127] Within the dark tent of the branches they would eat lunch before taking long midday naps. On really hot days Larry, wearing only a straw hat, would sleep in the sea.[128] Sometimes he brought an old typewriter along, wrapped in a mackintosh against the spray, and seated cross-legged under the fig tree, turned out pages of *The Black Book*. One day they found 'Angli' written in charcoal on the rocks and decided that the 'fisherboys' had spied them out. 'We have responded with

"Hellenes" which is fair enough. . . . N. draws a little head in a straw hat with a great nose and moustache.'[129]

On summer nights Larry sometimes suggested swimming parties far out in the open water. Dark Pantokrator reared up behind them and the mountains of Albania loomed across the straits. Sea phosphorescence was especially brilliant during August and September; Larry dived time after time to see the greenish-white sparks surround him 'like a nimbus'. Once, while on a bathing excursion, Larry, Nancy and Theodore were startled to hear a loud hissing, snorting sound like an expiring breath, repeated every five or six seconds. The swimmers scrambled into the boat and stared into the moonless night as the sound moved closer. All that could be seen was a faint phosphorescent ripple to seaward. They were frozen speechless as the blowing became more and more intense. Finally the sound retreated without the source revealing itself. 'It was probably a harmless grampus (the expression "snorting like a grampus" is well known), but we decided to be on the safe side & we did no more swimming that night,' commented Theodore.[130]

Larry may have taken to the sea like a dolphin, but he was also a careful observer onshore, quizzing Theodore about the two common types of cypresses, the tall, needle-like, almost black ones and the spreading, tamer variety. He gathered armfuls of wild flowers, noting that their bright, natural colours never clashed, as similar dyed colours might in a woven rug. He collected driftwood, and by a few deft cuts with a knife and a splash of coloured ink transformed the weathered shapes into a parade of mythic beasts that soon perched on ledges and tables all over the White House. He sketched everything, although he usually destroyed the drawings. One day he discovered on the beach the largest beetle Theodore had ever seen, three and a quarter inches long and somewhat resembling the European water scorpion. Unable to identify the monster, Theodore sent it to the Vienna Natural History Museum where it was declared a *Belostoma niloticum* from north-east Africa, never before recorded in Europe. Larry's specimen was alive when he discovered it, unlike the two his brother Gerry found later.

Other visitors were less stimulating than Theodore Stephanides. Larry was not one to remain alone for long, so when Nancy went away for a few days he would invite casual acquaintances to Kalami, sometimes to stay for a while and work. In the summer of 1936 he met Robert Burnett, who was writing a biography of Gauguin; Ralph Henry Brewster, author of *6,000 Beards of Athos*; and 'a few Huns who loathe Hitler but are scared shitless to say a word'. English or German, this crew annoyed Larry: 'All these young men are so sort of nice and malleable, but no fire, simply no original hate and brightness. It depresses me, coz I feel such a boor amongst them. But I will not think Stein is "quite sweet" or Breton such a "so absolutely amusing poseur". It kind of dilutes my sperm. . . . I must hate insincerity and emotional flabbiness of every sort or I can't go on with it. So I quarrel quite dreadfully with everybody.'[131]

Quarrelsome or not, Larry's gift for friendship and the swiftness with which he became fluent in demotic Greek aided his acceptance by the local herdsmen and fisherfolk. He acquired a reputation as a discriminating wine drinker that ensured his being served the best at peasant homes and *tavernas*. Having discovered from sad experience that the haphazard nature of Corfiot winemaking caused vintages even from the same vineyard to vary wildly, he insisted on sampling each bottle before purchase. 'This had certain inconveniences if he wanted to buy more than 2 or 3 bottles at a time,' observed Stephanides.[132] Larry accompanied the fishermen on night ventures, trying his hand at spearing fish lured by a carbide lamp suspended over the bow. He was especially fascinated by squid and octopuses, and a story was long repeated around Kalami that he once wrestled with a huge octopus in an underwater cavern: true or not, he did enough to lay the grounds for myths, and he incorporated into *Panic Spring* an anecdote of a giant octopus feared by fishermen.

Stephanides was an important contact for the Durrells within several cultures: Indian-born, Greek father, English mother, educated in England, France and Greece, an aspiring poet of a stubbornly Georgian cast, fluent in demotic Greek but with an English accent – a combination that led to his being arrested several times as a spy, Larry claimed – Theodore was not only a substitute for the father Larry had lost, but he could meet the young man on various cultural fronts and outmatch him in science. Theodore was a true Renaissance figure in the range of his interests, among them freshwater biology, folklore, myth and astronomy, and he would become a pioneer translator of Palamas and other Greek poets. Theodore was certainly one reason why Larry at this time considered attempting a medical degree. Theodore in turn virtually adopted Larry and Gerry, introducing Larry to the local gentry and later to the Venizelist political élite of Athens: George Katsimbalis, the titan of Henry Miller's *Colossus of Maroussi*; George Seferis, later Ambassador to the Court of St James and Nobel laureate in literature; Niko Ghika, sculptor and painter. Larry met these and other members of the Athens intelligentsia on early trips to the capital, and he became intimate with the three named here after the war drove him south from Corfu.

It would be wrong to imagine Larry and Nancy consorting on the island mainly with country folk and chance visitors. Dr Constantine Palatiano, trained in law in England, developed a close bond with Larry, more than forty years his junior. He owned a narrow four-storey house on the sea front of Corfu town and extensive property in the country – Louisa Durrell was to rent her last home on the island from him, the 'Snow-White Villa' at Ypso, inland from Perama. Larry claimed that he kept the skull of his mistress on his writing desk. Palatiano was at work compiling a history of Corfu, left unfinished on his death in 1944. According to Theodore, Palatiano was the main inspiration for the composite figure of Count D. in *Prospero's Cell*. Larry also knew members of the Soufi family, who had a garden full of statues and who owned large estates in the fertile Plain of Rópa, as did his other friends the Abramis and the Theotockis. Countess Eleni Theotocki was to remain a close friend for many years, and Larry was still visiting her at her Paris apartment three decades later. Marie Aspioti would also maintain her association with Larry, and in 1965 would publish *Lear's Corfu*, an anthology of the painter's letters that Larry arranged and prefaced. Marie's brother Maki enjoyed an occasional carouse with the Durrells and the Wilkinsons. One night he became so fuddled with wine that he stalled his car and was unable to restart it. Larry delightedly organized a pushing party to bring him home like a centurion in triumph, his chariot propelled by captives.[133]

Many of the Durrells' closest friends, however, were fellow expatriates and refugees: Barclay and Jane Hudson; another American, the painter Maurice Koster; old Captain Severn, whose passions were roulette and the vain pursuit of Louisa Durrell; and of course the Wilkinsons. Pat Evans had come from England at Larry's invitation. Koster, who had saved his earnings from illustrating magazines in order to escape to Corfu, lived in a house south of Paleocastrizza, where the grottoes were 'ribbed with jewels which smoulder purple and yellow and nacre' – as Larry saw them. The wines from the vineyards near Paleocastrizza bubbled slightly, like Koster's company: 'Ask for red wine at Lakones and they will bring you a glass of volcano's blood.'[134]

To read Larry's correspondence with Henry Miller during this period, however, is to gain the impression that little of note was happening on the island, that writing projects, ideas and correspondence occupied Larry's energies and most of his waking moments, and that he had few interesting friends on Corfu. This was far from the truth, but Larry was indeed looking more and more towards his correspondents in Paris for inspiration and encouragement.

In mid-1936 Miller's *Black Spring* appeared, and Larry recommended it as an antidote to the depression Alan was suffering following the break-up of a romance. 'My dear Alan, what a bugger life is,' wrote the philosophic Larry. 'Women are like reels of cotton (I loathe this kind of generalization): you have to work hard to make them undress.' He again ordered Alan, 'my good panurgic long-nosed friend', to read Miller, 'the greatest modern writer':

In Black Spring you will find the rich loamy humanity of a Rabelais: and laughter. LAUGHTER! You said to me once, 'You must write a big laughter book one day.' Here is a laughter that come[s] from the Rabelaisian source of life, the penis, the shit, the pissoir, the dung and divinity, the cunt, the anus. It's tonic. I think it would be valuable to you, because you are essentially timid in your stroke. Every letter you write ends in despair: THIS IS ADOLESCENT.

Larry then explained what Miller had done for him: 'Please believe me when I say these books have released me, the essential me from the limitations of feeling imposed by an English upbringing more than anything else.'[135]

The essential Larry emerged more and more clearly in his correspondence with Miller. When Henry advised him to 'write only what you please', and then dealt sympathetically with Surrealism as 'a permanent thing in art' as well as a contemporary 'movement',[136] Larry responded with a discourse on his own independence. 'I have always wanted to be in with people, feel myself part of a band of people,' he wrote. 'It's chilly work sitting all by yourself in the dark.' Then he gave reasons why he could not be part of a group: the Surrealists, for instance, wanted to define the artist in terms of social and political responsibilities. 'I'm tired of political people,' Larry said, because 'They have confused the inner struggle with the outer one. They want to bread-poultice a primary chancre.' If the conflicts within could not be resolved, no societal solution imposed by edict could hope to succeed. 'Listen, Miller, what I feel about it is this,' Larry continued. 'To have art you've first got to have a big personality, pass it through the social mincer, get it ready for misery.' He would create his own interior space, his 'HERALDIC UNIVERSE', and do it 'quite alone', beyond time.[137] In the months to come Larry clarified and redefined his stance to Henry. For the rest of his life he would remain essentially apolitical and his chosen artistic realm would never change. He would even learn to suffer with a reasonably good grace.

FOR A YEAR AFTER WRITING his first letter to Miller, Larry was in the position of chela to guru: Larry praised Henry's writing and proposed schemes to help him break through the twin barriers of censorship and of inattention on the part of the public; Henry kept asking, largely in vain, to see something of Larry's, 'so that I can return some of the audacious compliments you pay me'.[138] Then in early November 1936, 'in a hell of a mess packing to move into town for the winter', Larry sat down 'among the wreckage' at the White House, took a couple of over-sized sheets of cross-ruled paper, and in red ink wrote an analysis of Hamlet: 'Why everyone is so puzzled by poor Hamlet is because they always try to see a relation between the external battle (the murder, Ophelia etc) and the internal one. A failure, because the inner and the outer reality move along separate planes, and only seldom meet.' He had been comparing the Quarto Hamlet, the putative acting version, against the longer Folio text, and had come to the conclusion that there were really two Hamlets, the Prince and the private Hamlet, and that for this second Hamlet, Ophelia is merely an 'external tragedy'.[139] Larry confided to Michael Fraenkel that he had what 'virtually amounts to a PROOF of this duality theory', textual evidence based on a detailed comparison of the first and second Quartos. Larry's discovery had been a serendipitous result of his now-abandoned Elizabethan researches.[140] It represented a shift from the familiar romantic interpretation of Hamlet's character that linked his failures in action to flaws in character or to excessive sensibilities. According to Larry, when Hamlet did not act it was because there were really two Hamlets, one living in the physical, political world of Denmark, and the other in the 'heraldic' world of the mind and spirit. This second Hamlet was the important, controlling one. Larry tried to see his own life in similar terms. Larry's own multi-faceted nature led him to view himself also as at least dual: the plodding journeyman writer in Corfu opposed within by a driven, tormented being, stifled and baulked nearly to the point of madness by his urge to create.

Henry immediately and without asking for Larry's permission typed out copies for Michael Fraenkel, his collaborator in the two-volume Hamlet philosophical correspondence (Fraenkel suggested that Larry's letter be incorporated – it was not), and for Philip Mairet, editor of the New English Weekly (who at once wrote to Larry directly, asking to publish the final version of the Hamlet 'essay'). The 'inner reality' is that state which the artist must enter, the 'Heraldic Universe', the term Larry derived from the symbolic and representational functions of mediaeval heraldry. In several letters studded with cross-outs and emphases and emendations he attempted to define his concept for Henry: 'The Heraldic Universe is just a name for that element in which that queer fish the artist swims. THE PRECISE ~~NATURE~~ <POSITION> OF THIS REALITY, WHICH DEMANDS AS YET A REAL PHILOSOPHIC PLACE IN THOUGHT, I WANT TO TRY AND FIX. !!!!!! <Each writer establishes the *nature* for himself. But I want a *philosophic admission of this reality.*> Now don't chuckle.'[141] The concern with different states of 'reality' was to remain vital to Larry's art, notably in *The Alexandria Quartet* and *The Avignon Quintet*.

Although the *New English Weekly* did not pay contributors, the acceptance of 'The Prince and Hamlet' was an important entry for Larry into a prestigious English publication: 'Payment, I said to Mairet, was the least of one's considerations. WHAT ONE NEEDS IS A PULPIT.'[142] Even more pleasing to Larry was that Henry was 'quite wrought up about it'.[143]

Meanwhile, other projects sprouted on Corfu under the heady influence of silver-maned Constantine Zarian, the self-proclaimed 'greatest poet' of Armenia: after a 'fine night with the bottles' he and Larry decided to collect a group of authors, including Miller, 'three, seven, or nine writers (any cabbalistic number)', and write a 'NEW BIBLE', to be published anonymously. 'I know Bragaglia, Unamuno, Saroyan . . .' shouted Zarian. Larry spent the next morning planning 'A NEW SONG OF SOLOMON, sans peur and sans reproche', 'THE NEW CRUCIFICTION', 'THE HERALDIC BOOK OF JOB'.[144] It hardly mattered that the New Bible was never written: what fun to dream it!

Zarian presided over fortnightly 'Ionian Banquets' held throughout 1937 at the Perdika Restaurant – The Sign of the Partridge – in Corfu town. The alleged purpose of these meetings was to found a journal, *Eos*, to which the thirty or so members of the coterie would contribute. There was a written 'Cérémonie-Questionnaire' in French for new members. During the ceremony the assemblage was to intone in chorus '*rétsina*' – one of Larry's favourite potations – and at the conclusion of the affair the inductee was obliged to 'PAYER TROIS BOUTEILLES' and to deliver a eulogy to the Solar Hymn 'en paroles poétiques et en un style allégorique'.[145] There were short after-dinner speeches, often delivered by Larry in English punctuated with phrases in colloquial Greek. Owing to the departure from Corfu of some key members and to the impending war, no issues of the proposed journal appeared, but the banquets themselves were highly successful.

Zarian passed his letters from Unamuno and Céline around the table. Larry was glad to reciprocate with Miller's 'rambling exuberant' missives. Smoke from the Papastratos cigarettes turned the cellar room grey-blue. During the talk, the food, the wine, and the letter-reading, Luke, a red-faced and blind guitarist, sometimes arrived led by his small son, a boy with the pallor of a Byzantine icon. The son accompanied his father on a violin in renditions of Greek jazz songs, and the refrains were sung by 'roystering Zarian', by the sober Stephanides, by the Russian Peltours, by Larry and Nancy. Around midnight Larry would hoist the jib of the *Van Norden*, start the auxiliary motor, and slice through the calm sea to Kalami.

Larry was proud of the *Hamlet* essay and amused by his wild flights with Zarian, but although he confided to Alan about *Panic Spring*, he felt that Henry would disapprove and so kept the writing of the novel, like a guilty secret, out of the letters he sent to Paris. When he finally admitted to Henry that he had written the book, the typescript was already at Faber and Faber, and Larry brought it up mainly as an example of publishers' censorship: 'A new and facile novel being castrated by big-wigs. First they agreed to let the word fuck stay in if it went thus: & f—k: then f— : now the libraries might get touchy so they want —. Or something milder.' He added that he felt ashamed for writing 'cheaply . . . knowing the book isn't worth a — either way.'[146] It was, he said months later to Henry, 'all dross'.[147] Reading the galleys was agony: 'Very depressed. My proofs of the shit novel have just come. WHY DOES ONE WRITE LIKE THIS?'[148] Larry was sure that his writing in *The Black Book* was much tighter, and this increased his dissatisfaction with its predecessor.

Panic Spring is a string of vignettes of an oddly assorted collection of castaways and misfits, guests from the outer world on Mavrodaphne. A few of the characters – Walsh, Gordon – are carried over from *Pied Piper of Lovers*. Despite the Charles Norden pseudonym with which Larry signed the novel, *Panic Spring* owes almost nothing to Henry Miller but a good deal to Norman Douglas and Aldous Huxley.[149] The evocations of island scenes are reminiscent of *South Wind*, and Larry's book has some of the urbanities and world-weariness evinced in Huxley's portrayals of genteel house parties. Larry genuinely admired Douglas, especially what he would call his 'writing personality', which Larry characterized as 'unsnobbish', possessed of 'delicacy and tact and the stylish gentlemanly thing'.[150]

Larry's provisional titles for *Panic Spring*, 'Phoenix and Nightingale' and 'Music in Limbo', were rather too archly appropriate – an artist rises from the ashes of his dead love to write music on vague Mavrodaphne – but then so is his final choice. It was Nancy, perhaps mindful of the various panics in their own lives, who suggested 'Panic Spring in Limbo', and Larry finally dropped the 'in Limbo'. He was also conscious that 'Spring' in the title echoed Godfather Henry's *Black Spring*, while Larry claimed Pan as his own deity.

Panic Spring represented a considerable advance over *Pied Piper of Lovers*. Larry demonstrated in *Panic Spring* that he had assimilated the Greek ambience, and the book contains vivid writing about scene and place: 'Wheat like gold foam; the ashy rectangles of oats, the mustard crop, spittle-bright: these were tantalising images of coolness and ease focused against the blue water and the distance that hid Epirus.'[151] The novel also contains what would become his characteristic melding of a light tone and dark, macabre humour: Dr Fonvisin's story of the embalmed wife is greeted with sceptical laughter, and is then set against the death of the island's owner, old Rumanades, who seems to mock Fonvisin by *not* allowing himself to be restored to life. His failure does not depress the doctor, however: 'Fonvisin turned back into the room, laughing with tenderness at the morning, and patted the dead cheeks of the old man, saying: "Now if you don't mind, I'll have a bath."'[152] Fonvisin's bath is a baptism into resurgent life, a rejection of death.

One of the flaws of *Panic Spring* is that it is a talky book. The events dwindle into settings for 'significant' conversations. In Larry's life at this time there were a lot of such conversations: exchanges under the stars with Theodore, arguments in the shade of the olives about art with Koster and about writing with Wilkinson, disputes with Hudson over Villon and science and statistics. Whatever their real-life counterparts, the dialogues in *Panic Spring* about love and independence and artistic integrity do not break into the new and the surprising. Part of the problem of unity in the book stems from Larry's attempt to link episodes and characters from his Bloomsbury days with his newer Corfu experiences. Walsh and Francis – a woman, despite the spelling – who had been down-and-out in London are, like Fonvisin, conventionally reborn under the Greek sun, rebaptized in the Greek sea and under the sign of Pan. The timid schoolteacher Marlowe reverses his inner dissolution by finishing his essay on 'Quietism'. The joining glue of circumstance and narration, however, does not quite hold.

Larry had been chagrined when *Janus* had lambasted *Pied Piper*: now he was furious when Harold Strauss of Covici-Friede, American publisher of *Panic Spring*, praised the book – and gave him some advice. '*Panic Spring* appears to me to be only the first step in the long and brilliant career as a novelist that is marked out for you,' intoned Strauss. The novel was 'caviar', but he had told Mr Covici that Larry's *fourth* novel 'will sell 50,000 copies in America'. Only, Larry still had 'something to learn about the organization of a novel', and he should make this his 'objective' in his next book. Finally, since several English critics had noticed a 'kinship' between *Panic Spring* and Huxley's novels, Larry should contrive to get a jacket blurb from him. Savage with rage, Larry typed a copy of the letter to send to Henry, adding only a single word in annotation after the sender's name: '*Jackass!*'[53]

Larry's response to Strauss's condescending but well-meant advice was highly revealing. Larry's pride and confidence in his ability were growing, and he scorned to settle for the kind of success dangled before him. Nor did a slow but sure path to modest wealth sound appealing. Perhaps most galling was the suggestion that he approach Aldous Huxley, hat in hand, to beg a jacket blurb. Larry had nothing against blurbs, but he considered himself of a higher order *qua* writer than the hard-working Huxley. Larry was not blind to the irony of his position: he had set out to write, in *Panic Spring*, a Huxley-Douglas type of entertainment. Now he had only himself to blame when he was compared to Huxley. Prey to a hundred conflicting thoughts, Larry was tempted to play the game of alliances and allegiances, of pandering to popular tastes, as he had admittedly tried to do in his first two novels, but something stuck in his craw: his pride. Perversely, his pride denied him shortcuts to acceptance.

Larry was unhappy with *Panic Spring*, and *The Black Book* was refusing to come out right. He was as cross as a teething child, and his anger often boiled over. Henry had sent on some letters he had received from Herbert Read, and Larry responded with a two-page diatribe against Read as one of 'THESE LITERARY WHOREMONGERS WHO PROFESS TO BE PROTECTING ART', but who in their attempts to define literary movements had driven a wedge between artist and receiver:

Before, when art was less organised, and had more of the original godhead in it there was a direct flow of personality between the Christ and the man. Understanding was never the important thing. One does not want to be understood, only experienced by men. But these bleeders who profess to be trying to find the artist a place in society are the very ones who have destroyed that vital connection.[54]

Then, for the first time to Henry, Larry referred casually to his new book-in-progress: 'I can't work any more these days. The Black Book rots. Parts of it are wonderful, but it never quite escapes being literature. But there's hope. I'm not an englishman, only an anglo-indian, and if I don't stop, I'm sure to write something amusing one day.'[155] He was apologizing for not being an Englishman; he was glad that he was not an Englishman; the fact that he was 'only' a despised Anglo-Indian bore promise of future accomplishment. As so often, he was both teasing and serious – on all counts.

By mid-December, Larry had finished what was perhaps the third draft of the book and was writing to Henry with more confidence: 'Actually I am up against the wall properly now, just finishing a Black Book which Fabers will reject and rupture the contract, because it is good – (I AM TERRIFIED OF IT IT IS SO GOOD IN LITTLE FLASHES) – BUT NOT POPULAR.'[156] This letter was apparently written over a few days, for Larry ended with a postscript: 'Fête day for me. I've finished *The Black Book*. I'm in love with it. Hurrah!' By the end of December he was again rewriting it, 'trying to demillerise as I go along', and promised Henry to 'Send you *The Black Book* on its way through to Fabers for a rejection.'[157] So sure was Larry that Faber and Faber would reject the novel that he wrote a slur against the man he had cast as a villain since the days of his conversations with Gawsworth in Denmark Street, referring to the best-known figure in the firm as 'Eliot, who may be defined briefly as Debility's Eldest Handmaid!'[158]

Henry had been touting Larry's 'Prince and Hamlet' essay to publishers and journals, and Larry worried that 'AT THE WORST' someone would 'demand to see work of mine which justifies your enthusiasm'. 'MY DEAR H.V.M.,' he lamented, 'I HAVE NONE!!!!' Faber had rejected his poems, 'which are not at all bad for a small boy like me', but had accepted *Panic Spring*, 'which is a leprous distilment'.[159] *Panic Spring* may not have been an especially good novel, but it would be Larry's first book to be published by Faber and Faber. On the strength of it they had given him a three-volume contract, 'not realising, poor people, what a phoenix lurked under the lamb's evening-clothes', Larry gloated.[160] It was February 1937, and at the age of twenty-five he had just emerged reborn, so he felt, from the fiery ashes of *The Black Book*.

Henry decided to take Larry in hand, and responded to his confession that he had little to show to publishers. 'About yourself. First of all, *order*! Why not put in a carbon when you write?' He was not concerned that Larry had produced little: 'How could you, at your age?' A more serious admonition, one Henry would make repeatedly, was that 'You can afford to speak your mind, do as you please. . . . Start now and give it from the guts.' Speaking from bitter experience, Henry added, 'No matter what you do to please the editors it will never please them.'[161]

Larry was silently struggling with the revisions – the rewriting, more accurately – of *The Black Book*, and perhaps as a release, perhaps because the style was in the air, he tried his hand at writing surrealist pieces that went beyond any experimental prose in his novel. Early in January he typed 'A Christmas Carol' 'straight onto the machine' and sent it to Miller. 'You notice', Larry wrote, embellishing his letter with a sketch of a stout woman with plumed bonnet and a rifle with a U-shaped barrel, 'I point my madness away from me like an old lady with a gun.'[162] Although 'Carol' had made him 'LUMINOUS' for a whole day, he was unsure of it. When Henry raved, calling Larry a 'stinking genius',[163] Larry protested, 'I never knew what I wrote in that Carol thing. I never do.' None the less, he said, 'I stagger a little as I walk and feel three stories high.' Larry's insecurity about his work was real enough, and he fell back on Nancy's judgement when it came to his new novel: 'Nancy says that Carol is not a patch on the BLACK BOOK. NOT A BLOODY PATCH.'[164]

A few months later Larry composed 'Zero', a companion piece to 'Asylum', as a gift for Anaïs Nin, but Surrealism was not for Larry. It made him uncomfortable: 'So far I've never managed to honestly become anything more than an ardent Durrealist,' he had already announced.[165] He was preoccupied with *Hamlet*, with insanity, and believed or professed to believe himself a bit unhinged: writing *The Black Book* had proved a terrific strain, a dive into 'ego and id', the heading he placed above two of the three sections of the typescript. Reading the Henry Miller-Michael Fraenkel *Hamlet* correspondence in the raw typescripts Henry sent had not helped. 'I'm a little punch drunk with those Hamlet letters,' Larry admitted; 'Frankly, I am a little crazy. . . . Do you ever feel cracked?'[166]

Miller and Perlès had embarked on a collaboration with Fraenkel, who when he was not in Ibiza, Mexico, Puerto Rico, or New York, resided in the right-hand of the two ground-floor flats at 18 Villa Seurat. He was an American writer of some independent wealth, founder of Carrefour Press to publish his own enthusiasms, and Henry's benefactor in times of difficulty. His book *Bastard Death* reflected what Henry saw as his mordant Jewish pessimism. *Hamlet* was intended to be an epistolary *tour de force*, a philosophical correspondence in the course of which they pledged to write a thousand pages, 'no more, no less'. They were to focus upon death, taking *Hamlet* as a talking point – Hamlet and his quest for identity, for self – but allowing themselves to range over any topic. Perlès dropped out after writing one letter, but Fraenkel, obsessed though he was with death, was agile enough to tangle with Henry on anything from D. H. Lawrence to Lourdes, from Gutkind's *Absolute Collective* to *Mein Kampf*, from the Jewish origin of Christianity to Marxist revolution. In the case of Hitler's book, it was a matter of '*Finis* Hamlet . . . Enter Laertes . . . a blustering, rough-and-tumble . . . *Naturmensch*,' wrote Fraenkel.[167] Larry read the letters with mounting excitement. Always concerned with death, Larry wrote to Fraenkel about the death motif:

I suppose this is really a paradox, that the positive work of death should have to be anchored in life to have its own independant [sic] existence. I'm not much of a casuist: but all art, all works of art are given birth to. They have to be made life. The problem is how to make death valid as art without life in it. Is this rubbish?[168]

Although he did not say this to Fraenkel, Larry was attempting to forge death into life through humour. This was the meaning of Fonvisin in *Panic Spring* and Gracie and 'Death' Gregory in *The Black Book*, and the linkage would be consistent in his future fiction. Meanwhile, Mairet had emblazoned THE PRINCE AND HAMLET on the cover of the *New English Weekly*. 'I'm as proud as a stallion,' Larry exulted.[169]

In mid-January Larry wrote Henry an immense and perceptive letter about the *Hamlet* correspondence: 'It's all Henry Miller, PRINCE OF DENMARK.'[170] Henry replied that Larry's was 'the finest letter I ever received in my life', and then lamented that, due to the many demands on his time, 'My letter-writing days are almost over. . . . It is a great pity because you deserve the fullest response.'[171] Meanwhile Henry surged on with the *Hamlet* correspondence: he had only 150 pages to go to complete his part.

By late January 1937 Larry was having second thoughts about his third novel: 'Please H.M. *Don't* crack up *The Black Book* until you see it yourself – will you? Because I don't want to let you down – and the book mightn't be so good after all.'[172] Then it was February and Kalami was still locked in winter: 'Cypresses moaning and the ships passing in the mist.' Larry sat at his typewriter, evoking the lower depths of Dulwich and Bloomsbury in the *Black Book* typescript: 'I've written over 150,000 words to the book: four rewrites,' he confided to Henry. He was not satisfied, and mused grimly on the cliché of the Author surrounded by discarded sheets. 'It's terrible, but it gets better each time so I ought to be pleased.'[173] Nancy, however, who had not liked *Pied Piper of Lovers* nor was much interested in Larry's poetry, thought the book was 'terrific' and was 'terribly pleased'.[174] Pat Evans, then working on a novel of his own, was permitted a reading of the manuscript, and 'stabbed huge passages as mock Miller'. Larry complained to Henry, 'Your influence is damnable on my so-called writing. Must stop it.'[175]

Another major influence standing behind *The Black Book* was D. H. Lawrence, whose *Psychoanalysis and the Unconscious* and *Fantasia of the Unconscious* had been very much a part of the intellectual cud chewed by Larry's circle in London: 'of course the young were very for him,' Larry said later, 'because they sensed his wavelength, which was a creative one.' Lawrence was a convenient stalking horse for Larry's approach to the Freudian psychology that underpinned the development of the characters in *The Black Book*. In particular, Larry introduced Lawrence through the person of Chamberlain, who damages his personal relations by an application of what he takes to be Lawrence's theories, his 'bowels of compassion' and his supposed approval of sexual licence. Speaking of Lawrence, Larry admitted, 'There's much to be muddled by. If you read *Fantasia of the Unconscious*, no more absurd interpretation of Freud has ever been perpetrated, but nevertheless it's probably one of the most important documents. It gives you a clue to Lawrence's own absurdity, and . . . they're absolutely marvellous books.'[176]

Lawrence's 'muddle' did not bother Larry: '[Lawrence] didn't understand Freudian theory at all; he just listened to some gossip by Frieda and her psychoanalyst friends from Vienna, and tried to sort of blend them together. It obviously impressed him sufficiently to do a couple of books to try and understand, although in a way he resented the rigidity of the Freudian system and reacted against it. But the books are very interesting because they give you a very good portrait of Lawrence's own inside.' Larry worked out his ambivalent feelings about Lawrence through the gullible Chamberlain, who swallowed Lawrence's 'muddled' psychology entire; but Larry had given Lawrence rather rough treatment in *The Black Book*. He explained,

I disagreed violently, all that . . . North Country, non-conformist thing is a most disagreeable side of him. Also the most untruthful to his own genius. Because he's not a Christian, and he had to go to the Mediterranean to discover it. I've never been a Christian, so I knew exactly what was wrong. Psychoanalysis could have helped him, but he made such a fuck-up of understanding it, from those two books. . . . They outlined his personality and his psyche, which remained a constant right up to *Chatterley* and beyond – as well as completely traducing the Freudian canon in the most glorious way.[177]

Finally Larry decided to stop revising *The Black Book*, and Nancy began 'working against time' correcting the spelling errors.[178] Larry prefaced the text with an epigraph from the Tibetan that he had discovered reading Alexandra David-Neel,[179]

Mös gus yöd na
Khyl so öd tung,

adding the rough translation, 'Where there is veneration,/ Even a dog's tooth emits light'. According to the legend, a Tibetan trader gives his aged mother a dog's tooth found by the trail, telling her that it had been a Buddhist holy man's. Worshipped by the mother and others, the tooth comes to give off rays of light. David-Neel explained that the concentration of devout thoughts gave power to the worshipped object. Larry hoped that the passage would challenge readers through their thoughts to draw light from his humble work. It would turn out to be a fitting epigraph to his entire *oeuvre*. Larry's view of the relative truth of observed phenomena was similar to the conclusion David-Neel drew from the dog's tooth story: 'Tibetan theories about all phenomena . . . are grounded on the power of the mind and this is only logical for people who consider the world, as we see it, to be but a subjective vision.'[180] This described Larry's Heraldic Universe equally well.

In a letter to Henry, Larry called his book, with tongue-in-cheek bravado, 'a good little chronicle of the english death, done in a sort of hamstrung tempo . . . . I think it's a book Huxley could have written if he were a mixture of Lawrence and Shakespeare.'[181] By the end of February he had drawn a deep breath and had posted 'the one and only' copy to Henry, typed on fine linen paper and with a black cloth binding done in Corfu town, with instructions to 'pitch it into the Seine' if he did not approve. Henry's response on 8 March was everything Larry could have wished for: '*The Black Book* came and I have opened it and I read goggle-eyed, with terror, admiration and amazement.'[182] And so on for two typed pages, to be followed by five more in a letter of 13 and 15 March: 'One of the best evidences of the great merit of your book is this, that I haven't yet finished it! . . . Even I, voracious as I am, find it too rich and savory to gulp down quickly.'[183] Henry immediately began to scheme towards publication, suggesting either Jack Kahane, his own Paris publisher, or Michael Fraenkel's Carrefour Press. As Henry quite accurately saw the problem, 'No commercial, legitimate publisher can possibly bring it out.' Kahane, an ebullient former Manchester businessman and founder of the Obelisk

Press, wrote blatant pornography under various pseudonyms. He was a touchy customer, Henry said, and apt to be prejudiced against Larry precisely because he, Henry, had praised him too highly: 'Sort of professional jealousy.' Still, Henry promised, 'I will wheedle and cajole and jig for him, if necessary', provided Larry would assent to offering Kahane *The Black Book*.[184]

Henry's approval of *The Black Book* was especially gratifying to Larry because this was the first of his novels that really *meant* something to him other than merely a small cash advance and evidence of his developing career as a writer. As Larry wrote in his preface to *The Black Book* when it was republished in 1960, 'in the writing of it I first heard the sound of my own voice, lame and halting perhaps, but nevertheless my very own.'[185] The book was to prove the most important step that Larry would take on Corfu towards the discovery of his artistic self.

WHILE PIED PIPER OF LOVERS had contained Larry's response to India and to the death of his father and *Panic Spring* recorded his early impressions of Greece, *The Black Book* was an attempt to sum up the artist that Larry had become, and how that being had been formed: Lawrence Lucifer in the book *was* Lawrence Durrell in 1937, as nearly as he could re-create himself. All three novels talk about the emergence of an artist, whether a musician or a writer, but the third volume defines the struggle, opening with the words, 'The agon, then. It begins.'[186] In this sense, *Tropic of Cancer*, Miller's attack on society, his own declaration of independence, is the true godfather to *The Black Book*. But Larry's *Black Book* is far more than merely an excoriation of 'the English death', that 'spiritual and sexual etiolation' that he saw eroding England, and his own 'birth cry of a newly born baby of letters'.[187] He had set out to celebrate English and European literature and culture, and the book seethes with the resonances of Larry's self-education: Baudelaire and Beethoven, Chaucer and Shakespeare and Rabelais, Wilde and Petronius, Osiris and Dido, Gibbon and Swinburne, Ruskin and Rimbaud, Lawrence and Blake, De Gourmont and the Bible – the list seems endless. The specialized diction of psychoanalysis, printing, medicine, toxicology slid naturally into Larry's text. Whether he mentioned alexia and aboulia or muscarine from 'the beautiful scarlet mushroom fly agaric', Larry seemed to know exactly what he was talking about. *The Black Book* incorporates what would prove to be the themes and methods of Larry's later fiction: the primacy of loving well, the desperate need for rebirth to staunch the death-drift of the cosmos, the multiple narrative points of view, the use of diaries and letters, and so on. As he was well aware, the very density of theme and image in the novel constituted a flaw, but Larry himself knew that in its scope and vigour the book was a triumph. When such people as Cyril Connolly, David Gascoyne and Anaïs Nin recognized the virtues of *The Black Book* too, he was ecstatic.

While the letters about *The Black Book* were flying between Corfu and Paris, *Panic Spring* appeared in England to mixed notices: a review in the *Times Literary Supplement* of 24 April found it 'affected, derivative and exuberant, but, in its power of observation and language, entertaining and full of promise'[188]; *The Times* praised the novel for 'fine writing, keen perception, gracious scholarship'[189]; and V. S. Pritchett in the *New Statesman and Nation* concluded that Durrell's strong point was 'horror'.[190] The *Nation* in America panned it for an ineffectual use of 'the "South Wind" formula'.[191] One review really stung: H. E. Bates in the *Morning Post* wrote that '"Panic Spring" is the kind of novel one expects from a neurotic undergraduate. It is superior, maddeningly clever, flippantly satirical, and, to my mind, as dull as a wet Sunday afternoon.'[192] Larry shot back to the *Post* a tongue-in-cheek rebuttal, signed Charles Norden: 'I am not a neurotic undergraduate. I am not even an undergraduate. . . . IT IS NOT A BAD BOOK AT ALL, AND BY NO MEANS SUPERIOR.'[193] Larry claimed that he was having 'great fun' with the reviews, but he was too preoccupied with Henry's and Anaïs's responses to *The Black Book* to pay much attention to what by then seemed the very stale past. He would always be ambivalent about reviews: he was upset by obtuse or negative ones, yet he tried consciously not to be influenced by them.

Publication of *The Black Book* was to prove a major effort for Larry's Paris friends. The 308-page typescript that Larry had sent was speckled with his minor corrections in reddish-orange, green and blue ink, plus a hundred textual emendations in red ink. Henry and Anaïs undertook the enormous task of typing out a clean copy, with carbons, and of proof-reading the final manuscript. By early April they had given up doing the typing themselves and Henry – or, more probably, Anaïs – was paying to have someone else retype the manuscript. Larry was always cavalier about orthography and typographical errors, and when Miller wrote that four people had 'broken down' proofing *The Black Book*,[194] Larry replied airily, 'I am sorry . . . . What a noble thing – I am grateful. I never correct – because the printer's devil is paid to edit the book afterwards anyway.'[195] It was not true that the text was uncorrected, since Nancy had error-spotted for him and Larry had made numerous changes, but he was indeed casual about textual minutiae. Larry was half-proud of his poor spelling, which he thought of as deriving from the 'sluttish Irish' side of his nature. 'It's a distinction I share with Shakespear – about the only one I might add', he told Henry.[196]

By early February 1937, before sending off *The Black Book*, Larry and Nancy had rented three rooms from a Corfiot peasant who owned a long, low house just south of Paleocastrizza. Stephanides took three other rooms in the house for himself, his wife Maria and his young daughter Alexia; and there was still room for Maurice Koster. Theodore worked in Corfu town and came out for the weekends. Nancy found Maria Stephanides too 'prim and proper' – she disapproved of her husband's boisterous romps with the Durrells – but Alexia was 'absolutely enchanting, like a little fairy'.[197] A dirt track plunged down from the main road to the house, and thirty metres away was a beach of granular yellow sand, unlike the foot-bruising shingles of the east coast around Kalami. On the headland of the bay stood the ruins of a Byzantine fortress, the old *castrizza* that gave the name to the town.

March drove the wet chill of winter from the rocks and from the bones of the inhabitants, and the Durrells could return to life out of doors. 'Well, sun today', Larry wrote to Henry, 'I've moved my machine out on to the terrace under the vine-leaves. Uneasy blue sea. Lizards sucking in warmth on the wall. Spring opening quietly. It is impossible to think of writing – my writing that is.'[198] Larry was going through a spring of discontent following the completion of *The Black Book*. It had taken him eighteen months, and the strain showed. 'I get over emotional and shaky and liable to rages and fears and psychological tics – all due to this damned writing,' he lamented to Henry. 'I used to be so healthy and full of a sort of gawkish je m'en foutisme. The summer inaction will bring it back.' Even Henry's praise unsettled him, or so he claimed: 'Buoyancy does me no good.' He puzzled over what there was within himself that had produced *The Black Book*: 'I look at myself in the mirror from time to time – no clue whatever. A short fat Obelisk with the features of a good-natured cattle driver.' Zarian was in Austria and had posted him a 'huge Viennese briar pipe'. Larry asked Nancy to photograph 'me at all angles, with it in me'. 'Perhaps some clue will emerge from the subsequent photographs,' he wondered – his father had smoked only a pipe, and aspects of their kinship might emerge. Larry outlined a simple remedy for his writer's malaise, but he was not to carry it out in all its aspects: 'Am planning a monastic summer. Boxing at dawn with Capt McGibbon. Diving. Swimming. No smoking. Actually the thing which will heal me is a visit to Calypso's grotto on the lonely island north of us. As soon as the boat's ready we go. No more books, no more writers, no more anything. I WANT A GOOD STEADY JOB WITH A LITTLE HOUSE LOTS OF CHILDREN A LAWN MOWER A BANK ACCOUNT A LITTLE CAR AND THE RESPECT OF THE MAN NEXT DOOR.'[199] Henry was not fooled. By August, Larry would be in Paris: no boxing, swimming or diving; a great deal of smoking, plenty of books, and almost too many writers to count. *The Black Book* was to be published and Larry would help edit *The Booster* magazine – and neither publication was likely to earn him either the little house or the respect of the man next door.

Meanwhile, Larry and Nancy were getting ready to rough it, to sail north-west of Corfu to Mathraki island: 'Leave for Athens Saturday to buy a tent etc. Then the black sleek douce Van Norden will be launched and off we go.'[200] On the way to Athens, Larry and Nancy evidently stopped at Ithaca, for Larry, awed by the Homeric isle, was soon to write 'On Ithaca Standing':

> Tread softly, for here you stand
> On miracle ground, boy.

It was indeed a magical place,

> Where the kestrel's arrow falls only,
> The green sea licks.[201]

The visit to Athens showed Nancy how unused they had become to large cities: 'We were quite a couple of yokels in the city traffic and spent ages dithering backwards and forwards before we could cross a main road,' she wrote to Alan Thomas. Eating had taken up most of their time, it seemed, but they had 'managed to crawl up the Acropolis and visit the Byzantine museums'.[202] Larry loved Athens: it was the 'most beautiful' city he had seen, with 'all the virtues of the big town, and none of the vices'. Larry and Nancy travelled back from Athens in the 'MAGNIFICENT' First Class of an Italian ship.[203]

Although he warned Henry, 'Maybe you won't hear from me very regularly this summer,' Larry was not going to be cut off for long during his forays with the *Van Norden*: 'I'm leaving a machine on the north point with Koster, and strict instructions about mail. Return each week and see what the drag-nets bring in.' He had read and sent on to Miller *Time and Western Man* by Wyndham Lewis, and was studying the newly arrived

Egyptian *Book of the Dead*. He found himself 'tremendously moved by the hymns to Ra' and continued, 'I want to swallow the sun and feel it in my navel this summer.'[204] 'Undress and run. The island has no tenant,' wrote Larry in an unpublished poem, 'Sun'. He called on Helios to penetrate even his verse:

> Gambol in Ra, whose torpor melts the body.
> Dissolve in poem as ink from heavy nipples.
> I am the blond page the dog-surf worries,
> The sea prints in ceriphs and ripples.[205]

Larry began to outline his own 'Book of the Dead'; twenty years and many changes of direction later it would emerge as *The Alexandria Quartet*.

ALAN THOMAS WAS PLANNING to get married, but had announced that first he would be coming to Corfu alone. 'The boat's in the water,' Nancy told him, and 'The sail's up back to front (By the way can you sail? We can't) and the old sea captain's sniffing the wind.'[206] Nancy was not entirely joking: more than once Larry had nearly wrecked the *Van Norden*, despite the counsel of their elderly friend Captain Severn. Alan's timing was excellent so far as Larry was concerned: 'I am lolling a bit, resting really for the 1st time in my writing life, content and at ease with myself,' he wrote. He outlined a programme of excursions in the *Van Norden*, of visits to secluded islands, Byzantine chapels, and the ancient theatre at Butrinto. Larry advised Alan to come Deck Class from Brindisi: 'Uncomfy: yes, but even if you travel first you won't escape the central european flea which is the size of a small polar bear, does fifty in top, and has a cruising speed of seven knots per trouser-leg.'[207]

Resting or not, Larry was reading Nietzsche, whom he declared had said 'MORE OR LESS EVERYTHING'.[208] So many of Larry's cherished ideas over the coming years would coincide with Nietzsche's pronouncements, if they were not indeed formed by them. Larry was finding confirmation of his belief in Manichaean dualism, in the efficacy of the tragi-comic mix that he had first experienced in the Jacobean dramatists, in the instability of truth that would characterize his artistic maturity. His rejection of Christianity, his approbation of the Gnostic assertion of the complementary nature of virtue and wickedness, his attitude towards women – all parallel the thinking of Nietzsche, who stressed the Christian *'hostility to life'*.[209] The aphorisms of Pursewarden in the *Quartet* and of Sutcliffe in *The Avignon Quintet* would have the ring of Nietzsche's epigrams. 'When a woman has scholarly inclinations there is usually something wrong with her sexuality,'[210] wrote the German philosopher; this would perfectly describe Larry's Constance before the consummation of her love affair with Affad in the *Quintet*. The *mnemons* and dicta of Caradoc in *The Revolt of Aphrodite*, Larry's satiric novel diptych and the deliberate inverse of his two 'serious' sequences, would be Spoonerisms crafted from sober epigrams: 'He has been slumming among the Gnostics, selling his birthright for a pot of message,'[211] says Caradoc of another character. Larry would create in Caradoc a comic version of a Nietzschean superman, a man beyond God and evil. These books were far in the future, but the 'EVERYTHING' that he attributed to Nietzsche shows Larry sensed that the creator of Zarathustra was vital to his own development. Nietzsche had written that against the 'terror and horror of existence' the ancient Greeks had set 'the Olympian *middle road* of art':[212] Larry recognized the horror and was attempting the same escape route.

Larry kept talking about visiting his own *Übermensch*. 'Perhaps this fall we can meet and arrange some sort of campaign to take the skin off the public's behind,' he wrote to Henry. These schemes ranged from the publication of the 'Banned Book' collection of encomiums on Miller to a set of advertisements: 'An eminent doctor says: "I always take *Tropic of Cancer* in a glass of water before going to bed. A marked tonic effect." A famous divine writes: "Sir, I have used *Black Spring* for a number of years and find it good for swollen joints. My wife's arthritis, for many years crippling, has vanished after a single application." '[213]

Like any careful potentate, in the late spring Larry sent a trusted ambassador, Alan Thomas, to reconnoitre. Alan set out on the Southampton-Paris-Rome-Brindisi route and stopped at 18 Villa Seurat to meet the new Messiah. Alan avowed himself a 'heretic' in that he admired Miller's ability 'without being swept off my feet', unlike some people for whom he was 'Jesus Christ, Villon, Rabelais rolled into one' – this was a dig at Larry and at Pat Evans.[214] None the less, Alan found Miller's manner pleasant, and over a lunch cooked by Henry and served with a bottle of red wine, a bottle of white and 'a small bottle of cognac', their conversation spanned Larry, painting, the artist Hans Reichel (who appeared to borrow money and food) and James Hilton's *Lost Horizon*. Thus Alan could whet Larry's appetite for his own coming pilgrimage to Paris.

Larry, Nancy and Pat Evans were on the quay to meet Alan and to introduce him to Spiro Americanos, who said that 'because you are likes my brothers Master Lawrence' he would only charge Alan 250 drachmae –

less than half an English pound – instead of the usual 300 for a day of chauffeuring. Spiro seized Alan's luggage, announcing to the customs agent who was about to inspect his kit, 'He has nothings to declares!'[215] Alan's visit was officially under way.

At the Villa Anemoyanni Leslie was in charge: Louisa Durrell had accompanied Margo to England where her daughter was being treated for a glandular condition that had caused her to gain a pound a day. Back in England, the family felt that Louisa had no control over her children – as she herself often admitted – and was not bringing them up properly, taking them out of school and whisking them off to Corfu. A council of sisters-in-law and aunts had met to discuss 'what to do about Lou'.[216] Nothing came of it: Louisa simply went her own way. Clearly, Larry's headstrong nature could have come from either of his parents.

Alan noticed a marked positive change in at least one of Louisa's children. Leslie had developed quickly in the freedom from nearly all restraints, the constant outdoor activity, the sun. Within two years the gauche adolescent had become poised and confident. It helped to be English and with money to spend in a country that still admired England. His skill as a hunter also counted, and he could box. He often got into fights, and in his best effort a private quarrel had exploded into a general village riot in which some sixty people took part with fists, sticks and even knives. Someone had tried to send for the police but they turned out to be already enthusiastically engaged on one side or the other in the mêlée, settling their own private scores. Larry, who valued a reputation for respectability even while he was loud in his dislike of English stuffiness and English *pudeur*, was not amused. He had no wish to be typecast by Leslie's behaviour, and he was scathing in his disapproval.

Spiro drove them all to Paleocastrizza across the Plain of Rópa. They passed orchards glittering with ripe cherries, and the strawberries and early figs were being picked. Alan was lodged in a room Koster could spare, and Larry and Nancy pitched a tent nearby. Pat, who in order to see Alan had delayed his departure on a walking tour through Albania and Macedonia, left the next day, and Alan was immediately caught up in a round of boating, swimming, eating, hiking. He went night-fishing for cuttlefish, octopus and *barbuni* with Leslie. Alan walked to the monastery a few minutes from the cottage and the senior monk showed him the Byzantine buildings and a fine twelfth-century icon of the Virgin. Rowing a dinghy, Alan explored a cave at Agios Giorgios – Saint George – Bay. There were boat trips with Larry and Nancy to the secluded beach of sand as white as refined sugar at Myrtiotissa, where they swam naked in the tepid water and, clothed, visited another monastery set amid orange trees heavy with fruit. They inspected a rock island off Paleocastrizza, a rival claimant with Pondikonisi as the Homeric Phaeacian ship petrified by Poseidon. 'It is grand to be back among the Durrells, with their vital personality, wit and gargantuan laughter,' he wrote in his travel diary. 'It suits me admirably to live in a community which is generally held to be mad or eccentric. I have borrowed, or practically appropriated, a red fez which I wear on all occasions.'[217] Sometimes he set the fez off with a green shirt. He took to the lazy evenings under the olives, to the *Van Norden* which sailed 'like a bird', to Spiro, who arrived flourishing his hat, 'like the entry of an opera star'. 'Indeed,' decided Alan, 'all the human element on the island is comic opera'.[218] On cue, Larry produced an accordion which he played, passably, while he and the others sang.[219]

Spiro was by this time very much a member of the family, idolizing Louisa Durrell, on first name terms with everyone else, although he often insisted on calling Larry 'Lord Byron'. He featured in many adventures: the time the Mediterranean nearly washed away his beloved Dodge, parked too near the waterline, and the whole party had to be rallied with great shouting and cursing to rescue it; his cooking an eel in red sauce on the beach; his wild plunging ride through a trackless olive grove to get ahead of a bus that would not let him pass on the dusty road to Paleocastrizza. Another essential figure in the Durrell ménage was Paradiso, the middle-aged maid whose main function seemed to be to carry pitchers of water on her head down from the spring, keeping the great earthenware jar in the house supplied. Fastidious Alan described her as 'solid and rough carved like a Piero della Francesca except for the smell'.[220] Koster had not mastered Greek, so Larry was often called upon to translate his needs for Paradiso. Finally Larry said in some exasperation, 'You can't go on like this, either Koster must learn Greek or you must learn English, Paradiso.' 'What, that dreadful language,' she replied, 'Blim-blim-blim'. She was so pleased with her phonetic rendition that she kept repeating 'Blim-blim-blim' to everyone she met. When her fellow villagers asked her what the devil she was up to, she would reply with finality, 'Talking English!'[221]

Alan brought with him news of the latest intellectual currents and the gossip of London and Bournemouth. Their discussions ranged over Havelock Ellis (whom Alan was reading at Paleocastrizza); the nature of genius and of the artist; the brain, religion, Lao Tzu, Henry Miller, *Hamlet*, writing. Despite the far-ranging discussions, Larry confessed later to Henry that Alan had been a 'disappointment' due to 'his stiff-necked literary way of looking at things'; in fact, he did not understand 'a word about anything any of us say'[222] – not a fair pronouncement on Larry's part. Alan may have disapproved of many of Larry's and Henry's ideas, but he agreed with Larry on a scheme to import Miller's banned books into England by having them sent to Grindlay's Bank, whence Louisa Durrell would retrieve them and hold them pending distribution. 'Damn funny if she's put in jail,' Larry wrote to Henry, 'just suit her sense of humour.'[223]

Theodore was an endless source of erudition and amusement. He was always coming up with some scientific discovery or oddity: an improved contraceptive that worked on rabbits; a discourse on suicide inspired by a patient who had shot himself through the temples but had survived, blinded (use a calibre larger than a .22, Theodore advised); a sandwich made from microscopic marine organisms that he claimed were 'rather nice' and were certainly high in protein. Someone they met by chance on the beach opened up a dialogue on Surrealism. 'That is typical of this place,' wrote Alan, 'we are so cut off from the world that we don't know if war is declared or not, and then we stumble on this outpost of sophistication'.[224] Indeed, a particularly imaginative rumour concerning the Spanish Civil War came to them at Paleocastrizza via Koster, who had got it from the village policeman, who had it via the wireless: Spain had sunk the battleship *Deutschland*, the story went, and in retaliation the Germans and the Italians were bombarding Spanish ports. By the next day the rumour had been expanded to have the pocket battleship *Admiral Graf Spee* sunk by a shore battery. 'I'm glad, Alan, that you've been here for at least one Corfu rumour,' said Larry.[225] No iota of this one was true, but they all knew that the next rumour might turn out to be the first signal of a general war.

Alan returned to England and, war scares or not, Larry tried to return to his writing. For the present, however, he kept finding reasons for *not* writing: 'I want to write a bit about Nancy's arse but no space,' he moaned. 'One minute room, four by four with two beds in it, three by three, paints, typeriter on the floor paper MSS, chinese white, sanitary towels, tooth-picks, cigarette ends.' Everything was 'helter skelter'. He and Nancy fought over the clutter: 'Nancy is in a filthy temper because no room to stroke her art,' Larry explained, taking his machine and fleeing to the silence of the olive groves. He was crammed full creatively, he was sure: 'Notebooks overflowing, dripping. A huge canvas waiting for me. By God, such a book!' It would not deal with mundane reality but with 'my cosmic life which has only just begun: perhaps the DIARY OF A GOD'. While he was 'intoxicated' with his 'arrogance' – 'I strike attitudes,' he confessed – he was also 'scared of paper really'. He found it easy to jot down 'pensées', but 'When I start to write seriously I get a pain in the brain,' he told Henry. Koster was also having trouble, attempting to fit his paintings to artistic theory. Turning his frustration away from himself, Larry quarrelled with Koster, telling him that he, Koster, would never be an artist unless he found God. 'Gee! I don't believe all that stuff. It's phoney,' Koster had replied.[226]

Back at the White House, Larry tried to resume his work routine, but there were still too many summer distractions. Stephanides came to visit, and was with Larry and Nancy on the beach at Mangkephali when they heard loud shrieks. They ran around a small promontory to find several village girls milling about in a panic: one of their number was drowning in deep water. Larry dived in and dragged the unconscious girl ashore, where he and the good doctor were able to revive her. 'Lawrence was, naturally, the hero of the hour & his reputation & prestige among the local inhabitants rose very considerably,' wrote Stephanides.[227] When Larry was concluding *The Alexandria Quartet* more than twenty years later, he would describe the rescue by his quondam double Darley, of a comatose Clea, with Dr Balthazar hovering in attendance.

Anaïs Nin had been writing to Larry since the beginning of the year, and she now sent him her *Winter of Artifice* manuscript plus a section of what would become *Ladders to Fire*. *Winter* he called 'lovely, beautifully proportioned and written with a hot poker', but he found the other 'bigger in scope', the 'first book in Europe which belongs to a female artist'. In giving herself totally in writing, the woman undergoes a 'crucifixion', one 'much worse for a woman artist than a man – because her world operates so intimately *through* man'. The woman's detachment is a detachment from the male, whereas, Larry said, 'for me it works differently': his 'prime detachment', he implied, came from 'a rift with humanity' that was, paradoxically, easier to bear. His own loneliness, then, derived from his need for artistic distance from his subjects, a need served by a conditioned inner indifference and coldness. 'Perhaps women have had more practice in involution,' he continued, 'perhaps the deep sensitive biological nerve of the woman is more hurt by the snapping of the cord.' For the moment, Larry gave up trying to think his way into a woman artist's soul: 'I'm glad I'm not a woman. How can you stand it?' he asked, closing the topic.[228] Within a year Larry and Nancy would be financing the publication of *Winter of Artifice*, and he would attempt for the rest of his life to pin down the nature of the creative woman: in Clea, Iolanthe, Constance.

All might be harmony where his literary *confrères* in Paris were concerned, but Larry complained, rightly or wrongly, of a lack of understanding on the part of his wife and friends on Corfu, and he was not getting much favourable news from England either. There had been 'not a chirp' out of T. S. Eliot, even though Curtis Brown had apparently forwarded *The Black Book* typescript to him at least a month previously. Then Larry received a volume of Nin's unpublished diary and he found it 'stupendous', with a 'rich luminous texture' and 'prose like a cataract': 'Too good for Eliot, all this: much too good for that mealy mouthed brimstone-and-treacle literary gent,' he growled.[229]

No sooner had Larry voiced his bitter words on Eliot than he received 'A CABLE FROM FABERS CONGRATULATING ME ON A FINE BOOK.' Eliot would be writing to him at once. Larry had in fact already submitted 'Asylum in the Snow' to the *Criterion* – even while he had been complaining about Eliot – and now he hoped to use the promised letter, sight unseen, as a 'handle' for getting 'ANAIS NINS LITTLE BIRTH THING' into the *Criterion*.[230]

Larry had been in agreement with Henry that on the grounds of obscenity his book was unpublishable in England, but then Eliot's cordial and thoughtful letter arrived: 'I am writing informally to tell you that I am very much impressed indeed by THE BLACK BOOK.' Eliot continued, 'It seems to me to have both promise and performance,' and with exquisite precision, he explained just what he meant: 'I say both, because the term "promise" used by itself is apt to be a disparagement of the accomplishment, and because one often has occasion to say about a book which is a good job in itself that the author is not likely to go any further. So I say that this is a book which ought to be published, but also that I think you ought to proceed from it to something still better.' He would like to see the novel put into a form in which it could be published by Faber, but did not press Larry to alter it against his conscience. 'Sometimes one feels about a thing of one's own that it has done its job just as it stands, and that alteration from such motives is a matter of indifference.' Whatever Larry's decision, Eliot made clear his support, and also that Larry's contractual obligation to Faber could be waived should he decide not to alter his text: 'I shall be glad,' wrote Eliot, 'first, if anything can be done to make this book publishable in England; if not, I shall be glad to see it published abroad; and in any case I look forward with keen anticipation to the next book you write after this.'[231]

Eliot's letter threw Larry into a quandary. He could safely forget his wicked comments to Henry about Eliot – they had not been noised about – but the temptation was tremendous to have a book that Eliot had singled out for praise published by Faber. With some misgivings, Larry wrote to Henry that he would stick to the Obelisk Press if Kahane demanded exclusive rights. Kahane had still not made a firm commitment. 'It's rather a fix,' Larry worried. 'If I refuse Faber and then this "weathercock" refuses me . . . . I'll be left with my first real book on my hands. No money. No edition. Nowt.'²³² To his surprise, Larry soon found himself in the midst of an artistic and ethical dispute with Henry over whether to allow Faber to bring out an expurgated *Black Book* in England.

A good-humoured letter just in from Spencer Curtis Brown did more than ruffle Larry's feathers: it inadvertently catapulted him into the arms of Henry and Kahane. Curtis Brown had spoken to Frank Morley at Faber. 'It seems to me,' wrote the judicious Curtis Brown, 'that unless you want to revise the Black Book, and I presume from your former letters that you don't, it would be best to get Kahane to publish it with the Obelisk.' They should make it clear to Kahane, however, that he would have no claim on future Durrell titles, since Faber 'do seem very genuinely to want to go on with your books'. Larry nearly exploded when he read what came next: 'WHAT FABER'S WANT FROM YOU, AND WHAT I WOULD LIKE FROM YOU, IS A NICE JOLLY BOOK THAT WOULD SELL SEVERAL THOUSANDS OF COPIES. COULDN'T YOU WRITE A NICE JOLLY BOOK?' To this, Curtis Brown added a short postscript: 'Don't be put off by my frivolity. WRITE A HIGHBROW BOOK IF YOU WANT TO, BUT I'D LIKE TO SEE PRIESTLEY BEATEN AT HIS OWN GAME. AND I'D MAKE *SO* MUCH COMMISSION OUT OF IT, PLEASE, IN YOUR KINDNESS.'²³³

The staccato of Larry's machine sounded through the ancient olives of Paleocastrizza as he answered his agent. 'Your letter inflames me and at the same time arouses my admiration,' he began.

I am writing to ask you for permission to quote it, along with other quotations from such notables as Webster, Marston, Sir Alfred Mond, and Bottomley, in an appendix to the Black Book. This section is to bear the simple but homely title DRIED VOMIT, by several hands. It will be an epitome of what happens to a writer when he becomes a writer: and will answer once and for all the Delphic riddle – when is an author not an author? Because you have been kind to me I shall not keep you waiting until you see the book: I shall tell you the answer at once. WHEN HE'S A PRIESTLY.

Larry would not complain if Faber published *The Black Book*, but if not, 'then I remain amoebic – Charles Norden will serve up an occasional piece of dried vomit for the British and American publics: while Lawrence Durrell moults in obscurity.' Meanwhile, Larry would offer options abroad on all books written under his real name 'Unless, as I say, Faber want me for better or for worse – Norden or Durrell.' He could not resist a parting shot: 'In the meantime I should like to say that I consider the Black Book an eminently JOLLY book.'[234] Larry typed out copies for Henry of Curtis Brown's letter and his own reply, annotating them in red ink, 'Destroy'. Henry carefully saved them.

Larry thought that he was risking the loss of both his agent and his English publisher, but he also knew that a popular success as a new Priestley would not satisfy him. Yet despite his indignation at Curtis Brown, he could not quite reject the silvery tones of that particular temptation.

For Larry this was a larger issue than simply *The Black Book*, which he said he was not concerned about: 'I KNOW THAT SOONER OR LATER IT WILL COME INTO ITS LITTLE OWN UNEXPURGATED.' To Henry, he argued defensively for his need to write two sorts of books, serious fiction and public-pleasers. He proposed to sign his 'real' books with his own name, but to attribute the others to 'my double Amicus Nordensis'. His alias was necessary as a link: 'I am so alone really that I'm a bit scared of going crazy; Norden would keep me in touch with the commonplace world which will never understand my personal struggle.' He carried on about his 'lonliness' – a word that he consistently misspelled. *The Black Book* had cost him an immense emotional toll; in fact, he claimed, had nearly brought on a nervous breakdown. He was quite certain that his mind *had* nearly cracked. 'I CAN'T WRITE REAL BOOKS ALL THE TIME,' he cried. In between soothing himself with 'literary gardening' – essays, travel books, one more Norden novel – he would write 'the Book of the Dead, the Book of Miracles etc.'[235]

Henry responded with three densely-packed typed sheets and, after a few business details, weighed in with a stiff lecture: 'Alors, "I want to begin here and now to talk about your future work!" . . . . (Ahem) Don't, my good Durrell, take the schizophrenic route!' The toll would be disintegration. Henry added up all the advantages Larry possessed: youth, a happy marriage, encouragement, enough funds and 'a boat to boot, be Jesus!' He ridiculed Larry's expectation of sympathy 'because you are *alone*!': 'That's in your favor. You can't be alone and be with the herd too.'[236] 'No', Henry had written in *Tropic of Cancer*, 'what the artist needs is *loneliness*'.[237]

Also, Larry should be able to remain silent when he had nothing to say: 'Lie Fallow.' With a sly dig at Larry's Greek world, he added, 'I can understand the phrase – Homer nodding. But that is different from Homer pseudonyming.'[238] After laying down the law, Uncle Henry made an offer: Fred Perlès had just been given *The Booster* magazine: would Larry like to be an unpaid contributing editor? Would he not! Thus was born one of the more hilarious adventures of the next two years.

Larry had done considerable flip-flopping over the past few weeks, but the truth was that his priorities kept shifting with the excitement of the moment. He wanted to write a novel that would please him more than *The Black Book* had, and that would justify, as he saw it, the praise that he was already receiving from Henry and Anaïs: this would require, he knew, concentrated effort. He wanted to write good poetry, but he could not be rushed: his poems had to form, he said, like stalactites. He wanted to live a completely independent life, yet he also wanted financial security. He was half-sincere when he threatened to study medicine and become a doctor: that might bring him life's secrets as well as security – the caduceus represented, to him, at once the sensibility of the serpent and the straight line of intelligence.[239] He wanted to be a vagabond, yet have a fixed centre. Even when he lamented that he was half-crazy with the strain, the voice within might accuse him of striking a fashionable pose – hadn't he, the public Larry, invoked mad de Nerval, orated on schizophrenic Hamlet? And, Larry could not forget, his father had lost his mind.

Wrenching himself away from introspection, Larry addressed the outer world. The great European cataclysm might be impending but there was still the censorship battle to be fought, and on 1 July Larry wrote to George Bernard Shaw asking for his help in getting Henry's books into England. Larry was rewarded with a letter from Shaw's secretary saying that Mr Shaw was 'quite unacquainted' with Miller's work and, further, that 'He does not think his interference would either reassure or intimidate the censorship.'[240] Larry, signing his letter 'Charles Norden', got a somewhat more satisfactory response from Edwin Muir, who replied evasively that he had read little Miller, but that 'perhaps Miller will have to come in' to a history of English literature since 1914 that Muir was writing. Then Muir praised *Panic Spring*.[241]

Correspondence, writing, publication plans, visitors, outdoor adventures, and above all, self-education – all these took time and energy, but Larry felt able to embrace everything. His mother and sister had returned from England; Pat Evans was back from Macedonia, and his 'homeric love' for Margaret had evolved into a 'huge emotional mess'[242] Larry said – although Margaret maintained much later that 'nothing really happened'.[243] Larry wanted to spend less time with the family and more at Kalami, and this encouraged him to begin a construction project. A summer pleasure enjoyed by Larry, Nancy and their guests at the White House was to sit out at night on the worn and warm stone shelves a few feet above the wavelets. In those pre-pollution days the stars seemed closer and were certainly far more numerous; and there were no electric lights within miles to interfere with one's night vision. The setting was ideal for conversation or for just musing in silence. 'Why not,' said Larry, 'add to the house a second storey with *big* windows so that we can enjoy this all year?' Totsa Athenaios was doubtful but Larry argued with eloquence, gestures, pencil and paper: he would plan the addition, would pay the costs, would help with the work – and Totsa would end up with twice the house for nothing. Soon Totsa agreed. He had built the present house himself, and within a short while he and a crony from the village set to work with stone and cement, aided by a small boy who carried innumerable pails of water. Larry was full of suggestions and advice, especially on the subject of the windows. Stephanides was present at the start of the project and recalled Larry's adamancy: 'I *insist* on two *big* windows. I *must* have two *big* windows so that I can look out on the sea & feel as if I were actually riding the waves. . . . each one must extend from here to here. See, I am marking it so that there should be no mistake.'[244] And so on at length. Gently and patiently Totsa explained that the eastern winter winds from snowy Albania would freeze the occupants behind the *big* windows, that storms would shatter the glass. Larry waved this aside; Totsa stopped arguing and picked up his mason's hammer and trowel.

There were even more exciting ventures in prospect than house construction. It was July and Paris was calling, with Anaïs and Henry sounding siren notes. England was tempting too: old friends such as Alan, John Gawsworth, and Peter Bull stood ready to welcome Larry back, and Faber looked encouraging. Soon Larry and Nancy would be boarding the Corfu-Brindisi ferry, but they would be leaving much behind. Larry's description of his domestic life at the time catches a serenity he would never quite recover:

At such moments we never speak; but I am aware of the brown arms and throat in the candlelight and the brown toes in the sandals. I am aware of a hundred images at once and a hundred ways of dealing with them. The bowl of wild roses. The

English knives and forks. Greek cigarettes. The battered and sea-stained notebook in which I rough out my poems. The rope and oar lying under the tree. The spilth of the olive-press which will be gathered for fuel. The pile of rough stone for the building of a garden wall. A bucket and an axe. The peasant crossing the orchard in her white head-dress. The restless cough of the goat in the barn. All these take shape and substance round this little cone of flame in which N. is cutting the cheese and washing the grapes. A single candle burning upon a table between our happy selves.[245]

CHAPTER 4

Henry Miller and the Villa Seurat

So one fine year to where the roads
Dividing Europe meet in Paris.
'Cities, Plains and People'

IN EARLY AUGUST 1937 Nancy and Larry Durrell appeared in Paris. There on the platform of the Gare de Montparnasse stood Anaïs Nin and Henry Miller, Anaïs with the pure cameo of her face set off by simple and dramatic clothes, Henry quintessentially the casual Brooklynite, grinning affably. They had a gift for Larry, a copy of Otto Rank's *Art and Artist*. The first stop was the Dôme for drinks.[1] Anaïs remembered her first meeting with the Durrells differently from Larry's account and perhaps more accurately – she might be 'a very adept, adroit prevaricator' in her reconstructions of her private life, but she was also a keen observer and had no reason to play the fabulist in this instance.[2] In her version, their encounter occurred a day or two after Larry and Nancy's arrival. Anaïs recorded in her diary: 'I walked to Henry's studio to meet Lawrence Durrell and his wife. What first struck me were his eyes of a Mediterranean blue, keen, sparkling, seer, child and old man. In body he is short and stocky, with soft contours like a Hindu, flexible like an Oriental, healthy and humorous. He is a faun.' Nancy she described as 'a long-waisted gamin with beautiful long slanting eyes'.[3] Anaïs commented in Nancy's hearing, 'She walks like a puma,'[4] and to Michael Fraenkel Anaïs wrote, 'and she paints like Debussy'.[5] Larry simply found Anaïs 'delectable'.[6]

However their first encounter took place, it seemed a meeting not of strangers but of old friends. Henry swept Nancy up in the embrace of his regard, and she too felt completely accepted. With English people he had never seen before, Larry might have been diffident, feeling his way, judging how he should behave. However, Anaïs and Henry were so unconventional, so un-English, that Larry felt suddenly euphoric, and all his hesitations vanished in a surge of anecdotes and laughter. He did not have to act a role.

After the nearly one hundred letters and various manuscripts that had been exchanged among the three, the photographs sent by Larry and the watercolours given by Henry, they were hardly strangers, but here was the immediate impact of eyes, bodies and voices. They fitted together like a jazz trio: Larry's musical cadences, Anaïs's strangely monotone non-national English with trace-accents of French and Spanish, Henry's sonorous Brooklyn buzz, in the role of string bass, punctuated by his companionable 'hmmm . . . d'you see?' Henry, photographed alone, always appeared a tall, thin man: in fact, he measured only about five feet eight inches, but he towered over Larry. Nancy noted Henry's 'rather feeble-looking pale blue eyes' behind thick lenses, and the baldness that made him seem older than his forty-five years. But she found him *enormously* welcoming' and his grin 'wonderful'.[7]

Henry installed Larry and Nancy temporarily in the flat below his at 18 Villa Seurat. It was Sunday when they arrived, and Alfred Perlès was away at his part-time job as 'a sort of tout', signing up new members at the American Country Club at Ozoir-la-Ferrière. His three-hundred-franc wages tinkling in his pocket, Fred arrived in the late afternoon to find, in his words:

Lawrence Durrell, fresh from Corfu, with the Ionian tan still on his face and hands. Of him, I first perceived the laughter, which kept reverberating through the high-ceilinged studio: an almost continuous laughter, loud and persistent: from the guts. He and Henry were gay. They were having a party that must have been going on for the better part of the day, and which was to go on, intermittently, for over a year. The place was littered with bottles and glasses, books, remnants of food and manuscript pages, the smoke of their cigarettes spiralling up to the ceiling, curling along the ceiling, like clouds of incense.[8]

Henry was in his customary mocha dressing gown, looking like 'an inquisitive friar straight from Tibet'[9] or an 'archangel in mufti',[10] staring in affection and amazement at Larry, and humming in agreement with his guest's chatter. Larry was curled compactly on the floor, his long hair golden from the sun and his limbs strong after two years of hiking, sailing and swimming. Fred 'recognized him at once from the ceiling frescoes in the Italian museums, picked him up from the floor and gave him the accolade'. The aroma of grilling steaks mingled with the cigarette smoke, and Nancy emerged from the kitchenette. To Fred she seemed an 'elegant flamingo'.[11]

Counting a tiny mezzanine inhabited by a tall ballerina, there were five flats in the building, a new Art Decco structure near the foot of the Villa

Seurat cul-de-sac. Henry lived in a large studio apartment that Anaïs paid about $25 per month for. Downstairs directly below Henry lived Betty Ryan, a young American painter who was studying with the *maître* of the Académie Ozenfant. She had moved in when Fraenkel departed for Mexico. Across the corridor was the Russian painter Chaim Soutine. Betty was away on Capri with her father during the Durrells' first visit to Paris, so Henry had arranged for them to stay in her flat. Even in such close proximity the two master correspondents exchanged notes. The first volley set the tone:

Dear Miller,
Two questions:
(1) What do you do with the garbage?
          AND (TWO)
(2) When you say 'to be with God' do you identify yourself with God: or do you
    regard the God-stuff reality as something *extraneous* towards which we
    yearn?

To which Henry replied:

d'en haut!
My dear Durrell –
    The first question is easier to answer than the second. The garbage you put in a
little can (under the sink) and about sundown, or thereafter, you deposit it in
front of your door, in the street. The noise you hear about 7:30 in the morning is
the noise made by Madame the Garbage Collector who rolls her little truck out of
the little hut at the end of the street (illuminated by a cross at night).
    As for the second question, being rather pressed for time, and slightly jocund at
the moment, I should say blithely – sometimes you approach and sometimes you
become! Gottfried Benn answers it nicely (via Storch) in an issue of *transition*
which I will dig up for you and show you. I could discuss it better over the table.
When do I eat with you downstairs? I am free for dinner this evening, if that says
anything.[12]

Fred recognized Larry's catalytic quality, that enormous energy and enthusiasm that sent others flashing about like piranha at feeding time:

From the moment of his entry on the scene, the rhythm of events accelerated, as
though all life had been switched into a higher gear. The days and nights grew
gayer and brighter, as if lit up by the approach of a comet. The world was clearly
racing towards another internecine slaughter while optimism and good cheer
reached an all-time high in the Villa Seurat.[13]

Everything seemed to be going well, whether or not Larry had a hand in it: the ambience was right. Henry was diplomatically negotiating the publication of Larry's *Black Book* with his own publisher, Jack Kahane of the Obelisk Press. Anaïs proclaimed Larry a kindred soul: 'With Durrell I had instant communication. We skipped the ordinary stages of friendship, its gradual development. I felt friendship at one bound, with hardly a need of talk.'[14] 'You won't write about me in the diary?' asked Larry. 'Of course not!' lied Anaïs. She had just recorded a 'marvellous description' of Larry in the pages of her 'Black Children',[15] as Larry christened her ebony-bound diaries.[16] Fred's love affairs were flourishing and his second novel, *Le Quatuor en Ré-Majeur*, was about to appear. Fred had been told to do as he liked with *The Booster*, stodgy house organ of the American Country Club, to 'turn it into a Paris version of *The New Yorker*'.[17] The only stipulation was that he print two pages of Club news. Here was a journal with some advertising revenue and a circulation of a few hundred. Henry wrote his letters on *Booster* stationery topped by the grand claim, 'The largest paid circulation and most influential English language monthly Sports journal published on the Continent.'[18] The French name of the magazine had a fine Gallic vigour: *L'Animateur*. Henry and Fred had the basic format and editorial direction of *The Booster* well in hand before Larry arrived.[19]

At first Fred and Henry did most of the editing work on *The Booster*, with Larry contributing ideas and advice and drawing the cork of an occasional bottle of Volnay. Nancy designed the cover, a woodcut of three superimposed abstract faces, open-mouthed and presumably boosting. Anaïs held herself aloof, disliking 'the Fred smell' of *The Booster*, the brash vulgarity, she thought, of the 'boosts'.[20] By mid-August circular letters advertising the journal had been typed and mailed.

The first *Booster* under the direction of the new troika contained an editorial announcing that the magazine would be 'serious but gay withal'. Behind the banter was an irony that was probably Miller's but that could have originated with any one of the three musketeers – as they called themselves – Larry, Henry or Fred: 'There are so many people who profess to be in the right that we see no harm in being wrong now and then.' They proclaimed an optimism that held that 'everything is excellent – including the high-grade bombers with ice-boxes and what not.'[21]

Pretending to have 'no aesthetic canons to preserve or defend', Fred, Henry and Larry none the less produced a first issue of considerable quality. Writing as 'Charles Norden', Larry led off with a 'Sportlight' column that discussed the Tunney-Dempsey and Farr-Louis fights in terms of Lao Tzu. 'For the sportsman', wrote Larry, 'a proper psychic attitude is necessary: an attitude in which time not only flies, but **ceases to exist.**' Larry had floated this time concept in *The Black Book*, and it would resurface throughout his career. The American boxers Tunney and Louis, according to Larry, had mastered the Taoist 'axioms of webbing and weaving, ducking and bobbing', while the English fighters understood only the dogged attack. In particular, 'The negro . . . adept at the Tao, realises that to get as near as possible to your man is the same as getting as far as possible from him.' Failing to grasp this, Larry concluded, 'The English heavyweight wears the anxious expression of [a] curate at a picnic, trying to avoid a wasp.'[22] He – whether boxer or curate – must lose.

This issue of *The Booster* would also include poetry by Larry and Patrick Evans, fiction in English by Miller and in French by Nin and Perlès. The water-colourist Hans Reichel and the photographer Brassaï received special 'boosts', and the issue was illustrated by one of the American Abe Rattner's feathery line drawings and Brassaï's photograph *Chair Prime*. The placid and unsuspecting advertisements invited readers to buy curaçao liqueur from Wijnand Fockink and 'UNE NOUVELLE BALLE DE GOLF' called 'SILVER KING (High Velocity)'.[23]

Henry, Larry and Fred radiated from their Villa Seurat epicentre, walking to the Brasserie Zeyer on the Avenue du Maine near the Alésia metro station, where they would find Hans Reichel, the 'mystic painter', as Henry termed him, sitting over his morning coffee and newspapers if it was a good day for him. If Reichel was on a binge, he would be standing morosely before a glass of wine at the long, clean zinc counter in Zeyer's or at a less reputable bar nearby. When they felt flush the Boosterites would go further afield to dine at the Dôme, the Select or La Coupole.

For an entire 'Durrell week', Anaïs reported, 'we had them all day and almost all night.' Her evaluation of Larry in some ways matched his own self-analysis: she saw a 'cataract of words' and a 'universe of nuances' beneath the bland exterior of 'a healthy young English boy'. She thought that Larry did not quite know what to make of the world of his imaginings: 'He is a little amazed at himself, as someone who has discovered a disease in himself.' He was like a shepherd or a sailor who had been 'illimined' without going through the artist's obligatory suffering.[24] Larry would hardly agree that he had not suffered, but he had already told Henry about his bafflement at what lay within. There was an element of the disingenuous in his confession to Henry, perhaps, but Larry was genuinely alarmed for his mental stability. Being embraced by the Villa Seurat circle had increased his self-confidence while it added to his internal tension: he had aroused expectations that he was not quite sure he could meet. He was introduced as a prodigy to André Breton, Herbert Read and Raymond Queneau – 'crazy people', he told Alan Thomas – Eugène Jolas had promised to publish 'Asylum in the Snow' in *transition*; and Kahane was reading *The Black Book*.[25]

Anaïs sensed that Larry was beginning to feel overwhelmed by Villa Seurat and the 'Dôme circus' and when she confronted him with her suspicion, he admitted that she was right. He was contemplating an escape to London, or even back to Corfu. 'It is not a moral revulsion,' he said, 'it is heraldic' – he did not wish to pollute his ideal world with too much crassness. 'I can't stand idiots very long,' he confided to Anaïs,[26] referring not to Henry but to some of their hangers-on.

Leaving quite a stir behind them, Larry and Nancy dashed off to London. To Larry's eyes, the citizens had not improved. His first letter back to Miller opened with a rant: 'Fuck the English eh? Henry the English are everywhere, all around me – like mutilated black beetles.'[27] After that, most of his news was good. At Faber and Faber he had met Frank Morley, 'a man after your own heart', who was interested in publishing Henry's *Max and the White Phagocytes*. Encouraged by Henry, Larry had also met the sexologist Havelock Ellis: 'Listen, I went down and bearded Havelock,' Larry reported. 'I should say rather that he bearded me. Magnificent beard. He is covered with hair like a wild boar – likes your work and promises to write you in detail about the books. Hasn't finished them yet – disagrees with you about *urination*!!! Lovely old man.'[28] Larry had also seen a friend from his earlier London days, Mulk Raj Anand – 'he's famous,' Larry announced parenthetically – and the Indian writer had promised a poem for *The Booster*. Another old friend, Count Geoffrey Potocki de Montalk, had given him a 'document' that '*proves* (I said PROVES) that Bach was a Potocki!!' The astounding revelation about Bach's Polish ancestry was not to appear in *The Booster*: in a thoroughly American access of *lèse-majesté*, Henry showed disrespect for Potocki's title by addressing a letter to him as 'Dear Mr. de Montalk'. Fulminated the royalist from New Zealand, 'It is *this* which has caused all the trouble ever since I came to Europe – not CUNT but COUNT.'[29] Potocki demanded the return of his Bach article. Larry also took a full charge of chain-shot from George Bernard Shaw, who had finally got round to reading Miller. A letter arrived from Sidmouth, penned in the old lion's indignant hand: 'This fellow can write; but he has totally failed to give any artistic value to his verbatim reports of bad language.' There was some personal advice: 'And you, Lawrence, must be careful. To be a convicted obscene author is a heavy handicap; but to be a commercial traveller in obscene literature is the very devil. I conclude that you are young and foolish – both of you. So you had better do what I tell you.'[30]

Meanwhile Larry was too busy to see all the people he had planned to, let alone write to Henry, who grumbled that he had gone silent. When he finally fired off a note, Larry said that he would ring up Rebecca West – Anaïs had urged him to call on her – 'if I have time'. He had executed a few commissions, buying Henry a velveteen coat and a Scotch tweed, but 'so far no pink shirts'. Despite all the good contacts, Larry's view of the London literary scene did not change: 'Been to the Café Royal a lot and confirmed the opinion I always had of English writers.'[31] One poet he *did* enjoy talking to was the outspoken Audrey Beecham, athletic niece of Sir Thomas the conductor. She also numbered Dylan Thomas among her friends, and recalled one night when, drunk and amorous, he had wandered into her bedroom: 'I told him to leave and when he did not I hit him, just once, and he went backwards through the door and collapsed on his own bed.' She described meeting Nancy, 'a tall, beautiful woman' accompanied by 'a short, pig-faced man'.[32] Despite this unflattering appraisal, she had liked Larry and wrote to him, 'I agree with all you felt . . . at the Café Royal.'[33] She sent him three poems which he later printed in *Delta*, the successor to *The Booster*.

Larry excused himself to Henry for not writing more often: 'I'm snowed under with things – proofs, engagements, work in the British Museum.'[34] Subsequent letters recounted meetings with friends such as Alan Thomas and George Barker, with Tambimuttu – who became a life-long ally – and with two men at Faber and Faber who were to become friends: Alan Pringle and T. S. Eliot. Larry was somewhat intimidated by Eliot's gravity, but sensed his underlying gentleness.[35] Larry quickly discovered the humour, modesty and sheer kindliness behind Eliot's direct but slightly asymmetric regard: the right side of his face seemed poised to break into a smile, the left was tinged with melancholy. As an earnest of his good intentions, Eliot gave Larry permission to use his comments on *The Black Book* for advertising, and later sent a special blurb, offering to 'try again' if it did not meet Larry's approval.[36] Eliot's written comment on *The Black Book* was more than Larry could have hoped for, and Kahane was to feature it on the flyleaf:

Lawrence Durrell's *The black book* is the first piece of work by a new English writer to give me any hope for the future of prose fiction. If he has been influenced by any writers of my generation, the influences have been digested, and he has produced something different. One test of the book's quality, for me, is the way in which reminiscences of it keep turning up in my mind: evocations of South London or of the Adriatic, or of individual characters. What is still more unusual is the sense of pattern and of organisation of moods which emerges gradually during the reading, and remains in the mind afterwards. *The black book* is not a scrap book, but a carefully executed whole. There is nothing of the second-hand literary about the material; but what is most unusual is the structure the author has made of it.[37]

That Eliot had singled out the structure for comment was particularly gratifying: the combination of direct story line and diary excerpts, the inclusion of a genuine letter to Alan Thomas, the parallel visions of a pair of narrators who never meet – in this careful juxtaposition of voices and of fiction and reality lay Larry's claim to originality. Remarks deeply critical of Eliot vanished henceforth from Larry's letters.

No one more unlike Eliot could be imagined than J. Meary Tambimuttu, the Sinhalese poet and editor who had arrived penniless on the London scene after Larry had departed for Corfu. Tambimuttu had long waving black hair, apparently jointless fingers that he could bend backwards, skin the colour of polished teak, wild dark eyes. No one could encounter Tambi and remain indifferent. Larry was no exception. Buffie Johnson, whom Larry would soon meet at 18 Villa Seurat, termed Tambi 'one of the most consistently outrageous people I have known'.[38] She might have added, also in the superlative, delightful, infuriating, naïve, calculating, resourceful, feckless. Tambi's diction and line of patter invited parody. Tambi, looking at his watch, might say to Larry in the Fitzroy Tavern: 'I must go! I am having lunch with T. S. Eliot. You know who is T. S. Eliot? He has been my benefactor. Do you have any money? Good! Give it to me! I am a prince in my own country, and princes never carry money.' There was a broad element of humbug in Tambi, but with him and according to him, anything and everything was possible: a show for this sculptor, a publisher for that poet, a new magazine, a *Festschrift* for some overlooked genius. A small yet significant percentage of Tambimuttu's schemes actually transpired. His *Poetry* magazine printed many distinguished poets, along with a lot whose names have faded out. Even those who suffered from his importunities and schemes forgave him. Larry cherished him, a *picaro* who reminded him of his unforgotten India.

The contradiction that had appeared to Larry in his youth remained: Pudding Island was a wretched, dull place but he made wonderful friends and found delicious characters there and enjoyed himself enormously – at times.

WITHIN WEEKS LARRY AND NANCY had boarded the boat train, headed once more for the excitement of Paris. Betty Ryan had returned from Capri, so Larry and Nancy moved in for a few weeks with Fred at No. 7 across the street from Henry's apartment. Betty was very much a member of Henry's circle: Nancy, somehow believing Henry's relationship with Anaïs to be merely platonic at this time – obviously she was not permitted a reading of the more steamy passages in Nin's diary – thought that he was in love with Betty; Hans Reichel certainly was; Soutine was rumoured to have seduced her;[39] and Fred proclaimed that she had 'the face and bearing of a Madonna'.[40] Nancy saw her as 'one of those very soft, gentle, rather fey sort of people . . . . *trembling* with sensitivity . . . . like a trembling Chinese flower.'[41] It would have surprised Nancy to know that Betty and Henry were talking of getting married – after Anaïs was no longer on the scene. Betty was a trained artist and an accomplished linguist, and would over the years learn Russian and Greek to add to the French and German she already spoke fluently. When Larry and Betty discovered they shared a hatred of Ingres, they resolved on a symbolic act. They tore down an Ingres poster pinned up in the Dôme and joyfully 'sent it floating down the Seine.'[42] She had a regular allowance from her father, enough to sustain her at the Villa Seurat and to pay the salary of a maid, and she gave small, elegant dinner parties for the hungry gang that pounded up the stairs to Henry's studio.

The long sessions of talk with Henry and Anaïs answered another kind of hunger: for contact with other artists as committed to ideas as Larry was. Writing was necessary to him wherever he happened to be, and the long sessions of talk spurred him on. He bought a fresh notebook, wrote on the front endpaper 'Lawrence Durrell/ Paris. 1937/ Summer/ "Thoughts! Beautiful thoughts!"' and proceeded to fill it with verse drafts, commentaries and quotations. First came eight pages of passages from Lao Tzu, with accompanying annotations – fuel for discussions with Henry – then some notes headed 'Psyche: the concept of soul' and a few pages on Rank's *Art and Artist*.[43] Fully half of the 160 pages were to be devoted to various drafts of 'The Death of General Uncebunke: A Biography in Little', the mock-heroic verse collection of fourteen 'Carols' that would be followed by the related 'Five Soliloquies Upon the Tomb of Uncebunke'. The tone is at once serious and satirical, affectionate and flippant: the very name of the title character precluded the heroic. Larry did not apparently have a specific relative in mind, but celebrated a generic colonial uncle and his consort Aunt Prudence. Prudence, to be sure, owed her name to Larry's second cousin Prudence Hughes, who was quite sure that Larry had taken her off to slow music.[44] 'My uncle sleeps in the image of death', began Larry, a refrain that would open several of the carols. He demanded that God, who keeps track of fallen birds, take note of his uncle's death:

> Here was a ruddy bareback man,
> Emptied his blood upon the frozen lake,
> Wheeled back the screaming mares,
> Crossing the Jordan.
>
> Excuse me, Lord God, numberer of hairs,
> Sender of telegrams, the poisoned arrow,
> Suffer your faithful hound, give him
> At least the portion of the common sparrow.
> [. . .]
>   he lies in the status
> Of death's dumb music, the dumb dead king
> On an ivory coast.

Larry's feeling for the dead Uncebunke comes through in the music of phrase, the ring of the Welsh *cynghanedd* in the repeated consonants of 'death's dumb music, the dumb dead king', sleeping a 'Botanical plant-pure sleep'. Prudence prays silly prayers – '"Thy will be done in Baden Baden./ In Ouchy, Lord, and in Vichy"' – and she 'Ate the white lie: "Happily ever after"'. Perhaps reflecting the many things Larry held against his mother, Prudence 'sweetly sang both crotchet and quaver', and seems to have missed the gravity of her husband's demise.[45]

Personally, emotionally, the Uncebunke poems were very important to Larry. He hoped to make a mark with them, to break into the mainstream poetry market. He also needed to lay the ghost of his dead father: to bury him in the family religion but without compromising his son's dispute with Christianity. Larry felt that he had accomplished this, through the ironic distance that he so carefully maintained in the fourteen carols and the soliloquies linked with them. 'Friends, Humans, Englishmen!' he wrote in the third of the 'Five Soliloquies', 'Officer at the bar and gentleman in bed'. Larry ridiculed the colonial life of this man who 'took first prize/ In the Regatta for men past menopause' and 'Shot his bolt in the Gobi'; and Larry demystified his death and funeral: 'Give us to God with slim and shining handles', he quipped wickedly. If in *The Black Book* Larry had vanquished the 'English death', in the Uncebunke poems he killed off and embalmed the White Man's Burden of colonialism. In an optimistic mood, he sent the Uncebunke poems to Eliot at Faber.

By September, William Saroyan had lent his name to the *Booster* venture and soon appeared in its pages, but he did not take an active part in running the magazine. Fred, Larry and Henry drew up an irreverent and apolitical manifesto calculated to displease the American Country Club:

Booster Placard

THE BOOSTER

is a non-successful, non-political, non-cultural review published in English and French from Paris once a month under the direction of the celebrated literary quartet:

First Violin Alfred Perlès
Also First Violin William Saroyan
Viola Lawrence Durrell
'Cello and Traps Henry Miller

18 Villa Seurat, Paris (xiv)

ON SALE HERE
5 francs 1 shilling 25 cents

WE ARE

For	*Against*
Food	Peace
Pocket Battleships	Poison Gas
Depressions	Fair Play
Plagues	Hygiene
Token Payments	Moderation
Epilepsy	Rheumatism and Arthritis
Taking the lead	All isms
Shangri-la	Schizophrenia

The editors sent copies of *The Booster* to all the influential literati they hoped might be helpful. Herbert Read replied that he found the magazine amusing, but that the notices attributed to the Club were a bit overdone. In fact, the Club advertisements were no joke. An incredulous but friendly Read came to visit the *Booster* crew, and Larry remembered him at the Deux Magots 'in the black muffin of a hat giving his young son an ice'.[46]

Two Durrells appeared between the covers of the October 1937 issue of *The Booster*, Gerald with a macabre 'prose poem' about an operating theatre, Larry with the final pages of *The Black Book*, dedicated as a 'Coda to nancy'.[47] Gerry sent another poem, 'Death', for the November issue, and Larry accused Evans, still his brother's tutor: 'You wrote this yourself, Pat.' 'If I could write as well as that,' snapped Evans, 'do you think I would be wasting my time as a tutor?'[48] Gerry's poem treated the invisible approach of death:

> on a mound a boy lay
> as a stream went tinkling by:
> mauve irises stood round him as if to
> shade him from the eye of death . . . .[49]

Larry felt an almost paternal pride in his eleven-year-old brother, whom he described as being 'at work on a monumental novel about the fauna and flora of the world'.[50]

Meanwhile, the staid advertisements and the Club announcements continued – 'Mme Joseph Lacorne recently entertained Mme Petit at tea'[51] – but people were beginning to take note of the excerpts from *Tropic of Capricorn* and *The Black Book*. Complaints began to arrive in the letter box of Elmer Prather, manager of the American Country Club. Larry claimed that his essay on boxing had brought in 'three hundred and four threatening letters from boxers all over the world', but that none the less circulation 'has just crept into double figures'.[52]

There was much more to Paris for Durrell the writer than hectic activity. 'Paris as usual was humming with ideas, like a beehive,' he recalled many years later, 'and here at last I found people with whom I could discuss these ideas.' Einstein had proved that matter, distance and time were not linear constants, but depended upon the relative motion of the observer. Larry was determined to apply the physicist's ideas to literature, particularly to the handling of time. 'In order to destroy time I use the historic present a great deal,'[53] said Larry, writing about *The Black Book* but also prefiguring his treatment of time in *The Alexandria Quartet* and in *The Avignon Quintet*. Larry had long been preoccupied with death – in other words, with the passing of biological time – as he had demonstrated in *Pied Piper of Lovers*. Time was the source of the Elizabethan frenzy, of the brutal onrush of 'Time's winged chariot', but in Einstein Larry hoped that he had found an answer: by embracing relativity, he could seize the moment *and repeat it at will*. He could reverse time, perform resurrections. Henry had solved his own time equation by personally participating, so he claimed, in three time frames simultaneously: 'I gloat over the past, I revel in the present, and I make merry in the future.'[54] Larry's attempt to control time, in contrast, depended more on his interpretation of physics and philosophy than his own ego.

Just as Einstein was transforming the understanding of time and physics, the studies of multiple personality disorders and the nature of the subconscious by Freud, von Feuchtersleben, Groddeck and others were changing the concept of the personality: while the physicists were busy subdividing that basic building block of matter, the atom, the stability of character was being called into question. Was a person's nature fixed, discrete, or could character shift, like atoms transformed by bombardment into other elements on the atomic chart? 'Could such material influence literary form, and provide a sort of frame?' Larry wondered. Could the novel, in fact, mirror the totality of character, its conscious and subconscious elements, viewed in associational and relativistic terms, with the different sections in motion across time like the hypothetical laboratories of theoretical physicists? 'I began to dream of a sort of novel-as-apparatus (*un roman-appareil*),' Larry would recall, 'which one could use as a historic or poetic "conscience", as portable as a pocket-compass!' Here was the germ of the future *Avignon Quintet* in which, Larry would write, characters could 'become one another, could circulate in each other's blood streams'. But as he would admit, 'It was years before I dared to begin on such a book.'[55]

The Villa Seurat group was made up of highly charged personalities, replete with complex relationships and animosities. Buffie Johnson, studying painting with Picabia, was just a few days older than Larry. She noted that Larry was always sketching, even while sitting in cafés, and found his drawings of Greek villages, done from memory, quite good. She felt instinctively close to Larry, identifying him with her twin who had died at birth. They were about the same height, but there the outward resemblance ended: Buffie was a large-eyed beauty, serious, soft-spoken. She was very definite in her opinions and admitted, 'I detested Henry, both the man and his writing,' although she branded him a 'trickster hero' and found the same element in Larry. More specifically, she said of Henry, 'I didn't like his ego-maniacal stance or his attitude toward women.' She was sure the feeling was reciprocated: 'I might say he disliked me quite as cordially.'[56] Fred Perlès did not spend much time working at the Club, but elected to be where the most fun, food and women were to be enjoyed – and that usually meant where Henry was. Nancy, somewhat rebelliously cooking for the Miller ménage, noted Fred's 'very thin mouse-like hands' and 'big black rather damp eyes'. He seemed to her 'utterly and completely corrupt – unreliable'. Anaïs frankly despised Fred, who had once been in love with her, and would later condemn his description of her long relationship with Henry as a 'caricature'. There was an element of jealousy in Anaïs's feelings: she considered herself one of the 'Three Musketeers of La Coupole' – to the exclusion of Fred – and she was annoyed whenever she found Larry and Nancy with him.[57] Yet between Anaïs and Fred the relationship was complex and partly financial: he did secretarial work for her at this time, and next year would retype her *Chaotica* manuscript. 'All the money I have comes from my job with Anaïs,' he explained to Henry.[58] Henry himself complained to Larry about Fred's dependence on him, yet Fred, in the Sancho Panza role he chose, was essential to Henry, sometimes as court jester, sometimes for financial support – for a time Fred had housed and fed Henry out of his slender earnings as a proof-reader for the *Chicago Tribune* Paris edition – and always as a loyal friend. He and Henry called one another Joe or Joey. In some ways a sincere *ingénu* yet in others disingenuous, Fred employed a deft irony to ridicule the foibles of humanity in so original a way that Betty Ryan named his flights *Perlèsiflages*, and the term stuck. Sharing his flat, Larry and Nancy liked to lie abed and watch Fred's morning antics, talking to his visage in the mirror as he shaved: 'Hullo, Joe! How are you this morning, Joe? You all right, Joe?'[59]

Fred alone was a sketch, but when he was with Henry anything could happen, anywhere. Sometimes, when they had come to an impasse in planning *The Booster* or merely felt restive, whether at 18 Villa Seurat or even at Zeyer's or the Dôme, one of them would ask, 'Take the lead, Joe?' The other would respond, 'Yeah, take the lead, Joe!'[60] Then they would leap to their feet and prance around the table hooting, each with one finger in his ear and another up a nostril. Finally they would subside into their seats and carry on the business – or fun – of the day. Once Henry was reading out loud from Confucius to a group that included Larry and the Chinese friend they always called 'Mr Chu'. Henry began to clown and urged Nien-Sien Tcheou to 'take the lead'. Tcheou turned 'the colour of an unripe cucumber', while Larry roared with laughter.[61] Tcheou, quiet in his

neat dark suit, endured the teasing to become the 'Oriental Department' of
The Booster.

'There was war in the offing, we laughed it off,' recalled Fred. 'Larry was
good at laughing; he laughed so loudly that he was sometimes turned out of
a cinema.'[62] Larry's laughter was open, ribald, hearty. Such was not
necessarily true of the others. 'Henry's laughter was not really Rabelaisian
laughter,' Larry said. 'It was nervous laughter. . . . And of course Joey used
to appeal to him, because Joey burst into even more nervous laughter,
hysterical laughter, like a Pekinese . . . barking.'[63] Laughter was one form
of escape; another was the extravagant romanticism of the film *Lost
Horizon*, which Larry, Nancy and some of the Villa Seurat crew saw three
or four times.[64] All the latest American and British films were presented in
English in the big cinemas along the Champs-Élysées, and Larry was
determined to see those he had missed by living on Corfu.

Anaïs disliked loud, boisterous fun, and even Nancy, who certainly
enjoyed a good laugh, had a somewhat inhibiting effect on the men, so the
Villa Seurat cronies saved their wildest flights for bachelor evenings. When
the 'Gostersool' mood was upon him, the serious Reichel could be a good
comic, but Henry and Larry awarded the palm to Fred. Once he shifted
into an Austrian accent and took Hitler off like a twin, his eyes glittering
wickedly, his voice straining in mock-German and then in passionate
recitations of German poetry. Glasses were smashed and Fred, barefoot,
was soon prancing on the table and leaving bloody tracks everwhere. This
inspired him to a new frenzy of bombast and invention, while Henry and
Larry became hysterical with laughter, singing 'Die Lorelei' and other
German songs along with Fred.[65]

The Booster, like a runaway train, was getting ready to jump the rails.
Fred and Henry fully intended to push the magazine beyond all limits, and
when one of them said, 'Come on, Joe, let's fuck it up, Joe,' the other would
reply, 'OK, Joe!'[66] The last straw was 'Nukarpiartekak', a story Larry had
located in a collection of tales from Greenland and printed in translation:
an aged Eskimo disappears entirely into the vagina of a young woman. The
only subsequent evidence of his existence is the small skeleton she passes
into the snow next morning. In the following issue the editors printed
Elmer S. Prather's 'Announcement' of the Club's 'complete disassociation
with the journal'. 'Congratulations!' wrote Henry to Larry, 'we are *free*
men!'[67] Fred, Larry and Henry kept the original name until the 'Air-
Conditioned Womb Number' of December 1937–January 1938, their
fourth. After this issue, the Club threatened a lawsuit if the editors

continued to use the *Booster* name. With the unapologetic notice that 'circumstances imposed upon us a title which we did our best to live down to', the cronies changed the name of the journal to *Delta* and continued publication for three numbers. The roster of authors published in the seven *Booster/Delta* issues would years later ensure high prices at book auctions: aside from the works of the 'celebrated quartet' of editors, poetry and prose by Mulk Raj Anand, Kay Boyle, Roy Fuller, David Gascoyne, James Laughlin, Artur Lundkvist, Anaïs Nin, Kostes Palamas, Raymond Queneau, Dylan Thomas and many others appeared.

SHARING LODGINGS WITH FRED PERLÈS might be hilarious, but from the first it had been regarded as a temporary measure. Anaïs took Nancy in hand to search for rooms, and within weeks they had arranged to rent a quite luxurious flat at 21 rue Gazan along the eastern edge of the Parc de Montsouris. After the spartan whitewash and crude, bright peasant décor of their various homes on Corfu, Nancy was delighted with the Parisian elegance of the apartment. It was above street level and overlooked the park through an enormous window – the kind Larry wanted for the new rooms Totsa was building for them in Kalami. The rue Gazan flat was on two levels: a kitchen and a large studio below, and up one flight a bathroom and a bedroom with a balcony. Fred took Nancy to the *marché aux puces* where for a small sum they bought a few pieces of furniture and some tableware. A stroll diagonally across the rolling lawns of the park brought Larry and Nancy to within a few streets of the Villa Seurat.

David Gascoyne, a young Surrealist poet, appeared at 18 Villa Seurat, tapping diffidently on Henry's door. Gascoyne was as pale as a denizen of a cloister or a crypt, a good foot taller than Larry, but emanating from him was the ethereal sensitivity of the Salisbury Cathedral chorister that he had been. Anaïs called him 'the English poet who looks just as an English poet should look'.[68] Larry immediately discovered common ground with this painfully tentative visitor: they were both determined to avoid the parochial in their poetry. David carried off a typescript of *The Black Book* to read. This put the seal on their friendship: although he found the journals embedded in *The Black Book* 'horrifying', he discovered that, like himself, Larry was 'engaged on a sort of adventure of experience to which documents of this kind are particularly relevant'. For this reason and 'because you are an expert on the English Death, and what I have written here seems to deal almost entirely in one way and another, even if not deliberately, with precisely that', David resolved to let Larry read his unpublished journal.[69] Larry responded with 'Paris Journal/For David Gascoyne', a poem that captured his new friend's juxtaposition of quotidian reality with psychological and romantic depth: his surrealism – and his struggle with despair and death, not unlike Larry's own:

> But today Sunday. The pit.
> The axe and the knot. Cannot write.
> The monster in its booth.
> At a quarter to one the mask repeating:
> 'Truth is what is
> Truth is what is Truth?'[70]

Not everyone was as willing as Larry to put up with David's moods. Anaïs pronounced him 'a mystical, poetic boy, but bound like a dead Arab by multiple tight white bandages'. She also read his diary, which she found 'full of reticences and evasions' – unlike her own, which was blazingly explicit in its unrevised form. 'I love Larry,' Anaïs confessed to her diary, 'but I have no warmth for Gascoyne. He leaves me cold in spite of his suffering.'[71]

David was poor to the point of going hungry, and the almost daily lunches at Larry and Nancy's flat probably saved him from malnutrition. Even more welcome than the food was the conversation. David and Larry engaged in a continuing argument about religion with Larry proclaiming himself a pagan, and David advocating Christianity 'in the tradition of Langland, of Dame Juliana – Julian of Norwich – of George Herbert, of Thomas Traherne, of Thomas Browne, and later of Gerard Manley Hopkins and Coventry Patmore'. David claimed that this was an 'English' Christianity, of which 'the whole point is love and forgiveness, "Love and do what you like"'.[72] Larry might agree with the last part of David's statement, but he was not about to strike his pagan colours.

Among the other visitors to Larry and Nancy's flat was Buffie Johnson. She chanced to arrive once when Count Geoffrey Potocki, in the full regalia of his self-proclaimed *ambassade* to France, was holding forth. He and Larry were discussing Gregorian music. Buffie listened quietly. She wondered whether Count Geoffrey were not at once a Catholic monseigneur and a secular prince. Then the conversation switched to the recent abdication of Edward VIII, and Potocki's halo exploded for Buffie when she heard him say, 'Well, of course, I was picketing Buckingham Palace when I was arrested. I was uneasy because I was afraid they would find the pornographic pictures in the bottoms of my sleeves.'[73] He indicated his soutane. She received a further jolt when Potocki switched to the subject of his favourite sexual ploy, conducted *à trois*, in which the third member was a servant whose sole function was to assist the principals in attaining the correct postures.[74]

Anaïs Nin had fallen under Larry's spell as quickly as had Henry and Fred, and new projects sprouted like dragons' teeth. Soon the Villa Seurat Series was launched to publish *The Black Book*, Henry's *Max and the White Phagocytes*, and Anaïs's *Winter of Artifice*. The £150 it cost to print the three titles came from Nancy's capital. 'I used to write to . . . the Midland Bank and say, "Sell another £200 worth of stocks,"' Nancy recalled.[75]

The publisher of the Villa Seurat Series was Jack Kahane of the Obelisk Press, and in his *Memoirs of a Booklegger*, published two years later, Kahane coolly took credit for having 'started' the whole project, mentioning Henry as editor but omitting the fact that Nancy had underwritten the cost. Passing over his early reluctance to publish *The Black Book*, Kahane hazarded a prediction, after *Time* magazine had devoted a page to Larry and Henry, that 'my two perhaps most notable writers, Lawrence Durrell and Henry Miller', would do well: Miller was already 'abundantly one of the most important of Americans', and Durrell would 'in a very short time' reach an equivalent position among 'living English writers'.[76] Larry called Kahane – to Henry, and with some justice – a 'weathercock'.

Perhaps the most unusual member of the Villa Seurat group was Hans Reichel. A year younger than Henry, he was short, broad-shouldered, with long arms and slender fingers; his heavy eyelids hooded eyes of an almost infinite sadness. There was something about him of the amphibian: his morose, thin-lipped stare suggested the regard of a wise frog or, to Larry, a watchful chameleon. Once he told Henry with great joy that he was sure that the fish in the pool at the Parc de Montsouris had spoken to him that day. 'More than anyone I ever knew Reichel lived almost entirely in the spirit,' wrote Henry.[77] He inhabited a tiny room at the Hôtel des Terrasses on the rue de la Glacière, painting his small, meticulous watercolours of fish and birds in the cramped space. Somehow, Reichel existed there for at least seven years. The summer of Larry's arrival in Paris, Henry took Betty Ryan to visit Reichel, and in October of the same year, on Henry's suggestion, Betty held an exhibition of the artist's paintings in her large flat. There were some substantial sales, and on the proceeds Reichel rented a large, square room at 7 impasse du Rouet. He moved his bed into a corner of the room and set up his painting table and chair in the centre. For a time, Perlès and David Edgar lived upstairs. Edgar, 'a secretive, anxious-looking man who almost never laughed',[78] was preoccupied with mysticism and spoke endlessly on Rudolf Steiner, Lao Tzu, yoga, Zen Buddhism to Henry, Larry, Reichel and anyone else who would listen.

Reichel hated to sell his oils and aquarelles, turning the walls of his room and even the back of the door into a personal museum. Accorded the recognition of major retrospectives after his death at the Museum of Modern Art in Paris, in Cologne, in his home town of Würzburg, and at the Guggenheim in New York, Reichel in the 1930s was virtually unknown and desperately poor. Nancy remembered him 'flap[ping] along the roads in an old overcoat', and thought that 'he gave the impression of being tragic, pathetic, and tremendously over-emotional'.[79] Nancy ignored a side of Reichel that Henry and Larry cherished, his Bavarian *Heiterkeit*, his gaiety. He could be a superb clown, but his laughter was sardonic, Larry remembered: 'Reichel had a laugh, at once mirthful and Faustian, a laugh that could tarnish a mirror.'[80] He was a study in absolute dedication, and refined his watercolours endlessly, painting his fish and faces with repeated tiny strokes, until the colours were set indelibly into the paper. 'You must work the paint right into the pores of the paper as if it were kisses penetrating human skin with the *idea* of love,' Reichel told Larry.[81] Reichel had a way of seeing objects and paintings as distinct worlds unto themselves and analysed one of Nancy's paintings in terms of geography: 'Yes. You see there is a way in *here*, and there is a way out *there*.'[82] He explained the concept similarly to Larry: 'In my paintings I try and leave a door to enter and a door to exit by.' 'Sometimes he would call me his "little golden mouse",' recalled Larry; 'at other times I was (he was right) an opinionated imbecile.' Reichel's utter sincerity disarmed Larry, who remembered him as 'Beloved Hans!' Reichel's gentleness belied the passion he felt for pure thought. 'Once he took a hammer and a nail with the intention of driving a perfectly simple idea into my youthful head,' Larry remembered, 'but of course when he placed the nail on my brow and I invited him to drive it home . . . he threw them both away. So I never learned what that vital idea was.'[83]

Miller wrote a celebratory essay, 'The Cosmological Eye', about Reichel, whose pictures often contain at least one eye. 'I want that the pictures should look back at me,' Reichel explained; 'if I look at them and they don't look at me too then they are no good.'[84] This communication should also go on between figures, even objects, said Reichel. In the 'Letter for the

Gostersools' – souls – Reichel wrote, 'Two flowers are looking mutual in each other's eyes – an understanding and they fly away as butterflies!' Appropriately, for his 'Letter' was to appear in the *Booster* 'Tri-lingual Womb Number', Reichel added in his trilingual patois, 'That what people calls "Gesunder Menschenverstand" n'exist pas. And insanity not more and not less than a new Dimension!'[85] The search for new dimensions in *The Alexandria Quartet*, the intermittently insane characters in the future *Avignon Quintet*, were prefigured by the German artist. The editorial trio of *The Booster* gave Reichel's 'Letter' the imprimatur of a note in boldfaced letters: 'Once again the artist proves that when a man has something to say it doesn't matter how he says it.'[86] Or where he went, including to Jimmy's Bar to hear Valaida Snow, the black 'Queen of the Trumpet' who was admired by people as diverse as Louis Armstrong and Queen Wilhelmina. Larry and Henry came away with an advertisement for *The Booster* touting Jimmy's Bar: 'Valaida Snow of Jimmy's bar/ Brings Gostersools from near and far . . . Say to the driver Cat Roo Igg Hens' – 4 rue Huyghens.[87]

Anaïs Nin was a more complicated person than Hans Reichel. She stood out as an individual even in the iconoclastic world of artistic Paris; she was as cosmopolitan as Reichel was self-confined to the subaqueous world of his twilight room and of the Brasserie Zeyer. Havana and New York, Spain and France mingled in Nin's cultural heritage. Her favoured meeting places were not the Dôme but the somewhat more patrician Deux Magots or the newer Coupole with its brilliant neon signs. Larry remembered her in a black cape floating homeward through the little park across from the Closerie des Lilas – always dramatically turned out, always on camera.

The delicate beauty of Anaïs's triangular white face and her genteel bearing masked a will of titanium, as well as a ruthless precision in writing that had already won Larry's awed admiration, particularly for the 'little birth passage' from the then-unpublished diary. When Larry and Nancy arrived in Paris, the diary already amounted to over forty-five notebook volumes. Anaïs made sure that her friends were all very aware of her notebooks: 'This diary was almost like another person,' Nancy recalled. 'She talked about it; Henry talked about it; everybody talked about it – everybody was afraid of Anaïs's diary.' It was 'a terrific *monster* of a thing lurking in the background', and the diarist's friends worried about what she would say about them. Nancy was astounded at the rapidity with which Anaïs could turn experience into art: 'I mean, she had an appalling abortion in the morning, and by the afternoon she'd written about it and transformed it into a work of art.'[88] As Anaïs's husband Hugh Guiler once said, wavering between pride and exasperation, 'I have an exaggerated wife.'[89]

In turn, Larry perplexed and intrigued Anaïs. 'I have known Lawrence Durrell for a thousand years,' she confided to her diary. 'He is a boy of ten playing in the Himalayas with the snow disease on him (the English disease of impersonality),' she wrote. In Larry's 'Asylum in the Snow', sent to Henry and Anaïs from Corfu, snow became a metaphor for madness, for isolation. Henry and Fred saw Larry as impulsive and spontaneous. Not Anaïs: her Larry was 'an old man in some ways, who does not live impulsively but cautiously, he is a spectator, he is a boy who laughs.'[90] Henry and Fred were right, but Anaïs was righter. Again, she wrote, 'This English obsession with impersonality makes him a spectator, makes him seem withdrawn, at the same time warm.'[91] Larry claimed that what seemed impersonality was really modesty, and that Anaïs believed him reserved because her nature made him quiet: 'You do not shout around fine china,' he recalled years later. Some assumed that Larry was carrying on an affair with Anaïs. 'No, I'm sorry to say,' testified Larry. He added, with a pensive downward glance, 'And it's too bad, since Henry told me she was a star performer.' At other times Larry merely said that he had not wanted to be 'one of the four hundred in Paris' to have bedded her.[92] Perhaps Larry shied away from an entanglement with someone as will-driven and consuming as Anaïs, someone he regarded as Henry's woman – a scruple that might then have restrained Larry. Nor did he want a starring role in her great sea monster of a diary. She christened him 'Peter Pan Larry' – an appellation revealing of their relationship, since he was to prove one of the few men close to her for whom she would never express a specific sexual interest.[93]

Larry, with Nancy as chaperone, spent long evenings on *La Belle Aurore*, the houseboat Anaïs kept tied up at the quai d'Orsay. On some of these occasions Conrad Moricand, Henry's astrologer and sometime parasite, arrived fastidiously decked out in a pressed suit, yellow gloves and cane, hair waved, trailing an effluvium of eau de cologne and baby powder, to deliver long monologues on his occult science. Anaïs presided like a high priestess in a holy fane, revelling in the rustle of the Seine and the slight creak and sway of the *Belle Aurore*, the soft candlelight, the precise French syllables of Moricand's discourse.

Henry was the most secure among the three of them in having found his artistic voice, but the Villa Seurat nexus was of inestimable importance to them all. Anaïs recognized 'how we mutually nourish each other, stimulate each other', and even claimed that Larry 'could have been, symbolically speaking, the writer child of Henry and myself'. Larry admired as 'anti-romantic' the unflinching way Henry described degradation, joy, sex, anguish. Anaïs saw Larry's 'impersonality', whether in his writing or in his relations with his friends, as stemming from his suppressed romantic inclinations.[94] Also, he was still insecure about his talent, as Anaïs realized: 'There is a miracle about his creation,' she wrote in her diary. 'He is a bit amazed. He walks the familiar streets with a vague uneasiness.'[95] Larry was also unsure about his direction. He stood hesitating between Anaïs's preoccupation with feelings and emotions, and Henry's ruthless explora-tion of the five senses. They agreed that Henry was the strongest of them all, because he was not afraid to be alone. 'Larry is afraid. I am afraid,' Anaïs said.[96]

The Villa Seurat friendships purported to be grounded in frank criticism, but although Henry had encouraged Anaïs to write the vivid truth from the very first, she complained that he 'attacked' her diary as 'anti-art'.[97] Sensing her need of faith in herself, Larry countered Henry's criticisms by urging him to get portions of the diary, 'the real red meat', for *The Booster*[98] and by praising her for 'writing as a woman, for not breaking the umbilical connection'. Contradicting himself, Larry also told her, 'You must make the leap outside of the womb, destroy your connections.' He and Henry joined forces in condemning her 'personal relation to all things' – an odd argument on Henry's part, since no one injected more of himself into his writings than Henry, but an understandable one on Larry's side, given his instinct for disguising the personal, even when he was employing the diary form in *The Black Book*. Anaïs admitted that 'Henry's respect is also reawakened by Durrell's admiration for me,' by his often-proclaimed understanding of her writing. On some occasions Anaïs noted a 'beautiful flow between Durrell, Henry, Nancy and me,' long, earnest discussions. She saw herself as speaking for all women against the allied pronouncements of Larry and Henry. Larry accused her writing of lacking form, saying that this was due to her female reliance on intuition, to her feminine sensibility. Finally, Larry and Henry agreed, 'We have a real woman artist before us, the first one, and we ought not to put her down.'[99]

Like Anaïs, Larry felt considerable self-doubt, and Anaïs's and Henry's approval gave him a tremendous boost: 'He is unsure of himself,' Anaïs said, 'but we are sure of him.'[100] The knowledge that his two main co-conspirators in Paris believed in him *artistically* was even more important to Larry than the thrilling discussions of Lao Tzu, Otto Rank, Proust, Spengler, Rousseau, and the avant-garde films.

Larry often picked up ideas for future work from his friends. In November he sent Anaïs a copy of 'Down the Styx', a strange surrealist prose piece that he had evidently just composed, a guide for the journey of Aunt Prudence into the underworld, an after-life depicted in terms hinting at a return to the womb. Anaïs found it 'both concrete, fleshly and fantastic . . . monstrous and possible'. Further, she told Larry, 'You have given us the WOMB for once and for all.'[101] She was reminded of Verne's *Voyage to the Centre of the World*, which she described to Larry as 'all about what happened to a party of people who went inside of the earth through the volcanic caverns'.[102] Apparently taking the hint from her, Larry drafted in the midst of the Aunt Prudence passages in his Paris notebook an outline for a drama to be called 'The Maze': the plot would be similar to that of his much later *Cefalû* or *The Dark Labyrinth* – a group of people become lost in a subterranean labyrinth.[103]

However much Larry may have tried to escape the political exigencies of 1937, they kept crowding in on him. Anaïs, assisted by her Spanish friends Helba and Gonzalo Moré, was collecting clothing for refugees from the civil war in Spain. Everyone recognized that Spain was the terrible prelude to a far wider conflict, yet Larry, Henry and Fred, disillusioned and sceptical about Allied leadership, seem to have been better than most writers at shutting out the world situation. Larry at least felt the helpless despair of the young at a future in grave doubt and at his own impotence. Fred and Henry, unmarried and without close family ties, could focus their energies on personal survival. Fred, Henry predicted, would prosper, 'like a bedbug'. Henry had wild fantasies: if he could only meet Hitler and make him *laugh*, world catastrophe could be averted. The Villa Seurat friends had a long history of being anti-military. Reichel was a pacifist who had been imprisoned in Germany in 1914 after announcing, 'I will not shoot at a living man.'[104] In this he resembled Fred, who had been court-martialled and subsequently committed to a mental hospital during the First World War for failing to give an order to fire on advancing enemy troops. Larry, sporadically conscious of being the head of two households and, despite his estrangement from Pudding Island, possessing stronger national loyalties than his companions, was reduced to anguished indecision.

Larry was not able to avoid conflict when he attempted literary criticism, however. T. S. Eliot delivered a metaphorical slap when Larry submitted his essay 'Poet's Horn-Book' to *The Criterion*. With exquisite tact, Eliot pointed out the impropriety of his publishing an article that praised his own – Eliot's – poetry while it 'dismiss[ed] Ezra Pound in a phrase'; that placed in the same category Wyndham Lewis, whom Eliot called 'one of the most living of living writers', and Huxley, 'one of the deadest'. Eliot warned Larry against too much 'critical activity', saying that there was 'a danger for you as a creative writer in critical work which is particularly concerned with making conscious the activity of your creative mind'. Eliot gave as an instance his own decision to 'leave Shakespeare alone for some time to come' after discovering that his recent lectures on Shakespeare were really concerned with his personal theatrical intentions.[105]

Larry defended and expanded his statements in 'Poet's Horn-Book' in a long letter to Eliot. He had known that his essay was both 'impertinent' and, at ten thousand words, too long, and had not expected Eliot to print it. His piece was really an attempt to set down 'in a single pill' what Henry Miller called 'this whole God business'. Larry had set out to write something 'that looked like reason and was really a defense of unreason', despite realizing, he said, that Bergson, Spengler and Nietzsche had already fully explored this territory. Miller's criticism of Lawrence was entirely 'creative', whereas F. R. Leavis seemed 'at bottom *uncertain of himself*': 'all his theses . . . soft cheese'. Larry was trying to sound a few chords in between the two, but his own pronouncements were grounded on passionate intuition: 'I feel always about art that it must rape me, as it were, squeeze me dry; like John Donne addressing Lord God in the religious sonnets.' 'Poet's Horn-Book' was very personal: 'With Pound I confess to a blind spot in me,' Larry admitted, although he was 'a very gifted literary gent'; 'Huxley has already demolished himself'; Wyndham Lewis might be 'POTENTIALLY . . . a very great man, but he lacks *pnevma*, somehow'. Yes, Larry had to agree that he and Henry attached too much importance to Lawrence. He might be 'a rotten artist at bottom', Larry admitted, but 'I like the struggle in him.'[106]

Larry was flattered by Eliot's interest, but warned his mentor, 'I do not intend to continue along the straight and narrow path very far. My job is to throw myself over precipices.'[107]

THERE WAS MUCH DISCUSSION in Larry's Paris circle about *The Black Book*, being passed around in typescript. Henry still found it alarming that it could be the work of one so young, and wondered what was going on inside Larry's sun-bleached boyish head. Fred, who like Henry was many years older than Larry, reacted similarly to him: 'To tell the truth, Larry never struck me as a child, not even a child prodigy. He baffled me from the very start . . . . it seemed as though he never had to go through a transition state, never had to break through a chrysalis, like most artists of genius. It frightened me a little because I couldn't understand it, it made no sense.'[108] In their artistic appraisals of Larry, Fred and Henry had to agree with Anaïs: somewhere inside lurked a wise old man. Larry's verse and fiction even before *The Black Book* often show a precocious control over his material, an astounding range of vocabulary; even, in embryo, many of the ideas that he would propound in his later fiction. Considered together, his first three novels form a trilogy centring on alienation, loneliness and death, and the development of the artist. But it was in *The Black Book* that Larry announced himself as a rebel, that he declared his true fictional colours.

In narrative technique, characterization, tone and ideas, *The Black Book* is the recognizable ancestor of the novels to follow. The story is told in a mélange of diary excerpts, flashback narrations and even a letter. The multiple points of view in *The Alexandria Quartet* are prefigured here by the use of two narrators to describe the same, or nearly the same, characters and events: Lawrence Lucifer, who has escaped from the 'English death' to live on a Greek island, and Horace 'Death' Gregory, the 'irrepressible dying diarist'.[109] Consequently the reader is given two distinct points of view.

Many of the characters are memorable: Gracie, casual prostitute dying of tuberculosis, rises above the cliché with her unflinching rejoinder, delivered with a husky chuckle from her 'wonky' lung: *'And the same to you with knobs on!'*[110] The aesthete Tarquin is brought to life, Henry Miller maintained, by the query, delivered in a conversational tone, 'Look, do you think it would damage our relationship if I sucked you off?'[111] *The Black Book* is a novel of personalities and ideas, not actions, a novel of exorcism, the laying of the ghost of the England Larry hated and rejected. He worried so much out loud that Gawsworth might recognize aspects of himself in Horace Gregory that Audrey Beecham felt moved to set Larry's mind at rest: 'Gawsworth is drinking himself into DTs. He'll be dead before he has time to sue you over your new novel.'[112] Larry said that Tarquin was drawn from life – but just whose, he declined to reveal.[113] The events are secondary: Gregory keeps a diary and befriends Gracie, the street girl he eventually marries and buries; Tarquin discovers that he is a homosexual and declares himself; a collection of medical students from Latin America, literary enthusiasts, whores, navvies and boiler-room caretakers make love and talk about it. Durrell's diatribe against the English death is imaged in the destinies that overtake his characters: Gregory gets married a second time, to a widow he plans to make sure will never experience an orgasm; Chamberlain tries to flee the English death by swallowing D. H. Lawrence uncritically, but he succumbs to paternity and meek domesticity; Tarquin lapses into a febrile state, playing 'the laughing record' over and over on his Victrola; the working poor, including Morgan the caretaker, may avoid the emotional sterility of the intellectuals, but their fates seem to be cancer, venereal disease and the Lock Hospital. Only Lawrence Lucifer, spokesman for the author, is able to escape at once England and the English death, finding creativity in the mainstream of European culture, 'From between your legs leaking, the breathing yoke', and in 'the enormous Now'.[114]

Even those aspects of his writing for which Durrell would later be castigated are already present in *The Black Book*: there is a rich profusion of language, a great lack of economy. Cut, admonished Henry. Larry, carried off in a flood of words, was unwilling or unable to delete much.

WITH THE WAR CLEARLY APPROACHING, the *Booster/Delta* editors swerved up to a more hysterical intensity, hammering out a new manifesto:

We are against strudel baths & fango packs, the slaughter of Chinese and Abyssinians, the killing of birds, particularly quail, and of defenseless snails, rabbits and oysters. We are against treaties & the breaking of treaties, against English wit and humor, the English sense of fair play, English diplomacy, English homosexuality. We are against all isms, including Taoism. We are against Social Credit or any form of credit. We are against all forms of torture, whether perpetrated by the English or any other nation, in the name of humanity. We are against any form of activity which might lead to success.

We are in favor of death on all fours – especially *now*.[115]

The sense of conflict intensified in Larry's personal life as well. On Corfu, Larry and Nancy had had arguments, but Nancy, frequently supported by Larry's mother and siblings, had stood up to him. In Paris it was different. Nancy bore the strain of constant ministration to his needs, of being repeatedly put down in conversation – Henry commented that 'Shut up, Nancy' was Larry's half-joking refrain. Anaïs too was sensitive to the secondary role Larry cast for Nancy. Besides, for Nancy the glow of Paris had worn off: she had had enough. From her point of view, part of the problem was Larry's possessiveness and his need to establish a persona suited to the accomplished artist of *The Black Book*. Nancy thought he resented it when she made friends on her own, and he specifically forbade her to accept Anaïs's invitation to have tea with her on *La Belle Aurore*. Nancy would also have liked to become involved with Anaïs's projects to aid refugees from the Spanish Civil War. However, Larry was jealous of his private life, his and Nancy's 'respectability': 'They are just a lot of bohemians,' he told Nancy, 'and we're not.'[116] To Anaïs he said, 'I hate Bohemianism.'[117]

Larry managed to slant his remarks to suit the audience: he wanted to prevent Nancy from indulging in sexual adventures, while he was appealing to that side of Anaïs that shunned chaos, dirt and disorder. 'The wine bottle has become symbolical,' Anaïs said of Larry. 'This expresses all he is fighting against. He does not want to lose the warmth, the flesh, the odor, the reality.'[118] With her, Larry and Nancy were content to sit in the Guiler apartment and drink coffee.

In December, Larry announced that he wanted to spend a couple of weeks alone in London; he had been corresponding with the psychologist Graham Howe and wanted to see him again, also T. S. Eliot – these were the reasons he gave. Nancy decided she needed her own holiday, especially a change from the city air – or so she said. Their reasons were more serious than either admitted. She wanted to get away from Larry, at least temporarily, and Larry told Buffie Johnson that his marriage was washed up, that Nancy was going away to obtain a divorce. He asked Buffie to accompany him to London and said that he wanted to marry her,[119] but did not confide fully in either Henry or Nancy. Nancy bought skis and a skiing outfit, knitted herself a sweater, and departed defiantly for Austria just after Larry had left for London. 'Saw Nancy off safely at the Gare,' wrote Henry. 'It's strange to see you going different directions.' He appended some advice: 'I hope you will be back soon and nestle down at 21 Rue Gazan. I rather think you'd be better off.'[120]

Marital rupture or not, Larry plunged back into the round of meeting other writers, boosting *The Booster*, and spending hours in the British Museum. He met a pair of ballerinas, Veronica Tester and Dorothy Stevenson, and invited them to Corfu. Veronica's brother Desmond, then a young man and Peter Bull's friend, had been famous as a boy actor, and Dorothy was an Australian who would later become an important dance promoter. Larry also encountered Anna Wickham, whom he dubbed 'the most amazing woman I have yet met in England'.[121] She introduced him to a poet Larry instantly recognized, under the conviviality at 'that squalid house of hers' in Hampstead, as burning with the sacred fire: Dylan Thomas. It was the slim, tidy young Dylan with closely cropped curls, self-possessed and with 'hidden reserves in him', whom Larry met.[122] He detected a jealousy in Caitlin for her husband's talent, and much later would condemn her as a 'bitch-wife' and a 'phallocrat' who had destroyed the tonal shades of Dylan's personality. Despite being 'poorly read' and an 'indeed rather stupid man', Dylan was 'really a *personnage*'.[123] Dylan wrote to Larry that he would have liked to continue their conversation 'in a clean pub . . . but Caitlin and I went away in a pantomime snow.'[124]

Larry took Buffie Johnson to a large party at a house outside London to see Alexander Calder perform a 'Circus' with his manikins. Larry had never met Calder, but there was much talk in avant-garde London and Paris about the sculptor's strange doings and Larry was intrigued. Although Calder's 'mechanical toys' are now part of the permanent collection of the Whitney Museum in New York, at the time it was considered very avant-garde or, worse, frivolous, for a serious artist to be so playful. And playful he was: the tall, lanky Calder sat on the floor surrounded by his mechanical cast, with perfect timing moving rods and touching triggers hidden on one or another figure. His creations would then leap high into the air, turn somersaults or jump through hoops. As Buffie said, Larry always knew what to do, and even though she lost her hat in the excitement, she had a marvellous time.

Nancy said that she had picked Austria for her adventure because everybody seemed to be going to Switzerland, and she wanted something different. She certainly did *not* want to meet anyone who might report back to a jealous Larry. She travelled to Innsbruck and stayed at the luxurious Goldener Adler, where she heard from some chance acquaintance of a place called Mutters – Mother's – high in the snow country. She sent Larry a postcard from Mutters saying it wasn't much fun, that she was moving on. She found a tiny lodge that she had to hike to, deep in a valley with no road. It was a haunt of young ski instructors and their friends, and they were very nice to Nancy. 'It was absolute bliss,' she recalled, a Shangri-La.

Meanwhile, in London Larry had lined up a number of subscribers and prospective contributors to *The Booster*, among them George Reavey, 'a fine nutty little chap', and Hugh Gordon Porteus, poet and Sinologist, who would turn up soon in Athens. Larry came to treasure Porteus for the elegant calligraphy of his letters, embellished with Chinese ideograms, and for his recollections of Wyndham Lewis, subject of a monograph he had written. Gawsworth, as designated heir to M. P. Shiel's disputed claim to the Caribbean island of Redonda, had proclaimed himself King Juan I and had dubbed Larry Don Cervantes Pequeña – a swipe at his shortness – and

Buffie Johnson he created Duchess de la Nueva Castilla de Redonda. Larry and Buffie visited Geoffrey Potocki in the attic that he shared with his brother Cedric. They discovered the two royalists still dividing Poland between them. He knew so many pretenders, Larry confided to Buffie, that he was going to write a book about them.[125]

Larry was enjoying himself, but he was in an emotional turmoil too. On the one hand, he found it daring to be in London with a beautiful woman not his wife. On the other, he imagined Nancy in bed with a succession of large, handsome ski instructors, and wondered if he had really lost her: possession dies hard. Then, too, Buffie insisted on separate rooms in the small hotel they had chosen, although she consented to take breakfast with him in his room, appearing domestically in a dressing gown. It was typically English of the chambermaid to scold them: 'But you aren't *allowed* to be in the same room!'[126] Both Buffie and Larry were angry, but he at least had the nagging feeling that he was at fault. Probably it was a combination of guilt and jealousy that in the end urged Larry to action. When Larry received Nancy's postcard from Mutters, he decided to cut short his visit to London and surprise her. He had already entrusted the editing of the *Delta* poetry number to David Gascoyne and Audrey Beecham. In a great rush Larry bought a couple of heavy art books as Christmas presents and caught the express for Innsbruck, pausing in Paris only long enough to dump Buffie unceremoniously in a hospital – she had collapsed after Larry had announced that it was all over between them.[127]

'Talk about detective-work,' Larry gloated to Henry after he had located his errant wife. 'I did not know her address, town, anything. Went on the hearsay of porters, hoteliers, etc.' He had climbed into bed with a startled Nancy at four in the morning on Christmas Day, 'snotty-nosed, up to the hips in thaw'.[128] 'I don't think my heart has ever sunk quite as much as [at] a cross, cold, damp Larry arriving just as I thought I was going to have a most wonderful time,' said Nancy years later.[129]

Larry ignored Nancy's 'jolly' companions and insisted on returning to Innsbruck after breakfast that very morning. They stayed at the Goldener Adler with its dark, cosy Goethe-Stube public room, candles flickering on the polished wood. 'Now we tear each other's hair out in the very room where the poet Goethe made his celebrated stay in this pearl of a town,' Larry wrote to Henry. Inspired by Goethe and by his own domestic turmoil, Larry bought a lined notebook, dated it 1 January 1938, headed it 'Jupiter in the Ascendant' after his favourite astrological indicator, and the following day drafted a poem entitled 'The Lucky Man'. The poem celebrates a sleep

'Deeper purer surer even than Eden', but hints at the quarrel with Nancy: 'What was bitter in the apple is eaten deep.' He imagined that in one of their reconciliations Nancy had conceived, for he wrote:

> Twin tides speak making of two three
> By fission by fusion, a logarithmic sea.[130]

Larry would not publish this poem until 1960, perhaps perceiving that it revealed too much of his private life, and even then he changed the title to 'The Cottager': the original title must then have seemed far too ironic.

Larry and Nancy went from Innsbruck up to Gris for a week of desultory skiing, which Larry had never attempted before and found he did not enjoy. 'Bloody snow,' he lamented to Henry, 'O bloody.'[131] Besides, he had acute tonsillitis and swollen gums. He and Nancy were still furious with one another; it was a miserable beginning for the new year.

THE JUPITER NOTEBOOK reflects the tensions of Larry's marriage over the next few months. 'Told me she'd be jealous', Larry began a short verse with the annotation 'Jazz Song'. He and Nancy still saw themselves as a joint creative venture, however. Larry wrote a poem entitled 'On Amanda Ros', beginning 'Compel the lion to speak' and illustrated by a wood-block print, evidently by Nancy, showing a lion speaking to a woman. Nancy was not after all pregnant, but Larry's thoughts kept returning to childbirth, with notes on Rank's *Trauma of Birth* succeeded by a poem draft headed 'Nursery Rhyme'. The final item in the short notebook is a press photograph showing birth defects: two generations of a Brazilian family born without hands or feet.[132] The womb, both in *The Black Book* and in his discussions with Anaïs on creativity, was a central symbol for Larry, but he was acutely aware that writers, like mothers, could bring forth monsters. The poet must strive to experience birth and death, Larry would say much later.[133]

Bad news arrived from Faber, and Larry wrote in mock outrage to Eliot, 'I WAS RIVEN BY THE REFUSAL OF UNCEBUNKE.' Larry added as a Parthian shot, 'I have dropped the Vicar of Stiffkey,'[134] referring to the satire he had been writing. On 10 January he and Nancy left Innsbruck for Paris.

Larry was seriously upset by the rejection of his poems, and Alan Pringle as well as Eliot discouraged him from attempting a book of essays. Eliot chided him for abandoning the 'Vicar of Stiffkey', 'just as we were beginning to get used to the idea': 'What bloody business are you going to be about next?'[135] The answer was determined by economics. Larry was having a 'row' with Pringle over money: he wanted an advance on a book of poetry, and was told that Faber would only consider a payment against a novel.[136] Therefore a novel was what Larry would write next. 'I scared up some monsters from my memories of London and fell to work,' he told Eliot. 'It goes stickily but quite powerfully so far.'[137] Although Larry did not breathe the title to Eliot, this was evidently the beginning of 'The Book of the Dead', progenitor of *The Alexandria Quartet*. When his draft stuck fast, Larry started over again, and yet again, writing in February to Alan Thomas, 'I am up to my ears in all kinds of work,' including 'three simultaneous novels', proofs of *The Black Book*, and essays for *The Aryan Path* of Bombay and for Dorothy Norman, about to launch *Twice a Year*. In the same letter Larry told Alan, 'I can't work' – he had too many friends.[138] Of his many projects only the essay, 'Tao and Its Glozes', written for *The Aryan Path*, would be completed and published.

The tone of his 'note' on Lao Tzu is in stark contrast to the pace and conflicts of Larry's life. Calm, reflective, measured, he set out to 'disentangle the conflicting fibres of doctrine and statement' in the *Tao Te Ching*, 'The Book of the Simple Way'. 'A huge and corrupt dogmatic theology' had sprung up around the '*practice* of Tao', Larry wrote, and this had obscured the denial of the striving ego that is at the heart of the Tao:

There is, to write nicely, no human entity; it is merged in the All. Here there is no trace of the rupture between the individual and his scenery. Fused, there remains only the gigantic landscape of the spirit, in which our Aryan problem ('To be, or not to be') is swallowed up, exhausted, sucked dry by the eternal factor, the Tao. The house admits its resident: the tenant is absorbed, like a piece of tissue, into the very walls of his spiritual house. The world of the definition is exploded.

Thus Larry turned to the Tao for support as he attempted to see his way through his frenetic activities to an inner space on a higher plane. Striving was self-defeating: 'When a man with a taste for reforming the world takes the business in hand, it is easily seen that there is no end to it. For spiritual vessels are not fashioned in the world. Whoever makes, destroys; whoever grasps, loses,' he quoted from Lao Tzu.[139] This statement of the primacy of the spirit seemed strikingly appropriate in 1938, with the war looming; it would remain current for Larry more than forty years later, when he chose to reprint his entire Tao essay as the concluding section of *A Smile in the Mind's Eye*, his brief philosophic autobiography.

The Tao was a soothing influence. Larry and Nancy called a truce, and he extolled marriage to Alan: 'It is a very blessed state indeed.' Then he added, wounds still fresh, stripping any hint of tender feelings from his praise, 'A real pivot from which a man can get to work.' Larry concealed the circumstances of his trip to London before Christmas, saying only that 'we' had considered living in a cottage in England for a year 'to be nearer our work and contacts', but that the need for sun was driving them back to Greece in April. 'As always happens when I leave people's interest in me evaporates,' he lamented. 'Everything caves in. Lousy world.' There were financial difficulties too: *Night and Day*, three months after printing 'Obituary Notice: A Tragedy' by 'Charles Norden', illustrated by Nancy, had collapsed, owing them £20, and to add to the insult, returned their manuscripts with postage due.[140] Now, when Reichel was especially hard up and was offering his painting *Pyramid of Fishes* for £6, Larry, who coveted the work, had no money: 'Broke, broke, broke.' Why did he not simply raid Nancy's bank account? Obviously there remained some strain between them, and money – or its scarcity – provided a focus for anger. Also, he and Nancy were caught up in the Villa Seurat Series publishing venture, and she was asserting herself. Her money was paying for the project, and she took an active part in it. Nancy basked in the approval both Henry and Hans Reichel expressed for her own art.

Larry escaped to view a pair of 'hallucinating' films, Cocteau's *Le sang d'un poète* and Dali and Buñuel's *Un chien andalou*. He also took in a René Clair film called *Ultra acte*. He wrote to Eliot, 'This is the form of the future,' adding, 'From now, if I have anything dramatic to do, I shall do it in a scenario.'[141] In particular, the easy time shifts of the cinema appealed to him.

On a cold spring day in March, Henry and David Gascoyne lunched at the Durrells' flat, 'arguing, futilely, about war and war-resistance', with Larry advocating involvement in the conflict. Henry took a qualified stand against David: 'Yes, Durrell's probably right; because he's a man, if ever there was one, who's so strongly favoured by Fortune, that even if he were fighting in the front line, he could be pretty certain of coming through without a scratch. But you're not like that,' Henry continued to David. 'You ask for trouble; your destiny can only be a tragic one.'[142] Gascoyne's trouble with Anaïs, when it came, was not of his seeking. Knowing that he desperately needed funds, she entrusted him with typing out a volume of her 'black children'. David had to return to London in the last week of March, and so he took her diary with him to finish the typing there. Larry had set out with David, planning a round of errands before returning to Greece, but he turned back at Gare St Lazare, crying, 'O God, I've forgotten something!' Larry followed on a later train. When Anaïs found out, said Gascoyne, 'that I had actually dared to take this precious journal across the Channel, she was *really* furious, and I'm afraid that was the end of a beautiful friendship.'[143]

On 8 April Larry flew back to Paris, and by the 10th he and Nancy were on the train heading for Corfu. She, at least, was glad to leave Paris, and looked forward to seeing Louisa Durrell and the rest of the family. Three young women, Buffie, Betty Ryan and Anaïs, noticed the strain in Nancy: Buffie still thought that the marriage would break up, whether or not she saw Larry again;[144] Betty noted that Nancy lacked 'spark'; and Anaïs recorded that Nancy had said to Larry, 'Perhaps you are dissatisfied with me,' to which he had responded, 'I am, but that does not mean I want to change, or that I want anyone else.'[145] In Betty Ryan's phrase, she was 'nice, but not *more* than nice',[146] and held herself somewhat aloof. Nancy did not entirely fit in, either with the wild crew at the Villa Seurat or in Anaïs's somewhat precious world of Oriental glass trees and esoteric conversations. And Larry's hectoring did not help Nancy's already low self-esteem. Henry had recognized her dissatisfaction and, in a rambling six-page letter to Larry written at the Castiglione Bar, included a line of advice to her: 'Don't let Larry browbeat you.'[147]

THEODORE STEPHANIDES WAS WITH Larry and Nancy when Spiro Americanos drove them from Corfu town to Guimari, and he walked with them down the donkey trail to Kalami. Larry was eager to move into the new rooms Athenaios had only half completed before their trip. From the distance they could see that the upper storey was finished, gleaming with new whitewash, tile-roofed. When they reached the beach and could see the seaward wall of the house, 'a roar of rage burst from Lawrence when it became evident that, although Athenaios had been worsted in *argument*, he had had the advantage of carrying out the *work* of building,' Theodore said. 'The seaward aspect of the upper storey had two *small* windows!'[148] Nancy and Theodore had difficulty in persuading Larry not to leave immediately, and for many weeks he would barely speak to Athenaios.

Eventually Larry became reconciled to the new rooms, with their white walls displaying Nancy's quiet paintings, framed by a few shelves of books. Larry made his peace with Athenaios after the autumn gales proved the Greek right about the need to have a tight seaward side. And their new quarters were really splendid. The sea below the windows 'runs golden on the ceilings, reflecting back the bright peasant rugs – a ship, a gorgon, a loom, a cypress-tree,' wrote Larry. Crude pottery gleamed on the table.

Nancy, 'calm eyes, calm hair,' sat reading 'with her legs tucked under her', her 'clear white teeth like those of a young carnivore'. Larry quoted Father Nicholas, their mason: 'What more does a man want than an olive-tree, a native island, and a woman from his own place?'[149] To be sure, Larry wrote these lines at a safe distance of more than five years after the marital tensions of 1938.

London and Paris had lashed Larry into frenzies of mental agitation and physical desire, neither drive centred on Nancy. Back in the calm of the White House, their marriage, although hardly tranquil, settled back into a companionable routine. Larry depended upon Nancy in many ways, from the handling of their domestic economy to her judgements on his writing. A part of him was convinced that he loved her, but clearly he still took her for granted.

Back in Paris, Anaïs and Henry were left to deal with the Durrells' landlord. They had departed owing him money, without giving notice, without even clearing out the flat – beyond holding a ceremonial burning of books they did not want. Anaïs and Henry made a daring raid to rescue a few valuable books, but finally they had to settle with the landlord to the tune of 1200 francs plus taxes owed to the government. Larry had left other loose ends to be tied up as well. In May the publisher James Cooney demanded an advance of $150 before starting to print 'Asylum in the Snow' and 'Zero'. This was paid, and soon Anaïs wrote that the manuscripts had been sent to him. Nothing happened: the project fell through. She and Henry were also proof-reading the galleys of *The Black Book* and haggling with the typesetter. 'It's been a devil of a time with the printer,' complained Henry.[150] On top of all this, Anaïs was finishing *Winter of Artifice* and Henry was working on *Tropic of Capricorn* and proof-reading *Max and the White Phagocytes*. No recriminations were sent flying to Corfu: in their view, Larry was worth all the time stolen from their own projects.

Working at breakneck speed on all fronts, Henry had an accident in June: he fell from the top of a ladder in the studio and cut himself on the skylight. Betty Ryan's friend Nicola Chiaromonte, staying in her flat, rushed to the rescue and carted Henry to the hospital to be stitched up. 'I always enjoy these little mishaps,' said Henry, thankful for the rest.[151]

WHILE LARRY AND NANCY WERE in Paris and London, Louisa Durrell had moved to her third house on Corfu, the 'Snow-White Villa' described in Gerald's *My Family* volume. The Palatiano family, who owned the place, knew it by the more poetic name of the Villa Cressida or Chrysida, and it was hidden in a copse of cypress and olive trees not more than a mile from the Villa Agazini. A tiny limewashed stone chapel stood in the grounds, and near it was a conical hillock suitable for violent fortress games. Larry and Nancy came to the Villa Cressida for a few days whenever the seclusion of Kalami became too much for them. Or, as Larry phrased it, 'you can have a little too much even of Paradise and a little taste of Hell every now and then is good for my work – keeps my brain from stagnating. You can trust Gerry to provide the Hell.'[152]

Suddenly it was full summer, and with the summer came visitors in the form of Larry's ballerinas, Dorothy Stevenson and Veronica Tester. He had been in the midst of writing 'The Aquarians' – 'a HUMOUR in the medieval sense'[153] – but he dropped it to organize a trip on the *Van Norden* to Agios Georgios beach, north of Paleocastrizza. Nancy was sure Larry was not in love with either of the girls, and they in turn looked with easy camaraderie on both Larry and Nancy. Nancy admired Dorothy Stevenson and thought that she was a very good dancer.[154] But it was still a time of high tension between Larry and Nancy – at twenty-six, he felt very much the jaded married man – and he did not help matters by insisting on sleeping under the stars on the sand between the two lithe girls. Neither did it help when, in emulation of the ancient satyrs, he danced naked with them on the beach. After Dorothy departed, Nancy and Veronica went off together to Athens, 'probably celebrating their escape from the tyrant,' Larry commented to Henry.[155]

Larry's discontent took the form of increased testiness. He was particularly hard on Leslie, who was still coddled by his mother: Larry accused him of wrecking his own life, of doing nothing but run about the fields and shoot off his guns with the *feelika*, the rural police. Leslie retaliated by taking Nancy's side in any quarrel, and would sometimes rush into the room and point a pistol at Larry. Nancy thought it quite possible that he *would* shoot Larry, and she blamed Louisa for letting her younger children grow up with a complete lack of discipline.[156] True, she did not have much control over her offspring, and it was easy to think of Louisa as weak, but that is not how she appeared to some outsiders. 'Larry's mother was a doll,' remarked their Greek friend Alexis Ladas, 'but *boy*, what a strong woman!' He saw that her strength lay in 'a kind of imperturbability'.[157] She would need all her serenity in the years to come.

Larry seemed able to switch himself on and off like a radio transmitter. While he was out 'camping on a sand-beach' he had not even written to Henry: 'I had nothing to write with, nor felt anything to write.' He broke silence in mid-August 1938 with a rambling letter. He was doing nothing, Larry said, but was 'as nerveless as an oyster'; 'everything lies and rots in a drawer'; W. T. Symons had rejected his Otto Rank essay for *Purpose* magazine. And what, he wondered, had happened to *The Black Book*? 'I feel I am just ready to know its faults,' he announced. He was still confident about his accomplishment, but was not sure what to try next: 'I am like a man with a cheque for a million in my pocket – but no legs to walk to the bank.' No matter, he continued, 'A little while and the miracle will happen again; I shall rise up on my stumps and run like a hare.'[158]

In fact, *The Black Book* had finally emerged from the toils of the Obelisk Press. Soon Larry held the first copy in his hands, grey wrappers with the title and his name emblazoned in black on the dull salmon front panel. Then, as he leafed through the book, he swore savagely: pages 115, 116 and 117 were mis-numbered and out of order – a printer's error. Henry said that he felt 'lousy' about the blunder that had crept in despite his many proof-readings. There was another disappointment: Kahane had not sent proofs to Eliot so that he could print an excerpt in *The Criterion*, and Larry had counted on the money. To make up the sum, Henry proposed to give Larry enough copies of *Tropic of Cancer* for him to smuggle into England for sale. Larry did not take him up on the offer. He was enough his father's son not to want to profit at the expense of a friend.

The Black Book was, moreover, getting enough favourable notices to please Larry. Paul Rosenfeld in *The Nation* called Larry's 'amazing performance' a successor to Kafka's in the genre of the 'irrational fable'. Rosenfeld also noted the 'parental' relationship of Eliot: *The Black Book* was a prose *Waste Land*. The *New English Weekly* was enthusiastic. Larry found his writing compared to Henry's in a *Time* magazine article with the lurid title 'Dithyrambic Sex': 'Less shocking than *Tropic of Cancer*, *The Black Book* follows a similar pattern, with realistic scenes giving way to tumultuous passages of invective and bitter rhapsody.' Completely missing the Rabelaisian gusto in both writers, the *Time* reviewer found mainly 'hopelessness and despair', beside which 'Joyce at his most pessimistic seems blithe and full of spirit'. *Time*'s errors must have amused Larry: the article had him born in Burma and 'working as a clerk in the Ionian Bank'.[159] Henry's friend Artur Lundkvist wrote a thoughtful piece about *The Black Book* for the Stockholm *Litterära Magasin*. Desmond Hawkins in *The Criterion* criticized the intrusiveness of the authorial voice, but compared Larry's achievement in prose to that of Auden's first poems. Henry reported that James Laughlin 'warmly admires' the book and would like to publish an excerpt in a New Directions anthology, or even print the whole book; 'And then, like an idiot, he adds – "Durrell is an Englishman, after all – " *Shit*!!'[160] By mid-November Kahane was complaining that *The Black Book* was 'scarcely selling at all'. He hoped to show the reviews around to boost sales. Henry was encouraging: *Tropic of Cancer* had sold fewer than 500 copies in the first year, but was now in its third printing. Larry himself mocked the excesses of *The Black Book*, calling it 'my O altitudo top note'.[161] His self-criticism was honest, but there were certain of his writings that he would always like despite their imperfections. *The Black Book* was one of these.

THE WORLD SITUATION KEPT INTRUDING. Hitler claimed the Sudetenland from Czechoslovakia, and at the Munich conference of 29 September 1938 British prime minister Neville Chamberlain capitulated to German demands. Believing that war was imminent, Henry fled in late September to Bordeaux and then to Marseille, telegraphing frantically for funds: to Jack Kahane, to James Laughlin, to Larry. All eventually cabled him money. Henry's feelings expressed one extreme of egotistical despair among Larry's friends: 'Nothing seems any good or worth while,' Miller lamented. 'Zero hour. I am completely eclipsed. I am sadder and blacker now than I was at 21 Years of age!!!' He projected his personal despair all over the map: 'I have seen a lot of towns and people – it all stinks to me. I imagine Corfu would stink too – *maybe even you*. You can't imagine to what a low point I have sunk. A black-out, as they say. If I were younger I would commit suicide again – but I am too old for that. I must live like a bed-bug for awhile – away from human society.' Henry saw the crisis and the coming war in terms of what they would mean to him as a writer, to all artists: 'What licks me, to put it simply, is this – how can people resume life after an experience such as we went through? How can they have the faith and the courage to take up their tools?'[162]

Larry's mood could not have been more different. With Nancy in Athens, he was immersed in the Greek-speaking world of Kalami. 'I wish I could mail you over a bit of the hallowed sangfroid I have felt today sailing the boat over to town and back,' he wrote to Henry. Usually Larry wanted Nancy and perhaps a friend or two around, but now the tranquillity suited him: 'For the last two days I have been happier than ever before in my life,' he wrote. That evening with the moonrise he was going to sail to the Bay of Fauns on the Albanian border, taking a child's *Odyssey* written in simple Greek for nourishment and a revolver 'in case Albanians stray over into the bay'.[163] In his fantasies he saw himself as a latter-day Odysseus, adventurous wanderer, confronting the brigands and the siren temptations of the Ionian. Many years later he would pour his daydreams into a 'sketch for a musical', *Ulysses Come Back*.

Quick to panic, Henry calmed down just as rapidly: by 11 October, although predicting an English and French defeat, he had decided to return to Paris to finish the *Hamlet* correspondence, *'with a vengeance'*.[164] Soon Anaïs, who had not allowed the war scare to upset her work, despite having been forced to move *La Belle Aurore* a few miles down the Seine to Neuilly, was reporting that Henry was writing 'magnificently' and that she was trying to finish *Winter of Artifice* for Kahane: 'It's your book you know,' she generously told Larry.[165] As Henry's mood rose, Larry's fell. There was a new reason for dissension at home: 'now, of course, nancy wants to have a child the slut,' Larry complained in exasperation to Henry. 'A little red general with fat legs, to ride into Czechoslovakia on a white horse? What sort of animal vegetable mineral is a woman's mind?'[166] Added to the logical arguments against producing a child on the edge of a war was Larry's instinctive rejection of fatherhood: he would have to grow up, to become financially responsible, to plan for the future – a future that looked increasingly grim. These considerations threatened his free life, his image of himself as an artist, one able to follow his whims, intuitions and madnesses to the limit.

World affairs notwithstanding, by 19 November 1938 Larry and Nancy were again on the train, heading for a flurry of London-Paris hops. Anaïs Nin went to London also, and Larry took her to the Faber offices, where, he claimed, 'Pringle made a sly face or two because he thought for a moment that she had MSS secreted in her blouse ready to launch at poor Faber once she was in.' Eliot was unable to see him on his visit to London, but Larry left behind for *The Criterion* a long 'prefatory letter from God' – part of the projected 'Book of the Dead'. On 29 November Larry bolted back to Paris because a general strike was threatened in England.

'I do feel, of course, that God uses the very characteristic idioms of Lawrence Durrell,' remarked Eliot of Larry's manuscript, 'but I suppose that He may be expected to speak to each of us in our own language.'[167] 'I'm sorry my impertinent accents creep in amongst God's dictums', Larry wrote in bristling justification, 'but being over-old in my young skin I always feel apologetic about speaking from my inner springs.' This 'ironic mask', Larry said, 'comes out of a bottomless sense of self-limitations; and from the fact that people see a bumptious boy in me more readily than a painful firework man.'[168] Eliot replied consolingly that he looked forward 'with much excitement' to seeing the entire manuscript, whereupon he would be better able to select a passage 'to exhibit' in *The Criterion*.[169] Eliot and Alan Pringle both asked Larry to give Faber first rejection rights on the book. Larry's problem was that he had written only two hundred pages, and a bare half of that was in polished form.

There is surprisingly little reference to political crises in the memoirs and letters left by Larry, Henry and most members of their circle. According to Larry, the desperate nature of the situation 'made us determined to ignore the coming holocaust and to use every second of time creatively. . . . I don't think we ever so much as mentioned the war in our conversations; certainly Reichel never did' – and the German artist, as a potential enemy alien in France and on bad terms with his native land, had the most to lose.[170] Henry hated the coming war on principle: 'I was always an out and out pacifist, and still am. I believe it is justifiable to kill a man in anger, but not in cold blood or on principle, as the laws and governments of the world advocate.'[171] Perlès wrote, recalling his chosen role of court jester, 'There was a war in the offing; we laughed it off.'[172] Laugh they did: hysterically, helplessly, sometimes grimly.

Larry himself was not sure just what he wanted to do about the war looming. At one time he and Leslie plotted a defence of Corfu against the Italians, an action to be based on bands of partisans roaming about the hills. When war seemed imminent in the summer of 1939, Larry would talk about joining the Greek Army to fight on the Albanian front. Later he considered offering his specialized knowledge of Ionian waters to the Royal Navy.

Impending slaughter or not, Larry was engaged in planning and editing the Xmas 1938 and Easter 1939 editions of *Delta*. Anaïs made good a promise to Larry: she commissioned Conrad Moricand to cast his horoscope and Nancy's for Christmas.[173] Apart from the astrological commonplaces associated with a Piscean nature – Larry, Moricand said, was creative, contradictory, mercurial, unreliable, vividly imaginative, a 'pure intellectual' – the astrologer made some astoundingly accurate remarks about Larry's inner being: he was committed to a 'systematic search for the ideal' and gifted with 'an almost "musical" sense of movement within knowledge'. He was subject to 'religious feelings in a rebellious heart', doomed to live in a 'constant state of revolt'. Further, he was a 'highly complex' person 'who deceives both himself and those around him as to his true nature'. The horoscope was a threatening one, said the astrologer, because Jupiter, 'the beneficient planet *par excellence*' and the one dominating Larry's chart, was in a 'perilous position' with respect to Mars, Mercury and the Sun. 'This means that the subject will need to call on all the vast resources of his mind in order to maintain a balance,' warned the sombre Moricand.[174] 'You see!' said Larry, who had for years told his confidants that he was half crazy. The fabled variableness of the Pisceans drew Larry on, especially with the temptations of his astrological sharers around: his 'twin' Buffie Johnson, and Anaïs. Anaïs was a frank sexual freebooter, and some of the others at 18 Villa Seurat hardly lagged behind: Henry talked a wild line, and Fred managed to bed a steady succession of young women – whom he generously offered to share with Henry – each one seemingly younger than the last. There had been a ticklish incident with an under-age girl and an irate father on the doorstep. Larry was caught, as usual, between conflicting emotions: he was driven frantic at the thought of Nancy falling a willing prey to one of the sexual predators, yet he himself was surrounded by temptation. If Moricand was correct in his assertion that Larry was an unreliable, variable aspirant towards the ideal, he was merely being true to his essence in searching for answers in sex as well as in philosophy and metaphysics.

There was more in Moricand's sketch for Larry to ponder: he combined a 'total emotional dependence with an acutely competitive sense'. Also, he 'enjoyed setting traps,' and he could shift suddenly from 'an apparent weakness of character' to 'boldness and even violence'. 'Pisceans are always at the extreme of Good and Evil,' pronounced Moricand.[175] He described Larry's patron deity as a '"protean" god of a thousand metamorphoses, who assumes all shapes to impregnate all goddesses'.

With the impetuousness of a lustful Greek god, Larry fell in love with an American journalist he met in Paris, Thérèse ('Tessa') Epstein. She had tremendous dash and directness, dark eyes, and she was Jewish. In fact, she was the first glimpse for Larry of the Justine character of his far-distant *Alexandria Quartet*.[176] She talked with reckless abandon, sitting in the Closerie des Lilas, and Larry was to write her as Teresa/Tessa into the most autobiographical of his poems, 'Cities, Plains and People'. In the poem he alternates between the first and the third person singular for the persona of the poet, but there is no doubt that he was remembering his affair with Teresa:

> Tessa was here whose dark
> Quickened hair had brushed back rivers,
> [. . .]
> In whose inconstant arms he waited . . .[177]

Nancy gave no sign of knowing the extent of Larry's infidelity.

By mid-December Larry and Nancy had returned to London, taking Fred Perlès with them. Fred claimed to have been kidnapped: 'Larry appeared in my room . . . "Pack! . . . you are going with us",' Larry had commanded. 'Certainly he saved my life,' recalled Fred.[178] As the holidays rushed upon them, Fred and Larry missed their Paris ringmaster, who had talked about joining them. For Henry Miller, Christmas had always been a time of despair, loss, poverty. The fact that Fred and Larry were enjoying themselves in London did not help his mood. His letters became increasingly despairing: his planned Christmas in London was dissolving like a mirage. 'Still no dough in sight,' he wrote. 'My fare back and forth, a visa, *pissgeld und trinkgeld*, all that would come to over a thousand francs' – more than £10. And he had so looked forward to seeing Veronica Tester and Dorothy Stevenson and going to 'the roller skating rink and the casinos and Covent Garden & the Café Royal'. Henry was bitterly certain that the trip would fade like a mirage: 'Thus far in my life I have never passed a jolly Xmas. Every Xmas has found me broke, balked and frustrated. And usually alone.'[179]

Larry and Nancy found enough ready cash for Henry's trip. Larry met him at Dover, to shepherd him 'trembling and swearing' through Customs[180] – Henry vividly recalling being denied entry in 1932. Henry was not sure he wanted to meet Eliot, who in turn had Grave Doubts about Miller. 'I get a message that Miller has landed,' Eliot wrote to Larry somewhat apprehensively. 'I am ready to arrange to meet him under whatever conditions you judge most propitious, if he is willing, or if he can be reduced to a state of anaesthesia in which he might be willing to meet anybody.'[181] They met on 29 December in the flat borrowed from Hugh Guiler at 140 Camden Hill Road, Eliot 'grave and composed',[182] Henry carefully dressed and on his best behaviour: each was wary, but soon there was 'a great deal of laughter', and Eliot promised a jacket blurb for Henry's next book.[183] With his note of thanks Eliot enclosed a cheque for £10, claiming that the sum was from an admirer of Larry's art who wished to remain anonymous. 'Don't try to find out where the money came from,' Eliot warned. 'You will oblige us, please, by cashing the cheque at the first opportunity.'[184] Most likely it came from his own account.

Bringing Henry and Dylan Thomas together proved more difficult. Nancy prepared a dinner in the Guiler flat, but hours after the appointed time there was no sign of their guest. Finally the telephone rang. It was Dylan: 'I can't find the flat so I'm not coming.' 'I'll come and get you,' offered Larry. Dylan turned out to be in a pub across the street, 'too frightened to move' and aggressive. He had changed in the intervening year into a 'sublunary golliwog', wrapped to the nose in an immense muffler. He was nervous about meeting an author whose work he admired, but Larry was able to win him over with 'a ludicrous picture of Henry walking round and round the dinner table cursing him'. In the end, it was a fine evening: Dylan read some of his verse in 'thrasonical' tones,[185] liked Henry 'enormously', and invited him to visit 'in the spring, in Wales, in the live quiet'.[186]

Larry managed several discussions about poetic theory with Dylan on this trip, and was disappointed to find that he wrote 'slowly and with difficulty', 'mutating' his nouns and adjectives to achieve the right colour. Larry judged him 'more interested in sound than in meaning', and lacking in modulation: 'Every stroke was a smash.' However, Larry respected Dylan's dedication, his self-assurance and his robust mentality.

Anaïs spent a quiet Christmas in Paris with Hugh Guiler, who came over to London just after the New Year. She sent with him the third part of her *Winter of Artifice* for correction, explaining to Larry that 'The other two parts I can't send because of Hugo . . . the Hans-Johanna-Father part.' Always terribly sensitive to criticism, she complained about Larry's comments: 'I went through a long grind with M. over every word – and I was simply discouraged . . . . The New Year was dismal . . . everything askew with Larry.' Anaïs was as usual balancing complicated relationships, and she instructed Larry, 'Give these [pages] to Henry please & tear up my letters if you're staying with Hugo.'[187] Larry was coming to understand that Anaïs had a very touchy side, that she demanded what she perceived as total loyalty from her friends, and accordingly he backed off from greater intimacy and from honest criticism. This was not what Anaïs wanted: 'I had a great fantasy about having a twin writer working with me,' she said much later. 'I was fixed on the need for the writer-companion, for the love of a fellow-writer.' She would describe her complicated relationship with Henry Miller, despite their intense discussions and their physical couplings, as being filled with 'contraries', and the wished-for harmony was to be even less complete with Larry. 'My friendship with Durrell was . . . almost vicarious,' she would recall.[188]

Looking back on his Paris friendships from the safe remove of a year, Larry used words that betrayed a certain caution in dealing with Anaïs. First he described Betty Ryan as 'a self-created miracle; she is sitting always over a tripod adding up oracles. I loved her.' He continued, 'And Anaïs, you know, is the first woman, really the *first*. That is why she is such a lovely monster, and my most adored of friends.'[189] But he did not say that he loved her.

Even as a *literary* conjunction, the contact between Anaïs, Henry and Larry could not produce a harmony, as all three eventually realized. 'I thought I shared a vision of writing with Henry Miller and Lawrence Durrell,' a disappointed Anaïs would confess. 'Time proved that the three of us went in totally different directions.'[190]

BY 11 JANUARY 1939 Henry was back in Paris. He particularly cautioned Larry to go easy on Anaïs's feelings over *Winter of Artifice*: 'We must handle her gently in all this.'[191] Even the buoyant Larry had become infected with pessimism, however, and he was finding it hard to console others. 'No humour in me these days much,' he confessed, 'the times are pressing inexorably in and people want the strong, tender words: and the ordinary thought.'[192] Eliot's dignified editorial in the last issue of *The Criterion*, announcing the cessation of publication, shocked and moved Larry. 'I have often cursed the Criterion in my black moods,' Larry wrote to Eliot, 'but now that it has ceased, I recognise the big part played in literature by its temperance and justice and quietness.'[193]

Meanwhile, Larry's correspondence kept expanding: in January a letter of criticism and advice on poetry magazines to Elizabeth Smart in Ottawa provoked a warm response. Unlike Anaïs, she plainly welcomed Larry's criticism: 'You're quite right about my technical equipment flopping on me.'[194] By the autumn of 1939 she had, in Larry's words, 'run away from home' to New York, and he added fatherly counsel to his usual publishing suggestions. 'I suppose you've seen enough films to know what the temptations are,' he lectured. 'AVOID THEM!'[195] She had a secret reason for cultivating Larry's acquaintance, but also for ignoring his personal advice: the year before she had happened upon a volume of George Barker's Apocalyptic verse in a Charing Cross Road bookshop, had fallen in love with Barker on the spot, and had resolved to marry him. Larry provided a tenuous connection with Barker. Smart was not to meet Barker until 1940 and they would never wed, although she would bear him four children.

Although Larry and Henry met with uneven results in their efforts to direct their friends, they were in a ferment of self-instruction. The names and topics coming up in their conversations and letters at this time show an idiosyncratic mix: Swedenborg and Keyserling, Balzac's *Louis Lambert* and *Séraphita* – which Henry proposed publishing in translation in the Villa

Seurat Series – Nijinsky's *Diary* and Dostoevsky, Rosicrucian cosmography and the Tarot, Bernard Bromage's *The Modern Mystic*, Suzuki and Alan Watts on Zen, translations from Lao Tzu. Larry encountered the philosopher Frederick Carter in a London pub and thought that 'on the whole [he] talked some annoying rubbish', calling the Tarot pointless 'when everyone knows,' Larry said, 'that it is a metaphysical system to which the key has been lost'.[196] Henry defended Carter, whom he pronounced 'an Apocalyptic man'.[197] Anaïs ordered Paracelsan alchemical texts from Zürich, and these too went into their discursive hopper. 'We all read with enthusiasm' the psychologist Graham Howe, Larry recalled; 'He influenced me much, was a Taoist but also a toughy.' Anaïs and Henry knew Otto Rank, and his writings, along with those of C. G. Jung and Richard Wilhelm, added to the ferment, to what Larry would refer to as their 'wide browsing ground'.[198] Larry wrote an essay on Rank that was never published. But it was Lao Tzu's *Tao Te Ching* especially that would have a lifelong concentrating effect on his thinking: the slim book would stand behind his *A Smile in the Mind's Eye* and would underpin the spirit of play in his 'Tibetan novel', *The Avignon Quintet*.[199]

Larry met Anne Ridler, Eliot's assistant and the sub-editor of the vanished *Criterion*, at the Faber offices. He had been proclaimed to her by Henry Miller as, in her words, 'the leaven that redeemed the lump of the English race'. Larry penned a mocking epitaph on the back of one of the first letters he wrote her:

> Ci-git LGD, a poet,
> His prose was verse,
> He did not know it.
> He never guessed
> His verse was prose,
> But worse than either was his Pose.[200]

From the first, Larry recognized Anne as a kindred poetic voice and gave her encouragement. He accepted three of her poems for *Delta* and had sent her 'pure lyric' to Nicholas Moore for *Seven*. He later suggested trying Tambimuttu and *Poetry* magazine. When the Easter 1939 *Delta* appeared, the final one, the lead poem in it would be Anne's, and the issue would conclude with Larry's long 'Sonnet of Hamlet', gracefully dedicated 'to Anne Ridler and to the lady in the painting, Ophelia'.[201] He kept writing encouragement to 'dear anne bradby alias ridler', telling her to find better titles, to strengthen endings, to submit poems to James Laughlin, to

Dorothy Norman of *Twice a Year*, to James Cooney of *Phoenix*. 'Now I really think you must sit up like an intelligent bunny on her tump and signal the outer world,' Larry told her. 'REMEMBER: REJECTION ALWAYS MEANS INFERIOR TASTE ON THE PART OF THE REJECTOR.'[202]

Larry came to depend on Anne Ridler's judgement. One of his early letters to her is addressed 'Dear Poetess': a manuscript of his own poems was being considered for publication, and he was worried. 'I begin to hear my defects roaring in my ears!' he lamented. 'I had no idea poetry went to the committee: what enemies I shall make! There should at least have been a legible Mss, even if unintelligible.'[203] He kept sending her copies of his latest poems for her comments: 'The Green Man', 'In Crisis'. He urged her to be ruthless: 'The self-liking is too deep for damage!'[204] He was not nearly as self-confident as he pretended. Respect for Anne's judgement led Larry to cultivate her friendship, and soon, with her husband Vivian, she was spending evenings with Larry and Nancy over wine and risotto and Marx Brothers films.

Larry was critical of several Faber poets: Auden was good, 'but like some passionate breed of sterile fly buzzing in a temple of Industry'; MacNeice was 'no good'; George Barker had 'only just begun'. Larry criticized himself as well, writing to Ridler that 'I buzz only for preference in jam-jars, where sweetness and misery is more or less relevant.' Then, somewhat disingenuously, he added, 'I am not a writer really . . . though exactly what I am or who I think I am I don't know.' Anne tried to interest Faber in Larry's poetry; he thanked her but protested that he had 'gaps in technique' because he was 'not trying to write "poetry"' but 'to find a poetic way to be myself'. 'I'm not really a Faber poet in this sense,' he reasoned. Jonathan Cape would publish his verse if Faber chose not to.[205]

Anne criticized Larry's lushness, his strings of adjectives, the obvious influence of such poets as Dylan Thomas and Barker. 'I dance inside, because these are my very real faults, and they are perhaps my greatest virtue . . . not in poetry but in self,' he replied. 'I find you very acute,' he told Anne. He thought of himself as crude, his gaucheness a 'defensive fun': 'Hence the caper sauce and huge adjectival sausages I ram into the blunderbuss before letting fly.' He saw Anne's verse as polished, gentle: 'As it is, I think you are probably the best critic to think upon, because being a woman you really are on the other side of the fence.' Larry defended his borrowings: 'In a sense, a poet doesn't have to write anything new; merely to organise his chips truly.' He had cribbed, he claimed, from Restoration poets as well. 'I confess I borrow directly what I want from other people because the total structure is what I try for first.'[206] Even T. S. Eliot came under Larry's scrutiny. Comparing the achievements of Eliot and Wyndham Lewis, Larry said that Lewis had started with a more brilliant natural endowment, 'yet', he added, 'look how much farther Eliot has got, with a plank and two bits of string'. Larry then expounded his theory of the relationship of artists to ambience:

People have their climatic flavour; Dylan Thomas is built out of suffocating coal from a Welsh mine; Barker out of a town boy's school primer – Piers Plowman say, where medieval England is green enough to make one weep for landscape, and where all the words are latin and morte d'arthur; Auden out of a hard concrete squash-court and swimming-bath, or a Silver Age tomb say; and MacNeice out of Birmingham Art Gallery; Spender out of the don's oak panelling, and windows looking out over the river, and books of geography for those who live in universities or asylums for the aged.[207]

Larry read other poets, he would much later admit, 'as a journeyman, and where I see a good effect I study it, and try to reproduce it'. Among those he had 'pinched' from was Auden, 'a great master of colloquial effects which no one before him dared to use'.[208]

Anne Ridler may have tried to interest Faber in Larry's poetry, but Eliot in his usual kindly manner kept trying to steer him in the direction of fiction. Eliot invited Larry to lunch at the Oxford and Cambridge University Club to discuss the publication of his poems and 'The Book of the Dead'. About the poems, Eliot wrote to Larry, 'I regard them as the by-products of a prose writer.'[209] This was not to say that Faber would not publish the poems: the question was when. He would prefer, he said, to see a major prose work published first, but if Larry wanted the poems to come out now, then he wished to hear his reasons. Eliot's letter was postmarked the date of the proposed luncheon, and Larry did not receive it until the following day.

Angry and baffled, Larry answered Eliot: 'I don't know what to say to you except to send the wretched by-products back. . . . I've no reason, as you say rather wickedly, for wanting them published; I think they are sufficient reason; this is really a strong conviction, and so far nothing can shake it.' He felt that this, his first real collection of poems, was at least as interesting as Auden's first volume, and 'would stand in relation to Barker's first book as Moby Dick stands to a red herring'. He was not about to haggle with Eliot, but he did say that 'Faber verse has really been mediocre in the last few years, and all with one accent, leading one way to the bottomless pit.' With self-mockery Larry concluded, 'It was as a tramline leading elsewhere that I so heroically interposed myself.' Larry complained that when he sent Eliot verse, he received a 'brilliant survey' of his prose career; when he sent fiction, Eliot discoursed on his poetry. 'Very well,' Larry wrote to him, 'I must stand on one leg if you wish it; but I propose to talk about one thing at a time!'[210]

Larry already had Pringle's assurance that only with novels would he be likely to receive advances. He still believed that Auden and Eliot were the most significant living poets writing in English, and to be told by Eliot that his poems were by-products really stung. 'Send the poems back,' Larry repeated to Eliot, adding bitterly, 'And I will never darken your door again.' He was planning a play, and he felt that he had to have an editor who believed his poetry worth publishing. 'I am absolutely convinced that, great man as you are, you have committed an error of taste in taking me art too lightly.' Larry closed the letter by saying rather wildly that he was exhausted, 'over the rim of myself, like a harvest moon covered in arterial blood'.[211] Larry was deeply shaken, and their correspondence evidently lapsed for over a year.

Meanwhile Larry was busy publishing other poets. Among those he had lined up for the *Delta* poetry number of Easter 1939 were Audrey Beecham, Dorian Cooke, David Gascoyne, Rayner Heppenstall, Anne Ridler and Dylan Thomas. A poet and a companion of this sojourn whom he did not print was Hugh Gordon Porteus, who signed his letters 'The Wombat'. Larry and Henry were still abuzz over the *Tao Te Ching*, yet Porteus, with enough Mandarin to read Lao Tzu in the original, parried: 'As to . . . the tao, we never mention it, because those who know do not say, and those who say do not know.'[212] He noted Larry's frenetic activity and accepted an invitation to dine in teasing terms: 'Dear Lorry, We feared engine trouble . . . *but we knew* our Lorry would not could not run out of gas.'[213]

Larry's most significant encounter in London was probably his meeting with Graham Howe, whose *Time and the Child* he had reviewed favourably for W. T. Symons's *Purpose*. Henry had also written an essay on Howe, 'a complete misinterpretation' like his own, said Larry after entertaining Howe at dinner in Hugh Guiler's flat. *Entertaining* was hardly the word. Howe had come in like a brooding cloud: 'Terrific egotism; nervous system screwed into a knot behind his eyes; almost depersonalised; but the mark of the beast on him. Surely a great and terrifying European.

Wow!' Howe, a 'real demoniac', tied the Tao to Einstein's theory of relativity, saying that it should be applied to metaphysics, not merely to mechanics. Eduardo Sanchez, Anaïs Nin's cousin, was 'knocked over like a ninepin; HE HAS FOUND HIS PLUTO-NEPTUNIAN.'²¹⁴ Larry must have felt his own shock of recognition: Einstein seen through the glass of Lao Tzu made sense to him, and he realized that if Howe could apply the conjunction to metaphysics, perhaps his own desire to join the ideas of the Taoist and the physicist in fiction might work.

England had been amusing but not especially productive, thought Larry. By February he was ready to return to Corfu. 'Why are you still in London?' Dylan Thomas asked him, recognizing his discontent. 'Has somebody moved Corfu?'²¹⁵ Larry was asking himself the same questions. 'Mewed in this isle so sweet', he wrote to Alan Thomas, 'I growl like a panther and gnaw the bars of voyage.'²¹⁶ He wanted to do so in his own boat, and preferably through the Rhine-Rhône canal system. He enlisted the aid of Desmond Tester to find a sailing craft that would carry half-a-dozen people in some ease and would cost no more than the remains of Nancy's inheritance. By the end of February he had found the ideal boat in Southampton, a fifty-foot Dutch ketch that promised to be stable and comfortable. Events on the Continent were becoming increasingly threatening, with the German invasion of Czechoslovakia on 15 March 1939. In the end he did not buy the ketch, partly because, with war impending, restrictions had been placed on travel by sea. He contemplated settling for the summer in Cornwall or going to America, but by 30 May Larry and Nancy were back on Corfu, after the usual ferry-train-ferry run south across Europe.

Before leaving England, however, Larry reported on the Stratford Festival in April for the *International Post*. Here he found an England that he could view with unreserved delight. Trinity Church was 'lovely, facing on the smoothest river in Christendom', over which 'the swans go suavely up and down'. He and Nancy saw *Othello* and *The Comedy of Errors*, and Larry rose early one morning to visit the site of New Place in Church Street: 'They have made a trim English garden where the house stood, with green lawns, and shining little trees.' It was here, sitting on a bench in the early sunlight, that Larry found Shakespeare, he told Henry: 'HERE IS THE KEY TO EVERYTHING HE WROTE. I don't think you can understand the old boy until you sit in this garden, and reflect how for those five years THE REST WAS SILENCE with him, living his small-town burgess life, cut off from the court and the London joys.'²¹⁷ Larry imagined Shakespeare a

Taoist in retirement, and he wrote to Anne Ridler, 'I think immediately of Lao Tzu going over the hills to the land of Dragons on his patient water-buffalo.' On the Avon, Larry observed, 'the swan does little cobbles with her horny black foot on the absolute water'.[218] The *International Post* folded after the first issue, and Larry's reportage on Stratford was not published: still, the visit left him with a new grasp of the bond between the great poet and his birthplace. Larry and Nancy paused briefly in Paris on their way south. With a sense of finality, Henry inscribed a copy of *Tropic of Capricorn* to them with the words, 'To Larry and Nancy from Henry – Paris 5/26/39 "last few days".'

BACK AT KALAMI, ON THE BLUE water of the strait Larry and Nancy saw not swans but 'boat-loads of costumes . . . sailing past the house bound north' for a peasant dance. Theodore Stephanides came to stay with them and in the evening they all walked the five miles to Kassiope for the festival. Larry and Theodore were translating Cavafy, 'who does marvellous and uncommunicable things'. They planned to sail over to Albania: Larry was growing a beard for 'protective colouring', and Theodore was already 'bearded as the pard'. The surrender to Greek rhythms lulled him, but Larry had not forgotten England and the poems that he hoped would appear in *Poetry* magazine, and in lines written in fractured syntax he commissioned Anne Ridler to hound Tambimuttu for a copy: 'I say, do try and ring Tambi will you and ask him to send me a new poetry if its out the dog with me anywhere.'[219]

Larry kept vowing that he wanted 'badly' to write but was 'mummer than a muffin'. He ascribed this to his recent trip to England and France:

I think I will write again and well when I get into my smooth native flow: at the moment I am a disjunctive mass of impressions and scars. I am always like that after six months in peopled places: people collide and hurt, and solitude nurses hurts up into little short circuits that electrify one's belief in oneself.[220]

He had returned with powerful and varied impressions: Howe's discourse on Einstein and Lao Tzu; Teresa Epstein's lovemaking in Paris and the temptations of 'the ballerinas' in England; the long talks with a demanding Anaïs; Henry's financial problems and hysterical laughter; Anne Ridler's encouragement; the idyllic experience of Stratford. The conflicting impulses of his possessiveness towards Nancy and his own desire for sexual freedom had brought on a few monumental quarrels. Principal among the hurts was certainly Eliot's rejection of his poetry, which shook his faith in himself.

'You're speaking to a poet manque it seems,' Larry wrote later to Elizabeth Smart. 'I have argued with Eliot until he turned green, I even *read* bits at him, right in the eye. But in England they think me no good. Yet I *can't* think them right, however much I try.'[221] Still, it was hard to open a poetry notebook with Eliot's critique echoing in his mind. There was much that he had to reconcile.

At Kalami many things distracted him from writing: seals were 'filching' fish from the nets in the bay; the corpses of Italians were being washed up after a recent bombardment; in imitation of Anaïs Nin, who had practised under Rank's guidance, Larry had acquired his first 'patient' for psychiatric counselling. He did have a few projects in hand, however. He had set out to prove that Shakespeare had come to Corfu before writing *The Tempest*, and he was trying to arrange for New Directions to publish his poems: James Laughlin had proposed buying sheets from Faber. Larry evidently saw a chance of finessing Faber into publishing his poems on a cost-sharing basis with Laughlin. Should he approve the scheme, Larry asked Anne Ridler – or 'Would it be another nail in Eliot's tea-cosy if I said so?' Larry was trying to get a job teaching English for the British Council on Corfu, and he asked Anne to sound Eliot out about writing a testimonial for him: 'I am not quite sure whether it's literary etiquette to apply for five lines saying I am [a] decent character (specially when I am so manifestly not).' By the middle of his letter he had decided *not* to ask Eliot.[222]

Despite all his plans for writing and work, Larry kept trying to entice people to Corfu who would be sure to distract him: the Barkers, the Ridlers. And he had been urging Miller to come since as far back as 1936. While realizing that he required solitude for his work, Larry was afraid of being alone with his thoughts, and he shrank from a situation that would leave him with no excuse for not writing. He was soon to have an excuse. Now, finally, Henry overcame his own hesitations and timidities and, despite the clear approach of war, in a burst of activity stored a trunk of manuscripts and papers with Jack Kahane, arranged to have funds sent to Greece, and boarded a train. His departure from Paris had the air of a carefree adventure. On 19 July Miller landed at Piraeus and three days later he was on Corfu. Larry and Nancy met his ship punctually: knowing the casual nature of Greek schedules, they arrived on the dock at noon the day after Henry was supposed to disembark, and were perfectly on time.

It was to be a holiday such as Henry had never experienced. Spiro Americanos drove the three friends straight to Kalami, where they swam from the steps of the White House before lunch. After a siesta they rowed south around the headland to the votive chapel of St Arsenius where, in Henry's words, 'we baptized ourselves anew in the raw'. For Henry it really heralded a rebirth: he was in bliss, lying about naked in the sun, free from money pressures, having merely to stretch forth his hand for food and drink, and to shrug himself alert for Larry's conversation. Henry did not even feel like reading. However, he would not have been Henry Miller had he not paid attention to the women around him. Whether it was the young maid at the White House who carried heavy jugs of water down from the well, or a powerful peasant woman locally regarded as a monster because of her six toes, or later on, George Seferis's regal sister Jeanne, Henry idolized Greek womanhood. Larry had great difficulty in persuading Henry not to take over the water-carrying from the maid: Henry wanted to share her humility, to feel the ache in his muscles. 'It just isn't *done!*' exclaimed Larry, horrified.

Larry was not always able to restrain Henry. He 'psychoanalysed' a young woman visitor, moving in on Larry's turf. And he offended Larry's sense of the holy nature of the place by having his 'first fuck with the English girl' at the little shrine to St Arsenius.[223] But Larry was forgiving: 'Walking or swimming', he noted, Henry had the 'peculiar lightness' of the eternal child.[224] In comparison, Larry often appeared the more serious: for despite the distraction of his guest – or perhaps because of it – Larry had resumed writing. Henry observed Larry on the balcony of the White House, 'with a pencil and pad, scribbling, scribbling, polishing style, rewriting, writing some more, bathing, drinking, singing, laughing, but always coming back to the pad and pencil'.[225] Or pen, which Larry preferred to pencil or typewriter. 'The intimacy of the touch is good,' Larry often said. 'It helps you shear off your prose.'[226]

Henry had long conversations in 'a broken-down French' with Nicola, the schoolmaster who lived in Kalami, and with the local policeman, Karamenaios, in 'a sort of cluck-cluck language made up largely of good will and a desire to understand one another'.[227] Henry even tried a rendition of Chinese – which he did not know – on a village mayor, and was astounded when the man answered him in something sounding like Chinese – which the mayor did not know either, but claimed that he had learned from the crew of a junk that had put in for repairs. The locals decided that the 'old man' was crazy, and they protected and adored him. Henry and Larry visited the Countess Helen Theotocki, exploring by canoe her 'beautiful little beach, the grottoes'.[228] Larry gave Henry the *Odyssey* to read and, acting out Homer, they spent a day at the beach near Paleocastrizza where, according to Larry,

'Ulysses was washed up naked and scared hell out of Nausicaa'.[229] Being around Henry was a lesson in enjoyment: 'Never did I meet anyone who appreciated Greece as much as he did, and who was drinking it from the right fountain, as they say in Greek,' Larry observed. 'He had come to Greece for a revelation and he got it!'[230]

Larry had been absorbing a revelation of his own from his earliest meetings with Henry – his 'mullah', as he sometimes described him. 'Day and night I was imbibing nuggets of information, spiritual information,' Larry would recall. 'He gave off such joy, and *joie de vivre*, about everything.' Henry was also a walking lesson in independence: 'He refused *absolutely* to be bulldozed by culture.' Larry strove to achieve a similar stance, saying late in his life that 'it's all very well to be knowledgeable about Shakespeare, but then you can't saw an olive tree correctly.' With the humility that for him was as genuine as it was unconscious, almost a matter of good manners, Larry claimed that he 'wasn't at the same level at all' as Henry, but that his service was to understand him. 'What he needed was someone who appreciated his value', Larry said, 'the intrinsic value of his insight.'[231]

With the German invasion of Poland on 1 September, the war became a fact, and Larry and Nancy decided to try to find work in Athens, having no desire to be trapped on Corfu by an invasion from Italy. Feeling angry with himself because he wanted more sun and more summer, Henry left Corfu with them. They disembarked at Patras and stayed at the Hotel Cecil, which Henry thought was the best hotel he had ever been in. They breakfasted in the solarium overlooking the sea. 'Here a terrible wrangle ensued between Durrell and his wife,' wrote Henry. 'It was really a private quarrel in which the war was used as a camouflage. The thought of war drives people frantic.' At this time Larry began talking about enlisting in the Greek army, and Henry did not attempt to dissuade him, fearing his intervention would have the opposite effect. Henry was sure Larry agreed with him about the war, but knew that 'being English despite himself, he was in a quandary'.[232] Henry was right about Larry, but there was even more to it: the powerful will of Larry's dead father was urging him towards the conflict. Unconventional though Larry was, scorning the political chicanery that underlay the war, he was still not able to escape entirely his father's conception of duty to the homeland. Men went to war: Larry felt that he should at least offer, as his father had offered, to become a combatant. But he procrastinated, quarrelling with Nancy and changing his mind a dozen times a day.

Larry found Athens 'beautiful and sculptural as ever, built on the curvature of little red dust hills'.[233] He and Nancy soon settled in a small fourth-floor flat at 40 Anagnostopoulou Street near fashionable Kolonaki Square. From their balcony they could see the Acropolis glowing through the haze, but the war made Larry feel too guilty to enjoy the city. He wrote to Anaïs that 'Life is very black for us all; no hopes, no solutions in sight.'[234] He would have to find a job soon or he would be forced to return to England. Luckily, he and Theodore were hired 'on probation' as temporary staff with the British Embassy Information Services.[235] While Theodore's duties involved mainly the translation into English of Greek newspaper articles and letters, Larry and several others were given the more interesting job of producing an official bulletin. The purpose was in part to counter a news-sheet distributed by the German Embassy: hostile propaganda, according to His Majesty's representatives. 'I have been working at the Legation here as a sort of Private Godfrey Winn, checking on opinion,' Larry explained to Anne Ridler.[236] Larry's group not only wrote most of the copy, but actually printed the sheets on a primitive mimeograph in the Embassy basement. The sheets came wet off the machine, and Larry spent a lot of time running about with masses of damp paper that had to be dried on clothes lines. Nancy helped edit these bulletins, but took a fairly inactive role as she had just discovered that she was pregnant. 'For my part I feel completely hopeless inside,' Larry confided to Anaïs Nin, echoing her feelings. 'It is so good to be working at the trivial all day and drinking retsina at night.'[237] He could not bear to think: either of paternity, his writing or the war. He felt like a fly stuck in molasses.

This was the time of the lull in hostilities following the rapid Nazi conquest of Poland, and Athens was in the grip of a nervous carnival spirit. Kolonaki society ladies, in black silk and girded with pearls, spoke of the dampening effect that refugees gathering at the Place Vendôme would have on the winter cultural season in Paris. There was a three-day frenzy at the British Legation when the vital Anglo-Greek Relations file was lost: it finally turned up hidden under a pile of 'Royal Visits' and 'Decorations' bulletins. In another opera-bouffe scandal, a timid English homosexual was fingered – incorrectly – by the Legation padre as a spy for the Vatican. 'People cut their German friends in public and played bridge with them in the evening,' recalled R. Romilly Fedden, who published poetry as Robin Fedden and was the Cultural Attaché at the British Embassy. All this unsettled Larry, who was supposed to be putting out an information bulletin. 'Do tell me', he said in anguish to Fedden late one night in the

Press Attaché's office, 'what the Greeks are thinking. No one has any idea, and I must say *something*.'[238] Fedden had first met Larry near midnight at a café on Syntagma Square adjacent to the parliament buildings. Larry was 'performing a curious parlour-trick, firing lighted matches from a roll of silver paper'.[239] Fedden, with his pale, serious face and noticeable stammer, made a sharp contrast with sun-cured Larry, whose words rang out if anything too assuredly. Many bottles of Samos wine were consumed and they bought cigars from an itinerant vendor. When the seats became too hard and the cold too penetrating, they repaired to the Argentina Cabaret, finally walking home through 'one of those rinsed and lucid Athenian dawns'.[240] Fedden's diary entry recorded that 'I talked a great deal too expansively, being drunk . . . . . . and remember nothing we said.' Drunk or sober, Fedden's power of observation was acute and he noted in Larry 'an elusive, almost feminine grace, deep-set eyes, and . . . an impression of great sensitivity balanced by composure.'[241] They parted friends.

The only member of Larry's circle who seemed completely detached from preoccupation with the war and the scramble to find employment was Henry Miller. Larry, Nancy and Theodore took him up the Acropolis and introduced him to their favourite tavernas in Athens and Piraeus. One of Larry's new friends was a very learned and witty young Englishman, the Honourable Edward Gathorne-Hardy. He was droll, sometimes outrageous, and an unabashed pederast. Sometimes in a fashionable restaurant he would scan the menu – and the crowd – with an appreciative eye, then announce perfectly deadpan to the waiter: 'Pour moi, les coquilles St Jacques, le canard à l'orange, les profiterolles' – then pointing – 'et puis, ce garçon-là!'[242] Larry thought that he and Henry, two of the most remarkable people he knew, should meet, so he invited Gathorne-Hardy and Robin Fedden to dine with him and Henry under the trees at a peaceful taverna. 'The setting and the food were right', recalled Fedden, 'the outcome was a disaster.' Dinner became a conflict of wit and words, with the incisive Gathorne-Hardy goading Miller, whom he thought brash and 'imprecise'. Finally Henry shouted, 'But I write my books here!', hitting the general area of his abdomen. 'Do tell me *just* where, my dear,' shot back Gathorne-Hardy with an expression of polite interest.[243]

Henry took to Larry's Greek friends instantly, while rejecting not only Gathorne-Hardy but every other Englishman, with one exception, that he encountered in Greece. That exception was Xan Fielding, a young Mediterranean hand with a formidable command of languages and a hawk's profile; they had a fine evening together in Larry's company.

Theodore Stephanides Henry pronounced 'the most learned man I have ever met, and a saint to boot',[244] the painter Niko Ghika he quoted as an oracle on the 'quintessential Greece', and George Seferis brought the Greek landscape alive for him, 'rhapsodizing on herbs, flowers, shrubs, rocks, clay, slopes, declivities, coves, inlets'.[245] But it was George Katsimbalis who stunned Henry with the sheer magnitude of his character, who inspired what many would term Henry's finest book, *The Colossus of Maroussi*. Only two other encounters had had such an impact on him, Henry said: his meetings with the one-armed French novelist Blaise Cendrars and with Larry.

Katsimbalis spoke passionately about everything: poetry, food, Greek history, his health. 'He saw the humorous aspect of everything, which is the real test of the tragic sense,' wrote Henry.[246] Katsimbalis portrayed himself as a wreck, the remnant of a human being, battered by the First World War, his arm damaged, his knee dislocated, one eye impaired. His liver was 'disorganized' and he suffered from rheumatism and arthritis, but this did not stop him from enjoying his meals: 'Between cavernous gulps of food he would pound his chest like a gorilla before washing it down with a hogshead of *retzina*.' The piney *retzina*, Katsimbalis said, was good for the liver, the lungs, the kidneys, the bowels, the mind. 'He always talked against a landscape, like the protagonist of a lost world,' Henry remembered.[247] Katsimbalis was passionate also about restructuring cities, and he reorganized Shanghai, London, Istanbul in his monologues. Larry listened and stored the memories, years later to create in Katsimbalis's shadow the city architect Caradoc in *The Revolt of Aphrodite*. Larry often compared Katsimbalis to Dr Johnson. On one of his limping rambles around Athens with Larry, the Colossus paused before a shop window, stabbed at the glass with his massive stick, and rumbled, 'Now there's a good book. It is a typical scamp of a book, a Greek book, full of good fun, bad taste, and laughter and irreverence.'[248] This was Larry's introduction to *Papissa Joanna* – Pope Joan – by Emmanuel Royidis, and years later he translated it.

By mid-September Miller, the Brooklyn boy who had once shunned rural life, claiming that his soul 'thrived on garbage cans', had gone back alone to Corfu. 'And the war is too big a thing for him to swallow; he must reject it,' Larry wrote to Anaïs. Margaret Durrell, then living with one of 'her' peasant families, fed Henry, and again he seemed content to do nothing but sit in the sun. Greece, Larry said, 'has made him dumb'.[249] Larry found himself unable to stop talking about the war. He wrote to Elizabeth Smart promoting his own apolitical stance, but without ducking the responsibility of the Allies: 'We are responsible down to the last man, and deserve to be massacred,' he told her. 'And if they ask you whether you believe in Chamberlain do not murmur under your breath "The yellow-bellied Birmingham rat". It gets you nowhere. Just sigh and say "As for me I'm neutral".'[250]

AFTER LARRY AND THEODORE had been working for the Information Services for about a month, a full complement of regular staff was supplied from England and the temporaries were dismissed.'[251] In Larry's sarcastic phrase, 'good English departmentalism has triumphed over those of us who knew Greece and Greek, and liked both.'[252] This would emerge as the prevailing tone of all Larry's work for the Foreign Office and the British Council: he would always see himself as the outsider, the maverick, striving at popular and intuitive levels against an entrenched and stodgy bureaucracy. There would be no escape from Pudding Island for as long as he took the King's shilling, and right now he desperately needed that shilling.

Larry wrote to Anaïs, now in New York, 'The money question is going to be a problem unless I find some other job.'[253] Her American husband had been ordered to return to the United States, and she pronounced a sad valedictory: 'I knew it was the end of our romantic life.'[254] Larry worried that his authorship of The Black Book might scare off the British Council, which he still hoped would hire him, and a rumour went around among his friends that Larry had surreptitiously bought and destroyed all the copies in Athens bookshops. Meanwhile on Corfu, Henry had spent some six weeks sun-worshipping; but then the autumn rains set in – so when Nancy made a quick trip to the island to collect household goods, he decided to return to Athens with her. Henry was again lionized by Greek intellectuals, including Seferis and Katsimbalis. Katsimbalis set out to conduct him around the Peloponnesus. In a series of swooping arcs, by ship usually but sometimes by train or car, the two set off with Seferis to visit Ghika on Hydra, then Katsimbalis took Henry on to Spetsai, to Nauplia, then to the great theatre of Epidaurus, and finally to Tiryns and Mycenae.

When a business emergency forced Katsimbalis to cut the tour short at Mycenae, Henry moved back into Larry's immediate circle. In October Theodore arranged for them to visit the Athens observatory, where the astronomers were amazed at their guests' reactions. Shown the 'splintered star world' of the Pleiades, Larry shouted 'Rosicrucian!', while the same image recalled the rose window at Chartres to Henry.[255]

By November Larry had been taken on as an English instructor by the

British Council: 'England's reply to Goebbels', as John Cromer Braun would sarcastically dub the Council.[256] The job meant regular work in the form of teaching and administration, but the pay was good and many of Larry's new colleagues were people of talent and accomplishment. He met Bernard Spencer, elegant and slender, a poet of the Auden and Spender cast, with fine, aesthetic features. Spender, who had been at Oxford with Spencer, had commented on his 'depressed or depressive quality',[257] and John Betjeman, a schoolmate at Marlborough, had called him a 'shy squirrel'.[258] Larry would concur on his personality: 'He was shy,' he recalled after Spencer's death in 1963, 'and one had to prise a laugh out of him, but when it arrived it was quite disarming.'[259] In most ways, Bernard and Larry were opposites, yet they were to become good friends despite Spencer's reticence and his 'formidable irony'.[260] Spencer's verse, spare and taut as the Greek landscape, won Larry's admiration. Robert Liddell was already on the staff when Larry joined it, and Larry soon met David Abercrombie, phonetician son of the poet Lascelles Abercrombie. Robin Fedden was part of their circle, and his opposite number at the Greek Ministry of Information was Seferis. Sometimes they were joined by a tall and fine-looking young diplomat, Bernard Burrows, who years later would ask Larry to stand godfather to his son Rupert.

Larry was much happier with the Council than with the Information Services. He was distressed by Britain's failure to help Czechoslovakia, he deplored the 'shabby let-down of Poland' by the 'political casuists', and he found the French 'beneath contempt as neighbours and allies'. 'Bang!' he wrote to Anne Ridler, 'These are the uncharitable sentiments which I have been hugging under my player's hide while I was a faithful servant of his majesty, writing wonderful articles in the Greek press, and conceiving wily schemes for the furtherance of our arms. Now as a teacher I breathe more freely.'[261] He would always feel uneasy when called upon to support a political stance that he could not agree with, and he would be called upon to do precisely this many times in the years to come. The tension between his political persona and his private thoughts would eat alike into his domestic temper and his creative life.

Henry Miller finally booked a passage for America on a ship due to leave in a vaguely specified number of days, but there seemed to be time for a final trip with Larry and Nancy in a small Morris loaned to them by Max Nimiec, a Polish count who announced to everyone that he was dying and that he intended to spend the remnants of his fortune first. Larry picked Henry up on 24 December at the King George Hotel in Athens and they drove by moonlight to Corinth, travelling on 'borrowed diplomatic privilege and his majesty's petrol'.²⁶² Contemplating old Corinth Larry said, 'I think of something fat, reddish and sensuous'²⁶³ – an impression confirmed by the squat, reddish pillars still standing. Nancy, Larry and Henry had a glum Christmas Eve dinner and wrote extravagant postcards to celebrities.

The sunrise began with Henry 'dancing about at dawn yelling Helios Helios like a madman'.²⁶⁴ They visited Mycenae, which Larry and Nancy had not yet seen. As they neared the ancient site, Larry said he was reminded of the hill country in India. 'Always voluble and articulate', wrote Henry, dangling his modifying clause but clearly referring to Larry, 'I observed with pleasure that he was silenced.'²⁶⁵

Larry recovered his tongue at the deep well at Mycenae and proposed that they should descend the slippery steps. He led the way down the narrowing dark passage, claustrophobic, a veritable journey into the womb of the earth. Henry followed timidly. Finally Larry was persuaded to abandon the attempt and Henry bolted to the surface. They dug out 'pieces of sentimental pottery' and met a shepherd in a cloak from whom they 'bartered an old coin for a cigarette in the tomb of Elektra the unhappy'. 'Attica is dull and suburban,' Larry continued, 'the adventure begins on the long roads into the vale of argolis. You begin to dance internally, the woods speak almost audibly. And off the route are strange unvisited valleys such as hold Nemea and the ghost of lions. . . . we climbed the pass where only angels could inhabit to get over into the fertile Spartan valley; and we went up in a cloud, lost for half an hour; and suddenly the whole miracle broke into view like Darjeeling gone symphonic.'²⁶⁶ Then Larry, 'juggling the loose wheel with the dexterity of a mountebank', drove them through terrific rain down the mountains to Sparta, discoursing all the while on Daphnis and Chloë. The lecture, Henry thought, he could well have done without. A rainbow pursued them into Tripolis. The magic broke, and Larry in a black mood brushed off a couple of Athens friends they met by chance, their dinner was 'abominable', the radio in the restaurant blared Wagner, German carols, and propaganda.²⁶⁷

'I felt perversely gay about Sparta', wrote Henry, 'for it had at last revealed to me the Englishman in Durrell, the least interesting thing about him, to be sure, but an element not to be overlooked.' Larry's uncharacteristic reserve and coldness began to infect Henry. 'To me at least it was really beginning to look like Christmas,' he recalled. 'That is to say, sour, moth-eaten, bilious, crapulous, worm-eaten, mildewed, imbecilic, pusillanimous and completely gaga.'[268] In the morning they parted on the steps of their hotel in Tripolis, Larry and Nancy to drive on to Epidaurus, Henry to catch the train to Athens. Henry's glasses were blurred with tears and rain. Both men were conscious that their free way of life was ending, and that they might never meet again.

On 28 December 1939 Miller sailed on the *Exochorda* for New York. After his dismal parting from the Durrells, he had a cold welcome in his native city: he was broke and he had begged Anaïs Nin to meet his boat. She did not, pleading influenza. In Paris, Henry had told Betty Ryan that he would marry her when he returned to the United States. Now she realized that he had no intention of doing so. The ruptures begun by the war were continuing.

'An awful mess up in Albania,' Larry wrote to Elizabeth Smart, referring to the winter troop deployments. 'In the meantime my wife is going home and I am staying on here.' Both must have known that there was a good chance Nancy would not be able to rejoin Larry, but he refused to consider leaving Greece until he absolutely had to. Nor did he harbour any illusions about the war situation. 'It is a deadly calm; wonderful, every day I sit and watch the sun go down behind the Acropolis, which, hackneyed as it may sound, is an appalling and weird sight,' he wrote. 'After you have been in Athens awhile, and awake to it (i.e. not a blinking Britisher), you begin to see what a part this symbol plays in the lay out of the town, and in the dim unstable consciousness of the Greek, who is one of the finest persons in Europe, internally divided and confused like the Irishman but with a greater traditional manner and poise.'[269]

Larry was seeing himself in the confused and divided Irishman. It was not so much the prospect of death that worried him as the false colouring being given it. He was hurt to see the young men being 'deluded', being told that they were dying 'for a lie'. Death was not trivial. In fact, he said, 'There is only a personal morality; that they cannot rob one of; which is not wanting to die but not turning one's back on death as a foolery. We should be willing to lay down what we have not to government and causes, but quietly to fate. Then our honour is our own and not in the service of the New Statesmen fairies or the unions or the economic mystics.' Death was too important to Larry for him to embrace it lightly, yet he had to envy the security of those who could: 'I would give anything for the comfort of owning a fighting-man's opaque and personal calm. It is we who are the lost ones, not the so-called butchers.'[270]

WITH SO MUCH IN THE BALANCE, Nancy's pregnancy was an unwelcome complication from Larry's point of view. She travelled to England on an Imperial Airways plane in February, planning to stay there at least until after the birth of their baby. But Larry, worried that travel to Greece might soon become impossible, asked her to return. She arrived on the Orient Express, and he reported to his mother that she was 'very well and calm'.[271] Larry arranged for a job with the British Council on Cyprus, and planned to leave Athens within weeks after the baby appeared.

Penelope Berengaria Durrell was born in Athens on 4 June 1940, and eight days later Mussolini declared war on Britain. Was it patriotism that prompted Larry and Nancy to give their daughter the name of Richard Lionheart's queen? Larry thought they would have to flee an Italian invasion, and he wired Miller for money; Henry complied, and later told Larry not to pay him back. Wallace Southam, a Shell Oil executive in Athens, and his wife Anna took Nancy and Larry into their home for a few weeks while Nancy was recuperating. George Seferis was among those at the baby's christening according to the Greek Orthodox rite, and he announced the event to Henry Miller: 'I saw the other day [Larry's] daughter christened Bouboulina-Berengaria.'[272] Larry may have seemed an unlikely parent, but 'after the first week', he recalled later, he actually enjoyed 'the nappies and the sun treatment and the fuss'. In fact, it was 'as good as having a new book out'.[273]

As the rumours of immediate invasion faded, Larry began working out variations on Penelope's name – the nickname Pinky stuck – and writing poems to her. In 'To Ping-Kû, Asleep', his love shines through:

> Invent a language where the terms
> Are smiles; someone in the house now
> Only understands warmth and cherish,
> Still twig-bound, learning to fly.[274]

When Anne and Vivian Ridler's child was born some eight months later, Larry wrote hoping that the Ridlers' baby would prove 'at least as much fun for you as Ping-Kêe is for us with four rabbit-teeth and a snub nose'.[275]

Fatherhood did not lead to a significant change in Larry's habits. In his midnight conversations at the Mykonos Taverna he would switch from hilarious repartee to hold forth on Pythagoras or make pronouncements about his own writing. 'One's aim is of no importance, one's manner of progressing towards it is everything,' he said to Robin Fedden. 'The poison of life is the desire for a permanent synthesis.' This rejection of permanence would become a motif in both *The Alexandria Quartet* and *The Avignon Quintet*. Prefiguring his attempts to apply Einstein's relativity to fiction, Larry stated, 'The problem of life is in the reconciliation of Time with Space.' In his own mind Larry had not definitively fixed the English, like beetles in amber, in *The Black Book*, and he now thought that 'The energy of the English is not spiritual but social.' As evidence he cited Shakespeare campaigning to procure a coat of arms and D. H. Lawrence 'stressing his parentage out of sheer annoyance that he was not a duke'.[276]

In midsummer 1940 the departure of foreign nationals for locations further away from the threats of Mussolini speeded up, and Fedden, having resigned from his Embassy post, moved to Cairo. During August, Larry, Nanos Valaoritis and Bernard Spencer sped off to Mykonos for a quick visit. It was partly a send-off for Spencer, who was departing for Cairo, where he moved in temporarily with Fedden. While on the island Larry drafted 'Fangbrand', the poem dedicated to his Mykonos friend Stephan Syriotis that would begin *A Private Country*. Two years later, discussing possible cuts with T. S. Eliot, Larry pleaded, 'But please leave dear old "Fangbrand" who is really the only piece of my personal mythology which comes off 100 percent.'[277]

The same month Larry, Nancy and Penelope also moved, not to Cyprus as he thought he had arranged, but to Kalamata in the southern Peloponnesus where the Council wanted him to start a school, the Institute for English Studies. The British Vice-Consul in Kalamata, a wealthy Greek banker named Panos Kostopoulos, had campaigned for a Council office in the town, and he lodged the Durrells on the waterfront near his consulate. There was apparently another reason for showing the flag in remote but strategically important Kalamata: a German official of considerable skill and sophistication was stationed there. Larry claimed that part of the justification for his own presence was to counter whatever propaganda the German managed to serve out.[278]

The invasion of Greece from Albania by the Italians on 28 October 1940 framed sudden new identities for Larry's friends. The gentle Theodore was mustered into the Royal Army Medical Corps and attached to the artillery, where he distinguished himself by lobbing into a hospital tent the practice shell needed to qualify for his commission – luckily, no one was hurt. The great raconteur George Katsimbalis instantly became 'a tall, tough lieutenant feeling the strain of youth again in his heart'. The poet Takis Antoniou took to sea as a captain, 'running the seas thoughtfully'.[279] Patrick Evans, son of staunch Quakers, joined the British Army and learned to drive a tank. Alan Thomas, also born into a Quaker family, served in the RAF until he was invalided out. Peter Bull slipped off the stage to command a small landing craft. True to his word, his fortune nearly spent, Max Nimiec died of his enlarged heart, appropriately enough at the Argentina Cabaret. 'Max is a great loss,' Larry mourned. 'Goodness and innocence were so deeply fused in him that from the surface he seemed vapid.'[280] Fred Perlès enlisted in the British Army under a programme for foreign nationals stranded by the war in the United Kingdom. Fred was amused to have changed sides for this war, and would say in years to come, 'I lost one and won the other.'[281] In one of the myriad ironies of the war, the shy pacifist Hans Reichel, a self-exile from Germany, was interned by the French as an enemy alien. Only Henry Miller managed to carry on as if the war were being fought on a distant planet, setting off in a 1932 Buick with his artist friend Abraham Rattner on a year-long tour of the United States.

The opening acts and the early triumph of the tragedy that was Greece were played out over the next six months. Three days after the Italian invasion, the Admiralty announced that Greek waters had been mined. In early November the RAF began bombing Brindisi and Bari. Greek land forces counter-attacked immediately and soon the Italians were in retreat, then in a rout. On 22 November the Greek forces, although ill-fed, severely outnumbered and outgunned, recaptured Koritsa in the north. In a few weeks they had pushed the Italians back into Albania, where the front stabilized until the German invasion of 6 April 1941. Meanwhile, however, the Greeks were jubilant, even though everyone knew that it would be only a matter of time before Hitler decided to take over the Greek campaign from Mussolini.

In February 1941 the British Council schools were closed due to the war situation, but by mid-March Larry had been given no new assignment. A fortune-teller had read in his coffee grounds 'You will cross water', and he deduced that his destiny would be Egypt.[282] 'We are sitting on the crater,' he told Henry, 'expecting Yugoslavia to cave in any day.' France too would fall soon, only with less honour: 'As we prophesied at the beginning of the war the arch-rat is France. You will see her declare for Germany before long: all she wants is an excuse.' In Greece, apart from 'one or two distant puffs and roars', they had seen nothing of the real war, although planes had buzzed Kalamata frequently and terrified the folk.[283] An Italian seaplane had seemed to be heading right into the room where Larry was sitting, and while he was writing of this incident to Anne Ridler, a tremendous concussion sent him racing to the beach where Penelope was being walked.

No one could say what had happened: perhaps a mine had detonated itself against the outer harbour breakwater. In this uncertain situation Larry applied to the RAF but was told he would be kept on, at least temporarily, by the Council. His earlier anger at Eliot forgotten, Larry was writing 'Dear TSE' and sending him additional poems for a projected volume: 'Epidaurus' and 'Letter to Seferis the Greek'.[284]

Mockingly, the season turned lovely. 'Now spring is coming this valley is getting beautiful and serene, encircled by big snow caps, and raving with oranges,' he wrote to Henry. 'Last Sunday we walked up the dizziest mountain path to the snowline of our range, and saw the great white snout of Taïgetos in the valley beyond.' Like an itinerant monk telling beads, Larry named the places that meant so much to him. 'I could shut my eyes and see it laid out like a relief map – Sparta under the wing of Mistra, Tripolis in the great Pear-Campus, Argos and Nauplia thawing slowly in the haze with the first anemones and asphodels, and Epidaurus like some afterthought – an appendix to the old world with all the revisions and false starts and erasures put in their place in one superb act of thought.' He had visited Athens recently and found the once-luminous city 'blacked out and grim, with planes patrolling over the statues', his friends dispersed: 'I get an occasional line from Seferiades who is working like hell; Katsimbalis is the most impressive officer in Greece I hear: and the young are surging forward. Stephan the bearded magician of Mykonos is up in the line. Daperis and Xipollitos too.' Larry sent his love to those Paris friends who now seemed so far off: 'To Anaïs and Betty and Eduardo and Hugo'. Penelope 'has grown enormously, has eight teeth, a vocabulary of two words, and a yell like a hungry starling'. This was to be the last letter Henry would receive from him for over a year, and Larry's closing evoked the world about to be lost to them all: 'I send you a leaf from a wild rose of Messenia picked beside the untamed and hero-loving gulf: and salute you in the name of Aphrodite the foam-born. love. larry.'[285]

THE GERMAN ONSLAUGHT CAME with dramatic suddenness on the cold Palm Sunday of 6 April. That night, half the port facilities at Piraeus were destroyed when the Luftwaffe blew up a munitions ship, the *Clan Fraser*. Thessaloniki fell on 9 April, and the Germans advanced steadily south-wards in the face of Greek and British resistance. Nancy cabled for the last £50 of her capital to have escape money. People were more annoyed than shaken when Koryzis, who had succeeded Metaxas as prime minister, died on 18 April of 'heart failure', as the papers reported his suicide: every

Greek knew the truth almost at once, and said that he had shot himself over the mismanagement of the war effort. Lárisa fell on 19 April and Ioánnina the next day, but Katsimbalis, attached to the Greek GHQ, told Theodore Stephanides that the Lamia-Thermopylae Line could still be defended. On the evening of the 21st Theodore had a splendid meal with some English officers at Costi's Restaurant, and Athens seemed nervous but optimistic. The next day he had lunch with George and Aspasia Katsimbalis, and the Colossus told him that the Lamia Line was cracking. Their meal was cut short by a telephone call ordering Theodore to return to his bivouac near Piraeus, and he ran out into the spring afternoon.

Various rumours reached Larry in Kalamata, but he had been given no definite evacuation orders. Within a few days he, Nancy and Penelope could expect to be interned – or worse, given the political aspect of Larry's British Council position. Refugees and combatants converged on Piraeus, Kalamata and anywhere else that held out hope of evacuation. Vice-Consul Kostopoulos arranged for a caïque to take the Durrells and others to Crete, and sent them by road 55 kilometres southwest to Pylos. They could take no belongings. Penelope was carried in a basket, like a loaf of bread. Alexis Ladas raced over from Athens in his cousin's Mercedes runabout, the car battered from dodging in and out of packed lines of trucks, military vehicles and carts jamming the roads leading away from Athens. Ladas joined the party on the tiny ship.

The caïque left on the night of 22 April, listing uncomfortably to port and emitting a trail of sparks from the diesel exhaust. Hugging the rocky coastline, the overloaded craft throbbed along, reaching a small inlet just short of Cape Matapan at the first sign of dawn. Theodore, who had never located his unit after parting from Katsimbalis, was aboard the antiquated Greek collier *Julia* setting sail from Piraeus at almost the same moment. 'The nights', Larry recalled, 'were starless and without moon,' the sea, mercifully, like silk.[286] The harbour would have been unsafe for Larry's caïque but for the great calm. The entire village near the bay came to see them tie up. The villagers' one radio had expired: 'What news?' they asked. The day was spent securing the boat as well as possible against the coming voyage in the open Aegean. In a secluded cove on nearby Cape Yerikos Larry, Nancy and Alexis Ladas swam, washed and sunbathed on the warm pebbles. 'Nancy and Larry dropped their clothes', recalled Ladas, 'and so did I, very discreetly behind a rock.'[287] Ladas, raised with Greek notions of modesty that dictated swimming almost fully clothed, never forgot Nancy's beauty.

The villagers killed their last pair of lambs and set out a feast, 'as if for a wedding'. No planes were spotted. 'So we sat in the warm, buoyant, late sunlight and toasted each other calmly and with love, for we did not expect ever to see each other again,' said Larry. 'We had no right to feel like this, for the world had come to an end. Why then this happy fulfilment of quiet talk and laughter?' It was, he thought, Greek pride at having resisted 'the Hitlerian menace' at a time when the great powers were temporizing.[288]

Just as the caïque was gathering way into the 'violet dusk', a crewman gave the alarm and all raised their heads to see Stukas in a tight wedge directly overhead. The captain turned the boat abruptly back under the cliffs. 'There was a moment of high excitement and near panic', Larry wrote, 'but it ended in roars of laughter, for the wretched aircraft above us turned out on closer scrutiny to be an arrowhead formation of wild duck.'[289] Theodore's ship, crawling along at a top speed of seven knots, met up with real German warplanes in full daylight, as two successive flights of eight and nine Junkers 87B Stukas attacked with bombs and machine guns. Theodore was too curious to take cover below decks. He observed that it was 'grimly fascinating to watch them as they roared up': 'As each plane arrived nearly overhead it flipped over on its side and then on its nose and seemed to fall vertically down on us.'[290] Although Theodore had to treat seventeen injuries from the strafing, and a bomb exploded close enough to blast two crew-members overboard to their deaths, the *Julia* could still amble at reduced speed towards Crete. She was to survive two more dive-bombing attacks that day. Theodore had the amused satisfaction of hearing a German radio report announce the sinking of the *Julia*.

There were real dangers ahead for Larry and Nancy as well: on Cythera, where they hid during the light of the second day, an armed party of Cretan deserters from the Albanian front, their own boat wrecked, wanted to take the caïque and maroon Larry's group. The Cretans, many of them battle-wounded, were in a savage mood and said they absolutely must get to Crete to execute a general who had turned traitor. A tense diplomatic discussion ensued: the fate of the women and children was pleaded, and the Cretans finally decided to allow them to leave on condition that they take three of the most seriously wounded. Several of the Cretan soldiers helped Nancy wash out Penelope's nappies: the baby's digestion was not taking kindly to irregular meals and unsuitable foods. The skipper of the caïque departed with some dispatch lest the Cretans change their minds. By coincidence, Theodore's ship also hid out for a day in one of Cythera's bays, but he saw neither Larry's caïque nor the Cretan warriors.

The night sea was alive with darkened caïques, all heading for Crete. An occasional glow was visible from other craft, but compared to them Larry's boat was like Halley's Comet. Luck and the old Greek gods must have been with them, however, for by the next day they were unbending their cramped legs on the streets of Chania. Larry found satisfactory lodgings for Nancy and Pinky with some kindly Cretans. There were a few air raids, and in Suda Bay the torpedoed cruiser HMS *York* lay beached, her stern awash, her single functioning gun still firing at the planes. But this was fairly far away, so that only a few stray shards of shrapnel came pattering down on the tin roofs of the makeshift tavernas where they paused to sip ouzo. Larry searched for Carnation milk for Pinky. Alexis Ladas reappeared in tailored riding breeches, 'manifesting a sang-froid which was rather out of place'. Although he missed Theodore, who had arrived at about the same time, Larry kept running into friends: all Athens seemed to be in Crete. The doctor would remain on the island during the violent days of the German invasion. He was lucky to have been dining with Katsimbalis when his unit had left the Athens area: on Crete he learned that most of his former companions were either missing or captured. Theodore was also fortunate to be off the *Julia*, for a bomb finally sank the old ship in Suda harbour. The Greek government was much in evidence, orbiting about King George and his entourage, which included George Seferis. The Minister of the Interior, Larry recalled, 'I saw emerging from a hole, clad in a tin helmet and looking like a giant rat'.[291]

An Australian transport materialized on the evening of 30 April as if by magic. Larry, Nancy and Penelope embarked under cover of darkness and the ship throbbed and surged into the night, racing to be out of easy range of the Luftwaffe by daylight. Larry's intellectual and emotional turmoil of the past few years was swept aside by the pure drive for survival.

CHAPTER 5

Egypt: Cairo

We are getting the refugee habit:
[. . .]
We are the dispossessed, sharing
With gulls and flowers our lives of accident:
No time for love, no room for love . . .

'In Europe'

THE PORT OF ALEXANDRIA must have loomed up before Larry and Nancy like Erebus. It was four o'clock on the first of May 1941, on what was definitely not an Ionian spring morning, when they slipped past the anti-submarine boom. The commercial Western Harbour of Alexandria smelled of spilt oil from ships holed or sunk by the Stukas, 'ships laid open in Caesarian section', he would write in *Clea*.[1] Owing to the black-out, little more than the silhouettes of nearby ships and buildings could be made out: no Fort Kait Bey, no Ras El Tin Palace. Nor was Egypt offering her traditional open-armed welcome: Larry was told that he was a 'refugee national' and that with all the passengers from their ship, he and his family would be interned under guard in a refugee camp until their identities could be established. There was a not unreasonable fear that German agents would infiltrate Egypt as refugees. A group of journalists, bursting to be off to file their stories, had shoved to the head of the gangway. Larry began to feel abused and bilious. Finally, one of the Field Security sergeants checking identities took his passport and read his name.

'Writer?'

'Yes.'

'Once of the Villa Seurat?'

'Yes.'

'Friend of Henry Miller?'

'Yes, anything wrong with that?'

'Not at all, would you step aside please.'[2]

The sergeant turned out to be John Cromer Braun, who published poetry under his middle name and who was eager to discuss writing, the Villa Seurat, Bloomsbury – anything literary from the lost pre-war world. Larry and Braun talked until daylight in a slit trench at the transit camp, while overhead streaked the tracers sent up by the anti-aircraft barrage.

With full light, Larry, Nancy and Penelope found themselves thrust out into the hazy, warm morning of coastal Egypt, the sun showing redly through the hint of fine sand in the air. Alexandria struck Larry as sticky, dirty, noisy. Yet that was not all: 'Going ashore in Alexandria', he wrote, 'is like walking the plank for instantly you feel . . . its backcloth of deserts stretching away into the heart of Africa.'[3] His deeper acquaintance with the city would have to wait, for soon they were handed into an army lorry for the gritty ride along the two-lane desert road to Cairo. Within minutes they left the reed-whipped shores of Lake Mareotis behind them and struck across the bare and level sand. Larry looked back, and years later would recall 'the flat mirror of the green lake and the broken loins of sandstone which marked the desert's edge'.[4] The last landmark dropped behind them, and only the staccato roar of the engine and the wind flapping the canvas covering of the truck gave an impression of motion: there were no trees, no buildings to mark progress. Several hours later, just before the truck jolted on to the streets of Cairo, the great pyramids of Cheops and Chephren rose up to their right. The heat acting upon Larry and Nancy's fatigue made them too drowsy to show more than a flicker of interest.

A spring *khamseen* had painted the skies, in Larry's phrase, 'as brown as buckram',[5] and the wind was blowing hot sand in from the desert, rendering buildings a uniform greyish beige. The grit sifted into closed drawers and sealed serving dishes, until everyone was in a state of depression or hysteria. The Cairo traffic was indescribably dense, and exhaust fumes assaulted eyes and throats. Rattletrap buses and trams, taxis, the tidy Fiats and Austins of the professional population, a few American limousines, military staff cars, lorries, motorcycles, bicycles, donkeys with panniers, two-horse gharries and goods wagons drawn by single emaciated horses, ice-carts, agile pedestrians, slow *gamoose* with huge curving horns, herds of sheep and goats, strings of drooling camels (prohibited in downtown Cairo but there nevertheless) – all seemed in desperate competition for the same strip of road, the same intersection, and every klaxon, bell, siren and voice claimed the right of way. Many animals and vehicles displayed blue beads to defeat the evil eye, while drivers kept one hand on the horn to ward off other threats. In the smaller streets and alleys the stench of refuse, sweat and urine gripped the nose with a physical violence.

LAWRENCE DURRELL

Egypt got off to a bad start with Larry. Alexander the Great had been twenty-four when he reached Egypt, Napoleon twenty-eight, and both had come with the optimism of youth and conquest; Larry was only twenty-nine, but he felt harried and disoriented. He had destroyed many files before leaving Greece and had stored some manuscript drafts and notebooks with Corfiot friends. Much of what he had been working on in Kalamata he had simply abandoned in his flight. He felt as if six years of his creative life had been casually lopped off. An immediate problem presented itself: having fled Kalamata with only the clothes they were wearing and with very little money, he and Nancy were forced to throw themselves on the mercy of the uniformed authorities, who took them to the Luna Park Hotel. The place was ramshackle, run-down, and the sybaritic tinsel of the cabaret downstairs coupled with the drab rooms above suggested that it had been, as was rumoured, a brothel. And of course it was thronging with other displaced persons. Still, they were lucky to have a room to themselves and a measure of security until Louisa could telegraph emergency funds.

Meanwhile the news from Greece cut like shattered glass. Athens radio had sent out a last message on 27 April as German forces entered the city: 'Last night with you – happy days with victory and liberty – God be with you and for you, good luck.'[6] Alexandria replied, 'We shall not forget you.' Foreseeing as they all did the coming Axis occupation of Greece, before leaving Kalamata Larry had written and posted to Eliot a long poem, at once consoling and celebratory, 'Letter to Seferis the Greek':

> O my friend, history with all her compromises
> Cannot disturb the circuit made by this,
> Alone in the house, a single candle burning
> Upon a table in the whole of Greece.[7]

Larry soon made contact with other friends from Greece, including Alexis Ladas, who had made a nervous passage from Crete on a three-hundred-ton caïque loaded with explosives: 'The British have such a predilection for shipping TNT from place to place,' he commented wryly.[8] David Abercrombie, now with the British Council in Egypt, sent Stephanides to Larry. Theodore was limping after having walked across Crete in borrowed boots several sizes too large. He had left the island with one of the last ships to run the gauntlet of German aircraft, and had come ashore at Alexandria at 2 a.m. on 1 June when, despite the black-out, the quays lining the harbour were inexplicably illuminated with bright lights.[9] Theodore told Larry that all who had been part of the evacuation from

234

Crete would receive a medal 'inscribed with the words EX CRETA'.[10]

By the time Theodore appeared at the Luna Park Hotel to greet Larry and Nancy, their money had arrived; they had located a flat in the Gezira Guest House and were merely waiting a day or so until their new abode could be made ready. The guest house was located in Zamalek, a haven of large houses in carved stone, stucco and brick on the exclusive Gezira Island between diverging branches of the Nile. Zamalek had wide streets shaded with plane trees, blue-flowering jacarandas and red flamboyants; many houses were set amid exotic gardens, and the great river flowed calmly towards the delta, imparting a slight coolness to the air. The island was reasonably quiet at night, and here most British civil and military personnel with families lived, enjoying a polo field, cricket pitches and even a golf course. Theodore was assigned to the General Hospital at Agusa, a suburb on the river a short walk away. Other friends displaced from Greece also lived in Zamalek, including Abercrombie.[11] In social terms it could almost have been Athens, yet the ambience was very different. For one thing, most of Larry's group had the temporary feeling that goes with being refugees: they expected soon to be sent *somewhere*: to another theatre of the war, to South Africa, to Britain. Most important for the hellenophiles, Greece had fallen, and the sense of exile – double exile – weighed upon them all. At the end of the year Larry would still be writing, 'We haven't collected ourselves after the loss of Greece.'[12]

When Larry arrived in Egypt, Rommel, who had only been in North Africa since 12 February 1941, was in the midst of a series of threatening but unsuccessful attacks on Tobruk. Lieutenant-General Sir Richard O'Connor's triumphs over the Italians in Egypt and Libya during late 1940 and the first two months of the new year had not been consolidated, owing to Churchill's insistence on a futile attempt to keep the Balkan Front alive. The German entry into the desert conflict had caught the British off balance and short of men and matériel, and soon O'Connor was in a German prison. It was not comforting for Larry to realize that he, Nancy and Penelope might shortly be forced to flee again. The earlier Italian night air raids on Cairo and Alexandria had been regarded by much of the populace as an entertainment: people sat on their rooftops to watch the searchlights probe for the planes and the tracers arc skyward. With the engagement of the Luftwaffe in the North African conflict, this attitude changed, and violent attacks on Alexandria during June resulted in a panic in which over a hundred thousand refugees fled to Cairo. Paradoxically, this was a great help to the British: the Egyptians became furious with the

Germans. The failure of Operation Battleaxe, launched by Wavell, the commander-in-chief, on 15 June 1941, led Churchill to replace him with Auchinleck. A new staff inexperienced in desert armoured warfare had to learn by costly trial and error: the field commander, Lieutenant-General Sir Alan Cunningham, fresh from victories in the scrubland of Ethiopia, had never even seen the virtually featureless northern desert before.

If these considerations bothered the brilliant international community in Egypt, there was little indication. For Cairo the war was a time of profit, excitement and privilege. There were vast new hotels, shops resplendent with glass and bright lights. True, some nights the black-out was in force, but the Arabist Freya Stark was not alone in the opinion that the condition 'improves a town's looks enormously . . . you can't think how pretty Cairo is with its dim lights blue and red and green'.[13] Bernard Burrows, recently arrived from Athens, introduced Larry to Freya, and there was instant mutual recognition of kinship. Although Freya was a bit older than the run of women in Egypt on official business, she had enough poise and dash for any three. With her flowing, feminine dresses and her hair coyly curled over her forehead to hide a scar, Freya looked ready for a genteel tea-party circuit. Only the roguish glint in her eyes hinted at the adventurous spirit that had sent her all over the Middle East, often alone, by car, camel, donkey and on foot. Fluent in Arabic, she had wangled official approval to form and direct her Brotherhood of Freedom cells, intended to counteract the anti-British effect of Communist and nationalist organizations.

Cairo made startling displays of the contrasts for which Egypt was notorious: alongside the glittering showcases thin children executed handsprings and cried for *baksheesh*, conjurers and flame-swallowers performed tricks. Black-veiled barefoot women in bedouin costume walked beside others, also veiled but in the elegant Paris manner and brilliant in silks and satins. In front of Shepheard's Hotel a man sold peerages for fifty piastres, half an Egyptian pound. A street vendor outside GHQ offered 'Chocolates? Cigarettes? OBE's?' while one enterprising pimp proclaimed, 'Mister, you want to sleep with my sister? She's clean and white inside like Queen Victoria.'[14] Prostitution flourished with the coming of the Allied armies. Major A. W. Sansom, the Chief Field Security Officer for the Cairo area, charged with reporting on the morale of the Allied troops, stated flatly, 'Morals and morale don't mix.' Morale, he asserted, 'depended mainly on the price, quality, and especially availability of prostitutes'.[15] The price at the professional end of the scale was one to five pounds, and availability was not in question; the quality, naturally, varied. The British were forced to make condoms available to the troops and to set up seven centres to treat venereal disease. When it came to writing about Egypt, Larry would emphasize a sexual licence and venality more appropriate to wartime than to the pre-war setting of the first three volumes of *The Alexandria Quartet*.

The British High Command flourished socially: General Wavell had attended a dinner with the American Ambassador, Mr Fish, on the evening when the winter offensive of 1940 was launched, and he gave away the bride at a smart wedding during another time of crisis in 1941. While Rommel was hammering the Eighth Army at El Alamein in June 1942, the British Ambassador, Sir Miles Lampson, would order the Embassy garden railings to be repainted.[16] Part of this display was aimed at building public confidence, as Larry would have been the first to appreciate: public and press relations – vulgarly called propaganda, for which Freya Stark liked to substitute *persuasion* – had been his main concern in Athens and Kalamata, and would employ him again in Cairo and Alexandria.

As soon as they could, Larry and Nancy fled from the Gezira Guest House to a three-bedroom flat at 14 Saleh Ayoub off Sharia Russell Pasha, not far from the Bulaq Bridge in Zamalek. The furniture was hired from a depot; there was no opportunity to make the walls cheerful with the bright peasant pots and fabrics of their Corfu days. The solid cut stone portals of Larry's building would not have been out of place in Bournemouth, but for the first time in his life, he was really on his own financially: his mother could not continue his allowance, and Nancy's inheritance had been used up. Money was a serious problem as he and Nancy tried to replace their abandoned wardrobe and survive in a war-inflated economy.

Neutral Cairo drew like a vortex an array of talent unequalled in variety and brilliance for a city of its size. Soon Larry's circle included Xan Fielding, now trained to parachute into German-held territories; Robin Fedden, back in Egypt after serving in a Quaker ambulance unit during the brief Syrian campaign; Gwyn Williams, burly, bluff and unmistakably Welsh, already teaching at Cairo University long before the war started and in Egypt since the mid-1920s; Bernard Spencer; Terence Tiller, a lecturer in English at Cairo University; Hugh Gordon Porteus; a protégé of F. R. Leavis named John Speirs, whose beautiful Latvian wife Ruth was engaged in translating Rilke. Although he was no longer working for the British Council, Larry kept up with his old Council friends. Through Abercrombie, he met Betsy and Jon Uldall, both phoneticians. Betsy was an American who wrote comic verse in the Ogden Nash manner, and Jon was Danish. Olivia Manning and her husband, R. D. ('Reggie') Smith, had arrived in Cairo from Athens shortly before Larry and Nancy, having made a direct passage on an old steamer. Olivia and Reggie had shared a two-berth cabin with British Council lecturers Robert Liddell and Harold Edwards and his lively and elegant Greek wife Eppy: there was a quarrel over the amount of space taken up by Eppy Edwards's large hat box, and by the end of the short voyage the two women were enemies. The Greek poet Elie Papadimitriou travelled on the same ship.[17]

The civilian hellenophiles and British Council folk were relatively few in number. In contrast, the invasion of uniformed authors seemed limitless. John Gawsworth turned up, no longer the Grub Street *mondain* Nancy remembered, but an untidy sergeant in the RAF. George S. Fraser, a private writing for *Parade* magazine, met Gawsworth at the grocer's shop off Soliman Pasha that was a favourite place among Fraser's acquaintance for cold beer and *mezes* of olives, peanuts and roasted fig-fed warblers. Gawsworth still pledged *Mon roi!* to the Stuart pretender or to Prince Rupert of Bavaria, when he was not toasting Sinn Fein or the French Republicans or Ernest Dowson. A trumpeter for all manner of causes, Gawsworth turned the Sunday at-home poetry gatherings of Keith Bullen, headmaster of the Gezira Preparatory School, into the Salamander Club, and Fraser's humble grocer's shop into an institution.[18] Larry disliked anything resembling literary clubs, and although he remained friendly with Gawsworth, he did not become a regular at either venue. Once a sergeant from Security, investigating reports of Gawsworth's wild talk, asked Larry if he was prepared to vouch for him. 'I said I was prepared to vouch – though with misgiving,' Larry recalled.[19] To his relief, Gawsworth was soon transferred to India, where he found a publisher and became a friend of Nehru.

Other poets-in-arms from Britain included Hamish Henderson, John Waller, Dorian Cooke and Keith Douglas. Larry liked Waller, 'an endearing character . . . and an awful ass', whose vaguely defined duties with a water supply unit seemed to leave him plenty of free time to write and publish.[20] The quality of his poems and the tragedy of his death would combine to make Douglas the most famous of the war poets. Eric de Mauny arrived with the New Zealand Expeditionary Force. One of Fraser's friends was William Campion, a learned enthusiast on Islam and Spain who was given to dramatic gestures and sardonic epigrams. He may have suggested to Larry the name and nature of Campion in Larry's *Dark Labyrinth*. There was enough talent for an entire expatriate movement, and it soon gave tongue in a variety of little magazines: the Army-based *Citadel* and *Parade*, John Cromer Braun and John Gawsworth's *Salamander*, Fraser and D. J. S. Thomson's *Orientations*, and *Personal Landscape*, the magazine founded by Larry, Robin Fedden and Bernard Spencer.

In the early months Larry supported his family in part by writing a humour column, based on a character named Aunt Norah, for *The Egyptian Gazette*. Beginning on 6 June and entitled 'Yorick's Column' – later he dropped the apostrophe – it ran irregularly at first before settling into a Sunday routine. The typesetting vagaries of the *Gazette* staff helped Larry's humour along. Yorick explains, 'My Aunt Norah is, of course, the window of Sir Percival Staggers, the only British general to die of a horse's bite.' Aunt Norah, a lady with a baritone voice and a wooden leg that turns out not to be wooden, volunteers for the balloon barrage: '"I will do anything to help" she is reported to have said, "and I just adore the balloons. I will help blow them up or let them down . . . Or I will simply hold the string. No sacrifice is too much."'[21] She is inadvertently carried off from Dulwich Park by a runaway balloon, and many of the later columns concern speeches in Parliament about her fate, official enquiries, and sightings of the balloon:

A Bremen broadcast on Friday night stated that a woman was seen on a stationary balloon eating a meal of cold chicken and claret with obvious zest; a German fighter pilot who approached the balloon was greeted by the woman, who leaned over the side and said: 'Pregnancy?'

'Pregnancy what?' the pilot shouted back.

'Pregnancy Deutsch?' asked the woman with an Australian accent.[22]

Yorick's Column included sketches apparently by Larry, as well as material under various sub-headings, among them 'Premature Epitaphs' – a title Larry used in a typed pamphlet circulated to a half-dozen friends – 'Misprint Dept.' and 'Untimely Ends'. This last was attributed to Stephanides. They do sound like Theodore's brand of humour, and were probably a collaboration. The reader is admonished to 'Think upon these untimely ends':

2 The parachutist with an impediment in his speech who counted the full ten before pulling the rip.
[. . .]
9 The man who complimented Hitler on his acting in 'The Dictator'.[23]

The scent of propaganda permeated 'Yorick's Column', and Larry threw in everything he could think of to make fun of Axis figures.

He also contributed some fifteen leaders to the *Gazette*, including one entitled 'Quo Vadis?' that gained a flurry of fan mail: it was 'a stupendously banal piece – but on the party line!' recalled Larry.[24] He made no claim to be producing art, but all his hack writing earned him around £10 a month. Later he did some broadcasting.[25]

The final Yorick entry appeared on 27 July, and at the beginning of August Walter Smart, the Oriental Councillor attached to the British Embassy, interviewed and hired Larry for the post of Foreign Press Officer in the Publicity Section. Spencer Brooke, a regular *Gazette* columnist whom Larry had lampooned in print, wrote that after 'carolling about the office like a young lamb' – this had the ring of truth – 'Poor Yorick has deserted journalism for WORK' of a 'hush-hush variety'. She added that 'His new bosses refuse to allow him to write one word for the Press'.[26]

Larry's knowledge of Greek and of the Greek temperament particularly recommended him to Smart, and Larry's especial charge was to influence the Greek press in Egypt to print stories supporting the Allied cause. For this he would receive £600 per annum, without perks. It sounded to Larry and Nancy like a lot of money, but an Egyptian pound, although worth a shade more than sterling, would buy far less in wartime Cairo than an English pound had in pre-war Corfu. None the less, it was a living wage: a Cairo policeman made only £50 per year, while the *fellahin* contrived to survive on £5.

The publicity people clearly needed Larry's help: the German propagandists had proved far more imaginative than the British, and a pitch was made to the Egyptian masses claiming that Hitler – 'Muhammad 'Ider' – was a Muslim out to liberate Egypt from the English infidels. Added to the propaganda put out directly from Berlin were anti-Allied statements from the 'Whispering Gallery', all those extreme Egyptian nationalists, Islamic fundamentalists, and members of the Hungarian, Romanian and Spanish legations favourable to the Axis.[27] According to an Egyptian estimate, 40 per cent of the population was anti-British, 15 per cent pro-British, and the rest, including the man-in-the-street, had no opinion.[28] After British losses in Greece and Crete, after Rommel's rapid advance, the Egyptians believed that while the British might be able to defeat the Italians, they were no match for the Germans. Also, many Egyptians asked, what were the stakes? Even so important a statesman as Nahas Pasha, who would become a wartime prime minister owing to the direct intercession of Sir Miles

Lampson, said that the British-German conflict was one 'in which we have neither a male nor a female camel': not our show.[29] Young King Farouk, surrounded by the Italian palace servants who had coddled him as a child, secretly favoured the Axis and gave tacit support to radical nationalist sentiments and actions. Lady Lampson was half Italian, and Farouk annoyed Sir Miles by saying, 'I won't get rid of my Italians till he gets rid of his.'[30]

It was Larry's poetry, not his propaganda, that gained him entry into Walter Smart's social circle. 'Smartie', as he was universally called, was a cherisher of artists, and his first visit to Larry's office occurred during an afternoon when his new press officer was late in returning from a luncheon with an Egyptian poet. 'I immediately concluded that Smartie was a low-down dog who had been testing my punctuality and general efficiency by a surprise visit,' recalled Larry. But no, Smart had merely wanted to talk to Larry about his poetry, and that evening Larry was invited to the hospitable home that he kept at 19 Sharia Ibn Zanki in Zamalek with his painter wife Amy Nimr, daughter of the founder of the Cairo newspaper *el Mokkatam*. Smart was a tall, thin man with a sculpturesque head and a 'long wide slanting nose' that reminded Larry of a Norman knight's, and he combined great erudition with an almost childlike enthusiasm and ingenuousness.[31] Perhaps he provided Larry with the first hint for the character of David Mountolive in *The Alexandria Quartet*,[32] but he was a man of greater intellectual distinction and humour than Larry would give to his creation.

Larry and Nancy were to be frequent guests at the Smarts', where they were apt to meet Freya Stark, fresh from Baghdad or Beirut on the business of her Brotherhood of Freedom; Bernard Burrows and his fiancée, Ines Walter; Elie Papadimitriou, whose *Anatolia* was much admired in Larry's circle; or some mystic, renowned scholar, or obscure eccentric. Amy Smart was especially warm towards Nancy, as one painter to another. Under a tree in the Smarts' garden in 1942 Larry met Patrick Leigh Fermor, an officer with the Special Operations Executive who as a youth had walked from Holland to Romania, and the two talked far into the night. Conversations with the Smarts and their guests, held in the comfortable rooms lined with brown-, silver- and gold-wrapped books in Arabic and Persian, French and Greek, the walls decorated with Amy's large thoughtful canvases, could range from theories about the Holy Ghost to the prosody of the Sufi poet Jalaluddin Rumi.

Amy, born into a Syrian-Lebanese Christian family, was as staunch a patron of young artists as her husband. Described by Lord Kinross as having a mind at once masculine, oriental and feminine, she was one of the extraordinary women who gave Larry hints for the characters of Leila Hosnani and of Justine in the future *Quartet*. Later, like Justine, Amy was to suffer the tragic loss of her only child, fatally injured by a battlefield explosive that the boy had picked up, an episode that Olivia Manning would use in her *Levant Trilogy*.

Not everyone was charmed by the Smarts. The photographer Cecil Beaton found their house 'rather slovenly' and Amy 'glib': 'by her stream of quite witty talk she prevents any good talk.'[33] With so many highly charged and ego-driven personalities crowded among the expatriates, friction was inevitable. Freya Stark judged Randolph Churchill, ostensibly in Egypt as a commando, although he seemed to spend most of his life at parties, 'a quite insufferable young man',[34] while Reggie Smith wrote satiric verses belittling Stark's Brotherhood of Freedom.[35]

Reggie Smith and Olivia Manning were among the people Larry was *not* likely to meet at the Smarts' home. Reggie, a large, burly, untidy man with thick, round, black-rimmed spectacles, was an excellent teacher and a tireless promoter of other writers. He was also incorrigibly congenial, and was a magnet at the Anglo-Egyptian Union for a crew seeking encouragement, advice and free drinks. One of those grateful for his friendliness was Fraser, who liked both his 'perpetual heartiness' and his strong principles.[36] Olivia tended to stay at home writing. She felt that her husband's talents and her own were not sufficiently recognized, and that Amy Smart should have offered them her patronage. It was not forthcoming. Olivia took her revenge by putting Amy into *The Levant Trilogy* as the foolish society gadabout Lady Hooper. Larry characterized Reggie's hangers-on as disreputable and tended to stay away from him, and he retaliated by referring sarcastically to Larry as 'the magician'.[37] Larry did not find attractive Olivia's tubular figure and oval face – set, typically, under a turban – and still less did he like her sharp, critical manner. In this, his opinion was shared by most people who knew her in Cairo.[38] Whatever his feelings about her, however, he did not object to the publication of her poem 'Written in the Third Year of the War' in *Personal Landscape*.

Walter Smart was a living link with Constantine Cavafy, the Greek poet who would become for Larry the ghostly voice of Alexandria. Larry and Theodore had translated his poem 'The Barbarians' and seen it published in the *New English Weekly* in 1939. Smartie told Larry how, as a novice diplomat, he had earned a rebuke for forgetting on his arrival in Egypt not only to Sign the Book but even to present himself for duty. He had been given an introduction to Cavafy, who lived above a brothel in Alexandria, and Smartie had been so entranced by the conversation of the old poet that he had spent several days talking literature with him before reporting to the Cairo Embassy. It had been well worth the reprimand, he said. His conversation was peppered with anecdotes about Cavafy, and Amy would later translate some of Cavafy's poems for *Personal Landscape*. Larry's own later translations of Cavafy were to form thematic accents in the mosaic of *The Alexandria Quartet*. Walking back to his flat from the cool, gracious home of the Smarts, Larry was hit as though with a physical blow by the solar inferno that was Cairo in the summer, a 'burning-glass of a city, wedged between its deserts'.[39] Curiously, Larry ignored the green, fertile delta and the Fayyoum oasis in fixing his heraldic image of Egypt: the country would remain for him 'flat and sandy – just these two cities in between sand dunes'.[40]

He was willing to suffer the desert inferno in a good cause, however. Knowing his instinct for nosing out interesting people, Stephanides was not surprised one day in September 1941 when Larry announced that the two of them had been invited by the great Harvard Egyptologist George A. Reisner for tea and a tour of the newly excavated 'Queens' Tombs'. They drove out to Giza, shimmering in the dry heat. Waiters in white flowing robes and red sashes served a marvellous tea under a marquee, and then Reisner took them to the small pyramid-tomb of one of the queens of Egypt. Biting the stem of his pipe in a snaggle of teeth, squinting at his guests through thick lenses – Reisner was approaching blindness after several failed operations for cataracts – he discoursed on the architecture of Egyptian tombs, the subject of the *magnum opus* that he had raced against blindness and death to complete. Larry, familiar with Wallis Budge's *Egyptian Book of the Dead*, was spellbound. He and Theodore followed the white head of their host inside a recently excavated burial chamber where the electric torch revealed a dado of scenes of commonplace life along the Nile, brilliant in colour that had never felt the bleaching light of the sun or the scouring of the *khamseen*. Here were fishermen, weavers, potters and housewives, painted by some humble recorder free from the pretensions of the artist. Reisner showed them where the ancient illustrator had skimped on details in places hidden by funeral furniture or statuary. He also pointed out a long-concealed niche containing the bust of a man not the queen's husband: was this the image of some earthly lover hoping for an eternity of adultery, Reisner wondered?[41] As Larry stood in this beautiful house of spirits, he must surely have thought of his long-planned 'Book of the Dead'. Reisner's own future was to be brief: in the coming June he would have himself carried from a Cairo hospital back to Giza, so that he could die among his beloved tombs.

Larry shared a large room at the Embassy with two other press officers, Mary 'Boo' Bentley and David Howarth. Larry and Mary hit it off at once, joking about the tribulations of life in Cairo; the earnest Howarth soon managed to shift himself to another office. 'We made his life miserable,' confessed Mary.[42] Larry announced to T. S. Eliot that he had found a 'lovely job', with a 'collection of extremely civilized people'. In fact, he added, 'Never seen a British colony so civilized – it would break Maugham's heart.'[43] Soon Mary had moved into a spare bedroom in Larry and Nancy's flat. At first Mary and Larry bicycled to the Embassy; later on, a gharry was sent to pick them up, along with other contract employees of the Embassy living in Zamalek. Larry acquired Princess Osmanoglou as a secretary and felt himself a potentate indeed.[44]

Sharing good fortune with friends was a way of life in wartime Cairo, where an inhabitable set of rooms was rare and costly. Mary's fiancé, Group Captain Dudley Honor, in charge of the air defences of Cairo, also stayed with them whenever he could leave his RAF squadron stationed in the Western Desert. 'We were as happy a family as you could wish for in wartime circumstances,' Mary remembered. Larry liked Dudley, who had been shot down while flying a Hurricane over Crete, and dedicated 'The Pilot' to him:

> This lovely morning must the pilot leaning
> In the eye of heaven feel the island
> Turning beneath him, burning soft and blue.[45]

They engaged a manservant, Abdullah, who could cook quite passably. He had casual notions about the ever-present Cairo insect life, however: once, Mary and Larry were checking on the preparations for a party when they noticed what appeared to be totally inappropriate date halves topping the canapés on a large platter. With their approach the dates fled – a platoon of cockroaches had been enjoying the offerings. Abdullah made a pitiable face and murmured '*Malesh, malesh!*' ('Sorry'), the universal Egyptian response to anything gone wrong, from a beetle in the soup to a rear-end collision. There was no time to produce replacements: 'We'll serve them and no one will be the wiser,' said the practical Mary. Larry would recall these 'cockroach-haunted rooms where I then lived' when he came to write *Justine* over a decade later.[46] Mary noted the strain between Larry and Nancy, but put it down to the disruption of their idyllic life in Greece and to what Nancy termed Larry's 'need for adulation' from their women friends. Then, too, there was the chronic shortage of cash: there was nothing in reserve, as there had been in pre-war days, for the occasional extravagances that they so much enjoyed.

And Cairo was an extravagant city: for those with money, the supply of pre-war hock and champagne served by white-robed waiters at the small square tables on Shepheard's terrace lasted into 1943. The cost was high, but the wicker chairs were comfortable; as a vantage point, set at head-height above street level, the terrace could not be beaten for seeing whoever was who in Cairo. The wartime austerity and rationing of England were virtually unknown in Egypt. From both the Groppi cafés issued the mingled aromas of roasting coffee and butter-rich pastry, people met for tennis and squash at the Gezira Sporting Club, and the Turf Club pampered the polo and gambling set, for whom the whisky never ran out in the upstairs bar. In the Kit Kat cabaret Hekmat Fahmy, 'the most rousing of all the Egyptian belly-dancers', quivered her lovely flesh for the benefit of officers on leave from the desert.[47] At the Badia, an *Opéra Casino*, Mme Badia appeared on stage, making up in vivacity for what she may have lacked in youth. There were also the Taverne Française, the Beba, and the Dolls. Sometimes these and the other nightspots had good floor shows, but the majority of the dancers were of very slight talent, and they often improved their incomes – and the take of the establishments – by a bit of prostitution on the side. Melissa, one of the heroines of Larry's *Quartet*, would be one of these. The great department stores, Chemla's, Cicurel's, Le Salon Vert and others, displayed every luxury. Even after quality wine and spirits vanished from the shops, the wealthy families of Egypt always managed to come up with good French and Italian wines and Scotch or American whisky.

Some of the pleasures available to young civil servants did not cost much, to be sure. The museums were closed for the duration of the war, but the time-traveller could visit the Sphinx and the pyramids at Giza for a powerful sense of Pharaonic Egypt, or penetrate Coptic Cairo to see the mediaeval Christian sector. A stroll through the vast Mousky bazaar evoked the ambience of the souks of all the Middle East: a labyrinth of alleys, lanes and aisles, a display of all the trade goods of east, south and west. The Birka, a bazaar in woman-flesh, was strictly Off Limits to Allied military personnel, and the uniformly dark, plump and squat whores seated before curtained booths serviced mainly the common soldiers of the Egyptian Army. Similar booths with their attendant muses would find their way into Larry's *Quartet*.

Transport to these entertainments came with risks: trams and buses were infested with lice, fleas and pickpockets; gharries were at least private, but they too came with vermin, and not uncommonly a wheel would fall off; Ford and Fiat taxis dating from as far back as the 1920s offered smashed windows, tyres bound up with bits of wood and metal, missing gears and usually no lights. Such a nervous effort of will was required to get about in Cairo that Larry and most other British residents – as distinct from the troops on leave – tended to stay on sheltered Gezira Island when their work did not take them into the area of banks and consulates. A favourite meeting place on Gezira was the Anglo-Egyptian Union, an agreeable low, green-shuttered building at 179 Sharia Fuad el Awal that had formerly been the residence of the commander-in-chief of the Egyptian Army. In fact, the Union shared with the Egyptian Officers' Club a garden shaded by tall trees. The Union was founded to promote rapprochement between English and Egyptian intellectuals, and there were lectures about Egypt and concerts featuring Arabic as well as Western music. As a social bridge the Union was not particularly successful: most young Egyptians felt that fraternization with the British would contaminate their nationalism and so, if they came at all, they usually clustered at separate tables and drank interminable cups of tea, while the foreigners at other tables took advantage of the low prices and the fact that the Union served alcohol an hour beyond the ten o'clock closing time of other legal establishments. For Larry, the Union was as close as anything in Cairo to the typical Greek taverna: a place where one could talk quietly over a drink. The bars in the city were packed with boisterous soldiers, while no Moslem café sold alcohol. The Union was also a haven for educated women who pursued culture rather than colonels, and Olivia Manning could sometimes be found there with her pale bird's face poised over a glass of Stella beer.

The Union was convenient for Larry and most of his friends. Here he relaxed with the Irish political journalist Keith Scott Watson and Nievis, his beautiful, eccentric Catalonian wife. It was in the shaded garden, Robin Fedden recalled, 'with ice tinkling in our glasses and bulbuls in the trees offering throaty comment', that he, Larry and Bernard Spencer planned *Personal Landscape* magazine.[48] A witness to this event was Mursi Saad el Din, one of the few Egyptian members of the Union. Fedden and Spencer were by this time teaching at the Fuad el Awal University. Bernard and

Larry 'first hatched the scheme' of the magazine.[49] The name came from Fedden's poem of the same title and was intended to emphasize the personal values, even pacifist ideals, in danger of being submerged by the war effort: those "personal landscapes" which obstinately continue to exist outside national and political frontiers.'[50] Like Fedden a declared pacifist, Spencer was not much in accord with the 'martial preoccupations' of most of the Cairo British. Larry's own attitude towards the war puzzled even his friend Robin, who recognized the 'high irony' with which Larry viewed the polished propaganda that he was paid to turn out. What seemed to bother Larry most, thought Fedden, was the 'canalization of thought and response' imposed by the war.

Many showed a friendly interest in *Personal Landscape*: the cheery Gwyn Williams; Terence Tiller, a precise, scholarly man with sharp features, 'like a mad policeman', as Larry described him[51]; Robert Liddell, compact, fussy, self-assured; and Dorian Cooke – 'the small, fell figure of Dorian/ Ringing like a muffin bell' in Larry's epigram. Thanks to the founding trio, the magazine looked towards Greek culture as represented by Cavafy, Elie Papadimitriou and Seferis. When Larry was sent to give instruction in English to Panagiotis Cannellopolous, president of the Greek government in exile, he came away with a pledge of support for *Personal Landscape*.[52]

Despite his complaints about Egypt to others, Larry described Cairo in favourable terms to Eliot. His main reasons for writing to Eliot were to announce that he had enough poems for a thick Faber volume, and to ask Eliot to contribute to *Personal Landscape*. A contingent of British poets, 'eating sand and beating off the mammoth Egyptian flies', desperately needed the encouragement of a poem or even a note in a letter from Eliot. Larry dismissed lightly the loss in his escape from Greece of '100,000 words odd of The Book of the Dead' and of the first act of 'Adam and Evil', 'the play I was sure you would not like'. Larry had come to terms with the disaster: 'It does one good to be stripped clean like that. I'm not sorry.' On the other hand, he continued with self-deprecating irony, 'The poems were saved by an error on the part of the British Council.' He was making up a collection: 'There is no doubt any more – I am writing poems at last: I think Faber will take them and like them.'[53] Eliot's reply was as friendly as always. 'Your attitude toward *The Book of the Dead* is heroic and right,' he wrote, and added that the novel 'will be all the better after such a painful mutation of the phoenix'. He permitted himself a faint touch of irony: 'As for the poems, if you say so I believe it, so all I want to know at present is when they are coming.' Eliot did not exactly refuse to send poems for *Personal Landscape*, but said that all he had at present were some 'verses' that he had written for an Indian Red Cross book.[54] Despite periodic prodding from Larry, Eliot was never to contribute to the magazine.

The first issue of *Personal Landscape* in January 1942 contained three poems by Spencer, three by Fedden and three by Larry – 'To Argos', 'To Ping-Kû, Asleep' and '"Je est un Autre"' – followed by a terse and ruthlessly honest review by Terence Tiller of his own Hogarth Press *Poems*. Larry saw his daughter Ping-Kû, Penelope, as a creation, like a poem or a primitive's fire. Tenderly he addressed her:

> . . . surely you won't ever
> Be puzzled by a poem or disturbed by a poem
> Made like fire by the rubbing of two sticks?[55]

Framed in a generous format, a slim copy of *Personal Landscape* cost five piastres, one shilling, less than the price of a drink at Shepheard's, and the printing was done by the press of the French Institute of Oriental Archaeology in Cairo. The magazine was distributed at the Anglo-Egyptian Union and at the Anglo-Egyptian and Renaissance bookshops. Bernard Spencer, lean and pale, would come through the gates of the Union bearing a stack of freshly printed copies to distribute to the various contributors. Every run of five hundred sold out: poetry was clearly at a premium, despite Fedden's deprecatory comment that most copies were bought up by 'friends and acquaintances'.

Each of the eight numbers of *Personal Landscape* would contain a contribution by Larry, usually poetry, but in the first two issues his 'Ideas about Poems' formed part of the manifesto of the magazine. In the beginning of the first issue he wrote:

1. Neither poet nor public is really interested in the poem itself but in aspects of it.
2. The poet is interested in the Personal aspect: the poem as an aspect of himself.
3. The public is interested in the Vicarious aspect; that is to say, 'the universal application', which is an illusion that grows round a poem once the logical meaning is clear and the syntax ceases to puzzle.

These theories, Larry thought, were all very well, but 'MEANWHILE./ the poem itself is there all the time.' 'Poems are Facts,' he concluded, and they needed to be aired, just like children.[56]

The other two editors, Fedden and Spencer, also appeared in nearly every issue of sixteen to twenty pages, which did not leave much room for other contributors, nor were uninvited submissions welcome: the landscape was not only personal, it was private. Almost everyone published was a non-combatant and a friend of the editorial troika. Tiller was published in every issue, Robert Liddell appeared five times, Elie Papadimitriou and Ruth Speirs three times each, and John Pudney twice. Then there were others among Larry's friends: Seferis, Dorian Cooke, Hugh Gordon Porteus, Gwyn Williams. Larry believed in the virtue of Speirs's translations of Rilke, but as Spencer's lover her welcome was assured in any case: while the editors flattered themselves that their literary standards were high, *Personal Landscape* was always intended to give voice to their group, not to an open field of writers. Larry would place in the magazine three clerihews by Diana Gould – later Lady Menuhin – after the ballerina's blazing passage through Alexandria.

The one important outsider was Keith Douglas, represented in three issues of *Personal Landscape*. Douglas had met Spencer in Cairo, and later in Alexandria Larry saw him twice during his leaves from the western desert and encouraged him to send poems. Douglas had vowed after the war 'to depart for sunnier and less hypocritical climates' than England,[57] so he was much in accord with Larry on two counts at least. At once boyishly exuberant and battle-wise, Douglas embraced his desert war with delight and pity. Larry thought that he was 'glad to have tested his courage',[58] and admired both the man and his poems. He was to tell George Fraser that he had in part modelled Johnny Keats in *Clea* on Douglas: the sun-blackened 'Greek god' who appears before a startled Darley to declare, '*Seriously*, life is wonderful,' and to assert that the desert must be seen. Suddenly Keats becomes grave and says, in the accents of Douglas's poem about death in battle, 'Vergissmeinicht', 'Nobody seeing [the war] for the first time could help crying out with the whole of his rational mind in protest at it: crying out "It must stop!"'[59] Darley never encounters Keats again, nor would Larry see Douglas after their second meeting in Alexandria. The soldier-poet appears to have had a premonition that he would die in battle, and Larry would apply this memorably to Keats: 'He sounded the empty coffin of his early death with patient knuckles.'[60] Douglas had been submitting his verse to *Citadel*, but he switched to *Personal Landscape* after meeting the editors, and when he left Egypt in November 1943 he gave most of his poems to them.[61] The final issue of the magazine would close with an announcement that Douglas had been killed in action in Normandy, the only such notice to appear in the entire run. Unique among the dead, Cavafy was very much a presence in *Personal Landscape*, both by way of

Amy Nimr's careful introduction for six of his poems and through Robert Liddell's 'Note on Cavafy'.

Fraser admired Larry's poetry and *The Black Book*, and tried to introduce the *Personal Landscape* contributors to the troops, using his pulpit at *Parade* magazine. Larry was reported to have torn up a piece Fraser had written about him, commenting with equal parts of acid and irony, 'Little poetasters making publicity for themselves out of their acquaintance with *great poets*!'[62] Larry confided to Eliot, 'the wretched Apocalyptics are a dreadful bore. G. S. Fraser is here as local representative; bad theory and worse art.'[63] Fraser sought out his company, and Larry was kind in manner although often sharply critical, once writing to him, 'The trouble with you, George, is your vulgar sub-editor's interest in whether the poet picks his nose or not'[64] – the confusion of biographical detail with literary quality would become Larry's frequent refrain about his critics. None the less, Larry was probably responsible for printing Fraser's 'City of Benares' in *Personal Landscape*. Fraser was rather an ambiguous figure, miserable in the barracks yet not at ease in the expatriate civilian set either. The jovial company of pink and blond John Waller, the future baronet, and of the soldier-poets Ian Fletcher and Eric de Mauny bruised him far less than meetings with Larry. Yet decades later Fraser would write a sympathetic book-length study of Larry's work. However, attention on this scale was far in the future, and Larry joked to Eliot, 'I am 30 and still obscure; who is the publicity man at Fabers; to whom do I complain?'[65]

Despite Larry's complaints, *Personal Landscape* was turning out well, enthusiastically supported by Smartie, and four issues appeared during 1942. Cyril Connolly, then a major arbiter of literary fortunes, wrote to Fedden offering to sell copies. In particular, Connolly wanted Fedden to write on Egypt and Larry to write on Greece for his 'Where Shall John Go?' series in *Horizon*. A year earlier Larry would have jumped at the chance, but he was too occupied now, and seven years were to elapse before he would be published in Connolly's journal. 'I think it is very important that writers like Durrell, Tiller & yourself', wrote Connolly to Fedden, 'should become absolutely steeped in the Aegean civilization.' This should provide 'a little taste & discipline' as antidotes to the 'windy nothings' being submitted to him in England. Larry had anticipated the directive on Greece by half a dozen years, but now he had switched focus, and by February 1942 he was already filling notebooks with details of Egyptian life.[66]

FEBRUARY WAS TO PROVE an exciting month. On the 4th, the massive six-foot-six Sir Miles Lampson, in response to the virtual collapse of the government and to King Farouk's encouragement of pro-German Egyptian nationalists, drove in the evening to the Abdin Palace and demanded the king's abdication. A battalion of British troops, supported by armoured cars and a few tanks, stood by to seal off possible escape routes and a warship was ready to spirit Farouk to exile in the Seychelles. Rather to Sir Miles's disappointment, Farouk gave in to his demand that Nahas Pasha be asked to form a government under him, and Egypt's neutrality effectively ended. It was a success in the short term, but a long-range disaster for Anglo-Egyptian relations and a tremendous boost to Egyptian nationalism. With each affront to the theoretical but in practice very limited Egyptian sovereignty, with each insult to Farouk personally, his popularity grew, while Sir Miles sped on his way towards earning elevation to the House of Lords as well as the title of 'most hated man in Egypt'.[67] Larry's job in public relations became harder, and he would remember Lampson, half affectionately but fittingly, as 'that old buffalo'. Larry was torn between the colonial's instinct to confront native 'recalcitrance' with efficient force, and his dislike of clumsy and costly gestures.

It was with relief that he turned back to poetry. Despite the limitation of the first issue of *Personal Landscape* to work by a mere three authors, and the declared intention to stress 'personal values' then in danger of being submerged by the war, the journal soon evolved into an organ for writers united more by the shared experience of exile than by a common purpose or outlook, as Fedden recognized in his introduction to the 1945 anthology compiled from it. To the usual connotations of the word 'exile' Fedden added 'stagnation', which he thought attacked writers who were placed in an 'alien context', the flaccid and enervating environment of Egypt. Larry felt this too, and it increased his discontent. He was by choice a *resident* in foreign lands, not a happy voyager, and he lacked the born traveller's delight in seeing unfamiliar places simply because they were there. Larry made quick judgements and usually stuck to them.

Cairo and indeed all Egypt nearly stunned Larry with the force of the contrasts and the horrors. He had come to hate 'this copper-pan of a blazing town with its pullulating stinking inhabitants'.[68] Larry and Nancy might often have longed for a cooling plunge, but they dared not swim in the river for fear of bilharzia. Neither could they sit in cinemas – showing the latest American films – without being nibbled by fleas. Larry could not walk the streets without having constantly to say 'No! Go away!' to an apparently endless string of pedlars and beggars. Children followed him in the streets, gleefully if uncomprehendingly shouting 'Fuckoff! Fuckoff!', the rebuff they had received from British soldiers.

Like a green branch borne to the Ark, Henry Miller's *Colossus of Maroussi* arrived, a message from a vanished world: 'A marvellous fantasy from beginning to end', Larry wrote Eliot, 'and thick with libels on me and everyone else'.[69] Larry, Nancy, Theodore, Seferis, Niko Ghika and of course Katsimbalis all appear under their real names in Henry's idiosyncratic vision of their times in Corfu, Athens, Epidaurus, Tripolis. Henry had printed without permission almost the entire text of Larry's August 1940 letter to him. Larry was not seriously upset.

In December 1941 Henry had written to Larry, having heard from Seferis that he was still in Cairo. Henry had considerable news. There was a chance that Larry's poems and *The Black Book* might be published in New York by a young couple Henry knew. Also, Anaïs Nin had bought a press and planned to print her diary herself. Henry had logged 25,000 miles in his Buick, priming himself to write *The Air-Conditioned Nightmare*. Now back in New York, he had seen Anaïs Nin and Elizabeth Smart, and had learned that David Edgar was in Harlem, Fred Perlès in Scotland. Betty Ryan seemed to have vanished. Henry was not to hear from Larry until the following September, when Larry's letter of 4 July 1942 finally arrived.[70] While a message or two might have been lost in transit, since he had fled Greece Larry had apparently not tried often, if at all, to contact Henry, and the uncharacteristic silence says more about his state of mind than about the pace of his life. He felt hopeless about writing when letters often took months to arrive. And he felt even more hopeless about the glorious pre-war Villa Seurat and Corfu worlds. Egypt was becoming synonymous with loss.

Also, Larry's marriage was steadily souring. There were two personal concerns that caused arguments between Larry and Nancy: shortage of money and assaults on their health. Flats in Zamalek that could have been rented for £10 per month before the war climbed to £60 in a few years, and although Larry had got in before the peak of the market, housing still consumed the major portion of his income, even when sharing expenses with Mary Bentley. While there was no rationing, imported goods cost at least five times what they did in England. Larry and Nancy had brought with them from Corfu a better set of intestinal antibodies than couples fresh from England could boast, but Penelope was a constant worry. The ubiquitous flies landed on the baby's eyes, nose and mouth, and she had a succession of minor ailments.

It all made Larry long for Britain, he confided to Anne Ridler, then in Scotland:

O I wish we are [*sic*] all in the Orkneys instead of in this terrible blinding sand-pan with its mocking hideous tombs and minarets. Such a country – cripples, deformities, ophthalmia, goitre, amputations, lice, flies. In the street you see horses cut in half by careless drivers or obscene dead black men with flies hanging like a curtain over their wounds and a crowd hemming them in with ghoulish curiosity. Dust in the air carrying everything miasmic, fevers, virus, toxins – One writes nothing but short and febrile like jets by this corrupt and slow Nile; and one feels slowly walked upon by the feet of elephants.[71]

Elephants! Given his youthful longing to return to India, Larry's dislike of Egypt – as a general colonial situation not so very different from India – would be surprising did it not illustrate what he had become: despite his disclaimers, he felt quite English, or at least British. Significantly, Larry was never to learn enough Arabic to converse freely, as he once could in Hindi. The pavement entertainments of baboons riding goats and scrawny bedouins manipulating snakes, the acrobats and *gulli-gulli* men who came up to terrace tables, the throngs in the Mousky, even the openness towards death that had fascinated him as a child in India, all these now filled him with proper English horror. His dead father had won after all, and Larry was at least partly pukka.

THERE IS NO EVIDENCE THAT Larry had intended *ever* to go to Egypt, before Hitler's advance catapulted him out of Greece. But the land was contributing more towards the evolution of Larry's writing than he knew. The 'Book of the Dead' that he had planned as far back as 1937 and lost in Kalamata was given a new skeletal framework by a country where, as Fedden put it, the earth 'bursts with corpses', where the crops are grown not in soil but in 'bone-mould and excrement'. The exile in Egypt 'must get accustomed to standing on people's faces'.[72] Cairo's necropolis, a city of the dead, a grisly palimpsest with a large community living in shanties and tents among the tombs and mausolea, must have impressed Larry by its frightful economy. In truth, he was fortunate that his first real experience of Egypt was in Cairo, where ancient Egypt was more insistently present than in Alexandria. As Larry's new friend Lord Kinross was to observe of Giza, 'No creation of man, no cathedral or temple or mosque, no tower or skyscraper, no fortress unsupported by any bastion of nature, so dominates a landscape as these three pyramids dominate the valley of the Nile before

Cairo.'[73] This sense of an immense past, reaching further back even than the antiquity of Greece, would provide both the historical cut stone of *The Alexandria Quartet* and a counter-balance to the sordid present.

Curiously, however, there was little sense of historical continuity, at least in the Europeanized cities: the Pharaonic past and the reinforced concrete apartment buildings jostled one another with few structures to represent intervening epochs. Time did not appear to be continuous, but shifted in jumps, like cinema vignettes. There was no eighteenth-century architecture such as so often marks the stage between the Renaissance and the modern in many European cities. 'To-day', wrote Fedden of Egypt in 1945, 'is ridiculously isolated and uncertain of itself.'[74]

The absence of clear continuity brought its own kind of instability, as if the populace were released from the logic of cause and effect. Freya Stark noted that in the East 'the unexpected happens so punctually that you are saved from the bondage of plans'.[75] Larry's observations bore this out, and he was to flout probabilities in character and event not only in the *Quartet* but also in the succeeding *Revolt of Aphrodite* and *The Avignon Quintet*. In the last sentence of *Quinx*, the final volume of the *Quintet*, the created novelist Blanford 'thought that if ever he wrote the scene he would say: "It was at this precise moment that reality prime rushed to the aid of fiction and the totally unpredictable began to take place!"'[76] It was Egypt all over again.

Knowing his penchant for seeking out unusual personalities, someone introduced Larry to Joseph McPherson, known familiarly in Cairo as 'The Bimbashi' – Turkish for 'Major'. Larry had seen McPherson 'ambling about Cairo on a white mule lost in thought and looking like God the Father', as a friend described him. McPherson had been in Egypt since 1901 and had held a variety of educational, military and government positions, including Acting Mamur Zapt, Head of the Secret Police, during the years 1918–20. After his retirement in 1924, McPherson had remained in Egypt, staying in his home near Giza and, occasionally, in his small flat near the Abdin Palace in the centre of Cairo. The year before Larry met him he had published *The Moulids of Egypt*, an account of religious fairs and festivals not unlike that written about Indian religions by Larry's uncle, C. H. Buck. McPherson was much loved by his Egyptian neighbours, who considered him a seer and a holy man. When Larry and Nancy visited him, McPherson was about seventy-six, 'white haired and frail',[77] 'of medium height and slightly built with a small and beautiful head which housed eyes of extraordinary luminosity and smiling kindness'.[78] McPherson received them in a room moving in its evocation of his personality: the small crucifix over the bed, a print of the Madonna, a photograph of his mother, a few cherished personal objects.

Much about McPherson marked him as an inspiration for Joshua Scobie in the *Quartet*, including his abiding love for the ordinary Egyptians, his adoration of his mother, his small-boned frailty, his spare, economical life, and even his surroundings: 'The furnishing of his room suggests a highly eclectic spirit', Larry would write of Scobie, 'the few objects which adorn the anchorite's life have a severely personal flavour, as if together they composed the personality of their owner.' Larry was recalling his visit to McPherson when he added, 'The shabby little crucifix on the wall behind the bed . . . . Nearby hangs a small print of the Mona Lisa whose enigmatic smile has always reminded Scobie of his mother.'[79] McPherson's was a saintly and monastic nature by contrast with the roguish character Larry was to create. Also, McPherson seems not to have exhibited the homosexual 'Tendencies' with which Larry would endow Scobie, nor did he go about in skirts and a Dolly Vardon bonnet. Larry carried off a copy of *The Moulids of Egypt*, inscribed in courtly fashion 'Compliments to Mr. & Mrs. Durrell', and stored it away for reference when he resumed work on 'The Book of the Dead'. The book was a tangible emblem of a figure so other-worldly and aesthetic that, without it, Larry could almost have doubted the old man's existence.

Even the war in nominally neutral Egypt seemed unreal, except when Rommel hovered like a raptor over El Alamein. That would come soon enough, but as late as May 1942 the British believed that their system of reinforced box-bunkers in Libya from Gazala to Bir Hacheim formed an impregnable barrier against German armour. Meanwhile, black-outs, inflation, rationing and parades bedevilled the civilians, but there was little sense of mission or of purpose: and it was Larry's business to convince the public that there *was* indeed a vital purpose. While he himself – and some others – commented unfavourably on his punctuality, he 'more than pulled his weight', according to his colleagues in the Publicity Section.[80] Still, he thought much of his work was devoid of purpose, and he once told Mary Bentley that he had just sent his tailor's bill on the Reuters tape to the Gezira Club. He proposed that they dash over to watch the brigadiers solemnly reading it.

From his post Larry watched the events in the Western Desert. Auchinleck in Cairo and General Alan Cunningham in the field had been goaded by Churchill into the premature Operation Crusader in the late autumn of 1941. Egypt seemed oblivious of the desperate battle going on: 'No one would guess anything was happening', wrote Freya Stark, 'in the almost peacetime liveliness of Cairo'.[81] Rushing to relieve beleaguered Tobruk, Cunningham by 21 November believed that he had Rommel in flight, and in Cairo, 'by a conspiracy of foolishness between press and public relations, the "victory" was announced to the world with vulgar flamboyance'.[82] In fact Rommel, with two panzer divisions, had shattered the British 7th Armoured Brigade at Sidi Rezegh, and his strategic victories continued. Rommel had stated that Shepheard's would be his Cairo headquarters – as it had been for the British in World War One – but at the hotel, where patrons waited interminably for drinks to arrive, they said, 'Wait 'til he reaches Shepheard's – *that* will slow him up!' In the desert, however, only the courage, resolution and sheer doggedness of the British Commonwealth troops, together with the leadership of Auchinleck, who took personal command in the field after Rommel's breakthrough, prevented the decisive German victory that would have led to the loss of Egypt. The desperate days of El Alamein were approaching, bringing with them telling personal consequences for Larry and Nancy.

A different battle was being waged in the fashionable night spots, the bars and brothels, and the boulevards and alleys of Cairo and Alexandria. When ten men stood at the bar at Groppi's, it was hardly an exaggeration to assume that three of them were spies. Overheard conversations of Commonwealth and British officers, even their love-letters to their mistresses, were apt to be transcribed and sold to the highest bidder. Jews schemed for Zionist goals, Greek royalists fought Greek republicans and communists, and the Copts were disappointed that the British had not given them the responsible government positions that they claimed as their ancient right. At the most venal level, officers and other ranks were decoyed with promises of women, clubbed and robbed; policemen who refused bribes were sometimes knifed. In the Kit Kat cabaret, Mac the barman was in the pay of British security while the captivating belly dancer Fahmy aided Johannes Eppler, the German master spy. Attempted arrests frequently led to shootings and stabbings. The terrorists were even more deadly: Lord Moyne, British Minister of State in Egypt, would be assassinated in 1944 by a pair of Zionist fanatics linked to the Stern Gang. Underlying everything was the Egyptian hatred of British control: King Farouk, encouraged by his Italian household staff, was barely held in check by the heavy hand of Sir Miles Lampson; young officers such as Gamal Abdel Nasser and Anwar Sadat plotted against the British; and even many seasoned politicians preferred the fox at the gates to the hounds within. Larry, with friends near the epicentre, got pungent whiffs of all these goings-on. Some assumed that he was in MI6, the Secret Service: he was so often on the spot just when things happened. 'No', said Larry, 'although to an extent we were all in the Secret Service, as employees of the Crown.'[83]

It was partly because of the phlegmatic national tradition, partly a deliberate pose of steadiness, that the British continued 'normal' life even as Rommel, by his series of deft strategies and bluffs in May and June 1942, raced across the desert towards Alexandria, capturing in rapid succession Gazala, Tobruk and Mersa Matruh. Pose or not, Stephanides's General Hospital No. 58 beat an undignified retreat from Mersa Matruh to Moascar on the Suez Canal. Cairo and Alexandria were thronging with refugees, deserters and combatants of all nationalities, and Larry's soldier friends, the poets Keith Douglas, Hugh Porteus, Erik de Mauny and John Waller, were among those who would dash to the cities for a bath, a night or two in a bed and a few good meals. A 'mad spirit of carnival' prevailed, Larry would write in *The Alexandria Quartet*; with 'furious gaiety' the soldiers threw themselves into 'a saddening and heroic pleasure-seeking which disturbed and fractured the old harmonies'.[84]

Rommel's threat to El Alamein in the summer of 1942 led to contingency plans for destroying fuel and war matériel, blowing up the Alexandria docks and scuttling the Vichy fleet, impounded in the Eastern Harbour, 'lying belly-down' and 'like a symbol of all that was malefic in the stars which governed the destiny of France'.[85] British dependants were evacuated by ship, rail and truck. On 29 June Alexandria was heavily bombed, especially the port areas, and at 3 a.m. on 1 July Rommel launched a probing attack on El Alamein, only sixty miles along the coast.

The pretence of normal life ceased abruptly. 'The Flap', as the civilian panic was called, produced the sort of dark comedy that Larry found irresistible. The Cairo streets were even more blocked with traffic than usual; the railway station was thronged with women and children trying to get out of Egypt. The first of July became known in Cairo as 'Ash Wednesday' because many embassies and consulates in Egypt sent tons of documents up in smoke from huge pyres in the courtyards. Some of these documents came down as 'black snow', but other papers marked MOST SECRET, carried off by strong updraughts before they had burned fully, were used by market vendors to make up little cones of peanuts.[86] On this day Larry was sent to Alexandria to inspect the offices of the Information Services and to destroy secret files, but he found that the building had already been seriously damaged by the bombing. All he was able to do was note down the addresses of the shops and businesses that had put up signs such as 'Welcome Rommel' and 'Please Advance, Rommel', so he could recommend that, in retaliation, they be declared Off Limits to Allied personnel.[87] The harbours had sustained damage: 'Gun-barrels split like carrots, mountings twisted upon themselves in a contortion of scorched agony', Larry would write. 'Human remains were being hosed along the scuppers by small figures with tremendous patience and quite impassively.'[88]

During the Flap, Nancy and Penelope left with Mary Bentley for Jerusalem on a refugee train. Olivia Manning gave Nancy and Pinky temporary lodging there. When Mary returned to Cairo a week later, Nancy stayed on in Jerusalem, a resolve easily justified by the war situation.[89] The first real battle for El Alamein would come between 13 and 17 July, when Auchinleck by three separate routs of Rommel's Italian contingent forced an Axis retreat. However, the German threat to Egypt was not yet over.

Although the immediate cause of their geographical separation had been Rommel, as the threat of invasion waned Nancy made it evident that she was in no hurry to return to Larry, and journeyed instead to Beirut. He thought of their separation as temporary, and he was preoccupied with his tasks at the Information Office. 'My wife's in Syria and my daughter, and my heart,' Larry wrote to Eliot. 'We are terribly rushed.'[90] As the memory of their conflicts dimmed, Larry became more conscious of his loneliness, and he missed the comfort of his small family. Still, the hectic pace of his official life kept him from dwelling on his own sorrows. When Theodore arrived on 14 August on a weekend leave to Cairo, he found Larry 'brisk, cheerful & optimistic', and next month Theodore pronounced Larry 'looking fit & brimful of energy'.[91]

A few weeks later Mary Bentley was present in the Information Office when Larry received a letter from Nancy, back in Jerusalem, in which she announced her intention never to return to him. He was shattered. Through all their quarrels, and despite his own discontent, Larry had never imagined that Nancy would – or even could – break away from him. Now, he told Mary in despair, she was gone and he could not even get to Jerusalem to talk to her. Mary tried to console him, and Dudley Honor came to his aid. Through one of those amazing manoeuvres that always seem possible for the truly resourceful, Dudley arranged to pilot a light bomber on an unspecified mission and flew Larry to Palestine.[92] Nancy had no warning of his arrival, but she did hear him out. There was a tense visit of a few hours between a pleading Larry and a tight-lipped Nancy: it was no go. Nancy intended to stay on her own. Soon Dudley's doctor friend, RAF Wing Commander Lorrie Newman, moved into the Zamalek flat, and the balance of the 'chummery' shifted further towards bachelor life.

Larry saw quite a bit of Gwyn Williams, who was also having wife problems and who lived at Mataria, north of Cairo. Gwyn was a marvellous companion: he was a good Shakespeare scholar, widely read throughout English literature; he was an accomplished draughtsman in ink and pencil; he could sing a store of French bawdy songs, accompanying himself on a banjo tuned like a ukulele; he spoke serviceable Arabic; best of all, he grasped whatever came his way with tremendous exuberance. He presented a marked contrast to Larry: his father had sold a house to send him to Oxford, where he and the poet Bryn Davies had very much followed their own bent in reading, sports, music and theatre. Both Gwyn's BA and MA degrees were awarded *in absentia*. Gwyn maintained that at Jesus College, 'I learnt how not to be bored and I have never been bored since'[93] – things that could not be said of Larry.

Larry enjoyed the company of Mary and of the two tall RAF officers, but without Nancy his domestic centre had cracked and he felt rootless. He still hoped to persuade Nancy to return to him, and he arranged to meet her on 15 September in Beirut. They had one night together, on the train to Jerusalem, and Larry again argued his case. 'I've only been unfaithful to you twice,' he told her, and she believed him.[94] That was not the main issue for her: she was revelling in her freedom, and was sure that she could not develop within the sphere of his possessive and demanding personality. She simply did not want to become what Larry wanted her to be. Nancy's steadfast refusal to return to him freed Larry: very well, his marriage was no longer an option. He would rise from the ashes, cast off whatever sackcloth he had donned, and resume life. Not all of Larry's friends were surprised at the break: George Wilkinson commented cryptically to Joseph Allen, 'You know what Nancy's like.'[95]

When Larry was reassigned to Alexandria, the others decided to give up the flat. Before he left Cairo for good, he stayed briefly with Bernard Spencer in what Larry and others called 'Orgy Hall'. Bernard, whose wife Nora was in England, was in love with Ruth Speirs, the Ice Maiden as her friends called her. Larry found her 'a very cool, cold girl', but he admired her sense of language and urged Eliot to publish her translations of Rilke.[96] There were parties, sometimes with dancing to a gramophone. At one of these Larry was holding forth, surrounded by women. The attention being shown this short, talkative man baffled a large Australian officer, fresh from the Front and new to their circle. He began to vent his anger with crude comments. Ordinarily, Larry would either have ignored the impoliteness or else responded with a cutting remark, but this time he must have been very much on edge. No one was prepared for what happened – for he flew at the man and in a flash the two were rolling on the floor in a tangle, 'little Larry and the big Aussie, spinning about, Larry hanging on fiercely'. Others had to pull them apart.[97]

Nancy was not having an easy time either. Faced with the necessity of supporting herself, she found a series of jobs: first with the official censorship, next as a sub-editor on the *Palestine Post*. Then Olivia Manning introduced her to Aidan Philip. Ironically, it was her connection with Larry and Henry Miller that attracted the interest of Philip, Director of the Near East Arab Broadcasting Station in Jaffa, who had learned that she knew Miller and wanted to hear a first-hand account of him. Philip offered Nancy employment, and she worked in broadcasting for the rest of her time in the Middle East.

Another line still sundered for Larry was his correspondence with Henry. Finally a letter dated 15 September 1942 reached Egypt. Henry had moved to Hollywood, where he so loathed the film people that he said he would rather be in Cairo – despite the dirt and the disease. He was trying to cut himself off from the war by reading the newspapers only once a fortnight, and then just the headlines. None the less, he wrote with fair prescience: 'I feel that Russia will dominate the whole continent. It may take till the end of this century to restore order.'[98] Henry tried to communicate again in two months, asking whether Nancy and Larry were 'still lambasting one another'.[99] In general, Henry's letters showed that he was largely successful in his efforts to ignore the war: writing *The Rosy Crucifixion*, reading about William Blake, and discussing books by Céline, Claude Houghton, Huxley, Frederick Prokosch and Wassermann occupied him, when he was not enjoying the company of Marlene Dietrich's eighteen-year-old daughter or of Melpomene Niarchos, a wealthy Greek woman living in Hollywood who knew many of Henry and Larry's Greek friends. The only direct effect the war seemed to have had on Henry's creative life was that he had withdrawn *The Air-Conditioned Nightmare* from prospective publication. He felt that he should not kick America in the teeth during a desperate conflict. The very detachment of Henry's letters served to increase Larry's discontent.

Larry's attention remained focused on England, and for once Henry's news seems not to have aroused much interest. Larry continued to importune Eliot on behalf of Bernard Spencer and Ruth Speirs, and praised Dorian Cooke and Elie Papadimitriou to him. Eliot replied that he could do nothing about Speirs's work, other than forward her Rilke translations to the Hogarth Press, holder of the translation rights.[100] The next year Eliot would oppose publishing Bernard Spencer: although Eliot liked Spencer's Mediterranean poems, he did not feel that there were enough really good ones for a book.[101] Larry's recommendations carried little weight.

During the early months of 1942 Larry sent Eliot four envelopes containing seventy pages of poems for the *Private Country* volume. It was June before Larry's manuscripts reached Faber. They were intended to form two collections, one headed by 'The Death of General Uncebunke', the other to be entitled *A Private Country*. Eliot immediately answered that it was 'time' for Faber to publish Larry's poetry, and that he was recommending this to the Board. He was not in favour of combining Larry's two manuscripts to make a single large volume: wartime paper shortages made small books desirable, but he advised adding selected poems from the 'Uncebunke' manuscript to the other to make up a substantial selection.[102]

Eliot's letter of acceptance took more months to reach Larry, who had meanwhile fired off missives to both Eliot and to 'Dear Sirs' at Faber, begging them to let him know whether the poems had arrived. As usual, he claimed to have 'no copy'. 'I am defending the Delta with all the old tenacity', Larry remarked with a flicker of his old Rabelaisian exaggeration, and admitted that the silence over the poems was 'beginning to obsess me'.[103] Over several months, despite the upheaval of his move to Alexandria and the activities of Rommel, Larry would badger Eliot with advice and admonitions. He listed eighteen of the shorter poems that were definitely to be included in the volume. At one point Larry suggested cutting the 'Uncebunke' sequence and 'The Sonnet of Hamlet', on the grounds that they had already been published, and despite his feeling that 'Uncebunke' was 'much the most original in shape but not in style'. The sonnet sequence was 'nice and taut but perhaps not so good as an idea', he thought.[104] In the end, Eliot opted to print both 'Uncebunke' and 'Hamlet', as well as all the other poems Larry had named.

Larry's feelings about his move to Alexandria were mixed. Gwyn Williams had just been appointed Head of the Department of English at the new University of Alexandria, so he would have at least one good friend at the outset.[105] As far as the climate went, Larry saw it as a draw: a climb out of the burning sand-pan and into the steam-bath. However, he had suffered emotionally in Cairo, the stage-set for the final act of his marriage to Nancy, and the bitterness that he certainly felt towards her was augmented by his regret over the loss of his daughter. He had given to his poetic *alter ego* Conon – 'he is one of my masks' – the confession that:

> We never learned that marriage is a kind of architecture,
> The nursery virtues were missing, all of them,
> So nobody could tell us why we suffered.[106]

Larry had to admit that it fitted his own misadventure, his dispossessed state. He had not paid enough attention to being a father and a husband. Perhaps, he must have worried, it was because it did not lie in him. On the other hand, in Cairo Larry had enjoyed his part in establishing *Personal Landscape*, and had confirmed friendships begun in Athens while adding to his acquaintance people such as Ines Walter, the Smarts, and Freya Stark, who would remain close friends for life. His experiences around the power centre of the Embassy had stocked his memory and notebooks with enough episodes and colour for a dozen novels.

CHAPTER 6

Alexandria

At the doors of Africa so many towns founded
Upon a parting could become Alexandria, like
The wife of Lot – a metaphor for tears.

'Alexandria'

LARRY WAS FORMALLY TRANSFERRED in October 1942 to Alexandria, where he lodged at the Cecil with its tiers of balconied rooms and dusty splendour, 'this moribund hotel' in whose vestibule, Larry wrote, 'the palms splinter and refract their motionless fronds in the gilt-edged mirrors'.[1] The Cecil faced the Place Sa'ad Zaghloul, but the best rooms were on the side bordering the Corniche, offering magnificent views across the Eastern Harbour. The hotel was too expensive for Larry's pocket so he soon moved in, briefly, with Gwyn Williams, who had leased a villa on nearby Embassy Hill.

Even though he hated Cairo, Larry must have viewed this change with mixed feelings. He was leaving the capital for the city of second rank in Egypt, and he would certainly miss the evenings with Bernard Burrows and Ines Walter, with the Smarts, and with the Anglo-Egyptian Union poets. On the other hand, he knew and liked two of Gwyn Williams's subordinates at Farouk I University: Robert Liddell and the Skelton specialist Harold Edwards. Also, rents were a fraction of Zamalek rates: Gwyn paid £6 per month for a six-room villa. Cheap and marginally potable wine came from the vineyards along Lake Mareotis, an ancient industry recently revived by the rich tobacco merchant Gianaclis. Never really happy far from salt water, Piscean Larry was especially glad to have so much sea the colour of copper sulphate instead of the Cairo desert, 'which lulls and dumbs'.[2]

Alexandria was a much smaller city than Cairo: there were then only about 750,000 inhabitants, and it could be taken in comprehensively, much more so than vast Cairo. Larry was to record Alexandria's 'captivating detail, its insolence of colouring, its crushing poverty and beauty'. The daily lives of the Egyptians had been at some remove from Larry when he

263

lived in the world of Zamalek and the Embassy, but in Alexandria a short excursion by foot or by tram displayed a panorama of small shops selling everything 'from live quail to honeycombs and lucky mirrors', of stalls with their 'warm gold of oranges lying on brilliant strips of magenta paper', of coppersmiths, leather-workers and potters. He was surrounded by a racial kaleidoscope: 'plum-blue Ethiopians', 'bronze Sudanese with puffy charcoal lips, pewter-skinned Lebanese and Bedouin with the profiles of kestrels'. Here lay, he was to write, 'The whole toybox of Egyptian life . . . street-sprinkler, scribe, mourner, harlot, clerk, priest – untouched, it seemed to me, by time or by war.'[3]

Amr, Moslem conqueror of Egypt in 641, had called the country 'a dusty city and a green tree': the Nile was the tree, and Alexandria was one of its greenest branches.[4] A would-be conqueror was pressing in on Alexandria in the early weeks of Larry's residence: from the western desert late at night came the flashes and crepitations of the duel between Rommel's and Montgomery's forces.

By 4 November 1942 Rommel was in stubborn retreat after the second battle of El Alamein, and Egypt was not again to be in serious danger of falling. The nightly German reconnaissance plane set into motion a sequence that Larry would describe in *Clea*. First began 'sirens which howled as the damned must howl in limbo'; then came 'searchlights . . . quivering and sliding in their ungainly fashion, like daddy-long-legs'; and finally the ack-ack batteries, the 'Chicago Pianos', would set up a furious and futile peppering. These were the main reminders of the shooting war, along with the smokescreen floated over the harbours by the defenders and the 'clouds of pink and yellow dust' shining upon 'the greasy buttocks of the barrage balloons'.[5] One of the gun batteries stood near Gwyn Williams's house, and the uproar may have hastened Larry's departure for a flat at 11bis rue des Pharaons, south of the British Consulate and within walking distance of his office at 1 rue Toussoum Pasha. As Public Information Officer he was now the head of his own small section, far from the supervising eyes in the Embassy.

Always a good walker, Larry carried out his explorations of Alexandria mainly on foot, following what he took to be E. M. Forster's advice.[6] To most readers of *Justine*, *Balthazar*, *Mountolive* and *Clea* almost a generation later, the choice of Alexandria as a location would seem inevitable, predestined. Like Corfu town but on a larger scale in both space and time, Alexandria, 'an earth so stuffed with precious historical relics',[7] as Larry called it, was a bewitching palimpsest. The older layers were poking through like teeth here and there if one knew where to look. Annotating his copy of Forster, Larry prowled the old districts and rode the crazy 'bucking, clicking trams'.[8] 'For two years I was able to walk about in the pages of this guide-book,' he would recall, 'using it piously as it deserves to be used, and borrowing many of its gleams of wisdom to swell the notes for the book I myself hoped one day to write.'[9] If Larry was not to *like* the city, he at least came to appreciate it, 'the ponderous azure dream of Alexandria basking like some old reptile in the bronze Pharaonic light of the great lake'.[10]

Ancient Alexandria was an idealist's dream, with her gates of the moon and sun, her Soma, Mouseion library and Hall of Justice; she was also a merchant's delight, with two sheltered harbours, a canal running to the Nile at Schedia, and a channel connecting the Mediterranean with Lake Mareotis. The city had seen Cleopatra's barge, had heard Mark Antony's infatuated sighs, and had witnessed his surrender of Roman duty to Egyptian passion. The city breathed life and sensuality.

Much of the Anfushi area where old Joshua Scobie was to reside in the *Quartet* had been under water until late mediaeval times. When Larry wove his way through the quarter in the noisy twilight city he found a tangle of irregular streets overhung by decaying mediaeval half-timbered houses of several storeys. Life spilled out of the dwellings into the alleyways: at benches and tables set in the dusty streets sat clusters of men and boys, drinking glasses of sugared coffee and heliotrope-hued water-and-syrup concoctions and playing checkers or versions of backgammon. Larry would remember the vivid ambience: 'The smell of the sweat-lathered Berberinis, like that of some decomposing stair-carpet. And then the street noises: shriek and clang of the water-bearing Saidi, dashing his metal cups together as an advertisement.'[11] Larry, although shrinking from the Arab population of the city, portrayed 'one-eyed Hamid' in the *Quartet* as the 'gentlest of Berbers' and gave to Scobie an appreciation of their virtues that he, Durrell, the young propagandist, did not then acknowledge.

To the west of the Anfushi sector, Larry would have come to the Ras el Tin ('Cape of Figs') Palace, where King Farouk seldom stayed, preferring the imposing Italianate structure at Montaza, fifteen miles to the east. Most of Ras el Tin was out of bounds to unauthorized persons, and it bristled with troops and anti-aircraft batteries emplaced to defend the Western Harbour. The tramlines and the avenues all curved inexorably back into the crowded city.

The desert *khamseen* roared in periodically, bent upon undermining thought: 'It gives the air a prattling, lustful sort of quality which, mingled with the sea, is very bracing and rather disorienting,' Larry decided. 'You could easily go mad here.'[12] Although in 1942 the modern city had done little to preserve what remained of her classical glory, Larry, walking along the rue Nebi Daniel towards the Mosque of the Prophet Daniel, would see a classical column to the right, said to have once supported the roof of the fabled Mouseion, standing quite casually amid shabby tenements like a fossil bone embedded in a cliff. Visible from what Larry would term 'the iodine-coloured *meidan*'[13] at the end of rue Nebi Daniel was Pompey's Pillar, which, although it had nothing to do with Pompey but had been erected by Diocletian as a commemorative monument, was too immense and solitary to be ignored. The shaft rose in polished red Aswan granite to eighty-four feet in height.

Half a mile west and slightly to the south of Pompey's Pillar were the Catacombs of Kom es Chogafa, the Hill of Tiles. Far more interesting than the bare Pillar, the Catacombs complemented it by plunging into the limestone, a wide staircase spiralling down to three underworld storeys of burial crypts. In an underground banqueting hall the relatives of the dead had once consumed ceremonial repasts. The ritual feast of *mummia*, the dried flesh of mummies, that Larry would write into *Monsieur* three decades later, may have been suggested to him by the easy communion of the living with the dead at Kom es Chogafa: a literal communion. A pair of magnificent bearded serpents flanked the entrance to the main burial chamber.

The outlines of the city Larry came to know clearly followed those of classical Alexandria: the same strip between the Mediterranean and Lake Mareotis, except that what had been Pharos Island now formed the top of a T connected to the mainland. The great Pharos, the lighthouse measuring 500 feet tall, had been one of the wonders of the ancient world. The base, or part of it, remained before Larry's eyes in the form of buff-coloured, turreted Fort Kait Bey, which Larry would recall as being battered by 'a mythology of yellow-maned waves attacking the Pharos'.[14] The narrow, mile-long causeway of the ancients, the Heptastadion, had been expanded by silting, landfill and the building of sea walls to become the Ras el Tin and Anfushi residential areas.

Larry found a townscape rendered in pastels, the colours softened by a pollen of dust, dimmed by the haze, by the vapours of Lake Mareotis, by the fine, blowing sand. The place assaulted all his senses at once: grit chafing the cuffs and neckband of his shirt, spice-heavy scents of the

1 Mahalia Tye (1818–94), mother of Samuel Amos Durrell, Lawrence George
Durrell's grandfather.
2 Major Samuel Amos Durrell (1851–1914)
3 Dora Maria 'Big Granny' Durrell (1862–1934)
4 Larry, Georgina 'Little Granny' Dixie, Leslie.

5 Larry Durrell (left) in school photograph at St Joseph's College, Darjeeling.
6 Left to right: Leslie, Louisa, Lawrence Samuel Durrell, Margaret and Larry.

7 Larry swimming in the Channel, c. 1926.
8 Larry setting out in his mother's Hillman, c. 1931.
9 Larry in London, c. 1932.
10 First passport photograph.

11 Nancy Durrell, c. 1935.

12 Corfu, c. 1938.
13 Larry and Nancy aboard the *Van Norden*.

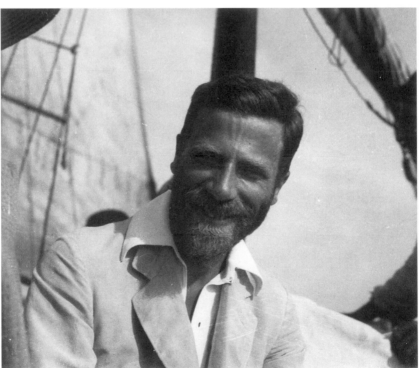

14 The White House, Kalami, showing the upper storey added by Athenaios for
Larry.
15 Dr Theodore Stephanides, Corfu, c. 1938.

16 Leslie Durrell, 1938.
17 Margaret Isabel Mabel Durrell.
18 Spiro 'Americanos' Chalikiopoulos cooking for Gerry Durrell.

19 Henry Miller in Paris, 1932.
20 Buffie Johnson, self-portrait.
21 Fred Perlès in England: from Larry's album.

22 Larry with Max Nimiec on Corfu, c. 1939.

23 Nancy and Penelope about the time of their departure for Palestine, 1942.
24 Portrait of Bernard Spencer by Amy Nimr.
25 Larry shooting on Lake Mareotis: 1940–44 album.

26 Office staff, Alexandria Office of Information: Miss Philpott, Larry, Milto Axelos, Miss Palli.

27 Military pass.

28 Yvette Cohen, later to become Eve Durrell: 'Gypsy Cohen burns black and fierce under her Tunisian eyebrows', Larry wrote.

29 The Villa Cleobolus.
30 In the garden of the Villa Cleobolus: Patrick Leigh Fermor, Joan Fermor, Xan
Fielding.

Mr and Mrs Lawrence G. Durrell who landed from the Brasil Star.

Mr and Mrs Hugh Ellis and their t... Brasil St...

"BEAUTY AND THE BEAST"

The Old, Old Story

31 The press welcomes Larry and Eve to Argentina over a fortuitous headline.
32 The Durrells' Argentine hostess, Bebita Ferreyra.

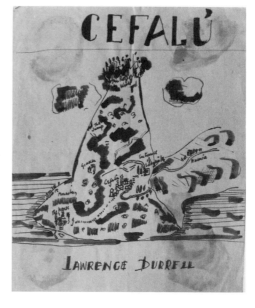

33 Mary Mollo, painted by Ella Mollo, her sister-in-law.
34 With George Katsimbalis, c. 1949.
35 Larry's cover design for *Cefalù*.

36 Larry and Eve at the Parthenon, c. 1949.

kitchens and bazaars cutting across the reek of decay, the dyed billowing silks, the repetitive Arabic quarter-tones of the vendors, the braying donkeys, the roasting coffee awaiting a translation into myriad milk-cloudy sweet cups: all these were timeless.

Forster had written to a friend in 1917, 'The Greeks are the only community here that attempt to understand what they are talking about', and although he found them 'dirty, dishonest, unaristocratic, roving, warped by Hellenic and Byzantine dreams', he thought that they were redeemed because 'they do effervesce intellectually, they do have creative desires'.[15] To Larry, the whole city was 'plangently Greek',[16] and the loyalty of the Greek population was his official charge. The Italians were the other major European-descended population, and Larry would develop important contacts there as well. A merchant class from all over the Mediterranean comprised a few French plus a wide representation of Levantine peoples, including Syrians, Lebanese and Armenians. The language of diplomatic and upper-level social discourse was French, and the bookstores displayed whole shelves of the Pléiade editions, but despite Egyptian nationalism English was gaining rapidly, thanks to British troops and American films. Alexandria was the headquarters for the British chamber of commerce for Egypt. In some of the more stylish shops, Arabic speakers and those wearing the robe-like *galibeya* would not be served: customers had to ask for goods in French or Italian and be dressed in European clothes.

Larry made a pilgrimage to 10 rue Lepsius, only a few blocks from his rue des Pharaons apartment, where Constantine Cavafy had lived out his last thirty years in a flat above a brothel. The small street, named after the great German Egyptologist, had a raffish reputation in Cavafy's time due to the courtesans who solicited from the windows. In their honour the less reverent among Cavafy's visitors renamed his street the 'rue Clapsius'. The old poet, who never had electricity installed, rated his visitors by candles: several for those who interested him, a lone flame for bores. Larry climbed up the square, dark stairwell to the poet's flat on the second floor, where Walter Smart had been, and where, over twenty-five years before Larry's visit, E. M. Forster had passed Cavafy's initiation rite – he had understood the poet's 'The City' read in Greek. Ecstatic, Cavafy had lit candle after candle until the room blazed with light.

Cavafy was fond of telling visitors, 'Where could I live better? Below, the brothel cares for the flesh. And there is the church which forgives sin. And there is the hospital where we die.'[17] In the next street was indeed the Greek hospital where Cavafy had died of cancer of the throat, and from the poet's windows Larry could catch a glimpse of St Saba, where his funeral service had been held. The presence of Cavafy himself, his curious, interested stare through perfectly round, thick-rimmed glasses, remembered from photographs, still lingered. Here, Larry would come to realize, dwelt the patron spirit of his own future *Alexandria Quartet*.

It was a fateful choice: Cavafy, although born in the city, knew little Arabic and was said never to have visited an Egyptian house. The Greeks of Alexandria yearned towards a Hellenic myth, even those who had never seen Greece, and scorned the Egyptians out of whom they made their living as tobacco and cotton factors, merchants and grocers. In fact, the cosmopolitan business and intellectual classes in Alexandria – French, Greek, Italian, Syrian, Armenian, Jewish, the European-educated Egyptian élite, and so on – rarely mixed with the Arabic-speaking, devoutly Islamic Egyptians, and Larry seldom did either. When he in a temper called the Egyptians 'apes in nightshirts', he was repeating the soldiers' tag for anyone wearing the *galibeya*, and he was also reflecting the prejudices of his circle. Arabic-speaking Egyptians would be banished from Larry's *Quartet*, or relegated to minor and usually demeaning roles.

A CONSIDERABLE FRENCH FLEET, Admiral Godefroy's command of a battleship and four cruisers, rode at anchor in the Western Harbour, adding to the inevitable tensions among Allied forces in Alexandria. Godefroy had been ordered by the Vichy government to return to France, but the British Admiral Cunningham had refused to permit him to leave. The French admiral acquiesced diplomatically at first, but that changed after the British sank a Vichy fleet at Mers el Kebir. Godefroy had prepared to fight his way out of the harbour, until the British agreed to feed the French sailors and to pay their salaries for the duration. This was the *status quo* during Larry's time in Alexandria. Godefroy had taken up tennis, and would send Cunningham polite messages of congratulation or condolence as British fortunes at sea warranted. Alexandria was also hostess to General de Gaulle's Free French, however, and fights in the streets of the city were frequent between the factions. '*Vous avez des moules ou des huîtres à vendre?*' taunted the Free French.[18] Godefroy's men were the real-life counterparts of the unruly French sailors who, in Larry's *Clea*, would wantonly shoot and kill Gaston Pombal's lover.

Larry had scarcely settled into the rhythms of Alexandria before he was sending poems to Eliot. 'Hope you'll accept them with good grace this time,' he needled his mentor. 'I'm sure they'll do you credit in the long run. Tra la tra la. Megalomania again.'[19] A dedication 'For Nancy' that had headed 'The Green Man' was crossed out. His regret at losing her was mixed with anger at what he regarded as her betrayal, her theft of their daughter. This last hurt seemed to strike deepest: Alexandria, where Larry moved only after Nancy's departure, became associated in his mind with the disappearance of his child. When Larry made the disappearance of Justine's daughter in the *Quartet* a vital *clou* to her character and motivation, he was thinking also of his own pain, his sense of loss over Penelope.

Nevertheless, Larry's well-being did not seem to be unduly affected by his separation from Nancy. 'I am very happy,' he wrote to Eliot early in the new year. 'My wife is being rather a nuisance at this moment, but apart from the fashionable domestic malaise I am here, and revolving a book in the back of what is left of my mind.' In the meantime, he added, 'I am still working like a pit-pony', running the Information Office and writing journalism, 'that last stage of decomposition'.[20] He returned to the attack on behalf of Bernard Spencer, warning Eliot not to be misled: 'Faber must be able to see the wood for the Treece,' Larry wrote, punning on the name of Henry Treece, one of the Apocalyptic poets then being published by Faber.[21] While on Corfu, Larry had complained about the unreliability of the mails when letters took ten days to reach him; now, he was driven to sending cables when months went by without answers to his letters: 'NEWSLESS ABOUT POEMS SPENCERS MANUSCRIPT UNACKNOW-LEDGED,' he wired Eliot in April.[22]

ALEXANDRIA WAS GRADUALLY GAINING a grip on Larry, despite his dislike of so much that was Egyptian. Much later he wrote: 'It is a place for dramatic partings, irrevocable decisions, last thoughts; everyone feels pushed to the extreme, to the end of his bent.'[23] The city was driving him into verse, and he was not the only one so catalysed: Gwyn Williams, who had written almost nothing before he arrived in Alexandria at the age of thirty-eight, under Larry's urging and in the freedom insidiously promoted by the city, became a translator of Welsh poetry and finally a poet. The impetus for Gwyn to compose a score of books 'all started in Alexandria', he said.[24] Gwyn's views of time and place were not unlike Larry's, for he too believed firmly that 'any moment has it all, past, present, and the possibilities of the future'. Yet Gwyn carried so much of Wales around in his mind that Larry said he expected him to write a novel about Alexandria entitled *Wild Wales*.[25]

Alexandria could have even stranger effects on its denizens, Larry claimed: 'People become monks or nuns or voluptuaries without a word of warning.'[26] One of his subordinates, a Copt, suddenly resigned to become a monk, arousing Larry's interest in the Copts: 'from him I learnt a little bit about them', Larry would recall.[27] A monastery was not for him, yet he was too self-conscious to become a true voluptuary either; none the less, he found the 'sexual provender' attractive.[28] 'It's funny the way you get woman after woman', he would confess to a tantalized Henry Miller, 'each more superficial than the last Gaby, Simone, Arlette, Dawn, Penelope.'[29] Leafing through a stack of photographs many years later, Larry paused over a snapshot of an Alexandrian society lady: 'That's Mrs – I can't remember – I *think* I had an affair with her.'[30] In the *Quartet* Larry would only half-jokingly dub the city the 'winepress of love'.

'Love, good food, music, swimming, we had it all,' Gwyn Williams realized. He and Larry, wifeless, were inducted as honorary members of the Rotor Arms, the club for young women in the Auxiliary Territorial Service. This gave the two men 'the right to sit in their armchairs and buy chits of books for drinks'.[31] The ATS provided secretarial and other office help for the armed forces, but it was not run with full military rigour and restrictions, and both *de facto* bachelors recognized the organization as being well supplied with beautiful girls 'ready to be interested in culture'. Larry gave several lectures on Miller's work 'chiefly to Jewish ATS here in Alexandria'. He described them as 'tremendous black-eyed big-bottomed girls, and all taking notes at terrific speed', adding incredulously, 'They study literature as if it were more interesting than sex.'[32] However, he thought that Alexandrian women in general took to love-making with abandon: 'Sex here is interesting; it's madly violent but not WEAK or romantic or obscure, like anglo-saxon women' – this was a jab at Nancy. He found it instead 'fierce and glaring, vulture and eagle work with beak and claws'.[33]

While Larry got to know Alexandria, Robin Fedden and Bernard Spencer in Cairo were working on the fifth issue of *Personal Landscape*. Bernard wrote to Larry that they were including his 'On First Looking into Loeb's Horace' and 'Mythology' poems, as well as verse by Keith Douglas, Robert Liddell, John Pudney and Spencer himself.[34] In addition, Fedden and Spencer had received a translation from Serbo-Croatian by Dorian Cooke and a 'paraphrase' from the Arabic of Shawqy by Herbert Howarth and Ibrahim Shukrallah. Terence Tiller had continued the theme of Larry's 'Ideas About Poetry' column with 'Seventeen propositions': poetry is a deliberate, analytical, intellectual process, and the imagination is itself intellectual. In fact, 'Poetry, NOT excepting music, is the most scientific of the arts.'[35] It was too clinical, too anti-romantic a view for Larry to endorse.

Larry's 'Horace' and 'Mythology' poems suggest an attempt to distance himself from Egypt and the war. He is concerned with a version of Horace who tried to 'escape from self-knowledge with its tragic/ Imperatives: *Seek, suffer, endure*',[36] useful watchwords for what Larry himself was going through – his sexual and metaphysical researches. In 'Mythology' Larry treated his imaginative realm, the one that a few years before he had attempted to explain to Miller as the Heraldic Universe, peopled with 'my favourite characters', those 'Out of all pattern and proportion'.[37]

This was to be the sole issue of *Personal Landscape* published in 1943, in part because of Larry's physical separation from his two co-editors and from the production centre in Cairo. While *Personal Landscape* continued to concentrate on work by the editors and their non-combatant friends, the rival *Salamander* group in 1943 made a focused effort to solicit poetry written by the troops. Three thousand poems arrived, and more than a hundred were printed in September in the *Oasis* anthology, with a foreword by Lieutenant-General Sir Henry Maitland Wilson. *Personal Landscape* would remain, like its trio of editors, stubbornly personal and private.

Larry's Paris sojourns had been spent largely in the company of autodidacts: Miller, Nin, Perlès. His London circle ranged from the intuitive Dylan Thomas and the wildly un-donnish Tambimuttu to the erudite Eliot. Now, in Egypt, Larry had established himself at the centre of precisely such a group of university literati as his father had imagined for him. And he had done it without attending a university. Spencer held a modern literature degree from Corpus Christi, Oxford; Tiller had won the Chancellor's Medal in English verse at Cambridge; Williams had earned an MA from Jesus College, Oxford; even Keith Douglas, young as he was, had spent two years at Merton; Fedden, Liddell and Harold Edwards were all university teachers. Nobody, in this circle, was about to condescend to Larry as a public school drop-out.

With the exception of Williams, none of Larry's close associates was in Egypt by choice, and they felt trapped. So did Larry, but more than any of them he seemed able to adapt to the situation, to produce, and to present a cheerful front. Under the stimulus of new friends and greater responsibilities, Larry gained, according to Fedden, 'a sense of wider reference', a 'vitality and sparkle which in wartime Egypt was . . . so striking and so welcome'.[38] Larry also discovered that he was an able administrator, and he wrote to Miller, more in quiet assurance than boasting: 'My office hums like a top; and the people working for me LIKE it.'[39] Larry's secretary and principal assistant was Miss Marjorie Philpott, a slender and pretty young woman with hair neatly piled on her head. Keeping track of the two English and two French newspapers of Egypt, along with other periodical publications, was the responsibility of 'the excellent Miss Palli'. 'I am in a service full of hysterical spinsters at the moment, who correct my punctuation and grammar with wonderful self-possession,' Larry confided to Eliot.[40] Milto Axelos, whose last name would appear prominently and with his consent in Larry's *Dark Labyrinth*, was the general factotum.

Larry's offices were in the imposing building that had housed the Banco di Roma, called by Forster 'the finest building in the city'.[41] A street away to the south-east ran the Sharia Fuad el Awal ('Fuad the First'), the renamed rue de la Porte Rosette, itself superimposed on the Canopic Way, the main artery of Alexander's original city. Two streets to the east of the Information Office Sharia Fuad el Awal was intersected by the rue Nebi Daniel to form the main crossroad of the modern city, in Forster's phrase, once 'one of the most glorious places' of the ancient world.[42] This was the Soma, traditionally the burial place of Alexander, and it was here that Larry would site in the *Quartet* the centre of information and pulse of the city, Mnemjian's timeless Babylonian barber shop, where the shrouded customers were shaved 'like dead Pharaohs'.[43] Fuad el Awal and Nebi Daniel were crowded thoroughfares, the Oxford Street and Charing Cross Road of Alexandria.

Larry viewed his official duties with a certain amount of cynicism, but he was effective when he had to be. Lesley Pares, remembered by Larry as 'so beautiful that the effect was like Hiroshima', was sent from the Ministry of Information in Cairo to secure press coverage for an RAF exhibition. She arrived a week early, met Larry for the first time and patiently explained what she thought should be done. There was plenty of time, he assured her, and entertained her lavishly with parties and beach picnics. Pares became more and more anxious at the work not touched, until on the day before the press review Larry said, 'Right! Down to business.' The two of them toured the commonplace and predictable exhibition, and then Larry gave the press such a glowing account of its importance that the show was lavishly reported and an abashed Pares was praised by her superiors.[44]

Amid crises and the ordinary crush of official duties, Larry negotiated with Tambimuttu for the publication of *The Black Book* in England, while in New York 'A nice nin', Larry quipped, was 'screaming for an American edition'. Changing his mind, Larry restrained Tambimuttu and asked Eliot if Faber would reconsider printing the book. He was turned down. Around the beginning of July, Larry proposed to his friend Dimitri Lambros and to Eliot that he write for the Greek Ministry of Information a short book on the Greek revolt from Turkey. He hoped that Faber would publish it in England, or that Tambimuttu would.[45] Eliot approved his resolve to treat Greek history 'from some other angle than the Byron one'.[46] Larry began research in the Patriarchal Library in Alexandria with the help of a friendly librarian, Moschorios, and called on his Greek contacts to supply him with material. He wrote to Eliot, 'I intend by my history an imaginative portrait of a national character and landscape', and 'embedded in this like flint an accurate and terse chronicle of the Greek War of Independence.'[47] With the resources of the ecclesiastical library before him, Larry found it hard to stick with recent history, however, and his readings included the Hermetica, Poemandres and various gnostic texts – more quarried stone for his future *Quartet* and *Quintet*.

Despite his disclaimer to Eliot, Larry could not help but see himself and Greece in Byronic terms. His projected history would be his service to modern Greece. Larry wrote a fairly long poem, 'Byron', in which a deliberate ambiguity in the references of the first person pronoun hints at Larry's identification with the great Romantic. Larry found many parallels with Byron's state: war, Alexandria as his own Missolonghi, their common despairs and dispossession. Larry listed the 'omens':

> Headquarters of a war
> House in a fever-swamp
> Headquarters of a mind at odds.

'Before me now lies Byron', Larry addressed a portrait of the poet, 'Shown in this barbered hairless man'. Byron, 'Tuned to women', turned to a series of love affairs to diminish thoughts of death:

> I helped these pretty children by their sex
> Discountenance the horrid fellow.

Many other selves of Byron found echoes in Larry: the lonely man 'searching for his mother'; Byron carving his name 'Under Sunium's white cliffs' while 'thinking softly of my daughter'; Byron trying to direct 'These unbarbered gangs of freedom'. Larry's concluding stanza confirms the identification:

> O watch for this remote
> But very self of Byron and of me,
> Blown empty on the white cliffs of the mind,
> A dispossessed His Lordship writing you
> A message in a bottle dropped at sea.[48]

Henry Miller had been Larry's guru of the pre-war days; but as Henry tried desperately to disengage himself from the implications of world upheavals, Larry turned to the dying Byron. Spiro Americanos had called him Lord Byron, and certainly he felt dispossessed, sundered from Nancy and Penelope, cut off from communication with his mother and his friends in England and America. Miss Nancy he did, yet her absence freed him even beyond his habitual independence.

Larry recognized the intensity of his pursuit of women and romance, as he rode the 'tram/ To horizons of love or good luck or more love – '. These words surged forward in his poem 'Alexandria' where he confessed:

> As for me I now move
> Through many negatives to what I am.

Without saying it, Larry was revising the Cartesian formula to fit his own case: I love, therefore I am. His ironic laughter was self-directed: 'and D./ Searching in sex like a great pantry for jars/ Marked "Plum and apple"', he wrote.[49]

More mundane excitement was provided when Operation Husky, the invasion of Sicily under the direction of General Eisenhower, began on 10 July 1943, and for weeks the Alexandrian harbours were chock-a-block with Allied ships of all classes. With the invading troops went Theodore Stephanides. Then in August there was a visitation from Cairo in the form of Sir Miles Lampson and Noël Coward, travelling with the ambassador and entertaining the troops and everyone else within earshot. Larry and Keith Scott-Watson went to see Coward on the 22nd around noon, and they found him with a breakfast tray on his knees. Coward noted in his diary only that 'I gave an interview to Larry Darrell [sic] who lived on Corfu and writes poems.' Coward was more interested in Scott-Watson because he could recount an anecdote about how much Coward had upset the Nazis while in Danzig.[50]

Soon there was news, both good and bad, for Larry from London. Tambimuttu wrote that he had 'run out' of the poems Larry had given him in 1939 and now wanted more, also reviews and an article on the Cairo poets. Anne Ridler reported that Larry's manuscript of a Greek fairy story had evidently been lost when her flat was bombed.[51] Eliot for the nonce sealed the fate of *The Black Book* with Faber – he still did not believe that it was publishable in England 'without a mutilation which would be worse than not publishing at all' – but he gave his blessing to Larry to place the book with Nicholson and Watson if he so desired. No, Larry decided, 'Let us shelve the question of the Black Book temporarily.'[52] Gratifying to Larry the poet, however, was Eliot's statement that he did not want a monopoly on 'anything but FUTURE POETRY'.[53] This was tremendously reassuring, coming from the man Larry considered one of the two greatest living English poets – he still thought Auden was the other.

ALEXANDRIA WAS ONLY A THREE-HOUR train ride from Cairo, and Larry's work necessitated occasional trips there. Thus he was able to visit the *Personal Landscape* poets and his other friends. By the autumn of 1942 Patrick, Lord Kinross, recently appointed Press Officer to the RAF, had shown up in Cairo. He moved in with David Balfour, successively a former Benedictine monk and a former Orthodox priest. At the turn of the year they were joined by Eddie Gathorne-Hardy, still lecturing for the British Council. The eccentric trio shared a house in one of the old sectors of the city, joined to the ninth-century mosque of Ibn Tulun.[54]

Closer to Larry's old flat in Zamalek, Xan Fielding, transformed into an agent with the Special Operations Executive, now camped intermittently at 'Tara', a mansion on Sharia Abou el Feda at the north end of Gezira Island. Patrick Leigh Fermor and William Stanley Moss had established Tara as the unofficial Cairo rest house of the SOE. Xan and Paddy had spent many months together 'in caves and goat-folds' on occupied Crete, and Xan had told Paddy about *The Black Book* and had regaled him with anecdotes about Larry, Katsimbalis, Ghika and Seferis in Athens.[55] Reginald 'Rex' Leeper, British Ambassador to the Greek Government in Exile in Egypt, was an adviser on SOE operations in the Balkans, and he probably heard stories about Larry that would cause him difficulties in the future.

The men of Tara passed most of their time incognito in Crete, Greece, France or elsewhere, but when they hit Tara it was with months of back pay and a great deal of pent-up exuberance to spend. For a few weeks at least they could forget the German reprisals on Crete, the civil war that was shaping up in Greece, or the coming conflict between Tito's Partisans and the royalists in Yugoslavia. Tara had many bedrooms, a grand ballroom with a parquet floor, and a piano borrowed from the Egyptian

Officers' Club. The resident spirit was the young Countess Sophie Tarnowska, separated from her husband. Among Larry's familiars who were often found there were Ines Walter, remembered by Moss as 'enormously *décolletée*, happy in the role of a Hungarian peasant', and Alexis Ladas, 'singing *Phillidem*' and recovering from an appendectomy.[56] Against heavy competition, Tara was arguably the site of the wildest parties held in wartime Cairo. At one of these, Countess Tarnowska's Polish friends shot out all the light-bulbs; at others, everything from golf-balls to sofas were thrown from the windows; once King Farouk appeared with a case of champagne. Such happenings became almost the norm in wartime Egypt.

Paradoxically, Tara was also a place where some of the best literary conversation in Cairo was available. Paddy had been translating Villon, and the books that he and Moss were later to take along on their seemingly suicidal but successful mission to kidnap General Kreipe, the Divisional Commander of Crete, indicate the range of their interests: Cellini, Donne, Sir Thomas Browne, Tolstoy, Marco Polo, *Les Fleurs du Mal*, *Alice in Wonderland*, Shakespeare.

Another port of call for Larry was the Roger Low house in Bulaq Dacrour, a cool suburb to the west of Cairo. The house was grand enough to have been designated by Rommel as his Cairo domicile, so the rumour went. After the Flap it had been rented by a consortium that consisted of David Abercrombie and his fiancée Mary; John Brinton, the American Military Attaché, and his wife Josie; Bernard Burrows and Ines Walter; Robin Fedden and his future wife, Renée Catseflis, an Alexandrian Greek. The garden was beautifully laid out, with clipped yews and a large pool; a midnight dip became a feature of the frequent parties. One of these was organized by Bernard Burrows to celebrate the marriage of Mary and David Abercrombie: an epic event, during which a male belly dancer performed. Mary remembered Larry folded into a knot and clinging 'like a lichen' to the edge of the pool, before he uncoiled to drift away.[57]

One friend who vanished from the Middle East picture in mid-1943 was Freya Stark, who set off on a campaign to counter the effects of Zionist propaganda on Anglo-American relations. Her highly placed friends in London were particularly afraid that the Zionists would succeed in branding the British as unreformed imperialists who were hopelessly pro-Arab on Palestine. From November until June of the following year she toured the United States and Canada, lecturing everywhere, from neighbourhood churches to the universities of Chicago, Michigan and

California. In all likelihood, she was the inspiration for Larry's later incorporation of Zionist plots into *Clea*.

A PRIVATE COUNTRY, Larry's first volume of poetry from a major publisher, appeared in late 1943, and the title, almost synonymous with that of the magazine he co-edited, drew attention to his personal landscape, to the Heraldic Universe that he inhabited. Most of the poems had been written in Greece, and nothing in *A Private Country* treated Larry's present situation, not even his 'Egyptian Poem', which dated from 1938. The physical emblem of Larry's private country was Greece, and his love showed in 'Matapan' and other lyrical poems:

> Here wind emptied the snowy caves: the brown
> Hands about the tiller unbuckled.
> Day lay like a mirror in the sun's eye.

This Faber volume demonstrated the broad scope of Larry's poetry. He followed Eliot's advice and included the 'Uncebunke' poems, composed over five years earlier and forming a satiric yet affectionate portrait of a generic Anglo-Indian progenitor, 'Officer at the bar and gentleman in bed'. 'My uncle has entered his soliloquy', Larry had written, looking back towards Hamlet. 'The Sonnet of Hamlet', composed shortly before the outbreak of war, is really a sequence of fourteen sonnets. Dedicated to '*Anne Ridler and the Lady in the Painting* Ophelia', it is the most demanding poem in the volume, probably the most difficult that Larry was ever to write – surreal, searing verse, printed in unrhymed couplets, fired by Larry's inner torment. Larry had worried often enough to others about going insane, and his words were not merely the rhetoric masking inspiration, so he thought. After all, his father had gone mad, he sometimes claimed. 'By the trimmed lamp I cobble this sonnet', the narrator's voice begins mildly enough. Soon all the themes of the great play are spread forth, the murder, guilt and metaphysical imaginings:

> Dumb poison in the hairy ear of kings
> Can map the nerves and halt the tick of hearts.

Hamlet's threatened madness becomes a shared thing for the poet's *persona*:

> I cool my spittle on the smoking hook.
> I take these midnight thoughts between a tong.

277

Ostensibly about Hamlet and 'Ophelia smiling at her chess', Larry's 'Sonnet of Hamlet' is also about poetic creation, his ancient subject: 'shall I marry/ The lunatic image in the raven frock?' he asks. For the earth-bound, mortal future, he writes of 'A red and popular baby born for the urn':

> For him I make a book by the moving finger bone,
> A rattle, cap and comedy of queens.[58]

The mood of dramatic tension established by the 'Sonnet' is countered in the book by 'A Ballad of the Good Lord Nelson', perhaps the most successful among Larry's few ribald poems: Nelson's 'empty sleeve was no mere excuse' and he well knew that 'a cast in the bush is worth two in the hand'.[59]

A Private Country received little notice, but what it garnered was mostly encouraging. Stephen Spender wrote a letter of appreciation to Larry and reviewed the book favourably in the New Statesman and Nation. Alex Comfort, recently down from Cambridge and preparing to launch New Road: New Directions in European Arts and Letters, praised the collection in the Tribune, and Larry's old friend Nicholas Moore wrote about it for Poetry Quarterly. Bernard Spencer applauded from Cairo.

Larry was still working on his Greek history. Stephanides was invalided back to Alexandria with dysentery in mid-October 1943, and his misfortune worked in Larry's favour. Theodore stayed with Larry for two weeks and plunged with characteristic enthusiasm into helping his host. While the two of them were joyfully recalling Greece, Anne Ridler wrote describing a poetry reading that she had participated in at the Wigmore Hall: Eliot, William Empson, S. I. Hsiung, Cecil Day Lewis, Desmond MacCarthy, Kathleen Raine, Edith Sitwell, Spender, Lady Wellesley. She was concerned that George Barker and Dylan Thomas had not been invited because they were apparently 'not respectable enough?'[60] If anything, Anne's report confirmed Larry's worst fears about literary England and intensified his conviction that he was right to be an expatriate. If admission to the company of poets hinged upon respectability, then better to be a renegade.

Compared with what Bernard Spencer called the 'frightening war-poetry' coming to Personal Landscape from Keith Douglas – 'Vergissmeinicht', 'Enfidaville', and 'Cairo Jag' – most of the verse being written in England seemed tame.[61] Larry excepted Eliot's verse, however, and was pleased in early November to repay a few debts by lecturing on Eliot to an audience of troops.[62] Then on 22 November 1943 Larry's friend Dimitri Lambros heard Day Lewis read Larry's 'In Arcadia' and 'At Corinth' on the BBC Home Service and wired Larry his congratulations from London. Larry must have felt that he was not after all only a voice speaking to himself in exile.

When he felt that he needed to escape, he caught the night train from Cairo to Aswan. Before arriving he would be served at dawn with 'marvellous coffee with Bath Oliver biscuits' and mango juice, followed by a full English breakfast. Larry would describe Aswan as 'an endearing mixture of Darjeeling and Bournemouth'.[63] It was a welcome relief from Lower Egypt to be among 'these rosy, golden hills'. 'This is the point at which the Nile, in its slow, oozing fashion, hit rock, bedrock,' Larry continued. The Nile he compared to a lotus, with the flower in the delta, 'And the root, of course, is darkest Africa.' He was keenly aware of the difference in the people:

You can already see on the faces the extraordinary change that's come about: a new dignity. Certainly, in the actual physical make-up, Africa is talking. The skin has become bluish, magenta-bluish, rather like carbon paper, and the eyes are glittering with – not exactly the kind of intelligence that is the cleverness of the Southern Egyptian (which is rather *racé*, rather fine, rather hysterical), but a kind of massive solemnity. And one can well understand that when Ancient Egypt visualized itself, it visualized this part of it as the head, and the north as the lower parts of the human body.[64]

He stayed at the old Cataract Hotel, with its Edwardian gun room, shelves of soothing Victorian novels, and nannies in wicker chairs.[65] Aswan was where one went for introspection, for recovery from an illness, and in Egypt it was fashionable to be ill.

Self-scrutiny was one thing, and *Personal Landscape* had been founded to give vent to private voices, but when outsiders presumed upon even well-intended analyses of the magazine, Larry reacted angrily. George Fraser attempted in 'Recent Verse: London and Cairo', an essay published in *Orientations* in September 1943, to define the tone of Tambimuttu's *Poetry in Wartime* as 'neoromantic' in contrast to the 'neoclassic' detachment of the *Personal Landscape* group. Tambimuttu responded tactfully enough to the effect that the categorization did not hold, and that Durrell and Tiller, at least, had published in both places. Much more forcefully, Larry wrote to *Orientations* accusing Fraser of 'self-advertising', 'ill-informed criticisms' and 'a battery of misquotations'. Larry was especially sensitive to the imputation that he, Spencer and Tiller were part of a clique. Far from being a group held together by shared ideas, he wrote, 'We have seldom been unanimous about anything.'[66]

Olivia Manning wrote a serious defence of the 'Poets in Exile' in Egypt in an article for *Horizon* magazine. The 'outbred' poetry of the exiles often gained from the contact with other cultures, she said, but then she committed the sin of praising Spencer's work at the expense of Tiller's and Larry's. 'Unlike Durrell's work', she wrote, '[Spencer's poems] never pretend to be more than they are; unlike Tiller's, they never give the impression of straining after something not quite realized.'[67] Tiller recalled that Manning's article had caused 'great annoyance' to many.[68]

SOCIAL INVITATIONS, BROUGHT ABOUT by his official position and his personality, cut into Larry's writing and editing time. As a friend remarked of Larry's arrival in a room, 'It's as though someone had uncorked a bottle of vintage champagne.'[69] His brother Gerry would claim that Larry's impact on a gathering was due to his ability to focus 'fifty million volts of charm' on the individual whom he happened to be addressing,[70] while Paddy Leigh Fermor said that Larry was 'a man who pumped the oxygen back into the air'.[71] On 13 November 1943 he boarded a train for ten days in Beirut to escape from friends, duties and Egypt. Even more important, he promised himself that before he returned he would complete 'Cities, Plains and People', the long autobiographical poem that would become the title piece of his next collection. In the stanzas about Corfu Larry wrote of 'the sad perfect wife' – which he personalized with a marginal 'Nancy' in a notation deleted before publication – and of her escape:

> Nets were too coarse to hold her
> Where the nymph broke through
> And only the encircling arms of pleasure held.[72]

Larry had a brief meeting with an old friend from the Corfu life he and Nancy had shared: Barclay Hudson was in Beirut. It was a further reminder of the Greek idyll that he had lost.

Amid the frenetic activity of Larry's life in Alexandria, the opening line of 'Cities', 'Once in idleness was my beginning', rang a poignant note for another vanished life, his childhood. Despite his situation, however, the prevailing tone of the poem is strong and assured as he summarizes his development and his spiritual progress. He names many of the writers who have meant much to him: Dante and Rabelais, Dostoevsky and Shakespeare, Lawrence and Blake; and in the published marginal notes, he lists those friends to whom he has felt especially close: Henry Miller, Anaïs, Nancy, Teresa Epstein, Katsimbalis, the Southams, Seferis, Stephanides. Tiny Penelope steps on stage: 'In her small frock walked his daughter'. The poem concludes with the implication that knowledge comes, finally, through non-striving and wise resignation. For Larry, already working on what would become *Prospero's Cell* – although he had not mentioned the title – the words were intended to have a personal application:

> For Prospero remains the evergreen
> Cell by the margin of the sea and land,
> Who many cities, plains, and people saw
> Yet by his open door
> In sunlight fell asleep
> One summer with the Apple in his hand.[73]

The poem was a triumph for Larry, evidence that he was still capable of sustained poetic effort, and he sent it confidently to Eliot on the last day of the year.

By late 1943 Larry had met in Alexandria 'a strange, smashing, dark-eyed woman . . . with every response right: every gesture; and the interior style of a real person – but completely at sea here in this morass of venality and money.'[74] Her name was Yvette Cohen, and she was the daughter of a small-time Jewish businessman and café proprietor from Tunisia. She would describe her father years later as rigidly moral, 'a simple, uncomplicated person with no intellectual background'. Her mother was a Jew of Spanish-Ladino ancestry, born in Constantinople.[75] Later, Larry liked to say that her father was a money-changer who operated sitting on the steps of public buildings: it suited Larry's heraldic vision of her past.

Eve, Yve, or Gipsy, as Larry variously rendered Yvette Cohen, had gone to school until she was sixteen, despite the poverty that kept the family constantly changing residences: Moharrem Bey, Bulkeley Bey, Sidi Gabr, Ibrahimiya, Camp Caesar, Sidi Bishr – a veritable catalogue of the tram stops that Darley and Melissa would pass through in *The Alexandria Quartet*.[76] Over her father's strenuous objections, Eve had gone to work after school: first typing for a film company, then for a time as a nurse. She found the conversation of her friends, young people sufficiently independent to move without chaperones from beach to café to cinema, insipid and unsatisfying. They in turn thought her an intellectual and called her 'Miss Psychoanalyse'.[77]

Eve was working as a journalist when she met Larry at a party; it was not a question of immediate attraction on her part, and they had separated without Larry finding out where she lived. Then one evening some time later, when she felt very depressed, she phoned Larry and he took her to Pastroudi's. He had not been sure that she would appear, and years later Larry would write his suspense into a rendezvous between Arnauti and Justine: 'Will she come, or has she disappeared forever?'[78] Larry and Eve sat at a lacquered wooden table under the low ceiling and devoured lavish pastries. This time they discovered they shared a disgust with the crass mercenary side of Alexandria and a lively interest in the workings of the inner self. Eve became a regular visitor to Larry's apartment. He said she was the 'only person I have been able to talk to really; we share a kind of refugee life'.[79] In fact, their conversations, in English and Alexandrian French, were more like cross-examinations, with Larry probing Eve's every experience, ambition and fear. Eve felt that she was being turned inside out, but she was mesmerized.[80] When the poet and diplomat Charles Johnston met Larry and Eve at the Union Bar, he pronounced her 'beautiful as a tigress, and about as articulate in English'.[81] She was small, with shining obsidian hair and eyes 'black and fierce under her Tunisian eyebrows', and alone with Larry, she was passionate in argument, intelligent, nervous. Emotionally and physically, Larry said, 'the flavour is straight Shake-speare's Cleopatra; an ass from Algiers, lashes from Malta, nails and toes from Smyrna, hips from Beirut, eyes from Athens, and nose from Andros, and a mouth that shrieks or purrs like the witching women of Homs or Samarkand. And breasts from Fiume.'[82]

One day Larry telephoned Paul Gotch, Regional Director for the British Council at Tanta, where he lived with his wife Billy and their infant daughter Linnet. 'Will you do me a favour, and look after this wonderful girl, Eve, for a week or so, while her domestic problems are sorted out?' It was their introduction to Eve, and they became fast friends.[83] Larry had been friendly with the Gotches in Athens, and when Paul was transferred to Alexandria soon after, Larry suggested that they share his rue des Pharaons flat.

Eve's parents were becoming increasingly alarmed at her behaviour and threatened her with a lunatic asylum, so Larry decided to try to separate her from them. He could not marry her – he was still legally married to Nancy – and her family was too respectable and too conservative to countenance their simply living together. Sometimes Eve was locked in her room and even struck by her father, and for a time she had left home to live with the family of her employer.[84] Larry persuaded her to take a desperate step: announcing that she had a newspaper assignment in Cairo, she boarded the train at the main Bab el Gedid station. But instead of continuing south along the delta, she got off at Sidi Gabr, only a few miles from the main station, and Gwyn Williams met her in his car. She hid at his villa on rue Sirdar until the first furor of the search for her and of her father's anger had subsided. Then Larry appeared in a taxi to take her to the rue des Pharaons. Her parents never found out that she was living with Larry, Eve claimed.[85] This was hard to credit in gossip-ridden Alexandria. Through his brother-in-law Cy Sulzberger of the *New York Times*, Alexis Ladas had recently met his future wife Diana Hambro, and the two couples spent a great deal of time in cafés, drinking and talking. Eve, Diana Ladas recalled, was 'completely polyglot', completely at ease.[86]

By December 1943 Larry had moved from the apartment on the rue des Pharaons and was living in the Ambron residence at 19 rue Mamoun in the Moharrem Bey sector between the main railway station and the El-Mahmudiya Canal on the southern edge of Alexandria. Since the 1930s Moharrem Bey had been the area of choice for the wealthy, but some had recently moved to country estates because of the bombing raids. The house was a late nineteenth-century mansion with features that were distinctive – wide marble formal front steps, a winding staircase inside a glass-topped well, and a tower rising two storeys above the roof terrace – but it was not architecturally distinguished as a whole. A garden the size of a small city block, with a swimming pool – disused – and magnificent trees, surrounded the house. The landlords were a delightful Italian-Jewish couple, Argo and Amelia Ambron, friends of the Smarts. The Ambrons had been chased out of Italy by the Fascists, and so had moved to their winter residence in Alexandria. Argo was a financier, while Amelia Ambron was a meticulously accurate artist who painted at her studio in the house and at an atelier in the city. So did her daughter Gilda, whom Larry especially liked. Another painter who was part of their circle was Clea Badaro, 'a very pretty blonde girl I was very keen on', Larry recalled.[87] She too came to the Ambron house to paint.[88] Badaro became known for powerful impressionistic paintings characterized by a deep shade of blue.

Larry invited the Gotches to move into the upper floor of the Ambron house with him, and soon they were joined by Harold and Eppy Edwards and Alexis Ladas: all congenial friends. There was plenty of room for guests, and occasionally Elizabeth David, later to become famous for her cookery books, and Charles Gibson Cowan, with his fine moustache, his strange airs and his teddy bears, joined the ménage. Friends on leave from the Western Desert were always welcome: Theodore Stephanides and the Nahoum twins, both majors, would drop in for a shower and an overnight.

Larry claimed the tower as his domain, and the others agreed never to disturb him there. A precarious outside wooden stair with an iron railing led to the upper room of the tower, a small octagon some eight feet across. From the tower he could see a mile along the rue Mamoun and could pick out the homes of prosperous Alexandrians. To the south, Lake Mareotis shimmered in the heat; and eastward the tall column of Pompey's Pillar rose as a reminder of the past. Although Larry wrote to Henry Miller, 'I . . . work in a little tower – very smart alec and quaint', he denied any accomplishment in the next phrase: 'but we are all so wormeaten by the war that I do no work at all.' Eve decorated the tower room for him. He was reading Henry's *Colossus of Maroussi* and trying to write his own 'Greek book', not the proposed Greek history but a project that he had mentioned to Miller on Corfu in 1939.[89] To Eliot he also described a 'book about a landscape', admitting that 'the hand-loom revolves with painful slowness'.[90] The story on the loom was *Prospero's Cell*. The news from Greece was terrible – 'famine, disease, and internal anarchy' – and he finally admitted to Henry that he and Nancy had separated, although he concealed the underlying reasons: 'Just the war I guess.' It was one of the great understatements of his life. The letter to Henry closes with the plea, 'Will you write some time – and disregard my bloody humours?'[91] Nothing seemed to be going right: not his writing, not the war, and certainly not his personal life – or so he said.

Larry found himself in the middle of another conflict, a light-hearted one for a change. Gwyn Williams's study of the history of Alexandria, his readings of Forster, Cavafy, Theocritus, Callimachus and the like, led him to believe that a verse war, a *flyting*, between Alexandria and Cairo would be much in the spirit of the cities. Alexandria would be represented by Larry, Harold Edwards, Robert Liddell and Williams, Cairo by Spencer, Tiller, Bryn Davies and Robin Fedden. 'Not since Troy was there such a bash-up,' wrote Larry to Tambimuttu.[92] Williams, Edwards and Davies, being Welsh, were steeped in the narrative verse traditions of their native land; Liddell was described by Larry as 'tart'; and Spencer could emerge from behind his quiet mask with a powerful irony. Robin Furness, translator of Callimachus and former head of the English Department at Cairo University, was persuaded by Williams to act as a referee, and this he did in verse. All seemed to enjoy themselves, and a few stanzas from Larry's 'Against Cairo: An Ode' capture the tone:

Dull by the brutish desert and the fens,
In Cairo all you prostituted pens
Flow slimy as the unchristian Nile
With logodaedely or bile:
In warts on prose, on poetry in wens.

Speak then, thou smart unbridled Fedden
Who doth with base iambic leaden
Stir the dark khamseen with thy verse,
And in full flush
Glide with sassoon-like rush
From poetry to pose – or something worse.

Tiller comes in for a more personal attack:

Next to the prurient one we bear –
That No Man's Land for women, Terence,
Whose verse by little napkins rinsed out
By beer and puberty goes reeling,
In clouds of local stout
To a great bouillabaisse of girlish feeling.[93]

In one of his replies Spencer scored a hit:

But oh what startled muse would not miscarry
when in the swollen verse of Durrell (Larry)
pornography and Greece and gaga marry.[94]

No one seemed much to mind what was said.

Firing off squibs was good fun, but Larry was finding it difficult to write seriously. 'You will bear with me, if on occasion I promise more than I perform,' he told Eliot. 'Egypt is simply lousy with material for good books', yet somehow, confronted with trivial obstacles, in this landscape one melted in 'apathy and boredom'. After more than half a year of talks and negotiations, Larry had just about given up on his Greek history: it 'still waits for cooperation from our gallant and maddening little allies', he complained to Eliot.[95] 'Of all the uncooperating, talkative, thankless, political races they are the worst.'[96] Larry was primed to write about Greece, and out of the grim wartime situation sprang the sunniest of his island books: 'In order to console myself I am writing a little book about Corfu to tide me over these dog-days,' he told Eliot.[97] By February he had pushed *Prospero's Cell* to 20,000 words.[98]

Larry had been reading D. H. Lawrence's writings about Italy while he was on Corfu, and they echoed in his mind as he worked on his Corfu memoir. 'Those travel books were absolutely unequalled,' he recalled.[99] He especially liked *Sea and Sardinia*: 'I read it as a revelation of Lawrence, not of Sardinia. I found the freshness, in a journalistic sense, so vivid I got a little jealous.'[100] He recognized Lawrence's ability to lift a few facts from a source book and puff life into them.

Larry's exasperation with the Greeks did not apply to Seferis, recently posted to Cairo. Soon Larry was helping him with English translations of his poems, intended for publication in *Personal Landscape*. This was to mark a high point in Larry's friendship with Seferis. Larry rated him alongside Eliot, but this did not prevent his covering Seferis's English version of 'Pretoria, Transvaal' with copious annotations in red ink. Good-naturedly, Seferis concluded his next letter with the request, 'So, please return this letter with your corrections (red ink, if possible).' If Seferis was sensitive about anything, it was 'the rights of my *personal* Country'[101] – Greece. This issue would cause friction between Larry and Seferis in the future. For the present, however, all seemed well and Bernard Spencer and Larry enlisted Seferis's aid in preparing an anthology based on *Personal Landscape* magazine, to be entitled *Personal Landscape: An Anthology of Exile*. He helped them with the 'bits and puzzles' section and with translations of Sikelianos.

Like that future bearer of his own initials in the *Quartet*, L. G. Darley, who would meet Justine at a lecture, Larry gained entry into some of the exalted circles of Alexandria through his cultural activities. Colin Keith-Johnson, then working for the Entertainments National Service Association (ENSA), enlisted Larry, Gwyn Williams, and Paul Gotch to help put on a few shows in mixed media for Gaston Zananiri's international cultural group. Zananiri's dream of reviving Mediterranean culture through such episodes was not taken altogether seriously by Larry and his friends, who seemed to find their inspiration more in Edith Sitwell, George Antheil and Dada than from the Med. They employed an epidiascope to project images in a darkened room, while from an adjacent room Paul played phonograph discs over a loudspeaker to blend with readings by Larry, Gwyn and Colin, also out of sight but co-ordinating their voices with the projections by spying through a peephole. Gwyn thought that it was 'all quite baffling for the Alexandria intelligentsia'. None the less, these entertainments brought them into the world of 'wealthy Jewish ladies and their salons, the Wednesday afternoons of Baron George Menasce'.[102]

Alexandria placed plenty of temptation before Larry. In February 1944, when Robin Fedden asked him to look out for Diana Gould, a ballerina who danced the role of Frou-Frou in *The Merry Widow*, then touring Egypt, he did not need further prompting. Larry attended a performance of *The Merry Widow* and sent 'naughty odes to the long-legged soubrette'.[103] He had always liked tall, elegant women, and when he discovered that Diana was also witty and irreverent, he happily appointed himself her guide. Larry may have complained to most of his correspondents about Egypt, but she thought he 'wore Alexandria like a cape' and was completely at ease in the city.[104] He also *felt* Alexandria, Diana realized, and she would later call him 'a masochistic onlooker'.[105] To experience and suffer – this seemed to Larry a fair summary of his life to date. He appeared to drive himself to suffer, yet he was quick to cast off his pessimism. There was nothing masochistic about the swerve and dash with which Larry escorted her about the city, from his favourite lowly Greek taverna to the roof of the Cecil, where Diana performed an impromptu *entrechat*,[106] her long black hair flying.

One luminous morning Larry and Diana walked by the shore of Lake Mareotis, and Larry said, 'One drop of rain, this winter, and in the Spring the whole place will be covered with asphodel.' Diana told Larry, 'I've never seen so much room in a sky before,' and he replied, 'I'll write you a poem for that.'[107] The result was 'Mareotis: For Diana Gould':

> Only we are held here on the
> Rationed love – a landscape like an eye,
> Where the wind gnashes by Mareotis,
> Stiffens the reeds and glistening salt.[108]

Perhaps disingenuously, Larry asked Diana to marry him – he had learned to use 'marriage' as a code word to invite further intimacy. She replied that it was 'sweet' of him, but turned him down: she had met and fallen in love with Fedden in Cairo, at a party given by Ines Burrows. 'Of course!' said a momentarily abashed Larry, 'How stupid of me not to realise.'[109] To make amends, he then used his Information Office position to arrange a lecture in Alexandria that would give Fedden an excuse to make the journey from Cairo.

Diana Gould's visit not only caused a flutter in Larry's circle of writers and diplomats, but led one amorous naval officer to present her with a huge box of chocolates, just as she was rushing to the theatre to don her costume. Larry commandeered a creaking gharry and climbed in beside her. The horse refused to start; in a fury, Diana opened the box and proceeded to pelt the horse's rump with confections. The bombardment had the desired effect: 'Up went its tail, out fell its dinner and off it went with a clatter and a snort . . . .'[110] Larry wept with mirth. They arrived at the theatre just in time.

Not on schedule, however, was Billy Gotch's baby, almost a month overdue. 'Bring her to the show, Larry darling, and I'll kick it out of her!' commanded Diana. Larry did – and Billy barely made it to the hospital after the curtain fell on *The Merry Widow*.[111] The Gotches asked Larry to be little Sheila's godfather.[112] Soon the theatre company left to entertain Allied troops in Italy. Mount Etna chose that moment to erupt, and Gwyn Williams fired an epigram after her:

> The proof that you're in Naples, not with us,
> Is the misbehaviour of Vesuvius.[113]

In April turbulence of another kind struck Alexandria when the last of three mutinies of Greek military units occurred. The trouble always seemed to begin with groups of dissident Greek liberals and the EAM – the communist-supported National Liberation Front – demanding the abolition of the monarchy and a radical reformation of Greek government. The mutinies of 1942 and 1943 had been put down by British troops with relative ease, but the formation in Greece on 29 March 1944 of a provisional government under the rubric of the Political Committee of National Liberation provided a focus for left-wing rebels. The most steadfast rebellions occurred in the First Greek Brigade at Bourg el Arab, among the merchant seamen under the union leader Karayannis, and on five ships of the Royal Hellenic Navy in Alexandria harbour. The first two were settled with no or few casualties, but Larry's house-sharer Alexis Ladas was among the royalist officers who spent the night of 24 April retaking the ships in desperate combat from bulkhead to bulkhead, Greek against Greek. Overwrought, streaked with grease, sweat and soot, Ladas staggered after daybreak into the house on the rue Mamoun. Larry and the Gotches were at breakfast and Larry greeted him jocularly: 'I hear you Greeks have been mixing it up!' 'Fuck your mothers!' shouted Ladas.[114] Although Larry's sympathies were really with the royalists, he found it difficult to take any Greek political aspirations seriously. He admired the Greeks as individualists, story-tellers, dancers, drinkers. He appreciated their generosity and their legendary love of freedom. But his colonial prejudice whispered to him that they could not run a country properly. The

English, perhaps because of that emotional sterility that he deplored, were better governors – this was his rooted opinion. As always with Larry, however, people came before politics; Ladas was tolerant; and there was no rift in the friendship.

Larry's work on *Prospero's Cell* was going well in the early spring, so well that he hesitated to admit it: 'I have been so long barren that I fear to tell you that I am *working* once more: for fear I shall blow up and fall into an Alexandrian frenzy of apathy,' he confessed to Henry Miller.[115] He tended to write fluently when he was in love, or at least in a state of emotional tension, and he hoped to finish the book by August 1944. The security, tenuous though it sometimes seemed, of his relationship with Eve made it possible for him to write about Nancy and Corfu without bitterness. Larry made the note of nostalgia in *Prospero's Cell* appear to be due simply to the coming loss of the freedom of youth. That the nostalgia was made bitingly poignant for Larry by the loss of both Nancy and Greece, he was able to conceal.

Where Larry would reveal more of his internal conflict was in his verse, and he forwarded to Eliot additional poems for the *Cities, Plains and People* volume.[116] Eliot liked the collection and agreed to eventual publication, but proposed waiting until 1945 since he thought it inadvisable to bring out a second volume of the poetry of any Faber poet within less than two years of the previous one. In fact, he would have preferred a prose work at once from Larry, 'but I gather from what you say about the Greek book that there is no prospect of this'.[117] Larry did not like this verdict, but he had to accept it. 'I was as usual rather pleased with myself, and still quite as unsure,' he said ruefully.[118]

Henry Miller was also in a state of personal turmoil. He and Anaïs had parted definitively, so he said – although a month later he would describe her as 'friendly' – and then he had sustained the 'worst defeat I ever suffered' at the hands of Sevasty Koutsaftis, a Greek woman in Hollywood.[119] Larry continued his exploration of Alexandrian women, and he described them to Henry in such terms as to drive him into a 'paroxysm' of desire. Perhaps deliberately rubbing pepper into Henry's wounds, Larry wrote:

But the women are splendid – like neglected gardens – rich, silk-and-olive complexions, slanting black eyes and soft adze-cut lips, and heavenly figures like line-drawings by a sexual Matisse. I am up to my ears in them – if I must be a little *literal*. . . . Now I think of the correct simile for the Alexandrians. When they make love it's like two people in a dark room slashing at each other with razors – to make each other feel _____?[120]

In sharp contrast, Henry lamented that in love 'All ends disastrously'. The stunning news that long-time bachelor and *bon viveur* Fred Perlès was planning to marry 'some Ann up in Dumfries' seemed a rebuke to his own womanless state. In his writing and his painting Henry had had a 'year of complete fulfillment and realization', yet he declared, 'I'd give it all up to wander with you through those streets and see those sloe-gin fizz eyes, drown myself in that abattoir of love.'[121]

No fewer than seventeen of Henry's books would be out in America and Britain by the end of 1944, he announced; in addition, he had sold twenty-four of his paintings before his show in Hollywood had even started, and Caresse Crosby, publisher and patroness to the Jazz Age, was going to feature his work at her Washington gallery. Henry was turning over the proceeds from the sale of his paintings to the artist Beauford Delaney and to Kenneth Patchen. Faced with all this evidence of his friend's successes, Larry rejoiced for Henry but complained of his own subsistence 'on a machine-made diet of gun bomb and tank – backed up by the slogan'. And it was Larry's business to create slogans, not art. He was acutely conscious of the near-impossibility of writing 'a single line of anything that had a human smell here', yet he knew that he was gaining in the raw stuff of fiction: 'I'm glad of this little death for all the material it's put in my way about people and affairs in general.'[122] He did not tell Henry that he was writing more poetry, because he knew that his American friend had little feeling for verse.

WHILE LARRY WAS EXPERIENCING the little death of Alexandria, his friend Paddy Leigh Fermor, together with William Stanley Moss, were confronting real death on Crete. Paddy had been parachuted into Crete on 4 February 1944, and Moss had followed him two months later. With the help of several bands of *andartes*, Cretan guerrilla fighters, they kidnapped General Kreipe, the commander of the German garrison, and kept him hidden on the island for eighteen days while the entire German force frantically combed the island. Finally a rendezvous was made with a fast patrol boat sent from Egypt. Then shortly after the Normandy invasion Xan Fielding was dropped into southern France, where he was captured by the Gestapo. He was due to be shot, but was rescued through the courage of a woman accomplice. Of course, Larry knew only in general terms what his friends were up to, but he realized that his life of routine was by comparison safe – and dull. He pretended to be blasé about the war, and he would sometimes terminate Paul Gotch's jazz and blues sessions by grabbing Paul's guitar and singing, 'He Played His Ukulele When the Ship Went Down'.[123]

Larry solaced himself for being stuck in Egypt by writing poetry and making love. 'The sloe-eyed people are still here,' he reminded Henry. 'There's a lovely English wren and a girl with the hips of an acrobat. But it's all really quite meaningless.'[124] He was tired of 'little people with little minds' – although he admitted that he was being unfair to Eve. Also, he was having a good time collecting linguistic absurdities under the heading 'Imbecility File – "This Egypt"': among his favourites were a Cairo laundry sign that proclaimed 'THE OXFORD IRONY'[125] and a café that requested clients to 'pay for all Consummations in advance'.[126] The *Egyptian Mail* provided a fine headline, 'BOOBS OF HEAVY CALIBRE DROPPED ON BERLIN', and an arresting caption about the army corps of South African women, 'W.A.A.F. SIN ACTION'. The Personal Column of the *Gazette* advertised: 'British officer in Zamalek urgently needs good plain cock.' A human interest story proclaimed that 'The husband greeted her with an ill-disguised rupture.' Even the High Command was not spared, and newspaper readers were told that 'General Auchinleck has assembled the greatest farce in history.' Soon Larry had a fat commonplace book of similar notes and press cuttings.[127]

Larry found Eve increasingly fascinating. According to Larry, Eve had grown up around the *souks* and back streets of Alexandria, and she was a natural story-teller: 'She sits for hours on the bed and serves me up experience raw,' he wrote to Henry, 'sex life of Arabs, perversions, circumcision, hashish, sweetmeats, removal of the clitoris, cruelty, murder.'[128] Eve would complain years later that Larry's version of her experience of Alexandrian life was fanciful and much exaggerated, but certainly she had seen far more than he of the lives the poor led in back streets and alleys.

Knowing Eve, Larry told Henry, 'has cured me for English women for good and all'. Eve, said Larry, 'like all people of the Tibetan sensibility' had thought she was going insane because no one understood her. Setting himself up as her psychoanalyst and 're-articulating her experience for her' had been 'fun'. Larry himself had discovered 'Sex now as a non-possessive form of friendship much more moving and infinitely more tender than the old anglo-saxon rout of ideas *about* everything.'[129] With the aid of a copy of Lao Tzu sent by Eliot, Larry had explained this view of sex to Eve, 'who understands every word – but it doesn't prevent her from scratching my face open for infidelities which in this landscape and ambience are as meaningless as she, I, or Pompey's Pillar are.'[130]

Larry was gradually evolving his understanding of love-making that he would years later ascribe to Pursewarden in the *Quartet*, that 'sex is a psychic and not a physical act'. In fact, Larry would add, 'The clumsy coupling of human beings is simply a biological paraphrase of this truth – a primitive method of introducing minds to each other.'[131] Larry might be able to convince himself that sex was psychic, but Eve was too practical an Alexandrian not to view his line of reasoning as a justification for infidelity, and Larry was often on the receiving end of jealous outbursts. Eve, with the eyes of an angry hawk, would storm on clicking heels into the Office of Information to demand of his subordinates in her clear, slightly French-accented English, 'Where's Larry?'[132] At the core of their relationship rested complementary needs: Eve craved escape from the stultifying world of her parents; Larry enjoyed the heady experience of introducing a beautiful innocent – in his view – to the world of his ideas. Larry had shared a thousand assumptions and cultural distinctions with Nancy, yet their marriage had fallen apart. Now he was willing to base a partnership on a supposed shared 'Tibetan sensibility' and a startling cultural difference.

He was probably thinking of himself when he later described Darley as 'weathered and seasoned by the disappointments of love in other places',[133] but this did not make him an undemanding lover. Larry in 1944 wrote out 'A Little Letter To Eve', a small holograph pamphlet of six pages, mainly in red ink, embellished with doodles and sketches, and stapled along one edge. 'Dear Yve,' he began, 'terrible fainéant and wicked black-eyed beast generally. . . . Why are you so perversely exacting? You do not know. Why am I so unsatisfactory as a lover? I do not know.' Then he proceeded to answer the first question: Eve was selfish – but he was even more so; and there was another reason: 'in love il faut avoir de confiance à soi-même and I haven't any – and you haven't though you pretend to have.' An angular doodle headed the next page. 'Thirdly you are terribly secret and I am too profound for expression.' Here, a labyrinthine abstract doodle in right angles intervened. Larry next addressed the writer's block that he was struggling against: 'I mean that my artistic difficulties as a writer are all reflected in my difficulties as a lover – expression, sincerity, style etc.' The greatest obstacle to their closeness was treachery: 'We are all traitors by the faiblesse of smiles or moues or by intention and we can't help it.' Knowing this, and with the pain of his separation from Nancy still throbbing, Larry tried to control his own jealousy by limiting his expectations: 'So my pessimism guards me against your smiles to other people and your bloody gipsy familiarity with tout le monde.' Language is a further barrier: 'Yr

English is not perfect – and you must feel as I would if I had to make love in Greek all the time: *nuance* is hard to understand.' None the less, he is 'devoted': 'I stand by your dark nut-brown gipsy face and flashy eyes and sombre sexy loveliness.' He added, 'the tendresse is the important thing'. The last line of the text is a printed question: 'What do you think?' Larry signed the letter with a profile self-portrait, but with his signature snub nose replaced with a long nose like an Italian carnival mask. On the back cover appeared more geometric abstractions framing 'The End.'[134]

Larry's 'Little Letter' is a self-consciously literary production sprinkled with French phrases and quaint expressions – the Elizabethan cliché 'nut-brown' was not a true description of Eve's complexion – but it accurately reflected their relationship. Both were self-absorbed, both insecure, both passionate. Their affair did not promise tranquillity.

Theodore Stephanides stayed with Larry during 11–25 July 1944 and Larry took advantage of his presence to follow Eliot's urging and press ahead on *Prospero's Cell*. Larry depended on Theodore for many of the folkways, for much of the biological and botanical detail, that he needed to give colour and verisimilitude to the book. 'I can't remember any of the wild flowers that I write about so ecstatically in the Greek islands,' Larry would later confess. 'I have to look them up.' This failing he called the 'defect of vision', a shortcoming that he would attempt to address by constantly rechecking his impressions.[135] To tell the truth, however, Larry was never so concerned with quotidian reality as with what he called the Heraldic Universe and 'reality prime'.

Larry had already given Theodore the formula for writing a travel book, and now he was putting it into practice himself. He had told Theodore to write 'Quite freely and easily bringing in your information in a given context. Invent some people, peasants and so on – and treat them quite boldly. Put them in and forget them just as you feel inclined; short sentences – no purple patches – no *Leacock*.'[136] In fact, Larry *did* invent quite freely: the dates in *Prospero's Cell*, for example, are not historically accurate but were included to give the book the form of a diary. Even one of the four people listed in the dedication as real, Count D – called 'Count C' in one draft – is not based on a single individual, but is apparently a composite character grounded on several of Larry's Corfiot friends,[137] despite the fact that Larry would identify the original of the Count to Henry Miller as his old friend Dr Palatiano.[138]

Prospero's Cell was to be an epitaph for Larry's lost youth. In the book he resurrected his marriage to Nancy – 'N.' in the narrative – in idealized terms, painting her as the gentle and graceful figure that she could be, with no hint of their rages and tensions. He brought to life the friends who had died – Palatiano, Max Nimiec and the chauffeur Spiro Americanos. *Prospero's Cell* is a tribute to island life, to the tranquil, bucolic idyll that was possible on pre-war Corfu, to the century-old tradition of friendship between Briton and Greek, to a pair of the nobler facets of Greek character: hospitality and generosity.

Corfu, fruitful as it had been for Larry, seemed even better in comparison with Alexandria. His opinions of the city were at least as harsh as those he had expressed over Cairo: 'I cannot think how to write or speak to you from this flesh-pot, sink-pot, melting-pot of dullness,' he confided to Diana Gould. He complained about the 'faces of the Arabs with their weakness and cupidity', and the 'thin exhausted lusts of the Alexandrians running out like sawdust out of dummies'.[139]

Larry felt too dispirited to begin a major undertaking: 'I need terribly to recover my sanity a bit – disoriented and bruised a bit still, and haven't seen anything but sand and palms for two years,' he told Henry Miller. Botanically this was not true, but it was how he felt. That very evening Larry had seen Seferis, just back from London. 'He is practically in the same state as I am', Larry reported to Henry, 'sort of exhaustion'. This, Larry felt, had affected all his friendships: 'In fact though he is my best friend in Egypt we almost never meet. It's as if meeting people who have real human demands to make of one is too tiring.'[140]

After finishing *Prospero's Cell*, Larry repaid a part of what he felt was his debt to Miller by writing 'The Happy Rock', an essay for inclusion in a book about Henry being compiled by Bern Porter. Henry recognized the title as one he had mentioned to Larry at Betty Ryan's flat, and now he suggested it to Porter for the whole book instead of the originally proposed 'I Am My Own God'. 'The Happy Rock' was a serious attempt to sum up Henry's achievement: admitting that Miller could on occasion write badly, make critical misjudgements, and be inaccurate and prejudiced, Larry proclaimed him 'a very great man' and praised his 'meticulous prose', the 'power and vehemence of his purely descriptive writing', and especially his health, sanity and undeviating honesty. Larry wrote that Henry had 'no correspondence with English literature', that he had never read Milton, Donne, Shakespeare, Swift, 'etc.'[141] This stung Henry like a critic's lash. He countered that Larry had 'made some queer errors about my reading!' He had indeed, Henry claimed, 'read Swift, Blake, most of the Elizabethans . . . when I was in my twenties'.[142] He had only himself to blame for Larry's statement. Back in 1936 he had told Larry of his ignorance of the Elizabethans and of a lot else: 'I know nothing of the classics – practically nothing,' he had written. 'I am ignorant. Even about English literature.'[143] Larry was not one to forget a statement like that – even if he sensed that it was an exaggeration dished out for effect, something he so often did himself.

Larry was being prodded from other quarters as well. Hugh Gordon Porteus, out in the desert with an RAF Fighter Control Unit, wrote with some glee that Kathleen Raine had called Larry 'a poor echo of Joyce'.[144] This Larry shrugged off as 'about the measure of applause one can expect from the English these days'.[145] Porteus had been digging latrines and was chagrined not to have found any artefacts. He turned his disappointment into verse:

> O to toil in Tibet
> Where there are no toilets yet.

Compared to his own life in the desert, Larry's complaints about his domestic misery struck Porteus as ill-founded and he chided his friend accordingly: 'I infer that you carry some of your affairs too far? Bad, bad.'[146]

Prospero's Cell and Faber's immediate acceptance of the book sharpened Larry's appetite at once for Greece and for an attempt at a major fiction. The planned 'Book of the Dead', originally to be set in Athens, was being translated in his mind to Alexandria. The new locale was connected in Larry's mind with Greece. In August 1944 he had confided to Miller, 'I have a wonderful idea for a novel in Alexandria, a nexus for all news of Greece, side by side with a sort of spiritual butcher's shop with girls on slabs.'[147] Soon he was writing to Henry, 'My notebooks are swollen like an amnion with notes for an Alexandrian novel.' The two central characters would be twins, and the book would be different in form from anything he had written: 'I want to strike a bold naturalistic note for once – tired of writing which is like the unwinding of intestines. I want a huge third person narrative this time, giving the whole range from the closet to the prie dieu.'[148] He felt 'stiff and out of practice' and, before tackling a major work, needed the 'sheer fun of writing a couple of books – bad books too'.[149]

One of these 'bad books' would be 'a straight narrative about some people who get lost in the womb'[150], which he had already described as 'a short anthropological study of the English tabus'.[151] This 'womb' would be the Cretan labyrinth. Almost from the start Larry called his new story 'The

Dark Labyrinth', the title under which it would resurface years later in Britain and, later still, in America. For sub-plot and episodes it would owe a lot to the Cretan adventures of his friends Paddy Leigh Fermor and Xan Fielding. Thus, right after *Prospero's Cell* Larry began the book that he first entitled *The Dark Labyrinth* and later *Cefalû*.

Through a bit of luck and some discreet lobbying – and 'with every wangle known to man also involved: the embassy, the army, the quakers and the pashas'[152] – Larry managed to secure the post of Public Information Officer for the Dodecanese Islands 'for the period of reconstruction'.[153] All that remained was to dislodge the Germans. Larry would begin his 'big book', he said, the reborn 'Book of the Dead', as soon as his posting to Rhodes was accomplished – 'and I am feeling a bit less hysterical'.[154]

There were other signs that Larry was coming back to life. He had met René Etiemble, 'a grand Frenchman', who was writing about Henry for some South American papers. Etiemble would supply names of people for Henry to canvass for book sales. Larry asked Henry to send him Melville's *Pierre*, Mumford's biography of Melville, and 'any well-documented' life of Emily Brontë – the last-named for a play he intended to write. The shortage of books, even 'the cheap edition classics which one had intended to save up and read at moments of crisis like these', was such that Larry had been reduced to reading French translations of Dostoevsky, 'despite my distaste for this futile logician's tongue'. Perhaps most important, he had really crashed into love with Eve Cohen, 'who says she is a burnt out soul from another planet, who is tired of everything except God; and he's tired of her!' The other women about were merely – and here he quoted Henry – 'beautifully groomed ponies'[155], but 'Gipsy Cohen provides a cyclone every day with a real generous and mad beauty which is touching and exciting.'[156]

While his poetry notebooks would not match the volume or variety of those he kept during his Greek days, in 1944 Larry filled many pages with drafts and occasional bawdy verses, including a limerick on 'A huge bearded lady from Giza' who made love like a great 'lemon squeezer'. Another was 'Zeus & Hera':

> Zeus gets Hera on her back
> But finds that she has lost the knack.
> Extenuated by excesses
> She is unable, she confesses.
> Nothing daunted Zeus, who wise is,

Tries a dozen good disguises:
Eagle, ram, and bull and bear
Quickly answer Hera's prayer.
I know a god must be prolix,
But – half a dozen different pricks?'[157]

Larry complained to Henry that since Nancy would neither return to him nor divorce him, 'My private affairs are still in an unholy muddle.' Nancy, 'who is behaving like a mad evangelist with a nice touch of anglo-saxon guilt', would not answer his letters, and there was 'No news of the child either to which I was perhaps too much attached.' His anger at Nancy boiled over into a general denunciation: 'These anglo-saxon women are all sphincter bound and spiritually unadventurous.'[158] Larry judged himself to be changed, 'tougher'. His writing would be different henceforth: 'I'm after good bleak effects this time – not going to froth over and bubble into nonsense merely.' An encouraging evaluation came in October from Anne Ridler, who sent an airgraph to say that *Cities, Plains and People* 'has yr usual brilliance, better integrated'.[159]

Larry had just met a master of bleak effects: the Egyptian writer Albert Cossery. He was a thin, morose man with long bony hands, but his dark eyes could lose their haunted look in good conversation. Cossery seemed to have reduced his needs to almost nothing: he lived in the poorest of rented rooms, had no possessions beyond a few books and a change of clothes, and wrote in French about the underdogs. Larry sent an English translation of Cossery's novel about the Egyptian poor, *The Men God Forgot*, to Henry, who wrote back that he was 'crazy about it', that it was 'quite unique', that he wanted a dozen copies to show around.[160]

Cossery was a strange figure, and he would remain an outsider, beyond Larry's regular circle of friends. For Larry there were always a number of good times to be had: an evening with Seferis; a session with Sir Walter Smart, in Alexandria for the October conference that would produce the Palestine Protocol; a meeting aboard a yacht with Henry Miller's friend Schumann; several trips with Gipsy Cohen for swimming and sunbathing at 'our deserted battlefield' at Abu el Sair, near Alamein. Larry drew the scene in ink and watercolours, and below the sketch he began a poem, 'By granite and seagulls remembering'.[161] He and Eve 'slipped down through the battlefields to a long beach where the real Mediterranean comes up in great green coasters and sky is smothered down to violet, all lambent and turning your body in water to a wonderful rose.'[162] They bathed naked and lay on the sand, and Larry felt that he was in Greece, despite being surrounded as they were with the shell casings and wrecks of war. Here Larry's fictional surrogate, Darley, would swim in the pages of the *Quartet* with Justine, with Clea.

As THE END OF 1944 APPROACHED, Larry had two books being prepared for the press at Faber. T. S. Eliot and Anne Ridler agreed that Larry's 'Prose Aphorisms about Poetry' should be dropped from *Cities, Plains and People*, but they had decided to allow illustrations in *Prospero's Cell* – if Larry would provide them.

Henry Miller's personal news was as good as his publishing triumphs, for a change: he had met a young Polish graduate of Bryn Mawr, Janina M. Lepska, in New York and was taking her back to Big Sur as his wife. The old anti-academic had visited universities in a half-a-dozen states, he told Larry.[163] Henry did not mention that he had been checked out by the FBI after telling a class of apprentice seamen at Dartmouth that there was little difference between them and the Nazis: 'They're fighting for the same things that you're fighting for.'[164]

Larry felt that his literary accomplishments were acceptable but modest: he wanted to produce his promised big book soon. More than he perhaps realized at the time, elements were crowding in that would help him to forge the characters and the philosophic underpinnings of *The Alexandria Quartet*. He had found in his lover Eve the 'Alexandrian Jewess' who would be a major inspiration for his heroine. He filled some fifteen pages in a small exercise book with notes in blue, green and red ink on Jung's *Integration of the Personality* and Louis Berg's *The Human Personality*. Two pages were devoted to comparing Einstein and Newton.[165] By October 1944 he had told Henry excitedly about a 'great undiscovered book – Groddeck's "The Book of the It"': 'He is a practising analyst in Germany – but *so* far above Howe and Rank as you will hardly believe until you read this astonishing thing. Please lose no time – *this* is the man we were looking out for in Paris.'[166] Georg Groddeck, to whom Freud owed his concept of the Id – so Groddeck's adherents claim – combined 'the Taoist identity of opposites' with a theory of disease that explained all illnesses and even accidents in terms of each patient's unconscious needs. These needs arise out of anxiety, fear, strain, overwork, as each operates on the interior 'It', the amalgam of conscious and unconscious, physical, spiritual and psychic forces that rules each individual. There is no sharp dividing line between body and spirit, said Groddeck.

Here was a theory, Larry felt, that went a long way towards explaining the variables in the human condition. 'I've had a wonderful time reading the book and testing each theory in my own experience,' he wrote to Henry; 'It rings like a dinner bell.'[167] Groddeck had died in 1934 and his books were mostly out of print: bringing his work before the public became a cause Larry would pursue energetically, and Groddeck was to be dumped wholesale into the *Quartet*. Larry asked Eliot to find a copy of *The Book of the It* and post it to Henry.[168]

'I shall have a novel for you very soon,' he wrote to Eliot in December about *The Dark Labyrinth*. 'It is a pot-boiler but has its points.'[169] He told his friends that he hoped it would make sufficient pounds to pay for his divorce from Nancy. The story took shape like a mediaeval morality with lashings of early twentieth-century psychology: a party of tourists with names suggestive of allegory – the Reverend Fearmax, the man of great fears; Graecen, the person seeking a state of grace; Truman, the decent and true man – become lost in a great subterranean labyrinth on Crete. The Minotaur is in residence, and each individual meets a version of the beast that corresponds to a personal psychic state. For Mr and Mrs Truman, for instance, the monster turns out to be a harmless and quite ordinary cow, while Fearmax meets what may be either his long-lost spirit-medium or a satanic beast.

In writing *Prospero's Cell* Larry had certainly mined Stephanides's tremendous knowledge of Corfu; for *The Dark Labyrinth* he would borrow from the wartime adventures on Crete of his SOE friends at Tara and, from stories told about the abbot of the Preveli Monastery and the village priest John Alevizakis, who had sheltered so many resistance fighters. John Baird, the central character in Larry's novel, is no casual tourist, but has joined the tour group to lay the ghost of a man he had been forced to kill during a wartime commando operation. He had buried this German, Böcklin – like Reichel, a Bavarian – under a poplar near the labyrinth used by his fifth columnists as a hide-out, but since the war this particular killing among many had preyed upon him, recurring in dreams and depriving him of peace of mind. A similar event had occurred during the kidnapping of General Kreipe by Leigh Fermor and Moss, when their Cretan accomplices had evidently killed the general's driver in cold blood some time after the actual attack. A more closely matching pattern for Baird's act came from Xan Fielding, who told Larry about the fate of a German deserter picked up by his *andarte* group on Crete. There was no immediate prospect of evacuating the prisoner to Egypt, Xan said, and the man might be a German plant. Xan had to think of maintaining the secrecy of his organization and of his clandestine radio transmitter, not to mention the safety of the peasant families sheltering the fighters: the prisoner would have to be killed. The German was young, thin, blond, and evoked in Xan a feeling of homesickness for western Europe; he felt 'an upsurge of disloyal fellow-feeling for this enemy'.[170] The deserter was pathetically friendly and co-operative. The next day, believing that he had to take personal responsibility, Xan shot the boy at the spot they had selected for his execution. Despite the point-blank range, distress made his aim bad, and the wounded man tumbled into a ravine, where he had to be followed and finished off. Years later Xan was still haunted, as he was too honest not to admit: 'I knew only too well that I had bungled the killing. Had I made a clean job of it I might soon have forgotten the expression in that German's eyes and the sight of his scalp on the rocks.'[171] In retelling the story, Larry retained the basic situation, extending the time the prisoner spends with the guerrilla band but absolving the killer, Baird, of bungling. In the novel, no second shot is needed.

Larry was expecting the proofs of *Cities, Plains and People* soon. 'They are really GOOD', he wrote to Henry Miller, 'for once I need not be ashamed.'[172] He was not so sure about his novel; he sent Eliot the typescript of *The Dark Labyrinth* and held his breath.

In mid-April 1945 Larry received right and left barrels from Eliot, in the form of a pair of air letters posted the same day and typed in block capitals since the wartime airgraphs were photographically reduced for transmission. Because half of the poems already set in type for *Cities, Plains and People* had just been published in Tambimuttu's *Personal Landscape* anthology, publication of the Faber volume would have to be delayed, *and* Larry would have to come up with some 'NOT TOO DISCREDITABLE POETRY' to add on at the end of the book.[173] 'What a mess. I am so sorry,' Larry apologized, blaming Robin Fedden, the editor of the anthology, for having included 'every mortal thing'.[174] Furthermore, Eliot rejected *The Dark Labyrinth*: it was neither a 'THRILLER' nor a 'SOUL-STRUGGLER'; 'TOO MUCH DURRELL FOR A NORDEN, AND NOT GOOD ENOUGH DURRELL FOR A DURRELL.' Larry had used the cooking pot metaphor, and Eliot deftly tossed the image back at him: 'THERE'S TOO MUCH MEAT IN IT FOR A POT-BOILING THRILLER, AND THE MEAT ISN'T WELL ENOUGH COOKED FOR SOMETHING BETTER.' And he was not through pummelling Larry yet, adding in type and handwriting, 'ARE YOU PRIMARILY A POET OR A PROSE WRITER? DO YOU KNOW which you wish to be?'[175]

Larry told Eliot that he agreed with his strictures, and pleaded that he had written both *The Dark Labyrinth* and *Prospero's Cell* 'straight out on the typewriter'. They were 'divorce books' cobbled together to earn him 'the odd hundred or so necessary' for his legal fees, and he did not think them worth more effort.[176] He would offer *Labyrinth* to Tambimuttu rather than try to revise it for Faber. Larry ignored the question of his writing identity, but it stuck in his hide, and he would respond at length later from Rhodes: it was too serious a question to answer in a facile phrase.

With the dawn of 1945 Europe seemed to be on the verge of returning to life, even to literary life. The Allies were steadily winning the war, and Henry's enthusiasms began to have more point. Fred Perlès, despite his demanding work for the military censorship, had found time to write *Alien Corn*, his first book in English. Fred, with a sensational sense of timing, managed to be at the Dôme on VE Day and he sent Henry an exuberant postcard. In a liberated Paris, Maurice Girodias was reviving his father's Obelisk Press as the Olympia Press, and had written to Henry about bringing out his books in French. Henry told Larry that he was receiving letters from American soldiers in Paris who reported seeing all the Obelisk Press books on display, especially in bookstores on the rue de Rivoli and the rue de Castiglioni: *The Black Book*, both *Tropics*, and Anaïs Nin's *Winter of Artifice*. He urged Larry to check with Maurice, who under the German occupation had wisely exchanged the Jewish-sounding Kahane for his French mother's maiden name. There might be royalties coming, and a chance of getting *The Black Book* out in a French translation.[177] In fact, said Henry, why not have the novel translated into 'a half dozen languages at least', including Arabic![178]

Larry was not one to be meanly jealous of a friend's good fortune, but Henry's description of his 'first good break . . . since I'm living in America' certainly invited comparisons that were to the detriment of life in Alexandria. 'I have a wonderful cabin, you know, dirt cheap – ten dollars a month,' wrote Henry. 'I have a young wife (21), a baby on the way probably, food in the larder, wine *à discrétion*, hot sulfur baths down the road, books galore, a phonograph coming, a radio also coming, good kerosene lamps, a wood stove, an open fireplace, a shower, and plenty of sun – and of course the Pacific Ocean, which is always empty.'[179] Perhaps it was the emptiness that most beckoned to Larry, jammed as he was with nearly a million other souls on a narrow strip of sand between the Mediterranean and reed-choked Mareotis. Larry was tied to the Information Office while Henry was able to follow a writer's life, geared to natural patterns:

I open the door in the morning, look towards the sun rising over the mountains, and bless the whole world, birds, flowers and beasts included. After I have moved my bowels I take the hound for a walk. Then a stint of writing, then lunch, then a siesta, then water colors, then correspondence, then a book, then a fuck, then a nap, then dinner, and so to bed early and up early and all's well except when I visit the dentist now and then.[180]

Henry was full of schemes to help Larry get published in the United States. He tried to persuade a small press in New York to bring out *The Black Book*, and when that came to nothing, he spoke to George Leite, editor and publisher of *Circle* magazine in Berkeley, about reprinting some poems from *Personal Landscape* in the magazine and about publishing *The Black Book* with a preface Henry offered to write. These proposals also fell through, but Leite was to publish *Two Excursions Into Reality*, consisting of 'Zero' and 'Asylum in the Snow', two years later. Henry also urged Leite to publish Cossery's *The Men God Forgot*; Ivan Goll of *Hemispheres* was another possible publisher for Larry's books; Larry should find an Egyptian publisher for his, Henry's, books; and so on and on. Larry did recommend Henry's writing to the Renaissance Bookshop in Cairo, with the result that Henry was soon delighted by a 'whopping order'.[181]

Henry's publication schemes did not particularly excite Larry, and the omens for *The Dark Labyrinth* were not good, since even his loyal friend Tambimuttu refused to commit himself to publishing the book without first seeing a promised new ending.

For all his frustrations, Larry's exile in Egypt was proving to be a godsend in a very real sense. Despite his complaints at the time about the stultifying effects of bureaucracy and the boredom of the military conflict, both Cairo and Alexandria were rich in human contacts for him, as he admitted in his verse:

> All indeed whom war or time threw up
> On this littoral and tides could not move
> Were objects for my study and my love.[182]

The people, indeed, could not be seen separately from Alexandria, 'a city of causes that were being lost even though militarily it was successfully defended', wrote Gwyn Williams. During the years 1942–5, the rise of Egyptian nationalism gradually eroded the European accents of the city. The exodus of ethnic and religious minorities would soon follow. On Corfu, Larry had identified with the genteel old aristocracy, the Palatianos, the Aspiotis, the Soufis, the Theotockis – cosmopolitans who looked to

Paris as their cultural Mecca. In Alexandria the social and intellectual upper level spoke French by preference and addressed their prayers northward, whether they were descended from Italians or Lebanese, Greeks or Syrians, Sephardic Jews or Copts, English or French. Williams, Larry's best friend in Alexandria, identified the cultural ambience:

Names of people I remember seeing there symbolise this mixture: Zananiri, Sachs, Baddaro, Menasce, Zogueb, Suarez, Salinas, Kerekreti, Barber, Perides, Fumaroli, Papasunessiou, Oumoff, Barukh, Baladi. Sects and philosophies flourished. There was Gaston Zananiri's dream of a new Mediterranean culture, rescued from World War II. It was out of this varied and dying ferment that Larry invented his *Alexandria Quartet*.[183]

Never really happy in Egypt, Larry was now bursting to get away. 'I have been like a prisoner writing on the wall with a rusty nail to keep sane,' he confided to Miller. Although he was sending some new poems and a copy of *Prospero's Cell*, he begged Henry not to judge him by this 'rubbish'. He blamed his inadequate productions on the censorship, which 'under the guise of military secrets has now become an instrument which successfully blankets ANY AND EVERY FREEDOM OF EXPRESSION that might seem a trifle unorthodox'. Run by 'nature's middle-men – the low-souled and the sneaking', this censorship 'makes one's work as a writer and a thinker useless'. The result is paralysis: 'Hence one doesn't write any more and tries hard not to think.' Larry judged, by contrast, that Henry's *Sunday After the War* contained some 'absolutely peak writing – the greatest of the age'.[184]

THE GERMAN GARRISON DEFENDING Rhodes was cut off from all resupply, and it would only be a matter of months before they capitulated. Larry's own spirits surged at the thought of leaving Egypt, and he began a play, *Black Honey*.[185] Then in April he received a cheque for £10 as an award from the Brazilian PEN association. Larry had submitted 'Cities, Plains and People' in competition for a prize of £50, which had gone to Robert Conquest, but Larry's poem had been praised for its 'exceptionally high level of accomplishment'.[186]

'They are liberating everyone everywhere,' said Larry. 'Soon it will be my turn.' Given 'a little Aegean sunlight and freedom', he would write 'The Book of the Dead'. In fact, he claimed, 'It's all written in my head.'[187] He was busy preparing to leave for Rhodes, where the sunlight and the freedom would be his. His main worry was how to get Eve out of Egypt: he was still married to Nancy, and Eve had no passport. When Robert Liddell walked into his office, Larry said quickly, 'Robert, will you marry Eve for me?' Liddell spun on his heel and rushed away.[188] Eventually, Larry was able to arrange to have Eve sent along as his assistant, although this was still tenuous when he departed on his first visit to the island. His headquarters would be in ancient Rhodes town, once site of the great Colossus, citadel of the Knights Hospitallers, haven for Crusaders, pirates, and conquerors. Meanwhile, he wrote to Henry, "I am dying, Egypt, dying" as Shakespear remarked."[189] He needed a holiday: 'I'm worn down to the size of a peanut."[190]

Egypt had seared Larry to the very soul. He felt that his life had been wrenched off its tracks, and the war had simply formed a backdrop to the chaos he felt within. The easy security of life on Corfu with a small income had vanished, and with it his wife and daughter. The sexual licence of wartime Egypt had excited him, but it had also increased his unrest. He was sundered from his mother and siblings – ties that meant far more to him than he admitted. He had been forced to assume financial responsibility, and he would never again cease to worry about money. The Greek culture and places that he had loved had given way to an Egyptian culture that bewildered and at times disgusted him, in a climate and landscape that he found violently antipathetic. Although he had seen the publication of his first important book of poems, he felt that he had lost five years of his creative life, and his ties with his writer friends of the glorious Paris days had loosened. He felt desperately the need for escape and regeneration.

One of the steps towards his liberation and rebirth was to ask Stephanides, in a letter written on the eve of his departure, to proof-read the galleys of *Prospero's Cell* for him – Larry never had much patience for such tasks. Larry delegated Theodore to 'vet the Greek and add any recipes you might remember'.[191] To Eliot, Larry wrote asking for a few changes in the text, in passages which 'might prejudice my return to Greece'. Cautious diplomat that he had become, he wanted to cut the phrase, 'They are our Bulgarian element', which he had attributed to Count D in speaking of the Royalists. Then in the Epilogue Larry requested substituting Eleftheria and Maro for the real names of Elie Papadimitriou and Miguett Averoff respectively. The two 'crazy but rather wonderful women' had been 'the core of the E.A.M. ideologists and . . . are in fearfully bad odour'.[192] Especially now that his tomorrows looked so promising, Larry did not want anything to cloud them.

Looming in his future, he hoped, was his next 'opus', and for Eliot's benefit he outlined the three major fictions and themes that he had planned during his days in Corfu:

Agon Ἀγων	Pathos Πάθοσ	Anagnorisis Ἀναγνώρϊσισ
The Black Book	The Book of the Dead	The Book of Time
The Dislocation	The Uniting	The Acceptance & Death

Parts two and three would not be written quickly: 'They must grow on me like frogs' eggs – and meanwhile I must write for practice for fun for money and for my girlfriends – no?'[193] Although Larry could not then have named either the title or the fictional bones of The Book of Time, it would eventually take shape as *The Avignon Quintet*.

On 1 May a Greek force liberated Rhodes, and soon Larry was given permission to make a reconnoitring trip to inspect his new domain. Leaning against the rail of the small Heavy Duty Motor Launch on the evening of 30 May, with the anticipatory ache of a lover for the Greece to come, Larry watched Alexandria recede, reflecting that Eve was his 'only tie with Egypt' and that she should soon be joining him on Rhodes. 'As we rounded the old fort I turned back to catch a last glimpse of E standing and waving to me from the corner of the esplanade before the mist began to settle and the whole scimitar-like sweep of minarets and belfries of the upper town dissolved in soft pearl and gold.'[194]

CHAPTER 7

Rhodes, *Paradise Terrestre*

The mixtures of this garden
Conduct at night the pine and oleander,
Perhaps married to dust's thin edge
Or lime where the cork-tree rubs
The quiet house, bruising the wall.
'In the Garden: Villa Cleobolus'

ULYSSES RETURNING TO Ithaca could hardly have felt greater elation than Larry landing at the beginning of June 1945 on a Greek island after his exile in Egypt. Elation rings through the early pages of the memoir that he started to write within months, *Reflections on a Marine Venus*, in which he describes how, awakening to his first Rhodian morning, he ran across the front garden of the Albergo della Rosa, 'and still half drugged with sleep, burst into the Aegean water, clear and cold as wine'. He and a chance travelling companion swam, 'speechless with gratitude', while 'before us across the straits the Anatolian mountains glowed, each one a precious stone'.[1] In *Reflections* Larry makes out this early sharer of his discovery of Rhodes to be Gideon, the one-eyed British officer who is one of the more memorable characters in the book: apparently he was a pleasant invention, from his monocle right through to his accidental death.[2]

It had not been a smooth passage for Larry, and like Ulysses, he had returned with misgivings. The trip on the powerful military launch, beginning with a rapid slice across the glazed waters off Alexandria, soon turned into a bone-shaking, roaring plunge through an Aegean storm. Friends in Greece had warned him: 'You will find it completely changed,' wrote one, while another lamented, 'The old life is gone forever.' A third counselled, 'Go to America.'[3] None the less, a lone dolphin, which had kept pace with the surging ship as the *café au lait* water of the Nile effluent gave way 'with the suddenness of an axe falling' to Mediterranean blue, lifted Larry's spirits with the power of augury.[4]

Larry's launch was blown off course by the storm, and the hour of the projected morning landfall passed without a glimpse of Rhodes. After a day punctuated by squalls and heavy seas, he began to doubt whether he would arrive at all. It was well after dark when the ship finally eased between the narrow jaws of Mandraki harbour. Larry shouldered his knapsack and stumbled off in the direction of the Albergo della Rosa, facing Turkey across a beach at the northern extremity of the town. On the way he plucked and crushed a leaf of eucalyptus to smell the oil: memories of Greece, of Kurseong.[5]

Following a breakfast of coffee, bully beef and biscuits that tasted delicious in his exalted state and to his sharpened appetite, Larry walked from the hotel past the Mosque of Murad Reis at the end of the Turkish cemetery, past the arcaded government buildings lining the waterfront, along the edge of the war-littered harbour, past more chipped and battered neo-classical buildings and the dome of the central produce market, now empty, and finally into the walled town of the Knights Hospitallers of the Order of St John. Somewhere behind the battlements the printing presses that were to be Larry's chief charge were said to lie. After some enquiry he found the linotypes in a cellar of the Castello, the rebuilt Palace of the Grand Masters, where they had been moved to be safe from Allied bombing. A young British officer was supervising the printing. From the ridge of Monte Smith above the town, puffs of purplish smoke followed by dull detonations marked the disposal of German and Italian landmines.[6]

Rhodes town, both within and without the walls, was quiet with the calm of exhaustion. Most of the inhabitants had long since fled to Symi and Casos, and those still around were foraging for food in the dustbins. The island had endured starvation owing to the blockade by Allied warships. After the surrender of Italy on 3 September 1943, a short but deadly battle was fought between the Italian troops, who had tried to gain control on behalf of the Allies, and the smaller German garrison. The Germans, having air power, had won, and had massacred most of the Italians; a successful invasion on 1 May 1945 by an Anglo-Greek force had contributed to the general destruction. Mandraki, the ancient harbour, was pocked and chipped with gunfire, and half of its surface was covered with the debris of wrecked boats and skiffs. To one side a disabled German launch leaked oil. Larry saw Indian infantrymen carefully coiling up the rusted barbed wire that the Germans had strung up as part of the coast defences. German prisoners, 'still whey-coloured from starvation', were filling up bomb craters and assisting in the delicate task of clearing the minefields that they themselves had laid. In the mediaeval town the statuary was 'truncated', the mosques empty, the market gutted.[7] It was as if the town had died.

Apart from the war damage and the destitution of the inhabitants, Larry was depressed by his first sight of the late 1930s Fascist attempts at restoring the ancient glories of Rhodes. 'The imposing waterfront lacks a single taverna or fruit stall,' he lamented, while 'dull faced public buildings . . . face the sky in a mock-medieval manner'. The great Castello had been embellished with the addition of battlements forked like falcons' tails. In fact, he thought, the Italians had shown themselves to be 'super perverters of scenery'.[8]

Those appendages of civilization that Larry had counted upon the Italians to perfect were wrecked. There were no public services, the buses had been sabotaged by the Germans, and the post office – so vital a part of Larry's life – was closed. Still, he was able to report back to Cairo that the news-sheet printed by the Army Propaganda Executive was being distributed and that basic electricity might yet be available 'this week'. He made comparisons between the present condition of the town and what it must have been like after the great sieges of Demetrius in the fourth century BC or of the Turks much later. Larry's technique in *Prospero's Cell* was to see the present in the mirror of the past, and he would continue to use the same formula in all his subsequent island books. Like the island after the great ancient invasions, this was 'a Rhodes dispersed into a million fragments, waiting to be built up again'.[9] This was not the Greece that Larry remembered or had hoped to find, but he was so glad to be out of Alexandria that he put a good face upon it. 'I have escaped from Egypt,' he told Eliot.[10] It was to be Larry's responsibility to raise enthusiasm for this rebuilding process among the people of Rhodes and indeed of the whole chain of fourteen Sporades islands that make up the Dodecanese. Larry was ready again to become part of the historical process.

BY 22 JUNE, LARRY WAS BACK IN Alexandria to close his office and to bring Eve to Rhodes. Another round of bureaucratic tangles had to be untied. Larry worked all the 'feints and dodges' that he could think of, including 'giving everyone the impression that someone else had engaged her'.[11] She was designated his Administrative Secretary. Finally, as Larry wrote afterwards to Gwyn Williams, he achieved the essential 'laisser passer' and 'we found ourselves on a filthy little Norwegian tanker in Alex harbour, with the inevitable last minute policeman trying to stop us, as in a film'. Also as in a film, the hero and heroine escaped – and Larry and Eve sailed out from under the 'misty eggshell blue' sky hovering over the city.[12]

This trip to Rhodes was much slower than the one Larry had made shortly before, but what a difference! It was 'very good fun', Larry wrote, to be 'locked up for two days with an assortment of Norwegian cut-throat sailors', and their first landfall was not Rhodes but Carpathos. Ordinarily, he would have been groaning with impatience; now, Eve was beside him, and it was a wonderful adventure, 'like one of my Mykonos dreams':

We went ashore and were led by ten little children, very clean and polite, through the warm scented morning through the bright crazy Douanier Rousseau town: no, Douanier is too harsh: Paul Klee. Rows of pastel pink blue yellow and sugar-white houses in the bowl of the harbour. The children led us deftly through a German minefield to bathe on a dazzling scorched beach where the sea was livid and nitric. Then we all went up the hill together hardly speaking, and lay under a big spreading olive in an almond orchard and here the children sat in a circle round us like druids and sang. It was beyond words clean and pure and life-giving.

The mountain spring water fetched for them by the children had the purity of a sacrament and, Larry noted, 'at every door in the village wonderful old wrinkled people blessed us and asked us in for a drink'. Eve was moved to tears. For two days a 'terrific' north wind pinned them to Carpathos, and then at last they were able to make the short hop to Rhodes.[13]

Larry and Eve moved into the grand but battered Albergo della Rosa, uninhabited except for 'too many' officers with their 'coarse sports and false moustaches'. The hotel was flanked by a garden the size of a small city park. The original late-Victorian façade had been drastically remodelled in dull reddish stone veneer to suit the predilection of De Vecci, the last of the Fascist governors, for geometric curves and squared corners, but the large public rooms and the black-and-white tiled floors hinted at its former elegance, as did even the smashed fixtures and cracked marble trim. None of this mattered to Larry in his euphoric mood, and he reported to Gwyn, 'Food is scarce and poor but we are living in a Cecil B. de Mille hotel and masses of fruit to eat: I have a bunch of yellow grapes by me as I write.' And that was not all: 'Bathe in green sea at six. Run on grass. Sunshine like the wand of Apollo.'[14] To Eliot, Larry said, 'It's so wonderful to feel large pieces of the sun wandering about inside one's cranium.'[15]

Larry's disappointment on his first visit to the battered town soon gave way to appreciation of its beauties. He frequently had the luck to land in places with many-layered histories, and on Rhodes the past was more intrusively present than it had been in Corfu, in Alexandria, or even in

Cairo. It was hard to walk the sloping cobbled length of the Street of the Knights, passing under the low-relief carved shields set high in the walls and identifying each of the orders, without feeling translated into mediaeval Rhodes. Larry's presses had been moved to an annexe of the knights' hospital, near the foot of the Street of the Knights. Like the remnants of a gargantuan game of *boules*, everywhere lay the round stone shot, weighing several hundred pounds each, of the formidable ballista used against the city in the classical sieges. The museum contained Mycenaean vases and carved Phoenician scarabees from long before the reign of Cleobolus, *tyrannos* of Lindos during the sixth century BC and one of the many claimants to be among the 'Seven Sages of Greece'. In 408 BC the three Dorian cities on the island had cooperated to build a new town and port on the northern extreme. This town would become Rodos, Rhodes, with five partly artificial harbours, complete with dry docks, that were to make it, according to Larry, 'the best equipped port in the Aegean'.[16] Gossip assigned the layout of Rhodes to Hippodamus, the same architect who had planned both Piraeus and Alexandria. When Larry walked the two and a half miles of fortified wall that surrounded the mediaeval town, he knew that he was standing on the site of the exploits of the Knights of St John of Jerusalem under the Grand Masters Pierre d'Aubusson and Villiers de l'Isle Adam, defenders in the great sieges of 1480 and 1522 respectively.

The many mosques Larry saw had been built by the Turks after they had driven out Villiers de l'Isle Adam in 1522, and the island had remained under Turkish control until 1912. There was still a considerable Turkish population, and in the old town the carved wooden lattices of the *misrebiahs*, from which the concealed women of the harems peered, overhung the roads. Three windmills stood then as now along the harbour mole.

Larry's command radiated out from his Ministry of Information headquarters on the sea front, a squat building of cut stone with a façade of six fine ogival arches, each framed with espaliered bougainvillaea. Above the arches was a smaller upper storey with two windows and a door opening on to the terrace. There was a tower in one corner, and above the windows, carved in stone and standing out in low relief from the wall, was a royal crown surmounting a shield bearing the Cross of St George. The walls were still pock-marked by small-arms fire. A black and white sign, in English and Greek, proclaimed the MOI Display and Reading Room.

Larry found that his job comprised two main aspects: he had the press to oversee, and he was also expected to escort visiting journalists. He had twice the responsibilities of his position in Alexandria. Again, he was fortunate in finding highly competent staff to handle much of the drudgery. While there must have been a few raised eyebrows in the Embassy in Egypt when it was whispered that Larry had taken his mistress to Rhodes as his secretary, Eve with her many languages and cheerful energy was in fact an excellent choice. Also from Alexandria Larry acquired Spiros Katexis, a Rhodian native who had been an agent for the Allies in occupied Rhodes until his cover had been compromised and he had been spirited to Egypt aboard an SOE launch. A powerfully built young man with a practical mind and a perfect command of English, he was soon able to handle every detail of the Information Office. This freed Larry to travel about his realm, the islands of the Dodecanese. He persuaded the Navy to let him declare himself an 'official passenger' on any military ship. Thus he became familiar with Carpathos: 'pale chalky, beautiful as an anemone, clean pre-historic picked bone – one wants to undress and climb trees'; with Cos: 'very . . . Hippocrates! Green verdant and mildly lenitive'; and with Patmos: 'straight middle ages stuff with the strangest atmosphere of any place I've visited', and with most of the other islands in the chain.[17]

Larry had scarcely settled in Rhodes before he began to project another island volume. 'In my magnesium flash way I have dug into the library here,' he told Eliot just weeks after his arrival. 'It's full of treasures. Italy has kept everyone out of here and there is masses of stuff for a book on Rhodes in the Prospero's Cell style.'[18] Eliot approved but with a cautionary note. 'Rhodes may make a good book', he replied, 'but I should think that unless you live there for several years first, it will have to be rather different from Corfu.' Specifically, Eliot warned Larry against 'the tripper who lurks in every man's soul' that would tempt him towards 'Baedeker values'.[19]

Larry was not so much concerned about his values as about Eliot's conception of them, and he answered his mentor, in a mixture of brash egotism and irony, on a point raised while he was still in Egypt. 'You ask whether I think myself a poet?' he began.

My dear TSE, I was never one to hang my head. I'm without doubt among the first three in contemporary England. You and Auden are the other two. At least if metaphysical disturbance tightly stated is the criterion all the others are decorators of each other's bed-sitters. I wish this would become clear to a great number of people. Do you think it ever will? Myself I doubt greatly. But I have struck the rift all right.

In fact, Larry believed that Eliot had made up his mind about him: 'I think that you know that I AM a poet really; certainly I have too poor a grasp for character to be a novelist, and my construction is always faulty and lazy.'[20] Larry attacked the point in another letter written about the same time in which he told Eliot, 'If your attitude is right, I'm not really a writer but an adventurer in writing – which makes it tedious.' However, Larry defended himself, 'when I strike a vein I think I strike it', whereas George Barker and Dylan Thomas do not, 'though they are streets ahead as performers'.[21]

Eliot's answer was brief and direct: 'I didn't ask you whether you were a poet. I wanted to know whether you were a poet or a novelist, which is not the same question. I am satisfied that you could be either: I don't believe that in 20 years' time you will find that you are both. That is incompatible with the laziness necessary for poetry.' Eliot warned Larry with the examples of Meredith and Hardy, who had tried to be novelists *and* poets. 'Scribble scribble scribble as George II said to Gibbon,' he taunted Larry.[22] 'As for scribble scribble and Mr Gibbon,' replied Larry, 'you should see this office. A daily Greek, Italian and English sheet and a weekly Turk. Very bad for my recording influence.'[23] Larry was not only editor and production director but chief writer for his daily, *Texhni* ('Art') which was published in English, Greek and Turkish.[24] None the less, he took Eliot's admonitions in good humour: 'I love your supulchral [*sic*] letters.'[25]

The trouble was that Larry still wanted to be at least two writers. Economics told him that there was perhaps a living to be made composing novels, but it was more than that: there were things that he wished to say in fiction. But he was not yet ready to return to 'The Book of the Dead': 'because I know the bloody thing won't be salable to an English publisher'.[26] Years later Barker would say that Larry had made the wrong choice and had missed his poetic calling, but Barker spoke with the fixity of purpose of someone who had never deviated from poetry.[27]

Larry's immediate response to Eliot's warning about compromising his quality by diversifying was to propose another tangent, 'DURRELLS GUIDE TO MODERN POETRY' in 10,000 words. 'I'm prepared to sell it to you for the sum of £5 down and a sliding scale of 99%,' he teased Eliot. Out of this would eventually grow his British Council lectures in Argentina and his only monograph on poetry. In contrast to his diligent pursuit of 'divorce money' through his fiction, Larry was consistently casual about the sale of his poetry. The following year he would not even realize that he had never received a contract for *Cities, Plains and People* until Eliot brought the matter up after the volume had been published. 'Yes, any contract you say', Larry replied, delighted at the production of 'Cities Plains and Purple'. He did not comment at all on the standard 10 per cent royalty proposed.[28]

By mid-August 1945 Larry had given up on his half-hearted attempt to revise *The Dark Labyrinth* in the hope that Faber would take it after all, and had sold the book to Tambimuttu. Tambi had just published the *Personal Landscape* anthology edited by Robin Fedden – 'the only affectionate link with horrible Egypt', Larry called it.[29]

He was to be as happy on Rhodes as he had been miserable in Egypt. The island was a small, friendly world just as Corfu had been, but now Larry was a relatively important person, with a title, a staff, a printing establishment and daily newspapers to produce. Soon he knew – and was known by – virtually everyone from the British Military Authority governor, Major-General Gormley, down to the washerwomen. It was a joy to have Eve with him, Eve who had never seen a Greek island and who had been inclined to be sceptical about his raptures. Faced with the ravening beauty of Rhodes and the comfortable warmth of the early island summer, she had to agree with him. It was through Eve that Larry made his most important friendship on Rhodes, a friendship that would last the rest of his life. Eve developed a persistent pain, so Larry took her to the Thermi Hospital where she was examined by the Chief Medical Officer, A. Raymond Mills, a young graduate of the University of Edinburgh. Dr Mills had married a Greek nurse born, like Eve, in Alexandria; and he already knew Larry's poetry, and had met Nancy Durrell two years before at Nuseirat in Gaza.[30] Ray was a robust blond Yorkshireman with the kind of forehead that a nineteenth-century phrenologist would have said promised great intellect: it seemed to be rounded out by pressure from within. Georgina Mills was a small, lively woman who could no more restrain her energetic husband than Eve could Larry.

Although Ray Mills had much more self-confidence than Stephanides, he was in many ways a younger version of Larry's other great doctor friend. Like Theodore, Ray had untold diverse interests that he was not content to contemplate idly. His quarters were stuffed with packing cases, each holding the specimens destined, he maintained, to be the subject of some future monograph: on sea shells, on ancient Rhodian pottery, on geology. He could sing songs in demotic Greek and talk knowledgeably on poetry, indigenous sexual practices, biochemistry and Elizabethan music. Just as Theodore's studies in freshwater biology, folk medicine and the *Karaghiosis* puppet theatre had found their way into *Prospero's Cell*, excerpts from Ray's paper on peasant remedies were to appear as an appendix to *Reflections on a Marine Venus*, and Ray was to be the only main character to appear in the book under his own name, while his wife would appear as Chloe. Ray had enough boisterous vigour to match Larry's. He needed the energy: his practice, in effect, took in all of Rhodes and the entire Dodecanese, and while he had other doctors to assist him on his staff, he seemed able to be everywhere himself. Sliding his powerful form into a small, open Fiat Balilla two-seater, Ray sped over the island, 'swerving about like a drunken hornet' on the mountain roads.[31] He was not naturally reckless: he was simply out to race time, to make it stretch to cover all that he wanted to accomplish.

Larry was still very full of his discovery of Groddeck's *Book of the It*, and to him Ray Mills, with his exuberant good health and the intense gaze of his blue eyes, seemed to epitomize the German psychoanalyst's theory of healing, of the patient's inner responsibility for sickness: 'One felt slightly ashamed of being ill in the presence of Mills,' Larry wrote. 'It was as if, staring at you as you stood there, he were waiting for you to justify your illness, to deliver yourself in some way of the hidden causes of it.' Ray was not about to let Larry escape blame for ill health. He apparently told Larry, 'Smoking and drinking are your two diseases. Cut them out and you'll live forever.'[32]

Ray and Georgina became Larry and Eve's frequent companions in the exploration of Rhodes. The Army gave Larry the use of a captured German Volkswagen jeep, 'which looked a total wreck but remained valiant, indestructible and faithful right to the end'. Driving this 'whizzing old thing', Larry searched out every safe antiquity and beach, every lovely village or spectacular outlook on Rhodes.[33] The archaeological sites were deserted, and erosion had laid bare potsherds and bits of statuary. Larry sent Eliot a fragment covered with writing that he had found at Cameirus.[34] In the first winter Larry, Ray and their womenfolk strolled along the marine drive at Trianda Bay, gazing at the snow-covered Taurus Mountains in Turkey.[35] The main concern for those straying off well-used roads and beaches was the chance of blundering into an unmarked minefield. Winter storms sometimes revealed 'the ugly white steel faces' of Teller mines in the sand, which the bold fishermen dismantled to extract the explosives for dynamiting fish. Once Larry went for a picnic of white wine and bully beef near Mount Phileremo with a staff officer who claimed to know all the minefields on the island, when they suddenly realized that they were in the middle of an uncleared zone. They tiptoed out 'with the most ludicrous and comical precautions', cursing their guide.[36]

A particularly valuable ally in touring the antiquities was Thomas W. French, a Cambridge-educated archaeologist who, after years as an officer performing mundane desk jobs, was granted his dream assignment: he was delegated to report on the war damage to antiquities throughout the Dodecanese, and he made Rhodes his headquarters. French shared a massive open Lancia with the army veterinary officer, who seldom needed the car for his duties. Larry quickly discovered that French, an exacting photographer with a wit that delighted in absurdities, was an ideal accomplice for excursions, trips that they both could justify as Official Business. In January and April of 1946 they combed the Acropolis in Lindos; after his exertions on the April visit, Larry stripped to his underpants and plunged into the chill sea while an amused Eve contented herself with taking off one shoe to test the water. They dined on olives, bread, cheese and Cypriot wine above the sea at Kastelos and gathered spring wild flowers in the plain at Thari.[37] Once Larry returned alone to camp out for a weekend on the Acropolis: he felt diffused and distracted in spirit by wartime Egypt, and the nights of thought in solitude produced an epiphany, a 'reaffirmation': 'I had a kind of confirmation that my own direction, though selfish, was OK,' he would recall many years later.[38]

John S. Hoyland, the chief British consular officer, a man with a chronically weak heart, became another of Larry's friends. Like Sir Walter Smart, Hoyland was an accomplished linguist and an encyclopaedia of esoteric information, and would sit for his portrait as Hoyle in *Reflections on a Marine Venus*.[39]

Everything on Rhodes seemed to need restoration, but it was the raising of the famous third-century BC Marine Venus from her wartime crypt that marked the rebirth of the island for Larry and Eve, for Ray and Georgina. The protective crate was carefully prised open, and the lovely wave-smoothed statue was raised, turning on the end of a rope, into the sunlight. It was her second rebirth into the air: the first had occurred years before, when workmen dredging the beach off the Albergo della Rosa had brought her up, foam-born in truth, after many centuries in the sea. The Venus was sucked smooth as a jujube, with a rust-hued beauty mark on one breast where some marine organism had clung. The statue became the talisman of Larry's stay on Rhodes.

LARRY'S EGYPTIAN CIRCLE WAS BEING dispersed as the wartime occupations ended. Soon his friends were writing to him from the United Kingdom, letters that made Larry trebly glad to be where he was. On the eve of Attlee's Labour victory, Gwyn Williams in Yorkshire described England under 'the mountebank Churchill'.[40] Gwyn had travelled back to England on the same ship with David Abercrombie and Harold Edwards. Robin Fedden and Robert Liddell had also been repatriated. Hugh Gordon Porteus reported from Lincolnshire that prices were high, good food and drink scarce, yet the Americans were burning surplus war matériel including 'serviceable ambulances'. The *Personal Landscape* anthology, he thought, compared favourably in content though not in production with 'homefront anthologies'.[41]

The editorial hands of Eliot and Anne Ridler were having a determining effect on *Cities, Plains and People*: Anne suggested moving 'Eight Aspects of Melissa' to the beginning and printing the other new poems Larry had supplied at the end. Eliot decreed the removal of 'The Cabala' from the volume; not only did he have doubts about it, but 'there is one word in your text which does not appear in Faber books'.[42] Larry drew his bow to the full and let loose:

I apologise for the un-British and un-Faber word – poor little thing. Only four letters and yet they carry such a wicked punch; I am struggling along with circumlocutions now: 'have carnal knowledge of' 'to know biblically' 'he entered in unto her' 'he took her' 'he awakened her'. So much jollier and healthier if he just puts one hand under her frock and fucks her – or not: just as he feels.

For Larry the issue went far beyond a single word. 'There must be something wrong with me,' he continued without the slightest note of contrition. 'I've become a Levantine. I find even the Lady Chatterly and Joyce approach disgusting.' Larry threatened to take his best books across the Channel to Maurice Girodias: 'It's such a relief. When I want to let fly again I feel that somewhere I have a home, even on the Seine is better than being bottled in a Leyden Jar of anglo saxondom.'[43]

Larry did not regret the omission of 'The Cabala', for it was really 'a sort of compressed sunopsis [*sic*] of the book of the dead'. 'Mr Balthazar would be furious anyway,' he explained, naming a man he had met in Beirut. 'He is one of a secret cult of Gnostics – only four or five left – who have persisted in the M.E. since Roman times.' The Cabala hypnotized Larry: 'It's a crazy system, The Great Chart of Eternal Forms – leaves you in a mist.' He gave Eliot fair warning. 'If you see me ride into Russell Sq on a yak one fine morning smiling the Longitudinal Smile you'll know I've had it.'[44]

Before he could devote himself in good conscience to the Cabala or to poetry or the book on Rhodes that he really wanted to write, Larry felt that he had to complete the revisions of his 'labyrinth book' for Tambimuttu, who had advised Larry to think up a new ending. Larry had also changed the title. 'Now I am racing through the Cretan novel at top speed for another 50 pounds for the divorce people,' he told Henry Miller. 'CEFALU it's called!!!'[45] Despite his disclaimers, *Cefalû* – 'head' in Greek, but also the name of a promontory on Crete – was becoming an important exercise for Larry. Into the novel he poured his gleanings from Groddeck, Freud, Adler and Stekel. Groddeck, however, was not only the psychoanalytic godfather of the book but the model for Hogarth, the eminent analyst who treats two of the main characters and propels them to their decisive encounters in Crete. Physically, Larry painted Hogarth as a double of Groddeck: the massive, blockish body, the 'coarse blunt nose',[46] the very large and hairy ears that on Groddeck gave added point to Freud's dismissal of his rival as a *Kauz* – an owl, an eccentric. More important, Hogarth's theory of the 'Inself', the inner being, is clear kin to Groddeck's It. In psychoanalytic terms, the labyrinth that most of the main characters enter is the domain in which each must confront the terrors of the unconscious. Larry also attempted to marry Classical myth to modern psychology: when Baird goes back to the scene of his crime intending to exhume and then re-inter Böcklin, he is also Odysseus returning to Circe's island to lay the ghost of Elpenor through a proper burial. Finally, *Cefalû* is about a descent into the underworld of death by a group of people obsessed with summing up their lives: the dying peer Lord Graecen records in his diary, 'What am I? What have I been? I can think of little on either score to interest a recording angel.'[47] Larry at thirty-three felt a similar consciousness of life and talent unfulfilled. If he was correct in his disparagement of the novel, it is in part because he had too obviously loaded a slender story with a vast weight of allegory, symbol and metaphor.

As if Freudian and Groddeckian psychology were not enough for some 250 pages to bear, Larry poured into the book his terrific cynicism about the war. His earlier ambiguity towards the conflict, noted by Robin Fedden and Henry Miller, had resolved itself. Larry's bitterness came through in *Cefalû*: to the painter Campion, like Pursewarden in the *Quartet* a frequent spokesman for the author, Larry gave the observation that the war had reached the *reductio ad absurdum* of 'a million imbeciles blowing each other's arms and legs off with incredible gallantry, and decorating each other with whatever members they have left'. The pundits even wanted war poets, Campion says, 'to justify their messy little rodent-conception of life'.

'What on earth have you or I to do with a war?' asks Campion rhetorically.[48] Transcending his cynical comments, Larry's final word on the war, ironically, was a German one, *Gleichgültigkeit* – indifference – spoken by the doomed Böcklin: 'that feeling of dreadful moral insensibility and detachment which is the peculiar legacy of wars'.[49] For both the military and civilians it all came down to 'pot hunting, the *laissez faire*, the idiocy'. Larry had found a succession of secure berths abroad, attached to the Ministry of Information; Campion had made the 'supreme sacrifice' and had joined 'the Ministry of Political War'.[50]

Larry was not much happier about post-war politics. From his present berth Larry wrote to Eliot, 'This island is lovely. Fruit and blueness and grey olive-crowned promontories. Only I wish we'd leave. I am so sick of our policy and our faces in Greece. The country is ruined – like a burnt-out whore.' Here we were, he said – he could not disassociate himself from British policy and actions – 'amiably distributing ersatz bread and butter and being prosy'. It was the 'self-satisfaction and piety and stupidity' that enraged Larry, who could see Greece rushing headlong into civil war while his countrymen pretended blandly that all was well. 'Do you remember', he asked Eliot, 'the advertisement of Earl Baldwin with his pipe? "My thoughts expanding in the pure aroma of Presbyterian Blend"?'[51]

IN NOVEMBER 1945 *Prospero's Cell* appeared in England, and Larry thanked Eliot for the 'lovely production'.[52] The reviews were good in the *Spectator*, the *New Statesman* and even the *Sunday Times*. *Punch*, Larry reported, said, 'Mr Durrell, whose ancestors ruled in Corfu . . . .' In some amusement, Larry wrote to Theodore Stephanides that he, Theo, had missed only one set of inverted commas, thus converting a speech by Count D into a part of Larry's ostensible diary, thus elevating his ancestors.[53] It was too good a mistake to correct!

Sir Walter Smart, recently knighted, wrote praising *Prospero's Cell*, and Larry replied that the old Corfu life was not quite possible on Rhodes 'under a military dispensation no matter how humane'. Although he conceded that the British Military Authority was doing a good job, many of the senior functionaries were 'ghastly' colonials. The Greeks, however, were 'delightful and unspoiled – troublesome, of course: argumentative, of course'. The best civic feature was the absence of 'party politics'.[54] Six months later, Larry's opinions of the native Rhodians had improved if anything – 'fishermen and farmers . . . as fine as Cornishfolk, only poorer' – but 'The administration has certainly finished me as far as the British are concerned.' The governor he considered a 'lugubrious neurasthenic' and his staff 'simpering comic opera'. Their manner towards the Greeks was condescending in the extreme: 'No greater collection of defrocked priests, ex-jockeys, haberdashers, and ruined boxers was ever gathered together to lord it over an innocent and peaceful people.' The police force had been 'recruited from people who have spent years arranging sprigs of parsley over the testicles of Canterbury Lambs in our shops at home'. All these types crowded into the British Club to drink their whisky and abuse the natives for being 'backward and dirty'.[55]

Not surprisingly, Larry and Eve spent many evenings alone with a small chess set and a case of books. Larry had laid in a supply of Proust, Dostoevsky and assorted poets.[56] He also possessed a collection of Sherlock Holmes stories, which he would later shamelessly claim to Eliot was his only reading that winter.[57] On Sundays they would take a pack of food and wine and walk into the hills. A new friend, Romilly Summers, 'round as the setting sun, ruddy with good humour, wine and food . . . a great walker and chatterer', was the 'perfect companion' for these excursions during the late autumn. In December he was going to be posted to Egypt: 'We are going to miss him terribly – a new sensation for me.' To Smartie, Larry wrote that he actually longed for the conversation and companionship of Cairo, 'with its exiled poets and ruffians, and its visiting secret agents'.[58] Being on an island lent a special delight to visits from friends, and among those who brought the outside world to Larry were the diplomat Patrick Reilly, the painter John Craxton, the architect J. M. Richards, then with the Ministry of Information in Cairo, and another Cairo friend, the millionaire Jean Tricoglou.

Towards the end of the year Larry was still grumbling about 'hastily recasting' *Cefalû* for Tambimuttu, after which he planned to spend 'about three years' writing 'the successor to the Black Book – the pathos to the agon'. At the age of forty-five he would tackle the 'anagnorisis', so he said. 'And somewhere in between I want to do a big FUNNY book.' This was the first hint of what would emerge more than two decades later as *Tunc* and *Nunquam*. For the present, his poetic muse was silent: 'The landscape has knocked me silly.'[59]

Larry might be grim about the labour of rewriting *The Dark Labyrinth/ Cefalû*, yet he found time to amuse himself in typeset verse. Partly as a tribute to Eliot, partly to indulge his pleasure in controlling an impressive array of printing equipment, Larry produced one of the items that would become the delight and despair of collectors. Using for the cover a print made from an ornate block that had been engraved for the Italian governor of Rhodes, Larry printed his poem 'The Parthenon' with the dedication 'For T. S. Eliot', issuing it in a limited edition of twenty-five copies that he sent as Christmas greetings to a select few.

Larry and Eve spent Christmas as guests of Father Porphyrios, Orthodox abbot of the monastery of St John on Patmos. From the port they walked up the path, doubling back upon itself, to the whitewashed monastery with its wide arches and roof terraces. Many islands appeared to float in the winter sea eight hundred feet below. Eve's warm interest and fluent Greek thawed any reserve the priests might have felt. The legendary haven of John Boanerges lived up to the Apostle's reputation as a 'son of thunder': as they sat eating lunch with the Abbot, 'the sky slowly darkened, swelled, became bitumen grey and then black with clouds; the sea like a lake of pitch'. Gusts of rain alternated with shafts of sunlight poking through tears in the storm-clouds. 'Thunder struck out of the silence', Larry wrote; 'the Abbot had his voice cut off – as though his tongue had been pulled out by the roots'.[60] Wine, good food and talk, an open fire in the hearth, a few choice illuminated manuscripts reverently shown, Eve's gaiety – the year that had opened in such uncertainty was ending magnificently.

LARRY'S FRIENDS WROTE HIM EPISTLES full of unhappiness that contrasted sharply with his own euphoric state. Diana Gould was experiencing feelings about England that Larry could appreciate: 'The trouble of this country is that there's no sex in the climate even.'[61] Gwyn Williams returned to his teaching post in Alexandria and found the city 'empty and ugly and full of ghosts'; he asked that Eve 'append the incoherent notes that console me a little for the loss of her direct friendliness and her beauty'.[62] Later, Gwyn wrote describing the rioting at the University of Alexandria. Larry had once been interested in teaching there; Gwyn's letters were not encouraging. Robert Liddell had found London 'very melancholy' and had also returned to Alexandria: 'I am thankful to be back even here.'[63] George Seferis in Athens was 'Very busy but not happy . . . . Fog, deadlock, cul de sacs, monkeys and goats everywhere.'[64] Harold Edwards was back in Greece but was finding life horrible. Of all Larry's correspondents, only Henry Miller seemed reasonably content: he was in San Francisco for the birth of his daughter Valentine, his first child since Barbara had been born to his then wife, Beatrice Wickens, in 1919. If Miller had any cause to complain, it was that he was low in funds yet had £3000 that he could not get at waiting for him in Maurice Girodias's account in Paris; Girodias was eventually able to get a couple of thousand dollars to Henry so that he could buy land at Big Sur. Girodias may have once wanted to become a priest,[65] but he was clearly showing sound business sense in running the Olympia Press. When Larry received his own royalty statement of £38 3s 9d for 1261 copies of *Cities, Plains and People*, the difference between the amounts must have stung.[66] Larry may have been acutely conscious of his luck at having an idyllic haven on Rhodes, but he still wrote to Henry about the possibility of emigrating to America. Henry was doubtful: 'So you still look to America with loving eyes!' was his response.[67]

Larry wrote to Theodore Stephanides around December that he was still 'hacking out the last pages' of his 'divorce novel'.[68] It was beginning to look like a photo finish: he expected that the papers would be served on him within weeks. Just before the new year began, he signed contracts for *Cefalû* in Britain and the United States, but only Tambimuttu's Poetry London publication would appear. 'Finishing the fucking thing at top speed', he wrote to Henry.[69] Larry was still unhappy with the book after he had sent off the typescript. 'Shit', he cautioned Henry, 'two good pages you might care to read / rest you can hang in the lavatory. Its chief virtue is that it paid for my divorce!'[70]

Larry had felt hurt by Nancy: now he was angry, and he had written her into the novel as Alice Lidell. The identification is unmistakable: Alice is described as tall, blonde, with 'long shapely fingers' and 'fine northern colouring'. She is also a Slade art student, and – here more than a tinge of irony becomes apparent – 'Her diffidence and breeding were charming.' She prides herself on her advanced opinions on everything cultural, but she has a tendency to repeat the pronouncements of her friends. She marries the protagonist, John Baird, who like Larry during his early days with Nancy, spends a lot of time in the British Museum reading room. Then there is a pregnancy scare which comes to nothing, and Alice flirts with Corèze, a Jewish painter. During a sharp quarrel Baird tells Alice, 'We are not Bohemians, after all'[71] – almost the exact words Larry had thrown at Nancy back in the Villa Seurat days. Nancy could not have missed the parallels – assuming that she read *Cefalû*. After Alice turns out to be pregnant after all, probably with Corèze's child, she has an abortion, and Baird nurses her back to health in a studio by the Parc Montsouris in Paris. Baird leaves his wife, to end up at a villa in Fez with a 'kohl-washed pair of dark eyes'.[72] A worldly-wise French lady asks Baird, 'No doubt you are beginning to enjoy love-making too, without all your silly Anglo-Saxon sentiment?'[73] Later in the novel, an adept young Italian woman is 'not like one of those English girls whose reactions to sex were, medically speaking, ear, nose and throat only'.[74] Larry had etched in the dark shadows of his marriage, right down to his complaints about Anglo-Saxon women. It was a sardonic circular joke: a novel based partly on his divorce to pay for that divorce.

In early February 1946 Larry visited Athens, an Athens buried under snow, for the first time since his flight from Greece in 1941. The meetings brimmed with emotion: the endemic Greek warmth heightened by elapsed time and suffering. 'For the first day I was in a whirlwind of embraces and tears and kisses,' he said. Everywhere he was greeted by friends: George Seferis, Captain Antoniou, the newspaper seller, the porter at the Institute of the British Council. He walked along beside a flourishing George Katsimbalis, 'his great voice filling in the span of years',[75] telling Larry how he had sung the Greek national anthem, forbidden under pain of death by the occupying Germans, at Palamas's funeral. The Colossus had sung the entire first stanza alone, but eventually the huge crowd of mourners had joined him, to the rage of the German embassy man officiating at the funeral. Fearing for his life, Katsimbalis had gone into hiding. For Larry's friends, the remembered moments of heroism were outnumbered by the humiliations and privations suffered, and Athens seemed sad, crowded, poor. None the less, Larry tried to find a position that he could move into when the Dodecanese islands were ceded to Greece. He found nothing.

Larry told Katsimbalis about his plans for his 'big book', which he still had half a mind to site in Athens. The Colossus rolled a prominent eye in his direction and told him that if he did, he could never live in the city again: Athens was too small a world, and his acquaintances, thinking themselves caricatured, would turn on him with vitriolic rage.[76] Besides, as Larry said in self-justification well after the fact, Athens 'lacked Alexandria's juxtaposition of races and cultures. And Alexandria is the starting point of our civilization.'[77] Alexandria it would have to be!

Larry's initial impression was that the Greeks were more 'gentle and friendly and sympathetic' towards one another than formerly – this observation would be revealed in all its unintended irony during the civil conflict that was even then building up to violence. Larry was alarmed at the 'muddled' political picture: there was 'no confidence in the centre', he wrote to Theodore, the communist EAM was very active,[78] and there was cynical infighting among Metaxists, Communists and Venezelists – egged on by Britain – 'It makes me glad I didn't join up and lose a leg for his Majesty, Glucksberg,'[79] King George. Within weeks, Larry was writing to

Henry that 'The bigots of the right and left are eager as ever to get killing again – not aggregates this time – France, Germany etc but their *sisters and brothers*.' In his pessimism, Larry predicted that the whole Middle East, after years of 'overeating and masturbating' would 'break into flames'; England he 'could not live in', and France was 'down the drain'. Despite his rejection of England, Larry trotted out his heritage as a fine thing: 'By God, you don't know how lucky we are in the type of civilization that bred us – Anglo-Saxons.' He was about ready to call it quits with Europe: 'No, if I come to USA it will be to become a citizen,' he concluded,[80] responding to Henry's cautionary words about the country.

Morally, Larry thought, the war had taken a toll even on 'the Georges': to Theodore he confided, 'I must also mention how very disappointed I am in George K. and George S; they have both done the frightened rabbit so fashionable among the Venezeli and become royalists.' Back on Rhodes, Larry was more than ever determined to stay on as long as he could, despite a recent infestation of foreign journalists 'boring hell out of me' in their eagerness to unearth 'anything to be political about' in the independence celebrations. Such social life as there was on Rhodes consisted largely of 'colonial administrators who talk shop in the back of their throats with a woeful imitation of an upper class accent' and pronounce the Greeks 'bloodsome'. He did not know what he would live on when his job ended, adding, 'but the world isn't much worth living in today is it?'[81]

Soon he was back in Athens, 'but found it full of mondaine [*sic*] people also hunting jobs'. Many wanted a comfortable Greek sinecure, and were desperate to escape war-damaged and shortage-haunted England. 'Our market value as poor teachers and beggars has sunk,' he told Eliot. 'Heavily endowed literary figures are now on the scene like wasps around a jam-pot.' There was a positive outcome of his visit, however. A couple of trunks stored in Athens had been faithfully saved for him, and he arranged to have them shipped to Rhodes. Thus he recovered 'most of my Book of the Dead' and had soon written some 5000 words of a new draft. If only he had time to work! 'This job is beastly,' he complained. He took philosophically the fact that his 'Adam and Evil' drama manuscript was still missing.[82]

In early April, Larry and Eve went on a tour of the Dodecanese islands, taking with them a young photographer and a journalist, both on the staff of *Parade* magazine. *Parade* was published in Cairo for the British armed forces, but there was nothing that suggested the military in Mary Mollo, the beautiful young woman behind the Rolleiflex camera. Born into an aristocratic Russian Jewish family that had escaped during the Bolshevik Revolution by the simple expedient of buying a train, Mary was a resourceful individual who had spent most of the war years in Africa and the Middle East. She had contracted tuberculosis in Brazzaville, journeyed by river steamer and overland from the Congo to Cairo for treatment, and had worked for *Parade* since 1943. Then she had married Henry Hadkinson, a British army officer stationed in Cairo. Best of all from Larry's point of view, she had been handed a copy of *The Black Book* by a friend when she was in her teens, and had been a Durrell fan ever since. When her editor had told her that the Public Information Officer, Lawrence Durrell, would be arranging a tour so that she and Stanley Maxton could report on the *Enosis* – Union with Greece – celebrations in the Dodecanese, she had felt shy. She need not have worried. She met Larry in the lobby of the Albergo della Rosa and each stared searchingly at the other: 'I felt I was drowning in the blueness of the bluest of eyes,' recalled Mary, while Larry later described Mary's dark-eyed regard as being like 'someone raking the bottom of a bird's cage'.[83] Mary was at once accepted by both Larry and Eve.

The party of four set out in a primitive fisherman's caïque manned by three Greek sailors who found their passengers very entertaining indeed. The toilet consisted of a *tanaké*, an old tin that had once held biscuits, and when one of the ladies retired with it below deck Larry kept up a volley of Rabelaisian ribaldry in Greek and English. Eve seemed to Mary to preside 'over our destinies like some Oriental goddess'.[84] The combined odours of petrol and oily cooking persuaded Larry and his party to sleep on deck, side-by-side under an old tarpaulin with the stars and the salt spray in their faces. For Larry, for them all, these were magical hours: no printers, no offices, no telephone. Just the dark night after a simple meal and a tot of cognac; the occasional ripple of laughter as one or another of them recalled some shared jest or prank; the sweet motion and sigh of the calm Aegean, the Zodiac pricked out overhead. With the dawn – they never tired of quoting Homer's 'rosy-fingered' epithet – Larry would slip alone over the side for a long cold swim.

Larry kept up a running commentary on the islands. Symi was a 'black honeycomb' and 'a great cobweb of stone', the town on Kalymnos was the work of 'an infant's paint-box', Leros was settled in a 'miasmic gloom' that might seem to be due to the extensive bomb damage but that really extended far back into antiquity, to the water 'cold as a polar bear's kiss'.[85] On Cos, which Larry called the 'spoiled child' of the Dodecanese, he showed them the ruins of the Aesculapium and the great tree of Hippocrates, decorated with votive offerings commemorating cured arms, legs, heads.[86] Mary photographed Larry perched over a broken column that he claimed was phallic.[87] So taken was Larry with Cos that he wanted to spend the night meditating amid the ruins. Later he would claim that he actually had slept two nights under the famous tree, but that it had been winter and all he had achieved was 'a touch of rheumatism'.[88] It was Patmos, however, that provided the climax of the tour.

They landed at the small harbour, Scala, and walked up the main street of the tiny town. The word *Enosis* was painted on the walls, flags were flying, and the entire island seemed in a delirium of happiness over the reunion with the motherland. Midway on the climb to the Monastery of St John, Larry paused to look down on the chapel dedicated to St Anne that guards the approach to what Larry called the 'heavenly cave'[89], the cleft in the rock where St John the Divine is said to have pressed his hand or laid his head when he received the vision of the Apocalypse. Years later Larry would refer to the same grotto as a 'lugubrious hole' – time had dimmed this particular memory.[90] Mary photographed the mediaeval turrets and parapets of the monastery and the equally magnificent bearded monks in their stovepipe hats. After showing off the architecture of the monastery, Abbot Porphyrios, delighted to see *kyrios* Larry again, gave his guests a candlelight supper with excellent wine. Larry jotted down lines in a small black notebook:

> Quiet room, four candles, red wine in pottery:
> Our conversation burning like a fuse,
> In this cone of light like some emulsion.[91]

That night they all slept splendidly in the guest rooms of the monastery where Larry 'waxed lyrical' over the bona fide flush toilet.[92]

Mixed in with the sightseeing were many long conversations – about life, death, love and Georg Groddeck. Larry converted Mary into a disciple of Groddeck. He also talked a lot about 'The Book of the Dead'. When the caïque finally throttled down to a measured *plam plam plam plam* for the re-entry into Mandraki Harbour, the regret at the ending of a perfect journey faded under the pleasant anticipation of hot baths, a lingering supper under the eucalyptus trees, and clean sheets.

THE MUNDANE WORLD, when it had to be faced, came as a shock. Larry measured his divorce fees in terms of writing – 'It costs about three novels or two novels and six short stories today to pay for a divorce.' He was angered by a review in the *Manchester Guardian* by Charles Morgan condemning Henry Miller for using 'gutter-words', and Larry applied this to his own next major effort: 'Now the only big subject left in English is sex!' he announced to Eliot. 'I want to do a book involving the attitude of the near-Levant to sex – it's so passionate and natural and really wonderful.' In the Levant 'sex informs and warms everything'. Paradoxically, this releases sage, hermit and artist alike. 'One is saturated and exhausted and bored to death with sex', Larry continued, 'consequently it is only here that one is ever free of it, as it were, and able to devote oneself to art or God or whatnot, and make the whole world an Eros . . . of contemplation and real biblical love.' But how to write it in English, because 'in England you bring the ceiling down if you talk above a whisper'? He could easily compose in French or Greek: in fact, he was 'seriously thinking' of writing in Greek 'or some other tongue where one is at ease, comfy, unbuttoned etc.'[93] Eliot responded, 'I have a letter from you which deserves and provokes an answer at some length and I don't know when I shall be able to get around to attempting an adequate reply.'[94] Alas, Eliot apparently never found the time.

Larry was using Greek in a more sophisticated way than ever before. On Corfu he had become fluent in casual demotic that sufficed for conversations with his rural neighbours, but in Rhodes he was actually editing the Greek edition of *Texhni*, and he continued to translate various Greek poets. Many evenings Larry, Eve, and Ray and Georgina Mills would sing Greek folksongs and declaim poetry. Larry would recite his own and others' verse, including Cavafy in Greek and English.[95] Early in 1946 he arranged for the printing at the Rhodes government press of his *Six Poems from the Greek of Sekilianos and Seferis* and he exchanged translations with Robert Liddell, who was translating Cavafy and Solomos. Liddell was critical of Larry's renderings of Cavafy, telling him bluntly, 'I'm afraid I don't like your ITHACA or your City any better than mine . . . . I find your versions wrong in FEELING – all that muddy romanticism – and the "sailors" terms.' However, although Liddell refused to 'collaborate with Amy Smart in massacring Cavafy', he offered to co-operate with Larry and Bernard Spencer in translating him.[96] Liddell summed up their different approaches succinctly: 'The thing is that we both, rightly, disbelieve in the possibility of translation . . . you want to produce "Thoughts on Reading Cavafy", I "A Crib to Cavafy".'[97] There would be no collaboration.

Larry felt full of Greek, and began translating a book that the Colossus had signalled to him in 1939. Now surrounded by the sleeping Turks, he set about rendering Emmanuel Royidis's *Papissa Joanna* into English. He was 'bursting with material' for a major novel, and Larry confessed that 'I make Cohen's life a misery acting scenes from the book I can't find time to write.'[98] Tom French had been repatriated to England, so there were fewer exploratory trips, and consequently Larry should have had more time on his hands. 'Your successor is a dreadful man and we are missing you bitterly,' Eve wrote to French.[99] By June Larry was 'racing through' *Black Honey*, a 'farcical piece of theatre' about Baudelaire's octoroon lover that he hoped would be staged and earn him some money. He was also planning a play on Sappho. 'As you see I am spinning like a weathercock,' he told Anne Ridler.[100]

In fact, his job was threatening to consume him. From her position behind a typewriter in the Public Information Office, Eve poured forth her news to Tom French, after chiding him for his own reticence:

> Well, I am not as bad as you are. Besides, I like writing letters in despicable english, I get a perverse relish in it. Therefore you shall suffer and be one more victim. . . .
> [. . .]
> You will be surprised to know that Larry is working awfully hard these days. This is due to the state of fine relations between the british and the Greek officials of the place. The things that go on, the fuss, the misplaced self-importance the incompetance, the refusal to cooperation, the stupidity profusely exposed make it all the funniest thing to hear (You should get Larry on the subject) but the most arduous task to have to be mixed in. However, everything, eventually comes out more or less right and as yet there has been no bloodshed, only a shower of resignations, Dagge is confined to bed. a part from having sinusites he has been bitten by a scorpion. (How symbolic!).
> I must end this horrible letter which has taken all my morning, while Larry kept rushing in and out to different conferences with a hord of people at his heels.

Eve's vigorous if unconventional prose mirrors her generous spirit and charm. Her postscript shows a wry humour: 'I am tired of excusing myself for the state of my letters. But to prove you that I try to improve it I will confess to you that I did the first page twice.'[101]

AFTER JUST OVER A YEAR in the Albergo della Rosa, Larry through delicate negotiations with the Mufti, spiritual leader of the Moslem population of Rhodes, obtained permission to move into the tiny house he had spotted long before across a lane from the great hotel, and in the eucalyptus-teeming garden of the Mosque of Murad Reis. 'Needless to say it was not without all sorts of difficulties, endless worries, intense hard thinking on both our parts, tremendous waste of money and unendurable waste of time,' Eve confided to Tom French.[102] The cottage consisted of a studio, a bedroom, a kitchen and a bathroom, and while one side was level with the road the rest sank into a cave of green bounded on three sides by a triple depth of oleanders. Larry began sleeping there on 31 July 1946. Eve kept her room in the Albergo della Rosa, but came and went at will: this suited her, as she did not really enjoy the domestic routine of cooking and cleaning. Larry had a 'little servant' to prepare meals and tidy the house.

He christened his retreat the Villa Cleobolus, after the intellectual tyrant of Lindos. Muffled sounds came from the adjacent road leading to the Mandraki waterfront, along which Larry could walk to his office in five minutes. In fair weather – which was most of the time – he dined at a table built around an immense baobab tree, kin to the Bo-tree sacred to Buddha. 'My table in the garden rotted with heat and spilt wine', Larry would write, 'sometimes I made notes on it or drew something. . . . Then visiting friends wrote messages on the table when I was absent, and finally started to write poems.'[103] The curved dry leaves of eucalyptus drifted through the garden and crackled fragrantly underfoot.

In the elongated trapezoid of the park containing the mosque, the Villa Cleobolus occupied one corner, while at the angle nearest the Albergo stood a pair of Turkish *turbe*, tall eight-sided mausolea, each sheltering the remains of some forgotten dignitary or holy man. Although sparse around the Villa Cleobolus, the white marble tombs of the lesser admirals and civil servants thronged near the mosque, the inscribed upright markers of the men topped with marble turbans, those of the women with cylinders resembling pineapples. On hot days a population of thin, languid cats dozed on the raised marble sarcophagi. Next to the mosque stood the tomb of the Imam Murad Reis, facing an arbour-shaded courtyard paved with tiny white and black pebbles cemented in stylized floral and geometric patterns, the traditional *hoklakia* of the island. Through their friendship with the Mufti, this too became part of Larry and Eve's living space.

Larry was not at all bothered to be living in the shadow of a mosque. Although sometimes young children in the Turkish quarter would spit and run away to avoid contamination by the 'infidels', causing Larry to remember Egypt and 'the suffocating beastliness of Islam and all it stands for, bigotry, cruelty and ignorance', he felt that Rhodes had softened and tempered the 'jagged edges' of the religion.[104] In the mornings, if he was not already awake, Larry was aroused by the call to prayer of the muezzin. Nor was Eve uneasy, despite her Jewish upbringing, but assumed the role here of comfortable companion and muse, 'dark-eyed E, whose shadow is somehow spread over all these – a familiar, a critic, a lover – E putting on a flowered frock in the studio mirror with her black hair ruffled'.[105] Both were eager to marry, as soon as Larry's divorce could be concluded. Eve burst forth excitedly to Tom French, '*Personal news*: SENSATIONAL! STUPENDOUS! We have just heard through the B.B.C. that the length of time after which one can safely get married following a previous divorce . . . is six weeks . . . instead of the six month regulation previously insisted upon.' She hoped that within two months she would be Larry's legal spouse. French had sent some photographs that he had taken shortly before leaving, and Eve teased him, 'How shall I forgive you this one? What a behind for a would-be poet's wife?'[106]

Soon after Larry had moved into the Villa Cleobolus, Mary Mollo returned to finish her photo-reportage on the Dodecanese. She was never to see Larry happier than when seated at the painted table under the baobab tree: he was writing well, he was his own master, and he was in love. He would take cane chairs into the garden by the pink oleanders and spread out his papers next to him on one of the Turkish tombs. Sometimes he typed with the machine next to him on another chair.[107]

In the late summer of 1946 several old friends showed up for a week of rollicking days of exploration and nights of talk and song around the baobab tree. Xan Fielding, Paddy Leigh Fermor and 'the Corn Goddess', as Larry called Paddy's wife Joan Eyres Monsell, burst upon the scene. During that 'first miraculous summer' after the war, Paddy had read *Prospero's Cell* on Corfu, and the trio had resolved to visit Larry. For Larry it was an orgy of talk about books: 'We sat up in my churchyard till three every morning reading aloud,' until the Mufti rattled his shutters in protest. Paddy had a vast repertoire of songs in at least five languages and Larry pronounced him 'quite the most enchanting maniac I've ever met'.[108] With full daylight they would plunge into the turquoise sea, pack some food and wine, and set off. Larry took them one day to the ruins of Cameirus, where 'wine-sprung curiosity' sent them into the vast network of the ancient plumbing, 'crawling on hands and knees through the bat-infested warren of underground water-conduits', to emerge covered with cobwebs and droppings.[109] At one point they came upon a sacrificial stone, and nothing would suffice but a re-enactment of an ancient ritual, with Paddy as the subject for a circumcision, Xan brandishing a large knife in one hand while extending the victim's member with the forefinger and thumb of the other,

Larry the officiating priest, and Joan recording the scene on film.[110] The climactic point at Cameirus came when Xan, inexplicably naked, leapt a couple of yards from a wall to the top of a column, which rocked sickeningly for some moments while the others froze. The column steadied and Xan posed, 'like a flying stylite'.[111] Never had they all felt so immortal, so invincible.

As if to remind himself that he was *not* invincible, Larry turned to the British White Paper on the Nagasaki atomic bomb blast. He was especially intrigued by the sterility that resulted from exposure to radiation, and tied it to Groddeck's claim about 'all human creations symbolising unconscious desires': here was a chance to 'set a positive term' on the human race. 'It's a great relief!' he wrote to Henry Miller; 'I was afraid they were going to go on like this forever.'[112]

In October, Larry's pessimism boiled over in a tirade to Eliot. The Foreign Office, 'repos[ing] like some filthy old pasha under an opium leaf thinking of oil wells', was ushering in the next big war. 'Greece has already started smouldering into civil war,' he continued, and the front line would extend from Salonika to Haifa. 'Greece is strategically indefensible and morally a total loss,' since 'hideous cynicism and expediency have replaced ordinary manly opportunism'. Egypt would blow up soon, and so would Palestine. In tune with the left-wing feeling sweeping across Europe, the British had 'greedily undermined the French in Syria' to make way for the Russians. Larry took Eliot to task for misdirected effort: 'And you, me dear sir, England's greatest poet, are writing long-visaged pamphlets about a "Christian society"! It won't do! It won't do!' Faced with hypocritical Labour politicians 'being measured for dress suits' and 'this brood of Catholic homo-sexual peers', Larry said, far better the 'opportunism of a Clive or a Nicholson, based somewhere in self-respect'. By invoking respectively the empire-builder and the fabled victor of the Punjab during the Mutiny, Larry showed that he still saw the world through Anglo-Indian eyes, but at present without hope. 'Dear TSE, I am dark, glum, dismal and very depressed,' Larry concluded with a sardonic edge. 'Meanwhile there is always a Good Time to have!'[113]

He was working hard at *Reflections on a Marine Venus*, but had become swamped with material, both human and archaeological, and his manuscript grew out of control. He had written *Prospero's Cell* from his exile in Alexandria, depending on memories, his notebooks, Atkinson's *An Artist in Corfu* and a few other more or less randomly chosen source books, and his conversations with Stephanides. Now, using Torr's two volumes on

Rhodes and Newton's *Travels and Discoveries in the Levant* for a base, Larry was attempting to write *Reflections* on the spot, while running the Department of Information and directing the Government Press. Adding to the tempting material at hand, the press was then engaged in printing and distributing the nine-volume *Clara Rodos*, a vast compendium of lore about the island.

Theodore Stephanides's restrained but vivid war memoir, *Climax in Crete*, appeared with a preface by Larry, the first of many prefaces he would compose for friends – or strangers whose books caught his fancy. Larry's introduction was a small repayment for Theodore's help with *Prospero's Cell* and various other projects, but more than that he genuinely admired the book, which he called 'a marvellous mirror of [Theodore's] quaint temperament'.[114] Larry wrote to congratulate him, but Theodore's pleasure in the publication of his book was tarnished by various woes: he had had to sell his house in England, and Larry divined something else: 'HOPE YOU ARE NOT HAVING DOMESTIC TROUBLE ARE YOU? IT'S IN THE AIR EVERYWHERE – POST WAR SYMPTOM.'[115] Larry urged Theo to see Maurice Cardiff in London and ask for a job with the British Council. Soon Larry heard from George Wilkinson that his guess had been correct: Theodore and Mary Stephanides were divorcing, and while Larry called it 'Miserable bad luck!', in the next paragraph he confessed that 'I am hastily writing my third divorce book.' Once again he turned to Theodore for help, asking him to send Lady Hester Stanhope's letters or at least to copy out 'any relevant passages for quotation'.[116]

Larry was prey to conflicting moods during his writing of *Reflections on a Marine Venus*. He was indeed glad to be on Rhodes and happy with Eve, but he was filled with pessimism for, in ascending order of magnitude, Greece, Europe, the world. 'It looks like a clear war within six years to me!' he wrote to Theodore. The adversary would be 'Russian totalitarianism' but the war would be fought 'all on behalf of the Shell Company!' The situation rated his strongest condemnation: 'O Lord O Lord what a bore!'[117]

Despite the Information Office and the many distractions of Rhodes, Larry was half-way through *Reflections on a Marine Venus* by October, and he continued to turn out poems. In October he sent Eliot a collection of poems that he wanted published as *On Seeming to Presume*, declaring modestly, 'I think some of them are OK some so-so and some wonderful.'[118] Eliot counselled 'a bit of ripening' first, but preferred to wait until he saw Larry face-to-face to explain his reasons: 'To say that with the appropriate reverence to an author takes a page and a half.'[119] Then Robert Fryer, a man with theatre connections in New York, asked Larry to write a play for him, and he began *Sappho* in a rush, working 'a whole winter', he would claim, 'on a play which is never destined to be published or played'.[120] Larry thought *Sappho*, while still in progress, at once 'good drama and very profound writing': 'A sort of mind-at-the-end-of-sex play'. He also tried to cast his Sappho material in novel form, typing out fifty-three pages before he abandoned the fictional treatment. His 'big book', Larry would assure Henry, was sitting patiently inside him, 'smoking a pipe and looking back at me'.[121]

At the end of October 1946 Larry flew again to Athens to search for a position. There were more wonderful times, with Katsimbalis, with Seferis. Henry Hadkinson had been transferred to Athens, and Larry introduced him and his wife, Mary Mollo, to his Greek friends, to the Leigh Fermors, and to Patrick Reilly at the Embassy. Mary was at one party in the Plaka that included Steven Runciman the historian, who was then on the staff of the British Council in Athens. The conversation had reached a stage of rather drunken hilarity when Runciman suddenly launched into 'a high-pitched warble of "Oh! the Fairy Queen".'[122] Larry laughed until the tears ran down his cheeks. Another evening in a humble taverna, flanked by a row of bright biscuit tins, Larry dined with Rex Warner and the aged poet Angelos Sikelianos, 'a sort of phoenix huddled in the ashes of his overcoat', according to Larry. John Lehmann, tall, patrician, with aloof eyes and a high, rounded forehead, was brought over to meet the Greek poet, whose *Death-Feast of the Greeks* he had published in *Penguin New Writing*. Sikelianos was witty, gentle, warm. Larry assumed a demeanour of grave and respectful deference, like an archdeacon at tea with a duchess, and later wrote to Lehmann about the 'smoky historic poignance' of the occasion.[123] But Larry still did not land a job.

EARLY IN 1947 *The Happy Rock* arrived, but Larry was displeased by the volume *in toto*: 'A wretched affair – quite unworthy of its object', he complained to Henry.[124] 'So this is the best that Americans can do with their great men; pissy little anecdotes about what he ate and drank – all unrevealing, uninspiring.' Then Larry qualified his outrage: 'There is one great man in America who I am sure will understand you and you him. . . . He is called Auden, and beside him and Eliot the rest of us poets are pygmies!'[125] Larry sounded a chord that he would apply and reapply over the years: 'What a talent you have for attracting the immortality-hunters, the moral crooks, to you!' To set matters straight, he promised eventually to write 'a decent book about you'.[126] Meanwhile, he fired a few barbs at his ancient foes, 'the Sitwells and their little crowd of flunkeys' and Cyril Connolly. Gerry was turning into a poet and, Larry said with some pride to Henry, thought him 'a bad writer and me *terribly* bad'. This Larry could accept with equanimity: 'At least that's preferable to writing us all day asking for contributions to papers which barely exist and to print works in 45 copies upside down!'[127]

Events kept crowding in on Larry. The smuggling of Jews into Palestine was in full spate towards the end of 1946, aided by the Jewish community on Rhodes. When some of Ray Mills's Jewish patients told him that an illegal refugee ship had been wrecked on Sirina, an uninhabited islet a hundred miles west of Rhodes, Ray informed Major-General Gormley, who immediately arranged a rescue mission. Ray, Larry and Eve were among the small party that rushed aboard the Royal Greek Navy destroyer *Kriti*. They surged toward Sirina at exhilarating speed, arriving at dusk. Eight of the refugees had died when the ship had run aground and sunk, but some eight hundred had reached land and were spilled about under the moonlight in a natural amphitheatre. The sight had a weird, ghostly unreality. Larry and Eve spent the next morning ashore, monitoring radio transmissions and talking to the refugees. They had boarded the ship at Split after coming by train, with the connivance of the Russians, from as far off as Romania. A few months later Larry's routine was again upset when King Farouk arrived in his royal yacht to scandalize Military Security by touring Rhodes on a motorcycle – when he was not attempting to mount a captured Italian naval gun on his ship.[128]

In the aftermath of the war, many couples were falling apart and the individuals were forming new combinations: Anne and Gwyn Williams were separating, so that 'I shall be free to make a bloody fool of myself again,' as Gwyn phrased it.[129] Larry told Hugh Gordon Porteus that he was ready to marry 'my latest and greatest nymph – Gipsy Cohen'. Larry sent Porteus a photograph of Eve with the comment, 'If she looks pensive it's because she wonders what is in store for her: address me Public Nymphomation Officer.'[130] According to Eve, he was already behaving like a husband, nagging her, 'Have you written to Tom? NO!! Have you done this? NO! have you done that? NO! Well? and what are you waiting for? may I ask?'[131] All this Eve seemed to take calmly, just as she did the icy conditions in the Public Information Office, where, with the cold pinching her toes, she sometimes typed with her gloves on – and her typing, never very accurate, worsened accordingly.

Recklessly, Larry wrote in January 1947 to his most regular correspondent, 'Dear Henry, I am very happy; being married some time this month to Gipsy Cohen.' He lacked confidence in himself to make the match work: 'Feel rather hysterical,' he added, 'Guess I haven't got over the loss of *my* small daughter yet.' He was nostalgic for the Paris days, and had written to Fred, Anaïs and Hans Reichel.[132] Writing to Tom French, Eve sounded far less hesitant about the match: 'First and foremost, as far as news goes', she began, 'we have the GGREATT PLLEASURRE to announce to you the wedding of Miss Cohen to Mr Durrell by the tenth of February'.[133] Eve had a practical reason to be glad: she was without a passport, being stateless, and would probably have been repatriated to Egypt otherwise. After various delays, on 26 February 1947, the day before his thirty-fifth birthday, Larry and Eve were finally wed. In a private ceremony before two witnesses, the formidable Colonel Gigantes of the Greek Sacred Brigade, now military commander of the Dodecanese, pronounced them united.[134] Eve was six and a half years younger than Larry but they had shared much, not least some of the war years in Alexandria. The difference between their backgrounds fascinated Larry. And they felt themselves very much in love. It seemed a promising match. Those who knew Eve, among them Robert Liddell and Eddie Gathorne-Hardy, congratulated Larry. Liddell wrote with cool irony to him, 'Of course I think Eve very sweet, even though I still doubt if her marriage to myself would have been in every way a success.'[135]

To all appearances, Larry and Eve were very content with their new state. The only problem was that their Rhodian idyll was about to end, and Larry did not have a job lined up. He still hoped for a Foreign Office posting to Athens, or failing that, he was considering rejoining the British Council with the object of getting himself sent to France or Italy. He thought he might go to England 'to interview the right people and wangle something out of them'.[136]

On 15 March 1947 Larry and Eve were in Athens to procure her a British passport. There was an emotional meeting with a handful of Larry's friends. Henry Miller had sent a 78 rpm disc of himself reading from *Tropic of Cancer*. Larry played it for Katsimbalis, Ghika, Seferis and Rex Warner. The Colossus and Seferis wept, and Larry presented Seferis with the recording when he left.[137]

Larry again drew a blank in Athens, so he took steps to get transferred from Foreign Office contract work back to the British Council. When Rhodes was handed over to the Greek government, Larry and Eve found themselves heading for England via Alexandria with nothing resolved. Eve did not inform her parents that she was coming to Egypt, and in fact did not see them. Larry was never to meet his in-laws.[138]

Larry and Eve were not the only ones soon to be heading towards Britain. Nancy's job as copy editor at the Near East Arab Broadcasting Station in Jerusalem had ended, and Edward C. Hodgkin, who had succeeded Aidan Philip as Director of the radio station in 1945, said in his mild, self-effacing way, 'Why don't you marry me?'[139] She agreed, and they departed together.

Despite his cavils about the burdens of his official position, Rhodes had been a time when writing, friendships, and the sheer joy of being in love amid natural beauty had come together for Larry. Now Rhodes was about to drift back into memory: the fecund smell of hot oil and ink and the precise clash of the presses, the winds in the pines of Cameirus, the quiet table sheltered by the oleanders and the baobab tree behind the Villa Cleobolus, the quick footfalls of Eve with her 'dark vehement grace' coming towards him over the eucalyptus leaves. 'Other futures?' Larry questioned in the Epilogue to the book that he was writing about the island. 'Not, I think, after one has lived with the Marine Venus. The wound she gives one must carry to the world's end.'[140]

CHAPTER 8

Exile: Cordova and Belgrade

Ulysses watching, like many a hero since,
Thinks: 'Voyages and privations!

The loutish sea which swallows up our loves,
Lying windless under a sky of lilac,

Far from our home, the longed-for landfall . . .
By God! They choose their time, the Sirens.'

'The Sirens'

LONDON IN APRIL 1947 was not as Larry remembered it: physically, the city was far grimmer. Bomb craters loomed like gaps in teeth; people looked pale and sour; there was still some rationing, and even the whisky was scarce. The Fitzroy Tavern was no longer popular, and Tambimuttu's crowd had gone over to the Wheatsheaf[1] or to the Hog in the Pound in Oxford Street, where Larry introduced Gwyn Williams to Tambi.[2] Nevertheless, coming from the unsettled Dodecanese and with Egypt still a vivid memory, Larry found himself lavishing praise on the England he had scorned. He found it 'really very pleasant, the easiest country in Europe to live in despite our groans'.[3] 'The Socialist Govt. has saved us,' he told Henry Miller in a surprising admission.[4] Unemployment was eliminated, and the socialists 'have done a wonderful job on food distribution and price control'. Goods were limited, to be sure, but they were apportioned justly and civil liberties were being protected.[5]

By mid-April Larry and Eve had moved in with Louisa Durrell at 52 St Alban's Avenue, Bournemouth. Aunt Prudence Hughes had advised Louisa to purchase London property – it was going for next to nothing – right after the war, but Louisa had listened to Leslie instead. Prudence would become a millionairess, while Louisa . . . . It was almost like old times: Louisa baffled by chaos, and Larry unwilling or unable to take matters in hand. Margaret, with two young sons to support, had just bought number 51 across the road and proposed to turn it into a lodging house: Larry volunteered helpful suggestions about burglar alarms, revolving baths and 'lavatory walls lined with bookshelves and a concealed radiogram'.[6] Leslie had left his mother's house to move in with his future wife Doris Hall, a booming-voiced, attractive woman, much taller than he, who ran an off-licence half a mile away, and he was paying for his keep by delivering beer. Doris had a wonderful sense of humour – she needed it – and she amused Larry by mispronouncing the town 'BourneMOUTH'. Gerry, slender, handsome, and at nearly six feet tall the giant of the family, was preparing for his first animal collecting expedition, the trip to the Cameroons that he would describe in *The Overloaded Ark*. 'You'd better pour me another gin,' said Louisa with a sigh. 'How I've managed to live so long with you children is a miracle.'[7] Not far away at 7A Wimbourne Road, Alan Thomas had bought a substantial house, and he was making a name for himself in the book world from his shop at 100 Old Christchurch Road.

Larry rejoiced in Gerry's venture, but he had the desperate caged feeling that he himself was back where he had started twelve years before: several books written, no recognition, older, with a different woman, but otherwise no further ahead. Nancy had been much loved by the family, but if Larry was worried about their reception of Eve, he did not show it. Probably he counted on their good nature and tolerance: after all, Margaret had recently separated from her first husband, and Larry teased her that the man was 'recuperating in a monastery'.[8] Eve was accepted without question,[9] and Larry enjoyed seeing the family after so many years. He set out to sell his siblings the virtues of Dr Groddeck, but Bournemouth still seemed 'a living graveyard'.[10]

As if to endorse the great proponent of psychosomatic pathology, within days Larry was writing to Henry, 'Here I am flat on my back with English 'flu.' Another annoyance surfaced when Henry wrote that the son of Spiro Americanos had told him Louisa Durrell had left debts for Spiro to pay on Corfu. Larry had investigated this on a return to Corfu before the war, and although 'some of the claims looked rather queer', he had told his mother to pay £110, and Spiro had signed a release. In any case, Larry was sure that Spiro, who had done all her purchasing, had skimmed a tidy percentage of the £120 per month that Louisa spent. Larry and Nancy had managed on £10 a month, buying everything themselves. Larry later encountered another example of Corfiot trickiness when the boatman entrusted at the outbreak of the war with the *Van Norden* tried to dun him to the tune of £100 for storing the sloop for six years, until Larry learned from the Navy that it had been confiscated by the Italians early in 1943 –

and soon sunk by the Italian harbour master. The Greeks really were short of food and clothing, Larry said, so he did not entirely blame them for trying an occasional dodge to 'raise a bit of dough'.[11]

A more serious cause of distress was that Larry had no idea where or when his next posting would be. He was well aware of the ponderous ways of the Foreign Office, and knew that he would simply have to out-wait the bureaucracy. He tried to push ahead with 'The Book of the Dead', which by the end of June would amount to some two hundred pages of text and a fistful of notes.

Larry made a quick trip to London to rattle the doorknobs of the Foreign Office in the hope of precipitating a decision. He missed Dylan Thomas, who had left for Italy, but had a good meeting with T. S. Eliot, whom he pronounced 'gentle, sweet, now older, more grey and worn-looking'. Once again, Larry had to revise his estimation of Eliot: 'He gives off a radiance now I didn't notice before – always felt he was like a senior civil servant.'[12] Larry tried to pin down Tambimuttu, 'who drifts from one idea to another', into mounting an exhibition of Henry Miller's paintings that Tambi had been sitting on for three years. 'Think I'll make it,' Larry concluded cautiously. Nothing happened. It was more upsetting to visit David Gascoyne. 'Still just the beautiful soft child he was', Gascoyne had been in and out of various asylums. Larry diagnosed 'an advanced persecution mania', since his friend heard 'voices denouncing him just behind his back' and named various people whom he claimed were after him. Larry thought that he could cure him given two months of contact, but there was so little time: 'Life has been a multicoloured rush of people and places.'[13] Among the demands made on Larry was a plea from Ruth Speirs to contact a 'dazed and exhausted' Bernard Spencer, whose wife Norah had died suddenly.[14] Larry wrote consolingly to Spencer, but every poet he knew seemed to be in trouble.

Finally a resolution of Larry's employment problem came, not from the Foreign Office but the British Council: he was to be offered a lecturing post. However, it would be in the wrong hemisphere – the Americas – and probably the wrong side of the Equator. The country was not named. Larry felt a bit like a Roman proconsul banished to outer Gaul, yet he reflected that he might be able to fit in a quick visit to Big Sur, or Henry could pop down for a rendezvous in Rio – to Larry, nowhere in the Americas could be too far from California. Larry gave a blanket acceptance to the Council. He hoped to finish 'The Book of the Dead' in South America. Meanwhile he turned to writing a critical essay on Henry Miller, focusing on the two

Tropics as the main theme, and asked Henry to send him a 'flimsy', a carbon copy, of his typescript of the unpublished *Rosy Crucifixion* so that he could take it into account.[15]

The next thing he knew, Larry had got into trouble with Sir Osbert Sitwell by writing an essay for *The Windmill* in which he referred to 'masses of Sitwelliana' and said that 'England is flooded with gentry-art – that is to say art without balls.'[16] Two years earlier, in 'The Happy Rock', Larry had referred to the 'amusing Sitwelliana of the twenties' among examples of work that would date with the epoch.[17] Then Larry compounded the insults – in Sir Osbert's eyes – by writing at Henry's request to ask his help in mounting an exhibition of Henry's paintings. Sitwell replied with 'a silly letter – like a big fatuous baby', said Larry.[18] 'I am amazed at your audacity and insolence in presuming, after offering me publicly the most gross of insults . . . that you should now write to me and ask my help on behalf of someone I admire, thereby making it impossible for me to refuse to answer you,' wrote Sir Osbert in his uneven, emphatic calligraphy. 'Though being a gentleman has greatly got in my way professionally', he continued, 'I begin to be glad of it when I consider your conduct.' Furthermore, he said, Larry's 'talents' were not such as to provide an excuse for his behaviour: 'I suggest you should read my books, and then your own!' After giving Larry a few more points of similar nature to ponder, Sitwell promised to do his best to serve Henry.[19] 'I answered it like a smaller but not less fatuous baby,' Larry told the *prima causa* of the uproar.[20] He had written to Sir Osbert saying that he assumed his anger was due to 'a recent article of mine – in which the word "Sitwelliana" occurs once', and then Larry had explained just why, although he admired some of his books 'very much', he thought a 'mild prod' was in order.[21] Sitwell never saw this letter: his secretary replied that owing to the 'insolent tone', 'I find myself unable to hand it to him'.[22] Larry sent Henry copies of the correspondence, with admonitions of strict confidentiality. 'Sorry I had to cross him', Larry said, 'but when you attack a man on literary grounds and he tries to intimidate you personally it's time to reach for the hatchet.'[23]

Larry was angry with himself over the futile quarrel, and he felt constricted by his mother's establishment. Recalling the period, Larry said, 'Life was solitary, poor, nasty, British, and short.'[24] It was a relief to get away from the literary infighting, the bruising memories, and the present tense of Bournemouth for a jaunt to Scotland to spend a week with Fred Perlès. Near the end of June, Larry and Eve took the train to Inverness, where they found Joey 'with his wrists up like a praying dormouse, bubbling and glugging like a child'. They set off in a small, rickety car for the sixty-mile drive to Ullapool, where they were to stay with Fred's friends, the writer John Pick and his wife Mary. The car broke down in Garve, but they finally made it to Rhue beyond Ullapool, where Larry basked in Scots hospitality and caught fish in Loch Broom outside the Picks' door. The beauty of the setting reminded him of Kouloura. John Pick was a tall, thin man with bristling eyebrows shading humorous eyes, and he told good stories. A conscientious objector, he had worked in a coal mine during the war until his health broke, and he had written a novel about his subsequent experiences as a hospital orderly. Larry was amazed at the change in Fred: 'He has become self-supporting, absolutely reliable, responsible, calm, unpanicky.'[25] In short, 'little Joe', with his marvellous chameleon ability, had left his raffish Viennese/Parisian self behind to become ineluctably British! Of course they spoke at length about Henry, and Fred convinced Larry that they should send a cable to Big Sur advising Henry to let them buy him a villa or a château in the south of France, using the untransferable Old Francs that Henry had amassed through the sales of *Tropic of Cancer* to Allied troops. Henry replied casually that he might ask Man Ray to buy him a few Picassos and Braques; later he suggested that Larry and Fred use the money to fly over for a visit.

Although Henry now had around four million francs in his account with Girodias[26], the exchange was preventing him from receiving funds. With his growing responsibilities – he had to provide not only for the needs of Lepska and Valentine, but was also trying to raise money to pay Moricand's fare to California from Switzerland – Henry said that he was more desperate even than during his hungriest days in Paris. Larry made enquiries about a legal channel for sending him a few pounds.[27] He had often chided Henry for squandering his funds on hangers-on, and warned him about the folly of entrusting his work to small presses and 'enthusiasts': 'They don't produce any *money* for one – and after one has had the fun of writing something, the next best thing is spend[ing] the money it brings on your girl.'[28] Meanwhile, Larry had a few pounds saved, but no fixed income, and Fred Perlès was trying none too successfully to live from his writing: the Villa Seurat trio languished under a pecuniary curse.

At last Larry knew that he would have a job. His sentence had come through: Argentina. 'Rather looking forward to it,' he said bravely. On the promise of future solvency, he and Eve crossed the Channel in July for three weeks of high living in Paris on £50 borrowed from Maurice Girodias.

Larry found young Girodias 'very nice', but worried that 'he is sadly like his father, tight, wolfish, and queer'. Girodias promised to put them all back into print as soon as printing costs fell, but Larry did not trust him: 'I'm afraid the future is black', he told Henry.²⁹ Still, Larry and Eve enjoyed Paris, even though dinners cost them £3 and they had resigned themselves to a cheap hotel on the rue Notre Dame des Champs at £35 per week.

In the midst of packing for Argentina, Larry posted the typescript of *Sappho* to Eliot, 'only because I can't bear to have it lying around on my desk any longer'. He had no 'clue' by which to judge the play: 'If you write and say this is abominable, gross, vulgar and stupid I shall believe you,' he told Eliot. He had aimed to create credible characters, and the verse was deliberately rough. 'I have tried to avoid the iambic line because something terrible happens to actors when they see an iambic. Their eyes roll. The[y] begin to freewheel down the slopes of the rich pedal-vowels, and consequently forget to act.' Larry concluded, 'Dear TSE, how I make you suffer.' Larry had neglected to type anything other than 'Bournemouth' on the letterhead, so Eliot merely annotated the letter, '*Not* ack. owing to lack of address.'³⁰

Continuing his campaign for Georg Groddeck, around the beginning of October Larry sent off a long article on him for Connolly's 'Studies in Genius' series in *Horizon*. In his essay Larry revealed not only why he found Groddeck's theories so attractive, but in the process defined his own view on the nature of the artist: '[Groddeck] is the only psycho-analyst for whom the artist is not an interesting cripple but someone who has, by the surrender of his ego to the flux of the It, become the agent and translator of the extra-causal forces which rule us.' These extra-causal internal forces control all humankind, since 'we are lived by a symbolic process, for which our lives provide merely a polished surface on which it may reflect itself'.³¹ Human free will recedes in importance as the It, a compound of all the subconscious influences acting upon the individual, controls our lives and our death. Larry's occasionally outrageous behaviour must have seemed to him the irresistible products of his It.

His interest in psychology also led Larry to write on Greek peasant superstitions for the BBC magazine *The Listener*. He met the burly South African poet Roy Campbell, then a producer for the BBC's Third Programme, and the two men, sharing a fondness for Dylan Thomas, tall stories, John Gawsworth, drink, Tambimuttu, and selected conservative prejudices, quickly became friends. During September Larry gave a talk on the BBC about his dream-experiences in Greece, which was published in

The Listener as 'Can Dreams Live On When Dreamers Die?' He was pleased when Rom Landau, then writing his monograph *Human Relations*, asked for permission to quote. The dream article also provoked an excited letter in December from Carl Jung, who claimed to have had experiences similar to those Larry described. Later Jung wrote to Larry his impressions of Groddeck, 'a man of abject ugliness and a peculiar, not altogether sympathetic originality of mind . . . . Groddeck's book had no influence to speak of'.[32] Larry's belief in Groddeck remained unshaken. All this activity was stimulating, but financially it did not even amount to treading water.

Larry and Eve moved to London in the autumn to prepare for the trip to Argentina. Ines and Bernard Burrows gave Larry the use of their elegant home at 10 Orme Square near Lancaster Gate, and one day Eve cooked lunch for T. S. Eliot and Gwyn Williams.[33] Eliot had recently met the Chilean poet Gabriela Mistral, totally unknown to Larry and Gwyn. Larry said, 'Mistral. Wasn't he a man and a Provençal poet?' Eliot responded in his level manner, 'Well, she was dressed like a woman.'[34] Always friendly towards Larry, even while taking him to task, Eliot dropped his formality of address and henceforth began his letters 'Dear Larry'.[35]

On 7 October an officious clerk in the Argentine Consul-General's office in London inscribed the model number of Larry's Remington portable in his passport, but he was not yet ready to travel. What with one delay and another, he and Eve did not embark on the *Brasil Star* at Liverpool until the last day of the month.

LARRY AND EVE CROSSED THE LINE and made their New World landfall at Rio de Janeiro, 'dead white, rising like a dream'. Larry thought Rio 'astounding: the most fantastic place I have ever seen' with its huge skyscrapers rising out of the tropical jungle amid the dramatic stage set of the 'noble harbour'. Not since he had stood on Eagle's Crag in Kurseong, said Larry, had he seen a spectacle to match that from the famous look-out mountain. The city was a 'geometrical Chirico' of immense boulevards, granite precipices and marble skyscrapers. 'Like going through a series of mad looking-glasses', Larry wrote, marble-lined tunnels led from one centre of immense buildings on wide bays to another equally fantastic cityscape. 'Rio is the dream of an ant bound hand and foot and delivered over to one of its own nightmares.'[36] Larry and Eve sat under the awnings of a café and sipped green coconuts, 'patrimony of the ape', through straws: coconuts 'Broken, you think, from some great tree of breasts,/ Or the green skulls of savages trepanned', he wrote in his poetry notebook.[37]

Inspired by the city, Larry in a few days finished a pair of poems that he hoped were good, 'Green Coconuts: Rio' and 'Christ in Brazil'. 'The journey was worth it if only to see this hallucinating spectacle,' he told Anne Ridler. Ominously for his future happiness, Larry added, 'After this B.A. will doubtless be very small beer.'[38]

Larry and Eve docked in the low-lying coffee port of Santos, a day's travel along the coast from Rio, before they sailed on to Montevideo, which Larry noted as the birthplace of 'poor Laforgue' – he was reading Laforgue's *Hamlet* and Mallarmé's *Igitur* – and pronounced the capital of Uruguay 'a fly-blown Neapolitan town as flat as a pancake on a dirty estuary'. And he had heard that Buenos Aires was worse.[39]

In less than a day's sailing they reached Argentina, then in the green summer season. The dock area of Buenos Aires, lined with grain elevators, projected a tough, utilitarian ambience. Wartime prosperity fairly glittered on the large cars and the well-dressed businessmen of Spanish, Italian, German and English descent. Jon Uldall met Larry and Eve and shepherded them through the Customs formalities. Larry seems not to have been impressed by the impressive heart of the city, the mile-long Avenida de Mayo, running from the Plaza del Congreso to the great Plaza Mayo, setting for the French Renaissance designs of the Government Palace, the Cathedral, the Capitol, the opera house. Their arrival was heralded with a photograph in a major Buenos Aires paper, coincidentally printed over a screamer in large capitals: 'BEAUTY AND THE BEAST'.

Larry was struck by the endless flat pampas outside the city, 'studded with oversexed cattle and gauchos'.[40] Larry was still impressed, but . . . . He tried to set down both his interest and his reservations:

This is a perfectly fantastic country: but then so is the whole continent. The interesting thing is the queer lightness of the spiritual atmosphere: one feels buoyant, irresponsible, like a hydrogen balloon. One realises too that the personal sort of European man is out of place here: one cannot suffer from angst here, only cafard.

Larry was sure that place determined character, and he thought that the Americas militated against the formation of a discrete personality and in favour of mass man. He simply could not bring himself to believe in Yankee individualism; not, at least, at mid-century:

So much is explained here about the American struggle, the struggle not to get de-personalised. Because this is a communal continent; the individual soul has no dimensions. In architecture, in art, religion, it is all community – skyscrapers, jitterbugging, hyperboles – it is all of a piece.

343

He was discovering, Larry said, why Henry and other typically American artists wrote as he claimed they did, formlessly:

I understand now why the American artist has no sense of form – because his soul is continually being siphoned off into the communal soda water fountain, and his struggle is to concretise it enough to suffer. . . . The fury, the destructive fury which you inveigh against so much comes from the European soul trying to gain a slippery footing in this oxygenated air and getting panicky because nothing – nothing has any value here: break it, break it. All this is quite understandable the moment you hit Rio.[41]

Henry completely ignored everything that Larry had to say about formlessness – his or any other American's – and Larry was never to alter substantially his first impression of the hemisphere. The Americas lacked form; therefore it was understandable that Henry's writing should lack form. However, so Larry thought, Henry should be enough of a European to overcome this intrinsic American shortcoming. The hemisphere was particularly dangerous to the artist: 'But what sort of white ant's dream is the art of this continent?' he asked rhetorically. 'The Maya, the Inca, you can see the sort of thing which is possible; the rest is European panic, European guilt. But there is something quite new and strange about the atmosphere here. It is a spiritual vacuum flask: I am not sure Tao is not like that. Maybe the Indians can tell us? Have they said anything yet? Have they spoken? Human faces, clouds, the Andes, the pampas – it is all somehow unqualifiable in European terms.'[42] Despite his distant roots in Old India, Larry knew himself to be a European artist: here he felt threatened.

Although he had been delighted with Rio, Larry remained apprehensive about the Americas, and when around the beginning of December he visited the relative backwater of Cordova, where he was to be based, he was thrown into a panic. The 'whale of a time'[43] that he and Eve had spent in Paris formed a glittering contrast with the dry, dusty, 'hideous', 'dull' Argentine town. Cordova was four hundred miles across the pampas from Buenos Aires, and on the lower slopes of a minor range of mountains. Everything – Europe, the Mediterranean, even Buenos Aires – seemed impossibly far away. People were very friendly and the educated Cordovans spoke English, but Larry still felt like a Laplander trying to communicate with the natives of Tobago: they shared so few frames of reference. The *norte* wind, worse than the *khamseen* of Cairo, tore at the shutters and coated everything with terra cotta dust.

Meanwhile, an oblivious Henry Miller wrote that 'Cordova-in-the-hills sounds wonderful.'[44] Larry, however, was finding it impossible to work on 'The Book of the Dead', as he had promised himself he would in Argentina, and Henry unwittingly galled him by announcing in pleased tones that he had nearly reached page 1000 of *The Rosy Crucifixion*. Before leaving Buenos Aires for the hinterlands, Larry had typed out a final draft of a collection of poems to be published as *On Seeming to Presume*.[45] 'The Anecdotes' – originally referred to as simply 'Conon' – he had composed in a Buenos Aires hotel while running a 103° temperature and 'cribbing pretty freely from Mallarmé'.[46] Larry as usual approved of his poems and was pleased when Eliot, while suggesting the elimination of eight of the 'Conon' sub-sections, accepted the collection for publication.

From his perch 'in the dull sierras of this dull flat featureless Golgotha of good living', Larry's aria of complaints sounded across the oceans to his friends. Surface mail 'takes ages', so he pleaded with his correspondents to spend seven pence on air postage. 'O dear how far away everything seems', he wrote, adding with an attempt at philosophical acceptance, 'but perhaps one needs that.' Larry hoped to make good use of the isolation to finish *Reflections on a Marine Venus* and to write a play about Rome, 'if the Lesbian interests anyone' – he was hoping for a London staging of *Sappho*.[47] Larry would later name Evelyn Laye, his father's favourite actress, as his ideal for the title role.[48] There was even talk of a production in English at a major Buenos Aires theatre.[49] Desperately, Larry reached back towards England. 'It may give you a grim pleasure to know that I am booked to lecture on your Quartets', he told Eliot, 'from coast to coast of this fearful bawling brash provincial sub-continent where everything but mostly the art smells of the stockyard and of pressed beef.'[50]

Although Larry may not have viewed it that way, the course he planned to teach on modern British poetry, and the anthology of Henry's work that he was preparing, were both cries of nostalgia for the English-language world he had left. The crisis occasioned by the February takeover of Czechoslovakia by the Communists convinced Larry that, in any case, there would be a short war, probably an atomic one, that would devastate all the major cities of Europe before he and Eve returned. Despite Larry's fear of war, his hatred of Argentina was such that he saw a malicious irony in his posting: 'It is characteristic too', he lamented to Henry, 'that two protesting Latin American specialists have been posted to Athens while I, no less protesting, find myself here'.[51] It was especially maddening, since he was trying to firm up his mass of writings about Rhodes into *Reflections on a Marine Venus*. The flesh of personal experience in his Rhodes material tended to be overpowered by the narrative skeleton of the great sieges. Also, he was indulging himself in a lengthy excursus on vampires that somehow refused to lie down peacefully with the history and the bucolic scenes at the Villa Cleobolus. Larry advised Theodore Stephanides, then working on the book that would eventually emerge as *Island Trails*, to round out his characters fully, then 'kill one off with a sob at the end for good measure'.[52] Spiro Americanos and Max Nimiec, who appear under their real names in *Prospero's Cell*, had both obliged by expiring well before he had finished the book, so he had victims ready for sacrifice. In *Reflections* he decided to knock off Gideon crossing a minefield – no emotional loss, since Gideon was pure invention.

Meanwhile, Larry could not resist aiming a jab at Henry: Fred Perlès had suffered the rejection of his latest effort, and Larry told Henry that Fred might eventually learn '*construction*' if he would only:

(1) Never read anything by Henry Miller.
(2) Study Stendhal.[53]

This may have been good advice, but Larry himself was rereading all the Miller that he could lay hands on, in preparation for editing what would be published years later as *The Henry Miller Reader*. He had proposed the project to Henry, telling him that a judiciously selected and uncensorable omnibus volume would gain him a wide American readership. Larry jotted down a list of essays, character sketches, and excerpts from the novels that would introduce the Master to the world. Soon Henry was responding with alternative lists that stressed *his* favourite pieces.

South of the equator Larry's genius for friendship still functioned. He met a young Argentine writer, Enrique 'Quique' Revol, and spent evenings of talk with him in Cordova. Revol introduced Larry to Jorge 'Monono' Ferreyra, a member of the Argentine aristocracy, who invited Larry and Eve to live at Casa Norman, his summer home at Cruz Chica, in the hills not far from Cordova. Monono Ferreyra and his lovely and much younger wife 'Bebita' became friends of Larry and Eve. The Ferreyras spoke English as well as they did Spanish. Indeed, Larry soon decided that all Argentines spoke English – at least, in his circle they did. He discovered that he could still ride a horse, and he and Eve spent hours galloping across the 'burnt sierras'. 'We overeat and ride lovely horses,' he told Alan. 'The horses are the best thing in the Argentine, beautiful and swift creatures.'[54] Larry's own horse was Fósforos ('Matches'). Larry's only published poem directly inspired by Argentina mentions Fósforos and celebrates the uplands:

The grass they cropped converting into speed
Made green the concert of their hooves
Over the long serene sierras turning
In the axle of the sun's eye
To legs as delicate as spiders' . . . .[55]

By contrast, Rio, experienced only for a few days, produced three finished poems.

Before the regular classes began at the British Council Institute at 137 Boulevard San Juan in Cordova, Larry lectured not only there but in Cruz Chica, La Plata and other towns. He spoke extemporaneously for the most part, yet never seemed to hesitate for a word or phrase. All this time he was writing out the notes that would be expanded into his *Key to Modern Poetry*. To Ferreyra he said, 'I am an Elizabethan scholar, my dear.'[56] Larry was much taken with the role of the artist in shaping society, and he poured out his ideas to the composer Sir William Walton, whom he evidently met at the Ferreyras' home.

Larry gave the typescript of his *Horizon* essay on Groddeck's *Book of the It* to Monono Ferreyra to read. Ferreyra had the secretary of the Golf Club type out copies for his friends, and believed that his conversion to Groddeck's theory of health saved his life – he was then fighting tuberculosis.[57] Larry later had the satisfaction of seeing his essay published as 'El Pensamiento de Groddeck' in the Buenos Aires *Réunion Publicación Trimestral*.

After a couple of months in South America, Larry summed up his impressions. 'Argentina is a large flat melancholy and rather superb-looking country full of stale air, blue featureless sierras, and businessmen drinking Coca-Cola,' he wrote to Mary Mollo. He found the people 'quite nice' but in a 'superficial and childish way'.[58] The diet was mainly beef, and he was offended by the 'loaf-sized' steaks.[59] Withal, 'one . . . is so bored one could scream'. The *cafard* had hit him all right. 'It is the most lazy-making climate I have struck: not as bad as Egypt, of course: but I'd give a lifetime of Argentina for three weeks of Greece, fascist or no fascist.'[60] Larry's discontent with Argentina was probably increased by the encouraging news from England; in early February he heard from Eliot that '*On Seeming to Presume* is now a good job, likely to promote the Durrell reputation.'[61]

With the end of school summer holidays in March, Larry and Eve knew that they would have to leave the hospitable Ferreyra home up in the hills at Cruz Chica. Larry in *The Alexandria Quartet* would have Pursewarden write a book entitled *God Is a Humorist*, and only One who enjoyed a joke would have sent Larry to live in Cordova. The city was probably the most conservative in Argentina, proud of its heritage as an important colonial centre, proud of its fine limestone buildings, among them the so-called Palacio Ferreyra, constructed of stone from the family's vast quarries. Cordova was also the site of the oldest university in Argentina and of dozens of fine churches. Typical Cordobeses adored strings of family names and as many titles and academic degrees as they could with any legitimacy attach to them. Raúl Víctor Peláez, one of Larry's students, called the local disease 'Bronzemia': 'the continuous assimilation of bronze particles entering the blood stream, gradually transforming or transmuting every Cordobes into a living statue or public monument with varying degrees of solemnity, pomp and circumstance'.[62] This was the society, valuing decorum and tradition so highly, in which Larry found himself, like Don Giovanni surrounded by stern *commendatóri*.

In early March, Larry and Eve moved into a house on the Boulevard Chacabuco in Cordova. Ferreyra noted that 'Larry was quite incapable of dealing with material things, even such trifles as money', and that he let Eve handle all practical matters.[63] Larry also seemed rather offhand about working at the British Council. He would come in at around 9 a.m. and vanish for a few hours, carrying away an office typewriter. Eventually the typewriter disappeared, and there was a ripple of scandal when it turned up again in Larry's possession. Despite his casual manner, he was working hard on his lectures and trying to get back to *Reflections on a Marine Venus*, still stuck at mid-point. He wrote to ask Lawrence Clark Powell, a librarian at the University of California at Los Angeles, about the influence of Giordano Bruno on authorship in Elizabethan days, saying that after taking notes for ten years, he only needed six months of free time to write his long-planned Renaissance study.[64]

Compounding the fuss made over the missing typewriter was a conflict of personalities. The Director of the British Council Institute when Larry arrived was Alec Clifford, a very religious and gentlemanly Anglo-Argentinean of strong Christian Evangelical persuasion. He and Larry took one another's measure and their dislike was instant, fervent and mutual. Clifford had approved of Larry's immediate predecessor, George Darrell Blackburn, a devout Oxford scholar who had taken as his *unofficial* literary span Congreve to Chesterton while he was supposed to be reading Chaucer to Milton. Not surprisingly, he had been sent down without a degree, and then he had converted to Catholicism in Rome in 1922.[65] Blackburn's passionate Catholicism had been a distinct asset to his acceptance by the Cordobeses. Blackburn was as long, skinny, dry and aesthetic as Larry was compact, sanguine and pithy. Larry's lectures always began with some outrageous anecdote or fact, and he would then progress without notes or convoluted sentences to an explication of Eliot's 'Gerontion' or to The Essence of the Decadence.

By April 1948, Clifford had resigned from the directorship, although he consented to stay on in a part-time capacity. 'No doubt, Clifford's resignation had a great deal to do with Larry's presence in his domains,' asserted Raúl Víctor Peláez, who knew Blackburn and who became a friend to both Clifford and Larry. Clifford valued decorum too much to spread rumours, but he made it clear that while he admired Larry's poetry, he disapproved of his attitudes towards love and sex.[66]

Eve, whether or not she was reflecting Larry's feelings in her letters, certainly agreed with his evaluation of Argentina: 'Here we are in the dreary corner of the Argentine and hating almost every moment of it', she confided to Ella Thomas, 'somehow the place has nothing to give to us that we care to have, in spite of the plentifulness of everything, the friendliness of the people, the climate is getting us steadily down.' The rest of Eve's letter detailed the items still rare or unobtainable in Britain that Eve proposed to send to Ella: Nestlé's chocolate, lobster in tins, cocoa, butter, nylons.[67] Soon Larry and Eve had posted several parcels of food and nylon stockings, an inversion of the Corfu days when Alan was Larry's supplier. They were also sending food to Louisa Durrell.

Larry proposed to write an article on P. G. Wodehouse, whom he contacted about the genesis of his character Jeeves. Wodehouse answered in cordial fashion, but Larry's piece was apparently never finished.[68] Nearly ten years later Larry paid Wodehouse the ultimate tribute of admiration when he composed the Antrobus stories in a Wodehousian manner. The Jeeves novels were good escape reading for Larry.

One of his fellow-teachers at the Institute was Norma Campbell, a shy young woman of great charm, who turned up at Larry's regular classes. She had come from Britain as an English tutor. Soon Norma was seen everywhere with Larry, and there was inevitable gossip.[69] She was not the only woman in Larry's orbit. Only half in jest, one of Alec Clifford's friends exploded when reminded of how 'poor Larry' had suffered in Cordova. 'What do you mean poor Larry, poor Larry . . . what a miserable life he had in this ass of the world of Córdoba? What do you mean by that! . . .

the s.o.b. was always drinking the best wines . . . and eating the best food and riding the best horses and screwing the best senoritas in town . . . You call that fellow poor Larry?'[70]

Whatever his own sins of commission or omission, Larry was quite capable of criticizing his friends for their errors in domestic judgement. He twitted Henry Miller for having saddled himself with Conrad Moricand: the astrologer had moved in with Henry and Lepska at their small Big Sur home – Moricand, the archetypal Parisian, elegant in three-piece suit and cane, among the cedars and golden-mantled ground squirrels of Big Sur! A desperate Henry asked Larry to find a position for Moricand in Argentina. Larry wrote back that Argentina was filled with 'tough go-getting tycoons' and that Buenos Aires was 'climatically an inferno, and morally the final circle of hell'. A bit overdrawn perhaps, but it had the desired effect of keeping Moricand away. For himself, by the end of March Larry was saying, 'I think I would rather risk the atom bomb than stay on.'[71] He attempted to keep his nerves under control with liberal doses of valerian.[72]

Larry confided to Anne Ridler that the solemnity with which he was delivering his public lectures on English poetry was bogus, and he pretended to see all his efforts as comic. So did a number of his students at his regular Institute classes, and Larry in fact encouraged that view with a series of 'Special Seminars on the Limerick's Metric System', held while drinking tea around a table in the library of the Asociación Argentina de Cultura Británica, as the Institute was called. Larry started off each class with a limerick of his own, and then spoke on any writer he wished. Larry seemed to Peláez never to slow down: 'He was always on the move, going from his office to the library, talking to two people standing on opposite corners of the room, and always saying, saying, saying something shocking or funny or unique.' His students would especially remember 'his ever-changing expression; his face, so round, with a smile in the middle; his eyes so alive, so pure; his voice'.[73]

People heard Larry's voice all over the 'bitterly cold' country. He was sent '300 miles through a wall of yellow dust' to lecture at Tucumán, then flown to Mendoza 'at the foot of the fucking Andes', then to Rosario 'in the heart of the dust-bowl'. 'Me one time lecture man,' Larry wrote to Mary Mollo. 'Me givvy lecture Shakespear. Shakespear him velly fine big-speak sing song man, velly wise, velly pure, velly clean.'[74] Twice he lectured on Henry Miller, 'but I had to be a bit cagey because of the Catholics!'[75]

He may have spoken cavalierly about his efforts, yet the lectures that Larry delivered in Argentina are not only a serious assessment of the subject: they are also a retracing of his own literary and philosophical roots. Despite its title, Larry's *Key to Modern Poetry*, based on these lectures, contains the ideas at the core of his fiction as well as of his verse. His aim in the series of lectures was ambitious. He began with an attack on critical method, which he said was rooted in a tendency of lecturers to consider literature in isolation. 'All the arts and sciences are simply different dialects of the same language', the same culture, he proclaimed.[76] In an effort to grasp this 'culture', Larry had read deeply in the anthropologists Taylor, Frazer and Rivers; in the psychologists Freud, Groddeck, Jung, Rank and Stekel; in the scientists Eddington, Whitehead and Einstein. However, it was not false modesty when Larry wrote disparagingly of 'my own thinking (if I may, for want of a better word, call it that)'. He admitted freely that his 'bias' in *Key* had been heavily influenced by Wyndham Lewis's *Time and Western Man* and Edmund Wilson's *Axel's Castle*,[77] and he had always turned to the *Encyclopaedia Britannica* when he needed a quick summation of a philosophic or scientific point. Out of the writers Larry named and a few hundred that he did not, he was creating his own institution of higher learning.

In fact, Larry had the same educational inferiority complex that he attributed to his father, and there is at once irony and a touch of pardonable human weakness in his appending 'Oxford' to the foot of his preface to *Key to Modern Poetry*. True, he would be temporarily residing in the town when he was preparing *Key* for the press, but his being there would have everything to do with the birth of his second daughter and no connection at all with the university.

Considering the book from the standpoint of its more appropriate American title, *A Key to Modern British Poetry*, it is a well-reasoned if idiosyncratic view of the course of English poetry up to 1939, a view given its peculiar bias by his adoption of little-known savants such as Georg Groddeck and an even more obscure psychologist he discovered during the revision process, Francis J. Mott. In fact, the book is a 'Key to Lawrence Durrell', although he did not intend it as such.

A Key to Modern Poetry would have earned Larry a doctorate in literature at most universities. In it he formulated his ideas about physics, time, culture and art. He presented an ingenious attempt to unify the sciences and the humanities. Lacking the mathematics to follow Einstein's proofs, he turned to Giordano Bruno in order to come to terms with 'the new space-time idea'. He seized upon Bruno's claim that 'in every point of duration is beginning without end and end without beginning'. From this he deduced that, just as 'time as history received its death-blow from geology and from Darwin', so 'time as process, as extension along a series of points, has been halted . . . dammed up'. This damming-up of time has had a disruptive effect on linguistics, which has led to *Finnegans Wake*, and in philosophy has changed our 'death-consciousness'. 'It is one of the paradoxes of the new space-time', Larry wrote emphatically, 'that if time is really spread out in this way, *we can just as easily situate death in the present as in the future*.' Thus, 'birth-life-death' becomes a 'multiple state' rather than a sequence.[78]

'Time and the ego are the two determinants of style for the twentieth century,' Larry decided. 'If one grasps the ideas about them one has, I think, the key to much that has happened.'[79] The problem of time he had resolved to his satisfaction: in relativistic terms and in literature, different times could be made to coincide. The ego, that ancient Homeric unity, could no longer be considered as discrete – so Larry had long ago decided, following D. H. Lawrence. Two inversions, then: seemingly diverse times became unity; the ego was no longer fixed but splintered into limitless states. Out of this line of reasoning would come the multiple-state structure of the volumes of *The Alexandria Quartet* and the superimposed, nested *gigogne* of *The Avignon Quintet*; and each set would contain non-discrete, variable characters.

Larry turned his key to unlock the difficulties in the poetry of Eliot, Auden and a host of other poets, including his friends George Barker, Anne Ridler and Dylan Thomas. Eliot he described in terms of film – 'Tiresias is the camera-man', moving freely in history and time.[80] Larry gave an extended illustration of how *The Waste Land* could be readily understood if scripted for radio drama, with a variety of voices – '*A Woman's Voice*', '*A younger Voice, eagerly*', '*a hoarse, plump voice, that of a rich middle-aged Jewess, shall we say?*', and so on. For Auden, Larry evoked jazz images: 'He strums on a very dry, a very highly strung, banjo', austere, unsentimental, honest.[81]

One wonders what the young Argentine students and society ladies who came to Larry's public lectures made of his theories. Peláez thought Larry absolutely clear, through his skill in illustrating concepts with startling examples. Consciously or not, Larry was using his British Council talks as a germinating ground for his future novels. Hating the *locus*, he was driven inward. In landlocked Cordova, and despite his amatory adventures, his mermaids were mostly in the mind.

Larry also worked steadily on the Miller anthology throughout his stay in Argentina. There was talk of a co-editorship with Malcolm Cowley, or of giving the entire project to someone else. Finally, Larry was made the sole editor, and he was grateful to James Laughlin of New Directions for the 'compliment' of having been entrusted with the task. Larry decided that Henry had developed an American style that was inferior in 'critical control' to his earlier 'European style', though it had 'gained vastly in power and flight'. Unless Henry regained some control, he would be in danger of taking off on a 'Bergsonian rampage' and producing 'muddled' books.[82]

Larry attempted to restart a stalled project by reminding Theodore Stephanides of his promise to proof-read the translation of *Pope Joan* that Larry had toiled over intermittently since 1945. Larry had more in mind for Theo than a mere vetting of commas and spelling: he asked him to check the pages against the Greek text and to alter 'as best you can' anything that was 'plain WRONG'. Larry did not, however, want Theo to concern himself with 'haunting absolute literals': 'a certain flowing art went into my translation'. Larry recommended to Theo as a possible resource George Borodin's *Loves of Joanna*, which he called a 'botched' version of the story, with parts 'stolen' from an earlier literal translation patched together with passages of the supposed translator's invention. Theo should ask Spencer Curtis Brown to procure a copy of Borodin's text, 'but for Godsake don't tell him how much of Royidis is printed in it'. Apparently both Curtis Brown and the publisher were under the impression that Borodin's version was only based on Royidis and was not a full translation, and Larry did not want to jeopardize the future of his own book: 'MINE IS THE FIRST FULL PURE AND GOOD REPRODUCTION OF ROYIDIS IN ENG-LAND.' He was sure that through his translation Royidis would become recognized as a classic, full of 'sunny lascivious Mediterranean charm'.[83] To streamline the book for the English reader, Larry had omitted most of the ponderous scholarly notes that Royidis had intended for his Greek audience, and had cut most of the original introduction and all elements of 'theological polemic', keeping only those parts that treated the genesis of Royidis's text. Larry had been at some pains to retain those annotations that showed Royidis to have founded his novel on fact: the saints, monks and monasteries really did exist.

Theodore soon wrote expressing his approval of *Pope Joan*. 'I'm glad we capture Royidis a bit,' Larry replied. 'What a master the man is!' Theodore was still very depressed over his divorce, and for that too, Larry had a solution: remarry.[84] Nor should Theo blame himself too much for the failure of a seventeen-year union: 'Atomic unrest', the last war and the fear of the next, had affected women's glands![85] Realizing this, Larry lectured Theodore, he should forge ahead. 'A creative man needs a bedworthy housekeeper, I think.' Theo should not rule out falling in love again: 'You might meet Papissa Joanna! And who could resist her?'[86]

Finally, everything seemed ready: Theodore completed his proof-reading, Larry sent out the typescript, John Buckland-Wright designed superb Kelmscott-style plates worthy of William Morris, and the type was set. Secure in his belief that *Pope Joan* was about to appear, Larry settled down to tackle *Reflections on a Marine Venus* again, after which he intended to write another verse play without waiting for a verdict from Eliot on *Sappho*. Then the publisher, Rodney, Phillips & Green, went bankrupt. It was infuriating.

Alan and Ella Thomas went to Paris in early spring, and even staunchly pro-English Ella admitted that she could now understand Larry's enthusiasm for France. 'You thought me jist plain unpatriotic no doubt when I said how dull and arranged life in England was,' Larry replied. Mounting his podium, he continued by saying that the English could learn about 'French food, Italian sweetness and sensuality, Greek intellectual animation' – without losing their own 'dogged domestic and civic virtues'. Argentina, alas, had no virtues worthy of imitation, 'unless torpidness is a virtue'. Larry felt himself afflicted by that torpidity. He had 'some muck on the stocks', he confessed, 'but nothing very sparkling'. Whenever he could, Larry escaped into sleep or violent activity. He and Eve were about to head off for a riding holiday in the sierras, he told Alan.[87] Careening over the rolling grasslands might sound romantic, but Larry tried to disabuse Theodore: 'Argentina is beef-bound and very hot,' he wrote. '*Not* a nice country.'[88] A plague of sighing and grief: he was getting fat.

Unhappy with Argentina, Larry was also distressed by the lack of advertising for *Cefalû*: 'One certainly suffers from selling Tambi books,' he complained. 'Better burn them or sell outright to Hodder for a fiver.' In this he was forgetting for the moment that he had been glad when Tambimuttu had accepted *Cefalû* after Faber had rejected the novel. His latest collection of verse, *On Seeming to Presume*, appeared in April, but Larry did not express any pleasure. His desperation showed even in his punctuation and typing, never perfect but now worse: 'I am hacking at the Rhodes book. God what a horrible climate here.. Can't concentrate.., Coming home soon even England is better than this. However. . .' A spark of the old Larry appeared in his postscript to Theodore: 'Just heard from

Zarian. He is in Rome, and delighted with his portrait in Prospero, unlike you, you devil.'[89]

Several good friends from Larry's Cairo days turned up in Argentina. Dudley Honor was appointed Air Attaché at the Embassy in Buenos Aires, and he and Mary entertained the Durrells when Larry could escape from Cordova for the capital city.[90] Dudley had the use of a twin-engined aircraft, and could fly up to Cordova for an occasional weekend with Larry and Eve. The Uldalls also appeared for evenings of reminiscence about Cairo, as did the Abercrombies and the Smarts.

At the end of April Larry received one of Eliot's typically sly letters, which began by chiding Larry for an undated letter. 'As, however, your usual alternative to omitting the date altogether is to date your letter the wrong month, I think I prefer it this way,' Eliot added. Furthermore, he had not yet had an opportunity to read the *Sappho* typescript. Larry would have to be patient, 'and you have dealt with me long enough to have a good deal of training in patience'.[91]

Larry made no secret of his dislike of Argentina, even with his local friends. One hostess reported that he had taken to his bed for six days, after phoning the British Council headquarters in Buenos Aires to say that he would not rise until he was given a ticket back to England.[92] Even for Argentina, it was a long siesta. 'Green tea, big belly, much sleep, no exercise', Larry lamented.[93]

Greece was constantly on Larry's mind. A confused but bloody civil war was staggering on between the Communist-backed EAM and the Populists, supported by republicans, monarchists, the British and the Americans. He was stung when Mary Mollo 'harangue[d]' him 'as if I were a communist', and he exclaimed, 'O of course I know that Russia is to blame and that now we MUST fight to keep her out.' Larry continued, 'I was a republican-Sophoulist', naming the venerable Liberal who had become premier under King Paul the year before, 'and I believed in REAL INTERVENTION, not this mealy mouthed disgraceful shambles we've created.' The British and American policy was a half-measure, based on the 'pathetic belief that the Greeks are not natural bandits at heart'. Certainly they were, Larry said, without condemning them for it, but stating flatly that Britain should either take a strong hand or 'LEAVE THE BLOODY PLACE'.[94]

Many of Larry's publications during 1948 looked towards Greece. *On Seeming to Presume*, although it contained two of his New World lyrics, 'Christ in Brazil' and 'Green Coconuts: Rio', mostly dealt with Greek themes: 'Patmos', 'Blind Homer', 'Phileremo', 'Rodini'. The dedications

'For George Seferis' and 'For Paddy and Xan' evoked Greece, and so did the six portraits in 'Eternal Contemporaries' and the settings in 'The Anecdotes'. John Lehmann produced Seferis's *The King of Asine and Other Poems*, translated from the Greek by Bernard Spencer, Nanos Valaoritis and Larry, and introduced by Rex Warner. Larry saw *Asine* as an homage to Seferis and the Greek world, and if anything it served to increase his discontent at being stuck in Argentina.

Larry had heard no more from Eliot about *Sappho*, but he had persuaded a local theatrical company to hold a dramatic reading. Soon the players were on their feet acting the parts. 'They ended with tears in their eyes,' Larry told Eliot. 'They were knocked cold, and so was I.' If these Spaniards had 'twigged' the play, surely a skilled English theatre director could win acceptance for it. 'My dear TSE,' Larry continued, 'you have a good play here, a very good play', in the tradition of Sartre and of Camus's *Le Malentendu*. 'I feel disposed to allow you to congratulate me on having done something worth while.' For the first and only time in his dealings with the firm, Larry offered to split publication costs with Faber and Faber. 'By the dark abdomen and the bones of Becket I conjure you to PRINT,' he concluded.[95]

At long last, in mid-July, Larry received word on *Sappho*. 'Your undated letter was a masterpiece,' began Eliot. So was his reply. 'I always believe it a good thing', Eliot said, 'to encourage authors to believe that their work is a little better than it is – not much better than it is, but a little.' Conversely, he continued reasonably, it was normal for authors to believe that some other publisher might be more understanding than their current one. Turning to *Sappho* at last, Eliot declared that 'The author is a little pretentious, and sometimes makes the mistake of trying to emulate Shakespeare in gnomic utterances put in a queer way, but on the whole he does know his onions, and plants them right side up.' Also, it was 'refreshing' to encounter a poet who understood that 'poetry is merely prose developed by a knowledge of aeronautics'. To conclude, Eliot wanted to publish *Sappho*, theatre production or not, although Faber would certainly lose money on the book if there was no staging of the play. The book would have to cost a lot, since printers and binders earned 'much more than authors'.[96] Here was a remark calculated to get under Larry's skin!

Eliot appended a score of specific comments. In *Sappho*, Larry had written 'Palpable rape', to which Eliot replied, 'Are not all rapes palpable, if any?' Finally, he advised, 'Read ANTONY AND CLEOPATRA and *simplify*.' We do not have the luck that Shakespeare had: 'We have got to make plays in which the mental movements cannot find physical equivalents.' Therefore we must deal in fundamental emotions easily understood.[97] 'Many thanks for your rather acid letter,'[98] Larry wrote, to which his mentor responded, 'It seemed to me an extremely sweet one. But if you like acid, I will see what I can do.'[99] Relieved that Eliot was not, as Larry had understood earlier, making stage production a condition for publication, he agreed to most of Eliot's suggestions. Especially, Larry did not want to turn *Sappho* into a Tennysonian reading script. 'Me, I'm a romantic', he cried, 'at the moment we need a sort of Stendhal for the stage'.[100]

Larry enjoyed repartee with Eliot, but he still had Argentina to contend with. He wrote to Henry Miller in terms reminiscent of his old feelings about Egypt: 'Hate this place and am waiting like a leashed greyhound to run for Europe. A rather *fat* greyhound albeit – one eats too much here to compensate for the continuous nervous suffering imposed by the beastly climate. . . . I can't work or think with this perpetual wind and dust.'[101] For Monono Ferreyra he composed a comic song called 'I'm So Sad'.[102] He sounded even more desperate in his letters to Mary and Dudley Honor. 'Come and rescue me for God's sake,' he begged. 'I am going quietly mad due to the deadness of everything and everyone here.' They drove north-west from Buenos Aires the next weekend to find Larry miserably depressed. Sitting in dry, landlocked, dusty Cordova, he was painting Greek harbour scenes in ink. 'The loo walls are covered with my efforts,' he told the Honors.[103] In his despondent mood, Larry wrote to Anne Ridler to congratulate Vivian on his appointment as Assistant Printer to the University of Oxford. 'I'm very glad,' he said. 'I want Vivian to be rich and respected. I must have a few friends who are good for a touch in later life, when I reach the obviously seedy period which lies ahead.'[104]

Despite his low spirits, Larry was still working on *The Henry Miller Reader*. He was convinced that there was money to be made from such projects – not a lot, but if he should break his contract with the British Council he might be glad of small commissions. Larry had no way of guessing it, but the *Reader* would become Henry's best-seller among all his titles published by New Directions.[105] Near the beginning of August, Larry asked Alan Thomas to buy the memoirs and letters of Edward Trelawney, friend of Byron and Shelley, for an omnibus volume to be aimed at Faber. Nothing came of this project.

By August Larry knew that he had had enough of Cordova, enough of Argentina. 'We have had no rain for seven months. . . . I dream of English drizzle and green oaktrees,' he wrote to Alan.[106] Romantic that he was, Larry judged all the Americas by his experience of Argentina, writing to Henry, 'It is much blacker, much darker than I ever imagined possible.' He did not blame the people, who were 'at the mercy of the influences': 'The soil and climate are talking the whole time – saying ugly swinish things.'[107] Larry convinced himself that he was collapsing: 'Enjoying a sort of nervous breakdown, which has had the good result of making me resign from the Council', he told Eliot.[108] He and Eve hoped to be out of the country in a month or two.[109] Although medical examination turned up nothing radically wrong, a sympathetic doctor gave Larry what amounted to a medical discharge. At least, it was a document to countenance his resignation after only seven months with the British Council in Cordova. Even if the British Council were never to employ him again that possibility did not look like too much of a problem 'from this end of the telescope'. He would teach until the end of the year but that was all. 'Probably we shall starve in England but *anything* would be better than the winter we have suffered here,' Larry wrote to Jon and Betsy Uldall. 'It has been terrible – everyone ill three days a week. . . . Behind me lie stomach ulcer, nervous insomnia, aphasia, etc.' Worst of all was the depression: 'Apart from illness one loses one's sense of *values* here – there is a very strong wicked emanation from the soil which pushes one towards *forgetting* how real people think.'[110] He was a Mediterranean animal rejecting a foreign habitat.

Larry and Eve fled to Buenos Aires to stay with the Ferreyras at their apartment at Posadas 1053. Monono introduced Larry to the writer Eduardo Mallea, who lived nearby at Posadas 1120 and who would later become Argentine ambassador to UNESCO. There were the inevitable cocktail parties, and at one of these Larry shocked the correct Buenos Aires folk by taking off his shoes and 'improvising a toe dance'. Monono recalled that 'It was a good party.'[111] Larry met Jorge Luis Borges briefly at another party; Larry was suitably complimentary, Borges polite.[112] Larry had probably read Borges's essay on the *Thousand and One Nights* which mentions the 'Chinese spheres that fit one into the other', the dolls that nest. In future, Larry would often name Borges among those writers with whom he was most in sympathy. At any rate, Borges's philosophic flight accurately prefigured Larry's declared application of the *gigogne* image to his future *Avignon Quintet*.[113] As far as Larry was concerned, he was marking time until departure.

By 4 DECEMBER 1948 LARRY AND EVE were running – by sea – for Bournemouth, like badgers to earth. Larry felt that he was returning from another exile. He was also returning without prospects. His royalties did not bring in nearly enough money to live on, and he had hardly endeared himself to the British Council by cutting short his projected two-year stay in Argentina. A period of casting about for a new position ensued. Larry's credit was still good enough with the Foreign Office, thanks to his record in the Mediterranean and to his medical chit, for him not to be blacklisted; still, he evidently had to be given the Rebuke Indirect for his un-British weakness in succumbing to the doldrums of provincial Argentina. His sentence, when it finally came, would be Belgrade, to all appearances firmly under the control of Marshal Tito. Here was a precious irony: as if divining his fear of the Bomb, the Foreign Office would maliciously post Larry to a buffer zone between the missile-brandishing USSR and bristling Western Europe.

All this was hidden in the future when Larry and Eve, tired travellers, collapsed at his mother's house in Bournemouth, where Larry resolved to hide for a month or two of 'resting up'. He convinced himself that he had been unwell for the past six months, a case of 'bad nerves', a 'frightful melancholia' that he said was 'due to Latin America as much as anything'. When his cousin John Dixie, on furlough from the Park Prewitt mental hospital, came to visit Louisa Durrell, Larry must have wondered whether he was headed there himself. 'England is wonderful after Argentina – the damp particularly & the cold,' he decided, singling out two traits of his adopted country that he had earlier especially detested. He managed to rouse himself for one good snarl: 'England is fatuous and apathetic as usual – the sweaty Christians are out in force – publishers demand a strong pietistic note.'[114] If they wanted Christian pabulum, however, they would have to look elsewhere, for he settled himself to write a long essay, 'Studies in Genius: VIII/Henry Miller', for Connolly's *Horizon*. 'It's to brush up interest in you here,' he told Henry.[115]

Larry may have been ambivalent about England during this visit, but there was no doubt about his joy at seeing Penelope again. She had been placed at Lytchett Manor School, just west of Bournemouth, in September 1947, not long after Nancy's marriage to Edward Hodgkin. When Nancy had discovered that she was pregnant, she had decided that with both a new marriage and a baby to adjust to, she could not cope with Penelope. Larry got Nancy's permission to take Penelope from the school for visits to St Alban's Avenue, and he immediately sensed the child's feeling of being abandoned. As much as he could, and backed up by Eve and by his mother, Larry tried to make Penelope feel welcome. He wrote happily to Henry Miller that he was seeing 'quite a bit' of Penelope, 'eight and lovely now'.[116] Penelope on her part looked upon Larry as her knight on a charger, and fully expected him to deliver her from bondage.[117] His own memories of loneliness and abandonment in his youth gave Larry an anguished empathy with his daughter. Still, he did not see how he could provide her with a home, even supposing Nancy would agree to his custody. He shied away from taking responsibility, and added another personal failure to his internal log. He was still sunk in 'blank gloom' after two months in England, and even a 'marvellous weekend' visit from Fred Perlès, now become 'a sort of little saint', failed to bring more than a temporary lift to his spirits. Larry thought that he could handle having 'no job, no money' if only his mood would change: he was quite convinced that it was something beyond his conscious control that, like an attack of sciatica, could 'end soon' – or might not.[118]

By 14 March, Henry was rereading Larry's 'Studies in Genius' essay, pleased with it but picking at details in an immense letter to his friend. Henry liked Larry's application of the term 'Lord of Misrule' to him, and could accept 'literary *clochard*', but he attacked Larry's 'ambivalent attitude' towards what he termed Henry's 'formlessness'. Larry and Eve were both reading Albert Cossery's 'marvellous' *Les Fainéants dans la vallée fertile*, set in Egypt. 'Eve adores it,' Larry wrote to Henry. 'What can I tell you about her? She's perfectly grand. I couldn't have been luckier nohow.'[119] Larry's spirits were reviving.

Larry's posting to Yugoslavia came through in April, and he and Eve moved to London where the Burrows again loaned them their Orme Square house. 'I am very happy at the idea of seeing the Balkans again,' Larry announced.[120] His passport was amended to read 'Government Official' and Eve's occupation was altered from 'Civil Servant' to 'Housewife'.[121] Larry was given a wad of brownish Roneoed sheets of the Belgrade Press Summary, some 300 legal-sized pages outlining the reportage of the Yugoslav press from 7 January to 4 November 1948. He groaned as he sat scanning the blurred typing. The combined efforts of the stilted propagandists of Marshal Tito's regime and the hostile Yugoslavian translators employed by the Embassy gave a ludicrous cast to serious news that Larry would later transform into pure Antrobus.

It was probably during this sojourn in London that Larry saw the astrologer Arthur Gauntlett to have a horoscope cast. Larry felt that he was losing control of his life, and hoped for at least a few clues about the future. Gauntlett forecast 'disappointment through the affections', including marital turmoil and strained relationships with mother and siblings. Larry would move around a lot, be financially solvent, probably follow a career in government service, and would experience a physical decline and a gain in weight beginning in 1968. (At this, Larry must have demurred: he had already added many pounds in Argentina, and he was still overweight.) His sixty-ninth year would be one of great crisis. Gauntlett predicted the general circumstance of Larry's death: 'The end of life, when it comes, will be quite sudden.'[122] The gist and tone of Gauntlett's reading certainly represented a sobering come-down from Moricand's Jupiterian flights of more than a decade earlier.

Finally everything was ready for their departure for Belgrade, and Larry and Eve took the familiar train to pass through a 'wonderful' Paris with 'all its old charm' regained.[123] Then it was on to Switzerland, from which they swerved into Trieste instead of continuing south to Brindisi and the Corfu ferry as Larry had so often done before the war. On 20 May 1949 Larry and Eve had their passports stamped in Trieste on leaving the British/ United States Control Zone, a vestige of the war, and entered Tito's domain.

Larry's first impressions of Yugoslavia were mixed: he found 'conditions' to be 'far from pleasant though much better than Latin America'. He was referring to the quality of life possible on a diplomat's salary and perks, a life largely protected from police interference. The Yugoslavs themselves seemed tattered, pinched, cowed. Any lingering interest in Communism that he might have retained from the political freethinking of his early Bloomsbury period was quickly quenched by Tito's variety. The reality was 'so much more horrible than you can imagine', he wrote to Henry Miller, 'systematic moral and spiritual corruption'.[124] Yugoslav officialdom was not friendly: 'As you know we are all Fascist pigs and imperialist beasts – and they try to make us feel it.'[125] He would be in charge of the British Council Reading Room on Kneza Mihaila in Stari Grad, the Old City, at the juncture of the Sava and the Danube, 'two damnably dirty and moist rivers'.[126] In addition, he was assigned an office in the Embassy on Generala Zdanova, a mile and a half away from the Council building. His responsibilities would be twofold: cultural affairs and press briefings.

His Argentine experience had been expensive, and he was negotiating at long distance the shoals of an overdraft at his London bank. Larry asked Theodore Stephanides for a supply of tincture of valerian ('I commend it to you'), his favourite sedative, and sal volatile. He noted with grim foreboding, 'There are several ugly similarities between this place and Argentina – notably a cold, or sort of 'flu which makes one angoissie – sub-normal temp – aching limbs and head buzzing so you can't stand.' Larry added that 'one imagines it is the onset of infant. paralysis'. Everyone was sick in Belgrade, he claimed, appending a request for 'a biggish bottle of "Chlorodine" for a friend'. All in all, Yugoslavia was a *chute totale*: 'Not writing, not thinking, working too hard.'[127]

Larry and Eve moved soon after their arrival into a house at 3 Puskinova Street, in a fashionable residential sector a few miles south-west of Stari Grad. The place needed a lot of repairs and paint to make it inhabitable, and Larry asked Alan to send him prints by Picasso and Henry Moore to enliven the walls. He painted one entire wall with a fresco of his own. Larry could not however complain, as in Cordova, about the lack of green: tall trees were everywhere around the widely spaced homes, and the forested area across the street from Larry's house gave him one of the best views in Belgrade.[128] Yet with the rain and, soon, the shortening of the days, these trees contributed to the darkness and gloom. Larry had arrived with a good impression of the Yugoslavs owing to his acquaintance with Radmila Djukić, Betty Ryan's friend during their Paris days, but he thought that the character of the populace had changed: 'The people have become brutish and ugly and *Marxist* – which is for me synonymous with pigs and fools.'[129] Nor did he feel any better about most of his diplomat colleagues. Larry claimed that he had 'always been instinctively anti-left', and he complained that his Chancery was 'full of little socialist vipers accusing me of misreporting and blimping'.[130] Despite his distress, he had unearthed a *Dictionary of National Biography* in the British Council offices, and with it as a reference he thought that he could perhaps write his long-planned Elizabethan study next year. He asked Alan to start sending out his Elizabethan books via the Foreign Office Bag, beginning with the Marprelate Tracts. This project would come after he had finished *Reflections on a Marine Venus* – a labour of love that had deteriorated into a bore. Larry must have noted with chagrin that he always seemed to be one or two countries behind when it came to writing about them.

Henry had told Larry that Radmila Djukić's sister Nadežda lived in Belgrade, and that he should look her up, but she had married and Larry did not know her husband's name. He probably did not try very hard to find her: he had heard that a visit from a British diplomat might bring police reprisals down upon any Yugoslav. For the protection of their local friends, foreigners routinely ignored them in public or picked them up away from their homes, but Larry was not disposed to cultivate local friends and he evinced no interest in learning Serbo-Croatian.[131] Already Larry yearned for escape: 'When our car arrives we may feel a bit better about life, however . . .' he conceded grudgingly. On the Autoput, the new highway, Belgrade was only a day's drive from Trieste, 'which represents our nearest civilised point of reference'.[132]

Larry's complaints reached something of a crescendo, and his ordinarily clear and ordered handwriting – now lapsing into irregularities and cross-outs – mirrored his mood. 'It is impossible to describe how awful life is here: you must turn to the very right wing papers for a true picture,' he told Alan. 'This is real slavery on a scale one cannot imagine until one's been here. Keep away!' The summer heat was turning out far worse than he had expected: 'The weather is quite intolerable here and it's impossible to do any work either private or official.'[133] By September he was referring to 'this dull country' and was looking forward to the 'relief' of a projected visit to Salonika. 'There's nothing I can offer to send you from here – you even have the good weather which we were told to expect,' he wrote to Theodore.[134] And an exceptionally severe winter was being predicted.

Perhaps Larry's mood had something to do with the reception that he gave Henry's next book. Larry had long disapproved of what he saw as Henry's lack of structure and form, but when he received *Sexus* from Girodias in September 1949, he got half-way through the second volume before he blew up at Henry. 'I'm bitterly disappointed in it, despite the fact that it contains some of your very best writing to date,' he began, mildly enough. But he also found the 'moral vulgarity' to be '*artistically* painful'; the book was full of 'silly, meaningless scenes' that struck him as 'childish explosions of vulgarity' and 'painfully disgusting'; perhaps worst of all, it was 'written so badly'. 'Henry, Henry, Henry,' he lamented. 'Ten minutes' thought would have saved the book.' Comparing *Sexus* with the 'wild resonance of *Cancer* and *Black Spring*', Larry found 'new mystical outlines' but ranted that 'they are lost, lost damn it in this shower of lavatory filth which no longer seems tonic and bracing, but just excrementitious and sad'.[135] Five days later, having finished *Sexus*, Larry cabled Henry: 'SEXUS DISGRACEFULLY BAD WILL COMPLETELY RUIN REPUTATION UNLESS WITHDRAWN REVISED.'[136] 'I know you'd feel better if I did get angry with you, but I can't,' Henry replied to Larry's letters and cable. 'I laugh and shake my head bewilderedly, that's all.' He tried hard to justify his style in *Sexus*, but his argument, spread over several typed sheets, could be

LAWRENCE DURRELL

summarized in a few of his lines: 'I want this book to contain "life's traces".
Whether it is in good taste, moral or immoral, literature or document, a
creation or a fiasco, doesn't matter.'[137]

Soon the third musketeer, Fred Perlès, opened fire when Larry sent him a
copy of his first letter criticizing *Sexus*. Joey, 'shocked and terribly sad',
attacked Larry for having adopted a tone certain to wound Henry, an ill-
tempered tone that was far more damaging than his actual complaints
about the book. 'Your quarrel is with the author of one particular book',
Fred continued, admitting that he had not yet seen *Sexus*, 'and I am not
defending an author but trying to shield a man from injury.' 'Yes', Larry
annotated the first half of Fred's sentence, adding 'You're right' to the
second. Fred ended with a plea for Henry: 'I can only love him. Please tell
him that you do, too.' Larry responded that Fred was mistaken in
suggesting that Henry might be written out, or might 'never recover' from
Larry's criticism. 'He is far more robust than you imagine,' said Larry
perceptively, and he expected Henry to become 'Riper and Riper', like a
Titian or a Goethe. More than that, 'He has the energy of a spring lamb –
I'm saying that he's misdirecting it.'[138]

By 29 September Larry was sending Henry apologetic cables and letters.
'Of course it upset me bitterly to write to you,' he told Henry. 'I shouldn't
have done it really – Little Joe is right. . . . I should have written differently.
I was so god-damned hopping mad with you however, and so god-damned
anxious to try and boost English interest in you that I nearly died of blood
pressure.' Larry's agitation was evident in his language: rarely during what
would become a forty-five-year correspondence with Henry would Larry
god-damn anything. Now that correspondence and the friendship itself
seemed at risk: 'If you were a lesser sized man you would punish me by
breaking contact', he wrote to Henry.[139] Fred, having finally read *Sexus* 'in
one sitting', agreed that the book had all the faults Larry had noted, 'but
somehow they don't go against *my* grain': if the book was true to Henry's
vision, that was good enough for him.[140] Fred was not a Booster for
nothing.

Sexus was causing Larry embarrassment in other ways as well. On the
strength of his *Horizon* article, he had been asked by a number of papers to
review the novel. He was to write eight reviews, including one for *Horizon*,
in which he set forth his reservations, although less forcefully than he
already had to Henry and to Girodias. 'It is what I feel; it is terribly
unkind,' was his simple explanation to Henry. He could not simply do
what 'fashionable critics' do and praise a friend's work, because he knew

364

Henry had a right to expect honesty from him. There were a few tremors from the Foreign Office as well: Larry's name had appeared in the *Herald Tribune* in a blurb advertising *Sexus*, and protocol had been violated. Embassy staff were not supposed to get their names into newspapers in such contexts; and besides, anything they published was supposed to pass censorship. Larry *had* run his *Horizon* essay through channels, 'but if *Sexus* had been the sort of book I hoped for I would have skipped that'. Larry asked Girodias to remove his name from blurbs, which he would never have done for a good Miller title such as *Tropic of Cancer*. 'But Henry I simply couldn't defend *Sexus* to myself, let alone anyone else,' he wrote in acute distress. While Fred still thought Henry should be petted and 'indulged', Larry refused to condescend to him: 'I DON'T THINK YOU ARE WRITTEN OUT,' he declaimed. 'I THINK YOU ARE AT THE EDGE OF THE MOST FERTILE PERIOD OF YOUR LIFE.'[141]

The author of the offending book was puzzled and disappointed by Larry's reactions, but he kept his sense of humour. 'Joey looks forward to my going gaga soon,' he said in a letter sent jointly to his two *vieux copains*. 'Hold your horses, lads!' he cautioned. 'True, I am approaching the grave, but I don't feel finished yet.'[142] If Henry was really hurt by the *Sexus* criticism, he did not admit it to Larry and Fred: 'In these matters friendship can only be asserted and maintained by the strictest probity,' he wrote, closing the letter, '"Fratres Semper"'.[143] Larry could only be relieved.

He enjoyed meeting Malcolm Muggeridge, who came through Belgrade towards the end of September, but it seemed to Larry that if good things were happening, they were taking place elsewhere. He was delighted when Gerry's trip to the Cameroons rated a 'very handsome write-up' in *The Times*, but was anxiously awaiting the publication of *Sappho*.

His job became more interesting when he was able to travel around Yugoslavia. In early September he was in Zagreb, and in the beginning of October he drove to Sarajevo, spotting magnificent white eagles in flight. The town he found a welcome contrast to grimy Belgrade:

Sarajevo is a strange place – a narrow gorge full of rushing waters; granite-red mountains and the town perched up a cliff in a series of coloured bubbles of minaret and mosque; veiled women. Narrow streets full of mountaineers and mules. Wild crying of eagles in the air above it and all around a petrified ocean of rock with roads bulging round mountains, coiling and recoiling on themselves.

At one of the many small humpbacked bridges in the town the Archduke

Franz Ferdinand had been assassinated back in 1914, and local inhabitants were proud to point out the spot. Back in Belgrade, Larry felt that 'Life is an awful bore,' and he predicted political trouble for the spring.[144] By the end of the month he and Eve were ready again to leave 'this filthy echoing rambling town, full of sodden Serbs', travelling by jeep for a week in Salonika and the Macedonian hills.[145] He would be on duty, but it would be sheer joy to stand on Greek soil once more.

Although in terms of latitude Belgrade lies south of Venice, the winter climate suggested Outer Mongolia to Larry. Towards the end of December a heavy snowfall smothered the city, 'so we shall have a white Xmas – if a dour one – what a horrible place this place is!' he wrote to Theodore.[146] Despite the holiday season, the shelves in the stores were mostly bare, and Larry had to ask Theodore to send him candles and vitamins via the diplomatic bag. Larry wrote across the bottom of an Embassy card, embossed and gilded 'With the season's greetings', 'Larry and Eve in blasted Belgrade 1949', and sent it off to the Thomases.[147]

Larry entered the new year occupied with a projected monograph which he outlined for Alan: 'A study of the Elizabethan writer, economic, social, political, and cultural which will combine a lucid arrangement of the factual material plus a readability and warm[th] of colouring that makes the books readable.' Larry identified 'the two gaps in my documentation': McKerrow's 'Introduction' to Nashe, and Fuller's *History of the Worthies of England.*[148]

During the first week of 1950 Larry and Eve left a snow-bound Belgrade to drive nearly due west through Brod and Zagreb to Trieste for a spell of sitting at café tables, gazing at smiling faces, and shopping in stores with goods to sell. Trieste struck Larry as having a 'curious sedateness', despite its partly Italian population; but he set that down to the sizeable Croatian and Slovenian minorities. 'The character of these Middle Europeans is dull, self-pitying and Slav – like the Poles; heavy as gunmetal,' he told Henry.[149] The contrast with Belgrade provoked another diatribe against Communism: the corruptness of the officials who live well while the populace starves and goes without coal, the scramble for foreign exchange to buy equipment from the West, the pervasive police system. The people were 'like moles – frightened to death'.[150] Accepting as a necessary evil the McCarthyite anti-Communist witch hunts then going on in America, he was 'grateful' to the United States for 'taking it seriously'.[151] In reply, Henry ventured a prediction: 'Communism will be knocked out not by an *opposing* ideology but by force of circumstance. Our "inventions" will upset the present order – of permanent conflict.'[152] Forty years later his prophecy would prove reasonably accurate. Larry was not then convinced, and applauded as the Americans 'bounded into Korea'. 'My heart leaps when I see that the USA has really tumbled to Communism', he wrote, declaiming that 'while our milk and water liberal cryptos are havering . . . the god-damned old Yankees have woken up with a start to what this really means . . . But you will disapprove.'[153]

Larry was reading J. W. Dunne on the nature of time and corresponding with Theodore in March about flying saucers and the Rhine experiments in paranormal cognition. It provided some escape from the Yugoslavian present, which he and Eve continued to see at first hand, 'travelling around this god-visited/or rather Lucifer-visited country drinking in the ugliness and the apathy'. He worried about what would happen if such a 'gang of fanatical ruffians' were to take over England.[154] Correcting the proofs of *Sappho* provided another escape. He was pleased with the play and sent a copy of the proofs to Henry, telling him it was an 'essay'.[155] Meanwhile, Gerry was happily off on another expedition, Xan Fielding was inviting contributions on travel for a newspaper, and some friends on Corfu had started up a journal called *Prospero* – Larry was pleased to take it as a compliment. Although most of the news was good, a distressing letter came from George Wilkinson, who had just been diagnosed as having tuberculosis.

In June 1950 Larry and Eve sought relief from the heavy atmosphere of Belgrade with a holiday on Ischia, island of pumice and good food and quiet, exquisite beaches, where they were guests of Larry's old friends of his Corfu days, Constant Zarian and his painter wife. Their spirits rose as the train clacked and squealed into Trieste and Immigration stamped their passports with the now-familiar 'FTT BR/US ZONE/Docks/Rail'. Larry had been planning the trip all year, and back in February, Zarian had written describing a white beach with a nearby mineral hot spring dating back to Roman times, vineyards terraced down to the sea, 'Pizzi Napoletani at Maria's', and a hospitable landlord who would demand no rent but would ply Larry with wine 'marvellous and icy cold' from his own 'mammoth' barrels.[156]

Larry and Eve spent a rollicking time with Zarian: much wild talk, their host's characteristically outlandish schemes, overeating and, yes, plenty of wine. Ischia, rich in vines, olives and fruit, was the perfect place for such a reunion. The vintages were excellent, the figs and apricots were in season, and Larry felt no obligation to work. He poured all this into a two-page letter in iambics to Anne Ridler:

> Together we have tasted every wine,
> Most of the girls (I mean the Muses Nine)
> And some small favours accident affords
> To such poor chaps as we – as deal in words.

Were Eve not with him, Larry boasted, he would have had many offers of marriage, 'Despite advancing years and stoop and paunch'. Zarian, a vigorous sixty-three, 'scales a mountain like a wild chamois', albeit a very large one:

> The Master with his silver flying hair
> Cooks like a saint and eats like a Corsair,
> In octopus and scampi and red mullet,
> In hen and hare and cuttlefish and pullet
> We've eaten round through past and present tense
> Right through the heart of time's circumference.

A month of this, Larry lamented, and he resembled

> Old Mercator's Projection
> That used to hang upon the schoolroom wall
> And puzzle us when we were very small.

After the cultural deprivation he felt in Yugoslavia, Larry even revelled in the throngs of artistic types. 'Capri is finished,' Larry announced somewhat prematurely; Ischia had become 'The Spot' for writers as well as for

> Poets and painters too from all the nations,
> And some of curious sexual persuasions.

Auden was living on the island and Larry once more paid tribute to him as 'the great peer/ Of all us little moderns'. 'We've met the great man more than once or twice,' Larry reported.[157] They even had dinner with him.[158] 'Eve is indifferent,' Larry continued in his verse letter to Anne; 'I thought him nice.'[159] Auden wrote to Larry in the same terms – 'It was nice to meet you.'[160] Neither man had struck sparks on the other. Larry was more excited at encountering the author of *South Wind*:

> Jogging to Panza yesterday who should I see
> A man I'm sure you reverence as much as me,
> Old Norman Douglas, worn as if by sea
> Like some old whorled and rubbed-out ocean shell
> Still holding shape and life and living well.

Returning to Belgrade, Larry sighed, would be hell.[161]

'Just got back to this hellhole from Ischia,' wrote Larry to Henry, confirming his prediction.[162] Now he was complaining about 'heat and work both of which I hate when I'm away from the sea'.[163] Larry tried to combat the heat by bathing, with a party that included the lovely Mariana Petrovich and another girl, in the Sava near where it joins the Danube at Belgrade. He brushed off any hint of a romantic attachment: the young women 'don't figure – they're old friends', he would recall.[164]

Larry had brought back from Ischia a tangible accomplishment in the form of *Deus Loci*, a poem of ten stanzas that he had commissioned to be handset and printed by Di Maio Vito on the island. 'Cities, Plains and People' might be the story of Larry's development, his odyssey; *Deus Loci* is his tribute to Spirit of Place, that mystical communion with ambience that stood in relation to Larry as Christianity to a Crusader:

> All our religions founder, you
> remain, small sunburnt *deus loci*
> safe in your natal shrine,
> landscape of the precocious southern heart.

The 'panic fellowship' of the little god 'is everywhere', in 'love's first great illness known', 'in the exile of objects lost'. The poem is Larry's hymn of gratitude for his Mediterranean return:

> So today, after many years, we meet
> at this high window overlooking
> the best of Italy, smiling under rain.

Dreary Yugoslavia seemed determined to wrest from Larry and Eve the memory of their month with the Zarians. In late July they were in their car again for a 'harrowing' ten-day official swing through Zagreb, Split, Dubrovnik and Sarajevo. He had to admit that there was 'lovely landscape' in the mountains of Montenegro and Bosnia and along the Dalmatian coast, but his impression was that 'everyone is starving more or less in this ideal Socialist state'. To add to their distress, 'the epoch of Balkan Belly' – the local equivalent of 'gippy tummy' – had come around again, and Larry begged Theodore to send a 'tidy packet' of Entero-Vioform medication. Larry was finding it impossible to write, given the importunities of an unending succession of boring, carbon-copy reporters: 'I feel like a very old bone unearthed each time for another gnaw by incoming journalists.'[165]

Given his constant complaints about Life as a Diplomat, why did Larry stick it? Henry kept telling him to cut loose: after all, *he* had been his own man, a professional writer, since leaving Western Union in 1924. To be sure, he was often on the edge of eviction, and sometimes over it; and he was sometimes really hungry. Larry was moulded from different clay: he had always feared an uncertain tomorrow, and he certainly did not like the thought of going hungry – *that* he had never really tried. 'I haven't adopted this profession for love,' he explained patiently to Henry, 'but because it's a useful means of getting into position to buy a house in a country I like.' Setting his friend straight, Larry wrote with perhaps unconscious under-statement, 'I'm unlike you: I plan things as carefully as possible, trying to curb my Irish impulses.'[166] If he could only secure a posting to Greece or Italy! After the month with Zarian, Larry looked for someone on Ischia willing to take pounds sterling for a house: then he would pay with the small capital he had in England, cut loose from the Foreign Office, and become once again a full-time writer.

There was another side to Larry's experiences in Belgrade that did not come out in his complaints to many of his old friends. For one thing, he had become genuinely fond of Ambassador Sir Charles Peake, 'one of nature's more delightful weathercocks, holding the ring and being amiable'. 'I did love him', Larry admitted, 'but he was so absent minded I nearly went mad working for him.'[167] Lady Peake, gentle and unassuming, he adored as well. A few years later he would caricature Sir Charles affectionately as Sir Claude Polk-Mowbray, the British ambassador in his series of humour sketches. Larry also threw himself into the amateur theatricals put on around Christmas by the embassy staff. He appeared as one of the dwarfs in a comic skit based on *Snow White and the Seven Dwarfs* one year, and he wrote *Little Red Riding Hood*, a twenty-four-page verse 'Pantomime', as he called it, for an Embassy performance. A satire on Yugoslav Commun-ism, the farce probably did not endear Larry to his left-leaning colleagues.[168]

In his serious drama *Sappho*, Larry considered matters of a more philosophical nature, the relationship of the ideal to reality. He wrote to Anne Ridler:

What I am after is the Spanish Tragedy or Tamburlaine. It will have to be as coarse as that until we get our hands in and until the bastards surrender the film to us as our proper medium. But even then we have to face the psychological problem of individual responsibility; whereas to really purge and satisfy[,] drama should not be a slice of life, or a morality done in terms of psychology, but a piece of mechanism reflecting the unearthly diversity of the real, which points, *at each and every step*, at the repose and structure of the ideal; and this done in terms of action, not tableaux and tricks and monologues.[169]

Sappho gained an important fan in Margaret Rawlings, who wrote to Larry in August requesting a one-year option to produce the play. Next month she wrote him to say that 'Your play is not formless. . . . it is perfect'.[170] Later Henry weighed in enthusiastically to praise the 'symbolism' of Sappho, Phaon and his brother Pittakos, the Greek general, the revelation of how the poet could affect the warrior.[171] Larry was delighted: 'Our literature is so full of either-or's; peace or war; mystic or warrior. It would be easy to load the scales *for* contemplation against action, for peace against war.' But he had become distrustful of 'generalised judgements', and would not become too excited until someone actually staged the play.[172]

In fact Larry was still 'playing around' with another drama, but given the 'mess' that Europe was in, he was taking his job as Press Officer seriously, consoling himself 'with all the experience of public affairs and behaviors' that was coming his way. 'The writing of the future will be Stendhalian and not Proustian,' he told Henry. 'I think you've exhausted the whole *subjective* cycle of contemporary literature.' For drama the pattern would be *Oedipus Rex*; for prose, Suetonius.[173]

Towards the end of the summer Larry and Eve were invited for dinner at the home of Toder Obradović, an Agence France Presse journalist. The police-state atmosphere was easing somewhat, but this was the first time Larry and Eve had been in a Serbian home. The conversation turned to books, and Mrs Obradović handed him one of Henry Miller's books, inscribed to her by the author when she had stayed at the Villa Seurat on her way through Paris in 1937. At once Larry realized that he was speaking to the Nadežda – Nadja – Djukić whom Henry had asked him to locate. She also brought out copies of *The Booster* and Anaïs's *House of Incest*. Larry pronounced Nadja and her husband 'Delightful people' – almost his first good word about any Serbians.[174] Nadja in turn found Larry 'very social and friendly': he entertained foreign diplomats and Yugoslav nationals alike in his home.[175] Nadja taught English, so like her husband she had a professional reason for speaking to foreigners, and to see Larry they were willing to risk official displeasure. Since he made no secret of his extreme anti-Communism, there was an extra element of risk in knowing him.

371

At the end of November 1950, Larry asked Alan to send a few items – including three fountain pens and three diaries for his staff, a couple of shaving brushes, and a dozen Christmas cards – and also requested a list of Elizabethan reprints from Hardings across from the British Museum. Larry remarked blandly in a postscript to Alan, 'eve proposes to have a child she says.'[176] Later he requested four titles on classical dance for a Yugoslav ballerina who had become his friend.[177] This marked the advent of Smilja in his life. She was considered a great beauty: dark-haired, with luminous black eyes. Soon gossips were referring to her as 'Larry's mistress', and Smilja later claimed to recognize herself in Larry's Justine. Then she broke with Larry and married the diplomat Sir Ronald Preston. 'Oh Ronnie, he pinched Smilja from me!' Larry said casually a few years later.[178] With just a touch of wickedness, Larry would reflect her situation through the peripheral Grishkin, Mountolive's Balkan dancer, in the future *Alexandria Quartet*.[179]

'We are sinking slowly into the frozen mush of a Central European winter,' Larry wrote to Theodore.[180] Eve was struggling through the early stages of pregnancy, and Larry drove her to Zagreb where he left her for a few days of rest in air purer than that of Belgrade. Larry had a friend in Zagreb, Joe Torbarina, with whom he sometimes sat up half the night talking. A more tangible danger to health than the vapours of Belgrade were the Soviet tanks massed on the border. 'We're in a sort of trap here, a killing-box!' Larry complained to Henry.[181] He and his colleagues were living 'in the lap of a positively pre-war luxury', but round about were 'the dirty streets, the shaggy, forlorn crowds', the hungry Yugoslavs. Larry found his world just as dreary, although in a different way: 'To change into a dinner jacket and motor to a reception where the combed and scented ladies of the Diplomatic corpse (sic) await, is to experience the pleasures of Babylon (the surfeit of which is hellish).'[182] A few years later Larry wrote his hatred of embassy receptions into *Justine*: 'They are simply bottom-sniffings raised to the rank of formal ceremonies.'[183] At one of these Larry found himself being presented to Marshal Tito, who was then known to be studying English. 'Goot evenink,' said Tito carefully. Without a flicker Larry replied, 'Goot evenink, your Excellency.'[184]

In January 1951 Larry gave three lectures on modern literature as part of a seminar on English studies at Belgrade University. On a more informal level, he often gathered groups of students and teachers of English together for discussions. At one of these, he asked Nadja Obradović, 'How would you start writing and what would you write about? Tell me!'[185] His question was not entirely Socratic: Larry knew that he should begin another major effort, but he felt as blocked as he had been in Argentina.

Larry recognized a certain irrationality in his gloom: 'Don't know why it is that we dislike most of the countries we get sent to – never happy unless we are in Greece.' His discontent was increased by his seemingly eternal need to revise *Reflections on a Marine Venus*, which the Faber editors had told him lacked shape and pace and must be cut by almost half. His staunch friend Anne Ridler, still Eliot's assistant at Faber, would eventually come to his rescue, but in the meanwhile he swore and sweated over it. 'I suffer from terrible nausea about my work', Larry would confess in an interview several years later, 'purely physical nausea' – a sensation that hit him whenever he was forced to reread his work and see its imperfections dancing before his eyes.[186] He hated revising, yet he had not the heart to rewrite *Reflections* from the beginning, as he might otherwise have preferred to do. The Rhodes idyll formed such a stark contrast with the grey life of Belgrade; the 'sodden Serbs' were not the volatile Greeks; the gay, cheerful Eve of the Villa Cleobolus was not the anxious expectant mother who was now his consort. As a distraction, Larry worked on the play that would eventually become *Acte*, but worried that 'it will just bog down like the Rhodes book.'[187]

Another distraction for Larry was the enormous car he had found hiding in a garage in Trieste and bought 'for a song'. It was a silver-grey Horch said to have belonged to Hermann Goering; the in-line eight-cylinder engine could have powered a locomotive, and it used so much petrol that only someone with access to subsidized diplomatic fuel could afford to run it. The car even had two horns, one bass and the other tenor. Nearly forty years later a retired car mechanic who had been assigned to the British Embassy in Belgrade would remember the car but not Lawrence Durrell.[188] 'We call it Herman and are planning one mad summer of plutocracy in it,' Larry wrote to Anne Ridler. 'As a matter of fact you have often seen Herman in the newsreels – do you remember the entry into Prague etc. with one of the big shots standing up in the front and giving the boys the salute. That's how I go to the office now. Everyone is speechless with rage, and few will speak to me these days.' The Belgrade police, however, were 'deeply respectful'.[189] Larry liked to claim that even Tito was jealous of his Horch, which was bullet-proof while the Marshal's limousine was not.

Eve seemed to be adjusting to the idea of her pregnancy. She had decided that their child should be born in Britain, where the medical attention promised to be far better than any available in Yugoslavia. Eve went alone to England in the early spring of 1951 to look for a suitable house to rent. She and Louisa Durrell visited Mary Mollo in London. By this time Eve's state, Mary thought, approached 'serene beatitude', and she seemed confident that having a baby would be the easiest thing imaginable. Louisa tried to warn her that childbirth *was* a bit painful, but added that she was sure Eve would manage it well. Soon Eve settled into a two-storey stuccoed house at 84 Old Road, Oxford, a few streets from the Nuffield Hospital in the suburb of Headington. Mary Mollo, herself in the early months of her first pregnancy, spent a few days with Eve before Larry's arrival. Eve and Larry were so convinced that she would have a son that they had discussed only boys' names. Eve in her 'exaltation' waxed 'quasi-mystical, expect[ing] a sort of messiah!'[190]

Larry arrived on 22 May from Belgrade, and on the 30th, after protracted labour, the baby appeared. It was a girl, with beautiful olive skin and a full head of black hair. Eve alarmed Mary with descriptions of her sufferings: 'Such terrible pains, Mary, you can't imagine.' Larry, Eve and Mary spent an evening discussing and rejecting name after name. Mary, who had been reading Larry's play, suggested Sappho as a joke. Larry and Eve were delighted and brushed aside Mary's objection that Sappho would be a difficult name for a girl to carry, especially in English school life, where any hint of lesbianism could mean social torture. 'Nonsense', said Larry, 'it's perfect, it's a beautiful name.' In desperation, Mary suggested Jane as a prosaic second name. 'Fine', agreed Larry, 'Jane is a nice, plain name.'[191] Mary became Sappho Jane's godmother. Henry Miller liked the Greek name too, writing to Larry, 'I'm delighted the girl is called Sappho, and not named after some new British man-of-war!'[192]

Larry seemed now as always to be short of money, but Mary and her husband Henry Hadkinson had recently returned to Europe after a failed venture in Canada, and Larry unhesitatingly loaned them £100. Although Larry never mentioned the debt, Mary paid him back over the years.[193]

Larry could only be away from his job for three weeks, so he set off for Belgrade, planning to return later for Eve and Sappho. 'I leave on Monday morn – with a sinking heart as I really dread those dreary arrogant ignorant Yugoslavs and my own colleagues are for the most part snakes,' he confided to Alan Thomas. Despite a 'terrific headcold', before departing on 11 June Larry played a slow blues rhythm on the piano and sang his latest composition in eight verses, 'Iron Curtain Blues'. He cut a unique 78 rpm disc and gave it to Alan. Buried in the humour was a fairly accurate rendition of Larry's feelings about life in Belgrade:

374

> Posted away, behind the Curtain,
> Life was a gay one,
> Now it's uncertain –
> I've got those Iron Curtain Blues.

The city was a wet billet, with plenty of cheap liquor from the Commissary accompanying the heavy rainfall in the low-lying river valley.

> Life diplomatic
> Once was ecstatic,
> As sweet as a serenade;
> Now though you keep drinking
> Your spirits keep sinking –
> They're sinking like New Belgrade.

Depression was no joke:

> The Naval Attaché's
> Hung himself on the stairs,
> We brush past his body now,
> Nobody cares –
> We've got those Iron Curtain Blues.
>
> [. . .]
>
> With allowances falling,
> Life's so appalling,
> We hardly know where to turn;
> There's a suicide daily –
> We do it quite gaily,
> The ashes look nice in an urn.[194]

During his brief visit Larry had seen Anne and Vivian Ridler and had met an eccentric philosopher to place in his pantheon above Graham Howe and Georg Groddeck. He was Francis John Mott, an American settled in Oxford and the self-proclaimed prophet of a strange set of theories intended to explain man's nature: it was largely a matter of fluid flow, said Mott, and in his *Universal Design of the Oedipus Complex* (1950) a schematic diagram showed the circulation of the body's juices through all of mankind's orifices and tubes, all rendered in colour-coded sketches of a cherubic child drawn in cut-away and marked like a traffic map with curving arrows. After reading Mott's *Universal Design of Birth* and

Oedipus Complex books, Larry had raved to Henry Miller that Mott had leapt beyond Freud, that he 'knocks Rank, Jung and Groddeck cold by the breadth of his vision and the simple outlines of his new psychology which he calls "biosynthesis"'.[195] Larry had been eager to meet the 'great man'.

Larry returned to Oxford on 9 August. For a time Larry, Eve and baby Sappho stayed with the Motts, Larry excitedly discussing his new guru's theories. The slender, wiry Mott resembled Henry – 'the same puckish sense of humour' – and Larry found him 'one of the most remarkable men I've come across'.[196] Larry was particularly taken with Mott's lucubrations on the Oedipus Complex, which ranged widely to include the relationship of the individual consciousness to the cosmos, as represented by a 'configurational sympathy' with 'the human organism in its various stages and organs'. Mott had a lot to say about the erotogenic nature of the non-sexual organs, about 'male nuclear sperm', the 'female peripheral egg', and dream interpretation.[197] Among his other beliefs, Mott held that the lingering vestiges of the birth shock could be reduced by re-enacting the experience of birth. This he demonstrated for Larry and Eve by pouring his two young and unruly children head-first out of a tube fashioned from a rolled-up carpet. Both Larry and Eve found this fascinating psychodrama, but Mary Mollo distrusted a psychologist who could not control his own offspring. John Mott became Sappho's godfather.

Where Mott was concerned, Henry was not having any: 'No, that Mott book is not for me, sorry.' Henry found Mott too pessimistic – 'it's time to stop worrying about the destruction of life' – and countered with Gutkind's *Choose Life*. He tried to discourage Larry from attempting to organize an 'Ark' survivalist group along the lines that Mott had proposed, but concluded mildly enough, 'I believe all you say about the man and wish him well.'[198] Lepska had just walked out on Henry, leaving him to manage, temporarily, the two rambunctious children, and he was too exhausted for another Cause. Then within a month a jubilant Henry announced that he had found his own Eve: Eve McClure, who would become the fourth Mrs Miller, had moved in. But as far as Henry was concerned, it was too late for him to embrace Mott.

Larry had a meeting in London with George Seferis, then Counsellor at the Greek Embassy, and he saw Anne and Fred Perlès. Larry, who had not met Anne before, pronounced her 'lovely and very charming'.[199] Eliot took him to lunch at the Garrick. With his *Key to Modern Poetry* nearly ready for the press, Larry seems to have tried to pin Eliot down on the seriousness with which he intended the Buddhist references in *The Waste Land* and elsewhere. 'You see', Larry recalled, 'I was aware that this Catholicism thing was really so shallow in his case, and all the epigraphs to his poems are Epictetus, Greeks, Buddhists of one sort or another. It seemed silly to be in the same posture as Graham Greene because he wasn't, intellectually and psychically. . . . I asked him point-blank once – when you are young you *are* tactless.' Larry mentioned Eliot's references to Heraclitus and other ancient Greeks, to the Pythagoreans and Buddhists. 'Oh yes,' Eliot answered with a smile, 'I do it just to get near to people.' Larry cut in quickly, 'May I publish that?' 'Certainly not!' he was told,[200] but Larry pressed on, as usual joining Eliot's Anglicanism to Rome: 'How can an intelligent man be a Christian, much less a Catholic?' With all of Eliot's non-Christian references, Larry concluded, 'I can't think how they let you into the Church.' Eliot assumed his most sober expression: 'Perhaps they haven't found out about me yet?'[201]

On 1 September Larry, Eve and Sappho, 'after a boiling trip on the Simplon Orient', were back in Belgrade.[202] A few weeks later, Larry was 'trying in the midst of a 1000 distractions to finish the Rhodes book', and he wrote to Theodore asking him to go to the British Museum and copy out passages by the fifteenth-century historian John Kay on an early siege of Rhodes.[203] Larry's goal was to finish *Reflections on a Marine Venus* by the end of the year.[204]

Soon after Sappho's birth, Larry finally found himself making real progress on a book inspired by his life with her mother: 'All of a sudden after two years' groaning and straining the dam has burst and I find myself working like a beaver on the Rhodes book.'[205] He asked Alan Thomas to rummage among the books being stored for him and to forward his copies of Torr and Bileotti on Rhodes, along with a manilla envelope of miscellaneous notes. Larry declared *Reflections on a Marine Venus* finished before Christmas 1951: at least, he sent off a swollen typescript, resolved to leave any editorial cutting to Anne Ridler. He had another pressing task: Margaret Rawlings had given a successful public reading of *Sappho* and Larry had promised to 'tailor the text to her character' so that she could arrange a full-scale production. This he would try to complete over the winter. He sent an urgent request to Alan for several titles, including two books by Arthur Weigall, *Sappho* and *Nero*, so that he could brush up on the background.

With the resurgent prospect of seeing *Sappho* on stage and his own reviving writing plans, Larry decided that his central dramatic problem was 'to reconcile naturalistic narrative with verse on the one hand, and verse with prose dialogue on the other'. The solution, he decided, lay in the choice of medium. To defeat 'sophisticated inattention' Larry proposed to turn to film methods:

The camera can wander throughout the longest soliloquy and provide the sort of musical notation you hint at through the power of visual images. While one man speaks you can study the *effect* of his speech on another's face. The prose passages which jerk continuity apart and make sudden transitions necessary never disrupt the film because motion is in the nature of the eye, and you can get a smooth transition by a track shot or a mixing shot into the next bit of your story.

Larry pleaded with Eliot to give the film scenario his artistic imprimatur by publishing his next play initially as a film script. Later Larry would claim to be using the film technique of 'jump-cutting' to achieve rapid transitions in his fiction, and he thought that he had *unconsciously* exploited the ploy in *Sappho*. He was really asking for something Elizabethan, 'an adult [medium] where drama poetry and spectacle can all co-exist without stealing from each other'.[206]

Despite his continued grumbling about Yugoslavia, Larry found happiness creeping up on him. He was delighted with his new daughter, whom he found 'charming and very dark like Eve'.[207] She also promised to be 'good-tempered and pretty'. To Theodore he said, 'The baby is frightfully amusing and a definite addition to one's life despite the piddle and bother, and at present shows signs of turning out rather a beauty.'[208] Larry wrote her a 'Cradle Song', telling her to 'go/ mimic your mother's lovely face'.[209] A few months later he was boasting that 'We are having enormous fun with Sappho-Jane, who is a great comedienne and most intelligent.'[210]

Larry sent Alan and Ella Thomas his usual Christmas shopping list of pens, lipsticks, safety razors and 'a couple of Oxford dictionaries' for his local staff. However, the season was different this year with tiny Sappho in the house. Larry asked Ella to buy 'trimmings plus candles' for the tree, and a few small dolls and toys to hang on it for the neighbourhood children. Larry cautioned against spending too much: 'I suppose about four or five pounds would meet the case. Heavens how broke we are with the new cuts!' Larry and Eve planned a lunch party for Christmas day.[211]

The salary reductions were in fact draconian. Larry's pay plus residence allowances and other perks had climbed to a very substantial £5000 per annum; under the new dispensation they had plummeted to a mere £1500. This would still have been a satisfactory wage in Britain, but in Belgrade anything approaching a respectable standard of living cost the sky. 'It's going to become almost impossible to live here, let alone save!' Larry complained to Alan. 'Or *spend*,' he added. 'So you'll be losing one of y^r best patrons alas!'[212] Larry's major reason for remaining in the employ of the Crown had vanished.

He might have been willing to stay on with the Foreign Office if he had been able to procure a posting that he really wanted, but to his intense chagrin he again missed out on Greece, 'chiefly through not being successful enough as a bum-sucker'.[213] The rumour was that he had made an enemy of Rex Leeper, the British ambassador in Athens. Some of his friends among the Embassy personnel dismissed this as the determining factor: Larry was simply not the sort to make a career diplomat, he would never have been seriously considered, his life was too irregular.[214] They meant this as a compliment.

In 1952 Larry's discontent with life as a servant of the Foreign Office came to a head: he must cut himself loose or perish – at least artistically. He selected a pristine printer's dummy for his drafts and wrote on the front endpaper:

Epitaph for L G Durrell

Hated Cant

Revered Cunt

Either criterion, he thought, disqualified him from continuing in the diplomatic service. On the facing page he wrote 'chute totale'. In the first few pages Larry drafted parts of the poems that would be published as 'Niki', 'Letters in Darkness' and 'Lesbos', but by the fifth page he had begun to intersperse prose passages annotated 'Justine' and 'Balthazar': he had finally begun *The Alexandria Quartet*. Under a heading '*Alexandria – The ground plan*', he sketched out a version of the story in which Justine commits suicide. Pages along in the same notebook, he outlined two scenes of a projected play to be entitled 'Diplomacy and a Woman of Thirty': a diplomat telephones his lover, a citizen of an enemy country; he is packing to leave, and she wants to escape with him . . . . Larry did not carry the story line beyond a page.[215] But escape was certainly on his mind.

The big book that he had been planning to write since at least 1938 refused to give birth to itself, and he found his duties too distracting and too time-consuming to permit him to work on anything requiring uninterrupted concentration. Larry decided to resign from the Foreign Office. First, however, he wanted one more holiday in Greece while he still had his press officer's salary. He and Eve planned some glorious weeks camping on the beach in Macedonia. They drove in a day from Belgrade to the Greek border, and then prospected the sea coast between Salonika and Volo for a small white village that they could use as a base. For a month, until 8 July, they camped 'on the wild savage peninsula of Chalcidice' opposite the island of Thasos. They had two tents, a small one especially for Sappho-Jane, who seemed delighted with the novelty. An old woman cooked for them and helped care for the baby. It was camping, but in 'lovely' style, with no housekeeping cares and complete comfort. They were offered an island called Olympiada for £60.[216] Why did Larry not buy it? He said that he was broke, but he probably found it too isolated for Eve and Sappho.

Larry was back in Belgrade for only a few weeks before he slipped off to northern Yugoslavia for another spell of camping, this time beside the lake of Bled, the only part of Yugoslavia that he said he might be tempted to visit again. It was not exactly a holiday: the Yugoslav government was moving there for the month of August. Then on 23 September he drove to Trieste for a day of errands. 'By the way I'm quitting the service in December', he wrote early in October to Henry, sounding more offhand about his plans than his state of mind warranted. 'We are setting off to Cyprus I think.' It would be a gamble, he admitted: 'No money. No prospects. A tent. A small car. I feel twenty years younger.'[217] Larry said much the same thing to Alan, telling him that they would 'starve splendidly', and asking for Stendhal's *Letters* 'as a wind-up to my three year buying spree'. His departure may not have been entirely voluntary: 'Looks as if I am getting the push for a year or two from the F.O.', he wrote to Alan. 'Gorgeous relief!'[218] To be sure, he was not entirely penniless: he had saved enough out of his salary to be able to buy a small house on Cyprus – so he hoped – and to live for a year without taking a job that would separate him from his writing desk.

His old money worries would not let him rest, however, and he asked Alan Thomas about opening a bookshop on Cyprus. An unnamed friend there, very likely George Wilkinson, had told him that the island boasted nothing beyond a couple of W. H. Smith-type shops, and Larry thought that by judicious buying of out-of-print Penguins, second-hand Collins Clear-Type classics, guide books, language and technical manuals, and school texts he could make a fair living. It would be a Middle Eastern bookshop 'for people marooned there'.[219] Cyprus was becoming the Army headquarters for the Middle East, and consequently was flooded with soldiers – the sort he had known in India, in Egypt – and he saw himself with a steady clientele. Larry was proposing for himself the kind of life that Alan had tried to tempt him with back in 1935. This time Alan tried hard to discourage him. Larry answered Alan's objections in spirited fashion, but a dramatic crisis burst forth to deflect his energies.

During the late autumn, Eve began to show symptoms of acute nervous tension, with periods of euphoria alternating unpredictably with bouts of the deepest depression. 'In other words, I had gone haywire,' as Eve herself summed up the various diagnoses.[220] Her black depression was characterized by a silent, catatonic state. Larry could get no response from her when she was like that, and he was more frightened by her silence than he would have been by a wild rage. Perhaps it was the upheaval of preparing to leave Belgrade and the diplomatic life, or perhaps it was a reaction to the double demands of being mother to Sappho as well as wife to Larry – neither occupation an easy task. Eve herself thought it was due to the let-down she felt on weaning Sappho, whom she had been breast-feeding for eighteen months. There were hints that some trouble already existed between Larry and Eve: Larry wrote a guarded account of his marriage in a partial draft, dated 8 November 1952, of a poem entitled in a later manuscript version 'The Hanover Letters', although it would be published as 'Letters in Darkness'. In retrospect, the poem is an analysis of his marriage and of Eve's breakdown:

> So marriage can, by ripeness bound,
> From over-ripeness qualify
> To sick detachment in the mind – .[221]

Fearing for her life as well as for her sanity, Larry rushed Eve to the British Military Hospital in Hanover, where she was admitted into the Psychiatric Division on 4 December. The psychiatrists were pessimistic about her chances of recovery, let alone of an easy cure. For several days they too feared that she might die. Soon, however, the immediate danger receded. When the doctors assured Larry that his presence would not help Eve, he returned to Yugoslavia. The staff at the hospital diagnosed her condition as being an 'ACUTE SCHIZOPHRENIC THOUGH[T] DISORDER WITH DEPRESSIVE FEATURES'.[222] Again, Larry must have been thinking of Eve's condition when he wrote, in a later section of 'Letters in Darkness',

Dear [. . .]
I watch the faultless measure of your dying
Into an unknown misused animal
Held by the ropes and drugs; the puny
Recipe society proposes when machines
Break down. Love was our machine.[223]

Larry was feeling a bit fragile himself: at forty, he felt old and unfulfilled. After dissecting his marriage, in the same poem he turned to the first person plural to analyse his condition:

So at last we come to the writer's
Middle years, the hardest yet to bear.

Then he stepped back further, rhetorically:

You cannot guess how he has been waiting
For these years, these ripe and terrible
Years of the *agon* . . . .[224]

No less than Eve, Larry felt that he was going through a dangerous crisis. His premonition turned out to be correct: with Eve at Hanover, Larry 'completely wrecked' his beautiful Horch, although he suffered only a few minor cuts himself.

Eve was in Hanover a week before Larry admitted her condition to anyone apart from those friends and associates in Belgrade who had to know. Finally he wrote to Alan on 10 December: 'All our plans awry again.' He was hoping for 'a brief cure and rest' that would have Eve back to him in early January. Larry stressed the need for confidentiality: 'Don't mention this to my family or I'll be inundated with letters and I'm too busy to think.' He had lost his cheque book, but he asked Alan to buy on his account some presents for Sappho. 'She loves dolls,' he said; a bright book 'preferably about dogs' would also be welcome. There were no other commissions. 'Going to be a dismal Xmas without Eve,' Larry added in closing.[225]

Before Christmas Larry received encouraging news from Hanover and reported somewhat prematurely to Alan that 'Eve is O.K. again.' He asked Alan to send her a copy of Kazantzakis's *Zorba the Greek* at the hospital.[226] Larry now thought that the three of them would be able to go to Cyprus in late January as planned. He got through Christmas all right with Sappho and a few friends, and in the last days of the year he began to pack for the move. On Cyprus he would be staying at the Villa Christina, a small guest house that George Wilkinson and his present wife had bought in Kyrenia. The parallel with Larry's earlier move to Corfu struck him: George had preceded him on Cyprus as well. George had divorced Pam in 1947 and the next year had married Iris Flavia Antoinette Mantura, a Middle Eastern beauty who had been Nancy Durrell's superior at the Near East Arab Broadcasting Station in Jaffa and Jerusalem. The chain of coincidences did not end there, for Larry had known Iris before she met George, when Larry had visited Jerusalem during and just after the war. They had occasionally gone out to lunch together. Larry had written to George, who promised to have his brother-in-law Guy Mantura meet Larry's ship.

Quitting the Foreign Office had filled Larry with fear and euphoria in equal portions: 'Facing poverty! Destitution!' he cried to Theodore, all the while packing for his move, taking care of Sappho, and trying to restart his Alexandria book. He asked Theodore to write up some notes that would illustrate the prowess of a really marvellous chess player, and in the next sentence rejoiced that 'Gerry and I will be cheek by jowl in Faber's Spring list – two Durrells where only one grew before.'[227] *The Overloaded Ark* and *Reflections on a Marine Venus* would appear together – and Gerry's would be a best-seller.

Eve had confounded the early gloomy prognosis, but she was in no hurry to return to Larry. She had long shared Larry's interest in psychology, and even during her breakdown she had remained fully lucid, so she maintained, and could analyse her own symptoms. While some psychiatrists might find this annoying in a patient, the young staff at Hanover, recognizing Eve as an intelligent ally in her own cure, listened to her and patiently explained their theories. She herself decided that 'manic depressive' described her illness better than the label given it at the hospital. She also accepted the hospital gladly: 'I was constantly aware of *all* parts of the maelstrom which was terrifying me', she recalled, 'with the result that I only felt safe in the hospital.' Having such confidence in the doctors and nurses at Hanover, she was able to focus her energies on her recovery: in her own words, to 'plunge' down to her inner 'rock bottom' before coming up 'for air' in the everyday world.[228]

By 5 January 1953 Lieutenant-Colonel Pozner, the psychiatrist who had taken over her case, was writing to Larry that she had made a 'gratifying recovery'. 'As you have already discovered', Pozner said, her 'delusions and ideation' were 'bound up with her early auto-erotic guilt feelings, her marked ambivalence towards her parents, and her craving for love-objects.'

He cautioned Larry that she was 'still vulnerable to stress, liable to become over-emotional, and is at the present moment concerned with the future relationships between her, your daughter, and yourself.'[229] On 13 January, Eve was given leave from the hospital and the next day, escorted by a nurse, she was reunited with Larry and Sappho in Trieste.

Larry's delight at seeing his beautiful Eve apparently in full command of herself was quickly tempered by the proposition she made. Eve asked for a year away from him in which to resolve her conflicts: the hospital experience had churned up her innermost self and she needed desperately to rediscover her own character. 'And this not just for my benefit, but for the welfare of the family as a unit, not least for Saph's!' she argued.[230] She wanted to take Sappho with her to England, but this Larry would not agree to. He proposed instead that Sappho accompany him to Cyprus, where he would establish a home for the three of them. If she must, Eve could have her year alone in England. Eve decided to return to Hanover as a voluntary patient in the Psychiatric Division, a status that would permit her to refuse medication. An order for her discharge was put through in January by Captain D. Sherret of the Royal Army Medical Corps, and eventually, by 9 April, she was ready to leave her refuge and was 'repatriated' to the United Kingdom.[231]

Meanwhile, acquiescing to circumstance, Larry resolved to go to Cyprus alone. It was not an easy decision. He had often feared for his own sanity: now, here he was, as he thought, racked by a mad wife, responsible for his young child, heading for a place he had never even visited. Mixed with his sympathy and deep concern was an irrational rage that told him she had taken refuge from him in her disease. He was seared to the core, and it would be years before his wounds would find solace in his art: in the brilliantly unstable Justine of *The Alexandria Quartet*, in the madness-haunted Benedicta of *The Revolt of Aphrodite*.

He and Sappho left Yugoslavia for good on 19 January and a few days later they embarked at Venice for the cruise to Limassol. From the deck of the ship Larry watched 'a Venice wobbling in a thousand water-reflections, cool as a jelly. . . . Cloud and water mixed into each other, dripping with colours, merging, overlapping, liquefying, with steeples and balconies and roofs floating in space, like the fragments of some stained-glass window seen through a dozen veils of rice-paper.' Larry invoked Stendhal and imagined a farewell to Europe as the ship sailed towards the Levant.[232]

CHAPTER 9

Cyprus: Paradise Regained and Lost

In an island of bitter lemons
Where the moon's cool fevers burn
From the dark globes of the fruit,

And the dry grass underfoot
Tortures memory and revises
Habits half a lifetime dead

Better leave the rest unsaid.
                                    'Bitter Lemons'

'I HAVE ESCAPED to this island with a few books and the child – Melissa's child,' Larry was soon to write in the opening page of *Justine*. All that he would have to do to turn this first page of his manuscript into autobiography would be to imagine Eve's name in place of Melissa's; to see his situation as private myth, he had only to imagine himself as Prospero cast adrift with his daughter Miranda. 'The villagers say jokingly that only a sick man would choose such a remote place to rebuild. Well, then, I have come here to heal myself', Larry continued.[1] True, he would be speaking of the sharer of his initials, L. G. Darley, but in a very real sense he, Lawrence G. Durrell, had come to Cyprus to heal himself – of the shock of Eve's crack-up, of the years in dusty Cordova and grey Belgrade, those outposts he saw as hiatuses in his creative career, interruptions that in fact went back to 1939, when he had been forced to give up a life dedicated solely to literature. Darley's progenitor, the poet George Darley, held appropriate resonance for Larry: he was Irish, his lyrics recalled Larry's beloved Elizabethans, and he had advocated a balance between metaphysical speculation and sensuous living. However, Larry would deny that Darley spoke with the author's voice: the similarities in names and situation amounted to 'a private joke with myself, as it were'.[2] With the turn of the new year, Larry adopted a now-or-never attitude. The principal quarry for the events of the future *Quartet* had been Egypt; let Cyprus now be the crucible.

385

On 26 January 1953, towards sunrise, Larry watched the flat, unprepossessing port of Limassol materialize, a jumble of warehouses and docks. He landed from a bumboat, carrying Sappho in his arms as he had carried Penelope at the end of another sea journey twelve years before. He cleared Customs, where the officials answered firmly in English every question he asked in Greek. Then he changed money and was met by Guy Mantura, who drove him to Kyrenia. Larry was happy to see George Wilkinson again, glad to have someone to smooth his passage into life on Cyprus. He stayed at the Wilkinsons' Villa Christina, and George's wife Iris helped care for Sappho.

The stories George had to tell seemed to imply a criticism of Larry's own rather comfortable war. George had spent most of the war disguised as the Greek corsair-skipper of a caïque supplying various SOE operations in the Aegean. With a transmitting antenna concealed in the mast and a belt of gold sovereigns around his waist, George had acted a part that took real courage and required little dramatization. When Force 133 of the SOE had been disbanded at the end of the war, George, knighted by the Greek government and promoted to major by the British, had been recruited by the Secret Intelligence Service, MI6, but had been invalided out by 1949. By next year George and Iris had established the Villa Christina.[3] George could still tremendously arch his left eyebrow and strike an attitude, and he was still determined to write, this time of his war experiences, but his former resilience had vanished. All he seemed to be able to produce was children: four during his Cyprus years, to add to the two he had fathered on Pam. Political hack writing, discouragement, ill health, more drinking than was good for him, a sense of failure – all got in the way of his projected novels. He was often paralysed by his meticulous bent. 'I'm the sort of person who would find it difficult to describe a mountain even if you put me in front of one,' he told his son Endymion. 'Before making up my mind, I would have to walk around it, then see it at different seasons and finally do some library study.'[4] It probably did not help George that Larry, weathered by adversity but if anything more cocky than he had been in the Little Songhurst Cottage and Corfu days, was once more in his orbit.

Only days after his arrival, Larry wrote to Alan Thomas to acknowledge the notebooks Alan had sent on ahead, and to ask that other material from the loft, including Lane's *Modern Egyptians* and a black notebook he had started on Corfu, be forwarded right away.[5] Clearly, Larry was bursting to get on with 'The Book of the Dead'.

Although Larry warned Alan that Eve might 'drift in your direction' and could also need a year of psychoanalysis, he thought there was a good prospect of her full recovery, and with that, her return to him on Cyprus. There seemed a chance for them to carry out their original intention of settling on the island. Still, Larry's mood was rather grim. His planned 'golden year off to work' was fading as the costs of providing for Eve and paying his own expenses on Cyprus were eating into his savings.[6] Eve, in the hospital in Hanover, had meanwhile written confidently to Alan and Ella Thomas that 'I am quite myself again, if a bit on the skinny side, but otherwise not very different.' She told them that she planned to come to England and would see them; she did not mention even the possibility of joining Larry on Cyprus.[7]

Larry remained preoccupied with the problems of finding lodgings and of caring for Sappho. He leased a bungalow on the main street of Kyrenia, on the road out to the hospital, hired a woman to cook, and began to search for a house attractive enough to live in and cheap enough to buy. Taking full advantage of his Greek, Larry sought out a Cypriot acquaintanceship. He made a firm friend of Clito, a quiet man but a sturdy drinker who loved a rambling, humorous discussion. He was a wholesale wine merchant but he also served customers at a few small tables. Clito's taverna was a convenient place for genial topers to compare the vintages of Cyprus, for men dodging their wives, for all manner of gossip. Here Larry learned about the black Stroumbi wine, the vintages from Paphos, Lefka and Limassol. A quite acceptable table wine drawn from the barrels directly into the customer's pitcher or bottle cost sixpence a litre.

Once on secure ground in the prosaic present, Larry gradually moved outward in space and back in time. The town was dominated by Kyrenia Castle, a sixteenth-century Venetian fort built over and around earlier Lusignan and Byzantine structures. Probably a Roman fortification had previously occupied the site. The castle had never been breached by force, although starvation and threats had variously led to conquests by Guy de Lusignan in 1191 and by the Ottomans in 1570. Ominously, it had been used as a prison during the Lusignan period, and would again be turned to penal service in 1954 as the Cypriot rebellion flared. Larry did not find the castle an especially interesting antiquity, but watching the evening sunlight fade away on the ancient stones became a ritual for him, sipping ouzo or Commandería, the tipple long ago of the Commandery of the Knights of St John of Jerusalem, the Hospitallers. This same sweet Cypriot wine, once drunk by de Musset, Lamartine and Rimbaud, had found favour with Larry's new Cypriot friends, the bookseller, the harbourmaster, the grocer, the schoolteacher. Cypriots, Larry discovered, were if anything even more hospitable than mainland Greeks, and any greeting to acquaintance or stranger alike at a café table provoked the inevitable '*Kopiaste!*' – sit down and share.[8] With them, he sounded out the methods and risks of buying a house.

Kyrenia, a focus of ancient sieges and saintly relics, contained numerous shrines and chapels. Larry walked up from the harbour to the small, plain Church of Chrysopolitissa with its Gothic doorway and Byzantine icons; he unearthed a shrine to St George amid a vegetable garden; he jotted down the anonymous verses of a local Turkish song:

> If you should come to Kyrenia
> Don't enter the walls.
> If you should enter the walls
> Don't stay long.
> If you should stay long
> Don't get married.
> If you should get married
> Don't have children.[9]

Kyrenia already had too many English residents, more than three thousand of them, for Larry to consider staying, and he knew that during the summers a pestilential tourist population would move in. He began to search in the outlying villages. Finally Larry threw himself on the mercy of Sabri Tahir, a Cypriot of Turkish extraction, and within a week Sabri had driven him to the abbey village of Bellapaix, four miles from Kyrenia, to inspect a house. Leaving Sabri's car in the square where the road ended, they walked two hundred yards, slipping on stones and boulders, up a steep lane impassable for cars. Their guide inserted a monstrous key into the tall, carved double doors, and Larry with rising excitement inspected a dark hallway and the four rooms along it. At the far end of the hall a window gave upon a tiny garden dense with bitter lemons, pomegranates and mulberry trees. A few banana plants proclaimed that frost had not touched Bellapaix during the past winter.

Then Larry ascended an outside staircase to find a roof balcony and another room: and he knew that he had found his home. Below lay the tree-crowded hamlet of Bellapaix and on the edge of the village the magnificent ruin of the fourteenth-century Augustinian abbey, called by Sir Ronald Storrs, a former governor of the island, 'the most remarkable monument of mediaeval art surviving in Cyprus, or the Levant'.[10] Larry's friend Sir Harry

Luke was to place Bellapaix in an even grander context: the structure had been compared to Tintern Abbey, he said, 'but with what can Tintern match the sweeping curve of mountains, the blue sea and distant Asian ranges, the groves of oranges and lemons and the stonework tinged with gold?'[11] The balcony also looked down upon the lower slopes of the coastal range and, in the distance, Kyrenia and the sea. Tiny on the shore, the Venetian castle jutted out from the coast like a forgotten toy. It was early spring, and the white puffs of almond blossom lit the courtyards, while the flowering cherries, peaches, apricots and tangerines promised a rich fruit crop. The village was famed for honey, and in the still air the hum of bees sounded like distant surf. Not even on Corfu had the sheer fecund beauty of a place so struck Larry.

Sabri's genius presided over the purchase of the house, and Larry would tell the story in *Bitter Lemons* in flamboyant terms, but there was no need to exaggerate his joy in ownership and reconstruction, 'the most intoxicating of all manias', he admitted.[12] By 3 March he was writing to Alan Thomas that he had bought a 'small Turkish house'.[13] It was fifty-five years old, with earth floors, an osier-and-packed-clay ceiling, no indoor lavatory, no running water and no electricity. Never mind: this was his, and he had never owned a house before. Nor, despite his modest adjective, was the house really small: the rooms were large, the ceilings high. Soon he engaged a Cypriot builder, Andreas Kallergis, and planned an ambitious project. On the lower floor a modern bathroom and a kitchen would be created, with water run in from the soon-to-be-installed government standpipe outside the door. There would be a great fireplace in the downstairs study. The master bedroom would also be on the entry level. The existing clay roof would be replaced by a poured cement one, on which Larry wanted another bedroom and a hall with a small fireplace added next to the original tall, irregularly shaped second-storey room, which would become his studio. The remainder of the upper storey would consist of what Larry called the 'indescribable terrace', with miles of coastline below, and Turkey lying magnificently spread along the horizon. Larry designed the upstairs bedroom with Sappho in mind: by sitting up in bed she could see the same marvellous view towards Turkey, 'framed like a water-colour' under the pointed arch of a large window. Larry told Kallergis how much money he had to spend, and together they sketched out the alterations. Electricity would have to wait: it had not reached the village yet. All the building material would have to be carried from the square on the backs of mules, donkeys or men, since the streets were not passable for wheeled vehicles. The preparations took on the aspect of a Crusader's siege train.

The living heart of Bellapaix was the square bordered by the abbey church, Dmitri's taverna and a few shops. Here men sat in the warm spring sunlight to gossip and conduct business over endless small cups of coffee, and from among the workmen congregated around the tables Kallergis recruited the carpenters, masons, and plumbers who would rebuild Larry's house. Their names would have graced a rosary of saints: Michaelis, Andreas, Marcos. As a foreigner who had bought a house in Bellapaix, Larry was the focus of considerable polite curiosity and speculation. He moved fluently into the life of the village, calling on the *muktar* or mayor, joining the men for a drink at Dmitri's. Larry disarmed and made a friend of Frangos, one of his more vociferously nationalistic neighbours, by claiming to have lost a brother fighting the Germans at Thermopylae.[14] Somehow the villagers picked up a pronunciation of Larry's name that came out as 'Mr Darling' and for a long time that is what they called him. It sounded like the Darley of the future *Alexandria Quartet*.

Larry was taken on his first tour of the abbey by the official antiquity warden Kollis, a stocky man with the 'round good-natured face of a Friar Tuck'.[15] In the chancel the votive tapers burned with long, ragged flames and oil lamps flickered beneath the gilded icons, for the little church was still the village place of worship. Worshippers strolled in, and each taking a pinch of the rising incense, made the Orthodox sign of the Cross. The ribs of the surviving pointed arches stood fragile and exposed, while bits of the delicate stone tracery of the cloister formed patterns against a sky alive with the flight of swallows. The view east and west from the vantage points of the remaining Gothic galleries replicated the one from Larry's balcony. 'I had begun to feel guilty of an act of fearful temerity in trying to settle in so fantastic a place,' Larry later wrote.[16] The mediaeval stone quoins and tracery floated as if by magic above the Levantine valleys.

In the central square to the south of the abbey was an ancient mulberry tree known as the Tree of Idleness: legend said that if you sat underneath its rambling, gnarled branches, you would be seized by the spirit of pure idleness. Larry knew that he could not remain idle for long, and already he was planning to look for a paying job. He asked Alan to let him know how his book account stood: 'Want to clear the decks.'[17] After fortifying himself with a glass of ouzo among the villagers under the Tree, Larry would cross his fingers with superstitious dread and hurry on up the hill, past the dark plumes of cypresses punctuating the gardens.

Larry hoped to re-create on Cyprus the Rhodean idyll he had shared with Eve. Although he would have said that he was too old and too life-scarred to harbour such illusions, he also wanted to recapture the magic of his youth on Corfu. But with Eve in Hanover 'swollen under luminol' – in Larry's verse[18] – and the baby on his hands, he had to assume precisely those mundane responsibilities he detested: equipping a home, arranging the domestic chores, coping with tradespeople. To complicate matters, the reconstruction of his Bellapaix home was taking longer than original projections had suggested, and the lease on his Kyrenia bungalow would run out in mid-June. Also, his overall impressions of Cyprus were not very good: although he admitted that the island had a distinctive cast, he found it 'weird and rather malefic', the climate 'not at all sexy', and the people 'listless' and with an 'Outer Mongolian' demeanour.[19] The humidity reminded him of Alexandria, not 'the champagne-dry, cooled airs of the Aegean group' to the north.[20] The only large bookshop was eighteen miles away in Nicosia, and Larry set about encouraging a friendly stationer in Kyrenia to expand his stock.

THE ORTHODOX PRIESTHOOD HAD become very powerful on Cyprus, and while Larry was settling into Bellapaix, Archbishop Makarios was helping found EOKA, the National Organization of Cypriot Fighters, with the aim of forcing *énosis* or union with Greece.[21] EOKA violence was in the shuttered future as Larry focused his attention on the joys of house construction and the travails of writing. He started work on his long-delayed big book about Alexandria, writing at night after Sappho had gone to sleep or by the light of candles before day broke. For the frame of his tale he took what was more or less his own situation, that of a man living alone on an island with a baby girl.

Larry reread the few books about Egypt that he had brought with him, and asked Alan Thomas to buy and forward others. Soon he had to hand Anthony de Cosson's *Mareotis* for material on the Western Desert; Robert Talbot Kelly's *Egypt Painted and Described*; S. H. Leeder's *Desert Gateway*, *Modern Sons of the Pharaohs* and *Veiled Mysteries of Egypt*; and Mary Louise Whately's *Ragged Life in Egypt*. He went through his books quite systematically, underscoring in pencil or blue ballpoint and occasionally making his characteristic mark in the margins: a small circle from which radiated a sunburst of lines. He listed significant pages on the back flyleaf, but seldom bothered to annotate, counting instead on his memory. He pored over *Modern Sons of the Pharaohs*, a study of the Copts, but found less of interest in Leeder's other two books, dealing respectively with Islam in Egypt and life around Biskra. De Cosson's *Mareotis* rated underlining throughout, as did Kelly's *Egypt*. It was not to be an extensive bibliography, and Larry tended to deprecate the number of even his relatively few published sources. 'With the help of [Joseph McPherson's *Moulids of Egypt*] and Leader [i.e. Leeder] on the Copts I constructed my book,' Larry would much later write to McPherson's nephew.[22] He sifted through his 'quarry' notebooks for impressions and ideas. From his memory of *Shem el-Nessim* – The Smelling of the Zephyr, a festival celebrated throughout Egypt by Copts and Muslims to commemorate the cooling Nile breeze[23] – Larry appears to have picked the name of the dignified, gentle Coptic financier, 'Prince' Nessim, important to the *Quartet* both as a key figure and, symbolically, as a descendant of the ancient Pharaonic rulers of the land. However, a day of looking after Sappho usually left him 'dead beat', despite the fact that she was 'such an angel'.[24] Louisa Durrell was planning to arrive by May to stay for six months and help with the child. 'Eve will be at least a year waking up – if ever,' he confided to Alan.[25]

On 9 April 1953 Eve was formally discharged from the hospital in Hanover and flown to England aboard a military plane.[26] She would need time to 'simmer down', Larry thought: 'Schizophrenia leaves a psychological over-hang for nearly a year after the patient is well.'[27] He realized that Eve's recovery would not necessarily alter her decision to live apart from him. 'At the moment', Larry wrote to Fred Perlès early in May, '[Eve] says we are washed up. Don't know if it's the crack-up or sanity – she seems fine – quite okay in fact.' More than anything, Larry felt emotionally drained: he wanted Eve to recover fully and return to him, but he could count on nothing. 'What I am going to do I don't know,' he agonized to Fred. 'I've never been in such a spot.'[28] Suddenly Eve decided to rejoin Larry, then without explanation reversed her decision and announced that she would come next year.

In England, Eve would support herself resourcefully by taking short-term live-in jobs, early on at Pinewood School, until Lady Ines Burrows helped her obtain a permanent position as an under-matron at Bedale's, a progressive co-educational boarding school at Petersfield, Hampshire. Eve moved to Bedale's in September and wrote almost at once to the Thomases, 'I simply love it!' She had not been keeping Larry informed of her plans, for at the same time he was still wondering to others just what Eve intended to do.

A friendship older than Larry's marriage also came under strain. George

Wilkinson's always dry sense of humour was shifting into sarcasm, 'the refuge of the weak', as he put it himself: 'And I tend to be sarcastic.' Larry and George had argued often enough in the past, but their disputes and the envy George felt for Larry's literary productions did not seem to be insurmountable barriers to their continued friendship.[29] What caused the rift was an affair that Larry started at the Villa Christina with the attractive godmother of one of George and Iris's children. Iris insisted on a complete break with Larry.[30]

By late spring the projected reappearance of another old friend was hovering over Larry. On a snowy 31 December in 1952 Henry Miller had arrived in Europe with the woman who would become his fourth wife, Eve McClure. Later they were joined by Eve's sister and brother-in-law, the painter Bezalel Schatz, for a motor tour. For Henry it was at first a disappointing trip, despite emotional reunions in Paris. Henry complained about the prices, the cold, his arthritis and the war scares. Soon he was threatening to land on Cyprus with his whole entourage, and Larry promised to put them up somehow.

Many of Larry's other friends and acquaintances began to seek him out. In April 1953 John Lehmann spent a few days in his company. Together they sat on the deserted beach at Pachyammos, talking about new writing. Larry did complain to Lehmann that he could not work because Eve's mental breakdown had saddled him with the care of Sappho, but he seemed in 'very good spirits' and full of ideas for books that he should write and that Lehmann should publish. The political situation in Cyprus did not seem threatening to Larry: he blamed the 'implacable priests' for stirring up the Enosis flames, the demand for union with Greece, an 'emotional fantasy' which he judged superficial rather than a firmly-held conviction. The peasants were so friendly towards him, and so 'uninhibited' in broadcasting their political views.[31] Sometimes Rose Macaulay would swoop by to pick up Larry and Sappho in her old car, and he would thrill to see the Lion Mount 'as if for the first time' through Macaulay's 'cool rare eyes'.[32] She joined Larry to celebrate the second birthday of 'the attractive Sappho' at the end of May.[33] Larry's impression of Cyprus was improving. The island 'has something strange of its own', he wrote, 'and after feeling disposed to hate it . . . I am now slowly feeling my way into its landscape – weird sort of place really'. One worry he had not yet resolved was the care of Sappho: 'Handling children is hell,' he confided to Henry Miller.[34]

Larry was in desperate need of a good conversation, he said. When Henry wrote to him from Toledo in Spain, recounting a wonderful reunion with Fred Perlès, Larry swore with frustration and regret. Almost every letter to Henry contained a plea that he come to Cyprus. Henry kept talking about it, but fatigue and the added complication of travelling with another couple made him hesitate. And much as Larry wanted to see Henry, the house was still a chaos of plumbers and masons, and Larry must have breathed more easily when Henry headed back north instead to see John Cowper Powys in Wales. Then in July Henry decided to make a run for America: it looked to him as though a mighty conflict between the Soviet Union and the West would break out in weeks or months, and he had no wish to find himself trapped on Cyprus or indeed anywhere in Europe. Henry was almost as jittery as he had been in 1938. It would be the Russians this time, he predicted, but they would both live to see a *Chinese* invasion![35] The reunion that Henry and Larry looked forward to was postponed indefinitely.

Although he continued to complain about the lack of stimulating company, Larry soon made valuable new acquaintances. Freya Stark's friend Austen Harrison, who had boarded for a time with her in Egypt, had taken up residence on Cyprus. Larry was delighted when the casually elegant Pearce Hubbard arrived in early June to drive him along the coast to Lapithos to meet Harrison. A renowned architect, Harrison had designed the Government House in Jerusalem, which Freya called 'the expression and climax of its landscape': 'perhaps the most beautiful modern building of the Middle East'.[36] Hubbard, also an architect, lived near Harrison. Larry called them the 'hermits of Lapithos' and plied them shamelessly with questions about his restoration project. The advice was willingly given: one glance at the Bellapaix house and Hubbard told Larry, 'By the way, go a bit deeper, another ten foot for the end of the balcony. . . . You don't want the whole thing to sit down one rainy day in the sludge and refuse to move – or to turn over on its side when you are giving an *ouzo* party on the roof.' Larry described Harrison in terms reminiscent of his word portrait of Sir Walter Smart: Harrison 'was a noble personage, with his finely minted Byzantine emperor's head and the spare athletic repose of his tall figure'.[37] Over their first candlelit dinner together, Larry, Austen and Pearce discovered various friends in common, including Sir Harry Luke and Lord Kinross, both soon to visit Cyprus. Marie Millington-Drake, blonde daughter of Sir Eugen Millington-Drake, founder of the Hudson Institute for Latin American Studies and former Minister in Montevideo, would by the end of the year become part of the circle of friends that gathered at Lapithos.

When Larry saw the beautiful ogival arches in Harrison's house, he cursed the masons for making his round. His project became daily more ambitious, and sometimes he was on the point of selling the house in despair. He figured that it would cost £1500, nearly five times the purchase price, to modernize 'skillfully and unobtrusively'. He wanted stained glass for some of the windows and a Turkish bed with a carved balustrade for Sappho.[38] All this would take money – much more than he had planned to spend on the house. 'What a passion building can become,' he confessed to Harrison, 'it is like gambling fever – and poor men should really be prevented by law from embarking on it with inadequate capital.'[39]

Architecture became the subject that would most fascinate Larry throughout his time on Cyprus: the two English architects took their places among his close friends and stimulated his speculations. 'I was . . . talking to Austen Harrison about the tomb, the temple, and architecture in general . . . when I suddenly began to see that the proportion of windows to the content of air in a room was like the human lungs,' he would recall. 'The dining room represented the head; the lavatory, the bathroom, and the septic tank were the bowels and cloaca . . . the receiving rooms were the arms and neck.'[40] The architecture of a place extended his pattern of correspondences, a warp and woof of person and structure, so that Larry would measure the *pneuma*, the breathing of a man, as an inhabited locus; would, in *The Alexandria Quartet*, treat the killing space of Narouz's violent courtyard as an extension of his personality; would describe in the future *Quintet* the cesspits of Avignon as the Augean stables of a culture.

But the mundane focused Larry's attention on Bellapaix. Through his own builder, Kallergis, he soon knew a score or more skilled artisans. Larry prided himself on being able to get to the core of another person in minutes or hours of a single conversation. He would locate an opening gambit – this man kept bees, that man had a son at the Gymnasium in Nicosia or owned a grove of pomegranates or gathered wild herbs, the beautiful Lalou raised silkworms – and few could resist the intelligent thrust of Larry's questions or the attentive manner of his listening, a murmured 'Ye-es, hmm', a slight, encouraging smile over the rim of a glass. Soon he had brief histories of many of his neighbours, and a thorough grounding in construction with stone, cement and timber. It was also part of Larry's social genius that he could pull back to a safe distance without causing offence – he had no desire to spend his evenings discussing bee-keeping once he had heard all that he wanted on the subject.

By the end of May, Louisa Durrell arrived on Cyprus, with Eve's blessing, to help her son care for Sappho. Louisa appeared just in time to take part in the move from Kyrenia to the unfinished house in Bellapaix. Larry planned to do some of the painting himself. Louisa had been through too much with her family not to take camping out among plumbers and plasterers as the most normal thing to do, but she did get a bad fright when bold Sapphy, playing with a cat beside the abbey walls, came within inches of a poisonous viper that the animal was hunting. This worried Larry too: there was no snake-bite serum on Cyprus. Louisa was reassuring in her letters to Eve, writing 'wonderful news' to her, and Eve confided to Ella Thomas, 'I have great hopes on being able to count on some moral support from her.' Eve ended her communication with a postscript: 'Larry is also getting to be far nicer too which is also hopeful, I thank God for it!'[41] God was invoked often these days in Eve's correspondence.

In his small car Larry began to make sorties to explore the island, the towns like irregular gems around a corona, their names a soft poetry: Limassol, Larnaca, Famagusta, far-off Paphos. In the centre was set the largest jewel, Nicosia, with the fantastic rosette of the Venetian walled city and at its heart the splendour of the Cathedral of Saint Sophia, visible from afar across the Mesaoria plain. Cyprus had the kind of past, the historical and literary associations, that he liked: Bronze Age and Iron Age Greeks, Roman road-builders, Byzantine monks, Crusaders, Templars, Knights of St John, Turks – all had landed, built cities and fortifications, fought and died. Cicero, to his intense annoyance, had once been appointed governor of Sicilia, which placed the island under his jurisdiction, and he had given the Cypriots a reprieve from heavy taxation. St Paul had visited Cyprus and, although legend said that he had been chained to a stone pillar and whipped, he had converted Sergius Paulus, the Roman proconsul, to Christianity. Cyprus thus became the first country to have a Christian ruler.[42]

Most of the antiquities that Larry saw dated from the Christian and Islamic eras. All over the island were Gothic churches set among green cypresses and thorny date-palms, Byzantine monasteries and Venetian fortifications. The Venetian period was marked by the construction of the eleven bastions with their connecting fortifications that encircle Nicosia, walls that Larry would soon be entering almost daily for work. In 1571 Mustapha Pasha completed the conquest of Cyprus for the Turks. The great Islamic power would govern the island until the British took control in 1878, and under the Turks many of the Christian churches sprouted minarets. There was also the famous architectural reference to Shakespeare: while it had required some fanciful mental gymnastics for Larry to claim *The Tempest* for Corfu, on Cyprus he had only to wander along the Famagusta harbour to see Othello's tower, where the Moor had lain dying. Larry set about sifting through the layers of the past, in his hand Mrs Lewis's *A Lady's Impressions of Cyprus* and Sir Harry Luke's *Cyprus Under the Turks*. Lord Kinross had published *The Orphaned Realm*, also about Cyprus, just two years before Larry landed at Limassol.

Cyprus was a way-station for both Turkey and Greece, lying geographically and culturally between them, and physically nearer Alexandria than Athens. The Orient and the West, the Islamic and Orthodox worlds, were still represented all over the island, and a handful of Larry's circle shared this double orientation. Among them was Zarian, who crashed upon the scene in mid-summer, working on a 'korzmic' book. He joined Larry in forays around the island, now changing hues with the season. In Bellapaix the blue jacaranda trees were in glorious florescence, while below on the plains the harvests of linseed and barley were over and the fields were turning tawny, buff, and rich brown under the burning sun. Sometimes a train of draught camels appeared on the cracked surface of the Mesaoria plain among the dust-devils, the men swathed like bedouin against the biting sand, their carmine, cobalt, or aqueous blue turbans dancing in the haze. Larry hoped that Zarian would settle in Cyprus. Members of the Cypriot Armenian community gave Zarian and his wife Frances Brooks a monastery on a bluff beyond Buffavento for their residence, but the three-hour muleback ride to the place must have seemed daunting even to Zarian. Before long they left Cyprus.[43]

With his savings running low, Larry began seriously to search for work. He would take almost anything. Briefly he received a pound a day plus a packed lunch as 'call boy for a film company'.[44] His old friend Maurice Cardiff returned to Cyprus to head the British Council, and he proposed to find Larry a teaching job. Cardiff had been the founder and co-editor of the *Anglo-Hellenic Review*, and his credit stood high with Greek intellectuals. He introduced Larry to Nikos Kranidiotis, poet and secretary to Archbishop Makarios, and to the painter G. Pol Georghiou. Soon Larry was contracted to begin lecturing in the autumn at the Pancyprian Gymnasium, a prestigious academy for Greek Cypriots set in a sprawling neo-classical building inside the Venetian walls of Nicosia. Like a school-boy trying to crowd as much activity as possible into the waning days of summer, Larry played and worked harder than ever. Part of the play involved visiting brothels in Nicosia, where Larry, combining research with pleasure, quizzed the whores on the sexual practices of the Cypriots.[45]

He tried to entice Theodore Stephanides to move to Cyprus and take up a general practice: a good living could be made, since he would be the only bilingual doctor. Eve was talking about coming for a 'trial flight', and this filled Larry with 'Grey foreboding!' 'Honestly', he confessed to Theodore, 'it's so much fun to live alone though I love the girl – there seem to be so many other irresistible ones. A series of temporaries is a good arrangement!'[46]

Marie Millington-Drake became a staunch friend and not a mere temporary. She combined a soft Botticelli beauty with a cosmopolitan experience and an intelligence sharpened by education and wide travel. 'I found that I was becoming hopelessly spoiled by money, birth, and upbringing,' she told Larry. 'I decided to stop being a fashion plate and start trying to realise myself.'[47] Larry was only too happy to assist her in the formation of a new self. She was in the process of buying a tract of land on a little bay east of Kyrenia, and Larry translated for her in her negotiations with the many co-owners.[48] Marie's mother was Lady Effie Mackay, daughter of the Earl of Inchcape of the great shipbuilding family, and her fortune provided Marie with the funds to indulge her wanderlust and her house-building mania. She and Larry became friends of the lonely *hodja*, a gentle black-robed figure who trailed about the nearby mosque-tomb of Hazaret Omer followed by his small tan cat. Marie was planning to write on the Balinese and Chinese shadow theatres, and Larry proposed to collaborate on a book with her, adding material on the Greek Karagheosis puppet shows – after he had finished his novel. Marie was journeying to England in September, and Larry commended her to Theodore in language that meant complete acceptance: 'Embrace Marie warmly from me. She's a good girl – .'[49] Larry suggested that he hand Marie his Karagheosis material to bring back with her to Cyprus, and join them in the proposed co-authorship. Eventually the project lapsed.

With good friends for company and lovers at his discretion, Larry had plenty of distractions. But he had resigned from the Foreign Office and come to Cyprus to write, not to be sociable. 'I'm full of beans and projects,' he told Theodore. 'This year was to be my "rest cure"! What a joke.'[50] He knew that he must shove along 'The Book of the Dead', even if only by a few pages at a time. He had long ago decided not to set it in Athens as originally planned. 'The important factor was that Alexandria was the source of our entire culture,' he would recall. 'All the religions met in a head-on crash there, all the metaphysics; our science was born there: the first measurement of the earth: Euclid. It was the birthplace of our mathematics.'[51] Alexandria it would have to be.

Towards the end of August 1953 he had completed a hundred pages of 'fine ferocious prose',[52] apparently a completely new version, rushing to set as many words as he could down on paper before his teaching at the Gymnasium began. 'I'm dying to finish this book – such a strange mixture of sex and the secret service!' he described it to Theodore.[53] Much later he claimed half-seriously that he had tried to 'beat Simenon up' in the *Quartet*.[54] Despite house-building and the first weeks of his teaching, he managed to write 25,000 words by the end of September, and he had hopes of finishing the book around the time of Marie's return in November. This time his instinct rang all the right bells: it seemed a 'corking novel' and although others might 'deplore' the story, 'it engrosses me', he said. Larry never could write well in uncongenial surroundings, and his progress showed that he had made up his mind about the island: Cyprus was now 'charming', and while he found the climate nearer to that of Salonika – which he did not rate very highly as regards weather – than Mykonos, his ideal, he decided that the place 'has a very real beauty of its own – it lies in the hush of the Levant'.[55]

LARRY BEGAN COMMUTING DAILY to the Pancyprian Gymnasium. In the absence of a university on Cyprus, the Gymnasium took on a greater importance in the intellectual life of the island than its relatively humble title would indicate.[56] A couple of generations earlier it had been the school attended by the military leader of the coming EOKA uprising, George Grivas, who would soon attain notoriety as Dighenis, taking his *nom de guerre* from the tenth-century Byzantine epic hero Dighenis Akritas – a brilliant choice, since for the Cypriot schoolboys who would be the principal auxiliaries for the terrorist campaign Dighenis carried the emotional allure of Robin Hood for an English boy. And Archbishop Makarios, a year younger than Larry yet the proven organizational genius behind EOKA, had also attended the gymnasium. Not surprisingly, Pancyprian was a hotbed of unionist sentiment,[57] and once the headmaster, although himself a supporter of Enosis, was beaten by his own sixth form students for opposing violent student demonstrations. Teaching there gave Larry daily contact with many of the young radicals of Cyprus: all ardent for Enosis, ritually anti-British, and invariably courteous to him. Larry met with English classes of sixth form boys and girls, segregated of course, and fourteen-year-old upper fourth form boys – cheerful 'incorrigibles' whom he could not persuade to listen to him. He described his girls' sixth as being 'united in only one thing . . . a passionate, heart-rending determination to marry their English teacher'. Larry had always been fond of malapropisms, and the students added to his stock. Asked by the girls why English had only one word for 'love' while Greek had many, Larry, in an attempt 'not to let the Empire down', offered 'dote' and 'adore'. It was a disaster. For months he was treated to essays describing the King and Queen of Greece as 'doting at each other' and to confessional epistles proclaiming, 'I dote him and he dotes me.' More portentous were the signed petitions, politely handed to Larry, calling for the freedom of Cyprus.[58]

The young Cypriots found Larry an impressive teacher, and not only because he published poetry and knew T. S. Eliot. One of his pupils at Pancyprian remembered that 'his Greek was good, maybe it was even better than ours, with a very good Greek accent, not a Cyprus accent.'[59] The job was proving more onerous than he had imagined: seven in the morning until two in the afternoon. Larry did benefit in a way that he had not foreseen, however. Through the school he came to know many of the island's intellectuals. Unlike the British-staffed Council of Larry's earlier teaching experience, the Gymnasium lecturers were mostly Greek Cypriots, and Konstantine Spiridakis, headmaster of the Gymnasium, and Theodore Sophocleous, one of the senior instructors, had written books on the Byzantine and Frankish period of Cypriot history. Moreover, they were 'a nice crowd', Larry thought.[60]

Another new Cypriot acquaintance was Paul Xiutas, the sales manager of the KEO wine and spirits company, and on a part-time basis Larry helped him write and translate advertisements.[61] Together they worked on the 'Boating Song', an advertising jingle. Another KEO advertisement printed in the *Cyprus Review* extolled the claret ('light, clear and mellow'), the bonded brandies, and 'the incomparable "Commanderie St John"'. Whatever sum Larry may have picked up for his efforts was far less important than his friendship with Xiutas, classical scholar, poet, and former principal of the gymnasium at Yialousa. Xiutas made a circuit of the island each week in his large car, and took Larry along on a trip to Limassol: 'he stops off at all unusual places and interviews weird characters' – exactly the sort of poking about that Larry adored. Xiutas had a tremendous fund of folk legends and anecdotes, and with him the conversation was entirely in Greek: well into their friendship, Larry still had made no estimate of the extent of Xiutas's English. 'For me', Larry said, 'he is the key to Cyprus.'[62] Xiutas was also an authority on Dighenis Akritas, and he had a reputation for political radicalism. He embodied some of the traits of Panos, that lover of Cypriot village life in *Bitter Lemons*.

Larry was to take an entire book to set down what he saw as the truth about Cyprus. Part of it was that Cyprus was afflicted by the web of jealousies and sensitivities endemic to any closed and inbred community. Larry worried to Austen Harrison that being seen with Xiutas, 'much feared' by the Pancyprian hierarchy, could get him 'sacked' from the Gymnasium.[63] Since both Xiutas and Larry were paid by Constantine Pericles Manglis, Cypriot millionaire, owner of KEO, and partisan of Makarios and Enosis, there was little likelihood of his being criticized for knowing Xiutas. Larry was posturing for Harrison's benefit. But he may have had some reason to fret that *Pope Joan* would lead to the loss of his teaching job, should the ribald book come to the attention of the clerics. In the village Larry seemed to be completely accepted: he was waylaid by Bellapaix friends asking him to drink with them, invited to Lalou's wedding, and consulted about headstrong children. But even at Bellapaix, Larry was constantly soothing feelings and juggling loyalties.

While Larry kept lamenting to his friends that he was 'going mad with frustration' at having no quiet place and no time to write, he pushed *Justine* ahead in little bits.[64] He was painfully aware that fifteen years had passed since his first – and thus far only – serious novel had been published. Of course, there were plenty of practical reasons for the long bondage to the Foreign Office, for such peripheral productions as *Prospero's Cell*, *Cefalû*, *Reflections on a Marine Venus* and *A Key to Modern Poetry*, but the justifications were not strong enough to silence Larry's inner reproaches, or to obliterate the counsel and example of Henry Miller: write – starve if necessary – but write honestly you must! Larry told himself that he was waiting for his next big work to ripen within him: 'It's simply a sort of premonitory sense that one day one was going to put one's whole shoulder behind a particular punch,' he would rationalize. In a few years, looking back from the perspective of the just-completed *Alexandria Quartet*, Larry would remember: 'I suddenly felt this was it, and this was the moment, and bang – at least I hope, bang.'[65] Both the confidence and the insecurity were real.

By October Larry had resolved that his novel would be '4–*dimensional*' in form, 'like some strange animal suspended in a solution'.[66] With superstitious dread, Larry confided his delight to Alan: 'Hush! I'm writing a wonderful novel!'[67] He was 'possessed' by his book. Never had he tried to write under more difficult circumstances, often in odd midnight moments lit by candles, perched anywhere, since his study was not yet ready – and yet, he told Henry, 'I never felt in better writing form, free of angoisse etc.'[68]

None the less, Larry seemed to embrace interruptions. Paddy Leigh Fermor came to stay with him for a week in mid-November, and they went on long rambles across the hills where the seasonal rains had brought out the greyish leaves of the asphodels, the bright splashes of crocuses and celandines. Back at Bellapaix, they celebrated the predictable riotous evenings. Once as they went through Paddy's vast repertoire of Greek songs far into the night, the lane outside the house filled with quiet neighbours, among them the usually boisterous Frangos, who told Larry, 'Never have I heard Englishmen singing Greek songs like this!'[69] No matter how late the party, Larry had to rise at five to be on time for his first class.[70] Despite his tiring schedule, Larry was eagerly anticipating a visit from Seferis, and he kept encouraging Stephanides to come.

A source of aggravation to Larry was that his house *still* was not finished, but in early November he was able to report that 'we are on the lap but last'. Only a few details remained, including the pair of small fanlights to be glazed with bright cathedral glass coming from England. Hovering over every detail, Larry predicted that the house would be 'awfully pretty'.[71] He asked Alan to start sending out his Elizabethan books. He now saw Bellapaix as an ideal place to bring up his daughter: 'I want Sapphy to have a peaceful village childhood here before she kicks off into the world.' Larry set out to teach her Greek. As for himself, he added, 'I insist on dying somewhere along this holy and pre-Xian shore.'[72]

With the 'lovely blue autumn days' Larry's spirits rose, and in the orchards and vineyards round about he saw the 'figs, apples and grapes in full swing'.[73] When he awoke before daylight the shadowy Lusignan abbey looming in the moonlight reminded him of Christchurch Priory. His heart soared as he listened to the nightingales in the garden and watched the faint 'lilac dawn' coming up over Asia Minor.[74] Larry continued to speak optimistically about *Justine*, 'which I think and pray is going to be good – better than anything since *The Black Book* anyway'.[75]

At forty-one Larry felt old amid 'the writer's/ Middle years, the hardest yet to bear', as he wrote in a poetry notebook. Counting his grey hairs and wrinkles,

> He matches now
> Old kisses to new, and in the bodies
> Of younger learners throws off his sperm
> Like lumber just to ease the weight
> Of sighing for their youth, his abandoned own;

And in the coital slumber poaches
From lips and tongues the pollen
Of youth, to dust the licence of his art.[76]

When Larry was not sleeping well, there were plenty of 'human poultices'[77] to be had among the bored British army wives: 'But I am so enjoying being an artist again that I only occasionally and purely medicinally nibble at the fresh fruit lying about.'[78]

It was clear that Larry had reached a creative impasse. He lacked the impetus – call it inspiration, courage, drive, what you will – to put his full effort into *Justine*. And so he blamed the construction of his septic system, Sappho, his job, interruptions by friends and lovers for distracting him.

In the same breath as his disparagement of the women he claimed were besieging him, Larry described a wonderful reunion with Seferis, who had burst upon him with a bang on the door and a shout, 'still the graceful and lovely humour-man and poet'.[79] Larry and Seferis discussed Aphrodite at length, both fascinated by the concentration of hermaphrodites on Cyprus around Paphos – about two per month were brought to the Nicosia hospital for surgical alteration. Larry thought that Freudian psychology was the first system since classical Greek philosophy to pose a theory of 'the dual sexuality of the psyche'. The towering conical phallic stone at the shrine of Paphian Aphrodite might seem unequivocal enough for most, but Larry said to Harrison, 'For me Aphrodite holds a great mystery which I would like to unravel.'[80] In *Bitter Lemons* Larry would attribute to the schoolmaster Panos a disquisition on the goddess as symbol of the 'dual nature of man'.[81] Larry was delighted with Seferis's theory that the women attempting to practise sacred prostitution before the Temple of Mylitta, but prevented by their ugliness from attracting men, 'by the sheer force of their public shame and envy caused hermaphrodites to be born – as a sort of projected wish fulfillment.'[82] Larry would attempt to unravel the secret of the 'old confining foam-born hand' in his poem 'Near Paphos': 'The double axe, the double sex' of hermaphrodites had been accepted

Before men sorted out their loves
By race and gender. . . .[83]

Another day Larry and Seferis sat in the autumn sunshine talking to Cardiff, the Cypriot poet and painter Adamantios Diamantis, and his wife Antonette. Seferis's imposing bulk was dignified in a three-piece striped suit, while Larry wore the shapeless, baggy trousers of the Cypriot villagers, and with his elastic-sided boots and wind-breaker collar turned up he looked very much the squire of Bellapaix. On 30 November Seferis read his poetry to Larry's students and was given a 'huge ovation'. The familiarity with which the revered poet treated Larry enhanced his reputation with his pupils. Larry told Harrison that Seferis was 'writing me up as a philhellenese'.[84]

Although Larry tried to give the impression that he had regained his old familiarity with Seferis, there was a definite cooling on the part of the Greek poet and diplomat. Seferis took himself off to Famagusta for nearly two weeks to work, he told Larry, on a 'complicated piece of poetic machinery'.[85] Yes, Seferis had referred to Larry as a 'Philhellene', but in a poem and ironically. The two men did not meet often, although Seferis spent a good deal of his time on Cyprus with Larry's friend Cardiff. Already Larry was finding it difficult to reconcile his divided loyalties, torn as he was between his genuine affection for the Greeks and his firm conviction that they would make a mess of governing Cyprus. Instinctively, he was still a Tory. To at least some of the Greeks and Cypriots, he was also a hypocrite, cynically coasting over the political shoals. Rodis Roufos, poet, novelist and Greek Consul in Nicosia from 1954 to 1956, would ten years later sketch an unflattering portrait of Larry in the guise of a fictional English writer, Maurice Ferrell, suggestive of both Maurice Cardiff and Larry:

In private he would discuss the political situation with invariable equanimity, for he rarely disagreed with the person he was talking to at the moment. His Greek friends spoke well of him because he was reputed to be a philhellene and told them he personally favoured 'Enosis' . . . it seems he was equally amiable to his Turkish friends, to whom he said widely different things, while I am told that with British interlocutors he adopted the proper jocular tone about both varieties of 'Cyps'.[86]

Larry's cynicism encompassed the entire political front, and while he enjoyed an argument, he often preferred not to disrupt a convivial gathering by probing painful issues. And to many, Enosis was like a carbuncle. In fact Larry and Maurice sympathized with the various positions and attempted to be even-handed. As Cardiff rembered, 'When interviewed by journalists or politicians we both tended to put the British case to those who were pro-Greek and vice versa.'[87]

Cyprus marked a time of construction for Larry. Not only was there his own house to concern him, but he appointed himself chief counsellor to Marie Millington-Drake, who remained preoccupied with house-building:

she had completed a 'grandiose' home of two storeys that had cost 'at least 20,000', and now she was proceeding with what Larry saw as a Xanadu in a 'bog' near the coast – 'a platonic image' of 'myrtle groves, statuary, ponds and seraglios'. Larry fretted over Marie, worrying that she had inherited the tendency to 'folies de grandeur' of her father. 'In a floundering crazy way she is so nice,' said Larry. His emotions were dangerously engaged when he started using such language about a young woman. There was worse to come: 'Anyway she likes me because though I tell her how crazy and shallow she is I really do like her for herself.'[88] Much later Larry dismissed the suggestion that he might have married her, musing *sotto voce*, 'Why didn't I marry her – where would I be?' as if it had always been out of the question.[89]

Now, as Larry prepared for Christmas 1953, he lamented only that his novel had 'gone by the board'. 'Never mind', he added, 'Sapphy is well and my mother.' He looked forward to the 'hosts of people' whom he expected to descend on him next summer – Henry Miller, the Leigh Fermors, Ines Burrows – 'It will make the island perfect.'[90] At least, he would have a fifteen-day winter holiday. 'By the way, do you loathe Christmas?' Larry began his invitation to Harrison for dinner on 25 December. It would be informal: 'we never dress for dinner any more'.[91] Louisa Durrell and her well-named compatriot Mrs Cooke prepared a fine meal, and Larry's 'pretty and delightful' friend Diana Newall flew over from Beirut to spend the holiday with them. It had been raining and the track in front of his house had turned to mud, but the upper storey was truly finished and a fire crackled in the fireplace. A sense of well-being flooded Larry. His mother fussed about genially, spoiling everyone and 'smoking her 270th cigarette for the day'.[92] 'Art is nothing to *living* – just a painful pointing in the direction of life,' he said later to Harrison.[93]

When Larry felt like complaining about the 'savage grind' at the 'damned Gymnasium'[94] and all the other chores that he faced, he thought of Rimbaud, who had been a quarry foreman on Cyprus long after withdrawing from literature. 'How hard and sane and unselfpitying his letters are,' Larry concluded. He could perhaps have got by for longer without resorting to teaching, but two sides of his nature drove him to work: he always felt panicky when he saw his assets dwindling; and he wanted to be able to 'see and enjoy [his] friends properly' – which meant having a good house, and food and drinkable wine in quantity. He added, 'The perpetual nibbling of money-worry is the worst of curses when one has children or can't bear squalor.' He may have envied the money brought in by Gerry's 'tremendous' success with his first book, *The Overloaded Ark*, which had appeared not long before, but Larry showed only joy in his brother's good fortune: 'How marvellous to have one's career fixed at 25 or so and to be able to pay one's way.'[95] Next year Larry would boast to Henry that Gerry was 'a more famous writer than all of us put together', yet was 'completely unspoiled by his fame and just the same as ever'.[96] While Larry certainly hoped to make some money from his writing, he tried to give the impression of being indifferent about aesthetic responses to his work. He told Harrison that he did not mind if people disliked his poetry: 'You know all art for me is "secateurs" an instrument to cut away dead selves – I have so many, and live such complicated multiple lives – I have to lop them off and let the fruit grow.'[97]

Early in 1954 Larry decided to snip off a bit of his past in the form of a spy thriller about Yugoslavia. In any case, he confessed that his novel was 'alas stopped', still locked at 25,000 words.[98] He blamed the combined pressures of his job, of rebuilding his house, and of minding Sappho. His motive for attempting the spy book was to make a little money out of the rumours of rebellion against Tito and out of his own thousands of miles logged on the twisting roads from Belgrade to Sarajevo, from Split to Dubrovnik. He had seen white eagles soaring over the pine forests, and enough shaggy mountaineers for a legion of partisans. He raced through a draft of *White Eagles over Serbia*, a calculated attempt to appeal to the market for anti-Communist adventure yarns. Larry had already listed a series of 'awkward shop' yarns to be written around the exploits of Methuen, a British secret agent. He kept the language relatively simple and avoided the temptation to indulge himself in a romantic plot by killing off the only possible love object early in the book. Larry's plotters attempt to smuggle through the mountains a treasure hoard intended to finance a rebellion in favour of King Peter. Larry sent the typescript off to Curtis Brown and hoped for the best.

Larry needed the money. He estimated that his house restoration was only £50 away from completion, and he had given up his idea of opening a bookshop on Cyprus, realizing that he would 'break a blood vessel' if he added another venture to his frantic life. Nevertheless, he complained that Cyprus was 'terribly provincial', with 'no music, no theatre, no nothing', so that stimulating company became even more important than ever to him.[99] Larry's friendship with Austen Harrison was growing, and Freya Stark was in Kyrenia preparing for a trip to the Black Sea. Harrison claimed to be descended from Jane Austen, and he had a marvellous store of anecdotes from his long experience as an architect in the Middle East. The travel writer Adrian Seligman and his artist wife Rosemary were other visitors, and Sir Osbert Lancaster passed through from Beirut. Freya Stark and Sir Harry Luke came up to Bellapaix in March to see Larry and his 'lovely child'.[100] Larry found Freya very entertaining, and they enjoyed together a query from a bookseller who thought that Freya's latest book, *The Coast of Incense*, was really *The Cost of Incest*.[101] Larry told Freya about his troubles with Eve, and he was taken aback when she scolded him: 'Lawrence, you can't treat a woman as a cat treats a tree, sharpening his claws on it all the time!'[102]

Larry complained of a rumour that he lived in a ruined monastery with 275 concubines. 'It's shocking how people exaggerate,' he told Alan Thomas. 'I've only got 235.' He wrote his return address as Monk Durrell, Bellapaix Abbey, and threatened to have himself photographed in a Carmelite habit, 'tonsured like a mandril' and dictating *Pope Joan* to 'a couple of pretty nuns'.[103] Eve did not often write, and he reported laconically to Henry Miller, 'There is no news more of Eve, and if [it] were not for Sapphy I would not bother any more; it is so wonderful to possess yourself when you are working on a book.' 'Women', he continued, 'are merely a tiresome interruption'. In fact – here Larry took on the tone of Timon of Bellapaix – they were 'Best enjoyed when least cared about'.[104]

To complicate his existence still further, Larry found himself inexorably drawn into the political life of Cyprus. In January, Peter Wakefield arrived from the Foreign Office as Adviser on Arab Affairs to Governor Sir Robert Armitage, and he was followed the next month by his slender and beautiful wife, Felicity. Wakefield was a tall man with a matinée idol's features. Armed with an introduction from one of Larry's former diplomat colleagues in Yugoslavia, they visited Larry. Wakefield questioned Larry in detail about popular sentiment on Enosis, sometimes sitting up until two in the morning while Felicity drifted in and out of sleep in a chair.[105] In March the novelist Joan Pepper settled in Cyprus with her husband Dennis Wetherell-Pepper, a government official specializing in Commonwealth relations, and soon they joined Larry's circle in Bellapaix, their host sitting in lotus position on the floor in front of the fireplace, a black wrought-iron candlestick beside him, bottles of wine within easy reach. Joan Pepper remarked on the feeling of peacefulness in the island air, an ambience that lulled her into disregarding the premonitions of future trouble discussed by Larry, Wakefield and her husband.[106] The older colonial hands in Nicosia maintained that 'a little bit of knocking together of heads' would quiet the

'Cyps' and preserve the security of the British bases on the island. 'We younger ones I suppose were more in tune with the times and recommended . . . that an agreement could be made,' recalled Sir Peter. 'We were giving up the colonial empire, so what was the point of hanging on? Larry was one of those whose advice was along those lines.'[107]

By February 1954 Eve felt that she had regained her personal equilibrium sufficiently to be able to resume life with Larry, and he sent her fare via Alan Thomas. In April a brisk and confident Eve stepped from the plane at the Nicosia airport. Larry sounded pleased in a letter to Henry Miller: 'Eve has just arrived back from England, v. pretty and gay. She is enchanted by this crazy house and the child who is three now and very pretty and wise.'[108] With cautious irony, Larry noted that Eve was 'throwing herself into her new life of horrible domestic subjection with what looks like gusto'.[109] Sappho, a year and a half old when she had last seen her mother, was at first bewildered by this intense, black-haired woman who claimed rights over her. But she was a friendly child and she responded affectionately to her mother's passionate endearments. 'Sapphy is tremendously pleased,' Larry admitted, but he sounded if anything harassed: 'At the moment work and my novel have me hamstrung. It will be another year or so before I am free to think.'[110] Meanwhile he was too exhausted with the daily struggle to write 'anything decent'; however, he was delighted to see his wife and his books again, all within his own four walls.[111]

To Henry, Larry confided his view of Eve's breakdown: 'Everyone had the impression that she had left me because of my bad treatment of her but in fact she simply had a bout of Judeo mystical schizophrenia.' The Jews were an 'extraordinary people', he continued, but given to 'shallow hysteria' and 'the enormous sexual charges given by race-continence and intermarrying'. Larry thanked his stars that he was not a Jew but one of the 'equivocal, sluttish uxorious Irish'.[112] Larry was optimistic about Eve, but what he did not know was that she had prepared an escape route for herself and Sappho-Jane months before she returned to him. As far back as February she had written to Alan and Ella Thomas, begging them to provide 'a possible landing place If I come back with Sappho sooner or later'. She foresaw a confrontation with Larry, apparently doubting that a lasting reconciliation would be possible: 'It would arm me with a ready plan, in case Larry challenges me with an alternative.'[113]

A few weeks after her arrival Eve had to admit that Larry was behaving well. 'Larry has become an attentive and adoring husband', she wrote to the Thomases, 'and I still cannot believe my eyes.' She added, 'My feelings for me [sic] took an unexpected freshness which I thought I'd lost forever.' Eve thought that Larry's fear of losing her again was behind his new-found consideration, but she was not about to complain: 'We are blissfully happy together.' Sappho was a cheerful child, and 'she's grown *so* pretty and sweet', Eve said. Louisa Durrell had wept when they met, partly from relief: coping with Larry's moods and 'keeping Sapphy well and happy' had been a strain, Eve surmised.[114] Perhaps, instead, Louisa's tears came from the knowledge that she must soon surrender her son and granddaughter, who seemed 'enormously well and happy'.[115]

Larry thought Eve had recovered well from her breakdown, but the air was soon electric with tension, and he compared their relationship at times to the situation in Fitzgerald's *Tender Is the Night*: the despairing husband and the unbalanced, beautiful wife. Ines Burrows, who came with her children and a nanny to stay in Cyprus for a week in early June, tried to 'reason with Larry' about the state of his marriage. Louisa Durrell backed Ines. Larry was angry at what he regarded as meddling, and Eve thought that it had chilled his friendship with Ines. 'Larry doesn't take kindly to criticism except from Mother, perhaps', said Eve. She described the outcome to Ella Thomas as 'disastrous', but added, in seeming contradiction, 'there is no doubt it has brought great improvement on Larry'.[116]

As it became more and more apparent that Larry and Eve would separate, there were some tense passages in the struggle between Eve, Granny Durrell and Larry for the allegiance of Sappho. Eve accused Larry of 'putting words into [Sappho's] mouth' instead of fostering independent thought.[117] Small matters took on exaggerated importance. Scissors had never touched Sappho's hair, and Eve wanted it cut. Larry and his mother did not. There was a scene, and finally Larry agreed to let Eve take Sappho to a barber. Standing before them, Sappho was made to choose – and she could not have realized the importance of her choice. It came down to this: 'Go with your mother and have your hair cut, or stay here.' The child hesitated, then went over to Eve. It would later be thrown back at her that she had chosen her mother over her father.[118]

Eve seemed to be convinced that Larry was watching her critically, waiting for her to make a slip. She set out to win Sappho's affection. In this she had the advantage that Larry was still teaching in Nicosia. However, the spontaneous child in Larry had made for a close bond with Sappho, whether he was telling her stories or taking her out for a ride in the car or for a swim. Sappho was delighted by all the attention from both parents, and was probably not yet aware of the tension between them. 'Truth to tell', Eve confessed at the end of July to Ella Thomas, 'things are not as well between Larry & me as one would wish and I find it painfully hard to know what to say to friends; particularly after our so promising beginning.' Not surprisingly in an Alexandrian, Eve showed a chameleon quality toward the cultures in which she lived. Already her thinking had become English, Ella and Eve both realized: 'May be what you call my inclination to britishness Ella adds up to the trouble, but the fact remains that Larry has an uncanny way of driving [me] more to it, against my inclination.'[119] Since Larry had, so he said, sworn off English women after his separation from Nancy, he must have been staggered to find his Gipsy showing similar signs. 'Money troubles and other squabbles' had him 'in the dumps', Larry admitted. There was no longer any practical reason for Louisa to stay at Bellapaix, and she probably felt that her presence was not helping Larry and Eve to sort out their marriage. Besides, she thought she might have to help Margaret, whose husband Jack Breeze had absconded, taking only his trombone, to play jazz in Liverpool.[120] Louisa left for Bournemouth during July 1954. 'Life is still rather tough', Larry told Alan, 'but I'm in expectation of better things.'[121] In her letters to friends, Eve not infrequently thanked God and resolved to 'pray as hard as I am worth'.[122] Larry cannot have been much in sympathy with this overtly religious turn, but he ordered a copy of William James's *Varieties of Religious Experience* for Eve's birthday on 8 August. Increasingly she was becoming 'very much on the perimeter of his life', Joan Pepper observed.[123] Eve in turn concentrated her attention on Sappho and the house in Bellapaix.[124] Larry ceased mentioning Eve to his friends.[125]

By July 1954 Larry had acquired a complicated new responsibility: he was appointed Director of the Information Services of the Cyprus Government, the position George Wilkinson had been hoping to get for himself. The pay would be several times what Larry was receiving at the Pancyprian Gymnasium, and he would be in charge of government press releases, publications, and the Cyprus Broadcasting Service. Larry called it a 'quite decent job'[126] and Eve commented on the 'wide field' and 'good salary'.[127] 'With God's help', she said, he would make 'superb work of it'.[128] Since he would need a telephone, and would have to have easy access to the seat of government, he would have to move to Nicosia. Housing was scarce in the capital, but Larry found 'a shabby little concrete villa' at 1 Castellorizon in Ayii Logitades, one of the newer housing developments. He would be paid enough to permit him to keep up his Bellapaix home as well. It was the kind of job Larry thought that he had left for ever when he resigned from his position in Belgrade, but in Nicosia he would have a far broader scope. The British had annexed the island in 1914, when the Turks declared for the Axis. Ironically, Greece had turned down a British offer to cede the island to them in return for Greek entry into World War One. Now the British wanted to retain their bases on Cyprus to secure the northern approaches to the Suez Canal, and the government feared that the cry for Enosis would bring the Turks in to defend the Turkish-descended fifth of the population. Greece was considered a shaky ally, and the Turkish bloodying of British troops in the Dardanelles in 1915 lingered in too many memories. Larry was true to his heredity, in his fashion: while he was far too fair-minded to write off Indians as 'Wogs' or to apply seriously his own exasperated 'apes in nightshirts' condemnation of the Egyptian man in the street, he did not have much confidence in Greek rationality. He loved the Greeks for certain aspects of their character – their courage, generosity, humour, wiliness – but he did not quite believe that they could make a go of running a country. None the less, he stood up against those who believed that the unrest could be quelled if only force were employed to 'give the Cypriots a lesson'. Larry countered that 'we should lose by force everything that could be gained by diplomacy'.[129] His political predilections did not prevent Larry from lambasting the British colonial government for neglecting Cypriot needs and thus keeping the island in poverty. Government from Greece, however, might well mean high taxation – although Cyprus was already heavily taxed – inefficient administration, and military service.

LARRY ONCE AGAIN FOUND HIMSELF climbing the steps towards the seat of power, this time for consultations on his future job with Governor Sir Robert Armitage. Marie Millington-Drake drove Larry in her little green car up to the summer quarters of the government high on Mount Troodos for his first interview. The beautiful villages on the lower slopes gave way to 'rocky banality' and a mountainside 'clumsily raped' to extract asbestos, which powdered the surroundings with a thin white dust. Higher still, Government Lodge had been built by Rimbaud in around 1880, but Larry found 'nothing to commend it except the memory of its author'. Made of harsh quarried stone, the lodge reminded Larry of the solid institutional villas of the Indian hill stations, and it stood, dark and grim, amid dense pines in a ravine. Sir Robert listened with apparent understanding and sympathy while Larry warned him that any coercive measures or stern dicta by the British would be seized upon by the Greek press to inflame Enotist sentiment. What many in the administration seemed to regard as an old-fashioned colonial matter could then explode into a European and international problem. The island was still in the main quiet, the press was unmuzzled and there were no political prisoners. 'Those who work in sovereign territory have to cultivate a suppleness and dissimulation . . . because no issues can be forced,' Larry firmly believed. 'The difference', he continued, 'is between the craft of a fly-fisherman and someone who dynamites from a rowing boat.' At almost the same time as Larry would be writing these words of analysis in *Bitter Lemons*, he would also be revising his thriller about a fly-fishing secret agent in Serbia: and both situations, the real and the fictional, needed the finesse of an Izaak Walton. He was not reassured at the lunch party that followed his meeting with Sir Robert when one of the old hands told Larry in a condescending manner, 'You'll see, we'll let them go so far and then simply smack them down.'[130]

Larry's Greek friends were far from pleased by his elevation. Some Cypriots wondered at the sudden transmogrification of the mere writer and teacher of English into the head of information services, and hinted darkly that Durrell had been a plant from the beginning, his teaching at the Gymnasium a blind to bring his ear within range of the heady whispers of Enotist plotting. Letters were published in the local papers querying the manner of his appointment, and a challenge in Parliament in London was threatened.[131]

The policy of Whitehall was to keep Cyprus within the Commonwealth, where in theory the island would function as a tranquil troop base for the protection of the Suez Canal and the oil supplies of the Middle East. The best way to accomplish this was clearly to foster a Cypriot rather than a Greek identity: Cyprus allied to Greece, given the Greek passion for national integrity, would be subject to the winds of Balkan political change. Larry's charge was even more difficult than it had been in Egypt, where he at least had a German wolf at the gates. On Cyprus he would have to encourage Greek and Turkish Cypriots to identify with the island, since an appeal to either ancestral homeland would invite the intervention of the other power. Adamantios Diamantis, after speaking to Larry on 22 August, wrote warning Seferis that the new position of their friend was a 'dangerous one' involving 'delicate work'.[132]

Before signing on, Larry had gone to Maurice Cardiff for advice. 'Do what you like but you will lose all your Greek friends,' Cardiff told him bluntly. And Cypriot writer-friends, he might have added: Larry had received a warm welcome from most important local writers. Cardiff was very conscious that the effectiveness of the British Council depended on the extent to which his organization was viewed as being educational and cultural in purpose, not tied to British government policy, and he himself was well regarded by the Cypriots. The Department of Information could not make a similar pretence of non-alignment. Speaking confidentially to Diamantis, Cardiff said that something good might come of Larry's appointment: since the job would be given to an Englishman in any case, better that it be Durrell than someone less sympathetic to the Greeks. In fact, Cardiff had recommended Larry to Armitage for the position. Larry did realize that becoming the official spokesman for the British government would be viewed as a betrayal by many in Cyprus and Athens. Knowing that Seferis planned another visit to Cyprus, Larry sounded out Diamantis in a way that made it clear that he would understand if Seferis preferred to avoid him. Larry told Diamantis that he would be happy to see Seferis, but added, 'Now that I am a government servant, he might not want to see me.'[133] Seferis perhaps did feel that he might be compromised by visiting Larry. Whatever the reason, he stayed clear of Larry during his trips to Cyprus in 1954 and 1955. Years later, shaking his head sadly, Seferis confided to the novelist and translator of his poetry, Edmund Keeley: 'I just don't understand what Durrell was doing on Cyprus.'[134]

Diamantis for one was unable to get over his bitterness and feeling of betrayal. Writing to Seferis about Durrell and other artists who had, to his way of thinking, sold out, Diamantis said, 'What a tragedy it is when one realises that their love, enthusiasm and visions of Greek faith and life were only stimulating games, merely helping them to write poems and express ideas, that friendship and openness for them were nothing more than a ploy for systematic research and cool classification of ideas and feelings to be canned and served at the right moment.'[135] In the correspondence between Seferis and Diamantis, the Durrell name became a byword for friends who had disappointed them. Larry's friendships with Seferis and some other Greeks suffered, and it was a heavy price to pay for a modicum of prosperity and a few years of service to the Crown. The break with Seferis was particularly distressing to Larry, who would continue to refer to him as one of 'the three wise men in my life', the one 'who gave me my metaphysical Greek education'.[136] The Greeks would not forget either. More than forty years later, Diamantis was still saying, 'Durrell was not a straight person.'[137] In 1987 Larry would comment that the 'disgusting situation' in Cyprus was 'entirely engineered by us', and he would admit his part in the dissimulation, 'our double-facedness in politics'.[138] His Greek critics like to cite evidence of a condescending colonial attitude in *Bitter Lemons* – and it does exist – but there is also a great deal in the book that is critical of British policy. When Larry came to write *Bitter Lemons*, he implied that it was largely his own reluctance to subject his Greek friends to reprisals by the EOKA terrorists that made him avoid their company. Apparently there was more to it than that.

Larry's first meeting with Sir Robert had occurred in early summer. In August 1954, just before he was due to assume the duties of Director of Public Information, a document was posted in public places throughout Cyprus offering a vaguely worded constitution, but threatening punitive measures against all manner of disaffection in print and action – a very doubtful carrot and a very menacing stick. Larry was astounded: this ran counter to everything that he had said to Sir Robert, and with which the governor had seemed in agreement. Around the end of August Larry moved into the office of the Director of Public Information, just off Ataturk Square and opposite the Nicosia General Hospital, in an old building full of mirrors.

Seferis may have wondered what Larry was up to, but there was really not much to hide. He had to field and respond to local press reports and meet journalists, both Cypriot and foreign. His favourite venue for these activities was at the Ledra Palace Hotel in Nicosia over a few drinks. He undoubtedly received the Reproof Direct – a phrase that Larry would use in his diplomatic sketches – when an investigative journalist found the Information Office closed and eventually discovered the Director of Public Information in Bellapaix, 'sitting under the Tree of Idleness', an anecdote that was widely reported.[139] And he caused raised eyebrows by writing all manner of communications, including personal letters, in red ink, 'which only Governors and Ambassadors are allowed to wield' – and also Archbishop Makarios.[140] It was not hubris on Larry's part: red had simply been one of his writing colours since the early Corfu days.

Larry was also made responsible for the *Cyprus Review*, a journal published by the Cyprus Information Office since 1942, and for the British-owned Cyprus Broadcasting Station, CBS. 'I am working like a nigger getting the Information Service here on its feet and starting up all sorts of papers etc.,' he wrote to Alan Thomas.[141] From the beginning Larry was fortunate in his section heads. His Chief Press Officer, in charge of the Office of Press and Publications, was Achilles Papadopoulos, a young Cypriot from a rural peasant family, who had returned the previous May after completing a public relations course in London. Achilles had a Scottish wife, Joyce, and he managed to maintain the tightrope balance required to be at once an anglophile – he would move on to a career in the British Foreign Office that would include a term as Her Majesty's Ambassador to El Salvador – and a Cypriot patriot. The other division under Larry's supervision was the Cyprus Tourist Office, headed by Reno Wideson, another Greek Cypriot despite his English-sounding name: Wideson's extremely pro-British father had simply translated his name into English as 'wide son'. Wideson was an excellent photographer, and Larry would later write a preface to his book of Cyprus photographs. He went everywhere with his Hasselblad, which Larry admiringly dubbed 'a philosopher's camera'.[142]

Larry and his associates issued a succession of tracts, including *Why Are We in Cyprus?* and *The Monopoly of Enosis*. From his office came *Cyprus Radio*, the programme guide, and Larry arranged panel discussions on such topics as 'The Consequences of Enosis for Cyprus' and 'The Alternative to Enosis'.[143] In opposition to Larry were ranked much of the Cypriot press, Archbishop Makarios and his priests, and Athens Radio. When the pile reached critical mass, Larry knew that he could go up with it.

George Grivas had meanwhile received two caïque-loads of arms and explosives, smuggled from Rhodes, and he would spend most of 1954 organizing his EOKA fighting network. Grivas was an austere, abstemious man and a veteran of Greece's disastrous Asia Minor campaign in 1922–23 and of the repulse of the Italians on the Epirot front during 1940–41. In 1943 he had formed a resistance band known by the letter X – Khi – that was accused of collaborating with the Germans while exterminating socialists and Communists. Near the end of the European war, British troops rescued Grivas's small group after it had been surrounded in the Theseion district of Athens by a much stronger Communist force. Grivas was still ultra-right, uncompromising, fanatically anti-Turk – and he would prove a superb tactician.

Inevitably, Larry's daily associates shifted from being his Greek Cypriot neighbours to his fellow expatriates. Partly because of Larry's new job, his 'satrapy' as Athens Radio called it, he saw more of his friends in the upper diplomatic, business and administrative circles. Peter and Felicity Wakefield, Philip and Fay Nind, Joan and Dennis Wetherell-Pepper became his frequent companions. Joan worked for Larry as a temporary, meeting VIPs on his behalf at the Nicosia airport and occasionally writing for the *Cyprus Review*. Eve was very much on the periphery of this circle; in fact, Larry let her know that he would be glad to see his mother return to help manage the household.[144] When Larry had a woman with him in public, it was likely to be Marie Millington-Drake or, more often, an exceedingly pretty girl of nineteen or twenty, Sarah Wolton, who had sailed to Cyprus on her father's yacht. Larry greatly admired her unsophisticated innocence and found her a job as Reno Wideson's personal assistant.[145] But it was Fay Nind, a slight, delicate artist barely five feet tall, who most captivated Larry. She radiated a sympathetic understanding, and she seemed to him so vulnerable and in need of appreciation, like an untended flower. Larry set out to be her gardener, to enhance her self-esteem. His sister Margaret took a less benign view: 'Larry always ruined women. He would build them up, make them dissatisfied with their husbands, discontented.' He had a way of making women laugh yet also feel valuable, appreciated: a formidable combination for friendship – or seduction. He also turned his short stature to advantage. For one thing, he usually held forth sitting down in front of a glass, when his somewhat disproportionately long torso made him seem little different in height from men a foot taller. But it was more than that. Standing, he stood straight, and usually projected a superb confidence. His sister, his critical and cool-eyed observer, always maintained that 'I never felt he was small. He was always the tallest in the room.'[146]

Fay and her husband, a Shell Oil executive, often joined the Cardiffs and the Wetherell-Peppers for late evenings at a small nightclub on the outskirts of Nicosia, where Larry would sometimes take over the piano after the place had officially closed. He played such tunes as 'Mood Indigo' and 'Smoke Gets in Your Eyes', and everyone would sing along with him when he came to 'Believe it, beloved, because it's true, / You're all that I want you to be.' For a time Larry saw the Ninds often. He climbed up to the great rock-bound pinnacle castle of St Hilarion with Philip, to stand on the worn bastion overlooking the ridges of the coastal range. The Ninds' daughter Charlotte, who was Sappho's age, would sometimes spend the night at Bellapaix.[147] Larry took Felicity Wakefield and Fay Nind to a local pottery, where they each painted a few bowls and plates. Larry turned a finely wrought small vase on a wheel, glazed it, and gave the piece to Joan Pepper. He also painted a plate with a tracing of his hand in the middle, telling Felicity, 'That will be the cover of *Justine*.'[148] So it would be, for the English edition.

LARRY WAS STILL NOT FINDING it easy to work on *Justine*, although he wrote to Eliot that he had 'the guts of a good book on Alexandria out on paper'. The only problem was that he lacked the time – or the 'necessary nervous breakdown without which one can't get the little extra power into it which embalms'. 'Only things which really please me are making love and lying in the sun,' he confessed.[149]

How much did Eve know about Larry's emotional turmoil? Probably she suspected quite a bit, but she was certainly misstating the case when she wrote to Ella Thomas, 'As for Larry's job, he simply loves it.' She did however recognize that the position was '*most* important', and she added, 'Only someone like Larry could face up to such a task with the buoyancy and zest which he puts into it.' Her own relationship with Larry she described as 'polite and cool', which Eve welcomed because 'it maintains peace in the house'. Larry must have reflected that, after their passionate beginnings in Alexandria and Rhodes, it was a sad come-down. He never had been, never would be for long, peaceful and tranquil in love. Sappho, Eve thought, had 'weather[ed]' the discord 'splendidly', and had turned into 'a charmingly self-possessed little darling', with 'all the normal reactions of her age'. The girl spoke fluent 'village greek', and Eve planned to enroll her in a nursery school in Nicosia.[150]

Eve may have implied a calm acceptance of her situation in her letters to Ella Thomas, but she told quite another story to Maurice Cardiff's wife Leonora when Eve and Sappho stayed for a week with the Cardiffs. Eve spoke of Larry always with 'extreme bitterness', expressing her rage at him for constantly leaving her out of conversations and for attempting to 'psychoanalyse' her. At least once the inner tensions broke out in violence, revealed to Maurice Cardiff when Eve turned up with a spectacular black eye at a morning reception for journalists that Larry had arranged at Government House. When Cardiff asked the cause, Eve hissed, 'Larry – But wait till you see *him*!' Larry arrived late, muffled in a silk scarf that did not quite conceal the claw marks on his neck.[151]

Late in 1954 Eve went off to Egypt to see her parents. Larry was once more on his own, but he had too much work in hand to misbehave thoroughly. He became a familiar figure at the Nicosia Government House, a far more impressive edifice than the Lodge on Mount Troodos. Built of Yerolakko sandstone and Limassol limestone after the riots of 1931 – when the original wooden Government House was burnt down – it was intended to show off Cypriot crafts and arts. No pillar had gone uncarved, no window frame undecorated. Every period of Cyprus from the Lusignans and the Turks to the present was represented.[152] It was a fitting emblem for the assimilation of Cypriot history and aspirations that Larry was trying to bring to pass.

Perhaps the most time-consuming of Larry's new responsibilities was the reformation of the *Cyprus Review*. When Larry inherited the journal, it contained the most dull and blatant propaganda, and Larry's aim was to foster Cypriot pride and identity through thoughtful – and non-political – articles and good art. 'If I had time I would write it all myself,' he confided to Harrison, but he had the radio station and the press to contend with and he complained that he was 'still without competent staff'.[153] 'It is unbelievable the amount of work I've got through during the last 2 months,' wrote a fatigued Larry to Alan Thomas. The pace of his life showed in the brevity of the handwritten notes he sent off to his best friends during his years in the Cyprus Public Information Office: ten or twenty lines scrawled anyhow across a sheet of Government of Cyprus stationery, or on any scrap that came to hand. 'Trying to save Cyprus for the British at this late stage after so many years of total neglect is really a hard nut to crack,' he told Alan.[154] Through the information services, Larry said that he was 'trying to make our case against the united howls of Enotists, British pressmen and fact-finding M.P.s'.[155] Larry pleaded with Freya to write on a Turkish Cypriot subject, saying that the island needed 'important people' coming to Cyprus to write up an 'identity' and thereby to foster a culture for 'us Cypriots' – he was now identifying with the islanders. To a Cypriot, it would have sounded condescending, yet his purpose was complex: 'I am planning to give the government a really good Middle Eastern review.' He wanted not only to 'project Cyprus' but to 'give some standing to British culture'.[156] His aim, in other words, was to promote a sense of Cyprus as an independent cultural entity, with Britain as a friendly godparent: this sounded suspiciously like an unholy alliance between high art and low politics. That is exactly how Seferis and Diamantis viewed Larry's direction of the *Review*.

As Larry would describe his charge, he was supposed to turn the *Cyprus Review* into 'something to stand the government in good stead'.[157] In plain language, all that Larry had to do was to convince the Greek Cypriots to accept the perpetuation of a benevolent British mandate, rather than to press for Enosis, union with Greece. With the first issue he edited, in September 1954, Larry's hand was made clear. Rather than a magazine of the most blatant propaganda, filled with such heart-stopping items as 'Dhekelia Power Station', 'Cyprus flowers for Her Majesty' and 'Football Matches in aid of Anti-T.B. League', Larry set out to raise the intellectual level of the monthly journal while at the same time to maintain in a far more subtle manner the pro-British flavour. Cloying cover photographs of smiling English nurses with plump, smiling Cypriot toddlers gave way to such graphics as an architect's sketch of 'The House I Should Build in Cyprus' and a pen-and-ink drawing of the Iplik Pazzari Mosque. The Christmas double issue featured poetry by John Lehmann and a contribution from Stewart Perowne. In other issues would appear articles by Patrick Leigh Fermor, Lord Kinross and Sigmund Pollitzer, as well as a report on her latest book by Freya Stark and sketches by Fay Nind.

As he and his cronies had done with *The Booster*, Larry would turn the *Cyprus Review* into a significant cultural journal. In this he was aided by George Wilkinson, who did not seem to mind working with Larry despite the obvious cooling of their friendship. George, 'under whose hand the magazine grew, struck new roots and firmly established itself' – as the valedictory notice in the journal stated – was the sub-editor of the *Cyprus Review* until September 1955, when he quit the magazine.[158] Eventually, after Larry's departure from the island, George would become the deputy director and political editor of the Cyprus Broadcasting Service.[159]

Larry's success with the *Cyprus Review* was invoked by Seferis as a reason *not* to contribute to the similarly bicultural Athens *Anglo-Hellenic Review*. Seferis could explain away as crass ignorance the claims voiced in the British House of Commons to the effect that the Cypriots were not Greeks, but it hurt him when genuine artists prostituted themselves to compromised goals and masters: 'But when I see intellectual institutions – quite artfully, I agree – placed in the service of these gentlemen, I tend to become suspicious. And when I see intellectuals and friends (e.g. Durrell) become propagandists for these gentlemen and use the friendships they had in Greece in order to infiltrate and enslave consciences, then I become absolutely suspicious.'[160] If he had heard Larry's boast to Harrison, Seferis would have been even angrier: 'We have really dented the Archbishop's stove-pipe hat with one or two of our custard pies and if only Labour doesn't come in and the Tories don't wobble we may get through the next round all right.'[161] Then in December 1954 British troops opened fire on student demonstrators in Limassol, wounding three, and the public relations balance shifted again.

SPENCER CURTIS BROWN REJECTED the *White Eagles over Serbia* manuscript on the basis of a reader's report, and did not bother to submit it to Faber, despite the firm's option on all Larry's novels. Curtis Brown's reaction convinced Larry that the spy novel was 'no go as it stood', so he concentrated what little time he had on his Alexandrian book. Eventually in 1956 he would dump the *White Eagles* typescript on to Joan Pepper's desk, begging her, 'Put one of your platinum-haired heroines in it!' He proposed that they publish her version under a pseudonym 'which would suit our personalities'.[162] Meanwhile Larry was devoting every moment he could to writing *Justine*, 'on the edge of cliffs, all over the island – or he was reading it to some gorgeous girl,' Joan recalled.[163] By January 1955 Larry had completed 200 typescript pages of *Justine*, but his position as Director of the Information Services was turning out to be an enormous task – far worse than teaching the sixth form![164]

Larry described his new novel as 'poetry with the steam pressure held down just below boiling-point', and teased his publishers that his title would be 'Sex and the Secret Service'. His phrasing and indeed his writing were influenced by the manoeuvring going on around him, and by his own part in it. 'Cyprus is a crazy island with a sort of tropical languor – tropical laisser faire and tropical politics,' he wrote. 'I am deep in Stendhal as a guide to the darker human motives.' He asked Alan Thomas to send him Rolfe's *Hadrian VII* and Svevo's *Memoirs of Zeno*, as well as books on Zen Buddhism by Humphreys and Suzuki. Suzuki especially he found 'absolutely fascinating and such a rest from this incessant clatter of press-work'.[165] As a further counterpoise to Stendhal and stress, he was reading Robinson's *Chinese Buddhist Hymns*. Larry was so exhausted that it even showed in his handwriting: unfinished letters and uneven lines instead of his usual neat calligraphy. 'Henry I'm terribly tired,' he admitted. 'Last two months – I've never worked harder or lived longer. What a silly paternless [*sic*] affair life seems to be with the eternal struggle to pay for the baby's shoes.'[166]

The main consolation was that the 'baby', Sappho in her pretty white frocks, was 'a beauty – dark with enormous black eyes full of devil and whim'.[167] Achilles Papadopoulos arrived one weekend at the house in Nicosia to find Larry in his stockinged feet, sitting on the floor with poster-sized sheets of black paper and a large box of coloured crayons, drawing picture after picture for Sapphy and all the while explaining what he was doing. 'Sapphy was . . . jumping up and down and clapping her hands and it was quite obvious to me that there was a very special relationship,' Papadopoulos recalled. 'She *adored* him, and he adored her.' Larry's subordinate was also struck by the 'mismatch' between Larry and Eve, Larry who 'never stopped talking . . . intellectualizing . . . a man with a sense of fun, full of anecdotes', while Eve was 'quiet, withdrawn, uncommunicative' – although Papadopoulos sensed that she had the 'temperament' to be sociable.[168] Eve once agreed to model for a charity fashion show in Nicosia, but then pulled out when Larry objected.[169]

Meanwhile the political tensions kept building. Wren, the British director of police operations on Cyprus, scored a triumph on 26 January when he managed to capture the reception party awaiting the *Saint George*, a caïque loaded with explosives and arms that Grivas was counting heavily upon for his projected campaign. A British destroyer intercepted and seized the caïque itself. Among those arrested was one of Grivas's key lieutenants, Socrates Loizides, who was obligingly carrying a document detailing the existence of EMAK, the National Front for the Liberation of Cyprus, an organization allied to EOKA. Paddy Leigh Fermor arrived to cover the trial, held in the little dock-house at Paphos, where he and Larry sat listening to the execrations and glass-smashing of a mob outside. The irony of Paddy's role was lost on neither of them: although never caught, Paddy had once been on the other side of the fence. He remarked that he and about four other operatives, each with a small fighting group, had kept several German divisions tied down on Crete, and he doubted the likelihood of eventual British success. Larry questioned whether the Cypriots by themselves would have the stamina for a long conflict, but he knew that the mainland Greeks or the Cretans could supply any ideological stiffening or firepower that the Cypriots might lack.[170]

In different circumstances Larry would have thoroughly enjoyed directing the course of the *Cyprus Review*. He himself contributed a number of unsigned pieces, including 'Beccafico – a Tragic History' and 'Plus ça change, a Mental Excavation'. Larry's one signed work was a short reportage on the Paris exhibition of his friend Georgios Pol Georghiou. Equally significant were the omissions: of Larry's Greek friends, only Theodore Stephanides contributed, and only one living Cypriot wrote for the magazine. Among the literati at least, Cardiff's prediction was being vindicated. The *Cyprus Review* had become a medium for live Brits and dead Greeks.[171] When Larry used his acquaintance with Archbishop Makarios to arrange to have Joan Pepper interview him, her husband's bosses forbade it.[177]

The verbal broadsides were about to lose their relative impact, for in March 1955 Makarios gave Grivas the signal to begin the insurrection. All unsuspecting, Larry welcomed Gerry and his wife Jacquie on the morning of 31 March. They intended to film on Cyprus for the next two months, and to look for a rare earless bat indigenous to the island. From his balcony in the Archiepiscopal Palace not far away, the Ethnarch watched anxiously until the flashes and the dull concussions signalled the onslaught, scheduled for that very night. Larry and Gerry were sitting after midnight over drinks amid the scraps of a late candlelit meal when detonations sounded all over Nicosia. Gerry professed himself pleased at the salute: 'Believe me, I am honoured.'[173] A terrific blast came from the direction of the radio station. The house door flew open. 'My classical records!' wailed Larry as he bounded out into the night. 'Wait', Gerry roared after him, 'if you're going to be such a bloody fool as to get yourself blown up, I can't let you go alone!'[174] Although there was damage to the tune of £60,000, the prized discs had survived. Smoke poured also from the Secretariat: 'Dust', said Gerry, 'from under the administrators' chairs.'[175] He and Jacquie moved to Larry's house in more peaceful Bellapaix.

From then on the Enosis crisis could not be treated as a joke, even by the most condescending journalists. Grivas had agreed to Makarios's demand that people should not be targeted, but the nature of the blasts made casualties inevitable in the subsequent months. Lest anyone should have doubted the organizational skill of Grivas or the wide distribution of his saboteurs, bombs went off that memorable first day in nearly every corner of the island. This time, miraculously, there was no loss of life across Cyprus, except for one EOKA partisan who was electrocuted when he threw a damp rope over a power line.[176] What neither Larry nor anyone else in the British administration knew was that most of the EOKA explosives were home-made by a group headed by the deputy headmaster of the Pancyprian Gymnasium and a chemist associate: the school was even more of a hotbed than Larry had realized.[177]

Later the focus of the rebellion changed, and any uniformed member of the Cypriot police, who were usually Turks, or any British soldier was likely to be killed. For a time an eerie chivalry prevailed, and a policeman or a soldier out of uniform was not considered fair game, nor were women and children. EOKA went into a paroxysm of apologies when a pregnant Englishwoman was killed. There was no embargo on killing suspected informants, however: a Cypriot woman was shot and wounded, then finished off with more shots in the hospital; a man was doused with petrol and burned to death in front of his wife, and so on. Ledra Street in Nicosia acquired the sinister title 'Murder Mile' because there were so many assassinations along its length. Among the victims on the Mile was the watchmaker Andreas Lazarou, who had been with the British secret service in wartime Cairo, and who was recruited under duress by EOKA and later executed on Grivas's orders.[178] Larry chose to ignore all such events in his

Cyprus Review, leaving it to the readers to recognize the ironies implied by such articles as 'Quiet Corners in Kyrenia', possibly written by Larry himself. A secluded shrine to St George might have served as a refuge, the article concluded, 'For has not Kyrenia often been the centre of stormy sieges and bitter wars in the history of Cyprus?'[179]

Even with the almost daily bombs and ambushes, Gerry and Larry risked swimming in the chill April sea at Larry's favourite northern beaches. Sappho loved the water and was utterly fearless. She made much of Gerry, who entered into the spirit of play and cavorted for her like a tame walrus. Once he surfaced, threw Sapphy into the air, and caught her. Suddenly her joyous yells ceased, and Gerry was surprised to find himself fixed by an extraordinarily searching stare from inches away. 'You're just a big daddy', she told him.[180] In April Larry traced Sapphy's hands in the poetry notebook that he had begun in Belgrade and annotated them: 'Dear child/ Be happy/ Larry'.[181]

Cyprus was becoming a less and less happy place. On 24 May, Empire Day, hundreds of schoolboys with stones routed a police detachment, and a timebomb manufactured from a Coca-Cola bottle and placed near Governor Armitage's seat at a charity film showing in the Pallas Cinema exploded five minutes after the lights had come on and everyone had filed into the foyer. Sir Robert, a civilian, felt out of his depth as the situation came more and more to require military responses.

A phase of Cyprus's complicated history that was to find its way into *The Alexandria Quartet*, albeit with a shift in location and actors, was the part the Cypriots had played years earlier in running guns to Israel to arm the Irgun, the Stern Gang and the armed Jewish insurrection. A brisk trade in contraband weapons brought substantial profits to local merchants and smugglers. Larry would transfer this activity wholesale to the Copts of Egypt – who were innocent of the charge. Smugglers, bombs, hordes of foreign reporters and private visitors – but Larry was able to report, 'novel shaping well under inconceivable difficulties'. The house was *still* not entirely finished: he was 'hopelessly in debt' despite his 'princely salary'; there was too much work. Not the least of his worries was the domestic conflict: 'I have had rather a rough time since Eve came back', he confessed to Alan Thomas.[182] Larry's tormented relationship with Eve, with the backdrop of a revolt in progress, had an important bearing on the *Quartet*, in which most of the love relationships are doomed. Writing and fighting had taken over his life.

ON 3 JULY 1955 LARRY WAS RECALLED to London for secret consultations with the Colonial Office. He had two days in Athens en route, and he seized the chance to see George Katsimbalis at a taverna in the Plaka, gloriously forgetting the heartbreak of Cyprus, and the next day Larry spent at the summer villa of Sir Charles Peake, now Ambassador to Greece, happily recalling the bad old days of Belgrade. Then Larry was off for England. To his surprise, he was interviewed by Alan Lennox-Boyd, Secretary of State for the Colonies. Larry immediately sized him up as a gentleman of 'great style completely untouched by affectation', a person of sophistication and humour. Reassured, Larry spoke his mind, telling the Colonial Secretary that Cyprus was one case 'where sovereignty and security were not necessarily compatible': yes, the Turks would support a continued British presence, as an alternative preferable to either independence or union with Greece, but the British should seek a long-term solution and not shelter behind Turkish support. Larry argued for setting up a twenty-year time limit for resolving the issue – in one of those three ways. The next day Larry was told to prepare for a return to Cyprus that very afternoon with Lennox-Boyd's entourage.[183]

Larry was as delighted as a schoolboy to travel with an important diplomat: the trip to the aerodrome in the black, old-fashioned Bentleys of the Colonial Office; a somewhat raffish companion from Scotland Yard who told Larry that he did not carry a machine gun but that 'I manage with a good eye and a very small Colt'; drinks in the VIP lounge and passport formalities so smooth as to make Larry feel like the Aga Khan.[184] Cyprus quickly jolted him back to reality: on the second day of conferences a bomb destroyed a large segment of the roof of the Nicosia tax office, half a mile away – and there was widespread disappointment when it turned out that the records had survived. This marked the first daylight bomb attack since the explosions began on the night of All Fool's Day.

Larry flew back to London on 12 July to rush through his schedule of appointments. He met Juliet O'Hea, his new agent at Curtis Brown, and shocked her, careful spinster that she was, by demanding immediately, 'If you had to abolish one of the Commandments, which would it be?' She replied, after a moment's hesitation, 'That one about adultery – the sixth rule.' 'That's my girl!' exclaimed Larry. They were friends from that moment.

This trip he managed to slip away from his official rounds long enough to visit the Octagon Room in the National Gallery to see the Paolo Veronese portraits of the Pisano family. The result was a haunting poem in which Larry merged the silvery-grey tone of the 'Veronese grey' paintings with diction suggestive of the Foreign Office and of grey London: the 'cigar-ash', the 'pane of cockney sky', the paintings 'like all these glittering hostages/ We carried out of Italy'. Finally, it was a return to the Thames of his schooldays at St Olave's,

> To where the tugs still howl and mumble
> On the father river.[185]

Soon after Larry's return from London, Eve left Cyprus, taking Sappho with her. Larry had acquiesced in her departure because of the increasing danger, and he seems to have accompanied his family as far as Athens, where he spent a week in mid-August. He may have been thinking of his struggle with Eve, putative avatar of Justine in the *Quartet*, when he had Nessim say of his wife, 'this Jewish fox has eaten my life'.[186] By this time, Larry was probably glad to see her go, but he missed his daughter. 'As for unhappiness', Larry confided to Harrison, 'she has grown into a massive thing this year'. Larry was thankful for his 'hard crust': 'How else can one do a job like this, be in love with the wrong person, have children, mad wives, etc.'[187] Having nowhere else to go in England, Eve followed up on the request made even before she had left for Cyprus and accepted the hospitality of Alan and Ella Thomas in Bournemouth for a visit of several weeks that stretched into months. Alan read to Sappho from Beatrice Potter almost every evening; as headstrong as either parent, the little girl was furious when Alan had company and did not read to her.[188]

The final break was a double blow for Larry: hard crust or not, he had to face the dissolution of his marriage, and for the second time he had lost a child. He jotted down the title for a book he might write: 'Perdita: The Lost Daughters'.[189] He was thinking of leaving Cyprus in the spring: the once-loved island seemed 'under a curse'.[190] He fell into a 'bad patch of distress and apathy after Eve left',[191] and described himself to Freya Stark as 'a very dilapidated old dung-beetle poet treading away at the meagre resources of time at my disposal'. The beloved Bellapaix house was 'shut up, empty and dusty', with Sapphy's toys, including the doll given her by Freya – Lucia 'with the spastic knee' – lodged in the cellar.[192]

With Eve gone, and in such an unequivocal manner, Larry tried to persuade Fay Nind to leave her husband for him, and in this he was abetted by some of their common friends, including Joan Pepper, who believed that Nind was cold towards his wife.[193] When a rumour – untrue – flew about that Philip was an agent for the British secret service, Shell decided in

September that the Ninds would have to leave Cyprus immediately, before he was bagged by EOKA.[194] Their departure would not mark the end of Larry's yearning for Fay, whom he seems to have missed much more than he did Eve.

LARRY DID NOT HAVE LEISURE to chew over his own misery. The Tripartite Conference had opened in London on 29 August 1955, and although it was to end ten days later without producing an agreement for the self-government of Cyprus under a tri-national commission – as proposed by the Secretary of State for Foreign Affairs, Harold Macmillan – it was still a time of heightened expectations, and the Information Office in Nicosia was kept busy. The failure of the conference was followed by increased EOKA activity, and on 17 September the British Institute library, with the best English literature collection in the Middle East, was burnt to the ground by schoolboys – probably including some of those from his upper fourth, Larry thought with a shudder. Macmillan was known to favour a strong line, and the appointment of Field-Marshal Sir John Harding to replace Armitage as Governor meant a shift from a primary emphasis on negotiation to a trust in force. Harding would combine the roles of Governor and Commander-in-Chief. Larry described the new Governor, who took over on 3 October, as a 'francolin', moving and deciding with the 'trained power of the will', the crisp directness of a raptor. Larry's language was adulatory: 'The francolin fitted warmly and naturally into the great gallery of human beings whose portraits made up the history . . . of this marginal place.' 'That fine head', he wrote, 'belonged to the historical tapestry of Cyprus – very English in its warm colouring and lively composure. He belonged to that trace of forgotten captains whose sense of destiny had made them free men, committed to history.' Larry betrayed a note of envy for men of decision so little troubled by conflicting truths. Still, Larry's eulogy for what he saw as typically English virtues illustrated his personal paradox: his ambiguity towards England. He could not bear to live among the retired English colonials in Kyrenia, people so like his own aunts and uncles, yet he wanted Harding to succeed in 'draw[ing] EOKA's teeth' so that Cyprus could once more be safe for these same colonials. 'Wish him luck I did on the old culverin with wooden wheels,' Larry admitted, like an old crusader pledging upon his sword.[195] Grivas's campaign was not a pretty thing, but neither was it the brainchild of a demented and self-seeking man. In fixity of purpose and personal probity, Grivas appears to have matched Harding, but Larry was too much his father's son, too British, to admit this. Like Larry, Archbishop Makarios was far more complex than the two military antagonists.

Harding immediately requested a meeting with Makarios, and the day after Sir John's arrival Achilles Papadopoulos found himself pressed into service as translator in a series of talks between Field-Marshal and Ethnarch.[196] Doubtless Sir John was an admirable man, but the situation required more than any one man could be expected to give: perhaps, if this is not too contradictory, he needed to be a devout military humanist, and Sir John's estimate that only five per cent of the population truly supported EOKA betrayed a misreading of the emotional appeal of race, of language, of religion, of roots. Larry tried tactfully to supply a corrective to Harding's thinking, telling him that 'Enosis [is] really quite serious.' Looking startled though still incredulous, Harding replied, 'You don't say, Durrell!'[197] As the deaths of Britons went from zero during Armitage's tenure to twelve in the first three months of Harding's, and the government hangings in retribution for EOKA killings and infractions mounted from none to seven by the end of 1956, it became clear that the initial wedge of Enosis had produced a chasm of distrust, ill-will and hatred that the new Governor was unable to span. The cumulative statistics are telling: 24 killed in 1955; 214 in 1956, of whom over half were Greek Cypriots; and the majority of the killings were by EOKA.[198]

One direct result of Larry's trips to London was that the Information Services were restructured, and a Director General was placed in charge. Larry's new title was Director of Public Relations; he was relieved of his broadcast responsibilities but remained head of the publications section with its various magazines, and he moved into 'very posh' quarters at 3 Canning Street opposite the Nicosia stadium. It is not clear whether Larry regarded his new position as a demotion: perhaps it was only a reflection of the increasing complexity of the situation. Handling the mobs of hard-drinking foreign correspondents drawn by the Enosis crisis came to swallow up most of his time. He acquired as an assistant Viscount Richard Lumley, a friend of Marie Millington-Drake's, who would later become the twelfth Earl of Scarbrough. Lumley – Dickon to Marie, Larry and the Wakefields – was then a twenty-two-year-old on his way around the world. He had got as far as Cyprus when his money ran out, and Larry took him on as his night duty officer and gave him a room in his Nicosia house. Dealing with the press not only meant answering the telephone at all hours, but also involved entertaining foreign reporters. Once Larry phoned back to his home in mid-morning to speak to Lumley. The maid was unable to wake him and reported in panic to Larry, 'The Lord is dead!' 'Stale news!' Larry shot back.[199] Viscount Lumley was resurrected, however, and in 1956 would become one of three ADCs to Sir John Harding.

Athens radio, paraphrasing Archbishop Spyridon's statement at the beginning of the current Enosis campaigned, proclaimed that 'freedom is acquired only by blood', and exploited every possible incident to inflame Enotist sentiment.[200] In the summer Larry felt an unwelcome wave of notoriety when his name was broadcast. Kyrenia Castle was being used as a detention centre, and Athens challenged the Public Information Officer to confirm to the people of Cyprus the lack of proper latrines. 'It must be true, Mr Durrell,' cried Athens radio, 'unless our sense of sight and smell . . . deceive us.' He received a shove from the Colonial Secretary: Larry was to make an inspection, then tour with the press 'to show that though we may be Fascist beasts our sanitation is still sound'.[201] There was nothing for it but to don his best official face and make the inspection. Meanwhile the centre had been moved to Kokkino-Trimithia near Nicosia, and Larry was relieved when he found only two of his former students among the young prisoners. One of them greeted him delightedly, 'So they got you at last, Mr. Durrell? I told you you were too friendly with the Greeks.'[202] In one cell he saw a copy of Ilias Venezis's *Aeolia*, with his own preface translated into Greek. Larry was distressed to have to admit that EOKA attracted the best and bravest of the youth.

As 1955 wore on, Cyprus staggered from one crisis to another. Larry wrote that his job was 'killing' him. He saw that the situation was 'going from bad to worse slowly', and his administration, for once, was not working smoothly: 'I am surrounded by industrious insects with mild stings and have not made myself too popular,' he complained to Harrison. For intellectual relief, Larry was deep in Suzuki and other Zen masters, but there remained a very concrete chance that he would be blown up or shot. Whenever he could get away from Nicosia, he would drive to the *tekke* of Hazaret Omer and commune with the seven Muslim dignitaries in their tomb on the bare jutting peninsula. There he would swim, sip sweet coffee with the *hodja*, and help him fill out coupons for a football pool, smiling at the bafflement in the old man's halting Greek. Between the sagacious and energetic Sabri and the simple holy man with the lines of concern etched deeply in his face, Larry felt that he had the two extremes of Turkish Cypriots: the one quintessentially modern, the other lodged in the past. He felt a responsibility towards both, as he did towards his Bellapaix neighbours. If Marie Millington-Drake was on the island, Larry would walk over to the next bay to see whether she was there with Austen Harrison, who was taking his time building the graceful arches of her home, 'Fourtouna' ('west wind'). She lived in a makeshift and largely open temporary structure of canes and bamboos almost on the beach, a few straw-covered bottles of chianti hanging from the beams.

By NOVEMBER 1955 LARRY WAS proclaiming rather ambiguously both that he had 'nearly finished' his '*second* novel' and that he was 'half way through a book called *Justine*'. Larry still liked to maintain that *The Black Book* was his first real fiction, and that his life's work would be devoted to three '*real* novels', corresponding respectively to youth, maturity and old age. Evasively, he described his novel as being 'about Eve and Alexandria before the war', and then in almost the same pen-stroke he wrote, 'I think probably I shall divorce Eve this year and go and live in the mosque for a while.' His 'only real capital' was 'lonleliness' – the word always gave him trouble. 'Of course there are plenty of women and adventures still', he told Henry Miller, 'but inside I've reached a new stage – a very small advance upon my own true nature whatever *that* may be.'[203]

Larry certainly needed the rest. To Alan Thomas he characterized his 'bitter uphill struggle against this too-long neglected Enosis situation' in the terms of long-past football matches: 'I've scored a few goals but mostly it is saving shots. The pitch is greasy, ball muddy and Yours truly tired of it all.'[204] After six weeks of 'hell', around the middle of December he came down with a vague germ and took to his bed for a few days, grateful for the excuse to rest. He spent Christmas Eve until one in the morning on night duty at the Information Office, and from his desk he penned Henry a quick summary of the past year 'of bombs and boredom', with political and domestic crises pacing one another. Cyprus had become 'this fucking island', but he felt a 'perverse affection' for it 'because I've suffered so much here'. Eve, Larry continued, her personality now marked by 'Jewish hysteria and religious mania', was in England 'with the kidnapped daughter'. He was not disposed to be forgiving toward Eve: 'May she fry in a nice Jewish hell!' Meanwhile, Larry had 'nearly finished' *Justine*, set 'in the palmy days of the palmy people', and although his peace of mind was 'gone for ever', he said that he was 'Exhausted but Happy'.[205]

Curiously, around this time Larry started another novel, with the working title 'A Village of Turtledoves'. It was to deal with the Foreign Office and feature an architect named Caradoc – who would appear with the same name and similar characteristics in *Tunc* and *Nunquam* more than a decade later. Larry had apparently suffered a loss of confidence in his ability to finish *Justine,* and he thought that by playing with a new story he would help loosen his hand. Also, he probably hoped that this would turn into a money-spinner: some of the passages were closely related to the Foreign Office humorous sketches that he would write in 1957. Larry went so far as to complete seventeen pages of typescript in early 1956 before giving up.

He was not yet ready to retire to the mosque and the company of the silent *hodja,* however. After he had 'succumbed to a bad patch of distress and apathy' following the departure of Eve and Sappho, he had a 'stroke of luck' such as had happened to him before. And fittingly, his good fortune derived from Egypt, in the form of 'a lovely young Alexandrian', Claude-Marie Forde, who, Larry said, 'tumbled into my arms'. The distress and apathy had not lasted very long, although Larry continued to say that he missed his young daughter. By January he was more than ever dismissive of Eve: their marriage was 'washed up'.[206]

One of Larry's talents was his ability in times of crisis to find the right woman to be his companion, to look after him. When Claude-Marie Forde applied for a job at his office, the Public Information Director hired her at once to run the French section of the Cyprus Broadcasting Service. She spoke a brisk, slightly Irish-accented English and perfect French, as well as most of the commoner languages of Egypt: 'We could all speak a great number of languages badly,' she recalled, making light of her considerable talent.[207] Claude was '*totally* bilingual', a friend once said of her; when she was speaking English, 'you couldn't tell she was French'.[208] She seemed extremely businesslike and capable, and Larry registered that she was slim, blonde, lovely and only an inch taller than he. Quickly they discovered common ground: she knew socially some of the people Larry remembered from Alexandria. In fact, he was sure he had seen her at a few wartime parties.[209] She knew Alexandria and its high society from the inside, in a way that Larry did not. She had been born Vincendon and her mother, a well-known beauty as a young woman, was a Menasce, a family prominent in Egyptian banking. The rue Menasce ran through Moharrem Bey in Alexandria, not far from Larry's old abode on the rue Mamoun. She was married with two children, Barry and Diana, and her English husband was proposing that they all move to Bombay to open a hotel – this she was sure that she did not want to do. Around the time she met Larry she began living in an apartment away from her husband and family. Also, she was trying to write a novel based on her experiences as a publican in Ireland.

To some of Larry's friends, Claude appeared to have fallen passionately for Larry and to have pursued him without respite. Joan Pepper was visiting Larry when an agitated Richard Lumley entered the room: 'Oh God, Larry, Fordie's at the door! What are we going to do?' Lumley handed her in, clearly tipsy, and Larry attempted an introduction – 'This is Joan Pepper' – at which Claude fell flat at Larry's feet. 'That's what you do to women!' said Joan, caught between amusement and disapproval.[210]

With Claude's encouragement, Larry went back to *Justine*. Soon Larry and Claude were spending their off-duty evenings sitting at opposite ends of the dining table, clattering away at their respective typewriters, EOKA explosions rattling the window panes – Larry noted that between January and June 1956 the monthly average was one hundred bombings.[211] Larry pinned a large map of Alexandria to the wall, and taking full advantage of Claude's memories of the city, he traced the routes of Darley and Nessim, Scobie and Clea, Pursewarden and Justine, discussing the various land-marks: the Pastroudi and Baudrot cafés, the Bourse and St Mark's, Fort Kom el Dik and the Nouzha Gardens. Much that Larry thought he had lost was restored to his memory as Claude recalled Alexandria to him, providing those essentials in describing the city that he dubbed 'the capital of Memory', 'one of the great capitals of the heart'.[212] 'We drank red wine and worked like maniacs,' Larry recalled.[213] Claude became woven into the fabric in various ways, from the physical description of 'honey gold'[214] Clea to the name Claudia that Larry gave to the Justine figure in *Moeurs*, the fiction-within-fiction lodged in the core of the *Quartet*. Another name that came from Larry's current life on Cyprus was that of Arnauti, Justine's first husband and putative author of *Moeurs*, who was apparently named after a cape on the north-western extreme of the island.

Larry combed again through his books on Egypt for details. He still had his underscored copy of Forster's *Alexandria* which he mined for data and even quoted in his text. The theory of disease and injury operating in the *Quartet* was to come from Groddeck's *The Book of the It*. Larry's copy was to be signed, over the years, by the thirty-seven friends to whom he had loaned the book, a list indicating his commitment to spreading Groddeck's message. By December 1955 Larry was scanning Edward William Lane's *The Modern Egyptians* for details on Cairo and on the Copts.

It was not long before Claude and Larry were living together, sharing his house on Castellorizon and her small flat on Archangel Michael Street.[215] Cautiously exulting, Larry wrote to Henry Miller, 'Happiness is really within reach.' Claude was a bridge between the Levant and Europe, between the women of Alexandria, whom Larry identified as 'the loveliest and most world-weary women in the world', and the energetic, will-driven women of Europe.[216] With her cultural roots in France and her knowledge of Egypt, she was an ideal companion for Larry during his attempt to render the cityscape of Alexandria. Claude soon received the imprimatur of an introduction to Harrison at Lapithos. The ageing bachelor architect responded warmly to her beauty and her laughter.

Larry told Henry that *Justine* 'carries a series of sharp cartoons of the women of Alexandria'.[217] Those who enjoy the game of identifying the originals of the heroines in Larry's books have decided that Claude was the model for Clea, just as Eve was the presumed prototype for Justine. Both judgements are simplistic. True, golden, creative Claude was reflected in Larry's invention of blonde, artistic Clea Montis, and dark, passionate, Jewish Eve made a very tolerable model for Justine, but there were many other candidates for both characters. Larry's painter friend Clea Badaro may have been a more direct inspiration than Claude: 'I borrowed her name for Clea,'[218] he said. Larry's expressed affection for Clea Badaro may have suggested to him the Darley/Clea love affair. Then, too, the flawless Botticelli beauty of Marie Millington-Drake may also have influenced his portrait of Clea Montis. The fact is that Larry worked from the palette of his imagination, taking a shape here, a skin texture there, a tone of voice or style of expression from another of the many women he admired.

Justine had become the dominant character in the novel that Larry had long been calling by her name. Mythologically, he reached beyond Aphrodite to Astarte, Ishtar and her avatar, the lustful devouring Queen Semiramis. The marriage of Aphrodite to Adonis had been celebrated in classical Alexandria: very well, Larry's geographical Justine would be as timeless as Cleopatra, as Isis. To bring myth into modern focus, Larry invoked the Marquis de Sade's Justine, whom he reincarnated in gorgeous form and spirit, taking hints from dark-eyed Smilja, from the bold independence of Thérèse Epstein, possibly from the directness and courage of Diana Gould, probably from the beauty and intelligence of Mary Mollo, certainly from the passionate troubled psyche of Eve Cohen Durrell; and echoes from many others. Eve herself denied any single model:

The long and the short of it is: I do not identify with the character of Justine. Nor have I met anyone like it in Alexandria. Someone remarked to me that: if Justine resembled any living person most, it was Larry himself! which Larry found very witty at the time and demurred about it by commenting that, she was anyway a composite of many people and of course there must be something of him too, since he wrote it! So there you have it.[219]

Larry would have agreed.

When he was interviewed in Hamburg towards the end of 1959, Larry had more to say about de Sade. 'In a sense he is the most typical figure of our century, with his ignorance and cruelty,' Larry said. 'I regard him as both a hero and a pygmy.' He was heroic in having the courage 'to try and conquer his despair' by giving in to it, and a pygmy because he failed. 'He is the champion whiner of all time,' Larry continued. 'Yes, infantile as modern man is: cruel, hysterical, stupid, and destructive – just like us all. He is our spiritual malady personified.'[220]

For once, Larry did not feel under the spell of any spiritual malady. He was loving well and writing well, it seemed to him. As his spirits soared, he assumed that no one around him had a right to feel ill. When Achilles Papadopoulos developed debilitating headaches for which the doctors could assign no cause, Larry pounced upon him:

'When is your baby due?' – Joyce was expecting her first-born.

'In two or three weeks.'

'Dear boy,' exclaimed Larry, 'what you've got is sympathetic labour pains!'

The child was born on 7 December 1955, and Achilles's headache vanished. The next day Achilles was shot at from arm's length by two men while he was driving away from his home: the window inches from his head was shattered, but he miraculously escaped injury. The headaches, at least, never returned.[221]

If EOKA really was targeting Information Office personnel, it would only be a matter of time before Larry was killed or injured. Reluctantly, he borrowed a small pistol from a Scots major in the police. Handguns became part of the *tenue de ville*. 'We laid our pistols on the bar of the Homer Palace and called for a double with the air of bing-bing artists in a Western,' Larry remarked wryly.[222]

As political tensions rose, the demands on Larry's talents as the inspirer of 'several million miles of prose in praise of a highly questionable policy' increased in consequence.[223] Sometimes Larry was not successful in getting good press notices, even from correspondents who were his old friends. Shan Sedgwick turned up in Nicosia in rainy December, walking into Larry's office amid roars of laughter, a live turkey under his arm. Together they spent a glorious ten days touring, eating and chatting, and then

Sedgwick filed a dispatch to the *New York Times* that undercut the British claim that their administration was much better than any the island could expect from Greece. Sedgwick wrote that there was no appreciable difference between the rural poor in Greece and in Cyprus, and that the Cypriots under British rule were among the most highly taxed people anywhere. He even criticized his friend's Public Information Office, which he equated with the Ethnarchy of Archbishop Makarios: the two agencies 'throw statistical data at each other' – presumably like custard pies. The main difference seemed to be that 'the former does so at the expense of the Cypriote taxpayer, the latter at the expense of the church'.[224] In any case, Larry was exhausted, and after Sedgwick left, a 'nasty carbuncle' erupted that kept him down for ten days.

At this point, how much did Larry himself believe of the official line that he was helping to create? He probably took his carbuncle as a Groddeckian sign of his inner conflict. Writing a year later in *Bitter Lemons*, Larry would still state that 'of course, our moral and legal title to the island was unassailable.' Enosis? Well, 'one must deeply sympathize with anyone not wanting to be administered by Greeks,'[225] he said, without admitting that most Greek Cypriots did not envision union as administrative subjection. On the other hand, Larry continued to be adamantly opposed to the rawhide colonials who set their jaws over their whiskeys and said that the rebellion would end if they could only 'squeeze the Cyps till they squeak'.[226] No, Larry ruled out unlimited force, but almost with a note of regret: he 'doubted' that 'with wobbling electorates at home unable to stand bloodshed and terrified of force', anything beyond 'ordinary police procedure' would be tolerated. What Larry seemed to pin his hopes upon was that, provided the colonial administration could temporize for fifteen years, 'anything might happen', and that if Anglo-Greek friendship only held, 'a referendum might even give us the Cypriot vote outright' – membership of the Commonwealth.[227]

Claude brought a welcome light touch into Larry's life. She was a superb secretary, an irresistible hostess, a skilled manager of household affairs, but more important than that she had a sense of gaiety, of humour, of comic timing. She had a fund of tales gathered as a tavern-keeper in Ireland, and she could 'think English' – or French or Alexandrian, for that matter. A true polycultural, she had absorbed English literature and convulsed Larry by declaring that 'Lady C was written by a sexy Cromwell.'[228] Mary Mollo, although a staunch friend to Eve, would describe Claude as 'a gold and porcelain creature, delicate as a thrush, strong as a thoroughbred'.[229] As

Larry's companion, she would need these qualities. Richard Lumley, who was still sharing Larry's Nicosia house when Claude moved in, appreciated her, although he distanced himself from the violent arguments that flared between Larry and Claude even in the early days of their companionship.[230] Lumley was distinctly *not* amused by the ruse that Larry concocted to fool Claude's sailor husband, who abruptly announced his imminent arrival on the island. 'I'll tell him that Lumley and I are homos, and that Claude is merely a close friend,' said Larry. He neglected to tell Richard of the plan, and invited 'Mr and Mrs Forde' to dinner with them. All went well until Forde, on leaving, commented to Richard that he and Larry must have fine times together. Forde's meaning was unmistakable, and so was Lumley's shocked response. The whole truth about Larry and Claude came out, but Forde seemed not to mind, and simply sailed away.[231] Larry's luck held.

One of the intrepid friends who risked EOKA bullets to visit during January 1956 was Diana Gould, now married to Yehudi Menuhin. They had not met for a decade, but she was the same irrepressible Diana, and Larry seemed to her as effervescent as ever. With her came 'The Fiddler', as Diana called her famous husband. The compact, quiet musician liked Larry 'immensely'.[232] Menuhin would have appeared merely a prosperous businessman were it not for his extraordinary yogi's gaze, a look that seemed to see beyond three dimensions. The affection was beamed both ways. 'How like you to understand Yehudi at once with your kindly searchlight eye,' wrote Diana. Larry found in Menuhin the aesthetic repose of the religions of India. 'Yehudi is metaphysically of the Far East,' said Diana in agreement; 'His serenity, lack of materialism, possessiveness or pecuniary interest belongs to a Hindu, a Bodhisatva.' By the gentle power of his example he showed Larry a way back to the observed Eastern religions of his childhood, an alternative path to the Christianity that had terrified and failed him: 'Christianity is but a brilliant mosaic of half-truths,' Larry would write before the year was out.[233] Larry would eventually take up the practice of yoga, naming Menuhin as his inspiration; and he would turn towards Buddhism. Perceptively, Diana contrasted Yehudi's freedom of mind with the obstacles she maintained that she and Larry owed to their British upbringing: Yehudi, she said, 'thinks across the barriers you or I have had to climb or knock down because of our educational background and the dogmas we were taught'.[234] For Larry, at the time attempting to keep open a dialogue, however tenuous, between the British authorities and the Cypriots, this meeting with Yehudi Menuhin was particularly inspiring. They drove out to Larnaca's salt lake, 'where

Mahomet's aunt boiled her billy-can' in Diana's irreverent phrase – Uum Haram, the aunt, had broken her neck falling from her mule and was buried there – and tried hard to persuade a raft of flamingos to rise in flight. Larry needed the gaiety.

The Colonial Secretary, Lennox-Boyd, arrived from London on the last day of February 1956 for a second round of negotiations with Archbishop Makarios, and was greeted by nineteen bomb blasts in Nicosia. Since Makarios was in close communication with Grivas, it was obviously a planned welcome. Larry by virtue of his office and his past consultations in London was in constant attendance upon Lennox-Boyd. London and Sir John Harding decided that the Ethnarch could no longer be tolerated, and on 9 March he was seized boarding a plane for Athens and packed off unceremoniously to the Seychelles instead, where he was to endure thirteen months of genteel house arrest – with his own bridge foursome thoughtfully provided – in the governor's summer residence. Exiling Makarios and three of those closest to him among the clergy may not have been entirely wise, as Larry said: 'The deportation of the Archbishop which was operationally just was politically nonsensical.'[235] Grivas took over the political as well as the military direction of the rebellion, and his instincts were harsher than the Archbishop's: there were 246 EOKA attacks before the end of March.[236]

Even as the victims of the bombs and ambushes were dying, there were grimly humorous notes traceable to the cultural differences between the opposing sides. EOKA managed to plant an operative named Neophytos Sophocleus among Harding's household staff.[237] After Sir John had shrugged off an intelligence report that he had been marked for assassination, a bomb was planted under his mattress and connected to an erratic timer that needed warm temperatures to operate properly. Since all good Cypriots sealed the windows at sundown to keep out the evil night air, the conspirators trusted that Sir John would do likewise, and confidently expected that he would join Castor and Pollux in the heavens towards midnight. Nothing happened. The Governor, with an Englishman's fanatical devotion to cold fresh air, had kept all the windows wide open throughout the night. Sophocleus had vanished by next morning and the staff discovered the bomb, which went off with a terrific blast ten minutes after it had been removed to a bunker. 'That's funny,' said Sir John, 'I slept better than usual last night.'[238] Larry's critics were to complain that he mixed the comic indiscriminately with the tragic in his books: they had not lived through a Levantine crisis as he had.

WITH CYPRUS SHATTERING HIS concentration at every turn, Larry finally declared *Justine* finished and handed the typescript to Joan Pepper for a formal reader's report. Joan told him, 'The Americans will love you, you'll win the Prix de Goncourt if you go on like this, but the Boots reader won't know what you are talking about in England.' Larry accused her of being 'too enthusiastic', but he himself thought the book very good.[239]

Freya Stark came through in the first week in April, on her way to Cairo, as usual disregarding the conflicts of nations. Then Sir Harry Luke, who had spent part of his youth on Cyprus, showed up briefly for a ritual meal with Larry of moussaka and a bottle of red 'Ace of Hearts' wine, shared on a deserted beach 'while the old unchanging sea rushed and hissed upon the pebbled shore'.[240] The beauty remained but many of those who had enlivened Larry's world had gone: Fay Nind, Austen Harrison, Pearce Hubbard. Maurice and Leonora Cardiff were leaving soon. Larry began to feel like a soldier defending a shrinking perimeter. After Leonora departed for England, Maurice invited Larry and Claude for a last dinner in his courtyard. Late in the evening an argument broke out between Larry and Claude about London, which Claude said was her favourite city. 'What do you find so wonderful about London?' Larry demanded. Soon they were shouting at one another across the table, until Larry pulled a pistol from his pocket and fired several shots into the wall over her head. An armed patrol banged on the door with their rifles, but Cardiff was able to convince them that it had been a false alarm. Larry and Claude left together amicably.[241]

Meanwhile the war of slogans continued, the walls covered with competing acronyms and phrases in the preferred bright blue paint. The exhortations ran from the blunt 'Out with the English' through the grimly comic 'May Hardingk fall out of his helicopter' to the all-encompassing 'Death to Everyone'.[242] Equally unambiguous was the warning painted in contrasting red near unruly Paphos: 'We Will Shed Blood'.[243] In April the deliberate killing of British civilians began. 'The Cyprus experiment has failed,' Larry announced. 'May make a book,' he added tersely. He had already decided to call it *Bitter Lemons* – 'very bitter I'm afraid' he wrote to Sir Patrick Reilly, then Minister in Paris. Larry asked him about the possibility of some sort of cultural post in France.[244] Half seriously, Larry consulted an astrologer, who told him that if he wanted to stop working in 1956 he should advertise 'not more than twice' in a newspaper. Larry asked Alan to place his ad in *The Times*: 'Poet and author, established, needs patron for two year writing plan. Repayable.' How much in earnest was he? Larry hedged on his motives: 'It would be amusing to prove the astrologer wrong.' Larry told Alan that he did not expect a rich patron to turn up, but he considered his situation desperate enough: 'I see myself jobless and starving in Sept. I have not a clue as to what I might do for a living. Such a bore. Unskilled labour on a farm I expect – "Poet shovels shit".' He was 'frantic' to be in France, even if only for a few weeks, but he was faced by a 'cobweb of problems', among them how to pay Sappho's expenses.[245]

Larry made a desperate attempt to make a little money: he asked Sir William Walton, on the strength of having met him in Argentina, to hand a copy of *Sappho* to Sir Laurence Olivier, with a view to production. The letter of rejection that arrived in July boosted Larry's poetic ego if not his bank balance. Olivier praised the writing, but said that it was 'more for the ear than for the eye', and that he could not respond to the characters as 'real people'.[246]

In May a fellow poet arrived in the guise of a Red Cross nurse: it was Penelope Tremayne, sent to the island because of her command of demotic Greek. Slim, cheerful and utterly fearless, she was given a white Land Rover and the dangerous assignment of bringing health care to the villages in the Troodos range – where Grivas often maintained his peripatetic headquarters. Her introduction to the island on her first drive alone had been helplessly to watch the death, from multiple gunshot wounds, of a lorry driver. From then on she had been caught up, like Larry, in the delicate task of being British among people who hated the British in the abstract – and who sometimes hated them enough in the flesh to commit murder – and yet who responded with the warmth typical of Greek or Turkish Cypriots to any individual who helped them. Tremayne was to experience both extremes: she was several times threatened with death in reprisal for government actions, yet an EOKA representative appeared to thank her for ministering to the dying truck driver.[247] 'There is a streak of madness in Penelope, in a most endearing way,' said an admiring Achilles Papadopoulos.[248]

If there was a single defining act for Larry in 1956, it was the hanging by the authorities on 10 May of Michael Karaolis, a mild-mannered clerk in the Income Tax department. In June of the preceding year he had killed Police Constable Michael Poullis during a Communist meeting in Nicosia. Hundreds had witnessed the shooting, and Karaolis was captured. Although nearly everyone, Cypriots and English alike, anticipated the death sentence for the crime, there were island-wide riots when the verdict was announced on 28 October. The day Karaolis was executed, demonstrations occurred all over Cyprus, and in Athens seven people were killed and two hundred injured when police and troops suppressed the disturbances that broke out. Larry was worn out, he had finished *Justine* and needed time to write the sibling novels, and he felt that his public efforts were futile. Pointedly, Kranidiotis, secretary to Makarios, told Larry that it was time for him to leave. His polite counsel amounted to a warning that Larry would no longer be protected from EOKA – indeed, that he might be a serious candidate for assassination.[249] He resolved not to renew his contract with the government when his second year of service ended in August. Although Larry had some hope of a writing contract that would guarantee him an income against future books, he was still not confident that he would be able to survive by his typewriter, and wrote to the British Council enquiring about jobs. He even asked Jacques Vallette of the *Mercure de France* to look for someone in need of a caretaker for a large country house – 'this of course would be an ideal job to have!' he told Sir Patrick Reilly.[250]

Larry was sure that his neighbours in Bellapaix would not harm him, but for the first time since the troubles began they started to avoid him, although whether in sorrow, anger or embarrassment he could not be sure. He complained bitterly in Clito's wine shop that the villagers had turned on him. Once a watchdog barked while Larry was sitting in the lighted window of the Cosmopolitan bar in Nicosia having a late-evening drink, and the waiter surprised three men outside carrying what appeared to be a Sten gun. Larry was convinced that he had been the intended victim. Then in early June 1956 an incendiary bomb was placed in his garage. He began to think that he might really be murdered in Nicosia.[251]

Moments of companionship had to be snatched piecemeal. In Larry's company it was possible to gain a few hours of relief from incessant talking about 'the Cyprus situation'. Penelope Tremayne recalled a June evening when she, Larry and two others were sitting on the dark veranda of his house drinking coffee, enjoying the faint breeze and the starlight. The lights glowed in central Nicosia half a mile distant. Three slight youths evidently in their late teens strolled up and down the silent street, talking in low tones and giggling. Suddenly they doubled over in unison, like runners at a starting line, and Larry snapped out 'Bomb!' Instantly there was a terrific explosion, a flash of colour like a fireworks display, and the young men ran off. Larry had his pistol but to shoot at the boys, even had he been so inclined, would have been to risk killing someone in the nearby houses. He and his party ran through the garden to the house across the street where the door had been blown in and a hundred clay flowerpots smashed. Inside the door stood a hysterical young Englishwoman and two blond, naked children, unhurt.

While Penelope calmed the woman, Larry phoned the police, giving them in quick phrases the location of the house and the direction in which the suspects had fled. Soon the garden was full of British civilian and military police. At this point a pair of Cypriot Greeks, middle-aged and 'portly as penguins', wandered along the road and were promptly arrested. In broken English they tried to explain that they were merely civil servants coming home from a taverna. Because they seemed frightened and nervous, the police were sure they had the culprits. Larry took the senior policeman aside: 'I think these people are telling the truth. I saw the three boys who threw the bomb; we all did; and these don't look the least like them.' The policeman was unmoved: 'Dark trousers and white shirts, you said, sir. That's what they've got, ain't it?'[252] Never mind that nearly every male in Nicosia wore the same combination. After considerable argument, Larry won his point and the two Cypriots were freed.

Larry's eventual success with the police sergeant had not been matched at higher levels. His first advice two years before to Sir Robert Armitage about the need for tact and persuasion had not been heeded. Then Larry had misjudged the staying powers of the Cypriots when it came to open rebellion. He had told his brother that the bombings of police stations and public buildings would never shift to deliberate assassinations, and he had been wrong. When Sir John Harding had been sent to oppose EOKA violence with his Commandos, Larry had perforce to agree with the institution of a martial law that he had from the outset hoped would not be required. Now Englishman distrusted Cypriot, and the islanders feared one another as well as the occupiers. Grivas had achieved his end, knowing that once 'the slender chain of trust upon which all human relations are based is broken', Cyprus would be ungovernable except by the most self-defeating military force.[253] There was profound weariness and despair in Larry's summation. 'I was, I realized, very tired after this two years' spell as a servant of the Crown', he wrote. As the bombs and killings mounted, as Cyprus slipped into an ever-darker chaos, Larry came to a heartbreaking conclusion: 'I had achieved nothing.' There was indeed a bitterness in the lemons: 'It was good to be leaving.'[254]

Larry's disbelief in the efficacy of political engagement had been burned into his very soul by Cyprus. However, in his creative life, Larry had pulled through: despite his failure to achieve the peace, inner and outer, that he thought he required for accomplished writing, despite his self-doubt, he had achieved *Justine*. The artist whose birth cry had sounded in *The Black Book* had finally reached maturity in Bellapaix, in Nicosia. The Cyprus venture, begun in desperation, lived with chaotic intensity, and concluding in retreat, had turned out after all to be a wondrous crucible in which to smelt the raw ore of the *Quartet*.

JOAN AND DENNIS WETHERELL-PEPPER left Cyprus in June by ship, and Joan worked throughout the trip to complete her interlinear version of Larry's *White Eagles over Serbia*. Soon after reaching England, she took Larry's draft and hers to Alan Pringle at Faber, telling him to read Larry's first. The Faber editors perused both, rejected the joint version because they felt the styles did not match, and asked Larry to revise his draft as 'an adventure story for older boys (and girls)'.[255] An embarrassed Larry wrote to Joan that he was 'disappointed' because he had been 'look[ing] forward with great amusement' to a collaborative publication. He blamed Juliet O'Hea for the initial rejection, for causing 'a saleable object' to 'hang fire' for over two years, and proposed to share the advance with Joan.[256]

By July, Larry and Claude were attending to the last details before their departure. He sent 'a clutch of letters from writers and others worth keeping' and the first draft manuscript of *Justine* to Alan Thomas, saying that he might be amused to read it. Faber seemed 'quite excited' by the story,[257] and turned it over to Alan Pringle for 'pringling', as the staff affectionately called his meticulous editing. What was he to do about his home in Bellapaix? Larry wondered. It was virtually unlettable, given its isolation and the continuing turmoil. He knew that Penelope Tremayne was looking for a house in a remote hill village to use as a base of operations, and he offered it to her. When she objected that the Red Cross would not pay rent, he replied, 'I don't want any rent. They can have it for nothing.'[258] For the next six months she was to live the precarious balancing act Larry knew so well: being English in EOKA-dominated Bellapaix.

Larry asked if Alan could put him up for a few days in September. Larry had never mentioned Claude to his best friend in England. There were apparently two reasons for this. The first was obvious: Ella and Eve were close, and Larry did not want his estranged wife to know that he was living with another woman. The other was that Larry may not have been sure that he was going to take Claude with him. He had arranged to maintain contact with Fay Nind, telling her to write to him care of Anne Ridler. He had also told the Wakefields and the Wetherell-Peppers that he intended to dump Claude before he left Cyprus or else part company with her soon after. 'She's not going to win,' he had said to Felicity Wakefield. He may have been disingenuous: the Wakefields did not approve of Claude – she was outside their social circle, she 'talked too much', and they felt that Claude 'had pinched our friend'.[259] But it was obvious to Larry that Claude, with her flawless French and her friends in France, would be a terrific asset in that country, and Larry by himself would feel insecure. True, he had made his move to Cyprus alone, but he had planned the move counting on Eve's presence, and he knew that the Wilkinsons would help him become established. In France he lacked a network of friends. Most important, he really seemed to be in love with Claude.

On 26 August Larry and Claude left Nicosia for London. They hoped that, after a fortnight in England, Claude's connections would provide them with a place to live near Paris. After 'this long spell of Balkan service', Larry said, 'I need debarbarising and re-gilding'. A large part of the heartbreak was leaving behind all that Larry had hoped for on Cyprus, materially for himself and politically in terms of benefit to the island: he had come to love it. Larry maintained that his prospects now were nil. He had enough money to last three months only, he said. Then he would be 'on the parish'[260], 'on the streets quite literally'. 'For the first time in my life I shall be prospectless and dead broke,' he lamented to Henry Miller.[261] Henry had been in that particular pickle far too often to become very alarmed for his friend. When Henry had taken the leap into destitution at the age of thirty-two, it had been the beginning of his creative life.

CHAPTER 10

Sommières, *Anni Mirabiles*

And there, lying upon the table in the yellow lamp-light,
lay the great interlinear to *Justine* – as I have called it. It
was crosshatched, crabbed, starred with questions and
answers in different-coloured inks, in typescript. It
seemed to me then to be somehow symbolic of the very
reality we had shared – a palimpsest upon which each of
us had left his or her individual traces, layer by layer.

Balthazar

THE RETURN OF THE prodigal to England brought him a biblical welcome
from his family. After a round of London visits, Larry and Claude moved
into his mother's house in Bournemouth. On 6 September 1956 there was a
joyous reunion with Sappho, and Larry made a second tracing of her hands
in his Cyprus notebook. Eve had taken a job in London under conditions
that did not permit her to have Sappho with her, and she told Larry that he
would have to care for his daughter for a couple of months at least. Larry's
intended two-week stay had to be extended indefinitely when the hoped-for
lodging in France did not materialize. Then Freya Stark wrote from Asolo
offering Larry 'a quiet corner to write in' while she herself spent a projected
ten months working on *Alexander's Path*.[1] There was the question of What
To Do About Sappho, Larry answered. 'Much as I enjoy her', he told Freya,
'the strain of trying to write with a small child on one's hands is v. great.' In
fact, Larry continued, he was writing this 'dispersed and scrappy letter' on
his knee while reading Lewis Carroll to Sapphy.[2] Larry had not seen fit to
tell Freya about the break-up of his marriage. Sappho would be 'very
happy while you write' in Asolo, Freya thought.[3] Wisely for all concerned,
Larry declined Freya's invitation and finally mentioned Claude. 'I hope, my
dear Larry', replied Freya, 'you will love a lot but not marry any more.'[4]
Yearning for her own children, Claude was wonderful with Sappho,
teaching her the alphabet and guiding her first attempts to read.[5]

Larry still hoped for France, and Henry suggested everyone he could think of for help in finding housing, from Brassaï to his Russian friend Eugene Pachoutinsky, but nothing turned up. Larry complained about his plight to Diana Ladas, the English ex-wife of Alexis. He seemed to blame Claude for the limbo they found themselves in: 'That bloody woman said she would find us a place to live – and she hasn't!'[6] Diana Ladas offered them her holiday cottage very cheaply. Taking Sappho along, Larry and Claude settled into the small 'two up, two down' cottage, picturesque and hidden in a cul-de-sac near Donhead St Andrew in Dorset. A tiny trout stream bisected the garden and washed against the kitchen wall. The very address seemed a calculated insult to a drinking man: Stone Cottage, Milkwell. The cottage was built of rough-cut stone, but its name had originally been Stepping Stone Cottage.[7] Milkwell, fortunately, was not accurately descriptive either: a snug tavern once favoured by Churchill, The Castle, stood at the crossing of the lane and the metalled main road. It served good ale and whisky, and gave Larry a chance to listen to the local dialect, to people who talked 'in the identical tiresome moralising way they do in Hardy'.[8] Sometimes Larry would encourage one of the older locals to read aloud to him from Hardy, buying him glass after glass the while.[9] No Hardy cartoon but a true cosmopolitan, Henry Miller's novelist friend Jimmy Stern was living outside Tisbury, about four miles away, and in October he and his wife Tania met Larry for the first time. They knew the south of France intimately, and were able to advise Larry on his proposed move.

Although *Justine* had been accepted by Faber and publication was due in February, Larry was frantic about money and had promised a book on Cyprus by Christmas. He had committed himself to paying for Sappho's schooling, and Claude was contributing to the support of her children, then living with their father. In Stone Cottage Larry hoped to find the isolation and peace he needed to complete *Bitter Lemons*. Sappho might be 'adorable as ever', but Larry was discovering that 'a six year old is even more work than a baby in arms!' The constant questions were enough to drive him round the bend: 'Daddy, what does God look like? . . . What is a "sake"? (For Jesus' sake, Amen.)'[10] Sappho seemed to enjoy the local school, but Larry worried about her accent 'getting broader and broader' – just as *his* parents had objected to an Anglo-Indian accent. Still, being away from the Public Information Office, from the bombs and the tragedy of Cyprus, made the Stone Cottage interlude feel almost like a holiday to Larry.[11] A holiday it would have been, were he not working all day, every day, at *Bitter Lemons*. Cut off from radio, television and daily newspapers, 'exhausted by travel and women and divorces and alimony', Larry took refuge in Claude's care and observed that little had changed in England: 'Everything is serene and bland as suet.'[12] By 6 November Larry was able to report that he had produced 40,000 words of *Bitter Lemons*.[13] He told Jimmy Stern that he had finished the book in twenty-seven days.[14]

Soon the Cyprus typescript was at Faber, and Larry, Claude and Sappho went to Bournemouth to stay with Alan and Ella and to see Louisa Durrell and Margaret. Alan recalled that, 'relaxed and exhilarated by the relief of having finished the book', the whole Cyprus experience recast before his eyes, Larry held forth and his conversation 'leapt and sparkled like the fountains of Versailles'.[15]

Before long Larry was back at his Underwood, revising *White Eagles over Serbia*. By the end of December 1956, Larry's 'juvenile' was ready to enter the Faber lists. The novel is in Larry's Van Norden mode, but like the much earlier *Panic Spring* it contains flashes of scene and character that are pure Durrell: 'some snatches of landscape not too bad – all accurate', Larry said. It was based on the 'true recital' of one of his venturesome friends.[16] Larry was considering writing a series of twelve thrillers about 'The Awkward Shop', the Secret Service.[17] Larry also set down some passages of 'Justine II', as he called the second volume of the *Quartet*, and he dashed off 'Moulder of Minds', the first of his humorous sketches about life among diplomats, which was to be published in the *New Statesman* in January. He and Claude had cause for celebration when her *Mrs. O'* was accepted by Faber.

In the early weeks of 1957 Larry and Claude went to Paris, where they stayed in a small hotel near St Sulpice. Sappho was back with her mother. Larry sent a postcard to Alan Thomas, describing in euphoric terms 'the marvellous strong well balanced untravelled wine' at 1/1^d, the Gauloises Bleues at 1/10^d, and the '*tremendous*' *baguettes* of paté, salami and liver. They had 'radiated' to Montparnasse, the Louvre, and St Germain des Prés. 'I should never have been anywhere else,' he raved, 'I feel I could write 3 Justines in 3 weeks *here*.'[18]

They ran though their contacts but in vain: no free or affordable housing appeared. Larry in desperation tried to drop in on Richard Aldington, whom he knew only by reputation and a single exchange of letters back in 1933. He missed Aldington in Paris by minutes, but then fired off a message to Aldington's Midi address to ask for advice on housing between Montpellier and Banyuls. Aldington replied immediately with a letter full of information, and concluded with an offer to help on the spot should

Larry come south. Aldington called Larry's attention to Sète, Le Grau du Roi, Les Saintes-Maries-de-la-Mer, and to 'some most ancient villages in the hinterland here'.[19]

Larry returned to London for the publication of *Justine* on 1 February: if he was going to have to live by his writing, he knew that he must nerve himself for periodic publicity forays. To the many over the years who would meet Larry at book signings or see him interviewed on television, he would be smiling, gracious and to all appearances completely at ease. When he spoke at length it was in fluent paragraphs usually delivered without notes. Yet the public display was an agony for him. He hated to present himself, but made each effort because he felt that it was expected of him and because he thought that it would buy him free time in the form of income. One part of him would always remain the dutiful son of a conscientious father. It gave him a sick feeling to disappoint people, whether it was his publishers or his public.

Larry had sent advance copies of *Justine* to some of his friends, and he was cheered by a letter from Freya Stark complimenting him on his 'terrific visual grip': 'You make me feel how vague all my adjectives are.'[20] Diana Menuhin, herself a direct and passionate woman, was dissatisfied with Justine as a character, yet thought that the novel 'was tremendous but that one bogged down and longed for air'.[21] Another passionate woman, Anaïs Nin, no longer communicating with Henry, wrote to Eve Miller that she was crazy about *Justine*.[22] To Larry she praised 'the great tactile richness'. In an interesting flight of hindsight, Anaïs recalled 'the young Larry of twenty six or so who appeared in Paris . . . and with whom I should have then and there run away'. At this, Larry's eyebrows must have risen in alarm. Artistically, Anaïs continued, 'I was to be completely alone', and her much-vaunted intellectual partnership with Henry had been finally dissatisfying: 'It was the contraries, not parallelism of any kind.' To Larry she explained her polyandrous life, in New York with Hugh Guiler and in California with Rupert Pole, the tall, gentle professor of forestry and amateur musician who had become her West Coast companion.[23] Later Anaïs wondered whether the various diaries in *Justine* were not 'proliferations' of Larry's own.[24] No, he responded: he had never kept a diary, fearing that the form would swallow him.

Leaving *Justine* to fend for herself, on 7 February Larry landed at Le Havre and went on to Paris, where he and Claude stayed with her father at 4 boulevard des Invalides. After a short visit, they boarded the train for Provence. A few days later they met Richard Aldington at the Hotel du

Centre in Montpellier. The talk was not only about housing for Larry and Claude, but about Aldington's problems with the literary establishment. Aldington had published his debunking biography of T. E. Lawrence two years before, and had thereby brought down a torrent of criticism from the British Establishment. He claimed that B. H. Liddell Hart had handed to his publisher William Collins a letter on 10 Downing Street stationery and signed by Sir Winston warning him against bringing out *Lawrence of Arabia*. Robert Graves and Liddell Hart had both written negative reviews of Aldington's book. Worst of all, Aldington's publishers had stopped reissuing many of his titles, and his royalties had dried up. 'I wish it had been possible to talk more shop but Claude chatters so,' Larry apologized to Aldington.[25]

Busy as he was, Larry immediately wrote to the *New Statesman* asking to review Aldington's recently published *Introduction to Mistral*, wishing to make some recompense for Richard's generosity and also to right an injustice. His review was published as 'Poet's Kingdom' on 4 May 1957.

Meanwhile, envelopes containing press cuttings had begun to arrive from Curtis Brown. The early verdicts on *Justine* by the few English reviewers were of the 'all right, but – ' sort. The *Times Literary Supplement* praised the 'rare acuity' and the poetic style of the novel, and commented favourably on the multiple viewpoints, but worried that the author 'loses as much from the resulting complexity of his narrative as he gains from the "multi-dimensional effect"'. Justine herself was put down as 'demented'.[26] The next day the *New Statesman* lauded the 'prose-poetry', but grizzled over a perceived lack of drama, a weakness in character delineation and tired metaphors.[27]

If Larry was discouraged that *Justine* seemed to be faring little better with the reviewers than *Cefalû* had ten years before, he did not let on. The public at least was buying *Justine*, and Faber brought out a second impression within weeks. Besides, the judgements of his friends were so positive. Henry wrote to him that 'nobody can wield the English language like you,'[28] and named various European publishers for *Justine*, 'all good friends', among them Heinz Ledig Rowohlt and Raymond Queneau at Gallimard.[29] 'Your troubles have done you good,' Henry concluded.[30]

An important breakthough came on 25 March with Christopher Middleton's radio broadcast, 'The Heraldic Universe', for the BBC. He attempted to explain Larry's treatment of time, perspective and mythical symbolism in *Justine*. The heroine sees herself in triple and five-fold mirrors, and the multiple faces represent, in addition to a many-faceted personality, Middleton suggested, 'time past, time present, and time future'.[31] In addition, he pointed out, behind these mirror-images was hidden what the narrator Darley called 'the austere mindless primitive face of Aphrodite' – the mythic emblem of modern Alexandria.[32] Middleton referred to the chapter on Georg Groddeck in Larry's *Key to Modern Poetry* to clarify the psychologist's influence: Groddeck's explanation of the interdependency of sex and the imagination had suggested to Larry that his characters must win through the 'sackcloth' of experience to reach the underlying 'cloth-of-gold', the higher, heraldic plane of meaning. Unfortunately, Middleton's brilliant investigation of *Justine* would not appear in print until thirty years later, but it showed that a contemporary outside Larry's circle could realize part of what he had set out to accomplish.

Justine was at first passed over by the Book Society, and Gerry could not resist reminding Larry that 'as I have always told you, it is naughty to write about sex all the time'.[33] Soon, however, the Society *did* recommend *Justine*, and Larry could be fraternally superior.

The most immediate problem was housing, and Larry and Claude started looking around Nice and Cannes, which he found 'not very nice', too expensive and too reminiscent of Bournemouth, Poole and Eastbourne. Travelling by train and village bus, they inspected and rejected Marseille, Toulon, Arles, Montpellier, Sète, Perpignan: 'All this bit is flat alluvial marshy with some pretty villages on the coast,' Larry thought, but there was too much tourist claptrap. The tourist plague scarcely reached three miles inland, however, and they began to concentrate on the smaller towns and villages.

Before the end of February they had located and leased the Villa Louis in Sommières, set in rolling country on the Vidourle river. They wanted to live near enough to a population centre so that Claude could find a secretarial job should they find themselves *in extremis*, they wanted a river for summer bathing, and they wanted to be somewhere attractive – Sommières was a limestone-and-tile town of about three thousand inhabitants, and it was within commuting range of both Nîmes and Montpellier. The Villa Louis was situated on a disused gravel lane up a steep hillside from the branch railway cutting, and the small Sommières station lay a hundred yards below them. 'All the trains have post horns and make one feel like Louis Philippe on a progress,' Larry told Aldington.[34] The few short trains per day were not enough to fracture the blissful sense of rural solitude. There were two good-sized rooms, a kitchen, and a very primitive bathroom downstairs. The upstairs consisted of a large room opening on to a raised terrace. One long side of the house was windowless and faced the road. The other opened west towards the garden and, beyond it, the reddish tile roofs of Sommières and the valley of the Vidourle rested in the middle distance, with the snout of the Pic Saint-Loup on the horizon. The best feature of the garden was a fine linden tree that promised shade for summer dining. To the right of the property an Albigensian castle, full of crazy angles and a home for rooks and swallows, thrust its square tower above the Villa Louis and with a 'girdle of medieval walls and ravelins' overshadowed the town. The other ancient glory of Sommières was the Pont Romain, called by Larry the 'tumpy Roman bridge across the green Vidourle',[35] at the midpoint of the town. Immediately below the bridge was a V-shaped weir, a Roman flood-control dam.

In Languedoc, primitive meant no internal running water and no flush toilet: Larry and Claude showered under a watering can, and it was no joke in chilly March. He bought a Racasan earth closet, similar to the one that he had reluctantly emptied at Little Songhurst Cottage so many years before, and a bottle of 'delightful' blue disinfectant. 'I am of course a firm supporter of the Old English Humus group', Larry joked, 'and believe in giving nature back as good as I get.' At first Larry found plenty of Rabelaisian amusement in the fortnightly burials – 'It remains to see how long the vines stand up to this Rupert Brooke treatment ("corner of a foreign field that is forever England")' – but as a routine the operation became a bore.[36] Was he regressing to his indigent youth, Larry wondered? Despite the rustic conditions, by mid-March he had settled down and was 'wrestling with a brute, trying to throw it before the end of June'.[37] This was the first evidence that he had buckled down to *Balthazar*. 'I'm racing to finish a book so I can get some dough next month,' he told Aldington.[38]

Sommières lay mainly on the east bank of the Vidourle, behind the *jaquemart*, a jack-of-the-clock that struck with a comically leaden clonk from atop the town wall. In the first century AD the proconsul of the Emperor Tiberius had built the bridge with seventeen spans, after observing the broad reach of the river during the spring floods. The inhabitants of mediaeval Provence, huddling together for defence, had built fortifications to enclose seven of the eastern and four of the western arches of the bridge, and today some of the principal shops rest upon the venerable bridge itself, now paved with pumpkin-yellow tiles. The Roman road to the coast had passed within yards of the Villa Louis, and it still formed the main north-south thoroughfare of the town, running past a seventeenth-century former Ursuline Convent to emerge through the northern gate at the Place de la

République. With weathered stone buildings of three or four storeys on all sides, the streets were dim and cool, and so narrow that some were impassable for cars, while nowhere except in the squares could vehicles overtake each other. In the central Place des Docteurs Dax below the Roman road and shaded by the water-worn and eroded arches of the bridge, the Sommiérois held a Saturday farmers' market where they offered fresh oysters and fish, sausages and goat cheeses, local wines, mattocks and scythes, blue workmen's shirts and trousers, along with melons and aubergines and leeks and all the other succulent provender of the valley fields. Larry and Claude would come down their lane to the southern edge of the town, follow the row of great plane trees on the margin of the Vidourle to the clock tower, slip into the *marché* down the concealed steps of the *maison de Reilhe*, and for a very few francs return with their string bags holding a week's fresh provisions. They were in a land where good eating and copious drinking conceded nothing to Rabelais's Chinon on the Loire.

The comparison with Rabelais was justified in another important way: just as the old master's writing was as much about the joys of the spirit as about the pleasures of the body, the practical citizens of Sommières respected the arts, even those in languages and media that they did not understand. Larry was quickly discovering that he only had to say that he was *un écrivain* to be treated with respect and consideration. His calling was something that he had kept silent about in English shops and pubs, but it was a source of pride in France that artists were cherished, and nowhere was this more true than in the Midi. The *pâtisserie* where he picked up his *croissants* and *pain au chocolat* most mornings, the vintner, the butcher, the grocer, the café waiters along the Vidourle – everyone fussed over 'Monsieur et Madame Durrèll', firmly accenting the name on the second syllable. They had a fine native tact that prevented them from imposing upon Larry and Claude's privacy; 'These people have a marvellous reserve as well as being really friendly', he wrote to Henry.[39] Soon Larry had a wide acquaintance of respectable townsfolk and countrymen and friendly tipplers – the categories overlapped. Among them were Louis Legrand and Marcel Ramage, who had fought with the *maquis* during the war. When the time came for the annual dinner of the veterans of the Class of 1936, to which Legrand and Ramage belonged, they invited Larry to be inducted as an honorary member. The wine flowed like the Vidourle itself, and Larry donned a straw hat and sang songs after the manner of Maurice Chevalier. Finally the party was ending, and Legrand clearly was in no condition to make his way home alone. Larry, seizing the excuse to leave, volunteered to accompany him, but Legrand turned out to be past recognizing his own dwelling. 'That looks like it . . . no, it isn't,' he kept saying as they wove about the labyrinth of the dark town, passing under the stone buttresses that spanned the alleys.[40] After this evening, Larry was more securely an adopted son of Sommières than he had ever been of Bellapaix.

Larry was assured of a major American publisher when Dutton promised a handsome advance for *Justine*. 'All this of course doesn't mean much – but it's a ray of light under the door,' said a cautious Larry.[41] He felt that it would be bad joss to exult. He was already hoping to duplicate his Bellapaix feat: buy an old village house 'full of odd corners' and restore it. His prospects improved when Kenneth Rexroth, one of the most important arbiters of American literary taste, wrote a powerful double appreciation for *The Nation*, dealing with both *Justine*, not yet out in the US, and the 1956 Grove Press *Selected Poems*. Placing Larry at the top of his generation in Britain, Rexroth pronounced, 'No one writing verse today can better evoke a scene, a place, a room, a situation, the body of a woman, alive at just that fleeting moment when it lived, with all the meaning of its present and all the pathos of its vanishing.' *The Black Book* was 'so perfect, so deadpan', Rexroth recalled, and he thought that *Justine* was at least the equal of the early novel in its 'comic irony' and 'the tour de force of a tour de force that is its style'.[42] This might not have been the judgement that Larry would have preferred, but it was a welcome signal.

Larry gained another important ally in America when Buffie Johnson, now married to the novelist and *New York Times* reviewer Gerald Sykes, reopened contact. Sykes wrote to Larry that *Justine* was 'the most interesting new novel I have read in a long time', and wanted to review it.[43] He also admired *The Black Book*, and would later write the introduction for its first American appearance in 1960. Sykes's broadside in August for the *New York Times* proclaimed that *Justine* 'demands comparison with the very best books of our century', and he drew an especially strong parallel with Proust – one of the ancestors of his novel, as Larry was pleased to admit.[44] Most other American reviewers took their tone from Rexroth and Sykes, and Larry's sales were assured. True, there were some puzzled or acerbic critics, but their voices merely served as leaven to the praise. The *Saturday Review* found 'aesthetic decadence' that derived from the wicked French: Huysman's *A rebours*, Baudelaire's 'phosphorescence of putrescence', Rimbaud's 'personalized anguish'. Among the more facile reviewers, *Justine* provoked attempts to emulate his prose and imagery: *Time* declared his novel to be 'fleshed with verbal luxuriance and approached by a dozen roads as twisted and surprising as the narrow alleyways in the dense Attarine Quarter' of Alexandria.[45] By this time, Larry could afford merely to sigh or laugh. Amid all the turmoil he found time to read Herrigel's *Zen in the Art of Archery*: 'Tremendous!'[46]

An intensive correspondence had begun after Larry and Richard Aldington's first meeting. As a young man, Larry had admired Aldington despite not much liking his novels, including him with Roy Campbell and Wyndham Lewis among those writers possessing 'real balls'.[47] Larry had praised Aldington's satires and had depended upon his translations from the French. After settling into the Villa Louis, Larry and Claude visited Aldington at Les Rosiers, the solid stuccoed house on the northern edge of Montpellier where he lived in a small flat with his eighteen-year-old daughter Catherine, called Catha by everyone. Aldington's marriage to Netta Patmore, Catha's mother, had broken up in 1946, and after the financial troubles following the publication of *Lawrence of Arabia*, Aldington's personal space had been reduced to a single room, with his bed amid stacks and boxes of books. Larry recalled, 'It was a bad period for him and he badly needed friends.'[48] Over the next few years Larry would take up the cause of the 'Aldington boycott' and launch various ploys – usually frustrated by Richard himself – in an attempt to break it. A warm man who masked his feelings behind a barrage of half-humorous, half-serious invective, Aldington was nicknamed by Claude 'Top Grumpy'. Claude, with her deft impersonations, was the only one in their circle who could really make Richard laugh.[49] He adored her, and for her benefit he put on his most outrageous performances, cheerfully slandering 'Henrietta' James, 'Churchwarden' Eliot, 'Sir Water-closet' Churchill, Geoffrey Grigson: 'I hear Grigson boasts of eating insects – sheer cannibalism!' Aldington said.[50]

Larry's daemon was driving him hard, the voice of conscience that told him he had delayed too long before re-committing himself exclusively to writing. Midway in *Balthazar*, Larry gave Pursewarden a speech that expressed his own regret at lost time: 'I am ashamed of one thing only: because I have disregarded the first imperative of the artist, namely, create and starve. I have never starved, you know. Kept afloat doing little jobs of one sort or another.'[51] Now he was at once exhilarated and scared. He was his own man, and was afraid that he *might* starve. Constantly worried about money, Larry easily convinced himself that he had always lived more or less in penury.

Now, with substantial sums in hand and more promised by *Balthazar*, Larry was tempted by many opportunities to add to his income. Tambimuttu weighed in with a suggestion in March that he take over the editorship of *Poetry London-New York* from him. That would have been enough to drive Larry insane. Tambi, however, proved the vanguard of a trend, as other commissions trickled in: next month Stephen Spender wrote to request an article for *Encounter*, and 'The Shades of Dylan Thomas' was the result. Every now and then, to relax and to bring in a few pounds, Larry scribbled another 'Antrobus story', as he referred to his comic sketches about the Foreign Office narrated by a diplomat named Antrobus. He claimed to take only twenty minutes to write these 'Antrobi'. Usually he took care to disguise the characters and incidents, but into 'Drage's Divine Discontent' he slipped the name Smilija for the 'second housemaid' who falls in love with the bald butler Drage – himself named, quite likely, after a small town that Larry must have driven through not far from Belgrade.[52] Larry's memories of the Yugoslav ballerina who had dumped him years before apparently still rankled.

Of greater financial significance, and welcome because it did not mean extra work, was the awakening interest of non-English publishers. Thanks in large part to Henry's urging, Heinz Ledig Rowohlt had read *Justine* and immediately decided that he wanted to publish the *Quartet* in Germany. There was the problem of a German translation, and after one translator had broken down amid the complexities of Larry's prose, Ledig Rowohlt took over the revisions himself. He pleaded with Larry for patience: 'You will have to play with me a little, Larry.'[53]

From March on, Aldington wrote Larry a steady stream of letters, often two or three in a week. With the death on 8 March of Wyndham Lewis, who had been a friend of Richard's, a pattern developed: Richard would write commentaries on friends of his past – D. H. and Frieda Lawrence, Ezra Pound and Wyndham Lewis – and on his first wife, Hilda Doolittle. Another burst of reminiscence began when Roy Campbell, one of Aldington's best friends, was killed in a car crash in Spain. Although Larry had not maintained contact with Campbell after their few meetings in London ten years earlier, he could share Aldington's grief. Larry liked to drop a few strategic gambits in Richard's way and then 'let his memories run on . . . Middleton Murry Katherine Mansfield Eliot Ouspensky'. Larry exclaimed to Henry Miller, 'Imagine, as a young man he was corresponding with de Gourmont and Proust.'[54] Frieda and Lawrence had stayed with Richard at Ile de Port-Cros in 1928. Lawrence was then quite ill and consequently testy. When Frieda showed him a few chapters from Aldington's *Death of a Hero*, Lawrence had lashed out that within a year Richard would be 'dead or in a bug-house'.[55] Richard and Larry disagreed in a friendly fashion over Eliot: after being good friends and associates – to the point that Richard had helped edit Eliot's *Criterion* for two years – they had quarrelled and Richard had lampooned Eliot in *Stepping Heavenward*. This satire Larry had recommended to Henry Miller some twenty years earlier. Paradoxically, Richard, another self-exile from England, reminded Larry of his own lingering ties to English writers from the previous generation.

Larry and Richard contrasted sharply in the degree of their expatriation. While Larry still complained a lot about Pudding Island and made it clear that he did not want to live there, he kept his image as an author in focus with strategic visits for the publication of his books and with reasonably measured public comments. *Bitter Lemons*, although critical of British policy towards Cyprus, contains laudatory portraits of the key figures, including Armitage, Lennox-Boyd and Harding. Also, whatever his complaints to good friends about stiff and imbecilic associates in the Foreign Office, Larry had worked in one capacity or another for Their Britannic Majesties' governments for more than fifteen years, and he had not maintained that record through open opposition. Aldington, however, tended to lash out, and perhaps worse, he stayed away: 'Of course part of the trouble is that I haven't touched the soil of the Isle Dolorous for 20 years,' Richard admitted.[56]

Before meeting Aldington, Larry had already created in *Justine* the character Ludwig Pursewarden in the spiritual image of Percy Wyndham Lewis,[57] friend of D. H. Lawrence. Curiously, the physical description of Pursewarden was to change after Larry got to know Richard. The fictitious writer was depicted in *Justine* as being 'little, fattish and blond and gave the impression of a young man lying becalmed in his mother'; in fact, he was rather like Larry himself.[58] Already by the time of writing *Balthazar*, Larry had begun to portray Pursewarden in terms suggesting Aldington, and in the one-volume edition of the *Quartet*, revised for publication in 1962 while his friendship with Richard was flourishing, Larry would alter the description in *Justine* to read 'clever, tallish and blond'[59] – a closer approximation to the younger Aldington. In *Balthazar*, Larry made fun of Lawrence's emphasis on sex through Pursewarden, who has written to Lawrence, '*I am simply trying not to copy your habit of building a Taj Mahal around anything as simple as a good f—k.*'[60] A year after writing this, Larry said of Lawrence: 'I feel that to cut off the head and exclude the reason in order to locate the affective nature of man in the abdomen, as he did, is to make the river flow backwards.' Larry sited the emotions elsewhere: 'My notion of the affective flow is upwards, a notion I have borrowed from the Hindus.'[61] This concept forms a fair schema for Darley's love affairs with both Melissa and Justine; and in *The Avignon Quintet*, Hamayana and Tantric Buddhism would assume obvious centrality. At the time of writing the *Quartet*, Larry was already moving philosophically eastward.

An inestimable gift that Richard made to Larry early in their acquaintance was an introduction to a French poet and television executive named Frédéric-Jacques Temple, a powerfully built bearded man who gave the physical impression of being perhaps a lumberjack or a sea captain. Temple had heard a lot about Larry from Henry Miller during a shared 1953 visit to Joseph Delteil in Maussane, and he stood ready to help Larry with anything from mundane housing details to publicity for his books. Larry was glad to make French friends, and he soon met Delteil and others through Temple. As Larry moved into a new experience of France, some of the figures of the Paris that he had shared with Henry were dropping away: Michael Fraenkel, after a lifetime of fascination with death, died in Mexico, and the one-armed Blaise Cendrars became paralysed – on his good side.

Larry was so happy to be in France, even though he grumbled about having to 'shit with the wind blowing up our arseholes' at the bathroom-less Villa Louis, that he wasted little nostalgia on his lovely and plumbed-in Turkish house at Bellapaix. Penelope Tremayne wrote to him that the EOKA operatives in the village had considered shooting her, but had decided against it – and then had told her of their decision. The crazy, ingenuous Cypriot peasant nature still held. However, Larry's ties to Cyprus were rapidly loosening. By 19 April Penelope was writing to say that, while the Greek Cypriots were still friendly, 'the Turks grow more hostile daily'. She had arranged for Peter Storrs to rent the Bellapaix home for the summer, but she was shipping the pictures Larry had left behind, and would get his silver home 'somehow'.[62]

Larry was more concerned with settling into Sommières. The Villa Louis came with many fruit-bearing vines, and it was good to watch the buds put forth delicate leaves and, within weeks, clusters of tiny green pinheads that would become grapes. As spring arrived Larry and Claude planted a small *potager* in the yard sloping down towards the railway cutting. Soon they were eating fresh salads, *haricots verts* and shallots to supplement the market fare.

It was becoming increasingly clear that they would not need their garden to keep themselves from starving. By 1 May Larry was writing to Alan Thomas that he was on the last three or four pages of 'Justine II', and he was cautiously optimistic that the book 'may not be as bad as one always fears'.[63] Days later he told Henry Miller that he would begin writing the third of the *Quartet* 'after tea today'.[64] Soon he was speaking of *Mountolive* as a work in progress.

Probably the claim that Larry would make to future interviewers of having written *Balthazar* in six weeks was not far off the mark, but he was not being entirely straight when he averred that money shortages had made him send the novel 'to the printer as it was', full of slips and imperfections that he would otherwise have caught, or that all the parts of the *Quartet* had been 'done under terrific pressure, financial pressure'.[65] It suited Larry's sense of drama to make his plight sound more desperate than it was, and if he was able to convince himself that his back was to the wall, so much the better. Larry's fear of insolvency was, however, quite genuine, and money *was* tight, although he had a small cushion in Britain, and less in France. 'We have enough dough for about two more months here', he had written to Aldington near the end of March, 'by which time I hope the exchange control people will have done their stuff.'[66] Then on 24 May *White Eagles over Serbia* was published in England. What with the European and American advances for *Justine*, 'the baby won't be crying for bread before Xmas', Larry said.[67] His relief was palpable.

Larry worked at top speed to finish *Balthazar*, and by 6 May he was 'on the last few pages' of 'Justine II', as he still called the novel.[68] By 25 May Larry said that the 'typing out' of Justine II had begun. The heroic Claude was to hammer into clean copy 140,000 words in two weeks, despite a visit by Amy and Sir Walter Smart. Claude's reward was ten days alone in London in early July to see her children Barry and Diana. She also visited the Faber offices and sold her second novel, *The Rum Go*. 'She is an Alexandrian Becky Sharp', said an admiring Larry, 'gay resourceful and good tempered'. 'Luck!' he added.[69]

Over the same period, Larry rewarded himself with a few days in Ascona, where he wrote a Note to preface *Balthazar*. The Note was his Jolly Roger, a guide to readers and a challenge to critics, at once a signpost and an artistic justification. 'Modern literature offers us no Unities', he wrote, 'so I have turned to science and am trying to complete a four-decker novel whose form is based on the relativity proposition.' He was also careful to say what he was *not* attempting in the *Quartet*: 'This is not Proustian or Joycean method – for they illustrate Bergsonian "Duration" in my opinion, not "Space-Time".' Larry would attempt to incorporate Einstein in his portrait of human relations, just as Proust had exemplified the Bergsonian universe in his. Lest anyone miss his grand intention, Larry added that 'The central topic of the book is an investigation of modern love.'[70]

The unity Larry was searching for through the *Quartet* was a universal principle that would explain all the contradictions he had observed: the reported dead who turned up alive, the drastic personality changes in wives and friends, and nature's most distressing *truc*, the variability of love. At the heart of this instability Larry saw the ego. In *Key to Modern Poetry*, Larry had quoted D. H. Lawrence's warning that 'You mustn't look in my novel for the old stable ego of the character.'[71] Larry would explain later that 'Freud torpedoed the idea of the stable ego so that personality began to diffuse.'[72] Turning to the relativity theorem, Larry believed that he had found the appropriate scientific metaphor for the unstable ego: if the time, velocity and mass factors of a unique event had been shown to be variable, then must the ego not of necessity be similarly shifty?

The nature of time had to be of vital concern to the novelist. The Bergsonian concept that Larry was rejecting was the idea that time was a function of memory, which gave it 'Duration'. For Henri Bergson, being, the state of existence, could be equated to time itself. In response to Descartes's 'Je suis une chose qui pense,' Bergson had postulated, 'Je suis une chose qui dure.'[73] Bergsonian time moves forward and changes, but in step with human existence. This stands in contrast to the illusory time of Platonic philosophy, which considers the finite and the infinite as one, unchanging, and to Einsteinian relativistic time, which views time as simply another variable, dependent upon the frame of reference of the observer. Bergson advised writers to 'throw reason overboard and depend on "intuition"', Larry claimed. As he saw it, Conrad, Henry James, Joyce and Woolf had extended Bergson's ideas 'into the domain of literary form'.[74] Larry wanted to move in another direction, and he took just as much from Einstein as he needed – the conclusion that the observed nature of events depends upon the relative motion of the observer. To the physicist, this means that a kinetic event – say, the swing of a pendulum being timed in a laboratory apparently at rest – would be measured differently by scientists observing the event from a second laboratory moving at a stellar velocity past the first laboratory. Furthermore, the scientists in the second laboratory would be quite justified in concluding that the laboratory with the pendulum was passing them, and not the other way around. To Larry this meant that nothing that he as novelist wrote about – not time, not events, not even character – was fixed, stable, finite, but depended on the orientation of the observer: in *Justine*, Darley believes that Justine is in love with him; in the sequel to *Justine*, another observer, Balthazar, 'proves' that she had been in love with Pursewarden instead. Soon Larry began to receive letters from excited physicists and mathematicians, some saying that 'you can't create a continuum of words',[75] a four-dimensional relativistic continuum, others approving of his application of relativity.

In his own mind, Larry had long ago resolved the problem of flux: 'Time and the ego are the two determinants of style for the twentieth century', he had written in *Key to Modern Poetry*; 'if one grasps the ideas about them one has, I think, the key to much that has happened.'[76] *The Alexandria Quartet* would be his attempt to sweeten the scientific pill of the revelation of personality with a romantic coating.

Nearly everyone outside Greece and Cyprus liked *Bitter Lemons*. It was a Book Society Choice, and Larry wrote to Austen Harrison that the dedication to him had brought luck. Freya Stark found an 'extraordinary crisp quality' in so 'fair and clear an account', and Henry Miller enjoyed the prose. Larry's friends persisted in comparing him to writers of the previous generation. Hugh Porteus, 'The Wombat' of days gone by, said that 'You are doing the best writing since the heyday of pore old Wyndham'[77] – not exactly a compliment from Larry's point of view. More flattering was Aldington's claim that 'You have some of the mysterious DHL gift of making one feel one has lived personally your experience.'[78] Even Sir John Harding and his successor, Sir Hugh Foot, weighed in with letters of praise. Diana Menuhin gave a copy of *Bitter Lemons* to Prince Ludwig of Hesse, who decided that he would like to meet Larry. Larry caught a whiff of danger: suppose too many of his readers – frightful bores, no doubt – came to visit him? He would have to move to Baffin Land! Larry began to plead with his friends not to give out his address or telephone number. The curse of being unknown was rapidly being replaced by the greater curse of being famous. Eve Miller wrote complaining about the arrival of strangers at two in the morning in Big Sur, and Larry was determined that the same catastrophe would not happen to him.

He need not have anticipated gaining Greek fans with *Bitter Lemons*. Seferis and Diamantis were very angry about the book. To them it was a clever apologia for the continuation of British rule over Cyprus, a condescending denigration of Greek Cypriot aspirations for union with Greece. Although Seferis did not break off contact with Larry, it is doubtful that their relationship ever recovered fully. The Cypriot Kostas Montis and Larry's one-time Greek friend Rodis Roufos would each write a novel intended as a direct rebuttal of *Bitter Lemons*.[79] Roufos even composed a chapter of *The Age of Bronze* in which Maurice Ferrell, author of 'Sour Grapes', poses as a philhellene while assassinating the Cypriots with his clever pen. The identification with Larry is unmistakable: Ferrell 'writes brilliantly intellectual poems and enchantingly lyrical prose', he 'has an eye for the quaint and the comic in native customs', and 'One usually ran into him in some bar or tavern where he would be lounging comfortably, glass in hand.' Roufos accused Ferrell/Durrell of belittling Enotist sentiment and of cynically manipulating the sympathies of the readers by biased and inaccurate reporting. Roufos concluded, 'The book is not only very British – which is natural enough – it is Tory British.'[80] The 'Sour Grapes' chapter was cut before Roufos's novel was published by Heinemann, and in the other chapters the Ferrell character was renamed Harry Montague.[81] Larry in his comments on *Bitter Lemons* often mentioned British approval but passed in silence over Greek and Cypriot outrage. He would never return to Cyprus, and six years would pass before he revisited Greece.

In mid-July 1957 Aldington was in the process of moving to Maison Sallé, Sury-en-Vaux, in the Cher, where he had been offered free housing in a cottage owned by his Australian friend Alister Kershaw. In fact, Kershaw had bought the house so that Aldington would have a roof over his head, but he had tactfully not admitted this. Maison Sallé was a tiny hamlet inhabited by six *vignerons* and their families, situated on the edge of the Sancerre wine region, a two-hour drive south of Paris. It was an ideal retreat for one who, like Timon, had turned his back on the world. After all his complaints about maulings at the hands of English reviewers, Aldington found it even more annoying when he was commended: he had been ill following his move to Sury-en-Vaux, until he was 'galvanised into a simulacrum of activity by the blasted impudence of the Sodom-on-Thames reviewers who now have the fantastic impudence to praise me' – the *Times Literary Supplement* had quoted in a misleading context a remark of his about 'young boys and old boys', and he had written to the effect that he was 'not a crypto-pederast like their dear friend Henrietta James'.[82] 'I'm so delighted you are back on the field and in good fighting heart,' Larry responded.[83]

Larry continued his own energetic campaign to promote *Justine* and her

459

siblings, enlisting Miller's aid. Larry sent Henry the typescript of *Balthazar*, which he read before forwarding the parcel to Curtis Brown. Rather bafflingly, Henry announced: 'In some ways you remind me of Paul Valéry. Those aesthetico-religious-metaphysical speculations especially.'[84] Then Hans Reitzel, Henry's Danish publisher, requested the rights to the novel. Ledig Rowohlt asked Henry to draft a preface for the German *Justine*. With cavalier inaccuracy, Henry wrote, 'Like Balzac, Lawrence Durrell wrote his first novels under a pseudonym.'[85] As in the case of Larry's misstatements about Henry in *The Happy Rock*, the spirit counted more than bald facts. The German publisher did not in the event print Henry's preface, but Buchet-Chastel in France used it. Henry was full of schemes to boost Larry: he badgered Curtis Brown to secure a stage production of *Sappho*, and suggested that Buddhadeva Bose would be ideal to translate *Justine* into Bengali.[86]

Everything seemed to be going Larry's way in publishing, but he was still woefully short of cash. One day in the garden of the Villa Louis, Claude told Larry that she had arranged to take a highly paid secretarial job in Sète; she would have a small apartment there, and come back to Sommières on the weekends. Larry slapped her hard and she fell into a rose bush, but leapt back at him, swinging. Their fight was interrupted by a banging on the front door: it was a messenger from the *Poste* with an express letter. The advance for *Justine* had arrived from Dutton. 'Laughing and crying, we went at once to cash the cheque. Claude's face was scratched and we each had a shiner,' Larry recalled. 'But you see, I couldn't let her take a job – all the fight would have gone out of me and I could not have kept writing. And that was the marvellous thing about Claude – if I threw a plate at her, she threw one back!'[87] Larry thanked Henry, in emphatic capitals, for his success: 'THIS REALLY DOES OFFER ME THE CHANCE TO FREE MYSELF FROM DIRTY JOBS AND SEE AT LEAST A YEAR AHEAD. A VERY BIG TURNING POINT IN MY LIFE – THOUGH OF COURSE THIS ADVANCE WILL SOUND CHICKEN-FEED FROM THE U.S. POINT OF VIEW (about 1400 dollars). NOW THE REST IS UP TO ME AND UP TO BOOKS. MARVELLOUS. AND OF COURSE I REALLY OWE IT ALL TO YOUR HARD HITTING CHAMIONSHIP OF ME. WAS EVER A WRITER LUCKIER IN A TRUE FRIEND I WONDER?'[88]

During the second half of July the invasion of 'MASSES OF CHILDREN' began: Sappho, Barry, Diana, then sister Margaret and one of her two sons.[89] 'Saph the baby is seven, black as a sloe and sly as a mascot, and full of anti-social drives!' Larry would boast to Henry Miller.[90] Living conditions at the Villa Louis came to resemble 'CENTRAL MACEDONIA'.[91]

They still had no hot running water, and Larry cooled the wine by lowering the bottles into the well. What with swimming in the Vidourle, the *course libre* in the small bullring under the plane trees, and excursions to the Pont du Gard, Arles and Les Saintes-Maries-de-la-Mer, Claude and Larry kept the children entertained, but all writing had to cease. He complained loudly about the children, but it was largely *pro forma* or spoken for effect. The 'little beasts' put chewing gum in his typewriter: 'They drive me to my grave, but I love them.'[92] He was probably equally glad to see them arrive and to see them leave.

Larry would have been hounded to distraction without Claude. He had observed her skills as a broadcaster and an executive secretary, had watched her cope with bombing alarms on Cyprus and the family in Bournemouth. Now, with only the resources of a primitive cottage, she turned the children's summer into a marvellous adventure, directing their activities by gentle suggestion and her own tremendous enthusiasm: her laughter and her songs kindled them all. At timely intervals the wisps of cigarette smoke would give way to the aroma of a *gigot* of lamb rubbed with crushed rosemary and thyme roasting in the hearth, or a fish sautéing in butter and garlic. Claude's conjurings, wine glass in hand, always seemed effortless.

Finally the summer was over, the children were sent back to their schools, and Larry was able to return to the attack on the *Quartet*. As far back as April he had predicted that 'Justine III' would be easy to read, a 'big orthodox novella',[93] a 'naturalistic job'.[94] What with the continuing distractions of fine weather, swimming and visitors, by 10 October he was still only a hundred typescript pages into the book. However, Larry always felt that a hundred pages was a magic number, enough to give him the sense of the book, if it was to be any good at all. He cobbled together some 'fake Moscow scenes', justifying himself that 'anyway I didn't want things to be photographically right, nor . . . the absurdity of having my characters thought to be "real" which they aren't'.[95]

Claude's *Mrs. O'* appeared, and suddenly there were two published authors in the Villa Louis. Larry thought that she had spoiled the factual *donnée* with the addition of a love interest, but he found the narrative skilfully handled and predicted that she would eventually write something really good. Henry noted a similarity in writing between Larry and Claude: 'no hint of imitation – it's just there'.[96] With more money finally coming in than they required for their daily expenses, Larry and Claude allowed themselves an occasional jaunt to Nîmes for a film and an excellent meal at La Louvre.

Often the distractions sought them out. Cyprus had been a convenient pausing spot for the Eastern Med hands among Larry's friends, but for most people a trip to the island was too daunting. Sommières was another matter entirely. The great Paris-Marseille-Narbonne *autoroute* did not yet exist, but the old N7, the standard *route nationale* from Paris via Lyon to the Riviera, passed through Avignon, only about seventy-five kilometres away. Some friends already lived near by. In September David Gascoyne and his companion Meraud Guevara came over from Aix-en-Provence for a wonderful reunion: David still the same shy, gentle intelligence.[97] In October, Larry and Claude drove over to Arles to see Gascoyne again, and there was more esoteric talk and mundane punishing of the bottle.[98] Before long, Anaïs Nin wrote that she was planning to come to see Larry.

Treading on the tail of these old friendships came a new one that would continue for a score of years. Dr Arthur Guirdham, a psychiatrist living in Bath, had just read Larry's 1948 *Horizon* article on Groddeck, and on the strength of it caused his own *Theory of Disease* to be sent to Larry. He read it at once, 'WITH THE GREATEST INTEREST, INDEED WITH DELIGHT'. The problems that Guirdham addressed, Larry said, would have to be confronted 'IF THE ARTIST OF ANY SORT IS TO SURVIVE'. He recommended his own favourites to Guirdham: not only Groddeck, but Rank, Mott and Graham Howe.[99] Larry noticed a similarity between Hermann Keyserling's *Travel Diary of a Philosopher* and Guirdham's book. He peppered Guirdham with more titles: Herrigel's *Zen in the Art of Archery* and Orage's *On Love*. Larry was especially excited by Wu Wei Wu's *Fingers Pointing Towards the Moon*, which he described as being 'like a commentary on the novel-quartet I am trying to write between bouts of rubbish'.[100] Soon Larry was proposing schemes to get Guirdham published in America, to attract the sponsorship of J. B. Priestley and Cyril Connolly, and to get Juliet O'Hea to act as his agent. Clearly, Larry was on his way to adopting Guirdham as a new guru: confessing to the 'nerve-frazzling' aspect of the novelist's trade, Larry told him,

I try and behave as little like the neurotic I am and as much like the solid literary journeyman I would like to be. This is where works like yours and Groddeck's etc are such a help. They enable one to attack one's own weaknesses and the self-admiration and self-pity circuits which block up the current; and more important teach one to regard 'shaky nerves' and 'dizzy fits' – all the writer's unfortunate predispositions – as a form of *impertinence* really![101]

Larry suggested that Dr Guirdham's name might have been derived from the river Gardon or the surrounding region, the Gard. In his eagerness to claim Guirdham for Languedoc, Larry wrote to 'Onomasticos', author of a local newspaper column on names, 'Votre nom a son histoire'. Yes, the name could be Languedocien, replied Onomasticos, positing Ghirdam, Goudon, Gardon as variants.

Late in 1957 Larry received a letter on expensive embossed stationery announcing that *Bitter Lemons* had been awarded the Duff Cooper Memorial Prize. He was elated, thinking that it meant merely the deposit of a cheque in his account. A few days later Claude discovered him dancing about in the kitchen, wearing nothing but a deerstalker and a dressing-gown, shouting, 'I won't! I won't go!' He waved a peremptory cable from England. 'Oh, yes you will! Think of your two daughters!' replied Claude. There was nothing else for it: Larry would have to Face the Music. Only his long Foreign Office service kept him from dissolving in panic when he discovered that the prize was to be awarded by the Queen Mother. He and Claude travelled from Nîmes in a *couchette*, and Larry was amused by the contortionist antics of 'commercial travellers' in upper berths wriggling into their blue pyjamas 'in a complicated simian way with their balls swinging around in mid-air'. On Sunday, the day after their arrival, they spent a 'wonderful evening' with Fred Perlès, who drank a good deal and became exceedingly amorous towards Claude. Monday 9 December was the big event.[102]

Larry wrote out his brief speech in large letters so that he could scan the text without his glasses: 'Vanity, thy name is man,' commented Claude.[103] She would miss the ceremony: Larry did not wish to read in *The Times* about 'Durrell and his French companion'. For support he took along Penelope, whom he had not seen since she was eight – 'very pretty . . . and quite a "highbrow" in taste', judged her father.[104] The break in contact had not been his choice: Nancy had not wished to have any dealings with him. Now Penny was a tall, slender seventeen, shy and intensely uncomfortable in a black velvet dress purchased for the occasion. Claude described her as 'an ice maiden, ravishing'. Penelope had not heard of Claude before and asked bluntly, 'Where exactly do you fit in?' Larry explained. He fussed and fretted, 'I shall be sick in the Queen Mum's lap, I know.'[105] Larry, well-starched and wearing a lounge suit on Faber's advice, saw to it that they presented themselves, far earlier than need be, at Hyde Park Gate. The audience room was overheated, stuffy and cramped, 'stiff with earls and dukes'.[106] Larry was horrified to spot Cousin Prudence Hughes and Aunt Fan, decked out in enormous flowered and feathered hats, among the crowd, Aunt Fan as formidable as an aircraft carrier and to Larry's eye nearly as large.[107] Larry claimed that his mother had refused to come because 'the chimpanzee couldn't spare her', for which he thanked God.[108] Penelope was presented to the Queen Mother and attempted a curtsy. She had been studying ballet seriously for years, and every ballet session had ended with four curtsies, so this should have been easy for her, except that she now found herself standing with her bottom pressed hard against an extremely hot radiator.[109] If Larry noticed her discomfort he gave no sign; he pronounced the Queen Mother 'jolly sexy',[110] a 'charmer' with a 'mischievous eye' and 'the pink warm complexion of Eleanor Rumminge (Skelton's ale-wife)',[111] and she said that she had enjoyed his book. Larry gave his little 'mock modest' speech of acceptance and felt uneasily like a poseur, like T. E. Lawrence, he confided to Aldington. There were gruff cries of 'Hear, hear'. Lord Salisbury, who as a guiding spirit of the Conservative Party had been one of the architects of the Cyprus policy dissected in *Bitter Lemons*, 'made me a tender little speech', Larry said. Other diplomats who had read the book 'professed to be deeply moved and repentant', now that 'the damage had been done'.[112] The moment was pure Antrobus, and Larry enjoyed himself enormously.

While *Bitter Lemons* would remain popular and many would prefer it among all Larry's 'island books', the high-profile official recognition accorded the volume, over and above the Duff Cooper award, suggests that Colonial Office policy was still a factor in Larry's life. For the government, Cyprus remained an embarrassing issue, much in the news, and here was a personal memoir by a respected and rising popular author that portrayed the British overlords as well-meaning idealists attempting with considerable restraint to put down the rebellion of a small terrorist minority. Larry's claim in his preface that he was not writing a 'political book' but merely a personal memoir of the times was disingenuous. He was still Director of Public Information when he began the book, and the entire thrust of *Bitter Lemons* makes the evolution of the British stand seem just and inevitable. He implies that the initial British error had been the failure to temporize, to promise an eventual referendum on union with Greece, instead of saying at the outset 'Never!' Then, when Larry has the EOKA terrorists kill his gentle teacher-friend 'Panos' near the end, some cried foul, seeing this as a ploy on Larry's part to deflect criticism from the British for hanging Karaolis, a convicted EOKA killer. The original of Panos, undeniably identifiable as the schoolteacher Larry lodged with early in his stay on Cyprus, was unharmed by EOKA and was still alive in 1996.[113]

No, *Bitter Lemons* is certainly a political book, and HMG was grateful to Larry for having written it. Over the next few years, the Cyprus situation would generate at least seventeen books, but only Larry's would gain and retain a wide readership.

Larry and Claude enjoyed even more spending some of the £200 prize money on a three-day spree in Paris. They stayed in the luxurious suite that Fox Movietone had provided for Paddy Leigh Fermor, bathed three times a day, ate *châteaubriands* and browsed the Quai Voltaire bookstalls. They saw no one but Claude's father – Paddy was away – walked along the Villa Seurat, patronized the Closerie des Lilas, the Dôme, the Deux Magots and the Flore, and bought recordings of Bartók and of Menuhin interpreting Mozart to play on the small gramophone they had just acquired. During the long winter evenings Larry and Claude could now sit alone in the candlelit villa while Mozart cascaded from the machine. 'Music at last!' exulted Larry. 'What bliss it is in this silence.'[114]

Awaiting them were copies of Roger Giroux's 'marvellous' French translation of *Justine*, with a preface by Henry, a 'terrific accolade'.[115] Larry was twice lucky: in having a translator as in tune with his style as Giroux was, and in having Henry, popular and famous in France, to preface the book.

The new currency of the Durrell name meant that others started to seek him out to write prefaces for their books. Penelope Tremayne, back at her family home near Wadebridge in Cornwall, had finished *Below the Tide*, about her experiences in Cyprus. The Red Cross had insisted that she disguise the names of the dramatis personae, but she told Larry that he would recognize the Bellapaix characters. Larry complimented her for being able to 'tread the tight-rope of village diplomacy' in a job 'as arduous as it was dangerous', and for having told her story well.[116]

The year was ending wonderfully for Larry and Claude. It might be bad luck to gloat over successes, but even the cautious Larry had to admit that his gamble in cutting loose from the Foreign Office was working. Money was not exactly tumbling in, but advances and now royalties were in fact accumulating at Curtis Brown in an amount that freed Larry, temporarily at least, from the worry of being 'forced back into the Foreign Office'. For the first time in his life, everything that he wrote brought in money – not immense sums, but still gratifying amounts. *Justine* had earned Larry an advance against royalties of only £200, half on signing in May 1956, the other half on publication. Of this sum, 10 per cent had gone to his agent. After more than 2000 copies had been bought, Larry had begun to collect royalties of 15 per cent on each copy sold at retail prices. As the sales of *Justine* mounted, the publishers' purse-strings loosened a bit, and in July 1957 Faber offered Larry £500 each on the next two volumes of the *Quartet*. Still, Larry's continuing worried plaints to his friends were not entirely insincere. For one thing, he could hardly believe his good luck, and he was too instinctively Greek not to believe in hubris; and he had seen a tidy capital – his long-dead father's – dwindle to very little in a few years. He really did believe that he could suddenly fall into disfavour with the public and find himself destitute, with two children to educate, Claude to provide for, and the need to scuttle back to another distasteful job in the British Council or Foreign Office.

Osbert Lancaster had advised him that 'a cheap Xmas funny was a money spinner usually', so Larry collected a handful of Antrobus sketches into a slim book, *Esprit de Corps*. Aldington became Antrobus's greatest fan: 'This is Wodehouse born again and born greater,' he raved.[117] Richard, living in relative poverty, vowed that 'some copies SHALL go out as un-Xmas presents'.[118] Aldington said that Larry's agent 'should at once be crucified between A. S. Frere and T. S. Eliot' because, as he thought, these stories had been given no serial run. Larry had in fact done 'awfully well' from the serial publication of some of the *Esprit de Corps* sketches, earning more, he claimed, than he would ever make on a serious book: 'a tiny steady income', he wrote somewhat defensively to Henry. 'It is a basic wage. I always was a timid bugger about that basic wage.'[119] Six of the succeeding Antrobus stories appeared by contract in the *Sunday Times* at forty guineas each between February and May 1958, before being published under the volume title *Stiff Upper Lip* – which Larry dedicated to Richard in gratitude for his encouragement. Larry planned to follow *Stiff Upper Lip* with *Sauve Qui Peut*.[120] Claude had just sold her third novel, *A Chair for the Prophet*, to Faber, and an American publisher, Rinehart, was interested in her first two.

The Villa Louis might still lack indoor plumbing and hot water, but Claude had decorated the walls with Larry's bright gouache paintings and had pinned up photographs and, triumphantly, favourable reviews sent in fat packets by Durrant's cutting service. Clearly, the tide had turned in Larry's favour. Buoyed up by the Duff Cooper prize and filled with glowing memories of his days with Claude in Paris, Larry returned like a demon to the attack on *Mountolive*, which he regarded as the *clou*, the nail holding together the entire structure of the *Quartet*. He rose before daylight, stoked the fire and made coffee, and typed off page after page.

Perhaps to curb his own growing elation, Larry wrote in a bit of advice to his putative *alter ego*, Pursewarden: 'His one job is to learn how to submit to despair.'[121]

Once he settled down to the task, Larry wrote so fast, around five thousand words per day, that some people assumed that he was working from a detailed outline. This was not so. In the case of the *Quartet*, Larry said, 'I simply approached the three sides of space and one of time as a cook will open a recipe-book and say, "Let's cook this gigot." I had no idea what sort of gigot was going to come out of it.' He did 'very little deliberate plotting', but worked from 'data' recorded in the many pages of what he called 'Quarries', his fat notebooks in large format, kept in various colours of ink and occasionally pencil. He would cross out passages as he used them. One of his greatest fears was that his writing could become 'a mechanical exercise in a form', and whenever he sensed this to be in danger of happening to a novel, he said, 'I was prepared to throw all the data overboard and let it live its own life.'[122] None the less, he intended that *Mountolive* would be structured 'à la Stendhal'.[123]

Larry's style was very conscious as well. 'I'm with you about the Jap forms', Larry wrote in reply to Henry:

The trouble is with us[:] lack of a metaphysical resonance in proper nouns. Their impact in terms of affect is nearly always personal, or traditional. That is why Valéry flew to mathematics and chiselled out his stuff as fine as a cobweb, to achieve the *heraldic ideogram*. When a Jap writes 'cherry' 'moon' 'grass' the ideogram has a mystical-metaphysical ring quite different from the set of associations we stir by using them; hence the image making that we have to put into it; I work hot to cold like a painter. Hot noun, cold adjective ('mathematical cherry' rather than 'sweet cherry'). Or on a sour abstract word like 'armature' a warm and sweetish one like 'melodious'. . . The Chinese ideogram carries the 'given verb'; our syntax dictates a subject verb object copula in order to create a complex of affective sounds. Tough on us, isn't it?[124]

Often in Larry's work theory and experience came together. Part of the 'life' lived by David Mountolive was Larry's own past. While he may have encouraged critics to see his traits in Pursewarden and Darley, and would agree that there was something of himself in Justine, he was not in a hurry to admit that he was also Mountolive. Yet he gave to his English ambassador details from his own life: Mountolive had been born in India, had left it at age eleven, had had an affair with a Yugoslav dancer. Mountolive had not seen his father again after leaving India, and this Larry joined to his own myth of abandonment, a myth he came absolutely to believe, that he had not seen his father after coming to England.[125]

On 10 January 1958 Larry wrote to Henry that he had 'just finished' the third volume of the *Quartet*, and a few days later he sent it off to Faber. All told, he would claim, the book had cost him two months of actual writing.[126] This could be literally true only if he counted nothing but those days actually spent in the throes of composition, since he had begun the book towards the end of the previous April. He sent a copy of the typescript off to Sir Walter Smart for a libel reading: Larry guessed that some would see elements of Sir Walter in David Mountolive and a few others might think that they recognized themselves. 'And I didn't want dear old Peake, or that old buffalo Killearn to think that I was copying him from life,' he confided later to Sir Patrick Reilly.[127] More than anything, Larry did not wish to offend his old friends. The news arrived that Claude had sold *Mrs. O'* to Rinehart in America. Then a burst reservoir swamped part of the house and drove Larry and Claude with their typewriters into the kitchen, the only dry room. At least, Larry said, they could now afford Tavel Rosé.

AROUND THE BEGINNING OF 1958, Henry had a Danish astrologer friend cast horoscopes for Claude and Larry, and these confirmed that the pair were suited to one another – a conclusion that Larry had arrived at independently. Furthermore, Henry relayed, they could expect to move in October. This was news to Larry: he had no intention of leaving the Villa Louis, at least not before he had finished the *Quartet*.[128] Perhaps the astrologer spurred Larry on; at any rate, by February he was talking about selling the house in Bellapaix so that he would be able to put the funds into a place in France. In this Larry and Claude were encouraged by their 'hysterical landlord', who had decided to evict them so that he could have the Villa Louis for a relative. Claude asked Jacques Temple to keep his eyes open for a peasant *mas*, a small farmhouse, for them to lease or buy. They certainly did not wish to move at the beginning of the summer: they did not want to be settling into a new house when the children arrived for their holidays. By a 'fluke buy of marvellous value', for £15 Larry had picked up a used racing canoe for the children, complete with sail, tiller and centreboard, and he wanted to be near the Vidourle.[129] The hero of the affray over the Villa Louis turned out to be Temple: 'He brought a lawyer out and routed the landlord over five rounds!'[130]

Their victory over the landlord was still only a temporary one, and the astrologer was nearly right: Larry and Claude would have to vacate the house during September. This fitted nicely with Larry's view of astrology, as he explained it to me: 'It doesn't go far enough,' he said, but 'It's quite adequate as a general description of character.' As for the inaccuracies in the predictions, he continued, 'they say that it's my fault; that if I had the absolutely exact dates, they could be absolutely exact.' Larry added thoughtfully, 'The variation of a minute or two throws the whole universe awry in the architecture.' One astrologer had even run Larry's chart every five minutes over the five-hour span during which Larry figured that he might have been born, from 10 p.m. until 3 a.m. 'As far as I know it was ten o'clock at night, but I may be wrong.' He had originally told Henry Miller that he was born at one in the morning, but now he was not sure: 'Thank goodness I'm not', he said and, dropping his voice to a conspiratorial whisper, he added, 'so then we'll never know!' What Larry was indeed sure about was the influence of the nearer heavenly bodies, and from this by logical extension he derived his belief in astrology: 'Don't you feel the effect of the sun on you . . . or the moon?' he asked. 'When the sun comes out, I feel a radical change.' The conversation went from the distant gravitational pull of Mars and Mercury to that of a chestnut falling from a tree in the garden. Larry clung to his belief in the rationality of astrology: 'Theoretically, it doesn't seem as nutty as God the Father.'[131]

If Larry could not embrace God, he could not quite let Him alone either. In the *Quartet* Larry had Pursewarden write a novel sequence entitled *God Is a Humourist*. Speaking to an English interviewer in 1960, just after he had finished *Clea*, Larry referred to 'a question I have often asked myself: Was Christ really an ironist?' Many of Christ's supposed utterances did not square with the descriptions of his character; therefore, Larry said, 'I wonder how many of his sayings were perhaps irony? Because, strangely missing from his portrait is a smile, and I wouldn't have thought that a man could be as great as that and not have a smile somewhere. They allowed the babe to smile in the medieval paintings,' continued Larry, 'but there isn't a smile in the four New Testament portraits of the man.'[132] Here lay the unity of Larry's art: sober philosophy and wild humour, religion and sensuality, God and evil must coexist, and coexist without the intercession of moral judgement.

Larry himself had plenty to smile about. Even before the troubles with the landlord, Larry had announced that he would be 'resting' until April 1958, when he planned to tackle the final volume of the *Quartet*, but he was not entirely idle: he wrote several Antrobus stories, an article on Cyprus for *The Nation*, and 'The Disquieting American' for the *Evening*

Standard. Neither was Claude unproductive, for she launched herself into a manuscript on the customs of England and France. She threatened to call the book 'French Letters', until someone – Antrobus no doubt – convinced her to opt for the less prophylactic 'French Habit' and later *The French at Table*.

Larry was well aware that the fourth volume of the *Quartet* would be critical to his long-term success, and this may have been the underlying reason why he put off tackling it. Instead of working on *Clea*, as he had decided to call the book, Larry agreed with Fred Perlès on the joint authorship of a book about Henry. It would take the form of a correspondence between the two of them about their common friend. Larry had, so he said, been writing the first letter to Fred in his head since a lonely walk to the Villa Seurat on his way through Paris years before, heading to Yugoslavia. Recognizing amid the sounds of crepuscular Paris 'the little tin *vespasienne*' and the street-lamp under which Henry had read Nijinsky's *Diary*, Larry had been seized by his vision of the past.[133] He opened the exchange by suggesting that, since Fred had already painted a word-portrait of Henry, the two of them might address the gulf between the 'gentle, loyal and tender' man of their friendship and the figure of 'aggressions and savageries' thrown up by Miller's work. Then Larry stated the thesis and, inadvertently, the title of his and Fred's joint essay on Henry: '*Is art always an outrage* – must it by its very nature be an outrage?'[134] Fred countered that Henry's innocence precluded any intent to outrage: Henry no more *wished* to shock than a volcano spews its 'gems and ashes' by design.[135] For Larry himself, the answer was that art must by its very nature startle, shock and outrage. If life limped along behind art, so be it.

Soon Larry and Fred were happily pirouetting around and about Henry, until the *cher maître* could not resist joining the fray himself. Henry weighed in on 1 and 2 April with an eight-page typed epistle on his literary genesis that fairly blasted the other two correspondents off the field. He began with a friendly warning: 'Of course, you won't really get anywhere, you know. Take that for granted immediately – and you'll travel far and enjoy it.'[136] Henry later warned Larry not to accept blindly everything that he had said about himself: 'Remember the Tibetan business about the soul being . . . a thousand personalities.'[137] How could Larry forget this, since it was basic to his own ideas on the non-existence of the discrete ego? When that other believer in plural lives, Anaïs Nin, found out about *Art and Outrage*, she was outraged, and wrote to Larry, 'I'm sad that Perlès is getting another chance at misrepresenting Henry.'[138] She had still not forgiven Fred for what she called his 'shabby caricature of my ten-year relationship with Henry' in *My Friend Henry Miller*. Larry was ready to admit that 'little Joe was really rather a shit about Anaïs', but he blamed Henry for Fred's biographical treatment of Anaïs: 'His basic trouble was that he was so much under the influence of Henry that he used to fall into an imitation of his famous roughneck-treacherous attitude. When he isn't Henry, but a nice little mouse-like Central European of the genre of Schnitzler and Lifar, and a very good writer in his genre.'[139]

Always eager to do what he could for Larry, Henry drafted a preface for the projected English edition of *The Black Book*, and worried whether Larry would 'really like' it. Alan Pringle at Faber definitely did not like Henry's effort, and thought it might 'do harm': 'No, he has had great fun letting off his spleen,' Pringle told Larry. Henry took the rejection calmly enough, but *Esprit de Corps* occasioned a minor upheaval. Larry had not expected him to approve of the 'diplomatic sketches', so had not sent Henry the book. Then, emboldened by the British success of the stories, he mailed Henry a copy early in 1958. Henry was not amused: 'Don't write any more of that "Esprit de Corps" stuff,' he commented at once. 'That's really terrible. Not even for money!'[140] Larry replied that he had to buy shoes for Sappho. 'Don't buy any more shoes for the baby!' Henry growled. 'Believe me, they are better off without.'[141] Henry, who after neglecting his first daughter had become a most indulgent parent, was a fine one to talk.

Like a signal flare fired over a battlefield, *Justine* brought Larry both unwelcome and welcome notice. What he had feared came to pass, and reporters, admirers, critics and the merely curious tracked him down at the Villa Louis. As a veteran of Foreign Office public relations, Larry managed a campaign designed to bring him the most publicity possible with the least invasion of his privacy. He would meet reporters at the Café Glacier in Sommières, a humble establishment with a terrace precariously over-hanging the Vidourle, or try to crowd as many interviews as possible into his occasional trips to Paris. Sometimes an interviewer would really engage his ideas, and then Larry would take fire and emerge from behind his press patter of more or less canned explications and outrageous remarks.

Among those in whom Larry recognized shared ideals and ideas was the young French medical student and poet Jean Fanchette, who had chanced upon *Justine* at Blackwell's in Oxford a few months after publication. He had taken over *Lettres Suivent*, the literary supplement to a medical journal in Paris, and for it he wrote a long review which he sent to Larry near the beginning of March 1958. Larry replied that the piece was 'splendid' and 'quite overwhelming', and soon he was talking about meeting Fanchette on his coming trip to Paris. He seemed to be 'another of those amazing Frenchmen who speak perfect English', Larry decided.[142]

On the strength of Fanchette's essay, Larry asked Faber to send him *Balthazar* for review. There were echoes of Larry's own early discovery of Miller and *Tropic of Cancer*, only this time *he* was the *cher maître*. At the moment, Fanchette was planning to translate Caitlin Thomas's *Leftover Life to Kill* into French, but Larry came down hard on it, 'a vulgar shrewish little fishwife's book'.[143] Larry resumed his old campaign on behalf of Georg Groddeck, and he had soon persuaded Fanchette that he should instead translate *The Book of the It* into French – without even bothering to ask Fanchette if he knew German. Jean found the book 'extremely clever', but with some 'highly debatable' points. He took the Groddeck project up with four publishers: no one was interested. He did, however, unearth a book that Claude would later translate into English: Marcel Rouff's delightful minor classic about good eating, *La Vie et la passion de Dodin Bouffant, gourmet*. Loosely inspired by the career of the great chef Brillat-Savarin, the book sparkled with a charm perfectly suited to Claude's light touch.

Another ally, and closer to home, was Jacques Temple in Montpellier. He and Larry discussed Miller, about whom Temple would eventually write a book: Henry at the Villa Seurat was 'Miller-enfant', Temple claimed. 'Enfant, comme beaucoup d'artistes, parce que perpétuellement acharné à défendre l'individu contre le contexte social,' he explained. Henry's infantile behaviour was provoked by his need to defend his individuality against society. Fixing Larry with his wise eyes, Temple applied the same dictum to him. Their talk ranged from Cartesianism to poetry, to the Greco-Latin influences on French literature. He disagreed with Larry's assertion that French poetry tended to be '*claire*' while English was '*vague et obscure*'.[144] Larry was performing his chameleon role again, as he had with his Greek friends on Cyprus. Temple felt insecure in English, and Larry conversed and corresponded with him in French. Temple treated him with great respect, and perhaps on this account Larry tended to hold himself a bit in reserve.

On 11 April *Balthazar* appeared in England, and Larry waited anxiously to see whether the public would buy this version of *Justine*. Most of the critics were lavish in their praise, including Walter Allen who commended *Balthazar* in the *New Statesman* for the brilliant 'shake of the kaleidoscope', the retelling of Justine and Darley's story, and Paul Bowles who extolled Larry's epigrammatic prose. Larry pretended that he refused 'even to read the reviews' and simply had his publishers send them on to his agent. In fact he had wads of reviews in his personal files. 'It will sound unpatriotic but I really don't care *what* the English say,' he told Fanchette, a statement that should be weighed carefully, as he was writing to his most ardent advocate in France, and Jean was as much a rebel as the young Larry had been.[145]

When the English praised Larry, he grumbled, 'It is no consolation to be called a genius by someone who admires but really doesn't get the wavelength.' The English critics, he said, tended to score 'rather like boxing referees' at 'two points per good metaphor', while missing the idea content.[146] It would become Larry's greatest despair: that his books were not understood.[147] When the English offended him, he did not exactly turn the other cheek either, and when 'dear old Seaworthy' told Larry that he had 'grave reservations' about *Justine*, Larry bristled. His identification was with the rebels, those sometimes rejected by the English: with Aldington, Lawrence, Roy Campbell. Seaworthy, Larry said, was 'one of the foolish virgins of poetry', and although kindly, he was 'a sort of soft-boiled egg, who in some curious way feels that his role is that of Chief Aunt for literature', a literature characterized by 'mental snobbery' and 'laborious cartwheels'. Such people only feel comfortable with the likes of C. P. Snow and Ivy Compton-Burnett, Larry continued, and go to PEN Club meetings to spread 'the prettiest tail-feathers'. Not he, said Larry: 'I'm an angry old Camembert!' He had no sympathy with the literary Angry Young Men either: 'They need an enema.'[148]

Gerald Sykes was in a minority in feeling that *Balthazar* showed signs of haste, and he begged Larry to 'go slow' with *Mountolive* and *Clea* – Larry had confided the title of the final book of the *Quartet* to him, but had not admitted that *Mountolive* was already at the printer's. The news from Faber was good: *Balthazar* would go into a second impression almost immediately. Larry calculated that a steady readership of seven thousand would keep him out of the Foreign Office. *Balthazar* would top that figure in two months,[149] adding to his account £250 over and above the £500 advance. Larry had figured that he would need £800 a year to stay in France, and *Balthazar* quickly earned him that.

None the less, the uncertainty of his income plagued Larry, and he told Fanchette, 'I'd give my soul to be a doctor.' It was, Larry continued, an 'honourable profession', unlike 'this damned pen-pushing which lives in a sort of amo-odi relation to oneself!'[150] It was twenty years since Larry had told Henry Miller that he might break off writing and study medicine: how many of his protestations were voiced because Jean was a new doctor, and because Larry could name Keats and Céline as authors with medical backgrounds? No, Larry was spinning a yarn for Jean's benefit: he had had enough of day labour at the Foreign Office, and to have people dependent upon him night and day would have been intolerable.

In May, Larry accepted an invitation to edit and introduce a Henry Miller anthology for James Laughlin at New Directions. Fred Perlès wanted to co-edit the book but this did not transpire. Then Henry proposed that Malcolm Cowley should compile the volume jointly with Larry, yet this second plan fell through also – fortunately, as the egos were too large on both sides.

During April and May, Larry exchanged a number of letters with Anaïs about a possible meeting in Paris. She wanted to publish Larry's 1937 surrealist sketch 'Zero' and had a copy for him to approve. Anaïs and Hugh Guiler were in Europe for a film festival in Brussels, at which some of her husband's films were being shown. Anaïs had finished *Balthazar* and exclaimed, 'What a prodigious way of encircling all the relativities of truth.'[151] In a variety of ways, Anaïs was more of a *Doppelgänger* for Larry than he cared to admit. There was the fascination with psychoanalysis and what it might reveal about personality, and both had already counselled patients. Anaïs had practised in a formal way under Otto Rank's guidance, Larry casually – and with the devil only knew what responsibility for the consequences. In Egypt he had undertaken to explain Eve's psychological make-up to her; long before, he had treated an English girl on Corfu; and later there would be a young French pianist. He did not hesitate to diagnose David Gascoyne's breakdowns either, but most of his 'patients' were young women. Another point of contact was the degree of their expatriation, which would enable Anaïs to be equally at home in her native Paris or her adopted New York and Los Angeles, Larry to take root in various Mediterranean soils. And they were both sexual freebooters – for any number of reasons, not the least being a Faustian quest for knowledge and experience.

Perhaps their most striking similarity was that they shared a highly subjective approach to the truth. In the years following Anaïs's death in 1977 the extent to which she altered, revised and invented material in the allegedly factual diaries would be revealed. Malcolm Cowley – whom Nin detested because he distrusted the inner preoccupation of modern literature – would say dismissively of writers in general, 'All authors are liars,'[152] but the charge as applied to Anaïs and Larry was less damning than it sounded. The 'relativities of truth' that Anaïs recognized in *Justine* and *Balthazar* meshed with what she was trying to accomplish in her diaries.

By early May, Larry had not seen his way clear to coming to Paris, so Anaïs cut across his delays and offered to take the train south to Nîmes, to arrive early on 11 May. Larry picked her up at the Nîmes railway station shortly after daybreak. 'How gallant of you, my dear,' he greeted her. Larry and Anaïs had not seen one another for eighteen years, and there was a mutual stocktaking: at fifty-five, Anaïs's porcelain and unlined beauty had become almost Oriental, carefully maintained in the simplicity of black and white accents. Whatever she wore – stark cape, shawl, white blouse, delicate shoes – was chosen to set off her pale, aquiline visage and delicate form. Larry, who had scorned to look careless or bohemian in the early Paris and London days, now dressed entirely for comfort – loose trousers, a seaman's pea-jacket over a shirt and sweater, sturdy shoes. Even more noticeable was the change in his face: the nose thicker and more pronounced, wavy coruscations of his brow in smiling or frowning, the eyes harder in repose. They were not in repose, however, but were bright with welcome as he strode towards Anaïs. By seven they had collected Claude at the hotel where a room had been booked for their guest. Two days of continuous talk began immediately. Later in the evening Anaïs noticed that Claude, who seemed to her Irish rather than French, spoke more than Larry, and she found him 'impersonal', unresponsive, 'like a wounded person'. Anaïs told Henry that Larry had seemed subdued. More likely, he was on his guard, having learned from experience how easily Anaïs's feelings could be bruised. Larry said later that Claude had imagined Anaïs to be a 'humourless bluestocking' and had planned to prepare a few meals and then leave the two of them together – until Larry convinced her to stay. Claude, knowing both her man and, by reputation, their visitor, probably had private reasons for sticking around. But whatever her expectations, Claude loved Anaïs after the first few hours: 'No one ever knew how nice Anaïs was unless they talked to her,' Larry explained.[153] Even so, Anaïs's feelings *were* chafed by the picture that Larry had apparently painted of her to Claude: 'What distressed me was that Claude had expected a lady with a pearl necklace and a brooch . . . . He did not remember the special way I had of dressing, unconventional', Anaïs would write in her diary.[154]

None of her distress appeared in the note Anaïs sent to Larry and Claude, thanking them for her 'loveliest and deepest days in Europe'.[155] Two weeks later, trying to resolve in her mind her impressions of the meeting, Anaïs asked him, 'Larry, was it the red wine or did you really say: while we are discovering Justine it is Larry you will see and know?'[156] Larry

475

himself had cautiously admitted to Fanchette, 'I believe I am both Pursewarden and Darley, but intermittently in flashes; but different from either.'[157]

Larry's recapitulation to Henry of Anaïs's visit contained more than a little self-justification: 'Did anais find me so subdued?' he queried. Well, he might be 'a bit exhausted' after finishing in eighteen months three novels, *Bitter Lemons*, a volume of humorous sketches, and a batch of articles 'to keep wolf from the door', but he was 'in good heart underneath'. Beyond that, he told Henry, 'I have a very special attentiveness towards anais which prevents me from shouting and screaming in my normal way'. Larry remembered her dislike of boisterous scenes, and had acted accordingly: 'You don't shout at Dresden china do you?' Still, Larry was aware of a reserve between them: 'I think she has always found me a bit of a puzzle: strong watchful brain perhaps?' He spoke of the *ingénue* in Anaïs, a basic trait that coexisted comfortably with her varied sexual and emotional adventures. 'I see someone very young in her always, unmarked by experience, and feel like Uncle,' he told Henry.[158] To Fanchette he said, 'She's a Stendhal heroine!'[159] Larry had in all probability changed far more than Anaïs since the Paris days. She had known the eager young writer and talker, the Larry who tried to appear confident that he would fly a blazing trajectory across English literature. The experiences of the intervening decades had tempered his spontaneous exuberance and optimism.

Although Larry had been setting up a stalking horse when he described himself to Fanchette as 'totally unliterary and provincial', he came nearer the mark when he added that he was 'not so much of a barbarian as I'd like to pretend'.[160] He was well-read compared with his contemporaries, and he could discuss Beethoven with Eliot or *boules* and bulls with the Sommiérois under the plane trees. He knew and appreciated the virtues of Nuit Saint-Georges, Tavel and Dom Perignon, but most of the time he was quite content with red 'slosh', white 'plonk' or a bottle of local *pétillant blanc* for a few francs. More than ever, Larry had become a shape-changer, shifting personalities as the company or his own mood required.

Soon after Anaïs left, Larry and Claude drove to Paris in their matronly Peugeot 203 for a party in Larry's honour mounted by his publisher Corréa. They checked into the modest Hotel Royal on Raspail, and Larry sent Jean Fanchette a *pneumatique* suggesting that they get together for an *apéro* that evening, 20 May. They talked long over bottles of Tavel Rosé on the terrace of the Dôme, had dinner, then returned to the terrace for more Tavel and talk. The reason for Fanchette's excellent English was immediately apparent:

he had been born into a prominent Mauritian family and had, like Larry, grown up a colonial polyglot. He had come to Paris in 1951 to study medicine, and would soon receive his medical degree with a specialization in neuro-psychiatry. Jean had a superabundance of talent and energy: poetry, medicine, psychiatry – he was going to master everything. At present his *Lettres Suivent* supplement was thrusting aside the original medical orientation of the publication. Larry could not miss the parallel with *The Booster*. Jean was relieved to find that Larry did not have a Foreign Office manner to match the FO voice that he had used on the telephone; Larry immediately liked Jean and set himself to be warm and friendly. Claude's 'Alexandrine-Midi gaiety' rang like a chorus of bells over their talk.

Larry had scheduled a number of interviews during his visit. Seated in a café at ten in the morning before a glass of white wine – '*Excellent pour la santé*', he said – Larry spoke to Annie Brierre. In a few words he sketched his diplomatic career, including his arrival in Yugoslavia '*sans avoir lu Karl Marx*'. The weaving of fantasy and fact continued: Miller had revised *The Black Book* and had persuaded Eliot to read the typescript – neither of which was true. Asked about *Bitter Lemons*, Larry replied with fine irrelevance that he wrote satiric essays and detective fiction to pay for his daughters' education; poetry was still his chosen *genre*, but his poems had to form lazily, like stalactites, whereas his novels required fourteen hours a day of labour; his favourite author was Stendhal, his masters Miller and Eliot, and between those two he felt as if in the company of Balzac and Sainte-Beuve. Larry slipped in a strong boost for France: Anglo-Saxon writers – he named Lawrence and Miller – did their best writing in Latin countries, and for himself, '*J'aime la mesure française, et cette intellectualité qui ne dessèche pas le coeur.*' And he fixed Annie Brierre with a warm glance from his suddenly guileless blue eyes. He sent the resulting press cutting to Henry Miller with the annotation 'about 1/3 of this is true!'[161]

There were other encounters, and through Jean, Larry met the Israeli painter Zvi Milshtein; Larry's frequent protestations of poverty notwithstanding, he bought *The Clowns*, a large painting which he carried off to Sommières. As he did whenever he found someone whose work in writing or painting he really liked, Larry became an active partisan, telling Diana Menuhin to look up Milshtein, commanding Jean to take Anaïs around to visit the artist – 'She knows everyone of taste and could be of the greatest help.'[162]

After three days in Paris, Larry and Claude moved out to stay with Sir Walter and Amy Smart at Pacy-sur-Eure. Larry had to admit that he had done well with his friendships in Egypt: along with the delight of seeing the Smarts again, at a convenient hour's drive from Paris came the sybaritic pleasure of soaking in untold gallons of hot water, 'leaving terrible marks in their baths' after the primitive washing arrangements of the Villa Louis. To his surprise, Larry even enjoyed the big Corréa cocktail party on 28 May: 'Vanity surmounts every obstacle!' he told Aldington. 'After all, this party was for ME!'[163] Larry had paid for Sappho and Penelope to come to Paris, and Eve saw them off in London. Sappho, Penelope noted in her diary, 'was an angel'. Penelope had brought along her friend Jill Dawkins, a fellow ballet student. Claude met the girls on their arrival in Paris and whisked them straight to the Corréa reception. The Menuhins were there, and Diana, perhaps sensing the nervousness of the two young ballerinas, talked to them at length. Then followed a Chinese meal, after which Larry took his daughters and Jill to the Dôme to meet Jean Fanchette and his wife Martine. It was 2:30 a.m. before the girls got to bed, but Larry and Claude had given them a marvellous 'first glimpse' of Paris. The next day Jean took the older girls to a ballet master class, and Penelope was pleased to be offered a dancing role – which she turned down as she was on holiday.[164]

Two days later, Jean and Martine entertained the Durrell group and the Smarts for drinks at their rue Scipion bedsitter, where they sat on poufs under the light of 'bottle lamps with bread-basket shades'[165], and then Jean took the entire party out to dinner at a Chinese restaurant in the rue Claude-Bernard nearby. The following morning, not wishing to linger in Paris, Larry and Claude were going to drive the girls to Sommières. Larry scented trouble: de Gaulle was in the wings, about to return to power, and paratroopers from the regiments that had been serving in Algeria were threatening to occupy Paris and overthrow the government. Larry was only half joking when he complained that his mere arrival in a country was enough to cause catastrophe and mayhem: after all, it had happened in Greece, Yugoslavia, Cyprus! Jean was as usual irrepressible, supremely confident, full of plans. Claude matched him story for story, and Larry laughed and parried. Martine's pale, quiet sensitivity gave her the air of a hostess waiting for the punch bowl to crash. She was delicately beautiful, with an aristocratic, arched profile and immense, startled eyes – frightened in part because when the conversation shifted into English she was left behind. Recognizing her emotional fragility, Larry set himself to put her at her ease, and in her troubled future, Martine would always be at her best around Larry.

478

Jill, Penelope and Sappho watched and listened with amazement. When the bill came Jean found that he had barely enough cash to cover it. On the street outside, Jean saw Larry and his party into a taxi, announcing that he and Martine wanted to walk home – it was a lovely evening. In reality, he did not have the fare. Larry said nothing, but he grasped Jean's financial state. Weeks later, Jean received a package from Larry: it was the printer's proof of *Mountolive*, containing Larry's holograph corrections and emendations. Larry sent a note telling Jean to 'sell it to someone and take Martine to the movies . . . by taxi this time'.[166]

In those pre-*autoroute* days, Larry was content to make it a two-day trip from Paris to Sommières, and he stopped for the night at the Hostellerie Saint-Georges near Lyon. The next day, the first of June, he picked up the N7 and then paused in Orange to show his daughters the miraculously intact Roman arch, a smaller forerunner of the Arc de Triomphe. Then, secure on familiar territory, he took them to Avignon for a view of the broken bridge and a tour of the grey Palais des Papes, through Remoulins and across the stupendous Pont du Gard, past the pristine Roman arena in Nîmes, and finally – Larry tired but happy in his fatherhood – into Sommières.

The visit to Paris had given Larry his first taste of celebrity in France. Perhaps it was the challenge of the language, or the brilliance of the talk, or the excellence of the meals and wines – but whatever the reason, the women seemed extra beautiful, the conversations witty, the judgements on his writing among the best he had ever heard. His great gamble, he felt, was paying off. Paris had taken its toll, however: both Larry and Claude returned ill to the Villa Louis, but they still had the girls to entertain. They ate lunch daily in the patio under the linden tree, gazing at the splendid panorama below. Most days Larry led swimming parties among the lily-pads in the Vidourle beyond the Roman weir, where the local boys threw rose petals at Penelope and Jill. In the evenings they all gathered in the kitchen to dine by candlelight, talking endlessly, playing records, and 'generally horsing around'. Once they held a long discussion on 'the English way of life and how stifling it was to artistic and spiritual development'. '!' commented Penelope in her diary.[167]

Although the break-up of his marriages rendered Larry a father-at-a-distance most of the time, he enjoyed his offspring and had strong views on their upbringing. He was horrified by Henry's descriptions of *his* children's behaviour in *Big Sur and the Oranges of Hieronymus Bosch* and wrote giving his friend some good advice on handling young children, based on his experiences with Sappho, Diana and Barry:

I think kids need a sense of direction as well as the configurational development by a loving *family* – but mostly *mother*. She is the key – and she should devise the suitable disciplinary pattern for them; without her they topple inside. Every sweet pea needs a stick to grow up; and discipline that is purposeful and moral – *not* physical (i.e. the cane) gives them self-confidence. I must say our own three are marvellous all things considered; Claude has a knack of joining forces with them and leading them from the inside, so to speak. But we're fucked if we'll have bad manners or stupidity – and we seldom get it. They respect us, keep quiet while we're working – and we play as fair as we can by taking them all over the place and *really* working at awakening the little buggers up.[168]

In giving the primary importance to the mother, Larry was reflecting his own early life: he still blamed his mother for *not* disciplining his siblings, and he was not sure that the presence of a father was all that important, so long as there was a 'loving *family*'. At the centre of *Pied Piper of Lovers* it was precisely the lack of a sense of family in the motherless household that rendered Walsh Clifton so forlorn. When Larry set his hopes for the future of humankind on women with a new dignity and independent self-esteem, the root lay in his own experience.

Work with the children they did, especially Claude, but Larry helped energetically as well. For excursions there were trips to Les Saintes-Maries-de-la-Mer – 'the headquarters of all the Gipsies in Christendom'[169] – and to Aigues-Mortes, the intact walled town built in the thirteenth century by Saint Louis, Louis IX, as a port to service the Crusades. Because of silting, Aigues-Mortes is separated now from the sea by five miles of swampland and shallow *étangs*, but as Larry later wrote, 'Van Gogh's coloured boats still idle up and down the green canals among the dragonflies'.[170] The ochre sandstone of the unbroken walls surrounded the pure survival of a mediaeval townscape. Above the level of the other fortifications rose the Constance Tower, Louis's harbour keep, where the eighteenth-century Protestant Marie Durand was imprisoned for thirty-eight years, carving her deathless graffito 'Resister' into the stone. It was mainly to the mediaeval period of southern France from Avignon to the Pyrenees that Larry would turn for the historical underpinnings of his last major fiction, and Constance would be the name of his heroine: the *Quartet* still unfinished, he was already absorbing the Midi ambience of his works to come, and he was reading about the twelfth- and thirteenth-century Cathars. Inside the walls of Aigues-Mortes were several of the small open-air restaurants so beloved of Larry and Claude. After a long lunch, they drove the girls to the coast for sea bathing in wonderful waves.

Even the rustic conditions back at the Villa Louis made for adventure, and Penelope washed her hair on the terrace, with Claude pouring water over her head from a jug. They celebrated Penny's eighteenth birthday on 4 June with presents and champagne for lunch. Sappho came down with chicken pox two days later and then Claude followed suit; Penelope's attack was not to strike her until after she reached England. Claude also developed bronchitis, and there was a further scare when she turned out to have false appendicitis.

Larry, who did not fall victim to anything, naturally had no time to work, for he had to be 'male nurse to a prostrate household'. And he expected his German publisher Heinz Ledig Rowohlt to arrive within days. Somehow Larry found time to read the typescript of Arthur Guirdham's *Christ and Freud*, and to write an enthusiastic preface in which he announced that 'the doctor as artist is just beginning to emerge'. Concerned with the relationship between personality and disease, between religion and science, Larry asked, 'Could our illnesses be regarded as metaphysical extensions of our beliefs?'[171]

Penelope and Jill returned to Paris on the 21st, leaving Sappho in Sommières. Claude and Sappho had barely recovered from the chicken pox when Claude's Barry and Diana arrived. Then it was time for Rowohlt's visit. The tiny Villa Louis, satisfactory for a couple used to primitive conditions, soon palled under the pressure of children and visitors. 'God just wait till I'm rich!' Larry exclaimed.[172]

Ledig Rowohlt's visit was a considerable success. A warm person with a broad swathe of Germanic sentiment, his tremendous enthusiasm for *Justine* fired Larry to expatiate on his artistic conceptions and plans. Through it all, Barry, Diana and Sappho were as mute as rabbits. Rowohlt was very impressed with their good behaviour: 'They're so *English*, they're so *quiet*, they haven't spoken,' he marvelled. 'D'you know why?' Larry replied. 'I've given them each a hundred francs to shut up and stay shut up until you go away.' 'I thought it was *manners*,' said a crestfallen Rowohlt. 'No,' Larry pursued, 'It's *money*!'[173] Asked once whether he was a strict father, Larry answered ruefully, 'I try to be; but they make fun of me. "Education" does *not* exist.'[174]

He had returned from Paris to find a mountain of mail – Larry had committed himself to writing three prefaces and planning the Miller omnibus volume, and he was making a serious attempt to answer the 'surprisingly large' fan mail stirred up by *Balthazar*. Still, he was glad to be back at the Villa Louis and relieved that the threatened seizure of power by the French military had not occurred, that de Gaulle had come out of the events of the past week firmly in charge. During the coming months Larry would join his neighbours in nervously watching the approaching independence of Algeria. Over the years they would all feel the effects of the subsidies that Le Général lavished on the *pied noirs*, the French-descended Algerian colonials, to resettle them in Provence. Out of the influx of capital would spring the cement and lime plants, the quarries, the nuclear power stations, the *autoroute* and the blocks of workers' flats that now form such noticeable features of southern France. All this was hidden in the future as Larry and Claude settled into a countryside with folkways hardly different from those celebrated in the nineteenth century by Frédéric Mistral and in the first half of the twentieth in the plays and film scenarios of Marcel Pagnol. Larry himself was taking on a Pagnol reality – and why not, since his neighbours could have been impersonated without strain by Fernandel, Pagnol's favourite actor.

Henry was finding it impossible to stay on the sidelines while Larry was editing *The Henry Miller Reader*, and he kept weighing in with letters of advice – they should include a portrait category, and what about his 'Patchen' and 'Maurizius Forever' essays? – even while he wrote, 'I am almost ready to let you take over.'[175] He had already overbalanced and upended Larry and Fred's *Art and Outrage* correspondence about him, and said that it was 'too bad' that they had stopped writing. The book would be published, but it would not be the important expatiation on Henry's ideas that Larry had hoped for. He blamed Fred for refusing to 'get to grips' with Henry's work: 'He either gets *too pious* or too flippant.'[176] Henry felt pangs of conscience for taking up so much of Larry's time, and he wanted him to receive half the royalties for the anthology. Henry advised him, 'Do your own work first. MOST IMPORTANT. You're the rising star. Mine is sinking.'[177] Larry, however, still believed in Henry's excellence, and intended to repay his past generosity. Part of Henry's sinking feeling came from his own hectic situation: owing to the press of visitors, he had temporarily shelved *Nexus*; then the fog had shrouded Big Sur for a month, depressing his spirits and Eve's. Without a trace of irony, Henry lamented, 'I have a genius, I guess, for fucking up my life. My "serenity" is all above the eyes.'[178]

Larry did not have much serenity either. Before work could get properly under way on the Miller anthology, Fred and Anne Perlès arrived for a few days of explosive hilarity and sturdy drinking, despite Anne's attempts to restrain Fred. Jacques Temple joined the party for a day exploring Aigues-

Mortes; Larry felt that he had become a tour guide. For the rest of the summer the children had to be cared for. The holiday pattern continued: day trips to Arles, Les Baux, Saint-Rémy, Le Grau du Roi; swimming at the Pont du Gard and in the crashing blue waves of the Mediterranean; long discussions on art and politics in the evenings. The gravelly phrasing of Georges Brassens came from the gramophone, and Claude kept up a steady supply of succulent dishes. Often Larry and Claude sang along with Brassens.[179] In the midst of all the excitement a huge package of Henry's books arrived, and Larry started rereading them and making selections. 'It is quite frightening, the magnitude of your achievement – all stacked up on my desk,' he told Henry.[180] Henry found himself still unable to let Larry take over, and at the end of August he sent a list of some twenty-five titles and excerpts that he would like to see included, starring those 'especially dear to my heart'. 'Astrological Fricassee' he described as 'a killer-diller', 'Shadowy Monomania' he placed 'among my best essays'.[181] Henry was suddenly as happy as a child going through a trunk of his toys stored in the attic. Larry simply wished that Henry would let him get on with the job.

Anaïs Nin returned to Europe in June, staying with Hugh Guiler in Paris, nipping over to London to see Rupert Pole. This time Anaïs's meeting with Fanchette, urged by Larry, took place. 'Jean Fanchette is delicious!'[182] she told Larry, and dubbed him 'The Prince Delicious from Mauritius', the nickname that Sappho had already adopted for Jean. In late July, Anaïs came to Sommières for another visit, this time bringing Rupert Pole along. Again she stayed in a hotel in Nîmes – with the children visiting, the Villa Louis was packed to the windows – and they immediately launched into two days of continuous talk about *Balthazar*, which Anaïs had just bought in Brussels; about Argentina and Brazil, with Larry leaping on to his chair to convey the ferocious plant growth of the tropics; about Henry and why he did not move back to France; about *The Henry Miller Reader*, which Larry discussed in detail with Anaïs;[183] and, of course, a great deal of reminiscence. Larry seemed determined not to appear subdued this time. Anaïs and Larry slipped off together for a beach picnic at Les Saintes-Maries-de-la-Mer. The village was named after the two biblical Marys who, according to legend, had been washed up there in an unmanned boat along with Sarah, their black servant. The gypsies of southern Europe adopted 'Sancta Sará' as their patron, and they came in thousands for the black saint's festival on 24 and 25 May. Larry and Claude enjoyed the gypsy gatherings before commercialism and tourists smothered the gypsies, and, according to Larry, before an influx of hooligans and violent criminals had frightened most of them off. Larry looked with a benign eye on the bit of fortune-telling, whoring and pilfering carried on by the gypsies themselves.[184] They were a cheerful, raffish lot, and he put them wholesale into *The Avignon Quintet*. He showed Anaïs around the quiet village with its twelfth-century fortified church and the few surviving thatched peasant farmhouses of the sort that Van Gogh painted.

The other day of Anaïs's visit they sat in the hot afternoon under the plane trees in the small Sommières arena to watch a Provençal bullfight, which Anaïs found 'very gay'. The *course libre* does not end with the death of the bull, and only rarely with serious injury to the *razeteurs*, the men whose objective is to snatch the *cocade* tied between the animal's horns. Sometimes the bull pursues the *razeteurs* over the barriers and into the crowd, scattering spectators like skittles. Larry had become an *aficionado*, although he preferred to sit in the raised section reserved for dignitaries where he knew that he would not suddenly find a bull in his lap. Observant Anaïs noted, 'Larry has that curious quality of being immersed in experience, yet maintaining a constant control over its meaning.'[185]

In mid-summer Larry and Claude went to see a peasant *mazet*, a farm holding, available for lease or sale on the Uzès road leading north from Nîmes. They took an unmarked turning to the left just beyond the last houses of Nîmes, then followed a winding road up a shallow valley past a small country château; the road became a track, and less than a mile farther on they saw the low stone main building of the Mazet Michel blending into the rocky hillside. Surrounding the house were the frost-blasted trunks of what had been a grove of olives, hundreds of them; still, promising new green shoots were springing up from the roots. The place needed a lot of work: as with the Villa Louis, there was no proper bathroom, the place would be cramped for more than two people, and water came from a well with a very doubtful-looking electric pump. But there was space, blessed solitude and miles of open *garrigue* to the north, set aside as a military reservation but used only for occasional manoeuvres. Larry learned that he could count on some rough shooting – hare, grouse, quail and perhaps even *sanglier*, the savage wild boar of Languedoc. As they walked about the property their boots crushed fragrant rosemary and thyme. Larry was reminded of some of the wilder parts of Attica – that settled it! He wrote at once to Theodore Stephanides for advice on crops, and was told to consider wattles, kudzu, sisal, esparto grass, Chinese soya bean and carob – none of which sounded particularly edible. No matter: Larry and Claude would put in a kitchen garden. The bug of home ownership had bitten Larry again, and Claude was enthusiastic. Soon they had arranged a lease with an option to buy for the *mazet* and about twenty-two acres of stony olive grove, backed up a hillside against a square mile of scrubland. Across the hollow but still on the property was a small *mas*, a *maison de campagne*, where guests or a caretaker could stay.

On 27 August the Fanchettes arrived from Cannes for a few days, landing at the small station just below the Villa Louis. Jean fished in the Vidourle, and he and Larry discussed founding a journal with a Dickensian title, *Two Cities: La Revue Bilingue de Paris*. Jean proposed to make the first issue an 'Hommage à Lawrence Durrell'. Martine was pregnant with their first child, and Jean's volume of poetry, *Archipels*, was being published. '*I had the* baraka! *Nothing could fail!*' exulted Jean.[186] Larry was pleased that their stars seemed to be rising together.

With all this happening, Larry kept sorting and sifting Henry's enormous output, looking for the proper balance for the *Miller Reader*. Henry had been adamant that the book should not be advertised to the public as containing previously censored material, and he was not willing to risk a challenge in the courts. Larry had agreed to this, but he was none the less worried that Henry would slip in a few of the forbidden words and stick to them. Finally, on 6 September, the 'last brat' was airborne, and Larry felt like a châtelaine standing braced behind a dropped portcullis. Almost immediately he announced to Henry that the 'mock-up' of the *Reader* was finished.[187] Towards the end of October, Larry sent his preface to Henry, who responded, 'I do like it!' adding, 'And why not, since you flatter the shit out of me, as Joey would say.'[188] Larry had written that Henry's 'great tortured confession' ranges 'between marvelous comedy and grim tragedy', and that 'what he has tried to do is to accept and so transform the warring elements in the secret life of man'.[189]

One victim of Larry's terrific output since leaving Cyprus was his poetry. Eliot had once told him, 'A poet must be deliberately lazy.'[190] Larry had to admit that Eliot was right. He had drafted little or no verse since coming to France, but he would excuse himself that his poet's craft underlay his fiction: 'Poetry turned out to be an invaluable mistress,' Larry said just after he completed the *Quartet*. 'Because poetry is form, and the wooing and seduction of form is the whole game.'[191]

His correspondence, however, was all too flourishing, with Henry, with Richard Aldington, with a host of friends, acquaintances and fans stirred up by *Justine* and *Balthazar*. Larry sent the proofs of *Mountolive* to Richard, who was most enthusiastic. Then in Paris 'the old bitch *Justine*' was short-listed with Musil's *A Man Without Qualities* for Best Foreign Book. 'She didn't win, and justly', he wrote to Aldington, 'but what a compliment! Like being short-listed with Proust.'[192] Larry and Claude went to Grenoble, where he paid homage to Stendhal, who stood a shade above Proust in his regard. He had agreed to write on Grenoble for *Holiday* magazine, and to give focus to his article he tracked down the setting of *Henry Brulard*. He was thrilled to find it all there: Stendhal's uncle's house exactly as the writer had described it, in every detail, 'from *room* to *room*!' Even the vine that Stendhal mentioned and must have sat under was still growing, and Larry, *personne sentimentale*, picked two leaves 'to press in my *Rouge et Noir*!' Larry told himself that his essay was to be the last 'money spinner' of 1958. He visited an exhibition of Stendhal manuscripts, and found it most touching to see the 'florid handwritten title: "Connaissance *exacte* de l'homme"!' 'As if anyone could ever hope to . . .' added Larry, leaving the sentence incomplete.[193] He would knock out the piece in the next few days, he said, and then he would settle into the *mazet* and begin *Clea*. Suddenly he was swelling with optimism: after the *Quartet* he would 'drop all the peripheral rubbish which enables the children to holiday with us here', and then devote a whole year to a book that he really wanted to write. Perhaps he would even compose 'the missing chapters of the Satyrikon!'[194]

The furious pace of the year and a half in the Villa Louis had brought wonderful rewards. Two novels had reached the best-seller lists, and Larry had published in three genres new to him: comic fiction, the juvenile thriller and travel articles. He had met his bills, paid his daughters' school fees, and seen his bank cushion against the Poor House grow from a paltry three hundred to a few thousand pounds sterling. Larry had to admit even to himself that he had finally managed to consolidate his break from Foreign Office and British Council work, and he had gained a toe-hold in France. Sommières had been lucky for him.

CHAPTER 11

The Mazet Michel

Who told you you were free? What can it mean?
Come, drink! The simple kodak of the hangman's brain
Outstares us as it once outstared your world.
After all, we were not forced to write,
Who bade us heed the inward monitor?

And poetry, you once said, can be a deliverance
And true in many sorts of different sense,
Explicit or else like that awkward stare,
The perfect form of public reticence.

'Portfolio'

ON 15 SEPTEMBER 1958 Larry and Claude moved to the Mazet Michel. 'For all its primitiveness, it's a wonderful place, away from everything, smelling of sage and thyme and wild lavender, perfect for working and for relaxing', wrote Claude to Eve Miller.[1] A steep driveway rose to the right of the track that was the only road in, and then a dozen rough stone steps led from the shelf where they parked the old Peugeot to the terrace below the little fieldstone farmhouse. The dwelling, set flush with the ground, consisted of a living room with a fireplace facing the door, a bedroom to the left and a large kitchen to the right. In the back of the house were two more rooms, rather small.

For the rest of the month Larry and Claude were 'in the throes' of settling into 'Wuthering Depths', as Larry called the Mazet Michel. 'Very very Brontë,' he added. Although a mere fifteen miles from Sommières as the magpie flew, the terrain and 'colour tone' and even the sky around the *mazet* seemed to Larry pure Attica, not Languedoc at all. With the proceeds from a couple of 'reportages', as he termed them, for *Holiday* magazine and the security of a five-year lease on the *mazet*, he decided to plunge for a real bathroom, even though this meant an invasion of plumbers and masons who had 'feet like mastodons and carry mud sweat and tears all round the house on them'.[2] After the masons came the

487

carpenters, and Larry despaired of knocking out *Clea* before Christmas.

Claude picked up some sturdy old bookshelves for a few francs and had them plastered into one wall of the living room. Larry wrote to Alan Thomas asking him to start posting the books stored in the loft, saying that he could now afford 'a tenner's worth of sending'. He asked Alan to wrap his books singly, if possible, to spare the elderly postman who had to bicycle four kilometres to deliver them. 'I have to give him wine and fan him with my hat after every book,' Larry averred. He specifically requested his copy of de Sade's *Justine*. As storage cabinets and loaded bookshelves began to appear around them, Claude and Larry felt more settled than at any other time since they had come together. A 'symbol of homelessness for me', Larry said, 'is books on the floor, under the bed and in the granary'.[3]

Larry had sent out proofs and carbons of *Mountolive* to a few whose opinions he valued – Jean Fanchette, Richard Aldington, Henry Miller – and the approval was unanimous. Jean wrote a huge missive that was really a rave review, and Richard singled out for praise the long letter from Pursewarden and the mourning of the Coptic women, adding, 'I will confess that the scene of Mountolive and the child prostitutes hurt me – but then I am a sentimentalist about all children, and have an exaggerated respect for all ambassadors.'[4] To this, Larry replied that he had wanted 'something almost unbearably fierce' as a counterpoint to Leila's disastrous reunion with Mountolive, and he wanted to foreshadow the passage about Justine's lost child, still to come in *Clea*.[5] Richard later reported that his first wife, the poet H.D., was so moved by *Justine* and the sibling novels that her doctor had taken them away from her.[6] One of the most encouraging aspects of the responses of Larry's friends to *Mountolive* was that each picked out different passages to praise: Henry was bowled over by the slaughter of the camels, and Gerald Sykes found the fish drive 'in your best manner'.[7] A fine endorsement eventually came from Freya Stark, just back from Kenya: the first three novels of the *Quartet* 'are the actual *presence* of Alexandria',[8] she said.

The early reviews following the publication date of 10 October contained some amusing contradictions, but by and large confirmed the impressions of Larry's friends. The *Times Literary Supplement* pronounced *Mountolive* 'possibly the most significant of the series'.[9] Pamela Hansford Johnson in the *New Statesman* praised the style yet decried the absence of a 'moral and intellectual centre'.[10] *Time* magazine praised the imagery and 'penetrant thought', but judged the novel the weakest of the series to date.[11] Larry shrugged off kudos and blame alike.

To enhance the English sales of *Mountolive*, Larry proposed to Gerry that their mother, 'clad in a leopard-skin bikini, ride a camel through Trafalgar Square' – embellishing his tale with descriptions of Louisa's manifest propriety.[12] Perhaps the best evidence of Larry's new fame was a peremptory telegram from Hollywood, saying that he was the only man to write a film scenario on Cleopatra, and would he come immediately. 'Will I hell!' Larry exclaimed, and thought the offer a fine joke.[13]

Mid-October had arrived, and Larry still had not begun *Clea*. He and Claude were enjoying 'an amusing and wildly excited U.S. press on *Balthazar*', including one reviewer who called Larry a pompous prig and said that 'all his cornices are hung with rhetoric'.[14] Aldington proposed Larry for the Nobel Prize; Larry ignored the compliment. He was so happy with the *mazet* that he advised his friends to try the life. 'We live like peasants' became his repeated boast.[15] Of course, as he told Richard, 'you'd have to have someone as capable etc as Claude to help with the solitude'.[16]

Clea to write or not, Larry was aching to start building walls and terraces with the flat fieldstones scattered all over the property. He started building dry-stone walls two feet thick, carefully removing loose soil and pebbles to prepare a foundation and then stacking the slabs of stone without mortar, but settling each piece so that it would not wobble. The walls had a function – marking off borders, terrace from olive orchard, yard from kitchen garden – and they gave Larry a feeling of immediate accomplishment: it was 'nicer than writing, harder than walking!'[17] 'Larry liked to think of himself as a man of the earth', his sister remarked, 'but I think it was a part he played.'[18] He did enjoy using his hands, however, and made a lamp out of a curved, knotted olive limb, gloating that it was lovely but had cost a mere pittance.

Larry did not let the stress of writing or the isolation of the *mazet* keep him from reading his contemporaries. Henry tried to warm Larry to his latest discovery, Jack Kerouac. Larry sampled *The Dharma Bums* and pronounced it 'hick stuff': 'all those cute little fucks stolen in the name of Zen'. It was dirt for dirt's sake, on a nursery level, 'and gee when they open their little peepers to drink in the universe, gee how alloverish they come!' Larry blamed Anita Loos for what he saw as this 'breathless wondering lisp' in American fiction, and added that their old *copain* Saroyan had 'killed himself as a writer in this genre'. Although Larry conceded that he might later have to eat his words, he would not back down on Kerouac. Larry had just read *The Sergeant* by Dennis Murphy, and in contrast praised the 'melody as well as bite' of his prose.[19]

Isolated though the *mazet* was, on some mornings the air was shaken with detonations that suggested the activities of Larry's old EOKA antagonists or Rommel in the western desert: the French artillery was practising at a range just over the hill to the north. Nobody paid much attention, and Claude and Larry soon came to accept the occasional salvoes as they did thunder. They provided a fine backdrop for writing a novel about wartime Egypt. Larry was only mildly worried that a misdirected shell would land on his breakfast tray under the trees.

On 3 November Larry flew alone to London for meetings with publishers and the launching of *Stiff Upper Lip*. He had a six-hour night stopover in Paris, which he filled with a very late supper at the Dôme. It was an indication of his improving financial state that he would permit himself an expensive indulgence in mid-flight, so to speak. Larry's new Antrobus volume sold well in Britain, but the Americans tended to be unenthusiastic or worse. Kenneth Rexroth later pronounced the book 'unforgivable' and 'the most dreadful imitation of P. G. Wodehouse'.[20] Back in France, on 10 November Larry received a telegram from Juliet O'Hea at Curtis Brown with momentous news: *Mountolive* was an American Book of the Month Club selection, and that would guarantee him $20,000. He and Claude could live at the *mazet* for five years on such a sum!

Larry was still putting off tackling *Clea*, and he knew why: he reached back into pugilism and cricket for metaphors to explain himself. Having garnered considerable acclaim with the first two volumes and having 'scored an outer', a knock-out blow, with *Mountolive*, he hated to risk a leg-before-wicket, a weak finish to the *Quartet* that would undercut the whole series.[21] Not only that, but a poor showing now could ruin his earning power. He could imagine the critics saying, 'Durrell was unable to bring off his ambitious plan . . . a grandiloquent failure.' In mid-December he proposed starting *Clea* in ten days – like a desert mirage, the book kept slipping away as he approached. At the same time, he knew that he must keep up his momentum, in creativity and in sales.

Larry was elated when *Holiday* magazine offered him a contract to supply three more 'journalistic assignments' that would take him, he told Austen Harrison, to 'Italy, Spain; Gascony and Paris'[22] over the coming year, at $1000 each. 'An *income* pardy!'[23] he gloated to Aldington. Larry seldom lost sight of finances: 'I don't want to be stinking with money, just to have enough for a coup de rouge and a cigarette.'

With *Clea* still to come to finish the *Quartet*, Larry was already planning a comic novel. 'The Placebo', sprung from 'The Village of Turtledoves' and eventually to evolve into the *Tunc* and *Nunquam* volumes with the collective title *The Revolt of Aphrodite*, was to have a long seasoning. *The Alexandria Quartet* itself had been twenty years coming out of the quarry. Larry could work with furious rapidity once he decided where he wanted to take a story, but like some sculptors, he preferred to spend years feeling his way into the blocks of raw material. And whenever he could, as in the case of his poems, he went through many drafts and polishings. These days he did not have much time for poetry.

Larry was still settling into the Mazet Michel in mid-November when a rush request came from Anaïs for a preface for *Children of the Albatross*, due to be printed by the end of November 1958 for publication by Peter Owen. 'I ask hesitantly because I know Spy [*in the House of Love*] is your favored one', Anaïs said, 'and because you are overworked – yet it means a great deal to me and I hold my breath until you write'.[24] When she received a postcard from Larry agreeing, Anaïs replied with a cable to hurry him along. This she followed up with a letter saying that 'no one else can do it'.[25] In fact, Anaïs had written to Larry reluctantly, offended because Peter Owen had maintained that she *needed* a preface by a well-known author. Larry may have groaned, but he dropped everything, sat down at his typewriter, and punched out an affectionate appraisal, in which he wrote that her shimmering, poetic prose, 'iridescent as soap bubbles',[26] belonged to 'the great subjective-feminist tradition'. He mentioned what he considered her privileged background as the daughter of a famous pianist, 'embalmed' in grand hotels, and concluded that 'Those who care for finely-wrought musical writing shot through with clear insights into the inner world of human beings will not be disappointed.'[27] Larry thought that he had written a preface 'which Charlotte Brontë would have been glad of'.[28]

While Anaïs had felt a 'great humiliation' that her English publisher had felt she needed to be launched under someone else's colours, her annoyance at Peter Owen was nothing compared to her emotions when she saw Larry's preface. She was furious, especially about the soap-bubble metaphor and the references to her privileged upbringing. Larry did not really know her, understand her, nor care for her art: 'I am not using the preface,' she told him. 'I had the illusion that I occupied a special niche in your affection,' but the preface had 'utterly demolished' that illusion. 'The basic shock was the non-caring and the distortion.'[29] 'She made such an issue of these trifles', Larry recalled much later, 'that I suspected that there might be completely other reasons not concerned with myself.'[30] What these other reasons might be, Larry did not venture to guess, but he was staggered by her response: 'I thought that perhaps in me sleep I might have said something terrible', he wondered, but he reread the offending preface and could find nothing. 'I am absolutely blameless', he told Jean Fanchette, 'so I wrote and apologised for my lousy prose. She may be right there!'[31] On top of his distress over the contretemps with Anaïs was Larry's real guilt over work not done: 'I'm hovering about like a wet hen before beginning *Clea*,' he told Aldington. 'Ouf! I'm tired by the thought.'[32]

Nevertheless the year had been triumphant for Larry and Claude, a consolidation and a capping of the lucky breaks and winnings of the preceding year. Larry's fan mail had begun to arrive in sacks, causing his asthmatic postman to dismount and push his bicycle uphill to them. Claude saved the *facteur* a few grammes by slipping an unfranked postcard into Larry's pile of correspondence: 'Larry dear, I hope 1959 . . . . may be even better for you than 1958, and that I shall have the happiness of sharing it with you.'[33]

LARRY WAS RAPIDLY BECOMING an author with a French reputation, and Jean Fanchette assumed the role of chief booster. After two years as editor, Jean had lost control of *Lettres Suivent* and was definitely planning to launch *Two Cities* with a Durrell issue. While Larry felt some discomfort at the implied hubris of the thing, he sensed that the publicity would help him in France, where only *Justine* had been published in French. Larry was grateful whenever people said nice things about him. 'I must say the thought of people spending money to print homages to me is wonderful,' he wrote to Jean.[34] Typical of Jean's ventures, the plans were ambitious and he was in a terrific rush to see results: *Two Cities* would appear quarterly and would do for Larry 'what *transition* had done for James Joyce and *Nimbus* for Samuel Beckett', he promised.[35] Brother Gerry hazarded a prediction that Larry would soon be as well known as his own star chimpanzee, Cholmondely St John. 'Perhaps this isn't as inappropriate as it sounds!' noted Larry with some irony.[36] When Anaïs Nin agreed to become the New York editor, joining London editor Edwin Mullins, it became clear that Jean wanted to involve more than Paris and London. In his foreword to the first issue, he announced that the journal was taking its place in the top rank of literary reviews.

Like Larry's old friend Tambimuttu, there was an element of humbug and brash recklessness in Jean, but these were useful qualities when it came to launching a journal on no capital. Of course, he had the Durrell name, which he exploited adroitly to obtain contributions from Aldington, Henry

Miller, Fred Perlès and Jacques Temple; and he had enthusiastic support from the South African author Sinclair Beiles and from Elisabeth Janvier, Solange Pinton and a number of other French writers. The initial *Two Cities* would not be solely about Larry: Louis Aragon allowed himself to be interviewed, Loys Masson contributed a long poem, and there were other pieces without a Durrell reference.

The *Two Cities* editorial meetings were held at George Whitman's Shakespeare & Co. bookshop on the south bank of the Seine facing Notre Dame, named after Sylvia Beach's famous establishment of a generation earlier. André Malraux showed up at one of these meetings, and a small grant from the French government eventually resulted.[37] The comfortably cluttered Shakespeare & Co. became Larry's literary burrow in Paris, the equivalent for him of Bernard Stone's Turret Bookshop in London and, later, of Frances Steloff's Gotham Book Mart in Manhattan.

For his journal, Jean conducted a brief long-distance interview with Larry about *Justine* and his artistic genesis. Scores of journalists and others would grill Larry over the years, but he had already evolved his characteristic technique of using the interview form to play with his critics like a fly fisherman, deceiving them with artful fictions, tantalizing them with glimpses of truth – or versions of truth – and trailing them gasping into the shallows. Deliberately, Larry sketched the intellectual locus needed for his work to be understood in the way that he had envisioned it: to Jean he outlined his attempts to exploit the relativity theorem, the Freudian and Lawrentian attacks on the 'old stable ego', and his relationship as author to his 'invented' characters: 'Justine has everything to do with me, and nothing whatsoever.' Then Larry added enigmatically, 'I think Cleopatra was probably something like her.' Larry closed the interview with a typical touch: 'To all the questions you did not ask, I can only answer in the affirmative.'[38] For the rest of his life, he would be frustrated at the lack of understanding, for which his twists and turns would be partly to blame, but he was not being malicious in his evasions and riddles: he merely wanted people to enter into the spirit of play and of seeking. He would fan out his pack of truths like a magician, and his readers had only to select the right cards. He tried hard to help them, Larry maintained, and was he really at fault if his public chose to misread him?

Larry had not spent the better part of fifteen years as a press officer for nothing, and at the beginning of 1959 he jumped in with encouragement and advice on *Two Cities*. Anaïs was 'absolutely devoted' and a brilliant recruit to handle the American part: 'It's like having the Red Cross at one's side', he told Jean. The journal could become a 'cultural double-text crib' for students, and to alert British and French academics Jean should try for reviews in the *Times Literary Supplement* and *The Times*; also, he should contact Hilary Wayment of the British Council, Christopher Middleton, who had spoken on *Justine* for the BBC's Third Programme, Princess Caetani at *Botteghe Oscure*, Jacques Vallette of *Mercure de France* – 'a long standing fan of my poetry' – Heinz Ledig Rowohlt – 'He might be most useful, a delightful and generous man.' Jean should not neglect to place advertisements in *Encounter* and *London Magazine*. There seemed to be 'some kind of block chez Henry', and the old *cher maître* had not answered his latest letter, but if Henry failed to write for the *Hommage*, Larry would simply give Jean a long letter that Henry had written on *Mountolive*. After all, Henry had printed one of his letters in *Colossus of Maroussi* without permission, Larry said, and in any case, 'Henry does not bear grudges for long'.[39]

Larry was right about Henry, who could forgive him anything, but Anaïs tended to be less forgiving, and in the middle of the *Two Cities* planning Larry was relieved to receive a letter from her making peace over the *Children of the Albatross* preface. 'I don't want to go back to what hurt me – I value the alliance of the Three Musketeers too much,' she wrote. 'Let's just forget about it.'[40] Peter Owen still insisted on a preface, so with Larry's permission to eliminate anything that she felt 'detrimental', Anaïs cut half his preface before publication, although neither she nor the publisher sent the revised piece to Larry for approval.[41] Larry would refer to the preface incident as 'a storm in a tea cup',[42] but Anaïs's anguish was a good indication of just how much the friendship with Larry meant to her. Anaïs was aware that she tended to terminate even long-standing friendships when she felt betrayed, and she discussed this trait with her psychoanalyst friend Inge Bogner, who told her, 'Everybody sooner or later commits what you call treachery'.[43] Larry she had considered a soulmate since the 1930s: great elevation, great betrayal. Their correspondence diminished after 1959, and Nin's diaries reveal that on her side the hurt lingered to the end of her life. Larry gave no evidence of wavering: 'Of course I love the girl so much that I would do anything rather than upset her', he told Jean.[44] As it turned out, Larry did not have to risk upsetting Henry, who sent in a 'very glamorous article' on Larry during the *Black Book* days.[45]

A good reason for not wanting to ruffle Anaïs's feathers was that her assistance would be very important to the success of *Two Cities*; and in January, Jean received a cheque from Anaïs for $400 to guarantee four hundred copies – because, as she said, Americans expected free copies of a new magazine. Anaïs waved another olive branch by asserting that Larry's preface had helped *Children of the Albatross* in England. Early in January, Jean reported that subscriptions were being solicited in Japan, Germany and England as well as in the United States.

Larry's sales campaign in France was greatly aided by his good fortune in gaining a pair of excellent translators: Roger Giroux for *The Alexandria Quartet* and, later, Alain Bosquet for his poetry. *Justine* had cost Giroux a major effort, but *Balthazar* would take only half as long. By February, he was almost finished with the second volume, and he asked Larry for help with a few words and phrases.

Justine was taken up by the Club Française du Livre, and this new windfall prompted Larry to buy the Mazet Michel: he wanted to take root and he now had the funds. Larry located and engaged as sharecropper-cum-caretaker Monsieur Alphonse Tritignac, a 'partly disabled specialist in polyculture'. He would live in the dependent *mas*, plant a *potager*, and split the garden produce with them.[46] The man was a real son of the *garrigue*, knotty, lean, garrulous, 'chronically honest', but, Larry soon found out, 'What a grumbler! Jesus Christ!'[47] Water was always scarce, and Tritignac was quite capable of running the well dry to irrigate the lettuce, even if it meant depriving Larry and Claude of their baths. Limping, complaining, but absolutely loyal, he remained a fixture throughout Larry's time at the Mazet Michel.

WITH THE QUARTET THREE-QUARTERS COMPLETE, Larry analysed his public. He imagined that he would not appeal to the English, 'and don't specially want to', he claimed. He thought that because of their 'limited human experience', they tended to 'see life through a pinhole', and 'can't detect where romance leaves off and truth begins!' They were bound to accuse him of being too much like Pierre Louÿs or Marie Corelli! He accepted all this with equanimity: his 'extravagant and crude effects' were no accident.[48] He was more worried about what the French and the Germans thought of him – and so far, bless them, a noise of cheering filled the air. There was even going to be a *Collected Poems* in German next year.

Larry had virtually stopped talking about *Clea*: that meant that he was writing the novel, and he had an almost superstitious horror about being quizzed on his progress. At the end of January he was 'wrestling hard with poor Clea'[49] and had managed to shove the typescript along to page forty.[50] 'If only I don't fuck up this last book . . . Great expectations!' he agonized to Fanchette.[51] By the beginning of March he had completed the crucial first hundred pages.[52] When he received a letter in early March from Eve Miller, saying that she and Henry would be coming around 1 June, and that Henry's two *enfants terribles* would be with them, Larry knew that he could not let the book drag on into the summer. He secluded himself at the *mazet* and wrote in a windowless passage to avoid distractions. 'Artists', Larry believed, 'need to get away from people in order to get nearer to them.' He had selected the *mazet* as 'the best setting for writing', and he kept quite religiously to the pattern that he had evolved: 'I get up before dawn, brew several pots of coffee and enjoy them in bed by candlelight, have a peek at the dawn as it's coming up, and work uninterruptedly until around twelve,' he told Huw Wheldon. Later in the day he would be 'full of cigarette smoke and conversation, people, and anxieties, problems, overdrafts' – and unable to concentrate. 'I think the best way to tackle the day is just when it's on the horizon,' he stated axiomatically.[53] After lunch he would saw wood for the fireplace, harvest his almonds – his crop reached forty kilos – or build walls. The image of Larry stacking fieldstones, like some Wagnerian troglodyte with his short legs firmly straddled, forms the perfect complement to the bookman piling up titles: *Bitter Lemons, Justine, Balthazar, Mountolive.* Now he was trying the heft of *Clea*. The days were long gone when he would return later in the day to the typewriter, pour down more black coffee, and keep working until past midnight. Now his evenings were spent before the red heat of an olivewood fire, Mozart on the turntable, a glass of Arquebuse or cognac close by. Unless there was company, like good country folk he and Claude would turn in early.

When the writing was going badly, Larry might moan and swear and drink too much, but he was speaking no more than the truth when he told visitors how glad he was to be able to keep writing without too much fear, these days, of being driven back to the Foreign Office. The artist's function, Larry said, was to 'giv[e] a signal to the average chap' about how to live. In the course of his signalling, the artist if he was lucky might learn to fashion his own life well, might learn 'a secret which we evolve in solitude, with pain, and ink, and paper, and perhaps, later, we hope in our lives'. Always Larry would associate pain with the task of creation, like a woman giving birth. 'One is growing with one's books,' he concluded.[54]

Claude provided him with a crucial episode for the latter part of *Clea*. In *The Rum Go* she was mining her memories of Egypt when her woman narrator, sailing a 'cat-dinghy' in Alexandria's Eastern Harbour, is shot at by a sentry on the interned Vichy fleet for approaching too near a warship.

No one is hit but the sailing boat begins to sink. Claude's episode ends in comedy when the heroine and her lover are rescued by a navy launch. Larry turned the incident to tragedy as Fosca, Pombal's lover, is fatally shot in an almost identical situation. Larry in the space of two wives had thoughtfully covered extremes of the Alexandrian social spectrum: Eve had observed the rich, enviously, from the sidelines, whereas for Claude it had been the accepted thing to keep a sailing dinghy at the Yacht Club.

A ghost from Larry's past threatened to materialize through an acquaintance shared with Aldington. Count Geoffrey Potocki wanted to set up his printing press again, and Richard 'sent around the hat for tenners'.[55] Larry refused to contribute, and when Richard accused him of simply not wanting to put his hand into his pocket, Larry defended himself on political grounds. Having experienced Fascism in Greece under Metaxas and Communism under Tito, he judged that 'Ultimately both systems are the same. One-party government supported by a secret police and army.' The behaviour of the British police in Palestine and Cyprus had shown Larry 'the strong vein of brutish fascism the British have in their unconscious'. While he appreciated Potocki's writing, Larry considered him too close politically to the Fascist peer Sir Oswald Mosley. 'No', Larry continued, 'I can't go along with people who could wear Per Ardua Ad Buchenwald on their shoulder flashes.' He had loved Roy Campbell precisely because he had rejected the offer to become the British poet of Fascism. 'And if I am a Royalist', Larry concluded, 'it is in the biological sense – the only political creed possible to a poet I think, who is ultimately *only* interested in values and not politics at all'.[56]

Larry set himself to complete *Clea* before 10 April, when an assortment of editors and publishers – people he could not put off – was due to arrive from Paris. Also, Anaïs planned to land in Paris on 15 April, and he expected to see her during her stay in France. As the Millers' visit approached, Larry found a furnished flat for them on the place Docteurs Dax in the heart of Sommières, a safe distance from the *mazet*. True, they would have a car, and Larry would be happy to see them, but a little space as a buffer would not hurt. This suited Henry fine: he wanted privacy too. Then Anaïs came down with double pneumonia and had to cancel her projected visit. The gods were not protecting Larry's tranquillity, however, for Buffie Johnson and Gerald Sykes came in mid-April, followed on the 23rd by Julian Mitchell and Gene Andrewski from *The Paris Review*.

Larry lit one *Gauloise bleue* after another and talked through the afternoon and evening to the *Paris Review* people, who remarked upon his ability to turn 'stupid questions into apparently intelligent ones by assuming that the interviewer had meant something else'.[57] Thrown a banal query about the importance of *The Black Book* as a forerunner of the *Quartet*, Larry shifted ground to explain how valuable poetry had been to him in his efforts to learn finesse: when he had been at school in Darjeeling, only one boy had been able to catch the large green lizards intact, without their tails falling off. 'That strikes me as the best analogy I can give you,' he said. 'To try and catch your poem without its tail falling off.'[58] He was flattered by the interviewers' appraisal of him: 'When at rest he looks like Laurence Olivier; at other times his face has all the ferocity of a professional wrestler.'[59] The resulting interview for the *Writers at Work* series marked Larry's first serious treatment by a major literary journal, but he could not resist tossing off some of what would become his trademark exaggerations and flourishes. As a youth in London, Larry claimed, he had been leading a 'perfectly stupid puppy-clubman sort of life' of nightclubs and fast cars on the large allowance sent by his unsuspecting parents – contradicting his many complaints about having been strapped for cash and even half-hungry in his youth. Larry added that he had gone on a reading party to Switzerland to cram for perhaps his eighth attempt at the Cambridge entrance exams, had passed through Paris and fallen for the city, and *voilà*! he had become a European and a writer.[60]

After setting down the basic mythology of his early life that he would repeat over the years for other journalists, Larry dangled various plums of truth before the *Paris Review* folk. Had he possessed a very large private income, he confided to them, he would have 'domeciled' himself in a fine London flat and an English country house. However, faced with the prospect of 'shabby' digs in South Kensington or Woburn Place, he said, 'You have to make the vital decision as to whether you live in Europe and visit England, or whether you live in England and visit Europe.'[61] Wishing to do Aldington a good turn, Larry mentioned him as a major early influence more than once during the interview, and he continued to do this whenever the opportunity offered: it was his way of trying to help Richard win back his reading public. Larry acknowledged stylistic debts to Norman Douglas and to Lytton Strachey: 'It is condensation I admired in them,' he said. 'I have never really been a stylist deliberately. The stylists have taught me economy, which is what I very badly needed. Being naturally over-efflorescent, I have always probably learned more from the sort of writers I have never really imitated. They taught me, just as feature journalism told me to put the most important fact in the first sentence.'[62]

What really interested Larry most in the *Quartet*, however, was the form, and he thought that form concerned him more than it did most artists. In fact, he had already claimed to have been holding the pattern, though not the 'detail', of the entire *Quartet* in his head while writing *Justine*.[63] With quiet honesty, he voiced his self-doubt to the *Paris Review*: 'It may be that I haven't as much personality to deploy. My interest in form might be – I'm talking seriously now, not modestly – an indication of a second-rate talent. So one has to face these things.'[64]

Whatever one's talent, the important thing was to develop it to the fullest, said Larry. 'The theme of art is the theme of life itself,' he continued. 'This artificial distinction between artists and human beings is precisely what we are all suffering from.' True, he had written a book about writers, a *Künstlerroman*, and yet, he maintained, 'I'm not fundamentally interested in the artist. I use him to try and become a happy man, which is a good deal harder for me.' He ended with an epigram that echoed Oscar Wilde: 'I find art easy. I find life difficult.'[65] This bitter self-doubt intruded between Larry and the happiness and sense of fulfilment that might have flooded into his life had he been less introspective, less honest with himself.

Larry achieved his deadline on *Clea*, although he had a few weeks of tidying up to do. Now he could see his artist's dream coming true: 'Since I was 22 I wanted to live in France and write'. Thanks to advances from Dutton, Faber and Rowohlt, Larry thought that he would be able to live 'modestly' at the *mazet* for a while, and even 'forget the rest of Europe': 'For the first time I am doing the work I was invented for, and being paid for it.'[66] Larry gave Claude considerable credit, and would later claim that she had 'typed the Quartet complete four times and picked up numberless errors and false enjambements'. He was almost certainly exaggerating the amount of typing that Claude had done, but not her contribution to spotting errors in the text. 'I am dreadfully careless and hasty tho I try hard not to be,' he added ruefully.[67] He still felt poor and he cherished the notion that the *mazet* was utterly isolated, and therefore he asked Ray Mills to send him a set of dental picks – so that he and Claude could clean each other's teeth.[68]

Before he had even finished the polishing of *Clea*, Larry was mulling over his projected comic novel. He already saw a problem: 'I don't really think a comic novel is any good unless it's as vulgar as it is satiric,' he said, and he worried that it would be 'hardly permissible for me to be as vulgar as I would like'. Rabelais and the Elizabethans would be his models, 'coarse and vulgarly funny'.[69] 'I wish we could recapture the enormous range of feeling the Elizabethans enjoyed,' he said, 'from the utmost vulgarity and bawdry to the greatest delicacy, sophistication, and refinement.'[70] Optimistically, he promised himself that the new novel would be his 'project' for the coming winter. He was also excited at the prospect of a staging of *Sappho* by Gustaf Gründgens at the Deutsches Schauspielhaus in Hamburg. This would be his first true test in the theatre, and if it went well, Larry predicted that he would end up falling 'passionately in love with the play as a form'.[71]

Since the time of his early meetings with Henry Miller, Larry had been toying with the idea of visiting the United States. Now he could afford the trip; in fact, he could make it pay by accepting a few of the invitations to lecture that were flooding in. He held back. When he was in Argentina he had swept 'the Americas' together in a single condemnation. This he no longer did. North America he should reserve for his 'late fifties', he concluded, sizing up the venture: 'Experiences of continents are much bigger than experiences of small countries. Since both America and Russia between them are going to determine the shape of our future, one is obliged as a traveller in visiting those countries to stop travelling and start thinking.' He dodged into flippancy: 'Besides, if I went to America I'd immediately start falling in love with American girls – which would blind my vision. So I'll have to go there when all my passion is spent.'[72]

DURING THE FRENETIC YEAR of writing, publication and public appearances following the move to the Mazet Michel, Larry and Claude had gradually evolved a new social circle. Throughout his pre-war experience of Paris he had been an expatriate, consorting mainly with English and American residents and a few Continentals, such as Fred Perlès, Hans Reichel, and the Hungarians Brassaï and Tihanyi, who were themselves foreigners in France. Now, living with a French Alexandrian on the edge of a provincial town, dealing daily with local tradespeople, and being visited by French literary figures and publishers, Larry found his role shifting from that of expatriate to adopted son. This suited him both as a writer and an individual. 'This is one of our cardinal errors', he would say in autumn 1959, 'namely, to assume that art is a form of purely patriotic response to a given place. . . . I personally would like to feel that I was an English-European.'[73]

Deliberately, Larry was easing into Languedoc, and his talk became filled with images of the *garrigue* and the mistral, of woodsmoke and enormous meals. He was modern enough to purchase a petrol-powered chainsaw, but he paced himself so as to take years to work his way through his hundreds of frost-stunned olive trees. 'Olive is a delicious wood', Larry purred, as if savouring a termite's feast, 'but it burns tremendously fast.' As he spoke, the fire, more than the meal to be cooked on it or enjoyed before it, became a delight to the palate: 'But here also almond is delicious wood,' he continued. 'It's curious how it perfumes the atmosphere. One gets quite subtle about the different smells, a bit of olive, a bit of oak to keep it going, and perhaps a patch of almond or old cherry trees make a delicious flavour.'[74]

His daily life retained its essential simplicity and economy. When he invited friends to 'have another bottle of that slosh', or 'plonk', he was not being modest: it was still sure to be *gros rouge* rather than a choice vintage, or a bottle of what he sometimes called champagne, a cheap local fizzy white that could sneak up on the unwary and leave a spectacular headache. If he felt like indulging himself or wanted to entertain in some style, he might serve a ripe Saingorlon cheese and a bottle of Côtes du Rhône Gigondas. Larry also savoured a good Montrachet, a distinctive Blanquette or a Clairette de Bellegarde, but it was the conversation and the company that mattered most. He knew and appreciated good wines and champagnes, but the old nagging worry over money would not let him keep a good cellar. He even scolded friends who he knew were not wealthy when they brought good wines: 'Put that away – it's too *expensive*!' he would cry.[75] He never got over the fear of finding himself poor once more. This tension was often discernible: intermittent acts of generosity to daughters and friends, a miserliness towards personal expenses that would have done credit to Volpone. Like any careful *petit bourgeois*, M'sieur Durréll stumped into the *pâtisseries* and the *boulangeries* with his *filet à provisions*, his net shopping bag, becoming a familiar figure in the Nîmes shops. Larry and Claude had not detached themselves entirely from Sommières when they moved the twenty kilometres to the Mazet Michel. 'No,' wrote Larry, 'the little Roman town with its graceful bridge and ambling trout stream was certainly somewhere to linger.' He still loved the 'tiny medieval clock tower', 'the rabbit-warren streets and carved doorways with their battered 'scutcheons and masons' graffiti', the 'rooks calling from the old fort', the cafés under the plane trees alongside the east bank of the Vidourle.[76] Lest he bring down a horde of tourists, when he wrote these lines for *Holiday* magazine he disguised Sommières as Gaussargues, after the quai Gaussorgues along the river, named in honour of a Sommiérois historian and notable.

Larry was similarly circumspect in Paris. He maintained his early loyalty to the Hotel Royal on Raspail, where he always reserved Room 13, 'my lucky number'. At the Dôme, one of his favourite lunches was the humble *merlan en colère*, literally 'whiting in anger', the fish served biting its own tail. Always a good eater, Larry preferred a few substantial dishes to an elaborate spread of *haute cuisine*.

As the almond blossoms fell and the Provençal spring warmed towards summer, Larry's own fair weather showed every sign of holding. *Balthazar* in Giroux's translation won the Prix du Meilleur Livre Etranger, and the irrepressible Fanchette cabled Larry, 'CONGRATULATIONS I MYSELF WON THE FENEON PRIZE TODAY PARTY DUE FOR YOU SATURDAY.'[77] 'My glorious Copperfield', Aldington began his own generous note of 'gratters'. He had been out of sorts, yet he rejoiced in Larry's triumph as though it had been his own; he ended with the words, 'In health lousy, in temper testy, But ever your affectionate bedesman'.[78] As if Larry needed a reminder to thank his stars that he was in France, the continuing unrest in Cyprus struck him a glancing blow, causing the cancellation of a BBC radio dramatization of *Bitter Lemons*, carefully prepared by Xan Fielding.[79]

At this time, Jean Fanchette's fortunes seemed to be rising almost as precipitously as Larry's. Henry and Eve Miller, with the two children Valentine and Tony, were due in Paris, and Jean planned a launching party on 5 May for *Two Cities* that would feature the reunion of Larry and Henry. Henry said that he found Paris 'ghostly' and that it now meant nothing to him;[80] Larry did not agree, but he preferred his Paris in small doses. From a young American at the embassy in Paris, Jean borrowed a smart flat on the Boulevard Saint-Germain, cadged some bottles of scotch, and sent out myriad invitations. The affair was exactly the sort Jean relished, and he counted up the celebrities: Larry talking 'terrorist dialectics'; Henry escaping the effusive ladies to play with Frédérique, Jean's infant daughter; Buffie Johnson with her quiet, measured voice and her husband Gerald Sykes holding forth eloquently; the publisher André Bay and his wife Odette; Raja Rao, William Hayter, Sinclair Beiles; and the whole *Two Cities* crew.

After the party, Jean collected the Durrells, Millers, Sykeses, Beys and Raja Rao for a splendid dinner at the Chez Papille, paid for with the Fénéon Prize money. Later Jean remembered the scene in vignettes: 'Miller looking out of the window at the policemen chasing Algerians in the Paris dusk, Raja Rao the Hindu Brahmin trying hard not to look at the first course: "Queues de cochon grillées", Eve and that premonitory light in her beautiful dark eyes.'[81] Larry and Claude both loved Eve from the first: she launched herself into every new situation and meeting with enormous warmth and gusto. And on her part, Eve told them, 'You were both just as I hoped you would be.'[82] An elderly lady at a neighbouring table recognized Henry, and on the strength of a past acquaintance bought Dom Pérignon for the whole party. Elevated by the champagne, Henry produced a monologue on Lao Tzu, Keyserling, Kropotkin, and the days of *Tropic of Cancer* and *Black Spring*. The Millers and Durrells slipped away from the dinner 'to kiss Gerald and Buffie goodbye', and then fluffed a planned rendezvous with Jean through a misunderstanding – or so Larry claimed. To Jean, Larry called the party and dinner 'gargantuan', but after it all he was quick to scurry back to the *mazet* and be 'safe back in my fox-earth!'[83] He felt that he and Henry had been on display, and the threat of violence over the Algerian situation worried Larry. Fred Perlès missed Larry by a day and wrote to him from Paris, 'Why didn't you wait for me, espèce de couillons!'[84] Larry confessed afterwards, 'I feel like a cake that has been cut into a million pieces,'[85] and Gerald Sykes and Claude both felt that it had been an 'ill-fated dinner'[86] – too much posturing by Jean, too many enlarged egos, too little time for old friends.

The Villa Seurat cronies did not quite succeed in recreating the rollicking old times: Henry soon charged off to Copenhagen with Valentine and Tony; Eve stayed in Paris and bought a used Fiat; Fred left after a wonderful three days with the Millers, but returned later to drive south with Eve for a reunion in Sommières; Henry detoured to Die to see Albert Maillet. Anaïs came to Paris in early June after the others had left.

Like a flashback to the early Paris years, Maurice Girodias planned to republish *The Black Book* – it was still judged too hot for the English to handle. And Larry was threatening to return to an old literary love: at the end of the summer he wanted to drive his children back to England and then collect his Elizabethan books with a view to writing the study that had been haunting him for more than twenty years. Next year, he thought, 'I might steal a few months from money-grubbing to do a non-saleable.'[87] Aldington tried hard to dissuade him: 'Highbrow stuff knocks down novel sales,' he warned.[88] Larry had promised himself two months of pure holiday after completing *Clea*, but now his very success was refusing to let him rest. With the *Quartet* going into ten languages, he was bombarded with letters from his translators. 'GOD I WISH I HAD WRITTEN IT A BIT MORE SIMPLY AND NOT INVOLVED MYSELF IN ENDLESS QUERIES,' he lamented to Arthur Guirdham. 'NEMESIS! FROM NOW ON I'LL WRITE AS SIMPLY AS MAUGHAM.'[89] That, said Guirdham soberly, would be a mistake.[90]

Larry was reasonably satisfied with his accomplishment: 'I have the comfortable feeling of having done something to the top of my bent,' he would say a few months later. 'If it isn't good enough, I will try again. But I can't do any better at the moment.'⁹¹ With *Justine, Balthazar* and *Mountolive* holding places on the best-seller lists, to Larry's great joy Faber agreed to produce a *Collected Poems*. Larry leafed through his old notebooks for verses that could be tidied up or expanded for publication. He apparently had not produced a finished poem during the entire period of writing the *Quartet*. Now he unearthed a draft of 'The Lucky Man', dated 2 January 1938 in a notebook begun at the Goldener Adler, two wives ago. He made a few changes, gave it a new title, 'The Cottager' – the original one was too painfully poignant. He had written, 'Twin tides speak making of two three', but now he believed that he had lost both daughters created 'By fission by fusion'. One line fitted his situation perfectly: 'What was bitter in the apple is eaten deep.'⁹²

Another old poem cried out for rebirth: four lines from his 'Ballad of Kretschmer's Types' had appeared in the *New English Weekly* in 1937, but now he recognized in the completed poem a miniature autobiography, and he was quite serious in identifying himself as one of Kretschmer's two main types:

> (*pyknics are short, fat and hairy,*
> *leptosomes are thin and tall*).

He called on the reader to 'Pity the lanky leptosome', but to

> Salute the podgling pyknic then
> That gross and glabrous prince of men,
> Contriver of the poet's code
> And hero of the Comic Mode.

The poem ends with a prayer to the Lord:

> The pyknic who's half saint half brute
> O waft him in Thy parachute,
> And may his footsteps ever roam
> Where alcohol is Absolute.⁹³

Larry saw himself through a veil of irony, acknowledging the duality of his creative intent, both serious/heraldic and comic; realizing his saint/brute nature; and facing the special danger of alcoholism. Finally, he sent off some hundred and fifty poems to Faber, all but a handful previously published.

While Larry arranged the *Collected Poems* and toyed with the idea of a 'non-saleable', his brother Gerald took the immense financial risk of opening his own zoo on the island of Jersey. Gerry had always wanted a zoo, and he desperately needed a home for the two-hundred-odd animals he was keeping in Margaret's back yard in St Alban's Avenue and at his mother's house across the way. For a time Cholmondely St John shared Louisa's bedroom, until Gerry discovered that his mother no longer read at night lest the light disturb the petted ape. Louisa had adored Cholmondely from the time of his arrival, and knitted exotic sweaters for him, 'to keep the cold out, dear'.[94] After attempting vainly for eighteen months to persuade the Bournemouth and Poole authorities to help him establish a zoo for the twin towns, Gerry was offered a lease on the large Les Augrès Manor on Jersey to be his home and zoo headquarters. With Gerry leaving, Louisa Durrell knew that she would feel cut off in Bournemouth, where her only close friends were still the Browns. So when her son suggested that she sell her house and move to Jersey, she acted with the same casual air that had characterized her earlier momentous moves to Dulwich and to Corfu. As the youngest child, Gerry had always been very close to his mother; also, she was kindly, gentle, tolerant, and adored his animals, so it seemed an ideal arrangement.

Gerry might have a zoo at last, but Larry felt as though a circus troupe were moving in with him. After various delays and at least one breakdown of the old Fiat, the four Millers and Fred Perlès finally showed up at the Mazet Michel around 19 June, just as Larry was finishing the final revision of *Clea*. Larry installed them in the second-storey flat that he had reserved for them in Sommières. A few yards to the left of their open balcony they could see the stranded arches of the Roman bridge, and the sun pouring at midday through the plane trees made piebald patterns on the flags. Fred had only a week before he had to go back to his job in London, but for the next two months the Millers made Sommières their base. They found a ping-pong table at the Café Glacier and Henry played his expert game, easily beating Larry, besting Tony with more difficulty, and in fact usually defeating all comers. 'He was very good – he was practically unbeatable,' Larry remembered. 'You could see what a Buddhist he was when he played table tennis, because he never drove, you know, he always returned. But he could not be driven past. He was absolutely unparalleled. But always in a passive sense, a returning sense – he didn't slash or drive, he didn't have a winning style, but he had a negative style which was extraordinary. I never managed to beat him, and I played quite a good game.'[95]

Larry and Claude took the Millers into Nîmes and to Les-Saintes-Maries. Henry could not swim because of his perforated eardrums, but the rest of them plunged into the azure Mediterranean. Larry had set up a large tent at the Mazet Michel, and they sat out talking in the evenings, sipping *vieux marc* and stepping outside the circle of candlelight to gaze at the panoply of stars over the dark *garrigue*. Henry thought that while Larry had gained a pleasing undercurrent of gravity, he had lost none of the 'effervescence, enthusiasm, spontaneity, joy' of the young man he had known in Paris and Corfu.[96]

Aldington showed up in late July for one of his rare returns to the south, and Larry arranged a meeting with Henry. Jacques Temple was also present. Larry was not always successful in the introductions he made between his friends, but the gathering in Sommières produced expressions of mutual appreciation. It was a warm day, and the four men lined up on the Pont Romain for a photograph, one of the few late pictures of Aldington. Claude was in good form, and her mimicking of 'local characters in action' was much admired by Richard and Jacques. 'I liked Miller very much', said Aldington, 'and having read his Big Sur profess myself a humble disciple.'[97] Henry recognized the wounded man in Aldington, but he was clearly unsettled himself: he did not feel that he had been an 'utter failure', but 'close to it'. 'I'm going through some sort of crisis,' Henry admitted. The truth was that his relationship with Eve was collapsing, what with his nagging demands and her own need for serious companionship. Writing to Larry ten days after his return to Big Sur, Henry apologized: 'I must have been a sorry sight most of the time. A dud.'[98] Larry was discovering that it was nigh impossible to recreate the great memories of his life: places throbbed with different resonances and personalities had shifted, his own too. All the angles had changed. Instability and flux had long been part of his fiction, and they would dominate his future writing.

ON 2 SEPTEMBER 1959 Larry landed in England and this time even he could not complain about the warmth of his reception, despite his premonition that the *Quartet* was 'too sexy' for the English. Part of the time Larry and Claude stayed with the Thomases in Bournemouth. Larry was tense, drinking heavily, and Alan and Ella could hear their guests fighting in the bedroom. Claude grabbed Ella's wrist to demonstrate the power of Larry's grip, and left her with a deep bruise.[99] Claude underwent a 'small operation' in London, and Aldington queried, 'What has upset the girl? English food or the English mug?'[100] It was shaping into a trying visit.

While Claude recuperated – it would be a month before she could travel – Larry sped over to Paris for a few days on more PR business. 'I must go to Montmartre and meet a man called Worms! Worms!' Larry confided to Aldington.[101] Much of the time, Claude was running on sheer will: neither she nor Larry talked about her health, but it needed super-human stamina to keep up with Larry. This she simply did not have.

Larry arranged to have an article by Richard typed, and suggested to Hammond at Curtis Brown that he handle it, but Hammond said that Aldington's last letter to the agency announced that he hoped 'never to hear from such people again'. 'We laughed', Larry wrote to Richard, 'me ruefully'.[102] 'It was sad too,' Larry would recall, 'like watching a big fighter unaware that he is going blind, missing his lengths, losing his temper, swinging wildly'.[103] He tried hard to persuade Richard to return to England for a well-organized publicity campaign: the BBC had shown interest in a 'life and works' television programme. Larry called Richard 'our most distinguished elder of letters alive today', but said that he needed to face his public because some of his fans were saying, 'I thought he was dead years ago.'[104] Aldington refused to budge, remarking, 'My dear boy, it would be useless for me to appear before 9 million Brits (appalling thought to dwell on) for I should instantly offend 18 million.'[105] Larry was victim to no such hesitations, having just conducted a lightning attack on England: 'I have done 20 interviews and 3 television jobs,' he told Richard.[106]

Larry's visit to England produced some spirited interviews, as when he spoke to Kenneth Young for *Encounter* magazine. 'Would you say you were essentially a writer of ideas?' Young asked. Sensing a trap, Larry replied, 'I would rather say that I was a poet who had stumbled into prose, but of course ideas mean a great deal to me.' Next, Young tempted Larry to subscribe to D. H. Lawrence's idea 'that it is only through sex that you get close to the real universe'. 'I have been very much influenced by Lawrence as a writer', Larry replied, 'but not as a person of ideas.' There was a residual Calvinism in Lawrence, he explained, a refusal to employ science to back up his arguments for monogamy. When Young cast paganism before Larry, he ran up his ensign: 'I am afraid I am a pre-atonement, pre-redemption, and pre-original-sin man. I don't think Lawrence was.' A few days later Larry sent a postcard to Young saying that 'all answers to questions are *provisional* because I am still growing. Next year I might believe the opposite of all I believe to-day!'[107]

Everyone, both in England and on the Continent, wanted Larry to explain himself on love. Larry was happy to expand on his definition of modern love: 'But I hope to suggest that it itself is only a way of growing, a nourishment which prepares one for other problems, perhaps deeper ones.' Love, 'human and divine', was 'the *point faible* of the psyche', the vulnerable spot through which the soul's resistance could be breached.[108] His purpose was also to show the growth of the artist in self-knowledge and creative skill. In the final volume of the *Quartet* Larry intended to 'develop the idea that the sexual act is our "knowing" machine', 'the *point d'appui* of the psyche'. Larry justified his identification of sex as a primary fulcrum for his investigation: 'You can determine much about a culture or a civilisation from its approach to sex.'[109] This, Larry thought, explained why his reputation stood higher in France than in England: 'Above all, the French recognize that love is a form of metaphysical enquiry. The English imagine it has something to do with the plumbing.'[110]

Larry owed a lot to France. He claimed Stendhal and Proust as masters, and each volume of the *Quartet* was prefaced by at least one quotation from the Marquis de Sade. Was it merely a bit of calculated mischief on Larry's part to call attention to the link between his heroine and de Sade's? Anticipating the raised eyebrows, Larry included in the 'Obiter Dicta of Pursewarden' at the end of *Balthazar*: 'Why do I always choose an epigraph from Sade? Because he demonstrates pure rationalism.'[111] Larry later explained that 'What I meant was that I see in de Sade the literary twin of the French Revolution, and, of course, following from the French Revolution, of Marxism, which are both attempts to impose purely rationalized systems on the body politic.' No social revolutionary, Larry none the less defended de Sade from the charge of sexual excess: 'all de Sade's excesses were "voulus"', in other words, willed actions. 'They were a scientific investigation into sex,' attempts to prove that 'there is no morality in nature'. This was where Larry's own intense sexual curiosity and his speculations about human nature came together: 'I believe that human beings best reveal themselves through . . . the sexual relation'.[112] It sounded like a clever rationale for infidelities, but Larry apparently felt that he was justified in carrying his friendships with women into the bedroom. And he clearly expected his current wife or mistress to understand that for him to engage in the sex act with another woman who was intellectually stimulating to him did not mean a change in his allegiance. Even to himself, however, Larry probably did not maintain that all his affairs were conducted out of pure scientific curiosity. There was a Capodistria element in Larry: like the sensualist financier in the *Quartet*, his predatory eye flickered covetously towards casual strangers as well as at his companion across the wineglasses.

Larry had sent a copy of the proofs of *Clea* to Gerald Sykes, who advised him to delay publication and to 'rethink your last chapters'. The novel was 'not as poetic as the first book . . . but it makes a good, honest effort to pull the whole quartet together – and it succeeds on a *youthful* level.' Sykes particularly disliked 'Clea's weird and rather contrived maiming'. The criticism went both ways: Larry had read the typescript of Sykes's drama *The Eye of the Pyramid*, and against the counsel of the theatre critic Harold Clurman, persuaded Sykes to make the character Maggie 'not pathetic but horrible'.[113] Larry in contrast ignored Sykes's advice. Jean Fanchette also saw a pre-publication copy of *Clea*: he liked the 'perfectly controlled emotional capacity' of the novel, but on medical grounds he disputed the description of Clea's aborted foetus.[114] Larry did not change anything on Jean's say-so either.

In mid-November Larry took stock of his situation in a letter to Austen Harrison, written as an interlinear on a brochure advertising *Justine* and *Balthazar* by reprinting flattering nuggets from French and German reviews. He and Claude had decided to construct an annexe of several rooms at the rear of the Mazet Michel as a surprise for the children. Everyone wanted him to travel, but he felt 'travel-stained' and wanted instead to rest at home. Eventually, he would 'fill a chasm in my education and get to know Italy and Spain a bit'. He had turned down 'fifty' invitations to lecture in 'USA Germany Sweden Norway Spain etc etc', but would write articles on Gascony, Paris and so on for *Holiday* magazine. What seemed to excite him most was that *Sappho* would finally be given a full production. Larry seemed not to mind that it would appear in German, in Hamburg. He and Claude set off for the dress rehearsals and the 22 November opening night.[115] Margaret Rawlings, still eager to create the title role in an English production, flew in for the event. Larry's desire to have a *real* monkey appear as Diomedes's pet caused consternation. Actor-director Gustaf Gründgens refused categorically: what mere human actor could compete for attention with a live animal? Larry had to give in, and finally he admitted that Gründgens had been right.[116] Fortunately, the men took to one another: the saturnine, bald, autocratic German, and Larry, his opposite in almost every conceivable way.

Sappho was a considerable success, and it was filmed for German television. Not everyone liked the production, however, least of all Margaret Rawlings. While 'it was glorious to see you being applauded', she told Larry, 'it was so *badly* done . . . . static verse speaking . . . pants off boring'. She blamed the production: 'Your play is much better than they revealed.'[117] Still, Larry was tremendously pleased by the reception of *Sappho*, and soon began a drama about a Scythian princess named Acte who rebelled against the Romans. The story would pit Scythian idealism against Roman *Realpolitik*, with a cheerfully pessimistic Petronius – the author in disguise? – as referee and commentator. In *Acte*, Larry would explore the idea that 'reality' followed upon art: Petronius at the outset muses that perhaps his writing about a revolt in Scythia had 'provoked' what eventually happened. This idea became an article of faith for Larry in *The Avignon Quintet*. By March 1960 Larry had sent off the first two acts to Juliet O'Hea at Curtis Brown.

Whether or not he took proffered advice, Larry was usually grateful for any well-intentioned help, and he was generous in his efforts to assist others with prefaces, recommendations and suggestions. He wrote some twenty-two prefaces, mostly for friends, in the ten years following the publication of *Justine*. His importuning of Rowohlt was apparently responsible for Aldington receiving a commission to write the text for a picture book on D. H. Lawrence, and he continued his efforts to gain Richard both publicity and additional writing jobs. Then Harry T. Moore at Southern Illinois University asked Aldington to write a book-length critical study of Larry's work, and Richard proposed to drive south so as to discuss Larry's writing at length with him. It so happened that Huw Wheldon was coming on 8 January 1960 to interview Larry for the BBC *Monitor* Programme under the directorship of David Jones, and Larry suggested that Aldington be interviewed as well. 'Now don't be difficult this time and foul up this most important departure will you?' Larry demanded of Richard. 'Please believe me about the importance of this idiot's magic lantern; it doesn't matter if one mucks it up, the interview, gives offence, any damn thing; *the mere fact* of being on television puts one right into the ordinary news picture.' It was such marvellous publicity: 'Really, we ought to pay them,' Larry concluded.[118] Reluctantly, Aldington acquiesced.

Larry's scheme failed, however. 'It's no good,' Aldington wrote at the last moment. He had been against the English for forty years and still was, he said. 'During a feverish night I have realised that I have nothing to say to the British – apart from things they don't want to hear and the BBC wouldn't send out anyway.'[119] Larry was not nearly so rigid in his own quarrel with England: he recognized his artistic roots. When Wheldon asked him if he did not feel 'cut off from England', Larry replied, 'Oh, on the contrary. . . . language is one's passport. Anyone well grounded in the Elizabethans, and using the English language is an English writer, let's face it, however Irish he may be.'[120] Nevertheless, Larry did grumble about appearing on television for at least the fourth time since the publication of *Justine*: 'I'm tired of looking like a patient muffin; I wish I was Gary Cooper or even spade-bearded like Temple.'[121]

The Wheldon filming did not turn out to be easy for either interviewer or subject. Wheldon, a man of strong prejudices who prided himself on his judgements about novels, had doubts about Larry's writing and did not warm to the author when they met at the Mazet Michel. Visually, they made an odd pair: the burly, work-toughened Larry and the tall, thin man with the patrician profile, lipless mouth, cleft chin and elevated brow. Still, Larry was very much the gracious host on his home turf, in his usual casual trousers and pea jacket with the collar turned up, and he responded patiently and seriously when Wheldon asked him the old question about whether he saw himself primarily as a novelist or a poet. 'I think really I'm a poet,' he said. 'In poetry, perhaps, I'm not of sufficient size myself; but it leaks into my prose.' Economics drove him to novels, Larry continued, because you could 'rush a novel along by the scruff of its neck', whereas a poem had to grow through an autonomous process deep inside, slowly.'[122] In truth, Larry probably retained too much of his earlier self-doubt to commit himself entirely to poetry.

Wheldon showed his indifference by asking other stock questions, but Larry, perhaps because he liked Jones, who had startled him by reciting his – Larry's – poetry,[123] perhaps because he was thinking of his own reputation for eloquence, but most likely because he felt his usual obligation to give value, produced answers that saved the interview. Did Pursewarden and Darley have anything to do with Durrell? Wheldon wondered. 'Everything has got something to do with Durrell,' responded an obviously nettled Larry. 'I mean, I'm Justine as well as Mountolive,' he continued, 'You don't draw portraits from life. You just take the superficial things you observe about how an ambassador behaves, if you know how.' Wheldon switched to Pursewarden's ribald utterances: 'You take bawdiness pretty seriously, I think. Is it important to transgress prevailing opinion?' he asked. This stung too, and Larry spoke at some length:

I think I take it pretty naturally. I'm like Nelson, I turn my blind eye to it in the sense that I don't really know it's there. For me, there is no such thing. I think, in England, we do tend to confuse moral and aesthetic judgments. Because fundamentally, if you intrude a morality into everything you'll end up with your art becoming a series of morality plays. If you've ever had to be tortured by them you'll know what a relief it is to come on the Elizabethans because they have passed out of the narrow frame of the medieval morality plays. Ever since then with our two sort of lines of culture in England, it's been a running fight with puritanism the whole time, and puritanism is always trying to drag us back and strap us into moral patterns. Consequently, some sort of reaction is almost inevitable.

What Larry wanted in his ideal reader was a belief in his *sincerity*: this would free the author from 'petty moral judgments' and allow the author and reader to move together towards the 'apple' that the author is striving for.[124]

Early in the first session Wheldon had contradicted Larry, telling him, 'You don't realize what you've written.' Larry had stiffened.[125] In Nîmes the next day, on the steps inside the magnificent Roman amphitheatre, Larry got his own back. He cornered Wheldon on Taoism, asking whether the *Monitor* programme's star knew Chuang Tzu. 'No,' said Wheldon curtly.[126] Larry enlightened him: 'A philosophic comedian, a sort of hidden joke. He's really the basis of early Chinese religion'. When Wheldon quoted Pursewarden to Larry – 'The thing to do is to laugh until you hurt, and hurt until you laugh' – Larry replied, 'Yes. You have to,' adding pointedly, 'Yes – and you? . . . If you want to be a human being, you'd better learn.'[127] Larry's eyes took on a dangerous glitter. All but his first phrase was cut from the transmission.

Scenting heresy, Wheldon asked, 'What are you by religion?' Instead of parrying the question, Larry replied, 'I don't know. I'm trying to find out. . . . I'm for all religions, in a sense. . . . Perhaps the key there is that people don't want to become human beings really. I'm probably saying something which is not in our Christian canon, but I see Original Innocence rather than Original Sin as the foundation of the human character.'[128] In his annoyance at Wheldon, Larry had allowed himself to be surprised into candour. Equally angry, Wheldon pronounced Larry 'an impossible man'.[129]

The worst of all the television attention was that people began to track him down along the chemin d'Engances, and he was threatened with a mob of visitors. 'It's no fun at all,' he lamented. 'Fame attracts idiots like ordure flies.'[130] He posted a 'horrible churlish notice' on the gatepost of the Mazet Michel to scare off visitors.[131] It read: 'This is a workshop. If uninvited and unexpected, don't knock!' Something else that Larry did not want was the publication of his correspondence with Henry Miller, which Henry proposed for a joint collection of their letters: too many private matters would come out to suit Larry. People should buy his books, and then leave him alone to enjoy the royalties.

Usually Larry was handled quite handsomely by the press these days, as he himself often said, but a rather malicious account of his domestic situation, written by Jean-Paul Weber and published in the *Figaro Littéraire*, caused Larry's friends considerable anger. Larry had spent a day lavishing hospitality on Weber at the *mazet*, and thought that he had a tacit understanding with him that he would not broadcast the extra-legal nature of Claude's status. Aldington in particular resented 'the insult to Claude', and begged Larry to make a formal and dignified protest, from the *Figaro* editors up to André Malraux, then Minister of Culture. Larry was inclined to shrug it off, saying that even ten Webers would only serve to balance all the good notices that he had received. Richard was perhaps not joking when he then offered the services of two friends, 'one a good amateur boxer and the other late of La Légion': 'Shall I instruct them to waylay the bastard and knock his block off?'[132]

Clea appeared in England on 5 February, and *The Alexandria Quartet* was complete. Press attention reached a crescendo, first in Britain and then nearly two months later in the United States, after the US publication. Most of the reviewers praised the final volume and the *Quartet* as a whole, and many of those who disliked aspects of the series found much to appreciate. By now, major critics were assigned to review Lawrence Durrell: Granville Hicks's title pronounced *Clea* a 'Crown for a Majestic Work';[133] Gilbert Highet reaffirmed the comparisons with Proust, and thought that Larry had dramatized the concept of the relativity of truth;[134] V. S. Pritchett found that while the 'Decadent palls', 'the romantic inventor breaks through like a bursting flower';[135] Gerald Sykes wrote in the *New York Times* that the *Quartet* was an 'archetypal' tale, told in 'lyrical prose', of the growth of an artist;[136] Jacques Vallette stated in the *Mercure de France* that *Clea* was an inspiration to 'seeing clearly and braving suffering'.[137] Academics took diametrically opposing positions: Bonamy Dobrée saw in the prismatic points of view 'a freshly effective method for unraveling the subtle intricacies of character',[138] while Carl Bode thought Larry's characters hollow because they were so loaded with mythic and symbolic weight.[139]

A few strongly contrary voices sounded over the *Quartet*. Kenneth Rexroth, a self-proclaimed Durrell fan, asked rhetorically, 'What Is Wrong with Durrell?' and responded that in *Clea* Larry had written carelessly and had achieved only something flimsy and flashy. Rexroth excoriated Larry for 'childish meddling in the lives of the innocent' in positing a Coptic-Jewish plot to deal with the Nazis over Palestine.[140] Rexroth ended his review by saying that in the recently published Grove Press *Selected Poems* Larry made clear by his poetic accomplishment the extent of the failure of *The Alexandria Quartet*. These were 'great poems, lovely, temperate, with every subtle cadence so carefully controlled': 'There is little self-consciousness in them, and little Puritanism, but lots of the weary sensuality and fleshy joy of Greek and Turkish and Egyptian life and love and food and drink.'[141]

Every interviewer wanted Larry to place himself. With which modern writers was he most in sympathy? 'In France, with Montherlant and Proust,' replied Larry patiently; 'in America with Henry Miller; in Greece with Kazantzakis; in Argentina with Borges; in Italy with Svevo.'[142] He had already said about as much as he wanted to, for instance about his use of Freud and Einstein: 'I see Eastern and Western metaphysics getting jolly close together,' he had proclaimed back in April 1959.[143] None the less, he had invoked Einstein's name, and it would be the great physicist whom everyone wanted him to talk about. When in 1961 Jacob Bronowski interviewed Larry for the BBC about the relationship between science and literature, Larry explained, 'I was hunting for a form which I thought might deliver us from the serial novel, and in playing around with the notions of relativity it seemed to me that if Einstein were right some very curious by-products of his idea would emerge. For example, that truth was no longer absolute, as it was to the Victorians, but was very provisional and very much subject to the observer's view.' While other writers had been questing for a new form, he did not feel that they had succeeded. 'I don't know of course', Larry replied cautiously, 'I've only read deeply in French.' These other writers, he continued, 'hadn't expressed what I think Einstein would call the "discontinuity" of our existence, in the sense that we no longer live (if his reality is right) serially, historically, from youth to middle age, to death; but in every second of our lives is packed, in capsule form, a sort of summation of the whole'.[144]

Asked by the Paris magazine *Réalités* to rate his novels, he spoke with a mixture of confidence and irony: 'Objectivity is impossible, and writers, just like prima donnas, suffer from inexhaustible egoism. I dare to hope that what I have done is good, and even very good; if my present success continues long enough, I will end up believing it.' Larry was careful to differentiate between success and esteem: 'Success all by itself would be torture for a serious writer.' It was the esteem of a few of his 'fellow writers'

– Eliot, Miller, Nin – that really mattered. However, he continued, 'Success creates new responsibilities. It is more difficult to remain innocent. The public tries to force you to become an archimandrite. If one isn't careful, one ends up caught imitating Durrell in place of simply being Durrell.'[145]

Larry was delighted when the critical debate continued long after the initial flurry of reviews and articles: was Durrell 'a late Victorian decadent' or, as the French claimed, a major innovator to rank with Joyce and Proust? Was he merely pompous and difficult, or a conscious and skilled creator of gorgeous Byzantine mosaics?[146] D. J. Enright summed up his own response to the *Quartet*: 'When Durrell is good he is very, very good, and when he is bad he is horrid.'[147] Larry believed that a mixed press meant more sales than unmitigated praise, and that sheer column inches counted above all else. His tally stood high on both scores.

Larry really was becoming the English-European that he described himself as. His French friendships expanded to include Miriam Cendrars, daughter of Henry Miller's adored master-author; Dominique Arban, who wrote on Larry for *Preuves*; Alexandre and Nadia Blokh, both French but of Russian descent; the Avignon poet and *Reflets Méditerranéen* editor Robert Allan; *Etudes Méditerranéen* editor Jean Lacouture. The Blokhs became close friends. Nadia was a professional painter and Alex, a future president of French PEN, published poetry under the name Jean Blot. Both were wonderfully humorous, and Alex said modestly, 'My English is very fluent but I'm never quite sure of what I say.' The Blokhs lived in Colovrex, a suburb of Geneva, so they were within reasonable visiting range. 'We had of you the hang over magnificent,' wrote Alex after one of their early meetings; the Blokhs soon came back for more.[148] And there were old friends too. Larry had not lost contact with Mary Mollo and her husband Henry Hadkinson. They were living at Saint-Cloud on the northern edge of Paris. A friend who resurfaced in Larry's life from the Villa Seurat days was Cecily Mackworth, the Countess Chabanne. To his evident delight, she branded Larry a 'Romantic' in her essay, 'Lawrence Durrell and the New Romanticism'.

Meanwhile the convicted Romantic was keeping his pot boiling with journalism, cruising the Rhône and trotting off to Geneva on assignments for *Holiday* magazine. He said his latest subject was to be the United Nations – 'What duller subject could be imagined?' If he could make a few thousand a year from such hack work, he could, he said, write whatever he wanted the rest of the time. There was a limit, however: Larry turned down a commission that would have sent him 'up the Nile in a rowboat'! The *Quartet* was behind him and he no more wanted to return to Egypt than he had wanted to go there in the first place. Yet he was moving further East and turning mystical in his preoccupations. Along with Guirdham's books, Larry was reading Anagarika Brahmacari Govinda's *Foundations of Tibetan Mysticism* and following Johannes H. Schultz's advocation of yoga techniques in psychotherapy. Strangely, Lama Govinda was a German, 'hence the lucidity of the exposition'. Larry was still 'battling' to get Groddeck reprinted in Germany, believing as firmly as ever in his psychoanalytic method that used analysis as a 'springboard' for intuition.[149] Larry had been urging Guirdham to read Groddeck's *World of Man*, and by the autumn Larry would be able to tell Guirdham, triumphantly, that he had succeeded after a ten-year campaign in convincing publishers in Germany, Austria and France to print or reissue Groddeck.

At the end of March 1960 Richard Aldington dropped in with his Australian friends, the Geoffrey Duttons. Larry entertained them with songs from 'Scobie's songbook', a few sheets of scurrilous lyrics. From mid-April on, Larry was bombarded with messages from Henry Miller, posted from Rome, Lübeck or elsewhere, often with notes and signatures added by Fred Perlès or Heinz Ledig Rowohlt. Henry was having a glorious time on his circuitous way to Cannes, and would see Larry after the film festival. Eve Miller wrote from Big Sur to say that she was enjoying the peace and solitude. There was not much peace and solitude for Larry, however, when the small, determined Mai Zetterling and her husband, Larry's friend David Hughes, arrived to film gypsies for the BBC at Les Saintes-Maries-de-la-Mer. Zetterling's talk revived Larry's interest in film, and during May he went to Paris to work on a script for Rouben Mamoulian's *Cleopatra*. 'An ideal way of resting for me, playing with a new form,' he told Aldington. He pronounced the scenario 'a good discipline for a poet because film is the enemy of words . . . . In film the word does not get on well with the image.'[150] Larry looked upon the project as a money-spinner: he was living 'at hideous expense – luckily not mine but 20th Century Fox'.[151] In May his *Collected Poems* appeared; Larry did not overestimate his achievement, but he felt that the volume marked an important stage in his claim to legitimacy as a poet, and he was quietly pleased.

After the end of the Cannes Film Festival on 20 May 1960, Henry Miller arrived at the *mazet* with his latest woman friend, Caryl Hill Thomas, whom he had met while she was working as a waitress at Big Sur. It was not a very satisfactory visit. Larry was trying to finish *Acte*, and he knew that he would be leaving soon for London to resume work on the *Cleopatra* film script.[152] Henry himself had tired of Caryl. Both Larry and Claude were fond of Eve Miller – Henry was still married to her – and they thought that Henry was making a mistake. There was more to it than that: while in Reinbek on the way to Cannes, Henry had met Renate Gerhardt, English-language editor and translator for Rowohlt, his German publisher. Henry had fallen in love on the spot – with his usual teenage abandon. It all made for a distracted Henry, sighing like a bellows, and a cross Caryl. In the event, Henry would send her back to California a few days before he returned himself. A month later he learned that she was getting married: 'Lucky I didn't get caught,' he told Larry.[153] Eve was divorcing him: 'The next will have to be Japanese or Siamese', Henry proclaimed with what turned out to be prophetic accuracy.[154]

With Larry's increasing renown came a restoration of other ties. Henri el Kayem, an Egyptian author friend soon to Gallicize his name to Lecaye, wrote from Beirut to compliment Larry on his use of the novel form.[155] Lucy Schmick-Reichel, the artist's widow, asked Larry to speak at the opening of a Reichel retrospective at the Wallraf-Richartz Musée on 9 July.[156] This he was unable to do, but he sent a memoir that was published in a volume of Reichel's paintings. If any other evidence of the value of the Durrell name were needed, a collection of forged manuscripts and paintings turned up in London.[157]

This would turn out to be Larry's Cleopatra summer. By mid-June he was in London dictating more script for *Cleopatra*. He sat in a hotel suite, churned out 128 pages of typescript by 17 June, did major revisions or completely rewrote some 46 pages by 24 June. By early July he was back at the *mazet*, but throughout the first week of August Larry was again engaged to work on *Cleopatra*, mainly to rewrite his earlier script. Finally the stint came to an end, but he would return to it the following year.

Larry agreed to be interviewed for *Life* magazine by novelist and social critic Nigel Dennis. The meeting went well, and confirmed a friendship. Another friendship grew, one previously conducted through correspondence, when Arthur Guirdham arranged a meeting during the summer in Nîmes.[158] Guirdham himself was a tremendous presence: he and his wife Mary were gentle and kindly and unthreatening in manner, but the psychoanalyst projected an aura of uncanny psychic power. Larry could certainly turn an intimidating stare on others, but the look that came from Guirdham's eyes, set deep in his massive head, was so hypnotic that it could cause a feeling of vertigo in the person who met his gaze. Larry, who quickly shifted to Christian names with nearly all his friends, no matter how famous or dignified, would give Guirdham his professional title throughout most of their long correspondence. Their talk in Nîmes ranged from theories of healing to the future of civilization. Larry told him, 'We simply have to believe that something can be saved from the wreck, even at five minutes to midnight.'[159]

Larry was used to being present when celebrities were photographed, and on Rhodes and Cyprus he had commissioned others to take photographs for his magazines. Now he found himself the quarry, and he did not enjoy the experience. He was irked especially by the pair of photographers who arrived in July, after the Nigel Dennis interview, to photograph him for *Life* magazine; he resented the equipment, the lights, the fuss. He recalled that 'they had a thing like the periscope of a submarine, through which they took me from all sorts of angles.' He saw something sinister about it all: 'What they wanted was to demean me: by getting me farting, getting me drunk. . . . It's a subtle way of cutting me down to the size of *demos*. And of course it's our culture, it's the Anglo-Saxon culture. "We must cut him down to size. If we had a lovely picture of Goethe drunk, somehow, we'd've got him where we want him."' The resulting pictures were technically excellent, Larry admitted, but cold, 'like Coney Island'. The mania to show all had permeated society, he thought.[160]

As Larry was posing for the two *Life* cameramen, Henry's old friend Brassaï arrived by appointment to photograph him. Brassaï's method and philosophy contrasted sharply with the approach of the two younger men. His technique appealed to the spare, Buddhist side of Larry. Brassaï came with only a reflex camera on an ancient wooden tripod that kept collapsing 'like a kneeling camel'. 'Yes, if I limit myself to one film, that means twelve exposures,' he told Larry as he coaxed the tripod into standing firm, 'I usually get about three possible ones out of that lot . . . and it sharpens my sense of choice.' Brassaï sat looking at him for three quarters of an hour, chatting, without even touching his camera. Suddenly he said, 'Now! Do you think you could do that again?' Larry could, and Brassaï pressed the shutter once, twice, again. 'There's this particular look on the faces of the kids at a First Communion,' Brassaï mused. 'That's the look I always try for in my portraits: it's a look of realization.' Brassaï's photographs of Larry would be widely reproduced: by Rowohlt in Germany and by *Réalités* in France.

As evidence of his rising reputation, Larry was asked by Penguin whether he would be willing to testify in the courts on behalf of *Lady Chatterley's Lover*. Sir Allen Lane had just been haled into court for publishing the novel. 'You betcha!' Larry wrote to Richard Aldington, 'I've told them I'd take the first plane over to lend DHL any support I could.'[161] Hating conflict in the public arena, Larry was none the less willing to take a stand where he felt the issue really mattered. Lane won the case without requiring Larry's testimony.

For summer 1960, with its inevitable invasion of children, Larry and Claude had rented a flat and pitched a tent at Les Saintes-Maries-de-la-Mer, where the Blokhs and other friends came for days of swimming and feasting, and nights gathered around a bottle of Arquebuse, the Vulcanic brandy that had become Larry's favoured evening restorative. The incautious found themselves falling like skittles around his camp fire. Arquebuse certainly loosened tongues, and no one could remember next morning what had been said.

EVE DURRELL WAS NOW WORKING in Paris on public relations for an art gallery, and Larry began to receive reports on her from friends there. 'Eve . . . is also proud of you . . . . approves of Claude', Buffie Johnson told him.[162] It was both a wonder and a caution that Larry's wives and lady friends, current and ex, nearly all seemed to be on good terms with one another – and with him. Eve and Larry were still co-operating well over Sappho, arranging her schooling at Bedale's, giving her stimulating summers in the Midi. Larry mused about his varied love-life, 'In a novel which hasn't been published, one of my characters makes this remark: "One needs to know many women to know one of them; but is it sufficient to know a single man to know all of them?" Poor women! How boring the male world is! I am so happy to be a man and to be subjected to the obligation of which Caradoc speaks.' Claude accepted his occasional infidelities as more or less inevitable. Aside from the distraction of making love, Larry had resumed work on 'The Placebo'.

His creation, the architect and city planner Caradoc, had moved into his life just as Pursewarden had done a few years earlier. Architecture would be the art form featured in 'Placebo' and its offspring: the condition of modern architecture was symptomatic of the society: 'The mystery is how it's so ugly,' Larry would say a decade later. 'We have at our disposal 5,000 times more than King Solomon had to build a temple with, and where the hell is our architecture coming from? It must be coming from these little halitosis-ridden souls.'[163] Larry liked to quote Caradoc as an authority: 'Caradoc says: "There are secrets a thousand times more creative and a thousand times more destructive than the atomic bomb in the human heart. We artists are mere diviners."'[164] The division between his life and his art, always porous, was slowly dissolving. In personality Caradoc was close to George Katsimbalis: a great bear of a man, a raconteur, a lover of women, a formidable drinker, a fanatic about his personal independence. Although no architect, Katsimbalis too could discourse on city planning as easily as on poetry, as Henry Miller had written of him in *The Colossus of Maroussi*: 'He would take a map of London, say, or Constantinople, and after the most painstaking study would draw up a new plan of the city, to suit himself. Some cities he rearranged so thoroughly that later he had difficulty finding his way about – I mean in his own imaginative plan.'[165] It would be easy to visualize Katsimbalis as Caradoc in all the Blue Nube nightclub scenes in *Tunc*.

Larry was disappointed when Aldington backed out of his promise to Harry T. Moore to write a study of him; Richard still believed in him, but when he found out that a book was wanted of twice the length that he had proposed, he decided that neither his energy nor his health would hold up. Also, Bryher, Hilda Doolittle's companion, had offered him a stipend of £500 on condition that he stopped writing for a year.[166] Moore then approached Gerald Sykes to write a study of Larry, but Sykes was in mid-novel. Thus was born *The World of Lawrence Durrell*: Moore decided to edit a volume of essays on Larry, since he could not find the right person to compose a monograph. Larry told Moore that he had a 'fairly complete check-list' of essays in English, French and German, as well as long fan letters from both a physicist and a Cabalist. The German he could not read, but some of the French essays seemed interesting: 'Not all are convinced, of course, but that is all to the good.'[167] Larry sounded tender towards only one genre of his work: 'By the way, do you have to do more than mention the comic books?' he asked Moore. Larry may have felt especially vulnerable there, but it was more sentiment than embarrassment. 'I adore old Antrobus,' Larry admitted. 'It was he kept me alive while I wrote Balthazar and part of Mountolive.'[168]

As Larry's name and the fame of the *Quartet* were increasingly proclaimed in the world press and on television, everyone he had ever known seemed to be writing to him in December 1960. Claude Legagneux, who had met Larry on Cyprus, was now living in Caen, and wanted help in placing work. Ronimund von Bissing, who had been introduced to Larry in

Kyrenia, wrote inviting him to Blonay in Switzerland. A friendly request from Kimon Friar for a contribution to *The Charioteer* magazine showed that Friar did not hold any grudges against Larry for *Bitter Lemons*. Along with all the requests and invitations, Larry was delighted to receive an undemanding if enigmatic telegram from Salvador Dalí: 'DEPUIS MOIS THERAPIE GOUTTE A GOUTTE QUATRE VOLUMENS DARLEY MON FRERE . . . VENEZ MAISON ECRIRE EN PAIX ET JOIE STOP LOVE DALI.[169] Larry longed to be able to follow his advice.

He also received gratifying attention in the Midi press. Henri el Kayem wrote an article for *Etudes Méditerranéennes* that linked him with Cavafy and Forster. Then Robert Allan – who claimed kinship with Edgar Allan Poe – published a poem dedicated to Larry in *Les Cahiers de la Licorne*. Both were pleasant compliments, and more evidence of Larry's acceptance in the Midi.

Gerry had written to Larry the month before, employing the cheerful mockery with which he usually addressed his eldest brother: 'Now that I discover from all the critics that you are socially acceptable . . . come and spend Christmas with us.' To make certain that his motives would not be suspect, Gerry added a postscript: 'The report I saw in the "Telegraph" that you had received £17,000 for the Quartette has nothing whatsoever to do with this invitation.'[170] There was to be another reunion on 10 December when Larry and Claude had lunch at the Oustaloun in Maussane with Richard Aldington, in the south to visit Catha. She had adopted Larry and Claude as her family, and saw far more of them than she did of her own father.

Christmas in Jersey made a welcome change. Margaret – 'the scourge of the unwary' Larry called her[171] – flew over from Bournemouth. Larry and Claude were received with joyous affection and ribald comments, Claude then went to unpack, and the others drifted off to their various occupations, Larry and Gerry to drink and talk. Soon Claude found Louisa Durrell in the kitchen, holding a completely swaddled infant in the crook of one arm and stirring a large pot with her free hand. 'May I help?' enquired Claude. 'Well', replied Louisa somewhat vaguely, 'I suppose you could take him', and handed over the small bundle. Some minutes later the conversation was flowing easily when the peaceful baby in Claude's arms began to stir. Languidly and casually, a long hairy arm emerged from the blanket and encircled Claude's neck: the supposed human baby was a young chimpanzee from the zoo, in need of special care. Louisa often took over the nurturing of Gerry's nurslings and orphans, bedding them down in her chest of drawers. Claude cherished Louisa, and wrote out a verse 'For Dear Mother Who will understand':

> Durrell (Lawrence of that ilk)
> Thinks that gin is Mother's Milk,
> A View Sounder than any other
> If you know Lawrence Durrell's Mother.[172]

In founding his own zoo, Gerry had taken on a project that required the full application of his tremendous resourcefulness and energy. He had changed from capturing animals for other institutions to his own cherished goal: breeding endangered species with a view not to supplying zoos but to reintroducing them, wherever feasible, into their original habitats. The idea was revolutionary. Other conservationists laughed at him: many animals could not be made to breed in captivity; returning them to the wilds was not practicable; and so on. 'When mankind ceases to care about the loss of species, then man himself is doomed,' Gerry would say, his joking voice suddenly serious.[173] Soon Gerry was proving his critics wrong: through his combination of genius and patience, animals that had never before prospered in captivity ate, thrived, and mated. Larry professed himself terrified of Gerry's animals. Several times a day, at feeding times or during territorial or dominance displays, a terrific ruckus would sound from the chimpanzees or the Madagascan lemurs in the zoo surrounding Gerry's house. 'You see!' Larry would cry, 'They've broken loose, and we're all going to be *devoured*!'[174] This was part of Larry's own display, and while he did not share his brother's passionate commitment to animals, when Gerry hinted that one of his big cats needed a larger dwelling, Larry quietly sent him a handsome cheque 'to build a new cage for the lion'. What Larry admired in Gerry were his capacity for work and his successes. He and Gerry were united in their scorn of Leslie: they saw him as lazy, a sponge, a ne'er-do-well. Margaret? Well, the brothers would shake their heads. She was so like her mother, they thought. This Christmas Leslie was in Africa, and the rest looked amicable enough when a photographer from *Life* magazine showed up to record 'The Gathering of a Famous British Writing Clan'.[175]

The financial burden of the zoo was enormous, and Gerry found that he had to write two books a year, in addition to becoming almost a full-time fund-raiser, just to meet the basic expenses. Fortunately, everything Gerry wrote made the best-seller lists: Larry's old prediction to Henry Miller that Gerry would become a better-known author than either of them had come

37 With George Seferis in Cyprus, 1953.
38 Eve, Sappho and Louisa with Larry.

I had a look at the house. It was quite dry inside

Marie

39 Larry's report to Eve about the house in Bellapaix.
40 With Mr and Mrs Constant Zarian, Cyprus, 1954.
41 Marie Millington-Drake: LD album.
42 Austen Harrison.

I   The Echoes of Instinct

Landscape-tones : brown to bronze.
Steep skylines, low cloud, pearl ground with shadowed
oyster and violet reflections. The lion-dust of the desert:
the prophets' tombs turn to bronze and copper at sunset.
On the ancient lake, with its huge faults, green and
citron give to gun-metal, to a single plum-dark sail,
moist, palpitant — the sticky wings of a newly born
butterfly. Taposiris is dead — its columns sunk in sand.

Summer : buff sand, lilac skies,
Autumn : swollen bruise-greys
Winter : freezing snow-sand
           clear sky. panels
           washed delta greens
           magnificent starscapes

And Spring? There is no spring in
the Delta, no sense of renewal in things. One is
plunged out of winter into the wax effigy of a summer
too hot to breathe. But here at least in Alexandria
the sea-breaths save us from the tideless weight of
summer nothingness, creeping over the bar, to flutter the
striped awnings of the cafés upon the Grand Corniche.

. . . .

The city begins and ends in us.
Its roots are buried in our memory. But why must I
return to it night after night, writing here by the fire
of carob-wood while the Aegean wind clutches at the
house, bending the cypresses back like bows? Have I
not said enough about Alexandria. Am I to be

43 The opening page of *Balthazar* in draft, 1957.

44 Claude at the Villa Louis with her children, Diana and Barry.

45 Xan and Daphne Fielding.
46 Frédéric-Jacques Temple, Montpellier, 1981.
47 Richard Aldington and his daughter Catha in Moscow, June 1962.

48 Claudine Brelet, February 1969.
49 Margaret McCall in Alan Thomas's library, February 1971.

50 Christmas at the Mazet: Claude with Sappho.
51 Anaïs Nin at the Villa Louis, May 1958.

52 Watercolour by Oscar Epfs.
53 Sappho in a Greek wedding dress, c. 1966.
54 Larry in the lotus position, Rhodes, 1976.

55 Gerald Durrell, c. 1965.
56 Brassaï, Paris, c. 1969.
57 Larry and Henry with the bust of Bigot de Préameneu, Sommières, 1967.

58 In New York with Fiddle Viracola, 1970.
59 'Honey-gold' Claude Kiefer.
60 Ghislaine de Boysson, London, 1968.
61 Diane Deriaz, c. 1969.

DEAR HENRY A QUICK
BULLETIN OF NEWS FOR
XMAS ACCOMPANIED BY A
HOME MADE EPFS LETTER
HEAD TO REST YOUR EYE.
DID YOU KNOW THAT THE
GREAT EPFS NOW HAS TWO
 HUGE WATER COLOURS
HANGING IN THE WOMENS4
SECTION OF THE CASERNES
AT VERSAILLES ? HE GAV
THEM TO LITTLE ANNIE
VERNEUIL FOR WHOM I WRO
A COUPLE OF FINE LITTLE
NUMBERS ' Blonde
Cascadeur' and 'Annie
la MOme '. She got fed
up with singing and
joined the army and is
now a serjeant at the
Headquarters !

Little Buttons sends he
love for Xmas. She has
·re emerged briefly and
is just as mischevious
as ever abd still very
pretty ; what luck to
tumble into her arms on
a wet saturday . She
used to sign her lettrs

♥   but now with
maturity just round
the corner and a small
illegitimate child on
her hands she signs🐟

        which is perhap
more realistic. I tell
her that if ever she
wants to be a perfect
mistress she should
sign thus   🐟

 Ghislaine is fixing
up a flat in Paris. I
think with some regrets
but really we were not
suited -- her notion of
a foyer was the salle
des départs a Orly. She
wore me out with her
gambols and expense. What a huge error of judgement -- and costly too.
Just reading Brassai's solid documented and thoughtful book about you and
incidentally us. What he brings out so well is that our friendship and
admiration for each other was so firm that it withstood'every kind of harsh
test like changing ideas, chqnging notions of good and bad writing, It was
unique in that; down deep we firmly believed in each other as artists even
when being critical and feeling that the other had taken fausse route. The
book is good and has carefully followed your traces ;the bit I was lucky enuf
to live seems to me quite accurate and done with insight and kindness. What
en epoch to live through ... Now all that is left is senile seniority and
ennui. Can we throb to Mailer and Roth ? I cant . Bellow yes. This is where
one feels the arteries getting hard. HAPPY NEW YEAR HENRY. From Larry

62 Letter of 15 December 1975 to Henry Miller.

63 'Darley's tower': Larry returns to the Ambron house, Alexandria, 1977.
64 Sitting at Cavafy's desk in the Greek consulate, Alexandria.
65 Larry at Saint-Julien de Salinelles near Sommières, where Claude's ashes are in an unmarked grave.

66 Larry in front of Epstein's bust of Eliot at a Faber party.

67 With Fred Perlès outside the World's End pub.
68 Larry with Theodore Stephanides and Alan Thomas.

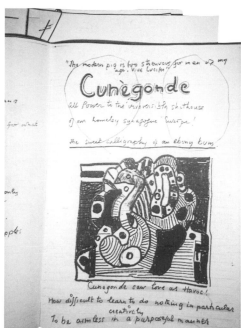

69 Gerry Durrell at the Mazet Michel, 1983.
70 Larry's 'Cunégonde' quarry notebook for *Caesar's Vast Ghost*.
71 With Ludo and Martine Chardenon.

72 Françoise and Larry at Le Glacier, July 1988.
73 Mme Tartes, shuttered.

to pass, at any rate for the English reading public. Larry was genuinely delighted by Gerry's successes, just as Gerry was with his, but each pretended to fulfil the roles that Gerry had assigned them in *My Family and Other Animals*. Still, each was a bit nettled when, as not infrequently happened, he was given one of his brother's books to sign. Once an Air France hostess, blushing prettily, handed Larry a pen and a copy of *My Family and Other Animals*. Without a flicker he wrote on the title page, 'Signed, in the absence of the author, by his brother, a better writer.'[176] It was sibling rivalry for public consumption.

Gerry was invariably grateful for Larry's support. 'He has the most extraordinary ability for giving people faith in themselves,' Gerry wrote in 1961. 'Throughout my life he has provided me with more enthusiastic encouragement than anyone else, and any success I have achieved is due, in no small measure, to his backing.' Larry admired all kinds of ambitions, the more outlandish the better. Once a London night porter confessed to him that he doubted whether he would ever achieve his ambition of crossing the Sahara on a bicycle. Larry set to work. 'For half an hour he talked with such infectious enthusiasm about touring Africa on a bicycle that you would have thought his one ambition in life was to undertake such a trip himself,' Gerry recalled. His warnings were brushed aside: 'Water's easy to get in the Sahara if you know where to look,' Larry said. By the time Gerry and Larry left, the night porter felt like Livingstone or Cecil Rhodes, and was making a list of the equipment he would require for his trip.[177]

After Jersey, Larry and Claude went to London for a few days on business: and to get married. He no longer believed in marriage, Larry said, but it would help his tax status. The marriage was performed at the Kensington Register Office where both D. H. Lawrence and James Joyce had been married, as Harry T. Moore pointed out to Larry. For him it was again a case of fox to earth: the World's End pub, an old haunt, was just ten minutes along King's Road. There was no ceremony, and Larry had hoped that the event would go unnoticed, 'but we got involved alas with Elizabeth Taylor's publicity and my fortuitous connection with the Cleopatra script made it "news"', said the chagrined former press officer.[178]

LARRY KEPT AN EYE ON WHAT his friends were composing. Henry Miller, emulating Larry's foray into drama, had just written, in three days, three acts of his first play, and was on the epilogue:[179] *Just Wild About Harry* would eventually be premièred at the Spoleto Festival, and would include in the cast Fiddle Viracola, who was to have a part in Larry's life a decade later. Henry was inclined to be modest about his drama: 'If I could, I'd write (plays) à la Beckett or Ionesco. . . . But I'll have to write my own kind of flapdoodle, I guess.'[180] From New York Gerald Sykes sent Larry the typescript of 'The Forbidden Tree', as he then called the book that would appear the following year as *The Hidden Remnant*, and Larry seemed genuinely enthusiastic. Alex Blokh wrote a novel that he said was inspired by Larry. The Blokhs and the de Rougemonts formed a nucleus of friends in Geneva for Larry and Claude, and the city became a frequent destination for them.

Larry wanted to make 1961 his year for drama and the producers were co-operating: *Sappho* would appear in Edinburgh in August, *Acte* in Hamburg in November. Gustaf Gründgens told Larry, 'If you knew how sick I am of being the most famous Mephisto of all time . . . why, you would write me a Faust with some humour in it!'[181] Inspired, by mid-February 1961 Larry had written half of *An Irish Faustus*. 'I'm trying a small break through on the front opened by Auden and Eliot', he announced, 'only using different criteria'.[182] Larry had himself trimmed the bulky *Sappho* to make an acting version for Edinburgh.[183] He was soon taken away from the drama when another onslaught of *Cleopatra* scripting hit, and Larry turned out wodges of typescript dated 24 February, 20 March, 28 March and so on until early April. For the six weeks, film director Walter Wanger guaranteed Larry $2,500 per week plus expenses. In the end, the direction of the film was taken over by Joseph L. Mankiewicz, who himself wrote much of the script that was eventually used. Larry's name would not appear among the credits.

Cautious Larry and practical Claude regarded the *Cleopatra* money as a windfall not likely to be repeated, and their habits did not change appreciably: they eventually bought a small Hillman Super Imp to replace the ageing Peugeot, and set about converting the narrow but deep open cistern behind the house into a swimming pool – in reality, a hot-weather plunge not much bigger than a very large bath. From the front, the most noticeable change in the appearance of the *mazet* was the broad dry-stone walls that Larry put in many recreational hours each week constructing. He seldom failed to show them off to visitors. His daughters and Claude's children teased him by calling the *mazet* 'Troy' in recognition of Larry's walls. Eventually the children would apply the name to 'their' annexe.

The fun of spending the money was in the future, however, as Larry and Claude set about answering mail and entertaining visitors. On 21 April 1961 they met Henry and Vincent Birge, Henry's factotum and chauffeur, in Avignon for a lavish luncheon. Then a French political crisis hit, and Henry took off like a dove for Switzerland, only to double back to Portugal on the advice of an astrologer. An amused Larry expected Henry back in France by the end of summer, since he would find Portugal 'boring' and 'not much fun foodwise'.[184]

In early May, Elliot Macrae of Dutton came to see Larry, bringing the good news that the paperbacks of the *Quartet* were selling well without taking the steam out of the hardbacks. At present, however, the theatre was still commanding Larry's attention. He began corresponding regularly with Gründgens about *Acte*, grateful for the suggestions of revisions. Gründgens objected that since *Akte* in German was the plural of 'act', the translation should be given a new title.[185] Larry proposed 'The Scythian Queen', provided it would sound well in German. This produced a sibilant 'Die skythische Königin',[186] so they settled on *Actis*. Soon Larry was busy writing a new final act on Gründgens's urging for the winter production planned in Hamburg. 'As I'm eager to learn I'm trying to comply,' said Larry. However, the season of summer callers was almost upon him: 'I'm expecting my family and other animals to descend on me,' Larry pretended to groan, 'so we are laying in stocks of food and wine against a Gargantuan week end.' Then he would try to get back to *An Irish Faustus*. He had written two acts, 'but owing to travel and the nibbling of visitors have rather lost the thread'.[187]

After several years of campaigning, Margaret Rawlings had finally succeeded in arranging backing for the English première of *Sappho*. The Bristol Old Vic Company would mount a lavish production at the Edinburgh International Festival, directed by John Hale and with Rawlings as the poet of Lesbos and Nigel Davenport as Pittakos. Larry had met Hale the year before after seeing *The Tinker*, a play directed by Hale, and the two had co-operated on preparing an acting version of *Sappho*. On 21 August the great event took place in the Royal Lyceum Theatre, where the play was scheduled for a one-week run. Larry's trip to Edinburgh, accompanied by Mary Mollo and Claude, did not provide favourable omens for the *Sappho* production: on the Channel crossing a woman began to scream that she had gone blind. 'Hysteria', commented Larry complacently; 'she should have read Groddeck.'[188] Then by mistake he was not booked on the luxurious Golden Arrow but on a slower train, and that one he nearly missed. For someone who usually insisted on being at an airport or railway station four hours in advance of the departure time, it was almost unmanning.

A reporter for the *Evening Standard* caught Larry at the Festival reception in the City Chambers. He put on his best bland face and announced, 'It was the wildest impertinence for me to write a play. When I did it I had seen only two plays, and one of them was *Charley's Aunt*.' Larry expressed a preference for Elizabethan plays, adding, 'I think people are heartily sick of the love affairs of isosceles triangles.'[189] Hale called Larry a 'frustrated Schiller', as Larry reported to Gustaf Gründgens with some amusement.[190] Larry liked Hale well enough to entertain him the following month at the *mazet*, and Hale helped out with advice on improving *Acte*.

Mary Mollo thought that 'Everything was rather flat and genteel; Sappho floated around the stage like a hostess in a Victorian drawing-room.' Compton Mackenzie, who met Larry for the first time at Edinburgh, liked the play but not the performance: 'I confess I was a little disappointed that Margaret Rawlings didn't throw herself off a cliff at the end', in emulation of the Sappho of legend.[191] Larry was fond of Rawlings as a person and therefore too loyal to say much. Asked what he thought of her performance, he balanced diplomacy with silence: 'Well, by the time she got to play it – you know, she waited about five years to do it, and she was good but – .' He did not continue.

By speaking well of a fellow writer, Larry gained another new friend. He received a warm letter from Claude Seignolle, diabolist and author of *Les Maledictions* and *Folklore de la Provence*: 'Would you be that: "... Irishman . . . very congenial . . . who lives in the Midi . . . loves the books of Seignolle"?'[192] Larry would indeed. Soon they had met and conversed happily about vampires, sorcery and Catharism. Seignolle was a balding, powerful man with oddly pointed ears, and he had been variously a gravedigger and an archaeologist, a tanner, and a newspaperman. 'I am *sorcier d'honneur* of a damned village', he said of himself, 'and maybe people think I am the Devil himself.'[193] Larry wrote a foreword for *Les Maledictions* in which he ranked Seignolle with E. T. A. Hoffman, Mary Shelley and Maturin. Soon Larry took on another task, accepting Kathleen Nott's invitation to edit *New Poems 1963* for PEN.

On 12 November 1961 Larry and Claude arrived in Copenhagen to visit Isak Dinesen, who wanted to meet Larry and had offered to pay his way. It was rare for Larry to obey a virtual command from a famous recluse, but he had admired her at least since his years in Alexandria, and in 1948 he had recommended her *Seven Gothic Tales* to Mary Mollo, then in Dinesen's Kenya. 'By the way', Larry had told Mary, 'look out for an astonishing woman writer . . . . Her real name is Baroness Blixen and she writes extraordinary short stories.'[194] Larry was profoundly moved by the old baroness, and impressed by the way she mounted the stairs in her home, touching the immense map of Africa on the wall, but what they spoke about was not recorded.[195] From Copenhagen Larry and Claude made the easy trip of a few hours south to Hamburg, where Gründgens was polishing *Acte/Actis* for the 24 November world première at the Deutsches Schauspielhaus. The beautiful Joana Maria Gorvin created the title role, and Werner Hinz was a convincingly insecure and treacherous Nero. Larry was delighted with the production, whatever he may have thought of the irony of seeing *Actis*, as had been the case with *Sappho*, performed for the first time in a language that he did not understand. The German press called the play 'spielbar und spannend' – stageworthy and gripping – and judged it better than *Sappho*.[196]

While he was in Hamburg, Larry recorded an interview that was eventually published in *The World of Lawrence Durrell*. Ignoring his reason for being in Hamburg, Larry concentrated on his novels to make one of his major statements about his work and the ideas behind them. Challenged to define Man, Larry at first evaded – 'How can I, how can anyone?' – but then he made the attempt anyway: 'An Eros-breath if you like; *amo ergo sum, sed cogito*.'[197] Larry's rephrasing of Descartes could serve as an epigram for that 'Investigation of Modern Love', the *Quartet*, and it would echo throughout his fiction to come.

Loving was as natural *and as necessary* as breathing, Larry thought, and he would constantly link the two. Clea not-breathing, drowning, is Clea unable to love or to create, Larry implied. 'You know what "breath" means in its Alexandrian connotation?' he asked. 'Sex and knowing become primal here where I try to symbolize the achievement of "artisthood" – the mysterious secret of which Pursewarden was trying to pass on to Darley.' 'Yes', Larry continued, it was very simple, 'in the Hermetic sense it is a matter of life and breath!' All those who were really alive were sun-worshippers: his entire life had been a series of flights towards the sun. Knowledge freed the way towards intuition. Larry attributed the determining epigram to Pursewarden: 'You must become a Knowbody before you can become a Sunbody.'[198]

After all the hard work and excitement, Larry and Claude decided to hibernate at the *mazet* instead of going to Jersey for the holidays. Their children were in England with various estranged spouses, so there was little pressure to have a family Christmas. Paddy and Joan Leigh Fermor passed through for an 'all-too-brief meeting'. Richard Aldington drove south from the Cher to be their only guest over Christmas, and Claude and

Larry were delighted to find Richard in such good form. 'He looks ten years younger and has recovered his laughter', Larry wrote to Harry T. Moore, who had met Richard during his researches on D. H. Lawrence.[199] Everything was going 'suspiciously well', said the superstitious Larry. A version of *Acte* was published in *Show* magazine in December 1961. He had sufficient funds coming in for the next five years, 'after which once more it's up to my typewriter and of course the public', yet he could not feel secure, having no pension 'and far too many dependents'.[200] Larry would *always* worry about money, but this did not prevent him from writing a 'non-saleable', an essay entitled 'Shakespear and Love', which included some animadversions around the identity of the elusive 'Mr. W. H.' Larry dated the typescript 'New Year '62' and sent it off to the magazine *Réalités*. Nothing happened.

With *The World of Lawrence Durrell* collection about to appear, Harry T. Moore now proposed to write a monograph on Larry and in fact had already signed a contract for the book. Larry immediately gave him deprecating advice: 'For goodness sake don't go to India,' he pleaded. 'Just read KIM and talk to my mother an hour in Jersey!' Neither should Moore bother with Alexandria: 'It's been invaded by the Arabs and the skyline changed by blocks of flats.' Instead, he should read Forster to obtain a grasp of Larry's Alexandria. The *Quartet*, he added, was 'atmospherically right but heavily invented'.[201] Despite his caveats, Larry was very pleased with Moore's proposed monograph, but worried about how much biographical probing he intended. He was acutely conscious of the problems faced by biographers, lamented that Kipling's family was refusing the publication of his letters, and noted that it was impossible to write 'an honest Rolfe', again because of the opposition of relatives. 'Personally I don't give a turnip,' Larry said, and he was not unduly worried over what might be revealed about others 'off the scene'. 'I am only concerned with the living, who goodness knows have had enough already to bear from me without being pilloried in prose.'[202]

When Larry received a copy of *The World of Lawrence Durrell*, he wrote to Moore that 'gasps of self-admiring egotism aside' he found the book 'balanced rather than partisan'.[203] A measure of balance came from Martin Green's negative appraisal of everything, from the poetry to the *Quartet* and even *White Eagles over Serbia*. He concluded that, because of living so long away from England, 'Durrell's mind is a museum-piece'.[204] Larry ignored this particular essay in his note of thanks to Moore. The whole book was 'a splendid present for my fiftieth birthday'. Larry told

Moore that a Benares astrology group had predicted the end of the world for the next day, and that if this turned out the case, 'why it won't seem quite so hard. I shall go under holding your book above my head!'[205] None the less, he developed 'a lovely Groddeckian rheumatism which makes typing agony' just as he was trying to finish *An Irish Faustus*. Perhaps it really was turning fifty that upset Larry, and his state of mind was not improved when Sappho commented, 'Daddy? O Daddy's so old he is almost DEAD.'[206] On top of everything, Languedoc was struck by 'the worst mistral on record': the roaring north-west wind cracked branches and rattled the roof tiles on the Mazet Michel.[207]

Larry was well aware of Moore's *The Intelligent Heart*, which was then the standard biography of D. H. Lawrence, and he knew that Moore was preparing a two-volume collection of Lawrence's letters that would be the most comprehensive to date. Larry had already referred to Moore as 'our senior Lawrence specialist'.[208] Thus when Moore wrote comparing Larry's books of foreign residence to Lawrence's travel writing, saying that 'Lawrence had a ferocity the rest of you simply don't have', Larry jumped as if slapped. He responded in a short letter that summarized at once his estimation of his own writing and his understanding of Lawrence's triumph:

Dear Moore;
    I'm going to come off badly if you set my travel stuff up against DHL! He found himself very early and learned to write badly, without pedantic care I mean, because he knew his personality carried a charge of feeling and he could really afford to do without language considerations. It's a question of self-confidence; mine grows slower and I tend to be word-bound, egg-bound. Consequently I often miss what you call the 'quickness'. It's really the immediacy of impact. Now when DHL was writing everyone complained about his wretched style! What set their teeth on edge are the very beauties we admire today. He subjugated language and harnessed it to his speaking voice. The only times I think I ever get near a comparison are in private letters; when I have to publish I get panicky and polish. Fortunately or unfortunately there wasn't time with the quartet. But I believe you could make a patchwork of extracts on landscape from private letters which could just bear comparison with the anthology RA [Aldington] made of DHL called The Spirit of Place. Anyway, what the hell; it's good of you to bother.[209]

Moore, as it turned out, would never write his study of Larry, but years later the faithful Alan Thomas would compile *Spirit of Place: Letters and Essays on Travel*, an anthology of Larry's work.

Larry's spring was comparatively leisurely, with visits from Richard

Aldington, Jacques Temple, François Erval, the Blokhs and their friends the Bouviers, and Claude Seignolle. Larry wrote another preface for a collection of Seignolle's occult tales, *Un corbeau de toutes couleurs*. Various old friends, reminded by the reviews of the *Quartet*, re-established contact: Archibald Lyall, a writer on Mediterranean subjects; Enrique Revol and Eduardo Mallea, both from the bad old days of Argentina. Part of the excitement of the early months of 1962 derived from Aldington's invitation to the Soviet Union for a celebration of his seventieth birthday. Richard sought Larry's advice, as a seasoned veteran of the Foreign Office. Richard's books were best-sellers in the USSR, and for the past few years he had been receiving royalty cheques from 'the Red Fiends of Muscovy'. But should he risk his conservative hide by accepting the hospitality of the Soviet Writers' Union? Larry told him that a 'long trip' would be good for him, and they both checked on protocol with their respective contacts in the diplomatic corps.

Aldington agreed to go to the Soviet Union, taking Catha along to prop him up. 'I have determined not to go dressed as a bohemian but as a pseudo-gent, with would-be impeccable black jacket and small-check trousers', he told Larry. 'A nylon shirt and silk tie should, added to this tenue, dispel any illusions of proletarian sympathies.' Still, Richard concluded, 'This Russ trip is a blind, and like Mr Weller Sr on another occasion, I don't take no pride on it, Sammy.'[210] Forewarned about the innumerable vodka toasts, Richard had let on that he was a teetotaller. Much to his surprise, Aldington was given by far the most splendid reception of his life, introduced to Tolstoy's grandson and to Gorki's widow, fêted everywhere, asked to sign countless copies of his books, showered with samovars, books and dolls by his official hosts as well as by humble people who had come long journeys to greet him. 'I found them the most cheerful and warm-hearted people I've ever met,' he confided to Larry. 'Such a pity they have to be communists.'[211]

With one small exception, the mainstream British press ignored both Aldington's birthday and his Russian triumph. He wrote to Larry that, 'to tickle my vanity', their common friend John Gawsworth proposed to send Hugh Oloff de Wet to sculpt heads of Larry and himself. Since Larry was to go to Edinburgh soon, Richard suggested that Oloff de Wet proceed to Scotland, and, he urged Larry, 'I feel sure you will consent *to sit for us both*. Who says the wisdom of Salaudmon died with him?'[212] The next day Richard dropped dead of a heart attack while sitting in the sun at Maison Sallé, and the joyously slashing letters of Top Grumpy ceased.

AFTER COMPLETING THE *Quartet* Larry had taken up painting again, and he found it more absorbing than ever. His favoured media were still water-colours, gouache and ink, laid on in brilliant combinations. The children were arriving for their summer holidays in mid-July, and Larry was doing nothing but painting ever larger canvases. He had perfected a drip method, so he said, for achieving a 'maculé' effect, 'but Jesus what a waste of paint, which is expensive'. He was again mulling over ideas for 'The Placebo', which he now tentatively subtitled 'an attic comedy'.[213] During the coming October he planned to do some poking around for background in Athens.[214]

On 20 August 1962 Larry and Henry were in Edinburgh for the International Writers' Conference. Henry had been dithering about whether to appear or not, but Larry persuaded him by saying that they would have no obligations and plenty of time for self-indulgence. Henry was in marvellous form, and for once he was not shy about being surrounded by eminent writers: Mary McCarthy, Norman Mailer, William Burroughs, Stephen Spender and Larry's old friend Dame Rebecca West. As a public intellectual exchange, the conference was largely a failure, although this was owing largely to the outburst of ill temper and political posturing displayed on the second day by Alexander Trocchi, Hugh McDiarmid and a few others. Henry said almost nothing in public, but Larry attempted to make a serious statement on the fourth day, when the Future of the Novel was the topic of discussion. With a hint of irony, Larry began: 'If I look a bit depressed it is possible that the future of the novel lies here in Edinburgh.' His depression was due not so much to the maunderings of his fellow writers as to the sonnet-writing computer that he had just seen in the linguistics department of the University of Edinburgh. His friend David Abercrombie had demonstrated the new wonder to him, a parametric talking machine known as PAT, that could 'speak' as programmed by Abercrombie and his colleagues. PAT represented a breakthrough in the electronic production of speech. Delighted to put one over on Larry, Abercrombie let him depart convinced that PAT could compose sonnets. Larry concluded that by Christmas it would be writing novels. With the breakdown of religion and metaphysics, the novelist, Larry told the audience, 'becomes a cosmologist, cosmologising'. The ancient market story-teller could write the nigh-endless *Thousand and One Nights*, but the modern writer has to search out form. 'Since Proust had thoroughly explored the Bergsonian universe in time, I wondered whether the only thing we might call a total metaphysic at the moment might offer us a form to explore, and this in fact is what the French novelists are doing: they are exploring the relativity idea through discontinuity and trying to build forms which satisfy it.'[215] This was what Larry was attempting to do as well, and these shared philosophic underpinnings were one reason why he was so well received in France.

To judge from the lack of response from his British audience, his extempore remarks were not understood in Edinburgh. Larry had picked up something from his visit to Scotland, however: the language computer would find its way into *Tunc* and *Nunquam* as the highly sophisticated word processor/thought machines Abel and Dactyl. An early draft of 'The Placebo', evidently written not long before Edinburgh, contains many eccentrics and Athens *demi-mondaines* who would appear in *Tunc* – Banubula, Caradoc, Charlock, Iolanthe, Koepgen, Sipple and Vibart – but neither Abel nor Dactyl. In *Tunc*, a 'Scots University' uses the machines to study phonetics.

In the autumn of 1962 Larry took up painting in oils, using tubes of paint bought for him by Claude and some old brushes provided by Amy Smart. 'Being the impatient bastard that I am', Larry confessed, he had started smearing paint 'like strawberry jam' with a palette knife. It was 'great fun', though not as 'nice' as building dry-stone walls.[216]

Another adventure came Larry's way in September when he went to Israel to research a proposed film scenario, *Judith*. Larry had drafted a story about a young Jewish woman doctor, scholarly and professional, to be played by Sophia Loren. 'Just finished tracing the border without anything to boast about', he wrote to Alan Thomas, 'rather hoped to be captured by drug-smugglers and carried off captive on a camel like this one to Damascus. How many small girls at public school could boast "My daddy is a slave in a harem. He gets forty lashes a day." '[217]

The Durrell name was riding high, and there was a rumour that he would receive the Nobel Prize in 1962. When it went to John Steinbeck, Larry seems not to have registered any disappointment, but he was well aware that his name had come up. More than twenty-five years later, on hearing that Artur Lundkvist had been on the prize committee, Larry said, 'He is a Com and received the Prize Lenin; it explains why I lost it that year to Steinbeck with his "preoccupation with the fate of the people" . . . . What the hell.'[218] He assumed that the Nobel owed more to connections and politics than to merit – since each country had writers of Nobel stature – and that no Communist would vote for him. During the summer he had been offered an OBE, which he had refused with the explanation, 'There must be many people who would appreciate it more than me.'²¹⁹ 'That was offered in malice,' Aldington had said. 'When they gave a cow like Dick Church & Spender! *Man!* a CBE!!'²²⁰ Larry gave no indication of feeling either pleased or slighted.

In early December, Larry was rushing to finish 'a draft of a scenario' for *Judith*.²²¹ Soon he would be leaving for a Jersey Christmas. He was also attempting some short plays to improve his technique. The year had not been very productive for him, but he had certainly enjoyed playing with old forms and new: painting, verse drama, and the film scenario. His old nemesis, boredom, was staying away.

CLAUDE WAS DIAGNOSED WITH a fibroid condition, and in March 1963 she and Larry went to Geneva for ten days of examinations and treatment. Larry was still wrestling with *An Irish Faustus*, which he sent to Curtis Brown in early April for typing. Then Larry took Claude in mid-April back to Geneva, for 'an operation on her insides'. Claude underwent a hysterectomy on the 24th, and seemed to be recovering quickly. Larry departed two days later for Madrid to meet Sophia Loren and discuss the *Judith* script with her. Larry pronounced Loren 'a sweet creature, great dignity and style'.²²² She convinced Larry that she was not suited for the role as he had conceived it: 'I am not an intellectual,' she told him.²²³ In fact, Larry liked her precisely because he saw her as a peasant, a simple person.²²⁴ Larry agreed to rewrite the story from beginning to end. On the 29th he was back in Geneva, lodged at his favourite Hotel Touring-Balances on the place Longemalle. After Claude was discharged from the clinic, they stayed on for ten days so as to have easy access to post-operative care. Larry returned with Claude to Nîmes on 14 May. A week later they sailed on the *San Marcos* for Piraeus: it was to be a convalescent trip for her.

They went to Spetsai to see George Katsimbalis and the photographer Dimitri Papadimos. 'My goodness how you would be enjoying every moment of this journey', Larry wrote to Henry Miller. 'Then to Mykonos – nowhere for a week – blue and hot', where they sat in a taverna drinking retsina.²²⁵ Claude's enthusiasm and Larry's laughter attracted attention. They started to talk to an American couple; the woman was a small, pretty brunette; her husband was a number of years older, his accent betraying his German origin – a witty man but shy, self-deprecating. The Americans recognized Larry Durrell, but there were no introductions and they never let on. Weeks later there was a chance encounter with the same pair, this time on Rhodes. Frances and Horst von Maltitz shared a rented car with Larry and Claude for a visit to the Acropolis at Lindos, where together they explored the temple of Athene Lindia and the ruins of the crusader castle. By the end of the day they were friends, and they all drank too much retsina, after Larry had showed them the trick of lowering wicker-covered demijohns on a string into the sea for cooling. Then the Durrells returned to Athens for a week of visiting old friends, but the next weekend they spent at Delphi with the von Maltitzes. By mid-July Larry and Claude were back at the *mazet*. Sappho arrived for her summer holidays, blazing with a thirteen-year-old's mixture of precocity and innocence. Sappho could be very critical of Larry and Claude and their quarrels, and pleaded with them, 'Please, *please*, don't drink any more Tavel.' The Wetherell-Peppers were visiting, and to Joan's amusement Sappho fell instantly in love with her husband Denis, 'who looked like a tall Laurence Olivier'.[226]

Larry's reputation in France continued to puzzle some English critics. When the *Times Literary Supplement* wrote that 'Mr Durrell and Miss Compton-Burnett meet with such praise in France as to raise many a lukewarm English eyebrow', Larry responded with the satirical 'Ode to a Lukewarm Eyebrow', in which he suggested that the reviewer 'Be dubbed forever a *pince-fesse* of English Lit.'[227] It had nettled him to be linked with Ivy Compton-Burnett, but Larry's return volley, alas, was neither clever nor funny.

The month of October was crowded with projects and crises. Ursula Schuh, wife of Oscar Fritz Schuh, the new director of the Deutsches Schauspielhaus in Hamburg, finished her translation into German of *An Irish Faustus*, and Larry was caught up with the revision process. Suddenly, with the fine sense of dramatic timing that had characterized his stage career, Gustaf Gründgens, for whom Larry had written the role of Faustus, died in a Manila hotel room on 7 October. It was a mystery: Gründgens left a note that said, 'I believe that I took too many sleeping pills. . . . Let me sleep long.'[228] Dr Schuh continued with his plans for the production. A segment of *Faustus* was due to appear soon in French in the magazine *Dire*, and Jacques Temple was just completing his translation of *Down the Styx* and asked Larry to vet some variants. Then a letter arrived from Ruth Speirs, giving an account of the death of Bernard Spencer: he had fallen, or jumped, from a moving train. This departure of one of Larry's circle of intimates from his Egyptian days seemed a pointed reminder of his own mortality. Peggy Glanville-Hicks had brought her ill-fated operatic version of Larry's *Sappho* to the point of orchestration. Financed by a Ford

Foundation grant, it would eventually get as far as rehearsals, but would never appear before the public.

As autumn chilled into winter, Larry completed a meticulous reading of the typescript of Arthur Guirdham's *The Nature of Healing*, and he sent the hapless author a detailed critique in which he said that the book needed to be 're-thought and re-felt – certainly re-tailored'. While the theme of the book, a study of four 'healers', was 'splendid', instead of launching into it Guirdham had opened up with seventy pages of 'vaguely generalised argument on the familiar vitalist versus mechanist lines which adds *nothing* to what even we laymen know and what has been so brilliantly said already in so many ways . . . Jung, Wilhelm, Graham Howe, Cruikshank – among doctors; but among philosophers there are *hundreds*'. Guirdham had treated the healers superficially, rather than bringing the full weight of his science to bear on them: he could have described everything from their horoscopes to the albumen in the urine, from the encephalograms to the graphologists' reports. Instead, everything was familiar: 'Even your "gestalt" of apparent coincidences has been included in a provisional system by Dunne' – his concept of the 'serial universe', Larry noted.[229] His criticism was well-meant and was taken as such by Dr Guirdham. It also showed how immersed Larry was in theories of disease and healing.

Within weeks Larry had reread Guirdham's manuscript, and while he held to his original strictures, he encouraged Guirdham to persevere, saying that his book could become 'as much a pioneering effort as FWH Myers' *Human Survival After Death*', which he praised for being 'anti-rational and anti-scientific (in the Victorian sense)'. Like Dostoevsky's Underground Man, Larry distrusted any system that purported to analyse the human condition on purely rational terms. He also referred Guirdham to Alan Watt's *Psychotherapy East and West*. What Larry wanted was a 'typology' to describe mankind, one that would go beyond Kretschmer's division of humanity into tall, lanky, introspective leptosomes and stocky, 'podgling', ebullient pykniks. Larry looked forward to the time when electricity would provide a 'Psychograph', so that the nature of an individual could be charted with the accuracy of a spectrum analysis. 'Today the nearest thing we have to a *comprehensive* typology of the human character, pace Kretschmer and Co, is astrology!' Larry concluded. 'No other system offers us the full range of psychological and physical types.'[230]

An Irish Faustus was published in London on 8 November 1963, and along with a few favourable notices it received a scathing review in the *New Cambridge*. The reviewer was offended by Larry's claim to be following 'Kit Marlowe' and offended by his supposed lack of 'any serious commitment to his subject', yet he also taxed Larry with portraying Faustus's triumph over Mephisto as a 'serious victory'. 'The choice of conclusion is between triviality and a serious failure of intelligence,' said the critic in summary.[231] This review was typical, Larry told Guirdham, of the 'trouble that I have always had from my compatriots'. Never mind: his German fans were all 'factory workers and teddy boys' who had not lost the capacity for 'cold shudders'. 'I wanted to try and recapture some of the silliness and wonder of gaslight melo as played in the village inn yard. . . . Why not use Frankenstein to say something serious?'[232]

For most of December, Larry was in Hamburg to oversee the production of *An Irish Faustus*. Even the recent death of Gustaf Gründgens had not snuffed out Larry's enthusiasm for the play, and he found that he could work well with Oscar Schuh, who made substantive textual suggestions. On his advice, Larry rewrote an exchange between Faustus and his assistant in order to clarify the conjuring powers of alchemist's gold, but he rejected Dr Schuh's urging that he change the protagonist's name to Dr Morienus to avoid the obvious Goethe comparison. Opening night came on Wednesday 18 December, and the 2500–seat Deutsches Schauspielhaus was packed. *Time* magazine claimed that Larry himself had been 'hooted from the stage', but the *New York Times* reporter said that, while there had been some catcalls, the cast, director and author were cheered for twenty minutes. Larry thought that *Ein irischer Faust* had garnered more curtain calls in Hamburg than either *Sappho* or *Acte*.[233] Alan and Ella Thomas had come over for the event, and with Larry and Claude they celebrated an 'improvised' Christmas.

On 28 December the Durrells flew to Paris to see 1964 in with actress Eleonore Hirt and stage designer Antonio Vargas. Together they went to Fauchon where they ordered 'champagne, caviar and a hundred and one delicacies and oddities'. Paris seemed 'so beautiful' under the lights, and the return to their hotel 'in a drunken taxi' turned into an adventure when they had to run a gauntlet of 'scullions from Maxims in their white steeples' who were stopping cars at the Place de la Concorde and pelting drivers with flour. 'We ignored all the red lights until we nearly collided with another taxi,' Larry told Alan Thomas. 'The drivers were about to castrate each other for sheer joy and had already begun a long alliterative insult with the highly insulting remarks "Tes cuilles" (Your balls!) when a lovely passenger leaned out and handed them a sprig of pine or holly and said "Bonne Année" so charmingly that they melted.'[234]

SOMEHOW, AMID ALL THE TRAVELS and the celebrations with old friends and new, Larry continued to work on 'The Placebo'. The story was to be no mere revision of earlier material.[235] Larry told Henry Miller that he was thinking of writing exactly what he wanted but not publishing anything else until he was, say, sixty. This might allow him to develop 'a pretty freehand style'. Why not, since for once in his life he did not need more money?[236]

Louisa Durrell had continued to live with Jacquie and Gerry on Jersey. It was fine with Gerry, but his wife eventually decided that she had had enough, and suggested to Louisa that she move back to the mainland for a while. Louisa left in January 1964 to stay with a friend in Bournemouth. Certainly the change upset Louisa and she felt rejected and lonely. She did what she had done earlier when hit by crises: she drank a bottle of gin. This time the shock was too much for her system, and she became irrational and disoriented. Margaret put her into a nursing home, planning to find a flat nearby for her. Within a week Louisa was dead. Larry and Claude flew to England for the funeral in Bournemouth. Larry was solemn, and gently lent his arm to Aunt Fan. Margaret was shocked and quiet: 'You sort of pull down a shutter and show a calm demeanour,' she said.[237] This Gerry was unable to manage. At first he refused to enter the church for the service, then finally he allowed himself to be half-carried to a back pew, supported by Alan Thomas. Alan too felt the loss intensely, but he hid his grief as best he could.[238]

After the burial the family and a few friends gathered at the Thomas home. Someone provided champagne, and Alan decided there was nothing for it but to start opening bottles, a great many of them. The atmosphere turned warm and friendly: just the sort of gathering Louisa had always loved. As the champagne and the release of tension acted upon the Durrells, they fell into their old habits of repartee and reminiscence. Aunt Prudence declared with satisfaction, 'Thank *God* that Louie died on British soil!'[239] For a couple of hours it was almost as if their mother had merely vanished into the kitchen to prepare a curry. 'Thank you for your rock-like support,' Gerry told Alan on leaving.[240] Later Gerry wrote, 'We were so glad you were there. Mother would have been too.' His humour flickered briefly: 'We can only hope that the popping of champagne corks did not deviate her spirit from its Heavenward course.'[241] Jacquie's note on their arrival in Jersey was more cryptic: 'Made the Zoo. Everything fine.'[242]

Larry scandalized Henry Miller by the flippancy of his tone, writing, 'I've just got back from England, and the dacent burying of my mother; she had an obsession about "being a trouble to people" and this time she performed her ploy to such good purpose that she almost slipped away before anyone knew where they were.'[243] Henry should have understood – it was so Durrellian to parry grief with flippancy. The death of the mother who had been such a centre of affection, of sibling rivalry in the early years, of both exasperation and fun, probably affected Larry internally much as it did Gerry and Margaret, but he did not show it. He had developed a more impervious shell than his youngest brother.

Larry returned to France to prepare a trick to spring upon the unwitting public. The painter Oscar Epfs burst into the Paris art world on 6 March 1964. The Epfs exhibition took place at the Galerie Connaître at 36 rue des Saints Pères and was presided over by the supposed sister of the artist in the person of Mary Mollo. The artist was represented by the photograph of a blond, bearded man of apparently Nordic origin. In fact, Mary had provided the portrait of a German geologist she had known in Brazzaville in 1941. Epfs, so it was given out to the press, had vanished in the Congo, and Lawrence Durrell was appearing at the exhibition merely to champion the presumed perished man. No one quite believed the ruse, although few identified Durrell as Oscar Epfs. There was some irony in the fact that the most artistically talented member of the family, Leslie, was at that moment beginning a new job at the Shimo-la-tewa School in Mombasa, and this was enough to give Larry a weave of truth as he spun yarns about Epfs. Nadia and Alex Blokh were in on the deceit, but not so Larry's friends Nanik and Denis de Rougemont. Mme de Rougemont, moved by Larry's harrowing tale of the missing artist, quizzed a stammering Mary about her alleged brother. Mary's embarrassment was taken for grief, and the compassionate Nanik de Rougemont bought one of the paintings. It did not help Mary that Claude stood by listening, scarlet with ill-suppressed mirth. When pressed on the significance of Epfs, Larry said variously that he had chosen the name because it sounded 'exactly like a fart', because the French could not pronounce it, because the name was so marvellous that Epfs deserved an Oscar.

Larry was not a very accomplished painter and he was a worse draughtsman: 'I can't even draw a cube right without a ruler,' he admitted.[244] Yet he had good colour sense and some of his Greek and Cypriot scenes, executed in a bold gouache medium, are pleasing. Painting had become important to him as a way of coming to grips with ideas. In 1988 he was to publish his artistic theory in 'Endpapers and Inklings', a series of notebook jottings:

Advice to his friend Epfs:
'First paint the rose in its physical form as
a pure flower. Next forget the physical form
and paint the perfume. Next forget everything
and paint the idea of the rose – any rose.
Remember that the rose was not created by
nature but by man – a compilation of
tensions like a wine or a water-color. Once
you become a painter you realize that everything
about it is imaginary except the thorns.'[245]

On 7 May 1964 Larry revisited Corfu for the first time since the war. He had bought a blue Opel Car-a-van, a small vehicle with a sliding side door that was ideal for camping at secluded beaches. He and Claude arrived by the time-honoured Brindisi ferry. On board the ship Larry was recognized by Joan Bird, wife of Group-Captain Peter Drewry Bird, military attaché at the British Embassy in Norway. Joan was a tall, striking woman with all the graces of a diplomatic wife coupled with a dramatic intensity of manner. Larry encouraged the Birds to look him up on the island.

Larry and Claude settled into a rented house on the sea near Paleocastrizza. Claude took to Corfu and the Ionian Sea like a nereid. This was to be their first long, relaxed holiday together, their reward for wagering Foreign Office security against the roulette game of literature. However, disaster struck almost immediately. Claude and Larry, both of them reckless with wine, quarrelled and Claude rushed from the house. She fell somewhere, perhaps into a ditch, went to bed in some pain, and awoke worse: the doctor said she had cracked two ribs. Bravely, Claude made light of the mishap.

Larry wrote to Alan Thomas, 'We have found a house for the summer here. . . . The place is more than ever magical!'[246] It was a small white cottage with a red tile roof and turquoise window and door frames, with a grape trellis in front that they could dine under. Pantocrator sloped up behind the house. Larry exclaimed, 'Amazingly little has changed.'[247] There were joyful reunions: Countess Heleni Theotocki was on the island, and Larry and Claude saw her often. The Countess, now resembling 'a very old parrot'[248] and as cutting as ever, entertained them with her wicked satirical observations on Corfu society and tried, possessively, to fend off other visitors. Niko the schoolmaster and Totsa Athenaios, his former landlord, embraced Larry most warmly. With the two men Larry revisited the shrine of St Arsenius, filling the tiny votive lamp with oil from his own olive trees at the Mazet Michel. 'Now you are drinking French,' Niko told the icon.[249] They sat under the cypresses to smoke and to talk 'idly, voluptuously about old times'.[250]

Larry slept one night in his ancient room at the White House at Kalami. His writing desk was still there, and the floor that he had stained himself was unchanged; only the fireplace had been walled in. Larry puffed a last cigarette, watching the play of the moonlight on the sea, before going to bed.[251]

In mid-July Larry and Claude went to Athens to pick up the children, Sappho and Claude's two. They had a week of visits, and by the 18th were back on Corfu. None of the young folk had been to Greece before, but as Larry observed, they soon 'dug their teeth into the summer': 'The children's first encounter with Greek scenery was well beyond expectation; they received that first terrific kick in the pants which we all felt the first time we hit Greece – or Greece hit us.'[252]

On 16 August, Larry flew to Israel to make a short film for CBS Television based on his showing Sophia Loren the tourist sights. This time Larry and Loren had a wonderful time together, laughing, talking, racing about on the foredeck of a speedboat. 'I acted her off her pretty little feet,' he boasted.[253] Moshe Dayan as Minister of Defence helped arrange the permits for both the CBS film and for *Judith*, since they were viewed as good propaganda for Israel.

The summer of 1964 was as close as Larry could come to the recovery of his youth: he had leisure, friends at hand, lovely women to admire, demijohns of retsina and solid, rich Greek cooking, the clear blue shock of the Ionian. There was even one aspect of his situation that was an improvement on 1939: he did not really need to worry about how much money he was spending. True, he was still careful, ordering wine by the metal carafe in restaurants, but he knew that he was not going to be broke at the end of the trip.

Larry's life seemed to be going well in every respect, and not merely when he was at leisure. He had become a world author, widely translated, admired in half a dozen genres, and his records at Curtis Brown showed royalties coming in from dozens of countries. Many people were wondering not whether but just when he would receive the Nobel Prize. Larry's personal life appeared never to have been better. When he and Claude were alone at the *mazet* it was even fairly tranquil: Claude was superb at the day-to-day management of the household. She kept his financial records, typed most of his manuscripts, absorbed his rages, kept herself attractive to him. 'Of course I make love to my wife every day,' he would claim to a friend a few years later.²⁵⁴ Larry probably did love her more than he had either of his other wives, and he certainly appreciated and depended upon her. With so much going so well for him, was Larry content? It was scarcely in his nature: he would not have been himself were he not continuously searching out new achievements, new lovers, new ideas. And fleeing boredom. Always, his happiness slanted over an abyss.

WITH LARRY'S ENCOURAGEMENT, Xan Fielding moved to Uzès towards the end of summer. In 1953 Xan had married Daphne Thynne, several years his senior, after her much-publicized divorce from the Marquess of Bath. Xan still looked as fit as the tough young commando Larry had known in Egypt, with his hawk-like profile and his smiling eyes. He needed his stamina to keep up with Daphne. Together they had set up house in Tangier and near Sabugo in the Valley of the Wolves, Portugal, before deciding to move to Uzès. Daphne wrote books, rode horses, had a predilection for short-legged dogs of Oriental pedigree, and knew such interesting people as Lady Diana Cooper, Dirk Bogarde and Evelyn Waugh.

Larry was delighted when the Fieldings rented a house north of Uzès, a mere fifteen miles up the Engances road from the Mazet Michel. This windswept pile Xan christened Wuthering Heights, in complement to Larry's Wuthering Depths. Larry found Daphne at once attractive and enormously amusing, and he had always been fond of Xan: they became the Durrells' most frequent company. Larry preferred to be a host rather than a guest, and hardly a week went by without his firing off a peremptory 'lewd postcard' or cable to Uzès: 'Come and have a glass and a jabber'; 'What about a stirrup lunch by the fire?'; or 'Duck on spit waiting to be eaten this minute!'²⁵⁵

There was literal truth in Larry's invitations. Some bird or animal would be browning nicely on a clockwork spit over an olive fire when Daphne and Xan arrived. Occasionally there would be other guests, such as Mai Zetterling and David Hughes. Before lunch, if the weather was cool, Larry and the Fieldings would sprawl around the open fireplace, Larry refilling the glasses with an unanswerable command: 'Just another touch of the stockwhip.' Claude would keep pace, drink for drink, popping in and out of the kitchen to stir the various pots and at intervals to launch a few anecdotes into the conversation. The 'jabber' would last until the ping of the clockwork spit summoned them to the deal table. Claude would usually begin the meal with a thick soup of lentils or chick peas, a favourite with

Xan. 'Have some butter in it,' Larry would say, showing the way with a huge dollop in his own bowl. Then followed slices of capon or lamb, with savory stuffing and gravy, side dishes of artichoke hearts, aubergines, sweet red peppers. Larry tended to be relatively silent and businesslike while eating, but he would get a second wind over the champagne or muscatel served with dessert. He would bound from his seat to mimic a friend or neighbour, or play a Greek record on the gramophone and nimbly lead the four of them in *syrto* or *sousta* folk dances. Finally, weak with laughter, all would collapse on easy chairs or 'The Elizabeth Barrett', as Claude called her sofa. Larry was still addicted to Brassens, and would listen attentively when the singer's deep voice and guitar sounded from the machine: 'The fellow's a real poet,' Larry would say. 'He ought to be elected to the Académie.'[256]

Very late one night, while the party was in the dancing phase and the stockwhip had been liberally applied, Daphne picked up Claude – she weighed nothing – and carried her around the room to Larry's cheers. All at once Daphne stumbled and, still carrying Claude 'like a battering ram', crashed into the glass door leading to Larry's study. Luckily, Claude's thick trousers saved her from injury, but some glass splinters struck Daphne's face. 'I'm afraid you have a few shaving nicks,' Larry said calmly. 'I'd better deal with them with my styptic pencil,' whereupon he poured on to his handkerchief a liberal quantity of the Arquebuse that they had been drinking, and proceeded to daub Daphne's cuts. Arquebuse, Larry explained, was 'a *vulnéraire* as well as a liqueur', and it had been used by the crusaders to heal their wounds. When Daphne tried to apologize for breaking the door, Larry replied, 'We've always hated it, haven't we, Claude? Been meaning to take it down for ages.' Whereupon he carefully kicked out another panel.[257]

IN 1964 GERRY DURRELL founded the Wildlife Preservation Trust, with headquarters at Les Augrès Manor on Jersey. As this meant becoming personally liable for a £20,000 loan, he set to work on a television series to be called *Two in the Bush*. A visit to Larry and Claude led to another project for Gerry: Larry convinced him that a terrific television documentary could be made around Provençal bullfighting.

Larry journeyed to Paris on 13 November 1964 to speak at a UNESCO gathering on 'Shakespeare and Love', delivering a revised version of the essay that he had drafted two years earlier. It was published the next year in *Réalités* in Pierre Singer's translation as 'L'Amour, clef du mystère'. A fanciful version of the public lecture would find its way into *Livia*, when Larry's creation and putative *alter ego* Sutcliffe 'behaved so outrageously at Unesco and fell into the big drum' during a celebration to honour 'the Bard'.[258] In the five years since the completion of *The Alexandria Quartet*, Larry had been very busy, but he had published only a few poems, two plays and occasional pieces. On 3 January 1964 he had admitted to Juliet O'Hea that he had a 'new novel' in hand, but when he announced hesitantly to Henry Miller just over a year later that 'I have started a novel of sorts',[259] he was still referring to the rewriting of the 'Placebo' material. Larry had gone so far as to send Curtis Brown a 'Placebo' typescript, but he had 'recalled it and started again from the beginning'.[260] He recognized that his new approach would lead to difficulties with the critics and the public. 'It's terrible to have a success; everyone wants you to repeat it by writing the same thing over again,' he told Henry Miller. 'I want to risk failure for a change by a new ploy.'[261] No matter, Larry said: 'I'm suffering from too much to say and a dislike of the novel form as a way of saying it; alas autobiography won't do either, nor poems.'[262] At the age of twenty-five Larry had drawn the figure of a man on a gallows in the margin of a letter to Henry, labelling it 'aut Caesar aut nullus': all or nothing. Now, feeling that he must finish the recast 'Placebo' or explode, he reached back into Petronius for a title: it would be *aut tunc aut nunquam* – either then or never. Into the new story Larry poured a weird concatenation of events and characters, of talking computers and inventors turned poets, of ribald humour and grim terror. Was it to be romance, farce, economic tract or science fiction? When the innocent coating of 'The Placebo' was stripped off to reveal *Tunc* and *Nunquam*, his reputation as a serious novelist would be at risk.

He let his fantasies run wild. First, Larry eliminated the ferocious bite of money-worries for Felix Charlock, the protagonist: an inventor, he signs a contract with the multinational firm Merlin's, guaranteeing fabulous wealth for himself in return for his inventive genius; and then he marries the heiress to the firm, Benedicta Merlin. How can a man have everything – wealth, accomplishment, power, beauty for a wife – and not be *felix*, felicity itself? When he has lost his freedom, when his wife turns out to be insane, when his son is killed, when . . . . As always, episodes from Larry's life were worked into the plot: the mad wife, Benedicta, takes away their son, Mark, as Felix Charlock watches helplessly – just so, Eve had wanted to take Sappho immediately after being released from Hanover; and just so, Larry had seen her actually take Sappho away from him on Cyprus.

Larry intended his novel to be read on several levels: it was to be a love story featuring two tormented women, a light and a dark; it was to be a fable about international corporate power; it was to be a parable about human values. As often as Larry restarted work on *Tunc*, he bogged down.

Larry kept up a fairly steady writing schedule, working from daybreak until noon, and then pottering about his property. Despite often chiding Henry Miller for wasting his time with unknown enthusiasts, Larry found himself unable to refuse a request made by a young South African lecturing at Aix-en-Provence. Stephen Gray arrived by arrangement one morning in early March with three French film amateurs. Claude provided her wonderful hospitality. Gray, recently down from Cambridge, was trying to write poetry, and Larry told him, 'Throw away and do it again if it's no good, don't tootle; hear the poem as a whole first, then write it down; you're the only one who knows when it's right.' For years the advice would echo like a mantra in Gray's head.[263]

During the spring and summer of 1965 the Fieldings were busy restoring La Galerie des Pâtres, the rambling old farmhouse that they had bought after abandoning Wuthering Heights. To Daphne's anguish, the builders had cut down an ancient grape vine. The vine was stubborn with life and soon poked a shoot through the new cement. Larry took Daphne's side against Xan and the masons, who wanted to cut it down again. 'You'll be destroying the spirit of the house,' Larry told Xan, who immediately relented. Daphne wanted to put up a plaque beside the vine: 'Saved by the Apostle of Love'.[264]

By the first of May 1965, Larry calculated that he had still only completed a third of *Tunc*. He hoped that another summer in Corfu would release the flow. Larry and Claude returned to the same cottage over-looking the sea at Paleocastrizza that they had rented the previous year. Mary Mollo came with her fourteen-year-old daughter Olivia and ten-year-old son Ian to live in a primitive gaslit cottage across the road. Sappho, only a few months older than Olivia, arrived after the term at Bedale's ended, and Claude's Barry and Diana soon joined the group. As a means of escape to isolated beaches and offshore islets where they could swim naked and unobserved, Larry had strapped to the top of the Opel a sizeable Zodiac inflatable boat, and he had brought along a powerful outboard motor.

Others were drawn into Larry's orbit. Catha Aldington arrived with her friend Ghislaine de Boysson to stay in a nearby hotel. Despite the fact that she was a blonde fashion model, Larry did not take much notice of Ghislaine and no one would have predicted that nine years later she and

Larry would be married. Colonel Gigantes, flamboyant as ever with his monocle and explosive laughter, and now metamorphosed into the Minister of Tourism for Greece, turned up with a young woman friend. Larry held long philosophical discussions with Evangelis, an elderly rubbish collector with the aesthetic face of a Byzantine saint. Larry loved the flow of the Greek syllables as they sat at a table in the patio, glasses of wine and a vase of flowers between them. 'That man is happy in his job,' Larry marvelled. 'He enjoys meeting people when he collects the garbage; they interest him. He is a person of great wisdom.'[265] Larry travelled to Athens, where he celebrated a reunion with Austen Harrison.

Larry expected Claude to perform her usual miracles in the kitchen, organize for the children events that would keep them entertained and out of the adults' hair, and be a star performer in his circle. Larry boasted so much about his good life that Henry wrote, 'What a wonderful organized, regulated, productive, happy life you lead. Bravo!'[266] Happy perhaps, but in the holiday atmosphere Larry and Claude drank even more than usual. Claude's temper could match Larry's, and Mary would sometimes have a tear-stained Claude join her at breakfast: heated words and dishes as well had flown the night before. Still, it was a good time for them all; Mary was devoted to Claude, and did not compete for Larry's affection.

For Larry this was to be a working holiday: he had agreed to co-operate with Ernle Bradford in making *The Search for Ulysses*, a two-part television film illustrating Bradford's thesis that the ancient hero's ten-year wanderings were not simply Homer's invention, but that they matched exactly both the winds and currents of the Mediterranean and the description of the places Ulysses/Odysseus visited. With his sandy-red pointed beard and sailor's squint to windward, Bradford must have seemed to Larry a reincarnation of Odysseus himself. Joan and Peter Bird were there during Bradford's filming, and together they downed glasses of local wine while Larry demonstrated his skill in skipping flat white stones over the sea. Larry led the vigorous Bradford, matching him step by step, up the steep climb to the Castle of St Angelo above the monastery at Paleocastrizza. Larry and Bradford argued the merits of the conflicting claims for the location of the Phaeacian ship turned to stone, but agreed that the mouth of the River Ermones must have been the spot where naked Odysseus had confronted the startled and impressed Nausicaa.[267] The two men shared a powerful identification with Odysseus.

BACK AT THE MAZET MICHEL, Larry did not know it but he was destined to move again. Claude felt they needed more space, room in which they and their offspring could live without getting in each other's way. The *mazet* was quite adequate for Larry and Claude, and with the rooms built in the rear annexe for the children they could conveniently sleep their combined families. There was no room, however, for civilized entertaining or for their burgeoning collection of books, papers, manuscripts and paintings. An additional inducement to move came from the French army, which was threatening to develop the Nîmes military reservation into the top gunnery school in France, and the chance of being bombed or shelled 'every day and all day instead of just ten minutes of a Tuesday morn' was too much for Larry.[268] Then Claude discovered that a great pile of a house on the flood plain of the Vidourle in Sommières, in a direct line with the old Roman bridge and across from the Villa Louis and the main part of the town, was being sold by the heirs of Mme Tartes, builder of the three-storey mansion. The latest flood of the Vidourle had swirled recently into the above-ground cellars of the house and had left a high water mark some two feet up the wall in the first-floor rooms. La Maison de Mme Tartes needed extensive repairs, a heating system, paint – but it could be purchased very cheaply. Meanwhile, Larry's best friend in England, Alan Thomas, had moved from Bournemouth to 16 Hobury Street, Chelsea. Parallel events seemed often to mark Larry's and Alan's lives.

Mme Tartes had placed the house in the centre of a trapezoidal acre of land along the route de Saussine. The house sat broodingly under a dark grey slate mansard roof that wrapped around the top storey and was pierced by a few inadequate *oeil de boeuf* windows. Larry was immediately attracted to the glassed-in back veranda, bright with huge expanses of clear glass softened by small green-tinted panes around the edges, which he said was 'straight out of old Darjeeling'. The rampant, overgrown garden itself Larry simply called Darjeeling. Sappho took one glance and pronounced the place a 'Charles Addams house', and Larry was forced to agree that 'it has a somewhat macabre look'.[269] Shuttered tight, standing amid the overgrown gloom of the thickets, and overtopped by old trees, it seemed a fit abode for vampires. The first two floors had magnificent high ceilings and tall windows. A gracious white marble staircase, accented by a cut crystal ball at the start of the centre handrail, spiralled up the full height of the house. Claude went to Paris to attend the auction of the property, returning with the deed in her handbag. The house had cost £6,000, but would soon be worth ten, then twenty and more times that.

For the third time in his life, Larry set about the major reconstruction of an old house, only this time he had sufficient funds, a comfortable dwelling to live in while the work proceeded, and the supremely capable Claude to prod the workmen and keep the accounts. Larry referred to the Mazet Michel as a 'hideout' and Daphne Fielding called it a 'snuggery'. These were not terms that fitted Mme Tartes's house: 'Not a château you understand', Larry wrote to Henry Miller, 'but a large comfortable solid vicarage type of thing – maison de maître in fact – such as a prosperous notaire or country doctor might own.' He thought the place 'rambling, ugly', but noted that it was set in 'a lovely parc, tall trees': hickory, chestnut, and palms.²⁷⁰ Here and there a few almond and cherry trees struggled for light. It was probably the largest house in Sommières, and the shrieking iron front gate stood at the top of a flight of steps above a surfaced road. There were old buildings across the way, but to the south only a large vineyard bordered the garden. The entire property was surrounded by a massive brick wall far taller than a man. The double iron gates of the drive were hidden in the turning of a lane off the route de Saussine, and the vegetation in the garden rendered the house almost invisible from the street during most of the year. Mme Tartes had built well: thick, solid walls, good slate from Angers on the roof. The floors, Larry discovered during the remodelling, were filled with a foot of sand for insulation against heat and noise. He and Claude resurfaced the floors with smooth tiles of a rich earth-red. The resulting surface was far from a true plane, but rose and fell with the pleasing undulations of a topographical map. The grand salon, running some thirty-five feet from the front of the house right back to the veranda, Larry lined with bookshelves along one inside wall.

Joyfully, Claude set about furnishing La Maison de Mme Tartes at second-hand shops and auction galleries. She and Larry picked up a magnificent Pleyel concert grand piano for £125 and paid a trifle for a neoclassical marble bust to grace a turning in the garden. Perhaps dating from the late eighteenth century but probably a more recent copy, the bust hauntingly suggested a younger Claude. Bits and pieces were moved over from the *mazet*: the 'Elizabeth Barrett' sofa and the lamp that Larry had fashioned out of a gnarled olive limb. Finally, Larry had enough wall space for his small collection of paintings – by Henry Miller, Zvi Milshtein, a portrait of Bernard Spencer by Amy Nimr, and, of course, his own gouaches. His bright *Turkish Women* painting went into the large kitchen. Claude picked out a dull red pineapple-pattern wallpaper, a relic of the nineteenth century, for the Darjeeling Room.

'It wasn't a very good year for me, I don't know why,' Larry pondered as autumn 1965 set in. 'Work piling up and a general paralysis setting in! Full of ideas but incapable of action. And far far too many visitors, too much talk talk talk.'[271] After the time-wasting 'strays' came some 'real friends': the Fieldings, and then George Katsimbalis for a few days. Together they picked up Jacques Temple for a session with Joseph Delteil. While Claude directed the platoon of masons, plumbers and carpenters installing a central heating system and otherwise refurbishing Mme. Tartes's mansion, Larry moved ahead in a dilatory fashion on *Tunc*. Early in the new year he wrote to Alan Thomas asking for various sourcebooks on Constantinople, explaining that 'I am only looking for fragments of atmosphere to pinch.' 'Loti Ayezayde and the Disenchanted are full of good optical stuff,' he continued. 'But useless to a modern traveller unless he takes a Turkish mistress.'[272]

Anaïs Nin finally received the fame that she always felt had been unfairly denied her when Volume One of her *Diary* was published. There were dozens of reviews, most highly favourable, none really nasty. However, after years of saying 'We want the diaries!', neither Henry nor Larry when approached would write a review for the *New York Times*.[273] They looked on with amazement as Anaïs became a public figure, lecturing, being interviewed on television, garnering honours. Larry was still enjoying considerable notice himself, but mainly in France. On 14 June 1966 his old friend Sir Patrick Reilly, now ambassador to France, held a black tie dinner at the embassy to celebrate the translation of Larry's poems into French. The guest list included the Duke and Duchess of Windsor, Lord Kennet, Baron de Rothschild and Cy Sulzberger of the *New York Times*. Larry ignored this event in a postcard written from Paris to Henry a few days later, saying only that 'Tous le monde parle de toi encore et me demande des nouvelles.'[274]

Larry and Claude would officially change their address to 15 route de Saussine on 15 July 1966, but with the renovations of the house still in progress, they decided on a quick trip to Corfu. As housekeeper they had hired Marcelle, an angular, maternal peasant type who adored Claude and cajoled, bullied and mothered Larry. Marcelle appeared to be competent and absolutely honest, so they confided the place to her care and departed. They drove through Italy to Brindisi in their new blue Volkswagen Microbus – christened L'Escargot by Larry – with the Zodiac strapped to the top. Once again they settled in Paleocastrizza, where they had agreed to meet Frances and Horst von Maltitz. Larry had become fond of them, and teased the quiet and scholarly Horst by ringing bawdy changes on the 'von Maltitz/small tits' rhyme. This Horst bore with a smile. Even in temporary digs, Claude was a remarkable cook, Frances thought: she was at once very fast and very good. 'How did you learn to do that?' asked Frances after witnessing one marvel of ingenuity and dispatch. 'Years of penury,' quipped Claude. The two women talked about Barry and Diana, and Claude's eyes watered. 'My husband got custody of the children,' sighed Claude. 'We were the guilty party.'[275]

One day while they were all swimming a small hired boat swung towards the beach, and in it were Joan and Peter Bird. Both Larry and the Birds professed surprise at the encounter, but Frances was certain that the meeting had been prearranged.[276] Joan's father Gabriel Couri was half-Lebanese, and her mother was English.[277] That she shielded her passionate nature behind the manners of a well-bred English lady made her all the more attractive to Larry. It was obvious to Claude and to Frances that Larry found Joan very attractive indeed.[278] Claude, nervous, 'never stopped talking – never!' Peter Bird recalled, and Larry reacted by calling her 'the toast of the British fleet'. He and Claude clowned in red-and-white hats advertising the *Judith* film, but there was a real edge to his teasing, and he talked to Joan about divorcing Claude. As in the case of his earlier threats to dump his wives, Larry may not have been serious – this was still part of his patter to a pretty woman – but he did strike the others as being hard on Claude. The two of them started drinking brandy at breakfast these days.

Still, a festive atmosphere prevailed. Larry turned everything into an adventure, and even pumping water from the cistern to flush the toilet became cause for hilarity, two at a time on the long-handled pump. He led them all on a vigorous hike above Lakones to a point overlooking a cluster of small blue bays.[279] He revelled in the role of star attraction and presided over long, slow meals. If they were at a restaurant with music, he would lead them in Greek and ballroom dances. He was, Frances thought, 'a *lovely* dancer, light on his feet and full of witty variations'. Claude seemed resigned to Larry's flirtation with Joan, simply telling Frances, 'I was promiscuous too, but not any more.' When Larry carried on too flagrantly, Claude would stay in her room.[280]

Often Larry was happy merely to talk to his friends. 'Do you know what they're saying about me, Peter?' he asked in mock outrage. 'That my prose is as sticky as nougat!' Sometimes Larry entertained them by reciting limericks:

> There was a young man of Calcutta,
> Who began to write 'fuck' on a shutter.
> He got as far as F U
> When a pious Hindu
> Knocked him ass over tit in the gutter.

Pretending to think that all Americans were rich, when the reckoning came Larry was as likely as not to say teasingly, 'Of course old Horst is rolling in dough – let him pay the bill.'[281]

Peter's holiday ended and the Birds returned to Norway, but within days Joan was back on Corfu, having driven from Oslo with her young daughter 'Bouf': the girl's best friend had died suddenly, and the trip to Corfu would be good for her, Joan said. The von Maltitzes departed for America, leaving the field to Joan. Then Claude's Barry arrived, and soon Bouf was 'seducing Barry into opening a wasp's nest over Larry's head'. Larry caught them at it, and laid the blame on the girl. Larry decided that Bouf was a brat, and she quite openly defied him. His passion for Joan and the squabbles with 'the children' kept him on edge, alternately exalted and miserable.

ALWAYS CONCERNED WITH KEEPING out of range of the tax-bandits, as he termed the Inland Revenue, Larry worked out a deal with Dutton in America that would guarantee him a relatively modest $5000 a year for fifteen years. Six years had passed since the appearance of *Clea*, and he knew that it was high time to publish another novel. By August 1966 he had returned to the attack on *Tunc*, although he implied to Henry Miller that it was a new creation: 'I've just started on a long and complicated (serious) novel which may work out all right if I can give it the high enema.'[282] Larry claimed to others that he was slaving at 'a slow beastly novel which has caused me a peck of trouble to visualise out and will probably be a flop'.[283] *Tunc* was turning out to be his most difficult birth yet. Although by mid-November Larry wrote to Henry that he had reached the half-way mark, he was probably exaggerating his progress.[284]

In the character of Vibart, a contract lawyer for the Merlin firm who has created for himself a purely fictitious career as a novelist, Larry parodied his own life. Vibart urges himself to 'Get out of diplomacy, where everything is so much smaller than life,'[285] just as Larry had once advised himself to leave the Foreign Office. Vibart discourses on the imaginary reviews of his imaginary novels – 'Subtle, thought-provoking and full of lovely mince' – finally giving himself 'the Nobelly Prize' because 'I became so thin.' Larry and his *alter ego* were in no danger of wasting away; quite the contrary: 'I'm putting on weight,' Larry wrote in Vibart's voice. 'Soon I shall be only fit to write the history of Adipose Rex.'[286] Nor did Larry seem to expect the Nobel Prize: it was something Henry Miller believed firmly in for himself, but Larry seemed quite genuine in his jokes about the award.

Although Claude's health had not been good for some months, as Christmas 1966 approached she and Larry decided to have 'a real English Christmas' with roasts, mincemeat and puddings. Alan and Ella Thomas, Mary Mollo and her husband Henry, Gerry and Jacquie Durrell, Catha Aldington and Theodore Stephanides were invited. Claude threw herself into the planning with her usual efficiency, intending to produce epic feasts on the open, waist-level fireplace-grill and gas stove of the great kitchen. Larry fussed about, checking the functioning of all the bathrooms and anxiously measuring the beds – to his mind Alan, at about three inches over six feet, was a giant. On 26 November Claude received Alan and Ella's acceptance and immediately wired to Theodore to say that he could travel with them. Mary was sent a note of brisk command: 'Mary, in this ghastly business could you legislate for enough mince (ugh!) for twelve? Ditto pubbing.'[287] Mary sent the supplies, but almost immediately, by 9 December, Larry wrote to everyone that the celebration had been called off: he was taking Claude to their usual clinic in Geneva. 'Of course she is livid; and the decision is really mine,' Larry told Alan. Claude in her gallant way would have carried on regardless of how she felt, so as not to disappoint the rest.[288] Fortunately, Diana Forde was working in Geneva, so she could give encouragement to her mother and Larry. Back in England, Penelope married an actor, Peter Ellis Jones, but Larry was apparently too preoccupied to notice the event.

Claude was placed on antibiotics for what Larry described as 'a sort of generalised septicemia based on the lungs'. Larry was very apologetic to his friends for 'having, I fear, buggered up your Christmas', but he did not sound especially worried: 'It's a fearful bore: but perhaps one should be glad it isn't something more serious like leukemia or cancer?'[289] He wrote to Alan that he was returning to Sommières to pick up some of the belongings Claude would need for a projected three-week stay in the clinic. Three days before Christmas Larry announced 'slow headway' and told Alan with wry humour that it 'seems Claude will have to have her Xmas dinner through a drip device!' His consolation was that 'at least it is a microbe and nothing worse'.[290] Then one morning when Larry arrived at the clinic he found a worried staff. An alarming diagnosis had been made: she had advanced pulmonary cancer, her blood chemistry was affected, and she was not reacting to the drugs. Larry stayed with her nights because, so he said, the night shift tended to neglect patients. Sitting in her lavatory sipping whisky and black coffee from a thermos, Larry overheard Claude asking the nurse to make up her face in death; she did not want Larry to see her not properly composed.[291] Barry Forde, lodging with the Birds, who were now in England, was summoned, but Sappho, who had looked upon Claude as a second mother, was not. Neither was Penelope. Diana was shocked and angered when Larry replied to her suggestion that Sappho travel to Geneva with Barry, 'It's not her mother who is dying.'[292]

Claude slipped away rapidly, and on New Year's Day 1967, with Larry sitting by her side, she died. 'She had died between shifts and was alone so I fulfilled her instructions,' he told me. 'She had left her make-up things in the side table for the job. It's strange to make up a dead face you know so well. It was like farding a dead infanta. Where had she gone? But almost smiling. Once she approved an adjective for the dead in a poem of mine – "the laughing dead". She explained, "I always feel they are laughing up their sleeves at us!"'[293]

CHAPTER 12

Larry in Revolt:
Cosmonaut of Interior Space

La mort avance
La vie recule
Ce soir j'épouse
La noctambule.[1]
  Red Limbo Lingo

'. . . in search of some fruitful perspective upon my own life here in the old château – the queer solitary life which I have at last adopted. Scribbling all this gives me something to do, I am resetting the broken bones of the past. Perhaps I should have begun it long ago. . . .'
  Monsieur

With saliva and patience, the elephant fucks the ant.
  LD in conversation with Buffie Johnson

AFTER CLAUDE'S CREMATION Diana and a friend returned with a stunned Larry to the massive dark house in Sommières. He left most of the heavy wooden shutters closed on all three floors of La Maison de Mme Tartes, allowing light to shine in only through the windows in his bedroom, the kitchen and the adjoining Darjeeling Room. Claude's death, he said to Henry Miller, 'sounds so improbable that I can hardly believe what I write: yet it *is* so';[2] her departure had 'left a huge hole in the pavement'.[3] He stopped the hands of the wall clock at 7.10, the time of Claude's death, and would never restart it.[4]

Had he felt more for Claude than for his previous wives? Mary Mollo, confidant to Eve, Claude and Larry, thought so.[5] It seemed to him that he had loved her most, perhaps because she had left him so suddenly and almost without notice – for these were Larry's phrases: Claude had departed, had deserted him. 'I've only once seen Larry very bad', recalled his sister, 'and that was after Claude's funeral. He was distraught. He started coming to family picnics – things that he would have scorned before.'⁶

Barry Forde was delegated to inform Larry's family and friends in England, but there was some confusion and Gerry and Jacquie Durrell did not find out about Claude's death for a week. Jacquie made her own assumption: 'It is quite obvious that Larry in his shock got everything mixed up in his mind.'⁷ Gerry, the most unabashedly sentimental of the siblings, was terribly upset on Larry's account. More than Larry's thoughts were tangled. Since most of his financial documents were in Claude's name, he found himself unable to complete the simplest transactions. Larry had come to depend on Claude as a household and business manager – even as a tax accountant – and as a secretary. For ten years she had presided over the increasing complexities of his growing financial success and public popularity. While he may have complained when she spent money, especially when she bought the Sommières house, he appeared to trust her absolutely. Latterly, he had not even asked Claude how much stood in his accounts.

Larry also made a serious misjudgement in excluding his daughters from Claude's death. Especially Sappho, but also Penelope, had loved Claude. Sappho's earliest memories echoed with Claude's laughter, and the long school holidays, presided over by Claude, had been what were perhaps the happiest moments of her childhood. Penelope had seen much less of Claude, but Claude had provided an acceptance and affection that Penelope was denied by Nancy. Indeed, a breach of several years between Penelope and her mother and stepfather had only been made up in 1966. Both girls felt that they had been deprived of a farewell from Claude, who had always insisted that they were as much part of the family as Diana and Barry. Excluded also from her funeral, they were denied even a part in Larry's grieving. Larry may have thought that he was sparing them distress. More likely he was beyond thought himself, and felt unable to cope with his daughters on top of his sorrow and worries. Irrationally, Sappho would blame herself for Claude's death, and her sense of guilt, mixed with anger at what she must have seen as her father's condescending treatment, would cast a shadow over her relationship with her father from then on.⁸ Larry would respond to her anger with rages of his own, and neither of them would be able – or have the courage – to track the anger to its source. This sad drama was to be played out in the years to come.

In the year after Larry's death, the London *Sunday Telegraph* printed a claim that during one or two years following Claude's death he had tried to replace her with his daughter Sappho, even to the point of incest. This claim appears to have been based for the most part on comments made years later by Sappho, and also on her 'recovered memories', a now largely discredited technique through which a few hints and clues were picked up from Sappho while she was under psychiatric care many years after the alleged incest occurred. Larry's accusers would point to the examples of incest – though rarely father-daughter incest – in his novels, and to the admittedly conflict-ridden relationship between Larry and Sappho.[9]

Claude had come close to satisfying all the roles Larry demanded of a woman: lover, intellectual companion, nurse, mother, cook, hostess, manager, critic, typist, proofreader . . . the list seemed endless. His attitudes towards women ranged from the frankest lust to unequivocal admiration. Anyone who had seen Larry sitting, for example, in an airport lounge staring at each attractive woman with naked desire would be reminded of the sensualist libertine Capodistria, his creation in the *Quartet*. At the other extreme, Larry idolized woman as the 'basic brick' of civilization, vowing that 'if we have any future it depends on her'.[10] Several factors restrained Larry in his pursuit of women, among them a socially conditioned propriety, a fear of boredom, and a genuine concern for the well-being of any woman interesting enough to attract his attention.

Facing the worst disaster that he had yet suffered, Larry tried to immerse himself in his writing. He returned to the troublesome manuscript that he had been unable to bring to a satisfactory conclusion over the past half-dozen years: 'Remember', he had written to Jean Fanchette years before, 'there's no consolation against death except a dirty three letter word . . . art'.[11] Now he had a special reason to put that consolation to the test. The most obvious action of *Tunc* revolves around various characters' attempts to join or to escape 'the firm', as the mega-corporation Merlin is referred to in the novel. The firm – tyrannically benevolent to its employees – is described in terms that suggest it as a metaphor for religion or civilization or society. In Larry's final version the narrator Felix Charlock moves closer and closer to Larry Durrell: in his loneliness, in his grief, in his bereavement – Charlock's former lover Iolanthe dies of cancer; his wife goes insane. He rescues his son from a suicide attempt and then breaks down: 'I wept my way right back to my solitary childhood, back to the breast, back into the very womb which is the only memory we know about.'[12] Larry, self-proclaimed solitary who thought he remembered his birth, was speaking personally.

Just over a month after Claude's death Ella Thomas disappeared, and Alan's life was thrown into an upheaval that prevented him from coming to Larry's support as he might otherwise have done. Ella's clothes and handbag were found above the White Cliffs facing the Channel, that emotive spot for Larry, but her body was never recovered. There was no clear indication of either suicide or murder, but each theory was postulated at length in the British press.[13] Hard work provided some solace for both men. Alan had already undertaken to compile and edit an anthology of Larry's prose to be called *Spirit of Place*, and on 23 February Larry came to stay with Alan in Chelsea, in part to discuss material for the volume. During his short visit Larry saw Wallace Southam and Bernard Stone, owner of Turret Books and founder of the Turret Books Steam Press, about plans to bring out some recordings of his poems set to music. Alan and Larry lived very quietly like two old bachelors, strolling the short distance along King's Road to the World's End Distillery for lunches. Sitting in the varnished Victorian pub, the two men felt as if their worlds were indeed crashing down. The new projects failed to turn Larry's spirits around. By the time he left London, he was suffering from an English cold and a toothache. 'I hope you are keeping your chin up,' he wrote to Alan from Sommières. 'Am just back with a raging cold and a large hole in my jaw which I had to get carved up in Paris.' He invoked Groddeck to explain the latter disaster: 'Guilt syndrome of psycho somatic origins.' It was an added vexation that 'lawyers' quibbles' – over settling Claude's estate – would put him in debt for the year.[14]

Worry over money made Larry more than ever determined to finish *Tunc* before 1968. At the time of Claude's death, he had been stuck at around mid-point. His long-intended 'Attic comedy' took on a darker undertone, became shadowed by regrets as he faced the futility and finality of her death. Wry, ambiguous phrases now dotted the typescript: hero and heroine are united 'For better or for hearse' and they go through 'the whole deathscapade of lovemaking'.[15] Living with a woman could mean trouble, as Felix discovers: 'Women cannot help being predatory – to take up with one is to inherit a mink farm.'[16] It was a reflection of Larry's own experience: one took a woman, loved her and lost her – in his present case permanently. 'I had never before actually feared to be parted from a woman,' Larry had Felix Charlock say. 'The novelty was overwhelming.'[17]

In the only new poem he published the year of Claude's death, Larry addresses her as the 'Confederate' of the title:

> My shutter croaks and now you tell me
> It is time for those last few words. Very well.

He hints that by finding his 'mislaid words' he may come to terms with his suffering:

> Very well; for not in this season will kisses
> Dig any deeper into the mind to seek
> The mislaid words we have been seeking,
> Delegates of that place which once
> The whole of suffering seemed to occupy – [18]

Was Larry regretting the words not spoken to Claude, the endearments and appreciation that he could not now express through kisses? It seems likely.

During the first three weeks of April, Larry had a series of visits from 'the children': Barry Forde arrived to stay for some weeks, and so did Sappho. Diana Forde was still working in Geneva and she came to Sommières some weekends. Xan and Daphne Fielding were Larry's only other regular company. Larry grumbled over how much the young folk ate, but admitted that he would regret his miserliness after he found himself rattling about in the empty house. The recent death of Eve McClure Miller – Henry had divorced her, in part because of her bouts of alcoholism – especially saddened Larry. He had called her Pocahontas, and said that she had 'won all hearts'.[19] Death was haunting his best friends, as if some obscene miasma hung about them all.

Finally Larry decided that he had finished *Tunc*. After the ease with which he had surged through the four volumes of *The Alexandria Quartet*, he had imagined that writing this 'comic novel' would be sheer play. In fact, it had taken him seven years, what with various false starts and some detours to write plays, film scripts and reportages. Claude's death had honed his humour to a sharper edge: he had come to realize that no amount of laughter could vanquish the Manichaean darkness. He dedicated the book 'For Claude-Marie Vincendon' and handed the typescript to Joan and Peter Bird, who had stopped by on their way to London, entrusting them with delivering it to Juliet O'Hea at Curtis Brown. She would in turn pass it on to Alan Pringle at Faber for 'wicket-keeping', as Larry called the editorial process. Larry pressed on the Birds a stiff jolt of the 'giver of life', his formidable Arquebuse. Peter was being transferred to Tel Aviv, and Larry gave them the names of his friends in Israel: Minister of Defence Moshe

Dayan, the painter-archaeologist Jean David, and General Avram Yoffe, a wildlife expert.[20]

As respite from the strain of finishing *Tunc*, Larry leafed through his old poetry notebooks, stopping at several pages that he had drafted in 1939, 'Solange', the rather surrealistic portrait of a prostitute of the 14th *arrondissement*. This he revised and doubled in length to ten printed pages. He retained the sexual/metaphysical identifications, the 'Whole doctorates granted in prime embraces' by Solange, 'working with pink tongue or tooth/ towards some mystical emphasis,/ a life without sanctions'. 'How can a love of life be ever indiscreet', Larry concluded near the end of the poem, punctuating the phrase as a statement, not a question.[21] He was writing his way back into life and preparing to live himself back into poetry. Still, apart from 'Solange', which would appear in 1969, he would not publish another poem until 1971.

Larry thought of selling La Maison de Mme Tartes, spending summers in Greece and Italy, and retreating to the Mazet Michel during the winters. Claude, Larry said, had been the one who hated to take long trips. Soon he had acted on his proposed second phase: he set off for Greece in L'Escargot, 'a dream to travel in'.[22] He also found it was a dream to hide in: even while he was in Sommières, Larry would sometimes drive a few miles from the house to camp for the night in a copse of oaks. He rejoiced in being out of range of the telephone and secure from chance visitors. Gerry pointed out that his brother no longer needed the Mazet Michel as a hideout and offered to purchase it. Larry refused, and Jacquie was sure she knew why: Larry had always loathed her, and she knew it and said so. If he would not sell Gerry the *mazet*, it was on her account.[23]

While Larry was indulging his wanderlust, Henry Miller was seeking domestic bliss in the person of a Japanese pianist and nightclub singer named Hiroko 'Hoki' Tokuda. After a long siege of amorous epistles and midnight telephone calls, Henry was successful, and he married Hoki on 10 September 1967 in California. A triumphal progress to Paris followed, ostensibly for a *vernissage* of Henry's paintings on 20 September. For Larry also it was turning into a busy year. He journeyed to Paris to be with Henry and Hoki. Larry had developed a very close but platonic friendship with Miriam Cendrars, and Henry, who had idolized her father, approved: 'I was surprised and delighted to see how well you ... got on together.'[24] Larry also entertained Margaret McCall, a blonde American-born film-maker for the BBC. Margaret was tall and dramatic, with a finely moulded face and clear skin – and Larry was powerfully attracted to her. Peter and

Joan Bird were in Paris too. Larry had a terrific quarrel with Joan: he wanted her to bear him a child, 'so that we would have something together'. She refused: whatever Joan's feelings for Larry, she was not willing to compromise her husband or unsettle her children's lives. A rupture of some years ensued.[25]

Travelling with Henry and his bride for fifty-three days were Robert Snyder and his cameraman Baylis Glascock, filming a documentary to be called *The Henry Miller Odyssey*. Henry had set down strict conditions for Snyder: no bright lights, no staging, no interruptions of the flow of talk, no replays of missed shots. Larry and Fred Perlès joined them for walks along the rue Villa Seurat, for bottles of Clos Vougeot at the Dôme, for reunions with Brassaï and the bear-like painter Michonze. Henry and Hoki followed Larry to Sommières, where Henry envied the 'beautiful house – and everything working so smoothly', which for him now meant central heating and plenty of hot water.[26] He now pronounced Larry 'one of the most considerate persons I ever knew', despite being restless, 'like a caged lion at times'.[27] The lively Hoki turned her attention on an intrigued Larry. They held jam sessions around the Pleyel: Hoki the professional nightclub performer, petite, with the enamelled perfection of an oriental doll,[28] Larry pattering out his easy jazz and swing. Larry had good talks with Hoki amid all the banter and innuendo, discussing the Japanese view of suicide: it fascinated him that the Japanese could kill themselves because something, a petal, for instance, was *too* beautiful.[29] 'I wondered', he asked, 'is the desire for it more a young man's thing?' While Glascock's camera snicked unobtrusively, Henry joined the discussion of suicide. Yes, he said, and he turned to methods: in his youth he had tried drowning and pills; neither had worked. To make sure that the poison he had obtained from a doctor would prove fatal, he had opened the windows on a particularly wintry night, swallowed the dose, and lain down naked on the bed, only to awaken next morning covered with snow, the sun streaming in, and with not even a sore throat. He had been double-crossed by his doctor, who had merely given him a sedative, Henry thought. Larry shook his head: 'I select a tree . . . one of these plane trees . . . .'[30] Suggestively, some of the massive plane trees lining the road between Sommières and Restinclières bore the scars of devastating collisions. Henry promised to send Larry a book on embalming. Still talking, Larry and Henry posed in the garden before a plaster copy of a bust of Bigot de Préameneu, a Napoleonic jurist with mutton-chop side-whiskers. Larry pronounced the bust horrible, but it was a gift from one of his favourites, a beautiful young writer named Paule

Wislenef – he was not ready to kill himself yet out of sheer boredom. In Paris, Diane, wife of Henry's amanuensis and eventual biographer Gérard Robitaille, had read Larry's future in the cards, and Henry, thinking back on the occasion, predicted a new marriage for Larry. 'No', responded Larry, it would be 'disastrous'. With some hyperbole he continued: 'I've been married since 23 and paying alimony since 27 and have passed through stupidity schizophrenia and death on a sort of ascending scale' – characterizing in one word each the respective failings of his three wives. 'I need four tedious mistresses and a good typist, that is all and I rather like the empty house echoing around me to the noise of a typewriter.' But Larry was not bitter: 'For the likes of us marriage is madness, although I have enjoyed mine, particularly the last.'[31]

Tailed everywhere by Snyder, Henry and Larry played the tourists in Nîmes, where they met one of Henry's admirers, the lovely Simone Perier, who would become a close friend of Larry's. Larry and Henry strolled into the centre of the deserted Roman arena, set up with red wooden barricades for a *mise-au-mort* bullfight. Just as Snyder heard the click that announced the end of a reel of 16 mm film, Larry ducked his head, aimed his index fingers from his temples, and charged Henry, who performed a nimble *veronica* with his jacket. It was a marvellous counterpoint to their verbal sparring. Snyder, stalling a moment to give Glascock time to prepare his camera, broke the rules and asked Larry and Henry for a repeat performance. To his delight they complied – but Glascock, on edge with indigestion and Larry's teasing him to 'loosen up', fumbled the reloading and missed the shot a second time. Snyder did not dare to ask again.

In another arena Hoki was playing Larry like a toreador. Sir Gawain was not pressed harder by the Green Knight's lady than Larry was by Henry's new wife, hugging, cajoling and tickling him. Larry quipped, 'Henry marries women for his friends to sleep with,' although he did not say whether he had been successful with Hoki. Henry and Hoki did not share a bed, a condition of their marriage, she would maintain, and Hoki bluntly told Snyder, 'Henry was old – we never touched one another at all.'[32] Later she would claim, 'All I had to do was sing for him.'[33]

Larry returned to Paris with the Millers and then stayed on for a few days after they left for America, lodging with Nadia and Alex Blokh and seeing Miriam Cendrars again. The Blokhs now lived in a light, cheerful house just off the Parc Montsouris, so that Larry felt the bitter-sweet ache of memories crowding upon him – of living there with Nancy during the heady days of the Villa Seurat nexus.

Back in Pacific Palisades, Hoki wrote increasingly urgent letters complaining about 'Larry who never writes me' and teasing him about his 'tummy'. Larry preferred to send her messages via Henry: 'Tell Hoki my stomach is as admirable as ever – never have I been admired for what we consider a serious blemish on our otherwise perfect beauty. I study it a lot and polish it with floor polish till it gleams in the sunset.'[34] Someone who attacked Larry less good-naturedly for his plumpness was Sappho, who referred scathingly to her father's 'wine belly' and his 'barrel belly'. Finally Hoki's patience wore out over Larry's silence, and she wrote to him in evident anger, 'You have just lost number one Japanese girlfriend.'[35] If Henry felt that anything untoward had happened, he never let on.

By MID-NOVEMBER 1967 Larry had the proofs of *Tunc* to correct: the novel seemed to him not to be 'too bad, as I feared'.[36] He was still struggling with the proofs into the New Year, but he was also working on *Nunquam*, the companion volume.[37] *Tunc* had ended with the accidental death or perhaps suicide of Mark – the boy had set off a booby-trap rigged to the computer Abel, a fatal encounter intended for his Uncle Julian. *Nunquam* would feature the creation of a robot version of Iolanthe: it is her revolt – first as a real woman, then as an autonomous robot – against male possession and domination by the Merlin firm, that would suggest the future title of the diptych, *The Revolt of Aphrodite*. The resurrection of Iolanthe is a failure: the robot has the intelligence of the real woman but not her warm affections; and the firm cannot control it either. Larry's meaning is clear: Aphrodite cannot be coerced or enchained.

Throughout his *Quartet* Larry had woven resurrections and rebirths. Capodistria's supposed death during the duck shoot in *Justine* is revealed in *Balthazar* to have been an elaborate ruse, while both Scobie and Pursewarden live again in the speeches and actions recalled by their friends. The duchess of Tu in the future *Monsieur* would return from death to dine with her lifelong admirer Blanford, who would ultimately find himself 'talking in whispers to an empty alcove'.[38] Now, with the image of Claude in death still vivid, Larry set about recreating in *Nunquam* the film star Iolanthe, whom he had killed off with cancer, mimicking life, in *Tunc*. Larry had invariably tried to mould his wives and women into idealized forms, often with results disastrous to his relationship with them. Buffie Johnson had once remarked on Larry's 'Pygmalion attitude' towards women, back in the Paris days.[39] Mary Mollo referred to this tendency in Larry, wickedly, as 'Guineapig-malion!'[40] But he would never quite lose his passion for shaping and reshaping his women. In the latex Cunégonde of the last chapter of his final book, *Caesar's Vast Ghost*, Larry would create the companion that he claimed to have desired all his life yet surely could not have tolerated, the totally compliant female.

Early in *Nunquam* Larry caused his invented inventor Felix Charlock to discuss his pattern of composition. 'Would you like to know my method?' Charlock asks rhetorically. 'While I am writing one book . . . I write another about it, then a third about *it*, and so on.' This is a deliberate prefiguring of the *gigogne* pattern of Larry's next fiction, *The Avignon Quintet*. Each book shoved the other along, so to speak: 'Like those monkeys in the Indian frescoes (so human, so engaging, like some English critics)', Larry wrote, 'who can dance only with their index fingers up each other's behinds.'[41] This was his answer to those who maintained that *Tunc* and *Nunquam* were outside the sequence of his major novels. They were not: they were variations on a theme, that was all.

Before creating the construct Iolanthe in *Nunquam*, Larry wanted to describe the embalming of the dead film star. Embalming – a simulacrum of life preserved – was becoming an important motif in the new novel, and he asked Nadia Blokh to find information on the subject in Geneva. To his annoyance all she turned up was an advertising brochure for Clarke's Fluid, 'The chemical that preserves the beauty'.[42] To extend life, even the appearance of life, through embalming! Of course the idea was Egyptian, was Roman, was universal. Larry had written a poem in his youth about Tulliola, Cicero's daughter, 'swimming in a kind of bath of precious oyle',[43] had treated embalming in *Panic Spring*, and had painted Claude's face in death. His lifelines were drawing shorter, and he probed the boundaries of love and death. Living alone in his creaking Charles Addams house, Larry drafted poems and prose jottings about vampires and bloody consummations:

> From a winter of vampires he selects one,
> Takes her to a dark house, undresses her:
> [. . .]
> A transaction where the words themselves
> Begin to bleed first and everything else follows.[44]

Never one to defer pleasure if he could help it, Larry now stressed a *carpe diem* note in his poetry:

Come, pretty little ogre
With the fang in your lip
Lest time in its turnings
Should give us the slip.[45]

In the novel he would complete ten years later, *Livia*, 'vampire' would be a code word for lesbians who bled men of their potency, but here he was ambiguous, curious.

The poems that Larry worked on concurrently with *Tunc* and *Nunquam*, published as *The Red Limbo Lingo*, are at once an epilogue to the pair of novels – 'In the Red Limbo Lingo hearts are flowers,/ Computers pick them through the sleepy hours' – and a transition to the Manichaean vision of *The Avignon Quintet*. The *Limbo Lingo* is subtitled *A Poetry Notebook*: 'In the beginning was the Word, and the word was blood,' Larry wrote, and he followed the bloody spoor of humankind from birth – 'First of all,/ He did not ask to be born' – to crucifixion, 'the common fate of the vampire in classical times', and the death of 'a Red Limbo Lingo poet-vampire'. He described 'The vampire's distress signal a thick bubbling sound ending in a sob' – his own. Like his much earlier 'Cities, Plains and People', *The Red Limbo Lingo* is autobiography, but more disguised and more obscurely allusive. In it Larry alluded to his early religious memories; to his created vampire Eric the Red in *An Irish Faustus*; to his recent experience of 'the blood-count with its red and white chromosomes . . . leukaemia' in Claude's clinical treatment and death. In a restatement of his early epiphany, Larry described religion, saw western civilization itself, in terms of blood-worship: 'What was he to do – indignantly finding himself born into a race which, despising the idol-worshipping savage, offered him in exchange the extraordinary blood-spattered figure of a man nailed to a wooden cross, like an expiring frog.' This Christ he recognized as 'a poor homeless vampire', the 'symbol of a cannibal sacrament'. Blood subsumed essences reached across Larry's lifetime: from his belief that he remembered his delivery among the bloody towels, to his horror of the Crucifix, to his preference for red ink, to his fascination with blood in every state: dark venous blood, menstrual blood, 'rich spagyrick blood'. Finally, Larry warned himself against becoming too serious, evoking 'A diplomat bitten by a frog in a lift' – blood, presumably, drawn.[46] But he *was* serious: blood was the Word, it was life.

With the critical acceptance of the Durrell canon came a string of doctoral candidates importuning the Master for literary and biographical data. In self-defence Larry suggested to Alan Pringle at Faber that someone be enlisted to write a bio-critical text, with emphasis on the work. His old wartime Cairo acquaintance George Fraser, now a professor of literature at Leicester, was signed up for the task. Alan Thomas, who already owned the most nearly complete collection of Larry's published work, readily agreed to provide a bibliography to be published as an appendix. By New Year's Day 1968, with his daughters and Claude's two children in the house, Larry had read the proofs of the book, and he wrote to Alan Thomas in gratitude for his detailed checklist: 'What a tremenjus piece of work – how can I thank you for rendering this splendid service?'[47]

Larry planned his first trip to the United States to coincide with the appearance there of *Tunc*. En route he proposed to stay with Alan Thomas, who in turn invited Larry to 'camp' in his wifeless house. Larry replied that he looked forward to 'drinking some strictly refundable booze chez vous'. While Larry had been entertaining an occasional woman but forming no steady ties, Alan had had a marvellous bit of luck. A few months after Ella's disappearance, he had hired Shirley Calentano, a tall and striking Californian living in London, to be his secretary and shipping clerk. Mrs Calentano had held a responsible position with an American defence contractor, and Alan discovered that she was absolutely reliable. Starting with no experience in the antiquarian book trade, Shirley learned so quickly that within six months Alan was able to leave his business in her hands when he travelled to New York to assess a major collection.

Larry's stopover in England became quite complicated. He had acceded to Alan Pringle's urging that he gratify George Fraser by speaking in the 'Poets in Person' series at the Leicester Arts Festival. Larry groaned privately over such affairs and usually refused to take part in them, but he accepted this one without hesitation and even tempted Alan Thomas: 'It might amuse to make ourselves a raree show.'[48] Alan accepted. Larry's appearance was billed as a 'programme of poetry and prose readings presented by one of our foremost novelists'.[49] Larry found that he could still present himself with polish and poise – he simply assumed his Antrobus mode.

Having once steeled himself to perform, Larry accepted one invitation after another. Alan gave Larry a large party at 16 Hobury Street, with Shirley presiding as hostess, and the narrow house 'echo[ed] to the clink of cans and the popple of corks'. Larry had taken over the top storey, three flights up from the street. The kitchen and dining room were at ground level, down from the street. Early each morning he would descend the groaning stairs, past Alan's mediaeval brass rubbings, to make himself coffee.

Alan had learned that Shirley was having a terrible time with the Italian husband she had recently married on impulse during a holiday in London. Alan was sympathetic – it was in his nature to be so – but had kept his relationship with her on a strictly professional level. It was Larry who played Cupid. Often he would be met in the evening by Margaret McCall or another of his friends, thus making Alan the odd man, and Larry would demand, 'Come on, Shirl, join us for dinner!'[50] Shirley was impetuous and irresistibly direct: Larry viewed her with considerable respect and a bit of alarm.

On 10 March Larry flew to Montreal, where he was lodged in the Ritz-Carlton, 'a gorgeous old hotel where I sit scratching my scrufola and meditating'. For some months he had been suffering from a distressing rash over a good bit of his body, but despite his discomfort, he signed books, gave interviews and appeared on television. He found the city 'rather beautiful', 'ever so slightly touched by San Francisco' – which he had never seen.[51] He was impatient with the mutual ignorance of the anglophone and French Canadians: 'Un bon théâtre pour un peu de cabotinage littéraire', he confided to Simone Perier.[52] Late on the morning of the 14th he landed in Los Angeles and was driven to Pacific Palisades for two weeks with Henry Miller. Larry found his old friend thriving amid a ménage that included at least four young Japanese women and, 'for balance', two Californian blondes. Henry's housekeeper-cum-secretary Connie Combs, Hoki, and Hoki's friend Puko took Larry to Disneyland on the 20th, where the child in him reigned: 'Haven't enjoyed a day so much since ages – it's bristling with marvellously inventive toys.'[53] He reported the event in a quick postcard to Alan Thomas: 'disneyland is absolutely marvellous – Spent 15 hours doing it and must quite certainly do it again/ Larry/ HAVING WONDERFUL TIME.'[54] Next he flew to New York and registered at the mouldering Algonquin Hotel in Manhattan. On All Fools' Day he gave a reading at the 92nd Street Young Men's Hebrew Association. During his visit Larry was accorded a reception by Frances Steloff at the Gotham Book Mart, where he met Marianne Moore, resplendent in her signature tricorne hat. For that single evening, Larry professed himself enchanted with her. 'You are the woman I should have married,' he told Moore.[55] 'You were a prodigious hit at the party,' she wrote to him later.[56] There was a poignant reunion one evening with Thérèse Epstein Marberry, whom he had not seen since the wild prewar days in Paris.

From the first, *Tunc* worried friends, publishers and public. Responding to Alan's doubts about *Tunc*, Larry cautioned, 'You must wait for the II part of *Tunc* before judging it. It is muy complicado.'⁵⁷ Larry was not about to back down before the adverse public criticism of *Tunc* and *Nunquam* either. Many reviewers took the easy route and complained that *Tunc* was not like the *Quartet*: *Newsweek* wrote that Durrell had lost his magic; the *Times Literary Supplement* found *Tunc* less concrete and less vigorous than the *Quartet*. The contrasting views of top-flight reviewers suggested that Larry had put one over on his critics: Kenneth Rexroth praised the sustained irony and satire,⁵⁸ while the *Atlantic Monthly* reviewer likened the author to a 'lazy satyr'.⁵⁹ Gerald Sykes, a friendly critic if ever Larry had one, called *Tunc* a failure, with its 'school boyish indecencies' and absence of lyricism,⁶⁰ but to another friend, George Fraser, the prose was poetic and the story had a 'fantasy-film vividness'.⁶¹

By 12 April 1968 Larry was back in London, tired but buoyed up by the excitement of new experiences and old friends. He sent *Holiday* magazine a poem that summarized his impressions of the 'land of milk and bunny':

> Land of Doubleday and Dutton
> Huge club sandwiches of mutton
> More zip-fastener than button
> Where the blue Algonquin flows
> Home of musical and mayhem
> Robert Frost and Billy Graham.

He ended with a promise: 'Rest assured I'll soon be back.'⁶² His intended title was 'Ode to America' but due to a printer's error the proofs read 'Owed'. Delighted with the mistake, Larry let it stand.

A WAVE OF RIOTS AND STRIKES by students and workers hit France in May 1968, virtually shutting down the country. Ignoring the political upheavals, Larry shut himself up alone in Sommières – the irrepressible Marcelle had finally broken down and was in the hospital for two weeks – and set about writing a musical to be called *Ulysses Come Back*. He turned out 'three smashing songs' and then got stuck.⁶³ The summer passed in a desultory fashion, and then Larry's luck turned when Claudine Brelet arrived at his door. Writer, anthropologist, photographer, she was a dark-eyed brunette with the most direct enthusiasms coupled with a mystic streak. Larry's spirits needed a lift: Claudine recalled that 'the blinds were all locked and an immense sadness impregnated the whole house'. She went around opening the shutters of '*la maison de Dracula*', as Larry had come to call the place. In future visits Claudine would collaborate with Larry on a translation of the poems published in English as *The Red Limbo Lingo*. Larry would try in vain to persuade his publishers to bring out a bilingual edition in which the French text was to be called 'Les Carnets d'un Vampire'.[64]

Margaret McCall swept into Sommières with all her plans and projects. She and Larry proposed to film *Lawrence Durrell's Paris* for the BBC, and with Larry she went to Paris on 23 September to scout locations and to conduct some interviews. They planned to return to Paris in October for the major filming. Larry wrote to the ambassador, Sir Patrick Reilly, for permission to film the embassy's great hall with the immense Wellington portrait: a return to the pomp that he had fled.

Larry travelled on to London where he had a meeting with Arthur Guirdham, now more than ever certain that he was the receptor of messages from ancient Cathars. Guirdham was convinced of the 'non-reality of time': all time existed simultaneously, so that he was not surprised at the congealed blisters on the back of a woman patient who had dreamed of being hit on the same spot by a flaming torch carried by a monk during extermination of the Cathars at Monségur in 1244. 'What will happen to us has already happened,' he would write in *A Foot in Both Worlds*. Larry was excited by this line of thought, which ran parallel to his own. Like Larry, Guirdham was fascinated by the number thirteen and courted association with it, although he was too much the scientist to believe in luck: he thought that his affinity with thirteen came from his earlier existence in the thirteenth century.[65]

Larry returned to Sommières to find that, while he and Arthur Guirdham had been rifling each other's minds, persons unknown had been busy during his absence: his house had been expertly burgled and his valuable Elizabethan books as well the paintings given him by Michonze, Milshtein, Brassaï and other established artists were taken. 'But they left *my* daubings,' said Larry in aggrieved tones.[66] This event shocked him into the realization that he was not completely anonymous, even in his secluded corner of Provence. He poured out his woes to a pair of new friends, Paule Wislenef and Tony Daniells, over dinner at the Hotel Pont Romain. While Larry and Paule clowned about, rolling bottles down the long hallway of the former textile mill, Tony, an artist, agreed to make up a block-printed sign, *Maison Piègé* – 'Booby-Trapped House' – to post on the doors of the house.[67]

Larry decided that he should take steps to safeguard his working notebooks, manuscripts and first editions, and if possible to convert them into a small capital before some thief did it on his own behalf, and he resolved to sell a part of his personal archive.

In between distractions Larry worked hard on *Nunquam*, so that by 16 February 1969 he was able to report to Henry that 'I've managed to push the second volume of *Tunc* to within about fifty pages of the end and if I can keep the heat on like this should be through in April some time. Ouf.'[68] Larry would caution against seeing in *Tunc* and *Nunquam* a polemic against any specific entity: 'You mustn't read this as though I'm writing about an individual life crippled by General Motors, or by the Catholic Church, or by Communism,' he told a pair of interviewers. He was playing a variation on the Faust theme in *Nunquam*; his Faust, Felix Charlock, sells his soul to the firm. The computer and its potential in artificial intelligence frightened Larry, so he had created the robot Iolanthe: 'I wanted to be funny and gruesome at the same time, and . . . to suggest that we are becoming computerized,' he said. Larry's pitiful Lucifer, Julian Pehlevi, orders his minions to build 'a perfect woman', and his fall in her embrace to his death from the dome of St Paul's Cathedral – the dome of Heaven – is the fall of Lucifer.[69] Larry's own identification with Lucifer reached back to his fictional avatar in *The Black Book*, Lawrence Lucifer, the putative generator of the story; and his despairing sympathy with creator-destroyers would extend to his final book, *Caesar's Vast Ghost*, with its invocation of another doomed conqueror, the great Julius.

Larry was trying to control his body and mind with yoga, which he now took up seriously. 'Click click go the bones when I do my Yoga,' he complained. 'Never mind.'[70] He was also attempting to combat his skin rash, 'rather like hives', he reported to Dr Guirdham, 'with which I have decorated myself on and off this winter'. He began to reread his volumes of Stekel, looking for the origin of his trouble. He noted with chagrin that the rash tended to appear whenever he settled down to write.[71] It also got in the way of his loving, and like an old bear, Larry said that he was 'getting used to' being alone: except for the occasional dinner-and-bed guest, he was content with solitude – 'if one can de mother fixate enough not to feel the need for mother substitutes around all the time'.[72]

Larry's solitude was broken by Claudine Brelet, who visited him again in February, and they discussed at length Guirdham's evidence of psychic phenomena. Claudine felt that there was some psychic influence operating on her as well, for frequently Larry would remark that Claudine had bought the *same* flowers to place in the *same* vase and in the *same* spot as Claude had. Then Claudine would make the fire in exactly the same way

Claude had. Larry and Marcelle also remarked on the Claudine/Claude name coincidence, until finally, Claudine recalled, 'It eventually frightened me and through meditation, I realized that I was not getting "mad" or "possessed by a ghost", but that I had simply a (karmic?) duty to "bring back life" around him, as if this was what Claude wanted, to keep him *alive*.'[73]

Then it was Easter, and despite the presence of Barry, Diana and Sappho, Larry managed to finish *Nunquam* by 4 April so as to be able to ride white Camargue ponies with them on Easter Sunday. He readily admitted that it had been 'laboured' writing; in fact, 'It was bloody agony.'[74] However, he thought that *Nunquam* had been worth the agony: 'To my surprise and relief it seems quite good – at least worthy as a successor to the Quartet,' he wrote to Henry Miller.[75] Larry expected the novel to 'get a good beating' at the hands of the critics, but consoled himself with the not-so-accurate thought that the *Quartet* had had to wait almost seven years 'before anybody took any serious interest in it'.[76]

Larry furnished *Nunquam* with a 'Postface' addressed to 'Dear C.-M.V.' – Claude-Marie Vincendon – but the actual ending of the novel describes Benedicta Merlin and Felix Charlock in bliss: 'There is some fine black jazz playing and we have been dancing, dancing in complete happiness and accord.'[77] Benedicta and Felix have buried their only child, and this reflects the childless life that Larry and Claude had lived most of the time. Larry's novels always had been, would continue to be, peopled with solitaries and childless couples: Justine deprived of her daughter, Constance childless in *The Avignon Quintet*. His lonely childhood-in-exile had left him uneasy when it came to describing happiness in terms of a settled family.

In the Postface Larry wrote to Claude as if she were alive, acknowledging the truth of her judgements: 'It was you who said once that all my novels were inquests with open verdicts.' In *Nunquam* he had written about 'the notion of culture – what is it?' Larry continued to his dead wife, 'I remember too that you remarked once about Spengler, "He's not pessimistic at all. He is a realist, that is all."' In the novel Larry had a formula for reversing the mechanistic sterility that had built up the mega-firm Merlin's, that had created the fatal robot Iolanthe: burn all the contracts and thus reassert simple trust. Realistically, it might not work, he said, but 'it will be now or never'.[78] The conflagration was worth proposing: the Luddite act of the century.

Towards the end of April 1969 Alan and Shirley drove to Sommières to see Larry for a week and to transport his archive to London so that Alan could prepare it for sale. They found him battered but in fairly good spirits. He had been to Geneva, where the German woman surgeon – she was beautiful, Larry said – who had cared for Claude had removed a cyst from his ear. Larry was still suffering from a painful eczema and anti-allergenics had been prescribed. Still, it was a shock one day to find a note on the table from their usually indefatigable host: 'Alan – so sleepy from histamine, have gone up to sleep – Hope you wont mind.'[79] Larry's archive was nearly lost when Alan's car burst into flames at Tain l'Hermitage, but it was saved through the quick action of a café proprietor. Back in Chelsea, Alan painstakingly typed out a detailed description of Larry's archive, and it was soon sold to Southern Illinois University for $75,000. With the promise of this windfall coming in, Larry decided to have a large swimming pool installed to the east of the house at the foot of the garden.

On 25 May 1969 Larry left Sommières for Greece, travelling with Margaret McCall. Their plan was to 'location-hunt' for a possible film.[80] His eczema kept plaguing him, but he hoped that the Greek sun and plenty of olive oil would clear his skin of rashes. He and McCall decided against the Greek film, but instead went ahead with plans for *The Lonely Roads*, about the wandering *clochards* of the Midi.

The swimming pool changed the pattern of Larry's life. The privacy was complete: the overgrown garden rendered the pool nearly invisible from the house, and the brick wall shielded him from the curious. Larry swam naked, and encouraged his guests to do likewise. He virtually stopped going to the sea to bathe, and claimed that he did not miss it. He kept a metal table and a few chairs under the immense chestnut tree beside the pool: a wonderful spot for dining, talking or simply musing with a glass in hand. But the sale of his archive, although giving him the pool, had, Larry felt, compromised his privacy in a way he had not foreseen. He would complain angrily in a published interview about 'the misuse of our letters and private papers by so-called scholars', and rail about 'graduate students' and 'kids' who were reading about 'the intimate details of our lives' so as to 'discuss them at cocktail parties'. This 'monstrous' situation had 'certainly stopped most correspondences'.[81] Was this genuine anger, a calculated outburst to attract curious scholars to the scandalous honey of his archive, or a burst of verbal pyrotechnics for a gullible interviewer? Both he and Henry had benefited financially from selling their manuscripts and letter files to university collections. They were caught between their need for privacy and their instinct to 'raise a bit of dough', as both would have phrased it, by selling off some old papers.

Thérèse Marberry stayed with Larry for a week in mid-August. He was very gentle with his old love, and brought her coffee in the morning, 'tray in hand'. She was especially moved by 'that surprise visit of yours around 4 a.m. the morning I left.' She added, 'I'd better stop now, for fear of bursting into tears in print.'[82] Tessa, very important to his creation of Justine, went to view the film *Justine*, just released. The attempt to tame the *Quartet* for the screen began almost with the publication of *Justine*, and many scriptwriters had struggled with the story. The original director, Joseph Strick, had been fired on location in Tunis, and the film had been completed by George Cukor, 'perhaps the most cultured and erudite of all Hollywood directors', according to one of his stars, Dirk Bogarde.[83] 'Larry, I saw the picture last night and came away depressed,' Tessa wrote, 'because Justine is dead . . . . a mere nympho. Please don't see this film if you can possibly avoid it.'[84] Larry appears to have taken her advice. The film was an object lesson in how a good book interpreted by famous actors – Bogarde as Pursewarden, Anouk Aimée as Justine – could fail on the screen. Even the script writer, Laurence Marcus, had despaired of his own final product and had written Larry a letter of apology. Larry's own comment, scrawled in anger across the cover of the script, wasted no words: 'A monument of illiterate shit!' The film soon vanished, and its failure tended to discourage other productions based on Larry's work.

Despite the disappointment of the silver screen, Larry co-operated fully in making *The Lonely Roads* for a BBC/Bavarian Television co-production. Margaret McCall arrived on the first of September, along with Diane Deriaz, Larry's trapeze artist friend, who was to be the 'questionmaster', interviewing Larry before the camera. Deriaz was a rare creature, one of those unusual people Larry seemed to be able to recognize by instinct. When he first saw her she was a hostess for Air France, and was being harassed by difficult passengers. Soon Larry had her life story: she belonged to a family of circus trapeze artists and had been a star attraction, photographed by Man Ray, friend to Paul Eluard, Picasso, Roland Penrose, Max Ernst. Then she had suffered a bad fall and could not perform again, but she had found a second career that would keep her aloft. When Larry met her she was about to be retired, owing to the airline's policy of keeping the stewardesses young. She was direct, fearless, articulate. Larry invited her to dine with him that evening as they landed at Orly.

The Lonely Roads, wrote Larry, was 'supposedly about me but in fact mostly about the landscape hereabouts, and more particularly about tramps – l'homme sans attachés'.[85] It was about freedom; it was even a crib for *Tunc.* The other main actor in McCall's film was a man known around Sommières simply as Blanco le Clochard. In his own way he was quite as extraordinary as Deriaz and, like her, he was a living embodiment of independence and a thinker about what that independence meant. Throughout the month, McCall, Deriaz, Blanco and Larry slogged about the sodden countryside: 'WE ARE FILMING AWAY MADLY HERE, BUT THE WEATHER IS ROTTEN,' Larry wrote to Alan Thomas.[86]

Larry was more intimately connected with this film than with any other. His affinity with *clochards*, with tramps, was rooted in his ideal of freedom. 'The enquiry in *Tunc* is Freedom I should say, no?' asked Diane. 'Yes, it really was, it's Freedom,' Larry replied. 'The Culture and the Freedom were the two notions in between which I was playing, because I wondered whether you could have a culture without a notion of Freedom.' When Julian Pehlevi crashes to the floor tiles of St Paul's in *Nunquam*, this query is answered in the negative. Larry identified with the *clochard*'s freedom: 'I am a tramp,' he told Diane, 'I believe in everything and nothing. But one is always in danger of being a croyant pratiquant out of politeness,' Larry said, alluding to the desire to please that had so often trapped him in situations and ideological positions that he abhorred. The tramp was not so easily trapped, he thought: 'These boys have been living at the end of my garden for ten years,' he said. 'They belong clearly to a fellowship which has no fixed beliefs. . . . It has helped me very much while I was fooling about with people who have fixed beliefs. I mean, I presume that General Motors has fixed beliefs. I know the Catholic Church does, I know the Communists have fixed beliefs. All these people are rigidified.' In fact, Larry believed, there was no such thing as freedom, but it was a 'fruitful illusion'. 'You mustn't ask what's right or wrong,' he continued. 'We must ask what's fruitful and what is unfruitful. The illusion of Freedom is important to civilization.'[87] That illusion was equally important to Larry himself: even though it kept him single, kept him lonely and discontented, kept him bouncing about the roads in L'Escargot.

ALAN THOMAS'S LOVINGLY COMPILED *Spirit of Place: Essays and Letters on Travel* appeared in May 1969, and Larry was pleased: Alan had done the arduous editing work with skill and humour. As a celebration of places and Larry's writing about them, the volume emphasized one side of his character, his response to a location. 'I have a theory about that,' Larry would say a year or so later to Marc Alyn. 'There are benign places and there are sterile places. Greece has always worked for me: Corfu, Rhodes, Cyprus.'[88] He could have named the Midi as well. Among locations that had not worked for him were England, Argentina, Belgrade, and paradoxically Egypt, whence he could derive material but not creative force.

Before Christmas Larry and Alan Thomas concocted a scheme to make a few pounds with a limited edition of *An Irish Faustus*, which Alan forwarded to Larry for signatures. Larry signed each title page and repackaged the books. By return post Alan noted that the signed copies had arrived safely, 'even though the string on one parcel had come undone; the immortality of everything you touch does not seem to have made sufficient impression on you, otherwise you would tie better knots'.[89] Unchastened, Larry hastened to Paris to bring in the New Year with his actress friend Eleonore Hirt – slender, elegant, wistful – and to drink a toast to Henry Miller at the Dôme. Before leaving, Larry delivered a tongue-in-cheek scolding to Alan for his 'immorality': Alan was being taken to court for alienation of affection by Shirley Calentano's estranged husband.[90]

Larry was reading about the Cathars and was already 'munching over ideas for a possible novel' in which the Templars would figure,[91] but with the *Nunquam* galleys long finished and the book about to appear, he decided to play for a while. Wallace Southam arrived in Sommières during early 1970 and spent a week setting on paper the tunes that Larry had composed for his proposed musical *Ulysses Come Back*. Larry felt that Ulysses' return to Ithaca after a long absence paralleled his own postwar landfall in Corfu; and Larry was wryly amused by Ulysses' problems with women. Circe, Nausicaa, Penelope must have blurred in the hero's mind, he thought. 'Yoohoo, Ulysses!' sang the siren Circe, sitting at her long black piano in her 'pad'; and then came the innocent Nausicaa on the beach, and finally the steadfast Penelope waiting 'patiently' in Ithaca.

> It's the same girl
> With the same damn face,
> And all her charms
> In a different sort of place,

Larry wrote in the principal refrain, adding, 'What's a poor sailor to do?/ It's anchors away.' 'I think it's funny and good in parts,' Larry confided to Henry.[92] Larry's many women must have sometimes run together in his memory as well, blending and recombining. No wonder he disbelieved in the discrete ego.

In an interview conducted more than a year later, Claudine Brelet would tease Larry about his several marriages and the 'good dozen' photographs of women on his mantelpiece. Then she came right to the point on *Ulysses*: 'Were you looking for the "same face" in all your women?' 'I don't know,' Larry replied. 'I was looking for a mother.' Claudine was someone Larry respected too much to humbug, and he continued, 'But a writer is a burden in a woman's life, because, while a writer is very strong in the realm of ideas, he remains very weak when it comes to the practical realities of life. Thus, a writer is a bit wrong, a bit twisted. He needs someone who would be a nurse for the love of art!' Claudine pressed on: 'A writer is an eternal adolescent, like you yourself?' 'Yes', Larry admitted, 'I believe it is essential.' Jean Giono had insisted years ago that he, Larry, 'had remained a nipper'.[93] *Ulysses Come Back* might have been composed as a lark, but he had surprised himself with the truth of his quest for a mother, for a nurse.

Larry was quite consistent these days in his view of himself as a writer first, an engager of life second. 'I live much more in the work than I do in real life, which makes me rather a failure in real life. My real life is rather a failure, rather hollow. I regard myself as diseased,' he had told Diane Deriaz and Margaret McCall.[94] Perhaps it was only natural that, as his once-powerful physique gradually subsided into middle-aged flabbiness under the assaults of overdrinking, overeating, too much smoking, and plain advancing eld, he should retreat more and more into his intellectual being. Yet it was also manifest that his preoccupation with writing, and his self-indulgence, made him a difficult person to live with. Early on, he had believed that he could succeed in both art and life. Now he was sure that he had not.

LARRY DID WHAT HE COULD to interest the public in *Nunquam*. The end of February 1970 found him in the air again, flying non-stop from Marseille to London, where he would arrive 'about seven for a stiff dose of porter' with Alan Thomas.[95] Gwyn Williams remembered these book parties, held at 'Alan and Shirley Thomas's treasure-house down in Chelsea, with the gentle and poetical Theodore Stephanides usually there'.[96] Theodore's once-golden beard had turned white and he had become quite deaf, but his lean profile retained the chiselled beauty of a Greek medallion. Theodore was sharing his house with his estranged wife, even though they had not spoken to one another for years. For Larry there were many visits and book signings, and then on 17 March, St Patrick's Day, he left for New York, where he again checked into 'my little dreamboat', the old Algonquin.[97]

The launching of *Nunquam* in America would not be until 23 March, so he had plenty of leisure to attend a private advance screening of Robert Snyder's *Henry Miller Odyssey*. Thus Larry met Fiddle Viracola, the Italian-

American stage and film actress and singer whose credits included countless appearances on and off Broadway, from *The Rose Tattoo* and *A Streetcar Named Desire* to *The Trojan Women*. She had even assumed the title role in a production of *Hello, Dolly!* in Tokyo. Henry had told her to show Larry New York, and she gathered him up like a pledge. Her ringing voice spanned octaves, and any hesitation on Larry's part was sure to evoke an irresistible 'Come o-on!' She had black hair, dark eyes, a complexion of white porcelain, and a voluptuous figure. She seemed to know everyone – Isaac Bashevis Singer, Irving Berlin, John Cage . . . Fiddle showed Larry Henry's Brooklyn, took him on the Staten Island Ferry, walked him around Greenwich Village at midnight, and sat with him in the Blue Room of the Algonquin. Larry was amazed by the tall, narrow wedge of the Flat-Iron Building, and later gave Fiddle an aquarelle of it, painted from memory. She became the muse of Larry's New York: he thought she was to the scale of the great city, and called her the 'Wow and Superwow Girl' and the Blithe Spirit. Soon Larry was cooking omelettes for Fiddle at her Tenth Street apartment. 'If a man really loved me, he'd do the dishes too,' Fiddle told Larry. Larry did the dishes. Setting aside his shyness with strangers, he even allowed Fiddle to introduce him to several of her many acquaintances in the art and theatre world.[98]

Together they visited a couple of Larry's friends: Frances Steloff at the Gotham Book Mart and Gerald Sykes, who became Fiddle's friend as well. Larry slipped away on his own for an evening with the recently widowed Thérèse Marberry. Mostly, though, he spent his time with Fiddle when he was not seeing publishers, being interviewed, giving a talk at Columbia University in the company of John Unterecker, or signing books. Larry was smitten, and Fiddle fell deeply in love with him. They walked in fresh snow, and on the Staten Island Ferry he took her hand and with a sweeping gesture announced, 'This could be Venice!'[99]

The Blue Room became Larry's unofficial office, and in its dim recesses, the smoke of his cigarette spiralling in the stale air, he held court for a pair of scholarly interviewers. *Tunc* and *Nunquam*, he said, had taken off from Spengler, whose 'armed Caesarism' – 'the colonels (it's always the Army) taking over in Latin America or Greece or Nigeria' – struck Larry as the perfect summation of the past forty years. Larry agreed with Spengler that Western civilization may be in its 'autumn', but he refused to give up entirely: 'In my guess there is a slender ray of hope, but the time is running out fast, and it's praying for rain.'[100]

The only game for the writer was language, writing with a 'fullness' sprung from the English Bible and the Elizabethans, so Larry often said. This robust language he saw in F. Scott Fitzgerald, in Faulkner, in Bellow. Larry was not word-shy precisely because language 'wears out': 'Already Shakespeare is practically unintelligible without notes.' If all you had was three hundred years 'at the very most', he concluded, 'You might as well have fun with the old violin.' He could not only hear the words, he could taste language: 'It's like an oyster: you squeeze a little lemon on it and it's delicious.'[101]

Together Larry and Fiddle went to Chicago for a round of interviews and book-signings. She had recently spent six months in Chicago with a revue, and so was recognized by many more people than Larry. Dick Cavett gave them a lift in his car, but Larry took an instant dislike to him, terming him 'a little insect'. Fiddle showed Larry the city from the elegant North Shore to Punchinella's, a café in the Loop where artists and actors talked and sang. One of his best memories was of the blues joints on Rush Street. Before they flew together back to New York, Larry defined the glittering city as 'a woman in a steel bra'.[102]

Despite the emotional lift he derived from being around Fiddle, Larry was often ill-tempered. It was not an easy period for him: he was drinking powerful spirits and his eczema had worsened, perhaps in consequence. Or his eczema was driving him to drink. Where he itched he could not help scratching, awake and asleep, and sometimes his trousers and shirt stuck to his skin in bloody patches. Fiddle pampered him and tried to find remedies to alleviate his suffering. His problem had finally been diagnosed as nervous urticaria, but he jokingly called it syphilis. He would be furious on his return to France when he discovered that Fred Perlès had suggested in an article that Larry had picked up a case of the clap in New York: 'Not very complimentary to Fiddle!' Larry fumed.

Larry was negotiating the publication of *The Red Limbo Lingo*, and his manner shifted back and forth from ingenuous delight in the New York cityscapes to moods savage and ghoulish. 'I could cut your head off,' he told Fiddle reflectively, sitting in the Blue Room. 'Sometimes it was like being with Count Dracula,' she recalled. When a grey mouse traversed the carpet, Larry was delighted. She saw Larry off at the airport with an impassioned hug and a brave 'Ciao!'[103] Back in Sommières, 'In a great hemisphere of loveless sky,' Larry sent a poem back to Fiddle:

> Somewhere perhaps in a cobweb of skyscrapers
> Between Fifth and Sixth musing I'll go,
> Matching some footprints in young snow.[104]

Larry's prediction that *Nunquam* would be mauled by the critics turned out to be an understatement. Anthony Burgess, writing for the *Saturday Review*, complained about the same failure to achieve rounded characters that he had disliked in the *Quartet*. For him, Durrell was a lyric poet who could not turn himself into a novelist. The *New York Times* stated that 'only' those who had enjoyed the 'wooden dialogue' and lushness of the *Quartet* would like *Nunquam*.[105] A review almost Durrellian in its humour appeared in the *New York Review of Books*, suggesting that the novel made sense as a feminist allegory once the reader realized that 'Lawrence Durrell' was 'the anagrammatic pseudonym of Ellen Ward Curler, a fragile relic of the Twenties'. Read as Durrell's, *Nunquam* 'would be no more than labored pretentious infantility, the resonance and crackle of hi-sci-fi'.[106] The novel fared just as badly in England: the *Times Literary Supplement* decried the slowed momentum following *Tunc*, and concluded that Durrell had failed to develop his ideas; the *New Statesman* claimed 'plain bad writing'.[107]

Larry thought that one source of critical unease was that he had been guilty of publishing in too many fields, and he brought up the examples of Lawrence and Hardy, who by publishing verse had confused readers accustomed to their novels. Only after their deaths did people realize that they had each left an integrated *oeuvre*. 'It will be the same with me,' said Larry, adding humbly, 'if there is a me, I mean, after the event.'[108] If he was upset by the reception of *Nunquam*, he gave no sign. Dutton, however, *was* upset, and Viking would soon become Larry's American publisher.

Fiddle accepted Larry's invitation to Sommières, and in late April she burst upon the quiet Midi town for a week: they spent an idyllic time, 'all solitary, with wood fires and walks across the garrigues in the rain, and visits to the old mazet to pick lilacs'.[109] Larry sat at the long black Pleyel, accompanying Fiddle on a wide range of 'old whisky songs' of the Jerome Kern variety, her rich voice filling the echoing house, her laughter matching his. 'You are like a crackling olive fire,' he told her.[110]

Fiddle got Larry to chant her Buddhist mantra, *Nam myoho renge kyo* – Reverence to the Sûtra of the Lotus of the Good Law. She had been raised a Catholic, but unlike Larry, she had kept her Christian faith, simply adding Buddhism to her spiritual stock. 'You are a *spiritual* being,' she kept telling him, then and over the following years. 'Fiddle, keep chanting!' Larry would write on the back of a letter to her.[111] Fiddle's visit was, Larry recalled to Henry Miller, 'such a perfect experience'.[112]

During the summer of 1970 Larry recorded a long-playing record of

Ulysses Come Back excerpts in London, with Belle Gonzales performing the female parts and Larry himself singing the recitative, in an edition of 99 copies produced by Bernard Stone. He sent the *Ulysses* record to an agent in New York to see whether there was any interest in expanding it into a full-length musical. One side of the recording sketches out the musical; the other contains some additional songs written, played and sung by Larry, including a tongue-in-cheek analysis of the generic hero:

> Every hero has a silver lining
> Every hero's soul is caviar
> That is what keeps all the ladies pining
> Even when he buggers off afar.[113]

There were no immediate takers for *Ulysses Come Back*, and Larry asked Fiddle to promote the musical sketch for him in the United States. Even she could raise no interest. He also said that Fiddle would be ideal to play the heroine in *Acte* and gave her the American rights to the play, but she found no sponsor for that either.

After London, Larry made a television film in Paris with Michèle Arnaud, a popular singer turned film producer. Their film included moments of comedy when Larry's outspoken cook/housekeeper Marcelle appeared in the middle of his monologues calling him 'un grand bébé'. *Spéciale sur Durrell*, with Larry showing off his French, would be broadcast by the Paris ORTF in February 1971. Michèle Arnaud was a small, intense, capable person who could at times seem vulnerable and in need of care. Larry was not taken in by this, but he became fond of her and welcomed her visits to the Midi. She inspired Larry to write songs in French. 'Sais Je Pourquoi?' queried his title. 'Plus jeune que moi, Ah, je le sais', went the lyrics. These he continued in another version in English, 'But much less lonely than I was those years ago/ During the earliest youth of our desire.'[114]

Within weeks Gerry arrived with a 'seraglio like a Turkish potentate',[115] to be followed by Miriam Cendrars, who also filmed an interview with Larry, and finally, in a group, the Fieldings, James Stern and Mai Zetterling. At around this time Margaret McCall came through on her way to film in Italy. Larry was entertaining himself writing 'pop tunes' for Annie Verneuil, whom Larry nicknamed Annie-la-Môme – the urchin. She was a wiry local *chanteuse* with a gay laugh, a frank, direct manner, a head of tight black curls, and 'a voice like a screwdriver'.[116] Larry admired her jauntiness, her independence, and recognized her strength: 'I have grave thoughts about nothingness, / Hold no copyright in Jesus like that girl.' She would stop by the house for a quick drink and a burst of repartee. He wrote:

> I am making her a small scarlet jazz
> For the cellar where they dance
> To a wheezy accordion, with a one-eyed man.
> Written to a cheeky begging voice.

> *Moi je suis*
> *Annie Verneuil*
> *Dit Annie La Môme*
> *Parfois je fais la vie*
> *Parfois je chôme*
> *Premier Prix de Saloperie*
> *De Paris à Rome.*[117]

With all the excitement, Larry's serious work was shoved aside and his drinking increased: 'the soft alcohols and the hard ones'[118] had long been indicators on the scale of his productivity. He tended to work on wine, lie fallow on gin and whisky. This was a fallow time, but his rationale was that 'All this distracting twaddle has enabled me to mark time and start trying to firm up the outlines of a new novel.' *Monsieur* was just around the corner.[119]

In September 1970 Fiddle Viracola was back in Sommières, and Larry pointed out the 'Favourite Actresses Wall' in his ground floor office in the old house. There were three 8-by-10-inch photographs: Sophia Loren, 'Ultra Violet' – an Andy Warhol protégée – and Fiddle. After about a week in Sommières, Fiddle helped Larry to deliver his paintings to Paris for an exhibition, sharing the driving with him in L'Escargot. They followed the *autoroute* north, stopping for the night in Auxerre, and the next morning pulled up at the luxurious Intercontinental Hotel. Clearly, Larry wanted to impress 'the adorable monster sweetheart', as he called Fiddle, for he would have preferred the modest Royal.[120]

The first night in Paris Larry went off with Michèle Arnaud while Fiddle visited friends. Michèle and Larry discussed her proposed production of *Les amis de Henry Miller* for television, for which she would eventually interview Brassaï, Belmont, Larry and even Marcelle again. Later, Fiddle took Michèle and Larry to a Buddhist service. Most of the time, however, he guided Fiddle around the city. They saw the cafés and bars where Larry and Henry and Anaïs had spent so many hours before the war: the Dôme, the Coupole, the Café Zeyer. They visited small restaurants and clubs. Fiddle, carrying her camera like a tourist, walked with Larry along Villa Seurat to number 18. On 10 September 'Larry & Fiddle' signed an exuberant postcard to Henry Miller, written in their two hands. Fiddle covered most of the card: 'Father GOOSE (L.D.) showed me all your old haunts yesterday, down to your favorite peeing places!! A souffle of a day – WINE, talk of you, AND dear, DEAR Larry.'[121]

Larry told Fiddle he wanted to marry her, but then said he was worried about growing old: 'You would hate me. I'd be an old man. I wouldn't want you to see me old.' He bought her two rings, one a tiny gold serpent, the other set with small rubies and an emerald.[122] There was a tearful parting, and Fiddle returned alone to New York.

Larry's health remained indifferent. He tried to put a good face on it, writing to Henry, 'I've had a short incubating period of bad health, which for me is always a prelude to getting an idea for a book – I've got it and will attack this winter when I settle back in Sommières.'[123] He gazed at his 'book-lined walls so scholarly', taking down volume after volume. 'I finger the sex of many an uncut book,' he wrote in his poetry notebook.[124] He added up his emotional balance sheet for 1970 and counted his trophies and his scars: Margaret, Thérèse, Fiddle, Michèle, Annie . . . . He had always feared boredom, and he agreed with Henry that sheer tension will keep one alive. Each romance seemed to end in a let-down, and with wry humour he wrote:

> She whooped him up with the Song of Songs
> then put him out like a stub.[125]

Larry was afflicted with moments of panic over his own isolation. His fictional bondsman of long ago, Lawrence Lucifer, had referred to himself as 'Hamlet's little godchild', suffering from 'the modern disease: the terrible disintegration of action under the hideous pressure of the ideal'. This paralysis came down to 'schizophrenic autism', a 'feeling of non-contact, which God knows even the most sane in our society begin to feel more and more'. Larry totted up all the broken ties that seemed to have begun with Claude's disappearance, and he must have linked them to his human failures, for he added, 'The further you go in the artistic world, and the more successful you are in communication, you often become more and more disembodied in your personal relations.' The better he wrote, the more unlucky he seemed to be in love. Henry Miller had 'come out the other end' of the vortex of his affairs, Larry said, 'as a sort of *Bonze*', but there was no guarantee that he would achieve the same: 'The intermediate stages . . . are extremely lonely-making, and you might never make it.'[126]

LARRY PASSED A 'WONDERFUL' Christmas 1970 with Penelope and Sappho, 'my two beautiful daughters,' he boasted to Henry. Larry ordered plum pudding from Paris and admired his offspring: 'Saph the baby is simply dazzling for beauty and brains and is going to be a poet I think – she already writes well at 18.' After their departure – Sappho to return to York, where she had matriculated that autumn at the university, Penelope to London – the house seemed sad and empty, and Larry sought distraction in a 'whole daisy-chain of love affairs', which left him finally indifferent.[127]

As January gripped the Midi, Larry stoked his kitchen fireplace with olive wood and dead vine stumps. 'I have started a queer sort of novel about the gnostic heresies, the Templars etc etc,' he wrote to Henry Miller. 'It's still all very fragile and may well jolt to a stop before I finish it. . . . I'm still alive, single, and living in the gaunt old house and trying to keep working – it's the only lifeline I think.' He bought his bread in the shadow of Sommières's Albigensian tower, and brought home books on the Templars, Cathars, Bogomils – persecuted heretics all. What he read reconfirmed all his youthful abhorrence of the main currents of Christianity.

Larry went to Paris towards the end of the month, and he sat in the Dôme sparring with Michèle Arnaud. This time Larry found Paris 'particularly annoying': 'You feel you ought to be in love and since you can't make it any more you feel frustrated and become cruel – "les caresses brutales".'[128] His health kept bothering him – the 'asthma-eczema complex' 'making a mess of my temper and my love making alike' – and he wondered if it might not be a 'fish allergy caught by eating too much scrod in Grand Central Station Oyster Bar – a favourite haunt of mine'.[129] Claudine Brelet saw him at the Blokhs' Parc Montsouris home 'entirely coated with some kind of white flour cream'. He discussed marriage with Claudine – who was already married and had a young daughter – but finally told her that he lacked the energy to help raise her child. She should have another child and a 'normal marriage', he said! Claudine thought that he was simply unwilling to risk his thinning emotional capital.[130]

In late February Larry scurried off to Geneva for a medical check-up and to arrange a meeting between Michèle Arnaud and Denis de Rougemont. After a lifetime of using alcohol as a therapy against depression, writer's block and boredom, Larry had been forced to suspect that too much alcohol was bad for his art and his heart. Now he had medical confirmation. 'I had my first medical check ever, nothing radical', he told Henry; 'alcohol gorged heart and ditto liver which means cutting down on the booze for a while, but nothing much else.' He defended himself by saying that the doctors he saw could not have performed the double lotus standing on their heads – 'which I now do for three minutes'.[131]

Larry had come to see de Rougemont's *Love in the Western World* as something of a bible on human sexuality. Making love properly had always been a subject for Larry to expatiate upon. Now it approached an obsession. An astrologer had predicted that his physical powers would begin to wane in 1968, and perhaps this spurred him on as the years passed. 'The reason that the Kama Sutra method fulfils one sexually more than the Western systems', Larry told the American college professor and poet Suzanne Henig, 'is that it puts you in tune with the sexuality of the partner.' Larry stressed the importance of breathing, especially during foreplay. 'You adjust your breathing to your partner's. You synchronise your orgasm by controlling your breathing; you keep count of your breaths,' he continued. Henig asked him how he kept his mind on the tally. Without a tremor Larry replied, 'It takes practice.'[132]

Despite his shaky health and his drinking and his adventures, Larry was optimistic about *Monsieur*. The theme was 'congenial':

I have always been intrigued by the catastrophic overnight collapse of the Templars, and the charges of heresy brought against them: also the mystery of WHY this order, so renowned for holiness, frugality – a huge army of 15,000 men, trained and armed and in perfect battle shape, and located in a chain of unbreachable fortresses stretching from France to Syria – why they should have allowed themselves to be disarmed, imprisoned, tortured and burnt at the stake, without uttering a word? They would have been capable of overturning France and Italy at a blow and taking charge. What happened? What was their sin? What turned them into rabbits? Everyone has their own view – mine is Syrian gnosticism with its roots in Alexandria or Oxyrhyncus. When I was idly reading about them I suddenly realised that in my travels I had unwittingly been posted always to one of their strong points, one of the places outremer where the so-called heresies were contracted. Taking Avignon as my apex, then, perhaps a modern novel with the sense of enchainment, of the complicity of Templar destiny? I don't know.

Larry thought that gnosticism was 'rich and sinister', 'very contemporary', even 'hippy'.[133] And like the *Quartet*, his new book was solidly rooted in places he knew well: Avignon and the heretic towns stretching towards the Pyrenees. Three months later Larry was saying somewhat nervously that his gnostic book 'may well be my best novel if only I can get it the way I want it'.[134]

Monsieur was to be the first of the 'Avignon quincunx' novels, but also the centre novel, the keystone of the projected five. Picture the five of a domino piece: this was the quincunxial pattern that Larry chose for what he envisioned as his final major effort. Trees were often planted in quincunx pattern in mediaeval parks, and Larry would work in patterns of fives throughout *The Avignon Quintet*: the five senses; the five-fold path of Tantric Buddhism; the five traps of Western Civilization, which he characterized in five M-words: 'Monotheism, Messianism, Monogamy, and Materialism', and 'The cornerstone of culture . . . another M – *merde*'. This final M he tied to materialism: 'The Freudian analysis of absolute value [is] based upon infantile attitudes towards excrement. Gold and excrement.'[135] *The Alexandria Quartet* had remained firmly entrenched in the plane of reality: the story of Darley's love for Justine is told in the first novel, and then he is twice disabused in the next two volumes; the final book moves the story on in time: but it is all real. *Monsieur* purports at the outset to be 'real', and the narrative is sketched in such vivid evocations of Provence in moonlit winter, of a desert oasis west of Alexandria, of mouldering Albigensian châteaux, that readers are drawn to accept the new narrator Bruce Drexel as they had once embraced Darley. Larry's difficulties in writing *Monsieur* enter into the narration: 'The Bruce that I was, and the Bruce that I become as I jot down these words, a few every day' reflects his hesitations. In his description of Bruce's train journey – in response to a telegram announcing the suicide of his best friend Piers de Nogaret – Larry, whether consciously or not, mirrored the course of his composition of the novel. The train is 'subject to unexpected halts, unexplained delays; it could fall asleep anywhere . . . and remain there, lost in thought'.[136] The novel begins in the later years of the principals in the Midi, quickly shifts to their youth in Egypt, traverses to mediaeval Europe through Piers's descent from Guillaume de Nogaret, who had engineered the extirpation of the Templars, finally returns to Provence – and then Larry would rip the narrative rug from under the reader by revealing that the entire story is the creation of the novelist Blanford, sitting in Venice watching the sun set 'over the loops of the Grand Canal'.[137] 'It's a groundplan,' Larry would later admit, the map to the entire *Quintet*.[138]

If Larry was finding *Monsieur* difficult to write, it was because he knew that so much depended on the structure that he was erecting. He was also intimately involved in the present tense: the 'famous death-map'[139] that

Piers keeps on the wall to record the passing of friends had its original in Larry's home, and Verfeuille, the dilapidated château inherited by Piers and his sister Sylvie, combines elements of several antiquities Larry knew as a guest, from that of Villevieille adjacent to Sommières to the Nuits-St-Georges home of Reynaldo Simony, his daughter Penelope's godfather. Larry set Verfeuille somewhere near Les Baux, 'high on the westward slopes of the Alpilles [where] from the highest orchard you can see not only misty Avignon in the plains below, but snatches of Arles and Tarascon as well'.[140] Near Les Baux wove the weird and hellish Val d'Enfer. At first Larry called his book simply 'Le Monsieur', but later he would subtitle the novel 'The Prince of Darkness' to emphasize the undercurrent of a death-drifting world. 'As an Englishman', he would explain piously, 'I've always assumed the devil was French.'[141] Among other local landmarks re-created in *Monsieur* is the sanatorium which becomes Sylvie's refuge, modelled on and named for the real Montfavet, 'the great straggling asylum'[142] south of Avignon, and faithfully reproduced in many details down to the small chapel in a hilltop grove of olives.

Larry had recently joined a 'lunch club' in Avignon that had provided him with 'a number of small savants . . . schoolmasters who have written a monograph, a mayor with an interest in ghosts and buried treasure'. It was really a form of lonely hearts club, and published a brochure in which widows and widowers printed their photographs and salient statistics. Larry advertised himself in this milieu not as a famous author but as 'un comptable' – an accountant – seeking companionship.[143] He was richly rewarded with background for the *Quintet*. Besides, he found the situation more amusing 'than anything Mr Pickwick thought up': 'Imagine lunching twice a fortnight outdoors under a tree with Raimu, Fernandel and company . . . and playing boules afterwards in a beret.'[144]

It had long been Larry's habit to drink his way through bouts of artistic sterility, to go through his rosary of wines – scarlet Fitou, red Corbières, Pic Saint-Loup, Pic Sainte-Barbare, Listel du Sable – far into the night. Now he was finding it impossible to heed the doctors' advice and reduce his drinking, as Joan Bird discovered when she reappeared in his life. Peter was retiring from the RAF at the end of their tour in Israel, and she proposed to see Larry on her way through Marseille. When he failed to turn up at the rendezvous, she rode with a French family as far as Lunel, where Larry finally came to fetch her. She found him so much the worse for drink that she did not think he could drive safely.[145]

His nose, barometer of his habits, was beyond returning to its youthful snub shape. Repeatedly, Larry found himself compared to W. C. Fields. Sappho, who seldom lost an opportunity to scold her father, went to a Fields film festival and told Larry that she would have recognized his nose anywhere.[146]

ONE OF THE BURDENS ON Larry's mind and exchequer was the upkeep of the Mazet Michel, and in May 1971 Gerry took this off his hands by leasing the property for a year. Larry did not like Jacquie any better, but he approved of his favourite sibling being in the *mazet*. Here was an echo of the old times in Corfu: the brothers Durrell within a few miles of each other, in easy range of a shared, rambling meal, a good booze-up or an argument. Gradually the two men were drawn closer together than they had ever been.

For all their similarities, nowhere was the difference in philosophy between the two brothers shown more vividly than in Larry's refusal to believe in the feasibility of *any* active intervention in the way things are, in contrast to Gerry's equally strong belief that one had to get out there and *do something*. Since the 1940s at least, Larry had renounced all belief in meaningful political or other public action: only in changing the way people thought did any hope for improvement lie. Gerry was certainly aware of the need to change thinking, but as a conservationist he was even more acutely aware that time was running out: a pink pigeon could not wait until the citizens of Mauritius could be educated on the importance of preserving habitats or of *not* eating the last few pink pigeons. Within a decade, from the time he first visited Mauritius, the last pink pigeon would have gone the way of the dodo, also indigenous to Mauritius, had not Gerry stepped in and established a captive breeding programme on Jersey. In their shared despair – black, mordant, sometimes cheerful – Larry and Gerry came together. Larry thought that time was running out: the 'divine entropy' that mandated the thermal extinction of the universe found its complement in the decay of human bonds and therefore of society, and the chance that he or anyone else could reverse this decay by teaching women and men to 'make love correctly' was slim indeed. Gerry knew with equal certainty the power of the forces arrayed against him: his cherished pink pigeons or St Lucian hutias or Madagascan lemurs would probably end up in someone's cooking pot the moment his back was turned, or at least they would become extinct when their habitats were destroyed by the inexorable crush of expanding human populations and industrial depredations. If Larry and Gerry both often drank for effect, it was at least in part to dull the edge of a pessimism each felt.

Larry was glad to be quit of the worry of the Mazet Michel, and the same month another burden left him, when he suddenly found himself indifferent to tobacco: he had smoked 'delicious Gauloises Bleues' all his life, had 'gone through the agony of wilfully trying to stop it', and now, without apparent effort of will, he was indifferent to tobacco. He credited yoga, since he had done nothing else that might explain his sudden release from the narcotic weed. He increased his *asanas* to an hour each day.[147]

For many years Larry's indulgences had been kind to him. He had pursued many women, but most did not seem to hold grudges, forgiving him his angers and his infidelities, and he had never been thrashed or shot at by irate husbands or rivals. Mary Mollo sometimes called him 'Old *mille-e-tre*'. This avocation at least showed no signs of impairing his health and it certainly did wonders for his inspiration, 'so long as I remain on the Gold Standard', he would add with a small chuckle.[148] He became quite proud of his double lotus headstand, which he performed naked in his bedroom, leaving the door open. 'Yehudi can play the violin standing on his head', said Larry of his friend and yoga master. 'When I can write a poem on my head I will have accomplished something.'[149] Also, by May his eczema had 'just departed', he hoped for good.[150] His optimism turned out to be ill-founded.

On 22 June 1971 Larry left for York to spend a week with Sappho. She drew a set of illustrations for her father's comic poem, *On the Suchness of the Old Boy*, to be published the following April in an edition of 226 copies by Bernard Stone. Larry began the poem in the tone of Lewis Carroll:

> Such was the sagacious Suchness of the Sage
> That all of a sudden in his old age
> [. . .]
> He became Umptious in the highest degree.

The Sage sounds suspiciously like Larry, for 'A heraldic uproariousness of mind possessed him'. Larry concluded with a paraphrase of the epigraph from de Sade that he had affixed to *Justine*:

> *I tell myself while pouring out a drink,*
> *Things are less complicated than you think.*
> *Dreams, therefore crimes, honey,*
> *Dreams, therefore crimes.*[151]

Sappho's illustrations are witty – a caricature of her father with a coiled serpent body – and suggestive: an anthropomorphic animal with a woman's breasts, a mouse with a head like a pen nib. Her cover drawing shows a frieze of female figures, not quite human but strongly suggesting human pregnancy. At about the same time Larry composed 'The Ophite', a poem named after the sect which identified the Holy Spirit as 'the first woman' and the serpent as man's benefactor. This poem he dedicated '*For Saph*'. In it he discusses 'the heartwhole'

> . . . whose cool apples conspire
> Against the serpent like all perverse fruit;
> Which identify with sin but remain innocent.

Larry concluded, 'Believe what you prefer./ No advice worth giving is worth taking.'[152] If Larry was counselling his daughter to 'remain innocent' despite her knowledge, he was certainly being ambiguous. But Larry did not believe in condescending to anyone; he saw the evolved woman as the means for the redemption of mankind, and he surely hoped that Sappho, bright and daring as she was, would develop into one of these paragons.

GRADUALLY, BY ALMOST IMPERCEPTIBLE shifts in attitude and acquaintance, Larry was becoming increasingly attuned to his adopted France. Towards the end of June he was in Paris at the home of Michèle Arnaud where he met Jacques Lacarrière, poet, hiker, environmentalist, writer on the gnostics. Larry had already discovered Lacarrière's *La cendre et les étoiles*, and had arranged to have copies sent to Henry Miller and Denis de Rougemont. Larry found Lacarrière a 'nice cool balanced Alan Wattish chap' with a 'petite amie' who struck him as a 'young Justine'. Lacarrière combined a formidable erudition, which included excellent Greek, with the stocky, powerful physique of a mountain guide. Later at the Coupole Larry remembered becoming 'rather drunk'.[153]

Larry returned to Sommières for a month with Margaret McCall, followed by ten days with Eleonore Hirt, and then in mid-August he motored off for 'a sort of International jamboree', his expenses paid, in Geneva. There he enjoyed further meetings with Denis de Rougemont. He also met Claude Kiefer, wife of a doctor in Geneva and friend of Salvador Dali who, Larry claimed, had painted her face in his crowd scenes. She was honey-blonde enough to remind him of the first Claude, wore white lace, and allowed her small green iguana to clamber across her golden hair. It seemed an excellent omen for *Monsieur* that she hailed from Périgord and could have come from a Cathar hagiography.

Larry always claimed to be one of the 'uxorious Irish', yet he seemed in no hurry to remarry after Claude's death. There were plenty of candidates, but either Larry rejected them or they him. Also, he seemed invariably to fall for married women. Always intrigued with the idea of suicide, Larry was perhaps only partially jesting when he confided to Henry Miller, 'If I can't write a novel or marry someone like Lou Andreas Salomé, I'll kill myself.'[154] As a safeguard, he was nearly always at work on a novel, and he kept searching for his own version of Salomé. His choice for 'someone like Lou' was devolving on Claude Kiefer. They celebrated a romantic meeting on 24 September 1971 at Orta, a lovely village on a peninsula projecting into Lake Orta, where Nietzsche had roamed the hills with the twenty-year-old Lou Salomé. The day before Claude arrived he picked up an obituary of George Seferis, 'a cruel piece of jump-cutting'. 'People', he said, 'have no right to do this to their friends.'[155] If anything, the news of Seferis's death heightened Larry's anticipation of Claude's arrival and his own musings about the Nietzsche/Lou, Durrell/Claude congruence.

So protective of Lou's memory did Larry become that he was furious over what he saw as the distortions in Rudolf Binion's biography of Salomé and wanted to write a rebuttal.[156] It was Lou Salomé's 'wicked sexy spirit', he said, that had 'started off the whole thing in Geneva'. In associating Claude with Lou Salomé, Larry was paying homage to another giant among his favourites, Rainer-Maria Rilke. In fact, Larry had once said there was 'only one thing' that he would have liked to have written: *The Notebook of Malte Laurids Brigge*.[157] To Larry's impassioned mind, the tryst with Claude brought him closer to the spirits of Nietzsche and Rilke.

Since the end of 1969, Larry had been aware that Arthur Guirdham was also writing on the Cathar and Templar heresies. Guirdham believed fervently in reincarnation, and in 1970 he had published a book, *The Cathars and Reincarnation*, in which he set forth evidence for anachronistic memories, remembrances that could not be explained in the contexts of the current lifetimes of patients he had psychoanalysed. Larry would later explain his characters in *The Avignon Quintet* as 'circulating in each other's bloodstreams', and this is what Guirdham believed his own character-set had been doing across time. The Cathar girl, burned at the age of eighteen in an *auto da fé* during the thirteenth century – whom he claimed that he had known in an early incarnation – this girl Guirdham had recently discovered resurrected in one of his young patients, 'Mrs Smith', who was able to describe the nature of her ages-past lover, the thirteenth-century proto-Guirdham: 'A little arrogant, possibly a little conceited, and liked to get his own way.' 'It is positively depressing', Guirdham commented in his deadpan manner, 'but I cannot see that I have changed a great deal over seven hundred years.'[158] Larry and Guirdham had a second meeting, and such was the gravity with which Guirdham spoke – seriously, yet with the passion of an old prophet – that it was quite impossible to laugh at him, even had Larry been so inclined. A few years later Guirdham would write another book about reincarnation, *We Are One Another*, which was also philosophically in tune with Larry's thinking on the breakdown of the discrete ego. Larry encouraged Claudine Brelet, as perhaps the most spiritual woman he knew, to contact Guirdham, who soon named Claudine to Larry as a possible translator of his work.[159]   Larry's life and his art were merging, despite the fact that there was no Nancy to fight the battles of *The Black Book* with, no Eve or Claude to inhabit the past and present while he shaped *The Alexandria Quartet*. Rather, *Monsieur* and its siblings sprang from a larger but less visible tapestry of Larry's life: from his imaginings as much as from his experiences, his conversations and his reading. In the interstices of the late nights of song, talk and laughter, the early morning plunges into river, pool and sea, the morning hours and days of writing, had always been the books of other writers. Larry had escaped formal education relatively untouched: for worse or better. His reading had been haphazard, but it had been fairly comprehensive despite his disclaimers. Asked in 1974 to introduce John Canning's *100 Great Books: Masterpieces of All Time* – which incidentally included Larry's *Quartet* – he confessed that it was a 'chastening experience to confront this log-book of the European voyage'. Unfortunately, Larry admitted, he was not one of the 'happy band' that had read everything on the list. He had 'several' gaps that greater industry might have plastered over, but he was not apologetic: 'I have not dealt as honestly with Aristotle as he deserves,' Larry admitted, and 'my antipathy to Milton has made me fearfully unjust to him because he bores me'.[160] Where Larry was not bored, however, he devoured idiosyncratic chunks. A speculation attributed to the novelist Sutcliffe in *Monsieur* fitted Larry with precision: 'Let us suppose a man world-weary and world-travelled, who has spent a lifetime hunting for a philosophy and a woman to match.'[161]

Out of loyalty to Henry Miller, Larry flew to California at the end of 1971, taking Margaret McCall along, for a gala celebration of Henry's eightieth birthday at the UCLA Research Library. Henry's helper, Connie Combs, met their plane and chauffeured Larry and Margaret to Pacific Palisades. 'All of a glorious drunken (or semi-drunken) evening', wrote Henry to Claude Kiefer, 'he was at the top of his form, never more subtle, boisterous, elusive and diabolically Irish'.[162]

From Los Angeles Larry and Margaret flew straight to Dublin for a belated first visit to the land he liked to claim as his own. A young man named Richard Pine, whose father had edited *Burke's Peerage*, was to speak on Larry's writing at Trinity College and Larry was to deliver a response. Larry had told Pine that he wanted a double room as he 'might bring a companion'. He and Margaret were nearly refused lodging at the Shelbourne when she refused to register as 'Mrs Durrell'. None the less, Margaret was very protective of Larry, very proprietary, steering him, hovering. Officially, Larry's sojourn was a rousing success, the whiskies 'tangy', and the people, 'while not specially beautiful', he found endowed with 'eyes of such heart-stopping blue candour'.[163] Larry was treating his eczema with Silcock Base, a preparation he had discovered in Dublin, and it brought considerable relief.[164] Pine and his companion drove Margaret McCall and Larry to the Wicklow Hills for a picnic in the wintry sunshine. Margaret grabbed Larry under the arm and ran off downhill with him, his short legs spinning frantically. He laughed and seemed in good humour, but later on Pine froze at the wheel of the car when he registered the words coming from the back seat: 'You aren't the woman I'm looking for. I want an *artist*, I want someone *young*.'[165] Although Larry wrote affectionately to Henry of 'this enchanting town' and of his visit with Margaret on 23 January to Joyce's Martello Tower 'under the most brilliant rainbow I've ever seen',[166] the sadness of his break with her echoes through his short poem 'Dublin', written soon after:

> That rainbow over Joyce's tower
> Was another rare deceit,
> Raising once more those vaulting hopes
> You soon proved counterfeit.[167]

The blame for the failure of their relationship, he felt, was hers, although he told Alan Thomas that it had been 'my decision and hard to make'.[168]

There was to be an epilogue to the break between Margaret and Larry. On their return from Ireland they spent a few days with the Thomases, and sat quarrelling and talking in the top-floor room. 'If I seemed a bit distrait the last morning it was because we didn't get a wink of sleep all night', Larry confessed to Alan and Shirley, 'having decided to break up the whole affair rather than drift on like a sort of minor Bulletin, carefully slotted into BBC programmes.' He continued, 'I rather like that girl despite . . . her infantile stagey notions about life and love.' She still refused to divorce her husband and marry him, Larry said, and he had become savage in his invective: 'After so long and persistent a pursuit I called her bluff (it wasn't bluff) and accused her of scalp hunting (very unjust).' 'Et voilà; how tedious all this love-bleat i[s]!' he concluded; 'I shall cure myself with green salads.' It was not like Larry to spill his romantic upheavals before even such close friends, but Larry knew that Shirley and Alan liked Margaret, and he felt a need to justify himself. But he also told the Thomases that in a few days 'my Circassian looking Frenchy comes down through the snows of Geneva to spend just two nights with me'.[169] He was at once melancholy and expectant.

It suited Larry's mood to be writing a note on Jules Laforgue for the *Mercure de France*: Larry singled out the 'unique ironic melancholy' and 'tremendous sadness' of Laforgue, which grew, he claimed, 'out of a deep insight into the tragic nature of things'. Deep within himself, Larry responded to Laforgue's ironic humour, towards which he too strove: 'Laforgue brought an irony which is the kind of tone that soldiers advancing into battle permit themselves. They have no hope, but they have a last minute gaiety.'[170]

DESPITE HIS LONELINESS and his various insecurities, Larry was not quite sure that he wanted to curtail his freedom with another marriage. Sometimes his solitude was noisily fractured by a visit from the young woman he called 'Buttons', an employee of the Department of Antiquities at the Sorbonne. She was almost thirty but she looked much younger, with a girl's small-breasted figure, as dark-haired as Claude Kiefer was blonde, and not languorous but tremendously energetic. Often she was none too fastidious either, and once Marcelle, with her French peasant's passion for cleanliness, had announced, 'She's not sleeping here!' but had relented after giving Buttons a sound scrubbing.[171] One day Larry drove Buttons to Vaumort, where they walked in the 'careless cemetery' and drank *vin nouveau*, watching the bees come and go from their hives in the half-exposed caskets: 'You pour some wine upon a tomb', Larry was to write in his poetry notebook; 'The bees drink with us, the dead approve.' Larry would, he said, remember Vaumort whenever he wanted to be 'perfectly alone' with her memory: 'In the long grass you found a ring, remember?'[172] Was this another lost ring, or was he consciously reliving the 'incident of the ring/ Lost in the grass: her laughter',[173] tossed almost as an aside into his much earlier poem 'The Octagon Room', written two years before he moved to France, and long before he met Buttons? Whatever the answer, Larry was certainly conscious of the reverberation, tricking time.

In his search for new companions, new adventures, Larry was still reluctant to relinquish past ties, and he kept seeing Margaret McCall who, on her part, was jealous of Buttons. 'Look at her – she's just a child!' Larry would say, taunting Margaret with her age. 'She's *thirty*!' Margaret would remind him.[174]

Scratching his hide, Larry kept awakening to the howling mistral. He was suffering also from insomnia, 'my old enemy', and, like his characters in *Monsieur*, he would set out into the darkness: 'Taken to walking at night now,' he wrote, 'long walks cross country; gives a wierd [*sic*] upside down feeling to the world – one with cats and foxes and night porters and criminals etc etc.'[175] Larry, proclaiming himself to be in 'the nadir of despond about this Margaret break – bodywork damaged and paintwork scratched',[176] fancied himself a hermit and he decided that what he needed as guardians of his hermitage were owls. They could live in his tower, a closed stuccoed structure at the south-east corner of the property, at one end of the swimming pool. The top part of the tower was a water tank, no longer needed because of improvements in the town water supply. Larry had his plumber cut a small hole in the tank and Gerry provided him with a special earth that owls like to have in their lodgings. Soon a pair of white barn owls moved in and Larry watched, delighted, as they raised their first family. The owls were silent and companionable. '*Mes dames blanches*', he called them.[177] Larry would often sit quietly under the trees to see them emerge in the evenings. Sometimes the young ones would fall into the pool and have to be rescued or would flutter softly against the glass of the Darjeeling Room, whewing in alarm.

As his sixtieth birthday approached, Larry decided that, despite his hatred of celebrating such signposts, he would throw a party. He couched the invitation in terms calculated to avoid taking anything for granted: 'Si je suis encore debout le 27 Février, DIMANCHE, j'aurai soixante ans.' 'If I am still around . . .' was becoming part of his cautionary formula. He would need sympathy on this occasion, so would his friends come to 'boire un verre (Champagne? Ciguë?)' and stay for lunch? He signed it, 'Lugubrement.'[178]

Larry's collected poems were being translated into French by Alain Bosquet, whom Larry visited at his Paris home. One evening he dined there with Ionesco, a most amusing man, Larry wrote to Henry Miller: 'What a clown he is, better than his own plays.'[179] Larry was not to develop his acquaintance with Ionesco, but when on the same trip he met Simone Lestoquard, a young Languedocienne artist working in Paris, he was smitten by her paintings, drawings and her beauty, and he invited her to visit him in Sommières.

He discovered that Simone Lestoquard knew the Cathar sites of the sub-Pyrenean region and enlisted her aid in searching out background for *Monsieur*. Together they drove in his blue Escargot to Lagrasse beyond Narbonne, then south through Mouthoumet, Duilhac and Cucugnan, before returning to Lagrasse via Félines and Laroque de Fa, names fragrant with heresy. Together they climbed to the breathless height of ruined Queribus, place of violent winds and site of the last siege of the Albigensian Crusade. They also visited Arques and Rennes-le-Château, inhabited towns that had gained notoriety during the late nineteenth century through the story that an obscure priest at the latter, Bérenger Saunière, had discovered the Holy Grail along with evidence that the wedding at Cana had been Christ's own.[180] In *Monsieur* Larry would weave the downfall of the Templars in 1307 with the Cathar heresies of the preceding century. Added to the pleasure of touring the Cathar lands with Simone was the fact that this was the domain of Corbières wines, one of Larry's standard table vintages. Larry saw Simone as a rare intelligence and an exotic creature, and he came to refer to her as 'my lovely long legged sand-leopard girl'.[181]

LARRY'S ECZEMA WAS back in force, and one day towards the end of March 1972 he stopped at a market stall in Arles to talk to a herbalist. He came home with an olive oil ointment and a tisane: burdock, lavender, wild hops, mixed with other medicinal plants. Larry had Marcelle brew up a potion. 'It's supposed to last three months the cure', he wrote to Henry, 'BUT AFTER TEN DAYS THE ECZEMA HAS COMPLETELY VANISHED. IT'S A BLOODY MIRACLE.'[182] Larry wrote to Ludovic Chardenon, the herbal doctor, describing the 'miracle' and asking to see him again. Soon Larry was back in Arles as guest of Ludo and his young wife Martine. Ludo was a large man with gargantuan appetites, a mane of unruly hair that had entirely abandoned the top of his head, and a store of amazing yarns, but he was completely serious about his calling, one that he had learned from his grandmother. He was also a man of some culture, with a theory that his cures went back to Roman and Greek medicine. Ludo claimed to be able to treat anything from a spider bite to emphysema. He was also a superb cook, and the marinated meats grilled outdoors over a fire of vine trimmings, served under a great fig tree, and moistened with several litres of good country wine 'fortified with a recipe from my grandmother', Ludo recalled, put them all 'in rare form'. Larry wanted to know every aspect of

Ludo's craft, and his new friend explained how, with only a quarter of an acre, he could subsist on his plants.[183]

Without telling Ludo what he intended, Larry quickly wrote a substantial article, 'The Plant-Magic Man', which he posted to the *New York Herald Tribune*. What Larry most admired about Ludo was how inherently he fitted into Provence, which he was constantly criss-crossing to collect herbs. 'By now the thyme will be best around Sommières', he had told Larry, 'and the wild bourdane around Les Baux.'[184] The essay appeared in July 1972, and Ludo's life was transformed as hundreds of orders and letters – mainly in English, which he did not know – poured in. Larry's 'Plant-Magic Man' soon appeared in the *Daily Telegraph*, and Jacques Temple translated it for the *Midi Libre*. Larry would maintain his commitment to Ludo's cause over the years, promoting the publication of Ludo's text in French, English and German, inveigling Gerry to compose a preface, and convincing Claudine Brelet's husband, Dr Rueff, to introduce Ludo's *Mémoires et recettes*. Through all the fame and considerable financial success, Ludo and Martine kept up the same hard-working peasant life, processing herbs and travelling to village markets. Ludo became one of Larry's most trusted friends – trusted except for his driving. Grimly, Larry described a trip he had made in Ludo's old Peugeot estate car 'at a hundred miles an hour' on the narrow roads. Suddenly Ludo had slammed on the brakes, got out, kicked and tugged at a front tyre, explaining, 'I thought I felt something – that wheel sometimes falls off.'[185] Satisfied, Ludo eased himself back into the car and roared off. He was reassuring evidence for Larry that 'everything with colour and sap and grace' had not vanished in the modernization of Provence,[186] and he would write Ludo into *The Avignon Quintet* as the Honey Man, an itinerant pedlar of natural products.

More excitement came to Larry's door when Fiddle Viracola, touring the Camargue with a friend, dropped in. 'I have to bear down rather hard on young Fiddle because she suffers from horrible jealousy,' Larry told Henry Miller. Larry was annoyed because, he said, Fiddle had told people the year before that he was marrying Michèle Arnaud – which he had no thought of doing, nor had Michèle any intention of leaving her husband. Now, to tease Fiddle, Larry claimed to be marrying Saroya, whom he had met on Corfu, 'at the end of the month'. Gleefully he reported Fiddle's response: 'She screamed: YIU *Cant* sell your body to that hooker.' Weaving deftly among his lady loves, Larry noted that Buttons was pregnant 'by person or persons unknown' – not by him *bien sûr*.[187]

By 2 May 1972 Larry was again at Orta, the lake 'girdle[d]' with snowy mountains, to await Claude Kiefer. He would plant a tribute to her inspirational quality towards the end of *Monsieur*: 'A writer big with book I hurried to Orta like a harvest in peril.'[188] He had brought *Daniele*, his own small boat, and planned to spend May on the Italian lakes. They held a rendezvous at Stresa on Lago Maggiore, for which their secret name was Vega:

> This we called Vega, a sly map-reference
> Coded in telegrams the censored name to
> 'Vega next tenth of May. Okay?'
> 'Okay.' 'Okay.' You came.

He wove fantasies about her claimed descent from the Cathar heretics, and they both pretended that neither her husband nor her two sons knew of their meetings. Larry courted discovery, naming first a poem and then his entire 1973 collection *Vega*. Claude Kiefer became his 'fixed star', 'another Vega'. There was a quiet perfection for Larry in these trysts held

> By this lake which parodies a new life
> With a boat outside the window, breathing.

It was the silence that he now craved:

> Ah! The beautiful sail so unerringly on towards death
> Once they experience the pith of this peerless calm.[189]

He had attained the kind of ease with her that had eluded him in most of his other relationships. She had a gentleness and a directness that precluded misunderstandings, and she did not set herself up to compete with him. When Henry Miller, turning lyrical over Larry's descriptions of Claude, would name her later as 'ésotérique' and 'mythologique', Claude brought 'Cher Henry' up short: she is not one of those who turns delirious over Shelley on the Acropolis under the full moon, she wrote to him, 'Mais je suis surtout bien simplement quelqu'un qui aime le bonheur et aimerait le répandre autour d'elle: ce qui n'est pas toujours facile.'[190] How could Larry not love this woman!

Larry had found a flat over a boathouse, and they dined in his rooms, with a single candle, 'watching sunset, until the evening star takes over with its queer palpitating glitter'. He was reading Catullus in a parallel text, joyful because his school Latin turned out to be still there. With Claude he made another Nietzschean pilgrimage up the Sacro Monte, talking of Lou

Salomé; 'A light silver rain fell and became dew as it landed on our clothes.'
Then the sun burst forth and a cuckoo sang. 'That night deep fog blown
apart by a thunderstorm as powerful as an artillery barrage,' Larry
recalled, while 'The lake slithered about and seethed and boiled.' The
storms were 'divinely Byronic'. He felt flooded with well-being, happy with
Claude and happy alone when she returned to Geneva. 'I light a fire and a
bit of joss', he wrote, 'and cook something simple. Then I read some Arthur
Waley Chinese poems, or Catullus or a life of Epicurus or beloved John
Donne and perhaps make some notes for this bloody book which wont
really get off the floor because laziness I suppose.'[191] He resolved to reread
Horace and Tibullus. Sometimes he composed a poem destined for the
Vega volume. Claude, Stresa, Orta, Vega – it was such perfect interludes
that restored his faith in himself, helped him return to his work.

IN MID-SEPTEMBER 1972 Larry was in Paris for a meeting with Anne and
Fred Perlès, on their way back to Cyprus. Larry invited Michèle Arnaud
along – one of his schemes was to enlist her help in placing Fred's work in
France. The party began at the Dôme, from which Larry and Fred wrote a
joint postcard to Henry: 'As usual you are the sleeping partner', said Larry
reproachfully, 'what a pity you aren't here'. The party moved to the
Coupole, floating on champagne and *fine à l'eau*.[192]

For several days Larry spent money lavishing food and drink on Anne
and Fred, but as soon as he was back in Sommières he heaped venom upon
Anne, complaining to Henry that she had opened up 'as usual with a lot of
stupid opinions – she really hates you, and says openly that Joe is a much
better writer; then she turns on him and says "Joe is going to do this, Joe is
going to do that" and Joe instead of smashing a bottle on her head sits there
cowed and larmoyant nodding and saying Ja Ja. It is heartrending to
watch.' Larry's main charges were that Anne abused Henry and had
muzzled Fred, stopped his art, 'sucked the life out of him', and that he had
only livened up when Larry could get him to the Dôme without his
'perambulating haggis'. Even then, Fred was not at ease, but kept 'sort of
looking over his shoulder until she looms into sight, when he makes a sort
of involuntary tidying up gesture, like doing up his flics or something'.[193]
Henry agreed about Fred '*and* that monster Anne!', adding 'D'accord avec
toi sur tous les points.'[194] The feelings of both men were largely
reciprocated by Anne: protective of Fred, she openly disliked Henry and
had little use for Larry.[195]

Larry did not exempt himself and Henry from criticism, but thought that

Fred had betrayed more than his person: his writing. 'I was thinking that we have all made disastrous choices as far as women are concerned, me particularly', Larry told Henry, 'but we have never surrendered our creative side to them.' What Larry did not add was that neither he nor Henry had surrendered his self-indulgence either. Ultimately, the women in their lives had always been less important than doing what each wanted to do – and that had been to write, to paint. Fred, far from feeling 'hollowed out like one of those insects in Fabre', as Larry suggested,[196] seemed quite content to burrow into the protective nest that Anne provided. To all appearances, Anne and Fred Perlès had achieved a balanced and affectionate marriage, and it would last for more than forty years. The other two musketeers were quite likely, on a subconscious level, pricked with a certain envy. Anne had a wonderfully wicked sense of humour, kept an immaculate house on very little money, and praised Fred to the treetops. She alternately egged on and reined in Fred; he twinkled and performed for visitors, ostentatiously playing the role of a husband who had slipped his chain.

Larry's creative side had not been very active during 1972, but he managed a flash of optimism: 'My novel has picked itself up and I'm getting a bit of traction at last and I hope to God I can finish it by Christmas,' he wrote to Henry in September.[197] He did not make it. Well into December he was still only on page 125 of *Monsieur*, 'this exasperating book which keeps trying to dictate to me like a bloody schoolmistress', and he had to confess 'it doesn't feel as if it is started yet'.[198]

Larry had just accepted an invitation to spend the first three months of 1974 at Caltech, the California Institute of Technology in Pasadena, a suburb of Los Angeles. He was offered a handsome stipend and full travel expenses in exchange for teaching a seminar on English literature and for giving a public lecture. Larry accepted, knowing that he would be living within easy visiting range of Henry and Anaïs. The trip a year hence would also give him a target date for finishing *Monsieur* – and he knew that he worked better under a strong threat.

Since at least 1971 Larry had been entertaining Catha Aldington's friend Ghislaine de Boysson, who had been to Hollywood and who knew a host of film people, who knew Aristotle Onassis and his moneyed circle. Ghislaine spoke a glib, accented English, laughed freely, and wore tight slacks and low-cut blouses. She allowed Larry to keep refilling her glass, and visitors noticed that she could not keep her hands off him.[199] Her love for Larry was evident, and while in private he would have enjoyed the attention, he found it irritating to be fondled possessively when others were present. He alternated being cruel towards her, then contrite and affectionate. Larry kept refilling his own glass also, far too frequently as he realized. He began to speak of his drinking in terms of illness, announcing to Henry that, thanks to yoga, he had had 'two good remissions'. His aim was not to stop drinking but 'at least limit and control my alcohol intake', which was 'wasteful moneywise as well as healthwise'. Since the red and white wines that were his house vintages at this time tended to cost under eight francs a bottle – about a dollar or fifty pence – cost was not really a factor. When he switched to whisky or gin, it was another matter. He valued 'healthy walking and easy muscles', but usually contented himself with yoga headstands.[200]

The year ended on a note of peaceful ease. Larry took the olives from the frost-stunted trees at the Mazet Michel to the mill for crushing. It was not for the money so much as for the pleasure of having his own olive oil, 'the green oil they call *vierge*', like any prosperous Midi husbandman. Claude Kiefer came down for a visit, and he loved her and the season: 'Log fires, champagne, roast chestnuts, music, candles, quietness, and long silent sleeps just waking and falling asleep like the deep sea breathing.'[201]

AT THE BEGINNING OF 1973 Michèle Arnaud's two-year-old ambition of interviewing Henry Miller in California for French television suddenly matured, and she proposed to take Larry along to Los Angeles. They planned to fly over on 10 February. 'Lay in a case of champagne (specify BRUT)', Larry scrawled in a quick handwritten note to Henry, 'and I'll refund you when I come – unless you've drunk it all.' Larry wanted Fred to join them, alone. 'I've told M. to try and detach [*sic*] Joe from that sad old scorpion for the occasion but . . . . I don't know if she can.'[202] Fred stayed at home. The filming was a great success, so Michèle and the cameraman thought, with Henry speaking discursively and both men spending half the time in French. 'You do it so easily and with such enjoyment – never showing off like me, the crazy actor,' said Larry.[203]

Larry was on such an ample champagne regime that Henry remarked that he would have been better off drinking Scotch. 'You can't keep this up forever, you know,' he told Larry. 'It's sheer suicide.'[204] Larry was too good a drinker not to have a string of extenuating circumstances and excuses: thanks to his 'strong tolerance' he was still in good shape; he wanted 'to control not abolish' his drinking, but hoped that this control would arrive naturally, 'not a torture coming from will power'; alcohol helped him cope with his eczema – which had returned, despite Ludo's treatments. 'I blot myself out at night to avoid scratching in my sleep – often awake in a pool of blood,' he said.[205] Almost certainly his drinking contributed to his eczema, but this he would not admit.

Henry amazed everyone with his 'wonderful athletic stamina'. In fact, despite his smoking and one almost useless leg – he kept postponing a hip replacement – he won 'those tremendous games of ping-pong!' On his return to Sommières, Larry said, 'I had to admit to the village that once more I had been thrashed, and so we couldn't ring the church bells as they had promised.' He had also caught a cold and lost his mackintosh with the mustard-yellow lining.[206] No matter. It had been a marvellous visit.

Larry found the return trip from Los Angeles 'astonishing' – apparently it was his first long flight in a jumbo jet, 'a sort of flying cathedral'. He flew 'north into Canada first and then across the frozen wastes of Greenland with a wierd [sic] moon among the icebergs'. Larry turned a hitch in the course of his homecoming to good account: a French air strike disrupted his connections in London, so he rerouted his flight to Geneva where he telephoned Claude. 'She rushed down in a taxi', Larry said, and like a pair of truant students, 'we spent the day together in the bookshops and pubs and walking by the frozen lake in a stiff bise which blew my cold away'. The next day he took the Catalan Express to Nîmes, and found his house warm despite the mistral and stocked with provisions by the maid. 'This morning I celebrated with a full yoga and a long walk in the garrigues,' he told Henry, full of a sense of well-being.[207]

Larry was optimistic about 1973: everything was going to change for him. 'I may find a girl more thrilling than the army of spectres I have now,' said he, being distinctly unfair to some very attractive women – as he knew: he kept telling people how wonderful Claude Kiefer was, but that she must not desert her family for him. Jacques Temple's *Entretiens* volume devoted to essays about him and photographs going back to the days in India was due to appear soon, a 'boost to flagging morale'. 'Feel like resuming my novel even,' he told Henry.[208] In April he went to London for the English publication of *The Black Book* – a mere thirty-five years after its appearance in Paris – and of the *Vega* poems.

Larry had seen relatively few films in the past twenty years. Indeed, not since his Paris and London days in the 1930s had he been a frequent filmgoer, and in 1960 he had denigrated the cinema industry to a pair of *Réalités* interviewers: 'It's a pity that sound was invented in film because it prevents film from ever becoming a great medium of expression.'[209] None the less, he agreed to be a judge at the Cannes Film Festival during May. When he was asked by a press interviewer whether he had the patience and humility to be a member of the jury, he replied, 'Non. C'est pourquoi on m'a invité, je pense.' Could he view twenty films with the innocence of a child seeing the cinema for the first time? 'Oui, imputresciblement!', incorruptibly, replied Larry, stretching the sense of the word for all it was worth. 'Je ne suis qu'un enfant invétéré', an eternal child.[210]

He took Ghislaine de Boysson along to Cannes, partly as a prop, since she knew so many film people. Larry appeared to be in a truculent mood. He drank fluently while flirting with various actresses, and often in his company were two women who had been his lovers, Michèle Arnaud and Fiddle Viracola. He was rude to Ghislaine, and alternately ribald and morose with others. Robin Livio attempted a serious interview for *Film Français*, the official organ of the Festival. Noting that sexuality was a 'powerful motivation and quest' in his works, Livio asked Larry to explain himself. Larry began extravagantly:

La seule chose qui a de valeur et qui ait une densité spirituel est ce tragique épisode dans la vie de tout le monde: aimer. Aimer – c'est se comprendre; et tout comprendre, c'est tout imaginer. Cosmonaute de l'espace intérieur, je pars pour la lune. Adieu Cannes![211]

Sex, in fact, was as fragile as life itself and twice as interesting! Was he in favour of the prevalence of sexuality in literature, drama, cinema? Larry shifted ground to pronounce approvingly on feminine liberation, a subject on which he had often attacked Sappho. 'On célèbre la liberté de la femme pour l'instant, et j'en suis très content. . . . Hourra!' But for himself, Larry continued, he deserved a Tibetan Sherpa as secretary. 'Elle dort devant ma porte et me protège contre la schizophrénie' – like his Burmese ayah, in Larry's fantasy she slept before his door to protect him. Desperately seeking firmer ground, the interviewer asked about his 'image' of tomorrow's woman. 'Je vois un gigantesque concombre en or massif' – I see a gigantic cucumber in solid gold, said Larry in perfect deadpan, 'portant la médaille du Mérite Agricole sur la poitrine.' Livio quickly switched to less controversial queries: What was happiness for Larry? An olive fire, Bach, a good wine, freedom? This produced an explosion of evident anger: 'Malheur! Nous sommes libres tous – mais tous, sans exception, mais sans le savoir!' Freedom came with a *déclic*, and departed, *Pouf!* 'Quel singulier emmerdement!' Larry concluded. Finally, in a tone of some exasperation, Livio asked whether he had been sincere in his responses. 'Je ne suis sincère en rien – et en tout à la fois,' quipped Larry, sincere in nothing and everything.[212]

After the Cannes Festival, Ghislaine joined Larry at Mme Tartes'. 'I have been sitting down in Sommières with a new girl who is rather a dear as well as an awful ass', Larry confessed to Henry. Ominously, he added, 'I may end in marrying her against my deep deep reservations. I have never seen such an ass.'[213] Even taking into account Larry's ingrained habit of disguising his feelings, his remarks did not bode well. However, he was no longer drinking 'so hysterically', and hoped to complete *Monsieur* before leaving for Pasadena in December. By late September he called the novel finished – prematurely, as it turned out.[214]

Larry and Ghislaine were married in November. For months her laughter had rung through the old house: 'She is a little firebrand,' Larry said.[215] 'Buckle me to a wedding ring/ And make me die of laughing,' Larry had written earlier that year in 'Apesong'.[216] Still, the marriage came as a shock to his friends. Larry announced the event in a cryptic postcard to Alan Thomas: 'Just married! very sad year in perspective. Hope you will have a better one. Happy everything/ Ghislaine/ Larry D.'[217] He embellished his initial with the snub-nosed profile sketch that he had rarely used since the 1940s. He had been saying, 'I'm done with this marriage ramp,' and people who saw him at the Cannes Film Festival in Ghislaine's company did not think they would be compatible. True, Ghislaine bore a distinct physical resemblance to Claude Vincendon, and she too loved vivacious company and social entertaining, but she appeared to lack Claude's ability to take Larry's criticisms and to deflect or absorb his rages. She had been married once before when she was quite young: to a cousin who left her ten days later. She committed herself entirely to the match with Larry, giving up her apartment in Paris and selling her furniture.

Larry was intrigued by Ghislaine's aristocratic de Boysson name – 'a French aristo', he called her. Here was a version of Constance, the 'duchess of Tu' character that he was creating in *Monsieur*. That Ghislaine was neither a haughty aristocrat nor a trained professional like the young doctor Constance did not matter to Larry. She was still 'the aristo' despite the scoffing of Wallace Southam and some of his other old friends.[218] Larry said that he married her because he couldn't take a 'mistress' to Caltech. His *pudeur* called on him to have a wife; his insecurity demanded that he have a companion. Also, Ghislaine was quite at home in Los Angeles, 'and once upon a time nearly married Bing Crosby', Larry claimed; 'It sounds most distressing, but a gentleman of my age learns to overlook mistakes.'[219]

She had declined Crosby's offer, she said, because she was unwilling to make her home outside France.[220]

ALTHOUGH LARRY WOULD HAVE SCORNED the suggestion, his visit to Los Angeles with Ghislaine was almost a honeymoon trip. At first, the reunion with Henry promised to be a great success. Larry checked into the nearby Santa Inez Inn, and arrived at Henry's home in Pacific Palisades with a case of Moët champagne. As the corks popped, the laughter kept pace. Ghislaine, with her pretty French face and her gaiety, made an immediate hit with Henry. He thought her charming and intelligent 'without being an "intellectual", thank God!'[221] His spirits seemed unabated, despite having recently lost the vision in his right eye during an artery replacement operation.

Larry and Ghislaine started out determined to be tourists. On 30 December they drove to San Diego where, Larry reported, 'I nearly fondled a real whale'. He dropped in unannounced to see Suzanne Henig but missed her. Two days later he, Ghislaine and a million others watched the great Rose Parade: Larry bought a postcard of the event and posted it to Alan Thomas with the comment 'At times my Pasadena hosts put on a small show in my honour – modest but noteworthy and I find it most touching.'[222]

Whenever Henry and Larry got together, they started to laugh: it was pleasure at seeing one another; it was the postures, pauses, gestures as much as the words themselves; it was a shared past that could be evoked with a phrase. They shared a strong element of the childlike: once they simply switched the television colour balance to green and watched professional wrestling, and this set them off laughing for hours.[223] Even a trip to Forest Lawn cemetery brought out the rogue in both men. Larry indicated Henry to a stern woman caretaker: 'He's shopping – he wants to see where they make up the stiffs!' She glowered at them: 'Not very funny – out!'[224] 'I actually went to Forest Lawn to mock', Larry claimed later to a Californian interviewer, 'and came away humbled. Despite the fairground atmosphere, the beauty of the landscape was touching.'[225] The truth was layered like a palimpsest: Larry's laughter at death had a genuine existential ring, yet he invariably responded positively to green beauty. Then too there were his polite and politic sides – he wanted to show appreciation to his hosts.

J. Kent Clark, the professor of English who had been largely responsible for bringing Larry to Caltech as an Andrew J. Mellon visiting professor, saw Larry and Ghislaine comfortably settled in the Athenaeum Club, a tile-roofed building of California Spanish architecture with a courtyard partially surrounded by a horseshoe structure two stories high. Larry pronounced it 'some strange Pasadena monastery created for the retirement of Rudolph Valentino', smiling at the reference to the great film lover.[226] Then Clark took them to dinner at Myako's, an excellent Japanese restaurant, where Larry was happy to settle on a low platform, cross-legged in a lotus position. The six-foot-four Clark performed a series of contortions all evening, attempting vainly to find a comfortable way of arranging his legs.

Two dining rooms, a library and various offices and public rooms occupied the ground floor of the Athenaeum Club. Up a fine spiral staircase were two score rooms for visiting scholars, and at the open ends of each wing of the building stood a two-room suite, each with a fireplace and a large balcony. Larry and Ghislaine were given one of these, Number 20. An earlier tenant had been Albert Einstein, a coincidence that delighted Larry. 'Sleeping in Einstein's bed was a sobering experience,' he would recall with only geographical accuracy.[227]

Below the balcony a brick-paved pedestrian avenue, shaded by olive trees, led to the many laboratories and classroom buildings. The ambience was reassuringly Mediterranean. The Einstein suite did not contain a kitchen, and all the residents were expected to take their meals according to a regular schedule in the dining rooms, where diners were subject to a dress code. This did not suit Larry at all, and before long he carried a small barbecue grill and a bag of charcoal up to his balcony. Soon a plume of smoke and the smell of steaks on the grill informed the management that the Rules were being abrogated. Would Mr Durrell please refrain from lighting fires on his balcony? The fire marshal was concerned. After about six weeks of the faculty club, Larry felt thoroughly claustrophobic, and when William Wyler, known to Ghislaine from her earlier visits, offered the Durrells the use of his summer home at Malibu, Larry and Ghislaine packed their suitcases into their leased Volkswagen Beetle and drove off. They found themselves in a millionaires' beach community, some fifteen miles on the superhighways from the campus. Larry soon decided that the light Volkswagen was too dangerous for the Los Angeles freeways, and he exchanged it for a yellow Ford Mustang: a more suitable car for snobbish Malibu, in any case.

The Wyler house was bright and airy, and Larry basked like a lizard in the sunlight pouring in. Ghislaine went to the local supermarket one day with a long shopping list, but had forgotten her glasses. As she was peering short-sightedly at the labels on the shelves, a handsome sun-browned man offered to help. He smiled a geometric smile at her obvious French intonation and ended up guiding her along the aisles, filling her shopping cart. A few days later, as Larry and Ghislaine were heading towards the beach they were hailed by a tall man leaning over the parapet of his roof. It was Ghislaine's samaritan of the supermarket, who turned out to be Burt Lancaster. The occurrence was quite typical of Malibu, but it revived Larry's old tics of possessiveness and jealousy.

Teaching at Caltech was hardly onerous. Larry's one class, 'Topics in Contemporary Literature', met three mornings a week: fifteen to twenty students seated around a huge oval table, with the emphasis on discussion rather than lecturing. The students dressed casually, while Larry favoured light suits and polka-dot ties – his insecurity made him feel the need to look respectable. 'You know one has to look ridiculously and hypocritically solemn at universities,' he would recall. 'It's part of the job.'[228] Despite his boast of having stopped smoking, he manifested with a short, curved briar pipe, the likes of which he had not touched since his youth on Corfu. This probably had more to do with image than tobacco: English poets were supposed to fondle pipes. He wanted to be intelligible to Americans, however. When he was interviewed by *Los Angeles Times* columnist Digby Diehl, he asked that 'Britishisms' be cut from his statements. Larry remained his father's son: he still worried about making the right impression.

He also took his teaching seriously. 'I'm very excited to teach literature at a great center of technology like this', he said, 'because rather than a vast separation between two cultures, I see science as a force that has greatly altered poetry, literature and our whole understanding of humanism.' The students were an élite selected on the basis of Scholastic Aptitude Test scores that placed them, academically, among the top one or two per cent in the nation. True, they were aspiring scientists rather than humanists, but they were articulate, eager, and they could be counted on to read assignments. 'I've been told that I am here to "humanize" these young scientists,' Larry explained, 'but more realistically I only hope to "tenderize" them.' He assigned such works as Wells's *The Time Machine* and Huxley's *Point Counter Point*, and he tried to foster philosophic debate about the purposes of technology. 'At nearly the same time, the atom was split and the ego was split – our age takes off from that point,' he said. 'Modern technology has caused a semantic disturbance, a sort of earthquake in syntax, and in my course we're attempting to unravel the apparent obscurity of modern literature. That ought to be easy for these very bright students because it is all rooted in Einstein anyway.'[229]

Larry moved rapidly. 'When I had lunch with Shakespeare at the Huntington Library yesterday', he began conversationally when he was explaining to the students Hamlet's 'whilst this machine is to him' letter to Ophelia. In the same period he took his listeners from the changing apprehensions of machinery as evil products of the devil to Freud's notion of 'the double-sexed nature of the individual psyche'. It was up to literature, he said, to resolve this duality. When a young woman, using Latin medical terms, tried to explain away schizophrenia as merely a 'scientific phenomenon', he appeared to parry: 'Isn't it strange that all the terms of ugly diseases sound like the names of beautiful Greek goddesses.' What he was really doing was illustrating duality: beauty which is the obverse of ugliness, health the inverse of disease. Larry was sensitive to the orientation of his students: 'They are programmed to make atom bombs, not write poetry,' he recognized.[230]

Larry persuaded both Henry Miller and Anaïs Nin to make guest appearances, and each time the numbers in attendance swelled. Anaïs made a tremendous impression, lecturing and answering questions for nearly two hours, despite the cancer that had attacked her intestines and weakened this most proud and fastidious of women. Finally she drew him aside: 'Larry, I have about eleven minutes before I must simply lie down or collapse; let us wind this up.'[231]

The old solidarity of the Villa Seurat crew still lived, for when Jay Martin alarmed both Henry and Anaïs by starting work on a Miller biography, Larry proposed that she head Martin off by taking on an *authorized* biography herself. No, Anaïs responded, Larry must write the book jointly with her: then she would accept. Fine, Larry replied. The project was intended mainly to scuttle Martin – it did not – and nothing came of the proposed collaboration. Anaïs, in any case, was much too ill.

Larry was expected to give a single public lecture, and when he did the circular, domed Beckmann Auditorium, for all the world like a structure out of science fiction by Edgar Rice Burroughs, was filled to the doors. Larry showed slides and spoke autobiographically, telling his audience what it had been like to be young on Corfu. He rambled on, picking up, dropping and returning to subjects: 'Occasionally they killed a lamb, Greek lamb isn't bad, it's – well, I suppose it was horrible, our diet . . . . there was only lamb for people with small incomes but good lamb and sometimes pork .... We roasted lambs on the spit and mopped up the blood.'[232] To the intellectuals who had come to hear Great Truths spoken, it seemed that Larry was having them on, and perhaps he was. He also gave a second public lecture, called 'Propaganda and Impropaganda', a *boutade* like the earlier lecture, at Claremont College in Pomona. This talk purported to be about his diplomatic career, and he trotted out an assortment of anecdotes of dubious veracity: about the German propagandist who suborned the mullahs 'to tell the Egyptians that once Rommel came they'd all have ice cream', and about Larry's Rhodes daily that sold magnificently because the islanders needed paper to wrap fish.[233]

Larry counted the lectures as triumphs, his audiences 'madly indulgent': 'They value one more for being natural than for being clever.' All one had to do to win their sympathy was to confess to lost notes or that one had sat on one's hat. 'It's just like life', Larry recalled, 'which itself is one long mishap.' If he realized that he was not pleasing all his listeners, he never said so. In fact, he commented airily that his 'babbling in public' netted him 'often far too much money for the effort involved', so that to earn easy money this way made him feel 'a bit dishonest', a charlatan riding on 'this damned Irish charm'.[234]

Larry was not always so well under control. There was one scene in Henry's house when Larry became furious at Ghislaine during dinner: his hand flashed across the table and he slapped her. Henry, in a voice shaking with anger, told Larry that if he touched her again he would not be welcome in his house. The ancient friendship seemed to hang in the balance. Then Larry collected himself, apologized to Henry, and a tense surface calm was maintained for the rest of the evening. Henry had often told Larry that tension was what kept one alive, but when the tautness broke out in violence, Henry did not wish to be a witness.[235] Six months after Larry had returned to France, Henry would confess that he too had lashed out, years before, and that therefore he should not criticize Larry: 'I omitted to say . . . that in my fury (or my drunken state) I tried to throw Hoki down a flight of stairs and break her neck – but I failed.'[236]

Larry and Ghislaine explored the Los Angeles area but made little contact with the Caltech faculty. To Kent Clark's subsequent chagrin, Larry did not meet Richard Feinman, the Nobel Prize-winning physicist then in residence at the school: Larry might have received an infusion of post-Einsteinian theoretical physics. Some faculty members thought Larry stand-offish, but it was probably more a case of others not seeking him out. He was working on *Monsieur* whenever he could drive himself to it; he was content to spend some of his free time with Henry and, occasionally, with Anaïs Nin and Rupert Pole. Clearly, Larry was not about to become a transplant to California, despite the near-Mediterranean climate and the olives and the vines and the presence of his old Paris friends. He claimed that he would have seen more of them but for the petrol shortage[237] – but since it took only a gallon to drive in the Mustang from Malibu to Pacific Palisades, this was hardly a valid excuse. 'Just winding up a most successful and pleasant trip,' he wrote to Alan Thomas. 'Fine country S. Calif. and the most hospitable and evolved people one could hope to meet. We had a "whale" of a time in both senses.'[238] But he was glad to head back to Sommières at the end of March after being on display for three months, and the visits had somewhat strained his friendship with Henry. Their letters continued to be affectionate, and Larry would often express worry about his friend's health, but he would never return to California.

As soon as Larry had settled back into his Sommières routine, he started painting with an eye towards an Oscar Epfs exhibition in Paris in the autumn. During the fourth week of April he went alone to Paris for the publication of *Pope Joan* in a French translation, launched with the obligatory cocktail party hosted by Chastel Buchet, his publisher. He returned, according to Ghislaine, with 'an enormous flew: spiting, coughing and groaning' [*sic*]. Chastened, he then decided to be 'pretty' for the summer, and went on a regime: only one bottle of wine per day, and light on the food.[239]

His drinking drastically reduced and his nerves calmed by painting, Larry returned to *Monsieur*. As much as ever, he was nagged by self-doubt. 'One gets less and less certain of one's effects as one grows older I find,' he confessed.[240]

Within less than a year of the wedding it was obvious that Larry wanted to cast off Ghislaine. To Alan Thomas he wrote, 'I am beginning to feel old and I have sad premonitions that this marriage is going to end in a mess like the others. I hope not.'[241] His comments to friends were often spoken to her face and they could be brutal: 'She's stupid . . . and she can do my taxes,' was one blunt explanation for the match, although neither part of this statement was true. 'And she likes money,' Larry would add as a parting shot.[242] To Alan he said, 'Ghislaine is driving me mad with fruitful irritation.' Part of the problem, paradoxically, was that Ghislaine evidently did love him and took a serious view of her role as a wife: it pained her to see his self-destructive drinking, to see him behaving in ways that did not reflect credit on the Great Writer whom she was sure she had married. And she did not hesitate to attempt to set Larry straight. Gerry did a marvellous imitation of Ghislaine clicking purposefully on her high heels to confront Larry with his latest outrage. She could be an irritation to him all right, but her attempts to influence his behaviour were fruitless. 'What hell other people are,' Larry concluded.[243]

He resumed his heavy drinking, and while he could still hold his liquor – he was seldom unsteady and he certainly did not confuse his syntax – he began to have seizures that he called epilepsy: he would fall, thrash about, be unable to speak, lose consciousness and sometimes lose control of his bodily functions. Ghislaine thought that these episodes followed a lunar cycle.[244] Perhaps his drinking also followed the phases of the moon; in any case, there was a positive correlation between the attacks and the amount that he drank.

Ghislaine, caught in an emotional cyclone, put up with the abuse: 'I was jealous, tortured, passionate and too much in love,' she said. Also, Larry could still be kind and gentle with her. Sometimes they walked together 'like tramps' along the railway lines that ran through Sommières, listening for the one goods train a day on the dying branch line. Larry wore shorts and ankle boots on these outings, and swung a heavy stick both as a prop and a protection against dogs. For Larry the dogs were no joke: he was afraid of them and once he fended off a shepherd's dogs with the point of an umbrella. 'I hate to disturb dogs when they are working,' he said to Ghislaine.[245]

In spite of his complaints about Ghislaine, and the fairly frequent visits to Gerry and Jacquie 'and Co' at the Mazet Michel, Larry kept at *Monsieur*, and in early June he sent the typescript off to Faber. He thought it 'a rather original novel', and was pleased.[246]

By September 1974 the first advance copies of *Monsieur* were out, and Henry Miller focused his good eye on its pages. He loved it as far as the Macabru ceremony, and wrote to Larry that it was 'pure magic, pure sorcelry[sic]', so gripping that it 'Makes me forget the sciatica, the arthritis, the deafness and blindness.'[247] However, six days later he told Larry that he was 'somewhat puzzled, bewildered', and that the book had 'seemed to fall apart' after the scene with Ophis, the albino serpent. The gnostics that Henry found so fascinating had vanished from the story with the introduction of the historian Toby and his Templar manuscript.[248] Larry was undisturbed by the criticism: Henry should not judge the 'shape' of the quintet by the first volume. 'My main stream is going to gradually expand through the lives of the "real" creator and his puppets,' Larry explained. He promised to send Henry the just-completed fifty pages of the novel that he was already calling 'LIVIA or BURIED ALIVE'.[249]

One reason why Larry could accept Henry's strictures with equanimity was that Viking had 'rushed in' with a $50,000 advance on *Monsieur*, and rights had already been sold in eight other languages.

Despite periods of temporary reconciliation, Ghislaine and Larry were in fact getting along worse and worse. By autumn a state of war existed. 'Ici, à Sommières nous ne sommes pas très sage et l'été à été très dur,' she complained to Henry. The evening before she and Larry had fought 'comme des fous' – like madmen – and despite her efforts to fight 'le plus professionellement possible', she had emerged with a swollen face and sprained neck, while Larry's 'doigt de l'écrivain' on his right hand had turned blue. With a note of humour and a pun, Ghislaine described Larry typing 'à "cloche-mains"', 'with hobbled hands', a distressing but not serious condition.[250] Larry ignored all this in his letters to Henry, who wrote, in a letter that crossed Ghislaine's, 'I'm also delighted to know you and Ghislaine are still together. Still in love, I hope?'[251]

In October Larry wrote to friends that he expected the break with Ghislaine to come around Christmas. They travelled to London early in the month for the appearance of *Monsieur*. He had called her 'Pig' in a newspaper interview, and Michael Parkinson, recording Larry for BBC Television, put him on the spot: 'I wonder if you could explain that term.' 'Yes', said Larry without hesitation, 'Shakespeare called his girlfriend "pigsnie". It was a traditional endearment of the strolling players . . . . it's a pretty word – P-I-G-S-N-I-E.'[252] But Larry had not called Ghislaine by this 'pretty word'. The same year he published a powerful poem about Van Gogh, 'A Patch of Dust', which refers to 'the French whore I live with'. Most people who knew them both defended Ghislaine, but Larry was simply through with her: she was 'too frivolous and silly',[253] a parasite, a tramp, 'a little man in girls' clothes', he claimed.[254] Perhaps he did not intend his charges to be taken literally; but their relationship had turned sour, so he lashed out at her and, when they were alone in the old house, sometimes threatened to shoot her with a handgun.[255] The trip to London was followed by a visit to Gerry's zoo, and then in November he was in Paris for an Oscar Epfs exhibition at Marthe Nochy's rue de Seine gallery. Anaïs Nin was in the city too, but their schedules kept them apart, so Larry said. He was, however, 'roundly ticked off by Anaïs' for mentioning in print Hugh Guiler as her husband – which was still true, but her mania for

LAWRENCE DURRELL

subterfuge and deceit remained, and she apparently continued to bear Larry a grudge for the ill-starred preface that he had composed years earlier for *Children of the Albatross*. Larry remained tolerant regarding Anaïs: 'About the "estrangement" theme, one must not exaggerate it,' he would recall. 'You know our friendship (between all four Musketeers) was so firmly based that we could afford to send each other to the dog house from time to time without breaking any expensive crockery. Each of us did it . . . and one just waited for the other to get over his or her spleen.'[256] Larry overestimated Anaïs's ability to forgive.

By December Larry and Ghislaine were back in Sommières and he could report that 'we are having a good friendly relationship and hardly quarrel seriously'.[257] A few days later Larry confirmed his tranquillity to Thérèse Marberry, who had not contacted him for a couple of years. He wrote with some sympathy of Ghislaine, but first he turned to Tessa's problems. She had fallen into a frightful depression following shock treatment, and Larry hastened to link her case to his, in terms that left no doubt that he still believed himself to be suffering from childhood wounds to his psyche: 'THE LONGER I LIVE . . . THE MORE I SEE THE FEARFUL RAVAGES OF CHILDHOOD IN ALL OF US. THE [m]UTILATION OF THE AFFECT BY OUR PARENTS FIRST OF ALL AND THEN OUR TEACHERS OPERATING UNDER THE UMBRELLA OF THE POISONED MUSHROOM OF OUR CULTURE. WE HAVE ALL BEEN RENDERED LOPSIDED BY THESE ELEMENTS.' Ghislaine was a fellow-sufferer: 'I HAVE GOT MYSELF MARRIED AGAIN TO A RATHER REMARKABLE AND QUITE IMPOSSIBLE WOMAN ARRANGEMENT genus epileptoid 666', he wrote, 'ANOTHER CASE OF A BRAVE IDEALISTIC AND GENEROUS SOUL BEDEVILLE [sic] BY A GHASTLY CATHOLIC YOUTH IN CONVENTS.' If everyone suffered from emotional disorders traceable to childhood, this shifted responsibility for behaviour a few degrees south – but this Larry did not say. He asked permission to quote in *Livia* from Tessa's '*ASTONISHING*' letter.[258] The sixteen letters that she wrote to Larry after his first reunion with her in 1968 form an eloquent case history of desuetude, of pain and suffering, of pills and broken bones, but also of courage in despair. Perhaps Larry, borrowing traits from her years previously for Justine, foresaw the collapse of her fine nervous sensibility. Four years later she would be dead, a shattered woman.

Larry and Ghislaine were still together in February 1975, and she was clearly trying to win back his affections, cooking good meals and dressing with meticulous care, acting the cheerful hostess. It was no use: Larry was

610

finished with her. He accused her of being a bitch and of drinking his whisky.[259] He dressed more carelessly than ever, lounging about in shorts and an old shirt most of the time, even in winter, when he would add a quilted vest to his attire. He touched the magnificent Pleyel infrequently these days, less than once a week: even playing slow jazz seemed to have lost its soothing power. Often he would sit from three to seven in the afternoon staring silently out of the kitchen window at the nearest chestnut tree.[260]

Larry returned to *Livia*, and by the end of March had completed the crucial first hundred pages. He had begun the 'merging': 'My "real" characters are beginning to interfere in the lives of my "imagined" ones,' he wrote.[261] He professed not to be concerned at the 'bloody' American reviews of *Monsieur*, balanced as they were, he said, by generally good ones in England. One wonders which reviews Larry was reading: while it is true that there were negative reviews in the *Christian Science Monitor*, the *New York Times*, and an 'exotic but' notice in the *Saturday Review*, such English arbiters of quality as the *New Statesman* and the *Times Literary Suplement* also panned *Monsieur*. Peter Prescott in *Newsweek* praised both the story and the descriptive richness of the language, but he was in a small minority. As usual, however, Larry's course appeared to be undeflected by the clamour.

Finally Ghislaine left for Paris and the old house fell silent. Larry sometimes complained to Mary Mollo, 'I don't know why my wives leave me – I'm so easy to live with!'[262] 'My brother destroys women,' was Gerry's comment: and he said it not in a condemnatory tone but simply as one states a fact. Ghislaine he liked: 'She is a sweetie but she was not in Larry's league.'[263] Larry pronounced his own sarcastic judgement: 'Ghislaine had a repertoire of 120 soufflés'.[264]

It was as if Larry courted disaster in many of his relationships. *The Revolt of Aphrodite* had in a curious way set the tone of his life since Claude-Marie Vincendon's death: he saw himself as having suffered from women in revolt – betrayed by Claude who had deserted him, by Margaret McCall who would not have him on his terms, by Ghislaine. But in a very real sense he, not Aphrodite, had been in revolt. Never one to be satisfied with the way things are, Larry's discontent had reached the dimensions of a rhinoceros. Towards the end of *Tunc* Felix Charlock is explaining to his son Mark that Abel the computer can reveal both his past and his future. He asks the boy, 'Do you see the different bays marked "When" "Who" "Why" "Where" and "If"?' 'Why "*If*"?' responds Mark, surprised. 'It's the most important question of all in a way', answers Abel's inventor. 'It can change all the others: just one tiny grain of *If*.'[265] The *if*s Larry faced were endless: *if* Claude had not died, *if* Margaret McCall had been younger or more compliant or . . ., *if* the second Claude had not been married, *if* Ghislaine had been different, *if* he had not been an ageing man afflicted with a horrible eczema during his search for a new mate. Larry had too much horror of pomposity, was too aware of the sin of hubris to phrase his revolt in the grandiose terms of the human condition. When he had written in valediction of Dylan Thomas that 'a poet's death is never wrong', he had wondered when his right time would come. The death with which, romantic that he was, he had always been half in love smiled at him from the corners of his gaunt house. The vampires of his poetry notebook, the vanished Templars and Cathars, the seduction of suicide, the entropic death-drift of the universe – all pulled against the cheerful tinted sunlight of the Darjeeling Room, against the quincunx of novels that he had set himself to complete, against his love of love, of living. His revolt may have shifted aim with each mood, but it was nearly always there, waiting to urge him to action – or inaction.

CHAPTER 13

Prospero's Cell

Though you a whole infinity may take
You'll not unravel the entire mosaic.
'Constrained by History'

For so long he had unconsciously thought that getting
old and dying were things that happened to others!
'Endpapers and Inklings'

The last breath and the last glass of wine
are the sweetest.
LD to Alfred Perlès

GHISLAINE AND LARRY did not part company conclusively. She came and went, sometimes spending extensive periods in Paris. When she was away, Larry barricaded himself in La Maison de Mme Tartes. At around five in the morning – six in winter – he would pad in heel-less slippers down the stairs, then cut across the corner of the Darjeeling Room into the kitchen. Then, if he had not provided himself with a thermos of Nescafé the evening before, he would turn on the gas under the kettle to make instant coffee. As soon as the kettle began to hiss, but before it was properly boiling, he would pour the water over the crumbled coffee extract. With daylight, he would raise the window and fold back the heavy painted shutters in the west wall of the kitchen. The wide glass expanse of the Darjeeling Room was always open, and if the sun was shining Larry would often move there. The rest of the house usually remained closed all day. 'It's the wind, you see, the mistral,' he would explain. 'People always complain because the shutters are always shut, but I don't want to keep going around to Lunel to find my shutters' – Lunel was the railway station eight miles distant. When a guest told Larry that a man had just been killed in Aix by a flying shutter, Larry said triumphantly, 'You see!'[1] The wind was just part of it, however – probably a very small part. The burglary of 1968 still frightened him, and

613

he now kept two pistols (loaded) and a cast metal popgun (fake) in his bedroom. Tony Daniells's woodblock print reading 'Maison Piège' was pinned to each outside door. Larry felt vulnerable, alone, like a boar at bay. It was not purely rational, he knew. He seldom complained to others – except about his taxes – and the booby-trap warning was pure bluff. In fact, the ambience suited his mood as he attacked *Livia*, sibling to *Monsieur*.

Larry may not have succeeded in finding the New Woman he said he craved, but he did hire Madame Mignon to do his cooking and cleaning, after Marcelle left to marry a policeman. She was grim-faced, very efficient, and not young, and from the first made it clear that she would Brook No Nonsense. Larry was rather intimidated by her, but he appreciated her solid virtues.

Larry embarked in July 1975 on a trip around Sicily in order to write on the island for *Travel and Leisure* magazine. Over the next year he would expand his essay into a travelogue, *Sicilian Carousel*. Meanwhile he continued to work on *Livia*, and watched the activities of his daughters from a cautious distance. Penelope had divorced her actor husband Peter Jones, and in August she married Roger Walker, a potter, and the pair moved to a dairy farm in Cornwall. Larry liked Walker and sent Sappho as his emissary with a dozen bottles of champagne for the wedding celebration.

Larry allowed himself to be talked into appearing in autumn 1975 in two films about his relationship with Greece. After all, the films meant expenses-paid travel around the Aegean and the Ionian, with a bit of cash thrown in. He planned to film on Corfu in September with Michèle Arnaud for French television, and then with Peter Adam, an Austrian-born film director, for the BBC, accompanied by Larry's old friend the photographer Dimitri Papadimos. Adam worked out a detailed script that required Larry to speak extemporaneously before the backdrop of many of his favourite locations: the Parthenon, Mykonos, the Lindos Acropolis, and of course various Corfu sites including Kalami, Paleocastrizza, Benitses for night-fishing, with Albania in the distance, and the Ionian Bar on the town esplanade for 'the happiest drinks, warmest sunlight'.[2] They also spent some days in Crete. A thin, aesthetic man with an encyclopaedic knowledge of literature and music, Adam proved equal to coping with Larry's moods and occasional stubbornness. He quickly grasped that Larry's 'natural modesty' and his 'shyness of producing himself' made each interview an 'ordeal' for him.[3] He often preferred to dodge serious subjects behind a screen of banter and jokes, but then, just as Adam had despaired of recording a useful segment of dialogue, Larry would come out with a vivid and poignant statement: 'Life is too important not to be taken lightly'; 'If you can love right, everything comes right'; and on the importance of locating the right place in which to live, 'Once you've found yourself thinking "I wouldn't mind *dying* here", then you've found it.'[4]

The best that came out of Adam's filming were Larry's retrospective insights. He had come to terms with the loneliness he had so often complained about to Henry Miller: like the Greek monks, he could now enjoy being alone – 'the word is marvellous in Greek – *monaxia*,' he said, 'Loneliness.'[5] The shrine of St Arsenius near Kalami had grown, if anything, in importance for Larry: 'It's my second birthplace,' he told Adam. 'You know, the old Indian notion that one is born twice – once physically and then once you sort of wake up to reality.'[6] Rhodes also had not been dimmed by time or new experiences: 'I was enormously in love,' Larry confirmed; 'Only three or four times did I strike really fruitful and happy places where I enjoyed a spell of real bliss, consciously,' and Rhodes had been one of those places. 'Here one lived it actually consciously day by day, and it was delicious like the honey.' What had fame done to him? 'Nothing really – it's made me drink a little too much, perhaps,' Larry remarked. Was he concerned with immortality? 'I don't think there's going to be any,' Larry said flatly; 'Try and perfect yourself before you croak.'[7] There was not a trace of self-pity.

After one long day of filming in the heat, Larry stripped off his clothes and plunged naked into the sea. Walking, Larry had the gait of an elderly sailor or a troglodyte these days, but in the water he still moved with the effortless ease of a dolphin. Adam, on a low cliff overlooking the beach, suddenly saw the ideal closing image for the film, and motioned to his cameraman. Just then Larry, floating on his back and blissfully relaxed, folded his legs into a lotus position, and Adam got his picture. *Spirit of Place: Greece* projected the lyrical beauty of one of Larry's early island books. To take advantage of the coming television exposure, Larry wrote the text for a illustrated large-format book, *The Greek Islands*, which would follow approximately the itinerary of the film. Wonderful memories crowded in, and soon he was putting weeks and months into the task.

Paul Gotch was staying at Kassiope on Corfu, and he brought Larry and the Birds together again. In 1971 Joan and Peter had bought an apartment in Athens on Larry's urging, but there had not been much contact in the interim. Peter Bull sometimes strayed over from his home on Paxos, and Larry introduced him to the Birds. The once-exuberant Bull of Larry's early

London days was now a rather sad, bulky man, surrounded by young men who took advantage of him.[8]

While he was in Athens, Larry managed to find time for a couple of evenings with George Katsimbalis, now a widower and a semi-invalid with arthritis and prostate trouble, largely confined to his lodgings. Larry judged him to be 'DYING for company', yet too proud and too frightened to encourage visitors or to get himself proper medical treatment. 'One gets panicky and infantile and hopeless when one is ill,'[9] remarked Larry: an observation as astute about the Colossus as it would turn out to be prophetic about himself.

A visitor characterized Larry's outlook around this time as being one of 'cheerful despair'. If he was not quite hopeless about his own situation, he was certainly not optimistic about the course being taken by civilization. The key to salvation, if one existed, rested with the role of women: 'The most critical part of our civilization is not an atom bomb at all but overpopulation,' he said in an interview in 1976. 'But basically, from an affective point of view, the kind of children that we're going to make are going to be pretty sterilised if women cannot be more respected and if their role cannot be more combined with complete freedom, with also a functional freedom as the matriarch of society.'[10] The failure of his latest marriage did not lessen his reliance upon women.

AMONG THE FRIENDS WHO cornered Larry in his Sommières lair even when he seemed most Timon-like were the Birds. When Larry made some scolding remark about Pudding Island, Peter asked him, 'What do you have against England?' 'You can't get a fuck on a Sunday!' he replied, as if that settled the matter. Together they went to dine with Tony Daniells in Uzès, and Larry seemed content to sit and listen attentively to the conversation rather than to lead it – the most startling evidence of an alteration in his nature.[11]

Agent and publishers alike urged Larry to write *Sicilian Carousel*: he did not seem able to finish *Livia*, and another title would keep his name before the public. He sent the typescript off in late 1976. The book was intended to be a response to Sicily in the manner of one of D. H. Lawrence's travel books. Larry had always admired Lawrence's evocation of the spirit of place, and his comments reveal his own aims. '*Twilight in Italy* is absolutely incomparable,' he said:

It doesn't matter if the facts are or aren't true, or if he got them out of a book; what he did with them is absolutely incredible. And of course when you go to Italy you realize what, hellishly, much of the writing about Italy is, and how photographic and electric his impressions were! . . . *Sea and Sardinia* is a marvellous one. . . . *Etruscan Places* was good but unfortunately it had a thesis, a thesis which didn't hold water. . . . Then he came back onto beam with *Mornings in Mexico*.[12]

Sicilian Carousel had for Larry elements of a sentimental journey with the spirit of a woman released for the occasion from Erebus. Marie Millington-Drake had moved from Cyprus to Sicily, and had often invited Larry to visit her new island. This he had put off from year to year, and then suddenly Marie had slipped unobtrusively away, to take her place on the 'Death Chart' that Larry kept on his wall. Very likely Larry was thinking of Marie when he wrote in *Livia* about how the death of a loved woman would affect his sometime *alter ego*, the novelist Robin Sutcliffe: should he be made to 'whimper in the novel like some ghastly dog?'[13] Larry himself preferred to recall good times. 'God, I have been *lucky*!' he would exclaim, gazing at Marie's picture. 'Such a beautiful woman!'[14] In the years since he had known her on Cyprus, Marie had made a 'correct marriage', produced two children, and, according to Larry, had died at the age of forty-one.[15]

From an artistic standpoint, *Sicilian Carousel* was not a very successful book. Larry had violated the mode of his earlier island books: he had never *lived* on Sicily, but he had travelled there on a tour bus with a group that included such neurotic and frantic women that, so he claimed, he had to disguise every character in *Sicilian Carousel* for fear of libel. So he fell back on the Antrobus trick of being funny where he could not be sensitive, ending the prose text of the book on the *opera bouffe* note of the faked plunge into Etna of one of his characters, the fleeing bankrupt Beddoes. The shortcomings of the book he fully realized. Henry Miller would send a rave, but Larry was not fooled. 'I'm afraid your reservations about the Sicilian book are very just', he wrote to me, 'it is rather fabricated and pot boiled.' Diana Menuhin, to whom, with her husband, the book was to be dedicated, 'put her long sharp finger on the meretriciousness of the book'. He had done far too much 'overproducing' recently, Larry thought, and it had been 'a real surprise to discover that Sicily would need a four year residence to take in and push out'. Even in his homage to Marie, he had not pleased himself: 'I rather funked the whole truth about Marie Millington Drake's end because of people still alive; there was nothing scandalous about it, it was simply tragic.' She had died, he claimed, of loneliness and drink.[16] He admitted that he had lacked the courage to visit Marie's home,

'In Naxos in Sicily where I didn't dare to go.'[17] He tried to make amends by closing the book with a poem of concealed homage, 'Autumn Lady: Naxos', in which 'My poor ship' is a metaphor for loss: 'She'll sink at moorings like my life did once.' He concluded,

> She will lie there in the calm cathedrals
> Of the blood's sleep, not speaking of love,
> Or the last graphic journeys of the mind.
> Let tides drum on those unawakened flanks
> Whom all the soft analysis of sleep will find.[18]

The loss of Marie was more grievous than any he had sustained since Claude's death.

In 1976 Simone Lestoquard arrived to paint Larry's portrait, a joyful occasion for him,[19] and early in the year he experienced a visitation from one of the long line of eccentrics that he cherished. Jolan Chang had been writing to him from Stockholm in his small, exquisite hand and equally meticulous English. Larry defined him as a 'Taoist-gerontologist', and Chang's subject seemed to be the Taoist preoccupation with approximating immortality in the here and now. Chang proposed to consult Larry on his latest manuscript, *The Tao of Love and Sex*. Larry's curiosity was piqued and he invited him to come, although he was honest enough to warn Chang that he was not an adept in the Tao. He was mildly alarmed when Chang telephoned him at once to say that he would be at the tiny Lunel station at daybreak next morning. Larry was even more surprised to see step from the train not a venerable sage but an almost boyish and sprightly youth. It turned out to be Jolan Chang all right, and he really was chronologically well past middle age.

Mme Mignon, tidying up the kitchen, was startled when Larry appeared with the delicate Chang, like some intelligent praying mantis.[20] Later, while Chang was preparing a vegetarian dinner for Larry and himself, the talk moved to Indian and Chinese yoga. Chang pronounced the latter 'more fluent, less static', and to demonstrate waltzed across the Darjeeling Room, waving a wooden spoon, while Larry tried to imitate his movements. Larry's part-time gardener, a 'morose existentialist', took one look through the window and fled, his nerves severely shaken.[21]

A long weekend of precise Oriental cookery – '"chinoiseries" of undercooked vegetables' sniffed Mme Mignon scornfully[22] – and happy philosophizing followed. Larry quickly identified his guest as a sexologist as well as a gerontologist, for Jolan Chang's treatise on extending human life was bound up with the concept of the *coitus reservatus*. Through the technique of withholding the orgasm, Chang, then in his sixties, proposed confidently to remain sexually active into his nineties and to live until at least 120. He allowed himself only one ejaculation in a hundred love encounters, but this enabled him to make love to several women in the same day. Further, Chang spoke of physical love in terms of cherishing rather than ravishing, which he saw as a Western fallacy in love-making. The 'sexual polarity' of the love partners was supposed to link them to the rhythms of the cosmos, not debase them into a conflict between egos attempting to dominate one another. For Larry, struggling with the complex love relationships of *Livia*, Chang's arrival was a real boon. Our 'sexual culture' was out of phase, and when Chang 'laid the blame at the door of Christianity – with its cult of the ego, of original sin, of the wrathful God', Larry knew that he had found a brother spirit. Larry announced that the cult of narcissism that is so essential to the Freudian explanation of homosexuality was 'vastly strengthened by the Christian code'.[23] Soon Larry was to build a long essay, *A Smile in the Mind's Eye*, around his talks with Jolan Chang.

Chang told Larry flatly, 'You are drinking too much; it makes you reason falsely and disturbs your yoga balance – not to mention making you fat.' All that Larry could do was agree – and open another bottle of St Saturnin. For one hilarious evening Chang set out to match Larry, glass for glass: what he was attempting to do was to 'meditate' Larry into a less destructive mode, 'like switching points on a railway'.[24] Chang became quite tipsy, but his ruse did not work on Larry.

Jolan Chang did however reinforce Larry's links with Buddhism, and early in February 1977, at Jacques Lacarrière's urging he accepted a long-standing invitation to attend the celebration of the Tibetan New Year at Kagyu-Ling, a Buddhist centre established three years before. A pair of 'quite penniless' young Parisians had discovered the Château de Plaige south of Autun and had raised the money to buy it for a dispossessed Tibetan group.[25] Larry turned suddenly daring and headed L'Escargot north into the white beard of a winter storm, through Valence, Lyon, Macon, Chalon-sur-Saône. The rivers had flooded parts of the Mâconnais to the rooftops, electricity pylons lay overthrown by the wind, deep snow smoothed the hills around his destination. 'It was appropriate, the snow', Larry wrote, 'to rediscover the ambience of my childhood by any other element would have left something lacking.' After nosing about for some time, Larry spotted the sodden prayer flags and pulled up before the

Château de Plaige, the symmetrical twin peaked turrets and gracious windows proclaiming it an eighteenth-century pastiche. 'It was precisely the sort of country-house-chateau which might be inhabited even today by a hill-Rajah,' Larry decided. In fact, he recalled similar edifices around Kurseong. 'I was glad that it was snowing,' Larry repeated, 'for in my memories it always snowed and always the white fangs of the Himalayan Alps across the valley held the blue glass-glitter of ice all the year around. Plaige was like a small yet faithful miniature of those grandiose landscapes of my extreme youth – it was the stage version, so to speak, of an epic scenery.'[26]

The sounds of the monks practising on their drums and trumpets for the services, 'this mixture of tooting and booming, of mice and elephants', Larry said, 'brought back so many forgotten impressions of the past – for this was the ordinary musical scheme of Nepal, Bhutan and all points north.' The music and the prayers evoked for him 'this galloping continuum – the natural force of the cosmos: the Tao!' Larry took his place early in the little chapel of the château and watched the minatory gestures and listened to the croaking prayers of the chief lama. 'It is quite impossible to describe the pleasure and reassurance this ordinary little service gave me,' he recalled. The drums and the 'squiffing' fifes brought back memories of mule trains in the mountains around Darjeeling, around Kalimpong. 'I could recover it all through this weird and tilting music,' Larry said. 'The drumming of hooves on rock!' In fact, he imagined that he could recover more than he had ever known: 'I had forgotten just how physically dirty one could become for lack of water, living at a lamasery at ten thousand feet.'[27] What mattered to Larry was the spiritual lift. He was returning to an imagined Tibet that he had never known in snow and stone.

BEFORE LARRY MET THE BUDDHISTS of Kagyu-Ling, Anaïs Nin died on 17 January 1977, after a tenacious battle with cancer. Larry hated any chipping away of his cherished circle, but he was able as usual to write the required consolations for the loss of 'this beautiful witch-like woman whom we called our third Musketeer'. 'She was our Aramis', he told Rupert Pole, 'the slim and delicate and aristocratic one, the born duelist. . . . And a world without real women in it to guide and nourish and inform its values will fall apart.' Still, Larry had been cut off from Anaïs for too long, and there was a hint of the familiar formula in his closing: 'I am so happy to have lived in the same small moment of time with her; and I hardly dare to mourn her death – I seem to see that mischevious [sic] small smile with its sardonic edge, and hear that quiet laugh.'²⁸ Larry mourned her, yes, but as a woman, and in the lavender way one laments an ancient flame. Nor did he rate her talent very highly – she had risen in part through her self-publicized associations with Henry, with Artaud, with Rank and so on.²⁹ Fred Perlès questioned her title to the musketeer circle: 'She lacks in muscularity,' he told Larry. 'If I were to give her name a military connotation, I'd call her a *vivandière*, though that's a bit catty.'³⁰

Back in Sommières, Larry worked on *The Greek Islands*, a 'bouquet garnis of isles and atolls', which he hoped would 'butter my parsnips this coming year which promises to be financially rocky'.³¹ He had taken a break from *Livia*, after completing two thirds of the novel, and was bracing himself against his intended divorce from Ghislaine and an expected heavy alimony.

Larry congratulated himself on his present good health, 'thanks to yoga', and held that he was 'lucky in my lovers – which is almost too good to be true at 65'.³² The most obvious benefit that Larry derived from yoga was improved breathing. Part of this was a secondary effect: yoga he would credit with enabling him to reduce and at times to stop his drinking. The deep breathing exercises certainly did help him with the shortness of wind that was the most noticeable symptom of the 'obstructive airways syndrome' traceable to his more than forty years of smoking. A vicious cycle developed: the more his breathing became laboured, the less walking he did; and the less exercise he got, the more his damaged lungs atrophied in his short, thick body.³³ Breath, *pneuma*, breathing control, became part of Larry's mantra, and his latest success in breathing or, conversely, shortness of breath came up frequently in his conversation.

Years earlier Larry had proposed Harry T. Moore as a possible editor of his correspondence with Richard Aldington, and Moore had invited me to collaborate with him. Larry went over the final typescript, and hoped that the resulting book, *Literary Lifelines*, would 'help Richard's image'. He worried that they might both appear '*un peu con*' – Richard because 'he wasn't quite his own stout self' during his last years. 'I trod warily not to inflame his wounds, so that I may sound a bit putain here or there.' Larry brushed aside opportunities to alter or delete unflattering passages, except where the living might be hurt. 'I am always against trying to arrange violets on my tomb,' he wrote. 'After all, whatever one suppresses will one day out; I used to irritate Anaïs about this, for she was always trying to subedit her own posthumous portrait.'³⁴ Larry was also aware that outrageous comments fired off for effect to a friend might carry unwelcome reverberations: 'Of course in private correspondence one can exaggerate etc.,' he remarked. 'It's a different matter when one prints.'[35] Larry worked fast: the day after acknowledging the receipt of the typescript in mid-April, he had read it and answered queries.

Larry had interrupted work on the manuscript of *The Greek Islands* to help with *Literary Lifelines*, and he went right back to his own book. Still, he was finding it difficult to keep at the task: 'I AM GOING THROUGH A RESTLESS PERIOD – OLD AGE I GUESS,' he confessed to Henry, 'AND MAY YET TAKE MY CARAVAN AND RUSH OFF TO CORFU FOR THE REST OF THE SUMMER.'[36] Then he changed his mind and stuck with *The Greek Islands*, completing it before 26 June. 'It was fun writing but too fast alas,' he told Fred Perlès. The islands book was 'no masterpiece', he realized, but 'it was written with feeling'.[37] Then in the early part of the summer he hid in a 'tiny workman's flat' at Le Grau-du-Roi on the coast so that he could escape the telephone[38] and 'get Livia pushed up a tone or two'.[39] In a sense he was hiding out literally: he had invited Ghislaine to stay in Sommières for the summer, and was finding living with her again a *cauchemar*, a nightmare. Anthea Morton-Saner, soon to succeed Juliet O'Hea as Larry's agent at Curtis Brown, came to Sommières for a brief visit, and she arrived just after Larry and Ghislaine had thrashed out the arrangements for the divorce. They all sat at the pool-side table, Larry and Ghislaine bantering with a giddy gaiety. While Juliet was tall, spare and spinsterish, Anthea was shorter than Larry, young, round-eyed, irreverent and utterly confident. She could also be tough-minded and ruthless on his behalf, as he would appreciate.

Larry let part of the middle floor of Mme Tartes's to a German family for a month beginning on 25 June: a chance to make a few francs, and it also improved the security against burglary. His Grau-du-Roi flat was no paradise, but was 'in a hideous group of tenement buildings on a mosquito ridden étang', and so unfinished that it still lacked an address: 'Perfect for what I need,' he wrote to Henry. Larry made weekly forays to Sommières to pick up mail and, presumably, to check on Ghislaine. Above all, he was determined to finish *Livia*.[40]

Although just east of the garishly modernistic Grande-Motte tourist centre, Grau-du-Roi was still a rough and ready fishing port where Larry could relax in open-air seafood restaurants and watch the fishermen surge up the Grande Roubine, a dredged channel bearing the Vidourle to the Mediterranean. There was also 'the proximity of a beach with quite a number of pretty Danes and Germans', Larry admitted to Henry. 'I really always preferred blondes, and always had trouble with brunettes. . . . One pretty child is coming to Avignon next month.' Simone Lestoquard was ill with cancer, and he was waiting for a remission in 'this foul disease' to see her again.[41] Larry was beginning to wonder when – 'if?' – he would ever manage to complete the projected 'Quinx', as he then called *The Avignon Quintet*. 'It's been a suicidal year!' he exclaimed.[42]

Well, perhaps not quite. One worry had been eased when Gerry had offered around the end of May to buy the Mazet Michel, and also to rent the middle flat in Mme Tartes' – 'SO THAT I WONT BE ALONE ALL THE TIME', Larry said, in capitals to spare Henry's eyes rather than for emphasis.[43] Separate plumbing and kitchen arrangements on each floor allowed the three living units to function independently. They shared the central staircase and the front and west doors, and that was all.

Sicilian Carousel appeared in England in July 1977, and Larry took a caning at the hands of the reviewers. The book 'shows Durrell's talent in tatters', said the *New Statesman*. It fared rather better in the United States, where the literary and social historian Paul Fussell judged *Carousel* 'more authentic Durrell and a better work of art than his pretentious and badly written novels' – a real backhander. No matter: by March of the next year *Sicilian Carousel* would have sold nearly 20,000 copies, 'which is a scandal really', Larry cheerfully admitted.[44]

IN AUGUST LARRY WROTE to Henry: 'I think very gently and in friendly fashion we shall push our divorce into action at the end of this month . . . . I have no other candidates for the sceptre and throne. I made a fearful and costly mistake here, though G is all right and full of charm – and will have no nasty deal from me cos I really like her. But what a terrible misjudgement I showed. It is all my fault.'[45] This humble pie being offered to Henry had perhaps a good deal to do with the fact that Larry was well aware Henry admired Ghislaine. Factors working in Larry's favour were that she was still fond of him and was not inclined to be vindictive: but she had given up her Paris life and contacts to marry Larry, and she felt that she was entitled to some compensation.

Peter Adam had persuaded Larry to make another film for the BBC on the *Spirit of Place* theme: this time it would be Egypt. Larry had been reluctant initially: he pleaded his health, he couldn't be bothered, it would get in the way of his writing. He was worried over his divorce from Ghislaine and the alimony that he would have to pay. And he really dreaded a return to Egypt: too many old scars, too many vanished friends, too many memories – and even the places that he remembered with pleasure would have been changed utterly, he felt. Finally, he simply lacked the courage or the will to refuse Adam.[46] There was another factor: the BBC *Spirit of Place: Greece* film two years previously had 'kicked the tombstones off books 30 years old', and Larry counted upon the Egypt film to resuscitate the sales of the *Quartet*. This, he hoped, would tide him over until he could finish 'THE QUINX',[47] *and* help pay for his divorce.

By September, when he was faced with the cold figures on the divorce papers, Larry lost his tolerant feelings towards Ghislaine and blew up to Henry: 'Our great love affair has entered the Hold Up stage, as marriages do, and I am planning to stake the papers for divorce on the 22nd. Before leaving. I cant take it no more. J'ai vécu un cauchemar et j'ai perdu une fortune.' He spoke wildly of being old and without a pension, even of needing to be coddled ('*dorloter*'), but said that he 'must be free even if bankrupt'. He reminded Henry of his comments in *Insomnia* about 'the black lustreless eye of Hoki' during their divorce proceedings. You should see Ghislaine's eye, Larry snarled, 'when money is discussed; it becomes black and dry as the anus of Time's dog!' But Larry still blamed himself: 'Well, I have really pulled the shit bucket over my own head this time and suppose that I formally deserve this set back.' Ghislaine was still at Mme Tartes's and was probably cooking his supper – one of her 120 soufflés – as he typed his tirade to Henry.[48]

As it turned out, Larry bought Ghislaine a modest top-storey flat in Paris and settled a small income on her. For all his laments, his finances were not seriously injured by his alimony payments. Gerry was also divorcing – Jacquie had left him to go off with Sophie, his secretary – and would soon marry Lee McGeorge, a zoologist from Memphis, Tennessee. They would spend their summers at the Mazet Michel, and their evident happiness and compatibility became a constant reminder to Larry of his unattached state.

On 7 October Larry arrived in London to spend ten days with Alan and Shirley Thomas while he completed arrangements with Peter Adam. Dimitri Papadimos would again come along as official still photographer. Even at this stage, Larry would have liked to find a reason to back out of the film, but he let inertia carry him along: 'Rather dreading the heat and the fatigue,' he admitted.[49] He was overweight, his face somewhat bloated, his temper testy. On the 16th Larry reviewed the *Spirit of Place: Greece* film and fumed, 'My god, what a lot of drivel.' He was worried that he had given away too many of his personal feelings.[50] However, the next day Larry filched Shirley's red bedroom slippers and set off with Adam.

Larry's first surprise on landing in Cairo was being able to admire the 'now uncovered' faces of the Egyptian women. During the three-hour drive through the desert twilight to Alexandria, Larry reminisced over his many wartime trips on the same dusty highway. They arrived at the Cecil to learn that the rooms reserved for the film party had not been held, but finally a grumpy Larry was bedded down in the single available room, along with the twenty-seven pieces of luggage required by the camera crew. It was not a very auspicious return to Alexandria.

The lavish breakfast next morning, presided over by grim-faced waiters in white brocaded gowns, was a feast ranging from croissants with honey to great copper cauldrons of fava beans sprinkled with cumin. Larry decided that the old Cecil had changed little. Then he set off with Adam, Dimitri and the others to prospect for filming locations. Larry soon discovered that what he had fondly recalled about Alexandria, the cosmopolitan atmosphere engendered by the five languages and more than five nationalities of the city, had vanished. 'It is a dispiriting exercise to bring the story up to 1977,' he wrote. The foreign population had left, and the posters and advertisements that were once in French, Italian, Greek and English were now mainly in Arabic. It was easy for someone remembering the city in 1945 to become lost in 1977: new government buildings had appeared, and ugly six-storey concrete tenements had replaced or grown up around many of the old structures. Moharrem Bey was no exception, and drab rectangular buildings crowded the surviving gracious older homes.

Larry had forgotten the address of the Ambron house, but like a dog let off the leash in a once-familiar neighbourhood, he cast about for a moment and shot away, Adam's film crew racing to keep up with him. Triumphantly, Larry pointed to the turreted mansion. They were let in by a friendly Egyptian family, and an excited Larry bounded up the creaking outside stairs of his old tower. The remembered view of Pompey's Pillar and Lake Mareotis had been cut off by blocks of flats, but he was elated to find the house and garden still extant. Later, in the Anfushi district near the harbours, they walked along Scobie's Tatwig Street. Larry shouted 'El Scob! El Scob!' at the passers-by, and told Adam, 'I'm sure they worship this old sod.'[51] He wanted to believe that his created Alexandria really existed. Some of it did.

Another joyous moment came with Larry's visit to the Cavafy Room set up in the echoing Greek Consulate. Larry sat at the poet's desk, surrounded by his books and a few pieces of furniture rescued from his old rue Lepsius flat, musing that on this surface Cavafy had written 'those famous poems, "Ithaca", "The Barbarians", "The God Abandons Antony", or best of all "The City", which is his real monument to modern Alexandria'.[52] Still at Cavafy's desk, Larry scribbled a postcard to Henry Miller: he was, in spite of everything, enjoying Alexandria, 'still full of Luciferian charm and magic'.[53]

However, Egyptianization had been a disaster, Larry thought. 'I spent a week there in the old familiar room at the Cecil, now stripped of all its finery and echoing like a barn with the seawind sweeping under the doors.' Once again he felt the pangs of exile. The great Eunostos Harbour was 'a mere cemetery' and he found the *commerçants* 'listless, spiritless'. The Egyptian nationalist garb seemed drab. 'The blue Chinese get-up of the female students at the University is rather fetching at first but soon palls,' he decided. The Pastroudi and Baudrot establishments were still open, yet there was 'no trade to set them twinkling with light and music'.[54] Some presences had not changed, however: at night Larry was bitten by fleas and mosquitoes. Mosquitoes may look innocent, Larry told Adam, but they have snouts of fire.[55] Larry did not feel well – in fact, he had a rather severe hangover – and he growled that even common medicines were known to the chemists only by Arabic names: 'Try and obtain some aspirin or throat tablets and see what happens!' Crossly, he blamed it all on 'the long flirtation of Nasser with Communism', but he was delighted rather than angered when a shopkeeper, asked for the most effective mosquito-repellent incense coils available, delivered a Vicks nasal inhaler. In sum, the city itself was 'depressing beyond endurance', although Larry permitted himself to hope for a future renaissance through some 'happy accident'.[56]

On 20 October Larry and Peter Adam were guests at the home of Dr Adham El Nakeeb for a dinner deliberately planned to resemble a gathering at the Hosnani town residence depicted in the *Quartet*. Larry, 'delightfully scruffy' in a tie and jacket, responded gracefully to the questions of elegant society women. With Larry, recalled Adam, 'Beautiful women can get away with anything. If I had put such silly questions, I would have had my head bitten off.' The next morning Larry was very amusing at the expense of his admirers: 'The beauty of these women is their low IQ,' he said. 'It's like making love to crème Chantilly.'[57] He was not scornful of all Alexandrian women, however, and proceeded to fall for a beautiful young married woman, tall and dark-haired. 'I ran into a new Justine in Alexandria who set my poor old heartstrings twangling,' he would confess – or boast? – to Henry.[58]

In love or not, Larry had eyes for every sort of woman. He was delighted when a pair of immense tarts in leather mini-skirts passed his table. He surmised to Adam that they had just been laid by an English sailor, and exclaimed happily, 'Thank you, thank you, Egypt! What magnetism, what magical wobble!' By this time, Larry had a severe cold that he was treating with potations of Scotch, and his manner ranged erratically from childlike joy to grumpy boredom. He complained loudly about Egypt, but when Adam criticized the deterioration of living conditions to an Egyptian journalist, Larry defended Egypt and attacked England, where, he said, 'Civilisation is measured in courtesies.'[59]

Some of Larry's most telling statements to Adam came at the least promising moments. After the 'Justine party' at Dr Nakeeb's home, as a tired Larry was getting ready for bed, Adam asked him why, in *The Alexandria Quartet*, his characters were 'so wounded by sex'. Instead of parrying, Larry responded thoughtfully:

It's obviously the weak point. It's not only Alexandria, it's the whole of Europe. And as they are the seminal part of a culture . . . You see, it's also a critique of our twentieth-century notions. What I was using, using as best I could, [was] the available psychology of our epoch, do you see? Under the terms of that, the double-sexed thing – which is an ancient gnostic thing – was a very important weapon that I tried to use. Because in talking about love, you make love with the opposite side of yourself, so to speak. The male has to mobilize the female in himself, and the female has to mobilize the male in herself, otherwise you don't get a love affair four square. You get it stunted in some way.

And that, by the grace of Freud and God combined, seemed to me suggestive and quite possible to achieve. At least it would be a sort of ideal worth expressing. So I tried to pass my characters a bit through the wringer of sex, so to speak, in the hope that the dice will fall out of their pockets and assume that sort of fortunate configuration.[60]

On their last day in Alexandria, Adam filmed Larry at Chatby, where the little tin tram of the *Quartet* still ran, and that evening in the Cecil, Dimitri photographed a clowning Larry in a pose that the subject called 'Elephant slicing feta'. Larry and Adam moved to the Mena House Hotel on the edge of Cairo, and from Adam's terrace they watched the sun set behind the pyramids. 'Too much talk in the world,' Larry said. 'When two people love each other, silence sets in.'[61]

In between film sessions, Larry and Adam visited Hassan Fathy, 85–year-old Egyptian city planner and master architect. Fathy had designed and constructed near Luxor the model village of Gurna on which Larry had

years before based his sketch for a novel, 'A Village of Turtle-Doves'.⁶²
While Larry listened intently, Fathy discoursed on the shape of minarets
and the beauty of trees and of other organic forms. Adam thought that
Larry seemed burnt out next to Fathy, twenty years his senior. 'It occurs to
me,' Adam recalled, 'that Larry, living alone in Sommières, has lost almost
all taste for intelligent conversation' – except with his own books.⁶³ Larry
compared himself unfavourably to an old friend, Moschorios, the
Patriarchal Secretary in Alexandria, 'whom I found as sprightly as ever at
84'. Moschorios had exclaimed, 'What – only sixty-six? How wonderful
my dear Durrell to be so young!' Larry wrote somewhat ruefully to Henry
Miller, 'He, like you, is a "Ripeness is all" man and knows the value of
things. I am learning, I suppose, but not fast enough.' The deaths in 1977 of
Anaïs Nin, Alan Pringle, John Gawsworth, Robin Fedden and Lord
Kinross, 'friends who decided to abscond', made Larry feel fragile. 'Never
mind, in a way, because life itself is simply an illusion – blown up like a
piece of Venetian glass for a few breaths – and then crack!'⁶⁴

Although Larry was usually able to pull himself together reasonably
well for the interviews on camera, he was still unreliable, quite capable of
wrecking a session with ill temper or a barrage of trivialities and
witticisms. After a few days of filming in Cairo, Peter Adam cornered
Larry in his room at 10 p.m. and told him bluntly that if he would not
consent to drink a good deal less, they might as well scrub the whole
project. 'I played the Dutch uncle, all right, and Larry took it quietly,'
Adam recalled.⁶⁵ The scolding worked. Larry promised to abstain from
drink.

He was delighted to return to Upper Egypt, revelling in the colonial
luxury of the old Cataract Hotel, bargaining vociferously for cheap gift
earrings and necklaces, seeing the feluccas mirrored in the morning Nile at
Aswan. Even the pervading squeal and thud of the sakkia, the primitive
water wheels, struck him as 'precious': 'If you sleep in the country, they
have to be got used to. The sound can be maddening at night,' he told
Adam. Larry had stuck to his word and was not drinking at all. His
breathing improved dramatically and with his health better, his mood had
brightened. Death on the Nile was being filmed at Abu Simbel, and two of
the stars, Mia Farrow and Lois Chiles, joined Larry, Adam and Dimitri for
a picnic. Larry's conversation glittered and flashed. Now all Egypt seemed
grand. 'I have to confess that I am terribly incurious,' Larry said to Adam.
'It sounds silly, but I am extremely incurious, and my real life seems to
pass either in books or in dreams. And if I weren't pushed, I don't think I

would have moved from A to B. Had the Germans not pushed me, I would never have moved from Greece. Pity, because look what I would have missed.'⁶⁶ Larry was none the less inclined to be irreverent about the great monuments: 'Abu Simbel was too big for comfort, as if it had been drawn on rubber and inflated; the sheer mass impresses but the aesthetic sense is poor,' he wrote later. 'It is institutional art – the kind of thing that Banks commission, as also at Luxor; but the massive weight and volume of stone strikes a chord.' He liked Kom Ombo better, a 'marvellous desolate palace full of engraved lovers in the middle of a mangrove (sugar beet) swamp'. A cobra or two appeared, as if to remind him of India.⁶⁷ 'Countries reflect their architecture in their obsessions,' Larry said, and the death-obsession of Egypt centred 'around the preciousness of the possession of the body'. This led, he thought, to a 'monumental type of architecture' that was heavy, stiff. Add to these tendencies the 'self-love' of some of the rulers, and excess results: Karnak was 'a Disneyland of the despots'.⁶⁸

On their next to last day in Egypt, Adam received a cablegram announcing the death of a close friend: Larry avoided the platitudes of consolation to discuss death and suicide, 'soothingly'. 'We are phantoms really,' Larry told Adam; we are not ego-stable but 'exist like old bits of cinema film – flap, flap, flap, 28 frames per second'. History and politics are meaningless. 'History is the endless repetition of the wrong way of living, and it'll start again tomorrow.' Life is 'terribly brief', so 'one should try and catch every scrap of wind in order to form oneself, so that death means something – that you're really used up when you die'.⁶⁹

Larry spoke so feelingly about the Copts – 'the original, first real Christians' – comparing their prayers to the 'pretty weak stuff' of European Christianity, that Adam felt encouraged to probe his religious beliefs. He got nowhere, as his subject dodged and parried, hiding his lifelong metaphysical bent:

ADAM: Are you a religious person?
LARRY: I don't think so. Do I look like it?
ADAM: You say you're not a religious person, but you have a great affinity to mystic qualities.
LARRY: Well, I'm simply trying to find out where I fit in the universe, you know.
ADAM: Where do you think you fit?
LARRY: Well, I'm trying not to show!
ADAM: Were you ever tempted by any monastic life?
LARRY: I think everyone is, don't you? . . .

ADAM: This search for truth, is that something which came to you through age or
have you always had it?

LARRY: No, everybody's got it. Don't talk as though I'm a leper!⁷⁰

The visit to Egypt gave Larry a useful shove, and he returned invigorated
and enthusiastic from the trip that he had undertaken with such dread.⁷¹ 'I
am glad I came along,' Larry told Peter Adam. 'I need this kick in the pants
to get me out of myself and sort myself out. Now I can return . . . I am off
drink.' He had lost weight and looked alert and fit. 'I was relieved to have
my feelings reassured by this visit,' Larry wrote in his notebook. He
thought that they had caught on film 'that wonderful feeling of stillness that
Egypt always conveys: the slow, green blood-time of the Nile'.⁷² It was a
sentiment quite different from the moods of decadence and frenetic passion
conveyed in *The Alexandria Quartet*.

Summing up his Egyptian venture for Henry Miller, Larry wrote:

The reality I had almost forgotten. I had been so often accused of overwriting it that
I expected it to be paler than my reflections of it. But . . . the flamboyance and
extravagance of Egypt cannot be exaggerated and beside the reality my versions
read like washed out and twice sucked jujubes. Of course one must except poor
dusty down at heel Alexandria – which however had the grace to put me up one
young Justine, just to prove that the old rose tree is not dead. But where the Arabs
go they take the dirt and the dust and fanaticism of the desert. Cairo is one horrible
sweat of mankind and cars. ALL the world is being devoured by the petrol engine –
what can we do? But once upriver the feluccas take over and their grave
manoeuvres colour everything. The Nile is not all that broad, and in some places
very narrow and calm like a village river. All life flows down it: the artery attached
to this narrow line of green and ending in the umbel, the lotus of the Delta. Down
below there on the sea all is sophistication, but once upriver gravity sets in; the
statues become enormous and grave and they sit pondering in deserted valleys
bathed in a solid pharaonic light and framed by the whistling desert with its winds
and odours. One walks in time and space as if in a thick solution of something
opaque, a jelly. The mind goes numb and people have to repeat questions twice
because you don't hear the first time.⁷³

By mid-November Larry was back in Sommières, burrowing in for the
winter. Ghislaine was still staying at the house and Larry counted the days
until the 27th, when she was to 'gallop off', 'with her saddle bags full of
gold and a "judgement" for an income'. Larry claimed that he could have
presented evidence that would have turned matters in his favour, but he did
not feel that it would have been right. This did nothing to assuage his
bitterness: 'I have never had such a terrible time, lack of confidence, feeling

of being sabotaged', he lamented to his old crony Henry; 'at least that is over with.' He was again talking about selling 'this unheatable house' and moving to Greece, 'about which I still dream'.[74]

He had still not finished *Livia* either, and another three volumes of the eventual *Quintet* were to follow it, but by the end of the month he was already proposing to write a book, hinted at even earlier, about Provence.[75] Inspired anew by Egypt he surged ahead on *Livia*: after a month he called it done, dedicated the book to Denis and Nanik de Rougemont, and sent the typescript off to Faber. 'I am frankly pleased', he told Henry; 'it presages the form of my quintet of short novels – the Q novels – a Quincunx which is the magic pentacle etc etc!'[76] Later he would claim that the book 'clears up all the queries in *Monsieur* and opens the way forward for Constance in Love, the next bloody book.'[77] Apart from the fact that most people he knew in the Midi were 'terrible bores', Larry said that he was 'happier' than he would be in Paris or elsewhere. 'I'm lucky in good health,' he added.[78]

'I have had a mediocre year with money troubles and a divorce and suddenly rocky health due perhaps to drink,' Larry summed up 1977 to Fred Perlès – he was being more truthful to Fred than he had been to Henry, whose health was so poor that Larry was ashamed to complain to him. 'And of course too much work – very much too much of that,' he continued. 'Two books coming in September and various other things on the way.' For most of the letter he vented his fury at Jacques Temple for having led him on to accept an appointment on the jury of the Académie Mallarmé, thinking it merely an honorary post on a body that would award annual prizes in poetry. Then, Larry claimed, it turned out to be a clever advertising scheme for Rochas perfumes. Larry vowed to stay away from promotional ploys after 'this one innocent gaffe'. 'How is life treating you?' he asked Fred, concluding:

Mine is much the same as ever, and on the whole I am enjoying living alone and doing my own cooking with just from time to time a fine strong love affair which is still within my means thanks to yoga. But old age is really an indignity and one should have the courage to push off when once the body starts to give in – I am counting the years now! Henry is so very optimistic that it is good for us all, but he is in a bad way compared to what he was some years ago. I often think of his ping-pong room when I am having a drink at the Glacier. Sommières hasn't changed too much; but many of the old characters have bitten the dust, as I suppose I myself must do one of these finely-fashioned sunset days. Are you writing anything? It's the only worth while thing left apart from fucking – I am on the last fond lap of both![79]

'I HAVE CELEBRATED THE SPRING by having a couple of teeth out and getting divorced from Ghyslaine', Larry reported early in March 1978, 'so that I have a convalescent sort of feeling.' Penelope and Sappho had been visiting, and there were no complaints from their father: 'It's a change from living alone and cooking for myself which I now do rather well however.'

A posthumous note was coming increasingly into Larry's phrases, even when he was reporting successes. After telling Henry that it was 'congenial' and 'exciting' that Faber was going to publish his *Collected Poems*, 'a real collected at last', he added, echoing Lord Nelson, 'Kiss me Faber and I die happy. . . . All my work to date is quite definitively gathered and placed between covers. It's a wonderful finalised feeling.'[80] On 12 May Larry met James Brigham at Alan Thomas's home to look over the great pile of photocopies that Brigham had brought from his own collection in Canada or had turned up in British libraries. There were poems Larry had forgotten that he had written, and others such as 'In Arcadia' that had been published in two or more versions. Brigham argued for the restoration of dedications, especially to Larry's wives. Larry agreed. But when Brigham suggested the re-insertion of the explanatory marginalia to 'Cities, Plains and People', Larry objected that he wished to distance his work from the personal contexts in which it had been written. This time Alan joined the fray, siding with Brigham, and they won Larry's reluctant acquiescence. After four or five sessions, Larry stopped Brigham in mid-query: 'Well, I think that's your choice . . . . After all, you're the editor of this book.'[81] Brigham had thought that he was merely assisting by assembling the poems, but once Larry decided that he could trust his editorial judgement, Larry's generosity took over.

It was not only his *oeuvre* that seemed to him to be drawing to a close: 'I am very mighty old and grey at sixty-six and all systems are slowed down or on the blink?' Larry answered his own question with some positive assertions: 'I still stand on my head a good deal and have mastered every vice except red wine.' He was also settling into a near-hermit routine. 'I have learned to cook extremely well,' he told Henry. 'It is a great relief as I am now quite independent of women? No longer helpless? And it will strengthen my resolve to live alone until if ever I find someone livable . . . I used to be so helpless on the practical front.'[82] As the question marks betrayed, Larry did not quite believe in his independence – he cast an evaluating eye on each of his women visitors – and at least some of his friends disparaged his culinary abilities. Mary Mollo, herself a superb cook, complained that he laced everything beyond recognition with garlic and ginger. Also, while he was talking independence, for about a week he composed on a tape recorder, a procedure that tied him to a transcribing secretary: 'A relief to scrap the typewriter,' he said. In this, he was merging with the life of his character in *The Revolt of Aphrodite*, Felix Charlock.[83]

Larry's posthumous mood deepened as he contemplated the disappearance of his friends: nearly all of his Alexandria and Cairo circle had gone, he said. 'And Argentina too' – he was mourning the death of Bebita Ferreyra. He spent ten days in May 1978 proofreading *Livia* in London, where his friends were also thinning out. Now he seemed to prefer London to Paris, but only as the lesser of two purgatories. 'Paris is a ghost,' Larry told Fred Perlès, good only for bringing in each New Year at the Coupole; 'Things aint wot they was.'[84] In fact, he had written to Henry the year before, 'PARIS IS HORRIBLE, FULL OF DIESEL FUMES AND FRENZY. LONDON IS MUCH LESS STRAIN, LESS PULLUTED [*sic*] AND NOISY.'[85]

Only Greece seemed to hold some of the old magic for Larry: 'It has changed of course as everywhere has, but I think the vibration down the spinal column is still there.' Indeed, as he summed up the places he had loved, he sounded like Timon – neither human society nor politics nor architecture nor literature pleased him:

Myself I feel rather stale with Provence and would welcome a chance to spend some time in Greece; perhaps this autumn I shall try. France has become so crowded and diesel-dirty and Paris is full of skyscrapers like Manhattan – an inconceivable ugliness is spreading everywhere. One is reminded that this wretched land spawned the worst architect in the world, Corbusier – and his blighted influence hangs on. Paris has become a vast RABBINAT of Jewish intellectuals chewing their own blankets and puffing each other. Between LOVE STORY and Barthes there is hardly a seam showing . . . It's terribly depressing, it's lost its magnetism and is imitating America more and more each day while professing to hate and despise it. Of England . . . there is nothing to say; it's in a mess, and financially bankrupt as well as intellectually. The poor young are trying desperately to find something worth saying or doing, but as in all places where le peuple is on top and has all the pocket money, there is nothing much to do except drug and demonstrate and fiddle money. It is depressing beyond words. O dear, I wish I could feel happier about things; but the future seems charmless really after what we have seen and known.

Partly, of course, Larry was the victim of nostalgia for his youth and of the crime-fear of the senior citizen; but it was true that the French cities that he had loved, even the smaller ones like Nîmes, Montpellier and Avignon, were developing a palisade of 'skyscraper graveyards' around the peripheries, while the seaside villages 'are shot to hell with jerry-building'.

People, Larry said, were now 'afraid to go out after dark just like Los Angelese [*sic*] downtown'. He dreamed of an even more secluded refuge than Sommières: 'Maybe I will find some little pension in Corfu or Mentone or Orta and dodder myself into the grave.' Larry's talk of doddering off had as usual to be taken with a dose of scepticism: at that very moment he was looking forward to a visit from a young Alexandrian student of his work 'who might swap a heartbeat with me'.[86]

Larry was trying to face up to *Constance*, the next volume of the *Quintet*, but by 4 June he was still merely hoping to begin it 'quite soon'.[87] He had always considered summers as playtime, and throughout August he was hanging fire: 'I am gathering my wits together for a final plunge to pivot this whole muddle of a book into a coherent *shape*. Will there be time? One doesn't care really.' His hedonism wrestled with his artistic ambition – and appeared to be winning: 'The last breath and the last glass of wine are the sweetest.' Despite 'material and love-success', 1978 thus far had been 'une année very néfaste', very unlucky.[88]

Larry's big coffee-table book, *The Greek Islands*, appeared in September 1978, and on the 21st he presided over a highly successful signing at Hatchard's in London for which five hundred appeared. The next day he went to Paris for another signing at Galignagni. While staying with the Thomases in Chelsea, Larry was visited by his Egyptian student, but he rejected her to go out with Margaret McCall. The Alexandrian was distraught and threatened to kill herself, until Shirley Thomas's daughter talked her into a less frenzied state.

In Paris Larry found excitement of an intellectual nature when he met Keith Brown, a professor of English at the University of Oslo and an occasional reviewer for the *Times Literary Supplement*. Brown had written to Larry after taking up the architectural construction of *Tunc* and *Nunquam* in his 1977 seminar on the Experimental English Novel. During the course of his studies Brown had attempted to approach the novels through Renaissance structure. Among other points, he had perceived patterns of circularity in physical structures (St Paul's Cathedral, the brothel scenes), in movements (falcons circle aloft, Benedicta and Felix travel around the world), and in plan. Everything about the two novels pointed to careful planning, Brown said. There are seven chapters in each novel, with 21 sections in *Tunc*, 23 in *Nunquam*. The first section in *Nunquam* is really the end of the story of *Tunc*; therefore, each story line by this count contains 22 sections, and the ratio of the smaller to the larger divisions is 22/7, the common mathematicians' approximation of π.

Viewed in terms of Renaissance numerology and symbolism, the two novels appeared to be as carefully put together as any Elizabethan or Jacobean play. It all seemed too neatly structured not to be true, so Brown had written a first letter to Larry: 'Have we gone completely mad, or . . . .' Larry replied that he had deliberately used 'the pi notion, which is really the sort of mason's sign of an architectural mathematic'. 'Come to breakfast,' he commanded, and the meeting occurred at a small café next door to La Coupole.[89]

Brown's breakfast with Larry lasted from 8 a.m. to 5 p.m. 'Durrell was like a boy who had been given a new train set,' Brown recalled. Larry kept interrupting himself to exclaim with a laugh, 'You can't know how marvellous for me this is – talking to somebody outside my own circle who doesn't just think I'm mad.' From structure, Larry shifted to rhythm in the novel form. Brown, the university-educated Renaissance scholar, listened in fascination as Durrell the autodidact delivered a complex exposition of the interrelatedness of rhythm and architectural structure: every work needed both, Larry said, 'like a wave – I don't claim to have invented the image – going through the legs of Brighton pier'. When these elements were not in proportion, the work was flawed. Behind Larry's eagerness Brown sensed his terrible loneliness, 'the loneliness of a man isolated by the strength of his commitment to a profession which others do not really take seriously', a man of critical intelligence who had 'thought long and hard about the basic aesthetics of this chosen trade'. Given the persistent misunderstanding of his writing by reviewers and critics alike, why had not Durrell spoken out, Brown wondered. If a writer was faced with misrepresentation, Larry replied, 'there's absolutely nothing you can do about it but sit tight, and try to have faith that you've done your work well enough for better perceptions to break through eventually'.[90] Larry was reflecting his own unease when he made his novelist creation Blanford in *Livia* worry: 'He always had a sneaking fear that what he wrote was too private to reach a reader.'[91] Larry told Brown to walk with him to meet 'a friend', but when the friend turned out to be Larry's Alexandrian graduate student, who had followed him to Paris, Brown excused himself. 'Metaphysical speculation and sexual curiosity' had not lost their powerful symbiosis for Larry. The two men were never to meet again, yet years later Larry was still referring on occasion to Brown as 'my one intellectual friend'.[92]

In early October 1978 Larry motored in L'Escargot to Orta for a rendezvous with Claude Kiefer, and while there he put the final touches to *A Smile in the Mind's Eye*: the place and the company seemed appropriate for writing about Taoism. But he remained blocked on *Constance*, still saying that he was 'shortly going to move into the centre-pin novel of the group'.[93] Compared with his old friends, Larry felt that he was doing reasonably well: Henry was getting 'potty' about respectability, and Larry told him that he was so 'superrespectable' that he stood a very good chance of being awarded the Nobel.[94] In fact, Henry had recently asked his famous friends to write letters nominating him to the Nobel committee; Larry had complied, although he thought that 'one must be a sort of UNESCO wirepuller and president of PEN' to cop the prize.[95] It was all very well for Henry to court the Nobel, but Larry relished his privacy too much to permit even such notice as might increase his sales. When he was told of a would-be American biographer in November, he cabled his response: 'NO BIOGRAPHY AUTHORISED OR DESIRED WILL OPPOSE.'[96] Larry felt seriously threatened, and contemplated a campaign: he would find a lawyer in New York to threaten suit 'at the least deviation from truth'; he would write an exposé in the *Times Literary Supplement*. The man backed off.

Larry pursued the subject of a biography, however. He had learned through an experience of Henry's two years previously that it was difficult to block a determined biographer. 'I have apparently attracted another of this breed of silverfish . . . . Not that there is anything to hide but the principle surely is that one does these things by consent whil[e] the people are alive?' he said. There was another factor: he hoped to write an autobiography. Larry wrote to me proposing a solution:

I think a so-called authorised biography should follow upon death and be part of the literary estate. To this end, as my executors will be my two daughters, I can if you wish appoint you the 'authorised' biographer. You can meet them when over and see what they think. . . . You could begin amassing material right now on the understanding that it would come out when I croak. Let me know what you feel about this.[97]

As Larry freely admitted, he had a 'selfish' motive: a 'definitively selected biographer' would provide him with something of a 'shield'. He feared subjectivity more than objectivity: 'I am not anxious to gild the lily but I am anxious not to fall upon some predatory French literary man like Josef Coprophage and have HIM interpret me – I have already had offers here from people who proudly say that they have known me for 15 years . . . so has the concierge of my hotel who may have interesting things to reveal about my night life.' Larry had another motive: if his story were to be told, those with the information to tell it were rapidly disappearing: 'While I was cogitating this', he continued, 'my eye happened to catch a glimpse of my death chart and I realised with a shock that nearly the whole of my Middle East friends have died in the last few years – Fedden, Kinross, Spencer, Wilkinson, Katsimbalis.'[98]

Larry judged himself to be sound in body and spirit these days, and claimed that he no longer really minded his loneliness. 'I have at last got on top of that terrible hippogriff – "unable to be alone",' he told Henry.[99] 'I am living alone now and adoring it,' he wrote in confirmation to Fred Perlès. His periods of self-confidence and boasting were matched by panicky moments when he felt unable to cope with the details of life and taxes, or when he was tempted by love: 'An occasional girl swerves in like a swallow to break the monotony – but not my heart. Too old I guess at 65 [sic] to fall in love any more. But still "valide" for pleasure and affection.' He was amused when one of his *vieux copains* showed signs of weakening: Fred had gout. 'It's the most aristocratic thing that you've done yet,' was Larry's not so sympathetic rejoinder.[100]

Larry had sounded less blasé in a letter written to Henry only the day before. It had been a 'wonderful autumn': 'I have been having an extraordinary adventure with a 19 year old Christian Canadian Arab; I fear I have run into another version of Zelda Fitzgerald. But an angel of light and love, with the kind of grasp of things which is given only to schizos! I shall be running for my life by the end of the week.'[101] So much for his protestations of indifference.

Larry ran as far as Jersey, where he spent a snowy Christmas listening to Gerry's lemurs and chimpanzees before flying to Paris and the Coupole. He said that he had intended to see in the New Year alone 'on the old bar seats where we so often sat long years ago, drinking a good champagne, glass after glass', but he was joined by Ghislaine and then, after he had sent her home in a taxi, by 'that little demon Buttons who turned up for a New Year TRINC and stayed the night with me finally, in my eternal little Room 13 at the Royal'[102] – Buttons aromatic with Anaïs-Anaïs perfume. 'I lay there in the dark smelling it and thinking and saying never a word,' Larry wrote to Anaïs Nin's ancient lover.[103] Larry's 'Arab Canadian' had been 'hauled back by the hair to her musician's arms', and Larry ventured a comparison of women along national lines. 'New world' women tended to be 'brutalised' and 'anaesthetic' due to the brutality of their men, and consequently they wallowed in '*sentimentality*'. 'Ugh!' he concluded, 'Flavour for flavour – French for American – the difference in soul (I am thinking of a night with Buttons compared to a night with X) is really extraordinary. I couldn't live with such robots I think.' Before he returned to the Royal he had listened to Dixieland played by rather tipsy American artists resident in Paris, 'Then midnight with its riots of actors in masks and drunks and ruined ladies riding on the backs of waiters, Yugoslavs being expelled for the wrong reasons and sleeping cinéastes,' followed by a stop at the Closerie des Lilas. Savouring the memory of the long evening, Larry decided that, after all, Paris, 'though grubbier and more expensive, has not changed at all and if you arrived one afternoon in a balloon you would find everything in place to supply a meal starting with oysters and ending with a prime Roquefort'.[104]

AT THE BEGINNING OF 1979 Larry was in Geneva to have two deep cysts removed from his back by one of the surgeons who had treated his dying wife Claude. As he lay under a local anaesthetic he recalled the roses and oleanders planted by Claude around the Mazet Michel, where he had sat far into the night with Henry Miller, with Xan and Daphne Fielding, with Paddy Leigh Fermor and other tried and tested friends. The snipping of the cysts reminded him of the pruning of a gardener, the signposts of the seasons. 'It was eerie to listen to the chat of the surgeon as he went to work slowly and patiently like a gardener,' he told Henry. 'And the noise of the scissors and the scalpel, snip snip; he was talking about the transplanting of roses, snip by snip, so to speak, so that finally I had the illusion that he was tailoring a rather unruly rose tree which was growing out of my back and setting it to rights. I remembered too that Claude wanted to drown the mazet in roses and oleander and indeed she went all over France for her cuttings.' Larry had planted a humble dog-rose where Claude's ashes lay in the cemetery of the Chapel St Julien, and this too must have been in his mind. 'Well, snip snip,' Larry continued, 'I thought of your life . . . and Claude's roses and Eve's laughter, and your last visit to the stony old garrigue where we drank so much. . . .'[105]

Soon he was back in Paris for a rendezvous with Françoise, a twenty-year-old concert pianist from Angers. 'This promises well, except for the difference in ages!' Larry wrote to Henry. 'She came all the way down and bust into the house with a load of questions and was so happy to be treated right and listened to with patience that I now can do no wrong.'[106] Henceforth Larry would keep the Pleyel meticulously tuned against the visits of his young performer.

He needed to get to work himself. As his sixty-seventh birthday approached, he still had not even begun *Constance*. He recognized it as a 'CRUCIAL NOVEL', the dramatic centrepiece of the series. He admitted that he was 'SHADOW BOXING LIKE'. Now that he was not especially driven by money pressure, he was finding it ever harder to get down to serious writing. Henry thought that Larry had liver trouble, and sent him information on remedies, but Larry replied in capitals, 'I AM AFRAID IT IS A MIXTURE OF AGE AND ALCOHOL WHICH I AM SLOWLY BRINGING TO HEEL. THAT AND A RATHER WEARY HEART WHICH I HAVE BEEN STRAINING BY TRYING TO MAKE LOVE TOO MUCH.' There were Buttons, aged thirty-five, Françoise the pianist, and two other young girls, 'FULL OF FEATHERS AND CURIOSITY'. 'SOME OF THESE CHILDREN DON'T KNOW HOW TO COME OFF AND HAVE TO BE SHOWN,' Larry explained. 'I AM RATHER OLD TO BE GIVING THESE SORT OF LESSONS.'[107] There was probably an element of vainglory in the line he took to his friends from pre-war Paris, companions of his prime. 'First time in my life girls of nineteen and eighteen give me the gaffer's call sign,' he told Fred Perlès. 'I am surprised and delighted to find I can render good service (and a tendresse lacking in today's louts),' he commented, but he was finding 'fucking a strain'. He figured that he might have only a year or two more in this line, and this he claimed to view with equanimity: 'I don't care – I can revert to yoga with happiness now I am getting so good at it. Better yogi than fogey!'[108]

Adventures or not, by mid-March Larry was finally attacking *Constance*, 'to clean up the mess I made in Livia and Monsieur and rearticulate my dolly, my Aphrodite, my one and only!'[109] He reverted to his old disciplined work habits. He would write from 6 to 9 a.m., then motor to the post office, shop and answer letters. Only then, these days, would he have 'a glass', followed by lunch, a nap, a long walk through the vineyards during which he plotted the next morning's task. 'A glass' again in the late afternoon, a light supper, and bed by 8.30 or sooner completed his usual day. He set out to firm up the links between the 'real' and the 'fictional' characters: in the early pages Larry described the arrival in Avignon of Freud's sofa, sent to the real Constance by the fictional Pia and Sutcliffe. 'I thought you told me Sutcliffe was invented,' Constance says accusingly to Blanford; he replies 'evasively'.[110] Larry was to throw in a thin sprinkling of autobiographical details: Blanford has an affair with a Slade student; Sutcliffe mentions 'a German Horch with bullet-proof windows';[111] the book abounds in lost daughters, Lord Galen's and Lord Banquo's; Blanford's refusal to enlist in the military reflects Larry's non-service. Larry kept casting about for sources, and Peter Bird recommended *The World at War* by Mark Arnold-Forster as background for *Constance*.

Larry allowed himself to be distracted from *Constance* by Jay Martin's biography of Henry Miller. While neither malicious nor containing serious errors, the book was lamentable, Larry said, because its appearance would for years prevent a better biography from being written. 'My growls about the French are due to perpetual arse-licking and quid pro quo trade,' he continued. 'Every time anyone writes a piece about you you are in honour bound to preface his next four books.' In fact, Larry told Fred Perlès that he was writing a satire about Coprophage to be called COMMENT ARRIVER SANS JAMAIS VOYAGER. Larry even called up old grudges, singling out Philip Toynbee because he had 'shat on us all consistently since the first appearance of the Tropics and then the Quartet'. Toynbee was 'British sludge', Larry said, 'I rate him as low as a packet of Players dropped in a lavatory.' Since Toynbee had aligned himself back in 1960 with Larry's friend Hilary Corke in admiring the *Quartet*, Larry's vehemence is puzzling. Only Brassaï he defended against Henry's anger over *Henry Miller: grandeur nature*: their old friend had written 'nothing we have not said about ourselves so where's the rub?'[112]

LARRY'S BEHAVIOUR SEEMED MORE ERRATIC than usual these days and his pronouncements extra harsh. In particular, his judgement in dealing with Sappho was hardly sound. Sometimes he would send letters from his lovers to her, imagining that they would amuse her. Instead Sappho was offended, but more than that, as she wrote in one of her journals, 'I feel very threatened by the fact that my father is sleeping with women who are my age or younger. I feel he is committing a kind of mental incest and that it is a message to me as his favourite daughter' – Sappho invariably assumed precedence over her half-sister.[113] On 5 April 1979 Sappho had begun irregular but fairly frequent visits to a London psychoanalyst, Dr Patrick Casement. As Casement probed her mind, Sappho set out to determine why her 'relationship' with her father 'is now so fucked up'. Sappho in her journal accused Larry of expecting her to assume Claude's role and absorb his aggressiveness. 'We quarrel over a shirt label,' Sappho admitted.[114] Others observed that her visits to Sommières would begin on a happy note, and that then Sappho would often systematically bait her father by attacking his conservative politics, his drinking, his figure – and by flaunting her feminism.[115] She did much the same to Gerald Durrell, once attacking him even when he arranged a party in her honour.[116] In September Sappho apparently suffered 'some kind of nervous breakdown', and by the next month she had embarked on a series of readings about incest.[117]

Larry may not have discussed the topic of incest, specifically, with Sappho, but he encouraged her treatment by Dr Casement, telling her that she could both relieve stress and have fun with psychoanalysis, although he warned her that the Freudian system, 'though marvellous . . . is very limited'.[118] Also, bearing in mind her mother's mental history, he feared for her stability. Sappho believed that her father had patterned Livia on her: Livia the lesbian, Livia 'Buried Alive', according to the subtitle of the book. Looking back over her life, Sappho thought that she had always been death-obsessed: 'Mantra during early adolescence: I'm dead,' she wrote in June 1979. 'Mantra during mid-adolescence: I don't exist.'[119] She noted that most of her 'female literary models' 'died young or tragically: Sappho, Sylvia Plath, Emily Brontë, Dickinson(?), V Woolf'.[120] Homosexuality and bisexuality had appeared in Larry's characters since before Sappho's birth, but she chose to see herself in Livia, while denying that she too was lesbian. After four abortions, 'approximately, and one miscarriage', Sappho wrote, 'Heterosexual sex is out for me.' She added, 'So, too, is lesbianism' – despite 'that tepid infatuation with the German girl'.[121] None the less, even casual acquaintances sensed a strongly lesbian attraction in Sappho, and she would spend some time with a lesbian crowd when she visited New York in 1981. Sappho claimed androgyny for herself.[122] She termed her name 'One more cross to bear *for which I hadn't been prepared by my parents*.'[123] Whatever her sexual make-up, Sappho was painfully insecure and unhappy, as Larry realized. But he lacked the patience or self-control to deal wisely with her.

He could not resist making caustic and half-joking observations on the progress of Sappho's psychiatric treatment, and probably did, as she claimed, accuse her of being lesbian and of 'trying to grow a prick in the wrong place' as a sort of 'masculine protest'. Men, he said, suffered from the obverse, and 'worry themselves into stitches about not having wombs'. The cysts that he had recently had removed, 'two large lumps of camel fat off my back'[124], he called them, he attributed to a subconscious androgynous impulse.[125] Women who rejected men and childbirth often did this from lesbian proclivities, he said.[126] His conclusions struck him as good Groddeck, good Freud. Language was always Larry's chosen weapon, and if Sappho reacted with blind fury, he felt that the accuracy of his probes was confirmed.

Larry showed more sympathetic understanding in dealing with Penelope than with her half-sister. The back-breaking work and harsh conditions on the Cornish dairy farm proved too much for Penelope, and Larry agreed to help his daughter and Roger Walker buy the semi-inhabitable remnant of a castle in County Cork. The property was very picturesque, with a stone arch leading into a courtyard, but it cost tremendous labour to restore several rooms and to set up Roger's pottery workshop. The strain levied a heavy toll on the relationship, and within a few years Penelope was to leave Ireland and divorce Roger.

Larry remained restless, and even as he tried one woman after another, he kept taking short trips, including one in late spring to Vienna, on an invitation that derived from his *Greek Islands* success. He detested the city, he told Henry Miller.[127] To Vienna-born Fred Perlès he sang a different aria:

A quick line in your direction to tell you that I have just come back after ten days in VIENNA, a really marvellous experience; the British Council asked me to read them to sleep: and I profited by the experience to visit this extraordinary place which I now realise would (had it not been for an unfortunate geographical position as a war-crossroads) [have] been *twice* as fruitful as Paris. *Here* we should have gathered to coax ourselves out of our individual cocoons . . . . Anyway I had a whale of a time. What painters! What monuments! What vistas! . . . . It's a Baroque dream and not a bit fulsome as I feared it might be. And such inns, such countryside, such good air . . . . In fact I have been rejuvenated for the next bloody chapter of my book.

Larry had appeared at the Literary Society, and had tried to interest them in Fred. Also, he had visited Freud's apartment, where he found portraits of Arthur Schnitzler and Lou Salomé. 'It made everything come real,' Larry concluded. 'It unrolled in a direct scroll from Nietzsche and Wagner to Freud and Jung via Mahler Mozart and the whole of that tremendous group of bright minds. Jesus what a place; it dims Paris and Venice.'[128] While praising the *place* to Fred, Larry said nothing about the people, and his silence on the subject probably meant that he had found them neither sympathetic nor especially attractive. At any rate, he was to be back in Vienna the next March, piqued by his need to isolate the strange attraction of the city: that time, he would have a 'delightful stay':

It's more than the beauty and the opulence of the architecture etc; more too than the wine and food and living doubles of Rubens's wife in every café. It's a lieu bénit – as Delteil used to say; once standing in the battered dusty shattered sordid squalid square at the Saintes I asked him why, in some curious way, it was still giving off real life magnetism he answered me laconically with that phrase.[129]

IN OCTOBER 1979 LARRY, Ray Mills and Anthea Morton-Saner drove in L'Escargot to Corfu, then Larry went to Paris in November and made yet another trip there towards the end of December. He spent Christmas Day 'virtuously' in bed with his 'private doctor', Nicole. 'I could get extremely fond of this girl if she were free for fondness', Larry confided to Henry, 'and less a slave to black psychiatry (the throwing of intellectual custard pies).' Larry could assure himself that courting 'beautiful and timid and resolute' Nicole[130] was splendid research for the character of his psychiatrist Constance, but his creation had a complicated ancestry. The name Connie had appeared in Larry's fiction as far back as *The Black Book*, but without a clear Lawrentian connection. In *The Avignon Quintet*, however, Larry definitely had Lady Chatterley in mind; in fact, he would admit to Carol Peirce, a visiting American professor, in 1985, 'It's the counter-proposition to Chatterley. Just as everything you've told me about the American, Pynchon, sounds negative, whereas I am positive: it seems to me, we are born into bliss, and we're looking at the wrong set of optics.' Pointing to a photograph of Marie Millington-Drake, Larry said, 'Well, it is Lady Chatterley; it is Constance – really.'[131] She may also have owed traits to Claude Kiefer and to Simone Lestoquard, the 'snow-leopard girl'. Constance, truth to tell, was an avatar of all the beautiful blonde women he had known or imagined.

Larry may have proclaimed Constance's kinship with Lawrence's Constance Chatterley, but in intellectual gifts and her capable yet vulnerable nature she was closer to Constance, the young psychiatrist played by Ingrid Bergman in Alfred Hitchcock's 1945 film *Spellbound* – which Larry almost certainly knew. There are a number of similarities in plot between the film and Larry's *Constance*, and the film dialogue contains the phrase 'Constance in love', Durrell's provisional title for the book.[132] Despite the sources and the inspiration, Larry's writing was not going well. 'I am having such trouble with this novel', he lamented. 'It is already written in my head, but just won't move on paper.'[133] *Constance* would treat the World War in a kaleidoscopic pattern: through the eyes of a Red Cross organizer, Constance, who would also function as the fixed star, the constant romantic centre of the novel; through the viewpoint of a Prussian general pining for the challenges of the Russian Front; through the experiences of Constance's sister Livia, who would become a pro-Nazi German citizen; through the cynical vision of the French Nancy Quiminal. Despite his claim that his outlook was positive, there was a dark side indeed to the *Quintet*: as Constance says, 'What good is a poor psychiatrist when the whole world has gone out of its mind?'[134]

Larry's biggest practical concern this winter was the high price of petrol, which had 'wrecked the whole economy' he said, and this again led him to shut down his oil-fired central heating system.[135] Thereafter he would depend upon the open hearth in the kitchen and several small bottled-gas space heaters that he wheeled from room to room. Consequently, during the winter he lived more than ever in only three rooms of his echoing house: he had moved his bedroom to the ground floor immediately to the right of the front door, which gave him a straight run down the hall to the kitchen and the adjoining Darjeeling Room. He would huddle over a gas heater to keep the chill from his bones, as though finally overtaken by the cold of the freezing dormitories of his youth. For a week at the end of February 1980 Larry warmed himself in Paris with Nicole, the 'pretty little alienist . . . who still believes in Freud and my sanity'.[136] Larry contemplated his love-life with amused irony: 'I have gone and fallen for a young doctor, Nicole, who keeps a dog the size of a piano and drives a racing car at 170 kilos an hour. I think after sixty one becomes really progressively dottier and dottier until one blows up like a paper bag.'[137]

In April the first academic conference devoted exclusively to his writing was held at the State University of New York Maritime College, and Larry responded to the invitation with his typical gratitude whenever anyone said something nice about him: 'I wish I could get over for it, simply to roll in the honey!' Fortunately, he had ready-made excuses – he was leaving in days for Vienna on a *Times* assignment, and then he would really have to get back to work on *Constance*. Larry's cordiality to university scholars placed him in rather a strained position. He had something of a chip on his shoulder about academics, due in part to his own failure to pursue a university education. On the other hand, he wanted to be understood, and he also knew that the presence of his titles on course reading lists was important to maintaining his sales. He was pleased that Buffie Johnson would 'reveal all' at the conference, and that John Unterecker, 'to whom I owe so much', would speak. He seemed grateful for the notice, yes, but he held rigidly to the belief that his name must rise or fall by the quality of his writing alone. However, if a writer he admired took notice of him he seemed really delighted. When Vladimir Volkov in the preface to the final volume of *his* quartet proclaimed *The Alexandria Quartet* the greatest novel of the twentieth century, Larry dropped his reserve: 'Wow, as Fiddle Viracola would say, and add on a higher note "and SUPERwow!"'[138]

At the time there was talk of forming a Lawrence Durrell Society in America, and Larry replied guardedly, 'If you think a society then okay form one, but it makes me think I feel the flowers growing over me as I lie in the grave.'[139] A year later he was still worrying: 'Please keep it Anglo Saxon or we'll have endless jealousies and back-biting.' Attention in France both threatened his privacy and aroused the mutual jealousies of his Gallic boosters, he thought.[140] A Durrell society in America was too far away to do him much harm. This attitude on his part, plus the size of the United States university system, ensured that he would receive far more scholarly attention in America than elsewhere.

Larry was not about to declare a truce with the reviewers, however, and he lashed out particularly against *New York Times* writer Anatole Broyard, 'a hero's name this', a man whose 'ballcrushing cognomen has clearly gone to his head – a big stupid head like a Turkish box kite with just about as much air (hot) flowing through it'. 'He writes as sweet and shrill as a nicolodeon,' Larry fumed. 'You hear him chewing gum as he types!'[141] Two years later Broyard would write as friendly a reappraisal of the *Quartet* as Larry could desire, but for the present he claimed that Broyard and an unnamed colleague at the *New York Times* had cost him 10,000 copies in lost sales. This was the division that Larry made: reviewers could endanger his livelihood, which was damned serious; he was more ambivalent about the academics: while he did not exactly trust their abilities or their insights either, what they said and wrote about him just might enhance the understanding of his books. And *that* meant a lot to him.

'So far it's been a wonderful year', Larry said in the spring of 1980, 'so many seminars and so few kicks in the pants'. He was casting about for some radical change in his life that would free him to work. 'I am only 100 pages up on Constance', he lamented, 'hobbled by 100 and 1 interruptions which are driving me mad; I can't find a woman to offer me the protection I need. Or perhaps don't any more? I am not so sure. But I regret the age of Claude where I was really free to work and to think of nothing else – Claude even wrote my love letters for me, so to speak.' He was hoping 'desperately' to finish *Constance* by mid-summer, and then press on: 'If only I can continue writing the books might round out into a sort of autobiographical whole one day.'[142] This sounded exactly like Henry Miller's lifelong intention, except that Larry as always wanted his autobiography to be interior, a life of the spirit, a life in disguise. By the time he had reached the mid-point of *The Avignon Quintet*, Larry was fading more and more into his fiction, blending into it, until all that remained was his ironic smile, like the grin of the Cheshire Cat – and even that sometimes faded. Larry was coming increasingly to eschew action, to avoid public movement. When he did venture from the shrouded house, it was likely to be to visit Tony Daniels, and then he would sit silently sipping his drink and gazing into the fire.[143] Partly to evade visitors, Larry was thinking of moving to Greece, and indeed had planned to make 1980 his last 'residential year' in France. However, Greece was not yet sufficiently integrated with the European Common Market to have a double taxation agreement – and he had no intention of paying both British and Greek taxes.

FOR YEARS HENRY MILLER HAD BEEN getting increasingly decrepit. A failed artery replacement had left him largely confined to a wheelchair, and he was blind in his right eye, totally deaf in his left ear, had a dislocated left hip, but was still 'merry and bright' and for three years had enjoyed a 'perfect' – if platonic – love affair with Brenda Venus, a former beauty queen. Henry had recently fallen victim to a money scare and had consented to be filmed once more by Robert Snyder. Henry told Larry, 'They want me to die on television – and I'm going to try, just to please them.'[144] Then Georges Hoffman, Henry and Larry's literary agent in Paris, arrived for a long-promised interview and very nearly did record Miller's death. Henry was bedridden but still eloquent, although reduced to a speaking head on the pillows. Hoffman was so moved that he wept after leaving Henry's room. Towards the end of May 1980 Larry received a letter from Henry, dictated to a friend, in which Henry said, 'I am truly dying now – or at least I think I am.' Henry wished Larry 'Most tender regards interim', and then added a postscript twice the length of the letter: it was Henry to the last. 'That's about it, Larry,' he concluded, 'All the best.'[145] Henry Miller died on 7 June, and Larry sorrowfully added his name to the Death Chart on the wall.

Larry had expected the news for so long that he did not register any shock, but when Fiddle called, asking if he would attend Henry's funeral, Larry reacted angrily: 'I don't want to go! There's going to be a bunch of bums hanging about. I know what my relationship is!'[146] His letter to the 'last but one of the Mohicans', Fred Perlès, poured venom on those 'literary pall-bearers we have inherited in France'. Larry's main targets were a pair of his own early supporters. 'Temple and Fanchette and others have come fully up to scratch,' Larry wrote. 'As a matter of fact Anais, operating from beyond the grave put a snuffer on Jean who at once mounted a society of Amis D'Anais Nin to "defend her memory" as he put it. Anais, who was something of a specialist in rising by literary association[,] told off her brother to snuff Jean as superpresident and inventor of Anais. There was a great huff all around.' 'Hardly are we over that', Larry continued, 'when Delteil dies and at once Temple sweeps into action; providentially Mrs Delteil went out of her mind so that she only has the vaguest grasp of what is going on. It remains for Jacques to pump out the body for his own greater glorification.' And so on at length. Larry did not seem to mind that Fiddle Viracola had arranged a memorial for Henry, but he said 'judge my surprise' when he learned that Norman Mailer, whose book on him Henry had especially hated, would open the proceedings, while New Directions had declined to participate. 'What an epitaph', Larry proclaimed; 'Mailer to read over one's tomb, and New Directions to piss as they have always pissed on Henry as a farewell gesture. . . . My advice to you my boy is just to refuse to die, or all these vultures will fly over to embalm you.'[147]

Fred concurred in Larry's estimate of Temple, but did not share his anger. 'That's it, Larry,' he wrote. 'We two don't need to comfort each other, we've been born comforted. Friends keep dying right and left, a normal process. Perhaps one of the beauties of life is that it is transient.'[148] Fred really believed this, and so lived with a contentment that inevitably escaped Larry.

Larry seemed, both immediately and in the long term, to view Henry's death philosophically, but this did not mean that he did not feel most deeply the loss of his longest standing literary friend, the last of his four inspirational 'uncles', as he liked to call Eliot, Katsimbalis, Seferis and Miller. Larry had armed himself against Henry's departure by thinking of him as done for years before his actual demise. As far back as 1975 Larry was referring to Henry as someone almost gone. Thus each letter from Henry was a surprise, a reprieve from the end that Larry had already vouchsafed him. Larry had accustomed himself to the idea of Henry's death, so that the news came almost as an anticlimax.

IN AUGUST 1980 LARRY went to Athens for over a month of visits with old friends, including Kimon Friar. On 16 September he received the National Greek Tourist Organization prize for the Best Book on Greece in 1979, a triumph for *The Greek Islands*, the book he had been pushed into writing as a pot-boiler. From Athens Larry came to England and lodged for six weeks with Celia and Rose Voelcker, neighbours of Anthea Morton-Saner's in Warbeck Road, Shepherd's Bush, west London. Larry christened the place 'the Brontë House'.[149] Sappho had offered him space in the house in Loraine Road, north London, that she and her companion Simon Tompsett had bought in 1977. Sappho warned him that it was 'knee-high in plaster dust' because of remodelling. Perhaps wisely Larry decided not to move in,[150] but one day he came over for kebabs and retsina with Sappho and Simon. Larry had helped her buy the place with a contribution of £5000. Additional funds had come from Simon's mother, and the arrangement was that Sappho would pay off the balance of the purchase price by taking in boarders.

In a curious way, Shepherd's Bush was a return to India, an India blended with the working man's London: Larry walked about the Shepherd's Bush Market set up permanently, indoors and out, between Uxbridge and Goldhawk roads below an elevated quarter-mile of the Metropolitan line. Muslim *halal* butchers hacked up portions of beef, lamb and goat in stalls; turbanned Sikhs offered silks and small carpets; cockney costers warned customers not to touch the fruit; Africans and West Indians bought and sold lengths of printed cloth. Larry found and patronized Jeffrey's, an Indian takeaway restaurant that offered oily onion bhajee, samosas and hot curries. There were better establishments closer to Anthea's street, but Larry would remain loyal to Jeffrey's.

Larry's excuse for the London trip was to launch his new *Collected Poems*. 'By some divine fluke' his poems would be graced with a Henry Moore etching on the dust wrapper, a 'consecration, quite unsolicited and undeserved', he said.[151] The moving force behind this was Bernard Stone, who was arranging for a limited edition at £750, each to be signed by Larry and prefaced by a signed original of the Moore etching.

He saw Fred and Anne Perlès under rather rushed conditions, but found it 'marvellous and reassuring' that they both looked well – so he told Fred. He disliked Anne as much as ever, but he maintained appearances for Fred's sake. What with Henry's recent death and his own wheezing, Larry expected all of his friends to have one foot in the grave. He wrote to Fred, 'I took my asthma to Edinburgh where I was gone over by the docs who found most organs in good repair.' He had stayed with Ray Mills, who introduced him to the best specialists. 'The asthma is not due to age', Larry reported; 'I could have got it any time. But I have decided to defeat it by a combination of science and witchcraft.'[152]

Reassured that he was not dying, at least for the present, Larry fled in early October to a rainy Paris, where he looked up Buttons. 'Little Buttons yawned dreadfully as she crawled out of bed at six to go to work,' he confided to Fred. 'I'm lucky – must not become gâteux with it.' He was recognized at the Select and pressed into accepting a free drink 'en honneur de M. Miller et ses amis'. Paris – and Buttons – were still good for his morale, but *Constance* was nagging at him: 'Tomorrow Sommières, silence, yoga, no drink, *work*!'[153]

In 1980 Sappho married Simon Tompsett, with whom she had been living for half a dozen years. Instead of bringing them closer together, the marriage contract seemed to drive a wedge between them, and they soon spent much of their time apart. Larry, who had found Tompsett rather a dull stick, complained, 'They were getting on perfectly well until they had to go and get married.'[154] By June 1981 Sappho was writing in her journal, 'Bitter bitter bitter thoughts about Simon.'[155]

Early in 1981 Larry came down with a mysterious ailment that stiffened his joints and deprived him of the use of his hands for 'nearly a month of thoroughly psychosomatic exhibitionism' and 'tedious side effects'. It was diagnosed as aspirin poisoning, but Larry suspected that part of the reason for his breakdown was his struggle with *Constance*, 'this novel which trails and trails'. Sappho arrived to stay for a week just as Larry recovered, and he spoke to her about his decision on his biography. She was planning a trip to New York in the spring, and Larry promised me, 'She will tell you *all*!'[156]

Larry evolved a firm theory about his illness: 'It was a real expiation . . . a purge,' he wrote. 'I must say I stage-managed it very well. I drove all the nurses crazy.' Then he reached back in time to assign a reason for his 'poisoning': 'It was Miller's death and my father's death.' Relieved by his recovery of the use of his hands and evidently liberated in spirit, Larry attacked *Constance* to such good effect that two weeks after Sappho left he was able to report, 'I've only got another fifty or sixty pages to go. It is such a relief.'[157] Then, turning his 'obscure psychosomatic illness' to good account, Larry reserved 15–30 May at a Corfu Club Méditerranée for 'a cheap rest in Greece'. He needed the rest before coming to grips with the conclusion of the novel: 'I think I see how which is a relief as I didn't.' His illness had been sent, he believed, 'to guide me to the solution'.[158] This was Groddeck rearing his owl's head: the It within Larry had brought on the paralysis of his hands for some good purpose. Groddeck was much on Larry's mind, and less than a fortnight later he would boast of his part in getting *The Book of the It* published in paperback in America, France and Italy. At the core of Larry's creative process was also his firm belief that the characters assumed an independence of action greater than that enjoyed by their creator. Larry might have a general idea of where his novel should go, but he was quite prepared to see his characters take matters into their own hands and up-end his original vision. If he lost control of his story in a way that he disliked, he would scrap it and start again.

Larry's innate caution led him to understate his progress to Alan Thomas: 'Constance is coming slowly to land – Ouf!' Alan had just purchased at his request a half-page fragment of prose in Stendhal's holograph and Larry responded that he was 'mad with joy to have his actual handwriting on my bedroom wall!' In some ways Stendhal was the patron saint of *The Avignon Quintet*: 'What encouragement he gives me with all his pains and mishaps and hopes and disasters!' Larry wrote his thanks to Alan on the back of a ribald card, for which he apologized with doubtful sincerity: 'I seem to have got into the dirty postcard business by mistake. They say my name is responsible – DUR-PUR-SUR – I'm not sure it hasn't something to do with an erection – it's dangerous to boast at my age. . . .'[159] Around this time Larry was caught up in a 'tremendous affair' with a young writer who called herself Mississipi with one p. 'The pace was too hot for me,' Larry confessed later. 'She's a glorious creature but a man a minute girl.'[160]

Larry interrupted his work on *Constance* to present an autobiographical address in French at the impressive Centre Pompidou, the Beaubourg, in Paris on 1 April 1981. This was his first, and would prove to be his only, public lecture in France, and he crafted it far more carefully than he had his pair of talks in California years before. After an introduction by Jean Fanchette, Larry gave the Pompidou audience an outline of his philosophic position three fifths of the way through *The Avignon Quintet*. His lecture was not only for the French: he would send an English version, 'From the Elephant's Back', to Tambimuttu to publish in his new venture *Poetry London/Apple Magazine*. He promised in his talk 'to discuss the theory and the practice of fiction in relation to myself', particularly that 'ambivalence of vision' that had him at times feeling 'more Asiatic than European'. He spoke at some length of the elephant-child Sadu that had been his playmate in a childhood lived in a stable, evolved colonial world. When he had set out to become a writer, Larry explained, he was struck by the instability of the modern world: 'What a gap stretched between Robinson Crusoe – the last novel of human isolation without loss of identity, without alienation, and Kafka's Castle.' The notions that the ego was not discrete, that matter was an illusion – these were Indian originally, and had only recently been corroborated in the West by Freud and Einstein in turn. The problem was vintage Durrell, but now he felt that he was working towards an answer. Curiously, he did not think that science had brought clarity: 'The universe had become a huge incomprehensible machine from which the only philosophy to be drawn was one of cosmic pointlessness.' If mankind mirrored the universe, then, 'Was he simply a succession of states, like an old movie?' Larry asked rhetorically. He was trying to approximate a portrait of the whole man by a technique of 'jump-cutting, like a modern film'. This was the essential clue to what he was attempting to illustrate in the *Quintet*: the relationship of reality to fiction, of creator to created, of abstract idea to concrete event. Thought becomes act; act becomes thought. 'Underneath the action will I hope be the Asiatic notion of a world renewed afresh with each thought', Larry said; 'therefore man as a Total Newcomer to each moment of time'. By entropic decay, the universe was moving ineluctably towards thermodynamic extinction; by the power of thought and of love, some individuals could win a personal reprieve. India had shown him the way – even before he knew what he was looking for; and Europe had given him his voice: in the poets Valéry, Eliot, Yeats and 'the greatest of them', Fernando Pessoa, and in his 'uncles': Henry Miller, Seferis, Katsimbalis and Stephanides – Larry substituted Stephanides for Eliot in this naming of his mentors. He maintained that 'there is a family feeling about my books', and explained that 'a character from an early book may stray into a later book without warning'.[161] Larry saw a unifying pattern. His hearers at the Beaubourg probably remembered best of all the elephant Sadu.

The great hall at the Centre Pompidou had been packed: 'They must like bad French and a lot of incomprehensible jokes,' Larry commented. He had followed that up with an 'extraordinary coup': 'I was invited to be the "honoured guest" for the 1 o'clock news programme – thirty minutes at peak viewing', he wrote, 'but the peak was made even peaker by the fact that it was the first bulletin to deal with the assassination of Reagan; fancy! I found myself upstaging the news of the hour, as one actor to another!'[162] As a former press officer, Larry appreciated the value of timing and coincidence.

Larry returned to Sommières and *Constance*. He felt that he needed an event that was powerful, savage and stunning to conclude the novel, a counterpoise to the earlier war passages. He found it in the murder of Nancy Quiminal, the Frenchwoman who had become the unwilling mistress of the Nazi administrator in order to protect her family and ailing husband. Very likely the scene had been suggested by Xan Fielding's account of the shaving of the heads of women who had accepted the embraces of German soldiers, a rite that had been carried out savagely throughout liberated France. 'The main participants were made to parade up and down in front of a jeering crowd,' wrote Fielding. 'Bedlam, I imagine, must have been much the same as this; for the object of the mob's derision – a handful of sullen creatures with shaven pates – looked like frightened lunatics.'[163] From this account Larry apparently fashioned the parade of lunatics from the asylum of Montfavet into Avignon, and then the humiliation and fatal shooting of Quiminal. Fielding had witnessed the head-shaving scene in Digne; Larry wrote it into Avignon. The drunken spree of the mob in *Constance* corresponds to the sprees with which each of the earlier Quincunx volumes ended: *Monsieur* with 'Dinner at Quartila's', *Livia* with 'The Spree', Prince Hassad's party. Larry deferred his own spree: on 23 April, Shakespeare's birthday, he announced, 'Good omen or bad I have this day *finished* Constance in a sort of teetotal haze of exhaustion.'[164] He had not been drinking since his illness in January, and he cautiously hoped that his abstinence might prove permanent.[165] He felt that he had earned a rest: 'I now am going to have a spell of rocking chair to see what the wild waves are saying.'[166]

Larry had his character Sutcliffe proclaim the pattern of a *roman appareil*, a novel of structure. 'Why not a book full of spare parts of other books, of characters left over from other lives, all circulating in each other's bloodstreams,' proposes Sutcliffe. Within the *Quintet*, character-echoes were becoming apparent: Dr Bruce Drexel/Piers/Silvie in *Monsieur* are reflected by the 'real' Blanford/Hilary/Livia triad in *Livia* and *Constance*. In the novel bearing her name, Constance discovers a parallel in Constanza, dead sister of the Nazi governor of Avignon, and so on and on. And there were links to earlier novels: the sardonic laughter of Pursewarden, the chuckle and wheeze of Scobie – Sutcliffe, in some ways reminiscent of the old transvestite rogue, has 'Tiresian tits' and occasionally wears earrings, yet he also embodies the ribaldry of Caradoc, the accents of Antrobus. 'To commingle and intersperse contingent reality – that's the game!' exclaims Sutcliffe, himself a fiction invented by the fictional novelist Blanford, invention of 'old D.'

A couple of years earlier Larry had suggested that his 'Quincunx' would follow a *gigogne* structure, the parts nesting one inside the other like a Chinese puzzle;[167] but a more useful pattern for *The Avignon Quintet* was the quincunx itself. Now, with *Constance* completed, it was becoming apparent that the first novel, *Monsieur*, stood last in straight chronology. In a conscious inversion of the usual reality-to-fiction sequence, the volume was a 'fiction' based on the 'reality' of its siblings, and in a further overthrowing of conventional expectation, the 'fictional' *Monsieur* was being revealed as the *thematic* centre of the *Quintet*: the violence and destruction of war,

Manichaean duality, the practice of psychiatry, the triune love relationships are all set forth in the first book, from which the others would radiate by association, not as temporal sequels. The inversions in chronology and in fiction/reality complement the evil/good inversions and the sexual inversions: brother-sister incest, lesbianism. *Monsieur* was the centre spot on the domino piece of Larry's quincunx pattern, and *Constance* would prove its most dramatic – and longest – satellite.

ON 3 MAY SAPPHO FLEW to New York for nearly a month's visit. 'I hope Saph creates a good impression!' Larry said.[168] She arrived without a return ticket and was held up by the immigration authorities, who went through her entire address book, quizzing her about various names. She stayed with a psychiatrist friend to the west of Central Park, was given a party by Buffie Johnson, and was introduced to New York theatre personalities by Fiddle Viracola. She asked some of Fiddle's friends to show her 'the seamy side' of Manhattan.[169] 'I'm writing a play on the Brontës', she told people, 'but don't let my father know.' She hinted that her father would be jealous if he knew that she was competing with him.[170] Shortly thereafter Larry said, with evident approval, 'Sappho is writing on the Brontës – but I'm not supposed to know.'[171] She had made sure that he *would* know: it was part of her game of teasing him.

Around the end of June Sappho visited her father in Sommières, and on her return to London wrote thanking him for a 'delightful refreshing week'.[172] Before writing to him, however, she had appended a rider to her will, requesting that she be buried in Steep churchyard. Then she added, 'In the event that my father should request to be buried with me – my wish is that the request be refused.'[173] Her feelings towards her father were more than ever fluctuating wildly.

In October 1981 Larry returned to Edinburgh for another physical examination: his 'asthma' was not improving. En route he saw Fred Perlès, but there were others present and the occasion turned into a 'ghastly . . . pub crawl' for which Larry apologized. Fred advised him to slow down, and Larry had to agree: 'But you always had the capacity to float and not to worry. Wish I had. I'll try and learn.' After their meeting, he explained, 'I ran away to Edinburgh so that I could have a fairly exhaustive check over on the cheap as Ray Mills is in charge of a big hospital with all sorts of machinery and drawbridges and portcullises and smashing nurses.' This time the doctors found something serious: 'They did their damnest [sic] to find me something with a nice name and finally came up with

EMPHYSYMA which is not at all bad, seeing that I am pro Greek.'[174] Larry really did seem rather pleased, and thereafter seldom failed to mention 'my emphysema' with a touch of rueful pride whenever he wheezed.

After his treatment Larry went to Corfu to try the effect of two-hour walks and a quiet hotel life 'with a suitcase full of philosophers and poets'. For a while he had the 'grave Saroyya' for company, but then he was alone, 'delectably so'. In his exhilaration at finishing a draft of *Constance*, Larry resolved to tackle the next *Quintet* volume before Christmas. But he was in no hurry, and he gave himself up to the magic of Corfu 'in delicious autumn weather, all crumbling into winter with high seas still warm for bathing'.[175] He stayed on the island until the last week in December.

When Leslie Durrell dropped dead of a heart attack in London, Larry did not attend the funeral: while he could speak with some affection about Leslie as a youth, the older man who appeared never to have been able to take hold had become a complete stranger. Gerry had shared Larry's exasperation with Leslie: they had each been asked to bail him out financially at various times, and that was simply unforgivable. In his last years Leslie had found employment as a caretaker near Hyde Park, and Larry used to joke, 'When I pass by in a taxi I get down on my hands and knees so I won't catch him dusting the Marble Arch.'[176] Apart from his daughters and Gerry, the only one in the family for whom Larry appeared to retain any affection was Margaret. Doris, Leslie's widow, lived on for many years in their small flat. When in her eighties she would sum Leslie up in her cockney voice with an appreciative chuckle: 'Aow, 'e was a proper buggah!'[177]

LARRY WAS NEVER ONE TO welcome birthdays, but his seventieth seemed especially to infuriate him. When Mary Mollo rang him up to congratulate him, he exploded: 'Damn cheek celebrating birthdays; it's like someone photographing you naked in your bath!'[178] Then he was badly frightened when he drove into Nîmes and was caught in a student riot around the Roman arena: combatants from two lycées having a 'carnival battle' with rocks and flour bombs swarmed over L'Escargot, grinning at Larry with painted 'Fellini faces'. He arrived home white with flour. On 3 March he posted off the 'proofed up' typescript of *Constance*.[179] He felt that the novel had gone well, and his judgement was supported when it was short-listed for the Booker Prize in 1982.

He was full of schemes to defeat ageing, and around this time he enjoyed telling friends that he planned to sell La Maison de Mme Tartes and live in a flat in Monaco or in a caravan at the beach, or else to resume his wandering life in L'Escargot. Another scheme that he investigated was the possible sale of his house under the *système viager*, a purchase agreement that would allow him to live in it rent-free for the rest of his life. The new owner would be responsible for maintenance. Larry dreaded especially the expense of keeping the slate roof reasonably watertight. In the end, he did nothing, and when the roof leaked – into a top-storey cubbyhole where some of Sappho's books were stored – he endured the damage rather than act.

He settled into a routine that resembled the half-housekeeping of his holidays in Greece. His work rhythm continued: he would try to write until noon, despite interruptions by visitors and the telephone. He had not found dictating into a tape recorder much of a success, and he still wrote mainly on his old manual typewriter. He was never to purchase an electric machine for himself. Most weekday mornings Ellen Buis, his Dutch part-time *bonne*, would appear around nine in the morning, do a bit of cleaning, cook a pot of rice and perhaps another dish, then leave shortly after noon. She would attempt to fend off casual intruders, but Larry's natural courtesy still left him open to much humbug. When the writing did not flow, a glass of wine would appear at his elbow very early in the day, and then he would welcome most visitors so long as they would share a bottle or two with him.

Larry became quite proficient at making simple baked meals for company: a whole chicken in a dish, sprinkled with olive oil, slices of raw ginger and garlic, dusted with paprika and any other spices to hand; a plate of halved *poivres rouges*, anointed with more olive oil and ground thyme. In season he liked a bisected avocado with a puddle of olive oil and soy sauce in the hollow. Dining was informal: 'Pick it up with your fingers, à la grec,' Larry liked to tell guests.[180] Sometimes he cooked with a flamy Madras curry, 'fresh from the armpits of Krishna'.[181] In fine weather he used a makeshift grill in the garden; the efficient clockwork spit of the Mazet Michel days had vanished.

The opening, a short stroll away, of a large supermarket with an excellent wine and cheese selection made shopping easy, but he still liked his customary circuit: to the post office, where he parked L'Escargot while he made a loop on foot inside the mediaeval walls, picking up a small orange-fleshed melon here, a *baguette* there, a *cervelle de petit nègre* – 'brain of a small Negro' – at his favourite *pâtisserie*. This confection, a meringue formed into two hemispheres and dipped in chocolate, did look astoundingly like an anatomist's model of a human brain. If it was a Saturday, Larry's progress would be slowed by numerous small conversations. Ludo Chardenon had moved to the edge of Sommières, setting up his 'Paradis des Plantes' business in a large house-and-barn complex. Ludo had become a real friend to Larry, inviting him for gargantuan feasts, and ploughing and planting his small *potager* at the back of Mme Tartes's or giving him free photocopying whenever he needed it. After a chat with Ludo, Larry would angle across the farmers' market in the main square, climb the steps of the hidden Reilhe passage and emerge by the Vidourle a few yards from the Café Glacier, where he would have coffee or a small carafe of *vin blanc*. The exquisite tact of the Sommiérois meant that he was neither sought out nor treated with an obsequious courtesy that would have embarrassed and angered him. The whole town knew M'sieur Durréll and seemed pleased by his presence, but the compliment of his residing there was accepted by people who were conscious of their own worth. To the stranger, he would appear hardly distinguishable from any farmer or townsman doing his errands. Only in the warm days of summer, when Larry lived in a pair of brief shorts and a cotton jersey, would he have stood out from his more conservatively clad neighbours.

In the summer of 1982 Larry was again on Corfu, this time as the guest of the Birds. For a while everything went well, but then his drinking became too much for Joan and she threw him out. He repaired to one of the Corfu Club Méditerranées, complaining loudly that he was forced to live in a 'mud hut'.[182] While he hated Club Med tourism, he liked the informality: food, wine and entertainment were laid on, no one knew him, and there was the occasional young woman to fall into his toils. It had been a 'wonderful holiday', he thought, and he had written a few thousand words of *Sebastian*, the fourth book of *The Avignon Quintet*. He decided that the final volume would be 'the True Confession of Jack the Ripper so to spk'.[183] Then, Larry said, he could 'retire from the ring with a clear con-science! There's a good Freudianism for you.' After that he would 'take to the chimney corner', where he would 'write chimneycorn'.[184] Meanwhile, he kept fairly steadily at *Sebastian*, pushing the novel along to forty thousand words by mid-September, sixty by the first week in December, although 'with all the usual panics and hot flashes'. Concurrently he was having adventures with 'the nymphs', among them Brigitte-the-astrologer whom he called La Sournoise and termed 'Not a woman but a fer de lance!' And then there was a Buddhist with rose madder hair who lived in a forest and wrote poetry. Larry justified himself in doggerel against the time a year or two hence when he would be off the 'gold standard':

When your bow has lost its twang
And your three friends rather hang
When the whole world seems to sag
There is nothing in the bag . . . .[185]

Larry had added a painter to his roster of acquaintances – not a lover, this one – and in October he sat for Barbara Robinson at her atelier-home in Quissac, just ten miles distant. A small, intense woman with a grown-up family, Mrs Robinson had been in the Midi since 1957, and Larry soon felt completely at ease with her, sitting quietly immobile for hours as she painted him in oils. The powerful, dramatic quality of Mrs Robinson's landscapes did not translate easily into her portrait of Larry, and he ended up looking rather like a sunburned Winston Churchill. None the less a friendship was confirmed, and Larry wrote an appreciation of her work in which he praised a 'pictorially impressionistic' technique that gave the 'effect of lightning-flashes of pure intuition'.[186] His piece would be printed as the preface to a volume on her work published in 1985.

It seemed that for each new friend, Larry lost two people from his past. Theodore Stephanides died quietly in London in the spring of 1983. There had not been much contact between the two men latterly, but Theodore had been adopted by Shirley and Alan Thomas as a sort of resident saint. Theodore was followed shortly by Nancy Durrell Hodgkin, who for some time had been courageously battling cancer. She maintained that she had never read anything of Larry's after *The Black Book*, and she had asked her second husband not to do so either. She never forgave Larry for her early sorrows, and died on 8 June 1983. Larry was deeply moved by her death, and shortly afterwards he spoke to a friend about Nancy and their Corfu life with tears streaming down his face.[187]

Sappho was still causing Larry worry: her life appeared to him to be disordered; he feared that she might have a narcotics or at least prescription drug addiction; her north London house depressed him. Flakes of paint hung from the living-room ceiling: Sappho had let the bath run over and the plaster was ruined. He felt helpless to intervene, and his attempts to give Sappho advice usually led to quarrels. Early in 1983 she was in hospital briefly because of a nervous crisis, and Penelope, despite being deeply involved in nursing the dying Nancy, had moved to her house temporarily to look after her half-sister. In sharp contrast to Penelope, who though eleven years her senior could have been taken for the younger sibling, Sappho seemed dull and despondent, her dark eyes at times both hostile and frightened, and she was overweight.[188] In October her stomach was pumped out after she had taken an overdose of sleeping pills and then telephoned her mother. Eve lived alone and very capably in her Holland Park flat, but Sappho felt that she should be caring for her mother rather than the other way around. Also, unbeknown to her father, Sappho had become a frequent visitor at Nancy's Dorset home, and her death had added to Sappho's distress. Guilt and loss loomed over her. Her attempted suicide shocked the family; Larry, distraught with worry, depended on Penelope for help.

To others, Larry complained about Sappho and spoke well of Penelope, but this did not mean he had been consistently an effective father to either daughter. Very trim, smartly dressed, very English, and with her mother's beautifully moulded face, Penelope certainly reminded Larry of Nancy – and that brought out the rogue in him. In spite of her periodic visits to Sommières, they were not at ease with one another. The loss of contact between Penelope's second and seventeenth years, bridged only by their brief meetings when she was eight, had left Larry out of her growing up, and they had never been able to close up the emotional distance. Then, too, Penelope did not like his great dark house, nor could she approve of her father's manner of camping in it, as she had let him know. Now their shared concern over Sappho drew them together. For the next fifteen months Penelope kept Larry informed of Sappho's state and consulted him at every turn.

Larry remained silent about his work these days, which as usual meant that the writing was going well. On 7 February he sent *Sebastian* to Faber, and on the 25th of the following month he departed for a holiday in Greece. He had continued to articulate the skeleton of the *Quintet*, moving Sutcliffe, the artistic *alter ego* of Blanford – Larry's surrogate prime – from his ambiguous 'real' existence in *Constance* to an established reality as a character on a par with Blanford, Constance, Prince Hassad and the others. In the fierce culmination of *Sebastian* the lunatic Mnemidis commits murder, believing erroneously that his victim is Constance. The book is suffused with the labyrinthine turnings of Avignon, with the other-worldly asylum at Montfavet, with the language of psychiatry. As so often, Larry's own health and the mental breakdowns that he had witnessed were reflected in the novel.

MORE THAN EVER LARRY'S LIFE was in his work, not in his human associations. He swung back and forth between maintaining that *The*

Avignon Quintet would be his last fiction, and saying that he felt another book coming. He thought that he had achieved a personal artistic breakthrough, in attitude at least, beyond *The Alexandria Quartet*, as he had tried to explain at the Centre Pompidou two years before. To Larry's mind, the *Quartet* was Western in cast and attitude, the *Quintet* Eastern. By this he meant that the *Quartet* was organized along the lines of Einsteinian physics: in other words, in four dimensions, and subject to the equations of relativity. With Einstein, time, matter and distance became unstable – relative – and when one added Freud to the mix, Larry had determined that he could make character shift as well. The range of shifts open to the ego in the Einsteinian universe of the *Quartet* was limited to the conscious and the subconscious, the male and the female, a 'perspex cube', Larry called it. In the *Quintet* he planned to break the confines of the cube by drawing on the five *skandas* of Buddhism – form, sensation, perception, conformation, consciousness – those elements of being that determine personality:

> By contrast to this attitude [in the *Quartet*], the five skanda pagoda mind . . . is perhaps equally full of traps though for us it seems to represent a blissfully calm view of reality. This is because it seems to offer a relief from materialist thought. The non-ego attitude is its ideal, and its science emphasises the insubstantiality of matter, and posits a kind of energy over mass state of mind which perhaps is what Einstein really meant, for he was as deeply religious in a pantheistic way as Newton!
>
> I am trying to move in my selfish and hesitating way from the fourth dimension to the five skanda view, using the same old equipment of the domestic novel, as a kaleidoscope uses the same bits of glass for different patterns. I would like to try and use the by-products of Asiatic philosophy as I tried in the Quartet to use the by-products of relativity philosophy . . . . And people? They will be spare parts of one another from the cosmic point of view, though quite real and discrete from a worldly, novelistic point of view. Underneath the action will I hope be the Asiatic notion of a world renewed afresh with each thought; therefore man as a Total Newcomer to each moment of time. . . . I would like to plant this Quintet at the point of tangence between these two cultural principles, so that it could be fruitful as well as entertaining.[189]

In the *Quartet* Larry had fractured the conventions of narrative truth by revealing contradicting versions of events, and he had shown characters changing their natures – Justine from society queen to outcast with drooping eyelid, then back to imperious queen, Scobie from *bimbashi* to transvestite – but Larry had treated the reader to plausible explanations. Far more explicitly than in the *Quartet*, in the *Quintet* he was denying both the discreteness of the ego and the concreteness of events: death was no longer final or even real, a belief Tibetan rather than Christian to his mind. Death was merely a shift from one form, one hull, to another.

Larry had always had designs on his readers, as he freely admitted. He would have liked nothing better than to change the way we think, to change the Western world by seducing it with his version of Eastern thought. The key to the reform of the Western personality was the grip of the ego, and here Buddhism's denial of a unique, discrete self was central to his thinking.

Larry's experience of the Tibetan New Year celebrations at the Château de Plaige had made a lasting impression on him. In *The Avignon Quintet* he was certainly moving back to the East, philosophically, but it still surprised many of his friends when in 1983 he accepted the presidency of a fund-raising committee dedicated to building a massive Buddhist temple at Kagyu-Ling. 'I accepted for a lot of vague reasons, not only Darjiling,' Larry said. He pronounced Kagyu Buddhism 'very aristocratic', and traced it back to Milarepa.[190] Most of the members of the committee were either Bhutanese, Tibetan or French. With Larry's encouragement, Anthea Morton-Saner and her father Robert Morton-Saner became official Friends of Kagyu-Ling. Morton-Saner had served with the Indian Civil Service, and his daughter was born at Naini Tal far north of Delhi. India, Larry's publishing and financial manager, and his spiritual life seemed to be drawing together in a tightening circle.

Larry had always disliked any sort of public group effort, yet here his name was, appended to a short article pleading on behalf of the construction project for support in cash and kind, and he also wrote letters to everyone he could think of, from French President Mitterrand to his then Minister of Culture Jack Lang. Part of the impetus had come from the continuing Chinese occupation of Tibet, which had spilled tens of thousands of Tibetans into northern India and indeed around the world. From the standpoint of religious history, Larry wrote, 'the invasion of Tibet and its fall could be compared only to something as momentous as the fall of Constantinople.' Larry quoted Milarepa, Tibetan sage of Henry Miller and the Villa Seurat days: 'The notion of emptiness engenders compassion!' Larry was one of many artists who donated paintings to be sold in support of the Kagyu-Ling foundation. 'What could be more desirable', Larry wrote, than to 'help our guests to plant the lotus of Buddhism successfully in European soil.'[191] He spoke of retiring to Plaige himself, to move into one of the tiny unheated meditation cabins – to live as a Buddhist monk as

Mountolive's father had done in the *Quartet*. When someone suggested that the ascetic life of the Tibetan monks already at Plaige might not mix well with his wine and women, Larry smiled: 'Oh, there are 180,000 varieties of Buddhism. It is a most tolerant religion.'[192]

The optimism with which Larry viewed the Tibetans at Plaige formed a complement to rather than a denial of his pervasive dark vision. Writing of his friend Henri Michaux, he said that they shared 'the poetry of comic despair,'[193] and in *Monsieur* Larry had already defined the relationship he saw between humour and death: 'Comedians are the nearest to suicide.'[194] Larry even joked about his haemorrhoids, which he called 'the occupational disease of the writer'.[195] In 1983 he had to add to his necrology the seemingly immortal Tambimuttu, who made a dramatic exit that fitted his hectic life, plunging headfirst from the iron fire escape that he favoured for access to his flat.

Lonely in the great house, Larry dropped cassettes into a cheap portable tape player: Greek songs, Rachmaninov piano concertos, French popular tunes. An American visitor once knocked and, though expected, received no answer, so he walked around to the back looking for Larry. In the Darjeeling Room stood Larry solemnly conducting to Greek *bouzouki* music coming from the tape recorder.[196] He would sometimes sing Charles Trenet's 'La Mer' and Brassens's 'Y'a plus de vin dans mon tonneau' into the small hours of the morning.[197]

BY MID-DECEMBER LARRY HAD 'The Ripper's Song', as he was thinking of calling the final volume of *The Avignon Quintet*,[198] well in hand. Showing a touch of his old insecurity and wanting reassurance, he gave me the first fifty pages to read, closely typed sheets that would print out to nearly half of the published text. The finished draft would differ only slightly. The writing of the *Quintet* had threatened to drag on for ever, and he was becoming increasingly eager to complete it.

Larry had been having falling fits for some years: with little or no warning, he would lose consciousness and drop in his tracks, but usually come to within minutes. Once, while staying with his agent in London, he was out for about eleven hours, and when he came round, he was blurred mentally for quite some time. Then in April 1984 he collapsed in Paris and was taken to the American Hospital in Neuilly: 'I woke up to find an Armenian neurologist peering into my eyeballs,' Larry reported. An encephalogram turned up the tracks of considerable electrical discharges, but no evidence of a brain tumour as he had feared. He was warned to stop drinking.[199] Gerry, also drinking heavily, was suffering from similar attacks: the brothers were convinced that it was not epilepsy, but surmised an hereditary tendency.[200] Larry, preferring the dramatic disease to the simple explanation, began to refer to his 'epilepsy'. Some of his symptoms *did* resemble epilepsy: he would fall, jerk spasmodically, bite his tongue, sometimes lose control of bladder and bowels. 'Scene of the epilepsy', he wrote in *Quinx: or, The Ripper's Tale*, 'the pearl saliva, / The tongue bitten in half, almost swallowed.'[201] By 11 June 1984 Larry called *Quinx* finished – 'the relief of doing the book is indescribable', he said. He was rewarded with a couple of dreams 'or even visitations' from Claude, who 'came to congratulate me and wanted to be made up'.[202]

With *Quinx*, Larry put the tail of the *Quintet* into its mouth, beginning the novel with a scene parallel to the opening of *Monsieur*: a train journey 'through the sluices and barrages of the Rhône' towards Avignon.[203] Larry felt that he had rounded off the task that he had set for himself forty years before in a letter to Eliot: *The Black Book* had been the *agon*, the struggle to be (re)born, as an artist, from the English death; it was the 'dislocation' from the artist's past. 'The Book of the Dead' – *The Alexandria Quartet*, in which Darley and Pombal are shaved 'like dead pharaohs' being prepared for the next world – had become the *pathos*, the suffering of the generations of living dead, and the 'uniting' of the artist with his calling: the defeat of death. Now, *The Avignon Quintet* finally stood clear as the *anagnorisis*, the recognition. Larry had predicted that his final major work would treat 'acceptance and death', and he had now shown, to his own apparent satisfaction at least, that the human personality did not exist as a distinct entity, and that *therefore* time and death could be defeated. People became one another, *were* one another: 'They *could* be each other by a simple slip of contingency,' Larry wrote shortly after completing *Quinx*. 'As for death which, like matter, rules the western novel, that doesn't exist either. Oriental thinking regards it as simply changing your violin case for another! Nor does reality itself have outlines, borders, because it is provisional and not fixed and demarcated. The multiplicity of possible lives in each of us is quite overwhelming – how to reduce it to an artistic formula is the problem? I have tried to do so while remaining a European.' Further defining his intentions, Larry wrote, 'The usual novelist wants to "tell how it [is]" but I want to "tell how it could never be unless you wanted it that way". No partition between reader and writer.'[204] As if to underline these near-infinite possibilities, he dedicated *Quinx* to Stela Ghetie, a young Romanian with whom he was then carrying on a passionate correspondence: 'We have never met and are not likely to', Larry wrote, 'but true love between artists can live on the shortest of commons; it will suffice to share the same sky!'[205] There was one near miss and no meeting occurred, so Larry's Beatrice remained elusive.

The *Quintet* certainly implies that death has no finality: Blanford at the end of *Monsieur* is able to defeat 'the chthonic darkness of unreason' through his conversations with the dead Duchess of Tu, Constance.[206] At the end of *Quinx* Blanford and Constance, young lovers again, enter the labyrinth as the proto-artist Blanford thinks, 'It was at this precise moment that reality prime rushed to the aid of fiction and the totally unpredictable began to take place!'[207] Thus Larry suggests that their cycle can be repeated in some other form. He had tried to free fiction from all the old verities of time, decorum, character and even from death. How well he was succeeding in his own life was another matter, but he certainly believed that, as he had often said, his art was even more important to him than his life. Larry often joked about his own death, sometimes saying that he thought suicide would be a good thing for him. He was delighted by the discovery of an embalmer in Marseille who – so Larry claimed – could 'glaze me like an eggplant in a saleable posture'.[208] This stuffed Durrell he said could be exhibited to American graduate students at fifty cents a head. He liked to introduce his biographer with the words, 'This is Ian MacNiven and I'm worth more to him dead than alive!'[209]

Perhaps it was the years of punishing his liver that finally caught up with Larry, or else simply a viral infection, but in 1984 he came down with hepatitis. He recovered fairly well, but it had been a 'serious bout', and he felt that he should lean on the ropes for a bit. Told that he simply must stop drinking, at least temporarily, Larry held off for more than a week, but when Michel Braudeau came to interview him for *Egoïste*, he seized the excuse to brace himself with a few pegs. 'I haven't had a drink for five days', he said to Braudeau, 'and I told myself that before talking to you I really had to have a slug of dry white. A lorry-driver's slug. . . . At seventy-two, oh yes . . . you can pray for me.' Larry rambled, repeated himself, gave more misinformation than usual, even apologized. 'This morning I was afraid of not knowing what to say. I was as dead as a battery, having taken my first slug of wine in a week.' Cruelly, Braudeau printed enough to make Larry's condition apparent. He projected his own condition on to his brother: Gerry would come over from the Mazet Michel, Larry said, 'to get pissed out of his mind several times a week'. This was an exaggeration for effect, but it was not like Larry to slander his brother over such matters.

'Alcohol, I believe, is a form of hysteria,' Larry said; fortunately, he added sententiously, he had got his own addiction under control through yoga.[210]

Finally Larry steadied himself to produce a few free-wheeling statements for Braudeau. 'It's Tibet which gave me the idea for a quartet and now a quintet,' he claimed. He had helped some Tibetans build a temple at Plaige, he continued, but this impulse had come more out of sentiment than religious fervour on his part. His talk mixed yoga, household chores, and his drinking problem:

I don't know that I'm the religious type. I'm more like Veda: after death, life doesn't stop; one simply changes costume. It's a dance of matter; we're comprised of such unstable elements, how can we not sense this motion? So, religious or not, I get up early, easy and lazy; I plug in the heat and the coffee pot, and while my coffee drips I sit in the bathroom, resting my head on a little cushion, in a pear-like headstand, save I have my legs in the lotus position, and I breathe regularly while thinking about the next chapter waiting for me. That's the good part of the morning. The bad is when I don't drink, that moment of the first glass which must be resisted.[211]

Larry certainly realized that alcohol was now bad for his art as well as his breathing: 'I have been feeling a trifle posthumous after my drunken exploits in Paris and somewhat chastened', he wrote to me, 'if one swallow dont make a summer two asthmas dont make a Proust neither.'[212] By the first of June 1984 he was seriously on the wagon, perhaps convinced by the lingering effects of the hepatitis or by his continuing falling fits. He tried acupuncture to control his desire to drink, and claimed that it really worked. When he said, 'Make mine fifty-fifty', he was now referring to half caffeine-free and half ordinary coffee. The sight of Larry drinking glass after glass of Perrier mineral water was amazing to his friends, but it certainly did have a positive effect upon his health: even his breathing improved, and he wheezed less after his walk the length of the house to answer the telephone. However, a teetotal regime affected his mood for the worse, and he sat for long hours staring morosely out of the kitchen window. In November he mused that he had failed as a poet: 'I remember Nanos [Valaoritis] saying once that when he asked Eliot if I wasn't a good poet he replied "Extremely good" and then added "But the *scale* is small." A devastating but perhaps just judgement.' Larry, contemplating his future silence, felt relief more than anything: 'Now that I am thru writing I feel wonderfully detatched [*sic*], and people can say what they feel about it all.' He prepared to sell off most of his remaining books and papers.[213]

For years Larry had sustained his establishment with only a part-time *bonne* and sporadic volunteer help with correspondence and in the garden. When Ellen Buis left for Holland temporarily in 1984, she suggested Françoise Kestsman, whom Larry already knew as a restaurant proprietor and Sappho's friend, to take over the housework, but very soon she was performing his secretarial work instead. 'I'll ask Françoise to find it,' became his response about misplaced documents.²¹⁴ Françoise Kestsman moved with quick, nervous energy, and she soon mastered not only his filing system but also Larry's relationship with each person in his address book. As no one had since Claude, she shielded him from interruptions and intrusions. She had the dramatic and hauntingly beautiful facial bone structure of a tragic actress, her skin taut over high cheekbones. Her parents came from a Jewish community in Poland, but she was French-born and had family in Brittany. Coincidentally, she had first seen Larry years before at an Oscar Epfs exhibition in Paris, but there had been no continuing contact. Then she moved to Sommières and opened a small restaurant near the western end of the Roman bridge. When her male partner in the restaurant venture absconded with the funds, she had been forced to seek employment to support her five children, three of whom were still living with her.

IT WAS A CHILLY MORNING on the first of February 1985 and Larry was sitting in the kitchen a few feet from a portable gas fire, his coffee on the black formica table before him. The telephone rang in his bedroom, and he scuffed along the cold hallway in his slippers, answering the phone with his slightly wheezing interrogative Hel-lo? A voice from London brought him the news he had been dreading for months. Sappho was dead. Larry said in a small voice, 'I'll come.' She had hanged herself during the night from the skylight of her attic bedroom – a 'hanging figure with its contrite downcast head, chapfallen now and pale from lack of blood', as Larry had written of Livia.²¹⁵ Larry was shocked and stunned, but he was hardly surprised. He rang Alan Thomas and asked if he could stay with him for a few days. 'Have you ever invented a story which . . . changed from fiction to reality for you?' Peter Adam had asked Larry years before. 'It is always doing that,' Larry had replied.²¹⁶ Here, as if to confirm his words, was his daughter dying as Livia had died. Sappho, believing that Larry had written her into the *Quintet* as Livia, had perhaps chosen this particular death so that her father would see a message in it. Did she intend in death to capture his attention in a more commanding way than she had been able to in life? Did she intend to punish him? She left no explicit indication. In a daze, Larry left for London.

The burial took place on 8 February at the Trent Park cemetery in Cockfosters. Snow lingered in patches, and an icy crust was frozen to the pavement. Larry stood with the scarf Sappho had knitted for him wrapped twice around his neck, a black woollen seaman's cap pulled down on his skull. The next day there was a brief memorial service at St Luke's Church in Chelsea of readings selected by Eve Durrell and Penelope's stepfather, Edward Hodgkin: Kahlil Gibran, Emily Brontë, Jeremy Taylor, Shakespeare. Eve, bravely composed, stood beside Larry. She wore a string of tiny ivory beads that Sappho had been wearing when she died. Larry was silent, grey-faced, 'like a little gnome, shrunk into himself'. After the service, Larry, Penelope, Shirley and Alan Thomas, Diana Forde Mitchell and a few others took the long walk to Edward Hodgkin's flat in Egerton Gardens for a small gathering.[217]

Gradually the story came out. Unable to face the divorce from Simon Tompsett, Sappho had flown to Australia to see her stepsister Diana. Sappho had cut the visit short when a relationship with a male travelling companion had gone wrong. She had returned to London at Christmas only to continue in a vortex of depression. The suicide was not a decision of the moment: she merely set out the suicide letter written to her mother on 24 January and made other preparations. Her four-page statement was controlled, simple, direct. She began, 'I'm sorry. I don't know what to say, and I still haven't really found ways of making you know how much I love you.' She was concerned about the few tenants in her Loraine Road house – she asked that one be paid the £100 she owed him for the installation of a telephone – and wanted to make sure that Simon received his fair share of the value of the house, but emphasized that he was entitled to no further claims on her small estate. She enclosed two keys, one for a trunk of books and papers, telling her mother, 'If you can't face it/them (papers etc) then leave them untouched. I'd rather NO ONE else went through them. I'm sorry.' She wrote that should Simon bring up her emotional problems, the solicitor should be informed that her first nervous breakdown had been in part precipitated by her fifth abortion, undertaken because she felt they couldn't afford a family. In her only reference to other members of the family she wrote, 'Give my love to Daddy and Pinks (& John).'[218]

SOON LARRY WAS BACK, alone, in Sommières. He could be very controlled when he wanted; his long practice in disguising his emotions in public told him not to let down his guard, so he continued to fulfil his publishing and other obligations. There was no question, however, about the depth of his sorrow. If a part of Sappho's intention had been to capture her father's attention, she certainly succeeded in that. 'I am dazed and wandering and think I must sleepwalk a bit,' Larry wrote. 'What irony! I feel as if the shade of Saph has preceded me into the Underworld.'[219] He came up with various explanations: 'She was living out her responses to the characters,' he said, referring to his own created fictions. 'Her suicide was an act of liberation.'[220] Whatever his reasoning, Larry was never to recover from her death.[221] Eve, he thought, saw their daughter's death in quasi-mystical terms: a final severing from him, a retribution for her mistake in marrying outside her parents' faith and culture.[222]

Some two months after Sappho's suicide, Larry went through a box of photographs with me. They were in no particular order, and 1930s snapshots taken on Corfu were intermixed with news photographs of the 1961 Edinburgh Festival and pictures of Larry and Henry Miller in California in the 1970s. From time to time pictures surfaced of Sappho at various ages. Larry never missed a syllable, nor did he linger longer – or less long – over pictures of his daughter than over those of other members of his family or of his good friends. In the same breath as talking about Margaret Rawlings in the role of Sappho at Edinburgh, Larry turned over a picture of his daughter and said, 'There's a lovely picture of Saph and me' – then added, after a pause that might have been either his emphysema or a slight catch in his voice 'in her Alice in Wonderland stage'. And again, later on, 'Some lovely pictures of Saph here, and Diana, together . . . and Saph on a horse.' He seemed very gentle, very subdued: sad beneath the quiet surface. Then he came upon a series taken at Gerry's zoo for *Life* magazine around Christmas 1960: 'Here's my family – and other animals. There's my sister, Leslie, and me.' Some sepia-toned photographs appeared: 'There's the brilliant boy' – himself, spoken with amused irony – 'I'm in a particularly aggressive mood, in India.' Larry picked up a portrait of a dramatically beautiful Eve in a Turkish costume borrowed from the Rhodes museum so that Mary Mollo could photograph her. 'That's the way she was,' he said quietly. 'That's before she went nuts.'[223]

Larry was not drinking when Sappho committed suicide, and his grief did not drive him back to the bottle. His abstinence made him more critical of his brother: 'I think Gerry should stop drinking,' he said, and told others that it was his brother's whisky intake that was causing his hip sockets to give out, 'rotting them out'.[224]

Larry himself felt increasingly frail, and the idea of quitting, shutting up shop, sounded more and more attractive to him. His library contained many Melville titles, and he admired the 'marvellous neurotic short stories', especially 'Bartleby the Scrivener', 'that man who refused everything, just lay against the wall'. Perhaps feeling a kinship with the scrivener's repeated denial, 'I would prefer not to', Larry expounded on the tale. '*What* a story!' he exclaimed. 'One *can't* do anything as good as that. . . . It must certainly have happened, and the chap *must* have been English. Only an Englishman could get himself into such a psychological fix.'[225] Often during his long siege with the Quincunx, Larry would have preferred not to sit at his writing table, and he was finding his planned Provence book even harder to grasp.

A part of his depression stemmed from his belief that his own creative life was ebbing like 'divine entropy', the running down of the universe that he had treated in *The Avignon Quintet*. He was not sure that his quincunx added up to what he intended. He also felt that he had slighted his poetic talent, although he was willing to concede that he had written 'five or six good poems'. Asked which they might be, Larry smiled quietly. 'That's for you to discover,' he replied. Only in learning to 'make love correctly' had he perhaps succeeded, Larry thought.[226] Mary Mollo, that long observer of Larry, disagreed: 'He was very sure of his own talent and very unsure of himself as a Don Giovanni.'[227] His failures in loving may have driven him to try so often. But it was more than that. Writing of his lovers, Larry said, 'If I list their names it is with the same mixture of reverence, nostalgia, sadness and curiosity as Stendhal did, recognising that they had brought him the choicest heraldic messages from the au delà; as women who opened pathways to self-realisation.' He was careful to place his wives in a special category among his lovers: 'The REAL ones never get a showing because you don't write to your wife, she's always there!'[228] Like Dowson to Cynara, he was faithful to them in his fashion.

In a larger, public sense, Larry certainly felt hopeless. To illustrate his pessimism, he brought up Samuel Beckett: 'How can you be Irish and forgive?' Larry asked, implying that his own Irishness gave him a like mandate to condemn.[229] He had tried in his books to point the way to the salvation of the ego-driven West through the acceptance of Eastern ideals of selflessness and non-possession: but no one was listening. Many years earlier, when he had read in the British White Paper that the Nagasaki atomic bomb appeared to cause human sterility, in his pessimism he had written, 'It's a great relief! I was afraid they were going on like this forever.'[230] According to Larry, Henry Miller too had sensed failure. Henry had always wanted to wake up America, to change it. Larry recalled a late conversation with Henry: 'When I said, "Do you think America has changed?" he said, "Jesus, d'you think England has changed? What they really want is to get a Buddha or a Christ and kick him to death in the streets."' The bitterness rang in Larry's voice as he repeated the exchange.[231]

Increasingly, Larry's pile of a house seemed to him an intolerable burden and a crushing expense. Tight-shuttered, the paint cracking on the woodwork, the roof leaking worse, the stucco flaking, surrounded by an increasingly dense tangle of briars and degenerate climbing roses, Mme Tartes' mansion added to his depression:

> Only of late have I come to see this house
> As something poisoned when I paid for it;
> Its beauty was specious and it hid pure grief.

He seemed to be addressing his lost wife Claude when he continued, 'Your absence, dearest, brings it no relief', but he could also have been referring in his loneliness to some more or less generic mate. He had given up his earlier struggle to escape from the house – it now possessed *him*:

> We have all died here; one by spurious one
> Of indistinct diseases, lack of sun, or fun,
> Or just our turn came up, now mine.[232]

In June 1985 Larry appeared on the prestigious Paris television programme *Apostrophe* to 'ooze sweaty charm and bad French'. He knew that his sales would rise: 'It's like having Ginger Rogers kiss you in public; after that everyone wants to!' Almost immediately he was served with a writ for a quarter of a million pounds for six years of back taxes, and he blamed his increased fame. Grimly, he debated either selling the house or a 'congruent suicide'.[233] Françoise Kestsman proved his salvation. She took charge of Larry's life with irresistible directness, brushing aside his hesitations and insecurities, filling the house with her slightly hoarse smoker's voice, her stories, her passions.

As always, Larry continued to be evasive about his private life, and did not appreciate detailed questions. 'The major things', Larry said in some exasperation when I asked for mundane facts, were 'obviously the books and the construction of them and the whole of my life is a sort of autobiography, but it's all written out, so to speak. It's printed out, as it were. Surely you could use that as a base without bothering too much about whether I smoked Camels . . . unless there's an obsessional thing which is interesting, indicating a deep fault in the character or a bias.' Just as Henry Miller had, Larry regarded his books as a spiritual and intellectual autobiography – only he had removed or disguised the personal physical presence that is so prominent a feature of Miller's books. Larry had always been writing about himself: 'Yes, of course! Isn't everyone?'[234]

Larry contemplated the important place that humour had always held in his work. 'Sympathy elicits humour.' He continued, 'Without sympathy I don't think you can have tragedy. . . . You can't get the tragic note unless you do it with a half-smile; otherwise you get melodrama.' Asked where this sympathy came from, Larry, incredulous, countered with a question, 'Where do you breathe from? I take yoga lessons.' Larry paused: 'Sympathy is oxygen.' Larry's own oxygen was running short – 'Everything's a bore when you can't breathe,' he often said – and he felt that Lawrence, another author with bad lungs, had in his writing often lacked both the sympathy and the humour. 'Yes, he's a nagger,' Larry said. 'Nag, nag, nag – he must have been frightfully insecure.' That had been Lawrence's great flaw: 'He had no humour, alas. . . . He could have presented his material in a less irritating way.' None the less, Larry remained an admirer of Lawrence the iconoclast, recalling his own youth, when 'of course, the young were therefore very *for* him, because they sensed his wavelength, which was a creative one. Opinions don't much matter once you hear that tone of voice; compared to all the other muddy tones, you see, what was available. Apart from the glorious dead there are very few glorious living that have anything much to say.'[235]

Larry's modesty and self-doubt prevented him from making a serious assessment of his own accomplishment, but with *Quinx* almost ready for publication, he was willing to talk about the pattern that he had sought to follow. A question about Caradoc, who had surfaced in Larry's notebooks years before his appearance in *Tunc*, provoked Larry to muse:

I mean it's a whole family, but a very limited family. But I did mean and I do hope, for what it's worth, that finally the whole thing would add up not as various as, let's say, Dickens and all his progeny, but with a family of perhaps seven or eight types – including a couple of clowns, a couple of diplomats, a couple of freaks, a couple of psychopaths – but reappearing under different guises and different names, sometimes performing the same functions, sometimes changing sexes, etc. And that the whole thing would present as what the French call an *oeuvre*, a work, with the *Quartet* and the *Quintet* holding the ring, so to speak, and the others just tossed in here and there, as waiting periods when I had to take in oxygen, waiting between fights.

Larry also hoped that his *oeuvre* would appear, as he had often said, 'pretty consistent as well as coherent philosophically from *The Black Book* onwards'.²³⁶

Even before Larry put *The Avignon Quintet* to bed by sending *Quinx* off to Curtis Brown, he had been planning the 'residence book' – with no prefixing adjective spelling out 'foreign' this time – that would become *Caesar's Vast Ghost*. Intended as his tribute to the region that had been his beloved home since 1957, Larry would also pour into the narrative echoes of all that he had lived through. From the 'rabid coarseness' of the Roman arenas at Nîmes and Arles, Larry shifted to the duality of human nature. 'The duality of the instinct is not split in the human soul,' he wrote; 'mother instinct, for example, and hatred of motherhood coexist in the human heart.' Sappho he had of course accused of being lesbian, and disturbed as he was by her abortions, he may well have had her in mind when he continued, 'The homosexual woman always shows her hatred of mother-hood because she cannot help it.'²³⁷ Sappho had variously justified her abortions by her poverty and her refusal to produce a grandchild for her father,²³⁸ so perhaps Larry was correct in assigning a psycho-sexual motive to her refusal to carry her pregnancies to term: lack of money was hardly a viable excuse for Sappho, and there is no evidence that Larry set much store by having grandchildren. The political upheavals that he had witnessed close to were a large-scale expression of the inner dislocations of modern humankind, he thought. 'Politics is simply the blueprint which encourages all these secret predispositions to evolve into action,'²³⁹ wrote Larry in explanation of the mass neuroses of the century. For supporting authority, Larry turned to history and to the volumes of Freud and Stekel in his library. But his heart was not in his writing: his tax situation was still not resolved; he was in a 'deadly mood'; he had a 'fixed conceit' that he would 'croak' before the end of the year.²⁴⁰

Larry continued to watch world events with a sardonic eye. Once sure that a nuclear war would soon devastate Europe while at the same time convinced that a sturdy opposition to everything with a Communist label was utterly necessary, Larry now decided that an even greater danger lay within: boredom. This was no new fear: it had been his ancient curse. At the rate that machines were taking over work, within fifty years man would not have to labour. Then, of course, 'the next problem is . . . How is he going to occupy his boredom?' Although humankind now had the easy capability for total self-destruction, Larry sensed a change: 'The realization is getting even to the political boys that no one can get anywhere with this massive buildup. It's a terrible waste of money and time.' 'A very simple change of air' might ensure the world twenty or thirty years of peace, 'but then the boredom would come up', he said, 'because this one world, this computer world, the electronic world, the television world' had arrived – such was Larry's hostility towards television that he still refused to have a set in his house. Nor were the young apt to rebel fruitfully: invoking Huxley, Larry mused that 'the *pompiers* would come and spray you with soma and everyone falls into a woolly sleep and comes out of the American Hospital renewed . . . not aggressive at all.' A different build-up was occurring: the young were 'over-populating' the globe, out of sheer boredom and insomnia. 'They're all taking pills and sleeping badly.' The options, he said, 'are really terrifying'. 'I'm leaving just at the right moment!' he concluded. 'Couldn't be better timed!'[241]

Still, Larry began to drop hints about another attempt at a major fiction. What would the subject be? After the collapse, he replied, after the universe had run down. 'Divine entropy' was still his phrase for this process.[242] On a practical level, he fretted over the burden of the house, saying quite ingenuously, 'I'd be much happier in a small hotel.' And he talked again about going away, even showing some interest in the West Indies. Greece was out for winter living, because except in Athens the restaurants were seasonal, he said.[243]

On 20 May 1985, less than three months after Sappho's death, Larry braced himself to go to London to launch *Quinx*. He stayed with his agent at Shepherd's Bush until 4 June. Surrounded by familiar pubs, Larry felt that he had better have a re-inoculation against alcohol from an acupuncturist, so he enquired after the best in London. 'It turned out to be a woman, a sinister old Chink,' Larry recalled. 'She stuck needles in me and *electrified* them! I was *fried*! After twenty minutes of this, I was so shaken that I rushed to the nearest pub for a glass.' A year of abstinence ended abruptly.[244]

Larry's fall from the grace of temperance probably had nothing to do with the acupuncturist: she made a good story. He had found it boring not to drink, but he had feared that he would not otherwise live to finish *The Avignon Quintet*. Now that he had met his goal, he would indulge himself. Very likely he also drank because he felt, as usual, that he might have written better. Criticism of the *Quintet* covered the widest possible range, from Larry's friend David Hughes who raved that 'Never has a novelist written with so scintillating an effort to put the world to rights,'[245] to Lorna Sage, who linked Larry unfavourably with Anthony Burgess: 'Both reflect a guilty obsession with words, words, words, in the absence, often, of matter.'[246] Most critics praised Larry's language and his power of description. A perceptive review came from Keith Brown, who wrote in the *Times Literary Supplement* that although Larry might not have succeeded entirely in writing a 'Tibetan' novel, 'There has always been in him a vein of unremitting philosophical curiosity about the way literature works, concealed by the fun that wells from his belief in the novelist as *homo ludens*.'[247] The French and German reviews were almost unreservedly laudatory.

LARRY HAD AGREED TO GO TO Pennsylvania State University in 1986 for a conference devoted to his writing. He went through an agony of hesitation, half hoping that his health would break down to give him an excuse for cancelling. It would be his first return to the United States since his stint at CalTech in 1974, and the first time that he had ever consented to listen to academics talk about him. The conference was to be the fourth devoted to his writing and was co-sponsored by the Lawrence Durrell Society. He got as far as London by 3 March and stayed once more with Anthea Morton-Saner at Shepherd's Bush until 8 April, when she suggested that he join the Lansdowne Club in Mayfair so that she could have some house repairs done. The club was centrally located, respectable, included a large swimming pool, and contained very cheap lodgings for members – but she forgot to warn him that the place was quite formal. He paid his dues and moved in. After a fine swim he enquired about the bar: it was not yet open. When it finally did open, Larry was informed that he must wear a tie to be served. He threatened to tie a bow tie around his neck – he was still wearing only his bathing costume and dressing gown – and return to the bar. After a week at the Lansdowne he departed for New York, never to resume London club life.

To save Larry a long walk from the plane at New York's Kennedy Airport, Anthea booked wheelchair service for him. Thus he returned to America grimly clutching his wallet, a leather affair the size of a large novel, and being wheeled along by a powerful black porter. Once he had been collected at the airport, Larry appeared content to let his hosts set the schedule. The drive through Pennsylvania two days later delighted him, especially the sight of Amish farmers ploughing with teams of three horses, and the peaked angularity of the nineteenth-century houses lining the streets in the smaller towns. Larry insisted on sitting in the back seat of the car, but he remained alert, commented on the style of the clapboard houses, and said that he would like to write on the architecture of Amish Pennsylvania. As the car approached a small octagonal brick schoolhouse near Aaronsburg, Larry let out a shout: it was Sodom School, now an historical monument. 'They must be joking!' he exclaimed. He got out of the car into the grey spring afternoon and walked up to the building, chuckling at such an amazing evidence of American naïveté.[248]

Larry attended every session of the two-day conference, and himself spoke at length the first day. His talk rang some changes on his earlier 'From the Elephant's Back' speech at the Centre Pompidou. He stood dwarfed behind a massive podium in his quiet grey-blue suit, with a blue-and-yellow barred scarf knitted for him by Sappho looped around his neck. Delivered extemporaneously and flawlessly, his address briefly traced his Indian and Greek roots, and launched into his intellectual and artistic ancestry. Summing up his writing, Larry stated, 'If I can have done one Tibetan-type novel, and one European-type novel, and left them to marry each other, and made a poetic equation which is a challenge which might offer a toehold to young poets and young thinkers, my job will have been done.' Larry said that Gerry had told him it was time to start thinking about what was to go on his plaque in Westminster Abbey. Recalling that he had seen a child's toy in Shepherd's Bush Market advertised as an 'Oriental Serpent – Authentic Wiggle', Larry said that the phrase 'Authentic Wiggle' would please him very much.[249]

One of the features of the Durrell conference was to be a dialogue with the novelist John Hawkes. Since the two men admired each other's work, the plan boded well, and when Hawkes appeared with his earnest familiarity and scuffed tennis shoes the two men seemed to like one another. The next day, when Hawkes tried to persuade Larry to tour a shanty town constructed by the Pennsylvania State students to protest against South African apartheid, Larry pulled back in horror: he wanted no part in a political action. Hawkes did not realize that Larry was serious, and tried to pull him bodily from the car. Larry braced himself like an octopus in a grotto.

The public dialogue that evening was not a signal success. Larry set out before him a tiny bottle of smelling salts, 'like a Victorian old lady', he said, to restore him should he lose his breath. This fascinated Hawkes, who seemed to want to talk about nothing else during their dialogue before the audience. Larry, now very pious and professional, kept trying to turn the conversation towards High Art: in vain, so he assumed a lotus position on stage. Finally Hawkes made an eloquent statement about the seminal importance of *The Alexandria Quartet* to his own work, and the audience settled back in relief.

As Larry was leaving the Nittany Lion Inn at Pennsylvania State University, he was followed by a chambermaid waving a hundred dollar bill, a tip half the amount of his room charge. Larry looked a bit puzzled: 'Yes, it's for you,' he said. When the girl insisted that it was too much, Larry, hovering between embarrassment and annoyance, shuffled a smaller note out of his wallet. He might drink cheap plonk, but he wanted to be generous, to do the right thing. He was still his father's son.

Larry had planned to spend a week after the conference in New York giving interviews, but when the time came he asked that several of them be cancelled. He also refused to move into the luxury suite provided by Viking Press at the New York Sheraton: Larry walked into the lobby, glanced around, and said, 'This place has no soul. I can't stay here!' He allowed himself to be driven to the Sheraton three times to meet a few photographers and reporters. He preferred to stay in my tiny home in Silver Beach Gardens, a Bronx community on the East River. The small settlement he pronounced, fancifully, to be 'just like a Greek village', and he enjoyed walking about in complete anonymity: no one recognized him.[250] He would rise at daybreak, make himself a cup of instant coffee, and read quietly – he finished a biography of Hilda Doolittle in a few days – often standing at the dining table, until we called him to breakfast. Then at about 9.30 in the morning, seated at the front table with the Empire State Building partially visible between rooftops, he would say, 'Do you think you could open a bottle of that good white wine?' Carefully, as if pacing himself, he would drink through the day, but only wine, and without ever a slurred word.

Claudine Brelet, in New York with UNESCO, came over for an evening of affectionate laughter and talk. Then Larry stayed overnight in Connecticut with Horst and Frances von Maltitz, alarming them that evening by suffering a blackout, one of his seizures. The next morning he seemed fine, but the warning was only the latest of many that had undermined his confidence in his ability to live or to travel alone.

One friend who refused to accept Larry's despairing moods was Fiddle Viracola. When she saw him in The Bronx she brought him gifts intended to reawaken his zest for life: a slingshot, a green bagel for St Patrick's Day in New York, a T-shirt proclaiming 'Backstage on Broadway'. For his breathing she gave him a crystal ball to be worn around his neck, and she suggested yoga and consultations with specialists. Maybe he did have emphysema, Fiddle told him, but he could not simply let it defeat him: all his life he had preached proper breathing, health through willpower and Georg Groddeck. Larry tried to put her off with banter, and when that did not work, withdrew into a sullen silence. At the reception and dinner that Fiddle arranged for him at New York's National Arts Club, Larry stood under the magnificent Tiffany glass ceiling drinking glasses of champagne and performing for the crowd of art patrons and dowagers. Clearly, the effort pained him. Towards the end of dinner he rose to make a short speech and toast, and Fiddle's professional eye noticed his unease: he did not know what to do with his hands. Immediately after the dinner he fended off an invitation to an intimate small party and bolted into the rainy night. He refused to see Fiddle for the rest of his stay. Later, from the safe distance of Sommières, Larry told her on the telephone that he had cut her 'because you reproached me'. He tried to tease her: 'We should have been in bed,' to which Fiddle replied, 'That's not what it's all about.' 'I know, I know,' replied Larry. 'No one knows the pain that I have within.' When she admonished him, 'Remember, you're a *spiritual* being within!', Larry replied, 'Oh, thank you! Thank you for saying that!'[251]

Larry left America as he had come, in a wheelchair, but he was clearly relieved that the conference had gone well, that it was *over*, and that no disasters had happened. A regime, usually adhered to, of seven or eight hours' sleep a night and nothing stronger than wine to drink had him looking well and feeling confident. He insisted on arriving hours early at the airport, and asked the attendant to wheel him to the First Class Lounge. The solicitous porter, believing Larry to be an elderly invalid, eased him through a series of locked doors and elevators. Near the destination, Larry spotted an airport bar and bounded from the still-moving wheelchair, calling over his shoulder to the astounded attendant, 'Be sure to call for me at 8.30!' Larry visited the Thomases in London, and was soon safely back in Sommières, where he proclaimed himself 'exhausted but jubilant and with a feeling of certitude about the Quinx which I had not had before setting forth'.[252] He was never to return to America or England.

The year continued to be a busy one for Larry. The French court had ruled against his appeal on his taxes while he was in America, and he offered his house for sale at £250,000 under the *viager* system: he would reserve the use of the top floor for his lifetime. Then on 20 May, Chili Hawes, who ran the October Gallery near Bernard Stone's Turret Books, arrived from London to spend three days interviewing Larry on film for *Quiet Days in Sommières*. The opening sequence showed her being picked up by Ludo Chardenon and driven to La Maison de Mme Tartes – Ludo as relaxed before the camera as if he were selling herbs in the market. The same day the mayor of Sommières, acting for Minister of Culture Jack Lang, solemnly invested Larry with the title Commandeur de l'Ordre des Arts et des Lettres and hung a heavy medal around his neck, already encircled with Sappho's scarf. Larry showed Chili a few of his recent paintings, including one of Sappho looking at the sea. This painting was liberally highlighted with metallic gold paint, and Larry commented, 'It gives a wonderful dead sort of feel to the centre of it.' He had been looking forward to seeing Chili, but he responded to her rather bland questions with quips and curt responses. 'I'm waiting to become one hundred,' he told her, 'then I'll know *everything*!' He was clearly not in a good mood: 'I don't know much about love,' he told her. 'Only once in my life was I loved uncritically.' 'By Claude?' Chili prompted him. He agreed. Had he been in love too? 'I never have – I've never loved,' Larry countered. His life had been a failure, he said, because he had not 'pulled off a sufficiently large trick'. It was not easy to judge Larry's sincerity, but he was disappointed in Chili, and it showed in his face as well as his answers. As much as anything, he was exhausted by repeated day-long film sessions. 'What's life?' she asked. 'Whatever you think it isn't,' he fired back with a taut smile.[253]

In July 'France Culture' sent a team to record Larry, and again he had to perform. That same month Penelope was married in Scotland to the artist John Hope, but Larry did not attend the wedding. Although he would come to like John, finding him quiet and well read, Larry's generic jealousy of his daughter's husbands led to a degree of cooling in his relationship with Penelope.[254]

Whenever he could bring himself to it, Larry worked at the mass of impressions of his nearly thirty years in Provence, trying to structure it all into *Caesar's Vast Ghost*. By October 1986 he had still only typed fifty pages: 'There is too much material', he complained, 'and I feel chopped out with Asthma etc!'[255] None the less, on 6 January he reported that he had finished the book. His elation turned out to be premature: Faber judged it not ready for publication.

IN FEBRUARY 1987 LARRY SUFFERED his worst health crisis to date when an influenza onslaught led into respiratory complications, and he was seriously ill for months. 'I think I may fade away this year,' he said.[256] He laboured at *Caesar's Vast Ghost*, even though he felt miserable much of the time, and by August he estimated that he had only twenty pages to go.

Françoise Kestsman kept him alive, he maintained, and her careful nursing made Larry more than ever dependent on her. 'What irony that my last girl – (I feel she is the last and best) – should be a Tartar princess with a mind like a battleaxe,' Larry wrote.[257] His self-sufficient lifestyle of only two years previously had vanished without a trace. Devoted to her children, Françoise moved with them into a small house across the Route de Saussines, so that she could balance the demanding roles of mother to her family and companion to Larry. There was no question of having the children live at Mme Tartes: Larry hated the noise and the fuss, and sometimes he seemed to resent the children.[258] 'The Polish cleaning lady lives with her kids across the street,' he told Fiddle Viracola. 'Thank God they're not here!'[259] To others he referred to her as 'The Polish Corridor'. Was it Larry's latent misogyny, his tendency to lash out at the woman at hand when he was unhappy about his health or anything else? Or did he simply resent his increasing dependency? Or was he unable to resist a few outrageous remarks? The answer was probably yes to all options. Beyond all other considerations, he wanted her love and devotion, but she rejected his offers of marriage. Late one evening, when an exhausted Françoise had fallen asleep on the Elizabeth Barrett, Larry exclaimed to his friends, 'Look, look at her! What can I do? She's so beautiful!'[260]

Larry remained concerned with the progress of the Kagyu-Ling Buddhist temple now nearing completion at Plaige, and his name still headed the *Comité de Soutien*. His vice-presidents were Gerry, Jacques Lacarrière, and Claude Lévi-Strauss. He attended the consecration of the temple on 22 August 1987, a day of ceremonies and dining organized by Lama Sherab, Larry's main contact among the Kagyu-Ling folk. Larry and Françoise were the guests of honour amid a large party that included many friends. The events began mid-morning and concluded near midnight with a *diaporama* on Buddhism projected on a giant screen. Sacred dances were performed by the lamas, and the Tibetan chants and drawn-out tuba notes reverberated across the green lawns. There was a theatrical and choreographic interpretation of the life of Milarepa. For Larry it evoked a palimpsest of memories and sensations reaching back to Darjeeling.

During the summer the writer Robin Rook and the painter Paul Hogarth visited Larry to discuss plans for *The Mediterranean Shore*, an undertaking that was to combine short excerpts from Larry's books with a text to be written by Rook and ink and watercolour sketches made especially for the book by Hogarth. Larry liked both men, and watched as Hogarth sketched scenes in Sommières.

Penelope Durrell had recently edited a new version of *An Irish Faustus*, slightly revised with Larry's help on the basis of an acting version that came out of a Durrell conference held at Muskingum College in Ohio during 1984. This new text was published by Peter Baldwin, a young Birmingham solicitor who collected rare Durrelliana and printed fine editions as a hobby. Penelope's text became the basis for a French production in Lyon in November 1987. Though unwell, Larry drove north with Françoise for the performance.

Larry's *oeuvre* was gaining increasing attention from academics, although their preoccupation remained and would continue to remain *The Alexandria Quartet*. Between 1980 and 1990 at least a dozen monographs and collections of essays on his work would appear, mainly in America. By 1987 there had been no fewer than thirty-six doctoral dissertations devoted entirely or in part to the *Quartet* alone. Larry would complain to his friends whenever he was approached by a graduate student, but he was reluctant to turn away anyone seriously attempting to fathom his work. Sometimes he would direct the seeker to Alan Thomas or to some university lecturer he knew. When Mary Byrne, after writing an M.Phil. thesis on the *Quartet* for Trinity College, Dublin, came to see him, he was cordial. Mary settled near by at St Jean de Fos, married Jean-Claude Vidal, and became a staunch friend to Françoise Kestsman.

Robin Rook returned to Sommières early in March 1988 to go over Paul Hogarth's pictures with Larry and to make the final revisions to captions and the commentary. The *Mediterranean Shore* volume was scheduled to appear in October. Larry was pleased to have a handsome book in prospect that had cost him very little effort. That Sunday, 13 March, Gerry came over from the Mazet Michel, bringing the lunch with him – Gerry walking with some difficulty after hip replacement surgery, Larry not walking well either, his face puffy from drink. Each was distressed by the other's condition. In April Larry had one of his seizures, and for a time he could not write coherently. Apologizing for missing a Durrell conference in Illinois, Larry wrote to me: 'I have tsarted contract these helipelhoid typle bits again and the dock totothinks it is sentible of me to test up until I manage to find which is causting (if anywhich more hritinaz that death of wheel . . . .' Conscious of his incoherence, he continued heartbreakingly, 'It is most depressing as a manifestation and I think af it hadnest been of Françoise Kestman I would have kicked the butchet a couple of month ado again.'[261] His usually flowing hand moved in crossouts and written-over words across the page.

In the summer of 1988 Anthea Morton-Saner found Larry more than ever retreating into his solitude. His health remained generally poor: his breathing was becoming progressively more laboured, he had dizzy spells, and his falling fits continued. He had become very jealous of Françoise's younger children, resenting the time that their mother spent with them, but he was relieved when Christophe, Françoise's oldest son, moved his photography studio into Larry's top floor. Françoise did not think that Larry should be left alone when she had to go out on errands.[262]

As the year advanced Larry wrestled with his old demons, despair and boredom. A glass of rosy Costière du Gard before him on the black kitchen table, he would stare out towards the chestnut trees and the vineyard beyond. 'Boredom is infinitely more powerful than love,' he wrote in the manuscript he sometimes called 'Provence Entire' and sometimes simply 'Caesar's Ghost'.[263] He saw the book as his Thank You note for three decades of Provençal hospitality. This time Larry had had far longer than in the cases of his island books to become familiar with the environs he was portraying. 'If you live in a place, I think you automatically imbibe it,' said Larry, judiciously choosing the right descriptive verb, 'if you feel it very strongly'. He continued the liquid metaphor: 'The great thing is to feel Vespasian, for example, our local emperor. He invented the public lavatory. Now once you know that, and you've had to do a pee into the arches, you know you are in tune with history.'[264] Larry was finding this book the most agonizing to write of any that he had attempted. He filled several quarry notebooks with jottings, but the problem of condensing and focusing his material seemed beyond him. He had experienced similar difficulties with *Reflections on a Marine Venus* and had given over the task to Anne Ridler, but now he neither had Ridler as editor nor the energy to perform the task himself. Still, he believed that he would not have got even this far were it not for Françoise, and he inscribed one of his *Caesar* quarry notebooks to her: 'For Françoise who brought me to life when nobody else could! "Onlie begetter"! from Larry Durrell 1988.'[265]

Larry, having difficulties with *Caesar's Vast Ghost*, kept tantalizing friends with hints of a book to come after it. 'If I ever write another book it will be a complete fantasia. It will be another Ship of Fools, a totally comic novel in which anything could happen, free association,' he said to Richard Pine, who had come from Dublin to see him. Pine brought Larry a copy of his book, *The Dandy and the Herald: Mind, Manners and Morals from Brummell to Durrell*, a bottle of whisky and a side of Irish smoked salmon. Françoise took these offerings and they drank Larry's standard cheap *pétillant* white wine while the two men discussed *The Avignon Quintet*. Richard Pine found it 'an extremely clever mirror-image book', folded in upon itself like a Rorschach blot, with *Constance* as the centre and the title character as the main consciousness. 'Constance', said Pine to Larry, 'is the monitor,' to which Larry replied, 'Tell me more.' 'Constance is the quiddity.' Larry unfolded his legs, got up and put his arms around Pine. Françoise looked on enigmatically. Larry seemed to lack the concentration to be interviewed, so Pine excused himself and left after arranging to return next morning. He had no sooner reached the Hotel du Nord across the Vidourle than the concierge appeared: 'Monsieur Durrell is on the phone.' Could Pine come back right away to continue their conversation? Crossing the bridge, Pine passed Françoise going the opposite way on her bicycle. She seemed very surprised to see him. At the house, Larry was sitting before a newly opened bottle of wine, looking smug and conspiratorial: a truant schoolboy who had outwitted his warden. For an hour the conversation flowed, but Larry was clearly exhausted. As Pine got up to leave, Larry handed him an advance copy of *The Mediterranean Shore*. 'Take this and read it – it will explain all! But guard it! Gerry is coming tomorrow and I must give this to him.'[266]

The next morning Pine found Larry slumped on one elbow in the kitchen. 'Go and see Avignon – come back next week,' he told Pine. He looked nonplussed when Pine told him that he had to return to Dublin. Françoise stood by, her manner clearly saying, 'Can't you see the man is ill?' Pine departed. Françoise tried to shield Larry not only from literary researchers from Dublin, but even from old friends such as Alan Thomas, who complained that he could not get through to Larry on the telephone. Alan had survived a severe stroke, but then had been diagnosed with cancer and leukaemia. Told that Alan would greatly appreciate hearing from him, Larry responded, 'We each know that the other is there. With friendships as old as ours, there is no need to speak.'[267] Only a few friends such as Mary Mollo, Ray Mills and the Birds maintained a fairly regular contact.

Not that Larry lacked company. Penelope and John Hope came for visits, and sometimes Tony Daniells would drive south from Uzès or Barbara Robinson would come over from Quissac. Most of the people he saw these days lived near by, and so could drop in for one of Françoise's excellent meals. Like Claude, she could prepare food deftly while remaining in the conversational circle, a cigarette and a glass of wine at hand, and a crush of her friends coming and going. Most of the conversation was now in French, unless there were guests who were seriously disadvantaged:

Françoise's English was good enough to translate Paul Auster into French, but she preferred to speak her native tongue.

Larry and Gerry were still affectionate with one another, but a note of weariness had invaded their banter. Larry kept urging Gerry to procure an elephant for the Buddhist temple at Plaige, until Gerry in some exasperation said, 'One elephant would suffer from loneliness.' 'Of course!' said Larry, as if suddenly stung by his own lifelong complaint, 'Then you must find *two* elephants.' Gerry groaned. 'Daddy said, "You are such a good dodger,"' he reminded his brother. 'Yes', replied Larry, 'I think I could even dodge God.'[268]

He began to dodge his brother too, or so it seemed, cutting himself off and refusing invitations to the Mazet Michel. 'We never see Larry,' Gerry remarked.[269] Larry still joked about the idea of death, which he linked to Bournemouth: 'It's the apotheosis of it, just the right place to die. . . . I should really go back there, if I had any sense of logic, and buy a flat next to my sister.'[270]

For years Larry had been saying that he was done with marriage. By the summer of 1988 he had added a codicil in Françoise's favour to his will. Now his line became, 'This woman won't marry me, although I keep asking her!'[271] If Françoise was within earshot, she would respond with a brusque rejoinder. Central among Françoise's motives for refusing him was her judgement that she could not combine a home for her children with one for Larry, so she still maintained the flat across the road.

The Durrell family kept shrinking. In the autumn of 1988 Prudence Hughes, after a lifetime of lawsuits and feuding with neighbours and tenants, died after bringing on a heart attack by throwing a brick at a neighbour's cat.[272] Larry had teased Prudence and her mother Aunt Fan since the 1930s, and losing 'Aunt Pru' was like seeing the extinction of an institution.

In 1989 a spirit from Larry's past arrived in the form of Simone Lestoquard, dropping in on her way to her country home in Narbonne. Larry roused himself to be lively and entertaining, but it clearly cost him an effort. He was once more considerably overweight, his jowls sagged, and he often could not be bothered to dress beyond his usual shorts or, in colder weather, old trousers topped with a jersey and a quilted jacket. He was conscious of the impression that he made, and he was still proud enough to resent it when others felt sorry for him. Probably he would rather that most people left him alone.

Caesar's Vast Ghost was still refusing to come right. The typescript had been returned by Faber: drastic revisions were needed to give the book coherence. Mary Byrne was often in the house, and Larry sensed that he could rely on her discretion and expertise. Finally he said to her: 'Look, I've got this appalling book. . . . If you can't do something with it, I'll have to return the advances.' Mary typed the text into her word processor and Larry went over the printed copy, crossing out, moving and inserting passages. Larry, the creator twenty years before of Abel and Dactyl, the marvellous word machines in *The Revolt of Aphrodite*, had no idea that technology could come to his aid so effectively.[273]

Amazingly, on the other side of his despair and gloom and ill-temper, the poet and the craftsman still functioned. Now, elated by the ease with which Mary was producing corrected text for him, he forced himself to concentrate on *Caesar's Vast Ghost*. The book contains some fine writing about place, the musical cadences about Les Baux – 'The stone-carved tombs of vanished Saracens are full of weeds and tall grasses, there the only moving things are the lizards avid for sunlight'[274] – and some of his best insights into the human heart: 'Unfortunately there is no medical cure for the pains of bereavement, unless it be drugs or alcohol, but neither really assuages the central wound, the hopeless sense of futile loss.'[275] Vintage Durrell too were Larry's comments on Christianity with its 'jealous god': 'What a contrast to the tolerant, easy-going pluralism of Roman pantheism with its generous outlines.'[276]

Caesar's Vast Ghost is not wholly the work of Larry's last years, however, but contains borrowings from his own earlier writings and from the works of others. A version of the first poem in the volume, 'Constrained by History', had done previous duty when Larry sent a draft under the title 'Omega Grey' for Fiddle Viracola to read at a memorial service for Henry Miller in 1980. And as Larry had done in other books, he lifted verbatim some passages to flesh out the history: much of the section on Antony's naval defeat by Octavian comes from Michael Haag's Notes to his edition of E. M. Forster's *Alexandria*. Perhaps, since Larry had written a preface for Haag, he felt that he had a right to the material.

Some of the poems, both the drafts in his *Caesar* quarry notebooks and the versions Larry finally published, suggest a plunge into the unconscious, into the turbulent Id. Discussing an 'Adipose Etipus', Larry followed 'Learning how to be old gratefully' with 'little coitus had never known a/ mother's tender care'.[277] And Larry was grateful for Françoise's care, even for the occasional scolding which allowed him to turn over the responsibility for himself to a woman at once lover and mother figure.

Not since his innocuous inscription 'To My Mother' of the poem 'A Dedication' in *Quaint Fragment*, published when he was nineteen, had he brought a persona even tangentially suggestive of his mother into the context of his poetry. Sheltering behind third-person address, Larry now wrote,

> One rapidly cooling corpse ago
> He heard his mother's angel go.

The ancient alleged rejections and betrayals seem to have welled up within Larry:

> She sank the knife home to the hilt:
> He felt the polar stab of guilt.
> This was her way of saying No.
> The treason was too much to bear
> In his heart's core.[278]

In the 'Women in Provence' section of *Caesar's Vast Ghost*, Larry outlined 'the triple notion of lover, wife and divinity' that the ideal mate must encompass. To that daunting trinity he added 'Mother, nurse, muse, despot, slave, confederate, conspirator, worshipper, judge!' In fact, he continued, 'The charter of love was limitless . . .'[279] This he really believed: small wonder that no one woman had been able to hold him. But had Larry, self-proclaimed expert on love, who had referred to *The Alexandria Quartet* as 'an investigation of modern love', in the deepest sense loved any of his women? The final chapter of *Caesar's Vast Ghost* Larry devoted to Cunégonde, 'a Latex doll of great beauty, resilience and simplicity'.[280] The great virtues that he attributed to her were acquiescence, passivity, silence. Was Larry indeed speaking for himself when he wrote of Cunégonde, 'I suddenly realized with her (I was not the only one) that I had never loved anyone. . . . I felt doomed'?[281] To many of Larry's women, it seemed likely that his powerful motor of self had effectively prevented the full realization of any Other. Mary Mollo thought that his sexual insecurity compounded the isolation.

'Le cercle refermé' Larry entitled the last poem in *Caesar's Vast Ghost*. In the first lines he looked back to his origins, to the 'Boom of the sunset gun/ In the old fortress at Benares', then noted the 'Corpses floating skyward'. This time he saw death as proximate and personal: 'Today they are coming to measure me for a coffin,/ So dying you begin to sleepwalk and regain your youth.' He knew it was not far off, although he could still get up in the morning, work if he felt like it, drink wine all day; yet he concluded that 'Mere time is winding down at last', that the 'harvest moon' was 'consenting'. He felt his pulse, 'a carotid . . . haunted by old caresses', and mused upon his youth,

> When young and big with poems
> Caressed by my heliocentric muse
> With lunar leanings, I was crafty in loving,
> Or jaunty as a god of the bullfrogs
> The uncanny promptings of the human I.

There is nothing in 'Le cercle refermé' the least bit self-pitying, complaining, or even angry. He ended the poem with

> A disenfranchised last goodbye,
> Goodbye.[282]

GRADUALLY FRANÇOISE TRIED TO CHANGE Larry's reclusive life. She introduced a cordless telephone, ending his traipsing shuffle from the Darjeeling Room to his bedroom to answer calls. Larry was amused by this innovation and promptly dubbed it 'The Martian'. Françoise also told Larry that he needed a dog for protection and company, and, ignoring his objections, acquired a female Alsatian puppy. Larry, who still disliked dogs, discovered that he did not mind the puppy, and eventually he allowed it to sleep on his bed, down by his feet. With his increasing dependency, Larry had not become easier to live with, and he quarrelled with Françoise as he had with most of the other women in his life. She answered him back with directness and spirit. Sometimes he would praise her lavishly to his friends, then reverse himself and rail against her when the mood was on him: she was a bitch and a tyrant, she spent too much of his money.

In October Larry became the first to receive the Antibes Literary Prize. Although Antibes was only a two-hour drive away, Larry decided that he was not well enough to go, citing constipation, so Françoise and Anthea Morton-Saner collected it for him. 'Une homme décoré – constipé? Never!' Annie la Môme teased him.[283] His reluctance to be seen in his run-down condition probably had more to do with his refusal to appear than his physical difficulties. When Georges Hoffman arrived in November to make a short film, Larry was able to pull himself together.

As 1990 began, Larry seemed in better health and spirits than he had been for several years, although he was operated on for a cataract in one eye and found the anaesthetic 'very wearing'.[284] For one thing, *Caesar's Vast Ghost* was about ready for the press, after costing him so much agony in the writing – and his editors almost equal pain. Larry had taken part in nearly every stage of the production, including advising photographer Harry Pecinotti, selecting the illustrations and going over the layout. It was a great relief to turn the typescript over to Faber for what he hoped would be the final editing. When Erica Jong, finishing her long-planned book on Henry Miller, *The Devil at Large*, asked to see him, he consented. He seemed pleased to be visited by someone who brought so much of the bright vibrancy of New York to provincial Sommières. Erica Jong appeared, full head of blonde curls, lively eyes, trim figure – and Larry cast off ten years of weariness and boredom in an instant.

On 8 June 1990 Larry was honoured in Sommières when the main building of the ancient Ursuline convent was declared 'L'Espace Lawrence Durrell': the site was converted into a cultural centre and the mayor presided over a dignified ceremony. His hand a bit uneven but quite legible despite cross-outs, Larry wrote in his verse notebook:

> With Espace Lawrence Durrell I feel
> [I] have inherited a piece of France
> for my very own. Adieu triste orphelinage
> de la literature anglo-saxon. Je deviens
> un European armé cap à pie avec la lange <langue?>
> Poète.
>
> Prêt à tout mais bonne à rien![285]

It showed that his 'orphanhood' in English literature still rankled. His gratitude to Sommières was genuine, and *Midi Libre* quoted him as saying, 'J'ai aimé ce patelin et le midi avec mon premier pastis!' – I have loved this village and the Midi from my first pastis.[286]

Although many stressed the flashes of wit and laughter Larry could still on occasion produce, his old friends knew he was fading; worse, that he was not at peace with himself. 'He is deliberately drinking himself to death,' Jean Fanchette said.[287] Joan and Peter Bird arrived on 24 September 1990. Ray Mills was staying with Larry. He was sitting hunched in the kitchen, his face fallen into slabs of caricature. 'Larry took ageing very badly,' Joan Bird thought. The Birds found his speech slurred, as if he had had a stroke. They were sure that it was not from drink. Together, they all went to Aigues-Mortes for lunch, and in a familiar café Larry's spirits bloomed fitfully. Back at the house, the telephone kept ringing, Larry answering each time, and becoming increasingly exasperated: after eight consecutive wrong numbers, he shouted 'Nyet! Nyet!' into the mouthpiece. That time it turned out to be the Dalai Lama's secretary, trying to arrange a meeting between Larry and his master.[288] Larry was willing, but Françoise cautioned him against accepting the invitation: the French government was wary of offending the Chinese, so it might not be wise to consort with the Tibetan holy man.

At supper, after a day of steady drinking, yet still apparently unwilling to attack those in the house, Larry lashed out at 'Bouf' Bird, Joan and Peter's absent daughter: her morals were a disgrace, she ought to be gassed, Larry ranted. Françoise told him to shut up, that he of all people had no right to say such things. He fell silent. The next day when the Birds came to say goodbye Larry had forgotten his outburst. He was melancholy, sad, pleading: 'Don't go! Have a glass!' The Birds left him standing in the doorway.[289] Ray stayed on a few more days, and accompanied Larry and a woman visitor to a restaurant. Larry had not wanted her along, but could not bring himself to tell her to go. Ray took a few photographs; Larry did not manage a smile for the camera, but sat morose, chap-fallen. 'I'm so bored,' he told Ray, 'I see no reason to keep on living.' 'Come off it!' Ray scolded, attempting to rally him.[290] On Rhodes, Larry had said that one felt ashamed to be ill in Ray's presence: but this time the healer's magic did not work. Larry kept puffing and wheezing, slouched with his elbows on the table, and Ray felt that he really did not want to live.

In October the Antibes Literary Prize was awarded to Jacques Lacarrière, and Larry, who had been unable or unwilling to make the trek the year before to collect the prize for himself, went with Françoise to see their friend be acclaimed. Larry had weathered so many crises of late that he was beginning to feel a bit reckless.

Françoise telephoned Penelope to suggest that she come to see her father soon. She arrived on 18 October for a five-day stay, dreading a repeat of Larry's hectic state of the preceding spring. Larry was tranquil, clearly pleased to see her. Penelope found in her father 'a new acceptance of what life brings; old age, disappointments, loss'. They spoke of old friends recently dead – Xan Fielding, Fred Perlès – of L'Espace Lawrence Durrell and of *Caesar's Vast Ghost*, of Françoise's idea for creating, eventually, a centre for Durrell studies in the house. Best of all, the tensions that had invaded their relationship seemed to have vanished.[291]

When Larry drafted the last lines of *Caesar's Vast Ghost*, death was a good distance away, but like any conscientious dramatist he seemed to be preparing his exit. His cue evidently was the appearance of the book. An advance copy arrived in the post, delighting him with its large format and coloured endpapers reproducing an Oscar Epfs felt-tip pen sketch. Larry was elated. The faithful Ray Mills phoned from Edinburgh to say that he had seen *Caesar* in several bookshops. Larry opened his working notebook and made a final entry: 'I went dead, monogamous and for keeps.'[292]

Late in the evening of 6 November Larry phoned Anthea Morton-Saner in London. He sounded exuberant and quite tipsy: 'Françoise says she'll marry me!' Anthea spoke to both of them; yes, it was true, Françoise confirmed, they had decided to get married. They were on their second bottle of champagne.[293] Why had she changed her mind? She had realized that Larry needed her so much that she would have to think of him over her own children, she told Anthea later.[294]

The next morning Larry was up as usual, his morning coffee soon followed by glasses of wine. Françoise departed to see her youngest, Edouard, off to school and to run errands. Pierre, her middle son, was in the house with Larry. Around 11.30 Larry shuffled into the bathroom; after some moments, Pierre heard a thump and called to him. When there was no response, he pushed the door open. Larry lay on the floor, unmoving. His face was a raspberry colour. Pierre fetched Françoise from her flat across the road, and the doctor was summoned: there was nothing to be done, he said, and Larry soon stopped breathing. It appeared that a massive cerebral haemorrhage had felled him. Larry had often said that he wanted to die 'on my feet, with all systems working': this would be the ideal Buddhist death, with the dying person alert and fully conscious of the process of death. Apparently Larry was cheated: the man who had prepared for death throughout his life was surprised by it, ignominiously, in the homely act of relieving himself. Perhaps it was not so inappropriate after all. God, as Larry and Pursewarden both appreciated, is a humorist.

Wearing a blue jacket and with Sappho's scarf knotted about his neck, Larry was laid out in the great salon. The only flower was a single red rose. Françoise closed the gates and the various house doors to keep out the merely curious, admitting only those who telephoned to identify themselves. Penelope sat long into the evening at his side in the glow of the candles. Larry's face, somewhat swollen yet looking peaceful, was set in a slight smile. His hands were crossed over his stomach. In death, Larry appeared as enigmatic as ever.

The body was taken to Orange for cremation. A party of seven waited for the ashes: Penelope, Françoise and her son Christophe, Georges Hoffman, Anthea Morton-Saner, Mary Byrne and her husband Jean-Claude Vidal. Then they went for a quiet moment to La Chapelle St Julien where Claude's ashes lay, and with his pocket-knife Hoffman mixed a handful of Larry's ashes into the hard earth. They returned to La Maison de Mme Tartes, but as Françoise said, the voice of the house had gone silent.[295]

Epilogue

Following Lawrence Durrell's wishes, Françoise Kestsman, his literary executor, set about creating Le Centre d'Etudes et de Recherches Lawrence Durrell in La Maison de Mme Tartes. Painstakingly, she collected copies of his rare early books and journal publications to replace those that Larry had given away, lost, or sold to Southern Illinois University. The salon was walled across the centre to form a secure room to hold the collection. Françoise's daughter Nadia, Mary Byrne and others helped her catalogue the manuscripts and the correspondence files still in the house when Larry died. Gerry Durrell unveiled an identifying plaque on the gatepost at a memorial ceremony on 18 September 1991. Since then, many have known the warm hospitality of Françoise, have heard her memories of Larry, and have benefited from her knowledge of his work and his associations. The spirit of the Darjeeling Room that Larry so loved, of the friendly kitchen where he packed the oven with capons roasting amid garlic and ginger, with baking *poivres rouges*, the black table where he so often sat with a glass of 'plonk', watching the magpies thieving among the branches – that spirit lingered about the Centre d'Etudes, until the house was put up for sale in 1995. The highway that Larry had so long feared was scheduled to be built across the foot of the garden. His remaining books, papers and manuscripts went to the University of Paris X at Nanterre.

The Durrells

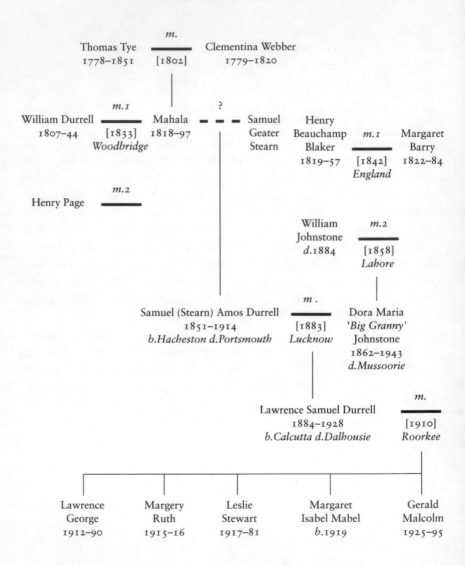

m.

Thomas Tye   Clementina Webber
1778–1851   [1802]   1779–1820

m.1   ?
William Durrell   Mahala   Samuel   Henry
1807–44   [1833]   1818–97   Geater   Beauchamp   *m.1*   Margaret
Woodbridge   Stearn   Blaker   Barry
                    1819–57   [1842]   1822–84
                         England

m.2
Henry Page

                    William   *m.2*
                    Johnstone
                    d.1884   [1858]
                         Lahore

                    m.
Samuel (Stearn) Amos Durrell   Dora Maria
1851–1914   [1883]   'Big Granny'
b.Hacheston d.Portsmouth   *Lucknow*   Johnstone
                    1862–1943
                    d.Mussoorie

                         m.
         Lawrence Samuel Durrell
         1884–1928   [1910]
         b.Calcutta d.Dalhousie   *Roorkee*

Lawrence   Margery   Leslie   Margaret   Gerald
George   Ruth   Stewart   Isabel Mabel   Malcolm
1912–90   1915–16   1917–81   *b.1919*   1925–95

The Dixies

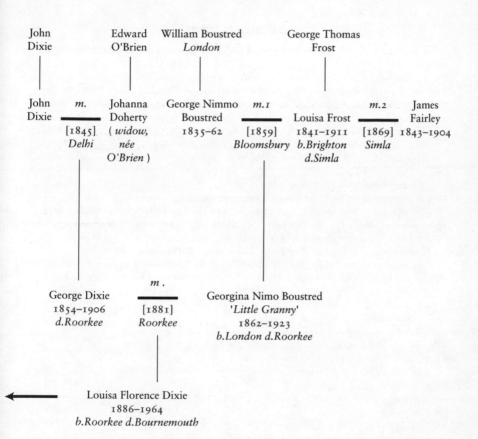

John Dixie		Edward O'Brien	William Boustred *London*		George Thomas Frost		
John Dixie	*m.* [1845] *Delhi*	Johanna Doherty (*widow, née O'Brien*)	George Nimmo Boustred 1835–62	*m.1* [1859] *Bloomsbury*	Louisa Frost 1841–1911 *b.Brighton d.Simla*	*m.2* [1869] *Simla*	James Fairley 1843–1904

George Dixie
1854–1906
d.Roorkee

m.
[1881]
Roorkee

Georgina Nimo Boustred
'*Little Granny*'
1862–1923
b.London d.Roorkee

← Louisa Florence Dixie
1886–1964
b.Roorkee d.Bournemouth

Notes

CHAPTER 1: India

1 Lawrence Durrell, 'From the Elephant's Back', *Poetry London/Apple Magazine* 2 (1982) 1.
2 H. G. Rawlinson, *India: A Short Cultural History* (London: Cresset, 1937) 405.
3 LD, 'Elephant's Back' 2. Durrell may have been referring to Cecil Henry Buck, his uncle, who wrote *Faiths, Fairs and Festivals of India*, and to his novelist second cousin, Richard Blaker.
4 LD to Henry Miller, c. 27 January 1937, *The Durrell-Miller Letters 1935–80*, ed. Ian S. MacNiven (London: Faber, 1988) 50. Hereafter cited as *DML*.
5 LD to HM, c. 12 December 1936, *DML* 30.
6 LD, 'Elephant's Back' 1–2.
7 LD interviewed by IMN, 6 May 1985.
8 LD interviewed by Paul Chutkow, 1 December 1988.
9 This was a recurring theme in Durrell's comments, to me and to others, about his father.
10 Lawrence Durrell, *The Big Supposer: A Dialogue with Marc Alyn*, trans. Francine Barker (London: Abelard-Schuman, New York: Grove, 1973) 30.
11 LD interviewed in *Réalités* (November 1960), trans. Earl G. Ingersoll.
12 I am greatly indebted to the late Cecil Noel Pearce, Durrell's cousin on his father's side, for much of the early family history. Mr Pearce made it a hobby in his retirement to haunt record offices and churchyards. A meticulous researcher, he gave me copies of all the documents that he unearthed.
13 LD interviewed by IMN, 7 May 1985.
14 LD in conversation with IMN.
15 Geoffrey Moorhouse, *India Britannica* (New York: Harper and Row, 1983) 239.
16 LD to HM, c. 27 January 1937, *DML* 50.
17 K. V. Mital, *History of Thomason College of Engineering (1847–1949)* (Roorkee: Univ. of Roorkee, 1986) 125.
18 LD, 'Elephant's Back' 3.
19 Moorhouse 203.
20 Cecil Henry Buck, diary (1909).
21 Margaret Durrell Duncan interviewed by IMN, 2 July 1989.
22 LD interviewed by Paul Chutkow, 1 December 1988.
23 IMN, conversations in Jullundur, March 1991.
24 Gerald Durrell, *Fauna and Family* (New York: Simon and Schuster, 1978) 95.
25 Moorhouse 219.
26 LD, *Spirit of Place: Letters and Essays on Travel*, ed. Alan G. Thomas (London: Faber, 1969) 43.
27 LD, among other places in an 'Autobiography' holograph notebook written for Alan G. Thomas (Coll. British Library).

28 Jeremy Mallinson, 'Ventures In the Animal Kingdom', unpublished manuscript 168.
29 Alan G. Thomas in conversation with IMN, 1 April 1991.
30 Gerald Durrell to IMN, 23 June 1993.
31 Gerald Durrell interviewed by IMN, 29 June 1992.
32 LD interviewed by IMN, 7 May 1985.
33 LD, *Pied Piper of Lovers* (London: Cassell, 1935) 8.
34 *Pied Piper* 3, 6, 25.
35 LD, 'Elephant's Back' 1. At other times Durrell claimed that he and his family spoke
    Urdu. There is not necessarily a contradiction: Urdu, spoken by Muslims in India and
    written in Arabic characters, is also called Hindustani, an Indic language of the Hindi
    group, widespread in northern India.
36 *Pied Piper* 16.
37 LD, 'Last Heard Of', *Collected Poems 1931–1974*, ed. James A. Brigham (London: Faber,
    1980) 320.
38 *Pied Piper* 17.
39 *Pied Piper* 24.
40 Sappho Durrell, 'Journals and Letters', *Granta* 37 (Autumn 1991) 71.
41 Lawrence Samuel Durrell, *Testimonials* (Calcutta: Edinburgh Press, [1926]) 19.
42 LD in conversation with IMN, May 1981.
43 G. Durrell, *Fauna* 85.
44 Margaret Durrell Duncan in conversation with IMN.
45 LD interviewed by IMN, 7 May 1985.
46 *Pied Piper* 43.
47 LD, 'Elephant's Back' 3.
48 LD, 'Elephant's Back' 3.
49 E. C. Dozey, *A Concise History of the Darjeeling District Since 1835, With a Complete
    Intinerary of Tours in Sikkim and the District* (Calcutta: Art Press, [1922]) 17.
50 *Pied Piper* 46, 48.
51 *Pied Piper* 46.
52 *Pied Piper* 114.
53 *Pied Piper* 78.
54 *Pied Piper* 54.
55 *Pied Piper* 51.
56 *Pied Piper* 39.
57 *Pied Piper* 45–46.
58 Mollie Briggs interviewed by IMN, 31 March 1991.
59 *Pied Piper* 77.
60 LD, 'Cities, Plains and People', *Collected Poems* 159.
61 *Pied Piper* 124.
62 G. A. Henty, Preface, *The Lion of St. Mark* (London: Blackie & Son, 1889).
63 *Pied Piper* 53–56.
64 *Pied Piper* 53, 59, 61.
65 *Pied Piper* 77.
66 Glory Dixie Wickenden interviewed by IMN, June 1993.
67 *Pied Piper* 40.
68 The admittedly tenuous evidence for Durrell's having attended the Jesuit-run Goethals'
    School rests on various passages in *Pied Piper of Lovers*. Durrell describes a visit that
    Walsh Clifton makes to an unnamed 'monastery' school with his father, and his
    subsequent schooling there. Goethals' was an easy walk from the Durrell homestead,
    and Durrell has Walsh Clifton stroll to his school with his Aunt Brenda. Also, in the

novel Durrell mentions the private hydroelectric generator that was a proud feature at Goethals'. The Cliftons' main contact at the monastery school was Father Calhoun, possibly based on Brother O'Brien, the guiding spirit behind Goethals' while the Durrells were in Kurseong. Durrell does not, however, appear on the roster of pupils, so that if he did indeed take classes there it may not have been as a regularly matriculated student. Goethals' was the only reputable school within easy commuting distance of Emerald Hall. In *Pied Piper* Durrell seems to have conflated his memories of Goethals' School and of Belgian Jesuit-run St Joseph's College – which young Larry definitely attended for two years, but which is not mentioned in the often closely autobiographical novel.

69 *Pied Piper* 133.
70 *Pied Piper* 138.
71 *Pied Piper* 137.
72 Glory Dixie Wickenden interviewed by Penelope Durrell Hope, 1985.
73 LD, *A Smile in the Mind's Eye* (London: Wildwood House, 1980) 33.
74 *Darjeeling and Its Mountain Railway: A Guide and Souvenir* (n.p.: Darjeeling-Himalayan Railway Co., 1921) 39–41.
75 *Pied Piper* 131.
76 *Pied Piper* 131–32.
77 Verrier Elwin, *The Story of Tata Steel* (n.p., 1958) 17.
78 Sardar Sohan Singh Sokhi interviewed by IMN, February 1991; information from Lawrence Durrell, Margaret Durrell Duncan and Gerald Durrell. Mr Singh was 102 years old, but clearly of sound mind and memory.
79 E. C. Dozey, *A Concise History of the Darjeeling District Since 1835* (Calcutta: Jetsun Publishing House, 1989 [c. 1916]), 123.
80 LD, 'Elephant's Back' 3.
81 LD, 'Elephant's Back' 2.
82 *Pied Piper* 60.
83 *Smile* 39.
84 *A Century Observed: Souvenir of St Joseph's College/North Point/Darjeeling 1888–1988* (n.p., 1988) 72.
85 *Pied Piper* 64.
86 LD to Father Stanford, 10 November 1960, *North Point Calendar* (1961).
87 *North Point Calendar* (1921) 12.
88 LD to Father Stanford, 10 November 1960, Calendar (1961).
89 LD, 'Elephant's Back' 1.
90 LD, *Supposer* 24.
91 Margaret Durrell Duncan in conversation with IMN, 29 March 1991.
92 Margaret Durrell, *Whatever Happened to Margo?* (London: André Deutsch, 1995) 37.
93 Margaret Durrell Duncan in conversation with IMN, 2 July 1989 & 14 June 1995.
94 LD, *Supposer* 26.
95 LD interviewed by Paul Chutkow, 1 December 1988.
96 J. K. Jha, 'Jamshedpur and Justine'. *Tisco News* 22:3 (June 1974) 20.
97 *Pied Piper* 95.
98 *Pied Piper* 72.
99 *Pied Piper* 63.
100 *Pied Piper* 110–11.
101 LD, *Supposer* 24.
102 *Construction Work in India 1921–1925* (Calcutta: Edinburgh Press, 1926). This 94-page illustrated brochure describing 'Durrell & Company/ Engineers and Contractors'

lists no author, but the only company officer named is 'L. S. Durrell, A. M. INST. C. E.', and it is dated 1 June 1926. It is likely that Lawrence Samuel Durrell wrote the text except for several testimonials.

103 L. S. Durrell, *Testimonials* 71.
104 *Construction Work in India* 6.
105 Jha, 'Jamshedpur and Justine' 20.
106 'Les Vies Singuliares de Lawrence Durrell', *Les nouvelles littéraires* 2629 (30 March-6 April 1978).
107 LD interviewed by Paul Chutkow, 1 December 1988.
108 G. Durrell, *Fauna* 87.
109 *Pied Piper* 96.
110 LD, *Supposer* 25.
111 *Pied Piper* 129.
112 LD, 'Elephant's Back' 2.
113 LD to Father Forestell, St Joseph's College, c. 1971.
114 *A Century Observed* 71.
115 *Pied Piper* 151.
116 LD, 'Elephant's Back' 3–4.
117 Margaret Durrell, *Whatever Happened to . . .?* (London: André Deutsch, 1995) 27. This speech was specifically accredited to Aunt Patience, MD's fictitious name for Prudence Hughes, her third cousin and the epitome of propriety.
118 *Pied Piper* 82.
119 LD, *Supposer* 26.
120 LD, 'Elephant's Back' 1.
121 LD, 'Elephant's Back' 1.
122 Sant Ram Chopra interviewed by IMN, Jullundur, March 1991.
123 LD, 'Elephant's Back' 3, 5.
124 LD to HM, c. 28 January 1937, *DML* 51.

CHAPTER 2: Pudding Island

1 LD, *Pied Piper of Lovers* (London: Cassell, 1935) 157.
2 *Pied Piper* 159–60.
3 *Pied Piper* 247.
4 LD, *Tunc* (London: Faber, 1968) 12.
5 LD interviewed by IMN, 8 May 1985. At least one of Larry's relations lived in Tunbridge Wells during the 1920s, but there is no agreement among the family sources on just who.
6 Durrell was unable or unwilling to recall the name of the school, but said simply that he had been 'at Tunbridge Wells'. No likely Tunbridge Wells school has a record of his attendance, but I was informed that as an unmatriculated student his name would probably not have appeared on the permanent records.
7 LD, *The Big Supposer: A Dialogue with Marc Alyn* (London: Abelard-Schuman, New York: Grove, 1973) 26.
8 LD, *Supposer* 25–26.
9 Gerald Durrell interviewed by IMN, 29 June 1992.
10 *Pied Piper* 251.
11 Ian Nairn, *Nairn's London* (Harmondsworth: Penguin Books, 1966) 196–97.
12 *Pied Piper* 192.
13 This is conjecture; but Dyson is an uncommon name, and in the relatively small circle of railway engineers in north-central India, nothing would have been more commonplace

than for Mr R. C. Dyson to say to Lawrence Samuel Durrell, concerned with the problem of his son's education, 'I have a relation in Dulwich who might take the boy as a lodger – a good, decent woman, y'know.'

14 LD to Keith Brown, Sunday 29 [October 1972?], Coll. Keith Brown.

15 LD quoted in Caroline Davies, 'Lawrence Durrell, Novelist with a Deep Passion', *Evening Standard* (8 November 1990).

16 *Pied Piper* 167–68.

17 LD interviewed by IMN, 6 May 1985.

18 LD to Keith Brown, Sunday 29 [October 1972?], Coll. Keith Brown.

19 LD interviewed by IMN, 6 May 1985.

20 LD, 'From the Elephant's Back', *Poetry London/Apple Magazine* 2 (1982) 3–4.

21 Durrell also told a version of this story in which a complete set of Dickens had arrived at their home in India loaded on a pack-mule. This sounds like one of his inventions: except perhaps in Burma, the family never lived in such isolated areas that pack-mules would have been used for parcel delivery.

22 LD interviewed by IMN, 6 May 1985.

23 School Report, 19 December 1924, St Olave's and St Saviour's.

24 Keith Brown, unpublished manuscript 2.

25 LD to Henry Miller, late March 1937, *The Durrell-Miller Letters 1935–80* (London: Faber, 1988) 65.

26 P & O Passenger List.

27 Glory Dixie Wickenden interviewed by IMN, 1993.

28 LD in telephone conversation with IMN, 22 Oct 1990.

29 School Report, June 1925, St Olave's and St Saviour's.

30 LD to Keith Brown, Sunday 29 [October 1972?], Coll. Keith Brown.

31 LD to Keith Brown, Sunday 29 [October 1972?], Coll. Keith Brown.

32 LD interviewed by IMN, 7 May 1985.

33 LD, 'Book of Travels', Coll. SIU-C.

34 LD, 'Elephant's Back' 3.

35 *Pied Piper* 177–78.

36 LD interviewed by IMN, 6 May 1985.

37 *Pied Piper* 176.

38 LD interviewed by IMN, 6 May 1985.

39 This was almost certainly a later addition on Durrell's part. A novitiate into *tumo* had to prove his control over his body temperature by drying successively seven small wet sheets placed over his bare back and shoulders. In Tibet this test was administered outdoors in sub-freezing weather. However, well into middle age Durrell assuredly did have excellent circulation and resistance to cold.

40 Harry Winter, *An Informal History of St Edmund's School, Canterbury* (n.p., 1982) 25.

41 *Pied Piper* 171.

42 The Rt Reverend Headley Sparks interviewed by IMN, Canterbury, 12 January 1984.

43 *Pied Piper* 171.

44 *Pied Piper* 230–31.

45 LD in conversation with IMN, 4 February 1975.

46 *Pied Piper* 180.

47 *Pied Piper* 219.

48 *Pied Piper* 173. This is the only example in Durrell's fiction in which a character clearly identified with the author is given even a hint of homosexual experience. I know of no evidence to support adolescent homosexual experience in Durrell's case: his schoolfellows, unlike most gentlemen, have told no tales. And at the end of his public

school time, Durrell has Walsh speak scathingly of the 'Lower V Sodomy Circle': 'God protect us from the taint of sodomy.'

49 The Rt Reverend Walter Fletcher Burnside, School Report, 1923.
50 Burnside, School Report, 1922.
51 LD, 'Elephant's Back' 3. Durrell is referring to G. P. Hollingworth, an English master who also taught French. He ran the Dramatic Society, and beginning in 1925 extended the scope of productions, previously devoted to Gilbert and Sullivan operettas, to include Shakespeare, Wilde, Shaw and other major playwrights.
52 LD interviewed by IMN, 6 May 1985.
53 *Pied Piper* 225.
54 LD interviewed by IMN, 6 May 1985.
55 *Pied Piper* 183.
56 *Pied Piper* 225.
57 LD to AGT, December? 1935, Coll. British Library.
58 LD, autograph manuscript, Coll. SIU-C. This quotation is from Durrell's handwritten draft response to the Kneller Tape, later published in revised form in *The World of Lawrence Durrell*, ed. Harry T Moore (New York: Dutton, 1964). One of Durrell's changes is significant: he had dropped the second sentence quoted here and had written instead, 'But I rather dread the word religion because I have a notion that the reality of it dissolves the minute it is uttered as a concept' (164).
59 LD interviewed by IMN, 6 May 1985.
60 *Pied Piper* 177.
61 *Pied Piper* 217.
62 LD interviewed by IMN, 6 May 1985.
63 Miss C. F. E. Davis, Registrar at St Edmund's, to IMN, 21 June 1995.
64 LD to HM, January 1937, *Lawrence Durrell/Henry Miller: A Private Correspondence*, ed. George Wickes (London: Faber, New York: Dutton, 1963) 48.
65 *Pied Piper* 221.
66 *Pied Piper* 225–26.
67 *Pied Piper* 201.
68 LD, 'Sonnet Astray', *Collected Poems 1931–1974* (London: Faber, 1980) 19.
69 St Edmund's School, Record.
70 LD interviewed by IMN, 6 May 1985.
71 Quite possibly Durrell never attempted entrance examinations for Oxford or Cambridge: the individual colleges had widely varying requirements and it is probable that he would have been accepted somewhere, given a modicum of perseverance. Neither university kept systematic records of failed candidates for admission during the years Larry might have applied. In some of the colleges, a student who could demonstrate that he had passed the Higher School Certificate or London Matriculation examinations with a sufficient score would have been exempted from all or part of either university's 'Previous Examination'. Nor were the requirements for admission uniformly stringent: in fact, according to E. S. Leedham-Green, Cambridge University Archivist, during the 1920s they were 'in some cases academically almost non-existent!' Durrell's protestations may have been merely a smokescreen behind which he fled formal education.
72 LD, *Supposer* 29–31.
73 Victor Brombert, 'Lawrence Durrell and His French Reputation', *World of Lawrence Durrell*, 170.
74 LD to Richard Aldington, January 1957, *Literary Lifelines: The Richard Aldington-Lawrence Durrell Correspondence*, ed. Ian S. MacNiven and Harry T. Moore (London: Faber, 1981) 3.

75 Joan Goulianos, 'A Conversation with Lawrence Durrell about Art, Analysis and Politics', *Modern Fiction Studies* (Summer 1971) 164.
76 LD in telephone conversation with IMN, 22 October 1990.
77 Margaret Durrell Duncan interviewed by IMN, 29 March 1991.
78 Margaret Durrell Duncan interviewed by IMN, 2 July 1989.
79 Margaret Durrell Duncan in conversation with IMN, 29 March 1991.
80 Margaret Durrell Duncan to IMN, 5 December 1987; also in conversation with IMN, 29 March 1991.
81 AGT in conversation with IMN, 1 April 1991; AGT had the story from Leslie Durrell.
82 Margaret Durrell Duncan in conversation with IMN, 1993.
83 *Pied Piper* 238.
84 LD to AGT, c. 1936, Coll. British Library. Salvarsan, professionally known as Arsphenamine, was an arsenic-based treatment for syphilis developed in 1909 by the German bacteriologist Paul Erlich.
85 *Pied Piper* 246.
86 Richard Pine, *Lawrence Durrell: The Mindscape* (London: Macmillan, New York: St Martin's, 1994) 149.
87 Conjecture of Cecil Noel Pearce, LD's cousin and son of his aunt, Muriel Florence Durrell. C. N. Pearce to IMN, 28 December 1990.
88 *Pied Piper* 101.
89 LD in telephone conversation with IMN, 22 October 1990. Margaret Durrell Duncan said essentially the same thing in conversation with IMN, 1993.
90 *Pied Piper* 215.
91 *Pied Piper* 246.
92 LD interviewed by IMN, 6 May 1985.
93 Nancy Myers (Durrell) Hodgkin, recorded memoir, Coll. Edward C. Hodgkin.
94 LD to AGT, 1937?, Coll. British Library.
95 Dorothy Brown Keep interviewed by IMN, 29 March 1991.
96 *Pied Piper* 262.
97 Nancy Myers (Durrell) Hodgkin, recorded memoir 1:30, Coll. Edward C. Hodgkin.
98 Cecil Henry Buck, diary 1929.
99 LD, 'Happy Vagabond', *Collected Poems* 18.
100 LD, 'Some Notes on My Friend John Gawsworth', *Spirit of Place*, ed. Alan G. Thomas (London: Faber, 1969) 17.
101 *Pied Piper* 268.
102 LD to HM, c. 27 January 1937, *DML* 51.
103 LD, 'The Art of Fiction XXIII', interview by Julian Mitchell and Gene Andrewski, *Paris Review* 22 (Autumn-Winter 1959–60) 39.
104 'Richard Blaker', *Dictionary of Twentieth Century Authors* 148.
105 LD to Alfred Perlès, pmk 17 July 1978?, Coll. Anne Barret Perlès.
106 LD to Alfred Perlès, pmk 17 July 1978?, Coll. Anne Barret Perlès.
107 LD, 'Finis,' *Collected Poems* 25.
108 Joseph A. Allen interviewed by IMN, 1993; Durrell's claim to AGT that only two copies were printed was not correct.
109 Margaret Durrell, *Whatever Happened to Margo?* (London: André Deutsch, 1995) 99.
110 *Pied Piper* 188.
111 Margaret Durrell, *Whatever Happened. . . ?* 174.
112 LD interviewed by IMN, 6 May 1985.
113 Phyllis Rickwood interviewed by Penelope Durrell Hope and by IMN.
114 Margaret Durrell Duncan in conversation with IMN, 29 March 1991.

115 Nancy Myers (Durrell) Hodgkin, recorded memoir, Coll. Edward C. Hodgkin.
116 Durrell held much against his mother: to various people he blamed her for allowing him to be sent away from India, for favouring Leslie, for wasting 'his' inheritance.
117 Nancy Myers (Durrell) Hodgkin, recorded memoir 1:3, Coll. Edward C. Hodgkin.
118 Lady Ottoline Morrell, *The Early Memoirs of Lady Ottoline Morrell*, ed. Robert Gathorne-Hardy (London: Faber, 1964) 178.
119 Pamela Wilkinson, unpublished memoir [2], Coll. IMN.
120 Endymion Wilkinson, 'George Curwen Wilkinson', unpublished manuscript, London (1993) 16.
121 *Pied Piper* 307.
122 Nancy Myers (Durrell) Hodgkin, recorded memoir 1:6 7, Coll. Edward C. Hodgkin.
123 *Pied Piper* 291.
124 Joseph A. Allen interviewed by IMN, 1992.
125 *Pied Piper* 327, 329.
126 Nancy Myers (Durrell) Hodgkin, recorded memoir 1:23, Coll. Edward C. Hodgkin.
127 Margaret Durrell Duncan interviewed by IMN, 29 March 1991.
128 'John Gawsworth', *Spirit of Place* 17.
129 Nancy Myers (Durrell) Hodgkin, recorded memoir, 1:15, Coll. Edward C. Hodgkin.
130 'John Gawsworth', *Spirit of Place* 18.
131 Nancy Myers (Durrell) Hodgkin, recorded memoir 1:15, Coll. Edward C. Hodgkin.
132 John Gawsworth to LD, 9 October 1932, Coll. British Library.
133 In 1865 Matthew Dowdy Shiell, a merchant on Montserrat, British West Indies, had declared his new-born son, Matthew, heir to Redonda, fifteen miles distant. There is no evidence that the elder Shiell had any legal claim to the island, but he considered it a pleasant addition to the family reputation to give his son a title. When Matthew was fifteen, Shiell brought his son to Redonda for a 'coronation', at which a friendly priest officiated. A fertilizer company was at work exploiting the guano or calcium phosphate deposits, and it does not appear that either father or son ever took part in the quarrying conducted on the island between 1865 and 1914. In 1885 Matthew left Montserrat for good, settled in London, dropped the second 'l' from his name, and began to move in a circle that included Wilde, Dowson and Machen.
134 LD, *Monsieur* (London: Faber, 1974) 141.
135 I visited George Barker late in his life at his home near Norwich. As adults and various children came and went in the chilly farm kitchen, I asked how many children he had fathered. 'Sixteen,' replied Barker. 'That's a lie, George,' said his wife. 'You've only fourteen.'
136 George Barker interviewed by IMN, 1983.
137 LD to Elizabeth Smart, January? 1940, Coll. National Library of Canada.
138 LD, 'Ballade of Slow Decay', *Collected Poems* 32.
139 Nina Hamnett, *Is She a Lady?* (London: Allan Wingate, 1955) 68.
140 LD, *The Black Book* (New York: Dutton, 1960) 173.
141 Nina Hamnett quoted in Hugh David, *The Fitzrovians* (London: Michael Joseph, 1988). The V and A: the Victoria and Albert Museum, London.
142 Nancy Myers (Durrell) Hodgkin, recorded memoir 2:68, Coll. Edward C. Hodgkin.
143 Geoffrey Potocki de Montalk to LD, 18 June 1933, Coll. British Library.
144 Geoffrey Potocki de Montalk to LD, 18 June 1933, Coll. British Library. The ellipsis is Potocki's.
145 LD, *Bromo Bombastes* (London: Caduceus Press, 1933).
146 *Bromo Bombastes* 7.
147 LD, *Supposer* 31.

148 Pamela Wilkinson interviewed by IMN, 16 January 1984.
149 LD, Argentina 1948 Notebook, Coll. SIU-C. Richard Pine conjectures that Dixie Lee was not a real person, but that Durrell invented her in honour of his Dixie-born mother. This seems quite likely, as I have not been able to find any independent confirmation of the existence of a singer of this name.
150 Nancy Myers (Durrell) Hodgkin, recorded memoir 1:32, Coll. Edward C. Hodgkin.
151 LD, *Livia* (London: Faber, 1978) 30.
152 Nancy Myers (Durrell) Hodgkin, recorded memoir 1:35, Coll. Edward C. Hodgkin.
153 Nancy Myers (Durrell) Hodgkin, recorded memoir 1:36, Coll. Edward C. Hodgkin.
154 Nancy Myers (Durrell) Hodgkin, recorded memoir 1:37, Coll. Edward C. Hodgkin.
155 A. J. A. Symons to LD, 15 August 1933, Coll. SIU-C.
156 Nancy Myers (Durrell) Hodgkin, recorded memoir 1, Coll. Edward C. Hodgkin.
157 Joan von Oettingen, 'Times with Lawrence Durrell and Nancy Myers – London. 1934 [sic]', unpublished manuscript enclosed with Joan von Oettingen letter to IMN of 7 March 1995.
158 Joan von Oettingen to IMN, 30 March 1995.
159 LD to Henry Miller, c. Autumn 1936, Coll. UCLA.
160 Pamela Wilkinson, unpublished memoir [1], Coll. IMN.
161 Endymion Wilkinson, 'George Curwen Wilkinson' 12.
162 Pamela Wilkinson, unpublished memoir [3], Coll. IMN.
163 *Pied Piper* 234.
164 *Pied Piper* 288.
165 Nancy Myers (Durrell) Hodgkin, recorded memoir, 2:7, Coll. Edward C. Hodgkin.
166 Reginald Hutchings to LD, 23 May 1934, Coll. British Library.
167 Pamela Wilkinson interviewed by IMN, 16 January 1984.
168 *Pied Piper* 107–108.
169 *Pied Piper* 227.
170 *Pied Piper* 216.
171 *Pied Piper* 233–34.
172 *Pied Piper* 232.
173 *Pied Piper* 240–41.
174 *Pied Piper* 231.
175 *Pied Piper* 336.
176 *Pied Piper* 367.
177 *Pied Piper* 369.
178 *Pied Piper* 99, 101.
179 *Pied Piper* 273.
180 *Pied Piper* 274–75, 300.
181 *Pied Piper* 310–11.
182 *Pied Piper* 371.
183 See Ray Morrison, 'Rémy de Gourmont and the Young Lawrence Durrell: A Creative Nexus', *Deus Loci* NS 1 (1992) 97–109.
184 *Pied Piper* 374.
185 *Pied Piper* 361.
186 *Pied Piper* 373.
187 LD interviewed by Paul Chutkow, 1 December 1988.
188 LD interviewed by IMN, 6 February 1975.
189 *Black Book* 211.
190 *Spirit of Place* 24.
191 Leslie Durrell to AGT, 7 March 1935, Coll. British Library.

192 Patrick Evans to AGT, 18 January 1935, Coll. British Library.
193 AGT in conversation with IMN, 13 February 1991. Thomas sang this verse to illustrate LD's type of comic lyric.
194 AGT in conversation with IMN, 13 February 1991.
195 Evelyn Lewton-Brain interviewed by IMN, 20 July 1992.
196 LD to AGT, pmk 1 October 1935, Coll. British Library.
197 AGT in conversation with IMN, 13 February 1991.
198 Nancy Myers (Durrell) Hodgkin, recorded memoir, Coll. Edward C. Hodgkin.
199 LD to AGT, 1935, *Spirit of Place* 36.
200 Alan G. Thomas to IMN, 4 November 1990.
201 LD, 'Faces', *Transition: Poems* (London: Caduceus Press, 1934) 12.
202 LD, 'Wheat-Field', *Collected Poems* 35.
203 George Wilkinson to LD, 7 September 1934, Coll. British Library.
204 LD, *Supposer* 37–8.
205 LD to George Wilkinson, October? 1934, *Spirit of Place* 29.
206 Margaret Durrell Duncan, Nancy Myers (Durrell) Hodgkin, Alan G. Thomas, and others have said that LD argued along these lines with his mother.
207 LD to George Wilkinson, October? 1934, *Spirit of Place* 30.
208 George Wilkinson to LD, 26 October 1934, Coll. British Library.
209 AGT in conversation with IMN, 13 February 1991.
210 George Wilkinson to LD, 15 January 1935, Coll. British Library.
211 AGT to IMN, pmk 21 January 1991.
212 LD in conversation with IMN, 8 May 1985.
213 LD, *Pied Piper of Lovers*, typescript, Coll. British Library.
214 AGT in conversation with IMN, 13 February 1991.
215 LD, inscribed for AGT in *Transition: Poems*, Coll. British Library.
216 LD, *Supposer* 26.
217 Nancy Myers (Durrell) Hodgkin, recorded memoir, Coll. Edward C. Hodgkin.
218 *Spirit of Place* 25.
219 *Black Book* 139–40.
220 LD, *Supposer* 24.
221 *Pied Piper* 372.
222 Nancy Myers Durrell to AGT, 2 March 1935, Coll. British Library.
223 *Pied Piper* 371.

CHAPTER 3: Corfu

1 LD to Alan G. Thomas, pmk 6 March 1935, Coll. British Library.
2 LD to AGT, pmk 14 March 1935, *Spirit of Place* (London: Faber, 1969) 30; unpublished portion of letter Coll. British Library.
3 LD, *Clea: AQ* (London: Faber, 1962) 877.
4 LD to Jeremy Mallinson, 5 September 1975, Coll. Jeremy J. C. Mallinson.
5 LD to AGT, pmk 20? March 1935, Coll. British Library.
6 LD, *The Greek Islands* (London: Faber, 1978) 16.
7 LD to AGT, 14 March 1935, *Spirit of Place* 30–31.
8 LD to AGT, pmk 20? March 1935, Coll. British Library. Eleutherios Venizelos, originally from Crete, tried to take control of the Greek government through a military coup on 1 March 1935. When the failure of the plot became evident, on 13 March he and the naval officers who had supported him fled to Rhodes. This ill-judged venture was to end Venizelos' political career within Greece; however, a number of respectable political

figures would continue to identify themselves as Venizelists. Venizelos continued to exert a tremendous influence on Greek politics until his death in Paris on 18 March 1936.

9 Charles Norden [pseud. LD], *Panic Spring* (London: Faber, 1937) 42.

10 LD, *Prospero's Cell* (London: Faber, 1945) 12.

11 The Corfiots had invited the Venetians to assume control over the island in 1386. The Venetians helped defend Corfu town against the Turks in 1431, 1537 and 1716, and the Italian heritage is seen in the names of some of Durrell's friends among the Corfiot aristocracy, such as the Abrami family, and by a few street names: Capodistria, Polila. Corfu was taken over by the French in 1797, by the British in 1814, and was finally ceded to Greece in 1864.

12 LD to AGT, March 1935, *Spirit of Place* 31.

13 *Prospero's Cell* 92.

14 LD to AGT, pmk 20? March 1935, Coll. British Library.

15 *Greek Islands* 29.

16 *Prospero's Cell* 107.

17 Thomas Dekker, *The Shoemaker's Holiday* II.iii.34.

18 LD to AGT, pmk 20? March 1935, Coll. British Library.

19 LD, 'Bitter Lemons', *Collected Poems 1931–74* (London: Faber, 1980) 238.

20 LD to AGT, pmk 20? March 1935, Coll. British Library.

21 Nancy Myers (Durrell) Hodgkin, recorded memoir, 2:37, Coll. Edward C. Hodgkin.

22 LD to AGT, before 20? March 1935, *Spirit of Place* 31–32.

23 LD to AGT, before 27? March 1935, Coll. British Library.

24 LD to HM, c. 28 January 1937, *The Durrell-Miller Letters 1935–80* (London: Faber, 1988) 51.

25 LD to G. Wilkinson, late 1934?, *Spirit of Place* 29.

26 LD in conversation with IMN.

27 Leslie Durrell to AGT, 10 March 1935, Coll. British Library.

28 LD to AGT, c. April 1935, *Spirit of Place* 32–33.

29 LD speaking in *Spirit of Place: Lawrence Durrell's Greece* (London: BBC, 1976), a film produced and directed by Peter Adam.

30 G. Wilkinson to AGT, 20 April 1935, Coll. British Library.

31 In his *Ulysses Found* (1963) Ernle Bradford argues convincingly, on the basis of place and voyage descriptions in the Homeric text, for the route Odysseus would most likely have followed in his wanderings. Durrell made a cameo appearance in *Search for Ulysses*, the BBC-TV film based on Bradford's book.

32 *Prospero's Cell* 12.

33 *Prospero's Cell* 16.

34 LD to AGT, c. 6 December 1935, Coll. British Library.

35 LD to AGT, c. July 1935, Coll. British Library.

36 LD to AGT, c. August 1935, *Spirit of Place* 34.

37 'A Lyric of Bodies', enclosed with LD to AGT, c. March 1935, *Spirit of Place* 33.

38 LD to AGT, pmk 4 June 1935, Coll. British Library.

39 LD to AGT, June? 1935, Coll. British Library. In the published version, 'went with a strange woman' was revised to read 'went with a woman.' Evidently *strange* was too strong!

40 Theodore Stephanides, 'First Meeting with Lawrence Durrell and The House at Kalami', *Deus Loci* 1:1 (September 1977) 3–4. This notation identifies published portions of Stephanides's journal, as distinct from the unpublished sections cited herein as 'journal'.

41 LD to AGT, pmk 20 July 1935, Coll. British Library.

42 *Panic Spring* 153.

43 Stephanides, journal 39, Coll. British Library.
44 W. Y. Evans-Wentz, Introduction to *The Tibetan Book of the Dead* (London: Oxford University Press, 1927, 1960) 2. It is not known when Durrell first encountered this book, but Tibetan Buddhism was clearly important to him while he was writing *The Black Book* in 1936.
45 LD, *The Black Book* (New York: Dutton, 1960) 229.
46 LD to AGT, pmk 1 October 1935, Coll. British Library.
47 Patrick Evans to LD, 1935, Coll. SIU-C.
48 LD, 'Bees': Patrick Evans's transcription of LD's unpublished poem enclosed with Evans's letter to AGT, after 17 October 1935?, Coll. British Library.
49 LD to AGT, late 1935?, Coll. British Library.
50 Gerald Durrell, *My Family and Other Animals* (Harmondsworth: Penguin, 1959) 55.
51 Pamela Wilkinson, unpublished memoir [4], Coll. IMN.
52 LD to Anne Ridler, spring 1939?, Coll. A. Ridler.
53 Durrell's friend Paul Hordequin would write in 1978, 'On devine que Larry a souhaité pour son jeune frère l'éducation aventureuse que lui-même n'avait pas reçue.' (*Les 23 siécles de Lawrence Durrell* [n.p.: Henri Veyrier, 1978] 45.)
54 Louisa Durrell to AGT, 29 May 1935, Coll. British Library.
55 Stephanides, 'First Meeting' 5.
56 Stephanides, 'First Meeting' 5.
57 John Gawsworth to LD, 5 August 1935.
58 LD to AGT, pmk 8 October 1935, Coll. British Library.
59 LD to AGT, pmk 1 October 1935, Coll. British Library.
60 LD to AGT, c. October 1935, Coll. British Library.
61 LD to AGT, pmk 3 January 1936?, Coll. British Library.
62 LD to AGT, late October? 1935, Coll. British Library.
63 LD to AGT, c. 9 December 1935, Coll. British Library.
64 LD to AGT, c. 6 December 1935, Coll. British Library.
65 LD to HM, 8 March 1937, Coll. UCLA.
66 Stephanides, journal 37.
67 Gerald Durrell in conversation with IMN, 29 June 1992.
68 Nancy Myers (Durrell) Hodgkin, recorded memoir 3:46, Coll. Edward G. Hodgkin.
69 LD, *The Big Supposer: A Dialogue with Marc Alyn* (London: Abelard-Schuman, New York: Grove, 1973) 39.
70 LD to AGT, pmk 1 October 1935, Coll. British Library.
71 LD, *Supposer* 39.
72 LD to AGT, pmk 15 October 1935, Coll. British Library.
73 LD to HM, August 1935, *DML* 2.
74 HM to LD, 1 September 1935, *DML* 3.
75 LD to AGT, summer? 1935, *Spirit of Place* 36–37.
76 LD to AGT, c. 6 December 1935, Coll. British Library.
77 Nancy Myers (Durrell) Hodgkin, recorded memoir 2:49, Coll. Edward G. Hodgkin.
78 LD to AGT, summer? 1935, *Spirit of Place* 36.
79 *Prospero's Cell* 13.
80 Stephanides, journal 26, Coll. British Library.
81 Stephanides, journal 19–20, Coll. British Library.
82 LD to HM, early September 1936, Coll. UCLA.
83 Stephanides, journal 21.
84 *Prospero's Cell* 19.
85 *Prospero's Cell* 12.

86 LD to HM, early 1936, *DML* 10.

87 LD, *Supposer* 38.

88 LD to Joseph A. Allen, pmk 6. March 1936, Coll. IMN.

89 LD to AGT, c. April 1936, *Spirit of Place* 45.

90 LD working notebook, 42/8/1, Coll. SIU-C; Richard Pine, *Mindscape* 115; LD to HM, early September 1936, Coll. UCLA.

91 LD, *Supposer* 37.

92 LD to AGT, May? 1935, Coll. British Library. Durrell is probably referring to Aldington's *Women Must Work* (1934).

93 LD to AGT, pmk 12 November 1935, Coll. British Library.

94 LD to AGT, November? 1935, Coll. British Library.

95 LD to AGT, November? 1935, Coll. British Library.

96 LD to AGT, December? 1935, Coll. British Library.

97 LD to AGT, pmk 3 January 1936, Coll. British Library.

98 Dorothy Brown Keep, interviewed by IMN, 29 March 1991.

99 LD to AGT, early 1936?, Coll. British Library.

100 LD to Joseph A. Allen, pmk 6 March 1936, Coll. IMN.

101 Apparently the postcard limerick was never sent, and in any case Durrell's anger had been misdirected: he had not known that Hutchings had resigned from the editorship of *Janus* in protest over John Mair's review of *Pied Piper*. Hutchings explained his role in a letter to Alan Thomas in 1966.

102 LD to AGT, early 1936?, Coll. British Library.

103 LD to Joseph A. Allen, pmk 6 March 1936, Coll. IMN.

104 John Mair, review of *Pied Piper of Lovers*, *Janus* 1:1 (1936) 29.

105 LD to Joseph A. Allen, pmk 6 March 1936, Coll. IMN.

106 LD to AGT, early 1936?, Coll. British Library.

107 LD to AGT, c. April 1936, Coll. British Library.

108 LD to AGT, c. 23 May 1936, Coll. British Library. Apparently Curtis Brown returned the short story and play manuscripts to Durrell, and they must have been among his papers lost during the war.

109 LD, 'The Art of Fiction XXIII: Lawrence Durrell', interview by Julian Mitchell and Gene Andrewski, *Paris Review* 22 (Autumn-Winter 1959–60) 48.

110 LD to AGT, end March 1936, *Spirit of Place* 43.

111 LD to AGT, c. 23 May 1936, Coll. British Library. Durrell's reference is to Luke 8:46, but he certainly was not claiming Christ as his master.

112 *Black Book* 208.

113 LD to AGT, c. June 1936, Coll. British Library.

114 LD to AGT, c. 23 May 1936, Coll. British Library.

115 LD to AGT, c. 23 May 1936, Coll. British Library.

116 LD to AGT, July? 1936, Coll. British Library.

117 LD, *Supposer* 38.

118 *Prospero's Cell* 21, 16.

119 *Prospero's Cell* 21. Although Durrell attributed the text of the letter to Nancy when he published it in *Prospero's Cell*, he had probably written it himself: the only extant manuscript of the letter is in Durrell's holograph and most likely dates from 1944. At this time, he was composing *Prospero's Cell* in Alexandria. My conjecture is that Durrell himself selected and purchased the *Van Norden* – but his version makes a pretty story, and it just may after all be the true one.

120 Patrick Evans to AGT, July? 1937, Coll. British Library.

121 Nancy Myers Durrell to LD, 1936, Coll. British Library. Quite likely written much later

by LD himself; the only example that I have been able to locate is a manuscript, c. 1944, in Durrell's autograph. Certain of the phrases support the later date and LD's composition of the decorated manuscript.

122 *Prospero's Cell* 120.
123 Leslie Durrell to AGT, 1936, Coll. British Library.
124 *Prospero's Cell* 16.
125 LD, 'Lesbos', *Collected Poems 1931–74* 226.
126 Stephanides, journal 4, Coll. British Library.
127 Nancy Myers (Durrell) Hodgkin, recorded memoir, 2:57, Coll. Edward C. Hodgkin.
128 LD to HM, c. 8 March 1937, Coll. UCLA.
129 *Prospero's Cell* 23.
130 Stephanides, journal 13, Coll. British Library.
131 LD to AGT, c. 23 May? 1936, Coll. British Library.
132 Stephanides, journal, 6, Coll. British Library.
133 Maki Aspioti interviewed by IMN, 18 July 1988.
134 *Prospero's Cell* 20.
135 LD to AGT, July? 1936, Coll. British Library.
136 HM to LD, c. August 1936, *DML* 17.
137 LD to HM, c. August 1936, *DML* 17–18.
138 HM to LD, October? 1935, *DML* 5.
139 LD to HM, early November 1936, *DML* 21.
140 LD to Michael Fraenkel, early December 1936, Carrefour Archives.
141 LD to HM, 20? November 1936, *DML* 27.
142 LD to HM, 20? November 1936, *DML* 27.
143 HM to LD, 15 November 1936, *DML* 26.
144 LD to HM, c. 12 December 1936, *DML* 29.
145 Stephanides, journal 10, Coll. British Library.
146 LD to HM, early 1936, *DML* 8–9.
147 LD to HM, 20? November 1936, *DML* 28.
148 LD to HM, c. 12 December 1936, *DML* 29.
149 The dust jacket copy of the American edition claims that *Panic Spring* 'bears a striking resemblance to the Aldous Huxley of *Those Barren Years* days'.
150 LD, 'The Art of Fiction XXIII' 53.
151 *Panic Spring* 99.
152 *Panic Spring* 353.
153 Harold Strauss to LD, 1937?, Coll. UCLA.
154 LD to HM, c. 27 November 1936, Coll. UCLA.
155 LD to HM, c. 27 November 1936, Coll. UCLA.
156 LD to HM, c. 19 December 1936, *DML* 31.
157 LD to HM, end December? 1936, *DML* 35.
158 LD to HM, c. 10 February 1937, Coll. UCLA.
159 LD to HM, c. 19 December 1936, *DML* 30–31.
160 LD to HM, February? 1937, *DML* 37.
161 HM to LD, 22? December 1936, *DML* 33.
162 LD to HM, c. 12 January 1937, Coll. UCLA.
163 HM to LD, 3 January 1937, *DML* 41.
164 LD to HM, c. 10 January 1937, Coll. UCLA.
165 LD to HM, c. October 1936, *Lawrence Durrell/Henry Miller: A Private Correspondence*, ed. George Wickes (London: Faber, New York: Dutton, 1963) 24.
166 LD to HM, c. 14 January 1937, Coll. UCLA.

167 Michael Fraenkel and Henry Miller, *The Michael Fraenkel-Henry Miller Correspondence called Hamlet* (London: Carrefour Press, 1962) 243.
168 LD to Michael Fraenkel, 1 February 1937, Carrefour Archive.
169 LD to HM, c. 14 January 1937, Coll. UCLA.
170 LD to HM, mid-January 1937, *DML* 42.
171 HM to LD, 20 January 1937, *DML* 46–47. Miller was then barely mid-way through an epistolary career that has been estimated at 200,000 letters.
172 LD to HM, c. 27 January 1937, *DML* 51.
173 LD to HM, February 1937, Coll. UCLA.
174 Nancy Myers (Durrell) Hodgkin, recorded memoir, 2:58, Coll. Edward C. Hodgkin.
175 LD to HM, February 1937, Coll. UCLA.
176 LD interviewed by IMN, 6 May 1985.
177 LD interviewed by IMN, 6 May 1985.
178 Stephanides, journal 44, Coll. British Library.
179 LD, poetry notebook, 1 January 1938, Coll. SIU-C. The text is found in David-Neel, *Magic and Mystery in Tibet*, trans. Claude Kendall (New York, 1932) 301. Durrell did not use David-Neel's French text, since the spellings in this passage are substantially different, and, rather typically, he had also differed in one word from the English text.
180 Alexandra David-Neel, *Magic and Mystery in Tibet*, trans. Claude Kendall (New York: Dover, 1971) 302.
181 LD to HM, February? 1937, *DML* 55.
182 HM to LD, 8 March 1937, *DML* 55.
183 HM to LD, 13 March 1937, *DML* 57.
184 HM to LD, 8 March 1937, *DML* 56.
185 LD, Preface, *The Black Book* (New York: Dutton, 1960) 13.
186 *Black Book* 21.
187 LD, Preface, *Black Book* (1960) 13.
188 *Times Literary Supplement* (24 April 1937) 307.
189 Reproduced as a blurb on the dust wrapper of *Panic Spring* (New York: Covici-Friede, 1937).
190 V. S. Pritchett, *New Statesman* 13 (1 May 1937) 741.
191 *Nation* 146 (1 January 1938) 753.
192 H. E. Bates, *Morning Post* (30 April 1937).
193 LD, 'An Open Letter to the Morning Post Press Cutting Agency', May? 1937, Coll. British Library.
194 HM to LD, 4 May 1937, Coll. SIU-C.
195 LD to HM, May 1937, *DML* 78.
196 LD to HM, late March 1937, *DML* 66. The spelling here follows Durrell's original in the UCLA collection.
197 Nancy Myers (Durrell) Hodgkin, recorded memoir 2:41, Coll. Edward C. Hodgkin.
198 LD to HM, late March 1937, *DML* 66.
199 LD to HM, late March 1937, *DML* 64.
200 LD to HM, late March 1937, *DML* 66–67.
201 LD, 'On Ithaca Standing', *Collected Poems* 111.
202 Nancy Myers (Durrell) Hodgkin to AGT, c. May 1937, Coll. British Library.
203 LD to AGT, April? 1937, Coll. British Library.
204 LD to HM, late March 1937, *DML* 67.
205 LD, 'Sun', unpublished poem, c. March 1937, Coll. British Library.
206 Nancy Myers (Durrell) Hodgkin to AGT, c. May 1937, Coll. British Library.
207 LD to AGT, c. April? 1937, Coll. British Library.

208 LD to HM, early May 1937, Coll. UCLA.
209 Friedrich Wilhelm Nietzsche, *The Birth of Tragedy* in *Basic Writings of Nietzsche*, trans. and ed. Walter Kaufmann (New York: Modern Library, 1968) 23.
210 Friedrich Wilhelm Nietzsche, *Epigrams and Interludes* in *Basic Writings of Nietzsche*, tr. and ed. Walter Kaufmann (New York: Modern Library, 1968) 279.
211 LD, *Tunc* (London: Faber, 1968) 90.
212 Nietzsche, *Birth of Tragedy* 42.
213 LD to HM, early March 1937.
214 Alan G. Thomas, 'Travel Diary: Corfu' [4].
215 AGT, 'Travel Diary'.
216 Molly Briggs and Phyllis Coulson interviewed by Penelope Durrell Hope, 29 January 1986. Both women are LD's cousins on the Durrell side.
217 AGT, 'Travel Diary' [16].
218 AGT, 'Travel Diary'.
219 AGT to IMN, 1987.
220 AGT, 'Travel Diary' [15].
221 AGT, 'Travel Diary' [23–24].
222 LD to HM, June? 1937, Coll. UCLA.
223 LD to HM, c. May 1937, Coll. UCLA.
224 AGT, 'Travel Diary' [34–35].
225 AGT, 'Travel Diary' [31].
226 LD to HM, June? 1937, Coll. UCLA.
227 Stephanides, journal 14, Coll. British Library.
228 A. Nin, *The Diary of Anaïs Nin*, Vol. 2, ed. Gunther Stuhlmann (New York: Harcourt, Brace & World, 1967) 204–205.
229 LD to HM, June? 1937, Coll. UCLA.
230 LD to HM, c. 28 June 1937, Coll. UCLA.
231 T. S. Eliot to LD, 28 June 1937, Coll. SIU-C.
232 LD to HM, mid-July 1937, *DML* 79.
233 Spencer Curtis Brown to LD, July? 1937, Coll. UCLA. Copy typed by LD and sent to HM in Paris. Very likely the sentences in block capitals and those in italic capitals were so emphasized by Durrell and not by Curtis Brown.
234 LD to Spencer Curtis Brown, July 1937, Coll. UCLA. This copy LD typed in red ribbon, a very unusual practice for him.
235 LD to HM, 21 July 1937, *DML* 81.
236 HM to LD, 29 July 1937, *DML* 84–85.
237 Henry Miller, *Tropic of Cancer* (New York: Grove Press, 1961) 63.
238 HM to LD, 29 July 1937, *DML* 85.
239 LD, working notebook, 42/8/1, Coll. SIU-C.
240 Blanche Patch to LD, 13 July 1937, Coll. SIU-C.
241 Edwin Muir to LD, 1 August 1937, Coll. SIU-C.
242 LD to AGT, pmk 8 February 1938, Coll. British Library.
243 Margaret Durrell Duncan in conversation with IMN, 14 June 1995.
244 Stephanides, journal 24, Coll. British Library.
245 *Prospero's Cell* 16–17.

CHAPTER 4: Henry Miller and the Villa Seurat

1 LD, 'From the Elephant's Back', *Poetry London/Apple Magazine* 2 (1982) 5–6.
2 Henry Miller, *The Complete Book of Friends* (London: Allison & Busby, 1988) 219.

3 A. Nin, *The Diary of Anaïs Nin* (New York: Harcourt, Brace & World, 1967) 2:223.

4 Nancy Myers (Durrell) Hodgkin, recorded memoir 2:102, Coll. Edward C. Hodgkin.

5 Anaïs Nin to Michael Fraenkel, 26 August 1937, *A Short History of Carrefour Press and Archives*, ed. Karl Orend and Constance Morrill (Paris: Alyscamps Press, 1994) 57.

6 LD, 'Elephant's Back' 5.

7 Nancy Myers (Durrell) Hodgkin, recorded memoir 2:93 Coll. Edward C. Hodgkin.

8 Alfred Perlès, *My Friend Lawrence Durrell* (Northwood, Middlesex: Scorpion Press, 1961) 10.

9 Perlès, *My Friend Lawrence Durrell* 11.

10 Alfred Perlès, *My Friend Alfred Perls* (London: Turret Books, 1973) 31.

11 Perlès, *My Friend Lawrence Durrell* 11.

12 HM to LD, early August 1937, *Durrell-Miller Letters 1935–80* (London: Faber, 1988) 90–91.

13 Perlès, *My Friend Lawrence Durrell* 12.

14 Nin, *Diary* 2:223.

15 A. Nin to LD, c. March 1958, Coll. SIU-C.

16 Nin, *Diary* 2:265.

17 LD, 'The Shades of Dylan Thomas', *Encounter* 9:6 (December 1957) 56.

18 HM to AGT, c. May 1937, Coll. British Library.

19 Patrick Mansur Freiherr Praetorius von Richthofen, *The* Booster/Delta *Nexus: Henry Miller and His Friends in the Literary World of Paris and London on the Eve of the Second World War* (Durham: University of Durham, 1987) 1:311. Doctoral dissertation.

20 A. Nin to Michael Fraenkel, 26 August 1937, *Carrefour Press* 57.

21 'Editorial', *Booster* 2:7 (September 1937) 5.

22 Charles Norden [pseud. Lawrence Durrell], 'Sportlight', *Booster* 2:7 (Septembre 1937) 8–9.

23 *Booster* 2:7 (Septembre 1937) 46–47.

24 A. Nin to Michael Fraenkel, 26 August 1937, *Carrefour Press* 57.

25 LD to AGT, mid-August? 1937, Coll. British Library.

26 Nin, *Diary* 2:237.

27 LD to HM, 1 September? 1937, *DML* 92.

28 LD to HM, 1 September? 1937, *DML* 89.

29 Count Geoffrey Potocki de Montalk to LD, 16 September 1937, SIU-C.

30 G. B. Shaw to LD, 9 September 1937, Coll. SIU-C.

31 LD to HM, 1 September? 1937, *DML* 93.

32 Audrey Beecham interviewed by IMN, 13 January 1983.

33 Audrey Beecham to LD, September? 1937, Coll. SIU-C.

34 LD to HM, 1 September? 1937, *DML* 93.

35 LD, 'The Other T. S. Eliot', *Atlantic Monthly* 215:5 (May 1965) 61.

36 T. S. Eliot to LD, 18 February 1938, Coll. SIU-C.

37 T. S. Eliot, on front flyleaf in Lawrence Durrell, *The Black Book* (Paris: The Obelisk Press, 1938).

38 Buffie Johnson, 'Personal Reminiscences of Lawrence Durrell', *Deus Loci* 1:5 (Fall 1981) 70.

39 Noël Riley Fitch, *Anaïs: The Erotic Life of Anaïs Nin* (Boston: Little, Brown, 1993) 202.

40 Bertrand Mathieu, *Betty Ryan, la dame d'Andros: La personne, l'oeuvre, le silence* (Charleville-Mézières, France: Editions du Museé-Bibliothèque Arthur Rimbaud, 1983) 14.

41 Nancy Myers (Durrell) Hodgkin, recorded memoir, Coll. Edward C. Hodgkin.

42 Betty Ryan in conversation with IMN, 1 June 1987.

43 LD, autograph working notebook, Summer 1937, Coll. SIU-C.
44 Prudence Hughes interviewed by IMN, 1983.
45 LD, 'The Death of General Uncebunke', *Collected Poems 1931–1974* (London: Faber, 1980) 45–50.
46 LD to HM, c. October 1945, *DML* 187.
47 *Booster* 2:8 (October 1937) 19–23.
48 AGT in conversation with IMN, 2 January 1984.
49 Gerald Durrell, 'Death', *Booster* 3:9 (November 1937) 11.
50 'Notes on new contributors', *Booster* 2:8 (October 1937) 49.
51 *Booster* 2:8 (October 1937) 32.
52 Charles Norden (pseud., LD), 'Sportlight', *Booster* 2:8 (October 1937) 9.
53 LD to HM, February? 1937, *DML* 55.
54 Michael Fraenkel and Henry Miller, *The Michael Fraenkel-Henry Miller Correspondence called Hamlet* (London: Carrefour Press, 1962) 338.
55 LD, 'Elephant's Back' 6.
56 Buffie Johnson, 'Personal Reminiscences of LD' 66.
57 A. Nin to LD, October 1937, Coll. SIU-C. Angered at finding the Durrells in Fred Perlès's company, 'I took you both away', she wrote in explanation to Durrell.
58 Alfred Perlès to HM, c. November 1937.
59 Nancy Myers (Durrell) Hodgkin, recorded memoir 2:89, Coll. Edward C. Hodgkin.
60 Nancy Myers (Durrell) Hodgkin, recorded memoir 2:93, Coll. Edward C. Hodgkin.
61 LD to HM, before 14 February 1947, *DML* 205.
62 Alfred Perlès, Preface to *Durrell-Miller Letters* x.
63 LD in conversation with Carol Peirce and IMN, 14 May 1985.
64 Nancy Myers (Durrell) Hodgkin, recorded memoir 2:106, Coll. Edward C. Hodgkin; Buffie Johnson, 'Personal Reminiscences of LD'.
65 HM, *Complete Book of Friends* 227–28.
66 Nancy Myers (Durrell) Hodgkin, recorded memoir 2:92–93, Coll. Edward C. Hodgkin.
67 HM to LD, October 1937, Coll. SIU-C.
68 Nin, *Diary* 2:126.
69 David Gascoyne to LD, 18 October 1937, *Paris Journal 1937–1939* (London: Enitharmon Press, 1978) 30.
70 LD, 'Paris Journal', *Collected Poems* 69.
71 Nin, *Diary* 2:267–68.
72 David Gascoyne, 'Remembering Larry', presentation, Avignon, 2 July 1992.
73 Buffie Johnson, 'Personal Reminiscences of LD' 67.
74 Buffie Johnson, 'Personal Reminiscences of LD' 68.
75 Nancy Myers (Durrell) Hodgkin, recorded memoir, Coll. Edward C. Hodgkin.
76 Jack Kahane, *Memoirs of a Booklegger* (London: Michael Joseph, 1939) 276.
77 Henry Miller, *Order and Chaos Chez Hans Reichel* (New Orleans: Loujon Press, 1966) 71.
78 Brassaï, *Henry Miller: The Paris Years* (New York: Arcade, 1995) 207.
79 Nancy Myers (Durrell) Hodgkin, recorded memoir 2:112, Coll. Edward C. Hodgkin.
80 LD, 'The Creation which Looks at You', in François Mathey, *Hans Reichel* (Zürich: Edition Scheidegger im Verlag Huber Frauenfeld, 1979) 51.
81 LD, 'The Creation which Looks at You' 53.
82 Nancy Myers (Durrell) Hodgkin, recorded memoir, Coll. Edward C. Hodgkin.
83 LD, 'The Creation which Looks at You' 53.
84 HM, 'The Cosmological Eye', *The Cosmological Eye* (Norfolk, Connecticut: New Directions, 1939) 358.

85 Hans Reichel, 'Letter for the Gostersools', *Booster* 3:9 (November 1937) 9. 'That what people calls the "sound mind" does not exist.'

86 *Booster* 3:9 (November 1937) 9.

87 Von Richthofen 1:426–28. The advertisement, featuring a photograph of Valaida Snow playing her trumpet, appeared in the November 1937 *Booster*.

88 Nancy Myers (Durrell) Hodgkin, recorded memoir, 2:95–96.

89 A. Nin to LD, c. March 1937, Coll. SIU-C.

90 Nin, *Diary* 2:226.

91 Nin, *Diary* 2:227.

92 LD in conversation with IMN, 7 May 1985.

93 Deirdre Bair, *Anaïs Nin: A Biography* (New York: Putnam's, 1995) 236–40.

94 Nin, *Diary* 2:231.

95 Nin, *Diary* 2:237.

96 Nin, *Diary* 2:231.

97 Nin, *Diary* 2:255.

98 LD to HM, early January 1938, Coll. UCLA.

99 Nin, *Diary* 2:231–33.

100 Nin, *Diary* 2:254.

101 A. Nin to LD, November 1937, Coll. SIU-C.

102 A. Nin to LD, November 1937 (second undated letter to Durrell of this month), Coll. SIU-C.

103 LD, autograph working notebook, Summer 1937, Coll. SIU-C.

104 François Mathey, 'The Painter Hans Reichel', *Hans Reichel* (Zürich: Huber Frauenfeld, 1979) 13.

105 T. S. Eliot to LD, 5 November 1937, published in LD, 'The Other T. S. Eliot' 62.

106 LD to T. S. Eliot, 'Saturday' 13? November 1937, Coll. Faber. *Pnevma*: Durrell's typed approximation of the Greek πνευμα, breath of life, soul..

107 LD to T. S. Eliot, 'Saturday' 13? November 1937, Coll. Faber.

108 Perlès, *My Friend Lawrence Durrell* 12.

109 LD to HM, February? 1937, *DML* 55.

110 LD, *The Black Book* (New York: Dutton, 1960) 80.

111 *Black Book* (1960) 172.

112 Audrey Beecham to LD, 27 June 1938, Coll. SIU-C.

113 LD interviewed by IMN, 7 May 1985.

114 *Black Book* (1960) 250.

115 *Booster* draft, typescript, Coll. SIU-C.

116 Nancy Myers (Durrell) Hodgkin, recorded memoir 2:96, 100, Coll. Edward C. Hodgkin.

117 Nin, *Diary* 2:238.

118 Nin, *Diary* 2:237.

119 Buffie Johnson interviewed by IMN, 6 March 1993.

120 HM to LD, 16 December 1937, Coll. SIU-C.

121 LD to HM, after 25 December 1937, *DML* 95.

122 LD to Tambimuttu, 2 February 1954, *Poetry London – New York* 1:1 (March-April 1956).

123 LD to Jean Fanchette, c. 24 March 1958, *Lawrence Durrell: Letters to Jean Fanchette 1958–1963* (Paris: Editions Two Cities, 1988) 24. Durrell in a letter to his daughter Sappho characterized Caitlin Thomas – along with Zelda Fitzgerald – as a 'phallocrat', a woman who attempts metaphorically to grow a penis as a 'masculine protest'. See 'Sappho Durrell: Journals and Letters', *Granta* 37 (Autumn 1991) 80.

124 Dylan Thomas to LD, c. December 1937, Coll. SIU-C.

125 Buffie Johnson, 'Personal Reminiscences of LD' 69.
126 Buffie Johnson in conversation with IMN, 6 March 1993.
127 Buffie Johnson interviewed by IMN, 1992.
128 LD to HM, after 25 December 1937, *DML* 95.
129 Nancy Myers (Durrell) Hodgkin, recorded memoir, Coll. Edward C. Hodgkin.
130 LD, 'The Cottager', *CP 1974* 250. The draft Ms is in Notebook A.3 (1 January 1938), Coll. SIU-C.
131 LD to HM, after 25 December 1937, *DML* 96.
132 LD, 'Jupiter in the Ascendant', autograph working notebook, Coll. SIU-C.
133 LD, 'The Asides of Demonax', Notebook, Coll. Univ. of Paris X/Nanterre.
134 LD to T. S. Eliot, before 10 January 1938, Coll. Faber.
135 T. S. Eliot to LD, 10 January 1938, Coll. SIU-C.
136 LD to T. S. Eliot, after 31 January 1938, Coll. Faber.
137 LD to T. S. Eliot, after 10 January 1938, Coll. Faber.
138 LD to AGT, pmk 8 February 1938, Coll. British Library.
139 LD, 'Tao and Its Glozes', *The Aryan Path* 10:12 (December 1939); reprinted in *A Smile in the Mind's Eye* (London: Wildwood House, 1980) 54–57.
140 LD to AGT, pmk 8 February 1938, Coll. British Library. *Night and Day*, edited by Graham Greene, ceased publication with the 23 December 1937 issue, due in part to a £3500 judgement for libel against the magazine, and another £500 levied against Greene personally. His crime had been to write a review of *Wee Willie Winkie* noting the seductiveness of the nine-year-old Shirley Temple's performance. Durrell commented to Alan Thomas, 'Then the paper went bust and the wretched author is being pursued for little Shirely's [*sic*] fucking damages. GRAHAM GREENE, the poor innocent.'
141 LD to T. S. Eliot, after 18 February 1938, Coll. SIU-C.
142 David Gascoyne, 18 March 1938, *Paris Journal 1937–1939*.
143 Gascoyne, 'Remembering Larry', 2 July 1992.
144 Buffie Johnson in conversation with IMN, 6 March 1993.
145 Nin, *Diary* 2:238.
146 Betty Ryan to IMN, 7 October 1990.
147 HM to LD, 5 May 1938, Coll. SIU-C.
148 Theodore Stephanides, 'First Meeting with Lawrence Durrell and The House at Kalami', *Deus Loci* 1:1 (September 1977) 10.
149 LD, *Prospero's Cell* (London: Faber, 1945) 19.
150 HM to LD, 24 June 1938, Coll. SIU-C.
151 HM to LD, early June 1938, *DML* 98.
152 Theodore Stephanides, journal 48, Coll. British Library.
153 LD to HM, late June 1938, Coll. UCLA.
154 Nancy Myers (Durrell) Hodgkin, recorded memoir 2:115, Coll. Edward C. Hodgkin.
155 LD to HM, mid-October 1938, *DML* 104.
156 Nancy Myers (Durrell) Hodgkin, recorded memoir 2:117–18, Coll. Edward C. Hodgkin.
157 Alexis Ladas interviewed by IMN, 1983.
158 LD to HM, mid-August 1938, Coll. UCLA.
159 'Dithyrambic Sex', *Time* (21 November 1938) 70.
160 HM to LD, 16 November 1938, Coll. SIU-C.
161 Anne Ridler, 'Recollections of Lawrence Durrell', *Twentieth Century Literature* 33:3 (Fall 1987) 296.
162 HM to LD, Saturday 8 October 1938, *Lawrence Durrell/Henry Miller: A Private Correspondence*, ed. George Wickes (New York: Dutton, 1963) 134–35.
163 LD to HM, mid-October 1938, *DML* 103–104.

164 HM to LD, 11 October 1938, *DML* 103.
165 A. Nin to LD, c. October 1938, Coll. SIU-C.
166 LD to HM, October 1938, *DML* 106–107.
167 T. S. Eliot to LD, 1 December 1938, Coll. SIU-C.
168 LD to T. S. Eliot, after 1 December 1938, Coll. Faber.
169 T. S. Eliot to LD, letters of 1 & 5 December 1938, Coll. SIU-C.
170 HM, *Order and Chaos Chez Hans Reichel* 9.
171 Henry Miller, 'Autobiographical Note', *The Cosmological Eye* 367.
172 Alfred Perlès, Preface to *DML* x.
173 A. Nin to LD c. October 1938, Coll. SIU-C.
174 Moricand's horoscope of Durrell is printed in *The Big Supposer: A Dialogue with Marc Alyn* (London: Abelard-Schuman, New York: Grove, 1973) 153–57, prefaced by the claim that Durrell was not to meet Moricand 'till years later' than the formulation of the study. This claim is insupportable, given the probable dates of the horoscope (December 1938) and of Durrell's meeting(s) with the astrologer on Nin's houseboat (1937 or 1938).
175 Moricand, *Supposer* 155–56.
176 LD in conversation with IMN.
177 LD, 'Cities, Plains and People', *Collected Poems* 162.
178 Alfred Perlès in conversation with IMN, 11 January 1984.
179 HM to LD, mid-December 1938, *DML* 109.
180 LD to Tambimuttu, 2 February 1954, *Poetry London – New York* 1:1. In 'Via Dieppe-Newhaven' Miller dramatized the story of his earlier aborted visit.
181 T. S. Eliot to LD, 28 December 1938, Coll. SIU-C.
182 LD to HM, early March 1950, *DML* 248.
183 LD, 'The Other T. S. Eliot', 61–62.
184 T. S. Eliot to LD, 13 January 1939, Coll. SIU-C.
185 LD to Tambimuttu, 2 February 1954, *Poetry London – New York* 1:1.
186 Dylan Thomas to LD, January 1939, Coll. SIU-C.
187 A. Nin to LD, before 3? January 1939, Coll. SIU-C.
188 'Anaïs Nin: An Interview with Daniel Stern and Dominique Browning', 1975, reprinted in *Conversations with Anaïs Nin*, ed. Wendy M. DuBow (Jackson: University Press of Mississippi, 1994) 221–22.
189 LD to Elizabeth Smart, January? 1940, Coll. National Library of Canada.
190 Anaïs Nin, 'Interview for Sweden', 1966, in *Conversations with Anaïs Nin* 18.
191 HM to LD, 19? January 1939, Coll. SIU-C.
192 LD to HM, late January 1939, *DML* 111.
193 LD to T. S. Eliot, after 13 January 1939, Coll. SIU-C.
194 Elizabeth Smart to LD, 15 January 1939, Coll. SIU-C.
195 LD to Elizabeth Smart, October-November? 1939, Coll. National Library of Canada.
196 LD to HM, after 21 March 1939, *DML* 121.
197 HM to LD, March-April 1939, *DML* 122.
198 LD to Keith Brown, Sunday 29 [October 1972?], Coll. Keith Brown.
199 Richard Pine, *Lawrence Durrell: The Mindscape* (London: Macmillan, New York: St Martin's, 1994) 97. According to Pine, 'The three main texts affecting [Durrell's] intellectual development were Kipling's *Kim*, Petronius' *Satyricon* and Lao Tzu's *Tao Te Ching*'.
200 LD, in Ridler, 'Recollections of LD', 293
201 *Delta* 3:1 [i.e. No. 3] (Easter 1939) 28.
202 LD to Anne Ridler, spring 1939?, Coll. Anne Ridler.

203 LD to Anne Ridler, 28 February 1939, Coll. Anne Ridler.
204 LD to Anne Ridler, February [1939], Coll. Anne Ridler.
205 LD to Anne Ridler, spring 1939?, Coll. Anne Ridler.
206 LD to Anne Ridler, early 1939, quoted in Ridler, 'Recollections of LD' 294.
207 LD to Anne Ridler, early 1939, quoted in Ridler, 'Recollections of LD' 294–95.
208 LD, 'The Art of Fiction XXIII: interview by Julian Mitchell and Gene Andrewski, *Paris Review* 22 (Autumn-Winter 1959–60) 52.
209 T. S. Eliot to LD, 26 March 1939, Coll. SIU-C.
210 LD to T. S. Eliot, after 26 March 1939, Coll. Faber.
211 LD to T. S. Eliot, after 26 March 1939, Coll. Faber.
212 H. G. Porteus to LD, 18 January 1939, Coll. SIU-C.
213 H. G. Porteus to LD, 23 February 1939, Coll. SIU-C.
214 LD to HM, mid-February 1939, *DML* 115–16.
215 Dylan Thomas to LD, c. February 1939, Coll. SIU-C.
216 LD to AGT, early March? 1939, Coll. British Library.
217 LD to HM, April 1939, *DML* 126.
218 LD to Anne Ridler, April 1939, Coll. Anne Ridler.
219 LD to Anne Ridler, June-July 1939, Coll. Anne Ridler.
220 LD to Anne Ridler, June-July 1939, Coll. Anne Ridler.
221 LD to Elizabeth Smart, January? 1940, Coll. National Library of Canada.
222 LD to Anne Ridler, June-July 1939, Coll. Anne Ridler.
223 HM to LD, Coll. SIU-C; also HM to 'Rico', 1967, Coll. British Library.
224 LD to HM, early March 1950, *DML* 248.
225 HM to LD, 21 April 1957, *DML* 286.
226 LD interviewed by Paul Chutkow, 1 December 1988.
227 Henry Miller: *The Colossus of Maroussi* (New York: New Directions, 1941, 1958), 16.
228 HM to LD, 27 May 1958, Coll. UCLA.
229 LD to HM, after 7 May 1958, Coll. UCLA.
230 LD interviewed by Paul Chutkow, 1 December 1988.
231 LD interviewed by Paul Chutkow, 1 December 1988.
232 HM, *Colossus* 25.
233 LD to Elizabeth Smart, October-November? 1939, Coll. National Library of Canada.
234 Nin, *Diary* 3:8.
235 LD to Louisa Durrell, pmk 27 September 1939.
236 LD to Anne Ridler, October 1939, *Spirit of Place* (London: Faber, 1969) 62.
237 LD to A. Nin, c. October 1939, Nin, *Diary* 3:6.
238 Robin Fedden, *Personal Landscape* (London: Turret Books, 1966) [6].
239 Fedden, *Personal Landscape* (1966) [5].
240 Robin Fedden, 'An Anatomy of Exile', *Personal Landscape: An Anthology of Exile* (London: Editions Poetry London, 1945) 13.
241 Fedden, *Personal Landscape* (1966) [5].
242 Xan Fielding interviewed by IMN, June 1990.
243 Fedden, *Personal Landscape* (1966) [9].
244 HM, *Colossus* 17.
245 HM, *Colossus* 46.
246 HM, *Colossus* 29.
247 HM, *Colossus* 30.
248 LD, Preface to Emmanuel Royidis, *Pope Joan* (London: Derek Verschoyle, 1954) 12.
249 LD to A. Nin, c. October 1939, in Nin, *Diary* 3:7.
250 LD to Elizabeth Smart, October-November? 1939, Coll. National Library of Canada.

251 Stephanides, journal 52–53, Coll. British Library.
252 LD to Anne Ridler, October 1939, *Spirit of Place* 62.
253 LD to A. Nin, c. October 1939, in Nin, *Diary* 3:8.
254 Nin, *Diary* 2:349.
255 HM, *Colossus* 102.
256 John Cromer Braun quoted by Dan Davin, *For the Rest of Our Lives* (London: Nicholson & Watson, 1947).
257 Stephen Spender to Roger Bowen, 4 December 1979, quoted in 'Introduction', Bernard Spencer, *Collected Poems*, edited and with an introduction by Roger Bowen (Oxford: Oxford University Press, 1981) xiii.
258 John Betjeman, 'Louis MacNeice and Bernard Spencer', *London Magazine* (December 1963) 63.
259 LD, 'Bernard Spencer', *London Magazine* (January 1964) 43.
260 Robin Fedden, *Personal Landscape* (1966) [4].
261 LD to Anne Ridler, late October 1939, *Spirit of Place* 63.
262 LD to Elizabeth Smart, January? 1940, Coll. National Library of Canada.
263 HM, *Colossus* 212.
264 LD to Elizabeth Smart, January? 1940, Coll. National Library of Canada.
265 HM, *Colossus* 215.
266 LD to Elizabeth Smart, January? 1940, Coll. National Library of Canada.
267 HM, *Colossus* 216–20.
268 HM, *Colossus* 221–22.
269 LD to Elizabeth Smart, January? 1940, Coll. National Library of Canada.
270 LD to Elizabeth Smart, January? 1940, Coll. National Library of Canada.
271 LD to Louisa Durrell, May? 1940, Coll. Penelope Durrell Hope.
272 George Seferis to HM, June 1940, *George Seferis to Henry Miller: Two Letters from Greece* (n.p., n.d.).
273 LD to HM, 1 January 1946, *Correspondence*, ed. Wickes, 215.
274 LD, 'To Ping-Kû, Asleep', *Collected Poems* 104.
275 LD to Anne Ridler, c. 17 February 1941, *Spirit of Place* 67.
276 Fedden, *Personal Landscape* (1966) [6–7].
277 LD to T. S. Eliot, after 1 September 1942, Coll. Faber.
278 LD in conversation with IMN, May 1985.
279 George Seferis to HM, 29 December 1940.
280 LD to HM, before 13 February 1941, *DML* 145.
281 Alfred Perlès in conversation with IMN, 11 January 1984.
282 LD interviewed by Peter Adam, 'Alexandria and after – Lawrence Durrell in Egypt', *Listener* magazine (20 April 1978), 497.
283 LD to HM, 13 March 1941, *DML* 147–48.
284 LD to T. S. Eliot, 15 March 1941, Coll. Faber.
285 LD to HM, 13 March 1941, *DML* 147–49.
286 LD, *The Greek Islands* (London: Faber, 1978) 106. The British authorities acknowledged that it was due to the darkness of the nights that so many of the expeditionary force, all but around 8000, could be evacuated.
287 Alexis Ladas interviewed by IMN, 1986.
288 *Greek Islands* 106.
289 *Greek Islands* 109.
290 Theodore Stephanides, *Climax in Crete* (London: Faber, 1946) 21.
291 *Greek Islands* 110.

CHAPTER 5: Egypt: Cairo

1 LD, *Clea: AQ* (London: Faber, 1962) 671.
2 John Braun, 'Lawrence Durrell's Arrival at Alexandria', *Return to Oasis: War Poems and Recollections from the Middle East 1940–1946*, ed. Victor Selwyn et al. (London: Shepheard-Walwyn and Editions Poetry London, 1980) xxviii.
3 LD, Introduction, E. M. Forster *Alexandria: A History and a Guide* (London: Michael Haag, 1982) xvi.
4 LD, *Balthazar: AQ* (London: Faber, 1962) 216.
5 LD, *Justine: AQ* (London: Faber, 1962) 121.
6 Rowland Langmaid, *'The Med': The Royal Navy in the Mediterranean 1939–45* (London: The Batchworth Press, 1948) 50–51.
7 LD, 'Letter to Seferis the Greek', *Collected Poems 1931–74* (London: Faber, 1980) 102.
8 Alexis Ladas interviewed by IMN, 1986.
9 The story of the fall of Crete and of Stephanides's march across the island in the midst of the German invasion is told in his book *Climax in Crete* (London: Faber, 1946).
10 Theodore Stephanides, *Climax in Crete* 165.
11 Mary Abercrombie to IMN, 28 June 1995.
12 LD to T. S. Eliot, December 1941, Coll. Faber.
13 Freya Stark to Flora Stark [mother], *Letters*, Vol. 4, edited by Lucy Moorehead (Salisbury: Michael Russell, 1977) 149.
14 W. S. Moss, *Ill Met by Moonlight* (London: Harrap, 1950) 183.
15 A. E. W. Sansom, *I Spied Spies* (London: Harrap, 1965) 40.
16 Freya Stark, *East Is West* (London: John Murray, 1945) 99.
17 Olivia Manning, 'Poets in Exile', *Horizon* (October 1944) 273.
18 G. S. Fraser, *A Stranger and Afraid: The Autobiography of an Intellectual* (Manchester: Carcanet Press, 1983) 164.
19 LD, Introduction, *Return to Oasis* xxvi.
20 LD in conversation with IMN, 6 May 1985.
21 LD, 'Yorick's Column', *Egyptian Gazette* (9 June 1941).
22 LD, 'Yoricks Column', *Egyptian Gazette* (29 June 1941).
23 LD, 'Yoricks Column', *Egyptian Gazette* (13 July 1941).
24 Alan G. Thomas and James A. Brigham, *Lawrence Durrell: An Illustrated Checklist* (Carbondale: Southern Illinois Univ. Press, 1983) 61–62.
25 LD to T. S. Eliot, December 1941, Coll. Faber.
26 Spencer Brooke, 'Passing By', *Egyptian Gazette* (2 August 1941).
27 Artemis Cooper, *Cairo in the War 1939–1945* (London: Hamish Hamilton, 1989) 101.
28 Dr Galal Aref of Alexandria in conversation with IMN, 3 September 1993.
29 Cooper, *Cairo* 48.
30 Cooper, *Cairo* 60.
31 LD, 'Thinking About "Smartie"', *Spirit of Place* (London: Faber, 1969) 71–73.
32 J. Fanchette, Foreword, *Letters to Jean Fanchette 1958–1963* (Paris: Editions Two Cities, 1986) 10.
33 Cecil Beaton, Diaries, 2 June 1942; quoted in Cooper, *Cairo* 183.
34 Freya Stark to Flora Stark, 30 June 1941, *Letters* 4:136.
35 Cooper, *Cairo* 99.
36 Fraser, *A Stranger and Afraid* 125.
37 Fraser, *A Stranger and Afraid* 124.
38 Manning's unpopularity is amply documented by Artemis Cooper in *Cairo in the War 1939–45* and by Roger Bowen in *'Many Histories Deep': The* Personal Landscape *Poets in Egypt, 1940–45* (London: Associated University Presses, 1995).

39 LD, Introduction, Forster, *Alexandria* xv.
40 LD interviewed by Michael Parkinson, BBC Television, 19 October 1974.
41 Theodore Stephanides, journal, Coll. British Library.
42 Mary Bentley Honor interviewed by IMN, June 1993.
43 LD to T. S. Eliot, December 1941, Coll. Faber.
44 Raymond Mills in conversation with Susan MacNiven, 1987.
45 LD, 'The Pilot', *Collected Poems* 133.
46 *Justine: AQ* 21.
47 Sansom, *I Spied Spies* 82.
48 Robin Fedden, *Personal Landscape* (London: Turret Books, 1966), [1].
49 Robin Fedden, 'An Anatomy of Exile', *Personal Landscape: An Anthology of Exile* (London: Editions Poetry London, 1945) 13.
50 Fedden, *Personal Landscape* (1966) [2].
51 Cooper, *Cairo* 152.
52 LD, Introduction, *Return to Oasis* xxvi.
53 LD to T. S. Eliot, December 1941, Coll. Faber.
54 T. S. Eliot to LD, 13 February 1942, Coll. SIU-C.
55 LD, 'To Ping-Kû, Asleep', *Collected Poems* 104.
56 LD, 'Ideas about Poems', *Personal Landscape* magazine 1:1 (January 1942) 3.
57 Douglas in *Keith Douglas: A Prose Miscellany*, ed. Desmond Graham (Manchester: Carcanet, 1985) 153.
58 Desmond Graham, *Keith Douglas 1920–1944: A Biography* (London: Oxford Univ. Press, 1974) 225.
59 *Clea: AQ* 793–94, 796.
60 *Clea: AQ* 756.
61 Bowen, *'Many Histories Deep'* 67.
62 Fraser, *A Stranger and Afraid* 124.
63 LD to T. S. Eliot, c. May 1942, Coll. Faber.
64 Fraser, *A Stranger and Afraid* 124.
65 LD to T. S. Eliot, c. May 1942, Coll. Faber.
66 Stephanides, journal 60, Coll. British Library.
67 Sansom, *I Spied Spies* 202.
68 LD to Anne Ridler, after 29 April 1942? *Spirit of Place* 74.
69 LD to T. S. Eliot, c. May 1942, Coll. Faber.
70 LD's letter of 4 July 1942 seems to have been lost by HM, although he referred to it in his reply to LD of 15 September.
71 LD to Anne Ridler, after 29 April 1942? *Spirit of Place* 75.
72 Fedden, 'An Anatomy of Exile', *Personal Landscape* (1945) 9.
73 Patrick Balfour, Lord Kinross, *Portrait of Egypt* (London: André Deutsch, New York: William Morrow, 1966) 15.
74 Fedden, 'An Anatomy of Exile', *Personal Landscape* 10.
75 Stark, *East Is West* 5.
76 LD, *Quinx* (London: Faber 1985) 201.
77 LD to John McPherson, 28 October 1975, Coll. John McPherson.
78 LD, Preface, *Bimbashi McPherson: A Life in Egypt*, ed. Barry Carman and John McPherson (London: BBC, 1983) 7.
79 *Justine: AQ* 105.
80 Mary Bentley Honor to IMN, 10 September 1991.
81 Freya Stark to Sir Sydney Cockerell, 23 November 1941, *Letters* 4:140.
82 Correlli Barnett, *The Desert Generals* (London: Allen & Unwin, 1960) 96.

83 LD interviewed by IMN, 7 May 1985. Durrell explained further that simply by virtue of holding a British passport and being committed to the Allied cause, he and his friends would be expected to keep their eyes and ears open, and to report back to the Embassy or other authorities.
84 *Clea: AQ* 732.
85 *Clea: AQ* 679, 670.
86 Cooper, *Cairo* 195.
87 Cooper, *Cairo* 194–95.
88 *Clea: AQ* 671.
89 Mary Bentley Honor interviewed by IMN, June 1992.
90 LD to T. S. Eliot, 25 August 1942, Coll. Faber. Nancy was still in Beirut: Lebanon was then part of Syria.
91 Stephanides, journal 60–61, Coll. British Library.
92 Mary and Group Captain Dudley Honor interviewed by IMN, June 1992.
93 Gwyn Williams, *ABC of (D.)G.W. A Kind of Autobiography* (Llandysul, Dyfed, Wales: Gomer Press, 1981) 166.
94 Nancy Myers (Durrell) Hodgkin, recorded memoir 2:116, Coll. Edward C. Hodgkin.
95 Joseph A. Allen to IMN, 6 April 1995.
96 LD in conversation with IMN, 11 May 1985; LD to T. S. Eliot, c. May 1942, Coll. Faber.
97 Ruth Speirs interviewed by IMN, 19 January 1984.
98 HM to LD, 15 September 1942, *The Durrell-Miller Letters 1935–80* (London: Faber, 1988) 155.
99 HM to LD, 21 November 1942, *DML* 158.
100 T. S. Eliot to LD, 19 June 1942, Coll. SIU-C.
101 T. S. Eliot to LD, 28 April 1943, Coll. SIU-C.
102 T. S. Eliot to LD, 19 June 1942, Coll. SIU-C.
103 LD to T. S. Eliot, 25 August 1942, Coll. Faber.
104 LD to T. S. Eliot, September? 1942, Coll. Faber.
105 Williams, *ABC* 30.
106 LD, 'Conon in Exile', *Collected Poems* 107–108.

CHAPTER 6: Alexandria

1 LD, *Justine: AQ* (London: Faber, 1962) 58.
2 LD to T. S. Eliot, 4 February 1943, Coll. Faber.
3 LD, *Clea: AQ* (London: Faber, 1962) 674–75.
4 Patrick Balfour, Lord Kinross, *Portrait of Egypt* (London: André Deutsch, New York: William Morrow, 1966) [9].
5 *Clea: AQ* 668.
6 Introducing Forster's *Alexandria: A History and a Guide* in 1982, Durrell misquoted Forster's suggestion about seeing the 'Turkish Town', applying the advice to the entire city: 'The best way to see the city is to walk about quite aimlessly.'
7 LD, Introduction, E. M. Forster, *Alexandria: A History and a Guide* (London: Michael Haag, 1982) xvi.
8 Forster, *Alexandria* 246.
9 LD, Introduction, Forster, *Alexandria* (1982) xvi.
10 *Clea: AQ* 660.
11 *Justine: AQ* 26.
12 LD interviewed by Peter Adam, 'Alexandria and after – Lawrence Durrell in Egypt', *Listener* magazine (20 April 1978) 497.

13 *Justine: AQ* 18.
14 *Justine: AQ* 101.
15 Forster, *Alexandria* 238.
16 LD, Introduction, Forster, *Alexandria* xvi.
17 Robert Liddell, *Cavafy: A Biography* (New York: Schocken Books, 1976) 180.
18 Artemis Cooper, *Cairo in the War, 1939–1945* (London: Hamish Hamilton, 1989) 53.
19 LD to T. S. Eliot, November? 1942, Coll. Faber.
20 LD to T. S. Eliot, 4 February 1943, Coll. Faber.
21 LD to T. S. Eliot, early 1943, Coll. Faber.
22 LD to T. S. Eliot, 11 April 1943, Coll. Faber.
23 LD, Introduction, Forster, *Alexandria* x.
24 Gwyn Williams, *ABC of (D.)G.W.: A Kind of Autobiography* (Llandysul, Dyfed, Wales: Gomer Press, 1981) 121.
25 Williams, *ABC* 11.
26 LD, Introduction, Forster, *Alexandria* x.
27 Peter Adam, '"Spirit of Place": Lawrence Durrell's Egypt', Post Production Script (BBC-TV production in association with RM Productions, Munich [23 March 1978]) 15.
28 *Justine: AQ* 17.
29 LD to HM, 23 May 1944, *The Durrell–Miller Letters 1935–80* (London: Faber, 1988) 172.
30 LD in conversation with IMN, 11 May 1985
31 Williams, *ABC* 30–31.
32 LD to HM, 22 August 1944, *DML* 173.
33 LD to HM, 23 May 1944, *DML* 172.
34 Bernard Spencer to LD, 28 May 1943, Coll. SIU-C.
35 Tiller, 'Ideas About Poetry: IV', *Personal Landscape* magazine 2:1 (1943) 2.
36 LD, 'On First Looking into Loeb's Horace', *Collected Poems 1931–1974* (London: Faber, 1980) 110.
37 LD, 'Mythology', *Collected Poems*, 115.
38 Robin Fedden, *Personal Landscape* (London: Turret Books, 1966) [7].
39 LD to HM, mid-May 1944, *DML* 168.
40 LD to T. S. Eliot, 5 July 1943, Coll. Faber.
41 Forster, *Alexandria* 111.
42 Forster, *Alexandria* 112.
43 *Justine: AQ* 35.
44 Cooper, *Cairo* 254–55.
45 LD to T. S. Eliot, 5 July 1943, Coll. Faber.
46 T. S. Eliot to LD, 2 October 1943, Coll. SIU-C.
47 LD to T. S. Eliot, 3 November 1943, Coll. Faber.
48 LD, 'Byron', *Collected Poems* 120–23.
49 LD, 'Alexandria', *Collected Poems* 154.
50 Noël Coward, *Middle East Diary* (London: Heinemann, 1944) 57, entry for 22 August 1943.
51 Anne Ridler to LD, 12 August 1943, Coll. SIU-C.
52 LD to T. S. Eliot, 7 October 1943, Coll. Faber.
53 T. S. Eliot to LD, 21 September 1943, Coll. SIU-C.
54 Cooper, *Cairo* 247.
55 Patrick Leigh Fermor, 'Observations on a Marine Vulcan', *Twentieth Century Literature* 33:3 (Fall 1987) 306.
56 W. S. Moss, *Ill Met by Moonlight* (London: Harrap, 1950) 52–53.

57 Mary Abercrombie to IMN, 28 June 1995.
58 LD, 'The Sonnet of Hamlet', *Collected Poems* 72–79.
59 LD, 'Ballad of the Good Lord Nelson', *Collected Poems* 113.
60 Anne Ridler to LD, 21 October 1943, Coll. SIU-C.
61 Bernard Spencer to LD, 23 October 1943, Coll. SIU-C.
62 LD to T. S. Eliot, 3 November 1943, Coll. Faber.
63 Peter Adam, 'Alexandria Revisited', *Twentieth Century Literature* 33:3 (Fall 1987) 405–406.
64 LD interviewed by Adam, 'Alexandria and after' 500.
65 Adam, 'Alexandria Revisited' 405–406.
66 LD, letter to the editors, *Orientations* (December 1943) 2.
67 Olivia Manning, 'Poets in Exile', *Horizon* (October 1944) 277. Roger Bowen gives a full account of the literary conflicts of Durrell, Fraser, Manning and others in *'Many Histories Deep': The* Personal Landscape *Poets in Egypt, 1940–45*, cited in Chapter 5.
68 Terence Tiller to John Lehmann, 7 November 1944, Lehmann Coll., Harry Ransom Humanities Research Centre.
69 Fedden, *Personal Landscape* (1966) [7]. Fedden is quoting an unnamed common friend on LD.
70 Gerald Durrell, 'My Brother Larry', *Twentieth Century Literature* 33:3 (Fall 1987) 264.
71 Leigh Fermor, 'Observations on a Marine Vulcan' 305.
72 LD, 'Cities, Plains and People', *Collected Poems* 165.
73 LD, 'Cities, Plains and People', *Collected Poems* 173.
74 LD to HM, mid-May [i.e., 11–25 July?] 1944, *DML* 169.
75 Eve Durrell to IMN, 24 August 1991.
76 Eve Durrell to IMN, 14 September 1991.
77 Cooper, *Cairo* 256.
78 *Justine: AQ* 60.
79 LD to HM, mid-May [i.e., 11–25 July?] 1944, *DML* 169.
80 Cooper, *Cairo* 256.
81 Charles Johnston quoted in Cooper, *Cairo* 257.
82 LD to HM, 23 May 1944, *DML* 172.
83 Eve Durrell interviewed by Paul Gotch on videotape, 10 May 1992. Coll. Paul Gotch. Paul Gotch to IMN, 21 August 1996.
84 LD in conversation with IMN, 8 May 1985; also Cooper, *Cairo* 256.
85 Eve Durrell to IMN, 14 September 1991.
86 Diana Hambro Ladas interviewed by IMN, 25 July 1987.
87 LD in conversation with IMN, 11 May 1985.
88 Adam, 'Alexandria Revisited' 397.
89 LD to HM, c. 25 December 1943, *DML* 159.
90 LD to T. S. Eliot, 31 December 1943, Coll. Faber.
91 LD to HM, c. 25 December 1943, *DML* 159.
92 Victor Selwyn, Preface, *Return to Oasis*, ed. Victor Selwyn et al. (London: Shepheard-Walwyn, and Editions Poetry London, 1980) xx.
93 LD, 'Against Cairo: An Ode', in Gwyn Williams, 'Durrell in Egypt', *Twentieth Century Literature* 33:3 (Fall 1987) 299–300.
94 Bernard Spencer, quoted in his *Collected Poems*, edited and with an introduction by Roger Bowen (Oxford: Oxford University Press, 1981), xxii.
95 LD to T. S. Eliot, 8 February 1944, first letter this date, Coll. Faber.
96 LD to T. S. Eliot, 8 February 1944, second letter this date, Coll. Faber.
97 LD to T. S. Eliot, 8 February 1944, first letter this date, Coll. Faber.

98 LD to T. S. Eliot, 8 February 1944 (Durrell's two letters of this date give similar information), Coll. Faber.

99 LD interviewed by IMN, 6 May 1985.

100 LD interviewed by Paul Chutkow, 1 December 1988.

101 George Seferis to LD, 8 February 1944, Coll. SIU-C.

102 Williams, *ABC* 30–31.

103 Diana Gould Menuhin to LD, 6 February 1945, Coll. SIU-C.

104 Cooper, *Cairo* 257.

105 Diana Gould Menuhin to LD, 30 July 1960, Coll. SIU-C.

106 Adam, 'Alexandria Revisited' 396.

107 D. Menuhin, 'Lawrence Durrell in Alexandria and Sommières', *Twentieth Century Literature* 33:3 (Fall 1987) 310.

108 LD, 'Mareotis', *Collected Poems 1931–74* 130.

109 D. Menuhin interviewed by IMN, 15 February 1991.

110 D. Menuhin, 'Durrell in Alexandria and Sommières' 310.

111 D. Menuhin, 'Durrell in Alexandria and Sommières' 309.

112 Paul Gotch interviewed by IMN, 10 August 1996.

113 LD to Diana Gould Menuhin, March 1944, *Spirit of Place* 75.

114 Alexis Ladas interviewed by IMN, 1985.

115 LD to HM, 8 February 1944, *DML* 159.

116 LD to T. S. Eliot, letters of 31 December 1943 and March? 1944, Coll. Faber.

117 T. S. Eliot to LD, 4 April 1944, Coll. Faber.

118 LD to T. S. Eliot, May? 1944, Coll. Faber.

119 HM to LD, 7 April 1944, *DML* 162.

120 LD to HM, 8 February 1944, *DML* 160–61.

121 HM to LD, 5 May 1944, *DML* 166.

122 LD to HM, mid-May 1944, *DML* 167.

123 Eve Durrell interviewed on videotape by Paul Gotch, 10 May 1992. Coll. Paul Gotch. Paul Gotch to IMN, 21 August 1996.

124 LD to HM, [i.e. 11–25 July] 1944, *DML* 169.

125 LD to Diana Gould Menuhin, March 1944, *Spirit of Place* 76.

126 'Art by Accident', *Personal Landscape: An Anthology of Exile* (London: Editions Poetry London, 1945) 63.

127 LD, 'Imbecility File' scrapbook, Coll. British Library.

128 LD to HM, mid-May [i.e., 11–25 July] 1944, *DML* 170. Eve Durrell gives a different account of her knowledge of the city, stating that 'of Alexandria's "seamy" side I was never aware' (Eve Durrell to IMN, 14 September 1991).

129 LD to HM, mid-May [i.e., 11–25 July] 1944, *DML* 170.

130 LD to HM, 23 May 1944, *DML* 172.

131 LD, *Balthazar: AQ* (London: Faber, 1962) 292.

132 Paul Gotch interviewed by IMN, 1985.

133 *Justine: AQ* 43.

134 LD, 'A Little Letter To Eve', Coll. British Library.

135 LD, 'The Art of Fiction XXIII', interview by Julian Mitchell and Gene Andrewski, *Paris Review* (Autumn-Winter 1959–60) 49–50.

136 LD to T. Stephanides, Spring 1944, *Spirit of Place* 74.

137 LD interviewed by IMN, 7 May 1985.

138 LD to HM, c. October 1945, *DML* 186.

139 LD to Diana Gould Menuhin, March 1944, *Spirit of Place* 76.

140 LD to HM, 22 August 1944, *DML* 174–75.

141 LD, 'The Happy Rock', in *The Happy Rock: A Book About Henry Miller* (Berkeley: Packard Press, 1945) 1–6.

142 HM to LD, 20 August 1944, Coll. SIU-C.

143 HM to LD, 22? December 1936, *DML* 34.

144 Hugh Gordon Porteus to LD, 9 August 1944, Coll. SIU-C.

145 LD to HM, 22 August 1944, second letter this date, Coll. UCLA.

146 Hugh Gordon Porteus to LD, 7 September 1944, Coll. SIU-C.

147 LD to HM, 22 August 1944, *DML* 174.

148 LD to HM, c. September 1944, Coll. UCLA.

149 LD to HM, September 1944, *DML* 176.

150 LD to HM, September 1944, *DML* 176.

151 LD to HM, 22 August 1944, *DML* 174.

152 LD to Gwyn Williams, c. June 1945, quoted in Gwyn Williams, 'Durrell in Egypt' 301.

153 LD to HM, early October? 1944, Coll. UCLA.

154 LD to T. S. Eliot, 1 December 1944, Coll. Faber.

155 LD to HM, 22 August 1944, second letter this date, Coll. UCLA.

156 LD to HM, 22 August 1944, first letter this date, unpublished portion, Coll. UCLA.

157 LD, 'Zeus & Hera', autograph working notebook, Coll. SIU-C. Durrell attributed essentially the same text to Pursewarden in *Clea: AQ* 755. Sometimes he referred to his more ribald productions as 'Pursewarden's incorrigibilia'.

158 LD to HM, 22 August 1944, first letter this date, unpublished portion, Coll. UCLA.

159 Anne Ridler to LD, 13 October 1944, Coll. SIU-C.

160 HM to LD, 25 February 1945, Coll. SIU-C.

161 LD's sketch annotated 'Sunbathing Abu El Sair/ 1944' appears in his autograph working notebook of 1944, Coll. SIU-C.

162 LD to HM, 23 May 1944, *DML* 172–73.

163 HM to LD, 13 December 1944, *DML* 177.

164 Robert Ferguson, *Henry Miller: A Life* (London: Hutchinson, New York: Norton, 1991) 291.

165 LD, autograph working notebook, A. 10, Coll. SIU-C.

166 LD to HM, c. October 1944, Coll. UCLA.

167 LD to HM, c. October 1944, Coll. UCLA.

168 LD to T. S. Eliot, March 1945, Coll. Faber.

169 LD to T. S. Eliot, 1 December 1944, Coll. Faber.

170 Xan Fielding, *Hide and Seek: The Story of a War-time Agent* (London: Secker & Warburg, 1954) 147.

171 Fielding, *Hide and Seek* 150.

172 LD to HM, c. October 1945, *DML* 186.

173 T. S. Eliot to LD, 5 April 1945, first letter this date, Coll. SIU-C.

174 LD to T. S. Eliot, pmk 13? April 1945, Coll. Faber.

175 T. S. Eliot to LD, 5 April 1945, second letter this date, Coll. SIU-C.

176 LD to T. S. Eliot, pmk 13? April 1945, Coll. Faber.

177 HM to LD, 18 February 1945, *Lawrence Durrell/Henry Miller: A Private Correspondence*, ed. George Wickes (London: Faber, New York: Dutton, 1963) 198.

178 HM to LD, 28 May 1945, Coll. SIU-C.

179 HM to LD, 18 February 1945, *DML* 179.

180 HM to LD, 18 February 1945, *DML* 179.

181 HM to LD, 14 August 1945, Coll. SIU-C.

182 LD, 'Alexandria', *Collected Poems 1931–74* 154.

183 Gwyn Williams, 'Durrell in Egypt' 301.

184 LD to HM, c. 1 March 1945, *DML* 179–80.

185 LD to T. S. Eliot, March 1945, Coll. Faber.

186 LD to T. S. Eliot, 16 April 1945, Coll. Faber.

187 LD to HM, c. 1 March 1945, *DML* 179–80.

188 Gwyn Williams to LD, 30 September 1985, Coll. IMN.

189 LD to HM, c. March-April 1945, Coll. UCLA.

190 LD to T. S. Eliot, pmk 13? April 1945, Coll. Faber.

191 LD to T. Stephanides, 30 May 1945, Coll. British Library.

192 LD to T. S. Eliot, 5 May 1945, Coll. Faber.

193 LD to T. S. Eliot, 5 March 1945, Coll. Faber.

194 LD, *Reflections on a Marine Venus* (London: Faber, 1953) 18.

CHAPTER 7: Rhodes, *Paradise Terrestre*

1 LD, *Reflections on a Marine Venus* (London: Faber, 1953) 23–24.

2 LD interviewed by IMN, 7 May 1985; confirmed in other interviews with Thomas W. French and Dr Raymond Mills.

3 *Reflections* 17.

4 *Reflections* 18.

5 *Reflections* 22–23.

6 *Reflections* 24–29.

7 *Reflections* 26.

8 LD to HM, 22 June 1945, *The Durrell–Miller Letters 1935–80* (London: Faber, 1988) 181. Durrell was careful, in *Reflections on a Marine Venus*, to distinguish between the tasteless restorations of 'the latest Italian governor' and the 'splendid thoughtful work' of Mario Lago, who as governor from 1922–1936 had brilliantly preserved or re-created many Rhodes landmarks. See John Hope, 'Rhodes Spa', *Architectural Review* (London, September 1977).

9 *Reflections* 27.

10 LD to T. S. Eliot, July-August 1945, Coll. Faber.

11 LD to T. Stephanides, c. December 1945, Coll. UCLA.

12 LD to Gwyn Williams, c. July 1945, in Gwyn Williams, 'Durrell in Egypt', *Twentieth Century Literature* 33:3 (Fall 1987) 301.

13 LD to Gwyn Williams, c. July 1945, in Gwyn Williams, 'Durrell in Egypt' 301–302.

14 LD to Gwyn Williams, c. July 1945, in Gwyn Williams, 'Durrell in Egypt' 302.

15 LD to T. S. Eliot, July-August 1945, Coll. Faber.

16 LD, *The Greek Islands* (London: Faber, 1978) 123.

17 LD to H. G. Porteus, c. December 1946, *Spirit of Place* (London: Faber, 1969) 87.

18 LD to T. S. Eliot, July-August 1945, Coll. Faber.

19 T. S. Eliot to LD, 2 September 1945, Coll. SIU-C.

20 LD to T. S. Eliot, July-August 1945, Coll. Faber.

21 LD to T. S. Eliot, c. July 1945, Coll. Faber.

22 T. S. Eliot to LD, 2 September 1945, Coll. SIU-C.

23 LD to T. S. Eliot, September? 1945, Coll. Faber.

24 Raymond Mills, 'With Durrell on Rhodes', *Twentieth Century Literature* 33:3 (Fall 1987) 313.

25 LD to T. S. Eliot, September? 1945, Coll. Faber.

26 LD to T. S. Eliot, July-August 1945, Coll. Faber.

27 George Barker interviewed by IMN, 1983.

28 LD to T. S. Eliot, April 1946, Coll. Faber.
29 LD to T. S. Eliot, pmk 20 August 1945, Coll. Faber.
30 Mills, 'With Durrell on Rhodes', 312.
31 *Reflections* 35.
32 *Reflections* 34–35.
33 *Greek Islands* 127.
34 LD to T. S. Eliot, 1 June 1946, Coll. Faber.
35 Mills, 'With Durrell on Rhodes' 313.
36 *Greek Islands* 119–20.
37 T. W. French interviewed by IMN, 6 June 1993.
38 Peter Adam, '"Spirit of Place": Lawrence Durrell's Greece', Post Production Script (BBC-TV production in association with RM Productions, Munich, and Télévision Française 1 [5 March 1976]) 31.
39 Spiros Katexis interviewed by IMN, June 1992.
40 Gwyn Williams to LD, 8 July 1945, Coll. SIU-C.
41 H. G. Porteus to LD, 9 July 1945, Coll. SIU-C.
42 T. S. Eliot to LD, 16 October 1945, Coll. SIU-C.
43 LD to T. S. Eliot, 22 October 1945, Coll. Faber.
44 LD to T. S. Eliot, 22 October 1945, Coll. Faber.
45 LD to HM, c. November 1945, Coll. UCLA.
46 LD, *Cefalû* (London: Editions Poetry London, 1947) 65.
47 *Cefalû* 87–88.
48 *Cefalû* 56–58.
49 *Cefalû* 64–65.
50 *Cefalû* 56–57.
51 LD to T. S. Eliot, 22 October 1945, Coll. Faber.
52 LD to T. S. Eliot, 17 November 1945, Coll. Faber.
53 LD to T. Stephanides, c. December 1945, Coll. UCLA.
54 LD to Sir Walter Smart, 5 December 1945, *Spirit of Place* 80.
55 LD to Anne Ridler, 15 June 1946, *Spirit of Place* 85–86.
56 LD to Diana Gould Menuhin, 15 December 1945, *Spirit of Place* 82.
57 LD, 'The Other T. S. Eliot', *Atlantic Monthly* 215:5 (May 1965) 64.
58 LD to Sir Walter Smart, 5 December 1945, *Spirit of Place* 81.
59 LD to T. S. Eliot, 17 November 1945, Coll. Faber.
60 LD to HM, 1 January 1946, *DML* 191.
61 Diana Gould Menuhin to LD, 11 January 1946, Coll. SIU-C.
62 Gwyn Williams to LD, 7 November 1945, Coll. SIU-C.
63 Robert Liddell to LD, 10 December 1945, Coll. SIU-C.
64 George Seferis to LD, 8 December 1945, Coll. SIU-C.
65 HM to LD, 8 February 1960, Coll. SIU-C.
66 C. A. Simmons to LD, 22 May 1946, Coll. SIU-C.
67 HM to LD, 21 April 1946, *DML* 197.
68 LD to T. Stephanides, c. December 1945, Coll. UCLA.
69 LD to HM, 1 January 1946, *DML* 191.
70 LD to HM, c. October 1946, *DML* 200.
71 *Cefalû* 34.
72 *Cefalû* 53.
73 *Cefalû* 50.
74 *Cefalû* 99.
75 LD to HM, mid-February 1946, *DML* 192–93.

76 Buffie Johnson, 'Personal Reminiscences of Lawrence Durrell', *Deus Loci* 1:5 (Fall 1981) 71.
77 LD, 'Becoming a Literary Tramp', interviewed by Dieter Zimmer. *Die Zeit* (27 November 1959) trans. Earl G. Ingersoll.
78 LD to T. Stephanides, 27 February 1946, Coll. UCLA.
79 LD to T. Stephanides, c. March 1946, Coll. UCLA.
80 LD to HM, 28 February 1946, *DML* 194.
81 LD to T. Stephanides, c. March 1946, Coll. UCLA.
82 LD to T. S. Eliot, mid-April? 1946, Coll. Faber.
83 Mary Mollo, 'Larry, My Friend', *Deus Loci* 7:2 (December 1983) 2.
84 Mollo, 'Larry, My Friend' 3.
85 *Greek Islands* 152.
86 *Reflections* 60–62.
87 Mollo, 'Larry, My Friend' 3.
88 *Greek Islands* 152.
89 LD to T. S. Eliot, mid-April 1946, Coll. Faber.
90 *Greek Islands* 164.
91 LD, 'The Anecdotes: In Patmos', *Collected Poems 1931–74* (London: Faber, 1980) 207.
92 Mollo, 'Larry, My Friend' 4.
93 LD to T. S. Eliot, April 1946, Coll. Faber.
94 T. S. Eliot to LD, 25 April 1946, Coll. SIU-C.
95 Mills, 'With Durrell on Rhodes' 313.
96 Robert Liddell to LD, 31 August 1946, Coll. SIU-C.
97 Robert Liddell to LD, 19 December 1946, Coll. SIU-C.
98 LD to Anne Ridler, 15 June 1946, *Spirit of Place* 85.
99 Eve Durrell to T. W. French, 2 August 1946, Coll. T. W. French.
100 LD to Anne Ridler, 15 June 1946, *Spirit of Place* 85.
101 Eve Durrell to T. W. French, 2 August 1946, Coll. T. W. French.
102 Eve Durrell to T. W. French, 2 August 1946, Coll. T. W. French.
103 *Greek Islands* 130.
104 *Reflections* 53.
105 *Reflections* 16.
106 Eve Durrell to T. W. French, 2 August 1946, Coll. T. W. French.
107 Spiros Katexis interviewed by IMN, June 1992.
108 LD to HM, c. October 1946, *DML* 199–200.
109 Patrick Leigh Fermor, 'Observations on a Marine Vulcan', *Twentieth Century Literature* 33:3 (Fall 1987) 306.
110 Xan Fielding interviewed by IMN, 4 June 1990.
111 Fermor, 'Observations on a Marine Vulcan' 306.
112 LD to HM, 25 September 1946, *DML* 199.
113 LD to T. S. Eliot, 20 October 1946, Coll. Faber. These passages were omitted from the version of this letter published in *Spirit of Place*, 86–87.
114 LD to HM, c. October 1946, *DML* 199.
115 LD to T. Stephanides, c. September 1946, Coll. UCLA.
116 LD to T. Stephanides, c. October 1946, Coll. UCLA.
117 LD to T. Stephanides, c. January 1947?, Coll. UCLA.
118 LD to T. S. Eliot, 20 October 1946, *Spirit of Place* 86.
119 T. S. Eliot to LD, 17 February 1947, Coll. SIU-C.
120 *Reflections* 180.
121 LD to HM, February 1947, *DML* 205.

122 Mollo, 'Larry, My Friend' 5.
123 John Lehmann, *In My Own Time* (Boston: Little, Brown, 1969) 445.
124 LD to HM, 20 January 1947, *DML* 200.
125 LD to HM, c. February 1947, *DML* 204–205.
126 LD to HM, 20 January 1947, *DML* 200.
127 LD to HM, c. February 1947, *DML* 204.
128 Mills, 'With Durrell on Rhodes' 314–15.
129 Gwyn Williams to LD, 22 August 1946, Coll. SIU-C.
130 LD to H. G. Porteus, c. December 1946, *Spirit of Place* 87.
131 Eve Durrell to T. W. French, 24 January 1947, Coll. T. W. French.
132 LD to HM, 20 January 1947, *DML* 201.
133 Eve Durrell to T. W. French, 24 January 1947, Coll. T. W. French.
134 Eve Durrell to IMN, 14 September 1991.
135 Robert Liddell to LD, 6 October 1946, Coll. SIU-C.
136 Eve Durrell to T. W. French, 24 January 1947, Coll. T. W. French.
137 LD to HM, 9 July 1947, *DML* 211.
138 Eve Durrell to IMN, 14 September 1991.
139 Penelope Durrell Hope interviewed by IMN, 20 May 1993.
140 *Reflections* 184.

CHAPTER 8: Exile: Cordova and Belgrade

1 Julian Maclaren-Ross, *Memoirs of the Forties* (London: Alan Ross, 1965) 156.
2 Gwyn Williams, *ABC of (D.) G. W.: A Kind of Autobiography* (Llandsyl, Dyfed, Wales: Comer Press, 1981) 152.
3 LD to HM, mid-June 1947, *DML* 209.
4 LD to HM, early May 1947, Coll. UCLA.
5 LD to HM, mid-June 1947, *DML* 209.
6 Margaret Durrell, *Whatever Happened to Margo?* (London: André Deutsch, 1995) 16.
7 Margaret Durrell, *Whatever Happened . . .?* 81.
8 Margaret Durrell, *Whatever Happened . . .?* 82.
9 Margaret Durrell Duncan in conversation with IMN, 20 October 1995.
10 Margaret Durrell, *Whatever Happened . . .?* 22.
11 LD to HM, 22 April 1947, Coll. UCLA.
12 LD to HM, mid-June 1947, *DML* 209.
13 LD to HM, mid-June 1947, Coll. UCLA. Unpublished portion of letter printed in *DML* 208–210.
14 Ruth Speirs to LD, 1 July 1947, Coll. SIU-C.
15 LD to HM, mid-June 1947, *DML* 208.
16 LD, 'From a Writer's Journal', *The Windmill* 2:6 (1947) 55.
17 LD, 'The Happy Rock', *The Happy Rock: A Book About Henry Miller* (Berkeley: Packard Press, 1945) 4.
18 LD to HM, 9 July 1947, *DML* 212.
19 Sir Osbert Sitwell to LD, 19 June 1947, Coll. UCLA.
20 LD to HM, 9 July 1947, *DML* 212.
21 LD to Sir Osbert Sitwell, before 14 July 1947, Coll. UCLA.
22 L. Shackleton to LD, 14 July 1947, Coll. UCLA.
23 LD to HM, 20 September 1947, Coll. UCLA.
24 LD in conversation with IMN, 7 May 1985.
25 LD to HM, 9 July 1947, *DML* 211.

26 Alfred Perlès, *My Friend Henry Miller* (London: Neville Spearman, 1955) 194.
27 LD to HM, mid-July 1947, *DML* 215.
28 LD to HM, June 1947, *DML* 210.
29 LD to HM, c. end-November 1947, *DML* 219.
30 LD to T. S. Eliot, September? 1947, Coll. Faber.
31 LD, 'Studies in Genius: VI/Groddeck', *Horizon* 17 (June 1948) 399. This essay was published as an introduction to Groddeck's *The Book of the It* (London: Vision Press, 1949).
32 C. G. Jung to LD, 21 April 1948, Coll. SIU-C.
33 Gwyn Williams, unpublished notes on *Premature Epitaphs and All*, Coll. British Library.
34 Williams, *ABC* 157.
35 T. S. Eliot to LD, 27 January 1948 and following, Coll. SIU-C.
36 LD to Anne Ridler, November 1947, *Spirit of Place* (London: Faber, 1969) 92.
37 LD, 'Green Coconuts: Rio', *Collected Poems 1931–1974* (London: Faber, 1980) 201.
38 LD to Anne Ridler, November 1947, *Spirit of Place* 92–93.
39 LD to Anne Ridler, November 1947, *Spirit of Place* 92.
40 LD to T. Stephanides, c. January 1948, Coll. UCLA.
41 LD to HM, c. end November 1947, *DML* 218–19.
42 LD to HM, c. end November 1947, *DML* 219.
43 LD to HM, c. end November 1947, *DML* 219.
44 HM to LD, 19 December 1947, *DML* 220.
45 LD to T. S. Eliot, January 1948, Coll. Faber.
46 LD to T. S. Eliot, February 1948, Coll. Faber.
47 LD to T. S. Eliot, January 1948, Coll. Faber.
48 LD to T. S. Eliot, March 1949, Coll. Faber.
49 LD to T. S. Eliot, c. February 1948, Coll. Faber.
50 LD to T. S. Eliot, January 1948, Coll. Faber.
51 LD to HM, December? 1947, *DML* 221.
52 LD to T. Stephanides, 1947, Coll. UCLA.
53 LD to HM, December? 1947, *DML* 222.
54 LD to Alan G. Thomas, pmk 17? April 1948, Coll. British Library.
55 LD, 'High Sierra', *Collected Poems*, 201.
56 Jorge Ferreyra, 'Durrell in Córdoba', *Twentieth Century Literature* 33:3 (Fall 1987) 330.
57 Ferreyra, 'Durrell in Córdoba' 330.
58 LD to Mary Mollo, 7 February 1948, *Spirit of Place* 94.
59 LD to Lawrence Clark Powell, March 1948, *Spirit of Place* 95.
60 LD to Mary Mollo, 7 February 1948, *Spirit of Place* 94.
61 T. S. Eliot to LD, 27 January 1948, Coll. SIU-C.
62 Raúl Víctor Peláez to IMN, 5 February 1987.
63 Ferreyra, 'Durrell in Córdoba' 330.
64 LD to L. C. Powell, March 1948, *Spirit of Place* 95–96.
65 George Darrell Blackburn to Sir Eugen Millington-Drake, 27 December 1943, Coll. Ian Clifford.
66 Raúl Víctor Peláez to IMN, 4 August 1987.
67 Eve Durrell to Ella Thomas, c. March 1948, Coll. British Library.
68 P. G. Wodehouse to LD, 19 May 1948, Coll. SIU-C.
69 Raúl Víctor Peláez to IMN, 5 February 1987.
70 Roberto Funes in conversation with Raúl Víctor Peláez, quoted in letter to IMN, 28 June 1987; Peláez in conversation with IMN, 2 April 1987.

71 LD to HM, end March? 1948, *DML* 223.

72 LD to R. Aldington, 26 March 1957, *Literary Lifelines: The Richard Aldington–Lawrence Durrell Correspondence* (London: Faber, 1981) 17.

73 Raúl Víctor Peláez, 'Larry's Long Siesta of 1948', *Twentieth Century Literature* 33:3 (Fall 1987) 333.

74 LD to Mary Mollo, June? 1948, *Spirit of Place* 98.

75 LD to HM, 22 January 1949, Coll. UCLA.

76 LD, *A Key to Modern British Poetry* (Norman: Univ. of Oklahoma Press, 1952) 1. The British title is *A Key to Modern Poetry*.

77 LD, *Key* xii.

78 LD, *Key* 34–36.

79 LD, *Key* 117.

80 LD, *Key* 146–49.

81 LD, *Key* 188.

82 LD to HM, September? 1948, *DML* 224.

83 LD to T. Stephanides, c. January 1948, Coll. UCLA.

84 LD to T. Stephanides, c. March 1948, Coll. UCLA.

85 LD to T. Stephanides, February? 1948, Coll. UCLA.

86 LD to T. Stephanides, c. March 1948, Coll. UCLA.

87 LD to AGT, pmk 17? April 1948, Coll. British Library.

88 LD to T. Stephanides, c. March 1948, Coll. UCLA.

89 LD to T. Stephanides, c. April 1948, Coll. UCLA.

90 Mary Bentley Honor to IMN, 4 June 1991.

91 T. S. Eliot to LD, 13 April 1948, Coll. SIU-C.

92 Peláez, 'Larry's Long Siesta of 1948' 333.

93 LD to Mary Mollo, June? 1948, *Spirit of Place* 98.

94 LD to Mary Mollo, June? 1948, *Spirit of Place* 97.

95 LD to T. S. Eliot, c. June 1948, Coll. Faber.

96 T. S. Eliot to LD, 11 July 1948, printed in LD, 'The Other T. S. Eliot', *Atlantic Monthly* 215:5 (May 1965) 62–63.

97 T. S. Eliot to LD, 11 July 1948, printed in LD, 'The Other T. S. Eliot', 63. Unpublished portions of this letter quoted here are in the Coll. SIU-C.

98 LD to T. S. Eliot, 6 August 1948 (possibly date of receipt), Coll. Faber.

99 T. S. Eliot to LD, 11 August 1948, Coll. SIU-C.

100 LD to T. S. Eliot, 6 August 1948, Coll. Faber.

101 LD to HM, July? 1948, Coll. UCLA.

102 Ferreyra, 'Durrell in Córdoba' 330.

103 Mary Bentley Honor to IMN, 10 September 1991.

104 Anne Ridler, 'Recollections of Lawrence Durrell', *Twentieth Century Literature* 33:3 (Fall 1987) 297.

105 Kathryn Winslow, *Henry Miller: Full of Life* (Los Angeles: Jeremy P. Tarcher, 1986) 300.

106 LD to AGT, August 1948, Coll. British Library.

107 LD to HM, c. November 1948, *DML* 226.

108 LD to T. S. Eliot, August 1948, Coll. Faber.

109 Eve Durrell to T. S. Eliot, August 1948, Coll. Faber.

110 LD to Jon and Betsy Uldall, c. August 1948, Coll. Betsy Uldall.

111 Ferreyra, 'Durrell in Córdoba' 330.

112 LD in conversation with IMN, 7 May 1985.

113 Jorge Luis Borges, *Seven Nights* (New York: New Directions, 1984; London: Faber, 1986).

114 LD to HM, 22 January 1949, *DML* 227.
115 LD to HM, 25 February 1949, *Lawrence Durrell/Henry Miller: A Private Correspondence*, ed. George Wickes (New York: Dutton, 1963) 260.
116 LD to HM, 25 February 1949, *Correspondence*, ed. Wickes, 260.
117 Penelope Durrell Hope in conversation with IMN, 21 May 1993.
118 LD to HM, 25 February 1949, *Correspondence*, ed. Wickes, 260.
119 LD to HM, 18? March 1949, Coll. UCLA.
120 LD to HM, pmk 14 April 1949, Coll. UCLA.
121 Passports of Eve and Lawrence Durrell.
122 Arthur Gauntlett, 'Interpretation of the Horoscope 375/A Mr Durrell', Coll. SIU-C.
123 LD to HM, c. July 1949, Coll. UCLA.
124 LD to HM, June 1949, *DML* 232.
125 LD to AGT, c. June 1949, Coll. British Library.
126 LD to T. Stephanides, end May? 1949, *Spirit of Place* 100.
127 LD to T. Stephanides, summer? 1949, Coll. UCLA.
128 Nadežda Djukić Obradović interviewed by IMN, 10 June 1995.
129 LD to AGT, c. July 1949, Coll. British Library.
130 LD to Sir Patrick Reilly, c. November 1958?, Coll. Sir Patrick Reilly.
131 Nadežda Djukić Obradović to IMN, 24 April 1995.
132 LD to AGT, c. July 1949, Coll. British Library.
133 LD to AGT, c. August 1949, Coll. British Library.
134 LD to T. Stephanides, after 14 September 1949, Coll. UCLA.
135 LD to HM, 5 September 1949, *DML* 232–33.
136 LD to HM, 10 September 1949, *DML* 233.
137 HM to LD, 28 September 1949, *DML* 234.
138 Alfred E. Perlès to LD, 21 September 1949, with marginal comments in LD's hand, Coll. UCLA.
139 LD to HM, early October? 1949, *DML* 238–39.
140 Alfred E. Perlès to LD and HM, October? 1949, Coll. UCLA.
141 LD to HM, early October? 1949, *DML* 239.
142 HM to LD, 15 October 1949, *DML* 241.
143 HM to LD, 3 October 1949, *DML* 238.
144 LD to HM, 12 October 1949, *DML* 241.
145 LD to HM, 27 October 1949, *DML* 243.
146 LD to T. Stephanides, before 25 December 1949?, Coll. UCLA.
147 LD to AGT, Coll. British Library.
148 LD to AGT, after 8 January 1950, Coll. British Library.
149 LD to HM, 27 October 1949, *DML* 244.
150 LD to HM, early March? 1950, *DML* 247.
151 LD to HM, 13 January 1950, *DML* 245.
152 HM to LD, 7 March 1950, *DML* 246.
153 LD to HM, July 1950, *DML* 251.
154 LD to T. Stephanides, 23 March 1950, Coll. UCLA.
155 LD to HM, early March? 1950, *DML* 248.
156 Constant Zarian to LD, 21 February 1950, Coll. UCLA.
157 LD to Anne Ridler, June 1950, *Spirit of Place* 104–106.
158 LD to AGT, June? 1950, Coll. British Library.
159 LD to Anne Ridler, June 1950, *Spirit of Place* 106.
160 W. H. Auden to LD, June? 1950, Coll. SIU-C.
161 LD to Anne Ridler, June 1950, *Spirit of Place* 107.

162 LD to HM, July 1950, *DML* 250.
163 LD to T. Stephanides, late July? 1950, Coll. UCLA.
164 LD in conversation with IMN, 11 May 1985.
165 LD to T. Stephanides, 18 August 1950, Coll. UCLA.
166 LD to HM, after 11 July 1950, *DML* 250.
167 LD to Sir Patrick Reilly, c. November 1958?, Coll. Sir Patrick Reilly.
168 Nadežda Djukić Obradović to IMN, 24 April 1995.
169 LD to Anne Ridler, quoted in 'Recollections of Lawrence Durrell' 296.
170 Margaret Rawlings to LD, 10 September 1950, Coll. SIU-C.
171 HM to LD, 4 November 1950, *DML* 252.
172 LD to HM, 1 December 1950, *DML* 253.
173 LD to HM, September? 1950, Coll. UCLA.
174 LD to HM, early September? 1950, Coll. UCLA.
175 Nadežda Djukić Obradović to IMN, 24 April 1995.
176 LD to AGT, before December 1950, Coll. British Library.
177 LD to AGT, c. December 1950?, Coll. British Library.
178 Felicity Wakefield interviewed by IMN, 30 May 1993.
179 *Mountolive: AQ* (London: Faber, 1962) 431.
180 LD to AGT, Winter 1950–51, *Spirit of Place* 107.
181 LD to HM, 1 December 1950, *DML* 253.
182 LD to T. Stephanides, Winter 1950–51, *Spirit of Place* 107–108.
183 *Justine: AQ* (London: Faber, 1962) 140.
184 LD in conversation with IMN, 16 April 1986.
185 Nadežda Djukić Obradović to IMN, 24 April 1995.
186 LD, 'The Art of Fiction XIII', interview by Julian Mitchell and Gene Andrewski, *Paris Review* (Autumn-Winter 1959–60) 47.
187 LD to T. Stephanides, winter 1950–51, *Spirit of Place* 107–108.
188 Belgrade British Embassy mechanic interviewed by IMN, 7 June 1988.
189 LD to Anne Ridler, 15 February 1951, *Spirit of Place* 108–109.
190 Mary Mollo, 'Larry, My Friend', *Deus Loci* 7:2 (December 1983) 6.
191 Mollo, 'Larry, My Friend' 6.
192 HM to LD, 22 October 1951, *DML* 256.
193 Mollo, 'Larry, My Friend' 6.
194 LD, 'Iron Curtain Blues', Coll. British Library.
195 LD to HM, March-April 1950, *DML* 248. The date of this letter is conjectural, and it may have been written a full year later, shortly before LD met Mott.
196 LD to HM, February? 1952, *DML* 259.
197 Francis J. Mott, *The Universal Design of the Oedipus Complex* (Philadelphia: David McKay, 1950) 123 and passim.
198 HM to LD, 10 March 1952, *DML* 259–60.
199 LD to HM, 2? September 1951, *DML* 254.
200 LD interviewed by IMN, 11 May 1985.
201 LD, 'The Other T. S. Eliot' 63.
202 LD to HM, 2? September 1951, *DML* 254.
203 LD to T. Stephanides, 21 September 1951, Coll. UCLA.
204 LD to HM, November? 1951, *DML* 257.
205 LD to AGT, pmk (Dip. Bag via London) 2 October 1951, Coll. British Library.
206 LD to T. S. Eliot, 1952?, Coll. Faber.
207 LD to HM, 2? September 1951, *DML* 254.
208 LD to T. Stephanides, 21 September 1951, Coll. UCLA.

209 LD, 'Cradle Song', *Collected Poems* 221.
210 LD to HM, February? 1952, *DML* 258.
211 LD to AGT, c. December 1951, Coll. British Library.
212 LD to AGT, c. December 1951, Coll. British Library. The Foreign Office had drastically reduced salaries of all contract employees such as Durrell.
213 LD to Anne Ridler, 1952, *Spirit of Place* 109.
214 Peter Wakefield interviewed by IMN, 30 May 1993; also interviews with H. T. Kennedy and John Priestman.
215 LD, holograph working notebook, Coll. SIU-C.
216 LD to HM, mid-July 1952, Coll. UCLA.
217 LD to HM, c. October 1952, *DML* 263.
218 LD to AGT, 15 October 1952, Coll. British Library.
219 LD to AGT, c. November 1952, Coll. British Library.
220 Eve Durrell, 'Notes on Life With Sappho', unpublished manuscript 2. An eleven-page document enclosed with ED letter to IMN of 9 July 1991, in response to IMN letter to ED of 25 June 1991.
221 LD, 'Letters in Darkness', *Collected Poems*.
222 Document, Psychiatric Division, British Military Hospital, Hannover, BAOR 5 [January? 1953], signed by Capt. D. Sherret, RAMC, Psychiatrist, Coll. Eve Durrell.
223 LD, 'Letters in Darkness', *Collected Poems* 227–28.
224 LD, 'Letters in Darkness', *Collected Poems* 230–31.
225 LD to AGT, 10 December 1952, Coll. British Library.
226 LD to AGT, mid-December 1952, Coll. British Library.
227 LD to T. Stephanides, 5 January 1953, Coll. UCLA.
228 Eve Durrell, 'Notes on Life' 3.
229 H. Pozner to LD, 5 January 1953, Coll. Eve Durrell.
230 Eve Durrell, 'Notes on Life' 3.
231 Document, Psychiatric Division, British Military Hospital, Hannover, BAOR 5 [January? 1953], Coll. Eve Durrell.
232 LD, *Bitter Lemons* (London: Faber, 1957) 15–17.

CHAPTER 9: Cyprus: Paradise Regained and Lost

1 LD, *Justine: AQ* (London: Faber, 1962) 17.
2 LD, 'A Poet Who Stumbled into Prose', interview by Kenneth Young, *Encounter* (December 1960).
3 Endymion Wilkinson, 'George Curwen Wilkinson', unpublished manuscript, London (1993), early draft 18.
4 Endymion Wilkinson, 'George Curwen Wilkinson' 16.
5 LD to AGT, pmk 2 February 1953, Coll. British Library.
6 LD to HM, 25 March 1953, *The Durrell–Miller Letters 1935–80* (London: Faber, 1988), 267.
7 Eve Durrell to AGT, 28 February 1953, Coll. British Library.
8 LD, *Bitter Lemons* (London: Faber, 1957) 29.
9 *Bitter Lemons* 28.
10 Sir Ronald Storrs and Bryan Justin O'Brien, *The Handbook of Cyprus* (London: Christophers, [1930]) 79.
11 Sir Harry Luke, *Cyprus: A Portrait and an Appreciation* (London: George G. Harrap, 1957, 1965) 105.
12 *Bitter Lemons* 84.

13 LD to AGT, pmk 3 March 1953, Coll. British Library.
14 *Bitter Lemons* 40.
15 *Bitter Lemons* 77.
16 *Bitter Lemons* 79.
17 LD to AGT, 3 March 1953, Coll. British Library.
18 LD, 'Letters in Darkness', *Collected Poems 1931–74* (London: Faber, 1962) 228.
19 LD to HM, May 1953, *DML* 269.
20 LD, 'Cyprus: Still Bitterness in the Lemons', *The Times* (29 April 1970) 15.
21 The organization founded by Archbishop Makarios and George Grivas would become known as the Ethniki Orgánosis Kypríon Agonistón, the National Organization of Cypriot Fighters. Cyprus had been under British control since the end of the Russo-Turkish War in 1878. Union with Greece was opposed by the considerable Turkish-descended population, horrified at the thought of becoming Greek citizens. Almost to a man, the Orthodox clergy on Cyprus supported EOKA: they administered the loyalty-or-death oaths required of all initiates, stored arms in the monasteries, and sheltered EOKA fugitives from the police and the military.
22 LD to John McPherson, 28 October 1975, Coll. John McPherson. Durrell's personal copy of *The Moulids of Egypt* was inscribed to him by the author, Joseph Williams McPherson, and is underscored throughout and highlighted with Durrell's characteristic markings.
23 Pennethorne Hughes, *While Shepheard's Watched* (London: Chatto & Windus, 1949) 29. I am indebted to Michael Haag for his clarification of the importance of Shem el-Nessim.
24 LD to HM, 25 March 1953, *DML* 268.
25 LD to AGT, 3 March 1953, Coll. British Library.
26 Eve Durrell, 'Notes on Life With Sappho', unpublished manuscript 4.
27 LD to AGT, pmk 8 May 1953, Coll. British Library.
28 LD to Alfred Perlès, pmk 2 May? 1953, Coll. Anne Barret Perlès.
29 Endymion Wilkinson, 'George Curwen Wilkinson', 15–16.
30 Endymion Wilkinson to IMN, September 1993.
31 John Lehmann, *In My Own Time* (Boston: Little, Brown, 1969) 534–35.
32 *Bitter Lemons* 96.
33 Rose Macaulay to LD, 13 April 1954, Coll. SIU-C.
34 LD to HM, May 1953, *DML* 269–70.
35 HM to LD, 21 September 1952, *DML* 263; 3 May 1953, *DML* 268–69. Similar comments appear in various other HM letters of this period.
36 Freya Stark, *East Is West* (London: John Murray, 1945) 99.
37 *Bitter Lemons* 99.
38 LD to AGT, pmk 8 May 1953, Coll. British Library.
39 LD to A. Harrison, 10 June 1953, Coll. E.L.I.A. (Greek Literary and Historical Archive), Athens.
40 LD, 'An Interview with Lawrence Durrell' by Eugene Lyons and Harry T. Antrim, 25 March 1970. *Shenandoah* 22:2 (Winter 1971) 52–53.
41 Eve Durrell to AGT, 20 September 1953, Coll. British Library.
42 Luke, *Cyprus* 32.
43 Leo Hamalian, 'Companions in Exile: Lawrence Durrell and Gostan Zarian', *Ararat* (1994).
44 LD to Sir Patrick Reilly, pmk July? 1956, Coll. Sir Patrick Reilly.
45 Maurice Cardiff to IMN, 31 August 1997.
46 LD to T. Stephanides, pmk 23 August 1953, Coll British Library.

47 LD, *Sicilian Carousel* (London: Faber, New York: Viking, 1977) 25.
48 *Bitter Lemons* 97.
49 LD to T. Stephanides, 30? September 1953, Coll. British Library.
50 LD to T. Stephanides, pmk 23 August 1953, Coll. British Library.
51 Lyons and Antrim, 'Interview with Lawrence Durrell' 47.
52 LD to T. Stephanides, pmk 23 August 1953, Coll. British Library.
53 LD to T. Stephanides, 30? September 1953, Coll. British Library.
54 Lyons and Antrim, 'Interview with Lawrence Durrell' 52.
55 LD to T. Stephanides, 30? September 1953, Coll. British Library.
56 David Roessel, 'Introduction' to the letters of Lawrence Durrell to Austen Harrison, *Deus Loci* NS 3 (1994).
57 Marc Dubin, *Cyprus* (London: The Rough Guides, 1993) 166.
58 *Bitter Lemons* 130–31.
59 Alexis Courtellas, interviewed by Frank Kersnowski, Summer 1990.
60 LD to A. Harrison, late 1953?, Coll. E.L.I.A., Athens.
61 Theodora Pavlidou, 'Another Dark Side of Durrell', *Cyprus View* 2 (October 1991) 5.
62 LD to A. Harrison, late January 1954, Coll. E.L.I.A., Athens.
63 LD to A. Harrison, late January 1954, Coll. E.L.I.A., Athens.
64 LD to AGT, pmk 15 October 1953, Coll. British Library.
65 LD, 'The Art of Fiction XXIII', interview by Julian Mitchell and Gene Andrewski, *Paris Review* 22 (Autumn-Winter 1959–60) 48–49.
66 LD to HM, pmk 24 October 1953, *DML* 272.
67 LD to AGT, 21 October 1953, Coll. British Library.
68 LD to HM, pmk 24 October 1953, *DML* 272.
69 *Bitter Lemons* 105.
70 *Bitter Lemons* 126.
71 LD to AGT, 22 December 1953, Coll. British Library.
72 LD to HM, 20 November 1953, *DML* 274.
73 LD to AGT, pmk 4 November 1953, Coll. British Library.
74 LD to HM, November? 1953, *DML* 275.
75 LD to HM, 5 January 1954, *DML* 276.
76 LD, 'Letters in Darkness', *Collected Poems* 230–31.
77 LD to HM, pmk 24 October 1953, *DML* 272.
78 LD to HM, 20 November 1953, *DML* 274.
79 LD to HM, 20 November 1953, *DML* 274.
80 LD to A. Harrison, 19 November? 1953, Coll. E.L.I.A., Athens.
81 *Bitter Lemons* 171.
82 LD to A. Harrison, 19 November? 1953, Coll. E.L.I.A., Athens.
83 LD, 'Near Paphos', *Collected Poems* 247–48.
84 LD to A. Harrison, 31 November 1953, Coll. E.L.I.A., Athens.
85 LD to A. Harrison, late November 1953, Coll. E.L.I.A., Athens.
86 Rodis Roufos, 'Sour Grapes', published in *Deus Loci:* NS 3 (1994) 135.
87 Maurice Cardiff to IMN, 31 August 1997.
88 LD to A. Harrison, late November 1953, Coll. E.L.I.A., Athens.
89 LD in conversation with Carol Peirce and IMN, 14 May 1985.
90 LD to AGT, pmk 22 December 1953, Coll. British Library.
91 LD to A. Harrison, after 1 December 1953, Coll. E.L.I.A., Athens.
92 LD interviewed by Chili Hawes, *Quiet Days in Sommières*, film produced by Peter Leippe, 1985.
93 LD to A. Harrison, late January 1954, Coll. E.L.I.A., Athens.

94 LD to A. Harrison, after 1 December 1953, Coll. E.L.I.A., Athens.
95 LD to HM, 5 January 1954, *DML* 276.
96 LD to HM, c. January 1955, Coll. UCLA.
97 LD to A. Harrison, late January 1954, Coll. E.L.I.A., Athens.
98 LD to AGT, 13 February 1954, Coll. British Library.
99 LD to AGT, 13 February 1954, Coll. British Library.
100 Freya Stark to John Grey Murray, 18 March 1954, *Over the Rim of the World: Selected Letters*, ed. Caroline Moorehead (London: John Murray, 1988) 325.
101 LD to AGT, 13 February 1954, Coll. British Library.
102 Alexander Maitland, *A Tower in a Wall: Conversations with Dame Freya Stark* (Edinburgh: William Blackwood, 1982) 93.
103 LD to AGT, 14 March 1954, Coll. British Library.
104 LD to HM, 20 November 1953, *DML* 273.
105 Sir Peter and Felicity Wakefield interviewed by IMN, 30 May 1993.
106 Joan Pepper interviewed by IMN, 4 June 1993.
107 Sir Peter Wakefield interviewed by IMN, 30 May 1993.
108 LD to HM, c. April 1954, *DML* 277.
109 LD to AGT, pmk 22 April 1954, Coll. British Library.
110 LD to T. Stephanides, c. April 1954, Coll. UCLA.
111 LD to AGT, pmk 22 April 1954, Coll. British Library.
112 LD to HM, c. April 1954, *DML* 277.
113 Eve Durrell to AGT, 2 February 1954, Coll. British Library.
114 Eve Durrell to AGT, 3 May 1954, Coll. British Library.
115 LD to Freya Stark, 1 June 1954, *Spirit of Place* (London: Faber, 1969) 124.
116 Eve Durrell to Ella Thomas, 8 September 1954, Coll. British Library.
117 Eve Durrell to Ella Thomas, 8 September 1954, Coll. British Library.
118 Penelope Durrell Hope to IMN, 17 June 1991.
119 Eve Durrell to Ella Thomas, 30 July 1954, Coll. British Library.
120 Eve Durrell to Ella Thomas, 8 September 1954, Coll. British Library.
121 LD to AGT, pmk 20? July 1954, Coll. British Library.
122 Eve Durrell to Ella Thomas, 30 July 1954, Coll. British Library.
123 Joan Pepper interviewed by IMN, 4 June 1993.
124 Felicity Wakefield interviewed by IMN, 30 May 1993.
125 Joan Pepper interviewed by IMN, 4 June 1993.
126 LD to AGT, 11 July? 1954, Coll. British Library.
127 Eve Durrell to AGT, 30 July 1954, Coll. British Library.
128 Eve Durrell to Ella Thomas, 8 September 1954, Coll. British Library.
129 *Bitter Lemons* 158–59.
130 *Bitter Lemons* 146.
131 Eve Durrell to Ella Thomas, 8 September 1954, Coll. British Library.
132 Adamantios Diamantis to George Seferis, 24 August 1954, *Allilografia* [Letters] *1953–1971* (Athens: Stigmi Press, 1985) 49.
133 Adamantios Diamantis to George Seferis, 24 August 1954, *Allilografia 1953–1971* 50.
134 David Roessel in conversation with IMN, 1 August 1993. Roessel was studying under Edmund Keeley at Princeton.
135 Adamantios Diamantis to George Seferis, quoted in Theodora Pavlidou, 'Another Dark Side of Durrell', (October 1991) 8.
136 Peter Collier, 'A Talk with Lawrence Durrell', *New York Times Book Review* (11 July 1968) 39.
137 Pavlidou, 'Another Dark Side of Durrell' 8.

138 LD interview, *Aegean Review* (Autumn 1987), quoted by Pavlidou, 'Another Dark Side of Durrell' 8.

139 Peter and Felicity Wakefield interviewed by IMN, 30 May 1993.

140 Achilles Papadopoulos interviewed by IMN, 20 July 1992; Durrell made fun of the exclusive use of red ink by the Foreign Office in 'Case History', the diplomatic sketch quoted here. *Esprit de Corps* 21.

141 LD to AGT, September? 1954, Coll. British Library.

142 Achilles Papadopoulos interviewed by IMN, 20 July 1992.

143 Pavlidou, 'Another Dark Side of Durrell' 7.

144 Eve Durrell to Ella Thomas, 8 September 1954, Coll. British Library.

145 Felicity Wakefield interviewed by IMN, 30 May 1993; Sarah Wolton Broad interviewed by IMN, 31 October 1997.

146 Margaret Durrell Duncan in conversation with IMN, 29 March 1991.

147 Philip Nind interviewed by IMN, 28 May 1993.

148 Felicity Wakefield interviewed by IMN, 30 May 1993.

149 LD to T. S. Eliot, 1954, *Spirit of Place* 125–26.

150 Eve Durrell to Ella Thomas, 8 September 1954, Coll. British Library.

151 Maurice Cardiff, *Friends Abroad: Memories of Lawrence Durrell, Freya Stark, Patrick Leigh-Fermor, Peggy Guggenheim and others* (London: The Radcliffe Press, 1997) 29–30.

152 Freya Stark, *Letters*, Vol. 4, ed. Lucy Moorehead (Salisbury: Michael Russell, 1977) 239; H. D. Purcell, *Cyprus* (New York: Frederick A. Praeger, 1968) 210.

153 LD to A. Harrison, October? 1954, Coll. E.L.I.A., Athens.

154 LD to AGT, October? 1954, Coll. British Library.

155 LD to Freya Stark, c. November 1954, *Spirit of Place* 126.

156 LD to Freya Stark, December 1954, *Spirit of Place* 127.

157 LD to Freya Stark, 31 March 1955, *Spirit of Place* 128.

158 *Cyprus Review* (September 1955) 6.

159 Endymion Wilkinson, 'George Curwen Wilkinson'.

160 George Seferis to G. P. Savvides, quoted in Pavlidou, 'Another Dark Side of Lawrence Durrell', 8.

161 LD to A. Harrison, December? 1954, Coll. E.L.I.A., Athens.

162 LD to Joan Pepper, 19 July 1956, Coll. Joan Pepper, Lady Carnwath.

163 Joan Pepper interviewed by IMN, 4 June 1993.

164 LD to HM, c. January 1955, Coll. UCLA.

165 LD to AGT, late 1955?, Coll. British Library.

166 LD to HM, c. January 1955, Coll. UCLA.

167 LD to HM, c. January 1955, Coll. UCLA.

168 Achilles Papadopoulos interviewed by IMN, 20 July 1992.

169 Joyce Papadopoulos interviewed by IMN, 20 July 1992.

170 *Bitter Lemons* 190.

171 David Roessel first made this observation in a talk entitled '"Something to Stand the Government in Good Stead": Lawrence Durrell, the *Cyprus Review*, and *Bitter Lemons*', presented at The Seventh International Lawrence Durrell Conference, Avignon, 1992.

172 Joan Pepper interviewed by IMN, 4 June 1993.

173 *Bitter Lemons* 180.

174 Gerald Durrell interviewed by IMN, 11 December 1983.

175 *Bitter Lemons* 181.

176 Purcell, *Cyprus* 260.

177 Purcell, *Cyprus* 266.

178 A. E. W. Sansom, *I Spied Spies* (London: George G. Harrap, 1965) 49; Purcell, *Cyprus* 263–64.
179 'Quiet Corners in Kyrenia', *Cyprus Review* (October 1955) 21.
180 Gerald Durrell interviewed by IMN, 9 July 1992.
181 LD, holograph notebook, Coll. SIU-C.
182 LD to AGT, 3 June? 1955, Coll. British Library.
183 *Bitter Lemons* 193–94.
184 *Bitter Lemons* 195.
185 LD, 'The Octagon Room', *Collected Poems* 248–49.
186 *Justine: AQ* 130. Durrell attributed the same words to Narouz in *Balthazar: AQ* 374.
187 LD to A. Harrison, September-December 1955?, Coll. E.L.I.A., Athens.
188 AGT in conversation with IMN, 19 September 1991.
189 LD, holograph notebook, Coll. SIU-C.
190 LD to A. Harrison, September-December 1955, Coll. E.L.I.A., Athens.
191 LD to HM, c. January? 1956, *DML* 279.
192 LD to Freya Stark, c. August 1955, Coll. SIU-C.
193 Joan Pepper interviewed by IMN, 4 June 1993.
194 Philip Nind interviewed by IMN, 28 May 1993.
195 *Bitter Lemons* 244.
196 Achilles Papadopoulos interviewed by IMN, 20 July 1992.
197 LD in conversation with Carol Peirce and IMN, 14 May 1985.
198 Purcell, *Cyprus* 270.
199 Richard Lumley, Lord Scarbrough, interviewed by IMN, 2 February 1984.
200 *Bitter Lemons* 185.
201 *Bitter Lemons* 198.
202 *Bitter Lemons* 199.
203 LD to HM, c. November 1955, *DML* 278–79.
204 LD to AGT, late 1955?, Coll. British Library.
205 LD to HM, 24 December 1955, Coll. UCLA.
206 LD to HM, January? 1956, *DML* 279.
207 Claude [Durrell], *The Rum Go* (London: Faber, 1958) 148.
208 Group-Captain Peter Bird, in conversation with IMN, 30 March 1991.
209 LD interviewed by IMN, 11 December 1983.
210 Joan Pepper interviewed by IMN, 4 June 1993.
211 LD, holograph notebook, Coll. SIU-C.
212 *Justine: AQ* 152.
213 LD to R. Aldington, after 11 October 1957, *Literary Lifelines: The Richard Aldington–Lawrence Durrell Correspondence* (London: Faber, 1981) 31.
214 *Justine: AQ* 128.
215 LD to Alfred Perlès, 3 January 1969, Coll. Anne Barret Perlès.
216 LD to HM, c. January 1956, *DML* 279.
217 LD to HM, c. January 1956, *DML* 279.
218 LD in conversation with IMN, 11 May 1985.
219 Eve Durrell to IMN, 24 August 1991.
220 LD, 'The Kneller Tape (Hamburg)', *World of Lawrence Durrell* (New York: Dutton, 1964) 165–66.
221 Achilles Papadopoulos interviewed by IMN, 20 July 1992.
222 *Bitter Lemons* 213.
223 LD to R. Aldington, c. 23–26 November 1958, *Literary Lifelines* 68.
224 A. C. Sedgwick, *New York Times* (18 December 1955) 38:1.

225 *Bitter Lemons* 176.
226 *Bitter Lemons* 191.
227 *Bitter Lemons* 176.
228 LD, holograph notebook, Coll. SIU-C.
229 Mary Mollo, 'Larry, My Friend', *Deus Loci* 7:2 (December 1983) 8.
230 Richard Lumley, Lord Scarbrough, interviewed by IMN, 2 February 1984.
231 Cardiff, *Friends Abroad* 32–33.
232 Diana Gould Menuhin to LD, 29 January 1956, Coll. SIU-C.
233 *Bitter Lemons* 212.
234 Diana Gould Menuhin to LD, 11 February 1956, Coll. SIU-C.
235 *Bitter Lemons* 243.
236 Purcell, *Cyprus* 283.
237 Purcell, *Cyprus* 283.
238 *New York Times* (2 April 1956) 33.
239 Joan Pepper interviewed by IMN, 4 June 1993.
240 *Bitter Lemons* 215.
241 Cardiff, *Friends Abroad* 33–34.
242 Penelope Tremayne, *Below the Tide* (London: Hutchinson, 1958) 16.
243 *Bitter Lemons* 170.
244 LD to Sir Patrick Reilly, c. June-July 1956, Coll. Sir Patrick Reilly.
245 LD to AGT, pmk 20? May 1956, Coll. British Library. Apparently Durrell's proposed advertisement never appeared.
246 Sir Laurence Olivier to LD, 25 July 1956, Coll. SIU-C.
247 Penelope Tremayne, *Below the Tide*; also Tremayne interviewed by IMN, 18 July 1992.
248 Achilles Papadopoulos interviewed by IMN, 20 July 1992.
249 Nikos Kranidiotis interviewed by David Roessel, 1994.
250 LD to Sir Patrick Reilly, pmk July? 1956, Coll. Sir Patrick Reilly.
251 Joan Pepper interviewed by IMN, 4 June 1993.
252 Tremayne, *Below the Tide* 33.
253 *Bitter Lemons* 215.
254 *Bitter Lemons* 246.
255 Alan Pringle to Joan Pepper, 17 July 1956, Coll. Joan Pepper, Lady Carnwath.
256 LD to Joan Pepper, 19 July 1956, Coll. Joan Pepper, Lady Carnwath.
257 LD to AGT, 13 July? 1956, Coll. British Library.
258 Tremayne, *Below the Tide* 85.
259 Felicity Wakefield interviewed by IMN, 30 May 1993.
260 LD to AGT, 20? May 1956, Coll. British Library.
261 LD to HM, 9 August 1956, *DML* 280.

CHAPTER 10: Sommières, *Anni Mirabiles*

1 Freya Stark to LD, 12 September 1956, Coll. SIU-C.
2 LD to Freya Stark, 20 September 1956, *Spirit of Place* (London: Faber, 1969) 135.
3 Freya Stark to LD, 16 October 1956, Coll. SIU-C.
4 Freya Stark to LD, 5 February 1957, Coll. SIU-C.
5 Penelope Durrell Hope to IMN, 31 July 1994.
6 Diana Hambro Ladas interviewed by IMN, 25 July 1987.
7 The present owners, Anthony De la Hey and Jo Barnes, claim that the shorter name, the one Durrell used, came from a farmer named Stone who had once owned the property;

Diana Ladas believed that the name was originally Stepping Stone Cottage, from the stream that flowed by the kitchen.

8 LD to HM, October 1956, *The Durrell–Miller Letters 1935–80* (London: Faber, 1988) 280.

9 Diana Hambro Ladas interviewed by IMN, 25 July 1987.

10 LD to Freya Stark, 21 October 1956, *Spirit of Place* 135.

11 LD to HM, October 1956, *DML* 281.

12 LD to HM, October 1956, *DML* 282.

13 LD to AGT, pmk 6 November 1956, Coll. British Library.

14 James Stern interviewed by IMN, 27 July 1987.

15 Alan G. Thomas, editorial notes, *Spirit of Place* 130.

16 LD comment written in a presentation copy of *White Eagles over Serbia*, quoted in Alan G. Thomas and James A. Brigham, *Lawrence Durrell: An Illustrated Checklist* (Carbondale: Southern Illinois University Press, 1983) 14. The 'venturesome friend' was probably Dorian Cooke, who had been under cover during the war in Yugoslavia.

17 LD, notebook, Coll. SIU-C. Tom Bevan's adventure story for boys, *One of the Awkward Squad*, may have suggested the series title to Durrell.

18 LD to AGT, January 1957, Coll. British Library.

19 R. Aldington to LD, 1 February 1957, *Literary Lifelines: The Richard Aldington–Lawrence Durrell Correspondence* (London: Faber, 1981) 5.

20 Freya Stark to LD, 5 February 1957, Coll. SIU-C.

21 Diana Gould Menuhin to LD, 22 March 1957, Coll. SIU-C.

22 HM to LD, 3 October 1957, Coll. SIU-C.

23 Anaïs Nin to LD, c. October 1957, Coll. SIU-C.

24 A. Nin to LD, c. March 1958, Coll. SIU-C.

25 LD to RA, c. 14–27 February 1957, *Literary Lifelines* 7.

26 Review of *Justine*, *Times Literary Supplement* (8 February 1957) 77.

27 Maurice Richardson, 'New Novels', *New Statesman and Nation* 53 (9 February 1957) 180.

28 HM to LD, 13 February 1957, *DML* 284.

29 HM to LD, 3 March 1957, Coll. SIU-C.

30 HM to LD, 13 February 1957, *DML* 284.

31 Christopher Middleton, 'The Heraldic Universe', *Critical Essays on Lawrence Durrell*, ed. Alan Warren Friedman (Boston: G. K. Hall, 1987) 17.

32 LD, *Justine: AQ* (London: Faber, 1962) 92.

33 Gerald Durrell to LD, 6 February 1957, Coll. SIU-C.

34 LD to RA, c. 14–27 February 1957, *Literary Lifelines* 7.

35 LD, *A Smile in the Mind's Eye* (London: Wildwood House, 1980) 4.

36 LD to RA, c. 12–18 March 1957, *Literary Lifelines* 9.

37 LD to RA, 18–21 March 1957, *Literary Lifelines* 12.

38 LD to RA, 26 March 1957, *Literary Lifelines* 17.

39 LD to HM, after 6 May 1957, *DML* 287.

40 Alan G. Thomas, editorial notes, *Spirit of Place* 131.

41 LD to HM, late February 1957, *DML* 285.

42 Kenneth Rexroth, 'The Footsteps of Horace', *Nation* (18 May 1957) 444.

43 Gerald Sykes to LD, 20 June 1957, Coll. SIU-C.

44 Gerald Sykes, 'It Happened in Alexandria', *New York Times Book Review* (25 August 1957) 4.

45 'Eros in Alexandria', *Time* (26 August 1957) 84.

46 LD to HM, late February 1957, *DML* 285.

47 LD to HM, early 1936, *DML* 11.
48 LD to IMN, 25 March 1977.
49 LD in conversation with IMN, 14 May 1985.
50 Most of these phrases appear in *Literary Lifelines*.
51 LD, *Balthazar: AQ* (London: Faber, 1962) 311.
52 LD, 'Drage's Divine Discontent', *Esprit de Corps* (London: Faber, 1957) 69.
53 Heinz Ledig Rowohlt to LD, 1957.
54 LD to HM, end April 1957, *DML* 288.
55 RA to LD, 14 February 1958, *Literary Lifelines* 42.
56 RA to LD, 18 April 1957, *Literary Lifelines* 21.
57 Curtis Cate, 'Lawrence Durrell', *Atlantic Monthly* 208:6 (December 1961).
58 *Justine:* (London: Faber, 1957) 54.
59 *Justine: AQ* 50.
60 *Balthazar: AQ* 284.
61 LD, 'A Dialogue with Durrell', interview by Kenneth Young, *Encounter* 13:6 (December 1959) 62.
62 Penelope Tremayne to LD, 19 April 1957, Coll. SIU-C.
63 LD to AGT, pmk 1 May 1957, *Spirit of Place* 141.
64 LD to HM, after 6 May 1957, *DML* 287.
65 Young, 'A Dialogue with Durrell' 65.
66 LD to RA, 26 March 1957, *Literary Lifelines* 17.
67 LD to Austen Harrison, pmk 15 June 1957, Coll. E.L.I.A., Athens.
68 LD to HM, 6 May 1957, Coll. UCLA.
69 LD to HM, mid-July 1957, *DML* 294.
70 LD, 'Note' to *Balthazar* (London: Faber, 1958).
71 LD, *A Key to Modern British Poetry* (Norman, University of Oklahoma Press, 1952) 49.
72 LD, 'The Art of Fiction XXIII', interview by Julian Mitchell and Gene Andrewski, *Paris Review* 22 (Autumn-Winter 1959–60) 57.
73 Descartes's formulation may be translated, 'I am a thing that thinks,' a variation of his better known 'Cogito, ergo sum.' Bergson's 'dure' suggests continuing, enduring.
74 LD, *Key* 117.
75 LD, 'The Art of Fiction XXIII' 56.
76 LD, *Key* 117.
77 Hugh Gordon Porteus to LD, 30 July 1957, Coll. SIU-C.
78 RA to LD, 24 August 1957, *Literary Lifelines* 28.
79 Kostas Montis's *Kleistes Portes* [*Closed Doors*] (1964) bears a note on the title page, 'an answer to *Bitter Lemons* of Lawrence Durrell'. At least seventeen books, largely in opposition to *Bitter Lemons*, have been written by Cypriots and Greeks treating the Cyprus situation.
80 Rodis Roufos, 'Sour Grapes', *Deus Loci* NS 3 (1994) 138.
81 David Roessel in '"Something to Stand the Government in Good Stead": Lawrence Durrell and the *Cyprus Review*' and 'Rodis Roufos on *Bitter Lemons*: A Suppressed Section of *The Age of Bronze*' discusses Durrell's career on Cyprus from a hellenic perspective and the Greek response to *Bitter Lemons*. These articles and the excised chapter of *The Age of Bronze* were published in *Deus Loci: NS* 3 (1994).
82 RA to LD, 11 October 1957, Coll. SIU-C.
83 LD to RA, after 11 October 1957, *Literary Lifelines* 31.
84 HM to LD, 31 July 1957, *DML* 294.
85 HM, Preface to *Justine*, typescript, Coll. SIU-C.
86 HM to LD, 9 September 1957, Coll. SIU-C.

87 LD interviewed by IMN, 16 June 1981.
88 LD to HM, August 1957, excerpt published in Ian S. MacNiven, 'A Critical Friendship: Lawrence Durrell and Henry Miller', *Into the Labyrinth: Essays on the Art of Lawrence Durrell* ed. Frank L. Kersnowski (Ann Arbor: U.M.I. Press, 1989) 21.
89 LD to RA, 22 August 1957, *Literary Lifelines* 25–26.
90 LD to HM, late February 1958, *DML* 307.
91 LD to RA, 22 August 1957, *Literary Lifelines* 25–26.
92 LD interviewed in *Réalités* (November 1960), trans. Earl G. Ingersoll.
93 LD to HM, late April? 1957, *DML* 287.
94 LD to HM, end April 1957, *DML* 289.
95 LD to Sir Patrick Reilly, c. November 1958?, Coll. Sir Patrick Reilly. Sir Patrick was then Ambassador to the USSR.
96 HM to LD, 23 October 1957, Coll. SIU-C.
97 David Gascoyne to LD, 30 September 1957, Coll. SIU-C.
98 LD to RA, after 11 October 1957, *Literary Lifelines* 30.
99 LD to Dr Arthur Guirdham, pmk 26 October 1957, Coll. Guirdham Estate.
100 LD to A. Guirdham, before 28 May 1958, Coll. Guirdham Estate.
101 LD to A. Guirdham, 1 January 1958, Coll. Guirdham Estate.
102 Claude Durrell to HM, 18 December 1957, *DML* 303.
103 Claude Durrell to HM, 18 December 1957, *DML* 304.
104 LD to HM, late February 1958, *DML* 307.
105 Claude Durrell to HM, 18 December 1957, *DML* 304.
106 LD to RA, c. 18–25 December 1957, *Literary Lifelines* 38.
107 Heather Teague to Zelide Cowan, 28 August 1952, Coll. Zelide Cowan.
108 Claude Durrell to HM, 18 December 1957, *DML* 304. Gerald Durrell had recently appeared on television with Cholmondely St John, the chimpanzee he had brought back from the Congo.
109 Penelope Durrell Hope in conversation with IMN, 21 May 1993.
110 Joan Bird in conversation with IMN, 30 March 1995.
111 LD to HM, before 20? January 1958, *DML* 306.
112 LD to RA, c. 18–25 December 1957, *Literary Lifelines* 38.
113 The Panos figure, who still lives in Cyprus, has remained resentful of *Bitter Lemons* and unforgiving towards Durrell. His name has been withheld by request, but he was interviewed in 1994 by David Roessel.
114 LD to RA, c. 18–25 December 1957, *Literary Lifelines* 39.
115 LD to HM, mid-December 1957, *DML* 300.
116 LD, Preface, Penelope Tremayne, *Below the Tide* (London: Hutchinson, 1958).
117 RA to LD, 1 December 1957, *Literary Lifelines* 35.
118 RA to LD, 13 December 1957, *Literary Lifelines* 37–38.
119 LD to HM, before 20? January 1958, *DML* 305.
120 LD to RA, c. 18–25 December 1957, *Literary Lifelines* 39.
121 LD, *Mountolive: AQ* (London: Faber, 1962) 440.
122 LD, 'The Art of Fiction' 43.
123 LD to HM, late February 1958, *DML* 307.
124 LD to HM, c. 27 February 1958, *DML* 308.
125 Durrell's face registered surprise when I reminded him that his father had visited England twice since he was placed at school in England. Then he looked down and said, very quietly, 'Yes, he came to my school at Canterbury.'
126 LD, 'The Art of Fiction' 43.
127 LD to Sir Patrick Reilly, c. November 1958?, Coll. Sir Patrick Reilly. The towering Sir

Miles Lampson, Ambassador to Egypt during LD's time there, had been made Lord Killearn.

128 HM to Claude Durrell, 22 January 1958, Coll. SIU-C.
129 LD to RA, 9? December 1957 [i.e. 10? February 1958], *Literary Lifelines* 36, 37.
130 LD to RA, c. 14 February-1 March 1958, *Literary Lifelines* 43.
131 LD interviewed by IMN 6 May 1985.
132 'Lawrence Durrell in Nîmes', interview by Huw Wheldon, *Monitor: An Anthology* (London: Macdonald, 1962) 124.
133 LD and Alfred Perlès, *Art and Outrage* (New York: Dutton, 1961) 7.
134 *Art and Outrage* 9.
135 *Art and Outrage* 13.
136 *Art and Outrage* 27.
137 HM to LD, 4 July 1958, *Lawrence Durrell/Henry Miller: A Private Correspondence*, ed. George Wickes (New York: Dutton, 1963) 337.
138 A. Nin to LD, after 23 June 1958, Coll. SIU-C.
139 LD to IMN, 9 August 1977.
140 HM to LD, 6 March 1958, quoted in IMN, 'A Critical Friendship' 20.
141 HM to LD, 3 April 1958, *DML* 317.
142 LD to J. Fanchette, 4 March 1958, *Letters to Jean Fanchette* (Paris: Editions Two Cities, 1988) 23.
143 LD to JF, c. 24 March 1958, *Letters to Jean Fanchette* 24.
144 Frédéric-Jacques Temple to LD, 30 April 1958, Coll. SIU-C.
145 LD to JF, c. 13 May 1958 [i.e. before 28 April], *Letters to Jean Fanchette* 28–29.
146 LD to JF, pmk 14 May 1958 [i.e. late April/early May], *Letters to Jean Fanchette* 30.
147 Anthea Morton-Saner in conversation with IMN, 15 July 1992.
148 LD to JF, c. 13 May [i.e. before 28 April] 1958, *Letters to Jean Fanchette* 28–29.
149 LD to RA, c. 10–14 June 1958, *Literary Lifelines* 48.
150 LD to JF, c. 13 May [i.e. before 28 April] 1958, *Letters to Jean Fanchette* 28.
151 A. Nin to LD, 19? April 1958, Coll. SIU-C.
152 Malcolm Cowley in conversation with IMN, 28 December 1979.
153 LD in conversation with IMN, 16 June 1981.
154 A. Nin, *The Diary of Anaïs Nin*, Vol. 6 (New York: Harcourt Brace Jovanovich, 1976) 162–63.
155 A. Nin to LD, 12–15 May 1958, Coll. SIU-C.
156 A. Nin to LD, 2 June 1958, Coll. SIU-C.
157 LD to JF, pmk 14 May 1958 [i.e. late April/early May], *Letters to Jean Fanchette* 30–31.
158 LD to HM, c. 2 August 1958, *DML* 323–24.
159 LD to JF, end July 1958, *Letters to Jean Fanchette* 36.
160 LD to JF, pmk 14 May 1958 [i.e. late April/early May], *Letters to Jean Fanchette* 30–31.
161 Press cutting, annotated in Durrell hand, 'Rencontré à Paris', publication unidentified.
162 LD to JF, pmk 28 June 1958, *Letters to Jean Fanchette* 34.
163 LD to RA, c. 10–14 June 1958, *Literary Lifelines* 48.
164 Penelope Durrell Hope, diary and letter to IMN of 26 November 1993.
165 Penelope Durrell Hope, diary.
166 LD to JF, c. 7 June 1958, *Letters to Jean Fanchette* 32; JF in conversation with IMN, May 1985, April 1990.
167 Penelope Durrell Hope, Diary.
168 LD to HM, early July? 1958, *DML* 321.
169 LD to HM, early July? 1958, *DML* 321.
170 LD, 'Ripe Living in Provence', *Holiday* 26:5 (November 1959) 184.

171 LD, Preface, Arthur Guirdham, *Christ and Freud* (London: Allen and Unwin, 1959).
172 LD to HM, c. 2 August 1958, *DML* 323–24.
173 LD in conversation with IMN, 11 May 1985.
174 LD interviewed in *Réalités* (November 1960), trans. Earl G. Ingersoll.
175 HM to LD, 27 May 1958, *Correspondence*, ed. Wickes, 335.
176 LD to HM, c. 20 August 1958, Coll. UCLA.
177 HM to LD, 11 June 1958, Coll. SIU-C.
178 HM to LD, 9 August 1958, Coll. SIU-C.
179 Penelope Durrell Hope, unpublished memoir, 20 February 1992.
180 LD to HM, early July? 1958, *DML* 320.
181 HM to LD, 29 August 1958, *DML* 324–25.
182 A. Nin to LD, after 23 June 1958, Coll. SIU-C.
183 LD to HM, c. 20 August 1958, Coll. UCLA.
184 LD in conversation with IMN, 7 May 1985.
185 Nin, *Diary* 6:163.
186 J. Fanchette, editorial note, *Letters to Jean Fanchette* 37.
187 HM to LD, 17 September 1958, Coll. SIU-C.
188 HM to LD, 30 October 1958, *DML* 331.
189 LD, Preface, *The Henry Miller Reader* (Norfolk, Connecticut: New Directions, 1958) xi.
190 LD, 'The Other T. S. Eliot', *The Atlantic* 215:5 (May 1965) 64.
191 LD, 'The Art of Fiction' 46.
192 LD to RA, c. 14–24 September 1958, *Literary Lifelines* 55.
193 LD to JF, pmk 12 September 1958, *Letters to Jean Fanchette* 37.
194 LD to HM, c. 20 August 1958, Coll. UCLA.

CHAPTER 11: The Mazet Michel

1 Claude Durrell to Eve Miller, 22 August 1958, Coll. UCLA.
2 LD to R. Aldington, 3 October 1958, *Literary Lifelines: The Richard Aldington-Lawrence Durrell Correspondence* (London: Faber, 1981) 57–58.
3 LD to AGT, pmk 15 October 1958, *Spirit of Place* (London: Faber, 1969) 148.
4 RA to LD, 6 October 1958, *Literary Lifelines* 58–59.
5 LD to RA, 9 October 1958, *Literary Lifelines* 59.
6 RA to Claude Durrell, 2 February 1959, Coll. SIU-C.
7 Gerald Sykes to LD, 26 November 1958, Coll. SIU-C.
8 Freya Stark to LD, 4 November 1959, Coll. SIU-C.
9 'His Excellency', *Times Literary Supplement* (17 October 1958) 589.
10 Pamela Hansford Johnson, review of *Mountolive*, *New Statesman* 56 (25 October 1958) 567.
11 Review of *Mountolive*, *Time* 73 (30 March 1959) 91.
12 Gerald Durrell, 'My Brother Larry', *Twentieth Century Literature* 33:3 (Fall 1987) 264.
13 LD to AGT, pmk 15 October 1958, *Spirit of Place* 149.
14 Quoted by LD to RA, 15–20 October 1958, *Literary Lifelines* 60.
15 LD interviewed by Stephen Gray, 3 April 1965.
16 LD to RA, before 6 November 1958, *Literary Lifelines* 61.
17 LD to RA, before 6 November 1958, *Literary Lifelines* 61.
18 Margaret Durrell Duncan in conversation with IMN, 29 March 1991.
19 LD to HM, c. 6 November 1958, *Durrell–Miller Letters 1935–80* (London: Faber, 1988) 332–33.
20 Kenneth Rexroth, *Assays* (Norfolk, Connecticut: New Directions, 1961).

21 LD to RA, 19 January 1959, *Literary Lifelines* 72.

22 LD to Austen Harrison, pmk 27 March 1959, Coll. E.L.I.A., Athens.

23 LD to RA, 10 January 1959, *Literary Lifelines* 71.

24 Anaïs Nin to LD, before 18 November 1958, Coll. SIU-C.

25 A. Nin to LD, 21 November 1958, Coll. SIU-C.

26 LD, draft preface for *Children of the Albatross*, in IMN, 'A Room in the House of Art', *Mosaic* 11:2 (Winter 1978) 54. This phrase and the word *embalmed* were cut by Nin from the published preface.

27 LD, Preface, *Children of the Albatross* (London: Peter Owen, 1959).

28 LD to J. Fanchette, pmk 26 January 1959, *Letters to Jean Fanchette* (Paris: Editions Two Cities, 1988) 44.

29 A. Nin to LD, December? 1958, Coll. SIU-C.

30 LD to IMN, 8 July 1977.

31 LD to JF, pmk 26 January 1959, *Letters to Jean Fanchette* 44.

32 LD to RA, 15 December 1958, *Literary Lifelines* 70.

33 Claude Durrell to LD, 1? January 1959, Coll. SIU-C.

34 LD to JF, c. 10 January 1959, *Letters to Jean Fanchette* 56.

35 Jean Fanchette, Foreword, *Letters to Jean Fanchette* 11.

36 LD to JF, c. 10 January 1959, *Letters to Jean Fanchette* 57.

37 Jean Fanchette, Foreword, *Letters to Jean Fanchette* 15.

38 'Lawrence Durrell Answers a Few Questions', *Two Cities* 1 (15 April 1959) 25–28.

39 LD to JF, c. 15 & c. 19 January 1959, *Letters to Jean Fanchette* 41–43.

40 A. Nin to LD, January? 1959, quoted in IMN, 'A Room in the House of Art', *Mosaic* 9:2 (Winter 1978) 55.

41 A. Nin to LD, January? & before 11 May 1959, Coll. SIU-C.

42 LD to JF, pmk 26 January 1959, *Letters to Jean Fanchette* 43.

43 Quoted in A. Nin, *The Diary of Anaïs Nin*, Vol. 6 (New York: Harcourt Brace Jovanovich, 1976) 203.

44 LD to JF, pmk 26 January 1959, *Letters to Jean Fanchette* 44.

45 JF to LD, 20 February 1959, Coll. SIU-C.

46 LD to RA, after 14 August 1958, Coll. SIU-C.

47 LD interviewed by IMN, 11 May 1985.

48 LD to A. Harrison, pmk 27 March 1959, Coll. E.L.I.A., Athens.

49 LD to J. Fanchette, c. 2 February 1959, *Letters to Jean Fanchette* 54.

50 LD to RA, between 26 January & 1 February 1959, *Literary Lifelines* 76.

51 LD to J. Fanchette, March 1959, *Letters to Jean Fanchette* 17.

52 LD to J. Fanchette, before 2 March 1959, *Letters to Jean Fanchette* 60.

53 LD, 'Lawrence Durrell in Nîmes', interview by Huw Wheldon, 14 February 1960, *Monitor: An Anthology* (London: Macdonald, 1962) 120–21.

54 LD, 'Lawrence Durrell in Nîmes' 121.

55 RA to LD, 25 February 1959, *Literary Lifelines* 84.

56 LD to RA, c. 14–24 September 1958, *Literary Lifelines* 54.

57 Julian Mitchell and Gene Andrewski, introduction to 'The Art of Fiction XXIII: Lawrence Durrell', *Paris Review* 22 (Autumn-Winter 1959–60) 34.

58 LD, 'The Art of Fiction XXIII', interview by Julian Mitchell and Gene Andrewski, 46–47.

59 Mitchell and Andrewski, introduction 34.

60 LD, 'The Art of Fiction' 34–39.

61 LD, 'The Art of Fiction' 36–37.

62 LD, 'The Art of Fiction' 53–54.

63 'Lawrence Durrell Answers a Few Questions' 28.

64 LD, 'The Art of Fiction' 61.
65 LD, 'The Art of Fiction' 55, 61.
66 LD to A. Harrison, pmk 27 March 1959, Coll. E.L.I.A., Athens..
67 LD to IMN, 15 April 1977.
68 Raymond Mills in conversation with IMN, 21 August 1995.
69 LD, 'The Art of Fiction' 60.
70 LD, 'A Dialogue with Durrell', interview by Kenneth Young, *Encounter* 13:6 (December 1959) 66.
71 LD, 'The Art of Fiction' 60.
72 LD, 'The Art of Fiction' 42.
73 Young, 'A Dialogue with Durrell' 61.
74 LD interviewed by Stephen Gray, 3 April 1965.
75 LD in conversation with IMN, 7 May 1985.
76 LD, 'Ripe Living in Provence', *Holiday* 26:5 (November 1959) 185.
77 JF to LD, 30 April 1959, Coll. SIU-C.
78 RA to LD, 14 May 1959, *Literary Lifelines* 90.
79 Xan Fielding to LD, 28 April 1959, Coll. SIU-C.
80 HM to LD, 8 March 1959, *DML* 341.
81 Fanchette, Foreword, *Letters to Jean Fanchette* 14.
82 Eve Miller to LD, 6 May 1959, Coll. SIU-C.
83 LD to JF, c. 10 May 1959, *Letters to Jean Fanchette* 63.
84 Alfred Perlès to LD, 8 May 1959, Coll. SIU-C.
85 LD to J. Fanchette, c. 10 May 1959, *Letters to Jean Fanchette* 63.
86 Gerald Sykes to LD, 8 June 1959, Coll. SIU-C.
87 LD to RA, c. 25–30 May 1959, *Literary Lifelines* 93.
88 RA to LD, 30 May 1959, *Literary Lifelines* 95.
89 LD to A. Guirdham, before 15 July 1959, Coll. Guirdham Estate.
90 A. Guirdham to LD, 27 March 1960, Coll. SIU-C.
91 Young, 'A Dialogue with Durrell' 66.
92 LD, 'The Cottager', *CP 1931–74* 250.
93 LD, 'Ballad of Kretschmer's Types', *Collected Poems* 253–54.
94 Jacquie Durrell, *Beasts in My Bed* (London: Collins, 1968) 97.
95 LD interviewed by IMN, 6 May 1985.
96 HM to LD, 2 September 1959, *DML* 348.
97 RA to LD, 29 July 1959, *Literary Lifelines* 96.
98 HM to LD, 2 September 1959, *DML* 348.
99 AGT in conversation with IMN, 19 September 1991.
100 RA to LD, 22 September 1959, Coll. SIU-C.
101 LD to RA, after 25 September 1959, Coll. SIU-C.
102 LD to RA, after 25 September 1959, Coll. SIU-C.
103 LD to IMN, 25 March 1977.
104 LD to RA, after 25 September 1959, Coll. SIU-C.
105 RA to LD, 7 November 1959, *Literary Lifelines* 105.
106 LD to RA, before 22 September 1959, *Literary Lifelines* 102.
107 Young, 'A Dialogue with Durrell' 61–68.
108 'Lawrence Durrell Answers a Few Questions' 26.
109 Young, 'A Dialogue with Durrell' 62.
110 LD, 'Letting the Book Breathe by Itself'.
111 *Balthazar: AQ* 386.
112 Young, 'A Dialogue with Durrell' 64.

113 Gerald Sykes to LD, 19 October 1959, Coll. SIU-C.
114 JF to LD, 8 December 1959, Coll. SIU-C.
115 LD to A. Harrison, before 22 November 1959, *Deus Loci* NS3 (1994) 27.
116 Mary Mollo, 'Larry, My Friend', *Deus Loci* 7:2 (December 1983) 8.
117 Margaret Rawlings to LD, 26 November 1959, Coll. SIU-C.
118 LD to RA, before 17 December 1959, *Literary Lifelines* 116–17.
119 RA to LD, 2 January 1960, *Literary Lifelines* 123.
120 Wheldon, 'Lawrence Durrell in Nîmes', 120.
121 LD to JF, pmk 3 December 1959, *Letters to Jean Fanchette* 76.
122 Wheldon, 'Lawrence Durrell in Nîmes', 120.
123 LD to RA, before 17 December 1959, *Literary Lifelines* 117.
124 Wheldon, 'Lawrence Durrell in Nîmes' 123–24.
125 Paul Ferris, *Sir Huge: The Life of Huw Wheldon* (London: Michael Joseph, 1990) 145.
126 Wheldon, 'Lawrence Durrell in Nîmes' 124.
127 Ferris, *Sir Huge* 145.
128 Wheldon, 'Lawrence Durrell in Nîmes' 125.
129 Ferris, *Sir Huge* 146.
130 LD to JF, pmk 3 December 1959, *Letters to Jean Fanchette* 76.
131 LD to JF, 15 December 1959, *Letters to Jean Fanchette* 76.
132 RA to LD, 2 February 1960, Coll. SIU-C.
133 Granville Hicks, 'Crown for a Majestic Work', *Saturday Review* 43 (2 April 1960) 15.
134 Gilbert Highet, 'The Alexandrians of Lawrence Durrell', *Horizon* 2:4 (March 1960).
135 V. S. Pritchett, 'The Sun and the Sun-less', *New Statesman* 59 (13 February 1960).
136 Gerald Sykes, 'A Tapestry Woven in Alexandria', *New York Times Book Review* (3 April 1960) 1, 28.
137 Jacques Vallette, 'Lettres Anglo-Saxonnes: Note sur *Clea*', *Mercure de France* 339 (July 1960).
138 Bonamy Dobrée, 'Durrell's Alexandrian Series', *Sewanee Review* 69 (1961).
139 Carl Bode, 'Durrell's Way to Alexandria', *College English* 22 (1961) 531–38.
140 Years after the *Quartet* appeared, the contacts between Avraham Stern, leader of the Stern Gang, and Hitler came to light. Stern had attempted to secure from Hitler the guarantee of a Jewish homeland in Palestine in return for Jewish support against Britain. This was reported by Christopher Hitchens, 'Minority Report', *The Nation* (7/14 August 1989) 159. I am not suggesting that Durrell had got wind of the Stern/Hitler negotiations; only that in having his Jewish financier Lord Galen attempt to bargain with Hitler for similar ends, Durrell had assessed the possibilities of international intrigue more realistically than his critics had.
141 Kenneth Rexroth, 'What Is Wrong with Durrell?', *Nation* (4 June 1960) 493.
142 'Lawrence Durrell Answers a Few Questions' 26.
143 LD, 'The Art of Fiction' 58.
144 LD to J. Bronowski, *Insight* (London: Macdonald, 1964) 107. This interview was broadcast by the BBC on 4 April 1961.
145 LD interviewed in *Réalités* (November 1960), trans. Earl G. Ingersoll.
146 George Steiner, 'Lawrence Durrell: The Baroque Novel', *Yale Review* 19 (1960) 488–95.
147 D. J. Enright, 'Alexandrian Nights' Entertainments: Lawrence Durrell's *Quartet*', *International Literary Annual* 3 (1961).
148 Alexandre Blokh to LD, 16 March 1960, Coll. SIU-C.
149 LD to A. Guirdham, c. March 1960, Coll. Guirdham Estate.
150 LD interviewed in *Réalités* (November 1960), trans. Earl G. Ingersoll.
151 LD to RA, after 28 May 1960, *Literary Lifelines* 138.

152 HM to The Henry Miller Literary Society, 15 July 1960, Coll. UCLA.
153 HM to LD, 24 July 1960, Coll. SIU-C.
154 HM to LD, 27 July 1960, Coll. SIU-C.
155 Henri el Kayem to LD, 26 June 1960, Coll. SIU-C.
156 Lucy Schmick-Reichel to LD, 27 June 1960, Coll. SIU-C.
157 H. Alan Clodd to LD, 30 June 1960, Coll. British Library.
158 A. Guirdham to LD, 29 June 1960, Coll. SIU-C.
159 A. Guirdham to LD, 2 August 1962, Coll. SIU-C. Reminiscing about their meeting, Guirdham quoted Durrell's words back to him.
160 LD interviewed by IMN, 11 May 1985.
161 LD to RA, after 20 August 1960, *Literary Lifelines* 152.
162 Buffie Johnson to LD, before 16 September 1960, Coll. SIU-C.
163 Peter Adam, '"Spirit of Place": Lawrence Durrell's Greece', Post Production Script (BBC-TV production in association with RM Productions, Munich and Télévision Française 1 [5 March 1976]) 22.
164 LD interviewed in *Réalités* (November 1960), trans. Earl G. Ingersoll.
165 Henry Miller, *The Colossus of Maroussi* (New York: New Directions, 1941, 1958) 58.
166 Although their marriage had broken up at the end of the First World War, Doolittle remained friendly towards Aldington, and her concern for his health had led to Bryher's offer. Born Winifred Ellerman, Bryher had inherited a considerable fortune from her father, an English steel magnate.
167 LD to Harry T. Moore, 16 November 1960, Coll. Beatrice Moore.
168 LD to Harry T. Moore, 9 December 1960, Coll. Beatrice Moore.
169 Salvador Dali to LD, 1960, Coll. SIU-C. 'After months therapy drop-by-drop four volumes Darley my brother . . . go home to write in peace and joy.'
170 Gerald Durrell to LD, 14 November 1960, Coll. SIU-C.
171 LD interviewed by Chili Hawes, *Quiet Days in Sommières*, film produced by Peter Leippe, 1985.
172 Claude Durrell, painted card, Coll. British Library.
173 Gerald Durrell in conversation with IMN, 1988.
174 AGT in conversation with IMN, 23 December 1983.
175 *Life* 50:4 (27 January 1961) 99–101.
176 AGT in conversation with IMN, 23 December 1983. The story was told, ascribing to Durrell exactly the same words, by Joan Bird in conversation with IMN, 30 March 1991.
177 G. Durrell, 'My Brother Larry'.
178 LD to Harry T. Moore, 16 May 1961, Coll. Beatrice Moore.
179 HM to LD, 5 January 1961, Coll. SIU-C.
180 HM to LD, 21 January 1961, Coll. SIU-C.
181 LD to IMN, 23 May 1984.
182 LD to Harry T. Moore, 15 February 1961, Coll. Beatrice Moore.
183 Nigel Dennis to LD, 26 November 1960, Coll. SIU-C.
184 LD to Harry T. Moore, 16 May 1961, Coll. Beatrice Moore.
185 Gustaf Gründgens to LD, 8 May 1961, 'Briefwechsel über *Actis*', *Die Zeit* (24 November 1961) 17. The exchange was published in German, although the correspondence was conducted largely in English, with Gründgens depending on the services of a translator.
186 LD to G. Gründgens, 12 May 1961, 'Briefwechsel über *Actis*' 17.
187 LD to Harry T. Moore, 16 May 1961, Coll. Beatrice Moore.
188 M. Mollo, 'Larry, My Friend' 8.
189 'That play of mine? Impertinent, says Mr. Durrell', *Evening Standard* (23 August 1961) 4.

190 LD to G. Gründgens, 18 September 1961, 'Briefwechsel ber *Actis*' 18.
191 Sir Compton Mackenzie to LD, 7 September 1961, Coll. SIU-C.
192 Claude Seignolle to LD, c. September 1961, Coll. SIU-C.
193 Claude Seignolle, biographical sketch, dust-wrapper, *The Accursed* (New York: Coward-McCann, 1967).
194 LD to Mary Mollo, c. June 1948, *Spirit of Place* 98.
195 Peter Adam, 'Alexandria Revisited', *Twentieth Century Literature* 33:3 (Fall 1987) 400.
196 Review of *Actis*, *Die Zeit* (24 November 1961) 17.
197 LD, 'The Kneller Tape (Hamburg)', *The World of Lawrence Durrell*, ed. Harry T. Moore (New York: Dutton, 1964) 162.
198 LD, 'The Kneller Tape (Hamburg)' 166–67.
199 LD to Harry T. Moore, 12 January 1962, Coll. Beatrice Moore.
200 LD to A. Harrison, 24 December 1961, Coll. E.L.I.A., Athens.
201 LD to Harry T. Moore, 12 January 1962, Coll. Beatrice Moore.
202 LD to Harry T. Moore, 3 February 1962, Coll. Beatrice Moore.
203 LD to Harry T. Moore, 3 February 1962, Coll. Beatrice Moore.
204 Martin Green, 'A Minority Report', *World of Lawrence Durrell* 138.
205 LD to Harry T. Moore, 3 February 1962, Coll. Beatrice Moore.
206 LD to IMN, 25 March 1977.
207 LD to A. Guirdham, 18 February 1962, Coll. Guirdham Estate.
208 LD to Harry T. Moore, 12 January 1962, Coll. Beatrice Moore.
209 LD to Harry T. Moore, 13 February 1962, Coll. Beatrice Moore.
210 RA to LD, 13 June 1962, *Literary Lifelines* 215.
211 RA to LD, 14 July 1962, *Literary Lifelines* 217.
212 RA to LD, 26 July 1962, *Literary Lifelines* 221.
213 LD, 'The Placebo', autograph manuscript, c. 1961–62, Coll. SIU-C.
214 LD to HM, 1 July 1962, *DML* 391.
215 LD, 24 August 1962, Transcript, International Writers Conference, Edinburgh, 7.
216 LD to A. Harrison, 18 December 1962, Coll. E.L.I.A., Athens.
217 LD to AGT, September? 1962?, Coll. British Library.
218 LD to HM, 6 January 1979, *DML* 501.
219 Group-Captain Peter Bird in conversation with IMN, 30 March 1991.
220 RA to LD, 13 June 1962, *Literary Lifelines* 215.
221 LD to A. Harrison, 8 December 1962, Coll. E.L.I.A., Athens.
222 LD to HM, 1 May 1963, *DML* 395.
223 LD interviewed by IMN, 7 May 1985.
224 Joan Bird interviewed by IMN, 30 March 1991.
225 LD to HM, pmk 21 May? 1963, Coll. UCLA.
226 Joan Pepper interviewed by IMN, 4 June 1993.
227 LD, 'Ode to a Lukewarm Eyebrow', *Collected Poems* 262.
228 G. Gründgens, Obituary, *New York Times* (8 October 1963) 43.
229 LD to A. Guirdham, mid-November 1963, Coll. Guirdham Estate.
230 LD to A. Guirdham, 25 November 1963, Coll. Guirdham Estate.
231 'An Irish Faustus', *New Cambridge* (1 November 1963).
232 LD to A. Guirdham, 25 November 1963, Coll. Guirdham Estate.
233 LD to HM, early February 1964, *DML* 400.
234 LD to AGT, New Year's Day [1 January 1964], Coll. British Library.
235 LD to Juliet O'Hea, 3 January 1964, Coll. Curtis Brown.
236 LD to HM, 15 February 1964, *DML* 401.
237 Margaret Durrell Duncan in conversation with IMN, 29 March 1991.

238 AGT in conversation with IMN, 1 April 1991.
239 Margaret Durrell Duncan in conversation with IMN & SMN, 29 March 1991.
240 AGT in conversation with IMN, 23 December 1983.
241 Gerald Durrell to AGT, pmk 3 February 1964, Coll. British Library.
242 Jacquie Durrell to AGT, 1 February 1964, Coll. British Library.
243 LD to HM, early February 1964, *DML* 400.
244 LD to HM, 6 February 1965, *DML* 406.
245 *Antaeus* 61 (Autumn 1988) 88–89.
246 LD to AGT, pmk 8? June 1964, Coll. British Library.
247 LD to HM, 6 October 1964, *DML* 403.
248 Group-Captain Peter Bird interviewed by IMN, 30 March 1991.
249 LD, 'Oil for the Saint; Return to Corfu', *Spirit of Place* 301.
250 LD to HM, 6 October 1964, *DML* 403.
251 LD, 'Oil for the Saint; Return to Corfu' 301.
252 LD to HM, 6 October 1964, *DML* 403.
253 LD to AGT, quoted in Alan G. Thomas and James A. Brigham, *Lawrence Durrell: An Illustrated Checklist* (Carbondale: Southern Illinois University Press, 1983) 101.
254 Frances von Maltitz in conversation with IMN, 21 November 1995.
255 Daphne Fielding, *The Nearest Way Home* (London: Eyre & Spottiswoode, 1970) 196–97.
256 D. Fielding, *The Nearest Way Home* 197–98.
257 D. Fielding, *The Nearest Way Home*, 198–99.
258 LD, *Livia* (London: Faber, 1978) 17.
259 LD to HM, 6 February 1965, *DML* 405–406.
260 LD to HM, 28 February 1965, *DML* 407.
261 LD to HM, 6 February 1965, *DML* 405–406.
262 LD to HM, 28 February 1965, *DML* 407.
263 Stephen Gray, *Accident of Birth: An Autobiography* (Johannesburg, South Africa: COSAW Publishing, 1993) 92.
264 D. Fielding, *The Nearest Way Home* 234.
265 Mollo, 'Larry, My Friend' 10.
266 HM to LD, 5 July 1965, *DML* 409.
267 Ernle Bradford interviewed by IMN, 1983; *Search for Ulysses* film; also Bradford's *Companion Guide to the Greek Islands* (London: Collins, 1963; Englewood Cliffs, NJ: Prentice-Hall, 1983) 37.
268 LD to A. Harrison, 27 November 1966, Coll. E.L.I.A., Athens.
269 LD to A. Harrison, 27 November 1966, Coll. E.L.I.A., Athens.
270 LD to HM, 6 October 1965, *DML* 410.
271 LD to AGT, pmk 14 February 1966, Coll. British Library.
272 LD to HM, 6 October 1965, *DML* 410.
273 Noël Riley Fitch, *Anaïs: The Erotic Life of Anaïs Nin* (Boston: Little, Brown, 1993) 373.
274 LD to HM, pmk 18 June 1966, Coll. UCLA.
275 Frances von Maltitz interviewed by IMN, 1986, 1992.
276 Frances von Maltitz interviewed by IMN, 1986, 1992.
277 Joan Bird interviewed by IMN, 30 March 1991.
278 Frances von Maltitz interviewed by IMN, 1986, 1992.
279 Group-Captain Peter and Joan Bird interviewed by IMN, 30 March 1991.
280 Frances von Maltitz in conversation with IMN, 21 November 1995.
281 Group-Captain Peter and Joan Bird interviewed by IMN, 30 March 1991.
282 LD to HM, 15 August 1966, Coll. UCLA.

283 LD to Juliet O'Hea, 1 November 1966, Coll. Curtis Brown.
284 LD to HM, 14 November 1966, Coll. UCLA.
285 LD, *Tunc* (London: Faber, 1968) 214.
286 *Tunc* 126.
287 Mollo, 'Larry, My Friend' 11.
288 LD to AGT, 9 December 1966, Coll. British Library.
289 LD to AGT, Sunday 11? December 1966, Coll. British Library.
290 LD to AGT, pmk 22 December 1996, Coll. British Library.
291 LD to IMN, 11 June 1984.
292 Penelope Durrell Hope to IMN, 31 July 1994.
293 LD to IMN, 11 June 1984.

CHAPTER 12: Larry in Revolt: Cosmonaut of Interior Space

1 Death advances
  Life retreats
  This eve I wed
  The noctambulist.
2 LD to HM, 17 January 1967, *The Durrell–Miller Letters 1935–80* (London: Faber, 1988), 416.
3 LD to HM, 13 February 1967, *DML* 416.
4 Jean-Pierre Graf and Bernard-Claude Gauthier, 'La galaxie Durrell', *Construire* (23 January 1985) 17.
5 Mary Mollo in conversation with IMN, 27 May 1995, and at various times previously.
6 Margaret Durrell Duncan in conversation with IMN, 29 March 1991.
7 Jacquie Rasen Durrell to AGT, 14 January 1967, Coll. British Library.
8 Penelope Durrell Hope to IMN, 31 July 1994.
9 The allegations of incest are discussed at greater length in the following chapter. To the best of my knowledge, no contemporaneous (1967–70) evidence for incest has surfaced.
10 Robert McDonald, 'Lawrence Durrell: Classical Puppeteer', *Descant* (Toronto) 14 (Summer 1976).
11 LD to J. Fanchette, 13 February 1962, 'Letters to Jean Fanchette', *Two Cities* 9 (Autumn 1964) 22.
12 LD, *Tunc* (London: Faber, 1968) 299.
13 The issue was never resolved, but Ella Thomas's personal difficulties and an accompanying severe depression make suicide appear the more likely alternative, according to Alan and Shirley Thomas. Conversations with IMN in 1987, 1991, 1993.
14 LD to AGT, pmk 8 March 1967, Coll. British Library.
15 *Tunc* 133, 137.
16 *Tunc* 298.
17 *Tunc* 142.
18 LD, 'Confederate', *Collected Poems 1931–1974* (London: Faber: 1980) 289. This poem first appeared in the March 1967 issue of the *London Magazine*.
19 LD to HM, 19 April 1967, *DML* 427.
20 Group-Captain Peter and Joan Bird interviewed by IMN, 30 March 1991.
21 LD, 'Solange', *Collected Poems* 293, 302.
22 LD to HM, 7 August 1967, *DML* 419.
23 Margaret Durrell Duncan in conversation with IMN, 29 March 1991.
24 HM to LD, 15 November 1967, *DML* 421.
25 Joan Bird in conversation with IMN, 30 March 1991.

26 HM to LD, 19 October 1967, *DML* 420.
27 HM to LD, 15 November 1967, *DML* 421.
28 Robert Snyder said in conversation to IMN, 6 January 1992: 'I don't think anyone could care for Hoki – cold.'
29 LD to HM, 5 March 1971, *DML* 447.
30 Robert Snyder, *The Henry Miller Odyssey* film, 1969.
31 LD to HM, 20 November 1967, *DML* 422–23.
32 Robert Snyder interviewed by IMN, 6 January 1991.
33 Andrew Ranard, 'Tropic of Roppongi: Mrs. Henry Miller's Nightclub in Tokyo'.
34 LD to HM, 2 December 1967, *DML* 424.
35 Hoki Tokuda Miller to LD, 1967, Coll. SIU-C.
36 LD to HM, 20 November 1967, *DML* 422.
37 LD to AGT, 1 January 1968, Coll. British Library.
38 LD, *Monsieur* (London: Faber, 1974) 295.
39 Buffie Johnson, 'Personal Reminiscences of Lawrence Durrell', *Deus Loci* 1:5 (Fall 1981) 73.
40 Mary Mollo in conversation with IMN, 1988.
41 LD, *Nunquam* (London: Faber, 1970) 16.
42 Advertising brochure for Clarke's Fluid, an embalming agent: 'Every time you see a pretty girl think of "Cintio" & "De Cage"/ The chemical . . .', Coll. SIU-C.
43 LD, 'Tulliola', *Collected Poems* 33.
44 LD, 'A Winter of Vampires', *The Red Limbo Lingo* (London: Faber, New York: Dutton, 1971) 29; also in *Collected Poems* 306.
45 LD, 'Avis', *The Red Limbo Lingo* 36; also in *Collected Poems* 312.
46 LD, *The Red Limbo Lingo* 9–19.
47 LD to AGT, 1 January 1968, Coll. British Library.
48 LD to AGT, 1 January 1968, Coll. British Library.
49 Brochure, Leicester Arts Festival, 8–21 February 1968.
50 Shirley Thomas in conversation with IMN, 1992.
51 LD to AGT, pmk 10 March 1968, Coll. British Library.
52 LD to Simone Perier, 11 March 1968, Coll. Simone Perier.
53 LD to Alfred Perlès, 21 March 1968, Coll. Anne Barret Perlès.
54 LD to AGT, pmk 21 March 1968, Coll. British Library.
55 LD in conversation with IMN, 7 May 1985.
56 Marianne Moore to LD, April? 1968, Coll. SIU-C.
57 LD to AGT, pmk 15 January 1968, Coll. British Library.
58 Kenneth Rexroth, 'A Steady Note of Mockery', *Nation* 206 (20 May 1968).
59 Edward Weeks, 'Durrell's Black Humor', *Atlantic Monthly* 221 (May 1968) 109.
60 Gerald Sykes, 'Durrell's 1984', *New York Times Book Review* (14 April 1968).
61 G. S. Fraser, 'By Courtesy of the Firm', *New Statesman* 75 (12 April 1968).
62 LD, 'Owed to America', *Collected Poems* 289–91.
63 LD to HM, 22 June 1968, *DML* 430.
64 Claudine Brelet to IMN, 7 March 1995.
65 Arthur Guirdham, *The Cathars and Reincarnation* (Wheaton, Illinois: Theosophical Publishing House, 1970) 19 & *passim*.
66 LD in conversation with IMN, 6 February 1975.
67 Antony Daniells interviewed by IMN, 18 September 1991.
68 LD to HM, 16 February 1969, *DML* 433.
69 LD, 'An Interview with Lawrence Durrell' by Eugene Lyons and Harry T. Antrim, 25 March 1970, *Shenandoah* 22:2 (Winter 1971) 48.

70 LD to HM, 16 February 1969, *DML* 434.
71 LD to A. Guirdham, 26? May 1969, Coll. Guirdham Estate.
72 LD to HM, 16 February 1969, *DML* 434.
73 Claudine Brelet to IMN, 7 March 1995.
74 Lyons and Antrim, 'Interview with Lawrence Durrell', 54.
75 LD to HM, 12 September 1969, *DML* 436.
76 Lyons and Antrim, 'Interview with Lawrence Durrell', 57.
77 *Nunquam* [283].
78 *Nunquam* [283], [285].
79 LD to AGT, c. April 1969, Coll. British Library.
80 LD to A. Guirdham, 26 May 1969, Coll. Guirdham Estate.
81 Digby Diehl, 'Tenderizer at Tough-Minded Caltech', *Los Angeles Times* (12 February 1974) Part IV: 6, 8. Around the time Durrell said this, I was corresponding with him about his archive at Southern Illinois University.
82 Thérèse Epstein Marberry to LD, 25 August 1969, Coll. University of Paris X/Nanterre.
83 Patrick McGilligan, *George Cukor: A Double Life* (New York: HarperPerennial, 1992) 309.
84 Thérèse Epstein Marberry to LD, 29 August 1969, Coll. CERLD.
85 LD to HM, 12 September 1969, *DML* 436.
86 LD to AGT, 29 September 1969, Coll. British Library.
87 Margaret McCall, '*The Lonely Roads*: Notes for an Unwritten Book', *Twentieth Century Literature* 33:3 (Fall 1987) 384–85. *Croyant pratiquant*: practising believer.
88 LD, *The Big Supposer: A Dialogue with Marc Alyn* (London: Abelard–Schuman, New York: Grove, 1973), 64.
89 AGT to LD, 29 December 1969. Coll. British Library.
90 The trial of the distinguished antiquarian bookseller was exploited aggressively by the tabloids. On the witness stand the aggrieved husband, Vittorio Calentano, made wild accusations against Alan Thomas and gave lurid descriptions of Shirley's alleged sexual proclivities. Alan was cleared on all counts, and the trial judge issued a rebuke from the bench to Mr Calentano, quoting an old precedent from a lawsuit dismissed as malicious. His words were featured in a banner headline: 'The Dirty Dog Shall Get No Dinner Here.'
91 LD to A. Guirdham, 12 January 1970, Coll. Guirdham Estate.
92 LD to HM, 10 February 1970, *DML* 437–38.
93 LD interviewed in French by Claudine Brelet, autumn 1971, for Michel Lancelot's 'Campus' programme on Europe 1. Translation by Claudine Brelet. Published in *Twentieth Century Literature* 33:3 (Fall 1987) 379.
94 McCall, '*The Lonely Roads*: Notes for an Unwritten Book' 391.
95 LD to AGT, pmk 20 February 1970, Coll. British Library.
96 Gwyn Williams, *An ABC of (D.) G. W.: A Kind of Autobiography* (Llandsyl, Dyfed, Wales: Gomer Press, 1981) 157.
97 LD to HM, 10 February 1970, *DML* 437.
98 Fiddle Viracola in conversation with IMN at various times between April 1986 and 11 June 1995.
99 Fiddle Viracola in conversation with IMN, 11 June 1995.
100 Lyons and Antrim, 'Interview with Lawrence Durrell' 46, 58.
101 Lyons and Antrim, 'Interview with Lawrence Durrell', 57.
102 Fiddle Viracola in conversation with IMN, 11 June 1995.
103 Fiddle Viracola in conversation with IMN, 11 June 1995.
104 LD, 'Nobody', *Collected Poems* 304. Fiddle Viracola's Manhattan apartment was on

10th Street between 5th and 6th Avenues.
105 Richard Boston, 'Those Who Liked *Alexandria Quartet* Will Love It, Those Who Didn't . . .', *New York Times Book Review* (29 March 1970).
106 Christopher Ricks, 'Female and Other Impersonators', *New York Review of Books* 15 (23 July 1970) 8.
107 Francis Hope, 'Strange Enough', *New Statesman* 79 (27 March 1970).
108 Lyons and Antrim, 'Interview with Lawrence Durrell' 55.
109 LD to HM, 12 May 1970, *DML* 440.
110 Fiddle Viracola in conversation with IMN, 11 June 1995.
111 Fiddle Viracola in conversation with LD and IMN, 16 April 1986.
112 LD to HM, 12 May 1970, *DML* 440.
113 LD, *Ulysses Come Back* recording.
114 LD, 'Sais Je Pourquoi?' Coll. British Library.
115 LD to HM, 4 October 1970, *DML* 441.
116 LD in conversation with IMN, 14 May 1985.
117 LD, 'Mistral', *Collected Poems* 319. 'Sometimes I am active/ Sometimes I am idle/ First Prize for Coarse Language . . . .'
118 LD to Suzanne Henig, 1973; Henig in conversation with IMN, 30 June 1994.
119 LD to HM, 4 October 1970, *DML* 441.
120 LD to HM, 4 October 1970, *DML* 441.
121 LD and Fiddle Viracola to HM, 10 September 1970, Coll. UCLA.
122 Fiddle Viracola in conversation with IMN, 16 April 1986.
123 LD to HM, 3 November 1970, Coll. UCLA.
124 LD, 'Rain, Rain, Go to Spain', *The Red Limbo Lingo* 26.
125 LD, *The Red Limbo Lingo* 21.
126 Lyons and Antrim, 'Interview with Lawrence Durrell' 49–50.
127 LD to HM, 28 January 1971, *DML* 443.
128 LD to HM, 28 January 1971, *DML* 443.
129 LD to HM, 19 February 1971, *DML* 445.
130 Claudine Brelet to IMN, 7 March 1995.
131 LD to HM, 5 March 1971, *DML* 447.
132 Suzanne Henig to IMN, 30 October 1994.
133 LD to HM, 19 February 1971, *DML* 445–46.
134 LD to HM, 5 May 1971, *DML* 448.
135 *Monsieur* 142.
136 *Monsieur* 7.
137 *Monsieur* 275.
138 James P. Carley, 'An Interview with Lawrence Durrell on the Background to *Monsieur* and Its Sequels', *Malahat Review* 51 (1979) 46.
139 *Monsieur* 35.
140 *Monsieur* 46.
141 Diehl, 'Tenderizer at Tough-Minded Caltech' 6.
142 *Monsieur* 12.
143 Claudine Brelet to IMN, 7 March 1995.
144 LD to HM, 5 May 1971, *DML* 448.
145 Joan Bird interviewed by IMN, 30 March 1991.
146 LD to HM, 11 August 1971, *DML* 452.
147 LD to HM, 5 May 1971, *DML* 448.
148 LD in conversation with IMN, 7 May 1985.
149 LD in conversation with IMN, June 1981.

150 LD to HM, 5 May 1971, *DML* 448.
151 LD, 'On the Suchness of the Old Boy', *Collected Poems* 325–28. The epigraph to *Justine* begins, '*There are two positions available to us – either crime which renders us happy, or the noose, which prevents us from being unhappy.*'
152 LD, 'The Ophite', *Collected Poems* 328.
153 LD to HM, 1 July 1971, Coll. UCLA.
154 Robert Snyder in conversation with IMN, 6 January 1992.
155 LD to HM, Thursday [23 September 1971], *DML* 452.
156 'Anaïs Nin: An Interview', by William McBrien, 1974, reprinted in *Conversations with Anaïs Nin*, ed. Wendy M. DuBow (Jackson: University Press of Mississippi, 1994) 211.
157 LD, 'Paroles avec Lawrence Durrell', interview by Hubert Juin, *Les Lettres Françaises* (17 December 1959), trans. Earl G. Ingersoll.
158 Guirdham, *The Cathars and Reincarnation* 117.
159 LD to AGT, 7 June 1970, Coll. British Library.
160 LD, Introduction, *100 Great Books: Masterpieces of All Time*, ed. John Canning (London: Souvenir Press, 1974) 13.
161 *Monsieur* 195.
162 HM to Claude Kiefer, 22 January 1972, Coll. Claude Kiefer.
163 LD to HM, 23 January 1972, *DML* 453.
164 LD to AGT, 14 February 1972, Coll. British Library.
165 Richard Pine in conversation with IMN, 1992.
166 LD to HM, 23 January 1972, *DML* 453.
167 LD, 'Dublin', *Collected Poems* 334.
168 LD to AGT, Thursday [3 February 1972], Coll. British Library.
169 LD to AGT, Thursday [3 February 1972], Coll. British Library.
170 LD, 'Jules Laforgue', *Mercure de France* (3 February 1972).
171 Shirley Thomas in conversation with IMN, 19 September 1991.
172 LD, 'Vaumort', *Collected Poems* 323.
173 LD, 'The Octagon Room', *Collected Poems* 248.
174 Shirley Thomas in conversation with IMN, 19 September 1991.
175 LD to AGT, 14 February 1972, Coll. British Library.
176 LD to Shirley Thomas, after 14 February 1972, Coll. British Library.
177 Mary Mollo, 'Larry, My Friend', *Deus Loci* 7:2 (December 1983) 12.
178 LD, 'Invitation', Coll. British Library. The whole text read: 'If I am still around on 27 February, Sunday, I will be sixty. In consequence I will need all your sympathies. Come, then, and drink a glass (Champagne? Hemlock?) in Sommières, and stay somberly for lunch after, if you wish. Eheu!'
179 LD to HM, Tuesday [11? April 1972], Coll. UCLA.
180 A popular book, *Holy Blood, Holy Grail* by Michael Baigent, Richard Leigh and Henry Lincoln, sets forth this legend in exhaustive detail. Durrell told me that he was familiar with this work.
181 LD to HM, 28 April 1977, Coll. UCLA.
182 LD to HM, Tuesday [11? April 1972], *DML* 457.
183 Ludo Chardenon, *In Praise of Wild Herbs: Remedies and Recipes from Old Provence* (Santa Barbara, Calif.: Capra Press, 1984; London: Century, 1985) 29.
184 LD, *The Plant-Magic Man* (Santa Barbara: Capra Press, 1973) 12.
185 LD in conversation with IMN and SMN, 6 May 1985.
186 *Plant-Magic Man* 24.
187 LD to HM, Tuesday [11? April 1972], Coll. UCLA.
188 *Monsieur* 268.

189 LD, 'Vega', *Collected Poems* 322.
190 Claude Kiefer to HM, 30 January 1973, Coll. UCLA. 'But I'm the kind of person who simply likes happiness most of all, and would love to spread it around her: which isn't always easy.'
191 LD to HM, 13 May 1972, Coll. UCLA.
192 Two postcards, Michèle Arnaud, LD, Anne and Alfred Perlès to HM, before 13 September 1972, Coll. UCLA.
193 LD to HM, 13 September 1972, Coll. UCLA.
194 HM to LD, 20 September 1972, Coll. British Library.
195 Anne Barret Perlès in conversation with IMN, 1989, 1992.
196 LD to HM, 13 September 1972, Coll. UCLA.
197 LD to HM, 13 September 1972, Coll. UCLA.
198 LD to HM, 11 December 1972, *DML* 460.
199 Suzanne Henig to IMN, 30 October 1994.
200 LD to HM, 11 December 1972, *DML* 460.
201 LD to HM, 11 December 1972, *DML* 461.
202 LD to HM, 29 January 1973, Coll. UCLA.
203 LD to HM, 5 April 1973, 2nd letter this date, Coll. UCLA.
204 HM to LD, 6 March 1973, Coll. British Library.
205 LD to HM, 13 March 1973, Coll. UCLA.
206 LD to HM, 25 February 1973, *DML* 464.
207 LD to HM, 23 February 1973, *DML* 463. *Bise*: north wind.
208 LD to HM, 13 March 1973, Coll. UCLA.
209 LD interviewed in *Réalités* (November 1960), trans. Earl G. Ingersoll.
210 Robin Livio, 'Qui êtes vous? Lawrence Durrell', *Film Français* (11 May 1973) 14.
211 'The only thing that has value and that gives a spiritual density to life is this tragic episode common to all the world: love. To love is to understand oneself; and to understand all is to imagine all. A cosmonaut of interior space, I am leaving for the moon.'
212 Livio, 'Qui êtes vous? Lawrence Durrell', *Film Français* (11 May 1973) 14.
213 LD to HM, 18 July 1973, Coll. UCLA.
214 LD to HM, 2 October 1973, *DML* 467.
215 LD to HM, 23 November 1973, Coll. UCLA.
216 LD, 'Apesong', *Collected Poems* 331.
217 LD to AGT, c. November 1973, Coll. British Library.
218 Joan Bird in conversation with IMN, 30 March 1991.
219 LD to HM, 8 October 1973, *DML* 468.
220 Ghislaine de Boysson Durrell in conversation with IMN, 1992.
221 HM to LD, 5 April 1974, Coll. British Library.
222 LD to AGT, pmk 2? January 1974, Coll. British Library.
223 Diehl, 'Tenderizer at Tough-Minded Caltech' 6.
224 Robert Snyder in conversation with IMN, 6 January 1992.
225 Diehl, 'Tenderizer at Tough-Minded Caltech' 6.
226 Diehl, 'Tenderizer at Tough-Minded Caltech' 1.
227 LD to HM, 12 May 1974, Coll. UCLA.
228 LD to HM, 14 April 1974, *DML* 473–74.
229 Diehl, 'Tenderizer at Tough-Minded Caltech' 1.
230 Diehl, 'Tenderizer at Tough-Minded Caltech' 1.
231 LD to Rupert Pole, 7 February 1977, Coll. Miller Estate.
232 LD, 'A Poet in the Mediterranean', *Blue Thirst* (Santa Barbara: Capra Press, 1975) 11–13. The Beckmann Auditorium and Claremont College lectures were collected in this

slim illustrated volume.

233 LD, 'Propaganda and Impropaganda', *Blue Thirst* 52.
234 LD to HM, 12 May 1974, Coll. ULCA.
235 Robert Snyder in conversation with IMN, 6 January 1992.
236 HM to LD, 23 October 1974, Coll. British Library. Enclosed with this missive of Miller's was a copy of a 16 January 1967 letter from him to his friend 'Riko' describing his courtship of Hoki Takuda.
237 LD to HM, Sunday, February? 1974, Coll. UCLA.
238 LD to AGT, pmk 6? March 1974, Coll. British Library.
239 Ghislaine de Boysson Durrell to HM, 28 April 1974, Coll. UCLA.
240 LD to HM, 12 May 1974, Coll. UCLA.
241 LD to AGT, 13 June 1974, Coll. British Library.
242 Mary Mollo in conversation with IMN, 1992.
243 LD to AGT, 27 June 1974, Coll. British Library.
244 Ghislaine de Boysson Durrell in conversation with IMN, 18 September 1991.
245 Ghislaine de Boysson Durrell in conversation with IMN, 18 September 1991 and 4 July 1992.
246 LD to AGT, 27 June 1974, Coll. British Library.
247 HM to LD, 13 September 1974, Coll. British Library.
248 HM to LD, 19 September 1974, *DML* 474.
249 LD to HM, pmk 23 September 1974, *DML* 475.
250 Ghislaine de Boysson Durrell to HM, 22 September 1974, Coll. UCLA. 'Here in Sommières we aren't getting along well and the summer has been very rough.'
251 HM to LD, 27 September 1974, Coll. UCLA.
252 LD interviewed by Michael Parkinson, BBC Television, 19 October 1974.
253 LD to HM, 4 October 1974, Coll. UCLA.
254 LD in conversation with IMN, 4 February 1975; also 1983.
255 Ghislaine de Boysson Durrell and Françoise Kestsman in conversation with IMN, 4 July 1992.
256 LD to IMN, 8 July 1977.
257 LD to HM, 19 December 1974, Coll. UCLA.
258 LD to Thérèse Epstein Marberry, 21 December 1974, Coll. University of Paris X/ Nanterre.
259 LD in conversation with IMN, 4 February 1975.
260 Ghislaine de Boysson Durrell in conversation with IMN, 18 September 1991.
261 LD to HM, 28 March 1975, *DML* 478.
262 Mary Mollo in conversation with IMN, 27 May 1995.
263 Gerald Durrell in conversation with IMN, 1988.
264 Joan Bird interviewed by IMN, 30 March 1991.
265 *Tunc* 293.

CHAPTER 13: Prospero's Cell

1 LD in conversation with IMN and others, 10 May 1985.
2 LD, *Blue Thirst* (Santa Barbara: Capra Press, 1975) 24.
3 Peter Adam, 'Alexandria Revisited', *Twentieth Century Literature* 33:3 (Fall 1987) 398.
4 Peter Adam, '"Spirit of Place": Lawrence Durrell's Greece', Post Production Script (BBC-TV production in association with RM Productions, Munich, and Télévision Française 1 [5 March 1976]) 32, 23.
5 Adam, 'Greece' 11.

6 Adam, 'Greece' 14.
7 Adam, 'Greece' 30, 25.
8 Group-Captain Peter and Joan Bird interviewed by IMN, 30 March 1991.
9 LD to HM, 3 November 1975, *The Durrell–Miller Letters 1935–80* (London: Faber, 1988) 480.
10 Robert McDonald, 'Lawrence Durrell: Classical Puppeteer', *Descant* (Toronto) 14 (Summer 1976).
11 Peter Bird in conversation with IMN, 30 March 1991.
12 LD in conversation with IMN, 6 May 1985.
13 LD, *Livia* (London: Faber 1978) 2.
14 LD in conversation with Carol Peirce and IMN, 6 May 1985.
15 LD in conversation with IMN, 7 May 1985.
16 LD to IMN, 6 March 1978.
17 LD in conversation with Carol Peirce and IMN, 14 May 1985.
18 LD, 'Autumn Lady: Naxos', *Sicilian Carousel* (London: Faber, New York: Viking, 1977) 219.
19 Simone Lestoquard to IMN, 6 October 1995.
20 LD, *A Smile in the Mind's Eye* (London: Wildwood House, 1980) 4.
21 *Smile* 11.
22 Mary Mollo to IMN, 23 June 1995.
23 *Smile* 12–14.
24 *Smile* 20–21.
25 LD, 'The Secret Chateau of Plaige', *Comité de soutien pour l'édification d'un temple himalayen* (Kagyu-Ling, 1983) 28.
26 *Smile* 34, 36.
27 *Smile* 36–38.
28 LD to Rupert Pole, 7 February 1977, Coll. Miller Estate.
29 LD to Alfred Perlés, before 23 June 1980, Coll. Anne Barret Perlès.
30 Alfred Perlès to LD, 24 June 1980, Coll. British Library. *Vivandière*: canteen-woman, sutler, camp-follower.
31 LD to IMN, 25 March 1977.
32 LD to IMN, 25 March 1977.
33 Raymond Mills in conversation with IMN, 21 August 1995.
34 LD to IMN, 14 April 1977.
35 LD to IMN, 15 April 1977.
36 LD to HM, 1 June 1977, Coll. Miller Estate.
37 LD to Alfred Perlès, pmk 17 July 1977?, Coll. Anne Barret Perlès.
38 LD to HM, 26 June 1977, Coll. Miller Estate.
39 LD to IMN, 8 July 1977.
40 LD to HM, 26 June 1977, Coll. Miller Estate.
41 LD to HM, 26 June 1977, Coll. Miller Estate.
42 LD to IMN, 9 August 1977.
43 LD to HM, 1 June 1977, *DML* 486; unpublished portion, Coll. Miller Estate.
44 LD to IMN, 6 March 1978.
45 LD to HM, 7 August 1977, *DML* 487–88.
46 Peter Adam interviewed by IMN, February 1983.
47 LD to HM, 7 August 1977, *DML* 488.
48 LD to HM, 10 September 1977, Coll. Miller Estate.
49 LD to HM, pmk 14 October 1977, Coll. UCLA.
50 Adam, 'Alexandria Revisited' 396.

51 Adam, 'Alexandria Revisited' 397.
52 LD, Introduction, E. M. Forster, *Alexandria: A History and a Guide* (London: Michael Haag, 1986) xix.
53 LD to HM, late October? 1977, *DML* 488.
54 LD, Introduction, Forster, *Alexandria* xviii-xx.
55 Adam, 'Alexandria Revisited' 401.
56 LD, Introduction, Forster, *Alexandria* xviii-xx.
57 Adam, 'Alexandria Revisited', 400.
58 LD to HM, pmk 3 January 1978, *DML* 492.
59 Adam, 'Alexandria Revisited' 400, 404.
60 Adam, 'Alexandria Revisited' 399–400.
61 Adam, 'Alexandria Revisited' 399–401.
62 David Roessel in conversation with IMN, December 1995. Durrell had not seen Gurna when he wrote the 'Village of Turtle-Doves' fragment in 1956, but Dimitri Papadimos, whom Durrell saw often at the time, had taken many photographs of Gurna for Fathy.
63 Adam, 'Alexandria Revisited' 404.
64 LD to HM, pmk 3 January 1978, *DML* 492.
65 Peter Adam interviewed by IMN, February 1983.
66 Adam, 'Alexandria Revisited' 406–407.
67 LD to HM, 25 November 1977, *DML* 491.
68 Peter Adam, '"Spirit of Place": Lawrence Durrell's Egypt', Post Production Script (BBC-TV production in association with RM Productions, Munich [23 March 1978]) 26.
69 Adam, 'Alexandria Revisited' 408–410.
70 Adam, 'Alexandria Revisited' 402–403.
71 Shirley Thomas in conversation with IMN, July 1992.
72 Adam, 'Alexandria Revisited' 408, 410.
73 LD to HM, 25 November 1977, *DML* 490–91.
74 LD to HM, 25 November 1977, unpublished portion, Coll. Miller Estate.
75 Adam, 'Alexandria Revisited' 408.
76 LD to HM, pmk 3 January 1978, *DML* 492.
77 LD to HM, 12 May 1978, *DML* 493.
78 LD to HM, pmk 3 January 1978, *DML* 492–93.
79 LD to Alfred Perlès, end 1977?, Coll. Anne Barret Perlès.
80 LD to HM, 12 May 1978, *DML* 493.
81 James A. Brigham, 'At Work in the Durrell Factory: Editing the *Collected Poems*', *Deus Loci* 5:1 (Special Issue, Fall 1981) 267.
82 LD to HM, 12 May 1978, *DML* 493.
83 LD to HM, 12 May 1978, unpublished portion, Coll. Miller Estate.
84 LD to Alfred Perlès, pmk 14 August 1978?, Coll. Anne Barret Perlès.
85 LD to HM, 1 June 1977, Coll. Miller Estate.
86 LD to HM, 4 June 1978, *DML* 495–96; unpublished portion, Coll. Miller Estate.
87 LD to HM, 4 June 1978, *DML* 495.
88 LD to Alfred Perlès, pmk 14 August 1978?, Coll. Anne Barret Perlès.
89 Keith Brown, 'Conversations with Durrell on the Structure and Background of His Novels', address presented at On Miracle Ground VII: International Lawrence Durrell Conference, 3 July 1992, Avignon.
90 Brown, 'Conversations with Durrell'.
91 *Livia* 3.
92 Françoise Kestsman in conversation with Keith Brown, 4 July 1992.
93 LD to HM, 16 October 1978, *DML* 497.

94 LD to Alfred Perlès, 6 November 1978, Coll. Anne Barret Perlès.
95 LD to HM, 16 October 1978, *DML* 497.
96 LD to IMN, 20 November 1978. I had been approached by the prospective biographer for an interview, and it turned out that this was the first Durrell knew of any such project afoot.
97 LD to IMN, 15 [i.e. 20?] November 1978.
98 LD to IMN, 25 March 1979. Joseph Coprophage was a name Durrell applied to those of his French partisans whom he judged to be especially sycophantic.
99 LD to HM, 16 October 1978, *DML* 497.
100 LD to Alfred Perlès, 6 November 1978, Coll. Anne Barret Perlès.
101 LD to HM, 5 November 1978, Coll. Miller Estate.
102 LD to HM, 6 January 1979, *DML* 501–502.
103 LD to HM, 10 January 1979, *DML* 504. Anais-Anais was a Cacharel perfume named after Anaïs Nin.
104 LD to HM, 6 January 1979, *DML* 501-502.
105 LD to HM, 10 January 1979, *DML* 504.
106 LD to HM, 6 January 1979, *DML* 503.
107 LD to HM, 16 February 1979, Coll. Miller Estate.
108 LD to Alfred Perlès, 16 March 1979, Coll. Anne Barret Perlès.
109 LD to Alfred Perlès, 16 March 1979, Coll. Anne Barret Perlès.
110 LD, *Constance* (London: Faber, 1982) 19.
111 *Constance* 138.
112 LD to Alfred Perlès, 16 March 1979, Coll. Anne Barret Perlès.
113 Sappho Durrell, 'Journals and Letters', *Granta* 37 (Autumn 1991) 70.
114 Sappho Durrell, 'Journals' 60–61.
115 Alan and Shirley Thomas, Anthea Morton-Saner in conversations with IMN.
116 Gerald Durrell in conversation with IMN, July 1992.
117 Sappho Durrell, 'Journals' 82, 87.
118 Sappho Durrell, 'Journals' 80.
119 Sappho Durrell, 'Journals' 75.
120 Sappho Durrell, 'Journals' 77.
121 Sappho Durrell, 'Journals' 69–70.
122 Sappho Durrell, 'Journals' 77–78.
123 Sappho Durrell, 'Journals' 70.
124 LD to Sappho Durrell, line quoted in Sappho Durrell, 'Journals' 80.
125 Sappho Durrell, 'Journals' 80; LD made similar statements about Sappho to IMN, 1981.
126 LD to Anthea Morton-Saner, per AM-S to IMN, 6 June 1995.
127 HM to LD, 9 June 1979, *DML* 505; Durrell's letter to Miller describing his trip has not been located.
128 LD to Alfred Perlès, 3 May 1979, Coll. Anne Barret Perlès.
129 LD to IMN, 26 March 1980. *Lieu bénit*: hallowed place.
130 LD to HM, 28 December 1979, *DML* 508.
131 LD in conversation with Carol Peirce and IMN, 14 May 1985.
132 Susan S. MacNiven, 'A Matinee Idyll?', *Deus Loci* NS 2 (1993) 163.
133 LD to HM, 28 December 1979, *DML* 509.
134 *Constance* 157.
135 LD to HM, pmk 16 November 1979, Coll. Miller Estate.
136 LD to IMN, 4 February [i.e. March] 1980.
137 LD to IMN, 26 March 1980.
138 LD to IMN, 26 March 1980.

139 LD to IMN, 4 February [i.e. March] 1980.
140 LD to IMN, 6 April 1981.
141 LD to IMN, 4 February [i.e. March] 1980.
142 LD to IMN, 26 March 1980.
143 Antony Daniells in conversation with IMN, 18 September 1991.
144 LD in conversation with IMN, 11 May 1985.
145 HM to LD, 8 May [pmk 15 May] 1980, *DML* 511.
146 Fiddle Viracola in conversation with IMN, 11 June 1995.
147 LD to Alfred Perlès, before 23 June 1980, Coll. Anne Barret Perlès.
148 Alfred Perlès to LD, 23 June 1980, Coll. British Library.
149 Anthea Morton-Saner to IMN, 12 December 1995.
150 Sappho Durrell to LD, 16 July 1980, 'Journals' 84.
151 LD to IMN, 4 February [i.e. March] 1980.
152 LD to Alfred Perlès, 8 October 1980?, Coll. Anne Barret Perlès.
153 LD to Alfred Perlès, 8 October 1980?, Coll. Anne Barret Perlès.
154 LD in conversation with IMN, 14 June 1981.
155 Sappho Durrell, 'Journals' 89.
156 LD to IMN, pmk 23 February 1981.
157 LD in telephone conversation with IMN, 8 March 1981.
158 LD to IMN, 22 March 1981.
159 LD to AGT, March? 1981, Coll. British Library.
160 LD to IMN, annotation on a letter from 'Mississipi', 2 January 1984.
161 LD, 'From the Elephant's Back', *Poetry London/Apple Magazine* 2 (1982) 1–9.
162 LD to IMN, 4 April 1981. Durrell is referring to the attempted assassination of the American president.
163 Xan Fielding, *Hide and Seek: The Story of a War-Time Agent* (London: Secker & Warburg, 1954) 252.
164 LD to IMN, 23 April 1981.
165 LD to IMN, 27 April 1981.
166 LD to IMN, 23 April 1981.
167 'An Interview with Lawrence Durrell on the Background to *Monsieur* and Its Sequels', James P. Carley, *Malahat Review* 51 (1979) 46.
168 LD to IMN, 23 April 1981.
169 Fiddle Viracola to IMN, April 1986.
170 Sappho Durrell in conversation with IMN, 3 May 1981.
171 LD in conversation with IMN, 14 June 1981.
172 Sappho Durrell to LD, 13 July 1981, 'Journals' 89.
173 Addendum dated 6 July 1981 to Sappho Durrell, Last Will of 13 October 1979, printed in 'Journals' 81.
174 LD to Alfred Perlès, FRIDAY 23 October [1981], Coll. Anne Barret Perlès.
175 LD to IMN, 3 November 1981.
176 AGT in conversation with IMN, June 1981.
177 Doris Durrell in conversation with IMN, July 1988.
178 Mary Mollo, 'Larry, My Friend', *Deus Loci* 7:2 (December 1983) 12.
179 LD to IMN, 4 March 1982.
180 LD in conversation with IMN, 11 May 1985.
181 *Smile* 20.
182 Joan Bird in conversation with IMN, 30 March 1991.
183 LD to IMN, 25 July 1982.
184 LD to IMN, 24 August 1982.

185 LD to IMN, 6 December 1982.

186 LD, 'Barbara Robinson vue par Lawrence Durrell', *Lumières de Barbara Robinson*
     (Toulouse: Tierra, 1985) 12.

187 Penelope Durrell Hope to IMN, 22 August 1996.

188 Penelope Durrell Hope and Sappho Durrell in conversation with IMN at 39 Loraine
     Road, February 1983.

189 LD, 'Elephant's Back' 8–9.

190 LD to IMN, 12 June 1983.

191 LD, 'The Secret Chateau of Plaige' 28–29.

192 LD to IMN, 14 December 1983.

193 LD, *Henri Michaux: The Poet of Supreme Solipsism* (Birmingham: Delos Press, 1990) 8.

194 LD, *Monsieur* (London: Faber, 1974) 271.

195 Raymond Mills in conversation with IMN, 21 August 1995.

196 Frank Kersnowski in conversation with IMN, 1990.

197 Jean Fanchette interviewed by Pepita Dupont, *Paris-Match* (November 1990).

198 LD in conversation with IMN, 23 April 1984.

199 LD in conversation with IMN, 23 April 1984.

200 Anthea Morton-Saner in conversation with Susan MacNiven, 11 June 1989.

201 LD, *Quinx* (London: Faber, 1985) 22.

202 LD to IMN, 11 June 1984.

203 *Quinx* 11.

204 LD to IMN, 15 December 1984.

205 LD to IMN, 11 June 1984. 'She is too important to me to leave out . . . . I will leave her
     letters to Sappho to whom I have shown only one. Astonishment!' Durrell wrote to me.
     He described Ghetie as 'a Brontë in the bud'.

206 *Monsieur* 305.

207 *Quinx* 201.

208 LD to IMN, 3 November 1984.

209 LD in conversation with IMN and others, 6 May 1985.

210 LD, 'Après ça' J'aurai Tunt Dit, interview by Michel Braudeau, *Egoïste* (June 1984) 51,
     trans. Earl Ingersoll.

211 Braudeau, 'Après ça' 51.

212 LD to IMN, 11 June 1984.

213 LD to IMN, 3 November 1984.

214 LD in conversation with IMN, 6 May 1985.

215 *Constance* 250.

216 Adam, 'Egypt' 33.

217 Shirley Thomas in conversation with IMN, 16 July 1992; Anthea Morton-Saner to IMN,
     15 May 1996; Penelope Durrell Hope to IMN, 22 August 1996.

218 Sappho Durrell to Eve Durrell, 24 January 1985. On 26 May 1991 Barbara Robson, who
     was co-executor with her husband Hugh of Sappho's will, made the charge in the London
     Sunday Telegraph that Durrell had committed incest with his daughter and implied that
     this had contributed to her suicide. In a later statement Robson claimed that the incest had
     taken place when Sappho was about eighteen, a year after Claude's death. Little evidence
     was produced other than Sappho's inconclusive journal entries and the frequency with
     which incest appears in Durrell's writing. While undergoing psychoanalysis in 1979,
     Sappho had begun to wonder if she had had an incestuous relationship with her father,
     and she discussed this 'buried' memory with her future husband Simon Tompsett and a
     few friends. After Robson had brought up an example of incest, she claimed that Sappho
     had told her that 'Something similar happened to me.' Sappho recalled later that her

grandfather had been sexually attracted to his daughter, her mother, but that this had not led to a consummation. Sappho recorded these recollections a decade after her incest experience with her father was alleged to have occurred. According to Tompsett, towards the end of her life Sappho concluded that the incest had not happened in any physical sense. This does not of course mean that there were not strong emotions running both ways between daughter and father, but as far as incest went, concluded Tompsett, 'physically, it was most unlikely' (*Independent* magazine, 28 September 1991).

To refute Robson's charge confronts one with the impossibility of proving a negative. However, the facts as established warrant the reasonable hypothesis that Sappho, in some ways obsessed with the father she had 'lost' through her parents' divorce, had in the manner of her suicide irrevocably linked herself to him and to his novels. The casebooks of the psychiatric community contain many such histories and even more examples of the power of suggestion under analysis. The technique of 'recovered memory' has been largely discredited as a reliable method for revealing events blocked out of the conscious mind.

Sappho was at once self-obsessed and highly responsive to suggestion, and her emotional life appears to have been focused on her father. Durrell was a passionate and compassionate man who could also be injudicious, selfish, cruel. Those who have charged him with incest have made much of the frequent mentions of incest in his books, but they fail to note that, with one or two relatively minor exceptions, it is always sibling incest. Further, these incestuous relationships invariably end disastrously, often with the insanity, death, or once the castration of one of the partners. Durrell had great hopes for Sappho, but knew the somewhat precarious nature of her heredity – he distrusted his own mental stability at times just as he did her mother's. Finally, he was intensely aware of the damage that could be caused by any incestuous relationship, and that, together with his own deep-rooted sense of propriety, would most probably have sufficed to prevent his committing incest.

219 LD to IMN, 29 February [*sic*, pmk 1 March] 1985.
220 LD in conversation with Jennifer Leonard, 23 July 1988.
221 Mary Mollo in conversation with IMN, July 1992.
222 LD in conversation with IMN, 14 May 1985.
223 LD in conversation with IMN, 11 May 1985.
224 LD in conversation with IMN, 14 May 1985.
225 LD in conversation with Carol Peirce and IMN, 14 May 1985.
226 LD interviewed by IMN, 7 May 1985.
227 Mary Mollo to IMN, 14 February 1994.
228 LD to IMN, 18 September 1982.
229 LD in conversation with IMN, 6 May 1985.
230 LD to HM, 25 September 1946, *DML* 198.
231 LD in conversation with IMN, 11 May 1985.
232 LD, 'Route Saussine 15', *Caesar's Vast Ghost* (London: Faber, 1990) 8.
233 LD to IMN, 1 July 1985.
234 LD in conversation with IMN, 6 May 1985.
235 LD in conversation with IMN, 6 May 1985.
236 LD in conversation with IMN, 11 May 1985.
237 *Caesar's* 75.
238 Barbara Robson, 'The Darker Side of Durrell', *Sunday Telegraph* (26 May 1991) xi.
239 *Caesar's* 75.
240 LD to IMN, pmk 24 September 1985.
241 LD in conversation with IMN, 11 May 1985.

242 LD in conversation with IMN, 7 May 1985.

243 LD in conversation with IMN, 11 May 1985.

244 LD in conversation with IMN, April 1986; Anthea Morton-Saner says that Durrell's account is a fabrication based on *her* visit to an acupuncturist to stop smoking.

245 David Hughes, 'The Master Goes Out to Grass', *The Mail on Sunday* (26 May 1985).

246 Lorna Sage, 'Soft Focus', *Observer* (26 May 1985).

247 Keith Brown, 'Up to the Pisgah-sight', *Times Literary Supplement* (31 May 1985) 597.

248 LD in conversation with IMN, April 1986.

249 LD address at Pennsylvania State University, 11 April 1986. Published in *On Miracle Ground: Essays on the Fiction of Lawrence Durrell*, ed. Michael H. Begnal (Lewisburg: Bucknell Univ. Press, 1990) 20.

250 LD in conversation with IMN, April 1986.

251 Fiddle Viracola in conversation with IMN, 1992.

252 LD to Susan MacNiven, 1 May 1986.

253 LD interviewed by Chili Hawes, *Quiet Days in Sommières*, film produced by Peter Leippe, 1985.

254 Penelope Durrell Hope in conversation with IMN, 14 June 1992.

255 LD to IMN, 23 October 1986.

256 LD in conversation with IMN, 10 March 1987.

257 LD to IMN, 31 October 1987.

258 Mary Mollo in conversation with IMN, 27 May 1995.

259 Fiddle Viracola in conversation with IMN, 11 June 1995.

260 Anthea Morton-Saner to IMN, 15 May 1996.

261 LD to IMN, pmk 11 April 1988.

262 Anthea Morton-Saner in conversation with Susan MacNiven, 11 June 1989.

263 *Caesar's* 203.

264 LD interviewed by Paul Chutkow, 1 December 1988.

265 LD, quarry notebook for *Caesar's Vast Ghost*, Coll. University of Paris X/ Nanterre.

266 Richard Pine in conversation with IMN, 9 December 1990.

267 LD in conversation with IMN, July 1988.

268 LD, Gerald Durrell, Lee Durrell and IMN in conversation, July 1988; GD in conversation with IMN, 18 September 1991.

269 Gerald Durrell to Fiddle Viracola, c. 1988.

270 LD in conversation with IMN, 6 May 1985.

271 LD in conversation with IMN, July 1988.

272 Anthea Morton-Saner in conversation with Susan MacNiven, 11 June 1989.

273 Information from Richard Pine and Mary Byrne, 1992.

274 *Caesar's* 160.

275 *Caesar's* 45.

276 *Caesar's* 135.

277 LD, Quarry notebook for *Caesar's Vast Ghost*, Coll. University of Paris X/ Nanterre.

278 LD, 'Sleepwalkers', *Caesar's* 47.

279 *Caesar's* 170.

280 *Caesar's* 188.

281 *Caesar's* 194.

282 LD, 'Le cercle refermé', *Caesar's* [205].

283 LD to IMN, telephone conversation, 27 January 1989.

284 LD to IMN, telephone conversation, 8 February 1990.

285 LD, Quarry notebook for *Caesar's Vast Ghost*, Coll. University of Paris X/ Nanterre. 'Goodbye sad orphanhood of Anglo-Saxon literature. I am becoming a European armed

head to foot with the swaddling-cloth <language?> Poet. / Ready for anything but nursemaid to nothing!'

286 Gérard Ducret, 'Le patelin rend hommage son écrivain', *Midi Libre* (11 June 1990).

287 Jean Fanchette in conversation with IMN, June 1990.

288 Group-Captain Peter and Joan Bird interviewed by IMN, 30 March 1991.

289 Joan Bird interviewed by IMN, 30 March 1991.

290 Raymond Mills in conversation with IMN, 21 August 1995.

291 Penelope Durrell Hope, diary entry for 18–22 October 1990; PDH to IMN, 22 August 1996.

292 LD, quarry notebook for *Caesar's Vast Ghost,* Coll. University of Paris X/ Nanterre.

293 Anthea Morton-Saner interviewed by IMN, 1990.

294 Anthea Morton-Saner in conversation with IMN, September 1995.

295 Georges Hoffman, Penelope Durrell Hope, John Hope, Françoise Kestsman, Anthea Morton-Saner in conversation with IMN, 1990–93.

Acknowledgements

I am most grateful to Lawrence Durrell, who encouraged me to undertake his biography and who cooperated with cheerful modesty, answering or parrying my questions as he saw fit, introducing me to his friends and lovers, welcoming my wife and me to his Sommières house and library. He gave me absolute freedom, and I hope that I have in some measure repaid his great kindness and trust with an objective yet sympathetic account of his life, aspirations and accomplishments.

Several members of Durrell's family have given me essential assistance: his surviving daughter Penelope made available to me her extensive researches into family history and, together with her husband John Hope, read drafts of various chapters and shared their detailed knowledge of Rhodes and much else; Durrell's late daughter Sappho told me a version of her relationship with her father; his sister Margaret and his late brother Gerald contributed their frank insights and memories, as did Gerald's widow, Lee McGeorge Durrell. Among Durrell's cousins who have been most generous in sharing information are Molly and Nigel Briggs, Phyllis Rickwood Coulson, Diana Knowles, E. Honeyfield Pearce, Glory Wickenden and Celia Yeo. Durrell's late cousin Cecil Noel Pearce, who made a hobby of haunting records offices, turned over his considerable material to me; second cousin Prudence 'Aunt Pru' Hughes, who accepted with good humour being the butt of Durrell's jokes, gave me invaluable genealogical data; so did Zelide Cowan, Richard Hughes and Michael Teague, Durrell's third cousins on the Fairley side. I have been most fortunate in having the assistance of Durrell's three former wives surviving when I began research towards the biography: Nancy Myers, Eve Cohen (who read and commented on four chapters) and Ghislaine de Boysson. Later, Nancy's widower, Edward C. Hodgkin, most generously made available to me a transcription of the tape-recorded memoir that she made in the last year of her life. I am grateful for the help of Maureen and Barry Forde, Durrell's stepson; of the late Doris Hall Durrell, Leslie Durrell's widow; and of Tracy Breeze, Durrell's grand-niece. Françoise Kestsman, who became Durrell's final companion, gave me the inestimable benefit of her memories and unlimited access to Durrell's papers, now part of a permanent Durrell collection at the University of Paris X/ Nanterre, under the supervision of Corinne Alexandre-Garner.

This book would not have been possible in its present form without the assistance and encouragement of the late Shirley and Alan G. Thomas, who most generously opened for me their archives, their home and innumerable bottles of wine. Alan Thomas was Durrell's lifelong friend and bibliographer, and his collection was willed to the British Library, which through the welcome cooperation of Roger Evans has permitted me full use of the material. The Lawrence Durrell Papers at Southern Illinois University at Carbondale, the most extensive collection of his published and unpublished writings and of his personal correspondence files, have been made available to me through the good offices of David V. Koch and Shelley Cox, library professionals whom I count as dear friends.

Mary Mollo, loyal friend to him but also clear-eyed critic of Lawrence Durrell, is in many ways the godmother of this book. Many of Durrell's friends or members of his circle have graciously accorded me access to their correspondence files: Ara Baliozian, Claudine Brelet, Keith Brown, the late Xan Fielding, the late Dr Arthur Guirdham, Claude Kiefer, Dr Raymond Mills and his late wife Georgina, the late Harry T. Moore and his widow Beatrice, Joan Pepper (Lady Carnwath), Simone Perier, Anne Barret and the late Alfred Perlès, Sir Patrick Reilly, Anne and Vivian Ridler, Betsay Uldall. I have been privileged to interview and/or correspond with many of Durrell's friends and acquaintances: Mary and the late David Abercrombie, Peter Adam, Catherine Aldington, Joseph A. Allen, Mulk Raj Anand (via C. Ravindran Nambiar), Marie Aspioti and her brother Maki, Arlette Aujoulas, Peter Baldwin, the late George Barker, the late Audrey Beecham, André Bey, Joan and Group-Captain Peter Bird, Radmila Djukić de Bloeme, Nadia and Alexandre Blokh, the late Kay Boyle, the late Ernle Bradford, Evelyn Lewton-Brain, Sarah Wolton Broad, François Bucher, Ellen Buis, the late Peter Bull, Sir Bernard and the late Lady Ines Burrows, Mary Byrne, Maurice Cardiff, Curtis Cate, Martine and Ludovic Chardenon, Paul Chutkow, the late George Cleyet, Beatrice Commengé, Veronica Tester Dane, Antony Daniells, Diane Deriaz, Martine and the late Dr Jean Fanchette, Joan and Patrick Leigh Fermor, Thomas W. French, Kimon Friar, Judy and David Gascoyne, Stela Ghetie, Paul Gotch and his late wife Billy, Stephen Gray, Chili Hawes, Mrs Hayball, Suzanne Henig, Eleonore Hirt, Mary Bentley and Group-Captain Dudley Honor, Buffie Johnson, David Hugh Jones, Erica Jong, Spiros Katexis, Dorothy Brown Keep, H. T. Kennedy, Jacques Lacarrière, Alexis C. Ladas, Diana Hambro Ladas, the late John Lehmann, Simone Lestoguard, the late Robert Liddell, Richard Lumley (Lord Scarbrough), Margaret McCall, Mary and Brian MacDermot, Cecily Mackworth (Comtesse Chabanne), Jack Macrae, Jeremy Mallinson, Frances and the late Horst von Maltitz, Lady Diana and Lord Yehudi Menuhin, Alexia (Stephanides) Mercouris, the late Henry Miller, Tony Miller, Robert Morton-Saner, Joaquín Nin-Culmell, Philip Nind, Patricia Nix, Marthe Nochy, Nadežda Djukić Obradović, Joan von Oettingen, the late Juliet O'Hea, Mr and Mrs Andonis Palatiano, Liana and the late Dimitri Papadimos, Joyce and Achilles Papadopoulos, Lady Peake (widow of Sir Charles), Mr and Mrs John B. Pick, Marie-Anne Pini, Rupert Pole, John Priestman, Barbara Robinson, Mrs Rodis Roufos, the late Lucy Schmick-Reichel, Gemma Salem, Annette and David Smith, Robert Snyder, the late Anna and Wallace Southam, the Rt Revd Headley Sparks, Ruth Speirs, the late Frances Steloff, Mary and the late Dr Theodore Stephanides, James Stern, Dorothy Stevenson, Bernard Stone, Sparrow and Harry R. Stoneback, J. Meary Tambimuttu, Frédéric-Jacques Temple, Penelope Tremayne and her husband Tony Willis, the late John Unterecker, Fiddle Viracola, Vladimir Volkoff, Lady Felicity and Sir Peter Wakefield, Sir John Waller, Katie and Web Wheelock, George Whitman, Reno Wideson, Endymion Wilkinson, the late Pamela Wilkinson, the late Gwyn Williams, Pauline Wright, Noel Young. I appreciate comments on Sappho Durrell by Barbara Robson and Simon Tompsett.

I have been lucky beyond bounds in gaining as my agent Durrell's own, Anthea Morton-Saner at Curtis Brown, who has shared with me her many years of Durrell-watching. Georges and Boris Hoffman, agents for Henry Miller, have been most helpful. I have been extremely fortunate in having as my senior editor at Faber John Bodley, whose warm feeling for Durrell found expression in his infinite patience in dealing with me throughout a series of long delays as distressing to both of us as they were unavoidable.

I must thank my institution, the State University of New York Maritime College, for supporting my research over the years with two sabbatical leaves approved by Vice President William R. Porter. Joel J. Belson and Karen Markoe, successive chairs of the Humanities Department, have given me consistent encouragement and some release time from classes. Profound thanks go to the staff of the Luce Library at the college, especially to Richard C. Corson, Jane Fitzpatrick, Alvina Kalsch, John Jong Jin Lee, Lisa Leschinsky, Filomena Magavero, Barbara Mastrandrea, Kathleen Pyzynski, Tereze Rancans, Pat Weisert. Dan Mastromarino and Robert Sasson have provided invaluable technical assistance.

ACKNOWLEDGEMENTS

Five friends have read and commented on the entire mauscript, and my debt to these individuals and to their advice is inestimable: Brewster Chamberlin, Michael Haag, Anthea Morton-Saner, Carol and Brooke Peirce. Betty Ryan Gordon discussed the Paris chapter; Peggy Fox and Jennifer Leonard read and critiqued the chapter on India; David Roessel placed at my disposal the results of his researches on Cyprus and reviewed my chapter on the island; James Rogers advised me on several chapters. My thanks to various other friends for generous advice and support: Terence S. Martin, who first suggested to me a serious study of Durrell; to James Fetzer, Richard Harris, Frank Leonard, Robert B. Sennish. These individuals have suggested many improvements to my text; where errors or infelicities remain, the blame is mine alone.

My thanks to the International Lawrence Durrell Society, whose members worldwide have been unfailingly helpful in my quest for Durrell. Principal among these is Carol Peirce, who for twenty years has encouraged my Durrell researches, and who has worked in an inspired way to promote the understanding of Lawrence Durrell.

I am in debt to many scholars, but especially to Richard Pine, whose *Lawrence Durrell: The Mindscape* is the most comprehensive attempt to date to delineate Durrell's intellectual and artistic growth. I am most grateful for the help freely given by Roger Bowen, James P. Carley, Virginia Carruthers, J. Kent Clark, Denis Constancias, Artemis Cooper, Noël Riley Fitch, Alan W. Friedman, Lawrence B. Gamache, Norman Gates, Leo Hamalian, Evelyn Hinz, Earl G. Ingersoll, Roger Jackson, Edmund S. Keeley, Jane Keller, Frank Kersnowski, Anna Lillios, Paul Lorenz, Bertrand Mathieu, Ray Morrison, Elizabeth Podnieks, Patrick Freiherr von Richthofen, Michael G. Satow, Avi Sharon, Susan Vander Closter, George Wickes and many others. For information and assistance I thank A. Artinian, Jo Barnes and Anthony De la Hey, the late Alan M. Cohn (SIU-C), John Ferrone, Lilace Hatayama (UCLA), Cathy Henderson (HRHRC), Kerin Hope, Elizabeth Kastor, Jelka and the late Alister Kershaw, David Lida, D. Malcolm Lakin, John McPherson, Einar Moos, Frank Paluka (Iowa), Lawrence Clark Powell, Brooke Whiting (UCLA).

My thanks for help to those in India without whose enthusiastic aid it would have been impossible to track down many of the facts of Durrell's heritage: Suresht Bald, R. R. Bhandari, S. K. Chatterjee, Sant Ram Chopra, V. J. Chopra, J. K. Jha, Susan Jootla, Ravi Khanna, Tshering Lama, Alakh Parkash Mayor, Veepak K. Mohanty, Nani Ardeshir Palkhivala, M. S. Rana, Anil Richharia, H. P. Sharma, Shakti Sharma, Jit Singh, Madan Singh, Magendra Singh, Dr R. G. Singh, Sardar Sohan Singh Sokhi, Mr and Mrs E. F. Surti, Mme Tendufla, P. Guha Thakurta, Ashok Tomar, Rev Walter.

Sincere thanks to the following who provided details of Durrell's schooling: Miss C. F. E. Davis and John V. Iyson (both of St Edmund's), Father John W. Whalen, SJ (St Joseph's), J. Arris (South London College, formerly St Olave's and St Saviour's), and many other school officials who helped me determine what Durrell did *not* attempt in education.

In Egypt I was given friendly assistance by Dr Galal Aref and his late wife Soad Hussein Sobhy, Naomi 'Moughee' Athanasian, Father Howard Levett, Hala Halim, Dr Adham El Nakeeb, Morsi Saad el Din, Gerald L. Vincent and many others. For information on Durrell in Argentina I thank especially Raúl Víctor Peláez, and also the late Jorge Ferreyra, Roberto Funes and Mrs Enrique Revol. On Cyprus I was greatly helped by several people who knew Durrell or the history of the island during his residence: Catherine and Alex Emmett, Deirdre Guthrie, Ioachim Ioachim, Ruth Keshishian, Julia Manglis, Peter Megaw, Sabri Tahir.

I am deeply concerned that I may have omitted mention of some who helped me. If indeed this oversight has occurred, I wish to assure these individuals that their contributions were deeply appreciated and ask that my apology be accepted.

My greatest debts, my greatest thanks, are due to Susan S. MacNiven, who has shared every research trip, has turned up limitless information, has been a party to nearly every interview, and has read several times over every word that I have written. But for her, this book would never have been completed.

For permission to quote from the letters, unpublished writings and notebooks of Lawrence Durrell, I wish to thank the Estate of Lawrence Durrell and his literary executor, Françoise Kestsman. For access to the letters of Lawrence Durrell to Michael Fraenkel, my thanks to Karl Orend, publisher, Alyscamps Press, Paris, and to the Carrefour Archive, repository of Fraenkel's literary remains. I extend my thanks to libraries, publishers and individuals not previously acknowledged for access to and, where relevant, permission to quote from material in their possession, and to use photographs: the Curtis Brown Archive; E. P. Dutton; E.L.I.A. (Hellenic Literary and Historical Archives Society), Manos Haritatos, President; Mrs Valerie Eliot; the Faber and Faber Archive; Mme Martine Fanchette; the Gennadius Library; *Granta*; Gunther Stuhlmann and the Estate of Anaïs Nin; Harcourt Brace Jovanovich; Harry Ransom Humanities Research Center, Austin; The Henry Miller Estate and Agence Hoffman; the India Office Library and Records; University of Iowa Libraries, Manuscript Collection; the National Library of Canada; New Directions Press; the Ohio State University Library; Department of Special Collections, University Research Library, UCLA; Southern Illinois University at Carbondale; the Viking Press.

Index

486, 490, 506, 528, 557, 566, 577, 589, 623, 626, 644, 661, 675; academic interest in, 679; and 'The Book of the Dead', 154, 196; Cavafy translations, 243; characters: Balthazar, 458, 569; Capodistria, 555; Clea, 432, 509, 527; Darley, 94, 286, 385, 432, 448, 455, 458, 467, 476, 511, 583, 662; Justine, 205, 242, 269, 379, 384, 425, 432, 446, 455, 458, 468, 488, 493, 511, 569, 583, 659; Lela Hosnani, 242, 488; Melissa, 245, 385, 455; Mountolive, 241, 432, 467–8, 488, 511; Nessim, 392, 395, 425; Pombal, 662; Pursewarden, 94, 292, 317, 348, 452, 454–5, 458, 467, 469, 476, 488, 511, 527, 561, 652, 688; Scobie, 255, 265, 561, 652, 659; different states of 'reality', 141; editions, 454, 524; the ending, 107; financial pressure claims, 456; Groddeck and, 299; intention, 457; international fame, 520; LD and Eve's relationship, 423; LD works on in Cyprus, 391–2; *Moeurs* (fiction-within-fiction), 431; moods of decadence and frenetic passion, 630; multiple points of view, 190, 352; Nietzschean influences, 154; rejection of permanence, 226; and relativity, 457, 458, 658; resurrections and rebirths, 561; reviews, 513–14, 515, 529; search for new dimensions, 185; seasoning process, 491; setting, 295; sources, 89, 94, 95, 159, 237, 246, 254, 273, 281, 286, 292, 298, 372, 385, 391–2, 431–2, 467–8, 476, 508; theory of disease and injury, 431; time, 177; translations, 453, 495, 503; as Western in cast and attitude, 658; writing approach, 467, 499; *see also Balthazar; Clea; Justine; Mountolive*
'Anabasis' *see The Black Book*
'The Ancient Britons', 131
'The Anecdotes', 345, 356
Antrobus stories, 349, 360, 429, 453, 466, 470, 490, 520
'Anubis', *see The Black Book*
'Apesong', 601
'The Aquarians' (abandoned), 200
Art and Outrage: A Correspondence about Henry Miller Between Alfred Perlès and Lawrence Durrell, 470, 482
'Asylum in the Snow', 88, 124, 146, 160, 171, 186, 199, 302
'At Corinth', 279
'Autumn Lady: Naxos', 618
The Avignon Quintet, 106, 254, 273, 305, 395, 583, 622, 623, 630–1, 633, 645, 650, 653, 656, 668, 672; the *anagnorisis* (recognition), 305, 662; Buddhism, 455; characters: 588, 652; Constance, 569; 642–3; Honey Man, 594; completed, 659,

671; dark side, 643; death, 663; different states of 'reality', 141; as Eastern in cast and attitude, 658, 660; endings, 651; and the five *skandas* of Buddhism, 659; the germ of, 178; *gigogne* image, structure, 352, 358, 562, 652; gypsies, 484; insanity, 185; Manichean vision, 563; mirror-image book, 681; *Monsieur* as the keystone, 583; Nietzschean influences, 154–5; and the 'perspex cube', 658–9; rejection of permanence, 226; reviews, 673; spirit of play, 209; Stendhal and, 649; time, 177; *see also Constance; Livia; Monsieur; Quinx; Sebastian*
'A Ballad of the Good Lord Nelson', 278
'Ballad of Kretschmer's Types', 504
'The Ballad of Slow Decay', 82
Balthazar, 264, 443, 445, 452, 453, 454–5, 458, 460, 475, 486, 495, 508, 509, 520; appears in English, 472–3; on bestseller lists, 504; completed, 456; fan mail, 482; Nin and, 474, 483; Note prefacing, 456–7; Prix du Meilleur Livre Étranger, 502; Pursewarden, 452, 454; reviews, 473, 489; royalties, 473
'Beccafico – a Tragic History', 421
Bitter Lemons, 84, 385, 389, 400, 403, 412, 414, 418, 434, 437, 444–5, 454, 458, 459, 476, 477, 521; Duff Cooper Memorial Prize, 463–4, 465, 467; as a political book, 464–5; popularity, 464; radio broadcast cancelled, 502
The Black Book: An Agon (working titles: 'Lover Anubis'/'Anubis'/'Anabasis'), 71, 72, 83, 97, 105–6, 112, 115, 118, 122, 124, 132, 135, 142, 144–5, 171, 181, 196, 221, 250, 305, 319, 324, 402, 429, 440, 477, 498, 589, 642, 657, 662, 671; appears in *The Booster*, 177; as autobiographical, 132; death in, 147, 175, 190–1; the diary form, 181, 187, 190; dispute over expurgated version, 161–2; Eliot praises, 160–1, 172–3; English edition, 471; excesses of, 202; influences, 132, 148, 150; Laurence Lucifer character, 150, 190, 191, 568; and LD's artistic self, 150, 202; LD's new direction in writing, 132; LD's Paris circle discusses, 189–90; Miller praises, 149–50; Nancy and, 147–8, 149; publication, 150, 151–2, 153, 160, 161, 162, 168–9, 183, 201, 252, 273, 275, 301, 302, 503, 599; reviews, 201–2; rewrites, 146, 147, 149; Rexroth on, 451; time concept, 170, 177; triumph in scope and vigour, 151; the womb symbol, 195
Black Honey (unpublished play), 303, 327
'Blind Homer', 355
'The Book of the Dead' (progenitor of *The*

LD's ambivalence towards, 106, 173, 359
LD analyses the English, 53, 226
LD determined to escape, 67, 106
LD's difficulties with, 51, 52, 73, 171, 326, 354, 573, 616
LD on his heritage, 323, 510–11
LD identifies with his father, 52
LD influenced by, 103
LD learns to put up with, 64
LD's opinion of, 51–2, 336
LD sent to, 7, 12, 20, 42, 47–50
and LD's experience in Argentina, 357–8, 359
English literature, LD's appreciation of, 55, 56
Enosis (Union with Greece), 324, 325, 391, 393, 399, 401, 404, 407, 411, 418, 422, 426, 427, 429, 434, 459
Enright, D. J., 515
EOKA (National Organization of Cypriot Fighters), 391, 399, 414, 420, 422, 425–8, 430, 433, 434, 435, 438, 439, 441, 455, 465, 490
Eos (proposed journal), 141
Epfs, Oscar (pseudonym of LD as a painter), 538, 607, 609, 665, 688
Epicurus, 596
Epidaurus, 221, 224, 228, 252
Eppler, Johannes, 256
Epstein, Thérèse ('Tessa'), *see* Marberry, Thérèse
Ernst, Max, 571
Erval, François, 530
Etiemble, René, 296
Études Méditerranéen, 515, 521
Euclid, 398
Eurasians, 22, 47
Evangelis (Corfiot rubbish collector), 545
Evans, Patrick (Pat), 98, 99, 107, 119, 131, 134, 138, 148, 155, 156, 164, 170, 177, 226
Evans-Wentz, W. Y., 36
Evening Standard newspaper, 470, 525

Faber and Faber Limited, 164, 171, 172, 196, 211–12, 247, 250, 357, 499
and *Balthazar*, 472, 473
and a bio-critical text, 564
and *Bitter Lemons*, 445
and *The Black Book*, 160, 161, 162, 273, 275, 471
and 'The Book of the Dead', 204
and *Caesar's Vast Ghost*, 677, 683, 686
and *Cefalû*, 354
and censorship, 316
and *Cities, Plains and People*, 289, 298, 300
Claude sells *The Rum Go*, 456
and *Collected Poems*, 504, 632
and *The Dark Labyrinth*, 301, 313
and *Justine*, 444, 447, 466

and Laughlin, 215
LD and Gerry appear together in the Spring list, 383
and *Livia*, 630
and *Monsieur*, 608
and *Mountolive*, 468
Nin and, 203
and *Panic Spring*, 116, 122, 142, 145
and *Prospero's Cell*, 295, 298
and *Reflections on a Marine Venus*, 373, 383
and *Sappho*, 356
and *Sebastian*, 658
and *Tunc*, 557
and the Uncebunke poems, 176, 195, 261
and *White Eagles over Serbia*, 419, 440
Fabre, Jean, 115, 124, 597
Fahmy, Hekmat, 245, 256
Fairley, Captain James H., 7, 8, 9, 12
Fairley, Louisa (née Boustred; LD's great-grandmother), 7
Famagusta, Cyprus, 396, 397, 404
Fan, Aunt, 464, 537, 682
Fanchette, Jean, 472, 473, 474, 477, 478–9, 646, 650
and *Clea*, 509
essay on *Justine*, 472
on LD's drinking, 686
and *Lettres Suivent*, 472, 477, 492
and medicine, 472, 477, 509
and *Mountolive*, 488
Nin and, 483
and *Two Cities*, 485, 492–5, 494, 502–3
at the Villa Louis, 485
Archipels, 485
Fanchette, Martine, 478
appearance, 479
emotional fragility, 479
at the Villa Louis, 485
Farouk, King of Egypt, 241, 251, 256, 265, 276, 333
Farquharson, John, 118
Farr, Tommy (boxer), 169
Farrow, Mia, 628
Fathy, Hassan, 627
Faulkner, William, 576
FBI (Federal Bureau of Investigation), 298
Fedden, R. Romilly ('Robin'), 218–19, 222, 225, 237, 239, 246, 248, 250, 251, 253, 270, 276, 284–7, 300, 313, 316, 317, 628, 637
on Egypt, 253, 254
'Personal Landscape', 247
Fedden, Renée (née Catseflis), 276
Feinman, Richard, 606
Fernandel (Fernand Contandin), 482
Ferreyra, 'Bebita', 346, 358, 633
Ferreyra, Jorge 'Monono', 346, 347, 348, 357, 358

Levant Trilogy, 242
'Written in the Third Year of the War', 242
Manor House, Roorkee, India, 7, 8, 10
Mansfield, Katherine, 454
Mantura, Guy, 383, 386
Marberry, Thérèse (née Epstein), 205, 214,
    281, 432, 565, 571, 575, 610
Marcelle (housekeeper in Sommières), 548,
    566, 569, 578, 579, 591, 593
Marcus, Laurence, 571
Marlowe, Christopher, 94
Marsh, Philip, 90, 130
Marston, John, 161
Martin, Jay, 605, 639
Marx Brothers, 210
Masefield, John: 'Cargoes', 94
Maturin, Charles, 526
Maugham, W. Somerset, 244, 503
    The Circle, 103
Maxton, Stanley, 324
Mazet Michel, near Nîmes, 486, 489, 490,
    491, 496, 497, 499, 500, 503, 512, 513,
    524, 527, 534, 539, 540, 546, 558, 586,
    655
    annexe, 509, 545
    Claude on, 487
    Claude's gardening, 638
    described, 484–5
    Gerry and, 585, 608, 622, 624, 663, 679,
        682
    LD buys, 495
    LD and Claude move to, 487
    LD takes his olives to the oil mill, 598
    LD works on his land, 500–1
    LD's daily life, 501
    Miller visits, 496, 497, 505, 506, 516–17
Melville, Herman, 296, 668
    'Bartleby the Scrivener', 668
    Pierre, 296
Menasce, Baron George, 286
Menuhin, Diana, Lady (née Gould), 249,
    287–8, 320, 432, 435, 446, 458, 477, 617
Menuhin, Yehudi (Lord Menuhin), 435, 465,
    478, 586, 617
Mercure de France, 438, 494, 513, 591
Meredith, George, 312
Merry Widow, The, 287, 288
Metaxas, Yanni, 229, 497
Michonze (painter), 559, 567
Middleton, Christopher, 494
    'The Heraldic Universe', 447–8
Midi Libre, 594, 686
Midland Bank, 183
Mignon, Madame (cook and cleaner), 614,
    618
Milarepa, 660, 678
Miller, Barbara, 320
Miller, Beatrice (née Wickens), 320
Miller, Eve (née McClure), 376, 393, 458, 483,

496, 502–3, 506, 516, 517, 557
Miller, Henry, 2, 88, 134, 157, 164, 232, 260,
    281, 302, 317, 393–4, 405, 442, 474,
    514, 515, 543, 579, 580, 587, 645, 651,
    667
    advises LD, 145–6, 401
    Les amis de Henry Miller 578 (proposed
        television film), 579
    appearance, 167
    and *Art and Outrage*, 470–1
    and astrology, 186, 468, 524
    and *Balthazar*, 460
    banned books scheme, 158
    belief in LD artistically, 187–8
    and *Bitter Lemons*, 458
    and *The Black Book*, 149–50, 151, 189,
        190, 199, 201, 471, 477
    and *The Booster*, 169, 170, 176, 179, 180,
        187
    Buffie Johnson and, 178–9
    and censorship, 85, 140, 163
    on Claude Durrell's writing style, 462
    on Claude Kiefer, 595
    condemned for use of 'gutter-words', 326
    and Cossery's *The Men God Forgot*, 297
    death, 646–7, 648, 649
    despairing state, 202, 206
    and Dylan Thomas, 206–7
    eightieth birthday celebration, 589
    and Eliot, 206
    on *Esprit de Corps*, 471
    essay on Howe, 212
    and Etiemble, 296
    and Fanchette's party, 502–3
    falls from a ladder, 199
    and the FBI, 298
    financial affairs, 320–1, 340, 370, 570, 646
    and Gascoyne, 197
    and Ghislaine, 602, 606, 609
    in Greece, 215–17, 219–20, 221, 223–4
    and 'The Happy Rock', 294, 332, 460
    health, 602, 608, 646
    'ignorance' of English literature, 294–5
    ignores the war, 227, 260, 274
    influences LD, 124, 132, 139, 148, 201
    at the International Writers' Conference
        (1962), 531
    on *Justine*, 447, 460, 465
    and Lawrence, 124–5, 189
    on LD, 2, 209
    LD on, 344, 353, 360, 363
    LD lectures on, 350
    lectures at Caltech, 605
    marries Hoki, 558
    marries Janina Lepska, 298
    Max and the White Phagocytes, 171, 183,
        199
    Mazet Michel visits, 496, 497, 505–6,
        516–17, 638